McDougal Littell

CLASSZONE

Visit classzone.com and get connected.

ClassZone resources provide instruction, practice and learning support for students and parents.

Literature and Reading Center

- Selection-specific content includes vocabulary practice, research links, and extension activities for writing and critical thinking

- Author Online provides information about each author, as well as in-depth author studies on selected writers

- English Learner support for a variety of languages includes audio summaries of selections and a Multi-Language Academic Glossary

Vocabulary Center

- Vocabulary practice and games reinforce skills

Writing and Grammar Center

- Quick-Fix Editing Machine provides grammar help in a student-friendly format

- Writing Templates and graphic organizers promote clear, orderly communication

Media Center

- Media Analysis Guides encourage critical thinking skills

- Project Ideas, Storyboards, and Production Templates inspire creative media projects

Access the online version of your textbook at **classzone.com**

Your complete text is available for immediate use!

McDougal Littell
Where Great Lessons Begin

McDougal Littell
LITERATURE

ACKNOWLEDGMENTS

INTRODUCTORY UNIT

Simon & Schuster: Excerpt from *The Old Man and the Sea* by Ernest Hemingway. Copyright © 1952 by Ernest Hemingway, copyright renewed 1980 by Mary Hemingway. Reprinted with permission of Scribner, an imprint of Simon & Schuster Adult Publishing Group.

Arte Público Press: "Los Ancianos," from *My Own True Name* by Pat Mora. Copyright © 2000 by Pat Mora. Reprinted by permission of Arte Público Press, University of Houston.

Flora Roberts Inc.: Excerpt from *The Miracle Worker* by William Gibson. Copyright © 1956, 1957 by William Gibson, copyright 1959, 1960 by Tamarack Productions, Ltd., and George S. Klein and Leo Garel as trustees under three separate deeds of trust, copyright renewed 1977 by William Gibson. Used by permission of Flora Roberts, Inc.

Little, Brown and Company: Excerpt from *Nisei Daughter* by Monica Sone. Copyright © 1953 by Monica Sone, copyright renewed 1981 by Monica Sone. Used by permission of Little, Brown and Co., Inc.

New York Times: Excerpt from "Japan Wars on U.S. and Britain; Makes Sudden Attack on Hawaii; Heavy Fighting At Sea Reported," by Frank L. Kluckhohn from *The New York Times,* December 8, 1941. Copyright © 1941 by The New York Times. Reprinted by permission of The New York Times.

Barbara Hogenson Agency: Excerpt from "The Secret Life of Walter Mitty," from *My World—And Welcome To It* by James Thurber. Copyright © 1942 by James Thurber, copyright renewed 1970 by Rosemary A. Thurber. Reprinted by arrangement with Rosemary A. Thurber and The Barbara Hogenson Agency. All rights reserved.

Continued on page R155

ART CREDITS

COVER, TITLE PAGE

Untitled (2002), Jerry N. Uelsmann. © Jerry N. Uelsmann.

Continued on page R161

ISBN 13: 978-0-618-94957-1   ISBN 10: 0-618-94957-7

Printed in the United States of America.

2 3 4 5 6 7 8 9—DWO—12 11 10 09 08

PENNSYLVANIA

McDougal Littell
LITERATURE

Janet Allen

Arthur N. Applebee

Jim Burke

Douglas Carnine

Yvette Jackson

Robert T. Jiménez

Judith A. Langer

Robert J. Marzano

Donna M. Ogle

Carol Booth Olson

Carol Ann Tomlinson

Mary Lou McCloskey

Lydia Stack

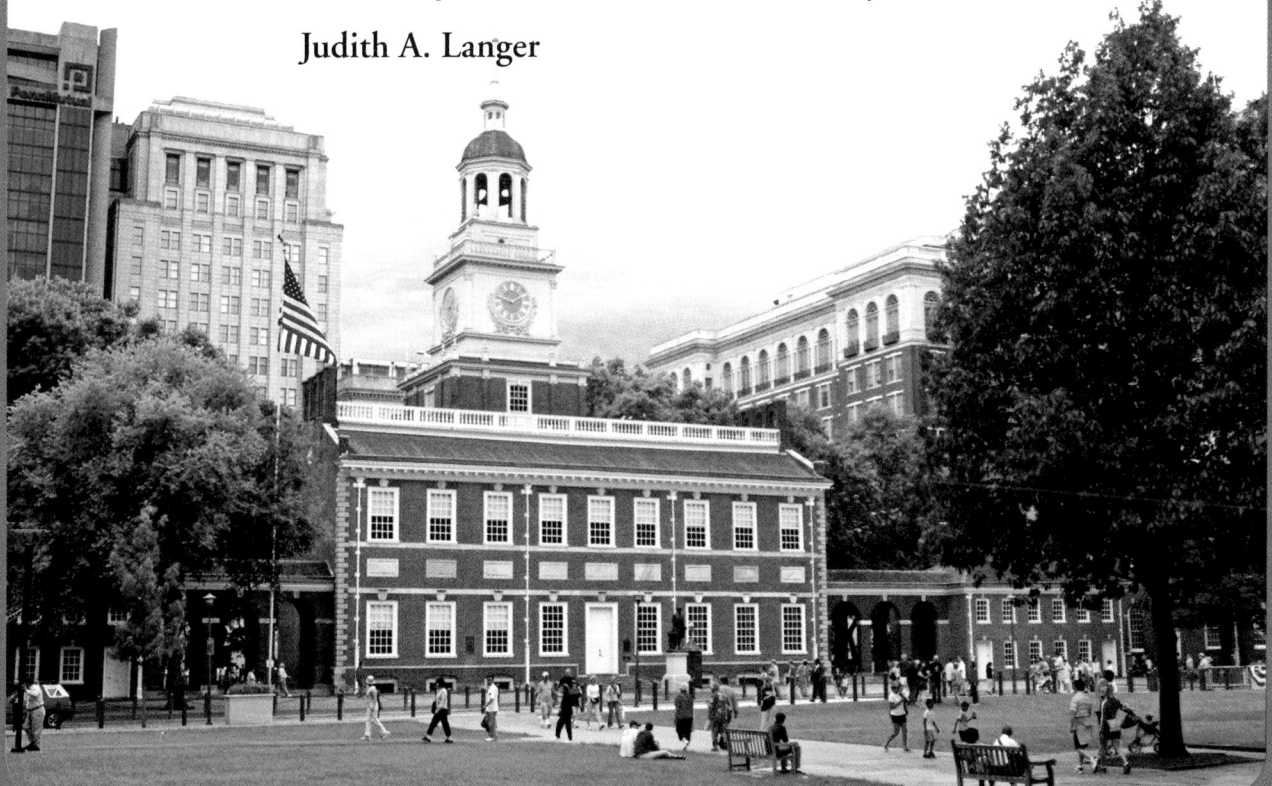

Independence Hall, Philadelphia, Pennsylvania © Steve Hamblin/Alamy

 McDougal Littell

EVANSTON, ILLINOIS • BOSTON • DALLAS

SENIOR PROGRAM CONSULTANTS

JANET ALLEN Reading and Literacy Specialist; creator of the popular "It's Never Too Late"/"Reading for Life" Institutes. Dr. Allen is an internationally known consultant who specializes in literacy work with at-risk students. Her publications include *Tools for Content Literacy; It's Never Too Late: Leading Adolescents to Lifelong Learning; Yellow Brick Roads: Shared and Guided Paths to Independent Reading; Words, Words, Words: Teaching Vocabulary in Grades 4–12;* and *Testing 1, 2, 3 . . . Bridging Best Practice and High-Stakes Assessments.* Dr. Allen was a high school reading and English teacher for more than 20 years and has taught courses in both subjects at the University of Central Florida. She directed the Central Florida Writing Project and received the Milken Foundation National Educator Award.

ARTHUR N. APPLEBEE Leading Professor, School of Education at the University at Albany, State University of New York; Director of the Center on English Learning and Achievement. During his varied career, Dr. Applebee has been both a researcher and a teacher, working in institutional settings with children with severe learning problems, in public schools, as a staff member of the National Council of Teachers of English, and in professional education. Among his many books are *Curriculum as Conversation: Transforming Traditions of Teaching and Learning; Literature in the Secondary School: Studies of Curriculum and Instruction in the United States;* and *Tradition and Reform in the Teaching of English: A History.* He was elected to the International Reading Hall of Fame and has received, among other honors, the David H. Russell Award for Distinguished Research in the Teaching of English.

JIM BURKE Lecturer and Author; Teacher of English at Burlingame High School, Burlingame, California. Mr. Burke is a popular presenter at educational conferences across the country and is the author of numerous books for teachers, including *School Smarts: The Four Cs of Academic Success; The English Teacher's Companion; Reading Reminders; Writing Reminders;* and *ACCESSing School: Teaching Struggling Readers to Achieve Academic and Personal Success.* He is the recipient of NCTE's Exemplary English Leadership Award and was inducted into the California Reading Association's Hall of Fame.

DOUGLAS CARNINE Professor of Education at the University of Oregon; Director of the Western Region Reading First Technical Assistance Center. Dr. Carnine is nationally known for his focus on research-based practices in education, especially curriculum designs that prepare instructors of K-12 students. He has received the Lifetime Achievement Award from the Council for Exceptional Children and the Ersted Award for outstanding teaching at the University of Oregon. Dr. Carnine frequently consults on educational policy with government groups, businesses, communities, and teacher unions.

YVETTE JACKSON Executive Director of the National Urban Alliance for Effective Education. Nationally recognized for her work in assessing the learning potential of underachieving urban students, Dr. Jackson is also a presenter for the Harvard Principal Center and is a member of the Differentiation Faculty of the Association for Supervision and Curriculum Development. Dr. Jackson's research focuses on literacy, gifted education, and cognitive mediation theory. She designed the Comprehensive Education Plan for the New York City Public Schools and has served as their Director of Gifted Programs and Executive Director of Instruction and Professional Development.

ROBERT T. JIMÉNEZ Professor of Language, Literacy, and Culture at Vanderbilt University. Dr. Jiménez's research focuses on the language and literacy practices of Latino students. A former bilingual education teacher, he is now conducting research on how written language is thought about and used in contemporary Mexico. Dr. Jiménez has received several research and teaching honors, including two Fulbright awards from the Council for the International Exchange of Scholars and the Albert J. Harris Award from the International Reading Association. His published work has appeared in the *American Educational Research Journal, Reading Research Quarterly, The Reading Teacher, Journal of Adolescent and Adult Literacy,* and *Lectura y Vida.*

JUDITH A. LANGER Distinguished Professor at the University at Albany, State University of New York; Director of the Center on English Learning and Achievement; Director of the Albany Institute for Research in Education. An internationally known scholar in English language arts education, Dr. Langer specializes in developing teaching approaches that can enrich and improve what gets done on a daily basis in classrooms. Her publications include *Getting to Excellent: How to Create Better Schools* and *Effective Literacy Instruction: Building Successful Reading and Writing Programs*. She was inducted into the International Reading Hall of Fame and has received many other notable awards, including an honorary doctorate from the University of Uppsala, Sweden, for her research on literacy education.

ROBERT J. MARZANO Senior Scholar at Mid-Continent Research for Education and Learning (McREL); Associate Professor at Cardinal Stritch University in Milwaukee, Wisconsin; President of Marzano & Associates. An internationally known researcher, trainer, and speaker, Dr. Marzano has developed programs that translate research and theory into practical tools for K-12 teachers and administrators. He has written extensively on such topics as reading and writing instruction, thinking skills, school effectiveness, assessment, and standards implementation. His books include *Building Background Knowledge for Academic Achievement; Classroom Management That Works: Research-Based Strategies for Every Teacher;* and *What Works in Schools: Translating Research Into Action.*

DONNA M. OGLE Professor of Reading and Language at National-Louis University in Chicago, Illinois; Past President of the International Reading Association. Creator of the well-known KWL strategy, Dr. Ogle has directed many staff development projects translating theory and research into school practice in middle and secondary schools throughout the United States and has served as a consultant on literacy projects worldwide. Her extensive international experience includes coordinating the Reading and Writing for Critical Thinking Project in Eastern Europe, developing integrated curriculum for a USAID Afghan Education Project, and speaking and consulting on projects in several Latin American countries and in Asia. Her books include *Coming Together as Readers; Reading Comprehension: Strategies for Independent Learners; All Children Read;* and *Literacy for a Democratic Society.*

CAROL BOOTH OLSON Senior Lecturer in the Department of Education at the University of California, Irvine; Director of the UCI site of the National Writing Project. Dr. Olson writes and lectures extensively on the reading/writing connection, critical thinking through writing, interactive strategies for teaching writing, and the use of multicultural literature with students of culturally diverse backgrounds. She has received many awards, including the California Association of Teachers of English Award of Merit, the Outstanding California Education Research Award, and the UC Irvine Excellence in Teaching Award. Dr. Olson's books include *Reading, Thinking, and Writing About Multicultural Literature* and *The Reading/Writing Connection: Strategies for Teaching and Learning in the Secondary Classroom.*

CAROL ANN TOMLINSON Professor of Educational Research, Foundations, and Policy at the University of Virginia; Co-Director of the University's Institutes on Academic Diversity. An internationally known expert on differentiated instruction, Dr. Tomlinson helps teachers and administrators develop effective methods of teaching academically diverse learners. She was a teacher of middle and high school English for 22 years prior to teaching at the University of Virginia. Her books on differentiated instruction have been translated into eight languages. Among her many publications are *How to Differentiate Instruction in Mixed-Ability Classrooms* and *The Differentiated Classroom: Responding to the Needs of All Learners.*

ENGLISH LEARNER SPECIALISTS

MARY LOU McCLOSKEY Past President of Teachers of English to Speakers of Other Languages (TESOL); Director of Teacher Development and Curriculum Design for Educo in Atlanta, Georgia. Dr. McCloskey is a former teacher in multilingual and multicultural classrooms. She has worked with teachers, teacher educators, and departments of education around the world on teaching English as a second and foreign language. She is author of *On Our Way to English, Voices in Literature, Integrating English,* and *Visions: Language, Literature, Content.* Her awards include the Le Moyne College Ignatian Award for Professional Achievement and the TESOL D. Scott Enright Service Award.

LYDIA STACK International ESL consultant. Her areas of expertise are English language teaching strategies, ESL standards for students and teachers, and curriculum writing. Her teaching experience includes 25 years as an elementary and high school ESL teacher. She is a past president of TESOL. Her awards include the James E. Alatis Award for Service to TESOL (2003) and the San Francisco STAR Teacher Award (1989). Her publications include *On Our Way to English; Wordways: Games for Language Learning;* and *Visions: Language, Literature, Content.*

CURRICULUM SPECIALIST

WILLIAM L. McBRIDE Curriculum Specialist. Dr. McBride is a nationally known speaker, educator, and author who now trains teachers in instructional methodologies. A former reading specialist, English teacher, and social studies teacher, he holds a Masters in Reading and a Ph.D. in Curriculum and Instruction from the University of North Carolina at Chapel Hill. Dr. McBride has contributed to the development of textbook series in language arts, social studies, science, and vocabulary. He is also known for his novel *Entertaining an Elephant,* which tells the story of a burned-out teacher who becomes re-inspired with both his profession and his life.

MEDIA SPECIALISTS

DAVID M. CONSIDINE Professor of Instructional Technology and Media Studies at Appalachian State University in North Carolina. Dr. Considine has served as a media literacy consultant to the U.S. government and to the media industry, including Discovery Communications and Cable in the Classroom. He has also conducted media literacy workshops and training for county and state health departments across the United States. Among his many publications are *Visual Messages: Integrating Imagery into Instruction,* and *Imagine That: Developing Critical Viewing and Thinking Through Children's Literature.*

LARKIN PAULUZZI Teacher and Media Specialist; trainer for the New Jersey Writing Project. Ms. Pauluzzi puts her extensive classroom experience to use in developing teacher-friendly curriculum materials and workshops in many different areas, including media literacy. She has led media literacy training workshops in several districts throughout Texas, guiding teachers in the meaningful and practical uses of media in the classroom. Ms. Pauluzzi has taught students at all levels, from Title I Reading to AP English IV. She also spearheads a technology club at her school, working with students to produce media and technology to serve both the school and the community.

LISA K. SCHEFFLER Teacher and Media Specialist. Ms. Scheffler has designed and taught media literacy and video production curriculum, in addition to teaching language arts and speech. Using her knowledge of mass communication theory, coupled with real classroom experience, she has developed ready-to-use materials that help teachers incorporate media literacy into their curricula. She has taught film and television studies at the University of North Texas and has served as a contributing writer for the Texas Education Agency's statewide viewing and representing curriculum.

PENNSYLVANIA

NATIONAL TEACHER ADVISORS

These are some of the many educators from across the country who played a crucial role in the development of the tables of contents, the lesson design, and other key components of this program:

Diana R. Martinez,
Treviño School of
Communications & Fine Arts,
Laredo, Texas

Natalie Martinez,
Stephen F. Austin High School,
Houston, Texas

Elizabeth Matarazzo,
Ysleta High School,
El Paso, Texas

Carol M. McDonald,
J. Frank Dobie High School,
Houston, Texas

Amy Millikan, Consultant,
Chicago, Illinois

Terri Morgan,
Caprock High School,
Amarillo, Texas

Eileen Murphy,
Walter Payton Preparatory
High School,
Chicago, Illinois

Lisa Omark,
New Haven Public Schools,
New Haven, Connecticut

Kaine Osburn,
Wheeling High School,
Wheeling, Illinois

Andrea J. Phillips,
Terry Sanford High School,
Fayetteville, North Carolina

Cathy Reilly,
Sayreville Public Schools,
Sayreville, New Jersey

Mark D. Simon,
Neuqua Valley High School,
Naperville, Illinois

Scott Snow,
Sequin High School,
Arlington, Texas

Jane W. Speidel,
Brevard County Schools,
Viera, Florida

Cheryl E. Sullivan,
Lisle Community School
District, Lisle, Illinois

Anita Usmiani,
Hamilton Township Public
Schools,
Hamilton Square, New Jersey

Linda Valdez,
Oxnard Union High School
District,
Oxnard, California

Nancy Walker,
Longview High School,
Longview, Texas

Kurt Weiler,
New Trier High School,
Winnetka, Illinois

Elizabeth Whittaker,
Larkin High School,
Elgin, Illinois

Linda S. Williams,
Woodlawn High School,
Baltimore, Maryland

John R. Williamson,
Fort Thomas Independent
Schools,
Fort Thomas, Kentucky

Anna N. Winters,
Simeon High School,
Chicago, Illinois

Tonora D. Wyckoff,
North Shore Senior High School,
Houston, Texas

Karen Zajac,
Glenbard South High School,
Glen Ellyn, Illinois

Cynthia Zimmerman,
Mose Vines Preparatory High
School,
Chicago, Illinois

Lynda Zimmerman,
El Camino High School,
South San Francisco, California

Ruth E. Zurich,
Brown Deer High School,
Brown Deer, Wisconsin

PENNSYLVANIA

OVERVIEW
Pennsylvania Student's Edition

LESSONS WITH EMBEDDED STANDARDS INSTRUCTION

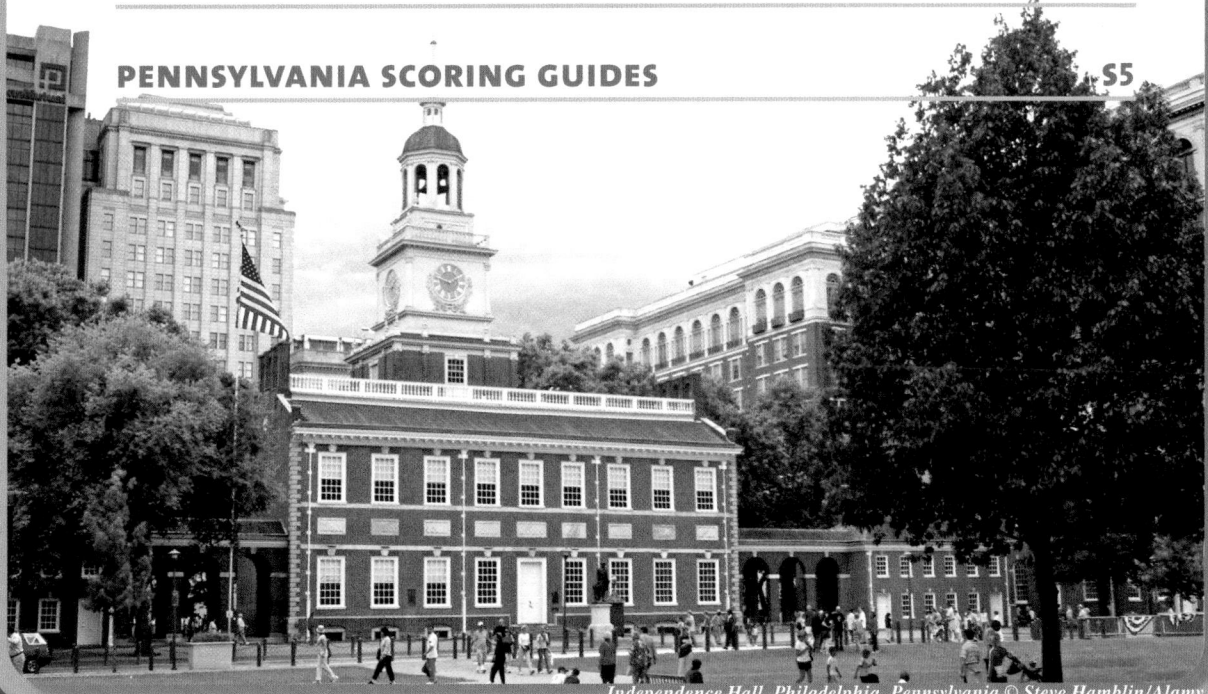 Look for the Pennsylvania symbol throughout the book. It highlights standards to help you succeed on your test.

Independence Hall, Philadelphia, Pennsylvania © Steve Hamblin/Alamy

PENNSYLVANIA CONTENTS IN BRIEF

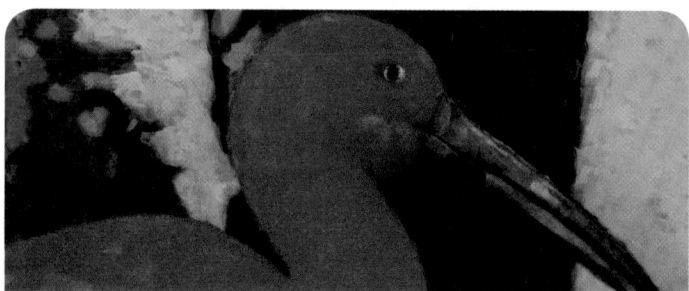

Online LITERATURE
CLASSZONE.COM

LITERATURE AND READING CENTER
- Author Biographies
- Additional Selection Background
- Literary Analysis Frames
- Power Thinking Activities

WRITING AND GRAMMAR CENTER
- Writing Templates and Graphic Organizers
- Publishing Options
- Quick-Fix Editing Machine

VOCABULARY CENTER
- Vocabulary Strategies and Practice
- Multi-Language Academic Vocabulary Glossary
- Vocabulary Flash Cards

MEDIA CENTER
- Production Templates
- Analysis Guides

RESEARCH CENTER
- Web Research Guide
- Citation Guide

ASSESSMENT CENTER
- PSSA Practice and Test-Taking Tips
- SAT/ACT Practice and Tips

MORE TECHNOLOGY

eEdition
- Interactive Selections
- Audio Summaries

WriteSmart
- Writing Prompts and Templates
- Interactive Student Models
- Interactive Graphic Organizers
- Interactive Revision Lessons
- Rubric Generator

MediaSmart DVD
- Media Lessons
- Interactive Media Studies

UNIT 1
PENNSYLVANIA

The Plot Thickens
NARRATIVE STRUCTURE

• IN FICTION • IN MEDIA • IN NONFICTION • IN POETRY • IN DRAMA

PENNSYLVANIA STANDARDS

VOCABULARY STRATEGIES

Latin roots: *mal, p. 49*
Denotation and connotation, *p. 76*
Latin prefixes: *in-, p. 92*

Greek roots: *chron, p. 104*
Synonyms and antonyms, *p. 118*
Word families: *aud, p. 131*

UNIT 2

PENNSYLVANIA

People Watching
CHARACTERIZATION AND POINT OF VIEW

- IN FICTION • IN NONFICTION • IN POETRY • ACROSS GENRES

PENNSYLVANIA STANDARDS

*Point of View,
Character Traits and Motivation*

*First-Person Point of View,
Draw Conclusions*

*Character Motivation,
Make Inferences*

*Third-Person Limited
Point of View, Monitor*

NONFICTION

*Characterization in
Autobiography,
Analyze Perspectives*

VOCABULARY STRATEGIES

Latin roots: *bene, p. 204*   Multiple-meaning words, *p. 248*
Latin roots: *spec, p. 219*   Specialized vocabulary, *p. 263*
Words from Greek culture, *p. 234*   Etymologies, *p. 282*

UNIT 3
PENNSYLVANIA

A Sense of Place
SETTING, MOOD, AND IMAGERY
● IN FICTION ● IN MEDIA ● IN NONFICTION ● IN POETRY

PENNSYLVANIA STANDARDS

Setting and Characters, Setting and Conflict, Imagery, Mood

ASSESSMENT SKILLS PRACTICE

VOCABULARY STRATEGIES

Connotation and denotation, *p. 324*
Latin roots: *quest, quer,* and *quisit, p. 340*

Word families: *clud, p. 354*
Context clues, *p. 371*

UNIT 4

PENNSYLVANIA

Getting the Message
THEME AND SYMBOL

• IN FICTION • IN NONFICTION • IN POETRY • ACROSS GENRES

PENNSYLVANIA STANDARDS

ASSESSMENT
SKILLS PRACTICE

VOCABULARY STRATEGIES

Suffixes: *-or, p. 421*
Connotation, *p. 444*

Using context clues, *p. 457*
Word origins, *p. 488*

Ideas Made Visible
AUTHOR'S PURPOSE

● **IN NONFICTION** ● **IN MEDIA** ● **IN FICTION**

**PENNSYLVANIA
STANDARDS**

*Author's Purpose and
Perspective, Organization
and Format*

*Diction, Analyze Patterns
of Organization*

*Tone, Identify Implied
Main Ideas*

Text Features, Take Notes

*Author's Purpose,
Interpret Graphic Aids*

VOCABULARY STRATEGIES

Word roots: *gen*, p. 532   Latin roots: *fract*, p. 555
Specialized fields: *"ologies,"* p. 545

UNIT 6
PENNSYLVANIA

Taking Sides
ARGUMENT AND PERSUASION

• **IN NONFICTION** • **IN MEDIA** • **ACROSS GENRES**

PENNSYLVANIA STANDARDS

Elements of Argument, Persuasive Techniques, Rhetorical Devices

Argument, Understand Rhetorical Devices

Persuasive Techniques, Summarize

Fact and Opinion, Recognize Bias

VOCABULARY STRATEGIES

Political words, *p. 609* Internet words, *p. 632*
Using a dictionary, *p. 618*

UNIT **7**

PENNSYLVANIA

Special Effects
THE LANGUAGE OF POETRY

• IN FICTION • IN MEDIA • IN NONFICTION • IN POETRY • IN DRAMA

PENNSYLVANIA STANDARDS

Form, Poetic Elements, Sound Devices, Imagery, Figurative Language

Lyric Poetry, Imagery, Make Inferences

Elegy, Diction, Paraphrase

PA24

A Way with Words
AUTHOR'S STYLE AND VOICE

• IN FICTION • IN MEDIA • IN NONFICTION • IN POETRY • IN DRAMA

PENNSYLVANIA
STANDARDS

VOCABULARY STRATEGIES

Prefixes: *in-, p. 762*   Homonyms, *p. 788*
Appropriate word choice, *p. 781*

UNIT 9

PENNSYLVANIA

Putting It in Context
HISTORY, CULTURE, AND THE AUTHOR
• IN NONFICTION • IN FICTION • IN POETRY

VOCABULARY STRATEGIES
Latin roots: *fid, p. 850* Idioms, *p. 887*
Greek words: *cosmo, p. 861*

UNIT 10

PENNSYLVANIA

Shakespearean Drama
THE TRAGEDY OF ROMEO AND JULIET

• IN DRAMA • IN MEDIA • IN POETRY

PENNSYLVANIA STANDARDS

Characteristics of Shakespearean Tragedy, The Language of Shakespeare, Reading Shakespearean Drama

Tragedy, Soliloquy, Aside, Allusion, Comic Relief, Blank Verse

Epic Poetry
THE ODYSSEY

UNIT 12

PENNSYLVANIA

Investigation and Discovery
THE POWER OF RESEARCH

Student Resource Bank

Selections by Genre

Features

 LITERATURE CENTER at **ClassZone.com**

 MEDIA CENTER at **ClassZone.com**

 **WriteSmart**

 **MediaSmart DVD**

VOCABULARY STRATEGIES

pages 49, 76, 92, 104, 118, 131, 204, 219, 234, 248, 263, 282, 324, 340, 354, 371, 421, 444, 457, 488, 532, 545, 555, 609, 618, 632, 762, 781, 788, 850, 861, 887, 1139, 1168

GRAMMAR AND STYLE

pages 50, 77, 93, 105, 119, 167, 205, 220, 235, 249, 325, 341, 355, 445, 465, 523, 533, 567, 619, 633, 683, 713, 763, 789, 851, 873, 1051, 1169

PENNSYLVANIA

STUDENT GUIDE TO PSSA SUCCESS

PSSA SUCCESS

Independence Hall, Philadelphia, Pennsylvania © Steve Hamblin/Alamy

Understanding the Pennsylvania Academic Standards and Assessment Anchors

What are the Pennsylvania Academic Standards?

The Pennsylvania Academic Standards outline what you should know and be able to do at each grade level, for success in taking tests like the Pennsylvania System of School Assessment (PSSA), as well as for everyday life and the workplace. Your teacher uses the standards to create a course of instruction that will help you develop the skills and knowledge you are expected to have by the end of grade 9.

What are the Pennsylvania Assessment Anchors?

The Pennsylvania Assessment Anchors are based on the Pennsylvania Academic Standards. The anchors clarify which standards are assessed on the PSSA. Currently, the anchors are only available for mathematics and reading, so while they will be the key to helping you prepare for the reading assessment, you will want to refer back to the standards to prepare for other assessments, such as writing.

How will I learn the Pennsylvania Academic Standards and Assessment Anchors?

Your textbook is closely aligned to the Pennsylvania Academic Standards and Assessment Anchors, so that every time you learn or practice a skill, you are mastering one of the standards. Each unit, each selection, and each workshop connects to a standard or anchor that is listed on the opening page of the section.

The Pennsylvania Academic Standards for Writing are divided into two strands:

1.4 Types of Writing

1.5 Quality of Writing

These two strands are further broken down by grade level, and then by standard. Standards describe what you must learn to master the strand. Pennsylvania uses a special code to identify the strand, the grade level, and the standard.

For a complete listing of Pennsylvania Academic Standards and Assessment Anchors, see page S1

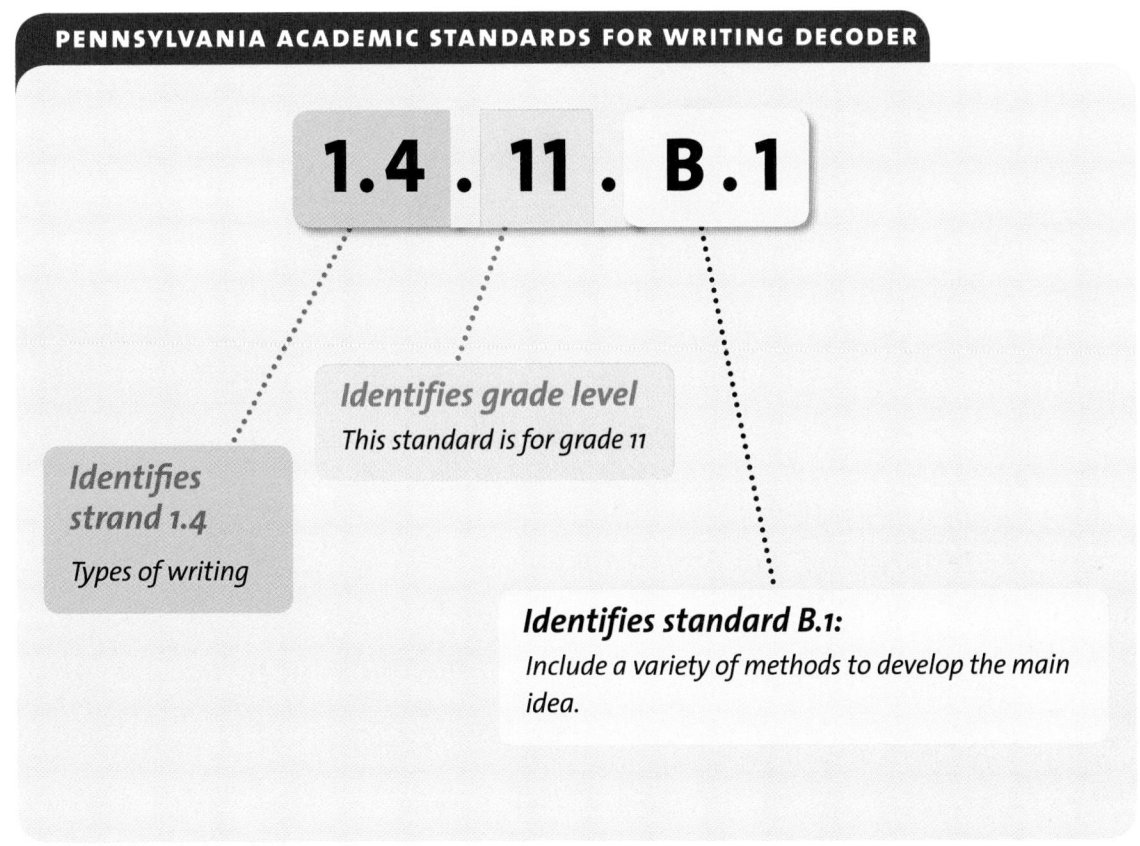

PENNSYLVANIA ACADEMIC STANDARDS FOR WRITING DECODER

1.4 . 11 . B.1

Identifies grade level
This standard is for grade 11

Identifies strand 1.4
Types of writing

Identifies standard B.1:
Include a variety of methods to develop the main idea.

The Pennsylvania Assessment Anchors for Reading are divided into two reporting categories:

A   Comprehension and Reading Skills

B   Interpretation and Analysis of Fictional and Nonfictional Text

The first reporting category is broken down into two assessment anchors:

A.1   Understand fiction appropriate to grade level.

A.2   Understand nonfiction appropriate to grade level.

The second reporting category is broken down into three assessment anchors:

B.1   Understand components within and between texts.

B.2   Understand literary devices in fictional and nonfictional text.

B.3   Understand concepts and organization of nonfictional text.

Assessment anchors describe what you must learn to master the standard. The assessment anchors are broken down into skills, and further broken down into eligible content. Pennsylvania uses a special code to identify the reporting category, the assessment anchor, the skill, and the eligible content.

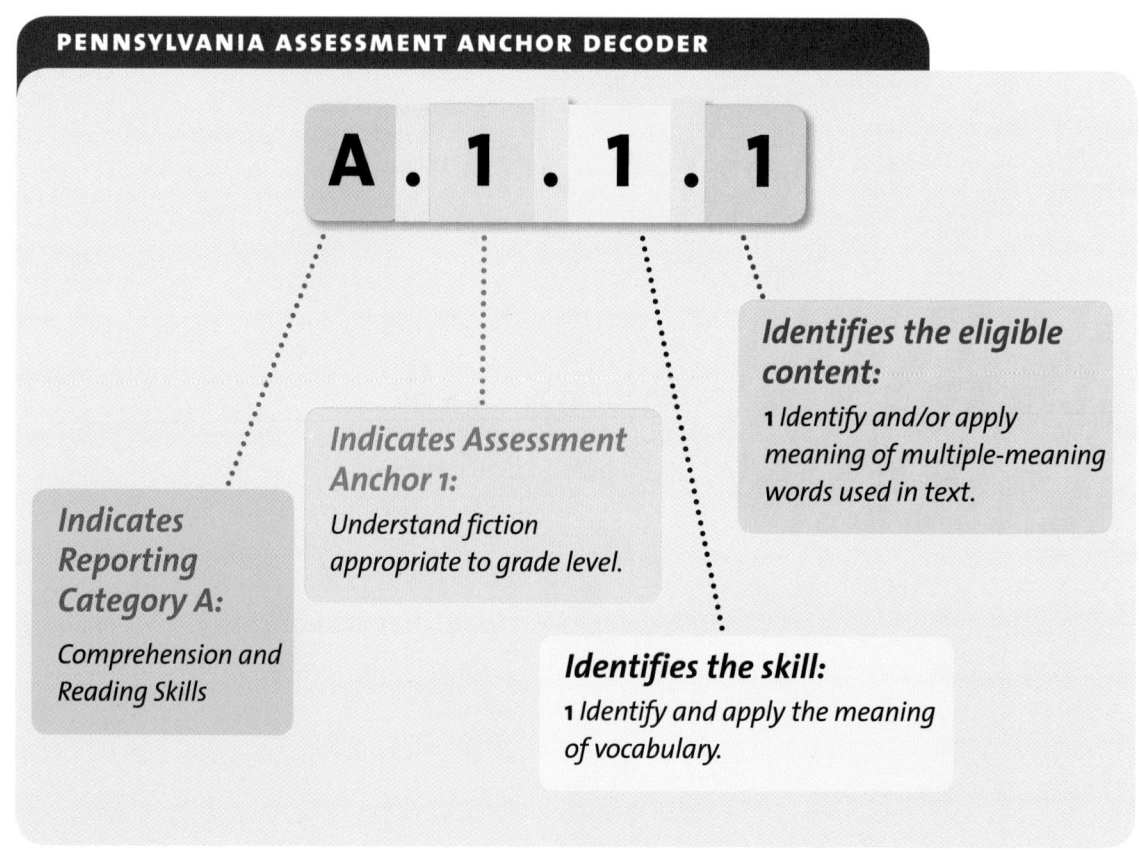

PENNSYLVANIA ASSESSMENT ANCHOR DECODER

A . 1 . 1 . 1

Identifies the eligible content:

1 *Identify and/or apply meaning of multiple-meaning words used in text.*

Indicates Assessment Anchor 1:

Understand fiction appropriate to grade level.

Indicates Reporting Category A:

Comprehension and Reading Skills

Identifies the skill:

1 *Identify and apply the meaning of vocabulary.*

Embedded Assessment Practice

Each unit has a formatted practice test that covers specific standards-based skills.

ASSESSMENT PRACTICE LOCATOR

UNIT 1 pg 176
Narrative Structure

- Plot Stages
- Conflict
- Sequence
- Predict
- Cause and Effect
- Synonyms and Antonyms
- Latin Word Roots
- Modifiers
- Precise and Strong Verbs

UNIT 2 pg 292
Characterization and Point of View

- Character Traits
- Character Motivation
- Point of View
- Draw Conclusions
- Make Inferences
- Monitor
- Multiple-Meaning Words
- Word Origins
- Supporting and Descriptive Details
- Words, Phrases, Clauses

UNIT 3 pg 392
Setting, Mood, and Imagery

- Setting
- Mood
- Imagery
- Analyze Details
- Make Inferences
- Paraphrase
- Connotation and Denotation
- Context Clues
- Present Tense
- Compound Predicates

UNIT 4 pg 498
Theme and Symbol

- Theme
- Symbol
- Make Inferences
- Draw Conclusions
- Context Clues
- Suffixes
- Independent and Subordinate Clauses

UNIT 5 pg 584
Author's Purpose

- Author's Purpose
- Patterns of Organization
- Text Features
- Make Inferences
- Main Ideas
- Media: Visual Information
- Word Roots
- Technical/Specialized Vocabulary
- Concrete and Abstract Nouns
- Adverbs
- Coordinating Conjunctions

UNIT 6 pg 658
Argument and Persuasion

- Elements of Argument
- Persuasive Techniques
- Rhetorical Devices
- Fact and Opinion
- Summarize Main Idea
- Specialized and Technical Vocabulary
- Dictionary
- Imperative Sentences
- Parallelism

UNIT 7 pg 734
The Language of Poetry

- Poetic Structure/Form
- Sound Devices
- Figurative Language
- Imagery
- Make Inferences
- Visualize
- Participles and Participial Phrases
- Infinitives and Infinitive Phrases

UNIT 8 pg 820
Author's Style and Voice

- Style
  - Word Choice
  - Sentence Structure
  - Tone
- Media: Visual Elements
- Homonyms
- Prefixes
- Sentence Types

UNIT 9 pg 916
History, Culture, and the Author

- Author's Background
- Historical and Cultural Context
- Draw Conclusions
- Synthesize
- Multiple Sources
- Idioms
- Greek and Latin Roots
- Gerunds and Gerund Phrases
- Vivid Verbs
- Coordinating Conjunctions

UNIT 10 pg 1078
The Tragedy of Romeo and Juliet

- Characteristics of Tragedy
  - Conflict
  - Character Motivation
  - Character Foil
  - Tragic Hero
- Shakespearean Language
  - Blank Verse
  - Word Play
- Paraphrase
- Parallelism

UNIT 11 pg 1178
The Odyssey

- Characteristics of an Epic
  - Setting
  - Conflict
  - Theme
  - Epic Hero
- Summarize
- Prefixes
- Latin Roots
- Figurative Language

UNIT 12 pg 1188
The Power of Research

Research Strategies pg 1188
Writing a Research Paper pg 1210

Preparing for the PSSA

What is the PSSA?

PSSA stands for the Pennsylvania System of School Assessment. All grade 11 students take the PSSA Reading Assessment and Writing Assessment. The PSSA Reading Assessment measures your understanding of the Pennsylvania Assessment Anchors for Reading. The PSSA Writing Assessment measures your understanding of the Pennsylvania Academic Standards for Writing. The PSSA consists of multiple-choice and open-ended items, as well as writing prompts for essay questions.

How can I be successful on the PSSA?

You can use the passages and questions on the following pages to prepare for the PSSA. This section will familiarize you with the format of test items. The tips and strategies in blue will guide you through reading the passages and answering the questions.

- Read the passages carefully, as well as the tips in the margins. The tips help you to focus on important points in the reading so that you will be better prepared to answer the questions that follow.

As you read, pay special attention to grammar, punctuation, and sentence structure, and keep an eye out for misspelled words or incorrect punctuation.

You may be tempted to read this passage quickly, skimming for errors in mechanics. Don't make this mistake. Pay attention to the overall message of the passage, and consider

Earth's System

1 A terrarium is a simple example of a system: an organized group of parts that work together to form a whole. **2** To understand a system, you need to see how all its parts work together. **3** This principle is true for a small terrarium, and it is true for planet Earth.

4 Both a terrarium and Earth are closed systems. **5** They are closed because matter such as soil or water cannot enter or leave. **6** However, energy can flow into or out of the system. **7** Just as light and heat pass through the glass of the terrarium, sunlight and heat enter and leave the Earth system through the atmosphere.

8 Within the Earth system are four connected parts: the atmosphere (Earth's air), the hydrosphere (Earth's waters), the biosphere (Earth's living things), and the geosphere (Earth's interior and its rocks and soils). **9** Each of these parts is an open system _____ both matter and energy move into and out of it. **10** The four open systems work together to form one large, closed

- Each question tests a particular standard or anchor. There are also strategies for answering the types of questions you will encounter on the PSSA.

1. **In a final revision, which title would better introduce the passage?**
   A Earth Is a Terrarium
   B The Open Systems of Earth
   C How Earth Is a Closed System
   D The Four Systems of Earth

Standard 1.5.11.E: Revise writing to improve style, word choice, sentence variety and subtlety of meaning after rethinking how questions of purpose, audience and genre have been addressed.

Strategy: Questions like this one remind you to proofread passages for content as well as errors in spelling and punctuation. You must understand what the passage is about to answer this question correctly. *C* is the best answer choice because it gives the passage a title that explains what is to come: an explanation of how Earth is a closed system. *A* only addresses a small detail of the passage—that Earth is like a terrarium. *B* and *D* indicate that the individual open systems of Earth are the most important parts of the passage, but they miss the larger message and should be eliminated.

PSSA Strategies and Preparation

The following section introduces you to how the Pennsylvania System of School Assessment (PSSA) will look and what kinds of items you may encounter on the Writing and Reading assessments. Look for tips and strategies in blue boxes throughout this section.

WRITING
INFORMATIONAL WRITING PROMPT

You will have up to 60 minutes to <u>plan</u>, <u>write</u>, and <u>proofread</u> your response to this writing prompt:

> **Failure is the condiment that gives success its flavor. —Truman Capote**
>
> **How does failure flavor success? Write an essay that explains your understanding of this quotation.**

Plan

Before you write:

- Read the prompt carefully so you understand exactly what you are being asked to do.
- Consider the topic, task, and audience.
- Think about what you want to write.
- Organize your thoughts on another piece of paper. Use strategies like mapping or outlining.

Write

As you write:

- Maintain a clear and consistent focus.
- Include specific details; use examples and reasons to support your ideas.
- Use a variety of well-constructed, complete sentences.
- Use a logical organization with an obvious introduction, body, and conclusion.

Proofread

After you write:

- Did you support your ideas with specific details?
- Do the point of view and tone of the essay remain consistent?
- Check for capitalization, spelling, sentence structure, punctuation, and usage errors.

Strategy:
To begin, concentrate on reading the directions and understanding what you need to do. Read the instructions about planning, writing, and proofreading first. Understand what you're being asked to do before you try to understand what you have to write about. Then read the prompt carefully. Ask yourself what the subject of the quote is: failure, but failure seen positively; failure as something that will prove useful (or flavorful) later. Have you ever failed in anything? How did that failure make your next success seem?

The PSSA Informational Scoring Guideline is a rubric that provides a way to evaluate your composition. The rubric outlines the level to which your writing demonstrates your ability to develop ideas, organize information logically, make appropriate word choices, and exhibit a unique style.

The PSSA Conventions Scoring Guideline on the next page outlines the level to which your writing demonstrates a mastery of grammar, usage, and mechanics. Your writing will be compared to both rubrics and scored appropriately.

Writing
PSSA INFORMATIONAL SCORING GUIDELINE

4	Focus	Sharp, distinct controlling point made about a single topic with evident awareness of task and audience.
	Content Development	Substantial, relevant, and illustrative content that demonstrates a clear understanding of the purpose. Thorough elaboration with effectively presented information consistently supported with well-chosen details.
	Organization	Effective organizational strategies and structures, such as logical order and transitions, which develop a controlling idea.
	Style	Precise control of language, stylistic techniques, and sentence structures that creates a consistent and effective tone.
3	Focus	Clear controlling point made about a single topic with general awareness of task and audience.
	Content Development	Adequate, specific, and/or illustrative content that demonstrates an understanding of the purpose. Sufficient elaboration with clearly presented information supported with well-chosen details.
	Organization	Organizational strategies and structures, such as logical order and transitions, which develop a controlling idea.
	Style	Appropriate control of language, stylistic techniques, and sentence structures that creates a consistent tone.
2	Focus	Vague evidence of a controlling point made about a single topic with an inconsistent awareness of task and audience.
	Content Development	Inadequate, vague content that demonstrates a weak understanding of the purpose. Underdeveloped and/or repetitive elaboration with inconsistently supported information. May be an extended list.
	Organization	Inconsistent organizational strategies and structures, such as logical order and transitions, which ineffectively develop a controlling idea.
	Style	Limited control of language and sentence structures that creates interference with tone.
1	Focus	Little or no evidence of a controlling point made about a single topic with minimal awareness of task and audience.
	Content Development	Minimal evidence of content that demonstrates a lack of understanding of the purpose. Superficial, undeveloped writing with little or no support. May be a bare list.
	Organization	Little or no evidence of organizational strategies and structures, such as logical order and transitions, which inadequately develop a controlling idea.
	Style	Minimal control of language and sentence structures that creates an inconsistent tone.

Writing
PSSA CONVENTIONS SCORING GUIDELINE

4	Thorough control of sentence formation. Few errors, if any, are present in grammar, usage, spelling, and punctuation, but the errors that are present do not interfere with meaning.
3	Adequate control of sentence formation. Some errors may be present in grammar, usage, spelling, and punctuation, but few, if any, of the errors that are present may interfere with meaning.
2	Limited and/or inconsistent control of sentence formation. Some sentences may be awkward or fragmented. Many errors may be present in grammar, usage, spelling, and punctuation, and some of those errors may interfere with meaning.
1	Minimal control of sentence formation. Many sentences are awkward and fragmented. Many errors may be present in grammar, usage, spelling, and punctuation, and many of those errors may interfere with meaning.

Passage 1

Read the passage below and then answer questions 1–3.

As you read, pay special attention to grammar, punctuation, and sentence structure, and keep an eye out for misspelled words or incorrect punctuation.

You may be tempted to read this passage quickly, skimming for errors in mechanics. Don't make this mistake. Pay attention to the overall message of the passage, and consider what other details might be included to make the argument stronger.

Earth's System

1 A terrarium is a simple example of a system: an organized group of parts that work together to form a whole. **2** To understand a system, you need to see how all its parts work together. **3** This principle is true for a small terrarium, and it is true for planet Earth.

4 Both a terrarium and Earth are closed systems. **5** They are closed because matter such as soil or water cannot enter or leave. **6** However, energy can flow into or out of the system. **7** Just as light and heat pass through the glass of the terrarium, sunlight and heat enter and leave the Earth system through the atmosphere.

8 Within the Earth system are four connected parts: the atmosphere (Earth's air), the hydrosphere (Earth's waters), the biosphere (Earth's living things), and the geosphere (Earth's interior and its rocks and soils). **9** Each of these parts is an open system _____ both matter and energy move into and out of it. **10** The four open systems work together to form one large, closed system called Earth.

1. **In a final revision, which title would better introduce the passage?**
   A   Earth Is a Terrarium
   B   The Open Systems of Earth
   C   How Earth Is a Closed System
   D   The Four Systems of Earth

Standard 1.5.11.E: Revise writing to improve style, word choice, sentence variety and subtlety of meaning after rethinking how questions of purpose, audience and genre have been addressed.

Strategy: Questions like this one remind you to proofread passages for content as well as errors in spelling and punctuation. You must understand what the passage is about to answer this question correctly. *C* is the best answer choice because it gives the passage a title that explains what is to come: an explanation of how Earth is a closed system. *A* only addresses a small detail of the passage—that Earth is like a terrarium. *B* and *D* indicate that the individual open systems of Earth are the most important parts of the passage, but they miss the larger message and should be eliminated.

2. **Which revision of sentence 5 is punctuated correctly?**

   A They are closed because matter, such as soil or water cannot enter or leave.

   B They are closed, because matter such as, soil or water cannot enter or leave.

   C They are closed because matter, such as soil or water, cannot enter or leave.

   D They are closed because matter such as soil or water, cannot enter or leave.

Standard 1.5.11.F.3: Punctuate correctly (periods, exclamation points, question marks, commas, quotation marks, apostrophes, colons, semicolons, parentheses, hyphens, brackets, ellipses).

Strategy: This is a complex sentence with a subordinate clause in the middle. In order for it to be correctly punctuated, commas must separate the subordinate clause from the rest of the sentence. *A* and *D* can be eliminated because they only contain the addition of one comma, so the subordinate clause is not completely separated from the rest of the sentence. *B* places the commas incorrectly. Remember that a complex sentence must make sense even if the subordinate clause is removed completely. *C* is correct.

3. **Which word best completes sentence 9?**

   A although

   B however

   C because

   D consequently

Standard 1.5.11.E: Revise writing to improve style, word choice, sentence variety and subtlety of meaning after rethinking how questions of purpose, audience and genre have been addressed.

Strategy: To best answer this question, first make sure you know what the paragraph is addressing. Then place each of the answer choices in the blank space and read the sentence again. Only one answer choice will make sense in the context of the paragraph. *A* may seem tempting, though if you read sentences 8 and 10 you'll soon realize that it doesn't make sense. *B* can be eliminated because it would create a meaningless sentence. *D* would also create a sentence without meaning. Only *C* makes sense in the sentence and in the context of the paragraph.

Passage 2

Read the passage below and then answer questions 4–6.

As you read this passage, ask yourself if the sentences are as clear as they could be. While you may be reading all the information you need to get the point, is that information effectively composed? If you were writing this passage, would you write it this way?

Anastasia

1 About a hundred years ago, a young girl named Anastasia appeared to be leading a charmed life. **2** Her father, Nicholas II, was the czar of Russia. **3** Anastasia lived in a palace with her mother, three older sisters, and a younger brother named Alexis. ▶ **4** Only the health problems of Alexis spoil their perfect world. **5** A blood disease that caused internal bleeding and sometimes left him crippled with pain, the young heir to the throne suffered from hemophilia.

6 But otherwise, Anastasia's family enjoyed the many pleasures their priviledged life offered. **7** Each summer, for example, they spent several weeks cruising on their huge yacht. **8** Aboard this luxury liner, Anastasia's family was attended by their regular servants, the ship's officers and crew, a platoon of marine guards, a brass band, and a balalaika orchestra. ▶ **9** In the eventing Anastasia and her older sisters danced and flirted with the ship's handsome young officers.

While there is nothing obviously wrong with this sentence, it could be constructed better. Read it again and imagine how you would rewrite it. What punctuation does it need to make its meaning clearer?

4. **In sentence 4, which form of the verb <u>spoil</u> is correct?**
    A spoiling
    B would spoil
    C have spoiled
    D spoiled

Standard 1.5.11.F.4: Use nouns, pronouns, verbs, adjectives, adverbs, conjunctions, prepositions and interjections properly.

Strategy: This passage is entirely in the past tense, so this verb should be as well. *A* and *B* are not correct, as they are not the past tense. The best answer choice is the simple past tense, *D*, which makes the sentence parallel to the other sentences in the passage.

5. **Which version best rewrites sentence 5 without losing or changing its meaning?**

   A The young heir to the throne suffered from hemophilia, a blood disease that caused internal bleeding and sometimes left him crippled with pain.

   B Hemophilia is a blood disease that caused internal bleeding and sometimes left him crippled with pain.

   C The young heir to the throne, Alexis, suffered from hemophilia.

   D Alexis, the heir to the throne, was often in pain from his blood disease that caused internal bleeding.

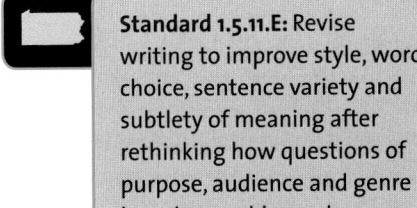

Standard 1.5.11.E: Revise writing to improve style, word choice, sentence variety and subtlety of meaning after rethinking how questions of purpose, audience and genre have been addressed.

Strategy: Sentence 5 might have struck you as awkward when you were first reading the passage. To answer this question, ask yourself which answer is more direct and clear in meaning. *D* can be crossed off because it is almost as awkward as the original. *B* and *C* are clearer, but now ask yourself if they contain all the same information as the original sentence. They do not, so they are not the best answer choices. *A* is the best revision, as it is more direct and contains all the necessary information from the original sentence.

6. **Which word is misspelled?**

   A <u>appeared</u> in sentence 1

   B <u>disease</u> in sentence 5

   C <u>priviledged</u> in sentence 6

   D <u>luxury</u> in sentence 8

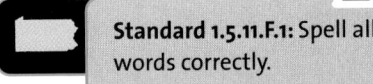

Standard 1.5.11.F.1: Spell all words correctly.

Strategy: You don't need to read the passage or understand its contents to answer this question correctly. You simply need to know how to spell the words in these answer choices. Don't waste time checking to see if the words are spelled in the passage the way they are here. Review the rules you know about spelling and choose the misspelled word from the answer choices. *A*, *B*, and *D* are all spelled correctly, but *C* is not. The correct spelling is privileged.

Read the passage below and then answer questions 7–11.

Remember to consider the passage content; don't just read it looking for errors in punctuation and spelling.

▶ Padre Hidalgo: A Cry for Freedom

▶ **1** Like much of Latin America in the early 1800s, Mexico was under Spanish rule—which meant that only those born in Spain could hold positions of power. **2** Padre Hidalgo wasn't born in Spain, but his parents were of Spanish descent, so he held a relatively high position in Mexican society. **3** The Indians who made up most of Hidalgo's parish were at the bottom of society. **4** They were treated harshly by the Spanish rulers and forced to pay a heavy tax. **5** Those who could not pay were imprisoned. **6** Unlike most other well-born people, Hidalgo cared about the Indians in Mexico. **7** He welcomed them into his home and helped them learn useful trades. **8** Still, Padre Hidalgo wanted to do more to improve the Indian's condition. **9** He believed in the ideals of freedom and equality that had emerged from the earlier american and French revolutions.

These words could be shortened into a contraction. Consider if you would use the contraction in this essay, and why. Some writers believe that a formal essay should never use contractions. However, they are generally acceptable if used sparingly.

Always pay attention to signal words such as *Unlike* or *However*.

7. **Which word uses capitalization incorrectly?**
   A <u>Indians</u> in sentence 3
   B <u>Padre</u> in sentence 8
   C <u>american</u> in sentence 9
   D <u>French</u> in sentence 9

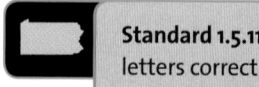

Standard 1.5.11.F.2: Use capital letters correctly.

Strategy: In order to answer this question, you must return to each sentence and check to see if all proper nouns mentioned in the answer choices are capitalized as they should be. *Indians* is a proper noun and is capitalized in sentence 3, so you may cross off *A*. *B* is not the right answer choice because *Padre* is a proper noun and should be capitalized in sentence 8. *French* and *American* are both proper nouns, but one is not capitalized in sentence 9, so the correct answer choice is *C*.

8. **Which word or phrase could replace <u>Unlike</u> in sentence 6 without changing the meaning of the sentence?**
   A Similarly
   B Because
   C As opposed to
   D For example

Standard 1.5.11.E: Revise writing to improve style, word choice, sentence variety and subtlety of meaning after rethinking how questions of purpose, audience and genre have been addressed.

Strategy: This question is basically asking for a synonym of the word *unlike*. You can eliminate *A* before rereading the sentence, as it is an antonym and therefore would certainly change the meaning of the sentence. Then replace the word *unlike* with each of the remaining answer choices to determine which one works best. *B* and *D* do not work in the sentence. *C* is a synonym for unlike and therefore is the best answer choice.

9. **Which is the correct contraction that could be used in sentence 5?**
   A couldnt'
   B couldnot
   C could'nt
   D couldn't

Standard 1.5.11.F.1: Spell all words correctly.

Strategy: Contractions place two distinct words together, normally using an apostrophe to mark the place where letters were deleted. You do not need to return to the passage to answer this question correctly; you simply need to choose the right contraction. *A*, *B*, and *C* are all incorrect. *D* is the only correct answer choice.

10. Which sentence could <u>best</u> be added to this passage?

    A This is why Padre Hidalgo is my hero.

    B Padre Hidalgo was one of the coolest guys in history.

    C I think there should be a statue of Hidalgo in Washington, D.C.

    D So he planned a revolt to win independence from Spain.

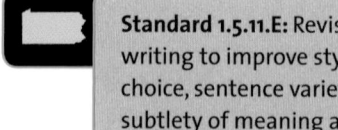

Standard 1.5.11.E: Revise writing to improve style, word choice, sentence variety and subtlety of meaning after rethinking how questions of purpose, audience, and genre have been addressed.

Strategy: To answer this question correctly, you have to consider the passage as a whole and then decide which answer choice best fits the genre and voice of the passage. The passage is not written from the first person, so the answer choices with words such as *I* or *my* should be eliminated right away. *B* can be crossed off because of the word *coolest* in the sentence. This does not fit with the tone of the rest of the passage. *D* is the best answer choice, as it matches voice and genre, as well as the subject of the piece.

11. What is the correct spelling of <u>Indian's</u> in sentence 8?

    A Indians'

    B Indians

    C Indians's

    D Okay as is

Standard 1.5.11.F.3: Punctuate correctly (periods, exclamation points, question marks, commas, quotation marks, apostrophes, colons, semicolons, parentheses, hyphens, brackets, ellipses).

Strategy: Reread sentence 8 to determine if the author is writing about one or many Indians. In this case, the author is talking about more than one. To show a possessive with more than one owner, the apostrophe is placed to the right of the *s*. Therefore, *A* is the correct answer choice.

READING

Read the passage below about Charles Dickens. Then answer questions 1–5.

Titles of passages often try to give a sense of the main idea, or theme, presented in the passage. At the end of the passage, ask yourself if this title was appropriate. Does it give a good sense of the main idea?

Charles Dickens: From Poorhouse to Mansion

The story of Charles Dickens's childhood reads like the plot of one of his novels. Forced to work at a young age, Dickens endured the long hours and unhealthy conditions common in factories in nineteenth-century England. Memories of his experiences haunted him for the rest of his life.

Dickens was born in southern England in 1812, when the Industrial Revolution in England was well underway. As thousands of factories opened for business, people left their farms for the cities. But their dreams of making more money and improving their lives didn't always come true. Men, women, and even children often exchanged back-breaking work in the fields for the boredom and danger of factory work.

Dickens's family moved to London when he was five. His father, John, worked as a clerk, so he was better off than many people in London. But with his large family and love of entertaining, he and his wife constantly lived beyond their means. When Charles was twelve, John was arrested for failing to pay a debt. He was sent to debtor's prison, where people were kept until they could pay back the money they owed.

To help support his family, Charles was taken out of school and forced to work in a shoe polish factory, wrapping and pasting labels on bottles. He worked from dawn to dark six days a week in a dirty room, listening to rats squeak beneath the rotting floorboards. His father finally inherited some money, settled his debts, and was released from jail. But Charles never forgave his parents for sending him to work at such a young age. He later claimed that the factory experience nearly destroyed him.

Pay attention to such strong language as this. What does it say about Dickens that he was unable to forgive his parents? These words send the passage in a certain direction, and you should take note of this cue.

Fortunately, Dickens overcame his unhappy childhood and became successful beyond his wildest dreams. He began his writing career as a journalist and then wrote short stories and essays. He developed a talent for writing character sketches, which eventually led to the humorous tales in his first successful novel, *The Pickwick Papers*. Other novels, like his much-loved *A Christmas Carol,* feature characters who are transformed from villains into kindly heroes. But Dickens's writing could also take a dark turn. His childhood experiences inspired novels like *Oliver Twist*, in which the young title character is abandoned and joins a gang of thieves.

In the late 1840s, Dickens began writing an actual account of his youth. But the memories were too painful, and he burned it. Instead he wrote *David Copperfield*, which blended fiction and facts from his own life. Like Dickens himself, the young David works in a factory. And a character named Micawber, a well-meaning but incompetent man who spends time in a debtor's prison, is similar to Dickens's own father.

The semiautobiographical writing helped Dickens come to grips with his past. His descriptions of working conditions also outraged his readers and helped bring about reforms in child labor and worker safety. By the time Dickens died in 1870, workers had formed unions, and Parliament had passed laws limiting child labor and the length of the workday.

Like most of his novels, Dickens's real-life story had a happy ending. When he was nine years old, Charles gazed in awe as he walked past a large mansion called Gad's Hill Place. His father told Charles that if he worked hard enough, he might live in such a house someday. For once, his father was right. Thirty-six years later, as the most successful and richest author of his generation, Dickens bought Gad's Hill Place and lived there until his death.

1. The description of the conditions under which Dickens had to work as a child shows his

   A   motivation to become successful and overcome his previous hardships.

   B   appreciation for his family and their support of his decisions.

   C   desire to write an autobiography that would clearly depict his circumstances.

   D   excitement over the purchase of Gad's Hill Place later in life.

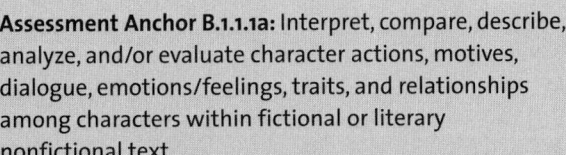

Assessment Anchor B.1.1.1a: Interpret, compare, describe, analyze, and/or evaluate character actions, motives, dialogue, emotions/feelings, traits, and relationships among characters within fictional or literary nonfictional text.

Strategy: First, read the question and each answer choice carefully, asking yourself which rings true as you do so. You will likely cross off *B* right away, as it is not an accurate statement about Dickens's feelings for his family. *C* can also be eliminated quickly, as Dickens found it too painful to write an autobiography. While *D* may seem like a strong answer choice at first, it is too specific. The description of Dickens's child labor experiences are used more broadly to describe his later motivations in general. *A* is the correct answer choice.

2. Which **best** describes Dickens's book *David Copperfield?*

   A   It is a book that accurately described Dickens's own life experiences.

   B   It is a light-hearted novel in which the villain turns kindly at the end.

   C   There is a character named Micawber who plays the part of his father.

   D   It is a combination of fiction and facts from Dickens's own life.

Assessment Anchor A.2.4.1: Identify and/or explain stated or implied main ideas and relevant supporting details from text.

Strategy: In order to analyze a supporting detail, return to the paragraph in question. You can skim the passage for the words *David Copperfield*, and then reread that paragraph. *A* is incorrect, as the paragraph states that he burned his only attempt to write an autobiography. *B* pertains to other books of his but not this one. *C* is partially correct—there is a character named Micawber, and he does share some traits with Dickens's father, but this is only a small part of the book. *D* is the correct answer choice; though Dickens included many facts about his own life in *David Copperfield*, it is still a work of fiction.

3. Why did people move from farms into the cities of England in the early 19th century?

   A They were seeking better jobs with higher pay.
   B They hoped to begin the Industrial Revolution.
   C They were tired of farm work and needed a change.
   D They hoped to find excitement and freedom in cities.

Assessment Anchor A.2.3.1: Make inferences and/or draw conclusions based on information from text.

Strategy: Rereading the second paragraph in the passage will help you answer this question correctly. It states that the Industrial Revolution was well under way in 1812, so *B* can be crossed off. While *C* and *D* could have been true in some cases, there is nothing in the text to support these conclusions. *A* is the best answer choice because the text supports this inference about the people's motivations.

4. Which would be the **best** alternate title for this passage?

   A Charles Dickens: Child Laborer
   B The Best Author of His Generation
   C Charles Dickens: Writer and Accidental Activist
   D Dickens: Son of a Debtor

Assessment Anchor A.2.5.1: Summarize the major points, processes, and/or events of a nonfictional text as a whole.

Strategy: Questions about alternate titles are really asking for a summary of the main idea of a passage. In this case, each of the answer choices provides a detail from the passage, but only one gives a fair summary of the entire passage. *C* would be the best alternate title for this passage, as it sums up the main idea. *A*, *B*, and *D* describe details, and therefore only apply to certain parts of the passage.

5. Identify at least two character traits of Charles Dickens described in the passage. Explain how each trait contributed to the fact that Dickens became a successful author in his own lifetime. Use details from the passage to support your answer.

Scoring Guide:

Score	In response to this item, the student—
3	demonstrates complete knowledge of understanding character traits by identifying two personality traits displayed by Dickens, and by explaining how each trait contributed to his success as a writer, using details from the passage.
2	demonstrates partial knowledge of understanding character traits displayed by Dickens. (Example: Student identifies two personality traits displayed by Dickens and uses an example from the passage to explain how one trait contributed to Dickens's later success.)
1	demonstrates incomplete knowledge of understanding character traits displayed by Dickens. (Example: Student identifies one personality trait displayed by Dickens and uses an example from the passage to explain how that one trait contributed to Dickens's later success.)
0	has given a response that provides insufficient material for scoring or is inaccurate in all respects.
Non-scorable	BLK—No response or written refusal to respond or response too brief to determine response OT —Off task/topic LOE—Response in a language other than English IL —Illegible

Assessment Anchor B.1.1.1.a: Interpret, compare, describe, analyze, and/or evaluate character actions, motives, dialogue, emotions/feelings, traits, and relationships among characters within fictional or literary text.

Strategy: Before you begin writing your response to this question, review the passage looking specifically for character traits. Try to ignore the other facts about Dickens and focus only on what kind of person you think he was, based on the passage. Now, write a response to the question, making sure to include two character traits. Also, don't forget to include ideas about how *each* trait contributed to the fact that he became a successful writer.

Read the closing procedures below for Uptown Music Store. Then answer questions 6–10.

Closing Procedures

Pay attention to how this passage is organized. You'll notice right away that this isn't a typical reading selection. The headers help to organize the information.

This word is in quotation marks, but the author is not denoting that someone is speaking. Think about why some words are in quotation marks and what that means about those words.

▶ **Closing Time**

The store closes at 9:00 p.m. Monday through Thursday, 11:00 p.m. on Friday and Saturday, and 7:00 p.m. on Sunday.

▶ **Security Staff**

The Security Captain should lock the front doors at the exact minute that the store closes. Security personnel will remain by the front doors to ensure that no new customers enter the store. Customers who are in line at the cash register after the doors have been locked will be politely let out of the store by Security after the purchases are completed.

Security personnel will make a "sweep" through the store, checking to ensure that no customers are in the aisles, the rest rooms, or anywhere else in the store. The Night Shift Manager will not close out the cash register until this "sweep" is done. After the Security Captain has ensured that there are no customers in the store, he or she will double-check the front doors to make sure they are locked and lower the security gate behind the front doors. The Security Captain will then turn on the electronic surveillance system for the front doors.

All other clerks and Security personnel should exit via the back door within 20 minutes of closing time. The Security Captain must remain in the store until the Night Shift Manager has finished all the closing procedures. The Security Captain and the Night Shift Manager must leave the store together, via the back door. The Security Captain will activate the electronic surveillance system for the back door as he and the Night Shift Manager exit. The Security Captain and the Night Shift Manager are *always* the last people to exit.

Cash Register Close-out

Note: The cash register should not be closed out until (a) all customers have left the store; (b) the Security staff has completed a "sweep" of the store; (c) the front doors have been locked, the security gate has been lowered, and the electronic surveillance system for the front doors has been activated; and (d) all employees—other than the Security Captain and the Night Shift Manager— have exited out the back door.

The Night Shift Manager is the only employee authorized to close out the cash register. A Night Shift Manager should never reveal his password to anyone.

To close out the cash register, enter the password for the Night Shift Manager. For security reasons, this password will be displayed on the screen as all asterisks.

Then locate the main lever on the right side of the cash register and turn it to the "Z" position. (Be sure the cash register is not in the "X" position; this is used by the Day Shift Manager only. If set in the "X" position, the cash register will only calculate transactions that took place between 10:00 a.m. and 4:30 p.m.) After the lever is set in the "Z" position, touch the CLOSE-OUT block on the computer screen. Wait for the cash register to calculate all the transactions of the day. All of the business day's transactions will be included on a multi-page printout that is called the nightly cash register receipt.

Carefully read the receipt to make sure that there is the correct two-letter code printed beside each transaction:

- "SL" should be printed beside every sale.
- "EX" should be printed beside every exchange.
- "RT" should be printed beside every return.

Count the money in the cash register drawer. Record all the amounts on the Night Shift Manager's Balance Sheet. Ensure that all the cash, coins, checks, and credit card/debit card documents are added correctly on the Balance Sheet. The amount in Line 7 of the Balance Sheet should match the amount listed as TOTAL on the nightly cash register receipt. If these two amounts match, place all the paperwork and money in the green pouch and lock it in the safe. If these two amounts do not match, please determine the reason and explain it in the DISCREPANCY section of the Balance Sheet. If you cannot determine the reason that the amounts don't match, write "Unknown Error" in the DISCREPANCY section of the Balance Sheet. Then place all the paperwork and money in the red pouch and lock it in the safe.

Ensure that the safe is locked. Exit the store with the Security Captain.

Take a minute to think about why this information is included in this passage. If the Night Shift Manager never works during the day, is this important for him or her to know? Consider why it is here and what purpose it serves in the passage.

Notice that this is the longest section of the passage. The directions are more complicated. Is this section intended for the Security staff or just for the Night Shift Manager? Think about why this information is grouped together in the same document.

6. Which is the correct definition for the word <u>sweep</u> as it is used in the passage?

    A to pass a broom over the floor in order to clean it

    B to remove soot from the inside of a chimney

    C to pass through and search a place for something

    D to win something easily and overwhelmingly

Assessment Anchor A.1.1.1: Identify and/or apply meaning of multiple-meaning words used in text.

Strategy: Don't rely on your memory of the passage to answer this question. Instead, return to the place in the passage where the word first appears and reread the paragraph. Next, eliminate all the incorrect answer choices. *A* is incorrect because security personnel are not in charge of cleaning up. *B* is incorrect because it refers only to the job of cleaning a chimney, which is not mentioned in this passage. *D* is incorrect because this passage is not about winning or losing anything. *C* is the correct answer choice, as it describes what the Security Captain should do at closing time.

7. The purpose of the boldfaced headers before each paragraph is to

    A organize the text into sections based on each section's intended audience.

    B alert the reader about closing times, personnel, and procedures.

    C explain which procedures need to happen before final close-out.

    D describe how the Night Shift Manager should cash out the register.

Assessment Anchor B.3.3.2: Interpret and/or analyze the author's purpose for decisions about text organization and content.

Strategy: To answer this question correctly, you must have already read the passage once. Now, return to the passage and read only the headers. Put yourself in the shoes of the people mentioned in the passage. If you were the Night Shift Manager, which sections would you read most closely? *A* best answers this question, as it explains the purpose of the headers. *B* is a good description of the main idea of the passage but does not explain the purpose of the headers. *C* and *D* are both details from the passage but do not explain the purpose of the headers.

8. Which statement from the passage best supports the idea that the Night Shift Manager is responsible for the accuracy of the cash close-out?

A "If set in the 'X' position, the cash register will only calculate transactions that took place between 10:00 a.m. and 4:30 p.m."

B "All of the business day's transactions will be included on a multi-page printout that is called the nightly cash register receipt."

C "Carefully read the receipt to make sure that there is the correct two-letter code printed beside each transaction."

D "Ensure that all the cash, coins, checks, and credit card/debit card documents are added correctly on the Balance Sheet."

Assessment Anchor A.2.3.2: Cite evidence from the text to support generalizations.

Strategy: The question states a generalization: The manager is responsible for the accuracy of the close-out. Assume that this generalization is true, and read each answer choice carefully to find out which one supports the generalization. Don't waste time returning to the passage for this type of question: everything you need to answer it is right here. *A, B,* and *C* all provide steps to the manager's process, but do not speak to the fact that this process must be accurate. *D* does, and therefore is the correct answer choice.

9. What is the main idea of the section titled "Security Staff"?

A Security personnel are responsible for the safe closing of the Uptown Music Store.

B Security personnel should exit the back door exactly 20 minutes after closing time.

C Security personnel and the Night Shift Manager must always be the last people to exit the store.

D Security personnel should lock the front doors even if there are people still in line at closing time.

Assessment Anchor A.2.4.1: Identify and/or explain stated or implied main ideas and relevant supporting details from text.

Strategy: As with questions about the main idea of entire passages, you need to distinguish between details from the paragraph and the main idea of the paragraph as a whole. *B, C,* and *D* are all supporting details from the paragraph. They all support the main idea that, as *A* states, security personnel are responsible for the closing of the store.

10. How would the Day Shift Manager close out his or her shift? Explain at least two steps he or she would need to take. Use details from the passage to support your answer.

Scoring Guide:

Score	In response to this item, the student—
3	demonstrates complete knowledge of drawing conclusions about the steps the Day Shift Manager would need to take to close out, based on the steps taken by the Night Shift Manager and details from the passage.
2	demonstrates partial knowledge of drawing conclusions about the steps the Day Shift Manager would need to take to close out. (Example: Student identifies two steps but only provides support for one of them.)
1	demonstrates incomplete knowledge of drawing conclusions about the steps the Day Shift Manager would need to take to close out. (Example: Student identifies one step and only provides support for that one.)
0	has given a response that provides insufficient material for scoring or is inaccurate in all respects.
Non-scorable	BLK—No response or written refusal to respond or response too brief to determine response OT —Off task/topic LOE—Response in a language other than English IL —Illegible

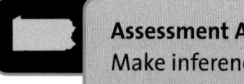

Assessment Anchor A.2.3.1: Make inferences and/or draw conclusions based on information from text.

Strategy: Before you begin writing your response to this question, review the steps to closing out and what the Night Shift Manager has to do. Now imagine how that would be different if the store were going to stay open for several more hours. Write a response to the question, making sure to include at least two steps.

The Power of Ideas

INTRODUCING THE ESSENTIALS

- **Literary Genres Workshop**
- **Reading Strategies Workshop**
- **Writing Process Workshop**

What Are Life's Big Questions?

Love and hate, freedom and responsibility, growing up and growing old—these emotions and experiences touch us all, and they are at the heart of the big questions that we ask about the world. This book is all about big questions like the ones shown here. Even though they are challenging to answer, such questions prompt us to think about key ideas that affect our lives. Through reading, discussing, and writing about literature, we can unlock the power of these ideas and come closer to understanding ourselves and the world.

How powerful is LOVE?

In the name of love, Romeo and Juliet risk everything to be together. Similarly, love drives a young wife in O. Henry's "The Gift of the Magi" to chop off her hair. Love is a powerful force, but is it strong enough to overcome all obstacles? You will read works by such writers as William Shakespeare, O. Henry, and Julia Alvarez that explore this age-old question.

What makes a HERO?

In Homer's epic the *Odyssey,* the hero bravely battles dangerous monsters. In 1955, Rosa Parks refused to give up her bus seat to a white passenger. As a young girl, Maya Angelou admired a more personal hero—the neighborhood woman who introduced her to the power of literature. We can find heroes in ancient stories, recent history, today's movies, and our own lives. What extraordinary qualities set heroes apart?

Does good always TRIUMPH?

In Hollywood movies like *The Lord of the Rings,* we expect satisfying endings—ones in which good characters prevail and evil forces are defeated. Literature, like real life, does not always have happily-ever-after endings. Read Edgar Allan Poe's classic spine tingler "The Cask of Amontillado" or Liam O'Flaherty's eye-opening story "The Sniper." Then ask yourself: Does good always triumph?

What is FAMILY?

Family can mean different things to different people. Relatives, friends, neighbors, and people who share similar cultural and religious backgrounds all can be considered family. You'll explore this idea further in Naomi Shihab Nye's "Hamadi" and in the ripped-from-the-headlines article "The Lost Boys."

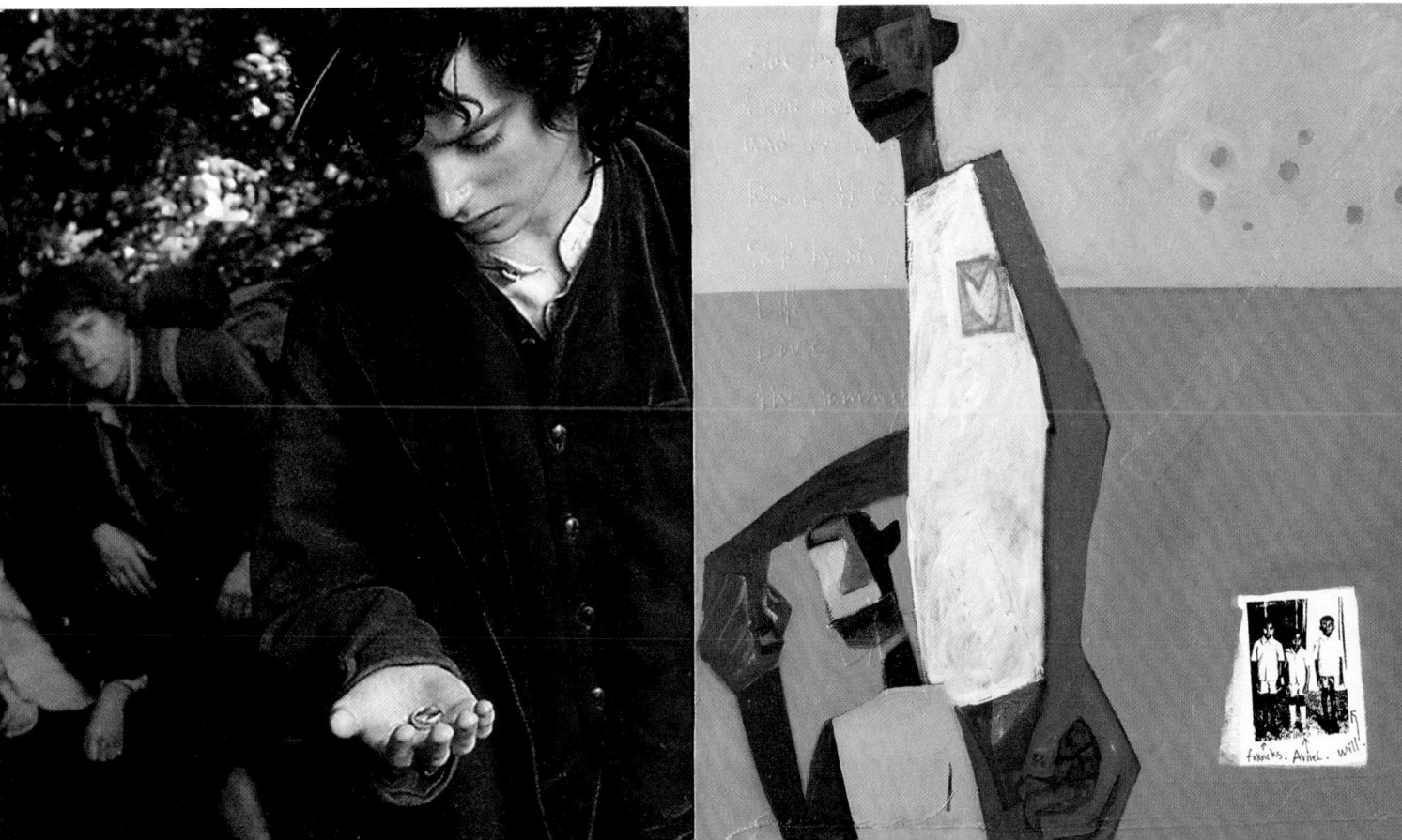

Exploring Ideas in Literature

At some point in your life, you have probably considered big questions and ideas like the ones on the preceding pages. For thousands of years, writers have also asked these questions, trying to make sense of the world around them. Many have left a written record of their lives and ideas: literature. Literature is writing that is worth reading, considering, and remembering, for both its ideas and the forms those ideas take.

The Genres

Literature encompasses a wide range of genres. Some are meant to be read; others are meant to be performed by actors on a stage. Media such as feature films are not technically literature, but they are similarly important to learn about today. Regardless of the genre, good literature allows readers to grapple with timeless questions and connect to other times and cultures.

In this book, you will explore questions and ideas in many genres. An ancient story, a news article, and a poem—despite their differences in form—can all help you explore a key idea, such as love or heroism. Before delving into the ideas in literature, familiarize yourself with the genres.

PENNSYLVANIA STANDARDS

READING STANDARDS
A.1.6 Identify, describe, and analyze genre (fiction)
A.2.6 Identify, describe, and analyze genre (nonfiction)
B.1.2.1 Interpret and evaluate connections between texts

GENRES AT A GLANCE

FICTION
Fiction is narrative writing that springs from an author's imagination.
• short stories   • novels   • novellas

POETRY
Poetry is the most compact form of literature. Words are chosen and arranged to create powerful effects.
• haiku   • sonnets   • narrative poems   • lyric poems

DRAMA
Drama is meant to be performed. Characters and conflicts are developed through dialogue and action.
• comedies   • tragedies   • farces

NONFICTION
Nonfiction is prose writing that deals with real people, events, and places.
• essays   • autobiographies   • news articles
• speeches   • biographies   • feature articles

TYPES OF MEDIA

Media are forms of communication that reach large numbers of people. They include many subgenres, each with its own forms and characteristics.
• feature films   • advertising   • Web sites

FICTION

At the heart of fiction is **narrative,** the telling of a story. Although fiction can be inspired by real events and people, it is mainly the product of a writer's imagination. A fiction writer shapes his or her narrative to capture and hold readers' interest, often creating memorable settings and characters who face challenging conflicts. Fictional stories can take any of a wide variety of forms, including science fiction, mystery, romance, and historical fiction. Regardless of the form, a work of fiction usually is one of three types.

- A **short story** often focuses on a single event or incident and usually can be read in one sitting.

- A **novel** is an extended work of fiction. Because it is much longer than a short story, a novel gives a writer space to develop a wider range of characters and a more complex plot.

- A **novella** is longer than a short story but shorter than a novel. Most novellas focus on a limited number of characters and a short time span.

Read the Model This excerpt is taken from a novella about an old Cuban fisherman named Santiago. After more than three months at sea, Santiago finally hooks a giant marlin. Can the old man muster enough strength to reel in the fish as it circles his boat? As you read, notice the elements of fiction that the author uses to hook readers and to explore the **key idea** of strength.

ACADEMIC VOCABULARY FOR FICTION
- plot
- conflict
- character
- setting
- theme
- narrator
- point of view

from

THE *Old Man* AND THE *Sea*

Novella by **Ernest Hemingway**

The fish was coming in on his circle now calm and beautiful looking and only his great tail moving. The old man pulled on him all that he could to bring him closer. For just a moment the fish turned a little on his side. Then he straightened himself and began another circle.

5 "I moved him," the old man said. "I moved him then."

He felt faint again now but he held on the great fish all the strain that he could. I moved him, he thought. Maybe this time I can get him over. Pull, hands, he thought. Hold up, legs. Last for me, head. Last for me. You never went. This time I'll pull him over.

10 But when he put all of his effort on, starting it well out before the fish came alongside and pulling with all his strength, the fish pulled part way over and then righted himself and swam away.

"Fish," the old man said. "Fish, you are going to have to die anyway. Do you have to kill me too?"

Close Read

1. Using terms from the Academic Vocabulary list, describe what is happening in this work of fiction.

2. **Key Idea: Strength** The old man's strength comes from his relentless will to catch the fish. In your opinion, what gives someone **strength?**

POETRY

The poet Robert Frost once wrote, "Poetry is a way of taking life by the throat." These words capture the impact of poetry on both writers and readers. In poetry, words and sounds are chosen to convey meaning and emotion.

What you'll most likely notice first about a poem is its **form,** or arrangement on the page. Usually, poems are divided into **lines,** which are arranged into groups called **stanzas.** While some poets follow fixed rules of form, others break with convention and invent unique forms to echo their subjects.

If you have ever read a poem aloud, you know that its impact depends on more than its form. The way a poem sounds—its brash **rhythms** or its predictable **rhymes,** for example—is part of its effect. Language delivers other powerful effects. **Imagery,** which consists of language that recreates sensory experiences, helps readers see, hear, and feel what a poem describes.

Read the Model Here, the love of an older couple—*los ancianos,* in Spanish—is described in striking detail. As you read, notice the poetic elements that help to paint a moving portrait of the couple. Also, consider what the poet is saying about the **key idea** of love.

ACADEMIC
VOCABULARY
FOR POETRY

• form
• line
• stanza
• speaker
• rhyme
• rhythm
• meter
• sound devices
• figurative language
• imagery

Los ancianos

Poem by **Pat Mora**

> They hold hands
> as they walk with slow steps.
> Careful together they cross the plaza
> both slightly stooped, bodies returning to the land,
> 5 he in faded khaki and straw hat,
> she wrapped in soft clothes, black
> *rebozo*[1] round her head and shoulders.
>
> Tourists in halter tops and shorts
> pose by flame trees and fountains,
> 10 but the old couple walks step by step
> on the edge.
> Even in the heat, only their wrinkled
> hands and faces show. They know
> of moving through a crowd at their own pace.
>
> 15 I watch him help her
> off the curb and I smell love
> like dried flowers, old love
> of holding hands with one man for fifty years.

---

1. *rebozo* (rĭ-bō′sō) *Spanish:* shawl.

Close Read

1. What characteristics immediately signal that this is a poem? Cite specific details.

2. **Key Idea: Love** The couple in this poem seem compatible and comfortable with each other. What other qualities of a relationship are essential for **love** to last over the years?

DRAMA

Characters in conflict are at the heart of drama, just as they are in fiction. But since drama is meant to be performed for an audience rather than read, the plot is carried by **dialogue** and **action**—what the characters say and do. Dramas are usually divided into **scenes,** with each scene set in a different time or place. In long plays, scenes are grouped into **acts.**

With their heroes, villains, and sets, dramas have been captivating audiences since ancient times. However, dramas also make good reading. To help yourself visualize a drama, you need to consider not only the dialogue but also the **stage directions**—the writer's instructions for the actors, the director, and the other people working on the play. Often printed in italic type, stage directions describe everything from the setting and the props to the characters' movements.

Read the Model *The Miracle Worker* dramatizes Helen Keller's relationship with Annie Sullivan, the teacher who taught Helen to use sign language and communicate with others. At this point in the drama, Helen has learned the mechanics of sign language, but she still does not understand the meanings behind the words. Here, Annie expresses her frustration to Helen's mother, Kate. How does Annie's attitude help you understand the **key idea** of determination?

ACADEMIC
VOCABULARY
FOR DRAMA

- plot
- character
- act
- scene
- stage
  directions
- monologue
- dialogue
- dialect

---

from

The Miracle Worker

Drama by **William Gibson**

from Act Three

Annie. . . . We're born to use words, like wings, it has to come.

Kate. How?

Annie (*another pause, wearily*). All right. I don't know how.
(*She pushes up her glasses to rub her eyes.*)

5 I've done everything I could think of. Whatever she's learned here—keeping herself clean, knitting, stringing beads, meals, setting-up exercises each morning, we climb trees, hunt eggs, yesterday a chick was born in her hands—all of it I spell, everything we do, we never stop spelling. I go to bed with—writer's cramp from talking so much!

10 **Kate.** I worry about you, Miss Annie. You must rest.

Annie. Now? She spells back in her *sleep,* her fingers make letters when she doesn't know! In her bones those five fingers know, that hand aches to—speak out, and something in her mind is asleep, how do I—nudge that awake? That's the one question.

Close Read

1. How do you know that Annie is exhausted? Cite specific details that reveal her state of mind.

2. **Key Idea: Determination** How do you think Annie's **determination** will eventually play out? Explain whether you think people can accomplish anything if they are determined enough.

NONFICTION AND INFORMATIONAL TEXT

When you see the word *nonfiction*—especially in a literature book— you probably expect to find what is considered **literary nonfiction,** such as biographies, speeches, and essays. Nonfiction also includes **informational texts,** such as news articles and train schedules, which provide factual information. Because you encounter informational texts all the time, you should know what to expect from them.

TYPE OF NONFICTION	CHARACTERISTICS	
AUTOBIOGRAPHY/ BIOGRAPHY The true story of a person's life, told by that person (autobiography) or by another person (biography)	• Provides details that give readers insights into a person's life • Is told from the first-person point of view (autobiography) or from the third-person point of view (biography) • Presents the person's own thoughts about his or her life experiences (autobiography) or information from a variety of sources (biography)	
ESSAY A short work that focuses on a single subject. Common types include personal essays and persuasive essays.	• May have the following purposes: to express feelings, to inform, to entertain, to persuade • May be **formal,** with an organized structure and an impersonal style • May be **informal,** with a conversational style	
SPEECH An oral presentation of the ideas, beliefs, or proposals of a speaker	• May have the following purposes: to express feelings, to inform, to entertain, to persuade • Achieves its power through effective language and a compelling delivery	
NEWS/FEATURE ARTICLES Informative writing in newspapers and magazines. A news article reports on recent events. A feature article focuses on human-interest topics.	• Are primarily intended to inform or entertain • May use statistics, quotations from sources, examples, and graphic aids to convey information • Usually are objective and balanced	The Daily New All Nine pu alive from
FUNCTIONAL DOCUMENTS Writing that serves a practical purpose. Types include consumer documents, such as instruction manuals, and workplace documents, such as memos and résumés.	• Are written for a specific audience (for example, the user of a product or a potential employer) • May present information in charts or other easy-to-navigate formats • Often include specialized jargon	

MODEL 1: AUTOBIOGRAPHY

This excerpt is from an autobiography by Monica Sone, a Japanese-American woman who grew up in Seattle during World War II. Here, Sone remembers the moment when she and her brother Henry found out from a classmate about Japan's attack on Pearl Harbor. Notice how Sone describes her feelings, and think about the **key idea** of identity as you read this text.

from

Nisei Daughter

Autobiography by **Monica Sone**

With that, Chuck swept out of the room, a swirl of young men following in his wake. Henry was one of them. The rest of us stayed, rooted to our places like a row of marionettes. I felt as if a fist had smashed my pleasant little existence, breaking it into jigsaw puzzle pieces. An old wound opened up again,
5 and I found myself shrinking inwardly from my Japanese blood, the blood of an enemy. I knew instinctively that the fact that I was an American by birthright was not going to help me escape the consequences of this unhappy war.

Close Read

1. How does Sone react to the news about the attack on Pearl Harbor? Cite details that reveal her feelings.

2. **Key Idea: Identity** Sone feels torn between her American upbringing and her Japanese blood. In your opinion, what forces shape a person's **identity?**

MODEL 2: NEWS ARTICLE

This article can help you explore the **key idea** of war. It was published in the *New York Times* on December 8, 1941, one day after the attack on Pearl Harbor.

DECEMBER 8, 1941

JAPAN MAKES SUDDEN ATTACK

NEWS ARTICLE BY **Frank L. Kluckhohn**

WASHINGTON, Monday, Dec. 8— Sudden and unexpected attacks on Pearl Harbor, Honolulu, and other United States possessions in the
5 Pacific early yesterday by the Japanese air force and navy plunged the United States and Japan into active war.

The initial attack in Hawaii, apparently launched by torpedo-
10 carrying bombers and submarines, caused widespread damage and death.

It was quickly followed by others. There
15 were unconfirmed reports that German raiders participated in the attacks.

Guam was assaulted from the air, as were Davao, on the island of Mindanao, and Camp John Hay, in Northern Luzom, both in the Philippines. Lieut. Gen. Douglas MacArthur, commanding
20 the United States Army of the Far East, reported there was little damage, however.

Close Read

1. How do the details in this article differ from those in Sone's account? Cite evidence from both texts to support your answer.

2. **Key Idea: War** Consider other wars you've studied or read about. For what reasons do countries go to **war?**

TYPES OF MEDIA

You may not think of media as literature, but learning how to "read" the media is a key part of being literate in today's world. From screaming headlines at the checkout counter to in-your-face advertising, all media messages have been constructed for a purpose—to grab your attention, entertain you, or influence your decisions. Becoming **media literate** starts with knowing the basics and thinking critically about *all* messages in this media-saturated age.

ACADEMIC VOCABULARY FOR MEDIA

• medium
• message
• purpose
• target audience

TYPE OF MEDIA	CHARACTERISTICS	
FEATURE FILMS Motion pictures that use narrative elements to tell a story	• Are intended to entertain and make money • Use camera shots, sound effects, music, actors, and sets to tell compelling stories • Are at least 60 minutes in length	
NEWS MEDIA Accounts of current events as presented on TV, in newspapers and magazines, on the radio, and on the Web	• Are intended to inform and entertain • Have varying degrees of accuracy and credibility • Medium (TV, radio, print) affects the presentation and delivery of information	
TV SHOWS Programs broadcast on television, including dramas, sitcoms, and reality shows	• Are usually intended to inform or entertain • Are financed by sponsors who pay to air ads during the programs • Use visuals and sounds to create programming that will engage viewers • Are typically 30–60 minutes in length	
ADVERTISING A sponsor's paid use of media to promote products, services, or ideas	• Is intended to persuade a target audience to buy a product or service or to adopt an idea • Uses persuasive techniques, visuals, and sounds to appeal to an audience • Is strategically printed or aired where a target audience is likely to encounter it	
WEB SITES Collections of "pages" on the World Wide Web. From a home page, users can explore other pages on a Web site by clicking hyperlinks or menus.	• Can be accessed at any time by anyone with a computer and an Internet connection • Are not always a reliable source of information (because anyone can publish on the Web) • Present content through text, graphics, video, sound, and interactive features	

Strategies That Work: Literature

❶ Ask the Right Questions

An important part of analyzing literature is knowing what questions to ask as you read. What should you be looking for when you are reading a drama? a news article? a classic novel? The following features will help you develop your own instincts for asking the right questions.

Where to Look	What You'll Find
Literary Analysis Workshops (at the beginning of every unit)	Interactive practice models and **Close Read** questions
Side notes and discussion questions	Questions (throughout and following each selection) that focus on the analysis of literary elements and key ideas
Analysis Frames (**Literature Center** at **ClassZone.com**)	Guided questions for analyzing different genres of literature

❷ Make Connections

"I can relate to the main character because ...," "This writer's view of love is different from ..."—connections like these are what make the ideas in literature meaningful. Here are some ways to tap into the selections in this book:

- **Big Questions and Key Ideas** Life and literature are both about exploring big questions and key ideas. Look for opportunities to connect what you read with experiences in your own life.

- **Discussion/Journaling** Share your insights with others or jot them down. Consider questions such as:
  - What does this mean to me?
  - Who or what does this remind me of?

❸ Record Your Reactions

Writing down your ideas in a **Reader's Notebook** can help you both remember and sort through your reactions and observations. Try a variety of formats.

GRAPHIC ORGANIZER

Set up a graphic organizer, such as a cluster diagram.

TWO-COLUMN NOTES

Divide each page into two columns, one for quotations and information from the text, and the other for your responses.

"Los ancianos"	My Impressions
"I watch him help her off the curb and I smell love" (lines 15–16)	Shows the power of the couple's love; also conveys how moved the speaker is by this sight

Becoming an Active Reader

To really explore ideas in literature, you need to open your mind to ideas that might be different from anything you've ever imagined. Learning how to be an active reader can help you do just that. The tools you need to be an active reader are already within your grasp. In fact, you use them when you are watching TV, surfing the Web, or curled up with a suspenseful page-turner. The skills and strategies shown here are ones that you will apply throughout this book.

SKILLS AND STRATEGIES FOR ACTIVE READING

Preview
Get a sense of a text before you start to read.
- Look for clues in the title, graphics, and subheadings.
- Skim the opening paragraphs.

Set a Purpose
Decide *why* you are reading a particular text.
- Ask: Am I reading to be entertained, to get information, or for another reason?
- Consider how your purpose might affect the way you approach a text. Take notes or just enjoy?

Connect
Relate personally to what you are reading.
- Think about whether you've encountered people or situations like the ones described.
- Ask: If I were in this situation, how would I react?

Use Prior Knowledge
Call to mind what you already know about a topic.
- Before reading, jot down what you already know.
- As you read, connect what you know to what you are learning.

Predict
Try to guess what will happen next.
- Note details about plot or characters that hint at where the story is heading.
- Keep reading to find out how accurate your prediction was.

Visualize
Form a mental picture of what is being described.
- Look for descriptive details about characters, settings, and events.
- Use this information to conjure up a vivid scene in your mind's eye.

Monitor
Check your own comprehension as you read.
- **Question** what is happening and why.
- **Clarify** your understanding by rereading difficult parts or asking for help.
- **Evaluate** how well you are understanding the text.

Make Inferences
Make logical guesses, using evidence in the text and what you know from experience.
- Record details about characters and events.
- Ask: How can common sense and my own experiences help me understand this character or situation?

Details in "Walter Mitty"	What I Know	My Inference
Mitty day-dreams a lot that he's a hero.	Daydreams are a way to escape real life.	Mitty is probably not content with his real life.

In this excerpt from James Thurber's classic story, exhilirating daydreams help save Walter Mitty from his own dull existence. As you move between Mitty's imaginary adventures and his ordinary routines, use the **Close Read** questions to practice active reading skills and strategies.

from

The Secret Life of Walter Mitty

Short story by **James Thurber**

"We're going through!" The Commander's voice was like thin ice breaking. He wore his full-dress uniform, with the heavily braided white cap pulled down rakishly[1] over one cold gray eye. "We can't make it, sir. It's spoiling for a hurricane, if you ask me." "I'm not asking you, Lieutenant Berg,"
5 said the Commander. "Throw on the power lights! Rev her up to 8,500! We're going through!" The pounding of the cylinders increased: ta-pocketa-pocketa-pocketa-*pocketa-pocketa*. The Commander stared at the ice forming on the pilot window. He walked over and twisted a row of complicated dials. "Switch on No. 8 auxilary!" he shouted. "Switch on No. 8 auxilary!" repeated
10 Lieutenant Berg. "Full strength in No. 3 turret!" shouted the Commander. "Full strength in No. 3 turret!" The crew, bending to their various tasks in the huge, hurtling eight-engined Navy hydroplane, looked at each other and grinned. "The Old Man'll get us through," they said to one another. "The Old Man ain't afraid of Hell!" . . .

15 "Not so fast! You're driving too fast!" said Mrs. Mitty. "What are you driving so fast for?"

"Hmm?" said Walter Mitty. He looked at his wife, in the seat behind him, with shocked astonishment. She seemed grossly unfamiliar, like a strange woman who had yelled at him in a crowd. "You were up to fifty-five," she said.
20 "You know I don't like to go more than forty. You were up to fifty-five." Walter Mitty drove on toward Waterbury in silence, the roaring of the SN202 through the worst storm in twenty years of Navy flying fading in the remote, intimate airways of his mind. "You're tensed up again," said Mrs. Mitty. "It's one of your days. I wish you'd let Dr. Renshaw look you over."

25 Walter Mitty stopped the car in front of the building where his wife went to have her hair done. "Remember to get those overshoes while I'm having my hair done," she said. "I don't need overshoes," said Mitty. She put her mirror back into her bag. "We've been all through that," she said, getting out of the car. "You're not a young man any longer." He raced the engine a little. "Why

---

1. **rakishly:** with a confident, carefree, and dashing look.

Close Read

1. **Visualize** Which details in lines 1–14 help you picture the excitement of the scene? Cite details about the setting and the conflict.

2. **Monitor** In the boxed text, the story shifts scenes, from a thrilling adventure to an uneventful car ride. Clarify your understanding by summarizing what is happening.

30 don't you wear your gloves? Have you lost your gloves?" Walter Mitty reached
in a pocket and brought out the gloves. He put them on, but after she had
turned and gone into the building and he had driven on to a red light, he took
them off again. "Pick it up, brother!" snapped a cop as the light changed, and
Mitty hastily pulled on his gloves and lurched ahead. He drove around the
35 streets aimlessly for a time, and then he drove past the hospital on his way to
the parking lot.

. . . "It's the millionaire banker, Wellington McMillan," said the pretty
nurse. "Yes?" said Walter Mitty, removing his glasses slowly.
"Who has the case?" "Dr. Renshaw and Dr. Benbow, but there are two
40 specialists here, Dr. Remington from New York and Mr. Pritchard-Mitford
from London. He flew over." A door opened down a long, cool corridor and
Dr. Renshaw came out. He looked distraught and haggard. "Hello, Mitty," he
said. "We're having the devil's own time with McMillan, the millionaire banker
and close personal friend of Roosevelt. Obstreosis of the ductal tract.[2] Tertiary.
45 Wish you'd take a look at him." "Glad to," said Mitty.
    In the operating room there were whispered introductions: "Dr.
Remington, Dr. Mitty. Mr. Pritchard-Mitford, Dr. Mitty." "I've read your
book on streptothricosis," said Pritchard-Mitford, shaking hands. "A brilliant
performance, sir." "Thank you," said Walter Mitty. "Didn't know you were
50 in the States, Mitty," grumbled Remington. "Coals to Newcastle,[3] bringing
Mitford and me up here for tertiary." "You are very kind," said Mitty. A huge,
complicated machine, connected to the operating table, with many tubes
and wires, began at this moment to go pocketa-pocketa-pocketa. "The new
anesthetizer is giving way!" shouted an intern. "There is no one in the East
55 who knows how to fix it!" "Quiet, man!" said Mitty, in a low, cool voice. He
sprang to the machine, which was now going pocketa-pocketa-queep-pocketa-
queep. He began fingering delicately a row of glistening dials. "Give me a
fountain pen!" he snapped. Someone handed him a fountain pen. He pulled
a faulty piston out of the machine and inserted a pen in its place. "That will
60 hold for ten minutes," he said. "Get on with the operation." A nurse hurried
over and whispered to Renshaw, and Mitty saw the man turn pale. "Coreopsis
has set in," said Renshaw nervously. "If you would take over, Mitty?" Mitty
looked at him and at the craven figure of Benbow, who drank, and at the
grave, uncertain faces of the two great specialists. "If you wish," he said. They
65 slipped a white gown on him; he adjusted a mask and drew on thin gloves;
nurses handed him shining . . .
    "Back it up, Mac! Look out for that Buick!" Walter Mitty jammed on the
brakes. "Wrong lane, Mac," said the parking-lot attendant, looking at Mitty
closely. "Gee. Yeh," muttered Mitty. . . .

---

2. **Obstreosis of the ductal tract:** Thurber made up this and other terms to
   sound like—and poke fun at—medical jargon.

3. **Coals to Newcastle:** an unnecessary task. This expression refers to Newcastle,
   England, which was a major coal-producing city.

Close Read

3. **Make Inferences** Given
   Mitty's actions in lines
   29–34, what can you infer
   about his personality
   and his relationship
   with his wife?

4. **Predict** Now Mitty
   pictures himself in an
   operating room with
   an important patient.
   What do you imagine
   will happen?

5. **Connect** Have you ever
   been the hero in your
   own dreams? Explain
   why you think many
   people have dreams in
   which they are stars.

Strategies That Work: Reading

❶ Read Independently

The best way to become a better reader is to read as much as you can, every chance you get.

What Should I Read?	Where Should I Look?
Novels 	▶ Experiment with different authors and genres. Also, consult the **Great Reads** feature (at the end of every unit) for suggested novels tied to key ideas.
Magazines Newspapers Web sites 	▶ Every time you check your favorite Web site or leaf through the daily newspaper, you are reading. Pick up whatever interests you, and keep reading.

❷ Use Graphic Organizers

Graphic organizers can help you track the action in a work of literature, recognize relationships, and understand what is happening. Look for suggested graphic organizers in each lesson.

Real Mitty	Fantasy Mitty
henpecked husband	commander, surgeon
boring life	series of adventures
meek, confused	courageous, confident
often yelled at or admonished	highly respected by many

❸ Build Your Vocabulary

Creating a personal word list can help you better understand not only a specific selection but also other readings throughout your life. Use these tips to get started:

- **List difficult words.** Consider listing vocabulary words from the selections, as well as other challenging terms you encounter.
- **Go beyond the definitions.** To help you remember each word and its meaning, list synonyms and antonyms, or write a sentence using the word.
- **Get some practice.** Visit the **Vocabulary Center** at **ClassZone.com** for interactive practice.
- **Try them out.** Using new words in your writing and discussions is one of the best ways to build your vocabulary.

Word	Meaning
haggard adj. "The Secret Life of Walter Mitty," line 42	**Definition:** having a worn appearance **Synonyms:** gaunt; worn **Antonyms:** lively, energetic Months of fierce battle had taken a toll on the <u>haggard</u> soldier.

Expressing Ideas in Writing

Writing is a way of reaching people—of telling them something they didn't know, stirring their emotions, or even persuading them to stand up for a cause. Whether you're writing for the millions (an entry in a blog) or one in a million (a love letter), the act of putting words on paper can have remarkable power.

Consider Your Options

Maybe you want to write a review of a movie, advising other viewers to avoid it at all costs. Maybe you've decided to write an essay on a character in literature whose conflict seems familiar to you. Maybe you're drafting a letter to apply for a job. All kinds of writing start as ideas long before they are transformed into words on a page. Whether you are responding to a prompt or writing in your journal, start by considering **purpose, audience,** and **format.**

PURPOSE

Why am I writing?
• to entertain
• to inform or explain
• to persuade
• to describe
• to express thoughts and feelings
• to inspire

AUDIENCE

Who are my readers?
• classmates
• teachers
• friends
• community members
• potential employers
• Web users

FORMAT

Which format will best suit my purpose and audience?
• essay   • speech
• letter   • research paper
• poem   • short story
• review   • journal entry
• script   • Web site
• power presentation

Continue with the Process

Every writer has a different process, and many use different processes at different times. But it's a rare writer who sits down with no plan in mind and types a final draft for publication. The **Writing Workshops** in this book are designed to help you develop and refine your own process for writing. Familiarize yourself with the basic process before you decide what works for you.

THE WRITING PROCESS

What Should I Do?

What Does It Look Like?

PREWRITING
Explore your ideas and determine what you want to write about. In addition to considering the questions on the preceding page, try some of these brainstorming strategies: **freewriting, clustering, listing.**

▶ **CLUSTER DIAGRAM**

- can be physical or emotional
- can surface unexpectedly
- Strength
- helps people overcome hard times
- not always visible at first glance

DRAFTING
Turn your prewriting ideas into a first draft without worrying about errors. If you are writing a formal essay, you might **draft from an outline,** such as the one shown. Another option is **drafting to discover**—writing with no set plan, letting the ideas develop as you go.

▶ **OUTLINE**

I. Emotional strength comes from a will to succeed in difficult circumstances.
   A. _The Old Man and the Sea_ (The old man doesn't let fatigue/age stop him.)
   B. _The Miracle Worker_ (Annie Sullivan perseveres in the face of failure.)

REVISING AND EDITING
Review your draft, making changes to content, structure, and style.
- Check your writing against a **rubric** (page 18).
- Get suggestions from a **peer reader.**
- Proofread for errors in grammar, usage, and mechanics.

▶ **PEER SUGGESTIONS**

In Ernest Hemingway's _The Old Man and the Sea_ and William Gibson's _The Miracle Worker_, the main characters display emotional strenth. ⁹

Suggestion: May want to begin with a more creative statement. Try: "Strength is much more than muscle for the main characters in . . ."

PUBLISHING
Let your idea loose on the world. Where you publish, of course, depends on your **purpose, audience,** and **format.**

▶ **PUBLISHING OPTIONS**

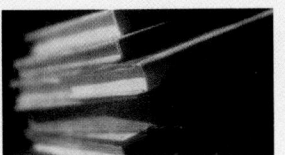

Do a Self-Check

Whether you're analyzing a short story or urging others to support a cause, being aware of the key traits of effective writing will help you stay on track. Use this rubric to evaluate how far you've come with your idea, and how far you have to go.

KEY TRAITS RUBRIC

	Strong	Average	Weak
Ideas 1	• centers around a clear, focused topic • is supported by vivid, well-chosen details	• has a topic, but it needs to be developed more • contains general statements with some details	• has no clear topic • lacks details or has unclear details
Organization 2	• opens in an engaging way and wraps up with a satisfying conclusion • flows in a logical manner	• has both an introduction and a conclusion, but they are uninteresting • lacks some transitions	• has no real introduction or conclusion • contains a confusing jumble of ideas
Voice 3	• conveys a strong sense of individual style • uses a tone that is well suited to the purpose and audience	• sounds "flat" in some places • lapses into an inappropriate tone at times	• has little or no "life" • employs a completely inappropriate tone for the intended purpose and audience
Word Choice 4	• uses words that are precise and colorful • conveys meaning in a powerful yet natural-sounding manner	• uses words that are correct, but ordinary • gets meaning across, but is not memorable	• uses words that are vague or incorrect • fails to convey meaning clearly
Sentence Fluency 5	• includes sentences of varied lengths and structures • creates a pleasing flow from one idea to the next	• has some sentence variety but not enough • lacks flow in some places	• includes mostly short or rambling sentences • is awkward or repetitious
Conventions 6	• shows a strong grasp of grammar and usage • has few problems with mechanics (spelling, capitalization, and punctuation)	• has minor grammar and usage problems • contains some mechanical errors	• has such poor grammar and usage that meaning is unclear • contains so many mechanical errors that the writing is hard to read

Strategies That Work: Writing

❶ Use Prewriting Strategies

Deciding on a topic and developing ideas can seem like the hardest parts of the process. Try these approaches to jumpstart your process:

- **Freewrite.** Write down anything that comes into your head.
- **Go graphic.** Use cluster diagrams, charts, and other graphic organizers to capture your thoughts.
- **Keep a journal.** Collect quotes, observations, song lyrics, photographs, freewrites, and other possible sources of inspiration.
- **Talk it out.** Brainstorm topics or supporting details with classmates.
- **Write from a prompt.** Consider the prompts in the **Writing Workshops.**

❷ Get Feedback from Peers

Other writers can help you at any stage of the process, from brainstorming ideas with you to proofreading your final draft. Consider these tips:

When You're the Writer	When You're the Reader
• Tell your readers what kind of feedback you are looking for. Should they focus on content, structure, or both? • Listen to their comments without arguing or explaining. • Let their suggestions sink in before you decide how you want to proceed.	• Be honest but kind. Offer positive reactions first. • Be specific. Don't say, "That character was unbelievable" without giving specific details to support your opinion. • Let the writer make the final decisions.

❸ Read, Read, Read

Reading other people's writing is one of the best ways to develop your own individual style. Consult these sources:

LITERATURE
For inspiration, look to the fiction, drama, poetry, and nonfiction in this book, as well as novels and periodicals that match your interests.

WRITING COMMUNITY
If you're serious about writing, form a writing group with others to share your efforts.

ONLINE RESOURCES
Consult the world of writing resources on the Web. Check out blogs, student publication sites, and the **Writing Center** at ClassZone.com.

UNIT 1

The Plot Thickens

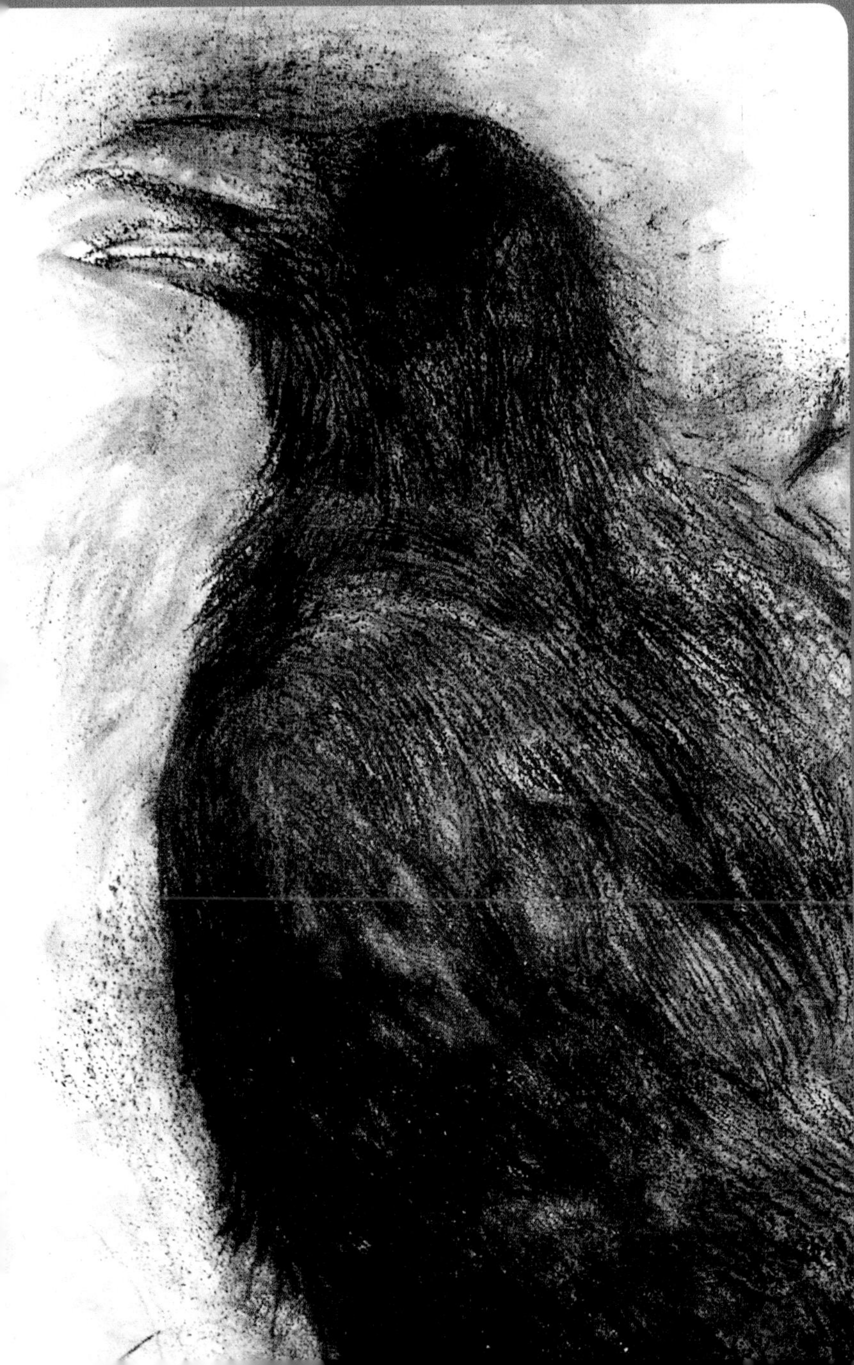

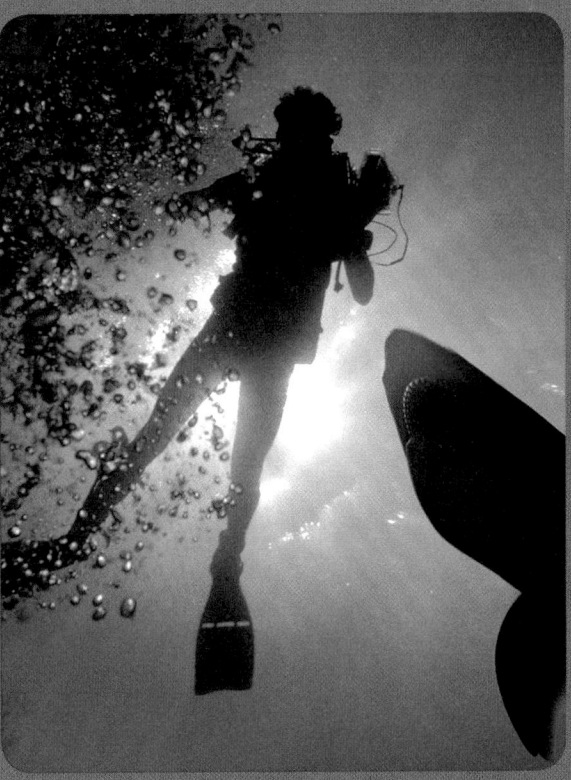

NARRATIVE STRUCTURE

- In Fiction
- In Media
- In Nonfiction
- In Poetry
- In Drama

UNIT 1 **Share What You Know**

What makes a GREAT STORY?

Whether you are riveted by the latest comedy at the local movie theater, caught up in the pages of your favorite novel, or transfixed by your grandparents' tales of growing up, what these **great stories** have in common is that each is told by someone who can capture your interest, hold your attention, and make you want to know how the story will end.

ACTIVITY Think of a story you have read or heard. It can be a favorite piece of fiction or a powerful true story, such as the saga of tragic events in *The Perfect Storm.* With a partner, share a summary of the story you chose. Then discuss the following questions:

- What made the story interesting?
- What emotions did the story evoke in you?
- Was the story told in any unusual ways?
- Did the story remind you of any other stories?

After answering these questions, think about what great stories have in common.

A TRUE STORY OF MEN AGAINST THE SEA
THE PERFECT STORM
SEBASTIAN JUNGER

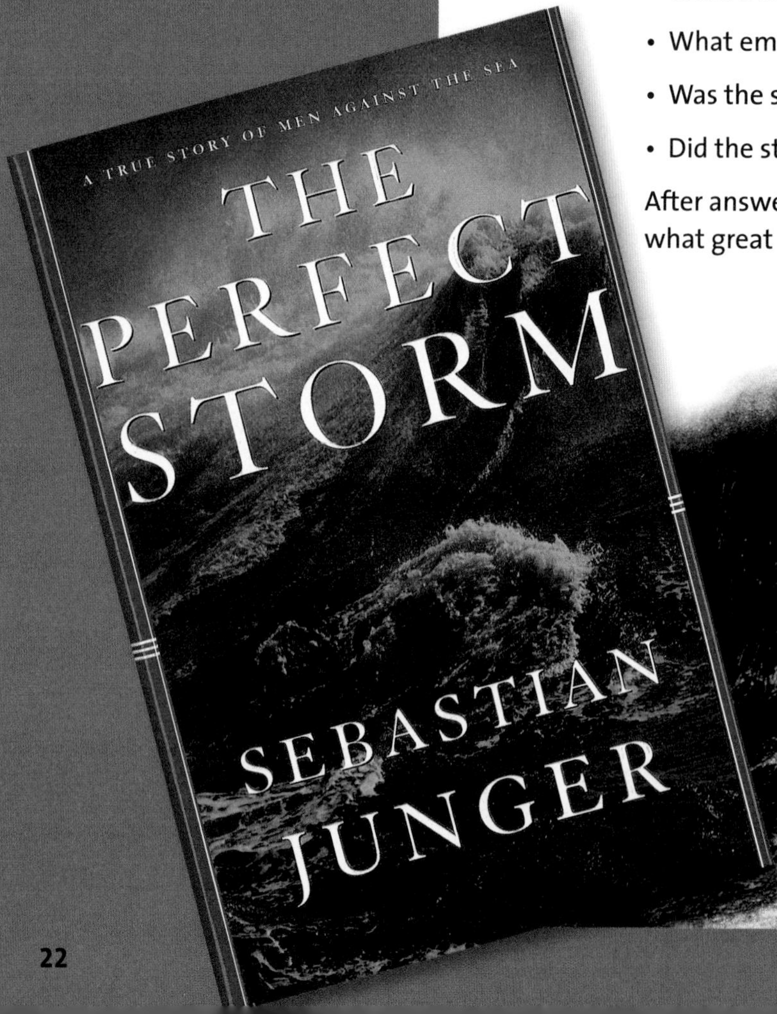

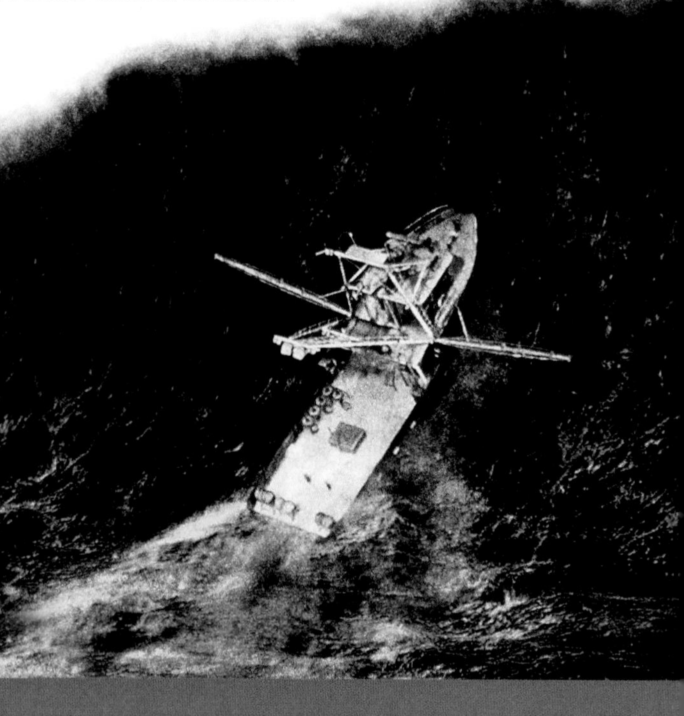

PENNSYLVANIA STANDARDS

Preview Unit Goals

LITERARY ANALYSIS
- Analyze stages of plot and plot development
- Identify and analyze conflict and its complications
- Analyze narrative techniques, including foreshadowing, irony, and suspense
- Identify narrative elements in poetry and drama

READING
- Use reading strategies, including predicting and visualizing
- Recognize sequence and cause-and-effect relationships
- Make inferences and draw conclusions
- Synthesize information from multiple texts

WRITING AND GRAMMAR
- Write a personal narrative
- Use realistic dialogue, descriptive details, and realistic characters to achieve a purpose
- Use precise verbs and modifiers

SPEAKING, LISTENING, AND VIEWING
- Identify the aesthetic qualities of film and evaluate the techniques used to create them
- Use a variety of media techniques to convey a cohesive story

VOCABULARY
- Use word roots to help unlock meaning
- Use synonyms and antonyms to understand meanings of words

ACADEMIC VOCABULARY
- complications
- conflict
- foreshadowing
- irony
- plot
- suspense
- synthesis

Literary Analysis Workshop

Plot and Conflict

Every good story is fueled by conflict. Can the hero survive the dangerous journey? Will the star-crossed lovers end up together, despite their feuding families? When a story grabs your interest, it's usually because the conflict is exciting and dramatic. Looking closely at how conflicts develop throughout the stages of a plot is a key part of analyzing a story and understanding *why* it hooks you.

Part 1: Plot Stages and Conflict

PENNSYLVANIA STANDARDS

READING STANDARDS
B.1.1.1.C.1 Interpret and evaluate elements of the plot
B.3.3.2 Analyze text organization

The series of events in a narrative is called **plot.** At the heart of any plot is a **conflict,** or struggle, between opposing forces. A conflict is internal or external.

- An **internal conflict** is a struggle within a character's mind. The struggle usually centers on a choice or decision the character must make. Should she tell the truth? Can he overcome his jealousy?

- An **external conflict** is a clash between a character and an outside force, such as another character, society, or a force of nature. Will the athlete defeat her bitter rival? Can the soldiers endure the war?

Whether internal or external, a conflict is usually introduced at the beginning of a narrative. As the characters attempt to resolve the conflict, "the plot thickens" at each stage. Will the characters succeed? You keep turning the pages to find out the answer to this question.

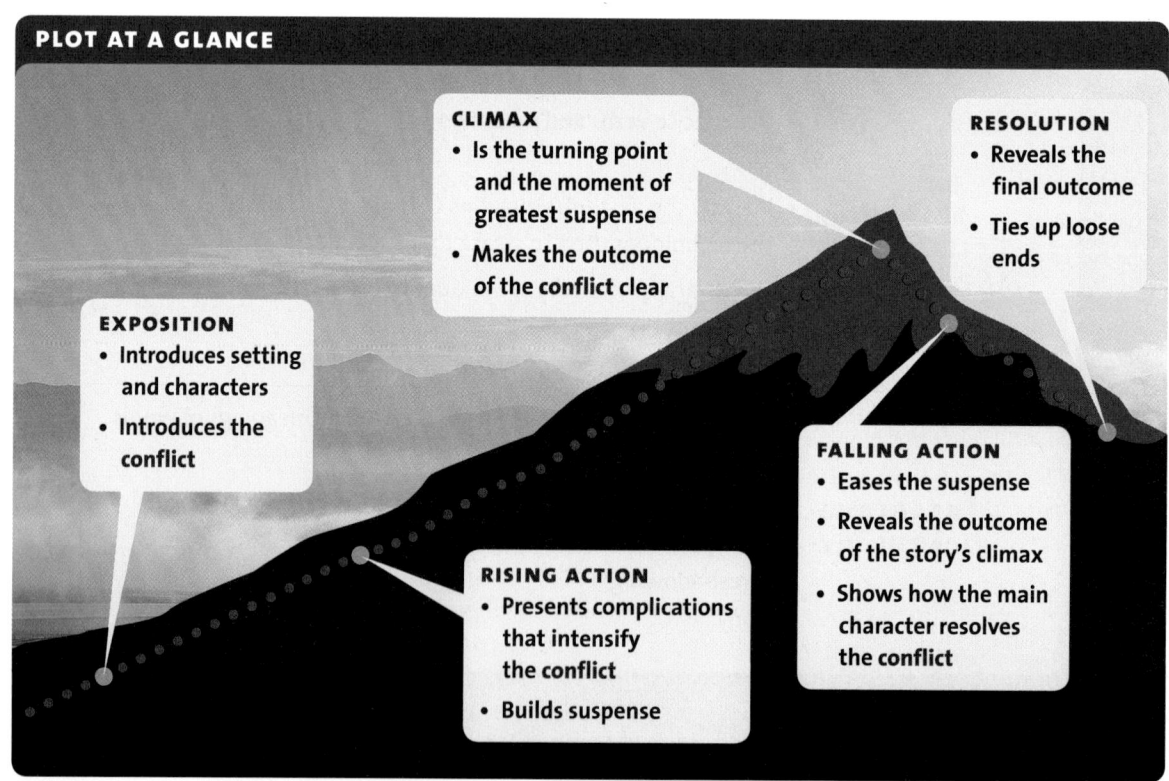

PLOT AT A GLANCE

CLIMAX
- Is the turning point and the moment of greatest suspense
- Makes the outcome of the conflict clear

RESOLUTION
- Reveals the final outcome
- Ties up loose ends

EXPOSITION
- Introduces setting and characters
- Introduces the conflict

FALLING ACTION
- Eases the suspense
- Reveals the outcome of the story's climax
- Shows how the main character resolves the conflict

RISING ACTION
- Presents complications that intensify the conflict
- Builds suspense

MODEL 1: CONFLICT IN EXPOSITION

In the exposition of this story, a young warrior named Temas is about to face a crucial test of adulthood in Masai culture—killing a lion. What conflicts emerge as Temas prepares for this pivotal moment?

from

BROTHERS ARE THE SAME

Short story by **Beryl Markham**

Yet in his mind Temas now trembled. Fear of battle was a nonexistent thing—but fear of failure could be real, and was. It was real and living—and kept alive by the nearness of an enemy more formidable than any lion— an enemy with the hated name Medoto.

5   He thought of Medoto—of that Medoto who lay not far away in the deep grass watching the same ravine. Of that Medoto who, out of hate and jealousy over a mere girl, now hoped in his heart that Temas would flinch at the moment of his trial. . . .

Close Read

1. Review the boxed detail. What does it tell you about the building conflict between Temas and Medoto?

2. In addition to his conflict with Medoto, what internal conflict is plaguing Temas?

MODEL 2: CONFLICT AT CLIMAX

Later, Temas learns that his rival is actually a friend. Find out how the conflict between Temas and Medoto changes at the story's climax.

During the test, Temas feels relieved when the lion attacks another hunter. Then Medoto throws a stone, causing the lion to charge Temas. Without hesitation, Temas kills the lion. Later, Medoto explains himself to Temas.

"If, until now, I have seemed your enemy, it was because I feared you would be braver than I, for when I fought my lion my knees trembled and my heart was white—until that charge was made. No one knew that, and I am called Medoto, the unflinching, but I flinched. I trembled."

5   He stepped closer to Temas. He smiled. "It is no good to lie," he said. "I wanted you to fail, but when I saw you hesitate I could not bear it because I remembered my own hour of fear. It was then I threw the stone—not to shame you, but to save you from shame—for I saw that your fear was not fear of death, but fear of failure—and this I understood. You are a greater warrior than

10   I—than any—for who but the bravest would do what you have done?" Medoto paused and watched a light of wonderment kindle in Temas's eye. The hand of Temas slipped from his sword, his muscles relaxed. Yet, for a moment, he did not speak, and as he looked at Medoto, it was clear to both that the identical thought, the identical vision, had come to each of them. It was the vision that

15   must and always will come to young men everywhere, the vision of a girl.

Now this vision stood between them, and nothing else. But it stood like a barrier, the last barrier.

Close Read

1. How has the conflict between Temas and Medoto changed? Support your answer with evidence.

2. What aspect of Medoto's and Temas's conflict still remains unresolved? Explain.

Part 2: Sequence and Time

From fairy tales, with their "once upon a time" beginnings and "happily ever after" endings, to modern classics, many great stories feature **chronological order.** The events follow a linear structure—that is, they take place one after the other.

Sometimes, however, a writer plays with time by interrupting the chronological order of events. He or she may suddenly focus on an event from the past or hint at future events. A writer may manipulate time for a variety of reasons—for example, to give you a deeper sense of the characters and conflicts or to keep you wondering what will happen next.

Flashback and **foreshadowing** are two common devices that writers use to introduce past and future events. By recognizing these devices, you can follow a story more closely and better understand your reactions to characters and events.

FLASHBACK	**FORESHADOWING**
What is it?	*What is it?*
An account of a conversation, episode, or event that happened before the beginning of the story, or at an earlier point	**A writer's use of hints or clues in early scenes to suggest events that will occur later**

What does it do?	*What does it do?*
• Interrupts the main action to describe earlier events	• Prepares readers for events that come later—often in the climax or the resolution
• Shows how past events led up to the present situation	• Creates suspense
• Provides background information about a character or event	• Makes readers eager to keep reading

How can I recognize it?	*How can I recognize it?*
• Look for possible clue words and phrases, such as "that summer," "as a young boy," or "her earliest memories."	• Pay attention to repeated or emphasized ideas and descriptions.
• Keep track of the chronological order of events so that you will be aware of events that interrupt this order.	• Notice when characters make important statements or behave in unusual ways.

MODEL: FLASHBACK

Moments after meeting the narrator in this story, you are transported to an earlier time in his life. As you read, notice what this flashback reveals about the narrator and his family.

from # Sweet Potato Pie

Short story by **Eugenia Collier**

From up here on the fourteenth floor, my brother Charley looks like an insect scurrying among other insects. A deep feeling of love surges through me. . . .

Because I see Charley so seldom, my thoughts hover over him like hummingbirds. The cheerful, impersonal tidiness of this room is a world away
5 from Charley's walk-up flat in Harlem and a hundred worlds from the bare, noisy shanty where he and the rest of us spent what there was of childhood. I close my eyes, and side by side I see the Charley of my boyhood and the Charley of this afternoon, as clearly as if I were looking at a split TV screen. Another surge of love, seasoned with gratitude, wells up in me.

10 As far as I know, Charley never had any childhood at all. The oldest children of sharecroppers never do. Mama and Pa were shadowy figures whose voices I heard vaguely in the morning when sleep was shallow and whom I glimpsed as they left for the field before I was fully awake or as they trudged wearily into the house at night when my lids were irresistibly heavy.

15 They came into sharp focus only on special occasions. One such occasion was the day when the crops were in and the sharecroppers were paid. In our cabin there was so much excitement in the air that even I, the "baby," responded to it. For weeks we had been running out of things that we could neither grow nor get on credit. On the evening of that day we waited anxiously for our
20 parents' return. Then we would cluster around the rough wooden table—I on Lil's lap or clinging to Charley's neck, little Alberta nervously tugging her plait, Jamie crouched at Mama's elbow, like a panther about to spring, and all seven of us silent for once, waiting. Pa would place the money on the table—gently, for it was made from the sweat of their bodies and from their children's tears.
25 Mama would count it out in little piles, her dark face stern and, I think now, beautiful. Not with the hollow beauty of well-modeled features but with the strong radiance of one who has suffered and never yielded.

"This for store bill," she would mutter, making a little pile. "This for c'llection. This for piece o'gingham . . ." and so on, stretching the money as
30 tight over our collective needs as Jamie's outgrown pants were stretched over my bottom. "Well, that's the crop." She would look up at Pa at last. "It'll do." Pa's face would relax, and a general grin flitted from child to child. We would survive, at least for the present.

Close Read

1. Explain what happens before the flashback.

2. At what point does the flashback begin? Explain the words or phrases that helped you identify it.

3. Find three details that describe the narrator's and Charley's family. One has been boxed. What do these details tell you about their childhood?

4. How does the flashback help you understand the narrator's feelings about Charley?

Part 3: Analyze the Literature

It seems like a familiar story. Girl meets and falls in love with boy. Boy falls in love with girl. After overcoming a few problems, they live happily ever after. Right? Wrong. This story traces a conflict, but that conflict is not resolved in a predictable way. As you read, use what you've learned about plot, conflict, and sequence to analyze the story.

Checkouts

Short story by **Cynthia Rylant**

Her parents had moved her to Cincinnati, to a large house with beveled glass[1] windows and several porches and the *history* her mother liked to emphasize. You'll love the house, they said. You'll be lonely at first, they admitted, but you're so nice you'll make friends fast. And as an impulse tore at her to lie on the floor,
5 to hold to their ankles and tell them she felt she was dying, to offer anything, anything at all, so they might allow her to finish growing up in the town of her childhood, they firmed their mouths and spoke from their chests and they said, It's decided.

They moved her to Cincinnati, where for a month she spent the greater
10 part of every day in a room full of beveled glass windows, sifting through photographs of the life she'd lived and left behind. But it is difficult work, suffering, and in its own way a kind of art, and finally she didn't have the energy for it anymore, so she emerged from the beautiful house and fell in love with a bag boy at the supermarket. Of course, this didn't happen all at once,
15 just like that, but in the sequence of things that's exactly the way it happened.
She liked to grocery shop. She loved it in the way some people love to drive long country roads, because doing it she could think and relax and wander. Her parents wrote up the list and handed it to her and off she went without

---

1. **beveled glass:** glass whose edges are cut at an angle.

Close Read

1. What do you learn about the setting and the main character's situation in the exposition of this story?

2. Reread lines 11–15, which set the stage for the main conflict. What do you think the conflict will be about?

3. Review the boxed details about the girl. What do they reveal about her personality?

20 complaint to perform what they regarded as a great sacrifice of her time and a
sign that she was indeed a very nice girl. She had never told them how much
she loved grocery shopping, only that she was "willing" to do it. She had an
intuition which told her that her parents were not safe for sharing such strong,
important facts about herself. Let them think they knew her.

25 Once inside the supermarket, her hands firmly around the handle of the
cart, she would lapse into a kind of reverie and wheel toward the produce.
Like a Tibetan monk[2] in solitary meditation, she calmed to a point of deep,
deep happiness; this feeling came to her, reliably, if strangely, only in the
supermarket.

30 *T*hen one day the bag boy dropped her jar of mayonnaise and that is how
she fell in love.
He was nervous—first day on the job—and along had come this fascinating
girl, standing in the checkout line with the unfocused stare one often sees in
young children, her face turned enough away that he might take several full
looks at her as he packed sturdy bags full of food and the goods of modern life.
35 She interested him because her hair was red and thick, and in it she had placed
a huge orange bow, nearly the size of a small hat. That was enough to distract
him, and when finally it was her groceries he was packing, she looked at him
and smiled and he could respond only by busting her jar of mayonnaise on the
floor, shards of glass and oozing cream decorating the area around his feet.
40 She loved him at exactly that moment, and if he'd known this perhaps he
wouldn't have fallen into the brown depression he fell into, which lasted the
rest of his shift. He believed he must have looked a fool in her eyes, and he
envied the sureness of everyone around him: the cocky cashier at the register,
the grim and harried store manager, the bland butcher, and the brazen bag
45 boys who smoked in the warehouse on their breaks. He wanted a second
chance. Another chance to be confident and say witty things to her as he threw
tin cans into her bags, persuading her to allow him to help her to her car so
he might learn just a little about her, check out the floor of the car for signs of
hobbies or fetishes and the bumpers for clues as to beliefs and loyalties.
50 But he busted her jar of mayonnaise and nothing else worked out for the
rest of the day.

---

2. **Tibetan monk:** a member of a Buddhist sect in central Asia that practices meditation.

Close Read

4. What event on this page sets the rising action in motion?

5. How would you describe the conflict faced by the girl and the bag boy? How does this conflict make the story more interesting?

Strange, how attractive clumsiness can be. She left the supermarket with stars in her eyes, for she had loved the way his long nervous fingers moved from the conveyor belt to the bags, how deftly (until the mayonnaise) they had picked up her items and placed them into her bags. She had loved the way the hair kept falling into his eyes as he leaned over to grab a box or a tin. And the tattered brown shoes he wore with no socks. And the left side of his collar turned in rather than out.

The bag boy seemed a wonderful contrast to the perfectly beautiful house she had been forced to accept as her home, to the *history* she hated, to the loneliness she had become used to, and she couldn't wait to come back for more of his awkwardness and dishevelment.

Incredibly, it was another four weeks before they saw each other again. As fate would have it, her visits to the supermarket never coincided with his schedule to bag. Each time she went to the store, her eyes scanned the checkouts at once, her heart in her mouth. And each hour he worked, the bag boy kept one eye on the door, watching for the red-haired girl with the big orange bow.

Yet in their disappointment these weeks there was a kind of ecstasy. It is reason enough to be alive, the hope you may see again some face which has meant something to you. The anticipation of meeting the bag boy eased the girl's painful transition into her new and jarring life in Cincinnati. It provided for her an anchor amid all that was impersonal and unfamiliar, and she spent less time on thoughts of what she had left behind as she concentrated on what might lie ahead. And for the boy, the long and often tedious hours at the supermarket which provided no challenge other than that of showing up the following workday . . . these hours became possibilities of mystery and romance for him as he watched the electric doors for the girl in the orange bow.

And when finally they did meet up again, neither offered a clue to the other that he, or she, had been the object of obsessive thought for weeks. She spotted him as soon as she came into the store, but she kept her eyes strictly in front of her as she pulled out a cart and wheeled it toward the produce. And he, too, knew the instant she came through the door—though the orange bow was gone, replaced by a small but bright yellow flower instead—and he never

Close Read

6. Review lines 29–68. Summarize the sequence of events that begins with the boy's dropping the jar. How do these events build suspense about what will happen?

7. What details in lines 69–78 tell you that the girl and the boy are enjoying the excitement of the building conflict? One has been boxed.

85 once turned his head in her direction but watched her from the corner of his vision as he tried to swallow back the fear in his throat.

It is odd how we sometimes deny ourselves the very pleasure we have longed for and which is finally within our reach. For some perverse reason she would not have been able to articulate, the girl did not bring her cart up to the bag

90 boy's checkout when her shopping was done. And the bag boy let her leave the store, pretending no notice of her.

This is often the way of children, when they truly want a thing, to pretend that they don't. And then they grow angry when no one tries harder to give them this thing they so casually rejected, and they soon find themselves in a

95 rage simply because they cannot say yes when they mean yes. Humans are very complicated. (And perhaps cats, who have been known to react in the same way, though the resulting rage can only be guessed at.)

The girl hated herself for not checking out at the boy's line, and the boy hated himself for not catching her eye and saying hello, and they most

100 sincerely hated each other without having ever exchanged even two minutes of conversation.

Eventually—in fact, within the week—a kind and intelligent boy who lived very near her beautiful house asked the girl to a movie and she gave up her fancy for the bag boy at the supermarket. And the bag boy himself grew

105 so bored with his job that he made a desperate search for something better and ended up in a bookstore where scores of fascinating girls lingered like honeybees about a hive. Some months later the bag boy and the girl with the orange bow again crossed paths, standing in line with their dates at a movie theater, and, glancing toward the other, each smiled slightly, then looked away,

110 as strangers on public buses often do, when one is moving off the bus and the other is moving on.

Close Read

8. Reread lines 79–86, which mark the story's climax. How do the characters resolve the main conflict?

9. In the falling action stage, lines 87–101, the characters reflect on their actions. Are they happy with the way they've handled the conflict? Explain.

10. Reread the resolution in lines 102–111. What are the results of the conflict for each character?

A Sound of Thunder

Short Story by Ray Bradbury

Would you visit the PAST *if you could?*

PENNSYLVANIA STANDARDS

READING STANDARDS
B.2.1.1 Analyze examples of foreshadowing

B.3.3.2 Analyze text organization

KEY IDEA Imagine that you could board a time machine and travel into the past. In "A Sound of Thunder," the main character does just that. His journey, however, has unexpected **consequences.**

QUICKWRITE If time travel were possible, what era would you most like to visit? Imagine one or two things you might do during your adventure. How would your actions affect the future? Create a cause-and-effect chart describing your actions and their possible consequences.

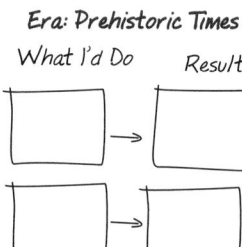

Era: Prehistoric Times

What I'd Do → Result

LITERARY ANALYSIS: FORESHADOWING

Foreshadowing is a writer's use of hints or clues to suggest events that will happen later in a story. By using this technique, Bradbury creates **suspense,** which in turn makes his readers want to know what will happen next. Foreshadowing often occurs when a character makes an unusual statement or issues a strong warning, as in the following example:

"So be careful. Stay on the Path. Never step off!"

Watch for other examples of foreshadowing as you read Bradbury's story.

Review: **Plot**

READING SKILL: ANALYZE SEQUENCE

A story about time travel presents some interesting challenges. If you were to create a timeline to track the characters' travels, it would go backward and then forward again. Yet the events in the story are presented in the order in which they happen to the characters. As you read the story, keep track of the **sequence** of events by creating a chart like the one shown. Record important events before, during, and after the time safari.

Before	During	After
Eckels prepares to travel back in time to hunt dinosaurs.		

Review: **Make Inferences, Predict**

▲ VOCABULARY IN CONTEXT

Bradbury builds an intensity in this story by using the following words. See which ones you already know. Place each word in the appropriate column. Then write a brief definition of each word you're familiar with.

WORD LIST		
annihilate	malfunctioning	subliminal
correlate	paradox	undulate
expendable	resilient	
infinitesimally	stagnating	

Know Well	Think I Know	Don't Know

Author Online

**Ray Bradbury
born 1920**

Social Critic for the Future
A major writer in the genres of science fiction and fantasy, Ray Bradbury explores the future, outer space—and the human heart. Over his long career, he has lived to see much science fiction become science fact. His most chilling stories comment on the human consequences of progress and often reflect the ironies of life.

A Library Education Bradbury fervently believes in the importance of reading. "I didn't go to college, but when I graduated from high school I went down to the local library," he has said. For ten years Bradbury spent two or three days each week reading in the local public library in Los Angeles, California.

Not Quite a Technophobe This master of science fiction writes his stories on a typewriter rather than a computer, scorns the Internet, and has never even driven a car. Still, Bradbury is a strong advocate of space travel because he views it as "life-enhancing."

 MORE ABOUT THE AUTHOR
For more on Ray Bradbury, visit the **Literature Center** at **ClassZone.com.**

Background

The Fourth Dimension Time travel has been a popular idea in science fiction ever since the British author H. G. Wells wrote his short novel *The Time Machine* in 1895. In the novel, Wells suggested that in addition to the three dimensions of length, height, and width, there was a fourth dimension of duration, or time. Wells speculated that if a machine could be invented to move along the fourth dimension, travel backward and forward in time would be possible.

A SOUND OF THUNDER

RAY BRADBURY

The sign on the wall seemed to quaver under a film of sliding warm water. Eckels felt his eyelids blink over his stare, and the sign burned in this momentary darkness:

TIME SAFARI, INC.

SAFARIS TO ANY YEAR IN THE PAST.

YOU NAME THE ANIMAL.

WE TAKE YOU THERE.

YOU SHOOT IT.

A warm phlegm gathered in Eckels's throat; he swallowed and pushed it
10 down. The muscles around his mouth formed a smile as he put his hand slowly out upon the air, and in that hand waved a check for ten thousand dollars to the man behind the desk.

"Does this safari guarantee I come back alive?"

"We guarantee nothing," said the official, "except the dinosaurs." He turned. "This is Mr. Travis, your Safari Guide in the Past. He'll tell you what and where to shoot. If he says no shooting, no shooting. If you disobey instructions, there's a stiff penalty of another ten thousand dollars, plus possible government action, on your return." **A**

ANALYZE VISUALS
Examine this picture. What information can you **infer** about the world it portrays?

A FORESHADOWING
Reread lines 13–18. What might the man's warning to Eckels foreshadow?

Eckels glanced across the vast office at a mass and tangle, a snaking and
20 humming of wires and steel boxes, at an aurora[1] that flickered now orange,
now silver, now blue. There was a sound like a gigantic bonfire burning all of
Time, all the years and all the parchment calendars, all the hours piled high
and set aflame.

A touch of the hand and this burning would, on the instant, beautifully
reverse itself. Eckels remembered the wording in the advertisements to the
letter. Out of chars and ashes, out of dust and coals, like golden salamanders,
the old years, the green years, might leap; roses sweeten the air, white hair turn
Irish-black, wrinkles vanish; all, everything fly back to seed, flee death, rush
down to their beginnings, suns rise in western skies and set in glorious easts,
30 moons eat themselves opposite to the custom, all and everything cupping one
in another like Chinese boxes,[2] rabbits into hats, all and everything returning
to the fresh death, the seed death, the green death, to the time before the
beginning. A touch of a hand might do it, the merest touch of a hand.

"Unbelievable." Eckels breathed, the light of the Machine on his thin face.
"A real Time Machine." He shook his head. "Makes you think. If the election
had gone badly yesterday, I might be here now running away from the results.
Thank God Keith won. He'll make a fine President of the United States."

"Yes," said the man behind the desk. "We're lucky. If Deutscher[3] had gotten
in, we'd have the worst kind of dictatorship. There's an anti-everything man
40 for you, a militarist, anti-Christ, anti-human, anti-intellectual. People called us
up, you know, joking but not joking. Said if Deutscher became President they
wanted to go live in 1492. Of course it's not our business to conduct Escapes,
but to form Safaris. Anyway, Keith's President now. All you got to worry
about is—" **B**

"Shooting my dinosaur," Eckels finished it for him.

"A *Tyrannosaurus rex*. The Tyrant Lizard, the most incredible monster in
history. Sign this release. Anything happens to you, we're not responsible.
Those dinosaurs are hungry."

Eckels flushed angrily. "Trying to scare me!"

50 "Frankly, yes. We don't want anyone going who'll panic at the first shot. Six
Safari leaders were killed last year, and a dozen hunters. We're here to give you
the severest thrill a real hunter ever asked for. Traveling you back sixty million
years to bag the biggest game in all of Time. Your personal check's still there.
Tear it up."

Mr. Eckels looked at the check. His fingers twitched. **C**

"Good luck," said the man behind the desk. "Mr. Travis, he's all yours."

They moved silently across the room, taking their guns with them, toward
the Machine, toward the silver metal and the roaring light.

B FORESHADOWING
What might the
conversation about
the election results
foreshadow?

C PLOT
What have you learned
about the characters'
situation in the
exposition?

---

1. **aurora** (ə-rôr′ə): a shifting, streaming display of light, like those sometimes seen in the sky in the northern
   and southern regions of the earth.

2. **Chinese boxes:** a set of boxes, each of which fits neatly inside the next larger one.

3. **Deutscher** (doi′chər).

First a day and then a night and then a day and then a night, then it was
60   day-night-day-night-day. A week, a month, a year, a decade! A.D. 2055.
   A.D. 2019. 1999! 1957! Gone! The Machine roared.

They put on their oxygen helmets and tested the intercoms.

Eckels swayed on the padded seat, his face pale, his jaw stiff. He felt the
trembling in his arms, and he looked down and found his hands tight on the
new rifle. There were four other men in the Machine. Travis, the Safari Leader;
his assistant, Lesperance;[4] and two other hunters, Billings and Kramer. They
sat looking at each other, and the years blazed around them. **D**

"Can these guns get a dinosaur cold?" Eckels felt his mouth saying.

"If you hit them right," said Travis on the helmet radio. "Some dinosaurs
70 have two brains, one in the head, another far down the spinal column. We stay
away from those. That's stretching luck. Put your first two shots into the eyes,
if you can, blind them, and go back into the brain."

The Machine howled. Time was a film run backward. Suns fled, and ten
million moons fled after them. "Think," said Eckels. "Every hunter that ever
lived would envy us today. This makes Africa seem like Illinois."

The Machine slowed; its scream fell to a murmur. The Machine stopped.

The sun stopped in the sky.

The fog that had enveloped the Machine blew away, and they were in an
old time, a very old time indeed, three hunters and two Safari Heads with their
80 blue metal guns across their knees.

"Christ isn't born yet," said Travis. "Moses has not gone to the mountain to
talk with God.[5] The Pyramids are still in the earth, waiting to be cut out and
put up. *Remember* that. Alexander, Caesar, Napoleon, Hitler—none of them
exists."

The man nodded.

"That"—Mr. Travis pointed—"is the jungle of sixty million two thousand
and fifty-five years before President Keith."

He indicated a metal path that struck off into green wilderness, over
streaming swamp, among giant ferns and palms.
90 "And that," he said, "is the Path, laid by Time Safari for your use. It floats
six inches above the earth. Doesn't touch so much as one grass blade, flower,
or tree. It's an antigravity metal.[6] Its purpose is to keep you from touching this
world of the past in any way. Stay on the Path. Don't go off it. I repeat. *Don't
go off.* For *any* reason! If you fall off, there's a penalty. And don't shoot any
animal we don't okay." **E**

"Why?" asked Eckels.

They sat in the ancient wilderness. Far birds' cries blew on a wind, and the
smell of tar and an old salt sea, moist grasses, and flowers the color of blood.

D MAKE INFERENCES
On the basis of details
presented so far, what
kind of person is Eckels?

E FORESHADOWING
What might Travis's
warning to the hunters
foreshadow? How
does his warning create
suspense?

---

4. **Lesperance** (lĕs′pər-äns).

5. **Moses . . . talk with God:** According to the Old Testament, God spoke directly to Moses several times
in mountainous locations, as when Moses received the Ten Commandments on Mount Sinai.

6. **antigravity metal:** a metal that counteracts the pull of gravity.

"We don't want to change the Future. We don't belong here in the Past.
100 The government doesn't *like* us here. We have to pay big graft to keep our
franchise.[7] A Time Machine is finicky business. Not knowing it, we might kill
an important animal, a small bird, a roach, a flower even, thus destroying an
important link in a growing species."

"That's not clear," said Eckels.

"All right," Travis continued, "say we accidentally kill one mouse here. That
means all the future families of this one particular mouse are destroyed, right?"

"Right."

"And all the families of the families of the families of that one mouse! With
a stamp of your foot, you **annihilate** first one, then a dozen, then a thousand,
110 a million, a *billion* possible mice!"

"So they're dead," said Eckels. "So what?"

"So what?" Travis snorted quietly. "Well, what about the foxes that'll need
those mice to survive? For want of ten mice, a fox dies. For want of ten foxes, a
lion starves. For want of a lion, all manner of insects, vultures, infinite billions
of life forms are thrown into chaos and destruction. Eventually it all boils
down to this: fifty-nine million years later, a caveman, one of a dozen on the

annihilate
(ə-nī′ə-lāt′) *v.* to destroy
completely

---

7. **pay big graft to keep our franchise:** pay large bribes to officials in return for their approval of the business.

entire world, goes hunting wild boar or saber-toothed tiger[8] for food. But you, friend, have *stepped* on all the tigers in that region. By stepping on one single mouse. So the caveman starves. And the caveman, please note, is not just *any* expendable man, no! He is an *entire future nation.* From his loins would have sprung ten sons. From *their* loins one hundred sons, and thus onward to a civilization. Destroy this one man, and you destroy a race, a people, an entire history of life. It is comparable to slaying some of Adam's grandchildren. The stomp of your foot, on one mouse, could start an earthquake, the effects of which could shake our earth and destinies down through Time, to their very foundations. With the death of that one caveman, a billion others yet unborn are throttled in the womb. Perhaps Rome never rises on its seven hills. Perhaps Europe is forever a dark forest, and only Asia waxes healthy and teeming. Step on a mouse, and you crush the Pyramids. Step on a mouse, and you leave your print, like a Grand Canyon, across Eternity. Queen Elizabeth might never be born; Washington might not cross the Delaware; there might never be a United States at all. So be careful. Stay on the Path. *Never* step off!"

"I see," said Eckels. "Then it wouldn't pay for us even to touch the *grass?*"

"Correct. Crushing certain plants could add up **infinitesimally.** A little error here would multiply in sixty million years, all out of proportion. Of course maybe our theory is wrong. Maybe Time *can't* be changed by us. Or maybe it can be changed only in little subtle ways. A dead mouse here makes an insect imbalance there, a population disproportion later, a bad harvest further on, a depression, mass starvation, and, finally, a change in *social* temperament in far-flung countries. Something much more subtle, like that. Perhaps only a soft breath, a whisper, a hair, pollen on the air, such a slight, slight change that unless you looked close you wouldn't see it. Who knows? Who really can say he knows? We don't know. We're guessing. But until we do know for certain whether our messing around in Time *can* make a big roar or a little rustle in history, we're being careful. This Machine, this Path, your clothing and bodies, were sterilized, as you know, before the journey. We wear these oxygen helmets so we can't introduce our bacteria into an ancient atmosphere."

"How do we know which animals to shoot?"

"They're marked with red paint," said Travis. "Today, before our journey, we sent Lesperance here back with the Machine. He came to this particular era and followed certain animals."

"Studying them?"

"Right," said Lesperance. "I track them through their entire existence, noting which of them lives longest. Very few. How many times they mate. Not often. Life's short. When I find one that's going to die when a tree falls on him, or one that drowns in a tar pit, I note the exact hour, minute, and second. I shoot a paint bomb. It leaves a red patch on his side. We can't miss it. Then I **correlate** our arrival in the Past so that we meet the Monster not more than

---

expendable
(ĭk-spĕn′də-bəl)
adj. not worth keeping; not essential

infinitesimally
(ĭn′fĭn-ĭ-tĕs′ə-mə-lē)
adv. in amounts so small as to be barely measurable

correlate (kôr′ə-lāt′)
v. to figure out or create a relationship between two items or events

---

8. **saber-toothed tiger:** a type of extinct wild cat that lived about 40 million years ago.

160 two minutes before he would have died anyway. This way, we kill only animals with no future, that are never going to mate again. You see how *careful* we are?"

"But if you came back this morning in Time," said Eckels eagerly, "you must've bumped into *us,* our Safari! How did it turn out? Was it successful? Did all of us get through—alive?"

Travis and Lesperance gave each other a look.

"That'd be a **paradox,**" said the latter. "Time doesn't permit that sort of mess—a man meeting himself. When such occasions threaten, Time steps aside. Like an airplane hitting an air pocket. You felt the Machine jump just before we stopped? That was us passing ourselves on the way back to
170 the Future. We saw nothing. There's no way of telling *if* this expedition was a success, *if we* got our monster, or whether all of us—meaning *you,* Mr. Eckels —got out alive."

Eckels smiled palely.

"Cut that," said Travis sharply. "Everyone on his feet!" **F**

They were ready to leave the Machine.

The jungle was high and the jungle was broad and the jungle was the entire world forever and forever. Sounds like music and sounds like flying tents filled the sky, and those were pterodactyls[9] soaring with cavernous gray wings, gigantic bats of delirium and night fever. Eckels, balanced on the narrow Path,
180 aimed his rifle playfully.

"Stop that!" said Travis. "Don't even aim for fun, blast you! If your guns should go off—"

Eckels flushed. "Where's our *Tyrannosaurus?*"

Lesperance checked his wristwatch. "Up ahead. We'll bisect his trail in sixty seconds. Look for the red paint! Don't shoot till we give the word. Stay on the Path. *Stay on the Path!*"

They moved forward in the wind of morning.

"Strange," murmured Eckels. "Up ahead, sixty million years, Election Day over. Keith made President. Everyone celebrating. And here we are, a million
190 years lost, and they don't exist. The things we worried about for months, a lifetime, not even born or thought of yet."

"Safety catches off, everyone!" ordered Travis. "You, first shot, Eckels. Second, Billings. Third, Kramer."

"I've hunted tiger, wild boar, buffalo, elephant, but now, this is it," said Eckels. "I'm shaking like a kid." **G**

"Ah," said Travis.

Everyone stopped.

Travis raised his hand. "Ahead," he whispered. "In the mist. There he is. There's His Royal Majesty now."
200 The jungle was wide and full of twitterings, rustlings, murmurs, and sighs. Suddenly it all ceased, as if someone had shut a door.

Silence.

A sound of thunder.

---

9. **pterodactyls** (tĕr'ə-dăk'təlz): extinct flying reptiles.

paradox (păr'ə-dŏks') *n.* a statement or an event that sounds impossible but seems to be true

F ANALYZE SEQUENCE
Up until now, the men have spent most of their time talking and arguing. Now, however, the action begins to pick up. As you read the next sequence of events, pay attention to what happens.

G GRAMMAR AND STYLE
Reread lines 188–195. Notice how Bradbury uses **sentence fragments** and **contractions** to create realistic dialogue.

Out of the mist, one hundred yards away, came *Tyrannosaurus rex.*

"It," whispered Eckels. "It . . ."

"Sh!"

It came on great oiled, **resilient,** striding legs. It towered thirty feet above half of the trees, a great evil god, folding its delicate watchmaker's claws close to its oily reptilian chest. Each lower leg was a piston, a thousand pounds of
210 white bone, sunk in thick ropes of muscle, sheathed over in a gleam of pebbled skin like the mail of a terrible warrior. Each thigh was a ton of meat, ivory, and steel mesh. And from the great breathing cage of the upper body those two delicate arms dangled out front, arms with hands which might pick up and examine men like toys, while the snake neck coiled. And the head itself, a ton of sculptured stone, lifted easily upon the sky. Its mouth gaped, exposing a fence of teeth like daggers. Its eyes rolled, ostrich eggs, empty of all expression save hunger. It closed its mouth in a death grin. It ran, its pelvic bones crushing aside trees and bushes, its taloned feet clawing damp earth, leaving prints six inches deep wherever it settled its weight. It ran with a gliding ballet
220 step, far too poised and balanced for its ten tons. It moved into a sunlit arena warily, its beautifully reptilian hands feeling the air.

"Why, why," Eckels twitched his mouth. "It could reach up and grab the moon."

"Sh!" Travis jerked angrily. "He hasn't seen us yet."

"It can't be killed." Eckels pronounced this verdict quietly, as if there could be no argument. He had weighed the evidence, and this was his considered opinion. The rifle in his hands seemed a cap gun. "We were fools to come. This is impossible."

"Shut up!" hissed Travis. **H**
230 "Nightmare."

"Turn around," commanded Travis. "Walk quietly to the Machine. We'll remit one-half your fee."

"I didn't realize it would be this *big*," said Eckels. "I miscalculated, that's all. And now I want out."

"It *sees* us!"

"There's the red paint on its chest!"

The Tyrant Lizard raised itself. Its armored flesh glittered like a thousand green coins. The coins, crusted with slime, steamed. In the slime, tiny insects wriggled, so that the entire body seemed to twitch and **undulate,** even while
240 the monster itself did not move. It exhaled. The stink of raw flesh blew down the wilderness.

"Get me out of here," said Eckels. "It was never like this before. I was always sure I'd come through alive. I had good guides, good safaris, and safety. This time, I figured wrong. I've met my match and admit it. This is too much for me to get hold of."

"Don't run," said Lesperance. "Turn around. Hide in the Machine."

"Yes." Eckels seemed to be numb. He looked at his feet as if trying to make them move. He gave a grunt of helplessness.

resilient (rĭ-zĭl′yənt)
adj. strong but flexible; able to withstand stress without injury

H MAKE INFERENCES
Why do you think Travis is annoyed with Eckels?

undulate (ŭn′jə-lāt′)
v. to move in waves or in a smooth, wavelike motion

"Eckels!"

250   He took a few steps, blinking, shuffling.

"Not *that* way!"

The Monster, at the first motion, lunged forward with a terrible scream. It covered one hundred yards in six seconds. The rifles jerked up and blazed fire. A windstorm from the beast's mouth engulfed them in the stench of slime and old blood. The Monster roared, teeth glittering with sun.

Eckels, not looking back, walked blindly to the edge of the Path, his gun limp in his arms, stepped off the Path, and walked, not knowing it, in the jungle. His feet sank into green moss. His legs moved him, and he felt alone and remote from the events behind. **I**

260   The rifles cracked again. Their sound was lost in shriek and lizard thunder. The great level of the reptile's tail swung up, lashed sideways. Trees exploded in clouds of leaf and branch. The Monster twitched its jeweler's hands down to fondle at the men, to twist them in half, to crush them like berries, to cram them into its teeth and its screaming throat. Its boulder-stone eyes leveled with the men. They saw themselves mirrored. They fired at the metallic eyelids and the blazing black iris.

I ANALYZE SEQUENCE
Reread lines 252–259. What important event occurs in these lines? What do you think might happen as a result of this event?

ANALYZE VISUALS
What qualities of
Tyrannosaurus rex are
emphasized in this
illustration? Explain.

Like a stone idol, like a mountain avalanche, *Tyrannosaurus* fell.
Thundering, it clutched trees, pulled them with it. It wrenched and tore the
metal Path. The men flung themselves back and away. The body hit, ten
270 tons of cold flesh and stone. The guns fired. The Monster lashed its armored
tail, twitched its snake jaws, and lay still. A fount of blood spurted from its
throat. Somewhere inside, a sac of fluids burst. Sickening gushes drenched the
hunters. They stood, red and glistening.

The thunder faded.

The jungle was silent. After the avalanche, a green peace. After the
nightmare, morning.

Billings and Kramer sat on the pathway and threw up. Travis and
Lesperance stood with smoking rifles, cursing steadily.

In the Time Machine, on his face, Eckels lay shivering. He had found his
280 way back to the Path, climbed into the Machine.

Travis came walking, glanced at Eckels, took cotton gauze from a metal box,
and returned to the others, who were sitting on the Path.

"Clean up."

They wiped the blood from their helmets. They began to curse too. The Monster lay, a hill of solid flesh. Within, you could hear the sighs and murmurs as the furthest chambers of it died, the organs **malfunctioning,** liquids running a final instant from pocket to sac to spleen, everything shutting off, closing up forever. It was like standing by a wrecked locomotive or a steam shovel at quitting time, all valves being released or 290 levered tight. Bones cracked; the tonnage of its own flesh, off balance, dead weight, snapped the delicate forearms, caught underneath. The meat settled, quivering.

Another cracking sound. Overhead, a gigantic tree branch broke from its heavy mooring, fell. It crashed upon the dead beast with finality.

"There." Lesperance checked his watch. "Right on time. That's the giant tree that was scheduled to fall and kill this animal originally." He glanced at the two hunters. "You want the trophy picture?"

"What?"

"We can't take a trophy back to the Future. The body has to stay right here 300 where it would have died originally, so the insects, birds, and bacteria can get at it, as they were intended to. Everything in balance. The body stays. But we *can* take a picture of you standing near it."

The two men tried to think, but gave up, shaking their heads.

They let themselves be led along the metal Path. They sank wearily into the Machine cushions. They gazed back at the ruined Monster, the **stagnating** mound, where already strange reptilian birds and golden insects were busy at the steaming armor.

A sound on the floor of the Time Machine stiffened them. Eckels sat there, shivering.

310 "I'm sorry," he said at last.

"Get up!" cried Travis.

Eckels got up.

"Go out on that Path alone," said Travis. He had his rifle pointed. "You're not coming back in the Machine. We're leaving you here!"

Lesperance seized Travis's arm. "Wait—"

"Stay out of this!" Travis shook his hand away. "This fool nearly killed us. But it isn't *that* so much, no. It's his *shoes!* Look at them! He ran off the Path. That *ruins* us! We'll forfeit! Thousands of dollars of insurance! We guarantee no one leaves the Path. He left it. Oh, the fool! I'll have to report to the 320 government. They might revoke our license to travel. Who knows *what* he's done to Time, to History!" **J**

"Take it easy; all he did was kick up some dirt."

"How do we *know?*" cried Travis. "We don't know anything! It's all a mystery! Get out there, Eckels!"

Eckels fumbled his shirt. "I'll pay anything. A hundred thousand dollars!"

Travis glared at Eckels's checkbook and spat. "Go out there. The Monster's next to the Path. Stick your arms up to your elbows in his mouth. Then you can come back with us."

malfunctioning
(măl-fŭngk′shə-nĭng) *adj.* not working or operating properly **malfunction** *v.*

stagnating (stăg′nā′tĭng) *adj.* becoming foul or rotten from lack of movement **stagnate** *v.*

J **PREDICT**
What do you predict might be the consequences of Eckels's action?

"That's unreasonable!"

330   "The Monster's dead, you idiot. The bullets! The bullets can't be left behind. They don't belong in the Past; they might change anything. Here's my knife. Dig them out!"

The jungle was alive again, full of the old tremorings and bird cries. Eckels turned slowly to regard the primeval garbage dump, that hill of nightmares and terror. After a long time, like a sleepwalker he shuffled out along the Path.

He returned, shuddering, five minutes later, his arms soaked and red to the elbows. He held out his hands. Each held a number of steel bullets. Then he fell. He lay where he fell, not moving.

"You didn't have to make him do that," said Lesperance.

340   "Didn't I? It's too early to tell." Travis nudged the still body. "He'll live. Next time he won't go hunting game like this. Okay." He jerked his thumb wearily at Lesperance. "Switch on. Let's go home."

1492. 1776. 1812.

They cleaned their hands and faces. They changed their caking shirts and pants. Eckels was up and around again, not speaking. Travis glared at him for a full ten minutes.

"Don't look at me," cried Eckels. "I haven't done anything."

"Who can tell?"

"Just ran off the Path, that's all, a little mud on my shoes—what do you

350 want me to do—get down and pray?"

"We might need it. I'm warning you, Eckels, I might kill you yet. I've got my gun ready."

"I'm innocent. I've done nothing!"

1999. 2000. 2055.

The Machine stopped.

"Get out," said Travis.

The room was there as they had left it. But not the same as they had left it. The same man sat behind the same desk. But the same man did not quite sit behind the same desk.

360   Travis looked around swiftly. "Everything okay here?" he snapped.

"Fine. Welcome home!"

Travis did not relax. He seemed to be looking at the very atoms of the air itself, at the way the sun poured through the one high window.

"Okay, Eckels, get out. Don't ever come back."

Eckels could not move.

"You heard me," said Travis. "What're you *staring* at?"

Eckels stood smelling of the air, and there was a thing to the air, a chemical taint so subtle, so slight, that only a faint cry of his **subliminal** senses warned him it was there. The colors, white, gray, blue, orange, in the wall, in the

370 furniture, in the sky beyond the window, were . . . were . . . And there was a *feel*. His flesh twitched. His hands twitched. He stood drinking the oddness with the pores of his body. Somewhere, someone must have been screaming one of those whistles that only a dog can hear. His body screamed silence in return.

subliminal
(sŭb-lĭm′ə-nəl) *adj.* below the level of consciousness

Blue Morpho Butterfly (1864–1865), Martin Johnson Heade. Oil on canvas, 12¼″ × 10″. © Manoogian Collection.

Beyond this room, beyond this wall, beyond this man who was not quite the same man seated at this desk that was not quite the same desk . . . lay an entire world of streets and people. What sort of world it was now, there was no telling. He could feel them moving there, beyond the walls, almost, like so many chess pieces blown in a dry wind. . . .

But the immediate thing was the sign painted on the office wall, the same
380 sign he had read earlier today on first entering.

Somehow, the sign had changed:

TYME SEFARI INC.

SEFARIS TU ANY YEER EN THE PAST.

YU NAIM THE ANIMALL.

WEE TAEKYUTHAIR.

YU SHOOT ITT.

Eckels felt himself fall into a chair. He fumbled crazily at the thick slime on his boots. He held up a clod of dirt, trembling, "No, it *can't* be. Not a *little* thing like that. No!"
390 Embedded in the mud, glistening green and gold and black, was a butterfly, very beautiful and very dead.

"Not a little thing like *that!* Not a butterfly!" cried Eckels. **K**

It fell to the floor, an exquisite thing, a small thing that could upset balances and knock down a line of small dominoes and then big dominoes and then gigantic dominoes, all down the years across Time. Eckels's mind whirled. It *couldn't* change things. Killing one butterfly couldn't be *that* important! Could it?

His face was cold. His mouth trembled, asking: "Who—who won the presidential election yesterday?"
400 The man behind the desk laughed. "You joking? You know very well. Deutscher, of course! Who else? Not that fool weakling Keith. We got an iron man now, a man with guts!" The official stopped. "What's wrong?"

Eckels moaned. He dropped to his knees. He scrabbled at the golden butterfly with shaking fingers. "Can't we," he pleaded to the world, to himself, to the officials, to the Machine, "can't we take it *back;* can't we *make* it alive again? Can't we start over? Can't we—"

He did not move. Eyes shut, he waited, shivering. He heard Travis breathe loud in the room; he heard Travis shift his rifle, click the safety catch, and raise the weapon.
410 There was a sound of thunder. ❧

K MAKE INFERENCES
What important discovery does Eckels make? Why do you think it horrifies him so?

Comprehension

1. **Recall** What does Eckels do in the past that has far-reaching **consequences?**

2. **Summarize** When Eckels returns from the world of dinosaurs, what is different about the present?

3. **Clarify** What is the "sound of thunder" at the end of the story?

Literary Analysis

4. **Make Inferences** How would you characterize the business practices of Time Safari, Inc.?

5. **Draw Conclusions** Why does Travis kill Eckels? Explain your answer.

6. **Understand Sequence** Look again at the chart you filled out as you read. Determine two points in the story where a character could have taken an action that might have prevented changing the future.

7. **Interpret Foreshadowing** Note three or four examples of foreshadowing in the story and the outcome of each example. Make a chart like the one below to record your results. An example has been filled in for you.

Foreshadowing	Outcome
"If you disobey instructions . . ."	Eckels steps off the Path.

8. **Analyze Theme** What theme, or message, is Bradbury conveying through this story? Cite evidence to support your answer.

9. **Evaluate Author** "A Sound of Thunder" is a work of science fiction, yet there are realistic aspects to the story. In your opinion, has Bradbury created a believable story? Cite specific examples to support your opinion.

Literary Criticism

10. **Critical Interpretations** In a review of *Dinosaur Tales*, a collection of Bradbury stories that contains "A Sound of Thunder," the critic Andrew Andrews remarked that Bradbury "gets to you—in simple ways he shows you how to marvel over these awesome, startling creatures." Reread Bradbury's description of *Tyrannosaurus rex*. What words and phrases convey its terrifying force?

PENNSYLVANIA STANDARDS

READING STANDARD
B.2.1.1 Analyze examples of foreshadowing

Vocabulary in Context

VOCABULARY PRACTICE

WORD LIST

annihilate

correlate

expendable

infinitesimally

malfunctioning

paradox

resilient

stagnating

subliminal

undulate

Answer the questions to show your understanding of the vocabulary words.

1. Which is more **expendable** in a jungle, a book or bug repellent?
2. Which is probably **stagnating,** a weed-filled pond or a flowing stream?
3. If I **correlate** information, do I throw it out or see how it fits together?
4. Would a **malfunctioning** phone never ring or have two choices of ring?
5. If a change happens **infinitesimally,** is it easy or difficult to detect?
6. What makes a person's body more **resilient,** exercising or reading?
7. Which might **annihilate** a bird species, a severe virus or a tasty plant?
8. Is a **subliminal** response an unconscious memory or a prepared speech?
9. Would ocean waves or broken glass be more likely to **undulate?**
10. Which is a **paradox,** a rose's blooming in snow or a tree's budding in spring?

VOCABULARY IN WRITING

Use at least three vocabulary words in a short paragraph that describes Eckels's thoughts when he steps off the path. You might start like this.

> **EXAMPLE SENTENCE**
>
> *Eckels was sure that the huge dinosaur would* **annihilate** *him.*

VOCABULARY STRATEGY: THE LATIN WORD ROOT *mal*

The vocabulary word *malfunctioning* contains the Latin root *mal*, meaning "bad" or "wrongly." When *mal* is used as a prefix with English base words, as in *malfunction* and *maltreat*, you can easily figure out meanings. To understand other words containing *mal*, you may need to use context clues as well as your knowledge of the root.

PRACTICE Use the meaning of the root, along with context clues, to figure out the meanings of the underlined words.

1. In his speech, the candidate <u>maligned</u> his opponents.
2. She was grateful that the tumor on her spine was not <u>malignant</u>.
3. Anyone who complains as much as he must be a <u>malcontent</u>.
4. Lincoln wanted to begin his second term as president "with <u>malice</u> toward none, with charity for all."
5. We now know that <u>malaria</u> is spread by mosquitoes, not through the air.

PENNSYLVANIA STANDARDS

READING STANDARD
A.1.2.1 Identify word meaning using affixes

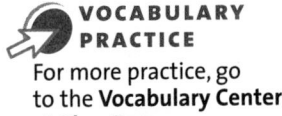

VOCABULARY PRACTICE
For more practice, go to the **Vocabulary Center** at **ClassZone.com.**

Reading-Writing Connection

Broaden your understanding of "A Sound of Thunder" by responding to these prompts. Then use **Revision: Grammar and Style** to improve your writing.

WRITING PROMPTS	SELF-CHECK

A. Short Response: Write Dialogue
What might the characters say to one another after the shooting of Eckels? Using Bradbury's style of dialogue as a model, write **one-half page** of dialogue to show how the characters react to the main incident in the story and its **consequences**.

A successful dialogue will . . .
- use informal, conversational language
- show an understanding of how the characters are likely to respond

B. Extended Response: Write Across Texts
What are the advantages and risks of time travel? Use "A Sound of Thunder" and "From Here to There: The Physics of Time Travel" on the next page to write a **three-to-five-paragraph response.**

A strong analysis will . . .
- state the pros and cons of time travel
- provide examples from the story and the article

REVISION: GRAMMAR AND STYLE

PENNSYLVANIA STANDARDS

WRITING STANDARD
1.4.11.A.3 Utilize dialogue

USE REALISTIC DIALOGUE Review the **Grammar and Style** note on page 40. Bradbury successfully crafts his dialogue by using the following techniques:

1. **Sentence fragments** Although seldom used in formal writing, sentence fragments are common in everyday conversation.

2. **Contractions** Using contractions, like *I've, we'll, hasn't,* and *don't,* makes dialogue sound less formal and more natural. Here is an example from the story:

> "A Tyrannosaurus rex. The Tyrant Lizard, the most incredible monster in history. Sign this release. Anything happens to you, we're not responsible. Those dinosaurs are hungry."
>
> Eckels flushed angrily. "Trying to scare me!" (lines 46–49)

Notice how the revisions in red make this dialogue sound realistic. Revise your response to Prompt A by using similar techniques.

STUDENT MODEL

"Why did'd you do that? Have you lost your mind?" Lesperance cried.

"He was a simpering idiot. He ruined it for all of us. The world's is better off without him," Travis shot back.

WRITING TOOLS
For prewriting, revision, and editing tools, visit the **Writing Center** at ClassZone.com.

MAGAZINE ARTICLE Will it ever be possible to vacation in the past? And if so, would the fate of a prehistoric butterfly really determine the course of a civilization? Questions like this have been the subject of debate among physicists.

From Here to There:
The Physics of
TIME TRAVEL
Brad Stone

TIME TRAVEL—it's the dream of every science-fiction hack who's ever picked up a pen, and the fantasy of many of the rest of us, too. How wonderful to go back and right the wrongs of the past! But time travel could also let you go back and cause an accident that kills your great-great-grandfather, negating your own existence and provoking a potentially universe-ending paradox. At least that's what armchair temporal theorists worry about. But not Paul Nahin. He's a professor of electrical engineering at the University of New Hampshire and the author of *Time Machines: Time Travel in Physics, Metaphysics, and Science Fiction.* And he's able to translate into plain English an ongoing, esoteric debate between some of the smartest minds in physics over whether time travel is actually possible. "The laws of physics as we know them now don't disallow time travel," explains the 57-year-old Nahin. "Anything that physics doesn't forbid must be considered."

Scientific consideration of time travel has its roots, with much of modern physics, in the genius of Albert Einstein, who married space and time in his theory of relativity. Doing further work on relativity in 1948, mathematician Kurt Gödel declared that it would actually be possible to travel through time under the right conditions. Serious scientists didn't give the matter much thought until the mid-'80s, when Carl Sagan's novel *Contact* sent its heroine on a journey through space-time via a wormhole (a theoretical hyperspace tunnel connecting two points of the universe). That intrigued researchers at Caltech, who three years later released a groundbreaking report on the plausibility of traveling through wormholes.

British physicist Stephen Hawking has been the most prominent skeptic, hypothesizing that any attempt at time travel would lead to a "back reaction," a massive buildup of energy that would rip space apart. His theory is called the Chronology Protection Conjecture, since it would make history safe from explorers who might meddle in important historical events. The best evidence against time travel, according to Hawking's writings, is that "we have not been invaded by hordes of tourists from the future."

Other physicists, hoping to prove that time travel is theoretically possible, have devised on paper four different ways to do it. But all require unrealistic quantities of energy under hugely improbable conditions.

Each proposal has supporters and detractors. But the one thing that physicists don't waste much time on is the paradoxes—like altering the present by killing someone in the past. Nahin says time-travel paradoxes are "manifestations of imperfect understanding." So whatever the resolution of the time-travel debate, rest assured that your great-great-grandpa is safe.

The Most Dangerous Game
Short Story by Richard Connell

What does it take to be a
SURVIVOR?

PENNSYLVANIA STANDARDS

READING STANDARDS
A.1.3.1 Make inferences and/or draw conclusions

B.1.1.1.C.1 Interpret and evaluate elements of the plot

KEY IDEA In a test of **survival,** what traits enable a person to succeed? That's the question posed in "The Most Dangerous Game," an adventure story that has thrilled readers since it was first published.

DISCUSS Brainstorm in a group to identify a situation that could be a test of survival. This could be as dramatic as a raging flood or as personal as losing a parent. Discuss the qualities and abilities that a person would need to meet the test, and provide reasons for each choice. Then list all the traits you generated and rank the top four, placing them in a diagram like the one shown.

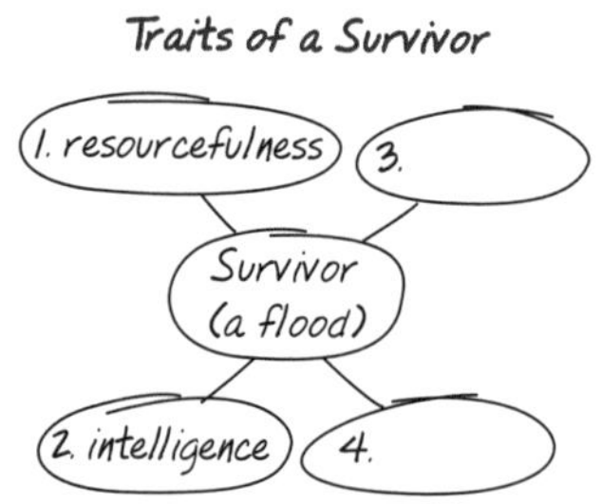

Traits of a Survivor

1. resourcefulness — 3.

Survivor (a flood)

2. intelligence — 4.

LITERARY ANALYSIS: CONFLICT

In the **rising action** of a story, a writer generally introduces one or more **conflicts** that the main character faces. As the rising action unfolds, complications arise that intensify the conflicts and add to the reader's sense of suspense. In "The Most Dangerous Game," Richard Connell expertly builds suspense as the main character encounters one conflict after another. As you read, identify the conflicts and note any complications that arise.

READING STRATEGY: VISUALIZE

Good readers constantly **visualize,** or use details to form a mental picture of the settings, characters, and events of a story. In this story, Connell includes details that help create an image of a dangerous island where strange things happen. As you read, practice the strategy of visualizing. Allow it to help you gain insight into the setting, characters, and events that surround this adventure. Use a chart like the one shown to record story details that form mental images for you.

Details from Story	What I Visualize
Dank tropical night . . . thick warm blackness	→ The dark, heavy air is almost like a blanket.

Review: **Predict**

▲ VOCABULARY IN CONTEXT

Use the context to help you figure out the meaning of each boldfaced word below.

1. real and **tangible**
2. the hunter's **quarry**
3. put at ease by his **disarming** smile
4. a charming, **cultivated** woman
5. a cruise ship offering every **amenity**
6. **condone** rather than condemn
7. a **droll,** self-mocking grin
8. felt no **scruples** about breaking traffic laws
9. asked **solicitously** about my health
10. recommended but not **imperative**
11. **zealous** support of the mayor's program
12. an **uncanny** coincidence

Author Online

A Writing Life
Even as a young boy, Richard Connell loved to write. When he was only 10 years old, he covered baseball games for his father's daily newspaper in Poughkeepsie, New York. By 16, Connell was city editor for the same newspaper. After graduating from Harvard and serving in World War I, Connell wrote more than 300 short stories, as well as novels and screenplays. Many of his short stories became successful films. Connell's success enabled him to travel the world and then settle comfortably in Beverly Hills, California, on the opposite side of the country from his previous hometown of Poughkeepsie.

**Richard Connell
1893–1949**

One-Story Legacy Although Connell became a prosperous writer during his lifetime, only one of his stories—"The Most Dangerous Game"—is widely read today. It won the O. Henry Memorial Prize in 1924. Because of its action-packed and suspenseful plot, it remains a popular and frequently anthologized work.

Background

Big-Game Hunting Hunting for big game, such as lions, rhinos, and leopards, was a popular sport among wealthy people in the early 20th century. These people had time and money to spend on travel and on satisfying their thirst for conquest, danger, and excitement. The two main characters in "The Most Dangerous Game" are experienced hunters in search of a greater challenge.

MORE ABOUT THE AUTHOR AND BACKGROUND
To learn more about Richard Connell and big-game hunting, visit the **Literature Center** at ClassZone.com.

The Most Dangerous Game

Richard Connell

"Off there to the right—somewhere—is a large island," said Whitney. "It's rather a mystery—"

"What island is it?" Rainsford asked.

"The old charts call it 'Ship-Trap Island,'" Whitney replied. "A suggestive name, isn't it? Sailors have a curious dread of the place. I don't know why. Some superstition—"

"Can't see it," remarked Rainsford, trying to peer through the dank tropical night that was palpable as it pressed its thick warm blackness in upon the yacht.

"You've good eyes," said Whitney, with a laugh, "and I've seen you pick off a
10 moose moving in the brown fall bush at four hundred yards, but even you can't see four miles or so through a moonless Caribbean night."

"Nor four yards," admitted Rainsford. "Ugh! It's like moist black velvet."

"It will be light enough in Rio,"[1] promised Whitney. "We should make it in a few days. I hope the jaguar guns have come from Purdey's. We should have some good hunting up the Amazon. Great sport, hunting."

"The best sport in the world," agreed Rainsford.

"For the hunter," amended Whitney. "Not for the jaguar."

"Don't talk rot, Whitney," said Rainsford. "You're a big-game hunter, not a philosopher. Who cares how a jaguar feels?"

20 "Perhaps the jaguar does," observed Whitney.

"Bah! They've no understanding." Ⓐ

ANALYZE VISUALS
What **mood** does the photo stir in you? Decide which details work to evoke this feeling.

Ⓐ **CONFLICT**
Reread lines 16–21. What can you conclude about Rainsford from his conflict with Whitney?

---

1. **Rio:** Rio de Janeiro (rē′ō dā zhə-nâr′ō), a city on the coast of Brazil.

"Even so, I rather think they understand one thing—fear. The fear of pain and the fear of death."

"Nonsense," laughed Rainsford. "This hot weather is making you soft, Whitney. Be a realist. The world is made up of two classes—the hunters and the huntees. Luckily, you and I are hunters. Do you think we've passed that island yet?"

"I can't tell in the dark. I hope so."

"Why?" asked Rainsford.

30   "The place has a reputation—a bad one."

"Cannibals?" suggested Rainsford.

"Hardly. Even cannibals wouldn't live in such a Godforsaken place. But it's gotten into sailor lore, somehow. Didn't you notice that the crew's nerves seemed a bit jumpy today?"

"They were a bit strange, now you mention it. Even Captain Nielsen—"

"Yes, even that tough-minded old Swede, who'd go up to the devil himself and ask him for a light. Those fishy blue eyes held a look I never saw there before. All I could get out of him was: 'This place has an evil name among seafaring men, sir.' Then he said to me, very gravely: 'Don't you feel
40   anything?'—as if the air about us was actually poisonous. Now, you mustn't laugh when I tell you this—I did feel something like a sudden chill. **B**

"There was no breeze. The sea was as flat as a plate-glass window. We were drawing near the island then. What I felt was a—a mental chill; a sort of sudden dread."

"Pure imagination," said Rainsford. "One superstitious sailor can taint the whole ship's company with his fear."

"Maybe. But sometimes I think sailors have an extra sense that tells them when they are in danger. Sometimes I think evil is a **tangible** thing—with wavelengths, just as sound and light have. An evil place can, so to speak,
50   broadcast vibrations of evil. Anyhow, I'm glad we're getting out of this zone. Well, I think I'll turn in now, Rainsford."

"I'm not sleepy," said Rainsford. "I'm going to smoke another pipe up on the afterdeck."

"Good night, then, Rainsford. See you at breakfast."

"Right. Good night, Whitney."

There was no sound in the night as Rainsford sat there but the muffled throb of the engine that drove the yacht swiftly through the darkness, and the swish and ripple of the wash of the propeller.

Rainsford, reclining in a steamer chair, indolently puffed on his favorite
60   brier.[2] The sensuous drowsiness of the night was on him. "It's so dark," he thought, "that I could sleep without closing my eyes; the night would be my eyelids—" **C**

B PREDICT
Reread lines 30–41. Notice that even a hard-boiled sailor is fearful of the island. What do you predict might happen on the island?

tangible (tăn′jə-bəl) *adj.* capable of being touched or felt; having actual form and substance

C VISUALIZE
Reread lines 59–62, trying to visualize Rainsford. What does the author's description tell you about Rainsford's mood?

2. **brier** (brī′ər): a tobacco pipe.

An abrupt sound startled him. Off to the right he heard it, and his ears, expert in such matters, could not be mistaken. Again he heard the sound, and again. Somewhere, off in the blackness, someone had fired a gun three times.

Rainsford sprang up and moved quickly to the rail, mystified. He strained his eyes in the direction from which the reports had come, but it was like trying to see through a blanket. He leaped upon the rail and balanced himself there, to get greater elevation; his pipe, striking a rope, was knocked from his
70 mouth. He lunged for it; a short, hoarse cry came from his lips as he realized he had reached too far and had lost his balance. The cry was pinched off short as the blood-warm waters of the Caribbean Sea closed over his head.

He struggled up to the surface and tried to cry out, but the wash from the speeding yacht slapped him in the face, and the salt water in his open mouth made him gag and strangle. Desperately he struck out with strong strokes after the receding lights of the yacht, but he stopped before he had swum fifty feet. A certain cool-headedness had come to him; it was not the first time he had been in a tight place. There was a chance that his cries could be heard by someone aboard the yacht, but that chance was slender and grew more slender
80 as the yacht raced on. He wrestled himself out of his clothes and shouted with all his power. The lights of the yacht became faint and ever-vanishing fireflies; then they were blotted out entirely by the night. **D**

Rainsford remembered the shots. They had come from the right, and doggedly he swam in that direction, swimming with slow, deliberate strokes, conserving his strength. For a seemingly endless time he fought the sea. He began to count his strokes; he could do possibly a hundred more and then—

Rainsford heard a sound. It came out of the darkness, a high, screaming sound, the sound of an animal in an extremity of anguish and terror.

He did not recognize the animal that made the sound; he did not try to;
90 with fresh vitality he swam toward the sound. He heard it again; then it was cut short by another noise, crisp, staccato.

"Pistol shot," muttered Rainsford, swimming on.

Ten minutes of determined effort brought another sound to his ears—the most welcome he had ever heard—the muttering and growling of the sea breaking on a rocky shore. He was almost on the rocks before he saw them; on a night less calm he would have been shattered against them. With his remaining strength he dragged himself from the swirling waters. Jagged crags appeared to jut up into the opaqueness; he forced himself upward, hand over hand. Gasping, his hands raw, he reached a flat place at the top. Dense jungle
100 came down to the very edge of the cliffs. What perils that tangle of trees and underbrush might hold for him did not concern Rainsford just then. All he knew was that he was safe from his enemy, the sea, and that utter weariness was on him. He flung himself down at the jungle edge and tumbled headlong into the deepest sleep of his life. **E**

D CONFLICT
Here the author builds **suspense** by introducing a complication. What do you think will happen next?

E VISUALIZE
Reread lines 93–104. Which details in this passage help you visualize the scene?

When he opened his eyes, he knew from the position of the sun that it was late in the afternoon. Sleep had given him new vigor; a sharp hunger was picking at him. He looked about him, almost cheerfully.

"Where there are pistol shots, there are men. Where there are men, there is food," he thought. But what kind of men, he wondered, in so forbidding a
110 place? An unbroken front of snarled and ragged jungle fringed the shore. **F**

He saw no sign of a trail through the closely knit web of weeds and trees; it was easier to go along the shore, and Rainsford floundered along by the water. Not far from where he had landed, he stopped.

Some wounded thing, by the evidence a large animal, had thrashed about in the underbrush; the jungle weeds were crushed down, and the moss was lacerated; one patch of weeds was stained crimson. A small, glittering object not far away caught Rainsford's eye, and he picked it up. It was an empty cartridge.

"A twenty-two," he remarked. "That's odd. It must have been a fairly large
120 animal, too. The hunter had his nerve with him to tackle it with a light gun. It's clear that the brute put up a fight. I suppose the first three shots I heard was when the hunter flushed his **quarry** and wounded it. The last shot was when he trailed it here and finished it."

He examined the ground closely and found what he had hoped to find—the print of hunting boots. They pointed along the cliff in the direction he had been going. Eagerly he hurried along, now slipping on a rotten log or a loose stone, but making headway; night was beginning to settle down on the island.

Bleak darkness was blacking out the sea and jungle when Rainsford sighted
130 the lights. He came upon them as he turned a crook in the coastline, and his first thought was that he had come upon a village, for there were many lights. But as he forged along, he saw to his great astonishment that all the lights were in one enormous building—a lofty structure with pointed towers plunging upward into the gloom. His eyes made out the shadowy outlines of a palatial château; it was set on a high bluff, and on three sides of it cliffs dived down to where the sea licked greedy lips in the shadows.

"Mirage," thought Rainsford. But it was no mirage, he found, when he opened the tall spiked iron gate. The stone steps were real enough; the massive door with a leering gargoyle for a knocker was real enough; yet about it all
140 hung an air of unreality. **G**

He lifted the knocker, and it creaked up stiffly as if it had never before been used. He let it fall, and it startled him with its booming loudness. He thought he heard steps within; the door remained closed. Again Rainsford lifted the heavy knocker and let it fall. The door opened then, opened as suddenly as if it were on a spring, and Rainsford stood blinking in the river of glaring gold light that poured out. The first thing Rainsford's eyes discerned was the largest man

F PREDICT
Answer Rainsford's question. What kind of men do you think Rainsford will encounter on the island?

quarry (kwôr'ē) n. the object of a hunt; prey

G VISUALIZE
Reread lines 129–140. Describe your mental image of the chateau. Does it seem like a warm and welcoming place? Explain.

Castle at Noon, William Low. © William Low.

Rainsford had ever seen—a gigantic creature, solidly made and black-bearded to the waist. In his hand the man held a long-barreled revolver, and he was pointing it straight at Rainsford's heart.

150   Out of the snarl of beard two small eyes regarded Rainsford.

"Don't be alarmed," said Rainsford, with a smile which he hoped was **disarming.** "I'm no robber. I fell off a yacht. My name is Sanger Rainsford of New York City."

The menacing look in the eyes did not change. The revolver pointed as rigidly as if the giant were a statue. He gave no sign that he understood Rainsford's words, or that he had even heard them. He was dressed in uniform, a black uniform trimmed with gray astrakhan.[3]

"I'm Sanger Rainsford of New York," Rainsford began again. "I fell off a yacht. I am hungry."

160   The man's only answer was to raise with his thumb the hammer of his revolver. Then Rainsford saw the man's free hand go to his forehead in a military salute, and he saw him click his heels together and stand at attention. Another man was coming down the broad marble steps, an erect, slender man in evening clothes. He advanced to Rainsford and held out his hand.

In a **cultivated** voice marked by a slight accent that gave it added precision and deliberateness, he said: "It is a very great pleasure and honor to welcome Mr. Sanger Rainsford, the celebrated hunter, to my home."

disarming (dĭs-är′mĭng) *adj.* removing or overcoming suspicion; inspiring confidence

cultivated (kŭl′tə-vā′tĭd) *adj.* refined or cultured in manner

---

3. **astrakhan** (ăs′trə-kăn′): a fur made from the curly, wavy wool of young lambs from Astrakhan (a city of southwest Russia).

Automatically Rainsford shook the man's hand.

170 "I've read your book about hunting snow leopards in Tibet,[4] you see," explained the man. "I am General Zaroff."

Rainsford's first impression was that the man was singularly handsome; his second was that there was an original, almost bizarre quality about the general's face. He was a tall man past middle age, 180 for his hair was a vivid white; but his thick eyebrows and pointed military moustache were as black as the night from which Rainsford had come. His eyes, too, were black and very bright. He had high cheekbones, a sharp-cut nose, a spare, dark face, the face of a man used to giving orders, the face of an aristocrat. Turning to the giant 190 in uniform, the general made a sign. The giant put away his pistol, saluted, withdrew.

"Ivan is an incredibly strong fellow," remarked the general, "but he has the misfortune to be deaf and dumb. A simple fellow, but, I'm afraid, like all his race, a bit of a savage."

"Is he Russian?"

200 "He is a Cossack,"[5] said the general, and his smile showed red lips and pointed teeth. "So am I.

"Come," he said, "we shouldn't be chatting here. We can talk later. Now you want clothes, food, rest. You shall have them. This is a most restful spot."

Ivan had reappeared, and the general spoke to him with lips that moved but gave forth no sound.

"Follow Ivan, if you please, Mr. Rainsford," said the general. "I was about to have my dinner when you came. I'll wait for you. You'll find that my clothes will fit you, I think."

---

4. **Tibet** (tə-bĕt′): a region in central Asia.

5. **Cossack** (kŏs′ăk): a member of a southern Russian people, many of whom served as fierce cavalrymen under the Russian tsars.

It was to a huge, beam-ceilinged bedroom with a canopied bed big enough
for six men that Rainsford followed the silent giant. Ivan laid out an evening
suit, and Rainsford, as he put it on, noticed that it came from a London tailor
who ordinarily cut and sewed for none below the rank of duke.

The dining room to which Ivan conducted him was in many ways
remarkable. There was a medieval magnificence about it; it suggested a
baronial hall of feudal times with its oaken panels, its high ceiling, its vast
refectory table where two score men could sit down to eat. About the hall were
the mounted heads of many animals—lions, tigers, elephants, moose, bears;
larger or more perfect specimens Rainsford had never seen. At the great table
the general was sitting, alone.

"You'll have a cocktail, Mr. Rainsford," he suggested. The cocktail was
surpassingly good; and, Rainsford noted, the table appointments were of the
finest—the linen, the crystal, the silver, the china.

They were eating *borsch*, the rich red soup with whipped cream so dear to
Russian palates. Half apologetically General Zaroff said: "We do our best to
preserve the **amenities** of civilization here. Please forgive any lapses. We are
well off the beaten track, you know. Do you think the champagne has suffered
from its long ocean trip?"

"Not in the least," declared Rainsford. He was finding the general a most
thoughtful and affable host, a true cosmopolite.[6] But there was one small trait
of the general's that made Rainsford uncomfortable. Whenever he looked up
from his plate, he found the general studying him, appraising him narrowly.

"Perhaps," said General Zaroff, "you were surprised that I recognized your
name. You see, I read all books on hunting published in English, French, and
Russian. I have but one passion in my life, Mr. Rainsford, and it is the hunt."

"You have some wonderful heads here," said Rainsford as he ate a
particularly well cooked filet mignon. "That Cape buffalo is the largest I
ever saw."

"Oh, that fellow. Yes, he was a monster."

"Did he charge you?"

"Hurled me against a tree," said the general. "Fractured my skull. But I got
the brute."

"I've always thought," said Rainsford, "that the Cape buffalo is the most
dangerous of all big game."

For a moment the general did not reply; he was smiling his curious red-
lipped smile. Then he said slowly: "No. You are wrong, sir. The Cape buffalo is
not the most dangerous big game." He sipped his wine. "Here in my preserve
on this island," he said, in the same slow tone, "I hunt more dangerous game."

Rainsford expressed his surprise. "Is there big game on this island?"

The general nodded. "The biggest."

"Really?"

"Oh, it isn't here naturally, of course. I have to stock the island."

amenity (ə-mĕn'ĭ-tē)
n. something that adds
to one's comfort or
convenience

---

6. **cosmopolite** (kŏz-mŏp'ə-līt'): a sophisticated person who can handle any situation well.

"What have you imported, General?" Rainsford asked. "Tigers?"

The general smiled. "No," he said. "Hunting tigers ceased to interest me some years ago. I exhausted their possibilities, you see. No thrill left in tigers, no real danger. I live for danger, Mr. Rainsford."

The general took from his pocket a gold cigarette case and offered his guest a long black cigarette with a silver tip; it was perfumed and gave off a smell like incense.

"We will have some capital hunting, you and I," said the general. "I shall be 260 most glad to have your society."

"But what game—" began Rainsford.

"I'll tell you," said the general. "You will be amused, I know. I think I may say, in all modesty, that I have done a rare thing. I have invented a new sensation. May I pour you another glass of port, Mr. Rainsford?"

"Thank you, General." **H**

The general filled both glasses and said: "God makes some men poets. Some he makes kings, some beggars. Me he made a hunter. My hand was made for the trigger, my father said. He was a very rich man with a quarter of a million acres in the Crimea, and he was an ardent sportsman. When I was only five 270 years old, he gave me a little gun, specially made in Moscow for me, to shoot sparrows with. When I shot some of his prize turkeys with it, he did not punish me; he complimented me on my marksmanship. I killed my first bear in the Caucasus[7] when I was ten. My whole life has been one prolonged hunt. I went into the army—it was expected of noblemen's sons—and for a time commanded a division of Cossack cavalry, but my real interest was always the hunt. I have hunted every kind of game in every land. It would be impossible for me to tell you how many animals I have killed."

The general puffed at his cigarette.

"After the debacle in Russia I left the country, for it was imprudent for 280 an officer of the Tsar[8] to stay there. Many noble Russians lost everything. I, luckily, had invested heavily in American securities, so I shall never have to open a tearoom in Monte Carlo or drive a taxi in Paris. Naturally, I continued to hunt—grizzlies in your Rockies, crocodiles in the Ganges,[9] rhinoceroses in East Africa. It was in Africa that the Cape buffalo hit me and laid me up for six months. As soon as I recovered, I started for the Amazon to hunt jaguars, for I had heard they were unusually cunning. They weren't." The Cossack sighed. "They were no match at all for a hunter with his wits about him, and a high-powered rifle. I was bitterly disappointed. I was lying in my tent with a splitting headache one night when a terrible thought pushed its way into my

H CONFLICT
Reread lines 228–265. The conversation between Rainsford and Zaroff hints at further plot **complications.** Use clues to predict future events.

---

7. **Crimea** (krī-mē′ə) . . . **Caucasus** (kô′kə-səs): regions in the southern part of the former Russian Empire, near the Black Sea.

8. **debacle in Russia . . . Tsar** (zär): a reference to the 1917 Russian Revolution, in which the emperor, Tsar Nicholas II, was violently overthrown.

9. **Ganges** (găn′jēz′): a river in northern India.

290 mind. Hunting was beginning to bore me! And hunting, remember, had been my life. I have heard that in America businessmen often go to pieces when they give up the business that has been their life."

"Yes, that's so," said Rainsford. **I**

The general smiled. "I had no wish to go to pieces," he said. "I must do something. Now, mine is an analytical mind, Mr. Rainsford. Doubtless that is why I enjoy the problems of the chase."

"No doubt, General Zaroff."

"So," continued the general, "I asked myself why the hunt no longer fascinated me. You are much younger than I am, Mr. Rainsford, and have not 300 hunted as much, but you perhaps can guess the answer."

"What was it?"

"Simply this: hunting had ceased to be what you call 'a sporting proposition.' It had become too easy. I always got my quarry. Always. There is no greater bore than perfection."

The general lit a fresh cigarette.

"No animal had a chance with me any more. That is no boast; it is a mathematical certainty. The animal had nothing but his legs and his instinct. Instinct is no match for reason. When I thought of this, it was a tragic moment for me, I can tell you."

310 Rainsford leaned across the table, absorbed in what his host was saying.

"It came to me as an inspiration what I must do," the general went on.

"And that was?"

The general smiled the quiet smile of one who has faced an obstacle and surmounted it with success. "I had to invent a new animal to hunt," he said. **J**

"A new animal? You're joking."

"Not at all," said the general. "I never joke about hunting. I needed a new animal. I found one. So I bought this island, built this house, and here I do my hunting. The island is perfect for my purposes—there are jungles with a maze of trails in them, hills, swamps—"

320 "But the animal, General Zaroff?"

"Oh," said the general, "it supplies me with the most exciting hunting in the world. No other hunting compares with it for an instant. Every day I hunt, and I never grow bored now, for I have a quarry with which I can match my wits."

Rainsford's bewilderment showed in his face.

"I wanted the ideal animal to hunt," explained the general. "So I said: 'What are the attributes of an ideal quarry?' And the answer was, of course: 'It must have courage, cunning, and, above all, it must be able to reason.'"

"But no animal can reason," objected Rainsford.

330 "My dear fellow," said the general, "there is one that can."

"But you can't mean—" gasped Rainsford.

"And why not?"

"I can't believe you are serious, General Zaroff. This is a grisly joke."

I VISUALIZE
As you read the rest of this page, visualize the expression on Rainsford's face as he listens to General Zaroff. How does his expression change over the course of the conversation?

J PREDICT
What "new animal" do you think General Zaroff likes to hunt? Support your answer with evidence.

"Why should I not be serious? I am speaking of hunting."

"Hunting? Good God, General Zaroff, what you speak of is murder."

The general laughed with entire good nature. He regarded Rainsford quizzically. "I refuse to believe that so modern and civilized a young man as you seem to be harbors romantic ideas about the value of human life. Surely your experiences in the war—"

340 "Did not make me **condone** cold-blooded murder," finished Rainsford, stiffly.

Laughter shook the general. "How extraordinarily **droll** you are!" he said. "One does not expect nowadays to find a young man of the educated class, even in America, with such a naïve, and, if I may say so, mid-Victorian point of view. It's like finding a snuffbox in a limousine. Ah, well, doubtless you had Puritan ancestors. So many Americans appear to have had. I'll wager you'll forget your notions when you go hunting with me. You've a genuine new thrill in store for you, Mr. Rainsford."

"Thank you, I'm a hunter, not a murderer."

350 "Dear me," said the general, quite unruffled, "again that unpleasant word. But I think I can show you that your **scruples** are quite ill-founded."

"Yes?"

"Life is for the strong, to be lived by the strong, and, if needs be, taken by the strong. The weak of the world were put here to give the strong pleasure. I am strong. Why should I not use my gift? If I wish to hunt, why should I not? I hunt the scum of the earth—sailors from tramp ships—lascars,[10] blacks, Chinese, whites, mongrels—a thoroughbred horse or hound is worth more than a score of them."

"But they are men," said Rainsford, hotly.

360 "Precisely," said the general. "That is why I use them. It gives me pleasure. They can reason, after a fashion. So they are dangerous."

"But where do you get them?"

The general's left eyelid fluttered down in a wink. "This island is called Ship Trap," he answered. "Sometimes an angry god of the high seas sends them to me. Sometimes, when Providence is not so kind, I help Providence a bit. Come to the window with me."

Rainsford went to the window and looked out toward the sea.

"Watch! Out there!" exclaimed the general, pointing into the night. Rainsford's eyes saw only blackness, and then, as the general pressed a button,
370 far out to sea Rainsford saw the flash of lights.

The general chuckled. "They indicate a channel," he said, "where there's none: giant rocks with razor edges crouch like a sea monster with wide-open jaws. They can crush a ship as easily as I crush this nut." He dropped a walnut on the hardwood floor and brought his heel grinding down on it. "Oh, yes," he said, casually, as if in answer to a question, "I have electricity. We try to be civilized here."

---

10. **lascars** (lăs′kərz): sailors from India.

condone (kən-dōn′) *v.* to forgive or overlook

droll (drōl) *adj.* amusingly odd or comical

scruple (skroō′pəl) *n.* a feeling of uneasiness that keeps a person from doing something

Detail of *Downtime*, Dale Kennington © Dale Kennington/Superstock.

"Civilized? And you shoot down men?"

A trace of anger was in the general's black eyes, but it was there for but a second, and he said, in his most pleasant manner: "Dear me, what a righteous young man you are! I assure you I do not do the thing you suggest. That would be barbarous. I treat these visitors with every consideration. They get plenty of good food and exercise. They get into splendid physical condition. You shall see for yourself tomorrow."

"What do you mean?"

"We'll visit my training school," smiled the general. "It's in the cellar. I have about a dozen pupils down there now. They're from the Spanish bark *Sanlúcar* that had the bad luck to go on the rocks out there. A very inferior lot, I regret to say. Poor specimens and more accustomed to the deck than to the jungle."

He raised his hand, and Ivan, who served as waiter, brought thick Turkish coffee. Rainsford, with an effort, held his tongue in check.

"It's a game, you see," pursued the general, blandly. "I suggest to one of them that we go hunting. I give him a supply of food and an excellent hunting knife. I give him three hours' start. I am to follow, armed only with a pistol of the smallest caliber and range. If my quarry eludes me for three whole days, he wins the game. If I find him"—the general smiled—"he loses."

"Suppose he refuses to be hunted?"

"Oh," said the general, "I give him his option, of course. He need not play that game if he doesn't wish to. If he does not wish to hunt, I turn him over to Ivan. Ivan once had the honor of serving as official knouter[11] to the Great 400 White Tsar, and he has his own ideas of sport. Invariably, Mr. Rainsford, invariably they choose the hunt."

"And if they win?"

The smile on the general's face widened.

"To date I have not lost," he said.

Then he added, hastily: "I don't wish you to think me a braggart, Mr. Rainsford. Many of them afford only the most elementary sort of problem. Occasionally I strike a tartar.[12] One almost did win. I eventually had to use the dogs."

"The dogs?"

410 "This way, please. I'll show you."

The general steered Rainsford to a window. The lights from the windows sent a flickering illumination that made grotesque patterns on the courtyard below, and Rainsford could see moving about there a dozen or so huge black shapes; as they turned toward him, their eyes glittered greenly.

"A rather good lot, I think," observed the general. "They are let out at seven every night. If anyone should try to get into my house—or out of it— something extremely regrettable would occur to him." He hummed a snatch of song from the Folies Bergère.[13]

"And now," said the general, "I want to show you my new collection of 420 heads. Will you come with me to the library?" 🄺

"I hope," said Rainsford, "that you will excuse me tonight, General Zaroff. I'm really not feeling at all well."

"Ah, indeed?" the general inquired, **solicitously.** "Well, I suppose that's only natural, after your long swim. You need a good, restful night's sleep. Tomorrow you'll feel like a new man, I'll wager. Then we'll hunt, eh? I've one rather promising prospect—"

Rainsford was hurrying from the room.

"Sorry you can't go with me tonight," called the general. "I expect rather fair sport—a big, strong black. He looks resourceful— Well, good night, 430 Mr. Rainsford; I hope you have a good night's rest."

The bed was good, and the pajamas of the softest silk, and he was tired in every fiber of his being, but nevertheless Rainsford could not quiet his brain with the opiate of sleep. He lay, eyes wide open. Once he thought he heard stealthy steps in the corridor outside his room. He sought to throw open the

🄺 **PREDICT**
Reread lines 419–420. What kind of heads do you think the general is referring to?

solicitously
(sə-lĭs′ĭ-təs-lē) *adv.* in a manner expressing care or concern

---

11. **knouter** (nou′tər): a person who whipped criminals in Russia.

12. **strike a tartar**: encounter a fierce opponent.

13. **Folies Bergère** (fô-lē′ bĕr-zhĕr′): a music hall in Paris, famous for its variety shows.

door; it would not open. He went to the window and looked out. His room was high up in one of the towers. The lights of the château were out now, and it was dark and
440 silent, but there was a fragment of sallow moon, and by its wan light he could see, dimly, the courtyard; there, weaving in and out in the pattern of shadow, were black, noiseless forms; the hounds heard him at the window and looked up, expectantly, with their green eyes. Rainsford went back to the bed and lay down. By many methods
450 he tried to put himself to sleep. He had achieved a doze when, just as morning began to come, he heard, far off in the jungle, the faint report of a pistol.

General Zaroff did not appear until luncheon. He was dressed faultlessly in the tweeds of a country squire. He was solicitous about the state of Rainsford's health.

"As for me," sighed the general, "I do not feel so well. I am worried, Mr. Rainsford. Last night I detected traces of my old complaint."

To Rainsford's questioning glance the general said: "Ennui. Boredom."

460 Then, taking a second helping of crêpes suzettes, the general explained: "The hunting was not good last night. The fellow lost his head. He made a straight trail that offered no problems at all. That's the trouble with these sailors; they have dull brains to begin with, and they do not know how to get about in the woods. They do excessively stupid and obvious things. It's most annoying. Will you have another glass of Chablis,[14] Mr. Rainsford?"

"General," said Rainsford, firmly, "I wish to leave this island at once."

The general raised his thickets of eyebrows; he seemed hurt. "But, my dear fellow," the general protested, "you've only just come. You've had no hunting—"

470 "I wish to go today," said Rainsford. He saw the dead black eyes of the general on him, studying him. General Zaroff's face suddenly brightened.

He filled Rainsford's glass with venerable Chablis from a dusty bottle.

"Tonight," said the general, "we will hunt—you and I."

Rainsford shook his head. "No, General," he said. "I will not hunt."

The general shrugged his shoulders and delicately ate a hothouse grape. "As you wish, my friend," he said. "The choice rests entirely with you. But may I not venture to suggest that you will find my idea of sport more diverting than Ivan's?"

---

14. **Chablis** (shă-blē´): a type of white French wine.

He nodded toward the corner to where the giant stood, scowling, his thick
480 arms crossed on his hogshead of chest.

"You don't mean—" cried Rainsford.

"My dear fellow," said the general, "have I not told you I always mean what
I say about hunting? This is really an inspiration. I drink to a foeman worthy
of my steel—at last."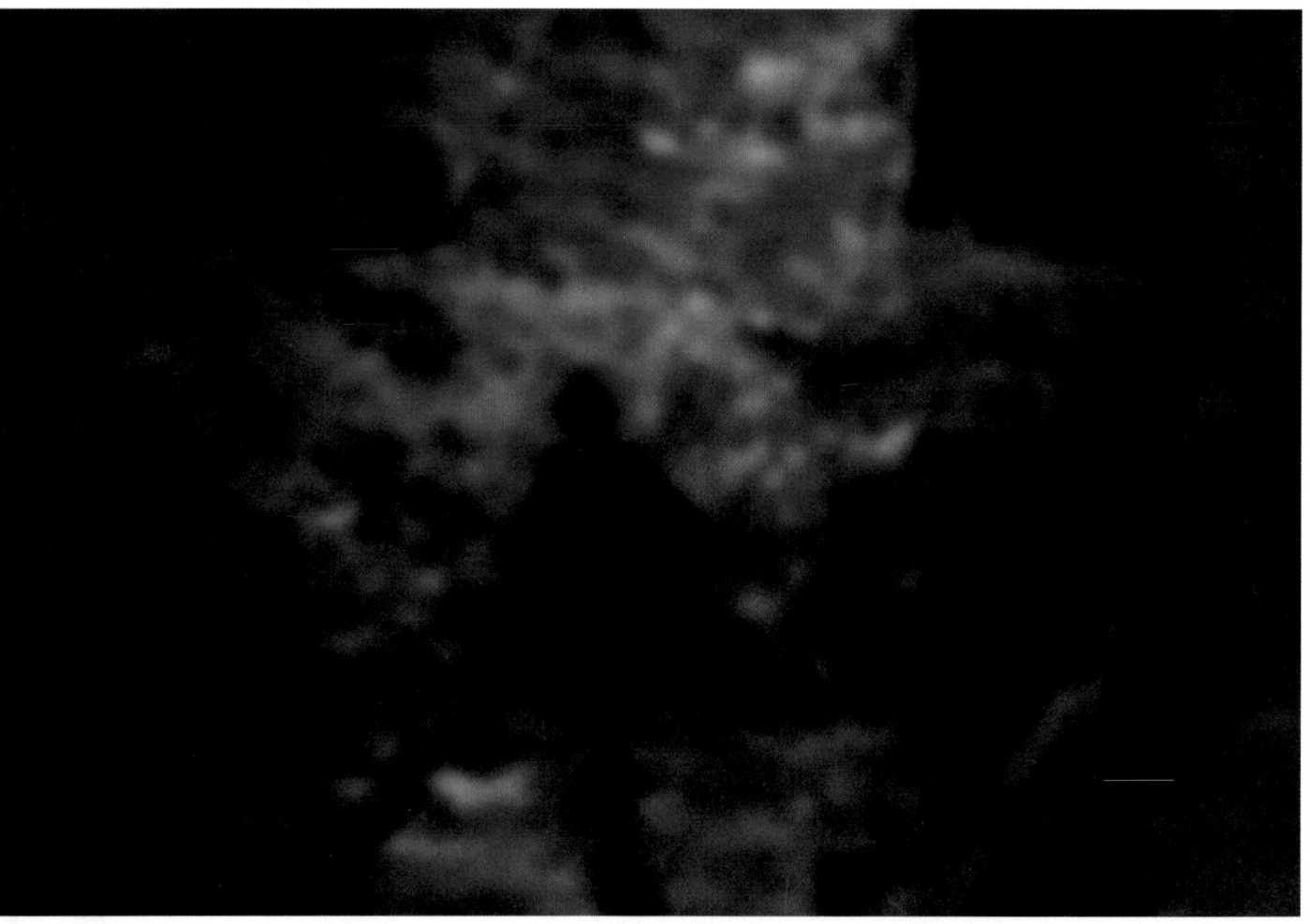

The general raised his glass, but Rainsford sat staring at him.

"You'll find this game worth playing," the general said, enthusiastically.
"Your brain against mine. Your woodcraft against mine. Your strength and
stamina against mine. Outdoor chess! And the stake is not without value, eh?"

"And if I win—" began Rainsford, huskily.
490 "I'll cheerfully acknowledge myself defeated if I do not find you by
midnight of the third day," said General Zaroff. "My sloop will place you on
the mainland near a town."

The general read what Rainsford was thinking.

"Oh, you can trust me," said the Cossack. "I will give you my word as a
gentleman and a sportsman. Of course, you, in turn, must agree to say nothing
of your visit here."

"I'll agree to nothing of the kind," said Rainsford.

L **CONFLICT**
The main conflict in the
story has now become
clear. What is it?

"Oh," said the general, "in that case— But why discuss that now? Three days hence we can discuss it over a bottle of Veuve Clicquot,[15] unless—"

500 The general sipped his wine.

Then a businesslike air animated him. "Ivan," he said to Rainsford, "will supply you with hunting clothes, food, a knife. I suggest you wear moccasins; they leave a poorer trail. I suggest, too, that you avoid the big swamp in the southeast corner of the island. We call it Death Swamp. There's quicksand there. One foolish fellow tried it. The deplorable part of it was that Lazarus followed him. You can imagine my feelings, Mr. Rainsford. I loved Lazarus; he was the finest hound in my pack. Well, I must beg you to excuse me now. I always take a siesta after lunch. You'll hardly have time for a nap, I fear. You'll want to start, no doubt. I shall not follow till dusk. Hunting at night is so
510 much more exciting than by day, don't you think? Au revoir,[16] Mr. Rainsford, au revoir."

General Zaroff, with a deep, courtly bow, strolled from the room.

From another door came Ivan. Under one arm he carried khaki hunting clothes, a haversack of food, a leather sheath containing a long-bladed hunting knife; his right hand rested on a cocked revolver thrust in the crimson sash about his waist. . . . ⓜ

Rainsford had fought his way through the bush for two hours. "I must keep my nerve. I must keep my nerve," he said, through tight teeth.

He had not been entirely clear-headed when the château gates snapped shut
520 behind him. His whole idea at first was to put distance between himself and General Zaroff, and, to this end, he had plunged along, spurred on by the sharp rowels of something very like panic. Now he had got a grip on himself, had stopped, and was taking stock of himself and the situation.

He saw that straight flight was futile; inevitably it would bring him face to face with the sea. He was in a picture with a frame of water, and his operations, clearly, must take place within that frame.

"I'll give him a trail to follow," muttered Rainsford, and he struck off from the rude path he had been following into the trackless wilderness. He executed a series of intricate loops; he doubled on his trail again and again, recalling all
530 the lore of the fox hunt, and all the dodges of the fox. Night found him leg-weary, with hands and face lashed by the branches, on a thickly wooded ridge. He knew it would be insane to blunder on through the dark, even if he had the strength. His need for rest was **imperative**, and he thought, "I have played the fox; now I must play the cat of the fable."[17] A big tree with a thick trunk and outspread branches was nearby, and, taking care to leave not the slightest mark, he climbed up into the crotch and, stretching out on one of the broad limbs, after a fashion, rested. Rest brought him new confidence and almost a feeling of security. Even so **zealous** a hunter as General Zaroff could not trace him

ⓜ GRAMMAR AND STYLE
Reread lines 513–516. Notice how Connell uses multiple **prepositional phrases**—such as "on a cocked revolver" and "in the crimson sash"—to add descriptive details.

imperative (ĭm-pĕr′ə-tĭv)
adj. absolutely necessary

zealous (zĕl′əs) *adj.* intensely enthusiastic

---

15. **Veuve Clicquot** (vœv′ klĭ-kō′): a French champagne.

16. **au revoir** (ō′ rə-vwär′): goodbye; farewell till we meet again.

17. **I have played the fox . . . fable:** In Aesop's fable "The Cat and the Fox," the fox brags of knowing many ways to escape an enemy. The cat knows only one, but is successful with it.

there, he told himself; only the devil himself could follow that complicated
540 trail through the jungle after dark. But perhaps the general was a devil—

An apprehensive night crawled slowly by like a wounded snake, and sleep
did not visit Rainsford, although the silence of a dead world was on the
jungle. Toward morning, when a dingy gray was varnishing the sky, the cry of
some startled bird focused Rainsford's attention in that direction. Something
was coming through the bush, coming slowly, carefully, coming by the same
winding way Rainsford had come. He flattened himself down on the limb, and
through a screen of leaves almost as thick as tapestry, he watched. The thing
that was approaching was a man.

It was General Zaroff. He made his way along with his eyes fixed in utmost
550 concentration on the ground before him. He paused, almost beneath the tree,
dropped to his knees, and studied the ground. Rainsford's impulse was to hurl
himself down like a panther, but he saw that the general's right hand held
something metallic—a small automatic pistol. **N**

The hunter shook his head several times, as if he were puzzled. Then he
straightened up and took from his case one of his black cigarettes; its pungent,
incenselike smoke floated up to Rainsford's nostrils.

Rainsford held his breath. The general's eyes had left the ground and were
traveling inch by inch up the tree. Rainsford froze there, every muscle tensed
for a spring. But the sharp eyes of the hunter stopped before they reached the
560 limb where Rainsford lay; a smile spread over his brown face. Very deliberately
he blew a smoke ring into the air; then he turned his back on the tree and
walked carelessly away, back along the trail he had come. The swish of the
underbrush against his hunting boots grew fainter and fainter.

The pent-up air burst hotly from Rainsford's lungs. His first thought made
him feel sick and numb. The general could follow a trail through the woods
at night; he could follow an extremely difficult trail; he must have **uncanny**
powers; only by the merest chance had the Cossack failed to see his quarry.

Rainsford's second thought was even more terrible. It sent a shudder of cold
horror through his whole being. Why had the general smiled? Why had he
570 turned back?

Rainsford did not want to believe what his reason told him was true, but the
truth was as evident as the sun that had by now pushed through the morning
mists. The general was playing with him! The general was saving him for
another day's sport! The Cossack was the cat; he was the mouse. Then it was
that Rainsford knew the full meaning of terror. **O**

"I will not lose my nerve. I will not."

He slid down from the tree and struck off again into the woods. His
face was set, and he forced the machinery of his mind to function. Three
hundred yards from his hiding place he stopped where a huge dead tree leaned
580 precariously on a smaller, living one. Throwing off his sack of food, Rainsford
took his knife from its sheath and began to work with all his energy.

N **PREDICT**
This is one of the most **suspenseful** moments in the story. What do you think General Zaroff will do to Rainsford? Why?

uncanny (ŭn-kăn'ē) *adj.* so remarkable as to seem supernatural

O **CONFLICT**
What **complication** is introduced to intensify the conflict and build **suspense**?

The job was finished at last, and he threw himself down behind a fallen log a hundred feet away. He did not have to wait long. The cat was coming again to play with the mouse.

Following the trail with the sureness of a bloodhound came General Zaroff. Nothing escaped those searching black eyes, no crushed blade of grass, no bent twig, no mark, no matter
590 how faint, in the moss. So intent was the Cossack on his stalking that he was upon the thing Rainsford had made before he saw it. His foot touched the protruding bough[18] that was the trigger. Even as he touched it, the general sensed his danger and leaped back with the agility of an ape. But he was not quite quick enough; the dead tree, delicately adjusted to rest on the cut living one, crashed down and struck the general a glancing blow on the shoulder as it fell; but for his
600 alertness, he must have been smashed beneath it. He staggered, but he did not fall; nor did he drop his revolver. He stood there, rubbing his injured shoulder, and Rainsford, with fear again gripping his heart, heard the general's mocking laugh ring through the jungle.

"Rainsford," called the general, "if you are within sound of my voice, as I suppose you are, let me congratulate you. Not many men know how to make a Malay man-catcher. Luckily for me I,
610 too, have hunted in Malacca.[19] You are proving interesting, Mr. Rainsford. I am going now to have my wound dressed; it's only a slight one. But I shall be back. I shall be back."

When the general, nursing his bruised shoulder, had gone, Rainsford took up his flight again. It was flight now, a desperate, hopeless flight, that carried him on for some hours. Dusk came, then darkness, and still he pressed on. The ground grew softer under his moccasins; the vegetation grew ranker, denser; insects bit him savagely. Then, as he stepped forward, his foot sank into the ooze. He tried to wrench it back, but the muck sucked viciously at his foot as if it were a giant leech. With a violent effort he tore his foot loose. He knew
620 where he was now. Death Swamp and its quicksand.

His hands were tight closed as if his nerve were something tangible that someone in the darkness was trying to tear from his grip. The softness of the

Tree Circle (1992), Peter Schroth. Oil on paper, 7½″ × 8½″.
© Peter Schroth.

---

18. **protruding bough** (bou): a tree branch that extends or juts out.

19. **Malay** (mə-lā′) . . . **Malacca** (mə-lăk′ə): The Malays are a people of southeast Asia. Malacca is a region they inhabit, just south of Thailand.

earth had given him an idea. He stepped back from the quicksand a dozen feet or so, and like some huge prehistoric beaver, he began to dig.

Rainsford had dug himself in in France when a second's delay meant death. That had been a placid pastime compared to his digging now. The pit grew deeper; when it was above his shoulders, he climbed out and from some hard saplings cut stakes and sharpened them to a fine point. These stakes he planted in the bottom of the pit with the points sticking up. With flying fingers he
630 wove a rough carpet of weeds and branches, and with it he covered the mouth of the pit. Then, wet with sweat and aching with tiredness, he crouched behind the stump of a lightning-charred tree. **P**

He knew his pursuer was coming; he heard the padding sound of feet on the soft earth, and the night breeze brought him the perfume of the general's cigarette. It seemed to Rainsford that the general was coming with unusual swiftness; he was not feeling his way along, foot by foot. Rainsford, crouching there, could not see the general, nor could he see the pit. He lived a year in a minute. Then he felt an impulse to cry aloud with joy, for he heard the sharp crackle of the breaking branches as the cover of the pit gave way; he heard the
640 sharp scream of pain as the pointed stakes found their mark. He leaped up from his place of concealment. Then he cowered back. Three feet from the pit a man was standing, with an electric torch in his hand.

"You've done well, Rainsford," the voice of the general called. "Your Burmese tiger pit[20] has claimed one of my best dogs. Again you score. I think, Mr. Rainsford, I'll see what you can do against my whole pack. I'm going home for a rest now. Thank you for a most amusing evening."

At daybreak Rainsford, lying near the swamp, was awakened by a sound that made him know that he had new things to learn about fear. It was a distant sound, faint and wavering, but he knew it. It was the baying of a
650 pack of hounds. **Q**

Rainsford knew he could do one of two things. He could stay where he was and wait. That was suicide. He could flee. That was postponing the inevitable. For a moment he stood there, thinking. An idea that held a wild chance came to him, and, tightening his belt, he headed away from the swamp.

The baying of the hounds grew nearer, then still nearer, nearer, ever nearer. On a ridge Rainsford climbed a tree. Down a watercourse, not a quarter of a mile away, he could see the bush moving. Straining his eyes, he saw the lean figure of General Zaroff; just ahead of him, Rainsford made out another figure whose wide shoulders surged through the tall jungle weeds; it was the giant
660 Ivan, and he seemed pulled forward by some unseen force; Rainsford knew that Ivan must be holding the pack in leash.

They would be on him any minute now. His mind worked frantically. He thought of a native trick he had learned in Uganda.[21] He slid down the tree.

---

20. **Burmese** (bər-mēz') **tiger pit:** a trap used for catching tigers in Myanmar, a country in Southeast Asia formerly called Burma.

21. **Uganda** (yōō-găn'də): a country in central Africa.

P PREDICT
Will the trap ensnare the general? Give reasons for your prediction.

Q CONFLICT
The introduction of the pack of hounds poses a new complication. What recourse does Rainsford have?

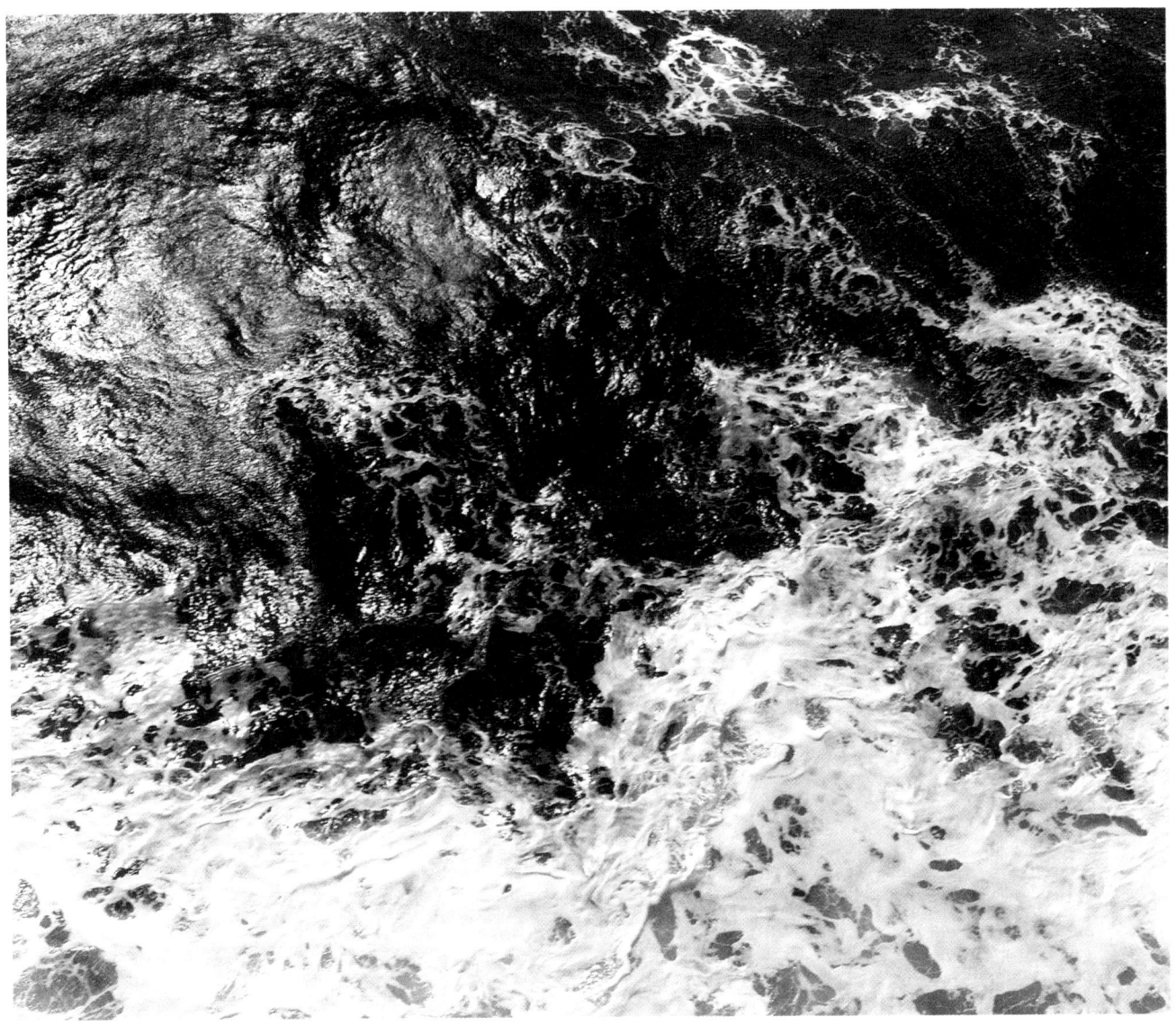

He caught hold of a springy young sapling, and to it he fastened his hunting knife, with the blade pointing down the trail; with a bit of wild grapevine he tied back the sapling. Then he ran for his life. The hounds raised their voices as they hit the fresh scent. Rainsford knew now how an animal at bay feels.

He had to stop to get his breath. The baying of the hounds stopped abruptly, and Rainsford's heart stopped, too. They must have reached the knife.

670 He shinned excitedly up a tree and looked back. His pursuers had stopped. But the hope that was in Rainsford's brain when he climbed died, for he saw in the shallow valley that General Zaroff was still on his feet. But Ivan was not. The knife, driven by the recoil of the springing tree, had not wholly failed.

Rainsford had hardly tumbled to the ground when the pack took up the cry again.

"Nerve, nerve, nerve!" he panted, as he dashed along. A blue gap showed between the trees dead ahead. Ever nearer drew the hounds. Rainsford forced himself on toward that gap. He reached it. It was the shore of the sea. Across a cove he could see the gloomy gray stone of the château. Twenty feet below him
680 the sea rumbled and hissed. Rainsford hesitated. He heard the hounds. Then he leaped far out into the sea. . . .

When the general and his pack reached the place by the sea, the Cossack stopped. For some minutes he stood regarding the blue-green expanse of water. He shrugged his shoulders. Then he sat down, took a drink of brandy from a silver flask, lit a perfumed cigarette, and hummed a bit from *Madama Butterfly.*[22] **R**

General Zaroff had an exceedingly good dinner in his great paneled dining hall that evening. With it he had a bottle of Pol Roger and half a bottle of Chambertin.[23] Two slight annoyances kept him from perfect enjoyment. One
690 was the thought that it would be difficult to replace Ivan; the other was that his quarry had escaped him; of course the American hadn't played the game— so thought the general as he tasted his after-dinner liqueur. In his library he read, to soothe himself, from the works of Marcus Aurelius.[24] At ten he went up to his bedroom. He was deliciously tired, he said to himself, as he locked himself in. There was a little moonlight, so before turning on his light he went to the window and looked down at the courtyard. He could see the great hounds, and he called "Better luck another time" to them. Then he switched on the light.

A man, who had been hiding in the curtains of the bed, was standing there.
700 "Rainsford!" screamed the general. "How in God's name did you get here?"

"Swam," said Rainsford. "I found it quicker than walking through the jungle."

The general sucked in his breath and smiled. "I congratulate you," he said. "You have won the game."

Rainsford did not smile. "I am still a beast at bay," he said, in a low, hoarse voice. "Get ready, General Zaroff."

The general made one of his deepest bows.

"I see," he said. "Splendid! One of us is to furnish a repast[25] for the hounds. The other will sleep in this very excellent bed. On guard, Rainsford. . . ."

710 He had never slept in a better bed, Rainsford decided. ❧

R VISUALIZE
Picture in your mind the contrasting images of Rainsford's dramatic escape and Zaroff's "civilized" actions at the edge of the water. What is the impact of this contrast?

---

22. *Madama Butterfly:* a famous opera by the Italian composer Giacomo Puccini.

23. **Pol Roger** (pôl′ rô-zhā′) . . . **Chambertin** (shăm-běr-tăɴ′): Pol Roger is a French champagne. Chambertin is a red French wine.

24. **Marcus Aurelius** (mär′kəs ô-rē′lē-əs): an ancient Roman emperor and philosopher.

25. **furnish a repast:** serve as a meal.

Comprehension

1. **Recall** Before arriving at the island, what is Rainsford's position on hunting?

2. **Recall** Why has Zaroff begun hunting human "game"?

3. **Clarify** What happens at the end of the story?

PENNSYLVANIA STANDARDS

READING STANDARD
B.1.1.1.C.1 Interpret and evaluate elements of the plot

Literary Analysis

4. **Draw Conclusions** In your opinion, why does Rainsford choose to confront Zaroff in the end, rather than simply ambush him? What does this reveal about his personality? Cite evidence.

5. **Compare and Contrast Characters** Use a Venn diagram to compare and contrast Rainsford and Zaroff. Start by listing each man's **character traits** in the appropriate circle. Then note their similarities where the circles overlap.

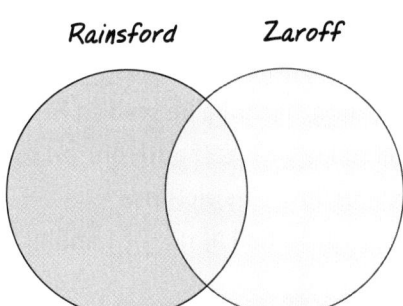

6. **Analyze Conflict** Reread lines 473–484. Connell does not reveal the main conflict until a good deal of the story has passed. Why? Support your answer.

7. **Examine Foreshadowing** Connell makes use of foreshadowing to help readers predict future events in the story. Find at least three examples of foreshadowing in the story. How does this technique add to the **suspense** of this story? Cite evidence.

8. **Visualize Description** Look back at the descriptive details you recorded as you read. Choose at least two details that evoked the most striking pictures in your mind. Which particular words helped make each of these images so vivid?

9. **Make Judgments** At the end of the story, do you think Rainsford has changed his mind about hunting? Support your opinion.

Literary Criticism

10. **Critical Interpretations** One critic has remarked that "ironically, Zaroff's belief in his invincibility as a hunter weakens him and causes his defeat." Cite evidence from the story to support or challenge this statement.

Vocabulary in Context

VOCABULARY PRACTICE

Choose the word from the list that best completes each sentence.

1. As Rainsford swam ashore, the air was so humid it was almost _____.
2. He spoke in a(n) _____ way in order to try not to anger Zaroff's guard.
3. For his own safety, Rainsford felt it _____ not to come across as an intruder.
4. Zaroff's love of fine food and wine made him seem a(n) _____ person.
5. His house offered every _____ that could make a guest comfortable.
6. In the morning, Zaroff inquired _____ whether Rainsford had slept well.
7. But Zaroff lacked the _____ that moral people have.
8. He saw nothing wrong with hunting a human _____.
9. In fact, with an odd, or a(n) _____, smile he stalked his prisoners.
10. Rainsford strongly disagreed with Zaroff and refused to _____ his hunting.
11. Zaroff was _____ in tracking down his victims.
12. Rainsford soon found that Zaroff had a(n) _____ ability to follow difficult trails.

WORD LIST

amenity
condone
cultivated
disarming
droll
imperative
quarry
scruple
solicitously
tangible
uncanny
zealous

VOCABULARY IN WRITING

Using at least four vocabulary words, write a paragraph characterizing either Rainsford or Zaroff. Here is a sample opening sentence.

> **EXAMPLE SENTENCE**
>
> Rainsford loved to hunt big **quarry**.

VOCABULARY STRATEGY: DENOTATION AND CONNOTATION

A word's **denotation** is its basic dictionary meaning; its **connotations** are the overtones of meaning that it may take on. For example, the vocabulary word *cultivated* means "cultured"; so does *highbrow*. However, *cultivated* has mostly positive overtones; *highbrow* has negative connotations of snobbishness.

PRACTICE Choose the word you would use to convey negative connotations. Then use the word appropriately in a sentence.

1. bold/reckless
2. conservative/reactionary
3. tightfisted/thrifty
4. unique/bizarre
5. outspoken/impudent
6. famous/notorious

PENNSYLVANIA STANDARDS

READING STANDARD
A.1.1 Apply the meaning of vocabulary

VOCABULARY PRACTICE
For more practice, go to the **Vocabulary Center** at **ClassZone.com**.

Reading-Writing Connection

Explore the themes of "The Most Dangerous Game" by responding to these prompts. Then use **Revision: Grammar and Style** to improve your writing.

WRITING PROMPTS

A. Short Response: Write a Diary Entry

In the dialogue at the beginning of the story, Whitney empathizes with hunted animals. What does Rainsford learn about the feelings of hunted animals from his experience of being hunted? Write **one or two paragraphs** of a diary entry that Rainsford might write on this subject after his experience.

B. Extended Response: Evaluate a Statement

Early in the story Rainsford says to Whitney, "The world is made up of two classes—the hunters and the huntees." Decide whether you agree or disagree, and write **two to three paragraphs** expressing your opinion. Support your position with evidence from your own experiences.

SELF-CHECK

A successful diary entry will . . .
- accurately reflect Rainsford's personality
- describe Rainsford's feelings during the experience
- tell what Rainsford learned from his experience

A strong evaluation will . . .
- explain what the statement means
- clearly state an opinion
- provide at least two examples from real life to support the opinion

REVISION: GRAMMAR AND STYLE

ADD DESCRIPTIVE DETAILS Review the **Grammar and Style** note on page 69. Writers often use **prepositional phrases** to add descriptive details that show what events are taking place and where, when, and how they are taking place. Here is an example from the story:

> *He executed a series of intricate loops; he doubled on his trail again and again, recalling all the lore of the fox hunt, and all the dodges of the fox. Night found him leg-weary, with hands and face lashed by the branches, on a thickly wooded ridge.* (lines 528–531)

Notice how the revisions in red add descriptive details that show how, when, and where in this diary entry. Revise your responses to the prompts by using the same techniques.

PENNSYLVANIA STANDARDS

WRITING STANDARD
1.5.11.F.4 Use prepositions properly

WRITING TOOLS
For prewriting, revision, and editing tools, visit the **Writing Center** at ClassZone.com.

STUDENT MODEL

Even though it's been several weeks, I still wake up, *in a cold sweat in the middle of the night,* trembling with fear. The feeling of panic is ~~intense~~ *like a chill in my veins*, and I can't move.

Daughter of Invention
Short Story by Julia Alvarez

What is a
GENERATION GAP?

PENNSYLVANIA STANDARDS

READING STANDARDS
A.1.3.1 Make inferences
B.1.1.A.2 Evaluate the relationship between characters and other components

KEY IDEA What causes **parent-child conflicts?** Is it inevitable that parents and teenagers disagree? In "Daughter of Invention," a father and his teenage daughter confront this issue head-on.

ROLE-PLAY With a small group of classmates, develop a list of subjects that may trigger disagreements between parents and teenagers. With a partner, role-play a dialogue between a parent and a teenager on one of these subjects. Then switch roles and have the conversation again. What insights do you gain?

● LITERARY ANALYSIS: PLOT AND CHARACTER

The plot of a story is shaped by the problems, or **conflicts,** that the main character faces. As the main character responds to the conflict—by making decisions, taking actions, and interacting with other characters—the plot moves forward and engages the reader.

The poet's words shocked and thrilled me.... That night, at last, I started to write, recklessly, three, five pages, looking up only once....

As you read "Daughter of Invention," notice how the narrator's actions and interactions influence the plot.

● READING SKILL: MAKE INFERENCES

Often a writer will not tell you everything that is going on in a character's mind. Instead, you may need to **make inferences,** or logical guesses, about what the character thinks and feels. To do this, you need to combine story details with what you know from your own experiences.

As you read, look for clues to how the narrator and her parents feel about living in the United States. For each character, use a chart like the one shown to record your observations and inferences.

Mother		
Details	My Own Experience	Inference
• She begins inventing in the U.S. →	New surroundings could lead to a fresh perspective. →	
•		
•		

Review: **Clarify**

▲ VOCABULARY IN CONTEXT

The following words all have negative connotations. Try writing definitions for as many of these words as you can.

1. disclaimer
2. inhospitable
3. insubordinate
4. misnomer
5. noncommittal
6. plagiarized

Author Online

**Julia Alvarez
born 1950**

Immigrant Experience Like the narrator in "Daughter of Invention," Julia Alvarez emigrated with her family from the Dominican Republic to the United States. As a ten-year-old in New York City, she felt out of place and was sometimes subjected to name-calling. It was at this time that Alvarez began to write, finding comfort in recording memories of her old life in the Dominican Republic. "I found myself turning more and more to writing as the one place where I felt I belonged," Alvarez has said.

Literary Success Alvarez has won many awards for her writing, which includes novels and poetry as well as short stories. Her fiction often centers on the grim political history of the Dominican Republic, as well as the experiences of Hispanic immigrants in New York City. Her poetry and short stories have appeared in numerous magazines and anthologies.

 MORE ABOUT THE AUTHOR
For more on Julia Alvarez, visit the **Literature Center** at ClassZone.com.

Background

The Dominican Republic Under Trujillo
In 1960, Alvarez's family fled the Dominican Republic after the discovery of her father's involvement in a plot to overthrow Rafael Trujillo (rä-fä-ĕl′ trōō-hē′ō). Trujillo, a brutal dictator, ruled the Dominican Republic from 1930 to 1961, staying in power by suppressing all political opposition. Those who criticized him simply "disappeared"—often after the black Volkswagens of the SIM, Trujillo's secret police, drove up to their homes.

Daughter of *Invention*

JULIA ALVAREZ

ANALYZE VISUALS
Examine the portrait. What details help you **draw conclusions** about the woman's personality?

She wanted to invent something, my mother. There was a period after we arrived in this country, until five or so years later, when my mother was inventing. They were never pressing, global needs she was addressing with her pencil and pad. She would have said that was for men to do, rockets and engines that ran on gasoline and turned the wheels of the world. She was just fussing with little house things, don't mind her.

She always invented at night, after settling her house down. On his side of the bed my father would be conked out for an hour already, his Spanish newspaper draped over his chest, his glasses, propped up on his bedside table,
10 looking out eerily at the darkened room like a disembodied guard. But in her lighted corner, like some devoted scholar burning the midnight oil, my mother was inventing, sheets pulled to her lap, pillows propped up behind her, her reading glasses riding the bridge of her nose like a schoolmarm's. On her lap lay one of those innumerable pads of paper my father always brought home from his office, compliments of some pharmaceutical company, advertising tranquilizers or antibiotics or skin cream; in her other hand, my mother held a pencil that looked like a pen with a little cylinder of lead inside. She would work on a sketch of something familiar, but drawn at such close range so she could attach a special nozzle or handier handle, the thing looked peculiar.
20 Once, I mistook the spiral of a corkscrew for a nautilus shell, but it could just as well have been a galaxy forming. **A**

A **MAKE INFERENCES**
Why might the mother spend her evenings sketching inventions?

It was the only time all day we'd catch her sitting down, for she herself was living proof of the *perpetuum mobile*[1] machine so many inventors had sought over the ages. My sisters and I would seek her out now when she seemed to have a moment to talk to us: We were having trouble at school or we wanted her to persuade my father to give us permission to go into the city or to a shopping mall or a movie—in broad daylight! My mother would wave us out of her room. "The problem with you girls . . ." I can tell you right now what the problem always boiled down to: We wanted to become Americans and my father—and my mother, at first—would have none of it.

"You girls are going to drive me crazy!" She always threatened if we kept nagging. "When I end up in Bellevue,[2] you'll be safely sorry!"

She spoke in English when she argued with us, even though, in a matter of months, her daughters were the fluent ones. Her English was much better than my father's, but it was still a mishmash of mixed-up idioms and sayings that showed she was "green behind the ears," as she called it.

If my sisters and I tried to get her to talk in Spanish, she'd snap, "When in Rome, do unto the Romans . . ."

I had become the spokesman for my sisters, and I would stand my ground in that bedroom. "We're not going to that school anymore, Mami!"

"You have to." Her eyes would widen with worry. "In this country, it is against the law not to go to school. You want us to get thrown out?"

"You want us to get killed? Those kids were throwing stones today!"

"Sticks and stones don't break bones . . ." she chanted. I could tell, though, by the look on her face, it was as if one of those stones the kids had aimed at us had hit her. But she always pretended we were at fault. "What did you do to provoke them? It takes two to tangle, you know."

"Thanks, thanks a lot, Mom!" I'd storm out of that room and into mine. I never called her *Mom* except when I wanted her to feel how much she had failed us in this country. She was a good enough Mami, fussing and scolding and giving advice, but a terrible girlfriend parent, a real failure of a Mom. **B**

Back she'd go to her pencil and pad, scribbling and tsking and tearing off paper, finally giving up, and taking up her *New York Times*. Some nights, though, she'd get a good idea, and she'd rush into my room, a flushed look on her face, her tablet of paper in her hand, a cursory knock on the door she'd just thrown open: "Do I have something to show you, Cukita!"

This was my time to myself, after I'd finished my homework, while my sisters were still downstairs watching TV in the basement. Hunched over my small desk, the overhead light turned off, my lamp shining poignantly on my paper, the rest of the room in warm, soft, uncreated darkness, I wrote my secret poems in my new language. **C**

B PLOT AND CHARACTER
Why was the narrator disappointed in her mother?

C GRAMMAR AND STYLE
Reread lines 57–61. Alvarez uses **modifiers** such as *poignantly, warm, soft,* and *secret* to convey the special atmosphere that surrounds the narrator as she writes.

---

1. *perpetuum mobile* (pĕr-pĕt′ōō-əm mō′bĭ-lē) *Latin:* perpetual motion (operating continuously without a sustained input of energy).

2. **Bellevue** (bĕl′vyōō′): a large hospital in New York City, with a well-known psychiatric ward.

"You're going to ruin your eyes!" My mother would storm into my room, turning on the overly bright overhead light, scaring off whatever shy passion I had just begun coaxing out of a labyrinth of feelings with the blue thread of my writing.

"Oh Mami!" I'd cry out, my eyes blinking up at her. "I'm writing."

"Ay, Cukita." That was her communal pet name for whoever was in her favor. "Cukita, when I make a million, I'll buy you your very own typewriter." (I'd been nagging my mother for one just like the one father had bought her
70 to do his order forms at home.) "Gravy on the turkey" was what she called it when someone was buttering her up. She'd butter and pour. "I'll hire you your very own typist."

Down she'd plop on my bed and hold out her pad to me. "Take a guess, Cukita?" I'd study her rough sketch a moment: soap sprayed from the nozzle head of a shower when you turned the knob a certain way? Coffee with creamer already mixed in? Time-released water capsules for your plants when you were away? A key chain with a timer that would go off when your parking meter was about to expire? (The ticking would help you find your keys easily if you mislaid them.) The famous one, famous only in hindsight, was the stick
80 person dragging a square by a rope—a suitcase with wheels? "Oh, of course," we'd humor her. "What every household needs: a shower like a car wash, keys ticking like a bomb, luggage on a leash!" By now, as you can see, it'd become something of a family joke, our Thomas Edison Mami, our Benjamin Franklin Mom.[3]

Her face would fall. "Come on now! Use your head." One more wrong guess, and she'd tell me, pressing with her pencil point the different highlights of this incredible new wonder. "Remember that time we took the car to Bear Mountain,[4] and we re-ah-lized that we had forgotten to pack an opener with our pick-a-nick?" (We kept correcting her, but she insisted this is how
90 it should be said.) "When we were ready to eat we didn't have any way to open the refreshments cans?" (This before fliptop lids, which she claimed had crossed her mind.) "You know what this is now?" A shake of my head. "Is a car bumper, but see this part is a removable can opener. So simple and yet so necessary, no?"

"Yeah, Mami. You should patent it." I'd shrug. She'd tear off the scratch paper and fold it, carefully, corner to corner, as if she were going to save it. But then, she'd toss it in the wastebasket on her way out of the room and give a little laugh like a **disclaimer.** "It's half of one or two dozen of another . . ."

I suppose none of her daughters was very encouraging. We resented her
100 spending time on those dumb inventions. Here, we were trying to fit in America among Americans; we needed help figuring out who we were, why these Irish kids whose grandparents were micks two generations ago, why they

disclaimer
(dĭs-klā'mər) *n.* a denial of responsibility or knowledge

---

3. **Thomas Edison Mami . . . Benjamin Franklin Mom:** Edison and Franklin were celebrated inventors.

4. **Bear Mountain:** a state park not far from New York City.

were calling us spics.[5] Why had we come to the country in the first place? Important, crucial, final things, you see, and here was our own mother, who didn't have a second to help us puzzle any of this out, inventing gadgets to make life easier for American moms. Why, it seemed as if she were arming our own enemy against us!

One time, she did have a moment of triumph. Every night, she liked to read *The New York Times* in bed before turning off her light, to see what the
110 Americans were up to. One night, she let out a yelp to wake up my father beside her, bolt upright, reaching for his glasses which, in his haste, he knocked across the room. "*Que pasa? Que pasa?*" What is wrong? There was terror in his voice, fear she'd seen in his eyes in the Dominican Republic before we left. We were being watched there; he was being followed; he and mother had often exchanged those looks. They could not talk, of course, though they must have whispered to each other in fear at night in the dark bed. Now in America, he was safe, a success even; his Centro Medico[6] in Brooklyn was thronged with the sick and the homesick. But in dreams, he went back to those awful days and long nights, and my mother's screams confirmed his secret fear: we had
120 not gotten away after all; they had come for us at last. **D**

"Ay, Papi, I'm sorry. Go back to sleep, Cukito. It's nothing, nothing really." My mother held up the *Times* for him to squint at the small print, back page headline, one hand tapping all over the top of the bedside table for his glasses, the other rubbing his eyes to wakefulness.

"Remember, remember how I showed you that suitcase with little wheels so we would not have to carry those heavy bags when we traveled? Someone stole my idea and made a million!" She shook the paper in his face. She shook the paper in all our faces that night. "See! See! This man was no *bobo*! He didn't put all his pokers on a back burner. I kept telling you, one of these days
130 my ship would pass me by in the night!" She wagged her finger at my sisters and my father and me, laughing all the while, one of those eerie laughs crazy people in movies laugh. We had congregated in her room to hear the good news she'd been yelling down the stairs, and now we eyed her and each other. I suppose we were all thinking the same thing: Wouldn't it be weird and sad if Mami did end up in Bellevue as she'd always threatened she might?

"*Ya, ya!* Enough!" She waved us out of her room at last. "There is no use trying to drink spilt milk, that's for sure."

It was the suitcase rollers that stopped my mother's hand; she had weather vaned a minor brainstorm. She would have to start taking herself seriously.
140 That blocked the free play of her ingenuity. Besides, she had also begun working at my father's office, and at night, she was too tired and busy filling in columns with how much money they had made that day to be fooling with gadgets!

---

5. **micks . . . spics:** derogatory terms for people of Irish descent and people of Hispanic descent, respectively.

6. **Centro Medico** (sĕn'trô mĕ'dē-kô): medical center.

D MAKE INFERENCES
What **internal conflict** does the narrator's father struggle with? Use details to support your answer.

She did take up her pencil and pad one last time to help me out. In ninth grade, I was chosen by my English teacher, Sister Mary Joseph, to deliver the teacher's day address at the school assembly.

150 Back in the Dominican Republic, I was a terrible student. No one could ever get me to sit down to a book. But in New York, I needed to settle somewhere, and the natives were unfriendly, the country **inhospitable,** so I took root in the language. By high school, the nuns were reading my stories and compositions out loud

160 to my classmates as examples of imagination at work.

This time my imagination jammed. At first I didn't want and then I couldn't seem to write that speech. I suppose I should have thought of it as a "great honor," as my father called it. But I was mortified. I still had a pronounced lilt to my accent, and I did not like

170 to speak in public, subjecting myself to my classmates' ridicule. Recently, they had begun to warm toward my sisters and me, and it took no great figuring to see that to deliver a eulogy for a convent full of crazy, old overweight nuns was no way to endear myself to the members of my class.

La Mère de l'artiste ["The artist's mother"] (1889), Paul Gauguin. Oil on canvas. Staatsgalerie, Stuttgart. © Staatsgalerie, Stuttgart. Photo © akg-images, London

But I didn't know how to get out of it. Week after week, I'd sit down, hoping to polish off some quick, **noncommittal** little speech. I couldn't get
180 anything down.

The weekend before our Monday morning assembly I went into a panic. My mother would just have to call in and say I was in the hospital, in a coma. I was in the Dominican Republic. Yeah, that was it! Recently, my father had been talking about going back home to live.

inhospitable
(ĭn-hŏs′pĭ-tə-bəl) *adj.* not welcoming; hostile

noncommittal
(nŏn′kə-mĭt′l) *adj.* not committing oneself; not revealing what one thinks

My mother tried to calm me down. "Just remember how Mister Lincoln couldn't think of anything to say at the Gettysburg, but then, Bang! 'Four score and once upon a time ago,'"[7] she began reciting. Her version of history was half invention and half truths and whatever else she needed to prove a point. "Something is going to come if you just relax. You'll see, like the Americans 190 say, 'Necessity is the daughter of invention.' I'll help you." **E**

All weekend, she kept coming into my room with help. "Please, Mami, just leave me alone, please," I pleaded with her. But I'd get rid of the goose only to have to contend with the gander. My father kept poking his head in the door just to see if I had "fulfilled my obligations," a phrase he'd used when we were a little younger, and he'd check to see whether we had gone to the bathroom before a car trip. Several times that weekend around the supper table, he'd recite his valedictorian speech from when he graduated from high school. He'd give me pointers on delivery, on the great orators and their tricks. (Humbleness and praise and falling silent with great emotion were his favorites.)

200 My mother sat across the table, the only one who seemed to be listening to him. My sisters and I were forgetting a lot of our Spanish, and my father's formal, florid diction was even harder to understand. But my mother smiled softly to herself, and turned the Lazy Susan at the center of the table around and around as if it were the prime mover, the first gear of attention.

That Sunday evening, I was reading some poetry to get myself inspired: Whitman in an old book with an engraved cover my father had picked up in a thrift shop next to his office a few weeks back. "I celebrate myself and sing myself . . ." "He most honors my style who learns under it to destroy the teacher."[8] The poet's words shocked and thrilled me. I had gotten used to the 210 nuns, a literature of appropriate sentiments, poems with a message, expurgated texts. But here was a flesh and blood man, belching and laughing and sweating in poems. "Who touches this book touches a man."

That night, at last, I started to write, recklessly, three, five pages, looking up once only to see my father passing by the hall on tiptoe. When I was done, I read over my words, and my eyes filled. I finally sounded like myself in English! **F**

As soon as I had finished that first draft, I called my mother to my room. She listened attentively, as she had to my father's speech, and in the end, her eyes were glistening too. Her face was soft and warm and proud. "That is a beautiful, beautiful speech, Cukita. I want for your father to hear it before he 220 goes to sleep. Then I will type it for you, all right?"

Down the hall we went, the two of us, faces flushed with accomplishment. Into the master bedroom where my father was propped up on his pillows, still awake, reading the Dominican papers, already days old. He had become interested in his country's fate again. The dictatorship had been toppled. The

E CLARIFY
Reread lines 185–190. The correct proverb is "Necessity is the mother of invention." Note that the title of the story is taken from the mother's misquotation.

F PLOT AND CHARACTER
Why do you think the experience of reading Whitman finally freed the narrator to write her speech?

7. **"Four score and once upon a time ago"**: Mami is misquoting President Abraham Lincoln's Gettysburg Address, which begins "Four score and seven years ago, . . ."

8. **"I celebrate . . . destroy the teacher"**: lines from the long poem "Song of Myself," by the American poet Walt Whitman (1819–1892).

interim government was going to hold the first free elections in thirty years. There was still some question in his mind whether or not we might want to move back. History was in the making, freedom and hope were in the air again! But my mother had gotten used to the life here. She did not want to go back to the old country where she was only a wife and a mother (and a
230 failed one at that, since she had never had the required son). She did not come straight out and disagree with my father's plans. Instead, she fussed with him about reading the papers in bed, soiling those sheets with those poorly printed, foreign tabloids. "*The Times* is not that bad!" she'd claim if my father tried to humor her by saying they shared the same dirty habit. **G**

The minute my father saw my mother and me, filing in, he put his paper down, and his face brightened as if at long last his wife had delivered a son, and that was the news we were bringing him. His teeth were already grinning from the glass of water next to his bedside lamp, so he lisped when he
240 said, "Eh-speech, eh-speech!"

"It is so beautiful, Papi," my mother previewed him, turning the sound off on his TV. She sat down at the foot of the bed. I stood before both of them, blocking their view of the soldiers in helicopters landing amid silenced gun reports and explosions. A few weeks ago it had been the shores of the Dominican Republic. Now it was the jungles of Southeast Asia they were saving. My mother gave me the nod to begin reading.

250 I didn't need much encouragement. I put my nose to the fire, as my mother would have said, and read from start to finish without looking up. When I was done, I was a little embarrassed at my pride in my own words. I pretended to quibble with a phrase or two I was sure I'd be talked out of changing. I looked questioningly to my mother. Her face was radiant. She turned to share her pride with my father.

But the expression on his face shocked us both.
260 His toothless mouth had collapsed into a dark zero. His eyes glared at me, then shifted to my mother, accusingly. In barely audible Spanish, as if secret microphones or informers were all about, he whispered, "You will permit her to read *that?*"

G MAKE INFERENCES
How has the mother changed since coming to the United States? Cite evidence.

Pedro Mañach (1901), Pablo Picasso. Oil on linen, 41 1/2″ × 27″; framed: 53″ × 38 7/8″ × 4″. National Gallery of Art, Washington, D.C., Chester Dale Collection. © 2004 Board of Trustees of the National Gallery of Art/2007 Estate of Pablo Picasso/Artists Rights Society (ARS), New York (1963.10.53).

My mother's eyebrows shot up, her mouth fell open. In the old country, any whisper of a challenge to authority could bring the secret police in their black V.W.'s. But this was America. People could say what they thought. "What is wrong with her speech?" my mother questioned him.

270 "What ees wrrrong with her eh-speech?" My father wagged his head at her. His anger was always more frightening in his broken English. As if he had mutilated the language in his fury—and now there was nothing to stand between us and his raw, dumb anger. "What is wrong? I will tell you what is wrong. It shows no gratitude. It is boastful. 'I celebrate myself'? 'The best student learns to destroy the teacher'?" He mocked my **plagiarized** words. "That is **insubordinate**. It is improper. It is disrespecting of her teachers—" In his anger he had forgotten his fear of lurking spies: Each wrong he voiced was a decibel higher than the last outrage. Finally, he was yelling at me, "As your father, I forbid you to say that eh-speech!"

My mother leapt to her feet, a sign always that she was about to make a 280 speech or deliver an ultimatum. She was a small woman, and she spoke all her pronouncements standing up, either for more protection or as a carry-over from her girlhood in convent schools where one asked for, and literally took, the floor in order to speak. She stood by my side, shoulder to shoulder; we looked down at my father. "That is no tone of voice, Eduardo—" she began.

By now, my father was truly furious. I suppose it was bad enough I was rebelling, but here was my mother joining forces with me. Soon he would be surrounded by a house full of independent American women. He too leapt from his bed, throwing off his covers. The Spanish newspapers flew across the 290 room. He snatched my speech out of my hands, held it before my panicked eyes, a vengeful, mad look in his own, and then once, twice, three, four, countless times, he tore my prize into shreds. **H**

"Are you crazy?" My mother lunged at him. "Have you gone mad? That is her speech for tomorrow you have torn up!"

"Have *you* gone mad?" He shook her away. "You were going to let her read that . . . that insult to her teachers?"

"Insult to her teachers!" My mother's face had crumpled up like a piece of paper. On it was written a love note to my father. Ever since they had come to this country, their life together was a constant war. "This is America, Papi, 300 America!" she reminded him now. "You are not in a savage country any more!"

I was on my knees, weeping wildly, collecting all the little pieces of my speech, hoping that I could put it back together before the assembly tomorrow morning. But not even a sibyl[9] could have made sense of all those scattered pieces of paper. All hope was lost. "He broke it, he broke it," I moaned as I picked up a handful of pieces.

<hr>

9. **sibyl** (sĭb′əl): a female prophet. (According to the Roman poet Virgil, the sibyl of Cumae recorded the words of her prophecies on tree leaves, which she arranged on the floor of her cave. If the wind scattered the leaves, the prophecies became unintelligible.)

---

plagiarized
(plā′jə-rīzd′) *adj.* copied from someone else's writings **plagiarize** *v.*

insubordinate
(ĭn′sə-bôr′dn-ĭt) *adj.* disobedient to a superior

H MAKE INFERENCES
Reread lines 269–292. What emotions besides anger might be behind the father's action?

Probably, if I had thought a moment about it, I would not have done what I did next. I would have realized my father had lost brothers and comrades to the dictator Trujillo. For the rest of his life, he would be haunted by blood in the streets and late night disappearances. Even after he had been in the states for years, he jumped if a black Volkswagen passed him on the street. He feared anyone in uniform: the meter maid giving out parking tickets, a museum guard approaching to tell him not to touch his favorite Goya[10] at the Metropolitan.

I took a handful of the scraps I had gathered, stood up, and hurled them in his face. "Chapita!" I said in a low, ugly whisper. "You're just another Chapita!"

It took my father only a moment to register the hated nickname of our dictator, and he was after me. Down the halls we raced, but I was quicker than he and made it to my room just in time to lock the door as my father threw his weight against it. He called down curses on my head, ordered me on his authority as my father to open that door this very instant! He throttled that doorknob, but all to no avail. My mother's love of gadgets saved my hide that night. She had hired a locksmith to install good locks on all the bedroom doors after our house had been broken into while we were away the previous summer. In case burglars broke in again, and we were in the house, they'd have a second round of locks to contend with before they got to us. ❶

"Eduardo," she tried to calm him down. "Don't you ruin my new locks."

He finally did calm down, his anger spent. I heard their footsteps retreating down the hall. I heard their door close, the clicking of their lock. Then, muffled voices, my mother's peaking in anger, in persuasion, my father's deep murmurs of explanation and of self-defense. At last, the house fell silent, before I heard, far off, the gun blasts and explosions, the serious, self-important voices of newscasters reporting their TV war.

A little while later, there was a quiet knock at my door, followed by a tentative attempt at the doorknob. "Cukita?" my mother whispered. "Open up, Cukita."

"Go away," I wailed, but we both knew I was glad she was there, and I needed only a moment's protest to save face before opening that door.

ANALYZE VISUALS
This painting depicts the execution of a group of Spaniards by Napoleon's occupying army. Why do you think a painting like this might appeal to someone like Papi? Explain.

The Third of May, 1808 (1814), Francisco de Goya y Lucientes. Oil on canvas, 266 cm × 345 cm. Museo del Prado, Madrid. Photo © Erich Lessing/Art Resource, New York.

❶ **PLOT AND CHARACTER**
Why does the narrator's father become enraged at her?

---

10. **Goya** (goi′ə): a painting by the Spanish artist Francisco de Goya y Lucientes (1746–1828).

350   What we ended up doing that night was putting together a speech at the last moment. Two brief pages of stale compliments and the polite commonplaces on teachers, wrought by necessity without much invention by mother for daughter late into the night in the basement on the pad of paper and with the same pencil she had once used for her own inventions, for I was too upset to compose the speech myself. After it was drafted, she typed it up while I stood by, correcting her **misnomers** and mis-sayings. **J**

    She was so very proud of herself when I came home the next day with the success story of the assembly. The nuns had been flattered, the audience had stood up and given "our devoted teachers a standing ovation," what my
360 mother had suggested they do at the end of my speech.

    She clapped her hands together as I recreated the moment for her. "I stole that from your father's speech, remember? Remember how he put that in at the end?" She quoted him in Spanish, then translated for me into English.

    That night, I watched him from the upstairs hall window where I'd retreated the minute I heard his car pull up in front of our house. Slowly, my father came up the driveway, a grim expression on his face as he grappled with a large, heavy cardboard box. At the front door, he set the package down carefully and patted all his pockets for his house keys—precisely why my mother had invented her ticking key chain. I heard the snapping open of the
370 locks downstairs. Heard as he struggled to maneuver the box through the narrow doorway. Then, he called my name several times. But I would not answer him.

    "My daughter, your father, he love you very much," he explained from the bottom of the stairs. "He just want to protect you." Finally, my mother came up and pleaded with me to go down and reconcile with him. "Your father did not mean to harm. You must pardon him. Always it is better to let bygones be forgotten, no?"

    I guess she was right. Downstairs, I found him setting up a brand new electric typewriter on the kitchen table. It was even better than the one I'd
380 been begging to get like my mother's. My father had outdone himself with all the extra features: a plastic carrying case with my initials, in decals, below the handle, a brace to lift the paper upright while I typed, an erase cartridge, an automatic margin tab, a plastic hood like a toaster cover to keep the dust away. Not even my mother, I think, could have invented such a machine!

    But her inventing days were over just as mine were starting up with my schoolwide success. That's why I've always thought of that speech my mother wrote for me as her last invention rather than the suitcase rollers everyone else in the family remembers. It was as if she had passed on to me her pencil and pad and said, "Okay, Cukita, here's the buck. You give it a shot." ∽

misnomer
(mĭs-nō′mər) *n.* an inaccurate or incorrect name

J MAKE INFERENCES
Why does the narrator's mother write the speech for her?

Comprehension

1. **Recall** How do the daughters respond to their mother's inventions?

2. **Recall** What difficulties do the daughters face in their new country?

3. **Clarify** How does the narrator's father react to his daughter's speech?

4. **Represent** Create a timeline showing key events in the order they occur. Circle the event that represents the **climax** of the story.

Literary Analysis

5. **Make Inferences** Review the inference chart you created for each character. How do the cultural differences between the Dominican Republic and the United States contribute to the **parent-child conflicts** between the narrator and her father? Cite evidence to support your answer.

6. **Plot and Character** What do you learn about the narrator from the way she resolves the conflict with her father? If she had acted differently, how might the conflict have been resolved?

7. **Make Judgments** Does the mother do the right thing by composing a flattering speech for her daughter to give? Explore this question in a chart like the one shown.

Pros	Cons
No one's feelings are hurt.	

8. **Compare and Contrast Characters** Compare the narrator's qualities with her mother's. Are mother and daughter more alike or more different? Support your interpretation with evidence from the story.

9. **Draw Conclusions** Reread lines 385–389. In what ways might the narrator's future be different from her past?

10. **Synthesize** Reread lines 378–384. A **symbol** is a person, place, object, or activity that stands for something beyond itself. What does the typewriter represent in this story?

Literary Criticism

11. **Critical Interpretations** One critic has said that at the end of this story, the reader is left with the impression that the narrator "is living in a new world where even the old obstacles of culture can be overcome." Do you agree with this interpretation? Support your answer.

PENNSYLVANIA STANDARDS

READING STANDARD
B.1.1.1.A.2 Evaluate the relationship between characters and other components

Vocabulary in Context

VOCABULARY PRACTICE

Write the word with a meaning closest to that of each boldfaced vocabulary word.

1. **inhospitable:** (a) inoperable, (b) unnecessary, (c) unwelcoming
2. **misnomer:** (a) mission, (b) misidentification, (c) misspent
3. **plagiarized:** (a) copied, (b) returned, (c) postmarked
4. **disclaimer:** (a) importance, (b) denial, (c) theory
5. **noncommittal:** (a) loyal, (b) cautious, (c) nonsensical
6. **insubordinate:** (a) inaccurate, (b) buried, (c) defiant

VOCABULARY IN WRITING

Write the opening paragraph of a speech that the narrator of this story might give in her school assembly. Use three or more vocabulary words. Here is a sample opening for such a speech.

> **EXAMPLE SENTENCE**
>
> When I first came to this school, it felt like an **_inhospitable_** jungle.

VOCABULARY STRATEGY: THE LATIN PREFIX *in-*

In- at the beginning of a word may be a prefix meaning "not," as in the vocabulary words *inhospitable* and *insubordinate*. If you can identify a root or a base word in words like these, you can easily figure out their meanings. (When the prefix *in-* precedes certain letters, it is spelled *il-*, *im-*, or *ir-*.)

PRACTICE Use a dictionary to help you find two words in each group that contain a prefix meaning "not." Then write a short definition of each word.

1. informal, internal, inedible
2. illegible, illegal, illness
3. imperial, immobile, improbable
4. irritate, irregular, irresistible
5. intellect, incapable, insufferable
6. imbalance, imagine, immature

PENNSYLVANIA STANDARDS

READING STANDARD
A.1.2.1 Identify word meaning using affixes

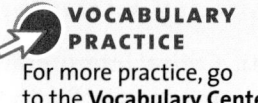

VOCABULARY PRACTICE
For more practice, go to the **Vocabulary Center** at **ClassZone.com**.

Reading-Writing Connection

Increase your understanding of "Daughter of Invention" by responding to these prompts. Then use **Revision: Grammar and Style** to improve your writing.

WRITING PROMPTS	SELF-CHECK

A. Short Response: Evaluate Characters

Early in the story, the narrator describes her mother as "a real failure of a Mom." Would the narrator evaluate her differently at the end of the story? Write **one or two paragraphs** expressing your opinion.

▶

A strong response will . . .
- clearly state an opinion
- include at least two examples from the text to support the opinion

B. Extended Response: Write a Scene

It's a year later, and the narrator has been asked to write another speech for school. Will the **parent-child conflicts** resume? Write **three to five paragraphs** describing the scene.

▶

A successful scene will . . .
- present events that are logical outcomes of the story
- effectively use modifiers

REVISION: GRAMMAR AND STYLE

SET THE SCENE Review the **Grammar and Style** note on page 82. Alvarez has carefully chosen **modifiers** that describe not only the physical details but also the atmosphere of the room.

Modifiers, which include **adjectives** and **adverbs,** are words and phrases that give information about other words. When describing a scene, incorporate modifiers that will paint a vivid picture for your audience. Here is another example of Alvarez's effective use of modifiers to enhance a scene:

PENNSYLVANIA
STANDARDS

WRITING STANDARD
1.5.11.F.4 Use adjectives and adverbs properly

> . . . *My father would be conked out for an hour already, his Spanish newspaper draped over his chest, his glasses, propped up on his bedside table, looking out eerily at the darkened room like a disembodied guard. But in her lighted corner, like some devoted scholar burning the midnight oil, my mother was inventing . . .*
> (lines 8–12)

Now study this model. Notice how the revisions in red help to make the images more vivid. Use similar techniques to revise your response to Prompt B.

STUDENT MODEL

As I sat down at the table, I slid my ^*trembling* fingers over the ^*black* typewriter keys. What was I going to write? Would my ^*well-meaning* father insist on reading every word again? I loaded a piece of ^*smooth, cream-colored* paper into the typewriter and stared ^*longingly* at its emptiness.

WRITING TOOLS
For prewriting, revision, and editing tools, visit the **Writing Center** at ClassZone.com.

The Gift of the Magi

Short Story by O. Henry

What are you willing to **SACRIFICE?**

PENNSYLVANIA STANDARDS

READING STANDARDS
A.1.3.1 Make inferences
B.2.1.1 Analyze irony

KEY IDEA Have you ever made a **sacrifice** in order to help others or make someone happy? In "The Gift of the Magi," a young couple have to decide what each is willing to do to show love for the other.

DISCUSS With a small group, list examples of sacrifices that people make for those they love. Consider examples in real life as well as those in books, movies, and television shows. Do all the sacrifices involve material items? Which are the hardest ones to make? Which sacrifice shows the greatest love?

Sacrifices for
Someone You Love

1. Spending a week's allowance to buy a gift
2.
3.
4.
5.

● LITERARY ANALYSIS: IRONY

Irony is a contrast between what is expected to happen and what actually occurs. There are three types of irony commonly used in literature:

- **Situational irony:** when a character or the reader expects one thing to happen but something else happens instead
- **Verbal irony:** when what is said is the opposite of what is meant
- **Dramatic irony:** when what a character knows contrasts with what the audience knows

O. Henry is well-known for writing stories in which situational irony results in surprising plot twists. As you read "The Gift of the Magi," be ready for the unexpected.

● READING STRATEGY: PREDICT

If a story is well written, it will keep you wondering what happens next. You may ask yourself questions and find yourself **predicting** possible answers. In this story, for example, what can you predict from the title?

As you read "The Gift of the Magi," jot down two or three predictions. Then see whether you were right—or whether O. Henry managed to surprise you.

▲ VOCABULARY IN CONTEXT

The following words are key to understanding this story of love and sacrifice. To see how many words you already know, substitute a different word or phrase for each boldfaced term.

1. **instigate** a rebellion
2. a package in the **vestibule**
3. as **agile** as a gymnast
4. **falter** in his determination
5. **ransack** the entire house
6. show **prudence** in her decisions
7. a face marked by the **ravage** of time
8. an **assertion** that can't be proved
9. win the **coveted** prize
10. a **chronicle** of the year's events

Author Online

A Life Like His Fiction
Using the pen name O. Henry, William Sydney Porter wrote hundreds of short stories. In some ways, his own life reflected the twists and turns of his stories. Born in Greensboro, North Carolina, and raised by his grandmother and aunt after his mother's death, Porter

O. Henry
1862–1910

left school at age 15 to work in a drugstore. At age 20, he moved to Texas and worked on a ranch. After he married and had a child, he went to work as a bank clerk. Then, after leaving this position, he was accused of having embezzled bank funds. Porter fled to Central America to avoid trial. When he returned to visit his dying wife, he was arrested, convicted, and imprisoned for three years. He always maintained his innocence.

From Prison to Fame Porter refined his short story style while serving time in prison. By the time of his release, he was already selling stories to magazines. Today the most renowned annual collection of new American short stories bears his pen name—the O. Henry Awards.

 MORE ABOUT THE AUTHOR
For more on O. Henry, visit the **Literature Center at ClassZone.com.**

Background

Bearers of Gifts In this story, O. Henry makes an **allusion,** or reference, to the Magi. According to Christian tradition, the Magi were three wise men or kings who traveled to Bethlehem, guided by a miraculous star, to present gifts of gold, frankincense, and myrrh to the infant Jesus. These gifts were prized possessions, having monetary, medicinal, and ceremonial value.

The Gift of the Magi

O. Henry

One dollar and eighty-seven cents. That was all. And 60 cents of it was in pennies. Pennies saved one and two at a time by bulldozing the grocer and the vegetable man and the butcher until one's cheeks burned with the silent imputation of parsimony[1] that such close dealing implied. Three times Della counted it. One dollar and eighty-seven cents. And the next day would be Christmas.

There was clearly nothing to do but flop down on the shabby little couch and howl. So Della did it. Which **instigates** the moral reflection that life is made up of sobs, sniffles, and smiles, with sniffles predominating.

10　While the mistress of the home is gradually subsiding from the first stage to the second, take a look at the home. A furnished flat at $8 per week. It did not exactly beggar description, but it certainly had that word on the lookout for the mendicancy squad.[2]

ANALYZE VISUALS
From this painting, what can you **infer** about the characters in this story?

instigate (ĭn′stĭ-gāt′)
v. to stir up; provoke

---

1. **imputation** (ĭm′pyŏŏ-tā′shən) **of parsimony** (pär′sə-mō′nē): suggestion of stinginess.
2. **mendicancy** (mĕn′dĭ-kən-sē) **squad:** a police unit assigned to arrest beggars.

The Kiss (1891), Édouard Vuillard. Philadelphia Museum of Art, The Louis E. Stern Collection, 1963. © 2007 Artists Rights Society (ARS), New York/ADAGP, Paris (1963-181-76).

Woman Combing Her Hair, Edgar Degas. Charcoal and pastel. © The Fine Art Society, London/Bridgeman Art Library.

In the **vestibule** below belonged to this flat a letterbox into which no letter would go and an electric button from which no mortal finger could coax a ring. Also appertaining thereunto was a card bearing the name "Mr. James Dillingham Young."

The "Dillingham" had been flung to the breeze during a former period of prosperity when its possessor was being paid $30 per week. Now, when 20 the income was shrunk to $20, the letters of "Dillingham" looked blurred, as though they were thinking seriously of contracting to a modest and unassuming D. But whenever Mr. James Dillingham Young came home and **A** reached his flat above, he was called "Jim" and greatly hugged by Mrs. James Dillingham Young, already introduced to you as Della. Which is all very good.

Della finished her cry and attended to her cheeks with the powder rag. She stood by the window and looked out dully at a gray cat walking a gray fence in a gray backyard. Tomorrow would be Christmas Day, and she had only $1.87

vestibule (vĕs′tə-byōōl′) *n.* a small entryway within a building

A IRONY
You might expect someone named Mr. James Dillingham Young to be rich. Is he?

with which to buy Jim a present. She had been saving every penny she could for months, with this result. Twenty dollars a week doesn't go far. Expenses
30 had been greater than she had calculated. They always are. Only $1.87 to buy a present for Jim. Her Jim. Many a happy hour she had spent planning for something nice for him. Something fine and rare and sterling—something just a little bit near to being worthy of the honor of being owned by Jim.

There was a pier glass[3] between the windows of the room. Perhaps you have seen a pier glass in an $8 flat. A very thin and very **agile** person may, by observing his reflection in a rapid sequence of longitudinal strips, obtain a fairly accurate conception of his looks. Della, being slender, had mastered the art.

Suddenly she whirled from the window and stood before the glass. Her eyes
40 were shining brilliantly, but her face had lost its color within twenty seconds. Rapidly she pulled down her hair and let it fall to its full length.

Now, there were two possessions of the James Dillingham Youngs in which they both took a mighty pride. One was Jim's gold watch that had been his father's and his grandfather's. The other was Della's hair. Had the Queen of Sheba[4] lived in the flat across the air shaft, Della would have let her hair hang out the window some day to dry and mocked at Her Majesty's jewels and gifts. Had King Solomon[5] been the janitor, with all his treasures piled up in the basement, Jim would have pulled out his watch every time he passed, just to see him pluck at his beard from envy. **B**

50 So now Della's beautiful hair fell about her, rippling and shining like a cascade of brown waters. It reached below her knee and made itself almost a garment for her. And then she did it up again nervously and quickly. Once she **faltered** for a minute and stood still while a tear or two splashed on the worn red carpet.

On went her old brown jacket; on went her old brown hat. With a whirl of skirts and with the brilliant sparkle still in her eyes, she fluttered out the door and down the stairs to the street.

Where she stopped, the sign read "Mme. Sofronie. Hair Goods of All Kinds." One flight up Della ran and collected herself, panting, before
60 Madame, large, too white, chilly, and hardly looking the "Sofronie."

"Will you buy my hair?" asked Della.

"I buy hair," said Madame. "Take yer hat off and let's have a sight at the looks of it."

Down rippled the brown cascade.

"Twenty dollars," said Madame, lifting the mass with a practiced hand.

"Give it to me quick," said Della.

Oh, and the next two hours tripped by on rosy wings. Forget the hashed metaphor. She was **ransacking** the stores for Jim's present.

agile (ăj'əl) *adj.* able to move quickly and easily

B PREDICT
What events might occur involving these prized possessions?

falter (fôl'tər) *v.* to hesitate from lack of courage or confidence

ransack (răn'săk')
v. to search or examine vigorously

---

3. **pier glass:** a large mirror set in a wall section between windows.

4. **Queen of Sheba:** in the Bible, a rich Arabian queen.

5. **King Solomon:** a Biblical king of Israel, known for his wisdom and wealth.

She found it at last. It surely had been made for Jim and no one else.
There was none other like it in any of the stores, and she had turned all of them inside out. It was a platinum fob chain[6] simple and chaste in design, properly proclaiming its value by substance alone and not by meretricious ornamentation[7]—as all good things should do. It was even worthy of The Watch. As soon as she saw it, she knew that it must be Jim's. It was like him. Quietness and value—the description applied to both. Twenty-one dollars they took from her for it, and she hurried home with the 87 cents. With that chain on his watch Jim might be properly anxious about the time in any company. Grand as the watch was, he sometimes looked at it on the sly on account of the old leather strap that he used in place of a chain.

When Della reached home, her intoxication gave way a little to **prudence** and reason. She got out her curling irons and lighted the gas and went to work repairing the **ravages** made by generosity added to love. Which is always a tremendous task, dear friends—a mammoth task.

Within forty minutes her head was covered with tiny, close-lying curls that made her look wonderfully like a truant schoolboy. She looked at her reflection in the mirror long, carefully, and critically.

"If Jim doesn't kill me," she said to herself, "before he takes a second look at me, he'll say I look like a Coney Island[8] chorus girl. But what could I do—oh, what could I do with a dollar and eighty-seven cents!"

At 7 o'clock the coffee was made, and the frying pan was on the back of the stove hot and ready to cook the chops.

Jim was never late. Della doubled the fob chain in her hand and sat on the corner of the table near the door that he always entered. Then she heard his step on the stair away down on the first flight, and she turned white for just a moment. She had a habit of saying little silent prayers about the simplest everyday things, and now she whispered: "Please, God, make him think I am still pretty."

The door opened, and Jim stepped in and closed it. He looked thin and very serious. Poor fellow, he was only twenty-two—and to be burdened with a family! He needed a new overcoat, and he was without gloves.

Jim stopped inside the door, as immovable as a setter at the scent of a quail. His eyes were fixed upon Della, and there was an expression in them that she could not read, and it terrified her. It was not anger, nor surprise, nor disapproval, nor horror, nor any of the sentiments that she had been prepared for. He simply stared at her fixedly with that peculiar expression on his face. **C**

Della wriggled off the table and went for him.

"Jim, darling," she cried, "don't look at me that way. I had my hair cut off and sold it because I couldn't have lived through Christmas without giving you a present. It'll grow again—you won't mind, will you? I just had to do it. My

prudence (prōōd′ns) *n.* the use of good judgment and common sense

ravage (răv′ĭj) *n.* serious damage

C PREDICT
What will Jim say about Della's hair?

---

6. **fob chain:** a short chain for a pocket watch.

7. **meretricious** (mĕr′ĭ-trĭsh′əs) **ornamentation:** cheap, gaudy decoration.

8. **Coney Island:** a resort district of Brooklyn, New York, famous for its amusement park.

110 hair grows awfully fast. Say 'Merry Christmas!' Jim, and let's be happy. You don't know what a nice—what a beautiful, nice gift I've got for you."

"You've cut off your hair?" asked Jim, laboriously, as if he had not arrived at that patent fact yet even after the hardest mental labor.

"Cut it off and sold it," said
120 Della. "Don't you like me just as well, anyhow? I'm me without my hair, ain't I?"

Jim looked about the room curiously.

"You say your hair is gone?" he said, with an air almost of idiocy.

"You needn't look for it," said Della. "It's sold, I tell you—sold and gone too. It's Christmas Eve,
130 boy. Be good to me, for it went for you. Maybe the hairs of my head were numbered," she went on with a sudden serious sweetness, "but nobody could ever count my love for you. Shall I put the chops on, Jim?"

Out of his trance Jim seemed to quickly wake. He enfolded his Della. For ten seconds let us
140 regard with discreet scrutiny[9] some inconsequential object in the other direction. Eight dollars a week or a million a year—what is the difference? A mathematician or a wit would give you the wrong

answer. The magi brought valuable gifts, but that was not among them. This dark **assertion** will be illuminated later on.

Jim drew a package from his overcoat pocket and threw it upon the table. **D**

"Don't make any mistake, Dell," he said, "about me. I don't think there's
150 anything in the way of a haircut or a shave or a shampoo that could make me like my girl any less. But if you'll unwrap that package, you may see why you had me going awhile at first."

assertion (ə-sûr′shən)
n. a statement

D PREDICT
What do you predict Jim's gift will be? Explain.

---

9. **discreet scrutiny:** cautious observation.

White fingers and nimble tore at the string and paper. And then an ecstatic scream of joy, and then, alas! a quick feminine change to hysterical tears and wails, necessitating the immediate employment of all the comforting powers of the lord of the flat.

For there lay The Combs—the set of combs, side and back, that Della had worshiped for long in a Broadway window. Beautiful combs, pure tortoise shell, with jeweled rims—just the shade to wear in the beautiful vanished hair. 160 They were expensive combs, she knew, and her heart had simply craved and yearned over them without the least hope of possession. And now, they were hers, but the tresses that should have adorned the **coveted** adornments were gone. **E**

But she hugged them to her bosom, and at length she was able to look up with dim eyes and a smile and say, "My hair grows so fast, Jim!"

And then Della leaped up like a little singed cat and cried, "Oh, oh!"

Jim had not yet seen his beautiful present. She held it out to him eagerly upon her open palm. The dull, precious metal seemed to flash with a reflection of her bright and ardent spirit.

170   "Isn't it a dandy, Jim? I hunted all over town to find it. You'll have to look at the time a hundred times a day now. Give me your watch. I want to see how it looks on it."

Instead of obeying, Jim tumbled down on the couch and put his hands under the back of his head and smiled.

"Dell," said he, "let's put our Christmas presents away and keep 'em a while. They're too nice to use just at present. I sold the watch to get the money to buy your combs. And now suppose you put the chops on." **F**

The magi, as you know, were wise men—wonderfully wise men—who brought gifts to the Babe in the manger. They invented the art of giving 180 Christmas gifts. Being wise, their gifts were no doubt wise ones, possibly bearing the privilege of exchange in case of duplication. And here I have lamely related to you the uneventful **chronicle** of two foolish children in a flat who most unwisely sacrificed for each other the greatest treasures of their house. But in a last word to the wise of these days let it be said that of all who give gifts these two were of the wisest. Of all who give and receive gifts, such as they are the wisest. Everywhere they are the wisest. They are the magi. ❧

coveted (kŭv'ĭ-tĭd) *adj.* greedily desired or wished for **covet** v.

E GRAMMAR AND STYLE
Reread lines 160–163. O. Henry uses the **precise verbs** *craved* and *yearned* to show Della's great desire for the combs.

F IRONY
Reread lines 175–177. What is ironic about the resolution of the plot?

chronicle (krŏn'ĭ-kəl) *n.* a record of events

Comprehension

1. **Recall** Why is Della unhappy when the story begins?

2. **Recall** What two possessions do Della and Jim treasure?

3. **Summarize** What **sacrifices** do the Youngs make to buy each other gifts?

PENNSYLVANIA STANDARDS

READING STANDARD
B.2.1.1 Analyze irony

Literary Analysis

4. **Predict** Reexamine the predictions you made as you read the story. Were you able to predict the outcome of the story, or were you surprised? Go back through the story to find passages that hint at the surprise ending.

5. **Analyze Irony** This story contains **situational irony,** in which characters, or the reader, expect one thing to happen but something entirely different occurs. To explore the situational irony in this story, make a chart like the one shown.

What Della Plans:	What Actually Happens:
What Jim Plans:	What Actually Happens:

   For each character, identify what is expected to happen and what actually does happen. There is a double irony here. How are the two ironies related?

6. **Draw Conclusions About the Narrator** Reread lines 22–24. In this and many other passages, the narrator speaks directly to the reader. How would you describe the narrator's personality? Cite evidence.

7. **Make Judgments** Reread lines 178–186. Here the narrator uses an **allusion,** or indirect reference to a person, place, event, or literary work. Why does the narrator compare Della and Jim to the Magi? What does this imply about the characters and the events in this story?

8. **Synthesize** What does this story seem to be saying about material possessions? Cite evidence to support your answer.

Literary Criticism

9. **Critical Interpretations** For several years in the early 1900s, O. Henry was one of the most widely read short story writers in the United States. Even today, some of his stories are considered classics. What elements in "The Gift of the Magi" might account for his continued popularity?

Vocabulary in Context

VOCABULARY PRACTICE

Write the letter of the word that is most different in meaning from the others.

1. (a) destruction, (b) ravage, (c) ruin, (d) creation
2. (a) stop, (b) stir, (c) urge, (d) instigate
3. (a) desired, (b) coveted, (c) craved, (d) unwanted
4. (a) cellar, (b) vestibule, (c) foyer, (d) entryway
5. (a) waver, (b) proceed, (c) falter, (d) hesitate
6. (a) assertion, (b) declaration, (c) denial, (d) statement
7. (a) limber, (b) clumsy, (c) flexible, (d) agile
8. (a) loot, (b) plunder, (c) organize, (d) ransack
9. (a) history, (b) record, (c) chronicle, (d) prediction
10. (a) carelessness, (b) caution, (c) prudence, (d) wisdom

WORD LIST

agile
assertion
chronicle
coveted
falter
instigate
prudence
ransack
ravage
vestibule

VOCABULARY IN WRITING

How might Della or Jim describe the events in this story? Assume the role of one of them and briefly retell the story as that character. Use three or more vocabulary words. Here is an example of an opening:

> **EXAMPLE SENTENCE**
>
> Here is my sad **_chronicle_** of the Christmas that almost wasn't.

PENNSYLVANIA STANDARDS

READING STANDARD
A.1.2.1 Identify word meaning using affixes

VOCABULARY STRATEGY: THE GREEK WORD ROOT _chron_

The vocabulary word _chronicle_ contains the Greek root _chron_, which means "time." This root is found in a number of English words. To understand the meaning of words with _chron_, use context clues as well as your knowledge of the root.

PRACTICE Write the word from the word web that best completes each sentence. Use context clues to help you or, if necessary, consult a dictionary.

1. A _____ illness is one that lasts a long time.
2. In a personal narrative, events are usually presented in _____ order.
3. The mayor kept a _____ to record events of his years in office.
4. If we _____ our watches, we'll be sure to meet at exactly noon.
5. A _____ in a ship is an aid in determining longitude.

VOCABULARY PRACTICE
For more practice, go to the **Vocabulary Center** at **ClassZone.com.**

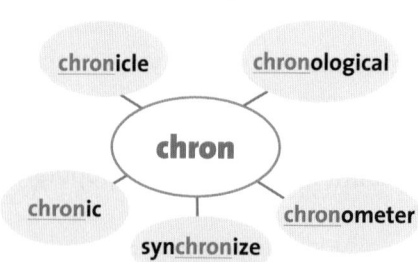

Reading-Writing Connection

Demonstrate your understanding of "The Gift of the Magi" by responding to these prompts. Then use **Revision: Grammar and Style** to improve your writing.

WRITING PROMPTS

A. Short Response: Understand Theme

"The Gift of the Magi" isn't simply a story about giving presents. O. Henry's main message concerns love and **sacrifice.** Write **one or two paragraphs** in which you discuss the theme of this story.

B. Extended Response: Write a Description

What do you imagine Jim's shopping trip was like? Write **three to five paragraphs** describing Jim's actions and thoughts as he sells his watch and buys the combs for Della.

SELF-CHECK

A strong response will . . .

- state the story's message about love and sacrifice
- cite specific details to explain the message

A successful description will . . .

- explain what Jim does and thinks as he shops for the gift
- include precise verbs that accurately reflect Jim's thoughts and actions

REVISION: GRAMMAR AND STYLE

MAKE EFFECTIVE WORD CHOICES Review the **Grammar and Style** note on page 102. Throughout the story, O. Henry uses **precise verbs** to descriptively convey the thoughts, feelings, and actions of his characters. By incorporating precise verbs into your own writing, you can give readers a greater and more accurate sense of your characters and their behavior.

In the following excerpts, notice how O. Henry uses verbs that help create vivid images for the reader:

> *With a whirl of skirts and with the brilliant sparkle still in her eyes, she fluttered out the door and down the stairs to the street.* (lines 55–57)

> *Instead of obeying, Jim tumbled down on the couch. . . .* (line 173)

Now study this model. Notice how the revisions in red help you to better visualize Jim's trip to the shop. Use similar methods to revise your responses to the prompts.

PENNSYLVANIA STANDARDS

WRITING STANDARD
1.5.11.E Revise writing to improve style, word choice

WRITING TOOLS
For prewriting, revision, and editing tools, visit the **Writing Center** at ClassZone.com.

STUDENT MODEL

                scurried
Jim ~~walked~~ to the shop; the store would close in just an hour. He reached

                              yanked   clasped
into his right pocket, ~~took~~ out the watch, and ~~held~~ it in his hands.

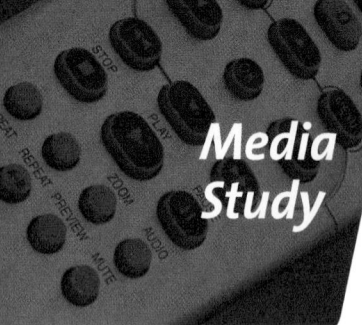

from The Lord of the Rings

Film Clip on **MediaSmart** DVD

What keeps you in
SUSPENSE?

**PENNSYLVANIA
STANDARDS**

SPEAKING/LISTENING STANDARD
1.6.11.F.2 Evaluate the role of media

KEY IDEA Have you ever been thrust into a situation that made your heart pound and your palms sweat? In this scene, Frodo Baggins, a young hobbit, has hardly started on a mission when he senses something ominous. Notice how the director builds **suspense** as danger reveals itself.

Background

Imagining Tolkien's World In 1999 the director Peter Jackson began to transform J. R. R. Tolkien's fantasy epic *The Lord of the Rings* into one of the most critically acclaimed movies of all time. As one reviewer stated, "This astounding movie accomplishes what no other fantasy film has been able to do: transport viewers to an entirely different reality, immerse them in it, and maroon them there...."

In the first installment, *The Fellowship of the Ring,* Frodo Baggins inherits a ring that has the power to destroy civilization. Frodo accepts the challenge of taking the ring to Rivendell, a place where a council will decide the ring's fate. He is joined on this mission by his loyal friend Sam and two other hobbits.

Media Literacy: Suspense in Movies

Suspense is a feeling of growing tension and excitement. Writers build suspense by making readers feel uncertain about what will happen next. Like writers, directors have the ability to make viewers feel excited or nervous as events unfold from one scene to the next. A skillful director can use basic filmmaking techniques, such as **camera shots, editing,** and **sound,** to create suspense and draw viewers into the action.

FILM TECHNIQUES	STRATEGIES FOR VIEWING	
A **shot** is a single, continuous view filmed by a camera. A director sets up shots that will advance a story's plot and tell the story in a compelling way.	• Pay attention to **point-of-view shots;** they show what characters see. In suspenseful scenes, they can make viewers sympathize with the characters and feel as if they are in danger themselves. • Notice how **high-angle shots,** in which the camera looks down on objects or persons, can make characters seem helpless. **Low-angle shots,** with the camera looking up, can make characters seem powerful or threatening.	
Editing is the process of selecting and arranging shots in a sequence. Editors and directors build tension by increasing the pace from one shot to the next.	Be aware of **pace,** which is influenced by the length of time each shot stays on the screen. As suspense increases, the length of shots gets shorter. **Quick cuts,** which may last no longer than a second, perhaps even less, are used to create excitement and build viewers' anticipation.	
Sound consists of the **music, sound effects,** and **dialogue** used in a scene. Sounds can be manipulated to increase viewers' emotional response to the scene.	• Listen for the use of **music.** Shrill tones or quick, steady beats often signal danger. • In particular, notice how any prolonged **absence of sound** affects you. Silence can heighten a tense moment.	

○ **MediaSmart** DVD
- **Film Clip:** *The Lord of the Rings*
- **Director:** Peter Jackson
- **Rating:** PG-13
- **Genre:** Fantasy
- **Running Time:** 4 minutes

Viewing Guide for
The Lord of the Rings

In this scene Frodo and the other hobbits take a peaceful break from their journey only to discover that a Black Rider is pursuing them.

As you watch this clip, pay attention to particular moments that draw you into the action and create suspense. Plan on watching the scene several times. To help you analyze suspense, refer to the questions that follow.

NOW VIEW

FIRST VIEWING: Comprehension

1. **Recall** How do the hobbits escape the Black Rider?

2. **Summarize** How does the setting change as the scene progresses?

CLOSE VIEWING: Media Literacy

3. **Make Inferences** What techniques does the director use to lead you to believe that the Black Rider is evil?

4. **Analyze Sound** How does the director use sound to increase tension in the scene? Think about sound effects, music, changes in volume, and absence of sound.

5. **Analyze Camera Shots** How does the director use **point-of-view shots** and **high-angle** and **low-angle shots** to influence viewers' perception of the events? Think about the following shots:
   - Frodo's view of the road
   - Frodo's view of the horse's mouth and bit and hoof
   - the shot of the Black Rider standing directly above the hobbits' hiding place

6. **Evaluate Editing** Toward the end of the scene, the Black Rider is closing in on Frodo and the other hobbits. What effect do the **pace** and the use of **quick cuts** have on viewers?

Write or Discuss

Evaluate Suspense A director's ultimate goal when filming a suspenseful scene is to make viewers feel the tension and anxiety that the characters feel. Evaluate the effectiveness of the director's portrayal of a suspenseful situation in the scene you viewed. Think about the following:

- the film techniques the director uses to create suspense
- specific emotions and reactions you think the director is trying to evoke
- your reactions to the clip

Produce Your Own Media

Create a Storyboard A **storyboard** is a device used to plan the shooting of a film and to help the director envision what the finished product will look like. Create a storyboard revisiting the beginning of the *Fellowship of the Ring* scene. Your storyboard should emphasize the Black Rider's point of view and should include between eight and ten shots.

HERE'S HOW Think of your storyboard as a set of rough sketches that includes descriptions of each shot. Here are some tips to get you started:

- Break down the incident shot by shot, in chronological order.
- Consider using a variety of shots and angles, including close-ups, high-angle and low-angle shots, and point-of-view shots.
- Once you establish the scene, use point-of-view shots to show what the Black Rider sees.
- Think about the sounds you want to accompany each shot.

MEDIA TOOLS

For help with creating a storyboard, visit the **Media Center** at ClassZone.com.

STUDENT MODEL

Shot type: LS (long shot)
Action: Black Rider races dangerously fast.
Audio: Horse screeches. Silence.

Shot type: MS (medium shot)
Action: Camera zooms in to show image of Black Rider. **Audio:** Music plays to indicate danger.

Production Tip

Use abbreviations of shot types in your storyboard.

POV = point-of-view shot
LS = long shot
MS = medium shot
CU = close-up shot
ELS = extreme long shot

The Rights to the Streets of Memphis

Autobiography by Richard Wright

What is worth
FIGHTING FOR?

PENNSYLVANIA STANDARDS

READING STANDARDS
A.2.6.1 Describe the author's purpose

B.3.3.2 Analyze text organization

KEY IDEA An important part of becoming an adult is learning to stand up for yourself and maintain your **convictions.** In "The Rights to the Streets of Memphis," Richard Wright recalls an episode from his early childhood when he was threatened by a neighborhood gang.

DISCUSS What would draw you to a rally or make you speak out in a crowd? With a small group, generate a list of issues or values that you would defend at any cost. Why is each one so important to you? Choose a spokesperson to present the one your group cares about the most.

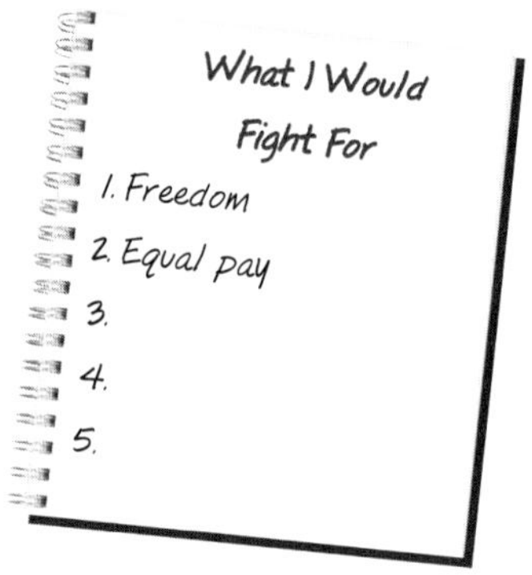

> What I Would
> Fight For
> 1. Freedom
> 2. Equal pay
> 3.
> 4.
> 5.

LITERARY ANALYSIS: AUTOBIOGRAPHY

An **autobiography** is the story of a person's life, written by that person. Writers of autobiographies generally use the same narrative techniques that are found in fiction. This makes the events they relate come to life for the reader. As you read "The Rights to the Streets of Memphis," notice how Richard Wright employs these and other narrative techniques:

• describes the **conflict** he faced
• builds **suspense** as events reach a **climax**
• uses realistic **dialogue** to reveal events and personalities

READING SKILL: IDENTIFY CAUSE AND EFFECT

Writers of autobiographies often explain the **causes** and **effects** of important events in their lives in order to help readers understand the full significance of their experiences. For example, to describe the magnitude of his hunger, Wright explains:

The hunger I had known before this . . . had made me beg constantly for bread. . . . But this new hunger baffled me, scared me . . .

As you read Wright's autobiography, jot down the cause-and-effect relationships he points out.

Cause	Effect
Father leaves.	Family is without food.

▲ VOCABULARY IN CONTEXT

Use an appropriate vocabulary word to complete each phrase.

WORD LIST	clamor	flay	stark
	dispirited	retaliate	

1. _____, absolute fear
2. a loud _____
3. _____ with a whip
4. _____, or get even
5. depressed and _____

Author On|ine

Richard Wright
1908–1960

A Hard Beginning
The son of a sharecropper and a teacher, Richard Wright grew up in poverty in the South. Because his family moved often and his mother became ill, Wright attended school irregularly. He dropped out of high school after only a few weeks and then traveled the country, working at odd jobs. Brilliant but troubled, he read widely. He also wrote powerful stories that earned him respect and recognition.

French Citizenship After establishing himself as a writer with the success of his novel *Native Son*, Wright moved to France in 1947 to get away from the racism he had experienced in the United States. He settled in Paris and became a French citizen, continuing to write until his death.

 MORE ABOUT THE AUTHOR
For more on Richard Wright, visit the **Literature Center** at ClassZone.com.

Background

Memphis in the Early 1900s This excerpt from Wright's autobiography *Black Boy* deals with a time when Wright was living in a tenement in Memphis, Tennessee. In the early 1900s, African Americans experienced harsh economic conditions in Memphis and other cities throughout the South. Federal welfare efforts, such as subsidized housing, food stamps, and aid to dependent children, did not exist. Most of the jobs available to black men and women paid very low wages. Like Wright's mother, many black women worked as poorly paid domestic servants.

THE Rights TO THE Streets OF Memphis

Richard Wright

ANALYZE VISUALS
What impressions of tenement life does the painting on page 113 convey?

Hunger stole upon me so slowly that at first I was not aware of what hunger really meant. Hunger had always been more or less at my elbow when I played, but now I began to wake up at night to find hunger standing at my bedside, staring at me gauntly. The hunger I had known before this had been no grim, hostile stranger; it had been a normal hunger that had made me beg constantly for bread, and when I ate a crust or two I was satisfied. But this new hunger baffled me, scared me, made me angry and insistent. Whenever I begged for food now my mother would pour me a cup of tea which would still the **clamor** in my stomach for a moment or two; but a little later I would feel
10 hunger nudging my ribs, twisting my empty guts until they ached. I would grow dizzy and my vision would dim. I became less active in my play, and for the first time in my life I had to pause and think of what was happening to me. **A**

"Mama, I'm hungry," I complained one afternoon.

"Jump up and catch a kungry," she said, trying to make me laugh and forget.

"What's a *kungry*?"

"It's what little boys eat when they get hungry," she said.

"What does it taste like?"

20 "I don't know."

"Then why do you tell me to catch one?"

"Because you said that you were hungry," she said, smiling.

I sensed that she was teasing me, and it made me angry.

"But I'm hungry. I want to eat."

clamor (klăm'ər) *n.* a noisy outburst; outcry

A CAUSE AND EFFECT
What cause-and-effect relationship did Wright begin to recognize?

Alley (1942), Jacob Lawrence. Courtesy of Clark Atlanta University Art Galleries. © 2007 Gwendolyn Knight Lawrence/ Artists Rights Society (ARS), New York.

"You'll have to wait."

"But I want to eat now."

"But there's nothing to eat," she told me.

"Why?"

"Just because there's none," she explained.

30 "But I want to eat," I said, beginning to cry.

"You'll just have to wait," she said again.

"But why?"

"For God to send some food."

"When is He going to send it?"

"I don't know."

"But I'm hungry!"

She was ironing, and she paused and looked at me with tears in her eyes.

"Where's your father?" she asked me.

40 I stared in bewilderment. Yes, it was true that my father had not come home to sleep for many days now and I could make as much noise as I wanted. Though I had not known why he was absent, I had been glad that he was not there to shout his restrictions at me. But it had never occurred to me that his absence would mean that there would be no food.

"I don't know," I said.

"Who brings food into the house?" my mother

50 asked me.

"Papa," I said. "He always brought food."

"Well, your father isn't here now," she said.

"Where is he?"

"I don't know," she said.

"But I'm hungry," I whimpered, stomping my feet.

"You'll have to wait until I get a job and buy food," she said. **B**

As the days slid past the image of my father became associated with my pangs of hunger, and whenever I felt hunger I thought of him with a deep biological bitterness.[1]

60 My mother finally went to work as a cook and left me and my brother alone in the flat each day with a loaf of bread and a pot of tea. When she returned at evening she would be tired and **dispirited** and would cry a lot. Sometimes, when she was in despair, she would call us to her and talk to us for hours, telling us that we now had no father, that our lives would be different from those of other children, that we must learn as soon as possible to take care of ourselves, to dress ourselves, to prepare our own food; that we must take upon ourselves the responsibility of the flat while she worked. Half frightened, we

Woman Worker (1951), Charles White. © 1951 The Charles White Archive.

B AUTOBIOGRAPHY
Reread lines 39–56. What life-changing event does Wright reveal through **dialogue**?

dispirited (dĭ-spĭr′ĭ-tĭd) *adj.* dejected

---

1. **deep, biological bitterness:** bitterness caused by the pangs of hunger.

would promise solemnly. We did not understand what had happened between our father and our mother and the most that these long talks did to us was to make us feel a vague dread. Whenever we asked why father had left, she would tell us that we were too young to know.

One evening my mother told me that thereafter I would have to do the shopping for food. She took me to the corner store to show me the way. I was proud; I felt like a grownup. The next afternoon I looped the basket over my arm and went down the pavement toward the store. When I reached the corner, a gang of boys grabbed me, knocked me down, snatched the basket, took the money, and sent me running home in panic. That evening I told my mother what had happened, but she made no comment; she sat down at once, wrote another note, gave me more money, and sent me out to the grocery again. I crept down the steps and saw the same gang of boys playing down the street. I ran back into the house. **C**

"What's the matter?" my mother asked.

"It's those same boys," I said. "They'll beat me."

"You've got to get over that," she said. "Now, go on."

"I'm scared," I said.

"Go on and don't pay any attention to them," she said.

I went out of the door and walked briskly down the sidewalk, praying that the gang would not molest me. But when I came abreast of them someone shouted.

"There he is!"

They came toward me and I broke into a wild run toward home. They overtook me and flung me to the pavement. I yelled, pleaded, kicked, but they wrenched the money out of my hand. They yanked me to my feet, gave me a few slaps, and sent me home sobbing. My mother met me at the door. **D**

"They b-beat m-me," I gasped. "They t-t-took the m-money."

I started up the steps, seeking the shelter of the house.

"Don't you come in here," my mother warned me.

I froze in my tracks and stared at her.

"But they're coming after me," I said.

"You just stay right where you are," she said in a deadly tone. "I'm going to teach you this night to stand up and fight for yourself."

She went into the house and I waited, terrified, wondering what she was about. Presently she returned with more money and another note; she also had a long heavy stick.

"Take this money, this note, and this stick," she said. "Go to the store and buy those groceries. If those boys bother you, then fight."

I was baffled. My mother was telling me to fight, a thing that she had never done before.

"But I'm scared," I said.

"Don't you come into this house until you've gotten those groceries," she said.

C AUTOBIOGRAPHY
Why do you suppose Wright includes such specific details about this experience?

D GRAMMAR AND STYLE
Reread lines 91–94. Wright uses **strong verbs in a series**—like *yelled*, *pleaded*, and *kicked*—to help readers visualize the attack.

"They'll beat me; they'll beat me," I said.

"Then stay in the streets; don't come back here!"

I ran up the steps and tried to force my way past her into the house. A stinging slap came on my jaw. I stood on the sidewalk, crying.

"Please, let me wait until tomorrow," I begged.

"No," she said. "Go now! If you come back into this house without those groceries, I'll whip you!"

She slammed the door and I heard the key turn in the lock. I shook with 120 fright. I was alone upon the dark, hostile streets and gangs were after me. I had the choice of being beaten at home or away from home. I clutched the stick, crying, trying to reason. If I were beaten at home, there was absolutely nothing that I could do about it; but if I were beaten in the streets, I had a chance to fight and defend myself. I walked slowly down the sidewalk, coming closer to the gang of boys, holding the stick tightly. I was so full of fear that I could scarcely breathe. I was almost upon them now.

"There he is again!" the cry went up.

They surrounded me quickly and began to grab for my hand.

"I'll kill you!" I threatened.

130 They closed in. In blind fear I let the stick fly, feeling it crack against a boy's skull. I swung again, lamming another skull, then another. Realizing that they would **retaliate** if I let up for but a second, I fought to lay them low, to knock them cold, to kill them so that they could not strike back at me. I **flayed** with tears in my eyes, teeth clenched, **stark** fear making me throw every ounce of my strength behind each blow. I hit again and again, dropping the money and the grocery list. The boys scattered, yelling, nursing their heads, staring at me in utter disbelief. They had never seen such frenzy. I stood panting, egging them on, taunting them to come on and fight. When they refused, I ran after them and they tore out for their homes, screaming. The parents of the 140 boys rushed into the streets and threatened me, and for the first time in my life I shouted at grownups, telling them that I would give them the same if they bothered me. I finally found my grocery list and the money and went to the store. On my way back I kept my stick poised for instant use, but there was not a single boy in sight. That night I won the right to the streets of Memphis. ꙮ 🄴

retaliate (rĭ-tăl′ē-āt′) *v.* to pay back an injury in kind

flay (flā) *v.* to whip or lash

stark (stärk) *adj.* complete or utter; extreme

🄴 **CAUSE AND EFFECT**
What effect did the fighting have on Wright's personality?

Comprehension

PENNSYLVANIA
STANDARDS

READING STANDARD
A.2.6.1 Describe the author's
purpose

1. **Recall** Why does Richard's mother have no food for him?

2. **Recall** What choice does Richard have to make?

3. **Clarify** What does the **title** refer to?

Literary Analysis

4. **Identify Cause and Effect** Review the cause-and-effect relationships you
   listed as you read. What are the main causes of Richard's predicament?

5. **Examine Language** Reread lines 1–10 and note the words and phrases
   that Wright uses to make hunger seem human. What effect does this
   personification have on the reader?

6. **Analyze Dialogue** Wright not only narrates events but also uses dialogue to
   bring a sense of reality to his narrative. Review the conversations between
   Wright and his mother. What does it suggest about their relationship and the
   way it changes?

7. **Predict** Reread the last paragraph of the selection. Will Richard be different
   after fighting the street gang? Cite evidence to support your prediction.

8. **Interpret Autobiography** In an autobiography, the writer must choose which
   life experiences to include and which to leave out. In your opinion, why did
   Wright choose to share this particular episode in his life? Support your opinion.

9. **Evaluate Narrative Techniques** Find
   examples of each narrative technique listed
   in the graphic shown. Which narrative
   techniques does Wright make the best
   use of in this autobiography? Explain your
   evaluation.

Techniques	Examples
• Describes conflict	
• Uses believable dialogue	
• Builds suspense	
• Develops personalities	

Literary Criticism

10. **Critical Interpretations** When this autobiography was published in 1945, a
    critic wrote, "It is not easy for those who have had happier childhoods, with
    little restraint or fear in them, to face up to the truth of this childhood of
    Richard Wright." Do you agree with this statement? Explain why or why not.

Vocabulary in Context

VOCABULARY PRACTICE

Write the word from the list that best completes each sentence.

1. Alone and hungry, Richard felt _____ as he walked the streets.
2. He knew it would be hard to rise above his family's _____ poverty.
3. He tried to concentrate amid the _____ as several older boys shouted at him.
4. If they tried to harm him, he intended to _____ immediately.
5. He would _____ them with his stick if necessary.

WORD LIST

clamor

dispirited

flay

retaliate

stark

VOCABULARY IN WRITING

Suppose you had been a neighbor of Richard's, watching the events in the street. How would you describe the encounter with the other boys? Write three sentences about what you saw, using three vocabulary words. Here is an example.

> **EXAMPLE SENTENCE**
>
> I saw a look of **stark** horror on Richard's face.

VOCABULARY STRATEGY: SYNONYMS AND ANTONYMS

Synonyms are words with the same, or almost the same, meaning. **Antonyms** are words with opposite meanings. Recognizing synonyms and antonyms can help you figure out the meanings of unknown words. For example, Wright says his mother felt "tired and dispirited." Though *tired* is not an exact synonym of *dispirited,* it is close enough in meaning to help you figure out what *dispirited* means.

PRACTICE In each sentence, the boldfaced word is either a synonym or an antonym of the underlined word. Use the boldfaced word to help you figure out the meaning of the underlined word. Then write a definition of the underlined word.

1. The table was **overflowing** with <u>bountiful</u> platters of food.
2. Though Alice was <u>nonplused</u> by his remarks, I was **unsurprised.**
3. The <u>affluent</u> Henleys were sometimes shunned by their **poorer** neighbors.
4. She wasn't **deceiving** anyone with her <u>prevaricating</u>.
5. <u>Intransigence</u> and **stubbornness** won't help us overcome this problem.

PENNSYLVANIA STANDARDS

READING STANDARD
A.1.1.2 Identify synonyms and antonyms

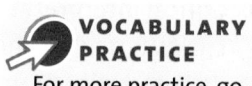

VOCABULARY PRACTICE
For more practice, go to the **Vocabulary Center** at **ClassZone.com.**

Reading-Writing Connection

Demonstrate your understanding of the characters in "The Rights to the Streets of Memphis" by responding to these prompts. Then use **Revision: Grammar and Style** to improve your writing.

WRITING PROMPTS

A. Short Response: Write a Different Conclusion

How might things have been different if Richard had not been victorious? Imagine that Richard lost the fight and the grocery money despite his strong **convictions.** Then write **one or two paragraphs** about his defeat and its consequences.

B. Extended Response: Interpret Motives

Mrs. Wright left her two young sons alone during the day. She ordered Richard to bring home groceries even if he must fight a gang to do so. Why did she act as she did? Write a **three-to-five-paragraph response,** describing her actions and explaining her motives.

SELF-CHECK

A strong conclusion will . . .

- provide details about how Richard lost the fight
- describe his and his mother's reactions to the loss

A successful response will . . .

- describe Mrs. Wright's actions
- explain the reasons for her actions

REVISION: GRAMMAR AND STYLE

EMPHASIZE ACTION Review the **Grammar and Style** note on page 115. There, Wright uses **strong verbs in a series** to emphasize the actions taking place. By incorporating similar techniques into your own writing, you can help readers to easily visualize events, as Wright does.

Here is another example from the story:

When I reached the corner, a gang of boys grabbed me, knocked me down, snatched the basket, took the money, and sent me running home in panic. (lines 75–77)

Now study this model. Notice how the revisions in red make the sentence much stronger, yet still concise. Revise your responses to the prompts by using the same techniques.

PENNSYLVANIA STANDARDS

WRITING STANDARD
1.5.11.E Revise writing to improve style, word choice

WRITING TOOLS
For prewriting, revision, and editing tools, visit the **Writing Center** at ClassZone.com.

STUDENT MODEL

To help her son survive, Mrs. Wright ~~used several tactics to make~~ *urged, commanded, and finally compelled*

him face his deepest fears. *to*

from **Seabiscuit: An American Legend**
Biography by Laura Hillenbrand

What makes a
WINNER?

PENNSYLVANIA STANDARDS

READING STANDARDS
A.2.6.1 Describe the author's purpose
A.2.6.2 Analyze examples that support the purpose

KEY IDEA In the heat of competition, what separates a **winner** from a loser? That's the question explored in *Seabiscuit,* the story of the legendary racehorse that won the hearts of millions of Americans.

PRESENT With a partner, choose someone you consider to be a winner. Create a "portrait" of the person in words and images, labeling the qualities that you feel led to his or her success. Share your portrait with the rest of the class.

LITERARY ANALYSIS: SUSPENSE IN BIOGRAPHY

A **biography** is a true account of someone's life. The biography you are about to read is unusual in that the author has chosen to make not a person but a famous horse the focus of her work.

Though biographers must research and report facts accurately, a good biographer is also a storyteller who engages readers. Through the use of **foreshadowing,** for example, the biographer can build **suspense** in the same way that a fiction writer does. Notice how the first sentence sets up a feeling of tension and concern about future events:

Quiet trepidation settled over the Howard barn in the week before the Santa Anita Handicap.

As you read this selection from *Seabiscuit,* pay attention to the various ways Laura Hillenbrand creates suspense.

READING SKILL: IDENTIFY AUTHOR'S PURPOSE

An **author's purpose** is the reasons the author has for writing a particular work. An author typically has one or more of these basic purposes in mind:

- to inform or explain
- to express thoughts or feelings
- to persuade
- to entertain

Understanding an author's purpose for writing can provide insight into the message, or theme, of a work. It can also help you decide *how* to read. For example, if you realize that an author is trying to inform or explain by including detailed information, you might decide to take notes as you read in order to revisit important content later on.

As you read this selection, try to decide Hillenbrand's purpose. Consider whether she might have had more than one purpose in mind. Record your findings, and be ready to discuss them.

Review: **Predict**

▲ VOCABULARY IN CONTEXT

Try to figure out the meaning of each boldfaced word.

1. felt **trepidation** waiting
2. mumbled **inaudibly**
3. looking for the **optimal** solution
4. tiny **increment** of speed
5. a slow, steady **cadence**

6. clumsy and **inept**
7. **inexplicably** dropped out of the race
8. finally reached an **unequivocal** decision

Author Online

Laura Hillenbrand born 1967

The Will to Overcome
At the age of 19, Laura Hillenbrand's life changed forever. Up until then, she had been physically active, swimming competitively, riding horses, and playing tennis. Suddenly, she was stricken with chronic fatigue syndrome, an illness that sometimes made her too weak even to feed herself. To find purpose in her life and "a way to endure the suffering," Hillenbrand started writing. As she wrote *Seabiscuit,* she found a link between herself and her subject—a horse who had the will to overcome obstacles.

A Thorough Researcher Although her illness sometimes left her bedridden, Hillenbrand meticulously researched the life of Seabiscuit. She placed ads in horseracing magazines, interviewed aging jockeys by phone, and sought information from the Library of Congress. Her research paid off in a best-selling biography filled with suspenseful events and memorable details.

 MORE ABOUT THE AUTHOR
For more on Laura Hillenbrand, visit the **Literature Center** at **ClassZone.com.**

Background

Horseracing Known as the sport of kings, horseracing is one of the oldest of all spectator sports. A popular type of horserace is the handicap, a race in which the horses carry different amounts of weight based on factors such as age and past performances. Faster horses carry more weight; slower horses carry less. The goal is to give all the horses an equal chance of winning. To ride a racehorse, a jockey needs balance, coordination, strength, and quick reflexes. According to Hillenbrand, "The extraordinary athleticism of the jockey is unparalleled."

Seabiscuit:
AN AMERICAN LEGEND

Laura Hillenbrand

Quiet **trepidation** settled over the Howard barn in the week before the Santa Anita Handicap.[1] Late in the week, a long, soaking shower doused the racing oval. When the rain stopped, asphalt-baking machines droned over the course, licking flames over the surface to dry the soil. Rosemont emerged from the barn three days before the race and scorched the track in his final workout. Reporters waited for Smith[2] to give his horse a similar workout, but they never saw Seabiscuit doing anything more than stretching his legs. Rumors swirled around the track that Seabiscuit was lame. Rosemont's stock rose; Seabiscuit's dropped.

10 Smith had fooled them. At three o'clock one morning shortly before the race, he led Seabiscuit out to the track and gave him one last workout in peace and isolation. The horse ran beautifully.

On February 27, 1937, Charles and Marcela Howard[3] arrived at Santa Anita to watch their pride and joy go for the hundred-grander. They were giddy with anticipation. "If Seabiscuit loses," mused a friend, "Mrs. Howard is going to be so heartbroken that I'll have to carry her out. If he wins, Charley'll be so excited that I'll have to carry him." Howard couldn't keep still. He trotted up to the press box and made the wildly popular announcement that if his horse won, he'd send up a barrel of champagne for the reporters. He went down
20 to the betting area, and seeing that the line was too long to wait, he grabbed a bettor and jammed five $1,000 bills into his hand. "Put it all on Seabiscuit's nose,[4] please," he told the bewildered wagerer before trotting off again. **A**

trepidation
(trĕp′ĭ-dā′shən)
n. nervous fear

ANALYZE VISUALS
Examine the photograph of Seabiscuit. What details convey his strength and will to win?

A AUTHOR'S PURPOSE
From what you have read so far, what do you think is the author's main purpose for writing?

---

1. **Santa Anita Handicap:** a race at the Santa Anita track in California, with a prize of $100,000.
2. **Smith:** Tom Smith, Seabiscuit's trainer.
3. **Charles and Marcela Howard:** Seabiscuit's owners.
4. **"put it ... nose":** bet all the money on Seabiscuit's coming in first.

At a little past 4:00 P.M. Pollard[5] and Seabiscuit parted from Smith at the paddock gate and walked out onto the track for the Santa Anita Handicap. A record crowd of sixty thousand fans had come to see eighteen horses try for the richest
30 purse in the world. Millions more listened on radio.

As Pollard felt Seabiscuit's hooves sink into the russet soil, he had reason to worry. The baking machines had not completely dried the surface. Rain and dirt had blended into a heavy goo along the rail; breaking from the three post,[6] Seabiscuit would be right
40 down in it. Far behind him in the post parade, jockey Harry Richards was contemplating a different set of obstacles for Rosemont. He had drawn the seventeenth post

Seabiscuit owner C. S. Howard, jockey Red Pollard, and trainer Tom Smith.

position. He was going to have the luxury of a hard, fast track, but his problem would be traffic. As a late runner, Rosemont would have to pick his way through the cluttered field.

The two jockeys virtually bookended the field as they moved to the post. Pollard feared nothing but Richards and Rosemont. Richards feared nothing
50 but Pollard and Seabiscuit. The two horses stood motionless while the field was loaded around them. **B**

At the sound of the bell, Seabiscuit bounded forward. To his outside, a crowd of horses rushed inward to gain **optimal** position. The field doubled over on itself, and the hinge was Seabiscuit, who was pinched back to ninth. In a cloud of horses, Pollard spotted daylight five feet or so off the rail. He banked Seabiscuit out into it, holding him out of the deep part of the track. He slipped up to fourth position, just off of front-running Special Agent. On the first turn Seabiscuit was crowded back down to the rail. As the field straightened into the backstretch, Pollard found another avenue and eased him
60 outward again, to firmer ground. Ahead, Special Agent was setting a suicidal pace, but Pollard sensed how fast it was and was not going to be lured into it. He sat back and waited. Behind him, Rosemont was tugging along toward the back of the field, waiting for the speed horses to crumble. **C**

B SUSPENSE IN BIOGRAPHY
Reread lines 32–51. What technique does the writer use to build suspense?

optimal (ŏp′tə-məl) *adj.* most favorable; best

C PREDICT
Which horse do you predict will win the race? Why do you think so?

---

5. **Pollard:** Red Pollard, Seabiscuit's jockey.

6. **the three post:** in the starting gate, the third position out from the railing.

With a half mile to go, Pollard positioned Seabiscuit in the clear and readied for his move. Behind him, Richards sensed that the moment had come to shoot for Seabiscuit. He began threading Rosemont through the field, cutting in and out, picking off horses one by one, talking in his horse's ear as clumps of dirt cracked into his face. His luck was holding; every hole toward which he guided his horse held open just long enough for him to gallop through. On the far turn he reached Seabiscuit's heels and began looking for a way around him. Ahead of him, Pollard crouched and watched Special Agent's churning hindquarters, waiting for him to fold.

At the top of the stretch Special Agent faltered. Pollard pulled Seabiscuit's nose to the outside and slapped him on the rump. Seabiscuit pounced. Richards saw him go and gunned Rosemont through the hole after him, but Seabiscuit had stolen a three-length advantage. Special Agent gave way grudgingly along the inside as Indian Broom rallied up the outside, not quite quick enough to keep up.

Lengthening stride for the long run to the wire, Seabiscuit was alone on the lead in the dry, hard center of the track. Pollard had delivered a masterpiece of reinsmanship, avoiding the traps and saving ground while minimizing his run along the boggy rail. He had won the tactical battle with Richards. He was coming into the homestretch of the richest race in the world with a strong horse beneath him. Behind them were seventeen of the best horses in the nation. To the left and right, sixty thousand voices roared. Ahead was nothing but a long strip of red soil.

The rest of the field peeled away, scattered across thirty-two lengths of track behind them. It was down to Rosemont and Seabiscuit.

Seabiscuit was moving fastest. He charged down the stretch in front with Pollard up over his neck, moving with him, driving him on. Rosemont was obscured behind him. He was gaining only by **increments.** Seabiscuit sailed through midstretch a full length ahead of Rosemont. Up in the stands, the Howards and Smith were thinking the same thing: Rosemont is too far behind. Seabiscuit is going to win.

Without warning, horse and rider lost focus. Abruptly, **inexplicably,** Pollard wavered. He lay his whip down on Seabiscuit's shoulder and left it there.

Seabiscuit paused. Perhaps he slowed in hopes of finding an opponent to toy with. Or maybe he sensed Pollard's hesitation. His composure, which Smith had patiently schooled into him over six months, began to unravel. Seabiscuit suddenly took a sharp left turn, veering ten feet across the track and back down into the deep going, straightening himself out just before hitting the rail. He had given away several feet of his lead. The **cadence** of his stride dropped. What had been a seamless union was now only a man and a horse, jangling against each other.

increment (ĭn'krə-mənt) *n.* a small, slight growth or increase

inexplicably (ĭn-ĕk'splĭ-kə-blē) *adv.* in a way that is difficult or impossible to explain

cadence (kād'ns) *n.* a balanced, rhythmic flow

From between Rosemont's ears, Richards saw Seabiscuit's form disintegrate. He looked toward the wire. It seemed close enough to touch, but Rosemont still wasn't past Seabiscuit's saddlecloth. He had been riding on instinct, reflex, but now his heart caught in his throat: *I am too late.* Desperate, he flung himself over Rosemont's neck, booting and whipping and screaming,
110 "Faster, baby, faster!" Striding high in the center of the track, Rosemont was suddenly animated by Richards's raging desire. He dropped his head and dug in. Seabiscuit's lead, stride by stride, slipped away.

For a few seconds at the most critical moment of their careers, Pollard and Seabiscuit faltered. For fifteen strides, more than the length of a football field, Pollard remained virtually motionless. Rosemont was some ten feet to his outside, leaving plenty of room for Pollard to swing Seabiscuit out of the rail-path's slow going, but Pollard didn't take the opportunity. From behind his half-moon blinker cups,[7] Seabiscuit could see nothing but an empty track ahead of him, nor is it likely that he could hear Rosemont over the roar from
120 the grandstand. Or perhaps he was waiting for him. His left ear swung around lazily, as if he were paying attention to something in the infield. His stride slowed. His mind seemed scattered. The lead was vanishing. A length. Six feet. A neck. The wire was rushing at them. The crowd was shrieking. **D**

D AUTHOR'S PURPOSE
Reread lines 113–123. What details make this passage not only informative but entertaining?

---

7. **blinker cups:** flaps put over a horse's eyes to keep it from seeing sideways.

Rosemont edges out Seabiscuit to win the Santa Anita Handicap by a nose.

ANALYZE VISUALS
What elements of the dramatic finish are captured by this photograph? What does the photo add to your understanding of the story? Be specific.

With just a few yards to go, Pollard broke out of his limbo. He burst into frenzied motion. Seabiscuit's ears snapped back and he dived forward. But Rosemont had momentum. The lead shrank to nothing. Rosemont caught Seabiscuit, then took a lead of inches. Seabiscuit was accelerating, his rhythm building, his mind narrowed down to his task at the urgent call of his rider. But Richards was driving harder, scratching and yelling and pleading for
130 Rosemont to run. Seabiscuit cut the advantage away. They drew even again.
Rosemont and Seabiscuit flew under the wire together.

Up in their box, the Howards leapt up. Charles ran to the Turf Club bar, calling for champagne for everyone. Voices sang out and corks popped and a wild celebration began.

Gradually, the revelers went silent. The crowd had stopped cheering. The stewards posted no winner. They were waiting for the photo. The exhausted horses returned to be unsaddled, and the fans sat in agonized anticipation. Two minutes passed. In the hush, a sibilant sound attended the finish photo as it slid down to the stewards. There was a terrible pause. The numbers blinked up
140 on the board.

Rosemont had won.

E SUSPENSE IN BIOGRAPHY
Reread lines 124–131. What words does the writer use to build excitement in this passage?

A howl went up from the grandstand. Thousands of spectators were certain that the stewards had it wrong, that Seabiscuit had been robbed. But the photo was **unequivocal:** Rosemont's long bay muzzle hung there in the picture, just a wink ahead of Seabiscuit's. "Dame Fortune," wrote announcer Joe Hernandez, "made a mistake and kissed the wrong horse—Rosemont—in the glorious end of the Santa Anita Handicap."

Charles and Marcela collected themselves. The length of Rosemont's nose had cost them $70,700. They continued passing out the champagne, brave
150 smiles on their faces.

Pollard didn't need to look at the tote board. He knew he had lost from the instant the noses hit the line. Wrung to exhaustion and deathly pale, he slid from Seabiscuit's back. He walked over to Richards, who was being smothered in kisses by his tearful wife. Pollard's face was blank, his voice barely above a whisper. All around him, people regarded him with expressions of cool accusation.

unequivocal
(ŭn′ĭ-kwĭv′ə-kəl)
adj. allowing no doubt or misunderstanding

ANALYZE VISUALS
What does this photo of Seabiscuit and Red Pollard show you about their relationship? Be specific.

"Congratulations, Harry, you rode a swell race," Pollard said.

"Thanks," said Richards, his face covered in lipstick and his voice breaking; he had shouted it away urging Rosemont on. "But it was very close."

160 "Close, yes," said Pollard almost **inaudibly,** "but you won."

Pollard saw Howard hovering nearby, waiting for him. The jockey went to him.

"What happened?" Howard asked gently. Ashen and spent, Pollard said that the rail had been slow, and that he had been unable to get outside without fouling Rosemont. If he and Rosemont had switched positions, he was sure Seabiscuit would have won.

It was a thin excuse. Pollard must have known that to save his professional standing, he would have to offer more that than, say something that would explain how he had allowed Rosemont to come to him without fighting back 170 until the last moment. Already, harsh words were being hung on him: *arrogant, **inept,** overconfident.* He could not have mistaken the reproach on the faces of those around him. His reputation was tumbling. But Pollard gave the public nothing to make them reconsider.

Perhaps he couldn't. He had a secret to keep, a gamble he had made years earlier and remade with each race. But he could no longer think that its risks affected only himself.

Perhaps Pollard didn't see Rosemont coming because of the blindness of his right eye. **F**

It is unlikely that he could have heard Rosemont over the din from the 180 crowd. Rosemont's surge, unexpected and sudden, may have eluded Pollard until very late in the race. Pollard did not begin urging Seabiscuit in earnest until Rosemont was alongside him, just forward enough for Pollard to see him with his left eye, upon turning his head. One good eye offers little depth perception, so he may not have been able to judge whether Rosemont was far enough to his right to allow Seabiscuit to move outward.

If this explanation is correct, then Pollard was trapped. He was publicly accused of inexcusable failure in the most important race of his career, but he could not defend himself. Had he let on that he was blind in one eye, his career would have been over. Like most jockeys in the 1930s, he had nowhere 190 else to go, nothing else to live on, nothing else he loved. For Red Pollard, there was no road back to Edmonton. If his blindness was the cause of the loss, his frustration and guilt must have been consuming.

Howard accepted Pollard's explanation without criticism. Neither he nor Smith blamed him.

Almost everyone else did. ‿

---

inaudibly (ĭn-ô′də-blē) *adv.* in a way that is impossible to hear

inept (ĭn-ĕpt′) *adj.* generally incompetent

F SUSPENSE IN BIOGRAPHY
Notice that the writer withholds this important piece of information from the reader until after the race is over. If the writer had revealed this information before describing the race, would the suspense have been greater or less? Explain.

Comprehension

1. **Recall** Which horse was Seabiscuit's main challenger in the race?

2. **Recall** How did the stewards determine which horse had won the race?

3. **Clarify** Why did Pollard keep the blindness in his right eye a secret?

Literary Analysis

4. **Identify Author's Purpose** Review your notes. What do you think Hillenbrand's main purpose was in writing this **biography?** What other purposes might she have had? Support your answer with evidence.

5. **Analyze Suspense in Biography** How does the author create suspense in this biography? In a chart like the one shown, give examples of each of her narrative techniques.

Narrative Technique	Example
Raising questions in reader's mind	• Rosemont's stock rose
Foreshadowing	
Withholding certain information	

6. **Compare and Contrast** Compare Seabiscuit and Pollard with Rosemont and Richards. What qualities made the difference between the **winner** and the loser of the Santa Anita Handicap?

7. **Make Judgments** Reread lines 186–195. Was it fair to blame Pollard for losing the race? Support your answer with reasons and evidence.

8. **Evaluate** Though not a short story, this selection reads like one. Identify the events that comprise the **falling action** and the **resolution** of the plot. How does the revelation about Pollard's blindness in his right eye affect your evaluation of Seabiscuit as a racing horse?

Literary Criticism

9. **Historical Context** Commenting on her biography of Seabiscuit, Hillenbrand said, "The subjects that I've written about—the men and the horse—were radically different individuals, but the one thread that pulls through all of their lives and through the events that they lived through together is this struggle between overwhelming hardship and the will to overcome it." When Seabiscuit was making racing history, the United States was reeling from the Great Depression, a catastrophic economic collapse that began in 1929 and continued through the 1930s. What might Seabiscuit have represented to the country at that time?

PENNSYLVANIA STANDARDS

READING STANDARD
A.2.6.2 Analyze examples that support the purpose

Vocabulary in Context

VOCABULARY PRACTICE

Write *true* or *false* for each statement.

1. A person who speaks **inaudibly** can easily be heard.
2. The **optimal** time to spot Mars is on a cloudy night.
3. To honor your ancestors, you might build an **increment.**
4. An **inept** person is not a good choice to manage a project.
5. If you have **trepidation** about heights, you may not like skydiving.
6. Troops might march to the **cadence** of a band.
7. If an event occurs **inexplicably,** it is hard to understand why it happens.
8. An **unequivocal** "no" answer indicates that you have not made up your mind.

WORD LIST

cadence

inaudibly

increment

inept

inexplicably

optimal

trepidation

unequivocal

VOCABULARY IN WRITING

Use three or more vocabulary words in a paragraph describing the last few seconds of the race. Here is an example of a sentence you might use.

> **EXAMPLE SENTENCE**
>
> The **cadence** of the two horses grew faster and faster.

VOCABULARY STRATEGY: THE *aud* WORD FAMILY

The word *inaudibly* can be traced back to the Latin root *aud,* which means "to hear." Many other words belong to the same word family as *inaudibly.* If you can recognize the root in these words, you can understand how they are related in meaning.

PRACTICE Use each word below in a sentence that shows its connection in meaning to *inaudibly.* If necessary, consult a dictionary.

1. audit
2. audiology
3. audience
4. audio-visual
5. auditorium
6. audition

PENNSYLVANIA STANDARDS

READING STANDARD
A.2.2 Apply word recognition skills

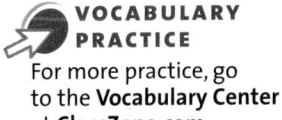

VOCABULARY PRACTICE
For more practice, go to the **Vocabulary Center** at **ClassZone.com.**

Horse of the Century

- Magazine Article, page 133
- Timeline, page 134
- Radio Transcript, page 135

Use with *Seabiscuit: An American Legend*, page 122.

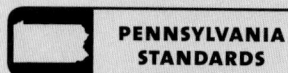

PENNSYLVANIA STANDARDS

READING STANDARDS
A.2.5.1 Summarize the major points
B.1.2.1 Evaluate connections between texts

What's the Connection?

In the selection from *Seabiscuit: An American Legend*, you read about one of the most famous horseraces of the 20th century. The following selections will help you get a sense of what it was like to actually be at that race and why many Americans practically held their breath as they listened to it on the radio.

Skill Focus: Synthesize

When you read different texts on the same topic, you **synthesize** information—that is, you put together the facts, ideas, and details you get from each of them. As a result, you gain a fuller understanding of the topic than you would from reading only one text.

Here's how you can synthesize the ideas and information in the pieces about Seabiscuit:

- Summarize the main ideas and details in each piece.
- Jot down any questions that come to you as you learn new information.
- When information in one source conflicts with information in another, jot down these conflicts as questions, too.
- Reread each piece to answer your questions and fill in gaps in your understanding.

For more help synthesizing, complete a chart like the one started here as you read the following selections.

Source	Main Ideas	New Information & Questions
From *Seabiscuit: An American Legend*	Jockey, owner, and fans were surprised by his defeat in the Santa Anita Handicap.	Why was this horse so popular?
From "Four Good Legs Between Us"	Even though Seabiscuit lost this race, he was fast becoming a celebrity.	Howard made him popular by racing him all over the country. What was going on in Europe?

from
Four Good Legs Between Us
Laura Hillenbrand

Though Seabiscuit had lost [the Santa Anita Handicap], he was rapidly becoming a phenomenal celebrity. Two factors converged to create and nourish this. The first was Charles Howard. A born adman, Howard courted the nation on behalf of his horse much as he had hawked his first Buicks, undertaking exhaustive promotion that presaged the modern marketing of athletes. Crafting daring, unprecedented coast-to-coast racing campaigns, he shipped Seabiscuit over fifty thousand railroad miles to showcase his talent at eighteen tracks in seven states and Mexico. The second factor was timing. The nation was sliding from economic ruin into the whirling eddy of Europe's cataclysm. Seabiscuit, Howard, Pollard, and Smith, whose fortunes
10 swung in epic parabolas, would have resonated in any age, but in cruel years the peculiar union among the four transcended the racetrack. **A**

The result was stupendous popularity. In one year Seabiscuit garnered more newspaper column inches than Roosevelt, Hitler, or Mussolini. *Life* even ran a pictorial on his facial expressions. Cities had to route special trains to accommodate the invariably record-shattering crowds that came to see him run. Smith, fearing Seabiscuit wouldn't get any rest, hoodwinked the press by trotting out a look-alike. Such fame fueled the immediate, immense success of Howard's Santa Anita and California's new racing industry, today a four-billion-dollar business.

A SYNTHESIZE
Summarize the two causes of Seabiscuit's popularity.

Timeline: Seabiscuit

1937 — *February 27:* In his first try at the Santa Anita Handicap, Seabiscuit loses to Rosemont by a nose, in a photo finish.

March 6: Seabiscuit draws a crowd of 45,000 excited fans and wins the San Juan Capistrano Handicap by seven lengths, smashing the track record.

May 6: The German airship *Hindenburg* bursts into flames as it is about to land in Lakehurst, New Jersey.

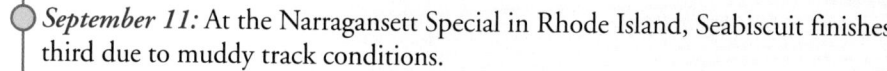

June 5: War Admiral captures the Triple Crown after a win at the Belmont Stakes.

June 26: Seabiscuit runs in the Brooklyn Handicap, beating rival Rosemont and local horse Aneroid.

July: Seabiscuit wins the Butler Handicap and the Yonkers Handicap easily, despite carrying far more weight than his competitors in both races.

September 11: At the Narragansett Special in Rhode Island, Seabiscuit finishes third due to muddy track conditions.

October 12: Seabiscuit wins the Continental Handicap in New York, gaining the top spot in the 1937 winnings race with $152,780 earned, $8,000 ahead of War Admiral.

October 30: Seabiscuit and War Admiral are slated to meet on the track, but Seabiscuit is scratched from the Washington Handicap due to muddy track conditions, allowing an easy victory for his rival.

December 7: War Admiral is named horse of the year by *Turf and Sport Digest*.

1938 — *October 30:* Orson Welles's radio broadcast of *The War of the Worlds,* the tale of a Martian invasion on Earth, creates panic among listeners who mistake it for news.

November 1: With 40 million listeners tuned in across the country, Seabiscuit beats War Admiral by four lengths in just over a minute fifty-six for the mile and three-sixteenths, a new Pimlico record.

1939 — *February 14:* Seabiscuit injures his suspensory ligament in a prep race for Santa Anita.

September 3: Britain and France declare war on Germany.

1940 — *March 2:* Seabiscuit wins in his third try at the $100,000 Santa Anita Handicap. He clocks the fastest mile and a quarter in Santa Anita's history, the second fastest ever run in the United States. The most people ever to attend an American horse race—75,000—watch as Pollard leads Seabiscuit from behind to victory.

April 10: Seabiscuit retires to Charles Howard's Ridgewood Ranch. **B**

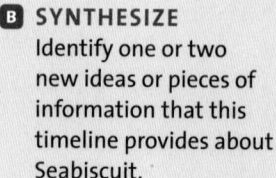

B SYNTHESIZE
Identify one or two new ideas or pieces of information that this timeline provides about Seabiscuit.

Races on the Radio
Santa Anita Handicap (1937) with Clem McCarthy and Buddy Twist

CLEM McCARTHY:

Eddy Thomas won't take the start until he's on his toes and the jockey is ready. Then he'll push that button, the bell will ring, and they'll be on their way. We don't have any starting barriers now, as you know. Here they go. And they're on their way down the stretch. The break was good; every horse got a chance just as they left there. **C**

As they come down here to the eighth pole, it is Time Supply and Special Agent. Special Agent is trying to force his way to the front and he's going to do a good job of it as they pass the stands. Here on the outside comes Rosemont in a good position. And as they go by me it is
10 Special Agent on the lead by one length. Special Agent has the lead and then comes Time Supply in second place right along beside him. Going to the first turn is Special Agent by a length. Time Supply is second and on the outside of him is Accolade. And Boxthorn is close up. Far back in the crowd, on the inside, in about twelfth place is Red Rain. Up there close is Rosemont in about sixth place.

They're going into the stretch; they've gone half a mile. And the time for the first quarter over this track was 22 and two fifths seconds, the half in 45 and four. They're turning into the backstretch with Special Agent on the lead. Special Agent has a lead now of one length
20 and a half. Right behind him comes Time Supply. And in there, slipping through on the inside is . . . Indian Broom is going up on the inside now in a good position. Around that far turn, there's still no change in the positions. Rosemont is having a hard time working his way through, he's now in sixth position going around on the inside, he's saving ground, he's got plenty left. If he's enough horse, he may get home.

C SYNTHESIZE
Read all or part of this transcript aloud, using the tone and style of a sports announcer. Where do you speed up the pace?

And on the outside, here comes the other one, Indian Broom. And Goldeneye is moving up from the rear. Here comes Accolade in second position. And Seabiscuit is now moving up and is challenging as they turn for home.

30   It's Special Agent and Seabiscuit challenging head-and-head as they swing into the stretch. And they've only got a quarter of a mile to come. They've stepped the first mile in 1:36 and four-fifths—and that shows you what this pace is. He can't live at it. Seabiscuit has got the lead half way down the stretch. But here comes one of the Baroni entries challenging on the outside, challenging boldly. And the battle is on. Indian Broom is coming fast and here comes Rosemont between horses. And Rosemont may take it all. It's gonna be a photograph finish. And it's anybody's race right to the end.

    I think Rosemont got the money. I think Rosemont was first. It
40 was an eyebrow finish. And Seabiscuit was the second horse. Seabiscuit was second and one of the Taylor entries; I think Indian Broom, was third. It was very close. That was an eyelash finish. Rosemont was closing strong, but Seabiscuit hung on. The time of the race was 2:02 and four-fifths, which makes the track almost identically like the track of two years ago . . .

BUDDY TWIST:

Oh boy, one of the most thrilling finishes I think that I've ever seen in a horse race in my life, Clem. The crowd down here has gone completely mad. The photographers are outside the charm circle, which is a white circle here, where the winner will come up in just a moment. Newsreel
50 photographers are setting up on every hand. The horses are just coming back now. And everybody, depending on who was their favorite, was shouting "Rosemont," "Seabiscuit"—one would call Rosemont, one Seabiscuit. There were half-a-dozen here who were just as sure Rosemont won as Seabiscuit, they don't know what to think of it. One of the most beautiful driving finishes I think I've ever seen.

CLEM McCARTHY:

Here's the photograph finish. Hold it now. Get ready for it. Just a few seconds and we'll know the winner of this race. I think Rosemont won it, but that's only my guess from where I stand. The photograph will tell us the actual winner. The naked eye is not as good as the photograph,
60 we'll have it in a second. They're looking at it down there. I know it was an eyelash finish. Either horse won by a whisker and that's all. Just about a quarter of an inch, I can't see any more between them. I really shouldn't express an opinion on a finish that close. And they're still waiting. That shows you what a difficult . . . There it is, Rosemont is the winner. Rosemont by a nose. Seabiscuit is second. Just a minute Buddy until I get it. Rosemont is the winner—I want you to get that jockey if you got him—Seabiscuit is second. And the Taylor entry finished third and fourth. They haven't put up the distinguishing numbers and they finished very close together. **D**

D SYNTHESIZE
What does this transcript reveal about the end of the race that was not included in the other texts?

Comprehension

1. **Recall** Which horse won the Santa Anita Handicap in 1937? What kind of a finish was it?

2. **Recall** How many times did Seabiscuit enter the Santa Anita Handicap before winning?

3. **Summarize** What major world events took place during Seabiscuit's rise to fame?

Critical Analysis

4. **Analyze Mood and Tone** What elements of the radio transcript contribute to the sense of excitement? Be specific.

5. **Synthesize** Review the ideas and information you noted in your chart. How did the world events of the day contribute to Seabiscuit's popularity? Use evidence from the texts to support your answer.

PENNSYLVANIA STANDARDS

READING STANDARDS
A.2.5.1 Summarize the major points
B.1.2.1 Evaluate connections between texts

Read for Information: Draw Conclusions

WRITING PROMPT

In a paragraph, state and support your conclusions about one of the following topics:

- horseracing as a spectator sport
- Seabiscuit's popularity
- jockeys

To answer this prompt, you will need to pick your topic and follow these steps:

1. Gather information about your topic from the three selections, as well as from Hillenbrand's biography of Seabiscuit.

2. Consider the main ideas and information you have collected. Ask yourself what conclusion(s) you can draw from them.

3. State your conclusion(s) in a topic sentence. Then, support those conclusions with ideas and information from the texts.

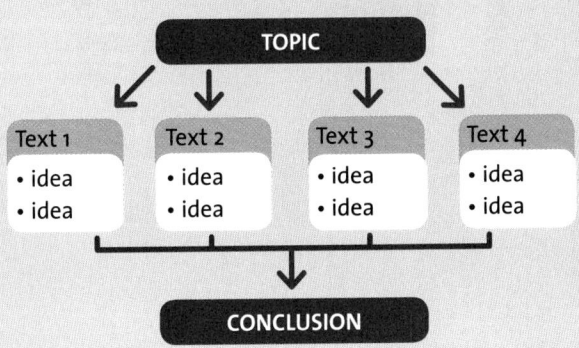

The Raven
Poem by Edgar Allan Poe

Incident in a Rose Garden
Poem by Donald Justice

Why are we fascinated by the UNKNOWN?

PENNSYLVANIA STANDARDS

READING STANDARDS
A.1.6.1 Identify and/or analyze intended purpose of text
B.2.1 Identify and analyze figurative language and literary structures

KEY IDEA Have you ever skimmed the strange headlines of a tabloid newspaper when standing in line at the supermarket? Do you channel-surf for television shows about strange phenomena? Our fascination with weird or unexplained events makes us part of a long tradition of writers and readers who enjoy speculating on the **unknown** or the unexplainable. The writers of the two poems you are about to read relied on that universal fascination when they introduced us to two strange, and perhaps imaginary, visitors.

DISCUSS With a partner, share the story of a movie, television show, or urban legend that you find fascinating or unbelievable.

LITERARY ANALYSIS: NARRATIVE POETRY

Like fiction, a **narrative poem** contains the elements of plot, conflict, character, and setting that combine to create a story. Because of the nature of poetry, these elements are often condensed into images and compact descriptions. For example, notice that this line contains information about setting, plot, and character:

Once upon a midnight dreary, while I pondered, weak and weary

In each of the following narrative poems, the **speaker,** or voice that talks to the reader, is also the main character in the story. As you read, note what events each speaker describes and how these create a compelling story in verse form.

READING SKILL: READING POETRY

When you read a narrative poem, certain reading strategies will help you understand the poem's story and meaning.

- First, read the poem silently to grasp the basic story line.
- Then read it aloud several times, and listen to how it sounds. Pay attention to sound devices, such as **rhyme, rhythm,** and **repetition.** Does the poem include **alliteration,** the repetition of consonant sounds at the beginning of words? How do these sound devices add to the effect of the poem? (To review the definitions of these sound-device terms, see the **Glossary of Literary Terms,** page R102.)
- Look for clues that reveal something about the **speaker.** What does the speaker feel about the poem's characters and events?

As you read each poem, record the most striking examples of sound devices in a chart similar to the following:

Sound Device	"The Raven"	"Incident in a Rose Garden"
alliteration	"nodded, nearly napping"	

Edgar Allan Poe: A Life of Tragedy
One of America's literary giants, Edgar Allan Poe has fascinated generations of readers with his haunting poetry and tales of horror. (See "The Cask of Amontillado" on page 344.) Poe suffered many tragic losses

Edgar Allan Poe
1809–1849

in his short life. He was orphaned at the age of 2 and taken in by foster parents, but never formally adopted. Poe later quarreled bitterly with his foster father. At the age of 27, Poe married a 13-year-old cousin, Virginia Clemm. She died about ten years later, after an agonizing battle with tuberculosis.

Death-Haunted Poetry Poe's poetry often deals with the subject of death. According to Poe, the "death then of a beautiful woman is, unquestionably, the most poetical topic in the world."

Donald Justice: From Music to Poetry Donald Justice originally intended to become a composer and studied for a degree in music before deciding to become a writer. He then earned a doctorate in creative writing, participating in the Iowa Writers'

Donald Justice
1925–2004

Workshop. A Pulitzer Prize–winning poet, Justice taught English at a number of universities.

MORE ABOUT THE AUTHOR
For more on Edgar Allan Poe and Donald Justice, visit the **Literature Center** at **ClassZone.com.**

The Raven

EDGAR ALLAN POE

Once upon a midnight dreary, while I pondered, weak and weary,
Over many a quaint and curious volume of forgotten lore—
While I nodded, nearly napping, suddenly there came a tapping,
As of someone gently rapping, rapping at my chamber door.
5 "'Tis some visitor," I muttered, "tapping at my chamber door—
    Only this and nothing more."

Ah, distinctly I remember it was in the bleak December;
And each separate dying ember wrought its ghost upon the floor.
Eagerly I wished the morrow;—vainly I had sought to borrow
10 From my books surcease of sorrow[1]—sorrow for the lost Lenore—
For the rare and radiant maiden whom the angels name Lenore—
    Nameless *here* forevermore. **Ⓐ**

And the silken, sad, uncertain rustling of each purple curtain
Thrilled me—filled me with fantastic terrors never felt before;
15 So that now, to still the beating of my heart, I stood repeating
"'Tis some visitor entreating entrance at my chamber door;—
Some late visitor entreating entrance at my chamber door;—
    That it is and nothing more."

Presently my soul grew stronger; hesitating then no longer,
20 "Sir," said I, "or Madam, truly your forgiveness I implore;
But the fact is I was napping, and so gently you came rapping,
And so faintly you came tapping, tapping at my chamber door,
That I scarce was sure I heard you"—here I opened wide the door;—
    Darkness there and nothing more.

ANALYZE VISUALS
What **mood** is conveyed by the style of the drawing?

Ⓐ NARRATIVE POETRY
With what **internal conflict** does the speaker struggle?

---

1. **from my books surcease of sorrow:** from reading, an end to sorrow.

25 Deep into that darkness peering, long I stood there wondering, fearing,
Doubting, dreaming dreams no mortal ever dared to dream before;
But the silence was unbroken, and the stillness gave no token,
And the only word there spoken was the whispered word, "Lenore!"
This I whispered, and an echo murmured back the word "Lenore!"
30   Merely this and nothing more. **B**

Back into the chamber turning, all my soul within me burning,
Soon again I heard a tapping somewhat louder than before.
"Surely," said I, "surely that is something at my window lattice;
Let me see, then, what thereat is, and this mystery explore—
35 Let my heart be still a moment and this mystery explore;—
      'Tis the wind and nothing more!"

Open here I flung the shutter, when, with many a flirt and flutter,
In there stepped a stately Raven of the saintly days of yore.[2]
Not the least obeisance made he;[3] not a minute stopped or stayed he;
40 But, with mien of lord or lady,[4] perched above my chamber door—
Perched upon a bust of Pallas[5] just above my chamber door—
      Perched, and sat, and nothing more.

Then this ebony bird beguiling[6] my sad fancy into smiling,
By the grave and stern decorum of the countenance[7] it wore,
45 "Though thy crest be shorn and shaven, thou," I said, "art sure no craven,[8]
Ghastly grim and ancient Raven wandering from the Nightly shore—
Tell me what thy lordly name is on the Night's Plutonian[9] shore!"
      Quoth the Raven, "Nevermore." **C**

Much I marveled this ungainly fowl to hear discourse so plainly,
50 Though its answer little meaning—little relevancy bore;
For we cannot help agreeing that no living human being
Ever yet was blessed with seeing bird above his chamber door—
Bird or beast upon the sculptured bust above his chamber door,
      With such name as "Nevermore."

B READING POETRY
Reread lines 25–30.
Identify examples of
alliteration, the repetition
of consonant sounds at
the beginning of words.
Notice how often this
sound device occurs in
this narrative poem.
What is the effect?

C NARRATIVE POETRY
What can you conclude
about the **speaker** from
the way he reacts to the
raven's entrance?

---

2. **saintly days of yore:** sacred days of the past.

3. **not the least obeisance** (ō-bā′səns) **made he:** he did not bow or make any other gesture of respect.

4. **with mien of lord or lady:** with the appearance of a noble person.

5. **bust of Pallas:** statue of the head and shoulders of Athena, Greek goddess of war and wisdom.

6. **this ebony bird beguiling** (bĭ-gī′lĭng): this black bird that is charming or delighting.

7. **grave and stern decorum . . . countenance** (koun′tə-nəns): serious and dignified expression on the face.

8. **art sure no craven:** are surely not cowardly.

9. **Plutonian:** having to do with Pluto, Roman god of the dead and ruler of the underworld.

55 But the Raven, sitting lonely on the placid bust, spoke only
    That one word, as if his soul in that one word he did outpour.
    Nothing farther then he uttered—not a feather then he fluttered—
    Till I scarcely more than muttered, "Other friends have flown before—
    On the morrow *he* will leave me, as my hopes have flown before."
60   Then the bird said, "Nevermore."

    Startled at the stillness broken by reply so aptly spoken,
    "Doubtless," said I, "what it utters is its only stock and store
    Caught from some unhappy master whom unmerciful Disaster **D**
    Followed fast and followed faster till his songs one burden bore—
65 Till the dirges of his Hope[10] that melancholy burden bore
        Of 'Never—nevermore.'"

    But the Raven still beguiling all my fancy into smiling,
    Straight I wheeled a cushioned seat in front of bird and bust and door;
    Then, upon the velvet sinking, I betook myself to linking
70 Fancy unto fancy, thinking what this ominous bird of yore—
    What this grim, ungainly, ghastly, gaunt, and ominous bird of yore
        Meant in croaking, "Nevermore."

    This I sat engaged in guessing, but no syllable expressing
    To the fowl whose fiery eyes now burned into my bosom's core;
75 This and more I sat divining,[11] with my head at ease reclining
    On the cushion's velvet lining that the lamp-light gloated o'er,
    But whose velvet violet lining with the lamp-light gloating o'er,
        She shall press, ah, nevermore!

    Then, methought, the air grew denser, perfumed from an unseen censer
80 Swung by Seraphim[12] whose foot-falls tinkled on the tufted floor.
    "Wretch," I cried, "thy God hath lent thee—by these angels he hath sent thee
    Respite—respite and nepenthe[13] from thy memories of Lenore;
    Quaff, oh quaff this kind nepenthe[14] and forget this lost Lenore!"
        Quoth the Raven, "Nevermore."

D **READING POETRY**
Reread line 63. Notice the **internal rhyme**—similar or identical sounds within a line—of the words *master* and *disaster*. Find examples of internal rhyme in other stanzas, and notice how they help emphasize certain words.

---

10. **dirges** (dûr'jǐz) **of his Hope:** funeral hymns mourning the loss of hope.

11. **divining** (dǐ-vī'nǐng): guessing or speculating.

12. **censer swung by Seraphim** (sĕr'ə-fǐm): container of burning incense swung by angels of the highest rank.

13. **he hath sent thee respite** (rĕs'pǐt) . . . **nepenthe** (nǐ-pĕn'thē): God has sent you relief and forgetfulness of sorrow.

14. **quaff, oh quaff this kind nepenthe:** drink this beverage that eases pain.

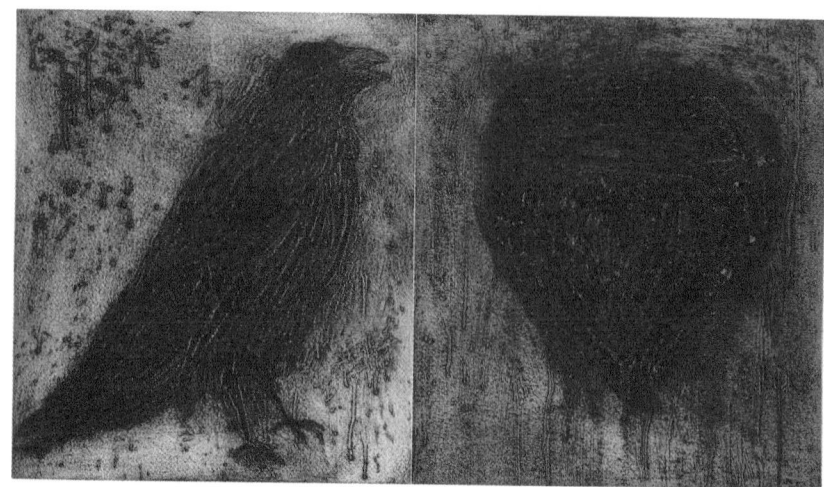

Red Passion (1996), Jim Dine. Cardboard relief intaglio. Image size 33 ⅛″ × 59″. Paper size 39½″ × 63⅞″. Published by Pace Editions, Inc. Edition of 12 © 2007 Jime Dine/Artists Rights Society (ARS), New York.

85 "Prophet!" said I, "thing of evil!—prophet still, if bird or devil!—
Whether Tempter sent, or whether tempest tossed[15] thee here ashore,
Desolate yet all undaunted,[16] on this desert land enchanted—
On this home by Horror haunted—tell me truly, I implore—
Is there—*is* there balm in Gilead?[17]—tell me—tell me, I implore!" **E**
90   Quoth the Raven, "Nevermore."

"Prophet!" said I, "thing of evil!—prophet still, if bird or devil!
By that Heaven that bends above us—by that God we both adore—
Tell this soul with sorrow laden if, within the distant Aidenn,[18]
It shall clasp a sainted maiden whom the angels name Lenore—
95 Clasp a rare and radiant maiden whom the angels name Lenore."
        Quoth the Raven, "Nevermore."

"Be that word our sign of parting, bird or fiend!" I shrieked, upstarting—
"Get thee back into the tempest and the Night's Plutonian shore!
Leave no black plume as a token of that lie thy soul hath spoken!
100 Leave my loneliness unbroken!—quit the bust above my door!
Take thy beak from out my heart, and take thy form from off my door!"
        Quoth the Raven, "Nevermore."

And the Raven, never flitting, still is sitting, *still* is sitting
On the pallid bust of Pallas just above my chamber door;
105 And his eyes have all the seeming of a demon's that is dreaming,
And the lamp-light o'er him streaming throws his shadow on the floor;
And my soul from out that shadow that lies floating on the floor
        Shall be lifted—nevermore! **F**

---

15. **whether Tempter sent . . . tempest tossed:** whether the devil sent or a violent storm carried.

16. **desolate yet all undaunted:** alone and yet unafraid.

17. **balm in Gilead** (gĭl′ē-əd): relief from suffering.

18. **Aidenn** (ād′n): heaven.

Incident *in a* Rose Garden

DONALD JUSTICE

The Back of a Man with a Rose, René Magritte.
Private Collection Bloch, Santa Monica, CA. © 2007
C. Herscovici, Brussels/Artists Rights Society (ARS),
New York. Photo © Superstock, Inc.

The gardener came running,
An old man, out of breath.
Fear had given him legs.
 Sir, I encountered Death
5 *Just now among the roses.*
 Thin as a scythe he stood there.
 I knew him by his pictures.
 He had his black coat on,
 Black gloves, a broad black hat.
10 *I think he would have spoken,*
 Seeing his mouth stood open.
 Big it was, with white teeth.
 As soon as he beckoned, I ran.
 I ran until I found you.
15 *Sir, I am quitting my job.*
 I want to see my sons
 Once more before I die.
 I want to see California. **G**
We shook hands; he was off.

G **NARRATIVE POETRY**
In lines 4–18, the gardener
(whose words are
italicized) describes
Death as a **character.**
What do these lines
suggest the **conflict** of
this poem will be?

20 And there stood Death in the garden,
Dressed like a Spanish waiter.
He had the air of someone
Who because he likes arriving
At all appointments early
25 Learns to think himself patient.
I watched him pinch one bloom off
And hold it to his nose—
A connoisseur of roses—
One bloom and then another. **H**
30 They strewed the earth around him.
  Sir, you must be that stranger
  Who threatened my gardener.
  This is my property, sir.
  I welcome only friends here.

35 Death grinned, and his eyes lit up
With the pale glow of those lanterns
That workmen carry sometimes
To light their way through the dusk.
Now with great care he slid
40 The glove from his right hand
And held that out in greeting,
A little cage of bone.
  Sir, I knew your father,
  And we were friends at the end.
45 *As for your gardener,*
  I did not threaten him.
  Old men mistake my gestures.
  I only meant to ask him
  To show me to his master.
50 *I take it you are he?* **I**

for Mark Strand

H READING POETRY
Read aloud lines 26–29, and note the **rhythm** created by the words. What effect does this add to the image presented?

I NARRATIVE POETRY
For most readers, this poem has a **surprise ending.** Did any clues hint at this outcome?

Comprehension

READING STANDARD
B.2.1 Identify and analyze figurative language and literary structures

1. **Recall** What is the **setting** of each poem?

2. **Recall** In "The Raven," what loss is the speaker trying to recover from?

3. **Recall** In "Incident in a Rose Garden," for whom has Death really come?

4. **Clarify** What happens at the end of each poem?

Literary Analysis

5. **Analyze** Reread lines 7–12 of "The Raven." The **speaker** has tried to forget his sadness and loss. What is his mental state at the end of the poem? Do you think the raven is real or just a figment of his imagination? Support your views with details from the poem.

6. **Identify Irony** Explain the ironies, or unexpected twists, in "Incident in a Rose Garden."

7. **Interpret Narrative Poetry** Use a chart to identify the narrative elements found in these poems. In each poem, which element plays the largest role? Support your answer.

Narrative Element	"The Raven"	"Incident in a Rose Garden"
Characters		
Setting		
Conflict		
Resolution (How does it end?)		

8. **Reading Poetry** Review the chart you filled in as you read the poems. Which poet depends more heavily on **sound devices** to help convey mood and meaning? Cite evidence.

Literary Criticism

9. **Critical Interpretations** With the publication of "The Raven" in 1845, Poe became famous overnight. More than 160 years later, the poem is still considered a classic. What accounts for its continued appeal? Be specific in your answer.

Sorry, Right Number

Teleplay by Stephen King

What sends a CHILL *down your spine?*

PENNSYLVANIA STANDARDS

READING STANDARDS
A.1.3.1 Make inferences and/or draw conclusions

B.1.1.1.C.1 Evaluate elements of the plot

KEY IDEA Not all horror stories give readers a fright by portraying gory scenes. Some present ordinary people doing ordinary things— until something creepy, or even **supernatural,** happens. In *Sorry, Right Number,* a family is puzzled by a mysterious phone caller pleading for help.

QUICKWRITE Supernatural events play a part in many stories of fantasy, mystery, and horror. Work with a group to generate a list of supernatural occurrences in stories, movies, and TV programs. Arrange them in a "chill factor" chart according to how powerfully they affect you.

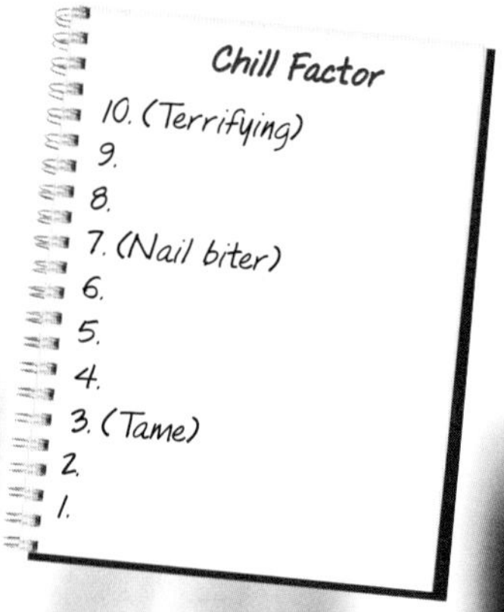

Chill Factor

10. (Terrifying)
9.
8.
7. (Nail biter)
6.
5.
4.
3. (Tame)
2.
1.

148

LITERARY ANALYSIS: PLOT IN DRAMA

As you probably know, a **drama** is basically a story told in dialogue form. Like a work of fiction, drama establishes a setting, presents a series of **plot** events, and centers around one or more **conflicts** that the characters must cope with. Because a drama does not use a narrator to describe what happens, the plot unfolds through the characters' words and actions. As you read this drama, note what the dialogue and camera directions reveal about the setting, the conflict, and the unusual events that surround the cast of characters. Also, be ready for Stephen King's special brand of suspense.

READING SKILL: READING A TELEPLAY

Reading a teleplay is different from reading a script for a stage play. Your mind's eye will be challenged to **visualize** what the camera is focusing on. For example, in *Sorry, Right Number,* when a camera direction calls for an extreme close-up and then takes you inside a telephone receiver, you have to imagine not only how this looks but also what effect it creates. In addition, in a teleplay, you don't have to wait for formal scene changes to have changes in setting, as you do with a regular stage play. You can be instantly thrown from one setting to the next, even from one time period to another, by a camera direction that reads "slam cut to."

Before you read, study Stephen King's note at the beginning of the teleplay to familiarize yourself with common teleplay terms. As you read, use your experience watching TV and movies to help you visualize what the camera wants you to see.

Author On[l]ine

From the Trash Can to the Bestseller List Stephen King nearly threw away his writing career before it began. He dumped the manuscript of his first horror novel, *Carrie,* into the trash, but his wife retrieved it and urged him to continue working on it. Later, after *Carrie* became a hit movie,

Stephen King born 1947

King went on to have six titles on the *New York Times* bestseller list at the same time. Credited with reviving the market for both horror fiction and horror films, King has been called a "one-man entertainment industry."

From Brain to Screen King has written that the idea for *Sorry, Right Number* came to him "one night on my way home from buying a pair of shoes." He wrote the script in two sittings and about a week later submitted it to a friend who produced a TV series called *Tales from the Darkside.* The friend bought the teleplay the day he read it and had it in production a week or two later; and it was broadcast a month after that—"one of the fastest turns from in-the-head to on-the-screen that I've ever heard of," King commented.

MORE ABOUT THE AUTHOR
For more on Stephen King, visit the **Literature Center** at ClassZone.com.

Background

Writing for Television Mixed in with the camera directions in *Sorry, Right Number* are passages in King's own voice. King acts as both author and "narrator" of the play, frequently addressing the reader. He explains abbreviations, points out things he wants the reader to know, and comments on situations.

SORRY, RIGHT NUMBER

Stephen King

CAST OF CHARACTERS

Katie Weiderman	Polly Weiderman
Jeff Weiderman	Operator
Connie Weiderman	Dawn
Dennis Weiderman	Minister
Bill Weiderman	Groundskeeper
	Hank

Author's note: Screenplay abbreviations are simple and exist, in this author's opinion, mostly to make those who write screenplays feel like lodge brothers.[1] In any case, you should be aware that *CU* means *close-up; ECU* means *extreme close-up; INT.* means *interior; EXT.* means *exterior; B.G.* means *background; POV* means *point of view.* Probably most of you knew all that stuff to begin with, right?

Act I

(*Fade in on* Katie Weiderman's *mouth, ECU*)

(*She's speaking into the telephone. Pretty mouth; in a few seconds we'll see that the rest of her is just as pretty.*)

Katie. Bill? Oh, he says he doesn't feel very well, but he's always like that between books . . . can't

sleep, thinks every headache is the first symptom of a brain tumor . . . once he gets going on something new, he'll be fine.

10 (*Sound, B.G.: the television*)

(*The camera draws back.* Katie *is sitting in the kitchen phone nook, having a good gab with her sister while she idles through some catalogues. We should notice one not-quite-ordinary thing about the phone she's on: it's the sort with two lines. There are lighted buttons to show which ones are engaged. Right now only one—Katie's—is. As* Katie *continues her conversation, the camera swings away from her, tracks across the kitchen, and through the arched*

20 *doorway that leads into the family room.*)

Katie (*voice, fading*). Oh, I saw Janie Charlton today . . . yes! Big as a *house!* . . .

---

1. **lodge brothers:** members of the same men's social organization. Lodges sometimes have special rituals or vocabularies.

(*She fades. The TV gets louder. There are three kids:* Jeff, *eight,* Connie, *ten, and* Dennis, *thirteen.* Wheel of Fortune *is on, but they're not watching. Instead they're engaged in that great pastime, Fighting About What Comes On Later.*)

Jeff. Come *onnn!* It was his first *book!*

Connie. His first *gross* book.

30 **Dennis.** We're gonna watch *Cheers* and *Wings,*[2] just like we do every week, Jeff.

(Dennis *speaks with the utter finality only a big brother can manage. "Wanna talk about it some more and see how much pain I can inflict on your scrawny body, Jeff?" his face says.*)

Jeff. Could we at least tape it?

Connie. We're taping CNN[3] for Mom. She said she might be on the phone with Aunt Lois for quite a while.

40 **Jeff.** How can you tape CNN, for God's sake? It *never stops!*

Dennis. That's what she likes about it.

Connie. And don't say God's sake, Jeffie—you're not old enough to talk about God except in church.

Jeff. Then don't call me Jeffie.

Connie. Jeffie, Jeffie, Jeffie.

(Jeff *gets up, walks to the window, and looks out into the dark. He's really upset.* Dennis *and* Connie, *in*
50 *the grand tradition of older brothers and sisters, are delighted to see it.*)

Dennis. Poor Jeffie.

Connie. I think he's gonna commit suicide.

Jeff (*turns to them*). It was his *first* book! Don't you guys even *care?*

Connie. Rent it down at the Video Stop tomorrow, if you want to see it so bad.

Jeff. They don't rent R-rated pictures to little kids and you know it!

60 **Connie** (*dreamily*). Shut up, it's Vanna! I *love* Vanna!

Jeff. Dennis—

Dennis. Go ask Dad to tape it on the VCR in his office and quit being such a totally annoying little booger.

(Jeff *crosses the room, poking his tongue out at Vanna White as he goes. The camera follows as he goes into the kitchen.*)

Katie. . . . so when he asked me if *Polly* had tested strep positive,[4] I had to remind him she's away at
70 prep school[5] . . . Lois, I miss her . . .

(Jeff *is just passing through, on his way to the stairs.*)

Katie. Will you kids *please* be quiet?

Jeff (*glum*). They'll be quiet. *Now.*

(*He goes up the stairs, a little dejected.* Katie *looks after him for a moment, loving and worried.*)

Katie. They're squabbling again. Polly used to keep them in line, but now that she's away at school . . . I don't know . . . maybe sending her to Bolton wasn't such a hot idea. Sometimes when
80 she calls home she sounds so *unhappy* . . .

(*INT. Bela Lugosi*[6] *as Dracula, CU*)

(*Drac's standing at the door of his Transylvanian castle. Someone has pasted a comic-balloon coming out of his mouth which reads: "Listen! My children of the night! What music they make!" The poster is on a door but we only see this as* Jeff *opens it and goes into his father's study.*)

(*INT. a photograph of Katie, CU*)

(*The camera holds, then pans slowly right. We pass*
90 *another photo, this one of Polly, the daughter away at school. She's a lovely girl of sixteen or so. Past Polly is Dennis . . . then Connie . . . then Jeff.*)

---

2. **Cheers and Wings:** popular television sitcoms of the 1980s and 1990s.

3. **CNN:** the Cable News Network.

4. **had tested strep positive:** had strep throat, an infection caused by bacteria called streptococci.

5. **prep school:** a private high school that prepares students for college.

6. **Bela Lugosi:** a Hungarian-born actor (1882–1956) best known for his roles in U.S. horror films of the 1930s and 1940s.

(*The camera continues to pan and also widens out so we can see* Bill Weiderman, *a man of about forty-four. He looks tired. He's peering into the word-processor on his desk, but his mental crystal ball must be taking the night off, because the screen is blank. On the walls we see framed book-covers. All of them are spooky. One of the titles is* Ghost Kiss.)

100 (Jeff *comes up quietly behind his dad. The carpet muffles his feet.* Bill *sighs and shuts off the word-cruncher. A moment later* Jeff *claps his hands on his father's shoulders.*)

Jeff. BOOGA-BOOGA!

Bill. Hi, Jeffie.

(*He turns in his chair to look at his son, who is disappointed.*)

Jeff. How come you didn't get scared?

Bill. Scaring is my business. I'm case-hardened.
110 Something wrong?

Jeff. Daddy, can I watch the first hour of *Ghost Kiss* and you tape the rest? Dennis and Connie are hogging *everything*.

(Bill *swivels to look at the book-jacket, bemused.*)

Bill. You sure you want to watch *that,* champ? It's pretty—

Jeff. *Yes!*

(*INT.* Katie, *in the phone nook*)

(*In this shot, we clearly see the stairs leading to her*
120 *husband's study behind her.*)

Katie. I *really* think Jeff needs the orthodontic work but you know Bill—

(*The other line rings. The other light stutters.*)

Katie. That's just the other line, Bill will—

(*But now we see* Bill *and* Jeff *coming downstairs behind her.*)

Bill. Honey, where're the blank videotapes? I can't find any in the study and—

Katie (*to* Bill). *Wait!*
130 (*to* Lois). Gonna put you on hold a sec, Lo.

(*She does. Now both lines are blinking. She pushes the top one, where the new call has just come in.*)

Katie. Hello, Weiderman residence.

(*Sound: desperate sobbing*)

Sobbing voice (*filter*). Take . . . please take . . . t-t-

Katie. Polly? Is that you? What's wrong?

(*Sound: sobbing. It's awful, heartbreaking.*)

Sobbing voice (*filter*). *Please—quick—*

(*Sound: sobbing . . . Then, click! A broken*
140 *connection.*)

Katie. Polly, calm down! Whatever it is can't be that b—

(*hum of an open line*)

(Jeff *has wandered toward the TV room, hoping to find a blank tape.*)

Bill. Who was that?

(*Without looking at her husband or answering him,* Katie *slams the lower button in again.*)

Katie. Lois? Listen, I'll call you back. That was
150 Polly, and she sounded very upset. No . . . she
hung up. Yes. I will. Thanks.

(*She hangs up.*)

Bill (*concerned*). It was Polly?

Katie. Crying her head off. It sounded like she was trying to say "Please take me home" . . . I knew that school was bumming her out . . . Why I ever let you talk me into it . . .

(*She's rummaging frantically on her little phone desk. Catalogues go slithering to the floor around*
160 *her stool.*)

Katie. *Connie did you take my address book?*

Connie (*voice*). No, Mom.

(Bill *pulls a battered book out of his back pocket and pages through it.*)

Bill. I got it. Except—

Katie. I know, dorm phone is always busy. Give it to me.

Bill. Honey, calm down.

Katie. I'll calm down after I talk to her. She is
170 sixteen, Bill. Sixteen-year-old girls are prone to depressive interludes. Sometimes they even k . . . just give me the number!

Bill. 617-555-8641.

(*As she punches the numbers, the camera slides in to CU.*)

Katie. Come on, come on . . . don't be busy . . . just this once . . .

(*Sound: clicks. A pause. Then . . . the phone starts ringing.*)

180 **Katie** (*eyes closed*). Thank You, God.

Voice (*filter*). Hartshorn Hall, this is Frieda.

Katie. Could you call Polly to the phone? Polly Weiderman? This is Kate Weiderman. Her mother.

Voice (*filter*). hang on, please, Mrs. Weiderman.

(*Sound: the phone clunks down.*)

Voice (*filter, and very faint*). Polly? Pol? . . . Phone call! . . . It's your mother!

(*INT. a wider angle on the phone nook, with* Bill)

190 **Bill.** Well?

Katie. Somebody's getting her. I hope.

(Jeff *comes back in with a tape.*)

Jeff. I found one, Dad. Dennis hid em. As usual.

Bill. In a minute, Jeff. Go watch the tube.

Jeff. But—

Bill. I won't forget. Now go *on*.

(Jeff *goes.*)

Katie. Come on, come on, come on . . .

Bill. Calm down, Katie.

200 **Katie** (*snaps*). If you'd heard her, you wouldn't tell me to calm down! She sounded—

Polly (*filter, cheery voice*). Hi, mom!

Katie. Pol? Honey? Are you all right?

Polly (*happy, bubbling voice*). Am I *all right?* I aced my bio exam, got a B on my French Conversational Essay, and Ronnie Hansen asked me to the Harvest Ball. I'm so all right that if one more good thing happens to me today, I'll probably blow up like the *Hindenburg.*[7]

210 **Katie.** You didn't just call me up, crying your head off?

(*We see by Katie's face that she already knows the answer to this question.*)

Polly (*filter*). Heck no!

Katie. I'm glad about your test and your date, honey. I guess it was someone else. I'll call you back, okay?

Polly (*filter*). 'Kay. Say hi to Dad!

Katie. I will.

220 (*INT. the phone nook, wider*)

Bill. She okay?

Katie. Fine. I could have *sworn* it was Polly, but . . . *she's* walking on air.

Bill. So it was a prank. Or someone who was crying so hard she dialed a wrong number . . . "through a shimmering film of tears," as we veteran hacks like to say.

Katie. It was not a prank and it was not a wrong number! It was someone in *my family!*

230 **Bill.** Honey, you can't know that.

Katie. No? If Jeffie called up, just crying, would you know it was him?

Bill (*struck by this*). Yeah, maybe. I guess I might.

(*She's not listening. She's punching numbers, fast.*)

Bill. Who you calling?

(*She doesn't answer him. Sound: phone rings twice. Then:*)

Older Female Voice (*filter*). Hello?

Katie. Mom? Are you . . . (*She pauses.*) Did you
240 call just a few seconds ago?

Voice (*filter*). No, dear . . . why?

Katie. Oh . . . you know these phones. I was talking to Lois and I lost the other call.

Voice (*filter*). Well, it wasn't me. Kate, I saw the *prettiest* dress in La Boutique today, and—

Katie. We'll talk about it later, Mom, okay?

Voice (*filter*). Kate, are you all right?

Katie. I have . . . Mom, I think maybe I've got diarrhea. I have to go. 'Bye.

250 (*She hangs up. Bill hangs on until she does; then he bursts into wild donkey-brays of laughter.*)

Bill. Oh boy . . . diarrhea . . . I gotta remember that the next time my agent calls . . . oh Katie, that was so cool—

Katie (*almost screaming*). *This is not funny!*

(Bill *stops laughing.*)

(*INT. the TV room*)

(Jeff *and* Dennis *have been tussling. They stop. All three kids look toward the kitchen.*)

260 (*INT. the phone nook, with* Bill *and* Katie)

Katie. *I tell you it was someone in my family and she sounded*—oh, you don't understand. I *knew* that voice.

Bill. But if Polly's okay and your mom's okay . . .

Katie (*positive*). It's Dawn.

Bill. Come on, hon, a minute ago you were sure it was Polly.

Katie. It *had* to be Dawn. I was on the phone with Lois and Mom's okay, so Dawn's the only other
270 one it *could* have been. She's the youngest . . . I could have mistaken her for Polly . . . and she's out there in that farmhouse alone with the baby!

Bill (*startled*). What do you mean, alone?

Katie. Jerry's in Burlington! It's Dawn! *Something's happened to Dawn!*

(Connie *comes into the kitchen, worried.*)

Connie. Mom? Is Aunt Dawn okay?

Bill. So far as we know, she's fine. Take it easy, doll. Bad to buy trouble before you know it's on sale.

---

7. **Hindenburg:** an airship that exploded, crashed, and burned spectacularly in 1937.

280 (Katie *punches numbers and listens. Sound: the dah-dah-dah of a busy signal.* Katie *hangs up.* Bill *looks a question at her with raised eyebrows.*)

Katie. Busy.

Bill. Katie, are you sure—

Katie. She's the only one left—it had to be her. Bill, I'm scared. Will you drive me out there?

(Bill *takes the phone from her.*)

Bill. What's her number?

Katie. 555-6169.

290 (Bill *dials. Gets a busy. Hangs up and punches 0.*)

Operator (*filter*). Operator.

Bill. I'm trying to reach my sister-in-law, operator. The line is busy. I suspect there may be a problem. Can you break into the call, please?

(*INT. the door to the TV room*)

(*All three kids are standing there, silent and worried.*)

(*INT. the phone nook, with* Bill *and* Katie)

Operator (*filter*). What is your name, sir?

Bill. William Weiderman. My number is—

300 **Operator** (*filter*). Not the William Weiderman that wrote *Spider Doom?!*

Bill. Yes, that was mine. If—

Operator (*filter*). Oh, I just *loved* that book! I love *all* your books! I—

Bill. I'm delighted you do. But right now my wife is very worried about her sister. If it's possible for you to—

Operator (*filter*). Yes, I can do that. Please give me your number, Mr. Weiderman, for the records.

310 (*She giggles.*) I *promise* not to give it out.

Bill. It's 555-4408.

Operator (*filter*). And the call number?

Bill (*looks at* Katie). Uh . . .

Katie. 555-6169.

Bill. 555-6169.

Operator (*filter*). Just a moment, Mr. Weiderman . . . *Night of the Beast* was also great, by the way. Hold on.

(*Sound: telephonic clicks and clacks*)

320 **Katie.** Is she—

Bill. Yes. Just . . .

(*There's one final click.*)

Operator (*filter*). I'm sorry, Mr. Weiderman, but that line is not busy. It's off the hook. I wonder if I sent you my copy of *Spider Doom*—

(Bill *hangs up the phone.*)

Katie. Why did you hang up?

Bill. She can't break in. Phone's not busy. It's off the hook.

330 (*They stare at each other bleakly.*)

(*EXT. A low-slung sports car passes the camera. Night.*)

(*INT. the car, with* Katie *and* Bill)

(*Katie's scared.* Bill, *at the wheel, doesn't look exactly calm.*)

Katie. Hey, Bill—tell me she's all right.

Bill. She's all right.

Katie. Now tell me what you really think.

Bill. Jeff snuck up behind me tonight and put the
340 old booga-booga on me. He was disappointed as hell when I didn't jump. I told him I was case-hardened. (*pause*) I lied.

Katie. Why did Jerry have to move out there when he's gone half the time? Just her and that little tiny baby? *Why?*

Bill. Shh, Kate. We're almost there.

Katie. Go faster.

(*EXT. the car*)

(*He does. That car is smokin.*)

350 (*INT. the Weiderman TV room*)

(*The tube's still on and the kids are still there, but the horsing around has stopped.*)

Connie. Dennis, do you think Aunt Dawn's okay?

Dennis (*thinks she's dead, decapitated by a maniac*). Yeah. Sure she is.

(*INT. the phone, POV from the TV room*)

(*just sitting there on the wall in the phone nook, lights dark, looking like a snake ready to strike*)

(*Fade out.*)

Act II

(*EXT. an isolated farmhouse*)

(*A long driveway leads up to it. There's one light on in the living room. Car lights sweep up the driveway. The Weiderman car pulls up close to the garage and stops.*)

(*INT. the car, with* Bill *and* Katie)

Katie. I'm scared.

(Bill *bends down, reaches under his seat, and brings out a pistol.*)

10 **Bill** (*solemnly*). Booga-booga.

Katie (*total surprise*). How long have you had that?

Bill. Since last year. I didn't want to scare you or the kids. I've got a license to carry. Come on.

(*EXT.* Bill *and* Katie)

(*They get out.* Katie *stands by the front of the car while* Bill *goes to the garage and peers in.*)

Bill. Her car's here.

(*The camera tracks with them to the front door. Now we can hear the TV, playing loud.* Bill *pushes the*

20 doorbell. *We hear it inside. They wait.* Katie *pushes it. Still no answer. She pushes it again and doesn't take her finger off.* Bill *looks down at:)*

(EXT. the lock, Bill*'s POV)*

(big scratches on it)

(EXT. Bill *and* Katie*)*

Bill *(low).* The lock's been tampered with.

*(*Katie *looks, and whimpers.* Bill *tries the door. It opens. The TV is louder.)*

Bill. Stay behind me. Be ready to run if something
30 happens. I wish I'd left you home, Kate.

(He starts in. Katie *comes after him, terrified, near tears.)*

(INT. Dawn *and* Jerry*'s living room)*

(From this angle we see only a small section of the room. The TV is much louder. Bill *enters the room, gun up. He looks to the right . . . and suddenly all the tension goes out of him. He lowers the gun.)*

Katie *(draws up beside him).* Bill . . . what . . .

(He points.)

40 *(INT. the living room, wide,* Bill *and* Katie*'s POV)*

(The place looks like a cyclone hit it . . . but it wasn't robbery and murder that caused this mess; only a healthy eighteen-month-old baby. After a strenuous day of trashing the living room, Baby got tired and Mommy got tired and they fell asleep on the couch together. The baby is in Dawn*'s lap. There is a pair of Walkman earphones on her head. There are toys— tough plastic Sesame Street and PlaySkool stuff, for the most part—scattered hell to breakfast. The baby*
50 *has also pulled most of the books out of the bookcase. Had a good munch on one of them, too, by the look.* Bill *goes over and picks it up. It is* Ghost Kiss.*)*

Bill. I've had people say they just eat my books up, but this is ridiculous.

(He's amused. Katie *isn't. She walks over to her sister, ready to be mad . . . but she sees how really exhausted* Dawn *looks and softens.)*

(INT. Dawn *and the baby,* Katie*'s POV)*

(Fast asleep and breathing easily, like a Raphael
60 *painting of Madonna and Child.[8] The camera pans down to: the Walkman. We can hear the faint strains of Huey Lewis and the News. The camera pans a bit further to a Princess telephone[9] on the table by the chair. It's off the cradle. Not much; just enough to break the connection and scare people to death.)*

(INT. Katie*)*

(She sighs, bends down, and replaces the phone. Then she pushes the stop button on the Walkman.)

(INT. Dawn, Bill, *and* Katie*)*

70 *(*Dawn *wakes up when the music stops. Looks at* Bill *and* Katie, *puzzled.)*

Dawn *(fuzzed out).* Well . . . hi.

(She realizes she's got the Walkman phones on and removes them.)

Bill. Hi, Dawn.

Dawn *(still half asleep).* Shoulda called, guys. Place is a mess.

(She smiles. She's radiant when she smiles.)

Katie. We *tried.* The operator told Bill the phone
80 was off the hook. I thought something was wrong. How can you sleep with that music blasting?

Dawn. It's restful. *(Sees the gnawed book* Bill*'s holding)* Oh Bill, I'm sorry! Justin's teething and—

Bill. There are critics who'd say he picked just the right thing to teethe on. I don't want to scare you, beautiful, but somebody's been at your front door lock with a screwdriver or something. Whoever it was forced it.

Dawn. Gosh, no! That was Jerry, last week. I
90 locked us out by mistake and he didn't have his key and the spare wasn't over the door like it's supposed to be. He was mad because he had to take a whiz real bad and so he took the screwdriver to it. It didn't work, either—that's one tough lock. *(pause)* By the time I found my key he'd already gone in the bushes.

---

8. **Raphael . . . Madonna and Child:** Raphael (1483–1520) was a well-known painter of mostly religious subjects in the period known as the Renaissance.

9. **Princess telephone:** an early type of compact telephone, popular in the 1960s.

Bill. If it wasn't forced, how come I could just open the door and walk in?

Dawn (*guiltily*). Well . . . sometimes I forget to lock it.

Katie. You didn't call me tonight, Dawn?

Dawn. Gee, no! I didn't call *anyone!* I was too busy chasing Justin around! He kept wanting to eat the fabric softener! Then he got sleepy and I sat down here and thought I'd listen to some tunes while I waited for your movie to come on, Bill, and I fell asleep—

(*At the mention of the movie* Bill *starts visibly and looks at the book. Then he glances at his watch.*)

Bill. I promised to tape it for Jeff. Come on, Katie, we've got time to get back.

Katie. Just a second.

(*She picks up the phone and dials.*)

Dawn. Gee, Bill, do you think Jeffie's old enough to watch something like that?

Bill. It's network. They take out the blood-bags.

Dawn (*confused but amiable*). Oh. That's good.

(*INT.* Katie, *CU*)

Dennis (*filter*). Hello?

Katie. Just thought you'd like to know your Aunt Dawn's fine.

Dennis (*filter*). Oh! Cool. Thanks, Mom.

(*INT. the phone nook, with* Dennis *and the others*)

(*He looks* very *relieved.*)

Dennis. Aunt Dawn's okay.

(*INT. the car, with* Bill *and* Katie)

(*They drive in silence for awhile.*)

Katie. You think I'm a hysterical idiot, don't you?

Bill (*genuinely surprised*). No! I was scared, too.

Katie. You sure you're not mad?

Bill. I'm too relieved. (*laughs*) She's sort of a scatterbrain, old Dawn, but I love her.

Katie (*leans over and kisses him*). I love *you.* You're a sweet man.

Bill. I'm the *boogeyman!*

Katie. I am not fooled, sweetheart.

(*EXT. the car*)

(*Passes the camera and we dissolve to:*)

(*INT.* Jeff, *in bed*)

(*His room is dark. The covers are pulled up to his chin.*)

Jeff. You *promise* to tape the rest?

(*Camera widens out so we can see* Bill, *sitting on the bed.*)

Bill. I promise.

Jeff. I especially liked the part where the dead guy ripped off the punk rocker's head.

Bill. Well . . . they *used* to take out all the blood-bags.

Jeff. What, Dad?

Bill. Nothing. I love you, Jeffie.

Jeff. I love you, too. So does Rambo.

(Jeff *holds up a stuffed dragon of decidedly unmilitant aspect.[10]* Bill *kisses the dragon, then* Jeff.)

Bill. 'Night.

Jeff. 'Night. (*as* Bill *reaches his door*) Glad Aunt Dawn was okay.

Bill. Me too.

(*He goes out.*)

(*INT. TV, CU*)

(*A guy who looks like he died in a car crash about two weeks prior to filming [and has since been subjected to a lot of hot weather] is staggering out of a crypt. The camera widens to show* Bill, *releasing the VCR pause button.*)

Katie (*voice*). Booga-booga.

(Bill *looks around companionably. The camera widens out more to show* Katie, *wearing a nightgown.*)

Bill. Same to you. I missed the first forty seconds or so after the break. I had to kiss Rambo.

Katie. You sure you're not mad at me, Bill?

---

10. **unmilitant aspect:** unaggressive appearance.

(*He goes to her and kisses her.*)

Bill. Not even a smidge.

Katie. It's just that I could have sworn it was one of mine. You know what I mean? One of mine?

Bill. Yes.

Katie. I can still hear those sobs. So lost . . . so heartbroken.

180 **Bill.** Kate, have you ever thought you recognized someone on the street, and called her, and when she finally turned around it was a total stranger?

Katie. Yes, once. In Seattle. I was in a mall and I thought I saw my old roommate. I . . . oh. I see what you're saying.

Bill. Sure. There are sound-alikes as well as look-alikes.

Katie. But . . . *you know your own.* At least I thought so until tonight.

190 (*She puts her cheek on his shoulder, looking troubled.*)

Katie. I was so *positive* it was Polly . . .

Bill. Because you've been worried about her getting her feet under her at the new school . . . but judging from the stuff she told you tonight, I'd say she's doing just fine in that department. Wouldn't you?

Katie. Yes . . . I guess I would.

Bill. Let it go, hon.

200 **Katie** (*looks at him closely*). I hate to see you looking so tired. Hurry up and have an idea, you.

Bill. Well, I'm trying.

Katie. You coming to bed?

Bill. Soon as I finish taping this for Jeff.

Katie (*amused*). Bill, that machine was made by Japanese technicians who think of near everything. It'll run on its own.

Bill. Yeah, but it's been a long time since I've seen this one, and . . .

210 **Katie.** Okay. Enjoy. I think I'll be awake for a little while.

(*She starts out, then turns in the doorway as something else strikes her.*)

Katie. If they show the part where the punk's head gets—

Bill (*guiltily*). I'll edit it.

Katie. 'Night. And thanks again. For everything.

(*She leaves. Bill sits in his chair.*)

(*INT. TV, CU*)

220 (*A couple is necking in a car. Suddenly the passenger door is ripped open by the dead guy and we dissolve to:*)

(*INT. Katie, in bed*)

(*It's dark. She's asleep. She wakes up . . . sort of.*)

Katie (*sleepy*). Hey, big guy—

(*She feels for him, but his side of the bed is empty, the coverlet still pulled up. She sits up. Looks at:*)

(*INT. a clock on the night-table, Katie's POV*)

(*It says 2:03 A.M. Then it flashes to 2:04.*)

(*INT. Katie*)

230 (*Fully awake now. And concerned. She gets up, puts on her robe, and leaves the bedroom.*)

(*INT. the TV screen, CU*)

(*snow*)

Katie (*voice, approaching*). Bill? Honey? You okay? Bill? Bi—

(*INT. Katie, in Bill's study*)

(*She's frozen, wide-eyed with horror.*)

(*INT. Bill, in his chair*)

(*He's slumped to one side, eyes closed, hand inside his*
240 shirt. *Dawn was sleeping. Bill is not.*)

(*EXT. a coffin, being lowered into a grave*)

Minister (*voice*). And so we commit the earthly remains of William Weiderman to the ground, confident of his spirit and soul. "Be ye not cast down, brethren . . ."

(*EXT. graveside*)

(*All the Weidermans are ranged here.* Katie *and* Polly *wear identical black dresses and veils.* Connie *wears a black skirt and white blouse.* Dennis *and* Jeff *wear black suits.* Jeff *is crying. He has* Rambo the Dragon *under his arm for a little extra comfort.*)

(*Camera moves in on* Katie. *Tears course slowly down her cheeks. She bends and gets a handful of earth. Tosses it into the grave.*)

Katie. Love you, big guy.

(*EXT.* Jeff)

(*weeping*)

(*EXT. looking down into the grave*)

(*scattered earth on top of the coffin*)

(*Dissolve to:*)

(*EXT. the grave*)

(*A* Groundskeeper *pats the last sod into place.*)

Groundskeeper. My wife says she wishes you'd written a couple more before you had your heart attack, mister. (*pause*) I like Westerns, m'self.

(*The* Groundskeeper *walks away, whistling.*)

(*Dissolve to:*)

(*EXT. A church. Day.*)

(*Title card: Five Years Later*)

(*The Wedding March is playing.* Polly, *older and radiant with joy, emerges into a pelting shower of rice. She's in a wedding gown, her new husband by her side.*)

(*Celebrants throwing rice line either side of the path. From behind the bride and groom come others. Among them are* Katie, Dennis, Connie, *and* Jeff . . . *all five years older. With* Katie *is another man. This is* Hank. *In the interim,* Katie *has also taken a husband.*)

280 (Polly *turns and her mother is there.*)

Polly. Thank you, Mom.

Katie (*crying*). Oh doll, you're so welcome.

(*They embrace. After a moment* Polly *draws away and looks at* Hank. *There is a brief moment of tension, and then* Polly *embraces* Hank, *too.*)

Polly. Thank you too, Hank. I'm sorry I was such a creep for so long . . .

Hank (*easily*). You were never a creep, Pol. A girl only has one father.

290 **Connie.** Throw it! Throw it!

(*After a moment,* Polly *throws her bouquet.*)

(*EXT. the bouquet, CU, slow motion*)

(*turning and turning through the air*)

(*dissolves to:*)

(*INT. The study, with* Katie. *Night.*)

(*The word-processor has been replaced by a wide lamp looming over a stack of blueprints. The book jackets have been replaced by photos of buildings.*)

Ones that have first been built in Hank's mind,
presumably.)

(*Katie is looking at the desk, thoughtful and a little sad.*)

Hank (*voice*). Coming to bed, Kate?

(*She turns and the camera widens out to give us Hank. He's wearing a robe over pajamas. She comes to him and gives him a little hug, smiling. Maybe we notice a few streaks of gray in her hair; her pretty pony has done its fair share of running since Bill died.*)

Katie. In a little while. A woman doesn't see her first one get married every day, you know.

Hank. I know.

(*The camera follows as they walk from the work area of the study to the more informal area. This is much the same as it was in the old days, with a coffee table, stereo, TV, couch, and Bill's old easy-chair. She looks at this.*)

Hank. You still miss him, don't you?

Katie. Some days more than others. You didn't know, and Polly didn't remember.

Hank (*gently*). Remember what, doll?

Katie. Polly got married on the five-year anniversary of Bill's death.

Hank (*hugs her*). Come on to bed, why don't you?

Katie. In a little while.

Hank. Okay. Maybe I'll still be awake.

(*He kisses her, then leaves, closing the door behind him. Katie sits in Bill's old chair. Close by, on the coffee table, is a remote control for the TV and an extension phone. Katie looks at the blank TV, and the camera moves in on her face. One tear rims one eye, sparkling like a sapphire.*)

Katie. I *do* still miss you, big guy. Lots and lots. Every day. And you know what? It hurts.

(*The tear falls. She picks up the TV remote and pushes the on button.*)

(*INT. TV, Katie's POV*)

(*An ad for Ginsu Knives comes to an end and is replaced by a star logo.*)

Announcer (*voice*). Now back to Channel 63's Thursday night Star Time Movie . . . *Ghost Kiss.*

(*The logo dissolves into a guy who looks like he died in a car crash about two weeks ago and has since been subjected to a lot of hot weather. He comes staggering out of the same old crypt.*)

(*INT. Katie*)

(*Terribly startled—almost horrified. She hits the off button on the remote control. The TV blinks off.*)

(*Katie's face begins to work. She struggles against the impending emotional storm, but the coincidence of the movie is just one thing too many on what must have already been one of the most emotionally trying days of her life. The dam breaks and she begins to sob . . . terrible, heartbroken sobs. She reaches out for the little table by the chair, meaning to put the remote control on it, and knocks the phone onto the floor.*)

(*Sound: the hum of an open line*)

(*Her tear-stained face grows suddenly still as she looks at the telephone. Something begins to fill it . . . an idea? an intuition? Hard to tell. And maybe it doesn't matter.*)

(*INT. the telephone, Katie's POV*)

(*The camera moves in to ECU . . . moves in until the dots in the off-the-hook receiver look like chasms.*)

(*sound of open-line buzz up to loud*)

(*We go into the black . . . and hear:*)

Bill (*voice*). Who are you calling? Who do you *want* to call? Who *would* you call, if it wasn't too late?

(*INT. Katie*)

(*There is now a strange hypnotized look on her face. She reaches down, scoops the telephone up, and punches in numbers, seemingly at random.*)

(*Sound: ringing phone*)

(*Katie continues to look hypnotized. The look holds until the phone is answered . . . and she hears herself on the other end of the line.*)

Katie (*voice; filter*). Hello, Weiderman residence.

(*Katie—our present-day Katie with the streaks of gray in her hair—goes on sobbing, yet an expression of desperate hope is trying to be born on her face. On some level she understands that the depth of her grief has allowed a kind of telephonic time-travel. She's trying to talk, to force the words out.*)

Katie (*sobbing*). Take . . . please take . . . t-t-

(*INT. Katie, in the phone nook, reprise*)

(*It's five years ago, Bill is standing beside her, looking concerned. Jeff is wandering off to look for a blank tape in the other room.*)

390 **Katie.** Polly? What's wrong?

(*INT. Katie, in the study*)

Katie (*sobbing*). Please—quick—

(*Sound: click of a broken connection*)

Katie (*screaming*). Take him to the hospital! If you want him to live, take him to the hospital! He's going to have a heart attack! He—

(*Sound: hum of an open line*)

(*Slowly, very slowly, Katie hangs up the telephone. Then, after a moment, she picks it up again. She* 400 *speaks aloud with no self-consciousness whatever. Probably doesn't even know she's doing it.*)

Katie. I dialed the old number. I dialed—

(*Slam cut to:*)

(*INT. Bill, in the phone nook with Katie beside him*)

(*He's just taken the phone from Katie and is speaking to the operator.*)

Operator (*filter, giggles*). I *promise* not to give it out.

410 **Bill.** It's 555-

(*Slam cut to:*)

(*INT. Katie, in Bill's old chair, CU*)

Katie (*finishes*). -4408.

(*INT. the phone, CU*)

(*Katie's trembling finger carefully picks out the number, and we hear the corresponding tones: 555-4408.*)

(*INT. Katie, in Bill's old chair, CU*)

(*She closes her eyes as the phone begins to ring. Her* 420 *face is filled with an agonizing mixture of hope and fear. If only she can have one more chance to pass the vital message on, it says . . . just one more chance.*)

Katie (*low*). Please . . . please . . .

Recorded voice (*filter*). You have reached a non-working number. Please hang up and dial again. If you need assistance—

(*Katie hangs up again. Tears stream down her cheeks. The camera pans away and down to the telephone.*)

430 (*INT. the phone nook, with Katie and Bill, reprise*)

Bill. So it was a prank. Or someone who was crying so hard she dialed a wrong number . . . "through a shimmering film of tears," as we veteran hacks like to say.

Katie. It was not a prank and it was not a wrong number! It was someone in *my family!*

(*INT. Katie [present day] in Bill's study*)

Katie. Yes. Someone in *my family.* Someone very close. (*pause*) Me.

440 (*She suddenly throws the phone across the room. Then she begins to sob again and puts her hands over her face. The camera holds on her for a moment, then dollies across to:*)

(*INT. the phone*)

(*It lies on the carpet, looking both bland and some-how ominous. Camera moves in to ECU—the holes in the receiver once more look like huge dark chasms. We hold, then:*)

(*Fade to black.*)

MEMOIR Stephen King wrote a memoir of his life as a writer. Here are a few words of advice from the book.

from

On Writing

Stephen King

If you want to be a writer, you must do two things above all others: read a lot and write a lot. There's no way around these two things that I'm aware of, no shortcut.

I'm a slow reader, but I usually get through seventy or eighty books a year, mostly fiction. I don't read in order to study the craft; I read because I like to read. It's what I do at night, kicked back in my blue chair. Similarly, I don't read fiction to study the art of fiction, but simply because I like stories. Yet there is a learning process going on. Every book you pick up has its own lesson or lessons, and quite often the bad books have more to teach than the good ones.

Good writing, on the other hand, teaches the learning writer about style, graceful narration, plot development, the creation of believable characters, and truth-telling. A novel like *The Grapes of Wrath* may fill a new writer with feelings of despair and good old-fashioned jealousy— "I'll never be able to write anything that good, not if I live to be a thousand"—but such feelings can also serve as a spur, goading the writer to work harder and aim higher. Being swept away by a combination of great story and great writing—of being flattened, in fact—is part of every writer's necessary formation. You cannot hope to sweep someone else away by the force of your writing until it has been done to you.

Comprehension

1. **Recall** At first, whom does Katie believe the sobbing caller to be?

2. **Recall** Why doesn't Bill return to bed after watching the movie?

3. **Summarize** What happens on the fifth anniversary of Bill's death?

4. **Clarify** Who is the sobbing caller?

READING STANDARD
B.1.1.1.C.1 Evaluate elements of
the plot

Literary Analysis

5. **Reading a Teleplay** Look back through the play. What clues do the camera directions give you for interpreting the play's **supernatural** occurrences?

6. **Analyze Plot in Drama** Create a plot diagram like the one shown. Then place the events of *Sorry, Right Number* in their correct positions on the diagram. More than one event may be placed in each position.

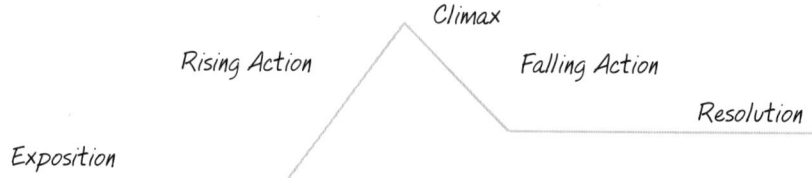

7. **Analyze Foreshadowing** In drama as in other fiction, foreshadowing can deepen a mood of suspense by hinting at future events. Go back through the teleplay and find examples of foreshadowing. For each example, provide a description of what eventually happens.

8. **Interpret** How would you explain the vague understanding—the "desperate hope . . . trying to be born"—that comes to Katie after she hears her own voice on the phone? Support your answer.

9. **Make Judgments** Could Katie be in any way responsible for her husband's death?

10. **Evaluate** Revisit the "chill factor" chart you created before reading the play. Where would you place *Sorry, Right Number* on a scale of 1 to 10? Support your answer.

Literary Criticism

11. **Author's Style** In the excerpt from *On Writing* (page 165), Stephen King lists what he considers the qualities of good writing: "style, graceful narration, plot development, the creation of believable characters, and truth-telling." Which of these qualities does this teleplay best exemplify? Cite details, including lines of dialogue and examples of camera directions, to support your opinion.

Reading-Writing Connection

Increase your understanding of *Sorry, Right Number* by responding to these prompts. Then use **Revision: Grammar and Style** to improve your writng.

WRITING PROMPTS

A. Short Response: Create Dialogue

Imagine that Katie tries to explain to her family what occurred with the phone call. What does she say? How does her family react? Write **one-half page** of the dialogue that you imagine would occur.

B. Extended Response: Write a Review

Imagine that you are reviewing *Sorry, Right Number* for your school newspaper. Write a **three-to-five-paragraph review** in which you summarize the plot and explain your reaction to the teleplay. Do not give away the surprise ending in your review.

SELF-CHECK

A strong dialogue will . . .

- consist of informal, conversational language
- reflect how the characters probably would respond

A successful review will . . .

- summarize the plot with correct use of grammar
- contain details that support a reaction to the teleplay

REVISION: GRAMMAR AND STYLE

CREATE REALISTIC CHARACTERS At various points, King uses **slang** to suggest the youth of a character. In writing dialogue, it is important to choose language that accurately reflects the characteristics of the people who are speaking; otherwise, your audience will find it difficult to believe what they are reading. Here is an example of King's use of slang in *Sorry, Right Number*:

> **Katie.** *Just thought you'd like to know your Aunt Dawn's fine.*
>
> **Dennis** (filter). *Oh! Cool. Thanks, Mom.* (Act II, lines 120–122)

Notice how the revisions in red make the following dialogue more accurately reflect the ages of the speakers. Revise your response to Prompt A by making the same kinds of revisions.

PENNSYLVANIA STANDARDS

WRITING STANDARD
1.5.11.B.3 Write fully developed paragraphs that have details

---

STUDENT MODEL

Katie. Now, I know you're going to think this couldn't have happened.

But five years ago, on the day Bill died, I got a call from myself.

Polly. ~~That sounds really odd.~~ *Whatever, Mom.*

Dennis. Mom, ~~that's a strange thing to say.~~ *you're freaking out!*

Hank. You're wrong, Katie. Let's talk about this.

WRITING TOOLS

For prewriting, revision, and editing tools, visit the **Writing Center** at ClassZone.com.

Writing Workshop

Personal Narrative

Your life is a series of stories, all of them uniquely yours. Each reveals something about you and the people and events that shape your life. When you write about yourself, you can begin to gain a deeper understanding of why certain experiences were important to you. In this workshop, you will write a personal narrative, a story that describes a memorable event from your past. Begin by studying the **Writer's Road Map.**

WRITER'S ROAD MAP

Personal Narrative

WRITING PROMPT 1

Writing from Your Life Write a personal narrative describing a meaningful experience in your life. Your narrative should explain the significance of the experience and include details that help the reader visualize the characters and unfolding events.

Experiences to Explore
- a memorable incident from your childhood
- a challenging experience that taught you a lesson
- an accomplishment you are proud of

WRITING PROMPT 2

Writing from Literature Incidents and conflicts that characters face can remind us of similar experiences in our own lives. Choose a character whose story you can relate to. Write a personal narrative describing the real-life incident or conflict you are reminded of.

Characters to Relate To
- the narrator in "Daughter of Invention"
- Richard Wright in "The Rights to the Streets of Memphis"

 WRITING TOOLS
For prewriting, revision, and editing tools, visit the **Writing Center** at **ClassZone.com.**

KEY TRAITS

1. IDEAS
- Focuses on an interesting, well-defined **experience**
- Re-creates the experience, using vivid and relevant **details**
- Uses **dialogue** and gestures to develop characters

2. ORGANIZATION
- Hooks the reader with an intriguing **introduction**
- Clearly shows the **order** in which events occurred
- Concludes by summarizing the **significance** of the experience

3. VOICE
- Uses a **tone** appropriate for the audience and purpose
- Reflects the writer's **personality and style**

4. WORD CHOICE
- Uses **precise words** to help the reader visualize the characters and action

5. SENTENCE FLUENCY
- Varies **sentence structures** to create a pleasing rhythm and flow

6. CONVENTIONS
- Employs **correct grammar and usage**

Part 1: Analyze a Student Model

WRITING STANDARD
1.4.11.B Write complex informational pieces

Rich Rosario
Franklin High School

KEY TRAITS IN ACTION

Facing My Fear: Riding the River

"A rafting trip through the Grand Canyon? For a week? Really?" I said, a grin pasted on my face. "That's a great idea, Dad." I felt a knot forming in my stomach.

Opens with an intriguing **introduction** that focuses on a clearly defined **experience.** This essay has a conversational **tone.**

My two brothers high-fived each other. "This is gonna be awesome!"
5 they hollered. My mother grinned her approval.

Uses **dialogue** and gestures to develop characters.

I'm not the best athlete at Franklin High, but I work hard, and I enjoy competition. However, I used to avoid rafting, sailing, kayaking, and similar sports. Here's why: When I was ten, I climbed a railing, slipped, and fell into the Dungeness River. My uncle jumped in
10 immediately and fished me out. I came up coughing and spluttering, with a brand-new fear of drowning. Rushing, churning water filled my nightmares.

Voice reflects the writer's **personality and style.** Varied **sentence structures** create a pleasing rhythm.

The night my father told us about the vacation, I looked through the expedition catalog from Western Adventures, and my worst fears
15 were confirmed. On the cover was a photograph of a huge orange raft vanishing into a giant rapid. The vacationers clung to the sides, tiny and powerless. Now, I'm an OK swimmer. But as I looked at the catalog, I wondered why anyone, even a champion swimmer, would want to go whitewater rafting. Does anyone really think that the guides can control
20 everything that happens during the journey? I asked myself.

Uses relevant **details** to explain the experience. The writer describes his thoughts and feelings. The question is an example of interior monologue (words the writer says to himself or herself).

I didn't say anything, of course, and in August we headed off for our adventure in Arizona. We joined our raftmates, four other families, at the point where the Colorado slices its way through the canyon.

"If you fall in, relax and go with the flow," one of the lean,
25 sunburned tour guides said. "We'll pull you out!" he added.

As our raft drifted down the river, the knot in my stomach grew larger and tighter. I could feel every bump and sway, and I could hear the whoosh of the river all around me. Within a few minutes, the whooshing sound began to seem more like a thunderstorm. Our guides ordered us to 30 grab the ropes and brace ourselves. The sound ahead resembled the roar of a jet engine. My heart thudded in my chest.

> Re-creates the experience for the reader with vivid sensory **details**. Describing the knot in his stomach is more effective than writing "I was scared."

Up ahead, the waters of the Colorado appeared to be boiling, bubbling up into the air and crashing back down. In the center was a trough that looked to be 30 or 40 yards long—and we were headed 35 right for it. I held on to the ropes until my fingers felt raw. The raft held 20 people, but the raging river tossed it around like a rubber toy in a bathtub. We flew up out of the water and crashed back down. The front of the raft was submerged in icy water. There was no doubt in my mind: I was going to drown.

> Uses **precise nouns** (*trough*), **verbs** (*flew, crashed*), and **modifiers** (*raw, raging*) that enable the reader to picture what is being described.

40 Seconds later, the front of the raft shot out of the water like a cannonball. And then, suddenly, it was all over. We had made it.

> Includes words and phrases throughout the essay that signal the **order** in which events occurred.

The rafters erupted in wild shouts, all of us laughing about how we were soaking wet and what a thrill the ride had been. The knot in my stomach eased a bit. We encountered many more rapids in the next five 45 days, but my fear was never again as knife-sharp.

During that vacation, I faced my worst fear not just once, but dozens of times. I learned that worrying about an experience can be worse than the experience itself. I realized that I am tougher than I thought. I found out that it's all right to express fear—even to scream if I need to. By the 50 end of the week, I had a real smile on my face, not a pasted-on grin. And the knot in my stomach was long gone.

> Strong concluding paragraph summarizes the **significance** of the experience. By using some of the same details as in the introduction, the writer gives his essay unity and coherence.

2

WRITING STANDARD
1.5.11.B.3 Write fully developed
paragraphs that have details

Part 2: Apply the Writing Process

PREWRITING

What Should I Do?

What Does It Look Like?

1. Analyze the prompt.
Study the prompt yo u chose on page 168. (Circle) the phrase that tells you what to write. Underline important details about the assignment.

▶ **WRITING PROMPT** Write a (personal narrative) describing a meaningful experience in your life. Your narrative should explain the significance of the experience and include details that help readers visualize the characters and unfolding events.

This should be about an event that's important to me. I have to include lots of vivid details and explain why I think the event is important.

2. Choose a story to tell.
Think back over your life, recalling memorable, challenging **experiences.** Create a timeline of peaks and valleys in your life. Include the great experiences and the ones that involved real challenges. (Circle) the experience that you want to write about.

▶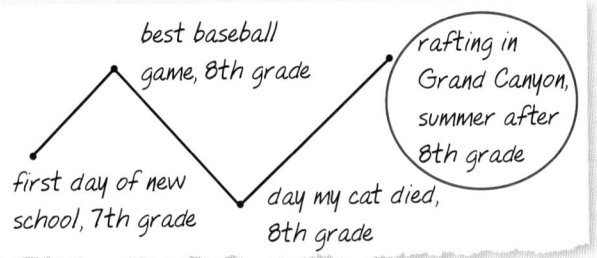

best baseball game, 8th grade

rafting in Grand Canyon, summer after 8th grade

first day of new school, 7th grade

day my cat died, 8th grade

3. Consider your audience and purpose.
Bring your narrative into focus. Make a chart that shows who your audience is and what particular information they might need to understand your story. Add a **statement of purpose** to your chart. This statement will help you explain why the experience is important.

▶

Audience	Information	Purpose
• Teacher • Classmates • Readers of an "outdoor" magazine?	• Why I was scared—the experience when I was ten • Details about rafting	I'll show that fears seem real but they can be faced and sometimes conquered.

4. List the details of your experience.
Think about the story you want to tell. Your narrative is like a short story, so think about ways to engage your reader, such as using **sensory details.**

▶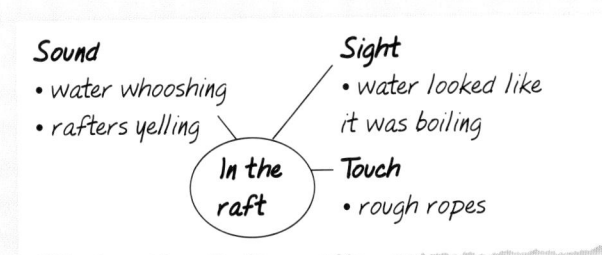

Sound
• water whooshing
• rafters yelling

Sight
• water looked like it was boiling

In the raft

Touch
• rough ropes

What Should I Do?	**What Does It Look Like?**

1. Prepare a story map.

Preparing a story map will help you make sure that your narrative includes all important details and events. The map will also help you put events in the proper order.

Most narratives use **chronological order,** also called time order—the sequence in which events happened. You may describe events in a different order, as long as you use transition words or other clues that help your reader understand the sequence.

STORY MAP

Title: *Facing My Fear: Riding the River*

Characters: me, Mom, Dad, Frank, Dave

Setting: home, Dungeness River, Colorado River

Problem: *My family is going whitewater rafting, but I am scared of drowning.*

Event 1: *Dad tells us we're going rafting.*

Event 2: *I remember the time I almost drowned.*

Event 3: *I look at the rafting catalog and get nervous.*

Event 4: *We get through the first rapid.*

Solution or Ending: *I learned that I can face my worst fear.*

2. Write an interesting beginning.

Grab your reader's attention with a strong start. You might use a question, a description, or some dialogue. Sometimes plunging right into the story will make your reader hungry for more.

A question

Have you ever stared fear in the face and lived to laugh about it? I have.

A bit of dialogue

"A rafting trip through the Grand Canyon? For a week? Really?" I said, a grin pasted on my face.

3. Include vivid details.

Create vivid pictures for your reader as you write. What details can you add that will help a reader see what you saw, hear what you heard, and feel what you felt?

TIP Before revising, consult the **key traits** on page 168 and the **rubric and peer-reader questions** on page 174.

From prewriting notes . . .

The rapids turned out to be fierce and challenging.

. . . to draft

Up ahead, the waters of the Colorado appeared to be boiling, bubbling up into the air and crashing back down. In the center was a trough that looked to be 30 or 40 yards long—and we were headed right for it.

REVISING AND EDITING

What Should I Do?

What Does It Look Like?

1. Show, don't tell.
Instead of telling your reader "I was scared" or "She looked happy," show your characters' emotions and reactions. <u>Underline</u> any statements in your essay that sound like these examples. Consider adding dialogue, or information about tone of voice, expressions, or gestures or other movements.

▶ ~~All of us were glad the scary part was over.~~ ~~I started to feel somewhat less nervous.~~
The rafters erupted in wild shouts, all of us laughing about how we were soaking wet and what a thrill the ride had been. The knot in my stomach eased a bit.

2. Consider your tone.
Is your narrative funny? bittersweet? scary? Highlight words and details that give the narrative its tone. If you have few highlights, or if you don't like the tone in certain places, ask a peer reader for help.

▶ ~~Are these idiots crazy or what?~~ I asked myself. ~~What are they thinking, anyway?~~
Does anyone really think that the guides can control everything that happens during the journey?

3. Include sensory images.
• (Circle) places where sensory images—words and phrases that appeal to sight, sound, taste, smell, and touch—seem to be missing.
• Add specific nouns, powerful verbs, and vivid adjectives and adverbs. Consider using figurative language, such as similes and metaphors.

See page 672: Figurative Language

▶ ~~The ride was starting to get really bumpy and noisy.~~
I could feel every bump and sway, and I could hear the whoosh of the river all around me. Within a few minutes, the whooshing sound began to seem more like a thunderstorm. Our guides ordered us to grab the ropes and brace ourselves. The sound ahead resembled the roar of a jet engine.

4. Don't forget the significance.
• Ask a peer reader to tell you why the experience was important.
• If he or she can't tell you, add information about the event's significance to the conclusion and at other points, if appropriate.

See page 174: Ask a Peer Reader

▶ ~~I'm glad we took that trip. It turned out to be a really good vacation after all.~~
During that vacation, I faced my worst fear not just once, but dozens of times. I learned that worrying about an experience can be worse than the experience itself. I realized that I am tougher than I thought.

Preparing to Publish

Personal Narrative

Apply the Rubric

A strong personal narrative . . .

☑ captures the reader's interest with an intriguing beginning

☑ focuses on a clear, well-defined experience

☑ uses dialogue to develop characters and add realism

☑ includes words and phrases that signal chronological order

☑ creates vivid descriptions through the use of precise language and strong sensory details

☑ maintains a consistent tone

☑ shows the writer's style

☑ uses a variety of sentence structures

☑ concludes by explaining why the experience mattered to the writer

Ask a Peer Reader

- What is the main incident or conflict in my narrative?

- How would you explain in your own words the significance of the experience to me?

Check Your Grammar

- When writing dialogue, enclose each speaker's actual words in quotation marks. Begin a new paragraph whenever the speaker changes.

> " A rafting trip through the Grand Canyon? For a week? Really? " I said, a grin pasted on my face. " That's a great idea, Dad." I felt a knot forming in my stomach.
>
>   My two brothers high-fived each other. " This is gonna be awesome! " they hollered.

- Unless the speaker's words are a question or an exclamation, use a comma to separate the speaker's words from the phrase identifying the speaker. Place the comma inside the closing quotation mark.

> "If you fall in, relax and go with the flow , " one of the lean, sunburned tour guides said.

- If the speaker's words are a question or an exclamation, use a question mark or exclamation point in place of a comma. Place the punctuation mark inside the closing quotation mark.

> "We'll pull you out ! " he added.

See page R50: Quick Reference: Punctuation

Writing Online

PUBLISHING OPTIONS
For publishing options, visit the **Writing Center** at ClassZone.com.

ASSESSMENT PREPARATION
For writing and grammar assessment practice, go to the **Assessment Center** at ClassZone.com.

Presenting an Informal Speech

Captivate your classmates with a **narrative presentation**—a retelling of the incident you described in your personal narrative.

Planning the Presentation

Adapt what you wrote. Here's how to turn your writing into an effective speech:

- Use shorter sentences.
- Eliminate minor characters and unnecessary dialogue.
- Be sure the sequence of events is clear.
- Focus on the descriptive details related to setting and characters. This will help your audience "live" the experience and understand its importance.
- If you are using notes, mark your text to show where you will use a different voice, a certain facial expression, a gesture, or sound effects. Notice how Rich Rosario adapted parts of his personal narrative.

Written Narrative	Informal Speech
"A rafting trip through the Grand Canyon? For a week? Really?" I said, a grin pasted on my face. "That's a great idea, Dad." I felt a knot forming in my stomach.	[grin] You should have seen the grin on my face when my dad told me about our next family vacation! [pause] It was a _fake_ grin. We were going on a rafting trip through the Grand Canyon. [frown] Yuck!
My two brothers high-fived each other. "This is gonna be awesome!" they hollered. My mother grinned her approval.	~~My two brothers high-fived each other. "This is gonna be awesome!" they hollered. My mother grinned her approval.~~

Delivering the Presentation

1. **Use a conversational tone.** Use some of the same inflections and gestures you use when you share an important event with a friend. You might speak at a faster pace to describe exciting events and at a slower pace to create suspense or drama.

2. **Find out your time limit, if any.** Pace your delivery so that you finish on time. (You might have a friend time you as you practice.)

See page R79: Evaluate a Narrative Speech

Reading Comprehension

ASSESS

The practice test items on the next few pages match skills listed on the Unit Goals page (page 23) and addressed throughout this unit. Taking this practice test will help you assess your knowledge of these skills and determine your readiness for the Unit Test.

REVIEW

After you take the practice test, your teacher can help you identify any skills you need to review.

- Plot Stages
- Conflict
- Sequence
- Predict
- Cause and Effect
- Synonyms and Antonyms
- Latin Word Roots
- Modifiers
- Precise and Strong Verbs

ASSESSMENT ONLINE

For more assessment practice and test-taking tips, go to the **Assessment Center** at ClassZone.com.

DIRECTIONS *Read the following selections and then answer the questions.*

Fish Cheeks

Amy Tan

I fell in love with the minister's son the winter I turned fourteen. He was not Chinese, but as white as Mary in the manger. For Christmas I prayed for this blond-haired boy, Robert, and a slim new American nose.

When I found out that my parents had invited the minister's family over for Christmas Eve dinner, I cried. What would Robert think of our shabby *Chinese* Christmas? What would he think of our noisy *Chinese* relatives who lacked proper American manners? What terrible disappointment would he feel upon seeing not a roasted turkey and sweet potatoes but *Chinese* food?

10   On Christmas Eve I saw that my mother had outdone herself in creating a strange menu. She was pulling black veins out of the backs of fleshy prawns. The kitchen was littered with appalling mounds of raw food: A slimy rock cod with bulging fish eyes that pleaded not to be thrown into a pan of hot oil. Tofu, which looked like stacked wedges of rubbery white sponges. A bowl soaking dried fungus back to life. A plate of squid, their backs crisscrossed with knife markings so they resembled bicycle tires.

And then they arrived—the minister's family and all my relatives in a clamor of doorbells and rumpled Christmas packages. Robert grunted hello, and I pretended he was not worthy of existence.

Dinner threw me deeper into despair. My relatives licked the ends of their
20   chopsticks and reached across the table, dipping them into the dozen or so plates of food. Robert and his family waited patiently for platters to be passed to them. My relatives murmured with pleasure when my mother brought out the whole steamed fish. Robert grimaced. Then my father poked his chopsticks just below the fish eye and plucked out the soft meat. "Amy, your favorite," he said, offering me the tender fish cheek. I wanted to disappear.

At the end of the meal my father leaned back and belched loudly, thanking my mother for her fine cooking. "It's a polite Chinese custom to show you are satisfied," explained my father to our astonished guests. Robert was looking down at his plate with a reddened face. The minister managed to muster up a
30   quiet burp. I was stunned into silence for the rest of the night.

After everyone had gone, my mother said to me, "You want to be the same as American girls on the outside." She handed me an early gift. It was a miniskirt in beige tweed. "But inside you must always be Chinese. You must be proud you are different. Your only shame is to have shame."

And even though I didn't agree with her then, I knew that she understood how much I had suffered during the evening's dinner. It wasn't until many years later—long after I had gotten over my crush on Robert—that I was able to fully appreciate her lesson and the true purpose behind our particular menu. For Christmas Eve that year, she had chosen all my favorite foods.

from Piedra

Gary Soto

Piedra. River of rock, place where our family went for a Saturday picnic. It was a fifteen-mile drive past plum and almond orchards, dairies, the town with its green sign, Minkler—Population 35, *Mexicanos* pruning orange trees on ladders, and our mother's talk that if our grades didn't improve we would be like *those* people. Past cows with grassy jaws, past fallen fences, groceries, tractors itching with rust, the Griffin ranch with its mowed pasture and white fence that proclaimed he was a gentleman farmer. We gawked at his ranch, and counted his cows, which seemed cleaner, better looking than the fly-specked ones we had passed earlier.

10   I dreamed about Griffin's daughters. I imagined that their hair was tied in ponytails and bounced crazily when they rode horses in knee-high grass near the river. They were the stuff of romance novels, sad and lonely girls who were in love with a stable boy, who was also sad and lonely but too poor for the father's liking, because he himself had once been poor but now was rich and liked to whip horses, cuss, and chase gasping foxes at daybreak.

My dreaming stopped when the road narrowed, gravel ticked under a fender, and we began our climb through the foot-hills.

Comprehension

DIRECTIONS *Answer these questions about "Fish Cheeks."*

1. What is the narrator's main conflict?

   A She is afraid that Robert won't like her when he sees how her family celebrates Christmas.

   B She wishes she had a slim nose like those of the American girls.

   C She doesn't like any of the foods that her mother is preparing for Christmas Eve dinner.

   D She doesn't want to spend Christmas Eve with people that she hardly knows.

2. Why is the narrator worried about her mother's Christmas Eve dinner menu?

   A She doesn't like any of the foods on the menu.

   B She thinks the food will seem strange to the guests.

   C She worries that her mother doesn't know how to prepare all the unusual dishes.

   D She wishes that the food choices were healthier.

3. In what part of the plot does the narrator describe the unusual food that awaits the minister's family?

   A exposition

   B rising action

   C climax

   D falling action

4. In the rising action, which of these events complicates the conflict?

   A The narrator ignores the minister's son.

   B The narrator cries about Christmas Eve dinner.

   C The narrator's relatives murmur with pleasure.

   D The narrator's father offers her the fish cheeks.

5. Which of the following would the narrator probably do when she sees Robert at school after Christmas?

   A wave at him and shout hello

   B say something rude to him

   C try to avoid meeting his eyes

   D invite him back to her house

6. The resolution of the plot occurs when

   A the narrator's father belches

   B the narrator's mother gives her a miniskirt

   C the narrator is in love with Robert

   D the narrator is an adult

7. In the resolution of the story, the narrator realizes that

   A she never agreed with her mother

   B her mother was a superb cook

   C she should be proud to be Chinese

   D she preferred Chinese food after all

DIRECTIONS *Answer these questions about the excerpt from "Piedra."*

8. Why does the mother tell her children to get better grades?

   A She wants them to do as well as the tree pruners they saw.

   B She wants them to have better-paying jobs than pruning trees.

   C She wants them to be smarter than their friends.

   D She wants them to learn how to run a ranch.

9. What do you learn about the main character in this excerpt?

   A He would like to get good grades.

   B He admires the Griffen ranch.

   C He and his family live in a city.

   D He wants to be a farmer.

10. The rising action of the plot begins when

   A they go through Minkler

   B they drive past Griffin's ranch

   C the narrator daydreams about girls

   D they climb through the foothills

11. What prompts the narrator to begin daydreaming?

   A seeing the green Minkler sign

   B passing the people who prune trees for a living

   C seeing a ranch that is better than all the others

   D feeling the car start its climb through the foothills

DIRECTIONS *Answer these questions about both selections.*

12. Which issue seems more important to the mother in "Fish Cheeks" than to the mother in "Piedra"?

   A money

   B tradition

   C school

   D friendship

13. In what way are the narrators of both selections alike?

   A Both narrators are parents who care about their children.

   B They are both students who want to get better grades.

   C Both narrators are children who disobey their parents.

   D They both long for something they do not have.

Open-Ended Items

14. How would the narrator of "Fish Cheeks" probably react if her parents invited the minister's family to dinner for the next holiday? Give evidence from the selection to back up your answer.

15. In "Fish Cheeks," how can you tell that the guests were embarrassed at the end of the meal? Give three pieces of evidence from the story.

16. In "Fish Cheeks," what does the narrator's mother mean when she says, "Your only shame is to have shame"? How does she want her daughter to feel? What does she do to change her daughter's feelings?

GO ON

Vocabulary

DIRECTIONS *Use your knowledge of synonyms to answer the following questions.*

1. Choose the word that is a synonym of the underlined word in the following sentence from "Fish Cheeks."

   And then they arrived—the minister's family and all my relatives in a <u>clamor</u> of doorbells and rumpled Christmas packages.

   A crowd
   B shabbiness
   C noise
   D offering

2. Choose the word that is a synonym of the underlined phrase in the following sentence from "Fish Cheeks."

   The minister managed to <u>muster up</u> a quiet burp.

   A hide
   B echo
   C produce
   D excuse

DIRECTIONS *Use your knowledge of antonyms to answer question 3.*

3. Choose the word that is an antonym of the underlined word in the following passage from "Fish Cheeks."

   Dinner threw me deeper into despair. My relatives licked the ends of their chopsticks and reached across the table, dipping them into the dozen or so plates of food. Robert and his family waited patiently for platters to be passed to them. My relatives murmured with pleasure when my mother brought out the whole steamed fish. Robert <u>grimaced</u>.

   A laughed   C growled
   B smiled   D gasped

DIRECTIONS *Use your knowledge of vocabulary and the Latin word roots given to answer the following questions.*

4. The root *pall* means "pale." Which word in "Fish Cheeks" may have something to do with making a person turn pale and probably comes from the Latin root *pall?*

   A disappear
   B appalling
   C polite
   D pleaded

5. The word *resembled* in line 15 of "Fish Cheeks" comes from the Latin root *simil.* What does this root probably mean?

   A like
   B inflated
   C tread
   D shame

6. The word *polite* in line 27 of "Fish Cheeks" comes from the Latin root *polit.* What does this root probably mean?

   A pretend
   B polish
   C pluck
   D platter

7. The Latin root *clam* means "cry out." Which word in "Piedra" likely comes from the root *clam?*

   A counted
   B gawked
   C climb
   D proclaimed

Writing & Grammar

DIRECTIONS *Read this passage and answer the questions that follow.*

> (1) Schools are adding outdoor learning experiences. (2) This is happening nationwide. (3) Kids can work in an edible garden. (4) They grow lettuce, tomatoes, and peas. (5) The students at one school built an oven. (6) They used clay, straw, and water to build it. (7) They mixed the materials together. (8) Kids also dig in the dirt, pull weeds, and remove pests from their plants. (9) Butterflies and bees fly around the plants. (10) Tomatoes hang over the garden wall.

1. Choose the best way to rewrite sentences 1 and 2, using a prepositional phrase.

  A Schools are adding outdoor learning experiences, and these schools are nationwide.

  B Schools across the nation are adding outdoor learning experiences.

  C The nation's schools are adding outdoor learning experiences.

  D Schools are adding outdoor learning experiences nationwide.

2. Choose the best way to add details to sentence 4, using modifiers.

  A They grow fresh lettuce, tomatoes, and peas.

  B They grow crunchy lettuce, juicy tomatoes, and green peas.

  C They grow crisp lettuce, tomatoes, and peas.

  D Lettuce, tomatoes, and peas grow well.

3. Which prepositional phrase would add details to sentence 5 that describe the oven the students built?

  A out of natural materials

  B with enthusiasm

  C in the sky

  D underneath the garden

4. Choose the best way to rewrite sentence 8, using strong verbs in a series. Choose D if no change is needed.

  A Kids also heave the dirt, yank out weeds, and exterminate pests from their plants.

  B Kids also hoe in the dirt and remove weeds and pests from their plants.

  C Kids also dig in the dirt, weed, nurture their plants, and remove pests.

  D No change is needed.

5. Choose the best way to rewrite sentence 9, using a precise verb or verbs. Choose D if no change is needed.

  A Butterflies and bees move around the plants.

  B There are butterflies and bees around the plants.

  C Butterflies flit and bees hover around the plants.

  D No change is needed.

6. Choose the best way to rewrite sentence 10, using a precise verb. Choose D if no change is needed.

  A Tomatoes lie on the garden wall.

  B Tomatoes are on the garden wall.

  C Tomatoes cascade over the garden wall.

  D No change is needed.

Ideas for Independent Reading

Which of the questions in Unit 1 intrigued you the most?
Continue exploring them through independent reading.

What does it take to be a survivor?

The Autobiography of Miss Jane Pittman
by Ernest J. Gaines

This unusual novel is written as an autobiography. A 110-year-old woman tells the story of her life, from her childhood as a slave in Louisiana to the civil rights era of the 1960s.

And Then There Were None
by Agatha Christie

At certain points, this mystery novel might bring to mind the sizzling plot elements of "The Most Dangerous Game." Ten strangers are lured to an island from which there is no escape.

In These Girls, Hope Is a Muscle
by Madeleine Blais

This true account goes behind the scenes as a basketball team tries to survive the state playoffs.

What is worth fighting for?

Shoeless Joe
by W. P. Kinsella

Against everyone's advice, Ray Kinsella builds a baseball diamond in a cornfield to give Shoeless Joe Jackson, a legendary outfielder done in by scandal and now dead, a chance to play.

All Quiet on the Western Front
by Erich Maria Remarque

This fictional antiwar classic follows Paul Baumer into the German army during World War I. While fighting the human enemy, Paul also fights a more deadly enemy—the hate that leads men into war.

The Pact: Three Young Men Make a Promise and Fulfill a Dream
by Dr. Sampson Davis, et al.

Three young men from the wrong side of the tracks in Newark, New Jersey, made a pact: they would all become doctors and they would do it together. Over-coming numerous obstacles, they all achieved their goal.

What makes a winner?

Bad Boy: A Memoir
by Walter Dean Myers

The author of many novels about black characters remembers his own childhood in Harlem. Surrounded by poverty and drugs, he seeks escape and adventure in books and succeeds in becoming a writer.

The Natural
by Bernard Malamud

Roy Hobbs, a talented athlete whose promising career is cut short by his own misdeeds, makes a comeback in middle age. He struggles to be a great player and to fulfill his dream.

The Miracle Worker
by William Gibson

This play tells the true story of the dedicated Annie Sullivan's struggle to free Helen Keller from the prison of her dark and silent world. Convinced that she can give Helen the gift of language, Annie applies herself with fanatical dedication.

UNIT 2

People Watching

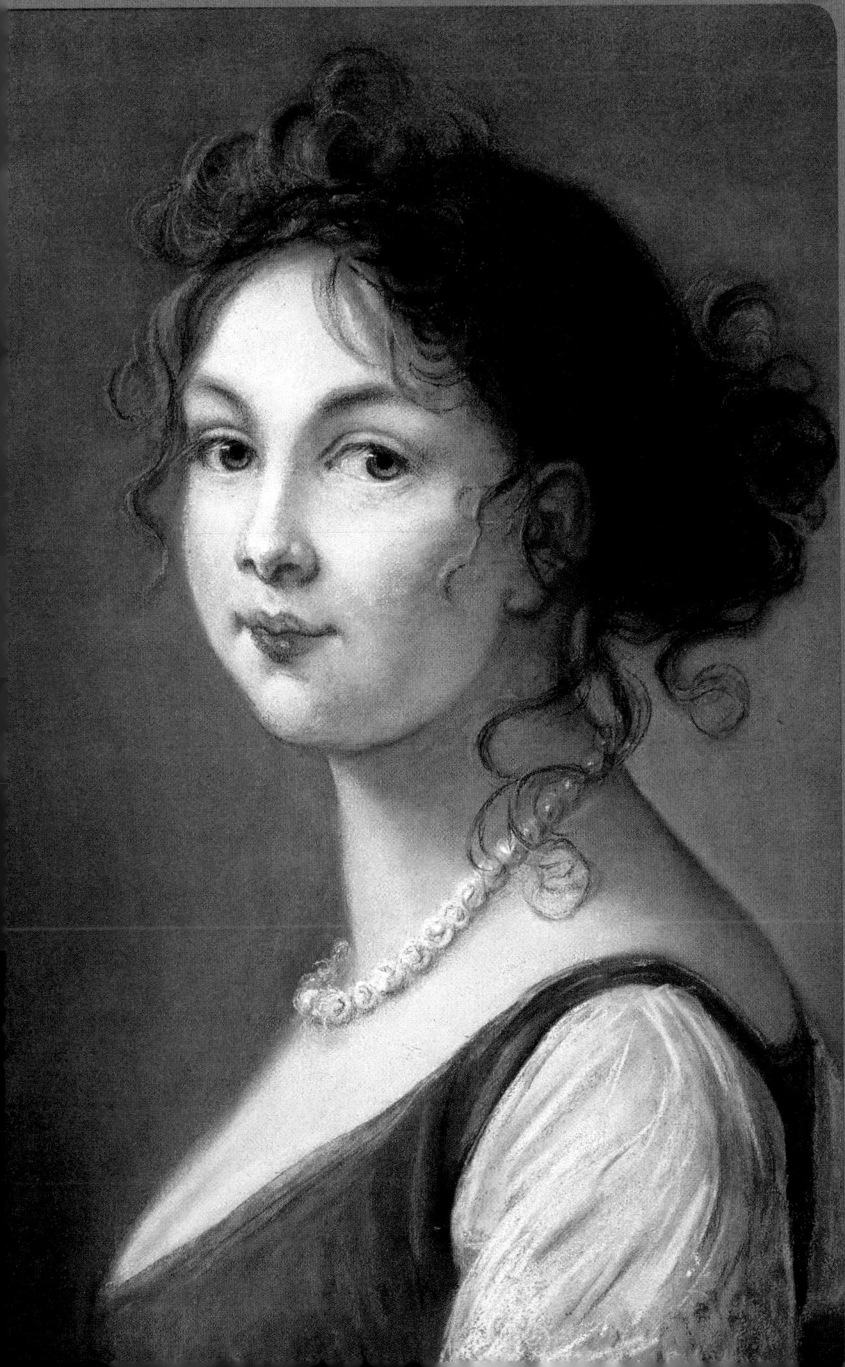

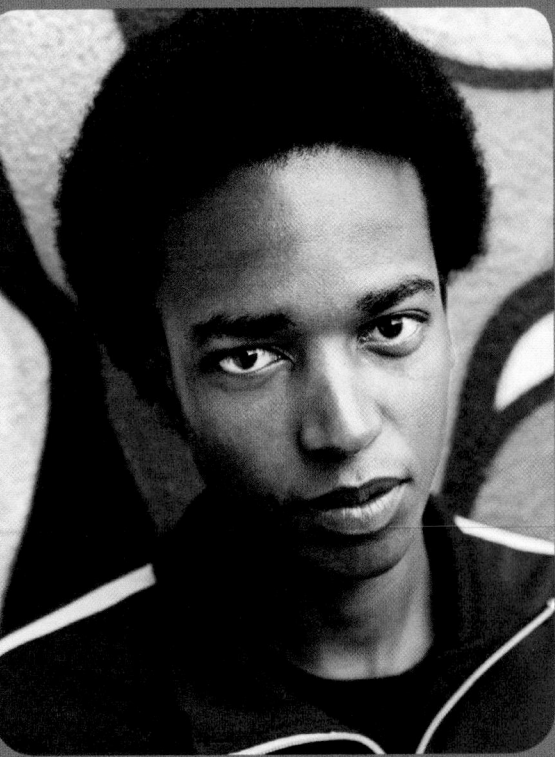

CHARACTERIZATION AND POINT OF VIEW

- In Fiction
- In Nonfiction
- In Poetry
- Across Genres

What makes a
CHARACTER
memorable?

Any skilled actor knows that it takes more than costumes and makeup to create a memorable **character.** Everything from the voice to the walk to the simplest of gestures and facial expressions must be considered and carefully chosen.

ACTIVITY With a group of classmates, think of several strong characters that you remember from TV shows, books, or movies. Describe each one, including details about both looks and personality. Then consider the following questions:

- On what details did you base your first impression of each character?

- How did your impression change as you got to know the character better? What details led to this change?

- Considering your discussion, what would you imagine a writer needs to keep in mind when creating a character?

Online LITERATURE CLASSZONE.COM

Literature and Reading Center
Writing Center
Vocabulary Center

LITERARY ANALYSIS
- Identify and analyze point of view
- Analyze character traits and motivation
- Identify different types of characters
- Understand the methods writers use to develop characters
- Analyze and compare characterization in a variety of texts

READING
- Make inferences and draw conclusions
- Make generalizations
- Monitor strategies while reading
- Recognize main ideas and supporting details
- Interpret graphic aids

WRITING AND GRAMMAR
- Write a compare-and-contrast essay; cite evidence
- Use supporting and descriptive details; use precise adjectives
- Vary sentence beginnings by using phrases and clauses

SPEAKING, LISTENING, AND VIEWING
- Create and present a power presentation

VOCABULARY
- Use knowledge of word origins to help unlock meaning
- Determine correct usage and meaning of multiple-meaning words and specialized vocabulary

ACADEMIC VOCABULARY
- character motives
- character traits
- first-person point of view
- third-person point of view (omniscient or limited)

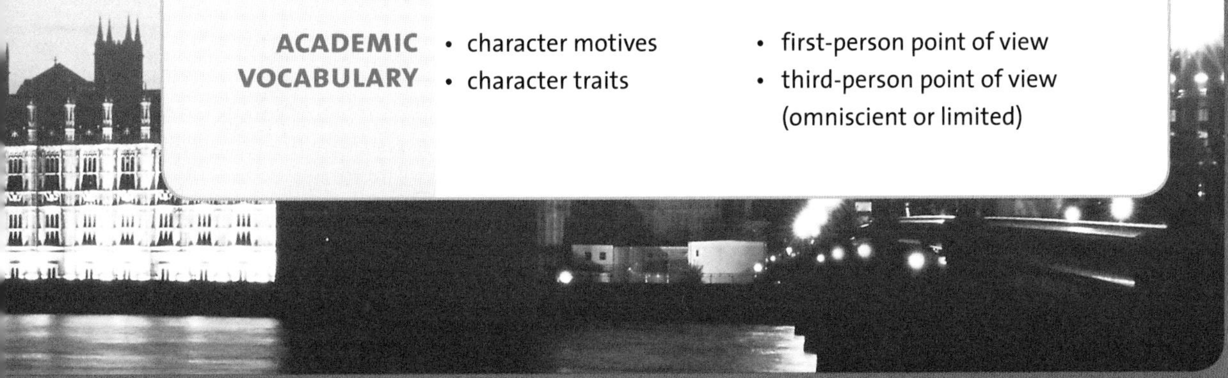

Character and Point of View

When you read a book or watch a movie, you become involved on an emotional level with the characters. Like real people, characters can win your sympathy, make your blood boil with anger, get on your nerves, or give you insights into human nature. By asking some pointed questions, you can better understand why you are reacting the way you are. For example, through whose eyes are you experiencing events? Which details are shaping your impression of each character?

PENNSYLVANIA STANDARDS

READING STANDARDS
B.1.1.1.A.1 Evaluate character
B.2.2.1 Identify and analyze point of view

Part 1: Point of View

The perspective from which a story is told is called **point of view.** Think of point of view as the lens that a writer chooses for his or her readers to look through. Point of view determines what you learn about the characters and may influence how you feel about them. It also affects the choice of the **narrator**—the voice that tells the story. Knowing a story's point of view can help you evaluate the details you receive about characters and events.

FIRST-PERSON POINT OF VIEW

The Narrator

- is a main or minor character in the story
- refers to himself or herself as *I* or *me*
- presents his or her own thoughts and feelings
- does not have direct access to the thoughts and feelings of other characters

▼

Impact on the Reader

- Your understanding of characters and events is limited to what this narrator reveals about them.
- You can't necessarily trust the narrator's interpretation of events.
- The story seems real, almost as if the narrator were talking to you.

THIRD-PERSON POINT OF VIEW

The Narrator

- is not a character in the story
- may not be an identifiable person but merely a voice that tells the story
- is called **omniscient** if he or she knows the thoughts and feelings of all the characters
- is called **limited** if he or she focuses on the thoughts and feelings of one character

▼

Impact on the Reader

- You are likely to learn more about characters and events than if the story were told by a first-person narrator.
- You might not feel as connected to the characters because the story is told in a less personal way.

MODEL 1: FIRST-PERSON POINT OF VIEW

A first-person narrator allows you to experience events from his or her perspective. Even though you are getting only one view of the action, you often feel as though you are right at the scene. As you read this excerpt, consider how the boy's thoughts affect the way you picture the room.

from GREAT EXPECTATIONS
Novel by **Charles Dickens**

    . . . I was half afraid. However, the only thing to be done being to knock at the door, I knocked, and was told from within to enter. I entered, therefore, and found myself in a pretty large room, well lighted with wax candles. No glimpse of daylight was to be seen in it. It was a dressing-room, as I supposed
5 from the furniture, though much of it was of forms and uses then quite unknown to me. But prominent in it was a draped table with a gilded looking-glass, and that I made out at first to be a fine lady's dressing-table.
    Whether I should have made out this object so soon, if there had been no fine lady sitting at it, I cannot say. In an arm-chair, with an elbow resting on
10 the table and her head leaning on that hand, sat the strangest lady I have ever seen, or shall ever see.

Close Read

1. How does the first-person point of view influence the way you visualize this scene?

2. How do you think this scene would be different if the lady were the narrator?

MODEL 2: THIRD-PERSON POINT OF VIEW

In a story told from the third-person point of view, an outside narrator tells you about the story's characters and events. As you read this excerpt, think about whether the character would describe himself in the same way the third-person narrator does.

from The Chocolate War
Novel by **Robert Cormier**

    The Goober was beautiful when he ran. His long arms and legs moved flowingly and flawlessly, his body floating as if his feet weren't touching the ground. When he ran, he forgot about his acne and his awkwardness and the shyness that paralyzed him when a girl looked his way. Even his thoughts
5 became sharper, and things were simple and uncomplicated—he could solve math problems when he ran or memorize football play patterns. Often he rose early in the morning, before anyone else, and poured himself liquid through the sunrise streets, and everything seemed beautiful, everything in its proper orbit, nothing impossible, the entire world attainable.

Close Read

1. Find an example of a direct comment about the Goober. Then find an example in which the narrator allows you to "see" his thoughts. An example of each has been boxed.

2. Identify a sentence that the Goober probably would not have used to describe himself and his running.

Part 2: Character Traits and Motivation

As a story develops, you might wonder why the characters act the way they do, question their choices, and feel satisfied when they learn from their mistakes. By analyzing characters' traits and motivations, you can develop a complete picture of the characters you meet and understand your reactions to them.

CHARACTER TRAITS

You have probably encountered characters who are athletic, shy, arrogant, or wise—words you might also use to describe people in your life. These words are descriptions of **character traits,** or qualities shown by characters. Sometimes a narrator directly identifies a character's traits, but more often, traits are revealed through indirect methods of characterization. This means that a writer *shows* you a character without telling you what kind of person he or she is. Using the clues in the text, you must form your own impression.

METHODS OF CHARACTERIZATION	EXAMPLES
 **1. PHYSICAL APPEARANCE** Descriptions of the character's • clothing • physical characteristics • body language and facial expressions • gestures or mannerisms	• A character who usually wears unmatched socks and stained shirts might be described as **slovenly.** • If a character is always smiling and making eye contact with others, you might infer that she is **warm** or **friendly.**
2. SPEECH, THOUGHTS, AND ACTIONS Presentation of the character's • speech patterns • habits • tastes • talents and abilities • interaction with others	• A character who speaks so quietly that others can't hear might be described as **timid.** • You might infer that a character who repeatedly misses softball practice without telling the coach is **irresponsible** or **unreliable.**
 **3. OTHER CHARACTERS** Presentation of other characters' • reactions to the character • relationships with the character • impression of the character's reputation	• If a character's girlfriend describes him as a "no-good lying jerk," you might infer that he is **insensitive** and **dishonest.** • If people often confide their troubles to a character, you might conclude that she is **trustworthy.**

MODEL 1: PHYSICAL APPEARANCE

Whether it is accurate or not, your first impression of a character may be based solely on his or her appearance. As you read this excerpt, consider how the narrator's description of her unique wardrobe affects your impression of her. How would you describe the narrator to others?

from Life Without *Go-Go* Boots

Personal essay by **Barbara Kingsolver**

. . . In fifth grade, when girls were wearing straight shifts with buttons down the front, I wore pastel shirtwaists with cap sleeves and a multitude of built-in petticoats. My black lace-up oxfords, which my parents perceived to have orthopedic value, carried their own weight in the spectacle. I suspected people
5 noticed, and I knew it for sure on the day Billy Stamps announced to the lunch line: "Make way for the Bride of Frankenstein."

Close Read

1. What do you learn about the narrator's traits from her own description of how she dresses? Find two details that reveal these traits.

2. Identify one trait that is revealed through Billy Stamps's reaction to the narrator.

MODEL 2: SPEECH, THOUGHTS, AND ACTIONS

In this excerpt from the novel *To Kill a Mockingbird*, the writer creates a distinct portrait of Miss Maudie by showing her in action. As you read, think about how the writer reveals Miss Maudie's personality.

from *To Kill a Mockingbird*

Novel by **Harper Lee**

Miss Maudie hated her house: time spent indoors was time wasted. She was a widow, a chameleon lady who worked in her flower beds in an old straw hat and men's coveralls, but after her five o'clock bath she would appear on the porch and |reign over the street in magisterial beauty.|
5 She loved everything that grew in God's earth, even the weeds. With one exception. If she found a blade of nut grass in her yard it was like the Second Battle of the Marne: she swooped down upon it with a tin tub and subjected it to blasts from beneath with a poisonous substance she said was so powerful it'd kill us all if we didn't stand out of the way.

Close Read

1. What do you learn about Miss Maudie in this excerpt? Describe her as completely as you can.

2. Miss Maudie is both elegant and energetic. Which details in the text reveal these traits? One has been |boxed.|

CHARACTER MOTIVATION

Why does a character move across the country, steal money from a friend, go to war, or live alone on a mountaintop? Figuring out a character's **motivation**—the reasons behind his or her actions—is a key part of understanding the character. Love, hate, vengeance, ambition, and desperation are some of the emotions that drive characters' behavior. Sometimes a writer will directly tell you about a character's motivation, but more often you must look for details in the story that reveal the motivation. As you read any story, consider the following clues:

- the narrator's direct comments about a character's motivation

- the character's actions, thoughts, feelings, values, and interactions with other characters

- your own insights into human behavior

In the following excerpt, why does the mother persuade her husband to make some changes? As you read, use the clues in the text to uncover the mother's motivation.

from
THE EGG

Short story by **Sherwood Anderson**

It was in the spring of his thirty-fifth year that father married my mother, then a country school-teacher, and in the following spring I came wriggling and crying into the world. Something happened to the two people. They became ambitious. The American passion for getting up in the world took possession of 5 them.

It may have been that mother was responsible. Being a school-teacher she had no doubt read books and magazines. She had, I presume, read of how Garfield, Lincoln, and other Americans rose from poverty to fame and greatness, and as I lay beside her . . . she may have dreamed that I would some day rule men and 10 cities. At any rate she induced father to give up his place as a farmhand, sell his horse, and embark on an independent enterprise of his own. . . . For herself she wanted nothing. For father and myself she was incurably ambitious.

Close Read

1. How does the narrator's birth change his parents?

2. Reread the boxed text. What does it tell you about the mother's motivation for convincing her husband to give up farming?

Part 3: Analyze the Literature

Use what you've just learned about point of view, character traits, and motivation to analyze this excerpt from a novel about Hana, a Japanese woman who comes to the United States in the early 20th century. In the excerpt, some neighbors visit the new home of Hana and her husband, Taro. As you read, notice how the writer reveals Hana's and Taro's personalities. How does the choice of the narrator affect your understanding of the scene?

from
Picture*Bride*
Novel by **Yoshiko Uchida**

The men glanced around the living room which Hana had taken great pains to decorate properly. A new flowered rug lay on the floor, and fresh white curtains that Kiku had helped Hana sew hung at the windows. The first tight buds of the flowering peach in their yard had begun to swell, and knowing
5　there would be callers, Hana had arranged a spray on the mantel.

"We'll come right to the point," a tall red-headed man said without bothering to sit down. "There've been some complaints from the neighborhood about having Japanese on this block."

Taro caught his breath. "I see. Can you tell me who it was that
10　complained?"

"Just some of the neighbors."

"What is it we have done to offend them?"

"Well, nothing specific."

Taro looked at each of the men in turn and tried to keep his voice steady.
15　"Gentlemen," he began. "My wife and I looked many, many months to find a home where we might raise our daughter. When the owner said there would be no objection to our moving in here, we trusted him. It was a dream come true for us. We have already spent much time and money to make this house our home. And now, you would ask us to leave?"
20　Taro dared not stop before he finished all he wanted to say. "I should like to meet those neighbors who object to us," he said. "Is it any of you gentlemen?"

The men looked uncomfortable. "We're just here to represent them."

"Then please invite them to come talk to me. If they can tell me why we aren't desirable or why we do not deserve their respect, I shall consider their
25　request. I am the proprietor of Takeda Dry Goods and Grocers on Seventh Street and I would be happy to have them visit my shop as well."

The men glanced uneasily at one another and had nothing more to say.

Close Read

1. From which point of view is this story told? Explain how you know.

2. What do you learn about Hana's traits from the description of the room in lines 1–5?

3. What kind of people are the men in Taro's and Hana's home? Find two details that reveal their traits. An example has been boxed.

4. Reread lines 14–19 and 23–26. What is Taro's motivation for bravely speaking his mind? Explain what his words tell you about his character.

5. How would the story be different if Taro were the narrator?

Pancakes
Short Story by Joan Bauer

Are you a PERFECTIONIST?

PENNSYLVANIA STANDARDS

READING STANDARDS
A.1.3.1 Make inferences and/or draw conclusions

B.2.2.1 Identify and analyze point of view

KEY IDEA The main character in "Pancakes" is a **perfectionist**—she needs everything to be perfect in order to be happy. Would you describe yourself this way? Take this true-false quiz to find out. If you answer "true" to three or more statements, you are flirting with perfectionism.

DISCUSS After you take the quiz, form a small group with two to four of your classmates to discuss the pros and cons of perfectionism. Is striving for perfection ever helpful or necessary? When might it be difficult to cope with this trait?

quiz ⦾⦿ HOW PERFECT IS TOO PERFECT?

Answer the following questions to discover if a perfectionist lurks within you.

1. I won't even attempt to do something unless I know that I will be able to do it without a mistake.
☐ TRUE ◯ FALSE

2. I am so competitive that my best friends won't play sports with me.
☐ TRUE ◯ FALSE

3. I know what I will be wearing every day for the next week.
☐ TRUE ◯ FALSE

4. I won't eat food unless it's prepared exactly the way I like it.
☐ TRUE ◯ FALSE

5. I can't sleep unless my CDs are correctly categorized and in alphabetical order.
☐ TRUE ◯ FALSE

LITERARY ANALYSIS: FIRST-PERSON POINT OF VIEW

"Pancakes" is told from a **first-person point of view.** Jill, the narrator, is a character in the story, and she describes events as she herself experiences them. You will see the other characters and the actions in the story through Jill's eyes and learn exactly what she thinks and how she feels. As you read "Pancakes," look for comments that reveal Jill's feelings about her life and help explain the causes of her perfectionism.

Review: **Character Traits**

READING SKILL: DRAW CONCLUSIONS

After reading a story, you often add up the details you've read about and develop your own ideas about what they mean. This process is called **drawing conclusions.** A conclusion is a logical judgment that a reader makes. In order to be logical, a conclusion must be based on

- evidence from the text
- your own experience and knowledge

As you read "Pancakes," use a chart like the one shown to record important details about Jill's thoughts, actions, and relationships. Include your own ideas of what these details reveal about Jill.

Details About Jill	My Thoughts
She refers to her mother as "Ms. Subtlety" after her mother tapes an article on perfectionism to Jill's mirror.	Jill is being sarcastic. She might feel her mother is picking on her.

After reading, you can use the information you've gathered to draw conclusions about Jill's perfectionism.

Review: **Predict**

▲ VOCABULARY IN CONTEXT

Joan Bauer makes use of the following boldfaced words to tell this amusing story. Try to figure out the meaning of each word from the context of the phrase given.

1. mustard and other **condiments**
2. a **degenerate** with no morals
3. the **benign** climate of Hawaii
4. ill-behaved and **crass**
5. **steel** yourself against insults
6. **rabid** with anger

Author Online

Joan Bauer
born 1951

Comic Relief From a very young age, Joan Bauer knew she wanted to have a career making people laugh. She remembers having an early fascination with things that were funny—especially the stories told to her by her grandmother, whom she calls her greatest creative influence. Bauer often crafts characters who share the same anxieties she felt as a teenager—apprehension about her parents' divorce, worry about her appearance—and chronicles the relief and inspiration that humor can bring to adverse situations. Describing her motivation to write, Bauer says, "I want to create stories that link life's struggles with laughter."

Accidents and Accolades Bauer's first novel, *Squashed,* began as a screenplay. When she suffered severe injuries in a car accident, however, she found herself unable to meet the tight schedule the film industry demanded. During her long recovery, she turned her screenplay into a prize-winning novel. "The humor in that story kept me going," Bauer explains.

 MORE ABOUT THE AUTHOR
For more on Joan Bauer, visit the **Literature Center** at **ClassZone.com.**

Background

Writing from Experience Like Jill in "Pancakes," Bauer, as a teenager, waited tables in a pancake restaurant. She vividly remembers the Sunday morning when she was the only waitress on duty, frantically trying to attend to all her customers. The memory still haunts her: "I remember the sheer terror of dozens of hungry people looking to me and me alone for breakfast. To this day, whenever I walk into a pancake house, I hyperventilate."

Pancakes

JOAN BAUER

The last thing I wanted to see taped to my bathroom mirror at five-thirty
in the morning was a newspaper article entitled "Are You a Perfectionist?"
But there it was, courtesy of my mother, Ms. Subtlety herself. I was instantly
irritated because Allen Feinman had accused me of perfectionism when he
broke up with me last month. The term he used was "**rabid** perfectionism,"
which I felt was a bit much—but then Allen Feinman had no grip on reality
whatsoever. He was rabidly unaware, if the truth be known, like a **benign**
space creature visiting Earth with no interest in going native. I tore the article
off the mirror; this left tape smudges. Dirty mirrors drove me crazy. I grabbed
10   the bottle of Windex from the closet and cleaned off the gook until the mirror
shined, freed of yellow journalism.[1]

I glowered at the six telltale perfectionist signs in the now crumpled article.

1. Do you have a driving need to control your environment?
2. Do you have a driving need to control the environment of others?
3. Are you miserable when things are out of place?
4. Are your expectations of yourself and others rarely met?
5. Do you believe if something is to be done right, only you are
   the one to do it?
6. Do you often worry about your performance when it is less
20   than perfect?

Number six had particular sting, for it was that very thing that Allen
Feinman had accused me of the day he asked for his green and black
lumberjack shirt back, a truly spectacular shirt that looked a lot more
spectacular on me than it did on him because it brought out the intensity
of my short black hair and my mysterious brown eyes. He had accused me Ⓐ
of numbers one through five as well, but on this last fateful day he said,
"The problem with you, Jill, is that if the least little thing goes wrong, you

ANALYZE VISUALS
What qualities of this
photograph convey the
fast-paced atmosphere
of a busy restaurant?
Explain how these
qualities work together
to convey a specific
mood, or feeling.

rabid (răb′ĭd) *adj.*
uncontrollable; fanatical

benign (bĭ-nīn′) *adj.* good;
kindly

Ⓐ **DRAW CONCLUSIONS**
Reread lines 21–25 to
draw a conclusion about
the narrator's sense of
self. Do you think Jill
has a strong or a weak
self-image? Record your
answer in your chart.

---

1. **yellow journalism:** journalism that exploits or exaggerates the news to create sensations and attract
   readers.

can't handle it. Everything has to follow this impossible path to perfection.
Someday, and I hope it's soon for your sake, you're going to have to settle for
sub-par performance and realize that you're imperfect like the rest of us." He
stormed off like an angry prophet who had just delivered a curse, muttering
that if I was like this at seventeen, imagine what I would be like at thirty.

"Good riddance," I shouted. "I hope you find a messy, inconsiderate
girlfriend who can never find her purse or her car keys, who has no sense of
time, no aptitude for *planning,* and that you spend the rest of your adolescent
years on your hands and knees looking for your contacts!"

I padded down the hall to my bedroom. It was Sunday morning. I was due
at my waitress job at the Ye Olde Pancake House in forty-five minutes. I sat on
my white down quilt, saw the chocolate smudge, quick got up and brushed the
smudge with my spot remover kit that I kept in my top dresser drawer, being
careful to brush the nap against the grain. I put the kit back in the drawer,
refluffed my two white pillows, plucked a dead leaf off my philodendron plant,
and remembered my second to last fight with Allen when he went completely
ballistic at my selfless offer to alphabetize his CD collection with a color-coded
cross-reference guide by subject, title, and artist. **B**

Males.

I put on my Ye Olde Pancake House waitress uniform that I had ironed and
starched the night before: blue, long-sleeved ankle-length dress, white apron,
white-and-blue flowered bonnet. I could have done without the bonnet, but
when you're going for the ye olde look, you have to sacrifice style. I was lucky
to have this job. I got it one week after my parents and I moved to town, got
hired *because* I am a person of order who knows there is a right way and a
wrong way to do things. I replaced a waitress who was a complete disorganized
slob. As Howard Halloran, the owner of the Ye Olde Pancake House, said
to me, "Jill, if you're half as organized and competent as you look, I will die
happy." I smoothed back my short clipped hair, flicked a sesame seed off my
just-manicured nail, and told him that I was. **C**

"I have a system for everything," I assured him. "Menu first, bring water
when you come back to take the order, call it in, bring coffee immediately to
follow. Don't ever let customers wait." Then I mentioned my keen knack for
alphabetizing **condiments,** which was always a bonus, particularly when things
got busy, and how a restaurant storage closet should be properly organized to
take full advantage of the space.

"You're hired," Howard Halloran said reverently, and put me in charge of
opening and setting up the restaurant on Saturday and Sunday mornings, which
is when nine-tenths of all pancakes in the universe are consumed and you don't
want some systemless person at the helm. You want a waitress of grit with a
strategic battle plan that never wavers. Sunday morning in a pancake house is war.

I tied my white apron in a perfect bow across my back, tiptoed past my
parents' bedroom, taking care not to wake them, even though my mother had
taken an insensitive potshot at me without provocation.

It's not like my life had been all that perfect.

B CHARACTER TRAITS
Both the narrator's
mother and her former
boyfriend have accused
her of perfectionism. In
what ways do Jill's own
actions and emotions
illustrate this character
trait?

C GRAMMAR AND STYLE
Reread lines 47–57.
Bauer's use of the **precise
adjectives** *short, clipped,*
and *just-manicured*
provide insight into Jill's
personality.

condiment (kŏn′də-mənt)
n. a sauce, relish, or spice
used to season food

Did I ask to move three times in eighteen months because my father kept getting transferred? Did I ask to attend three high schools since sophomore year? Did I complain about being unfairly uprooted?

Well . . . I did complain a little. . . .

Didn't I figure out a way to handle the pressure? When my very roots were being yanked from familiar soil, I became orderly and organized. I did things in the new towns so that people would like me and want to hire me, would
80 want to be my friends. I baked world-class cookies for high school bake sales, even if it meant staying up till three A.M.; I joined clubs and volunteered for the grunge jobs that no one wanted; I always turned in a spectacular performance and people counted on me to do it. I made everything look easy. People looked up to me, or down, depending—I'm five four. And I sure didn't feel like defending all that success before dawn! **D**

I tiptoed out the back door to my white car (ancient, yet spotless) and headed for work.

Syrup, I tried explaining to Hugo, the busboy, must be poured slowly from the huge cans into the plastic pourers on the tables because if you pour it fast, you
90 can't control the flow and you get syrup everywhere, which never really cleans up. It leaves a sticky residue that always comes back to haunt you. Syrup, I told him, is our enemy, but like Allen Feinman, Hugo was a male without vision. He couldn't anticipate disaster, couldn't cope with forethought and prevention; he let life rule him rather than the other way around, which was why *I* personally filled the syrup containers on Sunday mornings—maple, strawberry, boysenberry, and pecan. **E**

I had just filled the last containers and was putting them on the tables in horizontal rows. I had lined up the juice glasses and coffee mugs for optimal efficiency, which some people who shall remain nameless would call
100 perfectionism, but when the place gets busy, trust me, you want everything at your fingertips or you'll lose control. I never lose control. Hugo had set the back tables and I followed him, straightening the silverware. You'd think he'd been born in a barn. Andy Pappas, the cook, was making the special hash browns with onion and green pepper that people loved.

I **steeled** myself for the hungry Sunday morning mob that would descend in two hours. I always mentally prepared for situations that I knew were going to be stressful—it helped me handle them right. I could see me, Shirl, and Lucy, the other waitresses, serving the crowd, handling the cash register. Usually Howard Halloran took the money, but he was taking a long-needed
110 weekend off since his wife said if he didn't she would sell the place out from under him. I could see myself watching my station like a hawk, keeping the coffee brewing, getting the pancakes delivered hot to the tables. Do it fast, do it right—that was my specialty.

It was seven o'clock. Shirl and Lucy were late, but I knew that Lucy's baby was sick and Shirl was picking her up, so I didn't worry. They'd been late before. I myself was never late. I unlocked the front door, and a few customers

D POINT OF VIEW
Reread lines 72–85. How, if at all, do the thoughts and feelings of the **narrator** change your perception of her? Explain your answer.

E POINT OF VIEW
Reread lines 88–96. Think about the way Jill's point of view affects your impression of Hugo. How might this passage be different if Hugo were the narrator?

steel (stēl) *v.* to make hard or strong

came straggling in with their Sunday newspapers, settling into the booths. Nothing I couldn't handle. Things didn't start getting crazy until around eight-thirty. I had my system.

120   I took orders, walked quickly to the kitchen window. "Four over easy on eight with sausage," I said crisply. "Side of cakes." That was restaurant-speak for four plates of two eggs over easy with sausage and pancakes on the side. Andy tossed his spatula in the air, went to work. The man had total focus. He could have two dozen eggs cooking in front of him and he knew when to flip each one. **F**

A young family came in with three small children; gave them the big table by the window. Got them kid seats, took their order.

"Number three."

That was my waitress number. Andy called the number over the loudspeaker when my order was ready and I went and picked it up. A nice time-efficient

130 system. I walked quickly to the counter (running made the customers nervous), grabbed the eggs, sausage, and pancakes, carried them four up on my left arm to table six, smiled professionally. Everything all right here, folks? Everyone nodded happily and dug in. Everything was always merry and pleasant at the Ye Olde Pancake House. That's why people came. Merry people left big tips.

I checked the ye old wall clock. Seven forty-seven. Still no Shirl or Lucy. They'd never been this late. Allen Feinman had been more than an hour late plenty of times. Allen Feinman didn't care about time—his or anyone else's. I didn't understand the grave problems he had at first; I was so caught up in him—this cute, brainy, funny guy who really seemed to want a shot

140 of discipline. I put in my usual extra effort into the relationship—baked his favorite cookies (cappuccino chip), packed romantic picnics (French bread, brie,² and strawberries), thought about unusual things to do in Coldwater, Michigan, which was quite a challenge, but I went to the library and came up with a list of ten possible side trips around town that we could do for free.

"You're just so *organized*," he would say, which I thought was a true compliment. Later on, I realized, coming from him, it was the darkest insult.

Andy was flipping pancakes on the grill. I scanned my customers to make sure everyone was cared for, turned to dash into

150 the bathroom quickly when a screech of tires sounded in the parking lot. I looked out the window. A lump caught in my throat.

A large tour bus pulled to a grinding halt.

I watched in horror as an army of round, middle-aged women stepped from the bus and headed toward the restaurant like hungry lionesses stalking prey.

It was natural selection—I was as good as dead.

160   "Number three."

---

2. **brie** (brē): a soft French cheese.

F DRAW CONCLUSIONS
Think about Jill's description of Andy. Does he seem like someone Jill would admire? Cite evidence to support your conclusion.

ANALYZE VISUALS
As you examine the photograph below, think about why the photographer chose to take such an extreme close-up of the clock. What effect does this create?

I looked at Andy, who raised his face to heaven.

"Call them," I shrieked. "Call Shirl and Lucy! Tell them to get here!"

Andy reached for the phone.

I turned to the front door as the tour bus women poured in. They were all wearing sweatshirts that read MICHIGAN WOMEN FOR A CLEANER ENVIRONMENT. "A table for sixty-six," said a woman, laughing.

My lungs collapsed. Sixty-six hungry environmentalists. I pointed to a stack of menus, remembering my personal Waitress Rule Number One: Never let a customer know you're out of control.

170   "Sit anywhere," I cooed. "I'll be right with you." **G**

"If you wrote the menu on a blackboard you wouldn't waste paper," one said.

"Number three." I raced back to the kitchen. Pancakes for table eight. I layered the plates on my left arm, plopped butter balls from the ye olde butter urn on the pancakes. Andy said he'd tried Shirl and Lucy and no one answered. At least they were on their way. I raced to table eight. The little girl took one look at her chocolate chip pancakes and burst into tears.

"They're not the little ones," she sobbed.

"Oh, now, precious," said her father, "I'm sure this nice young lady doesn't

180 want you to be disappointed."

I looked at the environmentalists who needed coffee. Life is tough, kid.

"Tell the waitress what you want, precious."

Precious looked at me, loving the control. She scrunched up her dimples, dabbed her tears, and said, "I want the teeny weeny ones, pwease."

"Teeny weeny ones coming up," I chirped, and raced to Andy. "Chocolate silver dollars for the brat on eight," I snarled. "Make them perfect, or someone dies."

"You're very attractive when you get busy," Andy said laughing.

"Shut up."

190   The phone rang. I lunged for it. It was Lucy calling from the hospital. Her baby had a bronchial infection,[3] needed medicine. She couldn't come in, but Shirl was on her way, she should be pulling onto the interstate now.

"Are you all right there, Jill?"

"Of course," I lied. "Take care of that baby. That's the most important thing."

"You're terrific," she said, and hung up.

I'm terrific, I told myself. I can handle this because, as a terrific person, I have an organized system that always works. I grabbed two coffee pots and raced to the tour group, smiling. Always smile. Poured coffee. They'd only get

200 water if they asked. We're so glad you came to see us this morning. Yes, we have many tours pass through, usually we have more waitresses, though. It's a safe bet that any restaurant on this earth has more waitresses than the Ye Olde Pancake House does at this moment. **H**

G DRAW CONCLUSIONS
Consider the difference between what Jill is thinking and what she actually says. What does this indicate about her character? Explain how you came to this conclusion.

H PREDICT
Will Jill be able to handle the crisis at the pancake house? Make a prediction about what will happen as Jill struggles to cope with the teeming crowd of hungry customers.

---

3. **bronchial infection:** an infection of the bronchial tubes—the tubes that connect the windpipe to the lungs.

I took their orders like a shotgunner shooting clay pigeons.

Pull!

Pigs in a blanket.

Steak and fried eggs.

Buttermilk pancakes.

Betsy Ross (buttermilks with strawberry and blueberry compote).

210   Colonial Corn Cakes (Allen Feinman's favorite).

A round-faced woman looked at me, grinning. "Everything looks so good." She sighed. "What do you recommend?"

I recommend that you eat someplace else, ma'am, because I do not have time for this. I looked toward the front of the restaurant; six large men were waiting to be seated. Hugo was pouring syrup quickly into pourers to torture me, sloshing it everywhere. I said, "Everything's great here, ma'am. I'll give you a few seconds to decide." I turned to the woman in the next booth. The round-faced woman grabbed my arm. I don't like being touched by customers.

220   "Just a minute. Well . . . it all looks so good."

"Number three." I glared in Andy's direction. "And number three again."

A cook can make or break you.

The round-faced woman decided on buttermilk pancakes, a daring choice. I ran to the kitchen window. "Hit me," Andy said.

"I'd love to. You're only getting this once. Buttermilks on twelve. Pigs on four, Betsy's on three. Colonials on seven." I threw the rest of the orders at him.

"You have very small handwriting," he said. "That's often the sign of low self-esteem."

230   I put my hand down in one of Hugo's syrup spills, pushed back my bangs with it; felt syrup soak my scalp.

Andy said, "You're only one person, Jill." ❶

I scanned the restaurant—juice glasses askew, hungry people waiting at dirty tables. I could do anything if I worked hard enough. Shirl would be here any minute.

"Waitress, we're out of syrup!" A man held his empty syrup container up. I looked under the counter for the extra maple syrup containers I had cleverly filled, started toward the man, tripped over an environmentalist's foot, which sent the syrup container flying, caught midair, but upside down by a

240   trucker who watched dumbly as syrup oozed onto the floor in a great, sticky glop. I lunged for the syrup container, slid on the spill, felt sugared muck coat my exposed flesh.

"Hugo!" I screamed, pointing at the disaster. "Hot water!"

"Number three."

I moved in a daze as more and more people came. Got the tour bus groups fed and out. Had they mentioned separate checks, one woman asked?

Nooooooooo . . .

❶ **CHARACTER TRAITS**
Think about Andy's character traits and what he says to Jill in line 232. Would you describe Andy as a perfectionist? Why or why not?

Made coffee. More coffee. Told everyone I was the only waitress here, if they were in a hurry, they might want to go someplace else. But no one left. They just kept coming, storming through the restaurant like Cossacks.[4] People were grabbing my arm as I ran by.

"What's your name, babe?" asked a lecherous man.

"*Miss*," I snarled.

"Number three."

"I had a life when I woke up this morning! Everything was in place!"

Buckwheats on table three. The man looked at them. . . . He said, "You call these buckwheats? Buckwheats are supposed to be enormous and hearty." I'm the fall guy for everything that happens in the restaurant. It's my tip that's floating down the river waving bye-bye. I embraced my personal Waitress Rule Number Two: The customer is always right, even if they're dead wrong. I said, "That's the way we do them here, sir," and he said he can't eat them, he can't look at them, he'll have the buttermilks, not knowing the trouble he's caused me. Andy gets sensitive if someone sends the food back—he's an artist, can't handle criticism. You have to lie to him or he slows down. I raced back to the kitchen.

"The man's a **degenerate**," I said to Andy. "He wouldn't know a world-class buckwheat if it jumped in his lap. He doesn't deserve to be in the presence of your cooking."

The phone rang. I lunged for it. It's Shirl calling from someone's car phone on the interstate with impossible news. A trailer truck had jackknifed, spilling soda cans everywhere. There was a five-mile backup. She'd be hours getting to work.

"Are you all right?" Shirl asked.

I looked at the line of cars pulling into the parking lot, the tables bulging with hungry customers, the coffee cups raised in anticipation of being filled, the line at the cash register. I heard a woman say how the restaurant had gone downhill, and the people were looking at me like I was their breakfast savior, like I had all the power and knowing, like I could single-handedly make sure they were happy and fed. And I was ashamed that I couldn't do it, but no one could. **J**

Not even me!

I tore off my ye olde bonnet. "I'm trapped in a pancake house!" I shrieked into the phone, and, like in all sci-fi stories, the connection went dead.

"Number three."

I limped toward him, a shadow of my former self.

"We're out of sausage," Andy said solemnly.

degenerate (dĭ-jĕn′ər-ĭt) *n.* a corrupt or vicious person

J POINT OF VIEW
Reread lines 280–285. Consider how learning Jill's thoughts contributes to your understanding of her character. How would your reaction to Jill be different if you didn't know what Jill was thinking and feeling?

---

4. **Cossacks:** a people of southern Russia, known as fierce cavalrymen.

"Good. It's one less thing to carry." I stood on the counter, put my head back, and screamed, "We're out of sausage and it's not my fault!"

A man at a back table hollered that he needed ketchup for his eggs. I reached down in the K section under the counter. Nothing under K. I got on my knees, hands shaking, rifling through jams, jellies, lingonberries. *Hugo!* I shrieked.

He ran up to me.

"Ketchup, Hugo! Wake up! The sky is falling!"

He pointed to the C section. "Catsup," he said meekly.

300   I was falling down a dark, disorderly tunnel. There was no end in sight. Coffee grounds were in my eyebrows, my hands smelled like used tea bags. I was exhausted, syrup encrusted, I'd had to go to the bathroom for three hours. People were going to get their own coffee—the ultimate defeat for any waitress. I looked at my haggard reflection in the coffee urn. The only consolation was that I wouldn't live till noon.

"Waitress!"

I raced down the aisle to table twelve, seeing the hunted look in my customer's eyes. I wanted to be perfect for every one of you. I wanted you all to like me. I'm sorry I'm not better, not faster. Please don't hate me, I'm only one
310   person, not even a particularly tall person.

"I'm sorry," I said to a table of eight, "but I simply can't do everything!"

I felt a ripple of **crass** laughter in the air. I turned. Allen Feinman had walked in with his parents. **K**

No. . . . Anything but this.

Our eyes met. I could hear the taunts at school, the never-ending retelling of this, my ultimate nightmare.

"Can I help, Jill?" He rolled up his shirtsleeves. Allen Feinman was offering to help.

I grabbed his arm. "Can you work the register?"

320   "Of course." Allen organized the people into a line, made change, smiled. He had such a nice smile. Thanked everyone for their patience, got names on lists.

Mrs. Feinman took off her jacket and asked, "Can I make coffee, dear?"

"Mrs. Feinman, you don't have to—"

"We've always been so fond of you, Jill."

I slapped a bag of decaf in her sainted hands. Mr. Feinman poured himself a cup of coffee and went back to wait in the car.

We whipped that place into shape. All I needed was a little backup. My pockets were bulging with tips, and when Shirl raced in at eleven forty-five, I pushed a little girl aside who'd been waiting patiently by the bathroom door
330   and I lunged toward the toilet stall. Life is tough, kid.

By one-thirty the crowds had cleared. Lucy called—her baby was home and doing better. Allen Feinman and I were sitting at a back table eating pancakes. He said he'd missed me. I said I'd missed him, too. Hugo was speed-pouring boysenberry syrup, spilling everywhere—but somehow it didn't matter anymore. It was good enough.

And that, I realized happily, was fine by me. ❧

crass (krăs) *adj.* crude; unrefined

K PREDICT
Predict what might happen with the arrival of Allen. Give reasons for your prediction.

Comprehension

1. **Recall** List two reasons why Jill is upset at the beginning of the story.

2. **Summarize** What crisis does Jill face in this story, and how is her crisis resolved?

3. **Clarify** What does Jill fear will happen when Allen Feinman shows up at the restaurant? Why does Allen's behavior surprise her?

PENNSYLVANIA STANDARDS

READING STANDARD
B.2.2.1 Identify and analyze point of view

Literary Analysis

4. **Draw Conclusions** Review the chart you made as you read. What drives Jill to constantly strive for perfection? Cite evidence to support your conclusion.

5. **Analyze Character** A **static character** is a character who changes very little, if at all, during the course of a story. A **dynamic character** is a character who changes significantly as a result of his

Jill's Traits at Beginning of Story	Jill's Traits at End of Story
1. Critical of others	
2. Meticulous	

or her experiences. In a chart like the one shown, list the character traits Jill exhibits at the beginning of the story and those she shows signs of as the story ends. Would you describe Jill as a static character or a dynamic character? Cite evidence from the text to support your answer.

6. **Analyze Point of View** With a **first-person narrator,** you see the story unfold through one character's eyes. Would a **third-person omniscient narrator**— a narrator who sees into the minds of all the characters in a story—have presented a more accurate picture of the events? Support your opinion.

7. **Evaluate Character Traits** "Pancakes" clearly points out the downside of **perfectionism,** but it suggests that this trait can be a positive force as well. Citing evidence from the story, decide whether perfectionism is an asset or a fault. Then compare your answer with the ideas you had about perfectionism before you read the story.

Literary Criticism

8. **Author's Style** In an essay titled "Humor, Seriously," Joan Bauer explains that her technique for creating humorous characters involves "layering nutty traits over serious personalities and situations." How effective is Bauer at developing a quirky character who confronts real-life problems in a humorous way? Cite specific dialogue and descriptions from "Pancakes" to explain your opinion.

Vocabulary in Context

VOCABULARY PRACTICE

Write the word from the list that best completes each sentence.

1. Allen Feinman may have been critical of Jill's attitude, but that did not make him a _____.
2. He did not have a _____ temper, nor was he outrageous in other ways.
3. Jill had to _____ herself against panic when she saw Allen walking into the restaurant.
4. Perhaps it was a bit _____ when he snickered at her plight.
5. Seeing each _____ lined up precisely would have made him laugh.
6. Still, the way he and his mother helped Jill out of a jam was quite _____.

WORD LIST

benign

condiment

crass

degenerate

rabid

steel

VOCABULARY IN WRITING

Pretend you are Allen, and write a paragraph giving reasons why Jill should not hate you. Use at least three vocabulary words. Here is one way you might start.

> **EXAMPLE SENTENCE**
>
> I can't understand why Jill has such **rabid**, negative feelings about me.

VOCABULARY STRATEGY: THE LATIN WORD ROOT *ben*

The vocabulary word *benign* contains the Latin root *ben*, which means "well." This root and the related form *bene* are found in a number of English words. To understand the meaning of words with *ben*, use context clues as well as your knowledge of the root.

PENNSYLVANIA STANDARDS

READING STANDARD
A.2.2.2 Use context clues

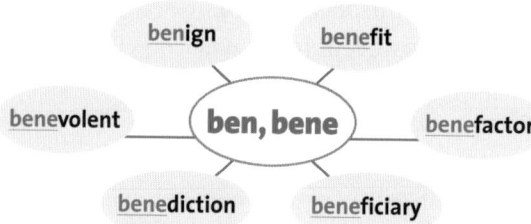

benign   benefit   benevolent   **ben, bene**   benefactor   benediction   beneficiary

PRACTICE Write the word from the word web that best completes each sentence. Use context clues to help you or, if necessary, consult a dictionary.

1. One _____ of a good night's sleep is feeling rested in the morning.
2. The minister offered a _____ at the end of the prayer service.
3. He assured us that his intentions were entirely _____.
4. There was only one _____ listed in Grandma's will.
5. Jennifer's _____ offered to pay her way through college.
6. Most charities involve themselves in _____ works.

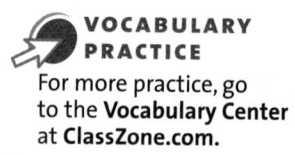

VOCABULARY PRACTICE
For more practice, go to the **Vocabulary Center** at **ClassZone.com.**

Reading-Writing Connection

Demonstrate your understanding of the characters in "Pancakes" by responding to these prompts. Then use **Revision: Grammar and Style** to improve your writing.

WRITING PROMPTS

A. Short Response: Write a Description
Imagine what Allen Feinman thought when he walked into the Ye Olde Pancake House and saw Jill, usually in control, surrounded by chaos. Write **one or two paragraphs** describing the scene from Allen's point of view.

SELF-CHECK

An effective description will . . .
- relate in clear detail what Allen sees
- convey what Allen thinks about Jill's situation

B. Extended Response: Compare Attitudes
Referring to details in the story, write **three to five paragraphs** comparing Jill's and Andy's attitudes toward their work at the restaurant. Make sure to include examples of Jill's **perfectionism**.

A strong comparison will . . .
- compare three aspects of Jill's and Andy's attitudes
- include explicit examples

REVISION: GRAMMAR AND STYLE

ADD SUPPORTING DETAILS Review the **Grammar and Style** note on page 196. Here, Joan Bauer uses **precise adjectives** to convey important physical details that support her characterization of Jill's personality. Revise your responses to the prompts by using similar techniques.

WRITING STANDARD
1.5.11.D.2 Use precise language

1. **Replace vague adjectives with more precise ones.** Some adjectives, such as *nice*, are too general. Instead, use adjectives that say exactly what you mean.

2. **Avoid using too many adjectives.** Too many adjectives can result in overwriting. Choose adjectives carefully, and you will need only a few.

Here are some additional examples of Bauer's use of precise adjectives:

> . . . *He went completely ballistic at my selfless offer to alphabetize his CD collection with a color-coded cross-reference guide.* . . . (lines 43–45)

> *I was exhausted, syrup-encrusted.* . . . (line 302)

Notice how the revisions in red improve the precision of this first draft.

STUDENT MODEL

Jill and Andy both have ~~good~~ *excellent* attitudes toward their jobs. They are both *diligent*, ~~hard~~, ~~fast~~ workers. Jill makes *careful* preparations for Sunday's crowd by arranging all of the condiments neatly in *alphabetical* order. Andy fries his hash browns ahead of time, so that when customers walk in, they are greeted with *an enticing* ~~a nice~~ aroma.

WRITING TOOLS
For prewriting, revision, and editing tools, visit the **Writing Center** at ClassZone.com.

The Necklace
Short Story by Guy de Maupassant

How important is STATUS?

PENNSYLVANIA STANDARDS

READING STANDARDS
A.1.3.1 Make inferences
B.1.1.1.A.1 Evaluate character

KEY IDEA What happens to people who place too much importance on **status,** or the standing they have in a group? In "The Necklace," you'll meet Madame Loisel, an unforgettable character whose pursuit of status costs her more than she could ever have imagined.

QUICKWRITE With a group, generate a list of factors that determine a person's status at your school. Add to or delete from the list that is shown. Then write a short paragraph explaining whether you think status should be determined by these factors.

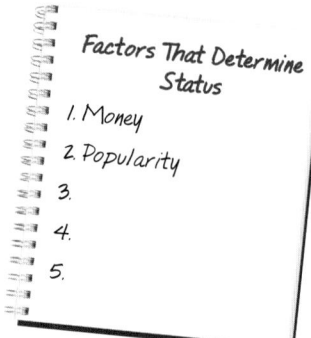

Factors That Determine Status
1. Money
2. Popularity
3.
4.
5.

LITERARY ANALYSIS: CHARACTER MOTIVATION

Motivation is the reason behind a character's behavior; it's what drives a character to think and act in a certain way. For example, a character might want the lead in a school play or perhaps to fit in with popular students. What the character says and does would reflect that desire. As you read "The Necklace," consider how Madame Loisel's words and actions reflect her motivation.

Review: **Point of View**

READING SKILL: MAKE INFERENCES

Instead of directly telling readers what a character is like, a writer often includes details that turn out to be clues to the character's personality. Readers can use these details, along with their own knowledge, to **make inferences,** or logical guesses, about the character's traits, values, and feelings.

In a chart like the one shown, record your inferences as you read, along with the details and experiences that helped you make them.

Details About Characters	Personal Experience	My Inference
Madame Loisel married her husband because she had no other prospects.	People are usually frustrated when they do something simply because they feel they have no choice.	She didn't really choose to marry her husband and probably feels frustrated.

Review: **Predict**

▲ VOCABULARY IN CONTEXT

Restate each phrase, using a different word or words for the boldfaced term.

1. few **prospects** for success
2. talked **incessantly** all day
3. **vexation** about their argument
4. a desperate **pauper**
5. **adulation** from her fans
6. **disconsolate** after losing his dog
7. **aghast** at her rude remarks
8. run the **gamut** of possibilities
9. a prisoner's **privation**
10. messy, with his tie all **askew**

Author Online

Master Storyteller
Guy de Maupassant (gē' də mō-pä-sän') is considered by many to be the greatest French short story writer. He created his characters with remarkable precision, focusing on the exact gesture, feeling, or word that defined each character. As a result, his stories

Guy de Maupassant
1850–1893

seem to be, in his words, "pieces of human existence torn from reality."

Reversal of Fortune Although Maupassant was born into an upper-middle-class family in France, the family fortune ran out early. He was forced to work for a time as a government clerk, the position that the main character's husband holds in "The Necklace." Eventually, though, Maupassant turned to writing and managed to achieve some wealth and fame through his hundreds of stories. Sadly, his success was short-lived. After suffering from mental illness, Maupassant died in a Paris asylum at age 42.

 MORE ABOUT THE AUTHOR
For more on Guy de Maupassant, visit the **Literature Center** at **ClassZone.com.**

Background

Status for Sale This story takes place in Paris in the second half of the 19th century. At the time Maupassant wrote "The Necklace," European societies were divided into upper, middle, and lower classes. Birth usually determined a person's class. Sometimes a man could buy his way into a higher class by acquiring wealth. A woman could improve her status by marrying into a higher class. One obstacle for women was the tradition of the dowry—money or property that a bride's family was expected to give her new husband, but that poorer families could not provide.

THE Necklace

Guy de Maupassant

She was one of those pretty and charming girls, born, as if by an accident of fate, into a family of clerks. With no dowry, no **prospects,** no way of any kind of being met, understood, loved, and married by a man both prosperous and famous, she was finally married to a minor clerk in the Ministry of Education.

She dressed plainly because she could not afford fine clothes, but was as unhappy as a woman who has come down in the world; for women have no family rank or social class. With them, beauty, grace, and charm take the place of birth and breeding. Their natural poise, their instinctive good taste, and their mental cleverness are the sole guiding principles which make daughters
10 of the common people the equals of ladies in high society.

She grieved **incessantly,** feeling that she had been born for all the little niceties and luxuries of living. She grieved over the shabbiness of her apartment, the dinginess of the walls, the worn-out appearance of the chairs, the ugliness of the draperies. All these things, which another woman of her class would not even have noticed, gnawed at her and made her furious. The sight of the little Breton[1] girl who did her humble housework roused in her disconsolate regrets and wild daydreams. She would dream of silent chambers, draped with Oriental tapestries and lighted by tall bronze floor lamps, and of two handsome butlers in knee breeches, who, drowsy from the heavy warmth
20 cast by the central stove, dozed in large overstuffed armchairs. **A**

ANALYZE VISUALS
Examine the portrait on page 209. What social class do you think the woman belongs to? Identify the details that helped you draw this **inference.**

prospects (prŏs'pĕkts') *n.* chances or possibilities, especially for financial success

incessantly (ĭn-sĕs'ənt-lē) *adv.* without interruption; continuously

A **MAKE INFERENCES**
Consider what you learn about Madame Loisel's situation in lines 11–20. Why do you think she feels the way she does?

---

1. **Breton** (brĕt'n): from Brittany, a region in northwestern France.

Louise Augusta, Queen of Prussia (1801), Marie Louise Élisabeth Vigée LeBrun. Pastel, 51 cm × 41 cm. Stiftung Preussische Schlösser und Gärten Berlin-Brandenburg. Photo by J. P. Anders.

She would dream of great reception halls hung with old silks, of fine furniture filled with priceless curios, and of small, stylish, scented sitting rooms just right for the four o'clock chat with intimate friends, with distinguished and sought-after men whose attention every woman envies and longs to attract.

30 When dining at the round table, covered for the third day with the same cloth, opposite her husband, who would raise the cover of the soup tureen, declaring delightedly, "Ah! A good stew! There's nothing I like better . . ." she would dream of fashionable dinner parties, of gleaming silverware, of tapestries making the walls alive with characters out of history and strange birds in a fairyland forest; she would dream of delicious dishes served on wonderful china, of gallant compliments whispered and listened to with a sphinxlike[2] smile as one eats the rosy flesh of a trout or nibbles at the wings of a grouse.

She had no evening clothes, no jewels, nothing. But those were the things she wanted; she felt that was the kind of life for her. She so much longed to please, be envied, be fascinating and sought after. **B**

She had a well-to-do friend, a classmate of convent-school days whom she would no longer go to see, simply because she would feel so distressed on 40 returning home. And she would weep for days on end from **vexation,** regret, despair, and anguish.

Then one evening, her husband came home proudly holding out a large envelope.

"Look," he said, "I've got something for you."

She excitedly tore open the envelope and pulled out a printed card bearing these words:

"The Minister of Education and Mme. Georges Ramponneau[3] beg M. and Mme. Loisel[4] to do them the honor of attending an evening reception at the Ministerial Mansion on Friday, January 18."

50 Instead of being delighted, as her husband had hoped, she scornfully tossed the invitation on the table, murmuring, "What good is that to me?"

"But, my dear, I thought you'd be thrilled to death. You never get a chance to go out, and this is a real affair, a wonderful one! I had an awful time getting a card. Everybody wants one; it's much sought after, and not many clerks have a chance at one. You'll see all the most important people there."

B MAKE INFERENCES
Think about Madame Loisel's dreams and desires up to this point. What can you infer about her values?

vexation (vĕk-sā'shən) *n.* irritation; annoyance

---

2. **sphinxlike:** mysterious (from the Greek myth of the sphinx, a winged creature that killed those who could not answer its riddle).

3. **Mme. Georges Ramponneau** (zhôrzh' rän-pô-nō'): *Mme.* is an abbreviation for *Madame* (mə-däm'), a title of courtesy for a French married woman.

4. **M. and Mme. Loisel** (lwä-zĕl'): *M.* is an abbreviation for *Monsieur* (mə-syœ'), a title of courtesy for a Frenchman.

A Paris Street, Rain (1877), Gustave Caillebotte. Oil on canvas. The Art Institute of Chicago.
© Erich Lessing/Art Resource, New York.

She gave him an irritated glance and burst out impatiently, "What do you think I have to go in?"

He hadn't given that a thought. He stammered, "Why, the dress you wear when we go to the theater. That looks quite nice, I think."

60 He stopped talking, dazed and distracted to see his wife burst out weeping. Two large tears slowly rolled from the corners of her eyes to the corners of her mouth; he gasped, "Why, what's the matter? What's the trouble?"

By sheer will power she overcame her outburst and answered in a calm voice while wiping the tears from her wet cheeks:

"Oh, nothing. Only I don't have an evening dress and therefore I can't go to that affair. Give the card to some friend at the office whose wife can dress better than I can."

He was stunned. He resumed. "Let's see, Mathilde.[5] How much would a suitable outfit cost—one you could wear for other affairs too—something 70 very simple?"

She thought it over for several seconds, going over her allowance and thinking also of the amount she could ask for without bringing an immediate refusal and an exclamation of dismay from the thrifty clerk.

Finally, she answered hesitatingly, "I'm not sure exactly, but I think with four hundred francs[6] I could manage it."

---

5. **Mathilde** (mä-tēld').

6. **francs** (frăngks): The franc was the basic monetary unit of France.

He turned a bit pale, for he had set aside just that amount to buy a rifle so that, the following summer, he could join some friends who were getting up a group to shoot larks on the plain near Nanterre.[7]

However, he said, "All right. I'll give you four hundred francs. But try to get a nice dress." **C**

As the day of the party approached, Mme. Loisel seemed sad, moody, and ill at ease. Her outfit was ready, however. Her husband said to her one evening, "What's the matter? You've been all out of sorts for three days."

And she answered, "It's embarrassing not to have a jewel or a gem—nothing to wear on my dress. I'll look like a **pauper:** I'd almost rather not go to that party."

He answered, "Why not wear some flowers? They're very fashionable this season. For ten francs you can get two or three gorgeous roses."

She wasn't at all convinced. "No. . . . There's nothing more humiliating than to look poor among a lot of rich women."

But her husband exclaimed, "My, but you're silly! Go see your friend Mme. Forestier[8] and ask her to lend you some jewelry. You and she know each other well enough for you to do that."

She gave a cry of joy, "Why, that's so! I hadn't thought of it."

The next day she paid her friend a visit and told her of her predicament.

Mme. Forestier went toward a large closet with mirrored doors, took out a large jewel box, brought it over, opened it, and said to Mme. Loisel, "Pick something out, my dear."

At first her eyes noted some bracelets, then a pearl necklace, then a Venetian cross, gold and gems, of marvelous workmanship. She tried on these adornments in front of the mirror, but hesitated, unable to decide which to part with and put back. She kept on asking, "Haven't you something else?"

"Oh, yes, keep on looking. I don't know just what you'd like."

All at once she found, in a black satin box, a superb diamond necklace; and her pulse beat faster with longing. Her hands trembled as she took it up. Clasping it around her throat, outside her high-necked dress, she stood in ecstasy looking at her reflection.

Then she asked, hesitatingly, pleading, "Could I borrow that, just that and nothing else?"

"Why, of course."

She threw her arms around her friend, kissed her warmly, and fled with her treasure. **D**

The day of the party arrived. Mme. Loisel was a sensation. She was the prettiest one there, fashionable, gracious, smiling, and wild with joy. All the

C CHARACTER MOTIVATION
What do you think is Monsieur Loisel's motivation for giving the money to his wife? Explain your answer.

pauper (pô′pər) *n.* a poor person, especially one who depends on public charity

D CHARACTER MOTIVATION
Why does Madame Loisel choose the diamond necklace? Explain her motivation.

---

7. **Nanterre** (näN-tĕr′): a city of north central France.

8. **Forestier** (fô-rĕs tyā′).

men turned to look at her, asked who she was, begged to be introduced. All the Cabinet officials wanted to waltz with her. The minister took notice of her.

She danced madly, wildly, drunk with pleasure, giving no thought to anything in the triumph of her beauty, the pride of her success, in a kind of happy cloud composed of all the **adulation,** of all the admiring glances, of all the awakened longings, of a sense of complete victory that is so sweet to a woman's heart.

She left around four o'clock in the morning. Her husband, since midnight, had been dozing in a small empty sitting room with three other gentlemen whose wives were having too good a time.

He threw over her shoulders the wraps he had brought for going home, modest garments of everyday life whose shabbiness clashed with the stylishness of her evening clothes. She felt this and longed to escape, unseen by the other women who were draped in expensive furs.

120

adulation (ăj′ə-lā′shən)
n. excessive praise or flattery

ANALYZE VISUALS
In your opinion, how well does this painting reflect the **setting** of the party? Describe the details that influenced your opinion.

The Ball, Victor Gabriel Gilbert. © Christie's Images/Corbis.

130　　Loisel held her back.

"Hold on! You'll catch cold outside. I'll call a cab."

But she wouldn't listen to him and went rapidly down the stairs. When they were on the street, they didn't find a carriage; and they set out to hunt for one, hailing drivers whom they saw going by at a distance.

They walked toward the Seine,[9] **disconsolate** and shivering. Finally on the docks they found one of those carriages that one sees in Paris only after nightfall, as if they were ashamed to show their drabness during daylight hours.

It dropped them at their door in the Rue des Martyrs,[10] and they climbed
140　wearily up to their apartment. For her, it was all over. For him, there was the thought that he would have to be at the Ministry at ten o'clock. **E**

Before the mirror, she let the wraps fall from her shoulders to see herself once again in all her glory. Suddenly she gave a cry. The necklace was gone. **F**

Her husband, already half-undressed, said, "What's the trouble?"

She turned toward him despairingly, "I . . . I . . . I don't have Mme. Forestier's necklace."

"What! You can't mean it! It's impossible!"

They hunted everywhere, through the folds of the dress, through the folds of the coat, in the pockets. They found nothing.

150　He asked, "Are you sure you had it when leaving the dance?"

"Yes, I felt it when I was in the hall of the Ministry."

"But if you had lost it on the street, we'd have heard it drop. It must be in the cab."

"Yes. Quite likely. Did you get its number?"

"No. Didn't you notice it either?"

"No."

They looked at each other **aghast**. Finally Loisel got dressed again.

"I'll retrace our steps on foot," he said, "to see if I can find it."

And he went out. She remained in her evening clothes, without the strength
160　to go to bed, slumped in a chair in the unheated room, her mind a blank.

Her husband came in about seven o'clock. He had had no luck.

He went to the police station, to the newspapers to post a reward, to the cab companies, everywhere the slightest hope drove him.

That evening Loisel returned, pale, his face lined; still he had learned nothing.

"We'll have to write your friend," he said, "to tell her you have broken the catch and are having it repaired. That will give us a little time to turn around."

She wrote to his dictation.

---

disconsolate
(dĭs-kŏn'sə-lĭt) *adj.*
extremely depressed
or dejected

E POINT OF VIEW
What is the impact of
having the narrator
explain what Madame
Loisel and her husband
each think?

F GRAMMAR AND STYLE
Reread lines 142–143.
Notice how Maupassant
varies his sentence
beginnings by using
words and phrases such
as *before the mirror*
and *suddenly*.

aghast (ə-găst') *adj.*
filled with shock
or horror

---

9. **Seine** (sĕn): the principal river of Paris.

10. **Rue des Martyrs** (rü' dā mär-tēr'): a street in Paris.

At the end of a week, they had given up all hope.

And Loisel, looking five years older, declared, "We must take steps to replace that piece of jewelry."

The next day they took the case to the jeweler whose name they found inside. He consulted his records. "I didn't sell that necklace, madame," he said. "I only supplied the case."

Then they went from one jeweler to another hunting for a similar necklace, going over their recollections, both sick with despair and anxiety.

They found, in a shop in Palais Royal, a string of diamonds which seemed exactly like the one they were seeking. It was priced at forty thousand francs. They could get it for thirty-six.

They asked the jeweler to hold it for them for three days. And they reached an agreement that he would take it back for thirty-four thousand if the lost one was found before the end of February.

Loisel had eighteen thousand francs he had inherited from his father. He would borrow the rest.

He went about raising the money, asking a thousand francs from one, four hundred from another, a hundred here, sixty there. He signed notes, made ruinous deals, did business with loan sharks, ran the whole **gamut** of moneylenders. He compromised the rest of his life, risked his signature without knowing if he'd be able to honor it, and then, terrified by the outlook for the future, by the blackness of despair about to close around him, by the prospect of all the **privations** of the body and tortures of the spirit, he went to claim the new necklace with the thirty-six thousand francs which he placed on the counter of the shopkeeper. **G**

When Mme. Loisel took the necklace back, Mme. Forestier said to her frostily, "You should have brought it back sooner; I might have needed it."

She didn't open the case, an action her friend was afraid of. If she had noticed the substitution, what would she have thought? What would she have said? Would she have thought her a thief?

Mme. Loisel experienced the horrible life the needy live. She played her part, however, with sudden heroism. That frightful debt had to be paid. She would pay it. She dismissed her maid; they rented a garret under the eaves.

She learned to do the heavy housework, to perform the hateful duties of cooking. She washed dishes, wearing down her shell-pink nails scouring the grease from pots and pans; she scrubbed dirty linen, shirts, and cleaning rags which she hung on a line to dry; she took the garbage down to the street each morning and brought up water, stopping on each landing to get her breath. And, clad like a peasant woman, basket on arm, guarding sou[11] by sou her scanty allowance, she bargained with the fruit dealers, the grocer, the butcher, and was insulted by them.

gamut (găm'ət) *n.* an entire range or series

privation (prī-vā'shən) *n.* the lack of a basic necessity or a comfort of life

G CHARACTER MOTIVATION
Consider why the Loisels don't tell Mathilde's friend the truth. What motivates them to go into such debt?

---

11. **sou** (sōō): a French coin of small value.

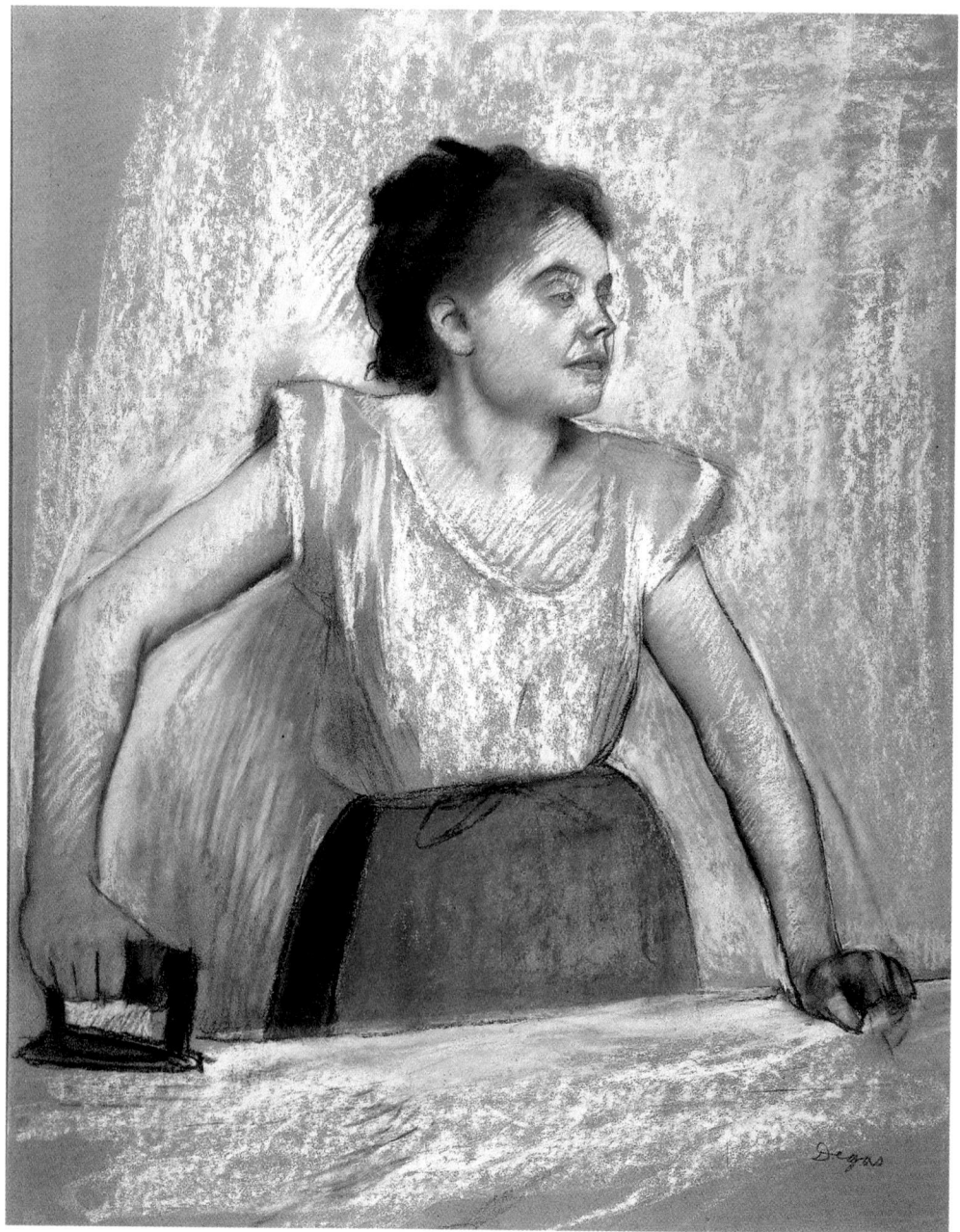

The Laundress (1869), Edgar Degas. Pastel, white crayon, and charcoal. Musée d´Orsay, Paris. Photo © Jean Schormans/Réunion des Musées Nationaux/Art Resource, New York.

ANALYZE VISUALS
Compare this artwork with the one shown on page 209. How do the details and styles of each reflect the changes that Madame Loisel endures?

210   Each month notes had to be paid, and others renewed to give more time.
  Her husband labored evenings to balance a tradesman's accounts, and at night, often, he copied documents at five sous a page.
  And this went on for ten years.
  Finally, all was paid back, everything including the exorbitant rates of the loan sharks and accumulated compound interest.

Mme. Loisel appeared an old woman, now. She became heavy, rough, harsh, like one of the poor. Her hair untended, her skirts **askew,** her hands red, her voice shrill, she even slopped water on her floors and scrubbed them herself. But, sometimes, while her husband was at work, she would sit near the window and think of that long-ago evening when, at the dance, she had been so beautiful and admired.

What would have happened if she had not lost that necklace? Who knows? Who can say? How strange and unpredictable life is! How little there is between happiness and misery!

Then one Sunday when she had gone for a walk on the Champs Élysées[12] to relax a bit from the week's labors, she suddenly noticed a woman strolling with a child. It was Mme. Forestier, still young-looking; still beautiful, still charming. **H**

Mme. Loisel felt a rush of emotion. Should she speak to her? Of course. And now that everything was paid off, she would tell her the whole story. Why not?

She went toward her. "Hello, Jeanne."

The other, not recognizing her, showed astonishment at being spoken to so familiarly by this common person. She stammered. "But . . . madame . . . I don't recognize . . . You must be mistaken."

"No, I'm Mathilde Loisel."

Her friend gave a cry, "Oh, my poor Mathilde, how you've changed!"

"Yes, I've had a hard time since last seeing you. And plenty of misfortunes— and all on account of you!" **I**

"Of me . . . How do you mean?"

"Do you remember that diamond necklace you loaned me to wear to the dance at the Ministry?"

"Yes, but what about it?"

"Well, I lost it."

"You lost it! But you returned it."

"I brought you another just like it. And we've been paying for it for ten years now. You can imagine that wasn't easy for us who had nothing. Well, it's over now, and I am glad of it."

Mme. Forestier stopped short, "You mean to say you bought a diamond necklace to replace mine?"

"Yes. You never noticed, then? They were quite alike."

And she smiled with proud and simple joy.

Mme. Forestier, quite overcome, clasped her by the hands. "Oh, my poor Mathilde. But mine was only paste.[13] Why, at most it was worth only five hundred francs!" ❧

askew (ə-skyoō′) *adj.* crooked; to one side

H PREDICT
Do you think Madame Loisel will tell her friend the truth? Why or why not?

I CHARACTER MOTIVATION
Think about what motivates Madame Loisel to approach her friend. Does this action surprise you, given Madame Loisel's earlier thoughts and actions? Explain your response.

---

12. **Champs Élysées** (shäɴ zā-lē-zā′): a famous wide street in Paris.

13. **paste:** a hard, glassy material used in making imitation gems.

Comprehension

1. **Recall** Why is Madame Loisel discontented at the beginning of the story?

2. **Recall** What causes the change in the Loisels' financial situation?

3. **Summarize** What twist occurs at the end of the story?

Literary Analysis

4. **Make Inferences** Review the inferences you wrote down during reading. How much do you think Madame Loisel has changed by the time the story ends? Explain your answer.

5. **Analyze Irony** The most common kind of irony is **situational irony,** which occurs when a character—or the reader—expects one thing to happen but something entirely different occurs. What is ironic about the ending of "The Necklace"?

6. **Compare and Contrast Characters** Does Monsieur Loisel long for **status** as desperately as his wife does? Cite evidence to support your opinions.

7. **Interpret Motivation** Consider what you know about the characters' feelings and goals. For each action described in the chart shown, decide on the character's motivation.

Action	Motivation
Mme. Loisel weeps when she receives the invitation. (line 60)	
Mme. Loisel borrows jewelry rather than wear flowers. (line 109)	
Monsieur Loisel advises his wife not to tell her friend about the lost necklace. (line 166–167)	

8. **Analyze Point of View** For most of "The Necklace," the narrator focuses on Madame Loisel's thoughts and feelings. However, since this story is told from the **third-person omniscient point of view,** the narrator also relays the thoughts of Monsieur Loisel. Did knowing Monsieur Loisel's inner thoughts affect your opinion of Madame Loisel? Explain your answer.

9. **Evaluate** Reread lines 199–201. Do you agree that Madame Loisel shows heroism in paying off her debt? Find examples to support your opinion.

Literary Criticism

10. **Critical Interpretations** The literary critic Edward D. Sullivan declared that "The Necklace" is not just a story pointing to a moral, such as "Honesty is the best policy," but a story showing that in people's lives "blind chance rules." Do you agree or disagree with Sullivan's argument? Cite evidence to support your opinion.

PENNSYLVANIA STANDARDS

READING STANDARD
A.1.3.1 Make inferences

Vocabulary in Context

VOCABULARY PRACTICE

For each item, choose the word from the list that relates in meaning.

1. dejected, miserable, low
2. irritation, displeasure, anger
3. opportunities, possibilities, chances
4. range, extent, scope
5. praise, worship, adoration
6. horrified, dismayed, appalled
7. loss, damage, hardship
8. slanting, sideways, crooked
9. beggar, debtor, have-not
10. steadily, ceaselessly, perpetually

WORD LIST

adulation
aghast
askew
disconsolate
gamut
incessantly
pauper
privation
prospects
vexation

VOCABULARY IN WRITING

Use each vocabulary word in a sentence of your own to describe one of the characters in "The Necklace." Here is an example.

> **EXAMPLE SENTENCE**
>
> *Madame Loisel ignores compliments from her husband, but she seeks* **adulation** *from wealthy acquaintances.*

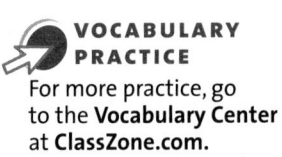

PENNSYLVANIA STANDARDS

READING STANDARD
A.1.2 Apply word recognition skills

VOCABULARY STRATEGY: THE LATIN WORD ROOT *spec*

The word *prospect* contains the Latin root *spec* or *spect,* which means "look" or "see." How is the root reflected in the meanings of the other words in the word family shown on the right?

PRACTICE This chart lists two additional roots and example words from "The Necklace." Use the roots and context clues to figure out the meanings of the underlined words.

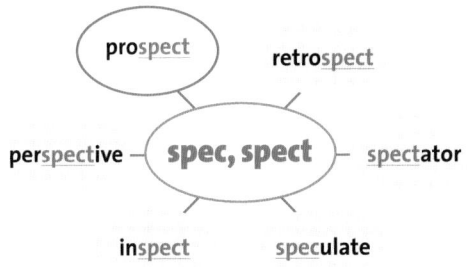

Root	Meaning	Example
dict = speak		**dictation** (line 168)
grat = thanks		**gracious** (line 115)

1. The courtroom was silent as the judge announced the <u>verdict</u>.
2. The actress expressed <u>gratitude</u> in her acceptance speech.
3. The confused defendant <u>contradicted</u> his earlier testimony.
4. What an <u>ingrate</u>! Sam didn't acknowledge our gift.
5. The subjects were afraid to defy the king's <u>edict</u>.

VOCABULARY PRACTICE
For more practice, go to the **Vocabulary Center** at **ClassZone.com.**

Reading-Writing Connection

Increase your understanding of "The Necklace" by responding to these prompts. Then use **Revision: Grammar and Style** to improve your writing.

WRITING PROMPTS	SELF-CHECK
A. Short Response: Analyze Characters How would you characterize the relationship between Monsieur and Madame Loisel at the beginning of the story? Using examples from the text, write **one or two paragraphs** to describe their marriage. Include details that show how they treat each other.	*A strong description will . . .* • list three characteristics of their relationship • cite specific details that support the conclusions
B. Extended Response: Write Across Texts Is it possible for a **status**-conscious person today to fall into the same financial situation as the Loisels? Use "The Necklace" and "Spending Spree" on page 221 to write a **three-to-five-paragraph response.**	*A successful response will . . .* • clearly state an opinion in the introduction • provide examples from the story, the article, and real life to support the opinion

REVISION: GRAMMAR AND STYLE

PENNSYLVANIA STANDARDS

WRITING STANDARD
1.5.11.D.1 Use different types and lengths of sentences

VARY SENTENCE BEGINNINGS Review the **Grammar and Style** note on page 214. Like Maupassant, you can vary your sentence beginnings to add interest to your writing. Revise your responses to the prompts by employing these techniques:

1. **Avoid using too many pronouns and articles.** Don't fall into the trap of beginning all your sentences with the words *he, she, it,* and *the.*

2. **Use words, phrases, and clauses that let readers know when, where, or how.** By using a variety of words, phrases, and clauses, Maupassant added descriptive details and avoided repetitive beginnings. Here are two examples:

   Finally, she answered hesitatingly . . . (line 74)

   As the day of the party approached, Mme. Loisel seemed sad. . . . (line 81)

Notice how the revisions in red improve the rhythm and flow of this first draft.

> **STUDENT MODEL**
> *Before the necklace is lost,*
> ᴧThe Loisels do not have a good marriage. Madame Loisel treats her husband
>   *Without a care for his feelings,* *At the party,*
> poorly. ᴧ~~S~~he frequently snaps at him. ᴧ~~S~~he ignores him ⊙ ~~at the party.~~
> *However,* *Sensitive to her needs,*
> ᴧ~~H~~e seems to always dote on her. ᴧ~~H~~e does everything she wants.

WRITING TOOLS
For prewriting, revision, and editing tools, visit the **Writing Center** at ClassZone.com.

MAGAZINE ARTICLE In "The Necklace," the Loisels borrow and buy their way into years of debt. Unfortunately, in their desire to achieve status, some teens today are falling into this same cycle.

$pending $pree

Been shopping lately? No matter which income bracket teens fall into, their general attitude stays the same: spend, don't save. On average, teens spend $100 a week on entertainment, clothing, and food. Perhaps this is why they're becoming the new target group of credit card marketers.

Pay or Play

While many teens might find the lure of a credit card to be irresistible, spending comes with a price. More and more often, young people are joining the ranks of those in debt.

What's the cause for this? Teens are often pressured to wear the same clothes, buy the same CDs, and own the same products. The credit card industry feeds off of this need to consume by offering credit cards to those who are barely out of high school.

Since most 18-year-olds are still unfamiliar with handling their personal finances, many don't pay their credit card bills on time, if at all. The result is a rapid build-up of debt.

Incentives for $aving

To help curb this financial downward spiral, one city has even established a "financial literacy" program. The Private Industry Council of Milwaukee County launched the pilot program, aimed at central-city teens. The training that

teens receive through the program encourages them to save and instructs them in how to open a bank account.

Payoff

Learning to handle money responsibly early on can reap great rewards down the line. Not only does it contribute to a person's peace of mind to know that he or she is financially secure, but it also helps to establish a good credit record. So count your pennies, and avoid becoming one of the many Americans who are currently in debt.

Convenient or Costly? The chart shows how credit card charges can accumulate, assuming you miss three monthly payments.

CD PLAYER	$40.00
CLOTHES	$100.00
DVDs	$28.00
Original total due:	$168.00
Credit card late fees and finance charges:	➕ $83.00
Credit card total due:	＝ $251.00

Hamadi

Short Story by Naomi Shihab Nye

What makes someone REMARKABLE?

PENNSYLVANIA STANDARDS

READING STANDARDS
A.1.4.1 Identify and explain main ideas and relevant supporting details
B.2.2.1 Identify and analyze point of view

KEY IDEA Whether it's an outrageous sense of humor or an aura of quiet confidence, some people have qualities that are hard not to notice. Susan, the main character in the short story "Hamadi," has a friend with a unique way of looking at the world. Susan finds Hamadi **remarkable;** she notices him because of his extraordinary personality.

PRESENT What makes individuals stand out to you? What traits give them striking personalities? Pick one remarkable person and list his or her traits. Then "introduce" this person to a classmate in a way that makes it clear why the individual is so extraordinary.

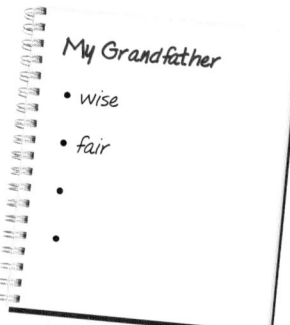

My Grandfather
• wise
• fair
•
•

LITERARY ANALYSIS: THIRD-PERSON LIMITED POINT OF VIEW

"Hamadi" is told from a **third-person limited point of view**. The narrator is an outside voice that tells what only one character thinks, feels, and observes. The narrator of "Hamadi" zeroes in on the thoughts and feelings of a high school freshman named Susan. As you read "Hamadi," pay attention to what the narrator reveals about Susan, and consider how this affects your perception of her.

READING STRATEGY: MONITOR

When you read, pause every few minutes to check, or **monitor**, how well you are understanding the story.

- **Visualize:** Picture characters, events, and settings.
- **Clarify:** Stop now and then to review what you understand.
- **Question:** Ask questions about the events and characters.
- **Predict:** Look for hints of what might happen next.
- **Connect:** Compare events with your own experiences.

As you read "Hamadi," use the "Monitor" annotations to help you gain insight into the characters.

Review: **Make Inferences**

▲ VOCABULARY IN CONTEXT

Which of the following words might be used to describe

1. an ornate piece of furniture?
2. an ancient language?
3. an empty room?
4. a subtle joke?
5. a meal after a long journey?

WORD LIST		
anthem	lavish	sustenance
archaic	spartan	wry
expansive	surrogate	

Author Online

More Than One Way to See
Naomi Shihab Nye was born in St. Louis, Missouri. Like Susan, the main character in "Hamadi," Nye grew up in an Arab-American family. In 1966 her family moved to the Middle East, and Nye spent her freshman year at a high school in East Jerusalem, then a part

Naomi Shihab Nye born 1952

of Jordan. Nye says her year in the Middle East changed her irreversibly. "This is one of the best things about growing up in a mixed family or community," she says. "You never think only one way of doing or seeing anything is right."

A Writer of Vision Best known as a poet, Nye is also a short story writer, essayist, children's book author, novelist, and songwriter. In all of her work, Nye honors diverse viewpoints and celebrates the mixing of cultures. Literature, she believes, gives us "insight into all the secret territories of the human spirit."

 MORE ABOUT THE AUTHOR
For more on Naomi Shihab Nye, visit the **Literature Center** at **ClassZone.com.**

Background

Seeking Refuge In this story, both the main character's father and her friend Hamadi come from a region torn by conflict. Hamadi is from Lebanon, a country devastated by a 16-year civil war. Susan's father is Palestinian. In 1947, the United Nations proposed a plan to partition what was then Palestine to create the state of Israel, a homeland for the Jewish people. More than 50 years later, the conflict between Israelis and Palestinians is still unresolved and often marked by violence. These situations have created millions of refugees—people who have fled their native lands in search of shelter and protection.

HAMADI

Naomi Shihab Nye

> *"It takes two of us to discover truth:*
> *one to utter it and one to understand it."*
>
> **KAHLIL GIBRAN,** *Sand and Foam*

Susan didn't really feel interested in Saleh Hamadi[1] until she was a freshman in high school carrying a thousand questions around. Why this way? Why not another way? Who said so and why can't I say something else? Those brittle women at school in the counselor's office treated the world as if it were a yardstick and they had a tight hold of both ends.

Sometimes Susan felt polite with them, sorting attendance cards during her free period, listening to them gab about fingernail polish and television. And other times she felt she could run out of the building yelling. That's when she daydreamed about Saleh Hamadi, who had nothing to do with any of
10 it. Maybe she thought of him as escape, the way she used to think about the Sphinx at Giza[2] when she was younger. She would picture the golden Sphinx sitting quietly in the desert with sand blowing around its face, never changing its expression. She would think of its **wry,** slightly crooked mouth and how her grandmother looked a little like that as she waited for her bread to bake in the old village north of Jerusalem.[3] Susan's family had lived in Jerusalem for three years before she was ten and drove out to see her grandmother every weekend. They would find her patting fresh dough between her hands, or pressing cakes of dough onto the black rocks in the *taboon*, the rounded old oven outdoors. Sometimes she moved her lips as she worked. Was she praying? Singing a secret
20 song? Susan had never seen her grandmother rushing. **Ⓐ**

Now that she was fourteen, she took long walks in America with her father down by the drainage ditch at the end of their street. Pecan trees shaded the

---

ANALYZE VISUALS
Susan daydreams about Saleh Hamadi to escape from the everyday. What aspects of this painting have a dreamlike quality?

wry (rī) *adj.* dryly humorous, often with a bit of irony

Ⓐ **MONITOR**
Reread lines 8–20. As you read, **visualize** the scene Susan remembers. Describe Susan's grandmother's **traits.**

---

1. **Saleh Hamadi** (sä´lĕкн hä-mä´dē).
2. **Sphinx at Giza** (gē´zə): a huge ancient statue with a man's head and a lion's body, near the city of Giza in northern Egypt.
3. **Jerusalem:** the capital of Israel and a holy city for Jews, Christians, and Muslims.

Inspiration (1994), Daniel Nevins.
Oil, acrylic, and collage on wood, 6.6˝ × 9.0˝.
Private collection. © Daniel Nevins/SuperStock.

path. She tried to get him to tell stories about his childhood in Palestine.[4] She didn't want him to forget anything. She helped her American mother complete tedious kitchen tasks without complaining—rolling grape leaves around their lemony rice stuffing, scrubbing carrots for the roaring juicer. Some evenings when the soft Texas twilight pulled them all outside, she thought of her faraway grandmother and said, "Let's go see Saleh Hamadi. Wouldn't he like some of that cheese pie Mom made?" And they would wrap a slice of pie and drive downtown. Somehow he felt like a good substitute for a grandmother, even though he was a man. **B**

Usually Hamadi was wearing a white shirt, shiny black tie, and a jacket that reminded Susan of the earth's surface just above the treeline on a mountain—thin, somehow purified. He would raise his hands high before giving advice.

"It is good to drink a tall glass of water every morning upon arising!" If anyone doubted this, he would shake his head. "Oh Susan, Susan, Susan," he would say.

He did not like to sit down, but he wanted everyone else to sit down. He made Susan sit on the wobbly chair beside the desk and he made her father or mother sit in the saggy center of the bed. He told them people should eat six small meals a day.

They visited him on the sixth floor of the Traveler's Hotel, where he had lived so long nobody could remember him ever traveling. Susan's father used to remind him of the apartments available over the Victory Cleaners, next to the park with the fizzy pink fountain, but Hamadi would shake his head, pinching kisses at his **spartan** room. "A white handkerchief spread across a tabletop, my two extra shoes lined by the wall, this spells 'home' to me, this says 'mi casa.' What more do I need?"

Hamadi liked to use Spanish words. They made him feel **expansive,** worldly. He'd learned them when he worked at the fruits and vegetables warehouse on Zarzamora[5] Street, marking off crates of apples and avocados on a long white pad. Occasionally he would speak Arabic, his own first language, with Susan's father and uncles, but he said it made him feel too sad, as if his mother might step into the room at any minute, her arms laden with fresh mint leaves. He had come to the United States on a boat when he was eighteen years old and he had never been married. "I married books," he said. "I married the wide horizon."

"What is he to us?" Susan used to ask her father. "He's not a relative, right? How did we meet him to begin with?"

Susan's father couldn't remember. "I think we just drifted together. Maybe we met at your uncle Hani's house. Maybe that old Maronite priest[6] who used to cry after every service introduced us. The priest once shared an apartment

B POINT OF VIEW
Reread lines 21–31. What important **character traits** of Susan's does the narrator reveal in this paragraph?

spartan (spär′tn) *adj.* simple, plain, and frugal

expansive (ĭk-spăn′sĭv) *adj.* outgoing; showing feelings openly and freely

---

4. **Palestine:** a historical region at the east end of the Mediterranean Sea.

5. **Zarzamora** (zär′zə-môr′ə).

6. **Maronite priest:** The Maronites are a Christian group allied with the Roman Catholic Church. They live primarily in Lebanon, the country to the north of Israel.

with Kahlil Gibran[7] in New York—so he said. And Saleh always says he stayed with Gibran when he first got off the boat. I'll bet that popular guy Gibran has had a lot of roommates he doesn't even know about."

Susan said, "Dad, he's dead."

"I know, I know," her father said.

Later Susan said, "Mr. Hamadi, did you really meet Kahlil Gibran? He's one of my favorite writers." Hamadi walked slowly to the window of his room and
70 stared out. There wasn't much to look at down on the street—a bedraggled flower shop, a boarded-up tavern with a hand-lettered sign tacked to the front, GONE TO FIND JESUS. Susan's father said the owners had really gone to Alabama.

Hamadi spoke patiently. "Yes, I met brother Gibran. And I meet him in my heart every day. When I was a young man—shocked by all the visions of the new world—the tall buildings—the wild traffic—the young people without shame—the proud mailboxes in their blue uniforms—I met him. And he has stayed with me every day of my life."

"But did you really meet him, like in person, or just in a book?"

He turned dramatically. "Make no such distinctions, my friend. Or your life
80 will be a pod with only dried-up beans inside. Believe anything can happen."

Susan's father looked irritated, but Susan smiled. "I do," she said. "I believe that. I want fat beans. If I imagine something, it's true, too. Just a different kind of true." **C**

Susan's father was twiddling with the knobs on the old-fashioned sink. "Don't they even give you hot water here? You don't mean to tell me you've been living without hot water?"

On Hamadi's rickety desk lay a row of different "Love" stamps issued by the post office.

"You must write a lot of letters," Susan said.

90 "No, no, I'm just focusing on that word," Hamadi said. "I particularly like the globe in the shape of a heart," he added.

"Why don't you take a trip back to your village in Lebanon?" Susan's father asked. "Maybe you still have relatives living there."

Hamadi looked pained. "'Remembrance is a form of meeting,' my brother Gibran says, and I do believe I meet with my cousins every day."

"But aren't you curious? You've been gone so long! Wouldn't you like to find out what has happened to everybody and everything you knew as a boy?" Susan's father traveled back to Jerusalem once each year to see his family.

"I would not. In fact, I already know. It is there and it is not there. Would
100 you like to share an orange with me?" **D**

His long fingers, tenderly peeling. Once when Susan was younger, he'd given her a **lavish** ribbon off a holiday fruit basket and expected her to wear it on her head. In the car, Susan's father said, "Riddles. He talks in riddles. I don't know why I have patience with him." Susan stared at the people talking and laughing in the next car. She did not even exist in their world.

---

7. **Kahlil Gibran** (kə-lēl′ jə-brän′): a Lebanese-American philosopher and mystic poet whose best known work is *The Prophet*.

C MONITOR
Reread lines 68–83. As you read, **question** whether Hamadi actually met Gibran in person. What does Hamadi's own answer to this question reveal about his character?

D POINT OF VIEW
Reread lines 87–100. Although the **narrator** does not directly convey Hamadi's thoughts, the narrator does give the reader clues about how Hamadi thinks and feels. What are these clues, and what do they tell you about Hamadi?

lavish (lăv′ĭsh) *adj.* extravagant; more than is needed

Healing (1996), Daniel Nevins. Oil on wood, 7.4″ × 9.0″. © Daniel Nevins/SuperStock.

ANALYZE VISUALS
Compare the mood of this painting with the mood of the painting on page 225. Consider the colors, lines, and textures in each painting, as well as each figure's facial expression and gestures.

S usan carried *The Prophet* around on top of her English textbook and her Texas history. She and her friend Tracy read it out loud to one another at lunch. Tracy was a junior—they'd met at the literary magazine meeting where Susan, the only freshman on the staff, got assigned to do
110 proofreading. They never ate in the cafeteria; they sat outside at picnic tables with sack lunches, whole wheat crackers and fresh peaches. Both of them had given up meat.

Tracy's eyes looked steamy. "You know that place where Gibran says, 'Hate is a dead thing. Who of you would be a tomb?'"

Susan nodded. Tracy continued. "Well, I hate someone. I'm trying not to, but I can't help it. I hate Debbie for liking Eddie and it's driving me nuts."

"Why shouldn't Debbie like Eddie?" Susan said. "*You* do."

Tracy put her head down on her arms. A gang of cheerleaders walked by giggling. One of them flicked her finger in greeting.

120 "In fact, we *all* like Eddie," Susan said. "Remember, here in this book—wait and I'll find it—where Gibran says that loving teaches us the secrets of our hearts and that's the way we connect to all of Life's heart? You're not talking about liking or loving, you're talking about owning."

Tracy looked glum. "Sometimes you remind me of a minister." **E**

Susan said, "Well, just talk to me someday when *I'm* depressed."

Susan didn't want a boyfriend. Everyone who had boyfriends or girlfriends seemed to have troubles. Susan told people she had a boyfriend far away, on a farm in Missouri, but the truth was, boys still seemed like cousins to her. Or brothers. Or even girls.

130 A squirrel sat in the crook of a tree, eyeing their sandwiches. When the end-of-lunch bell blared, Susan and Tracy jumped—it always seemed too soon. Squirrels were lucky; they didn't have to go to school.

Susan's father said her idea was ridiculous: to invite Saleh Hamadi to go Christmas caroling with the English Club. "His English is **archaic,** for one thing, and he won't know *any* of the songs."

"How could you live in America for years and not know 'Joy to the World' or 'Away in a Manger'?"

"Listen, I grew up right down the road from 'Oh Little Town of Bethlehem' and I still don't know a single verse."

140 "I want him. We need him. It's boring being with the same bunch of people all the time." **F**

So they called Saleh and he said he would come—"thrilled" was the word he used. He wanted to ride the bus to their house, he didn't want anyone to pick him up. Her father muttered, "He'll probably forget to get off." Saleh thought "caroling" meant they were going out with a woman named Carol. He said, "Holiday spirit—I was just reading about it in the newspaper."

Susan said, "Dress warm."

Saleh replied, "Friend, my heart is warmed simply to hear your voice."

All that evening Susan felt light and bouncy. She decorated the coffee can

150 they would use to collect donations to be sent to the children's hospital in Bethlehem. She had started doing this last year in middle school, when a singing group collected $100 and the hospital responded on exotic onion-skin stationery[8] that they were "eternally grateful."

---

8. **onion-skin stationery:** a thin, strong typing paper.

E MAKE INFERENCES
Consider what you know about Susan so far. Why does Tracy compare her to a minister? Explain your answer.

archaic (är-kā'ĭk) *adj.* very old or unfashionable

F POINT OF VIEW
Why does Susan find Hamadi so interesting? Decide whether you would be able to answer this question if Susan were not the point-of-view character.

Her father shook his head. "You get something into your mind and it really takes over," he said. "Why do you like Hamadi so much all of a sudden? You could show half as much interest in your own uncles."

Susan laughed. Her uncles were dull. Her uncles shopped at the mall and watched TV. "Anyone who watches TV more than twelve minutes a week is uninteresting," she said.

160   Her father lifted an eyebrow.

"He's my **surrogate** grandmother," she said. "He says interesting things. **G** He makes me think. Remember when I was little and he called me The Thinker? We have a connection." She added, "Listen, do you want to go too? It's not a big deal. And Mom has a *great* voice. Why don't you both come?"

A minute later her mother was digging in the closet for neck scarves, and her father was digging in the drawer for flashlight batteries.

Saleh Hamadi arrived precisely on time, with flushed red cheeks and a sack of dates stuffed in his pocket. "We may need **sustenance** on our journey." Susan thought the older people seemed quite giddy as they drove down to the
170 high school to meet the rest of the carolers. Strands of winking lights wrapped around their neighbors' drainpipes and trees. A giant Santa tipped his hat on Dr. Garcia's roof.

Her friends stood gathered in front of the school. Some were smoothing out song sheets that had been crammed in a drawer or cabinet for a whole year. Susan thought holidays were strange; they came, and you were supposed to feel ready for them. What if you could make up your own holidays as you went along? She had read about a woman who used to have parties to celebrate the arrival of fresh asparagus in the local market. Susan's friends might make holidays called Eddie Looked at Me Today and Smiled.

180 Two people were alleluia-ing in harmony. Saleh Hamadi went around the group formally introducing himself to each person and shaking hands. A few people laughed silently when his back was turned. He had stepped out of a painting, or a newscast, with his outdated long overcoat, his clunky old man's shoes and elegant manners.

Susan spoke more loudly than usual. "I'm honored to introduce you to one of my best friends, Mr. Hamadi."

"Good evening to you," he pronounced musically, bowing a bit from the waist.

What could you say back but "Good evening, sir." His old-fashioned
190 manners were contagious.

They sang at three houses that never opened their doors. They sang "We Wish You a Merry Christmas" each time they moved on. Lisa had a fine, clear soprano. Tracy could find the alto harmony to any line. Cameron and Elliot had more enthusiasm than accuracy. Lily, Rita, and Jeannette laughed every time they said a wrong word and fumbled to find their places again. Susan

surrogate (sûr′ə-gĭt) *adj.* serving as a substitute

G MONITOR
After you read line 161, stop to **clarify**. Why does Susan call Hamadi her "surrogate grandmother"?

sustenance (sŭs′tə-nəns) *n.* food or provisions that sustain life

loved to see how her mother knew every word of every verse without looking at the paper, and how her father kept his hands in his pockets and seemed more interested in examining people's mailboxes or yard displays than in trying to sing. And Saleh Hamadi—what language was he singing in? He didn't even seem to be pronouncing words, but humming deeply from his throat. Was he saying, "Om"?[9] Speaking Arabic? Once he caught her looking and whispered, "That was an Aramaic[10] word that just drifted into my mouth—the true language of the Bible, you know, the language Jesus Christ himself spoke."

By the fourth block their voices felt tuned up and friendly people came outside to listen. Trays of cookies were passed around and dollar bills stuffed into the little can. Thank you, thank you. Out of the dark from down the block, Susan noticed Eddie sprinting toward them with his coat flapping, unbuttoned. She shot a glance at Tracy, who pretended not to notice. "Hey guys!" shouted Eddie. "The first time in my life I'm late and everyone else is on time! You could at least have left a note about which way you were going." Someone slapped him on the back. Saleh Hamadi, whom he had never seen before, was the only one who managed a reply. "Welcome, welcome to our cheery group!"

Eddie looked mystified. "Who is this guy?"

Susan whispered, "My friend." **H**

Eddie approached Tracy, who read her song sheet intently just then, and stuck his face over her shoulder to whisper, "Hi." Tracy stared straight ahead into the air and whispered "Hi" vaguely, glumly. Susan shook her head. Couldn't Tracy act more cheerful at least?

They were walking again. They passed a string of blinking reindeer and a wooden snowman holding a painted candle.

Eddie fell into step beside Tracy, murmuring so Susan couldn't hear him anymore. Saleh Hamadi was flinging his arms up high as he strode. Was he power walking?[11] Did he even know what power walking was? Between houses, Susan's mother hummed obscure songs people hardly remembered: "What Child Is This?" and "The Friendly Beasts."

Lisa moved over to Eddie's other side. "I'm *so excited* about you and Debbie!" she said loudly. "Why didn't she come tonight?"

Eddie said, "She has a sore throat."

Tracy shrank up inside her coat. **I**

Lisa chattered on. "James said we should make our reservations *now* for dinner at the Tower after the Sweetheart Dance, can you believe it? In December, making a reservation for February? But otherwise it might get booked up!"

H MAKE INFERENCES
Compare how Susan answers Eddie's question in line 215 with how she introduces Hamadi in lines 185–186. Why does her attitude change?

I MONITOR
Think about how Tracy is feeling and why she acts the way she does. Can you **connect** her behavior to anything you've experienced?

---

9. **om:** a sacred syllable in certain Eastern religions, repeated to aid one's concentration while meditating.

10. **Aramaic** (ăr′ə-mā′ĭk).

11. **power walking:** fast walking with rhythmic swinging of the arms, done as a form of exercise.

Saleh Hamadi tuned into this conversation with interest; the Tower was downtown, in his neighborhood. He said, "This sounds like significant preliminary planning! Maybe you can be an international advisor someday." Susan's mother bellowed, "Joy to the World!" and voices followed her, stretching for notes. Susan's father was gazing off into the sky. Maybe he
240 thought about all the refugees in camps in Palestine far from doorbells and shutters. Maybe he thought about the horizon beyond Jerusalem when he was a boy, how it seemed to be inviting him, "Come over, come over." Well, he'd come all the way to the other side of the world, and now he was doomed to live in two places at once. To Susan, immigrants seemed bigger than other people, and always slightly melancholy. They also seemed doubly interesting. Maybe someday Susan would meet one her own age. **J**

Two thin streams of tears rolled down Tracy's face. Eddie had drifted to the other side of the group and was clowning with Cameron, doing a tap dance shuffle. "While fields and floods, rocks, hills and plains, repeat the sounding
250 joy, repeat the sounding joy . . ." Susan and Saleh Hamadi noticed her. Hamadi peered into Tracy's face, inquiring, "Why? Is it pain? Is it gratitude? We are such mysterious creatures, human beings!"

Tracy turned to him, pressing her face against the old wool of his coat, and wailed. The song ended. All eyes were on Tracy and this tall, courteous stranger who would never in a thousand years have felt comfortable stroking her hair. But he let her stand there, crying, as Susan stepped up firmly on the other side of Tracy, putting her arms around her friend. And Hamadi said something Susan would remember years later, whenever she was sad herself, even after college, a creaky **anthem** sneaking back into her ear, "We go on. On and on.
260 We don't stop where it hurts. We turn a corner. It is the reason why we are living. To turn a corner. Come, let's move."

Above them, in the heavens, stars lived out their lonely lives. People whispered, "What happened? What's wrong?" Half of them were already walking down the street. ∾

Detail of *Inspiration* (1994), Daniel Nevins.   Detail of *Healing* (1996), Daniel Nevins.

J GRAMMAR AND STYLE
Reread lines 235–246. Nye repeats the phrase "Maybe he thought about" to add emphasis to her writing.

anthem (ăn′thəm) *n.* an uplifting song or hymn

After Reading

Comprehension

1. **Recall** Why does Susan begin to feel interested in Hamadi?

2. **Recall** What does Susan invite Hamadi to do?

3. **Clarify** What happens to Tracy at the end of the story?

Literary Analysis

4. **Evaluate Monitoring Strategies** Review the monitoring strategies listed on page 223. Which strategy did you find most helpful as you read the story? Cite examples.

5. **Analyze Point of View** Think about how "Hamadi" might be different if it were told from a **first-person point of view,** with Hamadi himself as the narrator. How might your perception of Hamadi change?

6. **Draw Conclusions** Reread lines 257–261. Why do you think Hamadi's words have such a profound effect on Susan? Citing evidence from the text, explain why you think she finds Hamadi's words so meaningful.

7. **Analyze Characters** A **round character** is one who is complex and highly developed, displaying a variety of different traits in his or her personality. A **flat character** is not highly developed. He or she usually has one outstanding trait or role and exists mainly to advance the plot of a story. Identify one round character and one flat character in the story. Then explain how each fits the criteria above.

8. **Compare Literary Works** Compare Susan with Jill, the narrator of "Pancakes" on pages 194–202. Use a Venn diagram like the one shown to record Susan's and Jill's **traits.** Which character has the more **remarkable** personality?

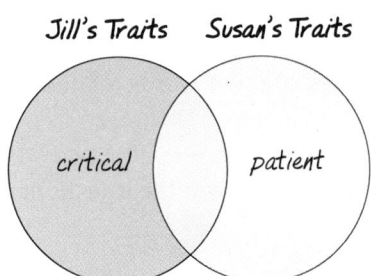

Jill's Traits   Susan's Traits

critical   patient

Literary Criticism

9. **Critical Interpretations** In reviewing *Habibi,* Nye's first novel, the critic Karen Leggett observed, "Adolescence magnifies the joys and anxieties of growing up even as it radically simplifies the complexities of the adult world.... Nye is meticulously sensitive to this rainbow of emotion...." Paraphrase this quotation. Then explain whether you think Leggett's comment applies to "Hamadi."

Vocabulary in Context

VOCABULARY PRACTICE

Indicate whether each statement is true or false.

1. It can be hard to tell when someone with a **wry** sense of humor is kidding.
2. **Spartan** hotel rooms are very elaborately furnished.
3. Someone with an **expansive** personality is usually rather shy.
4. Six courses and two desserts would constitute a **lavish** meal.
5. A poem filled with **archaic** words might be hard to understand.
6. Your **surrogate** grandmother would not necessarily be related to you.
7. Seeds and berries provide **sustenance** for many birds.
8. An **anthem** is a song written for an old person's funeral.

> **WORD LIST**
> anthem
> archaic
> expansive
> lavish
> spartan
> surrogate
> sustenance
> wry

VOCABULARY IN WRITING

Use at least four vocabulary words to write descriptive sentences about Saleh Hamadi. Describe his appearance or his personality or both. Here is an example.

> **EXAMPLE SENTENCE**
>
> *Hamadi is usually **expansive** in his talk, even with strangers.*

VOCABULARY STRATEGY: WORDS FROM GREEK CULTURE

The vocabulary word *spartan* originally referred to someone from the Greek city-state of Sparta, whose citizens were known for their rejection of luxury and comfort. Knowing the histories of other words related to ancient Greece can help you to understand their meanings.

PENNSYLVANIA STANDARDS

READING STANDARD
A.1.2.2 Use context clues

PRACTICE Read the chart and then answer the questions.

Character/Item	Description
Hercules	a mythological hero whose strength helped him perform almost impossible tasks
Colossus of Rhodes	an enormous statue of the Greek sun god
Narcissus	a mythological youth who fell in love with his own reflection
Titans	a race of mighty gods who preceded Zeus and his family

1. What is a modern-day example of something **colossal**?
2. What would a **narcissistic** person most likely talk about?
3. What might be an example of a **herculean** task?
4. By calling their ship *Titanic*, what were the ship owners suggesting?

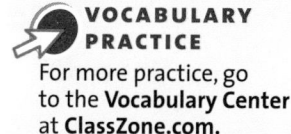

VOCABULARY PRACTICE
For more practice, go to the **Vocabulary Center** at **ClassZone.com**.

Reading-Writing Connection

Increase your understanding of "Hamadi" by responding to these prompts. Then use **Revision: Grammar and Style** to improve your writing.

WRITING PROMPTS	SELF-CHECK

A. Short Response: Interpret the Quotation

Reread the quotation from Kahlil Gibran at the beginning of "Hamadi." How does the quotation apply to the story? Which character utters the truth? Which one understands it? What is that truth and why is it important? Write **one or two paragraphs** that discuss the relationship between the quotation and the story.

A good interpretation will . . .

- explain the meaning of the quotation
- show how the characters and the story itself illustrate the quotation

B. Extended Response: Analyze Characterization

Analyze how Nye creates the character of Susan. In **three to five paragraphs,** identify the traits Susan exhibits, as well as the methods of characterization Nye uses to show the reader these traits.

A strong analysis will . . .

- discuss Susan's important traits
- identify at least three methods of characterization used to reveal these traits
- provide evidence from the text to support the analysis

REVISION: GRAMMAR AND STYLE

ADD EMPHASIS Review the **Grammar and Style** note on page 232. Throughout the story, Nye uses **repetition** to impress upon the reader the thoughts and actions of her characters. Use repetition in your own writing when you want to add emphasis.

Here are some examples from the story. Note that Nye repeats the same pronouns, nouns, and verbs:

> *Her uncles were dull. Her uncles shopped at the mall and watched TV.*
> (lines 157–158)

> *A minute later her mother was digging in the closet for neck scarves, and her father was digging in the drawer for flashlight batteries.* (lines 165–166)

Notice how the revision in red adds emphasis to this first draft. Use similar techniques to revise your responses to the prompts.

WRITING TOOLS
For prewriting, revision, and editing tools, visit the **Writing Center** at ClassZone.com.

> **STUDENT MODEL**
> Susan is a remarkable person. ⋀ She is observant and kind and curious about life.
> —*remarkable because*

from **I Know Why the Caged Bird Sings**

Autobiography by Maya Angelou

What is a TEACHER?

PENNSYLVANIA STANDARDS

READING STANDARDS
A.2.6.1 Identify and/or describe intended purpose
B.1.1.1.A.1 Evaluate character

KEY IDEA Your teachers at school are dedicated to helping you acquire knowledge, but are there individuals outside the classroom who teach you important things as well? In this selection, you'll meet Mrs. Flowers, a woman who acted as a **mentor**—a wise and trusted counselor or teacher—to a young Maya Angelou.

DISCUSS Think of people who have shared wisdom with you, helped you to see things in new ways, or pushed you when you needed encouragement. With a small group of classmates, discuss the impact a mentor can have, and then generate a word web detailing the most important traits of a mentor.

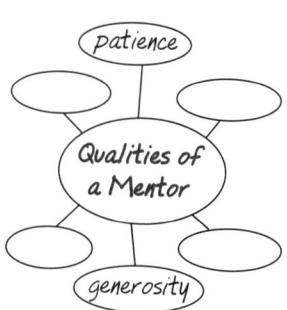

patience

Qualities of a Mentor

generosity

LITERARY ANALYSIS: CHARACTERIZATION IN AUTOBIOGRAPHY

When describing important individuals they have known, writers of **autobiography** often make use of the same methods of **characterization** that fiction writers do. These include

- description of a person's physical appearance
- examples of the person's speech, thoughts, or feelings
- the speech, thoughts, or feelings of other people
- the narrator's comments about the person

As you read, look for details that reveal Mrs. Flowers's personality **traits** and ways she influenced the young Angelou.

READING SKILL: ANALYZE PERSPECTIVES

Though autobiographies are written in first-person point of view, they often reflect two different **perspectives:**

- that of the writer at the time he or she experienced certain events
- that of the writer looking back on these events years later

As you read this selection, use a chart like the one shown to record Angelou's thoughts and observations about Mrs. Flowers from both her childhood and adult perspectives.

Child's Viewpoint	Adult's Viewpoint
"Why on earth did she insist on calling her Sister Flowers? Shame made me want to hide my face." (lines 25–26)	"She was one of the few gentle-women I have ever known, and has remained throughout my life the measure of what a human being can be." (lines 18–19)

Review: **Make Inferences**

▲ VOCABULARY IN CONTEXT

Make a chart like the one shown, placing each word in the column where it fits. Write brief definitions for the words in the first two columns.

WORD LIST	cascade	illiteracy	sacrilegious
	clarity	infuse	taut
	homely	leer	

Know Well	Think I Know	Don't Know

Author On⦿ine

Maya Angelou born 1928

Marguerite Moves South
Maya Angelou was born Marguerite Johnson in St. Louis, Missouri. The name Maya was originally given to her by her older brother, Bailey, who called her "mya sister" as a child. When their parents divorced, Marguerite and Bailey were sent to live with their grandmother in the small, rigidly segregated town of Stamps, Arkansas. Their grandmother, whom they called Momma, ran the only African American–owned store in her community, in a part of town referred to as Black Stamps.

Childhood Trauma After being abused by a family friend when she was eight, Angelou withdrew into herself and spoke to no one but Bailey for five years. It is at this point in her life that this selection takes place.

Never Defeated Angelou has come a long way since her early struggles. In 1993, when she read her poem "On the Pulse of Morning" to commemorate Bill Clinton's swearing in as president, she became only the second poet to speak at an inauguration. She served as a coordinator of Martin Luther King Jr.'s Southern Christian Leadership Conference and has taught in Africa and the United States. Her writings have achieved tremendous popularity, inspiring millions of people around the world. When asked what advice she'd like to pass on to her readers, Angelou replied, "You may encounter many defeats, but you must not be defeated."

 MORE ABOUT THE AUTHOR
For more on Maya Angelou, visit the **Literature Center** at ClassZone.com.

I KNOW WHY THE *Caged Bird* SINGS

MAYA ANGELOU

For nearly a year, I sopped around the house, the Store, the school and the church, like an old biscuit, dirty and inedible. Then I met, or rather got to know, the lady who threw me my first life line.

Mrs. Bertha Flowers was the aristocrat of Black Stamps. She had the grace of control to appear warm in the coldest weather, and on the Arkansas summer days it seemed she had a private breeze which swirled around, cooling her. She was thin without the **taut** look of wiry people, and her printed voile dresses and flowered hats were as right for her as denim overalls for a farmer. She was our side's answer to the richest white woman in town.

10 Her skin was a rich black that would have peeled like a plum if snagged, but then no one would have thought of getting close enough to Mrs. Flowers to ruffle her dress, let alone snag her skin. She didn't encourage familiarity. She wore gloves too. **Ⓐ**

I don't think I ever saw Mrs. Flowers laugh, but she smiled often. A slow widening of her thin black lips to show even, small white teeth, then the slow, effortless closing. When she chose to smile on me, I always wanted to thank her. The action was so graceful and inclusively benign.

She was one of the few gentlewomen I have ever known, and has remained throughout my life the measure of what a human being can be.

20 Momma had a strange relationship with her. Most often when she passed on the road in front of the Store, she spoke to Momma in that soft yet carrying voice, "Good day, Mrs. Henderson." Momma responded with "How you, Sister Flowers?"

ANALYZE VISUALS
Examine this portrait. How does it compare with Angelou's description of Mrs. Flowers? Cite details from the painting and the text to support your answer.

taut (tôt) *adj.* pulled or drawn tight

Ⓐ CHARACTERIZATION
Reread lines 4–13. What is distinctive about Mrs. Flowers's appearance and demeanor?

Woman with Umbrella, Bill Farnsworth. © Images.com/Corbis.

Mrs. Flowers didn't belong to our church, nor was she Momma's familiar.[1] Why on earth did she insist on calling her Sister Flowers? Shame made me want to hide my face. Mrs. Flowers deserved better than to be called Sister. Then, Momma left out the verb. Why not ask, "How *are* you, *Mrs.* Flowers?" With the unbalanced passion of the young, I hated her for showing her ignorance to Mrs. Flowers. It didn't occur to me for many years that they 30 were as alike as sisters, separated only by formal education.

Although I was upset, neither of the women was in the least shaken by what I thought an unceremonious greeting. Mrs. Flowers would continue her easy gait up the hill to her little bungalow, and Momma kept on shelling peas or doing whatever had brought her to the front porch.

Occasionally, though, Mrs. Flowers would drift off the road and down to the Store and Momma would say to me, "Sister, you go on and play." As I left I would hear the beginning of an intimate conversation, Momma persistently using the wrong verb, or none at all.

"Brother and Sister Wilcox is sho'ly the meanest—" "Is," Momma? "Is"? 40 Oh, please, not "is," Momma, for two or more. But they talked, and from the side of the building where I waited for the ground to open up and swallow me, I heard the soft-voiced Mrs. Flowers and the textured voice of my grandmother merging and melting. They were interrupted from time to time by giggles that must have come from Mrs. Flowers (Momma never giggled in her life). Then she was gone. **B**

She appealed to me because she was like people I had never met personally. Like women in English novels who walked the moors[2] (whatever they were) with their loyal dogs racing at a respectful distance. Like the women who sat in front of roaring fireplaces, drinking tea incessantly from silver trays full 50 of scones and crumpets.[3] Women who walked over the "heath"[4] and read morocco-bound[5] books and had two last names divided by a hyphen. It would be safe to say that she made me proud to be Negro, just by being herself.

She acted just as refined as whitefolks in the movies and books and she was more beautiful, for none of them could have come near that warm color without looking gray by comparison.

It was fortunate that I never saw her in the company of powhitefolks. For since they tend to think of their whiteness as an evenizer, I'm certain that I would have had to hear her spoken to commonly as Bertha, and my image of her would have been shattered like the unmendable Humpty-Dumpty. **C**
60 One summer afternoon, sweet-milk fresh in my memory, she stopped at the Store to buy provisions. Another Negro woman of her health and age would have been expected to carry the paper sacks home in one hand, but Momma said, "Sister Flowers, I'll send Bailey up to your house with these things."

---

1. **familiar:** a close friend or associate.

2. **moors:** broad open areas of countryside with marshes and patches of low shrubs.

3. **scones** (skōnz) **and crumpets** (krŭm′pĭts): Scones are small, biscuitlike pastries; crumpets are rolls similar to English muffins.

4. **heath** (hēth): another word for a moor.

5. **morocco-bound:** Morocco is a soft leather sometimes used for expensive book covers.

B ANALYZE PERSPECTIVES
Reread lines 39–45. Which parts of this passage are written from a child's perspective? Which are written from the viewpoint of an adult reflecting on the experience? Record your answers in your chart.

C MAKE INFERENCES
In lines 56–59, what can you infer about race relations in Stamps, Arkansas, in the 1930s? Consider whether you would be able to make these inferences if Angelou did not comment on her childhood experiences from her adult viewpoint.

She smiled that slow dragging smile, "Thank you, Mrs. Henderson. I'd prefer Marguerite, though." My name was beautiful when she said it. "I've been meaning to talk to her, anyway." They gave each other age-group looks.

Momma said, "Well, that's all right then. Sister, go and change your dress. You going to Sister Flowers's."

ANALYZE VISUALS
Does the girl in this painting look similar to how you envision Marguerite? Describe the **details** that influenced your answer.

Ancilla with an Orange (1956), Dod Procter. Oil on canvas. Royal West of England Academy, Bristol, UK. © The Bridgeman Art Library.

The chifforobe[6] was a maze. What on earth did one put on to go to
70 Mrs. Flowers's house? I knew I shouldn't put on a Sunday dress. It might be
sacrilegious. Certainly not a house dress, since I was already wearing a fresh
one. I chose a school dress, naturally. It was formal without suggesting that
going to Mrs. Flowers's house was equivalent to attending church.

I trusted myself back into the Store.

"Now, don't you look nice." I had chosen the right thing, for once.

"Mrs. Henderson, you make most of the children's clothes, don't you?"

"Yes, ma'am. Sure do. Store-bought clothes ain't hardly worth the thread
it take to stitch them."

"I'll say you do a lovely job, though, so neat. That dress looks professional."

80 Momma was enjoying the seldom-received compliments. Since everyone we
knew (except Mrs. Flowers, of course) could sew competently, praise was rarely
handed out for the commonly practiced craft.

"I try, with the help of the Lord, Sister Flowers, to finish the inside just like
I does the outside. Come here, Sister."

I had buttoned up the collar and tied the belt, apronlike, in back. Momma
told me to turn around. With one hand she pulled the strings and the belt fell
free at both sides of my waist. Then her large hands were at my neck, opening
the button loops. I was terrified. What was happening?

"Take it off, Sister." She had her hands on the hem of the dress.

90 "I don't need to see the inside, Mrs. Henderson, I can tell . . ." But the
dress was over my head and my arms were stuck in the sleeves. Momma said,
"That'll do. See here, Sister Flowers, I French-seams[7] around the armholes."
Through the cloth film, I saw the shadow approach. "That makes it last longer.
Children these days would bust out of sheet-metal clothes. They so rough."

"That is a very good job, Mrs. Henderson. You should be proud. You can
put your dress back on, Marguerite."

"No ma'am. Pride is a sin. And 'cording to the Good Book, it goeth
before a fall."

"That's right. So the Bible says. It's a good thing to keep in mind."

100 I wouldn't look at either of them. Momma hadn't thought that taking off
my dress in front of Mrs. Flowers would kill me stone dead. If I had refused,
she would have thought I was trying to be "womanish" and might have
remembered St. Louis. Mrs. Flowers had known that I would be embarrassed
and that was even worse. I picked up the groceries and went out to wait in the
hot sunshine. It would be fitting if I got a sunstroke and died before they came
outside. Just dropped dead on the slanting porch. **D**

There was a little path beside the rocky road, and Mrs. Flowers walked in
front swinging her arms and picking her way over the stones.

---

6. **chifforobe** (shĭf′ə-rōb′): a chest of drawers combined with a small closet
for hanging clothes.

7. **French-seams:** sew seams that are turned in and stitched on the wrong side so
that the unfinished edges of the cloth are not visible.

sacrilegious (săk′rə-lĭj′əs)
adj. disrespectful toward
a sacred person, place,
or thing

D CHARACTERIZATION
In addition to describing
her mentor in a
compelling way, Angelou
also presents a vivid
portrait of herself as a
child. List three **traits**
Marguerite exhibits.

110 She said, without turning her head, to me, "I hear you're doing very good school work, Marguerite, but that it's all written. The teachers report that they have trouble getting you to talk in class." We passed the triangular farm on our left and the path widened to allow us to walk together. I hung back in the separate unasked and unanswerable questions.

"Come and walk along with me, Marguerite." I couldn't have refused even if I wanted to. She pronounced my name so nicely. Or more correctly, she spoke each word with such **clarity** that I was certain a foreigner who didn't understand English could have understood her.

"Now no one is going to make you talk—possibly no one can. But bear in mind, language is man's way of communicating with his fellow man and it 120 is language alone which separates him from the lower animals." That was a totally new idea to me, and I would need time to think about it.

"Your grandmother says you read a lot. Every chance you get. That's good, but not good enough. Words mean more than what is set down on paper. It takes the human voice to **infuse** them with the shades of deeper meaning." **E**

I memorized the part about the human voice infusing words. It seemed so valid and poetic.

She said she was going to give me some books and that I not only must read them, I must read them aloud. She suggested that I try to make a sentence sound in as many different ways as possible.

130 "I'll accept no excuse if you return a book to me that has been badly handled." My imagination boggled at the punishment I would deserve if in fact I did abuse a book of Mrs. Flowers'. Death would be too kind and brief.

The odors in the house surprised me. Somehow I had never connected Mrs. Flowers with food or eating or any other common experience of common people. There must have been an outhouse, too, but my mind never recorded it.

The sweet scent of vanilla had met us as she opened the door.

"I made tea cookies this morning. You see, I had planned to invite you for cookies and lemonade so we could have this little chat. The lemonade is in the icebox."

140 It followed that Mrs. Flowers would have ice on an ordinary day, when most families in our town bought ice late on Saturdays only a few times during the summer to be used in the wooden ice-cream freezers.

She took the bags from me and disappeared through the kitchen door. I looked around the room that I had never in my wildest fantasies imagined I would see. Browned photographs **leered** or threatened from the walls and the white, freshly done curtains pushed against themselves and against the wind. I wanted to gobble up the room entire and take it to Bailey, who would help me analyze and enjoy it. **F**

"Have a seat, Marguerite. Over there by the table." She carried a platter 150 covered with a tea towel. Although she warned that she hadn't tried her hand at baking sweets for some time, I was certain that like everything else about her the cookies would be perfect.

clarity (klăr′ĭ-tē) *n.* clearness

infuse (ĭn-fyōōz′) *v.* to fill, as if by pouring

E **CHARACTERIZATION**
Reread lines 109–124. What does this passage reveal about the **conflict** developing in this selection? Summarize what you already know about Marguerite's conflict.

leer (lîr) *v.* to give a sly, evil glance

F **GRAMMAR AND STYLE**
Reread lines 143–148. Angelou uses the **adjective clause** "that I had never in my wildest fantasies imagined I would see" to convey with precision Marguerite's excitement.

Lemonade (2002), Michele Hausman. © Michele Hausman.

They were flat round wafers, slightly browned on the edges and butter-yellow in the center. With the cold lemonade they were sufficient for childhood's lifelong diet. Remembering my manners, I took nice little lady like bites off the edges. She said she had made them expressly for me and that she had a few in the kitchen that I could take home to my brother. So I jammed one whole cake in my mouth and the rough crumbs scratched the insides of my jaws, and if I hadn't had to swallow, it would have been a dream come true.

160   As I ate she began the first of what we later called "my lessons in living." She said that I must always be intolerant of ignorance but understanding of **illiteracy.** That some people, unable to go to school, were more educated and even more intelligent than college professors. She encouraged me to listen carefully to what country people called mother wit. That in those **homely** sayings was couched the collective wisdom of generations.

When I finished the cookies she brushed off the table and brought a thick, small book from the bookcase. I had read *A Tale of Two Cities*[8] and found it up to my standards as a romantic novel. She opened the first page and I heard poetry for the first time in my life.

illiteracy (ĭ-lĭt′ər-ə-sē) *n.* a lack of ability to read and write

homely (hōm′lē) *adj.* characteristic of home life; simple; everyday

---

8. ***A Tale of Two Cities:*** a novel by Charles Dickens, set in Paris and London during the French Revolution (1789–1799).

170   "It was the best of times and the worst of times . . ."⁹ Her voice slid in and curved down through and over the words. She was nearly singing. I wanted to look at the pages. Were they the same that I had read? Or were there notes, music, lined on the pages, as in a hymn book? Her sounds began **cascading** gently. I knew from listening to a thousand preachers that she was nearing the end of her reading, and I hadn't really heard, heard to understand, a single word.

    "How do you like that?"

    It occurred to me that she expected a response. The sweet vanilla flavor was still on my tongue and her reading was a wonder in my ears. I had to speak.

180   I said, "Yes, ma'am." It was the least I could do, but it was the most also. **G**

    "There's one more thing. Take this book of poems and memorize one for me. Next time you pay me a visit, I want you to recite."

    I have tried often to search behind the sophistication of years for the enchantment I so easily found in those gifts. The essence escapes but its aura remains.¹⁰ To be allowed, no, invited, into the private lives of strangers, and to share their joys and fears, was a chance to exchange the Southern bitter wormwood for a cup of mead with Beowulf or a hot cup of tea and milk with Oliver Twist.¹¹ When I said aloud, "It is a far, far better thing that I do, than I have ever done . . ."¹² tears of love filled my eyes at my selflessness.

190   On that first day, I ran down the hill and into the road (few cars ever came along it) and had the good sense to stop running before I reached the Store.

    I was liked, and what a difference it made. I was respected not as Mrs. Henderson's grandchild or Bailey's sister but for just being Marguerite Johnson.

    Childhood's logic never asks to be proved (all conclusions are absolute). I didn't question why Mrs. Flowers had singled me out for attention, nor did it occur to me that Momma might have asked her to give me a little talking to. All I cared about was that she had made tea cookies for *me* and read to *me* from her favorite book. It was enough to prove that she liked me. ❧ **H**

---

cascade (kă-skād') *v.* to fall or flow like a waterfall

G **CHARACTERIZATION**
What does Angelou mean when she says that speaking was both the least and the most she could do?

H **ANALYZE PERSPECTIVES**
Reread lines 183–198. In which lines is Angelou directly narrating her actions and experiences as a child? In which lines is she sharing insights she learned later, as she grew up? Explain your answers.

---

9. **"It was . . . the worst of times . . .":** the famous opening sentence of *A Tale of Two Cities*.

10. **The essence . . . remains:** The basic quality of a thing or event escapes, but the feelings or atmosphere that it creates remains.

11. **a chance to exchange . . . with Oliver Twist:** Angelou compares her existence as a black child in the bigoted South to wormwood, a bitter herb. Mead (a liquor made from honey) and tea with milk were common drinks in the respective eras of Beowulf and Oliver Twist, two characters from English literature. Angelou suggests that reading about such characters provided an escape from her racist Southern surroundings.

12. **"It is a far . . . than I have ever done . . .":** the final line of *A Tale of Two Cities*, spoken by a man who sacrifices his own life to save that of another.

Caged Bird   Maya Angelou

A free bird leaps
on the back of the wind
and floats downstream
till the current ends
5 and dips his wing
in the orange sun rays
and dares to claim the sky.

But a bird that stalks
down his narrow cage
10 can seldom see through
his bars of rage
his wings are clipped and
his feet are tied
so he opens his throat to sing.

15 The caged bird sings
with a fearful trill
of things unknown
but longed for still
and his tune is heard
20 on the distant hill
for the caged bird
sings of freedom.

The free bird thinks of another breeze
and the trade winds soft through the sighing trees
25 and the fat worms waiting on a dawn-bright lawn
and he names the sky his own

But a caged bird stands on the grave of dreams
his shadow shouts on a nightmare scream
his wings are clipped and his feet are tied
30 so he opens his throat to sing.

The caged bird sings
with a fearful trill
of things unknown
but longed for still
35 and his tune is heard
on the distant hill
for the caged bird
sings of freedom.

After Reading

Comprehension

1. **Recall** What is Mrs. Flowers's feeling about language?

2. **Summarize** What kinds of assignments does Mrs. Flowers give Marguerite?

3. **Clarify** What does Mrs. Flowers mean when she tells Marguerite that some people, though lacking formal schooling, are "more educated and even more intelligent than college professors"?

Literary Analysis

4. **Understand Motives** What motivates Mrs. Flowers to help Marguerite?

5. **Analyze Perspectives** Review the chart that you filled in while reading. How does Angelou's adult perspective help you to understand the long-range effect that Mrs. Flowers had on her life? Cite evidence.

6. **Evaluate Characterization in Autobiography** Skim the selection and find examples of the various methods of characterization used by Angelou in her autobiography. Which would you say is the most powerful method used to characterize Mrs. Flowers? Use the list shown to help you with your response.

> *Methods of Characterization*
>
> • *description of a person's physical appearance*
>
> • *examples of the person's speech, thoughts, or feelings*
>
> • *the speech, thoughts, or feelings of other people*
>
> • *the narrator's comments about the person*

7. **Compare Literary Works** Reread the poem "Caged Bird" on page 246. Does Mrs. Flowers teach the young Marguerite to "sing"? If so, in what way?

Literary Criticism

8. **Biographical Context** The title *I Know Why the Caged Bird Sings* is an allusion to the poem "Sympathy" by Paul Laurence Dunbar. The last stanza reads:

> *I know why the caged bird sings, ah me,*
> *   When his wing is bruised and his bosom sore,—*
> *When he beats his bars and he would be free;*
> *It is not a carol of joy or glee,*
> *   But a prayer that he sends from his heart's deep core,*
> *But a plea, that upward to Heaven he flings—*
> *I know why the caged bird sings!*

Why do you think Angelou refers to this poem in the title of her autobiography?

Vocabulary in Context

VOCABULARY PRACTICE

Determine the relationship between the first pair of words in each analogy. Then write the word that best completes the second pair.

1. *Drift* is to *snow* as _____ is to *water*.

2. *Smile* is to *sweetness* as _____ is to *wickedness*.

3. *Disease* is to *medicine* as _____ is to *education*.

4. *Fancy* is to *special* as _____ is to *everyday*.

5. *Toxic* is to *environment* as _____ is to *religion*.

6. *Bewilderment* is to *confusion* as *understanding* is to _____.

7. *Untied* is to *tied* as *loose* is to _____.

8. *Help* is to *assist* as _____ is to *inject*.

WORD LIST

cascade

clarity

homely

illiteracy

infuse

leer

sacrilegious

taut

VOCABULARY IN WRITING

What are some beliefs that Marguerite learned from Mrs. Flowers? Write three to four sentences about her beliefs, using at least five vocabulary words.

> **EXAMPLE SENTENCE**
>
> *Marguerite learned that **clarity** in speaking is essential.*

VOCABULARY STRATEGY: MULTIPLE-MEANING WORDS

Sometimes words, such as the vocabulary word *homely* in this selection, do not have the meanings you expect. Many English words have a number of meanings, and to understand what you are reading, you must decide which of these meanings the writer intends.

PRACTICE Write the letter of the best definition for each boldfaced word.

1. She **distinguished** herself from her friends by wearing all black.
(a) successful or commanding great respect, (b) set oneself apart,
(c) recognized differences among several choices

2. **Channel** your energies into some worthwhile project.
(a) direct into a particular course of action, (b) body of water connecting two larger bodies of water, (c) band of radio or television frequencies

3. The store sold **notions** as well as yarn and knitting needles.
(a) beliefs about something, (b) vague understandings of something,
(c) needles, buttons, and other sewing materials

4. Amassing **capital** was his primary goal.
(a) city where government is located, (b) punishable by death, (c) money

PENNSYLVANIA STANDARDS

READING STANDARD
A.2.1.1 Apply meaning of multiple-meaning words

VOCABULARY PRACTICE
For more practice, go to the **Vocabulary Center** at ClassZone.com.

Reading-Writing Connection

Broaden your understanding of this selection by responding to these prompts.
Then use **Revision: Grammar and Style** to improve your writing.

WRITING PROMPTS

A. Short Response: Compare Forms

An autobiography is the story of a person's life written by that person; a biography is the story of a person's life written by someone else. What advantages and disadvantages might an autobiography have as opposed to a biography? Use examples from this selection to write **one or two paragraphs** comparing these forms.

B. Extended Response: Analyze Traits

Think about the most important character traits Mrs. Flowers exhibits. Then review the word web you created detailing the qualities a **mentor** should possess. Write **three to five paragraphs** describing Mrs. Flowers's traits and analyzing how these traits compare with the qualities you listed.

SELF-CHECK

An effective comparison will . . .

- discuss at least two advantages and two disadvantages an autobiography might have compared with a biography
- use evidence from the selection to support your points

A strong analysis will . . .

- list at least three of Mrs. Flowers's traits, supported by evidence from the text
- compare the traits Mrs. Flowers exhibits with the qualities you discussed before reading

REVISION: GRAMMAR AND STYLE

ADD DESCRIPTIVE DETAILS Review the **Grammar and Style** note on page 243. In her writing, Angelou uses **adjective clauses** to add interesting, vivid details about her characters and their emotions. Adjective clauses are subordinate clauses that, like adjectives, modify nouns and pronouns. They are introduced by **relative pronouns** such as *who, whom, whose, that,* and *which* and **relative adverbs** such as *when, where,* and *why.* Here are some examples from the selection:

> . . . *It seemed she had a private breeze which swirled around.* . . . (line 6)

> . . . *From the side of the building where I waited for the ground to open up and swallow me, I heard the soft-voiced Mrs. Flowers.* . . . (lines 40–42)

Notice how the revisions in red make this first draft more descriptive. Use similar methods to revise your responses to the prompts.

PENNSYLVANIA STANDARDS

WRITING STANDARD
1.4.11.B.2 Use precise language and specific detail

STUDENT MODEL

Mrs. Flowers is a generous person. She invites Marguerite over to
who goes out of her way to make Marguerite feel at ease
^
her house and reads out loud from a book that captivates the girl.
, where she serves cookies and lemonade
^
that captivates the girl.

WRITING TOOLS
For prewriting, revision, and editing tools, visit the **Writing Center** at ClassZone.com.

Blind to Failure

Magazine Article by Karl Taro Greenfeld

When is STRENGTH
more than muscle?

PENNSYLVANIA
STANDARDS

READING STANDARDS
B.1.1.1.A.1 Evaluate character
B.3.3.3 Interpret and/or analyze
graphics and charts

KEY IDEA It's easy to think of people who are strong in body. Many famous athletes have tremendous physical strength. But some people are extremely strong in mind and spirit as well. In "Blind to Failure," you'll meet one such individual, Erik Weihenmayer, who was the first blind mountaineer to reach the top of Mount Everest. In scaling the world's highest peak, Weihenmayer became an inspiring portrait of **bravery** and determination.

QUICKWRITE Think of different types of strength—physical, emotional, spiritual, and so forth. Think of people who exemplify each type of strength and put them in categories in a chart like the one shown. Do any of the people belong in more than one category?

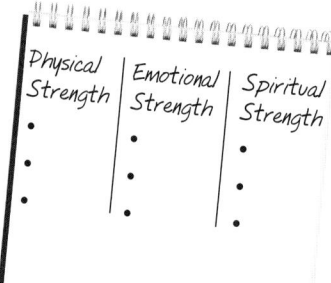

Physical Strength | Emotional Strength | Spiritual Strength

● ELEMENTS OF NONFICTION: CHARACTER STUDY

Some nonfiction writers provide insight into the personalities of individuals by writing **character studies.** A character study usually includes extensive details about its subject's appearance, speech, and actions. As you read "Blind to Failure," look for the following types of details about Erik Weihenmayer:

- actions that have made him newsworthy or famous and his own comments about those actions
- descriptions of his physical traits and facial expressions
- others' reactions to his accomplishments

● READING SKILL: INTERPRET GRAPHIC AIDS

Magazine articles like "Blind to Failure" often include **graphic aids**—charts, graphs, and maps—that present important information in visual form. This article features a **diagram,** a drawing in which lines, symbols, and words are used to help the reader picture a process, an event, or the way something works. As you read "Blind to Failure," turn back and forth between the text and the diagram to better understand the difficulties of the climb and to follow the climbers' progress. Use a chart to record the information you learn from the diagram.

Camp or Location	Elevation	Related Events/ Details of Climb	Other Information
Base Camp	17,600 feet	Below Khumbu Icefall	

Review: **Connect, Draw Conclusions**

▲ VOCABULARY IN CONTEXT

Which of these words do you already know? Write a sentence for each of the words. Then check your understanding after you've read the selection.

WORD LIST			
	acclimatization	crevasse	insurmountable
	aplomb	demeanor	paramount
	arduous	inevitability	transcend
	banal		

Author Online

Karl Taro Greenfeld born 1965

Striking Stories
Karl Taro Greenfeld was born in Kobe, Japan, and grew up in Los Angeles, California. As a journalist, he has made his home in Hong Kong, China, investigating everything from entertainment fads to economic disasters. In June of 2001, Greenfeld set out for Nepal to interview members of the Everest expedition that included Erik Weihenmayer, the climber you will read about.

Background

Reaching for the Peak At 29,035 feet, Mount Everest is the highest peak on earth. To reach the summit, mountaineers establish a series of camps at intervals up the mountain and then make numerous trips between them, carrying supplies from the base camp to the highest camp. When the highest camp is well stocked and the weather is favorable, the climbers make a push for the summit.

The Perils of Everest Climbing Mount Everest is incredibly dangerous, even for the most experienced climbers. Extreme cold makes frostbite common. Sunshine reflected off the snow can cause temporary blindness and fatal falls. Climbers often suffer dizziness and confusion due to lack of oxygen. The region above 26,000 feet is called the Death Zone. At that altitude, blood thickens, the heart speeds up, and the brain can swell, with serious injury or death a possible result. Ninety percent of climbers attempting to scale Mount Everest fail to reach the summit.

BUILDING BACKGROUND
To learn more about Mount Everest, visit the **Literature Center** at ClassZone.com.

BLIND to FAILURE

Karl Taro Greenfeld

ANALYZE VISUALS
Examine the photograph of Weihenmayer. Identify three character **traits** you would attribute to him solely on the basis of this picture.

When he saw Erik Weihenmayer arrive that afternoon, Pasquale Scaturro[1] began to have misgivings about the expedition he was leading. Here they were on the first floor of Mount Everest, and Erik—the reason for the whole trip—was stumbling into Camp 1 bloody, sick, and dehydrated. "He was literally green," says fellow climber and teammate Michael O'Donnell. "He looked like George Foreman[2] had beaten him for two hours." The beating had actually been administered by Erik's climbing partner, Luis Benitez.[3] Erik had slipped into a <u>crevasse,</u> and as Benitez reached down to catch him, his climbing pole raked Erik across the nose and chin. Wounds heal slowly at that altitude
10 because of the thin air.

crevasse (krĭ-văs′) *n.* a deep crack or split in a glacier

As Erik passed out in his tent, the rest of the team gathered in a worried huddle. "I was thinking maybe this is not a good idea," says Scaturro. "Two years of planning, a documentary movie, and this blind guy barely makes it to Camp 1?"

This blind guy. Erik Weihenmayer, thirty-three, wasn't just another yuppie trekker who'd lost a few rounds to the mountain. Blind since he was thirteen, the victim of a rare hereditary disease of the retina, he began attacking mountains in his early twenties. **Ⓐ**

But he had been having the same doubts as the rest of the team. On that
20 arduous climb to camp through the Khumbu Icefall,[4] Erik wondered for the first time if his attempt to become the first sightless person to summit Mount Everest was a colossal mistake, an act of Daedalian hubris[5] for which he would be punished. There are so many ways to die on that mountain, spanning

Ⓐ CHARACTER STUDY
Think about the endeavor Weihenmayer undertook and his fellow climbers' descriptions of the expedition to this point. What **inferences** can you make about someone who would attempt such a feat?

---

1. **Erik Weihenmayer** (wī′ən-mā′ər) . . . **Pasquale Scaturro** (päs-kwä′lā skä-tōō′rō).
2. **George Foreman:** a former heavyweight boxing champion.
3. **Luis Benitez** (lōō-ēs′ bĕ-nē′tĕs).
4. **Khumbu** (kōōm′bōō) **Icefall:** a stretch of glacier beginning at about 18,000 feet and extending to the area of Camp 1 at 20,000 feet.
5. **Daedalian hubris** (dĭ-dā′lē-ən hyōō′brĭs): excessive pride like that of Daedalus, a master craftsman in Greek mythology. When Daedalus fashioned wings for himself and his son from feathers and wax, his son flew too near the sun, the wax in his wings melted, and he fell into the sea and drowned.

the spectacular (fall through an ice shelf into a crevasse, get waylaid by an avalanche, develop cerebral edema[6] from lack of oxygen and have your brain literally swell out of your skull) and the **banal** (become disoriented because of oxygen deprivation and decide you'll take a little nap, right here, in the snow, which becomes a forever nap).

banal (bə-năl') *adj.* commonplace; trite

Erik, as he stumbled through the icefall, was so far out of his comfort zone
30 that he began to speculate on which of those fates might await him. For a moment he flashed on all those clichés about what blind people are supposed to do—become piano tuners or pencil salesmen—and thought maybe they were stereotypes for good reason. Blind people certainly shouldn't be out here, wandering through an ever changing ice field, measuring the distance over a 1,000-foot-deep crevasse with climbing poles and then leaping, literally, over and into the unknown.

The blind thrive on patterns: stairs are all the same height, city blocks roughly the same length, curbs approximately the same depth. They learn to identify the patterns in their environment much more than the sighted
40 population do, and to rely on them to plot their way through the world.

But in the Khumbu Icefall, the trail through the Himalayan glacier is patternless, a diabolically cruel obstacle course for a blind person. It changes every year as the river of ice shifts, but it's always made up of treacherously crumbly stretches of ice, ladders roped together over wide crevasses, slightly narrower crevasses that must be jumped, huge seracs,[7] avalanches, and—most frustrating for a blind person, who naturally seeks to identify patterns in his terrain—a totally random icescape.

In the icefall there is no system, no repetition, no rhyme or reason to the lay of the frozen land. On the other hand, "it is so specific in terms of where
50 you can step," Erik recalls. "Sometimes you're walking along and then boom, a crevasse is right there, and three more steps and another one, and then a snow bridge. And vertical up, then a ladder and then a jumbly section." It took Erik thirteen hours to make it from Base Camp through the icefall to Camp 1, at 20,000 feet. Scaturro had allotted seven.

A typical assault on Everest requires each climber to do as many as ten traverses through the icefall, both for **acclimatization** purposes and to help carry the immense amount of equipment required for an ascent. After Erik's accident, the rest of the National Federation of the Blind (NFB) team discussed letting him stay up in Camp 1, equipped with videotapes and food, while the rest of the team and
60 the Sherpas[8] did his carries for him. No way, said Erik. No way was he going to do this climb without being a fully integrated and useful member of the team. "I wasn't going to be carried to the top and spiked like a football," he says. The next day he forced himself to head back down through the icefall. He would eventually make ten passes through the Khumbu, cutting his time to five hours. **B**

acclimatization (ə-klī′mə-tĭ-zā′shən) *n.* the act of getting accustomed to a new climate or environment

B **CHARACTER STUDY**
Reread lines 55–64. What do you learn about Weihenmayer from his reaction to his teammates' idea?

---

6. **cerebral edema** (sĕr′ə-brəl ĭ-dē′mə).

7. **seracs** (sə-răks′): large, pointed masses of ice isolated by intersecting crevasses.

8. **Sherpas:** a Himalayan people who live around the Nepal-Tibet border and often assist climbers of Everest.

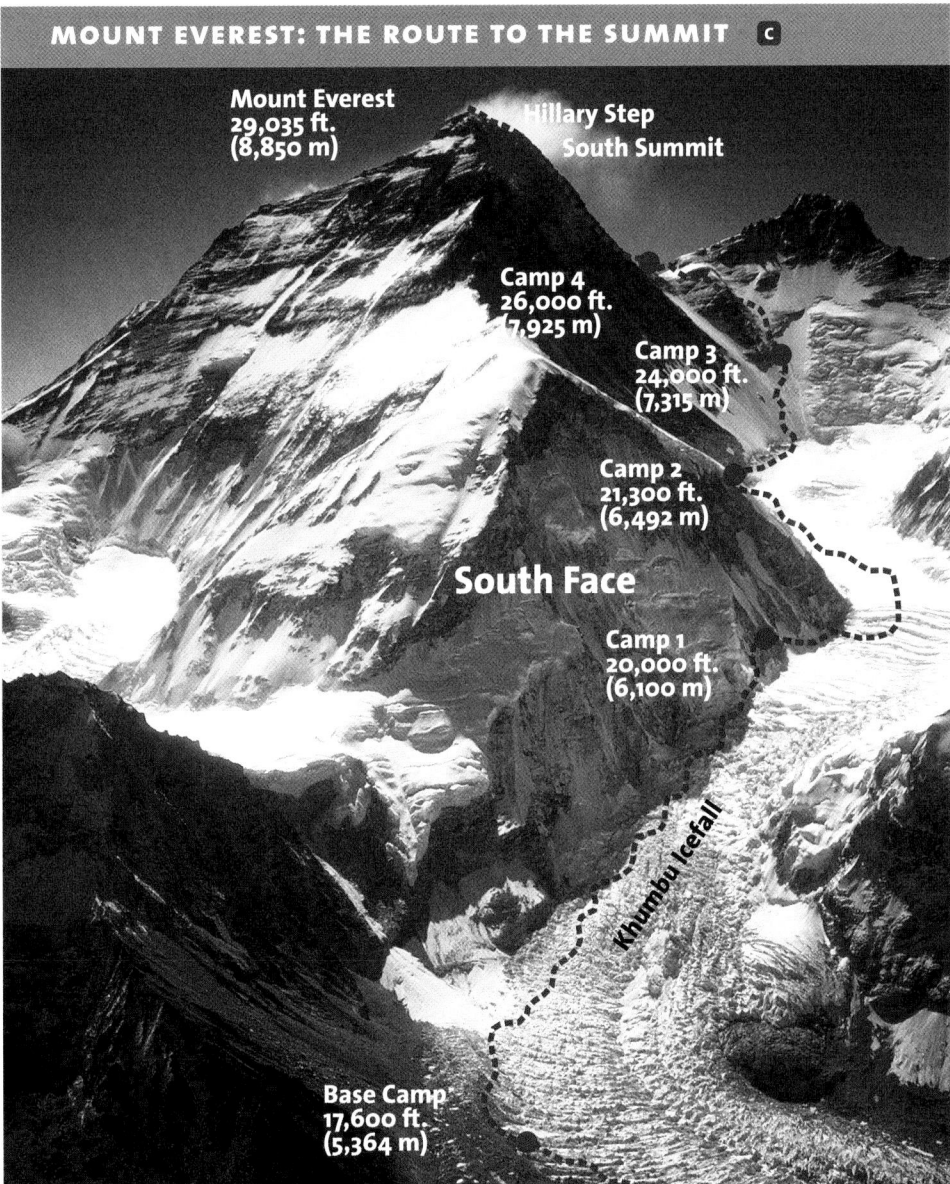

MOUNT EVEREST: THE ROUTE TO THE SUMMIT [c]

Mount Everest
29,035 ft.
(8,850 m)

Hillary Step
South Summit

Camp 4
26,000 ft.
(7,925 m)

Camp 3
24,000 ft.
(7,315 m)

Camp 2
21,300 ft.
(6,492 m)

South Face

Camp 1
20,000 ft.
(6,100 m)

Khumbu Icefall

Base Camp
17,600 ft.
(5,364 m)

[c] **INTERPRET
GRAPHIC AIDS**
What information about
Camp 1 do you learn from
this **diagram?** Record the
information in your chart.

    Sometimes, when Erik is giving a motivational speech for one of his
corporate clients . . . a fat, balding, middle-aged middle manager will approach
him and say, "Even I wouldn't do that stuff." Erik calls it the Even I Syndrome.
And he has to resist an impulse to say, "You're fat, out of shape, and you
smoke. Why would you even think of doing any of this stuff? Just because you
70 can see?" Erik is not impatient or smug, but he tires of people assuming that
sight will trump all other attributes and senses combined.
    By all accounts, Erik is gifted with strong lungs, a refined sense of balance,
a disproportionately powerful upper body, rubbery legs, and flexible ankles.
His conditioning is exemplary and his heart rate low. He is stockier than most
mountaineers, who tend toward lanky, long muscles. But he possesses an

abundance of the one indispensable characteristic of a great mountaineer: mental toughness, the ability to withstand tremendous amounts of cold, discomfort, physical pain, boredom, bad food, insomnia, and tedious conversation when you're snowed into a pup tent for a week on a three-foot-
80 wide ice shelf at 20,000 feet. (That happened to Erik on Alaska's Denali.[9]) On Everest, toughness is perhaps the most important trait a climber can have. "Erik is mentally one of the strongest guys you will ever meet," says fellow climber Chris Morris.

Everybody gets sick on Everest. It's called the Khumbu Krud, brought on by a combination of high altitude, dirty food, fetid water, intestinal parasites, and an utterly alien ecosystem. On Erik's team, at any given moment, half the climbers were running fevers, the others were nauseated, and they all suffered from one form or another of dysentery, an awkward ailment when there's a driving snowstorm and it's thirty below outside the tent. . . .

90 Scaling Everest requires the enthusiasm and boosterism of a physical-education teacher combined with the survival instinct of a Green Beret.[10] You have to want that summit. And if you whine . . . your teammates might discard you before you get there. Erik, beneath his beard and quiet **demeanor,** was both booster and killer. "He was the heart and soul of our team," says Eric Alexander. "The guy's spirit won't let you quit." **D**

E rik walks through these Kathmandu[11] streets with remarkable ease, his red-tipped cane searching out ahead of him, measuring distance, pitch, and angle. You give him little hints as he goes—"There's a doorway. Okay, now a right—no, left, sorry"—and he follows, his stride confident but easily arrested
100 when he bumps into an old lady selling shawls, and then into the wheel of a scooter. The physical confidence that he projects has to do with having an athlete's awareness of how his body moves through space. Plenty of sighted people walk through life with less poise and grace than Erik, unsure of their steps, second-guessing every move. And certainly most of the blind don't maneuver with Erik's **aplomb.** As he takes a seat in a crowded restaurant, ordering pizza, spaghetti, ice cream . . . —you work up an appetite climbing Everest—he smiles and nods as other diners ask, "Hey, aren't you the blind guy . . . ?"

With his Germanic, sculpted features and light brown hair, Erik looks a bit like a shaggy, youthful Kirk Douglas. He is a celebrity now: strangers ask for
110 his autograph, reporters call constantly, restaurants give him free meals. But is his celebrity the circus-freak variety—of a type with the Dogboy and the two-headed snake?

At its worst, Erik fears, it is. Casual observers don't understand what an achievement his Everest climb was, or they assume that if a blind guy can do it, anyone can. And indeed, improved gear has made Everest, at least in some

demeanor (dǐ-mē'nər) *n.* a way of behaving; manner

D CHARACTER STUDY
Think about how your perception of Weihenmayer would be different if his teammates' descriptions of him were omitted.

aplomb (ə-plŏm') *n.* poise; self-assurance

---

9. **Denali** (də-nä'lē): the highest peak in North America, also known as Mount McKinley.

10. **Green Beret:** a member of the U.S. Army Special Forces.

11. **Kathmandu** (kăt'măn-dōō'): the capital of Nepal.

people's minds, a bit smaller. In the climbing season there's a conga line[12] to the top, or so it seems, and the trail is a junkyard of discarded oxygen tanks and other debris. But Everest eats the unready and the unlucky. Almost 90 percent of Everest climbers fail to reach the summit. Many—at least 165 since 1953—never come home at all, their bodies lying uncollected where they fell. Four died in May. "People think because I'm blind, I don't have as much to be afraid of, like if I can't see a 2,000-foot drop-off I won't be scared," Erik says. "That's insane. Look, death is death, if I can see or not."

Everest expeditions break down into two types: those like Erik's, which are sponsored and united by a common goal, and those like the one described by Jon Krakauer in *Into Thin Air*,[13] in which gangs of climbers pay $65,000 each for the opportunity to stand on top of the world. But as conditions become more **arduous,** these commercial teams start squabbling, blaming weaker members for slowing them down and sometimes even refusing to help teammates in distress.

Many pros wouldn't go near Erik's team, fearing they might have to haul the blind guy down. "Everyone was saying Erik was gonna have an epic," says Charley Mace, a member of the film crew. ("Epic" is Everest slang for disaster.) Another climber planned to stay close, boasting that he would "get the first picture of the dead blind guy."

For Erik, who knew almost as soon as he could speak that he would lose his vision in his early teens, excelling as an athlete was the result of accepting his disability rather than denying it. Growing up with two brothers in Hong Kong and then Weston, Connecticut, he was always an athletic kid, a tough gamer who developed a bump-and-grind one-on-one basketball game that allowed him to work his way close to the hoop. He was, his father Ed says, "a pretty normal kid. While bike riding, he might have run into a few more parked cars than other kids, but we didn't dwell on his going blind."

His blindness was a medical **inevitability,** like a court date with a hanging judge.[14] "I saw blindness like this disease," he explains. "Like AIDS or something that was going to consume me." Think about that—being a kid, ten, eleven years old, and knowing that at some point in the near future your world is going to go dark. Certainly it builds character—that mental toughness his fellow climbers marvel at—but in a child, the natural psychological defense would be denial. **E**

When he lost his vision, Erik at first refused to use a cane or learn Braille, insisting he could somehow muddle on as normal. "I was so afraid I would seem like a freak," he recalls. But after a few embarrassing stumbles—he couldn't even find the school rest rooms anymore—he admitted he needed help. For Erik, the key was acceptance—not to fight his disability but to learn to work within it; not to **transcend** it but to understand fully what he was

---

arduous (är′jōō-əs) *adj.* requiring much effort; difficult

inevitability (ĭn-ĕv′ĭ-tə-bĭl′ĭ-tē) *n.* something that is certain to happen

E CONNECT
Reread lines 136–150. Do you agree that denial would be the natural response to a situation like Weihenmayer's? Explain.

transcend (trăn-sĕnd′) *v.* to pass beyond the limits of

---

12. **conga line:** The conga is a Latin American dance in which the dancers form a long, winding line.

13. *Into Thin Air:* a best-selling book about the 1996 climbing season at Mount Everest, during which eight climbers died.

14. **hanging judge:** a judge who always hands out very harsh sentences.

capable of achieving within it; not to pretend he had sight but to build systems that allowed him to excel without it. "It's tragic—I know blind people who like to pass themselves off as being able to see," Erik says.
160 "What's the point of that?"

He would never play basketball or catch a football again. But then he discovered wrestling. "I realized I could take sighted people and slam them into the mat," he says. Grappling was a sport where feel and touch mattered more than sight: if he could sense where his opponent had his weight or how to shift his own body to gain better leverage, he could excel using his natural upper-body strength. As a high school senior he went all the way to the National Junior Freestyle Wrestling Championship in Iowa.

Wrestling gave him the confidence to reenter the teenage social fray. He began dating when he was seventeen; his first girlfriend was a sighted
170 woman three years older than he. Erik jokes that he is not shy about using his blindness to pick up women. "They really go for the guide dog," he explains. "You go into a bar, put the guide dog out there, and the girls just come up to you." He and his friends devised a secret handshake to let Erik know if the girl he was talking to was attractive. "Just because you're blind doesn't make you any more selfless or deep or anything. You're just like most guys, but you look for different things," Erik says. . . . And the voice becomes **paramount.** "My wife has the most beautiful voice in the world," Erik says. Married in 1997, he and his wife Ellie have a one-year-old daughter, Emma. **F**

Erik first went hiking with his father when he was thirteen, trying to tap his
180 way into the wild with a white cane and quickly becoming frustrated stubbing his toes on rocks and roots and bumping into branches and trunks. But when he tried rock climbing, at sixteen while at a camp for the disabled in New Hampshire, he was hooked. Like wrestling, it was a sport in which being blind didn't have to work against him. He took to it quickly, and through climbing gradually found his way to formal mountaineering.

Watching Erik scramble up a rock face is a little like watching a spider make its way up a wall. His hands are like antennae, gathering information as they flick outward, surveying the rock for cracks, grooves, bowls, nubbins, knobs, edges, and ledges, converting all of it into a road map etched into his
190 mind. "It's like instead of wrestling with a person, I am moving and working with a rock," he explains. "It's a beautiful process of solving a puzzle." He is an accomplished rock climber, rated 5.10 (5.14 being the highest), and has led teams up sections of Yosemite's notorious El Capitan.[15] On ice, where one wrong strike with an ice ax can bring down an avalanche, Erik has learned to listen to the ice as he pings it gently with his ax. If it clinks, he avoids it. If it makes a thunk like a spoon hitting butter, he knows it's solid ice.

paramount
(păr′ə-mount′) *adj.* of highest importance

F CHARACTER STUDY
Reread lines 168–178, and think about Weihenmayer's **traits.** How do his own words affect your opinion of him?

---

15. **Yosemite's** (yō-sĕm′ĭ-tēz) **notorious El Capitan:** a 3,604-foot granite peak with a sheer cliff face, in Yosemite National Park, California.

Despite being an accomplished mountaineer—summiting Denali, Kilimanjaro in Africa, and Aconcagua[16] in Argentina, among other peaks, and, in the words of his friends, "running up 14ers" (14,000-foot peaks)—Erik viewed Everest as
200 **insurmountable** until he ran into Scaturro at a sportswear trade show in Salt Lake City, Utah. Scaturro, who had already summited Everest, had heard of the blind climber, and when they met the two struck an easy rapport. A geophysicist who often put together energy-company expeditions to remote areas in search of petroleum, Scaturro began wondering if he could put together a team that could help Erik get to the summit of Everest.

"Dude," Scaturro asked, "have you ever climbed Everest?"

"No."

"Dude, you wanna?"

210 Climbing with Erik isn't that different from climbing with a sighted mountaineer. You wear a bell on your pack, and he follows the sound, scuttling along using his custom-made climbing poles to feel his way along the trail. His climbing partners shout out helpful descriptions: "Death fall two feet to your right!" "Emergency helicopter-evacuation pad to your left!" He is fast, often running up the back of less experienced climbers. His partners all have scars from being jabbed by Erik's climbing poles when they slowed down.

For the Everest climb, Scaturro and Erik assembled a team that combined veteran Everest climbers and trusted friends of Erik's. Scaturro wrote up a Braille proposal for the Everest attempt and submitted it to Marc Maurer, president of
220 the National Federation of the Blind. Maurer immediately pledged $250,000 to sponsor the climb. . . . For Erik, who already had numerous gear and clothing sponsors, this was the greatest challenge of his life. If he failed, he would be letting down not just himself but all the blind, confirming that certain activities remained the preserve of the sighted.

He argued to anyone who would listen that he was an experienced mountaineer and that if he failed, it would be because of his heart or lungs or brain rather than his eyes. He wasn't afraid of physical danger—he had made dozens
230 of skydives and scaled some of the most dangerous cliff faces in the world—but he was frightened of how the world would perceive him. "But I knew that if I went and failed, that would feel better than if I didn't go at all," Erik says. "It could be like [the wrestling] Junior Nationals all over again. I went out to Iowa, and I got killed. But I needed to go to understand what my limits were."

insurmountable
(ĭn'sər-moun'tə-bəl) *adj.*
impossible to overcome

ANALYZE VISUALS
How does this photograph, which shows Weihenmayer and his teammates clambering over one of Everest's many crevasses, contribute to your understanding of Weihenmayer?

Oxygen deprivation does strange things to the human body. Heart rates go haywire, brain function decreases, blood thickens, intestines shut down. Bad ideas inexplicably pop into your head, especially above 25,000 feet, where, as Krakauer famously wrote in *Into Thin Air*, climbers have the "mind of a reptile." **G**

At that altitude, Erik could rely on no one but himself. His teammates would have to guide him, to keep ringing the bell and making sure Erik stayed on the trail, but they would be primarily concerned about their own survival in some of the worst conditions on earth. Ironically, Erik had some advantages as they closed in on the peak. For one thing, at that altitude all the climbers wore goggles and oxygen masks, restricting their vision so severely that they could not see their own feet—a condition Erik was used to. Also, the final push for the summit began in the early evening, so most of the climb was in pitch darkness; the only illumination was from miner's lamps.

When Erik and the team began the final ascent from Camp 4—the camp **H** he describes as Dante's Inferno with ice and wind[17]—they had been on the mountain for two months, climbing up and down and then up from Base Camp to Camps 1, 2, and 3, getting used to the altitude and socking away enough equipment—especially oxygen canisters—to make a summit push. They had tried for the summit once but had turned back because of weather. At 29,000 feet, the Everest peak is in the jet stream, which means that winds can exceed one hundred miles per hour and that what looks from sea level like a cottony wisp of cloud is actually a killer storm at the summit. Bad weather played a fatal role in the 1996 climbing season documented in *Into Thin Air*.

On May 24, with only seven days left in the climbing season, most of the NFB expedition members knew this was their last shot at the peak. That's why when Erik and Chris Morris reached the Balcony,[18] the beginning of the Southeast Ridge, at 27,500 feet, after a hard slog up the South Face,[19] they were terribly disappointed when the sky lit up with lightning, driving snow, and fierce winds. "We thought we were done," Erik says. "We would have been spanked if we made a push in those conditions." A few teammates gambled and went for it, and Jeff Evans and Brad Bull heroically pulled out fixed guidelines that had been frozen in the ice. By the time Base Camp radioed that the storm was passing, Erik and the entire team were coated in two inches of snow. Inspired by the possibility of a break in the weather, the team pushed on up the exposed Southeast Ridge, an additional 1,200 vertical feet to the South Summit.[20] At that point the climbers looked like astronauts walking on some kind of Arctic moon. They moved slowly because of fatigue from their huge, puffy down suits, backpacks with oxygen canisters and regulators, and goggles.

G INTERPRET GRAPHIC AIDS
Turn back to the **diagram** on page 255. In which camp or camps would the climbers have been subject to oxygen deprivation if they had run out of supplemental oxygen?

H INTERPRET GRAPHIC AIDS
As you read about the group's push for the summit, use the **diagram** on page 255 to follow the climbers' progress after they left Camp 4. How can you **infer** the locations of unlabeled features, such as the Balcony and the Southeast Ridge?

---

17. **Camp 4 . . . ice and wind:** Camp 4, at 26,000 feet, is compared to the hell described in the *Inferno*, the first part of Dante Alighieri's long poem *The Divine Comedy*.

18. **Balcony:** a natural platform where climbers often stop to rest.

19. **South Face:** the whole side of Everest on which Erik's group climbed to get to the summit.

20. **South Summit:** a peak several hundred feet below the true summit of Everest.

With a 10,000-foot vertical fall into Tibet on one side and a 7,000-foot fall into Nepal on the other, the South Summit, at 28,750 feet, is where many climbers finally turn back. The 656-foot-long knife-edge ridge leading to the Hillary Step[21] consists of ice, snow, and fragmented shale, and the only way to
280 cross it is to take baby steps and anchor your way with an ice ax. "You can feel the rock chip off," says Erik. "And you can hear it falling down into the void."

The weather was finally clearing as they reached the Hillary Step, the 39-foot rock face that is the last major obstacle before the true summit. Erik clambered up the cliff, belly-flopping over the top. "I celebrated with the dry heaves," he jokes. And then it was forty-five minutes of walking up a sharply angled snow slope to the summit.

"Look around, dude," Evans told the blind man when they were standing on top of the world. "Just take a second and look around."

t could be called the most successful Everest expedition ever, and not just
290 because of Erik's participation. A record nineteen climbers from the NFB team summited, including the oldest man ever to climb Everest—sixty-four-year-old Sherman Bull—and the second father-and-son team ever to do so—Bull and his son Brad.

What Erik achieved is hard for a sighted person to comprehend. What do we compare it with? How do we relate to it? Do we put on a blindfold and go hiking? That's silly, Erik maintains, because when a sighted person loses his vision, he is terrified and disoriented. And Erik is clearly neither of those things. Perhaps the point is really that there is no way to put what Erik has done in perspective because no one has ever done anything like it. It is a unique achievement, one
300 that in the truest sense pushed the limits of what man is capable of. Maurer of the NFB compares Erik to Helen Keller. "Erik can be a contemporary symbol for blindness," he explains. "Helen Keller lived one hundred years ago. She should not be our most potent symbol for blindness today." ❶

Erik, sitting in the Kathmandu international airport, waiting for the flight out of Nepal that will eventually return him to Golden, Colorado, is surrounded by his teammates and the expedition's seventy-five pieces of luggage. Success has made the group jubilant. This airport lounge has become the mountaineering equivalent of a winning Super Bowl locker room. . . .

In between posing for photos and signing other passengers' boarding passes,
310 Erik talks about how eager he is to get back home. He says summiting Everest was great, probably the greatest experience of his life. But then he thinks about a moment a few months ago, before Everest, when he was walking down the street in Colorado with daughter Emma in a front pack. They were on their way to buy some banana bread for his wife, and Emma was pulling on his hand, her little fingers curled around his index finger. That was a summit, too, he says. There are summits everywhere. You just have to know where to look. ✍

❶ DRAW CONCLUSIONS
What value might Maurer's idea have?

---

21. **Hillary Step:** a spur named for Sir Edmund Hillary, who, with the Sherpa Tenzing Norgay, was the first successful climber of Everest.

Comprehension

**PENNSYLVANIA
STANDARDS**

READING STANDARD
B.1.1.1.A.1 Evaluate character

1. **Recall** What was Erik Weihenmayer's goal, and why did he take on that challenge?

2. **Recall** Did Weihenmayer reach his goal? Explain your response.

3. **Summarize** What were Weihenmayer's advantages and disadvantages in comparison with the sighted members of his expedition?

Literary Analysis

4. **Analyze a Character Study** The purpose of a character study is to provide insight into the personality of an individual. In a chart, list Weihenmayer's three most outstanding traits. For each, cite examples from the text.

Outstanding Traits	Examples from Text
1.	
2.	
3.	

5. **Draw Conclusions** Think about the **conflicts** that Weihenmayer faced in "Blind to Failure." Which do you view as the main conflict—his internal struggle with his disability or his external struggle with the mountain? Support your conclusion with evidence from the text.

6. **Analyze Cause and Effect** How might Weihenmayer's presence have contributed to the great success of the expedition, with 19 climbers reaching the summit? Cite evidence from the selection.

7. **Evaluate Information from Graphic Aids** Review the chart you made as you read. How did the **diagram** help you understand this article? What other kinds of information, if any, would it have been useful to include in the graphic aid?

Literary Criticism

8. **Different Perspectives** Helen Keller once proclaimed, "No pessimist ever discovered the secret of the stars, or sailed to an uncharted land, or opened a new doorway for the human spirit." What might Keller say about Weihenmayer's **bravery** if she were alive today? Explain your answer.

Vocabulary in Context

VOCABULARY PRACTICE

Identify the words in each pair as synonyms or antonyms.

1. acclimatization/adaptation
2. demeanor/appearance
3. inevitability/certainty
4. banal/unusual
5. paramount/insignificant
6. arduous/simple
7. transcend/exceed
8. insurmountable/impossible
9. aplomb/awkwardness
10. crevasse/summit

WORD LIST

acclimatization

aplomb

arduous

banal

crevasse

demeanor

inevitability

insurmountable

paramount

transcend

VOCABULARY IN WRITING

Create five questions that you would want to ask Erik Weihenmayer in an interview. Use at least five vocabulary words. Here is a sample question.

> **EXAMPLE SENTENCE**
>
> *What was the hardest part of your **acclimatization** to Everest?*

VOCABULARY STRATEGY: SPECIALIZED VOCABULARY

Sports like mountaineering, as well as many occupations, have their own **specialized vocabularies.** A specialized vocabulary often includes words (like *crevasse*) that are used primarily within the particular field, as well as familiar words (like *face*) that are used with special meanings in the field. When familiar words have special meanings, it is often possible to figure out those meanings from the context. Otherwise, check a dictionary, looking for labels, such as *Mountaineering*, that may precede definitions giving special meanings of words.

PRACTICE Write the mountaineering term that matches each definition. If you need to, check a dictionary.

| ascenders | chimney | crampons | face | saddle |

1. devices attached to a rope to help one climb it
2. spiked iron plates on shoes to prevent slipping on ice
3. the sloping side of a mountain
4. a wide vertical crack into which the body of a climber can fit
5. a flat ridge connecting two higher elevations

PENNSYLVANIA STANDARDS

READING STANDARD
A.2.1 Apply the meaning of vocabulary

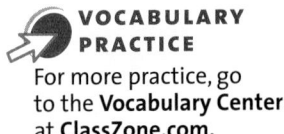

VOCABULARY PRACTICE
For more practice, go to the **Vocabulary Center** at **ClassZone.com.**

Reading for Information

A Different Level of Competition
Newspaper Article

Use with
"Blind to Failure," page 252.

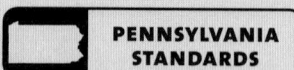

PENNSYLVANIA STANDARDS

READING STANDARDS
A.2.3.2 Cite evidence to support generalizations

A.2.4.1 Identify main ideas and supporting details

What's the Connection?

In "Blind to Failure" you read about Erik Weihenmayer, a mountaineer who successfully climbed Mount Everest despite having lost his vision as a teenager. Now, in "A Different Level of Competition," you will read about other intensely driven athletes who are taking the sports world by storm—despite their disabilities.

Skill Focus: Identify Main Ideas

The **main idea** of a nonfiction selection is the most important idea the selection expresses about its topic. It may be stated explicitly in a sentence in the text, or it may be implied. The main idea is often suggested by smaller key ideas, each developed in a paragraph or a longer section of the work. These ideas, too, may be stated or implied.

In the following article, various key ideas are developed one at a time over the course of several paragraphs. Use a chart like the one shown to note these key ideas.

Section	Key Idea
Title	"A Different Level of Competition"
Lead-in	Sports help people with disabilities.
Section 1 (paragraphs 1–5)	
Section 2 (paragraphs 6–9)	
Section 3 (paragraphs 10–16)	
Section 4 (paragraphs 17–20)	
Section 5 (paragraphs 21–24)	

Review: **Predict**

A Different Level of Competition

by Anne Stein

Sports for people with disabilities offer chances to build body and spirit Ⓐ

Champion skier Sandy Dukat's lower leg was amputated when she was four.

Here's a secret about young guys with disabilities who play team sports: They talk trash. And depending on the sport, they throw punches and crash into each other so hard that games can look like gladiator competitions.

In other words, a competitive athlete with a disability isn't any less intense than a competitive athlete without a
10 disability. Ⓑ

Take sled hockey, for example. A player balances on two ice-skating blades mounted beneath a molded plastic sled/seat. Sitting just inches above the ice, the athlete holds two small hockey sticks with metal teeth on one end to whip his body and sled around the rink; the other end is used for puck-handling. The stick is rotated to hit the puck.

20 "There are games that are rougher than others, but our team tries to focus more on the puck than the body," said Sylvester Flis, 27, a member of the 2002 U.S. Paralympic sled hockey team. Flis, who was born with spina bifida, lives in Chicago and practices with the RIC Blackhawks, sponsored by the Chicago Blackhawks and the Rehabilitation Institute of Chicago.

30 "We don't have big fights often, but there's lots of pushing and shoving. You've got to be very strong and athletic. You have to be in top shape to perform at the national level," Flis said.

But fighting and body checking aren't what draw people with disabilities to sports and competition. Besides the social aspects, there is an attitude of encouragement often lacking in able-
40 bodied athletics.

Matt Coppens, 30, of Richton Park lost both legs when a teenage driver ran into his car as Coppens set up roadside traffic cones.

Coppens wasn't much of an athlete before the accident. Now he trains full time and will join Flis on the sled hockey team. He also represented the United States at the 2000 Sydney Paralympics
50 in volleyball.

"There's so much camaraderie here," he said. "No matter what team you're on, you can't help but feel a closeness." Ⓒ

Whether it's competitive or recreational, sports serve an important role for people with disabilities, just as it does for the able-bodied.

"The benefits of participating in team sports have been studied a lot over the
60 years, especially in terms of what it does for youth and people without disabilities. [Team sports] does all the same things, and more, for people with disabilities,"

Ⓐ **PREDICT**
From the title and the lead-in, what do you think will be the main idea of this article?

Ⓑ **MAIN IDEA**
What key idea does Stein convey in her introduction?

Ⓒ **MAIN IDEA**
Identify the key idea introduced in this paragraph. How is the anecdote about Matt Coppens related to this idea?

said Jeff Jones, director of the Galvin Center for Health and Fitness at the Rehabilitation Institute of Chicago.

"Team sports teaches cooperation, sportsmanship, socialization and how to win and lose," Jones said. "It also teaches people with disabilities to challenge themselves. There's a phrase that's kicked around a lot among people with disabilities: 'If I can do this, I can do anything.'"

Jones said sled hockey players are some of the most conditioned, fit people he knows. They just happen to have a disability.

"They get what everyone gets out of team sports: a sense of accomplishment, enjoyment, satisfaction, conditioning and better health. And that makes everyday activities easier, just like it does for someone without a disability. They just don't happen to have as many opportunities as people without disabilities have to participate in sports," Jones said. "Our athletes are much more appreciative of the opportunities than those without disabilities. They can't just quit one team and go to another. The opportunities are few and far between."

Jerri Voda, who was born with cerebral palsy, races sailboats each summer through the Chicago-based Judd Goldman Adaptive Sailing Program.

"It's absolutely boosted my self-esteem," she said. "It's truly exhilarating for anyone with physical disabilities to participate in an activity that an able-bodied person can participate in. And the feeling of being out on the water driving a boat has totally heightened my independence and made me feel capable of achieving more in the future." **D**

Nearly every sport, recreational or competitive, can be adapted to the physical capabilities of participants.

Among the hundreds of sports available are wheelchair basketball, football and tennis; quadriplegic rugby; water and snow-skiing for the blind and visually impaired; and chair-based aerobics.

There are track and field and swimming events for every category of amputee, as well as blind softball and competitions for people with cerebral palsy and head injury. There is even a fledgling soccer league worldwide played by amputees on crutches.

Chicagoan Sandy Dukat, 29, is a member of the U.S. disabled ski team. Born without a femur, her leg was amputated at the knee at age 4, but the disability never stopped her from being a jock. Dukat competed against able-bodied kids in baseball, basketball and high jump, where she used one leg to clear a very competitive 4 feet, 11 inches.

Now Dukat's sport is alpine skiing, where she reaches speeds up to 50 m.p.h. perched on one ski and two poles with tiny ski-like attachments called outriggers. She didn't ski growing up in Ohio, but her fearlessness and speed caught the eye of coaches who encouraged her to train.

Though Dukat loves the thrill of sport, she would like to be seen as an elite athlete, not an athlete with a disability. She also would like people to stop clapping when she runs or skates along the lakefront path.

"People with disabilities are very capable," Dukat said. "We can work, have a family, a job, we can balance things."

She said someday people won't be shocked by the sight of her jogging with a prosthetic leg.

"It should be the norm. I don't look at someone with two legs and say, 'That's so cool.' It shouldn't be a surprise to see someone with disabilities doing this." **E**

D MAIN IDEA
What key idea is developed by the details in this section? Identify the sentence that states this idea.

E MAIN IDEA
What last point does the author make?

Comprehension

1. **Recall** Name three sports that have been adapted for disabled athletes.

2. **Summarize** How are athletes with disabilities similar to other athletes?

Critical Analysis

3. **Identify Main Idea** Review the key ideas you recorded in your chart. On the basis of these ideas, what would you say is the entire article's main idea? Explain your answer.

4. **Compare and Contrast** What do the athletes described in this article have in common with Erik Weihenmayer? Are they different from him in any way? Give examples to support your comparison.

Read for Information: Make Generalizations

WRITING PROMPT

What do people with disabilities gain from participating in rigorous sports and undertaking other physical challenges? Use information from "Blind to Failure" and "A Different Level of Competition" to support your response.

To respond to this prompt, you will have to make a generalization. A **generalization** is a broad statement about a category, based on a study of some members of that category. To make a generalization, follow these steps:

1. Gather evidence—anecdotes and direct statements—about what people with disabilities gain from playing sports.

2. Look for key ideas suggested by this evidence.

3. Make a general statement based on these key ideas.

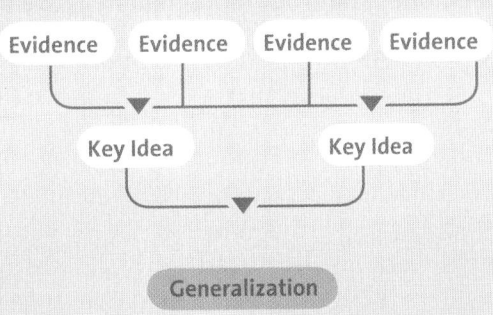

Review your evidence to make sure your generalization is true and fair; revise your generalization if necessary.

PENNSYLVANIA STANDARDS

READING STANDARDS
A.2.3.2 Cite evidence to support generalizations
A.2.4.1 Identify main ideas and supporting details

A Voice
Poem by Pat Mora

My Father's Song
Poem by Simon J. Ortiz

What makes a MEMORY?

PENNSYLVANIA STANDARDS

READING/SPEAKING STANDARD
B.2.2.1 Identify and analyze point of view

1.6.11.C.3 Adjust stress, volume and inflection to provide emphasis to ideas

KEY IDEA Whether they're once-in-a-lifetime occurrences or everyday experiences, some things remain imprinted on your mind long after they happen. In "A Voice" and "My Father's Song," two poets write about old **memories** that remain vivid many years later.

QUICKWRITE Think of a memory that remains very clear to you. Write a paragraph describing the memory in as much detail as you can. In a small group, try to generalize about the kinds of memories that retain their sharpness. Do memories of extraordinary events remain more vibrant than those of ordinary events? Do positive memories stand out more than negative ones?

LITERARY ANALYSIS: SPEAKER

The **speaker** in a poem is the voice that "talks" to the reader. Like the narrator in a work of fiction, the speaker relates the ideas or the story of the poem from a specific **point of view.** The speaker can be detached from or intensely involved with the experience or ideas expressed in the poem. It is important to keep in mind that the speaker is not necessarily the poet, even when he or she uses the pronouns *I* and *me.* As you read "A Voice" and "My Father's Song," ask yourself these questions about each speaker:

• Whom is the speaker addressing?

• What is the speaker's relationship to the subject of the poem?

• How would I characterize the speaker's attitude toward the person being described?

READING SKILL: READING POETRY

There are two ways to read lines of poetry:

• Read the lines continuously—paying attention to entire sentences, regardless of line breaks or stanzas.

• Read each line in isolation—noting the ideas and images in it, regardless of sentence structure.

Try both approaches with the following passage from "A Voice":

The family story says your voice is the voice
of an aunt in Mexico, spunky as a peacock.

When the lines are read together, they read like a regular sentence. When they are read with a pause at the end of each line, what gets emphasized?

Read "A Voice" and "My Father's Song" aloud using the first method, then silently using the second. Note how the line breaks help bring emphasis to certain words and ideas.

Author On·line

Pat Mora: The Power of Words

Pat Mora began writing poems while in elementary school in El Paso, Texas, where she was born and raised. Her mother, who dreamed of becoming a writer, won several speech contests while in school but was unable to continue her education when

**Pat Mora
born 1942**

the Great Depression hit. She passed on her ambition and her love of language to her daughter—gifts that have played an integral part in Mora's career. Discussing her motives for writing, the poet, essayist, and short story writer explains, "I am fascinated by the pleasure and power of words."

Simon J. Ortiz: A Voice of Inspiration

Simon J. Ortiz, an Acoma Pueblo Indian, was born in Albuquerque, New Mexico, and raised in the Acoma Pueblo homeland about 65 miles outside the city. He attributes his love of words to his father, who sang and talked to his son while working. Another

**Simon J. Ortiz
born 1941**

source of inspiration for Ortiz is his Native American heritage. His poems, short stories, and essays often center on themes of Native American history and culture. But they also explore more universal, personal subjects like identity and loneliness. Of his poetry, Ortiz says, "I tell you about me and my world so you may be able to see yourself."

MORE ABOUT THE AUTHOR
For more on these poets, visit the **Literature Center** at **ClassZone.com.**

A Voice

Pat Mora

Even the lights on the stage unrelenting
as the desert sun couldn't hide the other
students, their eyes also unrelenting,
students who spoke English every night

5 as they ate their meat, potatoes, gravy.
Not you. In your house that smelled like
rose powder, you spoke Spanish formal
as your father, the judge without a courtroom

in the country he floated to in the dark
10 on a flatbed truck. He walked slow **A**
as a hot river down the narrow hall
of your house. You never dared to race past him,

to say, "Please move," in the language
you learned effortlessly, as you learned to run,
15 the language forbidden at home, though your mother
said you learned it to fight with the neighbors.

You liked winning with words. You liked **B**
writing speeches about patriotism and democracy.
You liked all the faces looking at you, all those eyes.
20 "How did I do it?" you ask me now. "How did I do it

when my parents didn't understand?"
The family story says your voice is the voice
of an aunt in Mexico, spunky as a peacock.
Family stories sing of what lives in the blood.

A SPEAKER
What can you **infer** about the speaker's relationship with the person she describes?

B READING POETRY
By breaking the line after "you liked," what idea does the poet emphasize?

25 You told me only once about the time you went
to the state capitol, your family proud as if
you'd been named governor. But when you looked
around, the only Mexican in the auditorium,
you wanted to hide from those strange faces.
30 Their eyes were pinpricks, and you faked
hoarseness. You, who are never at a loss
for words, felt your breath stick in your throat

like an ice-cube. "I can't," you whispered.
"I can't." Yet you did. Not that day but years later.
35 You taught the four of us to speak up.
This is America, Mom. The undo-able is done **C**

in the next generation. Your breath moves
through the family like the wind
moves through the trees.

C SPEAKER
What is revealed in lines
35–36 about the speaker's
relationship to the person she
is addressing?

ANALYZE VISUALS
What do the sizes and
positions of the two women
in the painting suggest?

Girls from Guadalupita, New Mexico, Miguel Martinez. Oil pastel on paper, 30″ × 40″. Contemporary
Southwest Galleries, Sante Fe, New Mexico.

My Father's Song

Simon J. Ortiz

Wanting to say things,
I miss my father tonight.
His voice, the slight catch,
the depth from his thin chest,
5 the tremble of emotion
in something he has just said
to his son, his song: **D**

We planted corn one Spring at Acu[1]—
we planted several times
10 but this one particular time
I remember the soft damp sand
in my hand.

My father had stopped at one point
to show me an overturned furrow;[2]
15 the plowshare had unearthed
the burrow nest of a mouse
in the soft moist sand.

Very gently, he scooped tiny pink animals
into the palm of his hand
20 and told me to touch them.
We took them to the edge
of the field and put them in the shade
of a sand moist clod.

I remember the very softness
25 of cool and warm sand and tiny alive mice
and my father saying things.

D SPEAKER
From the description in this first stanza, what can you tell about the speaker's attitude toward the father?

Navajo Power Plant (1990), Shonto Begay. © Shonto Begay.

---

1. **Acu** (ä′kōō): the Acoma people's name for the Acoma Pueblo.
2. **furrow** (fûr′ō): a long, shallow trench made in the ground by a plow.

Comprehension

1. **Recall** Describe the incident related in "My Father's Song."

2. **Recall** What happens to the speaker's mother in "A Voice"?

3. **Clarify** In "A Voice," what is the speaker's mother referring to in line 20 when she asks, "How did I do it?"

PENNSYLVANIA STANDARDS

READING STANDARD
B.2.2.1 Identify and analyze point of view

Literary Analysis

4. **Compare Speakers** Review the questions listed on page 269. Then use a chart like this one to compare the two poems. What characteristics do they share?

	"A Voice"	"My Father's Song"
Person Being Addressed		
Relationship to Subject		
Attitude Displayed		

5. **Reading Poetry** Phrasing in poetry helps bring emphasis to certain words and ideas. It can also affect the interpretation of a poem. Why did Pat Mora choose to split certain sentences between lines or stanzas in "A Voice"? What does this call attention to? Cite specific examples.

6. **Interpret Imagery** Poets often make use of images that appeal to the five senses: sight, sound, touch, smell, and taste. In "My Father's Song," which of these senses does the poet evoke? What is the effect of using such images? Support your answer.

7. **Evaluate** In your opinion, which poem does a better job of characterizing the person being **remembered?** Support your opinion with details.

Literary Criticism

8. **Biographical Context** Both Mora and Ortiz are known for their efforts to preserve the cultures from which they come. To what extent does each of these poems fulfill that mission? Support your opinion.

Comparing Across Genres

from Rosa Parks

Biography by Douglas Brinkley

Rosa

Poem by Rita Dove

What is DIGNITY?

PENNSYLVANIA STANDARDS

READING STANDARDS
B.1.1.1.A.1 Evaluate character
B.1.2.1 Evaluate connections between texts

KEY IDEA Some people have it—quiet strength and an air of personal **dignity.** One such person was Rosa Parks. You are about to read two selections about Rosa Parks—a biography and a poem. Both pieces portray her dignity and courage and the important role she played in the civil rights movement.

DISCUSS With a small group, generate a list of real people, living or dead, as well as characters in books, movies, or TV shows, whom you consider to have dignity. Then discuss whether dignity comes mainly from within or from the approval of others.

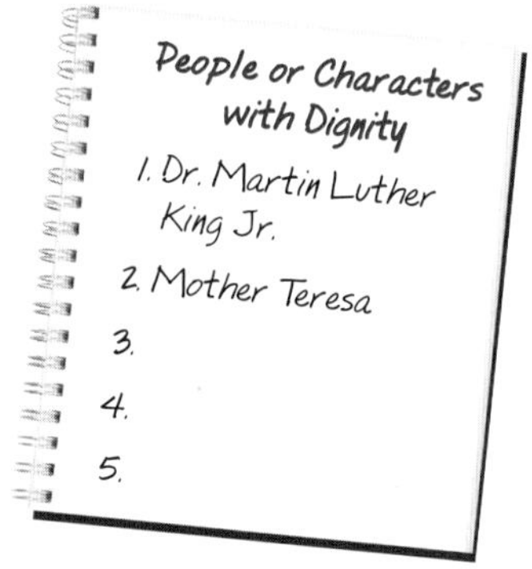
People or Characters with Dignity
1. Dr. Martin Luther King Jr.
2. Mother Teresa
3.
4.
5.

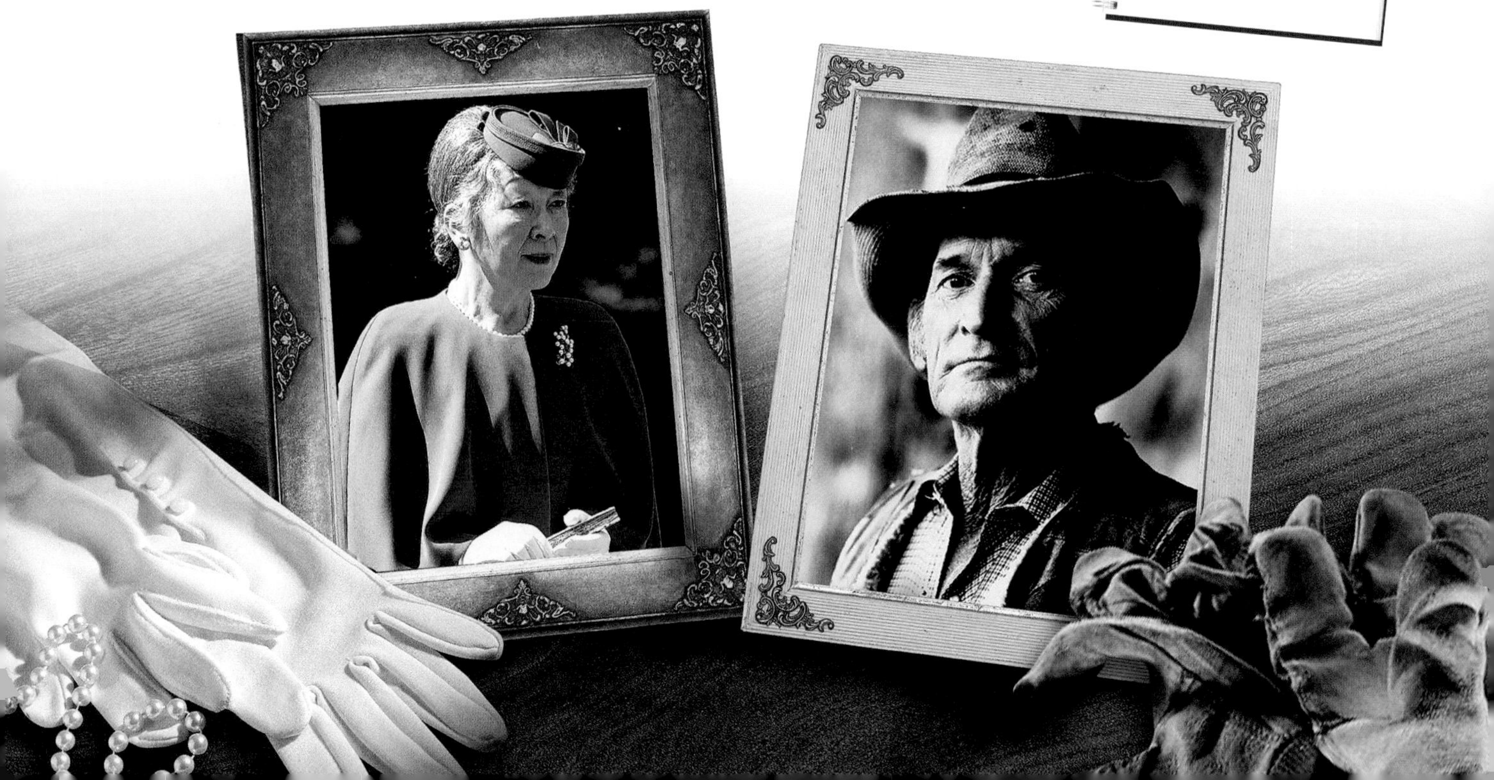

LITERARY ANALYSIS: CHARACTERIZATION ACROSS GENRES

As you know, fiction writers use methods of **characterization** to develop the made-up characters that populate their work. However, when writers of nonfiction and poetry portray real people, they cannot make up facts and details. Instead, writers in these **genres** shape readers' impressions of particular people by combining factual information with techniques unique to the genres in which they are working. The biography and the poem that follow both tell about Rosa Parks. The chart below shows the genre techniques each writer uses to characterize her.

Techniques Used in the Biography	Techniques Used in the Poem
• facts and details about Rosa Parks's actions, thoughts, and appearance	• word choice to describe Rosa Parks's actions and appearance
• quotations from Rosa Parks	• images to depict Rosa Parks's traits
• quotations from others who knew Rosa Parks	

As you read, notice the techniques each writer uses to portray this historic figure.

READING STRATEGY: SET A PURPOSE FOR READING

When you **set a purpose** for reading, you choose specific reasons for reading a work. In this lesson, you will read a biography and a poem in order to compare and contrast the ways they portray Rosa Parks. As you read, think about your impressions of Rosa Parks. After you read, you will use the **Points of Comparison** chart on page 281 to compare and contrast the two pieces.

▲ VOCABULARY IN CONTEXT

Restate each phrase, using a different word or words for each boldfaced term.

1. cheering **frenetically** during the final seconds of the game
2. a **protégé** of the company president
3. letting the mind wander in a pleasant **reverie**
4. an **exhortation** to try harder to win
5. as **serene** as a calm summer day
6. **retrieve** a lost scarf

Author Online

Douglas Brinkley: Historian and Educator Douglas Brinkley has written award-winning books about Henry Ford, Franklin Delano Roosevelt, and Jimmy Carter, among others. In 1993 Brinkley published *The Majic Bus: An American Odyssey.* In this first-person account, he described a class he

Douglas Brinkley born 1961

taught aboard a cross-country bus. Visiting 30 states, his students attended lectures, read widely, listened to American music, toured historical sites, and met celebrated authors.

Rita Dove: Honored Poet According to Rita Dove, "Poetry is language at its most distilled and most powerful." In 1993 she became the poet laureate of the United States—the youngest person and the first African American so honored.

Rita Dove born 1952

MORE ABOUT THE AUTHOR
For more on the authors, visit the **Literature Center** at ClassZone.com.

Background

Civil Rights Southern states once had laws that enforced racial segregation. Among other injustices, African Americans were forced to sit in separate sections of buses. In 1955, Rosa Parks's refusal to give up her seat on a bus triggered a 382-day bus boycott by African Americans in Montgomery, Alabama. The boycott brought Rosa Parks, Dr. Martin Luther King Jr., and their cause to national prominence. In 1956, the Supreme Court ruled that segregation on buses and other transportation was unconstitutional.

RosaParks

Douglas Brinkley

Rosa Parks headed to work on December 1, 1955, on the Cleveland Avenue bus to Court Square. It was a typical prewinter morning in the Alabama capital, chilly and raw, topcoat weather. Outside the Montgomery Fair Department Store a Salvation Army Santa rang his bell for coins in front of window displays of toy trains and mannequins modeling reindeer sweaters. Every afternoon when school let out, hordes of children would invade the store to gawk at the giant Christmas tree draped with blinking lights, a mid-1950s electrical marvel. But Rosa Parks saw little of the holiday glitter down in the small tailor shop in the basement next to the huge steam presses, where the
10 only hint of Yuletide cheer came from a sagging, water-stained banner reading "Merry Christmas and a Happy New Year."

   Not that many of Montgomery Fair's lower-level employees had the time to let the faded decoration make them sad. The department store rang up nearly half of its sales between Thanksgiving and New Year's Day, which turned the tailor shop into a beehive of activity every December. But even on days spent **frenetically** hemming, ironing, and steam-pressing, Parks's mind was more with the NAACP[1] than her workday duties. She was in the midst of organizing a workshop to be held at Alabama State University on December 3–4 and spent the morning during her coffee break telephoning H. Council Trenholm,
20 president of the university, applying enough quiet persuasion to be granted the use of a classroom over the weekend. "I was also getting the notices in the mail

ANALYZE VISUALS
What qualities of
Rosa Parks does the
photograph convey?

frenetically
(frə-nĕt′ĭk-lē) *adv.* in a
frenzied or frantic way

---

1. **NAACP:** a civil rights organization. The initials stand for National Association
    for the Advancement of Colored People.

for the election of officers of the senior branch of the NAACP, which would be [the] next week," Parks recalled. That afternoon, she lunched with Fred Gray, the lawyer who defended Claudette Colvin and was serving as Clifford Durr's[2] **protégé** at his law office above the Sears Auto Tire Store.

"When 1:00 P.M. came and the lunch hour ended, Mrs. Parks went back to her work as a seamstress," Gray would write in his civil rights memoir, *Bus Ride to Justice.* "I continued my work and left the office in the early afternoon for an out-of-town engagement." **Ⓐ**

30   Shortly after 5:00 P.M., Rosa Parks clocked out of work and walked the block to Court Square to wait for her bus home. It had been a hard day, and her body ached, from her feet swollen from the constant standing to her shoulders throbbing from the strain and her chronic bursitis. But the bus stand was packed, so Parks, disinclined to jockey for a rush-hour seat, crossed Dexter Avenue to do a little shopping at Lee's Cut-Rate Drug. She had decided to treat herself to a heating pad but found them too pricey. Instead, she bought some Christmas gifts, along with aspirin, toothpaste, and a few other sundries, and headed back to the bus stop wondering how her husband's day had been at the Maxwell Air Force Base Barber Shop and thinking about what her mother would cook for dinner. **Ⓑ**

40   It was in this late-day **reverie** that Rosa Parks dropped her dime in the box and boarded the yellow-olive city bus. She took an aisle seat in the racially neutral middle section,[3] behind the movable sign which read "colored." She was not expecting any problems, as there were several empty spaces at the whites-only front of the bus. A black man was sitting next to her on her right and staring out the window; across the aisle sat two black women deep in conversation. At the next two stops enough white passengers got on to nearly fill up the front section. At the third stop, in front of the Empire Theater, a famous shrine to country-music fans as the stage where the legendary Hank Williams got his start, the last front seats were taken, with one man left standing.

50   The bus driver twisted around and locked his eyes on Rosa Parks. Her heart almost stopped when she saw it was James F. Blake, the bully who had put her off his bus twelve years earlier. She didn't know his name, but since that incident in 1943, she had never boarded a bus that Blake was driving. This day, however, she had absentmindedly stepped in. "Move y'all, I want those two seats," the driver barked on behalf of Jim Crow,[4] which dictated that all four blacks in that row of the middle section would have to surrender their seats to accommodate a single white man, as no "colored" could be allowed to sit parallel with him. A stony silence fell over the bus as nobody moved. "Y'all

---

protégé (prō′tə-zhā′) *n.* a person who is guided or supported by an older or more influential person

Ⓐ CHARACTERIZATION
How did Parks's work for the NAACP differ from her job at the store? Why do you think Brinkley chose to highlight these differences?

Ⓑ CHARACTERIZATION
Reread lines 30–39. What do Rosa Parks's thoughts and actions reveal about her?

reverie (rĕv′ə-rē) *n.* a state of daydreaming

---

2. **Claudette Colvin . . . Clifford Durr's:** Claudette Colvin was an African-American teenager who had refused to give up her seat on a Montgomery city bus earlier in 1955. Clifford Durr was a white lawyer who worked for civil rights.

3. **racially neutral middle section:** a section of the bus where African Americans could sit, as long as no whites needed or wanted seats there.

4. **Jim Crow:** a term referring to the segregation of African Americans.

60 better make it light on yourselves and let me have those seats," Blake sputtered, more impatiently than before. Quietly and in unison, the two black women sitting across from Parks rose and moved to the back. Her seatmate quickly followed suit, and she swung her legs to the side to let him out. Then Parks slid over to the window and gazed out at the Empire Theater marquee promoting *A Man Alone,* a new Western starring Ray Milland. **C**

The next ten seconds seemed like an eternity to Rosa Parks. As Blake made his way toward her, all she could think about were her forebears, who, Maya Angelou would put it, took the lash, the branding iron, and untold humiliations while only praying that their children would someday "flesh out" the dream of equality. But unlike the poet, it was not Africa in the days of the
70 slave trade that Parks was thinking about; it was racist Alabama in the here and now. She shuddered with the memory of her grandfather back in Pine Level keeping watch for the KKK[5] every night with a loaded shotgun in his lap, echoing abolitionist John Brown's[6] **exhortation:** "Talk! Talk! Talk! That didn't free the slaves. . . . What is needed is action! Action!" So when Parks looked up at Blake, his hard, thoughtless scowl filled her with pity. She felt fearless, bold, and **serene.** "Are you going to stand up?" the driver demanded. Rosa Parks looked straight at him and said: "No." Flustered and not quite sure what to do, Blake retorted, "Well, I'm going to have you arrested." And Parks, still sitting next to the window, replied softly, "You may do that."
80 Her majestic use of "may" rather than "can" put Parks on the high ground, establishing her as a protester, not a victim. "When I made that decision," Parks stated later, "I knew I had the strength of my ancestors with me," and obviously their dignity as well. And her formal dignified "No," uttered on a suppertime bus in the cradle of the Confederacy as darkness fell, ignited the collective "no" of black history in America, a defiance as liberating as John Brown's on the gallows in Harpers Ferry. **D**

C CHARACTERIZATION
Reread lines 50–64. What do you learn about Rosa Parks from the way she reacted to the bus driver's commands?

exhortation
(ĕg′zôr-tā′shən) *n.* a communication strongly urging that something be done

serene (sə-rēn′) *adj.* calm; peaceful

D CHARACTERIZATION
How does Brinkley convey Rosa Parks's dignity and strength?

5. **back in Pine Level . . . KKK:** Pine Level is a town about 100 miles southeast of Birmingham. The KKK was the Ku Klux Klan, an extremist secret society that often violently terrorized blacks in the South.
6. **abolitionist John Brown's:** Brown, a white militant, performed radical acts to force the abolition of slavery, including a failed attempt to steal guns from the U.S. arsenal at Harpers Ferry, Virginia.

Rosa
Rita Dove

Rosa Parks

The only tired I was, was tired of giving in.

From *Americans Who Tell the Truth,* Robert Shetterly. Used by permission of Dutton Children's Books, a division of Penguin Young Readers Group, a member of Penguin Group, Inc. © Robert Shetterly.

How she sat there,
the time right inside a place
so wrong it was ready.

That trim name with
5 its dream of a bench
to rest on. Her sensible coat.

Doing nothing was the doing:
the clean flame of her gaze
carved by a camera flash.

10 How she stood up
when they bent down to **retrieve**
her purse. That courtesy. **E**

retrieve (rĭ-trēv′) *v.* to find and return safely

E CHARACTERIZATION
Which **images** portray Rosa Parks as a modest, unextravagant person? Which portray her as strong and serious?

Comprehension

1. **Recall** Where did Rosa Parks sit after boarding the bus in the evening?

2. **Recall** Why did the bus driver order her to move?

3. **Summarize** What decision did Rosa Parks make?

PENNSYLVANIA STANDARDS

READING STANDARD
B.1.1.1.A.1 Evaluate character

Literary Analysis

4. **Draw Conclusions** Rosa Parks, an ordinary person, helped launch the civil rights movement. Why was she able to wield such enormous influence?

5. **Analyze Characterization** In both the biography and the poem, what words and actions convey Rosa Parks's **dignity?**

6. **Make Inferences** A **paradox** is a statement that seems contradictory but is still true. Reread line 7 of the poem. In what way does this line express a paradox? Explain your thinking.

Comparing Across Genres

Now that you've read both selections about Rosa Parks, think about the similarities and differences you found in the ways Rosa Parks is portrayed. Create a **Points of Comparison** chart like the one shown, and respond in your own words to the questions. If a point of comparison is not covered in one of the selections, leave the box blank.

Points of Comparison	In the Biography	In the Poem
What did you learn about Rosa Parks's appearance?		
What did you learn about her daily life?		
What did you learn about her personality, thoughts, and feelings?		
What did you learn about her values and the things she thought were important?		
What genre techniques did the writer use to portray Rosa Parks?		

Vocabulary in Context

VOCABULARY PRACTICE

Write the word that best completes each sentence.

1. Boarding the bus, Rosa Parks was lost in a private _____ of memories and wishes.
2. She had been working _____ all day because it was the busy Christmas season.
3. She lunched with a lawyer who was a _____ of a famous civil rights lawyer.
4. She recalled her grandfather's _____ to act.
5. Her belief in the rightness of her refusal made her calm and _____.
6. She knew that if she lost her self-respect now, she might never _____ it.

WORD LIST

exhortation

frenetically

protégé

retrieve

reverie

serene

VOCABULARY IN WRITING

Imagine you are one of the other African-American passengers on the bus with Rosa Parks. Write a paragraph describing your reaction when she refuses to give up her seat. Use two or more vocabulary words in your paragraph. You might start like this.

> **EXAMPLE SENTENCE**
>
> *Rosa calmly refused to obey the driver, but I was feeling far from* **serene***.*

VOCABULARY STRATEGY: ETYMOLOGIES

Researching a word's **etymology**—that is, its history and origin—can give you insight into the word's meaning. One easy way to learn a word's etymology is to look the word up in a dictionary. Information about the word's origin will appear near the beginning or end of the dictionary entry.

> **se•rene** (sə-rēn′) *adj.* **1.** Unaffected by disturbance; calm and unruffled. See synonyms at **calm. 2.** Unclouded; fair: *serene skies and a bright blue sea.* **3.** often **Serene** Used as a title and form of address for certain members of royalty: *Her Serene Highness; His Serene Highness.* [Middle English, from Latin *serenus*, serene, clear.] —**se•rene′ly** *adv.* —**se•rene′ness** *n.*

PRACTICE Use a dictionary to answer these questions.

1. Through what languages can the history of *frenetic* be traced?
2. Does the Old French verb that gave rise to *reverie* mean "to be happy" or "to dream"?
3. From what Latin word does *exhort* derive, and what does it mean?
4. What language is the source of *protégé*?

PENNSYLVANIA STANDARDS

READING STANDARD
A.1.1 Apply the meaning of vocabulary

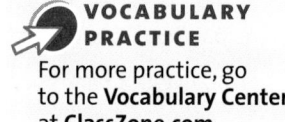

VOCABULARY PRACTICE
For more practice, go to the **Vocabulary Center** at **ClassZone.com**.

Writing for Assessment

1. READ THE PROMPT

In writing assessments, you will often be asked to compare and contrast how two writers treat the same subject. You are now going to practice writing an essay that requires this type of focus.

PROMPT

Like many people, Douglas Brinkley and Rita Dove seem fascinated by Rosa Parks and the courage she displayed when she defied racist laws and refused to give up her bus seat. In a four- or five-paragraph essay, compare and contrast the portrayals of Rosa Parks. Do they create the same impression of her? In what ways do they differ? Give evidence to support your response.

◀ **STRATEGIES IN ACTION**

*1. I need to write an essay that shows **similarities and differences** between the two works on Rosa Parks.*

*2. I have to consider how each writer **reveals Parks's traits** and personality.*

*3. I need to **include examples or quotations** from the two works.*

2. PLAN YOUR WRITING

• Review the **Points of Comparison** chart you created on page 281.

• Using your chart, find examples to use as evidence for the points you will develop in your essay. If necessary, review the selections to identify more examples.

• Create an outline to organize your main points. You might base this outline on the categories used in the chart.

3. DRAFT YOUR RESPONSE

Introduction Introduce the topic, Rosa Parks, and then explain that you will be comparing portrayals of her in a biography and a poem. Be sure to include the title and author of each work.

Body Use the topics in your comparison-and-contrast chart as a guide to the key points of your comparison. In one paragraph, for example, you might compare and contrast how each writer describes her appearance. Within each paragraph you write, give specific details to back up your points.

Conclusion Wrap up your essay with a restatement of your main idea and a brief summary of your main points.

Revision Check your use of transitional words and phrases to connect your ideas. Words and phrases such as *likewise, both,* and *in the same way* signal similarities. *On the other hand, instead, nevertheless,* and *however* signal differences.

Writing Workshop

Comparison-Contrast Essay

How does high school differ from middle school? Which video game should you buy? Why should you support one political candidate over another? You compare and contrast all the time in life—often to answer questions like these. In this workshop, you will write an essay comparing and/or contrasting two characters. Begin by consulting the **Writer's Road Map.**

WRITER'S ROAD MAP

Comparison-Contrast Essay

WRITING PROMPT 1

Writing from Literature Write an essay comparing and/or contrasting two characters from literature. Your essay should provide your reader with new insights into those characters.

Characters to Consider
- Madame Loisel and her husband in "The Necklace"
- Jill and Andy, the cook, in "Pancakes"
- Mami and Papi in "Daughter of Invention"

WRITING PROMPT 2

Writing from the Real World Write an essay about two people who exemplify strong contrasts within their profession.

People to Consider
- two athletes with different playing styles
- two musicians known for their distinctive sounds
- two comedians with unique approaches to their craft

 WRITING TOOLS
For prewriting, revision, and editing tools, visit the **Writing Center** at ClassZone.com.

KEY TRAITS

1. **IDEAS**
   - Clearly states the **subjects** being compared and/or contrasted
   - Presents a **thesis statement** that identifies similarities and/or differences
   - Uses specific **examples** to support key ideas

2. **ORGANIZATION**
   - Includes an engaging **introduction** and a satisfying **conclusion**
   - Follows a consistent **organizational pattern**
   - Uses **transitional words and phrases**

3. **VOICE**
   - Uses language appropriate for the **audience and purpose**

4. **WORD CHOICE**
   - Uses **precise adjectives** to convey similarities and differences

5. **SENTENCE FLUENCY**
   - Varies **sentence beginnings** for good pacing and variety

6. **CONVENTIONS**
   - Employs **correct grammar and usage**

Part 1: Analyze a Student Model

WRITING STANDARD
1.4.11.B Write complex informational pieces

Eve Zimmerman
Randolph High School

Madame Loisel and Della: Different Values

KEY TRAITS IN ACTION

What do you value in life? Madame Loisel in Guy de Maupassant's "The Necklace" and Della in O. Henry's "The Gift of the Magi" would answer this question differently. Madame Loisel dreams of living a life of luxury. Della wants to give her husband the perfect Christmas gift,
5 but she lacks enough money. Both women long for things they cannot afford, but their similarities end there. Their thoughts, treatment of their husbands, and responses to difficult situations reveal the differences in their values. While Madame Loisel equates happiness with her social status, Della looks to her husband and her quiet life for contentment.

Identifies the **characters** being compared and contrasted.

Introduction includes a focused **thesis statement** that presents the points that will be contrasted.

10 Madame Loisel's and Della's thoughts reveal a great deal about their values. Both women spend time reflecting on their situations. Madame Loisel's thoughts convey her selfish side. At the beginning of the story, readers learn that "she grieved incessantly, feeling that she had been born for all the little niceties and luxuries of living." Constantly fantasizing
15 about a life of wealth and attention, Madame Loisel is the star of her daydreams, and her husband does not even play a supporting role. Like Madame Loisel, Della grieves about her situation, but only as it relates to her husband. Della spends "many a happy hour" coming up with the perfect gift for Jim. Her thoughts show that Jim's happiness means more
20 to her than her own.

This writer uses point-by-point **organization.** This paragraph elaborates on the first point—the characters' thoughts. Varied **sentence beginnings** add sophistication.

Madame Loisel's and Della's values are also evident in the ways they interact with their husbands. Madame Loisel acts as if her husband is a nuisance to her. She is unappreciative and hot tempered when he brings home the invitation to the party. When her husband finally agrees to

Begins to examine the second point—the characters' treatment of their husbands. The formal tone is appropriate for the **audience and purpose.**

25 give her money to buy a dress, she does not even thank him. Later, she
   ignores him at the party and feels embarrassed by him when they finally
   leave together. Della, on the other hand, showers her husband with
   attention and love. After sacrificing her best feature, she does not spend
   time reflecting on her hair. Instead, she encourages Jim to look on the
30 bright side, saying, "My hair grows awfully fast. Say 'Merry Christmas!'
   Jim, and let's be happy." For Della, happiness is about Jim and their love
   for each other.

       In addition to their thoughts and treatment of their husbands,
   Madame Loisel and Della reveal their values through their responses to
35 difficult situations. To her credit, Madame Loisel repays her debt "with
   sudden heroism" and takes pride in her hard work. However, her values
   do not change. Even after everything she has been through, Madame
   Loisel often thinks back to the time "she had been so beautiful and
   admired." This response shows that she is still selfish and vain. Unlike
40 Madame Loisel, Della does not seem to mind the unfortunate situation
   she and her husband are in. At the end of the story, she and Jim do
   not dwell on their losses. They respond to the situation by saving their
   presents for a later time and enjoying each other's company over dinner.

       Madame Loisel's and Della's thoughts, relationships, and responses
45 to their circumstances show just how different they are. To Madame
   Loisel, happiness means wearing the best clothes, being admired, and
   living a privileged life. To Della, however, happiness means loving and
   being loved by her husband. Both women find themselves in similar
   situations, but their values—like most people's—have more to do with
50 their personalities than their situations in life.

Uses a **transitional phrase** to signal one difference.

Introduces the third point—the characters' responses to difficult situations.

Includes **examples** and **precise adjectives** that show the differences between the characters.

Conclusion summarizes similarities and differences and offers an observation about values.

2

WRITING STANDARD
1.5.11.A.1 Identify topic, task and audience.

Part 2: Apply the Writing Process

PREWRITING

What Should I Do?

What Does It Look Like?

1. Analyze the prompt.
Look again at the prompt you chose on page 284. Find words that state the **topics** you should compare and your **audience, purpose,** and **format.** If the prompt is not specific, then the choice is up to you.

> **TIP** Avoid choosing subjects that are too similar. Make sure there is a compelling reason to compare or contrast them.

▶ **WRITING PROMPT** Write an (essay) comparing and/or contrasting (two characters from) (literature.) Your essay should provide your reader with new insights into those characters.

Audience isn't stated, but I know that I'm writing for my teacher and classmates. My purpose is to analyze two characters and help readers understand them.

2. Brainstorm similarities and differences.
Use a Venn diagram, a chart, or another graphic organizer to record all the similarities and differences you can think of. Note the characters' looks, personalities, values, and relationships.

▶ **Madame Loisel**
* Values status
* Always thinks of herself
* Treats husband terribly

Both
* Want things they can't afford

Della
* Values her husband
* Thinks only about Jim
* Makes best of situation

3. Decide on a focus and write a thesis.
What are the most striking similarities or differences you noted? What conclusions can you draw about the characters? Using your answers to these questions, determine your focus and write a **thesis statement** that conveys your main idea. Then identify the points that will help you prove your thesis.

▶ **Working Thesis:** *Madame Loisel and Della both want things they can't afford, but they have different values.*

> **Points:** 1. Thoughts
> 2. Treatment of husbands
> 3. Responses to hard times

4. Collect evidence.
Use a chart to collect **examples** and **quotations** that relate to each point you identified.

▶

Point	Madame Loisel	Della
1. Thoughts	grieves "incessantly" about her financial situation	thinks only about Jim's gift

DRAFTING

What Should I Do?	**What Does It Look Like?**

1. Choose an organization.

Two ways to organize the body of a comparison-contrast essay are shown here. You may want to try out both before selecting the one that works best for your purpose.

- **Subject-by-Subject Organization**
  Discusses all the points relating to the first subject before moving on to the second subject

- **Point-by-Point Organization**
  Compares or contrasts both subjects, one point at a time

▶

SUBJECT-BY-SUBJECT ORGANIZATION

Subject A: Madame Loisel
  Point 1: Thoughts
  Point 2: Treatment of husband
  Point 3: Response to hard times
Subject B: Della
  Point 1: Thoughts
  Point 2: Treatment of husband
  Point 3: Response to hard times

POINT-BY-POINT ORGANIZATION

Point 1: Thoughts
  Subject A: Madame Loisel
  Subject B: Della
Point 2: Treatment of husband
  Subject A: Madame Loisel
  Subject B: Della
Point 3: Response to hard times
  Subject A: Madame Loisel
  Subject B: Della

2. Use transitions.

Transitional words and phrases, such as *like, also, similarly, but,* and *unlike,* are cues that signal similarities or differences.

See page 290: Check Your Grammar

▶

Like Madame Loisel, Della grieves about her situation, but only as it relates to her husband. Her thoughts show that Jim's happiness means more to her than her own.

    Madame Loisel's and Della's values are also evident in the ways they interact with their husbands.

3. Incorporate supporting details.

Show, don't tell, readers about the characters' similarities and differences. Use the evidence you collected earlier to help you prove your point.

TIP Before revising, consult the **key traits** on page 284 and the **rubric** and **peer-reader questions** on page 290.

▶

Madame Loisel's values do not change. —Key point
Even after everything she has been through, she
often thinks back to the time "she had been so —Support
beautiful and admired." This response shows that
she is still vain. Unlike Madame Loisel, Della does —Key
not seem to mind the unfortunate situation that she point
is in. At the end of the story, she and Jim decide
to enjoy each other's company and forget about —Support
the gifts.

REVISING AND EDITING

What Should I Do?	*What Does It Look Like?*

1. Improve your introduction.
- Put [brackets] around the first one or two sentences of your introduction.
- Review the bracketed text. If you are simply stating the obvious, try adding an interesting detail, such as a question or quotation, to hook readers.

▶ What do you value in life?
[Madame Loisel in Guy de Maupassant's "The Necklace" and Della in O. Henry's "The Gift of the Magi," ~~are very different people.~~]
  └ would answer this question differently.

2. Make sure you have included enough support.
- <u>Underline</u> the examples and quotations that you have used.
- If your essay lacks underlines, add examples and quotations to help readers understand the characters.

▶ Madame Loisel's thoughts convey her selfish side. She constantly dreams of a life of wealth and attention.
At the beginning of the story, readers learn that "she grieved incessantly, feeling that she had been born for all the little niceties and luxuries of living."

3. Monitor your tone.
- If you are writing an essay for class, use a formal tone. Read your draft aloud and highlight words and phrases that are too conversational.
- Replace words with ones more appropriate to your audience and purpose.

▶   ⌐ acts as if her husband is a nuisance to her.
Madame Loisel ~~is ridiculous. What's the deal with how she treats her husband?~~ She ~~gives him major attitude~~ when he brings home the invitation to the party.
  ⌐ is unappreciative and hot tempered

4. Check that your ideas flow smoothly.
- Draw [boxes] around the transitional words and phrases that signal the characters' similarities or differences.
- If your essay lacks boxes, add transitions where it makes sense to cue readers.

See page 290: Add Transition Words

▶ Madame Loisel treats her husband badly. She ignores him at the party and feels embarrassed by him when they finally leave together. Della showers her husband with attention.   , on the other hand,

Preparing to Publish
Comparison-Contrast Essay

Apply the Rubric

A strong comparison-contrast essay . . .

- ☑ opens with an engaging introduction that presents the subjects being compared and/or contrasted
- ☑ has a focused thesis statement
- ☑ supports the thesis with examples
- ☑ follows a consistent organization
- ☑ includes precise adjectives and varied sentence beginnings
- ☑ uses transitional words and phrases
- ☑ uses an appropriate tone
- ☑ summarizes the comparison and/or contrast in a satisfying conclusion

Ask a Peer Reader

- How would you summarize the similarities and differences between the characters I wrote about?
- Which examples are strong? Which are weak?
- Where do I need to include more supporting details?

Add Transition Words

For Comparing	For Contrasting
also	but
and	however
another	in contrast
both	instead
in addition to	on the other hand
like	unlike
too	yet

Check Your Grammar

- Use a comma to set an introductory transitional phrase off from the rest of the sentence.

  Like Madame Loisel , Della grieves about her situation.

- Use quotation marks around exact words cited from a story. Periods and commas should always go inside quotation marks.

  Madame Loisel repays her debt " with sudden heroism."

See pages R49–R50: Quick Reference: Punctuation

Writing Online

PUBLISHING OPTIONS
For publishing options, visit the **Writing Center** at ClassZone.com.

ASSESSMENT PREPARATION
For writing and grammar assessment practice, go to the **Assessment Center** at ClassZone.com.

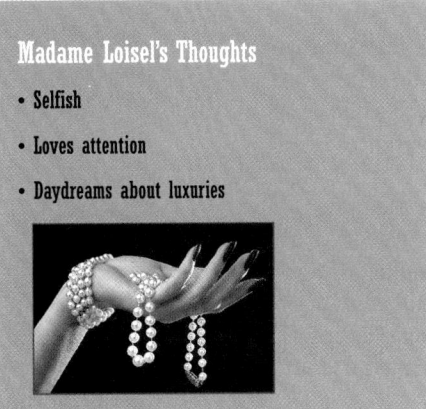

Creating and Presenting a Power Presentation

Most computers come equipped with software that lets users create slide presentations. Adapting your comparison-contrast essay to this format lets you express your ideas with extra style.

Preparing the Presentation

1. **Focus on the big ideas.** Your introduction and conclusion, as well as the main points, should get at least one slide apiece. Each slide should have one headline and three to five short bullet points.

2. **Choose a template.** If you have a flair for design, choose your own fonts and colors. If not, use one of the prefabricated templates provided in the software program.

3. **Use effects to complement your message.** Consider adding visuals or music. Avoid fancy effects and animations, as these detract from your main points. Each slide should be easy to read from the back of the room.

4. **Practice the presentation.** If you can, practice in the room you will present in, with the equipment you will use. Otherwise, print out your presentation and practice it in front of friends or family. Double-check that each point is logical, that any quotations you included are accurate, and that your spelling is correct.

> **Madame Loisel's Thoughts**
>
> • Selfish
>
> • Loves attention
>
> • Daydreams about luxuries

Delivering the Presentation

1. **Present to audience members—don't read to them.** Using each point as a reminder, elaborate on your topic so that your audience truly understands your opinions and evidence.

2. **Be respectful of other presenters.** Show them the same attention and consideration that you want them to give you.

3. **Find out how you did.** When you have finished, distribute a questionnaire to audience members. Ask for feedback about the content and style of your presentation.

Reading Comprehension

ASSESS
The practice test items on the next few pages match skills listed on the Unit Goals page (page 185) and addressed throughout this unit. Taking this practice test will help you assess your knowledge of these skills and determine your readiness for the Unit Test.

REVIEW
After you take the practice test, your teacher can help you identify any skills you need to review.

- Character Traits
- Character Motivation
- Point of View
- Draw Conclusions
- Make Inferences
- Monitor
- Multiple-Meaning Words
- Word Origins
- Supporting and Descriptive Details
- Words, Phrases, Clauses

DIRECTIONS *Read the following selections and then answer the questions.*

from Powder

Tobias Wolff

Just before Christmas my father took me skiing at Mount Baker. He'd had to fight for the privilege of my company, because my mother was still angry with him for sneaking me into a nightclub during his last visit, to see Thelonious Monk.

He wouldn't give up. He promised, hand on heart, to take good care of me and have me home for dinner on Christmas Eve, and she relented. But as we were checking out of the lodge that morning it began to snow, and in this snow he observed some rare quality that made it necessary for us to get in one last run. We got in several last runs. He was indifferent to my fretting. Snow
10 whirled around us in bitter, blinding squalls, hissing like sand, and still we skied. As the lift bore us to the peak yet again, my father looked at his watch and said, "Criminy. This'll have to be a fast one."

By now I couldn't see the trail. There was no point in trying. I stuck to him like white on rice and did what he did and somehow made it to the bottom without sailing off a cliff. We returned our skis and my father put chains on the Austin-Healey while I swayed from foot to foot, clapping my mittens and wishing I was home. I could see everything. The green tablecloth, the plates with the holly pattern, the red candles waiting to be lit.

We passed a diner on our way out. "You want some soup?" my father asked.
20 I shook my head. "Buck up," he said. "I'll get you there. Right, doctor?"

I was supposed to say, "Right, doctor," but I didn't say anything.

A state trooper waved us down outside the resort. A pair of sawhorses were blocking the road. The trooper came up to our car and bent down to my father's window. His face was bleached by the cold. Snowflakes clung to his eyebrows and to the fur trim of his jacket and cap.

"Don't tell me," my father said.

The trooper told him. The road was closed. It might get cleared, it might not. Storm took everyone by surprise. So much, so fast. Hard to get people moving. Christmas Eve. What can you do.
30 My father said, "Look. We're talking about five, six inches. I've taken this car through more than that."

The trooper straightened up. His face was out of sight but I could hear him. "The road is closed."

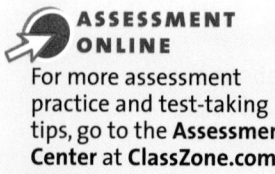
ASSESSMENT ONLINE
For more assessment practice and test-taking tips, go to the **Assessment Center** at **ClassZone.com.**

My father sat with both hands on the wheel, rubbing the wood with his thumbs. He looked at the barricade for a long time. He seemed to be trying to master the idea of it. Then he thanked the trooper, and with a weird, old-maidy show of caution turned the car around. "Your mother will never forgive me for this," he said.

"We should have left before," I said. "Doctor."

40 He didn't speak to me again until we were in a booth at the diner, waiting for our burgers. "She won't forgive me," he said. "Do you understand? Never."

"I guess," I said, but no guesswork was required; she wouldn't forgive him.

"I can't let that happen." He bent toward me. "I'll tell you what I want. I want us all to be together again. Is that what you want?"

"Yes, sir."

He bumped my chin with his knuckles. "That's all I needed to hear."

When we finished eating he went to the pay phone in the back of the diner, then joined me in the booth again. I figured he'd called my mother, but he didn't give a report. He sipped at his coffee and stared out the window at the 50 empty road. "Come on, come on," he said, though not to me. A little while later he said it again. When the trooper's car went past, lights flashing, he got up and dropped some money on the check. "Okay. Vamanos."

The wind had died. The snow was falling straight down, less of it now and lighter. We drove away from the resort, right up to the barricade. "Move it," my father told me. When I looked at him he said, "What are you waiting for?" I got out and dragged one of the sawhorses aside, then put it back after he drove through. He pushed the door open for me. "Now you're an accomplice," he said. "We go down together." He put the car into gear and gave me a look. "Joke, son."

Description of Maud Martha

Gwendolyn Brooks

What she liked was candy buttons, and books, and painted music (deep blue, or delicate silver) and the west sky, so altering, viewed from the steps of the back porch; and dandelions.

She would have liked a lotus, or China asters or the Japanese Iris, or meadow lilies—yes, she would have liked meadow lilies, because the very word

meadow made her breathe more deeply, and either fling her arms or want to fling her arms, depending on who was by, rapturously up to whatever was watching in the sky. But dandelions were what she chiefly saw. Yellow jewels for everyday, studding the patched green dress of her back yard. She liked their demure prettiness second to their everydayness; for in that latter
10 quality she thought she saw a picture of herself, and it was comforting to find that what was common could also be a flower.

And could be cherished! To be cherished was the dearest wish of the heart of Maud Martha Brown, and sometimes when she was not looking at dandelions (for one would not be looking at them all the time, often there were chairs and tables to dust or tomatoes to slice or beds to make or grocery stores to be gone to, and in the colder months there were no dandelions at all), it was hard to believe that a thing of only ordinary allurements—if the allurements of any flower could be said to be ordinary—was as easy to love as a thing of heart-catching beauty.

Such as her sister Helen! who was only two years past her own age of seven, and was almost her own height and weight and thickness. But oh, the long lashes, the grace, the little ways with
20 the hands and feet.

Comprehension

DIRECTIONS *Answer these questions about the excerpt from "Powder."*

1. You can tell the story is told from the first-person point of view because the narrator

   A   is a character in the story

   B   knows all the characters' thoughts

   C   doesn't take part in the story's action

   D   is a voice outside the story

2. How would the story be different if it were told from the third-person point of view?

   A   The story would give a more objective picture of the father.

   B   The mother would play a bigger role in the story.

   C   The story would have more descriptive details and more dialogue.

   D   It would be harder to understand the son's feelings.

3. What can you infer about the son's motivation for refusing to say "Right, doctor" in line 21?

   A   He is angry at his father.

   B   He is flattered that his father jokes with him.

   C   He is happy to be on a trip with his father.

   D   He misses his mother.

4. Reread lines 27–38 and monitor your understanding. Why does the father turn around with a "show of caution"?

   A   He wants the trooper to see how carefully he drives.

   B   He wants to see what the trooper is doing at all times.

   C   He doesn't want to damage his car.

   D   He wants to get around the barricades.

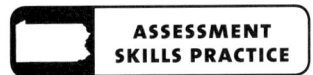
5. The father's motivation for driving on the closed road is to

A prove he's an excellent driver

B practice driving in the snow

C keep his promise to get his son home

D challenge the trooper's authority

6. Which pair of adjectives best describes the father's character traits?

A concerned and thoughtful

B awkward and unsure

C humorous and rebellious

D serious and cautious

DIRECTIONS *Answer these questions about* "*Maud Martha.*"

7. How do you know the selection is told from the third-person point of view?

A Maud Martha is the narrator.

B Maud Martha is the only character.

C Maud Martha is referred to as "I."

D Maud Martha is referred to as "she."

8. According to what the narrator reveals about Maud Martha, which adjectives best describe her character traits?

A lazy and conceited

B sensitive and sincere

C harsh and uncaring

D graceful and exotic

9. What can you infer about Maud Martha from lines 12–17?

A She loves only beautiful things.

B She works hard for a child.

C She wastes time on flowers.

D She feels like a special person.

10. What conclusion can you draw about Maud Martha's feelings for Helen?

A She sees Helen as a dandelion.

B She feels sorry for Helen.

C She admires Helen's beauty.

D She wishes Helen were prettier.

DIRECTIONS *Answer this question about both selections.*

11. How is Maud Martha like the son in "Powder"?

A Both show a sense of responsibility.

B Both act carefree most of the time.

C Both have sisters they admire.

D Both disagree with their parents' actions.

Open-Ended Items

12. Which character do you picture more clearly, the son in "Powder" or Maud Martha? Use the monitoring skill of visualizing to help you answer this question. Give examples of descriptive details in the text that help you visualize the character.

13. What is the father's motivation for calling his son an accomplice in line 57? What can you tell about the father from his words?

14. How are the father and son in "Powder" different? Are there any ways in which they are similar? Use story details to support your ideas.

GO ON

Vocabulary

DIRECTIONS *Use your knowledge of multiple-meaning words to answer the questions below.*

1. Which meaning of the word *gear* is used in the sentence below?

   The skiers gathered up their <u>gear</u> after the last ski run.
   A   the harness for a horse
   B   part of a car's transmission
   C   equipment for a sport
   D   a sailor's personal effects

2. Which meaning of *trail* is used in the sentence below from "Powder"?

   By now I couldn't see the <u>trail</u>.
   A   a course or path
   B   a scent or track of an animal
   C   something that hangs loosely
   D   a chain of consequences

3. Which meaning of *arm* is used in the part of a sentence below from "Maud Martha"?

   . . . and either fling her <u>arms</u> or want to fling her <u>arms</u> . . .
   A   an upper limb of the human body
   B   a forelimb of an animal
   C   something branching out from a large mass
   D   power or authority

4. Which meaning of *ways* is used in the sentence below from "Maud Martha"?

   But oh, the long lashes, the grace, the little <u>ways</u> with the hands and feet.
   A   roads or paths
   B   courses of action
   C   specific directions
   D   aspects or features

DIRECTIONS *Use the following Greek terms to help you answer the questions below.*

Item	Description
Iris	the Greek goddess of the rainbow
aster	a flower named after the Greek word for a star
Lotus-eaters	characters in the *Odyssey* who lost their memories when they ate lotus plants
Narcissus	a mythological person who fell in love with his reflection and turned into a flower

5. Which term is used for both a colorful flower and the colored part of the eye?
   A   iris
   B   aster
   C   Lotus-eater
   D   Narcissus

6. Narcissism is
   A   a love of bright colors
   B   a love of astronomy
   C   an excessive love of food
   D   an excessive love of oneself

7. Since the Latin prefix *dis-* can mean "the opposite of," what might *disastrous* mean?
   A   colorless
   B   under an unlucky star
   C   having an excellent memory
   D   hating one's reflection

Writing & Grammar

DIRECTIONS *Read the following passage and then answer the questions.*

(1) Mary Kingsley was an Englishwoman born in 1862. (2) She spent years traveling in Africa. (3) Her family expected her to stay home to care for her mother and younger brother. (4) Her mother was sick at the time. (5) Her parents died in 1892. (6) After their deaths, she went to West Africa. (7) Kingsley hacked through jungles in the heat. (8) Even then, she dressed like a proper English matron. (9) She always wore a dress made out of thick fabric. (10) She also wore boots and a hat. (11) Once she fell onto the spikes of an animal trap. (12) "It is at these moments you realize the blessings of a good thick skirt," she wrote later.

1. Choose the best way to rewrite sentences 1 and 2, using an adjective clause. Choose D if no change is needed.

   A Mary Kingsley, an Englishwoman, was born in 1862 and spent years traveling in Africa.

   B Born in 1862, Mary Kingsley was an Englishwoman who spent years traveling in Africa.

   C Mary Kingsley was an Englishwoman. Born in 1862, she spent years traveling in Africa.

   D No change is needed.

2. Choose the best way to vary the beginnings of sentences 3–5. Choose D if no change is needed.

   A Kingsley's family expected her to stay home to care for her mother and younger brother. Kingsley's mother was sick at the time. Kingsley's parents died in 1892.

   B Kingsley's family expected her to stay home to care for her mother and younger brother. Her mother was sick at the time. In 1892, her parents died.

   C Her family expected her to stay home to care for her mother and younger brother. Mary's mother was sick at the time. Mary's parents died in 1892.

   D No change is needed.

3. Choose the best way to rewrite sentences 6 and 7, using an adjective clause. Choose D if no change is needed.

   A After their deaths, Kingsley went to West Africa, where she hacked through jungles in the heat.

   B After their deaths, she went to West Africa. There, Kingsley hacked through jungles in the heat.

   C After their deaths, she went to West Africa and hacked through jungles in the heat.

   D No change is needed.

4. Choose the best way to rewrite sentences 9–10, using precise adjectives. Choose D if no change is needed.

   A She always wore a flowing black dress made out of thick fabric. She also wore buttoned black boots and a wool hat.

   B She always wore a long dress made out of thick fabric. She also wore black boots and a hat.

   C She always dressed all in black: long skirt, boots, and a hat.

   D No change is needed.

STOP

Ideas for Independent Reading

What makes a character grow and change? How many ways can you define strength? Find out by reading these additional works.

Are you a perfectionist?

Into the Wild
by Jon Krakauer

This true account of an idealistic young man tells of his wish to give up the trappings of wealth and privilege. He leaves a comfortable life to live a simple one in the wilderness. And he almost makes it.

The Chosen
by Chaim Potok

Two neighbor boys live with different sets of parental expectations. Reuven, the narrator, slowly comes to understand the weight of responsibility that rests on his best friend Danny's shoulders.

Pride and Prejudice
by Jane Austen

The mother of five daughters, Mrs. Bennet wants to find the perfect husband for each of them. As you read this Jane Austen novel, see if Mrs. Bennet and her daughters need to compromise their rather unrealistic standards.

How important is status?

The Outsiders
by S. E. Hinton

In this classic young-adult novel, the "greasers" are the poor kids' gang and the "socs" are a gang of rich kids. Tragedy forces Ponyboy, a greaser, to change the way he lives.

A Connecticut Yankee in King Arthur's Court
by Mark Twain

Hank Morgan lives in 19th-century Connecticut. After a head injury he wakes up in the England of King Arthur, where he is definitely not one of the privileged. Twain's social satire is still relevant to today's world.

Kaffir Boy
by Mark Mathabane

This is the true story of a black youth's coming of age under the apartheid policy in South Africa.

When is strength more than muscle?

Finding Fish
by Antwone Fisher

Fisher's autobiography tells of his life in a foster home, where he was humiliated and abused. Fisher escaped, first into the navy and then into a life of writing, where his talent flourished. His award-winning screenplay *Antwone Fisher* became a feature film.

Coming of Age in Mississippi
by Anne Moody

Moody's autobiographical classic describes her child-hood in the Mississippi of the 1950s. She was unwilling to accept the racist world of that time and challenged it through her work in the civil rights movement.

O Pioneers!
by Willa Cather

After her father dies, Alexandra inherits the family farm—over the protests of her brothers. She struggles to overcome tragedy and hardship while keeping her family together and forging a living on the hard Nebraska prairie.

A Sense of Place

3

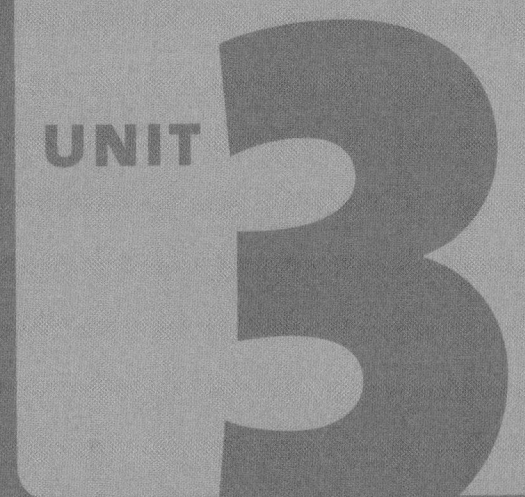

SETTING, MOOD, AND IMAGERY

- In Fiction
- In Media
- In Nonfiction
- In Poetry

299

UNIT 3 *Share What You Know*

How can you TRAVEL *without leaving home?*

We can experience the sights and sounds of a war-torn country long ago or a bustling city in the modern day. We can visit any place in the world—past, present, or future—because talented writers transport us to **settings** we have never seen and can only imagine.

ACTIVITY Recall a story you have read or a film you have viewed that you felt transported you to another place or time period. Concentrate on the setting of the story and think about all the ways in which the writer or director brought the setting to life. Then answer the following questions:

• How was the time period suggested?

• What details were used to portray the location?

• What information made the setting vivid and engaging?

• If the setting was completely imaginary, how was it made believable?

PENNSYLVANIA STANDARDS

Preview Unit Goals

LITERARY ANALYSIS
- Identify and analyze setting and its impact on conflict and character
- Identify and analyze imagery
- Identify mood and analyze ways in which writers convey mood

READING
- Analyze details
- Paraphrase
- Make inferences
- Identify author's perspective
- Distinguish between primary and secondary sources

WRITING AND GRAMMAR
- Write a short story
- Bring immediacy to writing by choosing an effective verb tense
- Write concisely by using compound predicates

SPEAKING, LISTENING, AND VIEWING
- Create a video presentation
- View and interpret a film production
- Analyze how film and design techniques convey meaning

VOCABULARY
- Use context clues to unlock meaning
- Understand and use connotative and denotative meanings of words

ACADEMIC VOCABULARY
- connotation and denotation
- imagery
- mood
- paraphrase
- primary and secondary sources
- setting
- symbol

Literary Analysis Workshop

Setting, Mood, and Imagery

A good story is much more than the events that happen or the conflicts between characters. When and where a story takes place also affects your reading experience. Consider, for example, a story about two lost hikers who are fighting for survival. It's the setting details—the towering trees, the stark winter sky, and the approaching snowstorm—that make you care about the conflict. By creating an unforgettable setting, a writer seizes your imagination and whisks you into the world of a story.

Part 1: Setting

You know that the **setting** of a story is the time and place in which the action occurs. The time could be a particular year, a specific season, a time of day, or a historical period. The place could be anywhere—from a bustling ancient city to a deserted tropical island.

In addition to describing the time and location of a story, setting details often reveal information about the characters' lives, their occupations, and their beliefs. Setting may also play a more active role by creating conflicts for the characters or by influencing their decisions and lifestyles.

PENNSYLVANIA STANDARDS

READING STANDARDS
B.1.1.1.B.1 Evaluate setting
B.1.1.1.E.1 Evaluate the tone, style, and/or mood
B.2.1.1 Identify and analyze imagery

ROLE OF SETTING	EXAMPLE SETTING
 *Setting can influence characters by* • determining the living conditions and jobs available to them • shaping their personalities, their dreams, and their values	***A poor, drought-stricken Midwestern farm town in the 1930s*** Despite months of grueling work, Joe's crops are failing again. Realizing that his life may never improve, he becomes bitter and angry.
 *Setting can create conflicts by* • exposing the characters to dangerous weather, such as a storm or a drought • making characters endure a difficult time period, such as the Great Depression	The drought has lasted seven years, and most of the farms are failing. People have begun to sell their most prized possessions because they need money. Recently, Mrs. Wilkes sold her wedding band to buy shoes for her daughter.
 *Setting can serve as a symbol by* • representing an important idea • representing a character's hopes, future, or predicament	Some people have planted a small flower garden in the town square. The garden is a symbol of their hope that their community can still thrive.

MODEL 1: SETTING AND CHARACTERS

Nervous Conditions takes place in a British colony in Africa during the 1960s. Nhamo has left his village to attend school at a mission. How has this opportunity affected him?

from Nervous **Conditions**

Novel by **Tsitsi Dangarembga**

. . . Nhamo was forced once a year to return to his squalid homestead, where he washed in cold water in an enamel basin or a flowing river, not in a bathtub with taps gushing hot water and cold; where he ate *sadza* regularly with his fingers and meat hardly at all, never with a knife or fork; where there was no
5 light beyond the flickering yellow of candles and homemade paraffin lamps to enable him to escape into his books when the rest of us had gone to bed.

All this poverty began to offend him, or at the very least to embarrass him after he went to the mission, in a way that it had not done before.

Close Read

1. Identify two details that help you understand Nhamo's life in both settings—the mission and the homestead. An example has been boxed.

2. How has Nhamo's experience at the mission influenced his perception of life on the homestead?

MODEL 2: SETTING AND CONFLICT

In George Orwell's novel *1984*, the country is run by a government that monitors citizens' every move and demands loyalty to its leader—Big Brother. As you read this excerpt, pay attention to the description of this society. How might the setting create conflicts for the characters?

from **1984** Novel by **George Orwell**

Outside, even through the shut window pane, the world looked cold. Down in the street little eddies of wind were whirling dust and torn paper into spirals, and though the sun was shining and the sky a harsh blue, there seemed to be no color in anything except the posters that were plastered everywhere.
5 The black-mustachio'd face gazed down from every commanding corner. There was one on the house front immediately opposite. BIG BROTHER IS WATCHING YOU, the caption said, while the dark eyes looked deep into Winston's own. Down at street level another poster, torn at one corner, flapped fitfully in the wind. . . . In the far distance a helicopter skimmed down between
10 the roofs, hovered for an instant like a blue-bottle, and darted away again with a curving flight. It was the Police Patrol, snooping into people's windows. The patrols did not matter, however. Only the Thought Police mattered.

Close Read

1. In what kind of world does this story take place? Identify four details that help you visualize the setting. One has been boxed.

2. What conflicts might this society create for Winston and other citizens? Explain your answer.

Part 2: Imagery and Mood

To create a setting that stays with you long after a story ends, a writer paints pictures with words. With the right choice of details and language, a writer can transport you to any scene and affect how you feel about a story.

IMAGERY

Imagery consists of words and phrases that recreate sensory experiences for readers. Rather than describing every aspect of a setting, a writer may use **sensory details**—words and phrases that appeal to the senses of sight, hearing, smell, taste, and touch—to help you visualize a scene. For example, in the *1984* excerpt on the previous page, Orwell uses phrases like these to appeal to the senses of sight and hearing:

- *"eddies of wind were whirling dust"*
- *"another poster . . . flapped fitfully in the wind"*

Armed with these details, your imagination fills in the rest of the scene. While Orwell does not mention anxious people and wailing sirens, you can picture these details as part of the setting.

MOOD

A writer also uses imagery and setting details to create the **mood,** or atmosphere, of a story. Whether it is lighthearted, hopeful, or mysterious, a story's mood can affect your emotional reaction to the characters and events. For example, the bleak, eerie mood established in *1984* might prompt you to sympathize with the characters as you are drawn into their unsettling world.

How do the sensory details in the graphic convey a mood of terror and fear?

SIGHT: "Flashes of lightning illuminated the **ink-black sky.**"

TOUCH: "Another cobweb stuck to her **cold, clammy skin.**"

TASTE: "She could not get the **metallic taste of fear** out of her mouth."

SOUND: "Her heart thumped wildly when she heard an **ominous scratching** on the door."

SMELL: "The **foul smell of dead mice** hung in the air."

MODEL 1: IMAGERY

This excerpt is from a chilling story by H. P. Lovecraft, a master of horror and suspense. As you read, pay attention to the sensory details he uses to describe an unusual street.

from

The Music *of* Erich Zann

Short story by **H. P. Lovecraft**

The Rue d'Auseil lay across a dark river bordered by precipitous brick blear-windowed warehouses and spanned by a ponderous bridge of dark stone. It was always shadowy along that river, as if the smoke of neighboring factories shut out the sun perpetually. The river was also odorous with evil stenches
5   which I have never smelled elsewhere. . . . Beyond that bridge were narrow cobbled streets with rails; and then came the ascent, at first gradual, but incredibly steep as the Rue d'Auseil was reached.
I have never seen another street as narrow and steep as the Rue d'Auseil. It was almost a cliff, closed to vehicles, consisting in several places of flights
10   of steps, and ending at the top in a lofty ivied wall. Its paving was irregular, sometimes stone slabs, sometimes cobblestones, and sometimes bare earth with struggling greenish-grey vegetation. The houses were tall, peaked-roofed, incredibly old, and crazily leaning backward, forward, and sidewise.

Close Read

1. The boxed detail appeals to the sense of smell. Find three more details and identify the sense each one appeals to.

2. What mood does this setting create? Point out specific examples of imagery that contributes directly to the mood.

MODEL 2: MOOD

The imagery in this excerpt evokes a very different atmosphere. Notice the specific sensory details that contribute to the mood.

from

Their Eyes Were Watching God

Novel by **Zora Neale Hurston**

It was a spring afternoon in West Florida. Janie had spent most of the day under a blossoming pear tree in the back-yard. She had been spending every minute that she could steal from her chores under that tree for the last three days. That was to say, ever since the first tiny bloom had opened. It had called her to
5   come and gaze on a mystery. From barren brown stems to glistening leaf-buds; from the leaf-buds to snowy virginity of bloom. It stirred her tremendously.

Close Read

1. How would you describe the mood of this excerpt?

2. Find four details that help to convey the mood. One has been boxed.

Part 3: Analyze the Literature

Using what you've learned in this workshop, analyze setting, mood, and imagery in these two short story excerpts.

The first excerpt is from a story that takes place in the mountains of New Mexico, where people tell tales about a legendary white horse that roams the wild. As you read, notice the details that the writer uses to describe the setting and create a distinct mood.

from

My Wonder Horse

Short story by **Sabine R. Ulibarrí**

I was fifteen years old. Although I had never seen the Wonder Horse, he filled my imagination and fired my ambition. I used to listen open-mouthed as my father and the ranch hands talked about the phantom horse who turned into mist and air and nothingness when he was trapped. I joined in the
5　universal obsession—like the hope of winning the lottery—of putting my lasso on him some day, of capturing him and showing him off on Sunday afternoons when the girls of the town strolled through the streets.

It was high summer. The forests were fresh, green, and gay. The cattle moved slowly, fat and sleek in the August sun and shadow. Listless and drowsy in the
10　lethargy of late afternoon, I was dozing on my horse. It was time to round up the herd and go back to the good bread of the cowboy camp. Already my comrades would be sitting around the campfire, playing the guitar, telling stories of past or present, or surrendering to the languor of the late afternoon. The sun was setting behind me in a riot of streaks and colors. Deep, harmonious silence.

15　I sit drowsily still, forgetting the cattle in the glade. Suddenly the forest falls silent, a deafening quiet. The afternoon comes to a standstill. The breeze stops blowing, but it vibrates. The sun flares hotly. The planet, life, and time itself have stopped in an inexplicable way. For a moment, I don't understand what is happening.

20　Then my eyes focus. There he is! The Wonder Horse! At the end of the glade, on high ground surrounded by summer green. He is a statue. He is an engraving. Line and form and white stain on a green background. Pride, prestige, and art incarnate in animal flesh. A picture of burning beauty and virile freedom. An ideal, pure and invincible, rising from the eternal dreams of humanity. Even
25　today my being thrills when I remember him.

Close Read

1. Describe the setting in this excerpt. Find details that reveal the season, the weather, and the narrator's lifestyle.

2. Find four examples of imagery in lines 8–14. One has been boxed. What mood do these details create?

3. How does the mood change in lines 15–19? Find three words or phrases that convey this change.

4. Which details in lines 20–25 help you understand how the narrator feels about the horse? Explain.

Now read this excerpt, taken from a story that is based on an experience from the writer's life. In 1897, Crane was a passenger on a ship that sank off the coast of Florida. He and three other men rowed back to shore in a flimsy lifeboat. How does Crane's use of imagery help convey a different setting and mood?

from

The

OPEN
BOAT

Short story by **Stephen Crane**

None of them knew the color of the sky. Their eyes glanced level, and were fastened upon the waves that swept toward them. These waves were of the hue of slate, save for the tops, which were of foaming white, and all of the men knew the colors of the sea. The horizon narrowed and
5 widened, and dipped and rose, and at all times its edge was jagged with waves that seemed thrust up in points like rocks.

Many a man ought to have a bathtub larger than the boat which here rode upon the sea. These waves were most wrongfully and barbarously abrupt and tall, and each froth-top was a problem in small-boat navigation. The cook
10 squatted in the bottom, and looked with both eyes at the six inches of gunwale which separated him from the ocean. His sleeves were rolled over his fat forearms, and the two flaps of his unbuttoned vest dangled as he bent to bail out the boat. Often he said, "That was a narrow clip." As he remarked it he invariably gazed eastward over the broken sea.

15 The oiler, steering with one of the two oars in the boat, sometimes raised himself suddenly to keep clear of water that swirled in over the stern. It was a thin little oar, and it seemed often ready to snap. The correspondent, pulling at the other oar, watched the waves and wondered why he was there.

The injured captain, lying in the bow, was at this time buried in that
20 profound dejection and indifference which comes, temporarily at least, to even the bravest and most enduring when, willy-nilly, the firm fails, the army loses, the ship goes down.

Close Read

1. Using details from the text, describe the setting as completely as you can.

2. Identify five sensory details. One has been boxed. What senses do they appeal to?

3. How would you describe the mood of this excerpt? Explain how the sensory details you found help to create this mood.

4. In which excerpt does setting play a more important role? Support your opinion with specific details.

A Christmas Memory
Short Story by Truman Capote

What do you look for in a FRIEND?

PENNSYLVANIA STANDARDS

READING STANDARDS
B.1.1.1.B.1 Evaluate setting
B.2.1.1 Identify and analyze imagery

KEY IDEA Think about your current friends as well as friends from the past. What draws you to someone and creates that special bond of **friendship?** Does a friend have to be your age? Do you always share the same interests and values? "A Christmas Memory" shows how important friendship can be to two very different individuals.

QUICKWRITE With a partner, write a "top ten" list of the key qualities you look for in a friend. Then compare your list with those of your classmates. Does everyone list similar qualities? Are physical traits and intellectual or emotional factors equally important?

Top 10 Qualities of a Good Friend
1. Sense of humor
2. Similar interests
3.
4.
5.

PEANUTS.

Peanuts: © United Feature Syndicate, Inc.

308

LITERARY ANALYSIS: DETAILS OF SETTING

In "A Christmas Memory," the adult narrator focuses on describing a particular period in his childhood. In fact, the narrator seems more interested in recreating the **setting** of this period than in telling about events. Through the use of **details,** the narrator describes not only the time and place of his childhood but also the historical era—the buildings, people, customs, and rituals that existed. The richness of the details makes the setting seem real and helps readers understand its importance to the narrator. Notice the vivid details used to describe walking through the woods:

Always, the path unwinds through lemony sun pools and pitch-black vine tunnels.

As you read, look for details that reveal the setting.

READING SKILL: ANALYZE IMAGERY

Good descriptive writing is usually filled with **imagery**— words and phrases that appeal to the senses. Capote gives readers a lasting impression of a holiday memory by creating descriptions that appeal to one or more senses. For example, note how this phrase appeals to your sense of hearing:

Lovely dimes, the liveliest coin, the one that really jingles.

As you read, use a chart like the one below to jot down words and phrases that you find especially striking. Check off the senses that are appealed to in each case.

Description	Sight	Smell	Hearing	Taste	Touch
Cracking open the pecans	✓		✓	✓	

Review: **Make Inferences**

VOCABULARY IN CONTEXT

To see how many words you know, restate each phrase, using a different word or words for the boldfaced word.

1. to **inaugurate** a project
2. a day that **exhilarates**
3. party **paraphernalia**
4. **squander** your money
5. ordinary, **prosaic** ideas

6. **suffuse** with perfume
7. a **potent** medicine
8. **goad** her to action
9. **cavort** in the park
10. **sever** all contact

Author On|ine

Truman Capote
1924–1984

Early Ambitions
Raised by elderly relatives in a small Alabama town, Capote started writing to fill the loneliness. He began publishing his short stories in his teens. As he later explained, "I always knew that I wanted to be a writer and that I wanted to be rich and famous." By the time his first novel, *Other Voices, Other Rooms,* was published in 1948, he was on his way to achieving these goals.

The Nonfiction Novel Capote enjoyed the celebrity that followed other successful publications, including the novel *Breakfast at Tiffany's* (1958). Then his career took a dramatic turn when he began what he called a nonfiction novel, a factual story written in the form of a novel. The result, *In Cold Blood* (1965), was an instant bestseller and made him a multimillionaire. Still, the six years he spent on this book took a toll on him.

Personal Decline Capote's life ultimately descended into a haze of addiction, illness, and writer's block. Although some critics contend he threw away his talent in the pursuit of celebrity, most acknowledge his talent as a storyteller.

 MORE ABOUT THE AUTHOR
For more on Truman Capote, visit the **Literature Center** at ClassZone.com.

Background
The Facts Behind the Fiction This story is based on Capote's childhood during the Great Depression of the 1930s. His friend was a much older cousin named Sook Faulk. Writing in the voice of an adult, Capote condenses years of experiences with his cousin into one memorable Christmas.

A Christmas Memory

Truman Capote

Imagine a morning in late November. A coming of winter morning more than twenty years ago. Consider the kitchen of a spreading old house in a country town. A great black stove is its main feature; but there is also a big round table and a fireplace with two rocking chairs placed in front of it. Just today the fireplace commenced its seasonal roar.

A woman with shorn white hair is standing at the kitchen window. She is wearing tennis shoes and a shapeless gray sweater over a summery calico dress. She is small and sprightly, like a bantam hen; but, due to a long youthful illness, her shoulders are pitifully hunched. Her face is remarkable—not
10 unlike Lincoln's, craggy like that, and tinted by sun and wind; but it is delicate too, finely boned, and her eyes are sherry-colored and timid. "Oh my," she exclaims, her breath smoking the windowpane, "it's fruitcake weather!"

The person to whom she is speaking is myself. I am seven; she is sixty-something. We are cousins, very distant ones, and we have lived together—well, as long as I can remember. Other people inhabit the house, relatives; and though they have power over us, and frequently make us cry, we are not, on the whole, too much aware of them. We are each other's best friend. She calls me Buddy, in memory of a boy who was formerly her best friend. The other Buddy died in the 1880's, when she was still a child. She is still a child.

20 "I knew it before I got out of bed," she says, turning away from the window with a purposeful excitement in her eyes. "The courthouse bell sounded so cold and clear. And there were no birds singing; they've gone to warmer country, yes indeed. Oh, Buddy, stop stuffing biscuit and fetch our buggy. Help me find my hat. We've thirty cakes to bake."

It's always the same: a morning arrives in November, and my friend, as though officially **inaugurating** the Christmas time of year that **exhilarates** her imagination and fuels the blaze of her heart, announces: "It's fruitcake weather! Fetch our buggy. Help me find my hat." Ⓐ

ANALYZE VISUALS
How does the woman in this painting compare with your image of Buddy's friend? Cite details from the story, such as those in lines 6–11, to support your answer.

inaugurate
(ĭn-ô′gyə-rāt′) v. to make a formal beginning of

exhilarate (ĭg-zĭl′ə-rāt′) v. to make merry or lively

Ⓐ **DETAILS OF SETTING**
Use the details on this page to figure out as much as you can about the setting.

Anna Kuerner (1971), Andrew Wyeth. Tempera on panel. © Andrew Wyeth.

The hat is found, a straw cartwheel corsaged with velvet roses out-of-doors
30 has faded: it once belonged to a more fashionable relative. Together, we guide
our buggy, a dilapidated baby carriage, out to the garden and into a grove of
pecan trees. The buggy is mine; that is, it was bought for me when I was born.
It is made of wicker, rather unraveled, and the wheels wobble like a drunkard's
legs. But it is a faithful object; springtimes, we take it to the woods and fill
it with flowers, herbs, wild fern for our porch pots; in the summer, we pile it
with picnic **paraphernalia** and sugar-cane fishing poles and roll it down to the
edge of a creek; it has its winter uses, too: as a truck for hauling firewood from
the yard to the kitchen, as a warm bed for Queenie, our tough little orange and
white rat terrier who has survived distemper and two rattlesnake bites. Queenie
40 is trotting beside it now. **B**

Three hours later we are back in the kitchen hulling a heaping buggyload of
windfall pecans. Our backs hurt from gathering them: how hard they were to
find (the main crop having been shaken off the trees and sold by the orchard's
owners, who are not us) among the concealing leaves, the frosted, deceiving
grass. Caarackle! A cheery crunch, scraps of miniature thunder sound as the
shells collapse and the golden mound of sweet oily ivory meat mounts in the
milk-glass bowl. Queenie begs to taste, and now and again my friend sneaks
her a mite, though insisting we deprive ourselves. "We mustn't, Buddy. If
we start, we won't stop. And there's scarcely enough as there is. For thirty
50 cakes." The kitchen is growing dark. Dusk turns the window into a mirror:
our reflections mingle with the rising moon as we work by the fireside in the
firelight. At last, when the moon is quite high, we toss the final hull into the

Wild Dog Mushroom (1974), Bob Timberlake. © Bob Timberlake.

fire and, with joined sighs, watch it catch flame. The buggy is empty, the bowl is brimful. **C**

We eat our supper (cold biscuits, bacon, blackberry jam) and discuss tomorrow. Tomorrow the kind of work I like best begins: buying. Cherries and citron, ginger and vanilla and canned Hawaiian pineapple, rinds and raisins and walnuts and whiskey and oh, so much flour, butter, so many eggs, spices, flavorings: why, we'll need a pony to pull the buggy home.

60   But before these purchases can be made, there is the question of money. Neither of us has any. Except for skinflint sums persons in the house occasionally provide (a dime is considered very big money); or what we earn ourselves from various activities: holding rummage sales, selling buckets of hand-picked blackberries, jars of homemade jam and apple jelly and peach preserves, rounding up flowers for funerals and weddings. Once we won seventy-ninth prize, five dollars, in a national football contest. Not that we know a fool thing about football. It's just that we enter any contest we hear about: at the moment our hopes are centered on the fifty-thousand-dollar Grand Prize being offered to name a new brand of coffee (we suggested "A.M.";
70   and, after some hesitation, for my friend thought it perhaps sacrilegious, the slogan "A.M.! Amen!"). To tell the truth, our only *really* profitable enterprise was the Fun and Freak Museum we conducted in a back-yard woodshed two summers ago. The Fun was a stereopticon[1] with slide views of Washington and New York lent us by a relative who had been to those places (she was furious when she discovered why we'd borrowed it); the Freak was a three-legged biddy chicken hatched by one of our own hens. Everybody hereabouts wanted to see that biddy: we charged grownups a nickel, kids two cents. And took in a good twenty dollars before the museum shut down due to the decease of the main attraction.

80   But one way and another we do each year accumulate Christmas savings, a Fruitcake Fund. These moneys we keep hidden in an ancient bead purse under a loose board under the floor under a chamber pot under my friend's bed. The purse is seldom removed from this safe location except to make a deposit or, as happens every Saturday, a withdrawal; for on Saturdays I am allowed ten cents to go to the picture show. My friend has never been to a picture show, nor does she intend to: "I'd rather hear you tell the story, Buddy. That way I can imagine it more. Besides, a person my age shouldn't **squander** their eyes. When the Lord comes, let me see him clear." In addition to never having seen a movie, she has never: eaten in a restaurant, traveled more than five miles
90   from home, received or sent a telegram, read anything except funny papers and the Bible, worn cosmetics, cursed, wished someone harm, told a lie on purpose, let a hungry dog go hungry. Here are a few things she has done, does do: killed with a hoe the biggest rattlesnake ever seen in this county (sixteen rattles), dip snuff[2] (secretly), tame hummingbirds (just try it) till they balance

---

1. **stereopticon** (stĕr′ē-ŏp′tĭ-kŏn′): an early slide projector that could merge two images of the same scene on a screen, resulting in a 3-D effect.
2. **dip snuff:** to place a small amount of finely ground tobacco (snuff) in one's mouth.

C ANALYZE IMAGERY
What words and phrases in this passage appeal to the senses and help you imagine the characters shelling pecans?

squander (skwŏn′dər) *v.* to spend or use wastefully

on her finger, tell ghost stories (we both believe in ghosts) so tingling they chill you in July, talk to herself, take walks in the rain, grow the prettiest japonicas in town, know the recipe for every sort of old-time Indian cure, including a magical wart remover. **D**

Now, with supper finished, we retire to the room in a faraway part of the 100 house where my friend sleeps in a scrap-quilt-covered iron bed painted rose pink, her favorite color. Silently, wallowing in the pleasures of conspiracy, we take the bead purse from its secret place and spill its contents on the scrap quilt. Dollar bills, tightly rolled and green as May buds. Somber fifty-cent pieces, heavy enough to weight a dead man's eyes.[3] Lovely dimes, the liveliest coin, the one that really jingles. Nickels and quarters, worn smooth as creek pebbles. But mostly a hateful heap of bitter-odored pennies. Last summer others in the house contracted to pay us a penny for every twenty-five flies we killed. Oh, the carnage of August: the flies that flew to heaven! Yet it was not work in which we took pride. And, as we sit counting pennies, it is as though 110 we were back tabulating dead flies. Neither of us has a head for figures; we **E** count slowly, lose track, start again. According to her calculations, we have $12.73. According to mine, exactly $13. "I do hope you're wrong, Buddy. We can't mess around with thirteen. The cakes will fall. Or put somebody in the cemetery. Why, I wouldn't dream of getting out of bed on the thirteenth." This is true: she always spends thirteenths in bed. So, to be on the safe side, we subtract a penny and toss it out the window.

Of the ingredients that go into our fruitcakes, whiskey is the most expensive, as well as the hardest to obtain: State laws forbid its sale. But everybody knows you can buy a bottle from Mr. Haha Jones. And the next 120 day, having completed our more **prosaic** shopping, we set out for Mr. Haha's business address, a "sinful" (to quote public opinion) fish-fry and dancing café down by the river. We've been there before, and on the same errand; but in previous years our dealings have been with Haha's wife, an iodine-dark Indian woman with brassy peroxided hair and a dead-tired disposition. Actually, we've never laid eyes on her husband, though we've heard that he's an Indian too. A giant with razor scars across his cheeks. They call him Haha because he's so gloomy, a man who never laughs. As we approach his café (a large log cabin festooned inside and out with chains of garish-gay naked light bulbs and standing by the river's muddy edge under the shade of river trees where moss 130 drifts through the branches like gray mist) our steps slow down. Even Queenie stops prancing and sticks close by. People have been murdered in Haha's café. Cut to pieces. Hit on the head. There's a case coming up in court next month.

Naturally these goings-on happen at night when the colored lights cast crazy patterns and the Victrola[4] wails. In the daytime Haha's is shabby and deserted. I knock at the door, Queenie barks, my friend calls: "Mrs. Haha, ma'am? Anyone to home?" **F**

---

3. **heavy enough to weight a dead man's eyes:** from the custom of putting coins on the closed eyes of corpses to keep the eyelids from opening.

4. **Victrola:** a trademark for a brand of old record player.

D MAKE INFERENCES
Reread lines 80–98. What do these details reveal about Buddy's friend?

E ANALYZE IMAGERY
Notice how imagery adds depth to ordinary objects such as coins and dollar bills.

prosaic (prō-zā′ĭk) *adj.* dull; commonplace

F DETAILS OF SETTING
Reread the description of Mr. Haha's café in lines 119–136. Which details indicate that the café is a dangerous and "sinful" place?

Footsteps. The door opens. Our hearts overturn. It's Mr. Haha Jones himself! And he *is* a giant; he *does* have scars; he *doesn't* smile. No, he glowers at us through Satan-tilted eyes and demands to know: "What you want
140 with Haha?"

For a moment we are too paralyzed to tell. Presently my friend half-finds her voice, a whispery voice at best: "If you please, Mr. Haha, we'd like a quart of your finest whiskey."

His eyes tilt more. Would you believe it? Haha is smiling! Laughing, too. "Which one of you is a drinkin' man?"

"It's for making fruitcakes, Mr. Haha. Cooking."

This sobers him. He frowns. "That's no way to waste good whiskey." Nevertheless, he retreats into the shadowed café and seconds later appears carrying a bottle of daisy-yellow unlabeled liquor. He demonstrates its sparkle
150 in the sunlight and says: "Two dollars."

We pay him with nickels and dimes and pennies. Suddenly, as he jangles the coins in his hand like a fistful of dice, his face softens. "Tell you what," he proposes, pouring the money back into our bead purse, "just send me one of them fruitcakes instead."

"Well," my friend remarks on our way home, "there's a lovely man. We'll put an extra cup of raisins in *his* cake."

Detail of *Winter Sun* (1971), Bob Timberlake. © Bob Timberlake.

Mrs. Dorsett's Kitchen (1973), Bob Timberlake. © Bob Timberlake.

ANALYZE VISUALS
What **details** in this painting evoke the scene described in lines 157–162?

The black stove, stoked with coal and firewood, glows like a lighted pumpkin. Eggbeaters whirl, spoons spin round in bowls of butter and sugar, vanilla sweetens the air, ginger spices it; melting, nose-tingling odors saturate
160 the kitchen, **suffuse** the house, drift out to the world on puffs of chimney smoke. In four days our work is done. Thirty-one cakes, dampened with whiskey, bask on windowsills and shelves. **G**

Who are they for?

Friends. Not necessarily neighbor friends: indeed, the larger share is intended for persons we've met maybe once, perhaps not at all. People who've struck our fancy. Like President Roosevelt. Like the Reverend and Mrs. J. C. Lucey, Baptist missionaries to Borneo[5] who lectured here last winter. Or the little knife grinder who comes through town twice a year. Or Abner Packer, the driver of the six o'clock bus from Mobile, who exchanges waves with
170 us every day as he passes in a dust-cloud whoosh. Or the young Wistons, a

suffuse (sə-fyōoz′) *v.* to gradually spread through or over

G GRAMMAR AND STYLE
Notice how Capote makes use of the **present tense** even though the memory is part of the narrator's past. This creates a sense of immediacy for the reader.

---

5. **Borneo** (bôr′nē-o′): a large island in the South China Sea, southwest of the Philippines.

California couple whose car one afternoon broke down outside the house and who spent a pleasant hour chatting with us on the porch (young Mr. Wiston snapped our picture, the only one we've ever had taken). Is it because my friend is shy with everyone *except* strangers that these strangers, and merest acquaintances, seem to us our truest friends? I think yes. Also, the scrapbooks we keep of thank-you's on White House stationery, time-to-time communications from California and Borneo, the knife grinder's penny post cards, make us feel connected to eventful worlds beyond the kitchen with its view of a sky that stops. **H**

180   Now a nude December fig branch grates against the window. The kitchen is empty, the cakes are gone; yesterday we carted the last of them to the post office, where the cost of stamps turned our purse inside out. We're broke. That rather depresses me, but my friend insists on celebrating—with two inches of whiskey left in Haha's bottle. Queenie has a spoonful in a bowl of coffee (she likes her coffee chicory-flavored and strong). The rest we divide between a pair of jelly glasses. We're both quite awed at the prospect of drinking straight whiskey; the taste of it brings screwed-up expressions and sour shudders. But by and by we begin to sing, the two of us singing different songs simultaneously. I don't know the words to mine, just: *Come on along,*
190 *come on along, to the dark-town strutters' ball.* But I can dance: that's what I mean to be, a tap dancer in the movies. My dancing shadow rollicks on the walls; our voices rock the chinaware; we giggle: as if unseen hands were tickling us. Queenie rolls on her back, her paws plow the air, something like a grin stretches her black lips. Inside myself, I feel warm and sparky as those crumbling logs, carefree as the wind in the chimney. My friend waltzes round the stove, the hem of her poor calico skirt pinched between her fingers as though it were a party dress: *Show me the way to go home,* she sings, her tennis shoes squeaking on the floor. *Show me the way to go home.* **I**

    Enter: two relatives. Very angry. **Potent** with eyes that scold, tongues that
200 scald. Listen to what they have to say, the words tumbling together into a wrathful tune: "A child of seven! whiskey on his breath! are you out of your mind? feeding a child of seven! must be loony! road to ruination! remember Cousin Kate? Uncle Charlie? Uncle Charlie's brother-in-law? shame! scandal! humiliation! kneel, pray, beg the Lord!"

    Queenie sneaks under the stove. My friend gazes at her shoes, her chin quivers, she lifts her skirt and blows her nose and runs to her room. **J**

    Long after the town has gone to sleep and the house is silent except for the chimings of clocks and the sputter of fading fires, she is weeping into a pillow already as wet as a widow's handkerchief.

210   "Don't cry," I say, sitting at the bottom of her bed and shivering despite my flannel nightgown that smells of last winter's cough syrup, "don't cry," I beg, teasing her toes, tickling her feet, "you're too old for that."

    "It's because," she hiccups, "I *am* too old. Old and funny."

H MAKE INFERENCES
Why do you think Buddy and his friend send their fruitcakes to strangers?

I ANALYZE IMAGERY
In lines 187–198, Capote appeals to four out of the five senses. Identify as many of these sensory details as you can.

potent (pōt'nt) *adj.* powerful

J MAKE INFERENCES
Reread lines 199–206. What impression do you get of the relatives?

Detail of *Another World* (1974), Bob Timberlake. © Bob Timberlake.

"Not funny. Fun. More fun than anybody. Listen. If you don't stop crying you'll be so tired tomorrow we can't go cut a tree."

She straightens up. Queenie jumps on the bed (where Queenie is not allowed) to lick her cheeks. "I know where we'll find real pretty trees, Buddy. And holly, too. With berries big as your eyes. It's way off in the woods. Farther than we've ever been. Papa used to bring us Christmas trees from there: carry them on his shoulder. That's fifty years ago. Well, now: I can't wait for morning."

220

Morning. Frozen rime[6] lusters the grass; the sun, round as an orange and orange as hot-weather moons, balances on the horizon, burnishes the silvered winter woods. A wild turkey calls. A renegade hog grunts in the undergrowth. Soon, by the edge of knee-deep, rapid-running water, we have to abandon the buggy. Queenie wades the stream first, paddles across barking complaints at the swiftness of the current, the pneumonia-making coldness of it. We follow, holding our shoes and equipment (a hatchet, a burlap sack) above our heads. A mile more: of chastising thorns, burrs and briers that catch at

---

6. **rime:** a white frost.

230 our clothes; of rusty pine needles brilliant with gaudy fungus and molted
feathers. Here, there, a flash, a flutter, an ecstasy of shrillings remind us that
not all the birds have flown south. Always, the path unwinds through lemony
sun pools and pitch-black vine tunnels. Another creek to cross: a disturbed
armada of speckled trout froths the water round us, and frogs the size of plates
practice belly flops; beaver workmen are building a dam. On the farther shore,
Queenie shakes herself and trembles. My friend shivers, too: not with cold but
enthusiasm. One of her hat's ragged roses sheds a petal as she lifts her head and
inhales the pine-heavy air. "We're almost there; can you smell it, Buddy?" she
says, as though we were approaching an ocean. **K**

240   And, indeed, it is a kind of ocean. Scented acres of holiday trees, prickly-
leafed holly. Red berries shiny as Chinese bells: black crows swoop upon
them screaming. Having stuffed our burlap sacks with enough greenery and
crimson to garland a dozen windows, we set about choosing a tree. "It should
be," muses my friend, "twice as tall as a boy. So a boy can't steal the star." The
one we pick is twice as tall as me. A brave handsome brute that survives thirty
hatchet strokes before it keels with a creaking rending cry. Lugging it like a
kill, we commence the long trek out. Every few yards we abandon the struggle,
sit down and pant. But we have the strength of triumphant huntsmen; that
and the tree's virile, icy perfume revive us, **goad** us on. Many compliments
250 accompany our sunset return along the red clay road to town; but my friend
is sly and noncommittal when passers-by praise the treasure perched in our
buggy: what a fine tree, and where did it come from? "Yonderways," she
murmurs vaguely. Once a car stops, and the rich mill owner's lazy wife leans
out and whines: "Giveya two-bits[7] cash for that ol tree." Ordinarily my friend
is afraid of saying no; but on this occasion she promptly shakes her head: "We
wouldn't take a dollar." The mill owner's wife persists. "A dollar, my foot! Fifty
cents. That's my last offer. Goodness, woman, you can get another one." In
answer, my friend gently reflects: "I doubt it. There's never two of anything." **L**

    Home: Queenie slumps by the fire and sleeps till tomorrow, snoring loud
260 as a human.

    A trunk in the attic contains: a shoebox of ermine tails (off the opera cape
of a curious lady who once rented a room in the house), coils of frazzled tinsel
gone gold with age, one silver star, a brief rope of dilapidated, undoubtedly
dangerous candylike light bulbs. Excellent decorations, as far as they go, which
isn't far enough: my friend wants our tree to blaze "like a Baptist window,"
droop with weighty snows of ornament. But we can't afford the made-in-Japan
splendors at the five-and-dime. So we do what we've always done: sit for days
at the kitchen table with scissors and crayons and stacks of colored paper. I
make sketches and my friend cuts them out: lots of cats, fish too (because
270 they're easy to draw), some apples, some watermelons, a few winged angels
devised from saved-up sheets of Hershey-bar tin foil. We use safety pins to
attach these creations to the tree; as a final touch, we sprinkle the branches

K DETAILS OF SETTING
Reread lines 222–239.
What is the effect of
including such vivid
details of this natural
setting?

goad (gōd) v. to drive
or urge

L MAKE INFERENCES
Reread lines 253–258.
What do you learn about
Buddy's friend from her
response to the mill
owner's wife?

---

7. **two-bits:** 25 cents.

with shredded cotton (picked in August for this purpose). My friend, surveying the effect, clasps her hands together. "Now honest, Buddy. Doesn't it look good enough to eat?" Queenie tries to eat an angel.

After weaving and ribboning holly wreaths for all the front windows, our next project is the fashioning of family gifts. Tie-dye scarves for the ladies, for the men a home-brewed lemon and licorice and aspirin syrup to be taken "at the first Symptoms of a Cold and after Hunting." But when it comes time for
280 making each other's gift, my friend and I separate to work secretly. I would like to buy her a pearl-handled knife, a radio, a whole pound of chocolate-covered cherries (we tasted some once, and she always swears: "I could live on them, Buddy, Lord yes I could—and that's not taking his name in vain"). Instead, I am building her a kite. She would like to give me a bicycle (she's said so on several million occasions: "If only I could, Buddy. It's bad enough in life to do without something *you* want; but confound it, what gets my goat is not being able to give somebody something you want *them* to have. Only one of these days I will, Buddy. Locate you a bike. Don't ask how. Steal it, maybe"). Instead, I'm fairly certain that she is building me a kite—the same as last year
290 and the year before: the year before that we exchanged slingshots. All of which is fine by me. For we are champion kite fliers who study the wind like sailors; my friend, more accomplished than I, can get a kite aloft when there isn't enough breeze to carry clouds.

Christmas Eve afternoon we scrape together a nickel and go to the butcher's to buy Queenie's traditional gift, a good gnawable beef bone. The bone, wrapped in funny paper, is placed high in the tree near the silver star. Queenie knows it's there. She squats at the foot of the tree staring up in a trance of greed: when bedtime arrives she refuses to budge. Her excitement is equaled by my own. I kick the covers and turn my pillow as though it were a
300 scorching summer's night. Somewhere a rooster crows: falsely, for the sun is still on the other side of the world.

"Buddy, are you awake?" It is my friend, calling from her room, which is next to mine; and an instant later she is sitting on my bed holding a candle. "Well, I can't sleep a hoot," she declares. "My mind's jumping like a jack rabbit. Buddy, do you think Mrs. Roosevelt will serve our cake at dinner?" We huddle in the bed, and she squeezes my hand I-love-you. "Seems like your hand used to be so much smaller. I guess I hate to see you grow up. When you're grown up, will we still be friends?" I say always. "But I feel so bad, Buddy. I wanted so bad to give you a bike. I tried to sell my cameo Papa gave
310 me. Buddy"—she hesitates, as though embarrassed—"I made you another kite." Then I confess that I made her one, too; and we laugh. The candle burns too short to hold. Out it goes, exposing the starlight, the stars spinning at the window like a visible caroling that slowly, slowly daybreak silences. Possibly we doze; but the beginnings of dawn splash us like cold water: we're up, wide-eyed and wandering while we wait for others to waken. Quite deliberately my friend drops a kettle on the kitchen floor. I tap dance in front of closed doors. One

Christmas Orange (1975), Bob Timberlake. © Bob Timberlake.

by one the household emerges, looking as though they'd like to kill us both; but it's Christmas, so they can't. First, a gorgeous breakfast: just everything you can imagine—from flapjacks and fried squirrel to hominy grits and honey-in-320 the-comb. Which puts everyone in a good humor except my friend and me. Frankly, we're so impatient to get at the presents we can't eat a mouthful.

Well, I'm disappointed. Who wouldn't be? With socks, a Sunday school shirt, some handkerchiefs, a hand-me-down sweater, and a year's subscription to a religious magazine for children. *The Little Shepherd.* It makes me boil. It really does.

My friend has a better haul. A sack of satsumas,[8] that's her best present. She is proudest, however, of a white wool shawl knitted by her married sister. But she *says* her favorite gift is the kite I built her. And it *is* very beautiful; though not as beautiful as the one she made me, which is blue and scattered with gold 330 and green Good Conduct stars;[9] moreover, my name is painted on it, "Buddy."

"Buddy, the wind is blowing." Ⓜ

The wind is blowing, and nothing will do till we've run to a pasture below the house where Queenie has scooted to bury her bone (and where, a winter hence, Queenie will be buried, too). There, plunging through the healthy waist-high grass, we unreel our kites, feel them twitching at the string like sky

Ⓜ **DETAILS OF SETTING**
What do the gifts received by Buddy and his friend tell you about the economic circumstances of the household?

---

8. **satsumas** (săt-sōō′məz): fruit similar to tangerines.

9. **Good Conduct stars:** small, shiny, glued paper stars often awarded to children for good behavior or perfect attendance in school.

fish as they swim into the wind. Satisfied, sun-warmed, we sprawl in the grass and peel satsumas and watch our kites **cavort**. Soon I forget the socks and hand-me-down sweater. I'm as happy as if we'd already won the fifty-thousand-dollar Grand Prize in that coffee-naming contest.

340   "My, how foolish I am!" my friend cries, suddenly alert, like a woman remembering too late she has biscuits in the oven. "You know what I've always thought?" she asks in a tone of discovery and not smiling at me but a point beyond. "I've always thought a body would have to be sick and dying before they saw the Lord. And I imagined that when he came it would be like looking at the Baptist window: pretty as colored glass with the sun pouring through, such a shine you don't know it's getting dark. And it's been a comfort: to think of that shine taking away all the spooky feeling. But I'll wager it never happens. I'll wager at the very end a body realizes the Lord has already shown himself. That things as they are"—her hand circles in a gesture that gathers 350 clouds and kites and grass and Queenie pawing earth over her bone—"just what they've always seen, was seeing him. As for me, I could leave the world with today in my eyes."

    This is our last Christmas together.

    Life separates us. Those who Know Best decide that I belong in a military school. And so follows a miserable succession of bugle-blowing prisons, grim reveille-ridden[10] summer camps. I have a new home too. But it doesn't count. Home is where my friend is, and there I never go. **N**

    And there she remains, puttering around the kitchen. Alone with Queenie. Then alone. ("Buddy dear," she writes in her wild hard-to-read script, 360 "yesterday Jim Macy's horse kicked Queenie bad. Be thankful she didn't feel much. I wrapped her in a Fine Linen sheet and rode her in the buggy down to Simpson's pasture where she can be with all her Bones . . ."). For a few Novembers she continues to bake her fruitcakes single-handed; not as many, but some: and, of course, she always sends me "the best of the batch." Also, in every letter she encloses a dime wadded in toilet paper: "See a picture show and write me the story." But gradually in her letters she tends to confuse me with her other friend, the Buddy who died in the 1880's; more and more, thirteenths are not the only days she stays in bed: a morning arrives in November, a leafless birdless coming of winter morning, when she cannot 370 rouse herself to exclaim: "Oh my, it's fruitcake weather!"

    And when that happens, I know it. A message saying so merely confirms a piece of news some secret vein had already received, **severing** from me an irreplaceable part of myself, letting it loose like a kite on a broken string. That is why, walking across a school campus on this particular December morning, I keep searching the sky. As if I expected to see, rather like hearts, a lost pair of kites hurrying toward heaven. ॐ

---

10. **reveille-ridden** (rĕv′ə-lē-rĭd′n): dominated by an early-morning signal, as on a bugle, to wake soldiers or campers.

Comprehension

1. **Clarify** How is Buddy's friend different from most people her age?

2. **Recall** What makes Christmas with his friend so memorable for Buddy?

3. **Summarize** What happens to the two friends after this particular Christmas?

Literary Analysis

4. **Examine Character** Think about your impression of Buddy's friend. What **details** helped create this character portrait?

5. **Draw Conclusions About Characters** Buddy is 7; his friend is over 60. Why are they such good **friends?** Give examples from the story to support your answer.

6. **Interpret Symbols** A symbol is a person, place, or object that represents something beyond itself. What might the kites at the end of the story represent, or symbolize? Give reasons for your interpretation.

7. **Evaluate Imagery** Look over the examples of imagery that you noted in your chart. Which example seemed the most vivid? What sense or senses did it appeal to? Explain your choice.

8. **Examine Details of Setting** Locate two passages in which the description of setting helps you understand something about the **historical era,** or time period, in which the story takes place. Then explain what the details tell you about the historical era.

9. **Analyze Influence of Setting** Think about the impact of setting on the events and characters in this story. What might change if the story were set in a city instead of the country or in contemporary times instead of the past? Choose one detail of time or place from the story and explain how the story would be different if this detail were altered.

10. **Make Judgments** In your opinion, is this story merely a vivid portrayal of a memory, or does it also convey a **theme,** or message?

Literary Criticism

11. **Biographical Context** Since its publication, "A Christmas Memory" has stirred debate among readers and critics. If it is based to a large degree on actual people and events, why is it called fiction? Explain why Capote might have chosen to call this work fiction as opposed to autobiography.

PENNSYLVANIA STANDARDS

READING STANDARD
B.1.1.1.B.1 Evaluate setting

Vocabulary in Context

VOCABULARY PRACTICE

Identify the word that is not related in meaning to the other words in the set.

1. (a) gear, (b) paraphernalia, (c) materials, (d) notice
2. (a) vigorous, (b) robust, (c) prosaic, (d) forceful
3. (a) start, (b) finish, (c) begin, (d) inaugurate
4. (a) destroy, (b) suffuse, (c) demolish, (d) consume
5. (a) depress, (b) invigorate, (c) energize, (d) exhilarate
6. (a) squander, (b) waste, (c) conserve, (d) misuse
7. (a) retreat, (b) urge, (c) spur, (d) goad
8. (a) potent, (b) mighty, (c) possible, (d) strong
9. (a) cavort, (b) prance, (c) frolic, (d) fight
10. (a) cut, (b) separate, (c) join, (d) sever

WORD LIST

cavort
exhilarate
goad
inaugurate
paraphernalia
potent
prosaic
sever
squander
suffuse

VOCABULARY IN WRITING

Write several sentences about how others in the household seem to regard the two friends. Use three or more vocabulary words in your sentences. Here is a sample.

> **EXAMPLE SENTENCE**
>
> *The others think that Buddy and his friend collect a lot of useless **paraphernalia**.*

VOCABULARY STRATEGY: CONNOTATION AND DENOTATION

A word's **denotation** is its basic dictionary meaning; its **connotations** are the overtones of meaning that it may take on. For example, the vocabulary word *goad* means "to urge," but it has connotations of physically forcing or bullying that *urge* does not have. When you choose words in writing, be sure to consider whether their connotations fit the context.

PRACTICE Choose the word that works best in each sentence.

1. Though the Smiths (spent, squandered) a lot of money, they thought putting their son through college was worth it.
2. It was (brave, foolhardy) of Karen not to study before final exams.
3. Al has a modest, (unassuming, groveling) manner that puts people at ease.
4. Anyone treating patients without a medical degree is a (fraud, pretender).
5. The haircut framed her (thin, emaciated) face quite nicely.

PENNSYLVANIA STANDARDS

READING STANDARD
A.1.2.2 Use context clues

VOCABULARY PRACTICE
For more practice, go to the **Vocabulary Center** at ClassZone.com.

Reading-Writing Connection

Increase your understanding of "A Christmas Memory" by responding to these prompts. Then use **Revision: Grammar and Style** to improve your writing.

WRITING PROMPTS	SELF-CHECK

A. Short Response: Rewrite a Scene
Imitation is a good way to learn from a master stylist like Truman Capote. Pick your favorite scene from the story and create a **one- or two-paragraph description** of it, using your own images.

A strong description will . . .
- clearly evoke the time and place
- include sensory details

B. Extended Response: Analyze a Character
Consider what you learn in this story about Buddy's **friend** and her values. Write a **three-to-five-paragraph response** in which you describe the kind of person she is, using quotations from the story to illustrate your analysis.

A successful response will . . .
- give a detailed description of the person's values
- include examples and quotations as support

REVISION: GRAMMAR AND STYLE

CHOOSE EFFECTIVE VERB TENSE Review the **Grammar and Style** note on page 316. By choosing to tell his story in the **present tense,** Capote invites the reader to relive the memory along with the narrator. Here is an example from the story:

PENNSYLVANIA STANDARDS

WRITING STANDARD
1.5.11.F.4 Use verbs properly

> *Long after the town has gone to sleep and the house is silent except for the chimings of clocks and the sputter of fading fires, she is weeping into a pillow . . .* (lines 207–208)

Notice how the revisions in red, changing past to present tense, bring an immediacy to the writing, as though the events were occurring now. Try using a similar technique as you revise your draft of Prompt A.

STUDENT MODEL

My friend jam~~med~~ⁱ her hat down on her head and recklessly navigateⁱ the

baby buggy across the frosty grass. The pecans we ~~sought were~~ *seek are* hiding under

rotting leaves and twigs.

WRITING TOOLS
For prewriting, revision, and editing tools, visit the **Writing Center** at ClassZone.com.

Through the Tunnel
Short Story by Doris Lessing

When is a R I S K *worth taking?*

PENNSYLVANIA STANDARDS

READING STANDARDS
A.1.4.1 Identify and explain main ideas and relevant supporting details

B.1.1.1.B.2 Evaluate the relationship between setting and other components

KEY IDEA In "Through the Tunnel," Jerry risks his personal safety. Sometimes people take such **risks** to prove something to themselves or others. The risks can be physical, emotional, or social. But when is an action too risky to attempt? More importantly, how do you calculate risk?

DISCUSS Think about a time when you or someone you know took a risk to prove something. Create a balance scale like the one shown to weigh that risk. In the base of the scale, write down the dangerous or risky activity. Jot down the risks in one box and the possible benefits in the other. Share your balance scale with your classmates, and discuss with them whether the possible benefits outweighed the risks of the behavior.

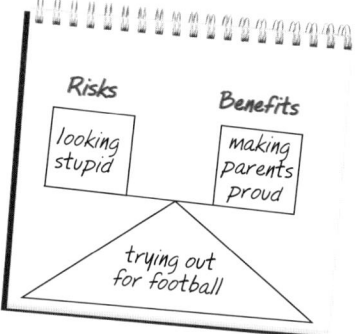

Risks   Benefits

looking stupid

making parents proud

trying out for football

LITERARY ANALYSIS: SETTING AS SYMBOL

A **symbol** is a person, place, object, or activity that stands for something beyond itself. For example, a star often symbolizes hope or excellence. A handshake communicates goodwill.

In "Through the Tunnel," various **settings** symbolize important ideas. As you read, think about what the beach, the bay, the tunnel, and the events that take place in each location might symbolize to Jerry.

READING SKILL: ANALYZE DETAILS

In order to understand the symbolic significance of each setting in "Through the Tunnel," you must analyze the **descriptive details** and pay attention to the larger meanings they imply. For example, the big beach is a familiar place where Jerry's mother goes. What might this represent to Jerry? As you read, keep track of words and phrases that describe each setting by using a chart similar to the one shown.

Beach	Bay	Tunnel
crowded	wild and rocky	
familiar		

Review: **Draw Conclusions**

▲ VOCABULARY IN CONTEXT

Lessing uses the numbered words in her story about coming of age. Try to match each word with a synonym.

1. contrition
2. incredulous
3. inquisitive
4. persistence
5. promontory
6. supplication

a. cliff
b. perseverance
c. regret
d. request
e. questioning
f. unbelieving

Author Online

Doris Lessing
born 1919

Distinguished Writer
Doris Lessing has been celebrated as one of the 20th century's "most powerful and compelling novelists." In sheer size and variety, her body of work is impressive: over 45 books ranging from novels and short story collections to essays, a thus far two-volume autobiography, and a book about cats.

Crossing Boundaries Born in Persia (now Iran), Lessing grew up on a farm in Southern Rhodesia (now Zimbabwe) with her British parents. As part of the small community of white settlers in Africa, she saw firsthand the injustices of white minority rule and racial segregation. In 1949, Lessing left Rhodesia for London to start a new life as a writer. Her first novel, *The Grass Is Singing* (1950), and many of her other early works are set in Rhodesia and deal critically with the colonial society she had known. Her best-known novel is *The Golden Notebook* (1962), a story about a woman writer in London struggling to come to terms with her life and times.

Child of Africa Lessing insists, "Whatever I am, I have been made so by central Africa." Her self-confidence, strength, and independence can be traced to her youth in the rough, unforgiving country of the African bush. There she could roam freely but, like other African children, had to deal at an early age with dangerous thunderstorms, droughts, snakes, scorpions, and insects. Survival—emotional, intellectual, and physical—is at the heart of her life and work.

 MORE ABOUT THE AUTHOR
For more on Doris Lessing, visit the **Literature Center** at ClassZone.com.

THROUGH THE
Tunnel

Doris Lessing

Going to the shore on the first morning of the vacation, the young English boy stopped at a turning of the path and looked down at a wild and rocky bay, and then over to the crowded beach he knew so well from other years. His mother walked on in front of him, carrying a bright striped bag in one hand. Her other arm, swinging loose, was very white in the sun. The boy watched that white, naked arm, and turned his eyes, which had a frown behind them, toward the bay and back again to his mother. When she felt he was not with her, she swung around. "Oh, there you are, Jerry!" she said. She looked impatient, then smiled. "Why, darling, would you rather not come with

10 me? Would you rather—" She frowned, conscientiously worrying over what amusements he might secretly be longing for, which she had been too busy or too careless to imagine. He was very familiar with that anxious, apologetic smile. **Contrition** sent him running after her. And yet, as he ran, he looked back over his shoulder at the wild bay; and all morning, as he played on the safe beach, he was thinking of it. **A**

   Next morning, when it was time for the routine of swimming and sunbathing, his mother said, "Are you tired of the usual beach, Jerry? Would you like to go somewhere else?"

ANALYZE VISUALS
What elements of this painting are emphasized by its **composition**—the sizes, shapes, and arrangement of its parts?

contrition (kən-trĭsh′ən) *n.* a feeling of regret for doing wrong

A ANALYZE DETAILS
From what you've learned so far, what contrast exists between the beach and the bay?

"Oh, no!" he said quickly, smiling at her out of that unfailing impulse of
contrition—a sort of chivalry. Yet, walking down the path with her, he blurted
out, "I'd like to go and have a look at those rocks down there."

She gave the idea her attention. It was a wild-looking place, and there was
no one there; but she said, "Of course, Jerry. When you've had enough, come
to the big beach. Or just go straight back to the villa, if you like." She walked
away, that bare arm, now slightly reddened from yesterday's sun, swinging.
And he almost ran after her again, feeling it unbearable that she should go by
herself, but he did not.

She was thinking, Of course he's old enough to be safe without me. Have I
been keeping him too close? He mustn't feel he ought to be with me. I must be
careful. **B**

He was an only child, eleven years old. She was a widow. She was determined to be neither possessive nor lacking in devotion. She went
worrying off to her beach.

As for Jerry, once he saw that his mother had gained her beach,
he began the steep descent to the bay. From where he was, high up among
red-brown rocks, it was a scoop of moving bluish green fringed with white. As
he went lower, he saw that it spread among small **promontories** and inlets of
rough, sharp rock, and the crisping, lapping surface showed stains of purple
and darker blue. Finally, as he ran sliding and scraping down the last few yards,
he saw an edge of white surf and the shallow, luminous movement of water
over white sand, and, beyond that, a solid, heavy blue.

He ran straight into the water and began swimming. He was a good
swimmer. He went out fast over the gleaming sand, over a middle region
where rocks lay like discolored monsters under the surface, and then he was
in the real sea—a warm sea where irregular cold currents from the deep water
shocked his limbs. **C**

When he was so far out that he could look back not only on the little bay
but past the promontory that was between it and the big beach, he floated
on the buoyant surface and looked for his mother. There she was, a speck of
yellow under an umbrella that looked like a slice of orange peel. He swam back
to shore, relieved at being sure she was there, but all at once very lonely.

On the edge of a small cape that marked the side of the bay away from
the promontory was a loose scatter of rocks. Above them, some boys were
stripping off their clothes. They came running, naked, down to the rocks. The
English boy swam toward them, but kept his distance at a stone's throw. They
were of that coast; all of them were burned smooth dark brown and speaking a
language he did not understand. To be with them, of them, was a craving that
filled his whole body. He swam a little closer; they turned and watched him
with narrowed, alert dark eyes. Then one smiled and waved. It was enough. In
a minute, he had swum in and was on the rocks beside them, smiling with a

B SETTING AS SYMBOL
Reread lines 21–30.
What might the beach
symbolize? The bay?

promontory
(prŏm′ən-tôr′ē) *n.*
a high ridge of land
or rock jutting out into
a body of water

C ANALYZE DETAILS
Reread lines 42–46. Why
might Jerry consider this
area "the real sea"?

desperate, nervous **supplication.** They shouted cheerful greetings at him; and then, as he preserved his nervous, uncomprehending smile, they understood that he was a foreigner strayed from his own beach, and they proceeded to forget him. But he was happy. He was with them.

They began diving again and again from a high point into a well of blue sea between rough, pointed rocks. After they had dived and come up, they swam around, hauled themselves up, and waited their turn to dive again. They were big boys—men, to Jerry. He dived, and they watched him; and when he swam around to take his place, they made way for him. He felt he was accepted and he dived again, carefully, proud of himself.

Soon the biggest of the boys poised himself, shot down into the water, and did not come up. The others stood about, watching. Jerry, after waiting for the sleek brown head to appear, let out a yell of warning; they looked at him idly and turned their eyes back toward the water. After a long time, the boy came up on the other side of a big dark rock, letting the air out of his lungs in a sputtering gasp and a shout of triumph. Immediately the rest of them dived in. One moment, the morning seemed full of chattering boys; the next, the air and the surface of the water were empty. But through the heavy blue, dark shapes could be seen moving and groping.

Jerry dived, shot past the school of underwater swimmers, saw a black wall of rock looming at him, touched it, and bobbed up at once to the surface, where the wall was a low barrier he could see across. There was no one visible; under him, in the water, the dim shapes of the swimmers had disappeared. Then one, and then another of the boys came up on the far side of the barrier of rock, and he understood that they had swum through some gap or hole in it. He plunged down again. He could see nothing through the stinging salt water but the blank rock. When he came up the boys were all on the diving rock, preparing to attempt the feat again. And now, in a panic of failure, he yelled up, in English, "Look at me! Look!" and he began splashing and kicking in the water like a foolish dog.

They looked down gravely, frowning. He knew the frown. At moments of failure, when he clowned to claim his mother's attention, it was with just this grave, embarrassed inspection that she rewarded him. Through his hot shame, feeling the pleading grin on his face like a scar that he could never remove, he looked up at the group of big brown boys on the rock and shouted, *"Bonjour! Merci! Au revoir! Monsieur, monsieur!"*[1] while he hooked his fingers round his ears and waggled them.

Water surged into his mouth; he choked, sank, came up. The rock, lately weighted with boys, seemed to rear up out of the water as their weight was removed. They were flying down past him, now, into the water; the air was full of falling bodies. Then the rock was empty in the hot sunlight. He counted one, two, three. . . .

supplication
(sŭp′lĭ-kā′shən) *n.* a humble request or prayer

◆ GRAMMAR AND STYLE
Reread lines 80–81. Notice how Lessing uses **a compound predicate** to concisely describe several actions taking place.

---

1. ***Bonjour! Merci! Au revoir! Monsieur, monsieur!*** (bôn-zhōōr′ měr-sē′ ō′rə-vwär′ mə-syœ′ mə-syœ′) *French:* Good day! Thank you! Goodbye! Sir, sir!

At fifty, he was terrified. They must all be drowning beneath him, in the watery caves of the rock! At a hundred, he stared around him at the empty hillside, wondering if he should yell for help. He counted faster, faster, to hurry them up, to bring them to the surface quickly, to drown them quickly—anything rather than the terror of counting on and on into the blue emptiness of the morning. And then, at a hundred and sixty, the water beyond the rock was full of boys blowing like brown whales. They swam back to the shore 110 without a look at him.

He climbed back to the diving rock and sat down, feeling the hot roughness of it under his thighs. The boys were gathering up their bits of clothing and running off along the shore to another promontory. They were leaving to get away from him. He cried openly, fists in his eyes. There was no one to see him, and he cried himself out. **E**

It seemed to him that a long time had passed, and he swam out to where he could see his mother. Yes, she was still there, a yellow spot under an orange umbrella. He swam back to the big rock, climbed up, and dived into the blue pool among the fanged and angry boulders. Down he went, until he 120 touched the wall of rock again. But the salt was so painful in his eyes that he could not see. **F**

He came to the surface, swam to shore, and went back to the villa to wait for his mother. Soon she walked slowly up the path, swinging her striped bag, the flushed, naked arm dangling beside her. "I want some swimming goggles," he panted, defiant and beseeching.

She gave him a patient, **inquisitive** look as she said casually, "Well, of course, darling."

But now, now, now! He must have them this minute, and no other time. He nagged and pestered until she went with him to a shop. As soon as she had 130 bought the goggles, he grabbed them from her hand as if she were going to claim them for herself, and was off, running down the steep path to the bay.

Jerry swam out to the big barrier rock, adjusted the goggles, and dived. The impact of the water broke the rubber-enclosed vacuum, and the goggles came loose. He understood that he must swim down to the base of the rock from the surface of the water. He fixed the goggles tight and firm, filled his lungs, and floated, face down, on the water. Now, he could see. It was as if he had eyes of a different kind—fish eyes that showed everything clear and delicate and wavering in the bright water.

Under him, six or seven feet down, was a floor of perfectly clean, shining 140 white sand, rippled firm and hard by the tides. Two grayish shapes steered there, like long, rounded pieces of wood or slate. They were fish. He saw them nose toward each other, poise motionless, make a dart forward, swerve off, and come around again. It was like a water dance. A few inches above them the water sparkled as if sequins were dropping through it. Fish again—myriads of

E DRAW CONCLUSIONS
Why is Jerry upset? Cite details that support your answer.

F ANALYZE DETAILS
What does the description of the boulders in line 119 suggest about the tunnel?

inquisitive (ĭn-kwĭz´ĭ-tĭv) *adj.* curious; inquiring

Reflections (1970), Ken Danby. Original egg tempera, 38″ × 52″. © Ken Danby/Gallery Moos, Toronto, Canada.

minute fish, the length of his fingernail, were drifting through the water, and in a moment he could feel the innumerable tiny touches of them against his limbs. It was like swimming in flaked silver. The great rock the big boys had swum through rose sheer out of the white sand—black, tufted lightly with greenish weed. He could see no gap in it. He swam down to its base.

150   Again and again he rose, took a big chestful of air, and went down. Again and again he groped over the surface of the rock, feeling it, almost hugging it in the desperate need to find the entrance. And then, once, while he was clinging to the black wall, his knees came up and he shot his feet out forward and they met no obstacle. He had found the hole.

He gained the surface, clambered about the stones that littered the barrier rock until he found a big one, and, with this in his arms, let himself down over the side of the rock. He dropped, with the weight, straight to the sandy floor. Clinging tight to the anchor of stone, he lay on his side and looked in under the dark shelf at the place where his feet had gone. He could see the hole.

160 It was an irregular, dark gap; but he could not see deep into it. He let go of his anchor, clung with his hands to the edges of the hole, and tried to push himself in.

He got his head in, found his shoulders jammed, moved them in sidewise, and was inside as far as his waist. He could see nothing ahead. Something soft and clammy touched his mouth; he saw a dark frond moving against the grayish rock, and panic filled him. He thought of octopuses, of clinging weed. He pushed himself out backward and caught a glimpse, as he retreated, of a harmless tentacle of seaweed drifting in the mouth of the tunnel. But it was enough. He reached the sunlight, swam to shore, and lay on the diving rock.

170 He looked down into the blue well of water. He knew he must find his way through that cave, or hole, or tunnel, and out the other side. **G**

First, he thought, he must learn to control his breathing. He let himself down into the water with another big stone in his arms, so that he could lie effortlessly on the bottom of the sea. He counted. One, two, three. He counted steadily. He could hear the movement of blood in his chest. Fifty-one, fifty-two. . . . His chest was hurting. He let go of the rock and went up into the air. He saw that the sun was low. He rushed to the villa and found his mother at her supper. She said only "Did you enjoy yourself?" and he said "Yes."

All night the boy dreamed of the water-filled cave in the rock, and as soon
180 as breakfast was over he went to the bay.

That night, his nose bled badly. For hours he had been underwater, learning to hold his breath, and now he felt weak and dizzy. His mother said, "I shouldn't overdo things, darling, if I were you."

That day and the next, Jerry exercised his lungs as if everything, the whole of his life, all that he would become, depended upon it. Again his nose bled at night, and his mother insisted on his coming with her the next day. It was

G DRAW CONCLUSIONS
Reread lines 155–171. How does Jerry's perception of the tunnel change? What does this tell you about him?

a torment to him to waste a day of his careful self-training, but he stayed with her on that other beach, which now seemed a place for small children, a place where his mother might lie safe in the sun. It was not his beach. **H**

190   He did not ask for permission, on the following day, to go to his beach. He went, before his mother could consider the complicated rights and wrongs of the matter. A day's rest, he discovered, had improved his count by ten. The big boys had made the passage while he counted a hundred and sixty. He had been counting fast, in his fright. Probably now, if he tried, he could get through that long tunnel, but he was not going to try yet. A curious, most unchildlike **persistence,** a controlled impatience, made him wait. In the meantime, he lay underwater on the white sand, littered now by stones he had brought down from the upper air, and studied the entrance to the tunnel. He knew every jut and corner of it, as far as it was possible to see. It was as if he

200 already felt its sharpness about his shoulders.

He sat by the clock in the villa, when his mother was not near, and checked his time. He was **incredulous** and then proud to find he could hold his breath without strain for two minutes. The words "two minutes," authorized by the clock, brought close the adventure that was so necessary to him.

n another four days, his mother said casually one morning, they must go home. On the day before they left, he would do it. He would do it if it killed him, he said defiantly to himself. But two days before they were to leave—a day of triumph when he increased his count by fifteen—his nose bled so badly that he turned dizzy and had to lie limply over the big rock like

210 a bit of seaweed, watching the thick red blood flow on to the rock and trickle slowly down to the sea. He was frightened. Supposing he turned dizzy in the tunnel? Supposing he died there, trapped? Supposing—his head went around, in the hot sun, and he almost gave up. He thought he would return to the house and lie down, and next summer, perhaps, when he had another year's growth in him—*then* he would go through the hole.

But even after he had made the decision, or thought he had, he found himself sitting up on the rock and looking down into the water; and he knew that now, this moment, when his nose had only just stopped bleeding, when his head was still sore and throbbing—this was the moment when he would

220 try. If he did not do it now, he never would. He was trembling with fear that he would not go; and he was trembling with horror at that long, long tunnel under the rock, under the sea. Even in the open sunlight, the barrier rock seemed very wide and very heavy; tons of rock pressed down on where he would go. If he died there, he would lie until one day—perhaps not before next year—those big boys would swim into it and find it blocked. **I**

He put on his goggles, fitted them tight, tested the vacuum. His hands were shaking. Then he chose the biggest stone he could carry and slipped over the

H SETTING AS SYMBOL
What does the big beach symbolize to Jerry now? Cite details in this paragraph that support your interpretation.

persistence (pər-sĭs′təns) *n.* the act of refusing to stop or be changed

incredulous (ĭn-krĕj′ə-ləs) *adj.* doubtful; disbelieving

I ANALYZE DETAILS
Reread lines 205–225. How dangerous is the tunnel? Point out details that reveal this.

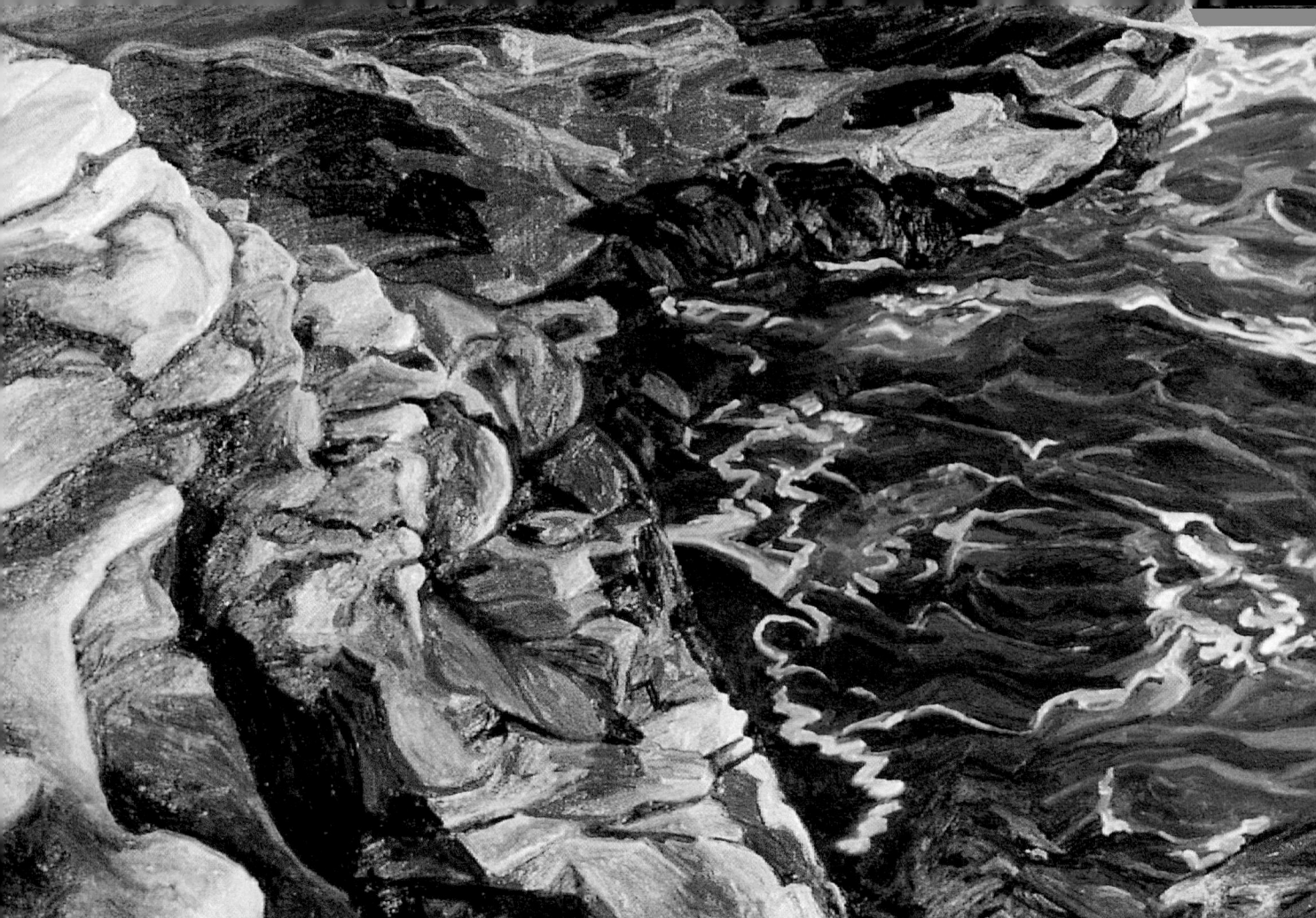

Ice Blue (1981), Susan Shatter. Oil on canvas, 40″ × 90″. Private collection. Courtesy of the Fischback Gallery, New York.

edge of the rock until half of him was in the cool, enclosing water and half in the hot sun. He looked up once at the empty sky, filled his lungs once, twice, and then sank fast to the bottom with the stone. He let it go and began to count. He took the edges of the hole in his hands and drew himself into it, wriggling his shoulders in sidewise as he remembered he must, kicking himself along with his feet.

Soon he was clear inside. He was in a small rock-bound hole filled with yellowish-gray water. The water was pushing him up against the roof. The roof was sharp and pained his back. He pulled himself along with his hands—fast, fast—and used his legs as levers. His head knocked against something; a sharp pain dizzied him. Fifty, fifty-one, fifty-two. . . . He was without light, and the water seemed to press upon him with the weight of rock. Seventy-one, seventy-two. . . . There was no strain on his lungs. He felt like an inflated balloon, his lungs were so light and easy, but his head was pulsing.

He was being continually pressed against the sharp roof, which felt slimy as well as sharp. Again he thought of octopuses, and wondered if the tunnel might be filled with weed that could tangle him. He gave himself a panicky,

convulsive kick forward, ducked his head, and swam. His feet and hands moved freely, as if in open water. The hole must have widened out. He thought he must be swimming fast, and he was frightened of banging his head if the tunnel narrowed.

A hundred, a hundred and one. . . . The water paled. Victory filled him.
250 His lungs were beginning to hurt. A few more strokes and he would be out. He was counting wildly; he said a hundred and fifteen, and then, a long time later, a hundred and fifteen again. The water was a clear jewel-green all around him. Then he saw, above his head, a crack running up through the rock. Sunlight was falling through it, showing the clean, dark rock of the tunnel, a single mussel shell, and darkness ahead.

He was at the end of what he could do. He looked up at the crack as if it were filled with air and not water, as if he could put his mouth to it to draw in air. A hundred and fifteen, he heard himself say inside his head—but he had said that long ago. He must go on into the blackness ahead, or he would
260 drown. His head was swelling, his lungs cracking. A hundred and fifteen, a hundred and fifteen pounded through his head, and he feebly clutched at rocks

in the dark, pulling himself forward, leaving the brief space of sunlit water behind. He felt he was dying. He was no longer quite conscious. He struggled on in the darkness between lapses into unconsciousness. An immense, swelling pain filled his head, and then the darkness cracked with an explosion of green light. His hands, groping forward, met nothing; and his feet, kicking back, propelled him out into the open sea.

He drifted to the surface, his face turned up to the air. He was gasping like a fish. He felt he would sink now and drown; he could not swim the few feet
270 back to the rock. Then he was clutching it and pulling himself up onto it. He lay face down, gasping. He could see nothing but a red-veined, clotted dark. His eyes must have burst, he thought; they were full of blood. He tore off his goggles and a gout of blood went into the sea. His nose was bleeding, and the blood had filled the goggles.

He scooped up handfuls of water from the cool, salty sea, to splash on his face, and did not know whether it was blood or salt water he tasted. After a time, his heart quieted, his eyes cleared, and he sat up. He could see the local boys diving and playing half a mile away. He did not want them. He wanted nothing but to get back home and lie down.
280 In a short while, Jerry swam to shore and climbed slowly up the path to the villa. He flung himself on his bed and slept, waking at the sound of feet on the path outside. His mother was coming back. He rushed to the bathroom, thinking she must not see his face with bloodstains, or tearstains, on it. He came out of the bathroom and met her as she walked into the villa, smiling, her eyes lighting up.

"Have a nice morning?" she asked, laying her hand on his warm brown shoulder a moment.

"Oh, yes, thank you," he said.

"You look a bit pale." And then, sharp and anxious, "How did you bang
290 your head?"

"Oh, just banged it," he told her.

She looked at him closely. He was strained; his eyes were glazed-looking. She was worried. And then she said to herself, Oh, don't fuss! Nothing can happen. He can swim like a fish.

They sat down to lunch together.

"Mummy," he said, "I can stay under water for two minutes—three minutes, at least." It came bursting out of him.

"Can you, darling?" she said. "Well, I shouldn't overdo it. I don't think you ought to swim any more today."
300 She was ready for a battle of wills, but he gave in at once. It was no longer of the least importance to go to the bay. ∾

Comprehension

1. **Recall** Describe Jerry's age and family situation.

2. **Summarize** What happens between Jerry and the older boys?

3. **Clarify** Why is it so important for Jerry to swim through the tunnel? Explain what he is trying to prove.

PENNSYLVANIA STANDARDS

READING STANDARD
B.1.1.1.B.2 Evaluate the relationship between setting and other components

Literary Analysis

4. **Identify Conflicts** Identify the external and internal conflicts Jerry faces in the story. How are these conflicts resolved?

5. **Analyze Suspense** Reread lines 234–267. How does Lessing build suspense in this passage? What other techniques does she use to build suspense in this story? Give examples to support your answers.

6. **Analyze Relationships** Explain Jerry's relationship with his mother. How has their relationship changed by the end of the story?

7. **Analyze Details** Look over the chart you made as you read. What are the major differences between the big beach and the bay? What does each place **symbolize** to Jerry?

8. **Interpret Setting as Symbol** What does Jerry's swim through the tunnel symbolize? Cite descriptions of the tunnel, its connection to the older boys, and Jerry's feelings about the tunnel to support your interpretation.

9. **Make Judgments About Motive** Does Jerry accomplish what he wants by swimming through the tunnel? To help you decide, create a two-column chart, briefly describing Jerry before and after his swim.

Before, Jerry is ...	After, Jerry is ...
anxious to please his mother lonely	

10. **Evaluate** Do the benefits of Jerry's accomplishment outweigh the **risks?** Base your decision on evidence from the story, such as Jerry's preparation, as well as on your own knowledge and experience.

Literary Criticism

11. **Critical Interpretations** The critic Martha Duffy once praised Lessing for the "unsparing clarity and frankness" of her writing. What evidence do you find in "Through the Tunnel" to support this assessment of Lessing's work?

Vocabulary in Context

VOCABULARY PRACTICE

Drawing on your understanding of the words, write *true* or *false* for each item.

1. If you feel **contrition** for something you did, you feel proud of your actions.
2. You should not live on a **promontory** if you are afraid of heights.
3. An **inquisitive** child will rarely ask why.
4. You might hear a **supplication** at a prayer service.
5. A person shows **persistence** by repeating a job until she gets it right.
6. If you are **incredulous** about a friend's advice, you likely will ignore it.

VOCABULARY IN WRITING

Using four vocabulary words, write a paragraph describing how one of the older boys might have reacted to Jerry's swim. Here is a sample opening.

> **EXAMPLE SENTENCE**
>
> The young English boy's **persistence** was amazing . . .

VOCABULARY STRATEGY: THE LATIN ROOTS *quest, quer,* AND *quisit*

The word *inquisitive* contains the root of the Latin word *quaerere*, meaning "to seek." Common forms of this root include *quest, quer,* and *quisit.* When the Latin prefix *in-* ("into") and the suffix *-ive* ("tending toward a specific action") are added to *quisit*, they make the word *inquisitive*, which literally means "inclining to seek into." Remembering the meaning of *quest, quer,* and *quisit* will help you understand words in this family.

PRACTICE Try your hand at writing a definition for each of these words in the *quest, quer,* and *quisit* family. Use a dictionary to confirm your definitions. Then, for each word, write a sentence that shows its meaning.

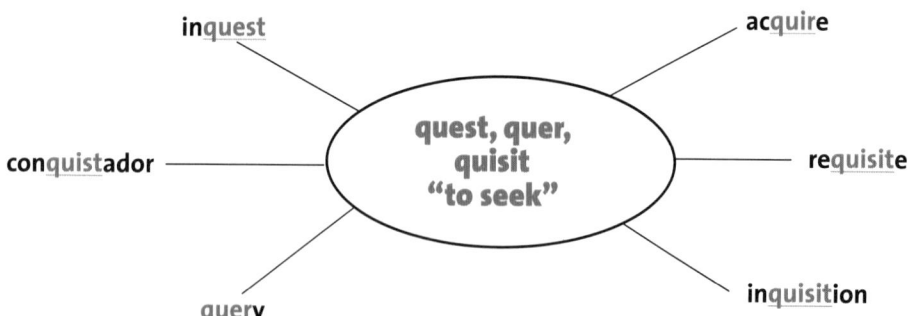

WORD LIST

contrition
incredulous
inquisitive
persistence
promontory
supplication

PENNSYLVANIA STANDARDS

READING STANDARD
A.1.2 Apply word recognition skills

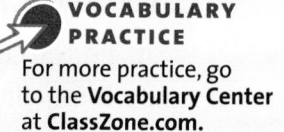

VOCABULARY PRACTICE
For more practice, go to the **Vocabulary Center** at **ClassZone.com**.

Reading-Writing Connection

Further explore the characters in "Through the Tunnel" by responding to these prompts. Then use **Revision: Grammar and Style** to improve your writing.

WRITING PROMPTS

A. Short Response: Analyze a Character's Actions

Do you think Jerry's mother is right to trust him by himself? Consider the **risks** Jerry takes, as well as his success, and then write a **one- or two-paragraph response** that explains your answer.

B. Extended Response: Create a Dialogue

Imagine a time when Jerry might tell his mother about his swim through the tunnel. How old would he be? What would he say? Using what you know about the characters, write a **one-page dialogue** in which Jerry tells his mother about his experience.

SELF-CHECK

A strong response will . . .

- clearly state your opinion
- include details and examples from the story to support your point

An effective dialogue will . . .

- show how each character thinks and feels
- include reactions and speech consistent with each character

REVISON: GRAMMAR AND STYLE

WRITE CONCISELY Review the **Grammar and Style** note on page 331. Like Lessing, you can use **compound predicates** to make your writing more concise and improve the flow of your sentences.

A predicate indicates what a subject is or does or what happens to the subject. By combining predicates, you can avoid writing a series of short, choppy sentences that begin with the same noun or pronoun.

Here is an example of how Lessing uses this technique:

He looked up once at the empty sky, filled his lungs once, twice, and then sank fast to the bottom with the stone. He let it go and began to count. (lines 229–231)

Notice how the revisions in red improve sentence flow.

PENNSYLVANIA STANDARDS

WRITING STANDARD
1.5.11.D.1 Use different types and lengths of sentences

> **STUDENT MODEL**
>
> I think Jerry's mom is a responsible parent. She pays attention to Jerry. ~~She~~
>   *and*
> tries to figure out what he wants. ~~He wants her to~~ give him more freedom, *when he asks for it*
>   *and*
> She knows he is a good swimmer. ~~She~~ decides to let him go to the bay.

WRITING TOOLS
For prewriting, revision, and editing tools, visit the **Writing Center** at ClassZone.com.

The Cask of Amontillado
Short Story by Edgar Allan Poe

Is REVENGE
ever justified?

**PENNSYLVANIA
STANDARDS**

READING STANDARDS
A.1.5.1 Summarize the key details
and events
B.1.1.1.E.2 Evaluate the relationship
between the tone, style, and/or mood
and other components

KEY IDEA Montresor, the narrator of "The Cask of
Amontillado," feels that **revenge** is necessary to right a
wrong. Some would argue that two wrongs never make
a right and that revenge leads only to more wrongdoing.
Do acts of revenge ever resolve conflicts?

PRESENT An act of revenge often causes a chain reaction,
and the repercussions can go on for months or years.
With a group, think of one act of revenge and chart
out the possible chain of effects. Share your chain of
events with the rest of the class.

Event
Girl makes fun of boy.

↓

Act of Revenge
Boy spills ink on her uniform.

↓

Effects
• Uniform is ruined. • Girl's parents have to buy a new one.

LITERARY ANALYSIS: MOOD

In "The Cask of Amontillado," Edgar Allan Poe creates an unforgettable **mood** of suspense and horror. From the beginning, the narrator's talk of injuries borne, unforgivable insults, and threatened revenge conveys a sinister feeling. Poe develops this mood by means of

- the sensory details and imagery used to convey the setting
- the repetition of words and the rhythm of the language
- words describing thoughts, feelings, and actions

As you read, notice how Poe's descriptions of the setting and his use of language combine to create a memorably dark tale.

READING STRATEGY: PARAPHRASE

Poe often uses long, complex sentences that are especially challenging to modern readers. To make sure that you understand the events in this story, try paraphrasing. To **paraphrase** is to restate information in one's own words. A paraphrase is about the same length as the original text. It includes all the details of the original but is written in simpler language. As you read this story, take time to paraphrase difficult passages. Here is an example.

Text	Paraphrase
"It must be understood, that neither by word nor deed had I given Fortunato cause to doubt my good-will." (lines 9–10)	You must understand that I said and did nothing to make Fortunato mistrust me.

Review: **Make Inferences**

▲ VOCABULARY IN CONTEXT

The boldfaced words help create a mood of horror. Use context clues to figure out the meaning of each word. Then use each word in a sentence. After reading the selection, check to see whether you used the words correctly.

1. to **preclude** pain
2. to lie with **impunity**
3. **immolation** of an enemy
4. **abscond** with money
5. everlasting **repose**
6. **termination** of a job
7. to help anger to **subside**
8. to close off an **aperture**

Author Online

The Genius of Poe

Edgar Allan Poe
1809–1849

Edgar Allan Poe started out as a poet but turned to writing short fiction to earn a living. His career in fiction officially began in 1833, with a $50 prize for his story "MS. Found in a Bottle." At the time he was living in poverty with his beloved aunt Maria Clemm and her daughter, Virginia. With the prize money came recognition and a job offer from a literary magazine. By 1838, Poe had married Virginia and moved the family to Philadelphia, where he worked for several leading literary magazines.

Master of the Macabre Poe may have started writing horror fiction because that's what the reading public wanted. Gothic tales were popular at the time, and newspapers regularly printed sensational reports of bizarre murders. Poe adapted elements of Gothic fiction, took a few story ideas from news headlines, added his psychological insights into the mix, and soon became the undisputed master of the genre.

 MORE ABOUT THE AUTHOR
For more on Edgar Allan Poe, visit the **Literature Center** at **ClassZone.com**.

Background

A Different Burial Ground Although this story begins during a time of carnival festivities, the setting soon shifts to the dark, cool burial vaults under the narrator's palace, where he also stores his wine. In such underground cemeteries, called catacombs, bodies were placed in carved recesses along the walls of burial chambers. The largest and most famous are those of Rome, in which early Christians were entombed.

The Cask of Amontillado

EDGAR ALLAN POE

The thousand injuries of Fortunato I had borne as I best could; but when he ventured upon insult, I vowed revenge. You, who so well know the nature of my soul, will not suppose, however, that I gave utterance to a threat. *At length* I would be avenged; this was a point definitively settled—but the very definitiveness with which it was resolved, **precluded** the idea of risk. I must not only punish, but punish with **impunity.** A wrong is unredressed when retribution overtakes its redresser. It is equally unredressed when the avenger fails to make himself felt as such to him who has done the wrong. **A**

It must be understood, that neither by word nor deed had I given Fortunato
10 cause to doubt my good-will. I continued, as was my wont, to smile in his face, and he did not perceive that my smile *now* was at the thought of his **immolation.**

He had a weak point—this Fortunato—although in other regards he was a man to be respected and even feared. He prided himself on his connoisseurship[1] in wine. Few Italians have the true virtuoso spirit. For the most part their enthusiasm is adopted to suit the time and opportunity—to practice imposture upon the British and Austrian *millionaires.* In painting and gemmary[2] Fortunato, like his countrymen, was a quack—but in the matter of old wines he was sincere. In this respect I did not differ from him materially; I
20 was skillful in the Italian vintages myself, and bought largely whenever I could.

It was about dusk, one evening during the supreme madness of the carnival[3] season, that I encountered my friend. He accosted me with excessive warmth, for he had been drinking much. The man wore motley.[4] He had on a tight-fitting parti-striped dress, and his head was surmounted by the conical cap and bells. I was so pleased to see him, that I thought I should never have done wringing his hand.

ANALYZE VISUALS
Would you describe the mood of this photograph as festive or sinister? Explain.

preclude (prĭ-klōōd′) *v.* to make impossible, especially by taking action in advance

impunity (ĭm-pyōō′nĭ-tē) *n.* freedom from penalty or harm

A PARAPHRASE
Paraphrase the opening paragraph. Why does the narrator vow revenge? What does he consider a successful revenge?

immolation (ĭm′ə-lā′shən) *n.* death or destruction

---

1. **connoisseurship** (kŏn′ə-sûr′shĭp): expertise or authority, especially in the fine arts or in matters of taste.

2. **gemmary** (jĕm′ə-rē): knowledge of precious gems.

3. **carnival**: a festival before the fasting period of Lent, characterized by fanciful costumes, masquerades, and feasts.

4. **motley**: the costume of a court jester.

I said to him: "My dear Fortunato, you are luckily met. How remarkably well you are looking to-day! But I have received a pipe of what passes for Amontillado,[5] and I have my doubts."

30 "How?" said he. "Amontillado? A pipe? Impossible! And in the middle of the carnival!"

"I have my doubts," I replied; "and I was silly enough to pay the full Amontillado price without consulting you in the matter. You were not to be found, and I was fearful of losing a bargain."

"Amontillado!"

"I have my doubts."

"Amontillado!"

"And I must satisfy them."

"Amontillado!"

40 "As you are engaged, I am on my way to Luchesi.[6] If anyone has a critical turn, it is he. He will tell me—"

"Luchesi cannot tell Amontillado from Sherry."

"And yet some fools will have it that his taste is a match for your own."

"Come, let us go."

"Whither?"

"To your vaults."

"My friend, no; I will not impose upon your good nature. I perceive you have an engagement. Luchesi—"

"I have no engagement;—come."

50 "My friend, no. It is not the engagement, but the severe cold with which I perceive you are afflicted. The vaults are insufferably damp. They are encrusted with niter."[7]

"Let us go, nevertheless. The cold is merely nothing. Amontillado! You have been imposed upon. And as for Luchesi, he cannot distinguish Sherry from Amontillado." **B**

Thus speaking, Fortunato possessed himself of my arm. Putting on a mask of black silk, and drawing a *roquelaure* [8] closely about my person, I suffered him to hurry me to my palazzo.[9]

There were no attendants at home; they had **absconded** to make merry in 60 honor of the time. I had told them that I should not return until the morning, and had given them explicit orders not to stir from the house. These orders were sufficient, I well knew, to insure their immediate disappearance, one and all, as soon as my back was turned.

B MOOD
Reread lines 27–55. How does Poe build a mood of suspense in this conversation between the narrator and Fortunato?

abscond (ăb-skŏnd')
v. to go away suddenly and secretly

---

5. **a pipe . . . Amontillado** (ə-mŏn′tl-ä′dō): a barrel of a wine that is supposed to be a type of pale, dry sherry, named for a town in southern Spain.

6. **Luchesi** (lōō-kā′sē).

7. **niter:** a white, gray, or colorless mineral, consisting of potassium nitrate.

8. **roquelaure** (rôk-lōr′) *French:* a man's knee-length cloak, popular during the 18th century.

9. **palazzo** (pə-lät′sō): a palace or mansion.

I took from their sconces two flambeaux,[10] and giving one to Fortunato, bowed him through several suites of rooms to the archway that led into the vaults. I passed down a long and winding staircase, requesting him to be cautious as he followed. We came at length to the foot of the descent and stood together on the damp ground of the catacombs of the Montresors.

The gait of my friend was unsteady, and the bells upon his cap jingled as
70 he strode.

"The pipe?" said he.

"It is farther on," said I; "but observe the white web-work which gleams from these cavern walls."

He turned toward me, and looked into my eyes with two filmy orbs that distilled the rheum of intoxication.[11]

"Niter?" he asked, at length.

"Niter," I replied. "How long have you had that cough?"

"Ugh! ugh! ugh!—ugh! ugh! ugh!—ugh! ugh! ugh!—ugh! ugh! ugh!—ugh! ugh! ugh!"

80 My poor friend found it impossible to reply for many minutes.

"It is nothing," he said, at last.

"Come," I said, with decision, "we will go back; your health is precious. You are rich, respected, admired, beloved; you are happy, as once I was. You are a man to be missed. For me it is no matter. We will go back; you will be ill, and I cannot be responsible. Besides, there is Luchesi—"

"Enough," he said; "the cough is a mere nothing; it will not kill me. I shall not die of a cough."

"True—true," I replied; "and, indeed, I had no intention of alarming you unnecessarily; but you should use all proper caution. A draft of this Medoc[12]
90 will defend us from the damps."

Here I knocked off the neck of a bottle that I drew from a long row of its fellows that lay upon the mold. **C**

"Drink," I said, presenting him the wine.

He raised it to his lips with a leer. He paused and nodded to me familiarly, while his bells jingled.

"I drink," he said, "to the buried that **repose** around us."

"And I to your long life."

He again took my arm, and we proceeded.

"These vaults," he said, "are extensive."

100 "The Montresors," I replied, "were a great and numerous family."

"I forget your arms."

"A huge human foot d'or,[13] in a field azure; the foot crushes a serpent rampant whose fangs are imbedded in the heel."

C MAKE INFERENCES
Reread lines 74–92. What is **ironic** about this conversation?

repose (rĭ-pōz´) *v.* to lie dead or at rest

---

10. **from their sconces two flambeaux** (flăm´bōz´): from their wall brackets two lighted torches.

11. **filmy . . . intoxication:** eyes clouded and glazed over from drunkenness.

12. **Medoc** (mā-dôk´): a red wine from the Bordeaux region of France.

13. **d'or** (dôr) *French:* colored gold. (Montresor is describing his coat of arms, the distinctive emblem of his family.)

"And the motto?"

"Nemo me impune lacessit." [14]

"Good!" he said.

The wine sparkled in his eyes and the bells jingled. My own fancy grew warm with the Medoc. We had passed through walls of piled bones, with casks and puncheons[15] intermingling, into the inmost recesses of the catacombs. I paused again, and this time I made bold to seize Fortunato by an arm above the elbow.

"The niter!" I said; "see, it increases. It hangs like moss upon the vaults. We are below the river's bed. The drops of moisture trickle among the bones. Come, we will go back ere it is too late. Your cough—" **D**

"It is nothing," he said; "let us go on. But first, another draft of the Medoc."

I broke and reached him a flagon of De Grâve.[16] He emptied it at a breath. His eyes flashed with a fierce light. He laughed and threw the bottle upward with a gesticulation I did not understand.

I looked at him in surprise. He repeated the movement—a grotesque one.

"You do not comprehend?" he said.

"Not I," I replied.

"Then you are not of the brotherhood."

"How?"

"You are not of the masons."[17]

"Yes, yes," I said; "yes, yes."

"You? Impossible! A mason?"

"A mason," I replied.

"A sign," he said.

"It is this," I answered, producing a trowel[18] from beneath the folds of my roquelaure.

"You jest," he exclaimed, recoiling a few paces. "But let us proceed to the Amontillado."

"Be it so," I said, replacing the tool beneath the cloak, and again offering him my arm. He leaned upon it heavily. We continued our route in search of the Amontillado. We passed through a range of low arches, descended, passed on, and descending again, arrived at a deep crypt, in which the foulness of the air caused our flambeaux rather to glow than flame.

At the most remote end of the crypt there appeared another less spacious. Its walls had been lined with human remains, piled to the vault overhead, in the fashion of the great catacombs of Paris. Three sides of this interior **E**

D MOOD
In lines 108–114, note the sensory details and imagery that help you visualize the setting. What mood do they create?

E GRAMMAR AND STYLE
Notice Poe's use of **formal language,** including complex sentence structures.

---

14. ***Nemo me impune lacessit*** (nā′mō mā ĭm-poo′nĕ lä-kĕs′ĭt) *Latin:* No one injures me with impunity.

15. **casks and puncheons:** large storage containers for wine.

16. **De Grâve** (də gräv′): a red wine from the Bordeaux region of France.

17. **of the masons:** a Freemason, a member of a social organization with secret rituals and signs.

18. **producing a trowel:** Montresor is playing on another meaning of *mason*—"one who builds with stone or brick."

ANALYZE VISUALS
What qualities of the catacomb are emphasized by the two arches? Explain.

crypt were still ornamented in this manner. From the fourth the bones had been thrown down, and lay promiscuously upon the earth, forming at one point a mound of some size. Within the wall thus exposed by the displacing of the bones, we perceived a still interior recess, in depth about four feet, in width three, in height six or seven. It seemed to have been constructed for no especial use within itself, but formed merely the interval between two of the colossal supports of the roof of the catacombs, and was backed by one of their circumscribing walls of solid granite.

It was in vain that Fortunato, uplifting his dull torch, endeavored to pry
150 into the depth of the recess. Its **termination** the feeble light did not enable us to see.

"Proceed," I said; "herein is the Amontillado. As for Luchesi—"

"He is an ignoramus," interrupted my friend, as he stepped unsteadily forward, while I followed immediately at his heels. In an instant he had

termination
(tûr′mə-nā′shən) *n.* an end, limit, or edge

reached the extremity of the niche, and finding his progress arrested by the rock, stood stupidly bewildered. A moment more and I had fettered him to the granite. In its surface were two iron staples, distant from each other about two feet, horizontally. From one of these depended a short chain, from the other a padlock. Throwing the links about his waist, it was but the work of a few seconds to secure it. He was too much astounded to resist. Withdrawing the key I stepped back from the recess.

"Pass your hand," I said, "over the wall; you cannot help feeling the niter. Indeed it is *very* damp. Once more let me *implore* you to return. No? Then I must positively leave you. But I must first render you all the little attentions in my power."

"The Amontillado!" ejaculated my friend, not yet recovered from his astonishment.

"True," I replied; "the Amontillado."

As I said these words I busied myself among the pile of bones of which I have before spoken. Throwing them aside, I soon uncovered a quantity of building stone and mortar. With these materials and with the aid of my trowel, I began vigorously to wall up the entrance of the niche.

I had scarcely laid the first tier of the masonry when I discovered that the intoxication of Fortunato had in a great measure worn off. The earliest indication I had of this was a low moaning cry from the depth of the recess. It was not the cry of a drunken man. There was then a long and obstinate silence. I laid the second tier, and the third, and the fourth; and then I heard the furious vibrations of the chain. The noise lasted for several minutes, during which, that I might hearken to it with the more satisfaction, I ceased my labors and sat down upon the bones. When at last the clanking **subsided,**

subside (səb-sīd') *v.* to decrease in amount or intensity; settle down

I resumed the trowel, and finished without interruption the fifth, the sixth, and the seventh tier. The wall was now nearly upon a level with my breast. I again paused, and holding the flambeaux over the mason-work, threw a few feeble rays upon the figure within. **F**

A succession of loud and shrill screams, bursting suddenly from the throat of the chained form, seemed to thrust me violently back. For a brief moment I hesitated—I trembled. Unsheathing my rapier,[19] I began to grope with it about the recess; but the thought of an instant reassured me. I placed my hand upon the solid fabric of the catacombs, and felt satisfied. I reapproached the wall. I
190 replied to the yells of him who clamored. I re-echoed—I aided—I surpassed them in volume and in strength. I did this, and the clamorer grew still. **G**

It was now midnight, and my task was drawing to a close. I had completed the eighth, the ninth, and the tenth tier. I had finished a portion of the last and the eleventh; there remained but a single stone to be fitted and plastered in. I struggled with its weight; I placed it partially in its destined position. But now there came from out the niche a low laugh that erected the hairs upon my head. It was succeeded by a sad voice, which I had difficulty in recognizing as that of the noble Fortunato. The voice said—

"Ha! ha! ha!—he! he!—a very good joke indeed—an excellent jest. We will
200 have many a rich laugh about it at the palazzo—he! he! he! —over our wine—he! he! he!"

"The Amontillado!" I said.

"He! he! he!—he! he! he!—yes, the Amontillado. But is it not getting late? Will not they be awaiting us at the palazzo, the Lady Fortunato and the rest? Let us be gone."

"Yes," I said, "let us be gone."

"For the love of God, Montresor!"

"Yes," I said, "for the love of God!" **H**

But to these words I hearkened in vain for a reply. I grew impatient. I called
210 aloud,

"Fortunato!"

No answer. I called again,

"Fortunato!"

No answer still. I thrust a torch through the remaining **aperture** and let it fall within. There came forth in return only a jingling of the bells. My heart grew sick—on account of the dampness of the catacombs. I hastened to make an end of my labor. I forced the last stone into its position; I plastered it up. Against the new masonry I re-erected the old rampart of bones. For the half of a century no mortal has disturbed them. *In pace requiescat!* [20] ❧

F MOOD
Reread this paragraph. What **details** make this description especially horrifying?

G PARAPHRASE
Restate what happens in lines 185–191. What emotions does Montresor experience at this point in the story?

H MOOD
Reread lines 192–208. Point out **images** and other **details** that convey the mood of the scene.

aperture (ăp′ər-chər) *n.* an opening, such as a hole or a gap

---

19. **rapier** (rā′pē-ər): a long, slender sword.

20. *In pace requiescat* (ĭn pä′kĕ rĕ-kwē-ĕs′kät) *Latin:* May he rest in peace.

THE STORY BEHIND
The CASK
of Amontillado
EDWARD ROWE SNOW

While at Fort Independence, Poe [who was a private there in 1827] became fascinated with the inscriptions on a gravestone on a small monument outside the walls of the fort. . . .

> *Beneath this stone are deposited the remains of Lieut. ROBERT F. MASSIE, of the U. S. Regt. of Light Artillery. . . .*

During the summer of 1817, Poe learned, twenty-year-old Lieutenant Robert F. Massie of Virginia had arrived at Fort Independence as a newly appointed officer. Most of the men at the post came to enjoy Massie's friendship, but one officer, Captain Green, took a violent dislike to him. Green was known at the fort as a bully and a dangerous swordsman.

When Christmas vacations were allotted, few of the officers were allowed to leave the fort, and Christmas Eve found them up in the old barracks hall, playing cards. Just before midnight, at the height of the card game, Captain Green sprang to his feet, reached across the table and slapped Lieutenant Massie squarely in the face. "You're a cheat," he roared, "and I demand immediate satisfaction!" . . .

The duel began. Captain Green, an expert swordsman, soon had Massie at a disadvantage and ran him through. Fatally wounded, the young Virginian was carried back to the fort, where he died that afternoon. His many friends mourned the passing of a gallant officer. . . .

Feeling against Captain Green ran high for many weeks, and then suddenly he completely vanished. Years went by without a sign of him, and Green was written off the army records as a deserter.

According to the story which Poe finally gathered together, Captain Green had been so detested by his fellow officers at the fort that they decided to take a terrible revenge on him for Massie's death. . . .

Visiting Captain Green one moonless night, they pretended to be friendly and plied him with wine until he was helplessly intoxicated. Then, carrying the captain down to one of the ancient dungeons, the officers forced his body through a tiny opening which led into the subterranean casemate.[1] . . .

His captors began to shackle him to the floor, using the heavy iron handcuffs and footcuffs fastened into the stone. Then they all left the dungeon and proceeded to seal the captain up alive inside the windowless casemate, using bricks and mortar. . . .

Captain Green shrieked in terror and begged for mercy, but his cries fell on deaf ears. The last brick was finally inserted, mortar applied, and the room sealed up, the officers believed, forever. . . .

[In 1905, workmen repairing the fort found a skeleton inside, shackled to the floor with a few fragments of an old army uniform clinging to the bones.]

---

1. **subterranean casemate** (sŭb´tə-rā´nē-ən kās´māt´): a fortified underground or partly underground room.

Comprehension

1. **Recall** Why does Montresor, the narrator, want **revenge?**

2. **Recall** How does Montresor trick Fortunato into joining him?

3. **Summarize** What does Montresor do to ensure the success of his plan?

4. **Summarize** What happens to Fortunato?

Literary Analysis

5. **Make Inferences About Character** What kind of man is Montresor? Think of four or five character traits that you can infer from Montresor's words and actions. Record your answers in a chart like the one shown.

Montresor's Character Traits	Words/Actions
1. shrewdness	He knows how to take advantage of Fortunato's pride.
2.	

6. **Analyze Mood** What is the overall mood, or atmosphere, of this story? In your opinion, what contributes most to the mood—the setting, the sound and rhythm of the language, or the descriptions of Montresor's thoughts, feelings, and actions? Provide details from the story to support your opinion.

7. **Make Judgments** Review your **paraphrase** of lines 1–8. Does Montresor achieve the kind of revenge he wants? Cite details to support your answer.

8. **Evaluate Narrator** Consider whether Montresor is a **reliable** or an **unreliable narrator.** Is the reader to believe, as Montresor does, that his revenge is justified? Give evidence from the story.

9. **Evaluate Dramatic Irony** A situation in which the reader knows something that a character does not is an example of dramatic irony. The first paragraph of the story prepares the way for dramatic ironies by giving the reader information that Fortunato does not have. Identify three examples of dramatic irony. What is the effect of the irony on your experience as a reader?

10. **Compare and Contrast** Poe often drew inspiration for his tales of horror from the real world. Compare the details of "The Story Behind 'The Cask of Amontillado'" on page 352 with the story of Montresor and Fortunato. How similar are these accounts?

Literary Criticism

11. **Critical Interpretations** In defining the short story as a literary form, Poe emphasized that every word should contribute to a "unity of effect or impression." He believed that a writer should first choose a "unique or single effect" to convey, then invent events "as may best aid him in establishing this preconceived effect." How well does Poe achieve a "unity of effect" in this story? Give examples from the text to support your answer.

Vocabulary in Context

VOCABULARY PRACTICE

Choose the situation that most closely relates to each vocabulary word.

1. **aperture:** (a) a crack in a building's foundation, (b) a large stack of lumber
2. **subside:** (a) two cars racing through traffic, (b) a heavy wind lessening in force
3. **impunity:** (a) getting away with a personal foul in football, (b) a tiny hole in a shirt
4. **termination:** (a) someone starting a new job, (b) someone being fired
5. **repose:** (a) lying on a deserted beach, (b) carrying a heavy load of books
6. **abscond:** (a) making a public announcement, (b) sneaking out of a meeting
7. **immolation:** (a) fatalities in a train accident, (b) cartons of spoiled produce
8. **preclude:** (a) getting vaccinated against polio, (b) planting bulbs in fall

WORD LIST

abscond

aperture

immolation

impunity

preclude

repose

subside

termination

VOCABULARY IN WRITING

How do you think Montresor feels after sealing up the wall? Using three or more vocabulary words, write a paragraph describing his feelings. You might begin as shown below.

> **EXAMPLE SENTENCE**
>
> *Montresor felt strange as he closed the final **aperture**.*

VOCABULARY STRATEGY: THE *clud* WORD FAMILY

The root of the word *preclude* can be traced back to a Latin word meaning "to close." This root—the spellings of which include *clud, clos, clus,* and *claus*—has given rise to a large word family. *Preclude*, in which the root is combined with the prefix *pre-*, literally means "to close before." If you can recognize the root in the family of words, you can understand how they are related in meaning.

PRACTICE Use each word in a sentence that shows the connection between its meaning and that of *preclude*. Then, using a dictionary, identify three additional words in the *clud* family.

1. include
2. recluse
3. foreclosure
4. exclusive
5. closet
6. clause
7. seclusion
8. conclude

PENNSYLVANIA STANDARDS

READING STANDARD
A.1.2.1 Identify word meaning using affixes

VOCABULARY PRACTICE
For more practice, go to the **Vocabulary Center** at **ClassZone.com.**

Reading-Writing Connection

Expand your understanding of "The Cask of Amontillado" by responding to these prompts. Then use **Revision: Grammar and Style** to improve your writing.

WRITING PROMPTS

A. Short Response: Interpret Ending

Montresor ends his story with a Latin sentence meaning "May he rest in peace." Does he mean these words in the usual sense? If not, what does he mean? Write a **one- or two-paragraph response** that explains your interpretation of his meaning.

B. Extended Response: Create a Monologue

What do you think goes through Fortunato's mind after he realizes what has happened to him? Why doesn't he try to reason with Montresor? Use what you know about Fortunato to write a **three-to-five-paragraph monologue,** retelling the last part of the story from his point of view.

SELF-CHECK

A successful response will . . .

- clearly state an opinion about the meaning of Montresor's words
- include details from the story to support that opinion

An effective monologue will . . .

- maintain a consistent point of view
- be consistent with Fortunato's character as revealed in the story
- clearly show Fortunato's feelings

REVISION: GRAMMAR AND STYLE

USE APPROPRIATE LANGUAGE Review the **Grammar and Style** note on page 348. Poe uses **formal language** to tell his suspenseful tale. This style of language contains challenging vocabulary, includes complex sentence structures and standard punctuation, and avoids contractions. Use formal language when you want your writing to have a serious quality. Here is an example from the story:

I continued, as was my wont, to smile in his face, and he did not perceive that my smile now *was at the thought of his immolation.* (lines 10–12)

Notice how the revisions in red make use of formal language that better reflects Poe's style. Use similar methods to revise your response to prompt B.

PENNSYLVANIA STANDARDS

WRITING STANDARD
1.5.11.B.2 Employ the most effective format for purpose and audience

STUDENT MODEL

I soon realized, to my horror,
~~It hadn't occurred to me~~ that Montresor ~~would~~ actually wall up the entrance
was   ~ing
Surely this was merely a jest. After all, how could
to the niche. ~~Where'd he think he was going? I couldn't believe~~ he ~~would~~
wretched, cavernous enclosure?
leave me in this ~~damp place!~~

WRITING TOOLS
For prewriting, revision, and editing tools, visit the **Writing Center** at ClassZone.com.

from **The Cask of Amontillado**

Film Clip on ⊙ *MediaSmart* DVD

What makes a setting
SINISTER?

PENNSYLVANIA STANDARDS

SPEAKING/LISTENING STANDARD
1.6.11.F.2 Evaluate the role of media

KEY IDEA In his writings, Edgar Allan Poe drafted a blueprint for spine-tingling effects that countless creative artists have followed. View a film adaptation of "The Cask of Amontillado" to explore how a team of filmmakers, guided by Poe's descriptions, evoked a time and place and a consistently **sinister** mood.

Background

Tale from the Crypt One could argue that had Poe been born in the 20th century, he might have enjoyed page-to-film success similar to that of the modern writer Stephen King. Beginning in the silent-film era of the 1920s, filmmakers saw potential in Poe's shadowy characters and in his haunting settings. Over time, Hollywood adapted a few of his horror classics into movies.

This version of "Cask" is part of a program called "Edgar Allan Poe: Terror of the Soul" that was first broadcast in 1995. The set design was based on actual 18th-century Italian catacombs. According to the production designer, David Wasco, "The descent into the catacombs was supposed to get spookier and spookier."

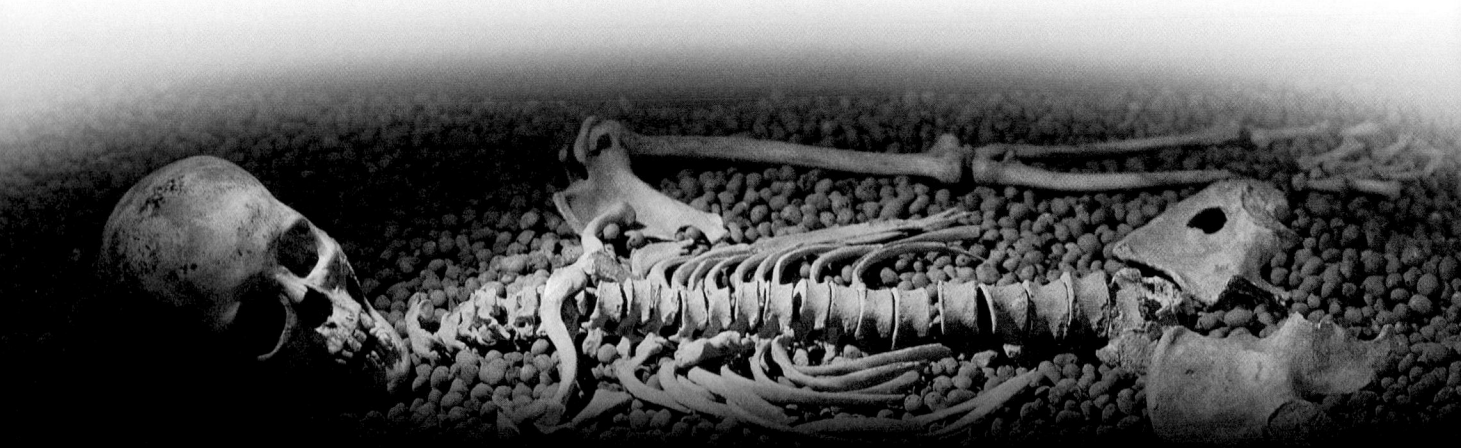

Media Literacy: Setting and Mood in Movies

To recreate settings of the past onscreen, filmmakers focus on representing the time and place of the story and the class, culture, and customs of the characters. After researching these areas, filmmakers select visual and sound elements that will accurately represent the period. These elements include **set design, costuming, props, music,** and **acting.**

When adapting a written work into a film, the director collaborates with other members of the filmmaking team. The art director, the production (or set) designer, the costume designer, the cinematographer, and the music composer all contribute ideas on how to make a setting vivid and how to convey the appropriate mood.

FROM PAGE TO FILM	STRATEGIES FOR VIEWING	
Creating Setting **Writers** reveal details of settings through description and dialogue. **Filmmakers** design specific sets and enhance them.	• Focus on the details of the **set design.** Are the **props**—the objects in the scene—appropriate to the time and place? • Look for distinctive details in the **costumes.** For example, an 18th-century character of high status would probably wear rich fabrics of velvet and silk.	
Creating Mood **Writers** often rely on word choice to describe vivid **details**—factual or sensory—that create atmosphere. **Filmmakers** create atmosphere primarily through visual and sound techniques.	• Be aware of the overall effect— lighthearted, gloomy, or mysterious— that **lighting** creates in scenes. • Notice how the **music** varies in tone. • Listen for **sound effects.** Creaking floorboards or hollow echoes can enhance an atmosphere established by the visual elements.	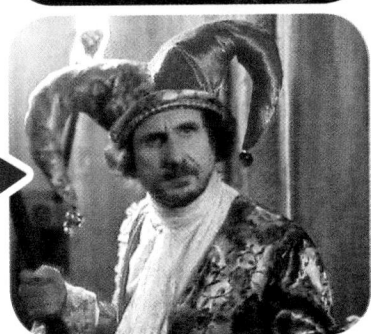
Creating Dramatic Irony **Writers** reveal to readers details that some characters don't know through **narration** and **dialogue.** **Filmmakers** use visual and sound techniques to reveal details.	• Look for clues in the **compositions.** A character might be placed deliberately in the foreground to suggest weakness or vulnerability. • Pay attention to **close-ups** that show characters' facial expressions revealing what other characters don't know. • Notice the tone of voice an actor might use in a line of **dialogue** to convey more than one meaning.	

Viewing Guide for
The Cask of Amontillado

This film excerpt from "The Cask of Amontillado" begins with the search for the Amontillado. You already know how this tale of revenge ends. So, as you watch the adaptation, focus on how film techniques create a sinister atmosphere and evoke a particular mood.

Watch the excerpt several times. To help you focus on elements of setting and mood, refer to the questions that follow.

NOW VIEW

FIRST VIEWING: Comprehension

1. **Recall** What did you see in the set design of the movie that made it clear that the characters are in the catacombs?

2. **Clarify** What type of shot do you see at the moment that Fortunato realizes he's caught in a trap?

CLOSE VIEWING: Media Literacy

3. **Analyze Setting and Mood** How does the director convey the sinister and claustrophobic setting of the catacombs? Think about the following:

   - the atmosphere of the **set design**
   - the use of **composition** and **lighting**
   - the **music** as the characters descend lower and lower

4. **Analyze Costumes** How does each character's **costume** reflect the role he plays in this cat-and-mouse tale?

5. **Analyze Dramatic Irony** To Fortunato, Montresor disguises his intentions. To viewers, he reveals them. How is the truth revealed? As you cite specific shots to support your response, think about

   - the use of **composition** and **close-ups**
   - the actors' facial expressions and behavior

Write or Discuss

Compare Film and Written Versions Edgar Allan Poe was a master at using words to create eerie and frightening story settings. In your opinion, does the film adaptation of "The Cask of Amontillado" effectively portray the story's sinister setting? To compare the film and written versions, note the following:

- Poe's description of the catacombs versus the visual presentation
- the sequence of events in the catacombs
- the film techniques used to enhance the scenes, including sound, lighting, and camera shots

Produce Your Own Media

MEDIA TOOLS

For help with creating a production design board, visit the **Media Center** at ClassZone.com.

Create a Production Design Board Imagine that you're part of a production team assigned to design sets for an adaptation of "The Cask of Amontillado." You'll use a production design board to present ideas for creating a sinister setting. A production design board visually represents different elements of a set, such as scenery, costumes, and props. The board displays small parts or drawings of these elements.

HERE'S HOW Work with a partner to review the short story and decide what scene (or scenes) to depict and how to present it. Consider these suggestions:

- Keep the presentation simple. Use labels to identify key elements.
- Using foam board as the background, apply photos or sketches of design elements and fabric samples (or magazine clippings of patterns).
- Attach quotations from the tale that inspired your selections.

STUDENT MODEL

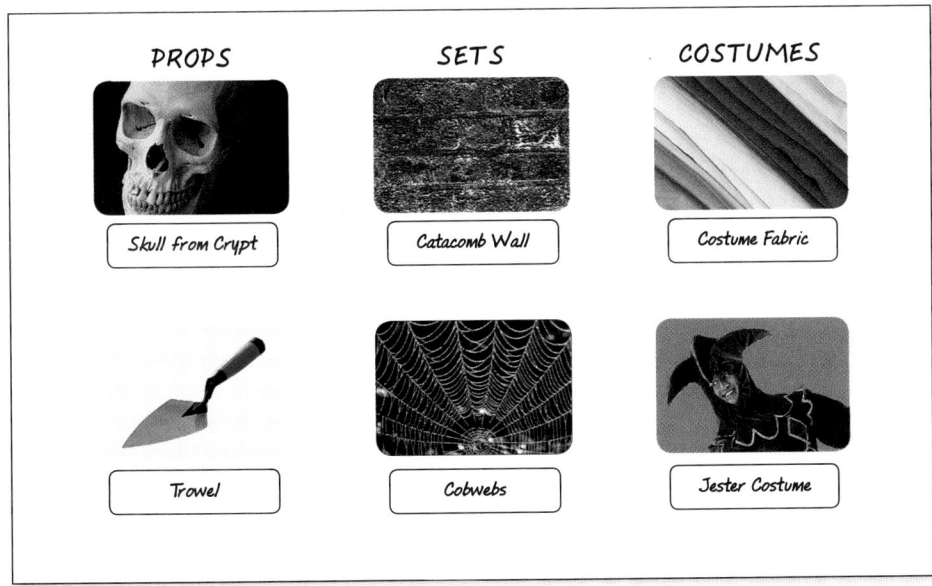

PROPS — Skull from Crypt

SETS — Catacomb Wall

COSTUMES — Costume Fabric

Trowel

Cobwebs

Jester Costume

Tech Tip

Use a clip-art program as a source of images of props and other elements of a set's design.

from **A Walk in the Woods**
Travel Narrative by Bill Bryson

Where do you find
ADVENTURE?

PENNSYLVANIA STANDARDS

READING STANDARDS
A.2.6.2 Analyze examples that support the purpose
B.1.1.1.B.2 Evaluate the relationship between setting and other components

KEY IDEA Do you find **adventure** in physically risky activities, such as rock climbing and skateboarding, or in everyday pursuits? In this selection, you'll read about the adventures of Bill Bryson, a well-known travel writer whose hike along the Appalachian Trail took some unexpected turns.

QUICKWRITE With a small group, generate a list of adventures you've had or would like to have. Then select one adventure and write a short paragraph explaining how you would prepare for it.

LITERARY ANALYSIS: SETTING AND MOOD

Setting can play an important role in creating a **mood.** In this selection, Bill Bryson describes the Appalachian Trail by using sensory details and precise verbs. These, in turn, convey a mood to the reader and help bring Bryson's experience to life. As you read, think about how the mood influences your impressions of the Appalachian Trail and those who travel it.

READING SKILL: IDENTIFY AUTHOR'S PERSPECTIVE

People often look at a subject from different perspectives. For example, a person living in Florida may react negatively to a 30-degree day, while a person raised in northern Minnesota might view such weather as a blessing. The combination of beliefs, values, and feelings that influence how a writer looks at a subject is called the **author's perspective.** In order to figure out an author's perspective, it's important to pay attention to

- statements of opinion
- details the writer chooses to include
- the writer's tone, or attitude (such as a humorous or serious tone)

As you read Bill Bryson's account of hiking the Appalachian Trail, try to figure out his perspective by completing a chart like the one shown.

Statement, Detail, or Tone	What It Reveals About Bryson
"Life takes on a neat simplicity...." (line 6)	He values a lack of complication.

Review: **Cause and Effect, Make Inferences**

▲ VOCABULARY IN CONTEXT

Put each vocabulary word in the appropriate column, and then write a brief definition of each word you're familiar with.

WORD LIST		
abysmal	reconnoiter	unnerving
buffeted	singularity	veneer
daunted	superannuated	

Know Well	Think I Know	Don't Know At All

Author Online

Bill Bryson born 1951

Native Son
Bill Bryson (brī′sən) is a popular travel writer whose hiking stories combine humor and human interest with a sense of adventure. Bryson spent more than 20 years of his adult life in England, touring the countryside and writing best-selling books. In 1995 Bryson returned to the United States and settled in New Hampshire near a branch of the famous Appalachian Trail. Soon after, he became inspired to hike the length of the trail, hoping to improve his fitness and become better acquainted with his homeland. *A Walk in the Woods* records Bryson's adventures with his friend Stephen Katz as they traveled the trail.

A Challenging Trip When he and Katz began their trip, Bryson was used to casual walks through the English countryside. He knew little about the rugged conditions to be found in the U.S. wilderness. As a result, Bryson and Katz were ill prepared for the many challenges they faced, including carrying 40-pound packs, making their own meals, and sleeping outdoors. Much of the humor and suspense in *A Walk in the Woods* stems from their lack of preparation.

 MORE ABOUT THE AUTHOR
For more on Bill Bryson, visit the **Literature Center** at ClassZone.com.

Background

A Path for the People The Appalachian Trail is a footpath that spans more than 2,100 miles from Mount Katahdin in Maine to Springer Mountain in Georgia. It passes through 14 states. The idea for the trail began in 1921 with a proposal by conservationist Benton MacKaye. On August 14, 1937, the trail was completed.

A Walk in the Woods

BILL BRYSON

Distance changes utterly when you take the world on foot. A mile becomes a long way, two miles literally considerable, ten miles whopping, fifty miles at the very limits of conception. The world, you realize, is enormous in a way that only you and a small community of fellow hikers know. Planetary scale is your little secret.

Life takes on a neat simplicity, too. Time ceases to have any meaning. When it is dark, you go to bed, and when it is light again you get up, and everything in between is just in between. It's quite wonderful, really.

You have no engagements, commitments, obligations, or duties; no special
10 ambitions and only the smallest, least complicated of wants; you exist in a tranquil tedium,[1] serenely beyond the reach of exasperation, "far removed from the seats of strife," as the early explorer and botanist William Bartram[2] put it. All that is required of you is a willingness to trudge.

There is no point in hurrying because you are not actually going anywhere. However far or long you plod, you are always in the same place: in the woods. It's where you were yesterday, where you will be tomorrow. The woods is one boundless **singularity**. Every bend in the path presents a prospect indistinguishable from every other, every glimpse into the trees the same tangled mass. For all you know, your route could describe a very large,
20 pointless circle. In a way, it would hardly matter. **A**

At times, you become almost certain that you slabbed this hillside three days ago, crossed this stream yesterday, clambered over this fallen tree at least twice today already. But most of the time you don't think. No point. Instead, you exist in a kind of mobile Zen mode,[3] your brain like a balloon tethered with string, accompanying but not actually part of the body below. Walking for hours and miles becomes as automatic, as unremarkable, as breathing. At the end of the day you don't think, "Hey, I did sixteen miles today," any more than you think, "Hey, I took eight-thousand breaths today." It's just what you do. **B**

---

1. **tranquil tedium:** calm and peaceful boredom.

2. **William Bartram** (bär′trəm): one of the first explorers of the Appalachian Mountains, who wrote about his experiences in a book published in 1791.

3. **mobile Zen mode:** walking, perfectly in tune with one's environment to the point of feeling at one with the surroundings.

ANALYZE VISUALS
How does the angle of this photograph affect the **mood** conveyed?

singularity
(sĭng′gyə-lăr′ĭ-tē) *n.* something peculiar or unique

A SETTING AND MOOD
Reread lines 14–20. What mood is created by Bryson's description of the woods?

B AUTHOR'S PERSPECTIVE
What was Bryson's attitude about hiking at this point? Cite details that helped you draw your **conclusion.**

And so we walked, hour upon hour, over rollercoaster hills, along knife-edge
30 ridges and over grassy balds, through depthless ranks of oak, ash, chinkapin,
and pine. The skies grew sullen and the air chillier, but it wasn't until the third
day that the snow came. It began in the morning as thinly scattered flecks,
hardly noticeable. But then the wind rose, then rose again, until it was blowing
with an end-of-the-world fury that seemed to have even the trees in a panic,
and with it came snow, great flying masses of it. By midday we found ourselves
plodding into a stinging, cold, hard-blowing storm. Soon after, we came to a
narrow ledge of path along a wall of rock. **C**

Even in ideal circumstances this path would have required delicacy and care.
It was like a window ledge on a skyscraper, no more than fourteen or sixteen
40 inches wide, and crumbling in places, with a sharp drop on one side of perhaps
eighty feet, and long, looming stretches of vertical granite on the other. Once
or twice I nudged foot-sized rocks over the side and watched with faint horror
as they crashed and tumbled to improbably remote resting places. The trail
was cobbled with rocks and threaded with wandering tree roots against which
we constantly stubbed and stumbled, and **veneered** everywhere with polished
ice under a thin layer of powdery snow. At exasperatingly frequent intervals,
the path was broken by steep, thickly bouldered streams, frozen solid and
ribbed with blue ice, which could only be negotiated in a crablike crouch. And
all the time, as we crept along on this absurdly narrow, dangerous perch, we
50 were half-blinded by flying snow and jostled by gusts of wind, which roared
through the dancing trees and shook us by our packs. This wasn't a blizzard; it
was a tempest. We proceeded with painstaking deliberativeness, placing each
foot solidly before lifting the one behind. Even so, twice Katz made horrified,
heartfelt, comic-book noises ("AIEEEEE!" and "EEEARGH!") as his footing
went, and I turned to find him hugging a tree, feet skating, his expression bug-
eyed and fearful. **D**

It was deeply **unnerving.** It took us over two hours to cover six-tenths of
a mile of trail. By the time we reached solid ground at a place called Bearpen
Gap, the snow was four or five inches deep and accumulating fast. The whole
60 world was white, filled with dime-sized snowflakes that fell at a slant before

C CAUSE AND EFFECT
Reread lines 29–37
and note the changes in
setting. How did these
changes affect Bryson
and his friend Katz?

veneer (və-nîr') v. to
cover with a thin layer
of material

D SETTING AND MOOD
Reread lines 38–56. How
does Bryson's description
of the setting and of Katz
influence the mood in this
paragraph? Cite details to
support your answer.

unnerving (ŭn-nûr'vĭng)
adj. causing loss of
courage **unnerve** v.

being caught by the wind and hurled in a variety of directions. We couldn't see more than fifteen or twenty feet ahead, often not even that.

The trail crossed a logging road, then led straight up Albert Mountain,[4] a bouldered summit 5,250 feet above sea level, where the winds were so wild and angry that they hit the mountain with an actual wallop sound and forced us to shout to hear each other. We started up and hastily retreated. Hiking packs leave you with no recognizable center of gravity at the best of times; here we were literally being blown over. Confounded, we stood at the bottom of the summit and looked at each other. This was really quite grave. We were caught

70 between a mountain we couldn't climb and a ledge we had no intention of trying to renegotiate. Our only apparent option was to pitch our tents—if we could in this wind—crawl in, and hope for the best. I don't wish to reach for melodrama, but people have died in less trying circumstances.

I dumped my pack and searched through it for my trail map. Appalachian Trail maps are so monumentally useless that I had long since given up using them. They vary somewhat, but most are on an **abysmal** scale of 1:100,000, which ludicrously compresses every kilometer of real world into a mere centimeter of map. Imagine a square kilometer of physical landscape and all that it might contain—logging roads, streams, a mountaintop or two, perhaps

80 a fire tower, a knob or grassy bald, the wandering AT,[5] and maybe a pair of important side trails—and imagine trying to convey all that information on an area the size of the nail on your little finger. That's an AT map.

Actually, it's far, far worse than that because AT maps—for reasons that bewilder me beyond speculation—provide less detail than even their meager scale allows. For any ten miles of trail, the maps will name and identify perhaps only three of the dozen or more peaks you cross. Valleys, lakes, gaps, creeks, and other important, possibly vital, topographical features are routinely left unnamed. Forest Service roads are often not included, and, if included, they're inconsistently identified. Even side trails are frequently left

abysmal (ə-bĭz'məl)
adj. very bad

---

4. **Albert Mountain:** a peak in western North Carolina.

5. **AT:** Appalachian Trail.

90 off. There are no coordinates, no way of directing rescuers to a particular place, no pointers to towns just off the map's edge. These are, in short, seriously inadequate maps. **E**

In normal circumstances, this is merely irksome. Now, in a blizzard, it seemed closer to negligence. I dragged the map from the pack and fought the wind to look at it. It showed the trail as a red line. Nearby was a heavy, wandering black line, which I presumed to be the Forest Service road we stood beside, though there was no actual telling. According to the map, the road (if a road is what it was) started in the middle of nowhere and finished half a dozen miles later equally in the middle of nowhere, which clearly made no sense—
100 indeed, wasn't even possible. (You can't start a road in the middle of forest; earth-moving equipment can't spontaneously appear among the trees. Anyway, even if you could build a road that didn't go anywhere, why would you?) There was, obviously, something deeply and infuriatingly wrong with this map.

"Cost me eleven bucks," I said to Katz a little wildly, shaking the map at him and then crumpling it into an approximately flat shape and jabbing it into my pocket.

"So what're we going to do?" he said.

I sighed, unsure, then yanked the map out and examined it again. I looked from it to the logging road and back. "Well, it looks as if this logging road
110 curves around the mountain and comes back near the trail on the other side. If it does and we can find it, then there's a shelter we can get to. If we can't get through, I don't know, I guess we take the road back downhill to lower ground and see if we can find a place out of the wind to camp." I shrugged a little helplessly. "I don't know. What do you think?"

He issued a single bitter guffaw and returned to the hysterical snow. I hoisted my pack and followed.

We plodded up the road, bent steeply, **buffeted** by winds. Where it settled, the snow was wet and heavy and getting deep enough that soon it would be impassable and we would have to take shelter whether we wanted to or not.
120 There was no place to pitch a tent here, I noted uneasily—only steep, wooded slope going up on one side and down on the other. For quite a distance—far longer than it seemed it ought to—the road stayed straight. Even if, farther on, it did curve back near the trail, there was no certainty (or even perhaps much likelihood) that we would spot it. In these trees and this snow you could be ten feet from the trail and not see it. It would be madness to leave the logging road and try to find it. Then again, it was probably madness to be following a logging road to higher ground in a blizzard.

Gradually, and then more decidedly, the trail began to hook around behind the mountain. After about an hour of dragging sluggishly through ever-
130 deepening snow, we came to a high, windy, level spot where the trail—or at least *a* trail—emerged down the back of Albert Mountain and continued on into level woods. I regarded my map with bewildered exasperation. It didn't give any indication of this whatever, but Katz spotted a white blaze twenty yards into the woods, and we whooped with joy. We had refound the AT.

E AUTHOR'S PERSPECTIVE
What is Bryson's opinion of AT maps?

buffeted (bŭf'ĭ-tĭd)
adj. knocked about or struck **buffet** v.

A shelter was only a few hundred yards farther on. It looked as if we would live to hike another day.

The snow was nearly knee deep now, and we were tired, but we all but pranced through it, and Katz whooped again when we reached an arrowed sign on a low limb that pointed down a side trail and said "BIG SPRING SHELTER."
140 The shelter, a simple wooden affair, open on one side, stood in a snowy glade—a little winter wonderland—150 yards or so off the main trail. Even from a distance we could see that the open side faced into the wind and that the drifting snow was nearly up to the lip of the sleeping platform. Still, if nothing else, it offered at least a sense of refuge.

We crossed the clearing, heaved our packs onto the platform, and in the same instant discovered that there were two people there already—a man and a boy of about fourteen. They were Jim and Heath, father and son, from Chattanooga,[6] and they were cheerful, friendly, and not remotely **daunted** by the weather. They had come hiking for the weekend, they told us (I hadn't
150 even realized it was a weekend), and knew the weather was likely to be bad, though not perhaps quite this bad, and so were well prepared. Jim had brought a big clear plastic sheet, of the sort decorators use to cover floors, and was trying to rig it across the open front of the shelter. Katz, uncharacteristically, leapt to his assistance. The plastic sheet didn't quite reach, but we found that with one of our groundcloths lashed alongside it we could cover the entire front. The wind walloped ferociously against the plastic and from time to time tore part of it loose, where it fluttered and snapped, with a retort like gunshot, until one of us leaped up and fought it back into place. The whole shelter was, in any case, incredibly leaky of air—the plank walls and floors were full
160 of cracks through which icy wind and occasional blasts of snow shot—but we were infinitely snugger than we would have been outside.

So we made a little home of it for ourselves, spread out our sleeping pads and bags, put on all the extra clothes we could find, and fixed dinner from a reclining position. Darkness fell quickly and heavily, which made the wildness outside seem even more severe. Jim and Heath had some chocolate cake, which they shared with us (a treat beyond heaven), and then the four of us settled down to a long, cold night on hard wood, listening to a banshee[7] wind and the tossing of angry branches.

When I awoke, all was stillness—the sort of stillness that makes you sit up
170 and take your bearings. The plastic sheet before me was peeled back a foot or so and weak light filled the space beyond. Snow was over the top of the platform and lying an inch deep over the foot of my sleeping bag. I shooed it off with a toss of my legs. Jim and Heath were already stirring to life. Katz slumbered heavily on, an arm flung over his forehead, his mouth a great open hole. It was not quite six.

daunted (dôn'tĭd) *adj.*
discouraged **daunt** *v.*

---

6. **Chattanooga** (chăt'ə-nōo'gə): a city in southeastern Tennessee.

7. **banshee** (băn'shē): in Gaelic folklore, a female spirit who wails as a sign that death is coming.

I decided to go out to **reconnoiter** and see how stranded we might be. I hesitated at the platform's edge, then jumped out into the drift—it came up over my waist and made my eyes fly open where it slipped under my clothes and found bare skin—and pushed through it into the clearing,
180 where it was slightly (but only slightly) shallower. Even in sheltered areas, under an umbrella of conifers, the snow was nearly knee deep and tedious to churn through. But everywhere it was stunning. Every tree wore a thick cloak of white, every stump and boulder a jaunty snowy cap, and there was that perfect, immense stillness that you get nowhere else but in a big woods after a heavy snowfall. Here and there clumps of snow fell from the branches, but otherwise there was no sound or movement. I followed the side trail up and under heavily bowed limbs to where it rejoined the AT. The AT was a plumped blanket of snow, round and bluish, in a long, dim tunnel of overbent rhododendrons. It looked deep and hard going. I walked a few yards as a test.
190 It was deep and hard going. **F**

When I returned to the shelter, Katz was up, moving slowly and going through his morning groans, and Jim was studying his maps, which were vastly better than mine. I crouched beside him and he made room to let me look with him. It was 6.1 miles to Wallace Gap and a paved road, old U.S. 64. A mile down the road from there was Rainbow Springs Campground, a private campsite with showers and a store. I didn't know how hard it would be to walk seven miles through deep snow and had no confidence that the campground would be open this early in the year. Still, it was obvious this snow wasn't going to melt for days and we would have to make a move sometime; it might as well
200 be now, when at least it was pretty and calm. Who knew when another storm might blow in and really strand us?

Jim had decided that he and Heath would accompany us for the first couple of hours, then turn off on a side trail called Long Branch, which descended steeply through a ravine for 2.3 miles and emerged near a parking lot where they had left their car. He had hiked the Long Branch trail many times and knew what to expect. Even so, I didn't like the sound of it and asked him hesitantly if he thought it was a good idea to go off on a little-used side trail, into goodness knows what conditions, where no one would come across him and his son if they got in trouble. Katz, to my relief, agreed with me. "At least
210 there's always other people on the AT," he said. "You don't know what might happen to you on a side trail." Jim considered the matter and said they would turn back if it looked bad.

Katz and I treated ourselves to two cups of coffee, for warmth, and Jim and Heath shared with us some of their oatmeal, which made Katz intensely happy. Then we all set off together. It was cold and hard going. The tunnels of boughed rhododendrons, which often ran on for great distances, were exceedingly pretty, but when our packs brushed against them they dumped volumes of snow onto our heads and down the backs of our necks. The three adults took it in turns to walk in front because the lead person always received
220 the heaviest dumping, as well as having all the hard work of dibbing holes in the snow.

reconnoiter (rē′kə-noi′tər) v. to make a preliminary inspection

F SETTING AND MOOD
Reread lines 176–190. Describe the mood in this paragraph. What details of the setting contribute to the mood?

The Long Branch trail, when we reached it, descended steeply through bowed pines—too steeply, it seemed to me, to come back up if the trail proved impassable, and it looked as if it might. Katz and I urged Jim and Heath to reconsider, but Jim said it was all downhill and well-marked, and he was sure it would be all right. "Hey, you know what day it is?" said Jim suddenly and, seeing our blank faces, supplied the answer. "March twenty-first."

Our faces stayed blank.

"First day of spring," he said.

230 We smiled at the pathetic irony of it, shook hands all around, wished each other luck, and parted. **G**

Katz and I walked for three hours more, silently and slowly through the cold, white forest, taking it in turns to break snow. At about one o'clock we came at last to old 64, a lonesome, **superannuated** two-lane road through the mountains. It hadn't been cleared, and there were no tire tracks through it. It was starting to snow again, steadily, prettily. We set off down the road for the campground and had walked about a quarter of a mile when from behind there was the crunching sound of a motorized vehicle proceeding cautiously through snow. We turned to see a big jeep-type car rolling up beside us. The

240 driver's window hummed down. It was Jim and Heath. They had come to let us know they had made it, and to make sure we had likewise. "Thought you might like a lift to the campground," Jim said. ❧

G MAKE INFERENCES
What does Bryson mean by "the pathetic irony" of its being the first day of spring?

superannuated
(sōō′pər-ăn′yōo-ā′tĭd) *adj.*
obsolete with age

Comprehension

1. **Recall** What have Bill Bryson and Stephen Katz set out to do?

2. **Recall** What stands in their way?

3. **Summarize** How do they survive the ordeal?

PENNSYLVANIA STANDARDS

READING STANDARD
A.2.6.2 Analyze examples that support the purpose

Literary Analysis

4. **Analyze Setting and Mood** What elements of setting most strongly contribute to the mood in this selection? Consider the time of day, the season, the weather, and the natural landscape. Cite details from the text to support your answer.

5. **Identify Author's Perspective** Review the chart you completed as you read. In a sentence or two, summarize Bryson's perspective on walking the Appalachian Trail. Explain whether you think his perspective changes in any way as the episode unfolds. Support your ideas with evidence from the text.

6. **Interpret Suspense** How do Bryson's poor preparations for his adventure contribute to the suspense of this selection? Explain.

7. **Evaluate Personality Traits** In what way do Bryson and Katz make unlikely heroes in this **adventure** story? Cite examples from the text.

8. **Make Judgments** In *A Walk in the Woods,* as in many outdoor adventure stories, nature is the **antagonist**—that is, the force that the central figure, or **protagonist,** struggles against. To what degree is nature really responsible for the troubles Bryson and Katz face? Use a graphic like this one in your evaluation.

Problem or Conflict	Caused by Nature	Caused by Hikers
Bryson and Katz are caught in a snowstorm.	✓	

Literary Criticism

9. **Critical Interpretations** Bill Bryson has been described by one critic as a writer "who could wring humor from a clammy sleeping bag." Judging by this selection, do you agree or disagree with that statement? Cite details from the selection to support your opinion.

Vocabulary in Context

VOCABULARY PRACTICE

Decide whether the words in each pair are synonyms or antonyms.

1. buffeted/battered
2. veneer/uncover
3. reconnoiter/inspect
4. superannuated/rejuvenated
5. daunted/inspired
6. unnerving/encouraging
7. abysmal/wonderful
8. singularity/commonality

WORD LIST

abysmal
buffeted
daunted
reconnoiter
singularity
superannuated
unnerving
veneer

VOCABULARY IN WRITING

What do you think was the worst thing about the situation Bryson found himself in? Write a paragraph explaining your opinion, using at least four vocabulary words. You might start like this.

> **EXAMPLE SENTENCE**
>
> What made Bryson's situation **unnerving** was that the snow wouldn't stop.

VOCABULARY STRATEGY: CONTEXT CLUES

Often you can figure out the meaning of an unfamiliar word by examining the words and sentences that surround it. Three types of context clues that can help you determine the meanings of unfamiliar words in *A Walk in the Woods* are

- **general context clues,** which allow you to infer the meaning of an unfamiliar word by reading information in the sentences that surround it
- **comparison clues,** in which the unknown word is likened to something known
- **example clues,** in which one or more examples are included in the text to suggest the meaning of the unfamiliar word

PRACTICE Use context clues to figure out the meaning of each word that follows. First identify the type of context clue that helps you determine the meaning of the word. Then write a definition of the word.

slabbed (line 21)
renegotiate (line 71)
topographical (line 87)
retort (line 157)

PENNSYLVANIA STANDARDS

READING STANDARD
A.1.2.2 Use context clues

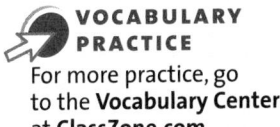

VOCABULARY PRACTICE
For more practice, go to the **Vocabulary Center** at **ClassZone.com.**

Wilderness Letter

Use with *A Walk in the Woods*, page 362.

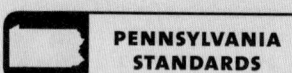

PENNSYLVANIA STANDARDS

WRITING STANDARDS
1.4.11.B.5 Use primary and secondary sources
1.4.11.C.2 Include cited evidence

What's the Connection?

In *A Walk in the Woods*, you read about some of the pleasures and perils of hiking the Appalachian Trail in a government-protected wilderness area. Now, in a letter from Wallace Stegner, you will read one of many arguments that have been made in favor of preserving such wilderness areas.

Skill Focus: Read Primary Sources

Primary sources are materials written by people who witnessed the events portrayed. These sources can give us unique insights into a subject. Letters, speeches, interviews, public documents, and other texts—whether published, archived, or only saved in someone's attic—are all types of primary sources. To get the most out of a primary source, consider

- the form and purpose of the text
- where and when it was written
- the intended audience
- the author's position in his or her family, society, or profession

To further analyze a primary source, complete a chart such as the one here. Try doing this as you read Wallace Stegner's letter.

What is the form and purpose of this document?	
What, if anything, do I already know about the author and his times?	
What seems to be the relationship between the author and his audience?	
What does the document tell me about life at the time it was written?	

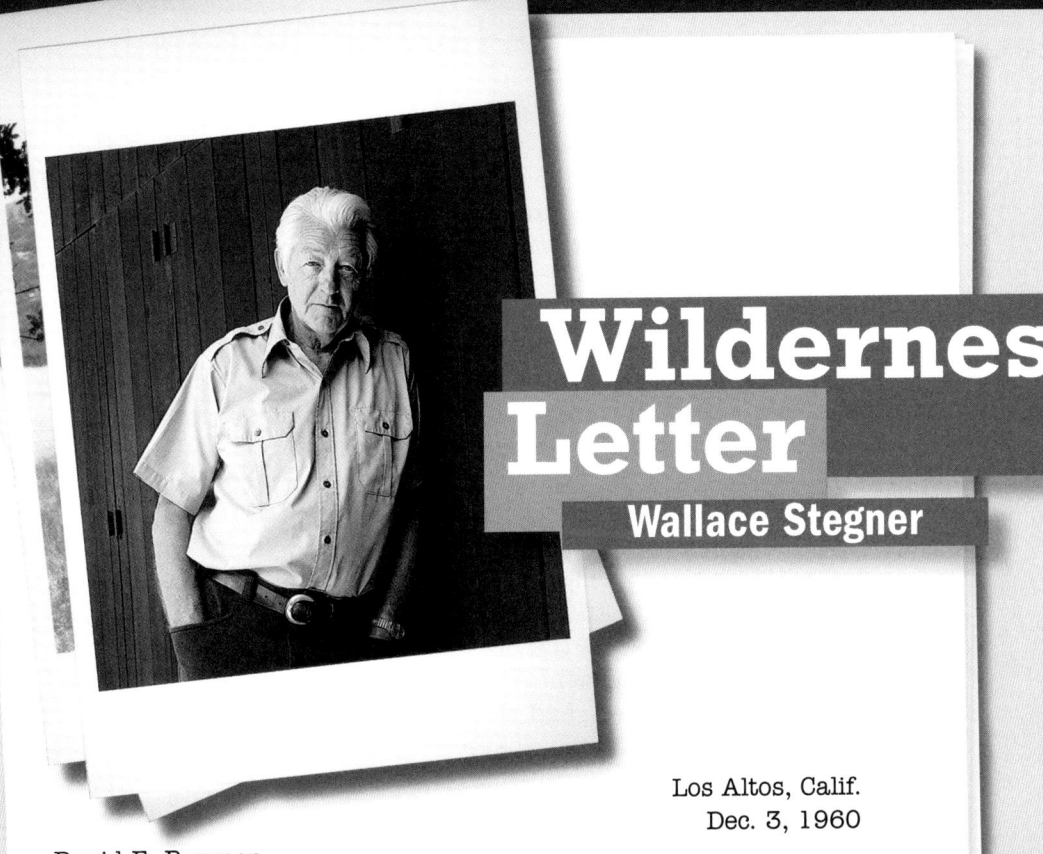

Wilderness Letter

Wallace Stegner

Los Altos, Calif.
Dec. 3, 1960

David E. Pesonen
Wildland Research Center
Agricultural Experiment Station
243 Mulford Hall
University of California
Berkeley 4, Calif.

Dear Mr. Pesonen:

I believe that you are working on the wilderness portion of the Outdoor Recreation Resources Review Commission's report. If I may, I should like to urge some arguments for wilderness preservation that involve recreation, as it is ordinarily conceived, hardly at all. Hunting, fishing, hiking, mountain-climbing, camping, photography, and the enjoyment of natural scenery will all, surely, figure in your report. So will the wilderness as a genetic reserve, a scientific yardstick by which we may measure the world in its natural balance against the world in its man-
10 made imbalance. What I want to speak for is not so much the wilderness uses, valuable as those are, but the wilderness idea, which is a resource in itself. Being an intangible and spiritual resource, it will seem mystical to the practical-minded—but then anything that cannot be moved by a bulldozer is likely to seem mystical to them.

I want to speak for the wilderness idea as something that has helped form our character and that has certainly shaped our history as a people. . . . Ⓐ

Ⓐ **PRIMARY SOURCES**
What does the beginning of this letter suggest about Stegner's purpose for writing?

Something will have gone out of us as a people if we ever let
20 the remaining wilderness be destroyed; if we permit the last
virgin forests to be turned into comic books and plastic cigarette
cases; if we drive the few remaining members of the wild species
into zoos or to extinction; if we pollute the last clear air and
dirty the last clean streams and push our paved roads through
the last of the silence, so that never again will Americans be free
in their own country from the noise, the exhausts, the stinks of
human and automotive waste. And so that never again can we
have the chance to see ourselves single, separate, vertical and
individual in the world, part of the environment of trees and
30 rocks and soil, brother to the other animals, part of the natural
world and competent to belong in it. Without any remaining
wilderness we are committed wholly, without chance for even
momentary reflection and rest, to a headlong drive into our
technological termite-life, the Brave New World[1] of a completely
man-controlled environment. We need wilderness preserved—as
much of it as is still left, and as many kinds—because it was the
challenge against which our character as a people was formed.
The reminder and the reassurance that it is still there is good for
our spiritual health even if we never once in ten years set foot
40 in it. It is good for us when we are young, because of the
incomparable sanity it can bring briefly, as vacation and rest, into
our insane lives. It is important to us when we are old simply
because it is there—important, that is, simply as idea. **B**

We are a wild species. . . . Nobody ever tamed or domesticated
or scientifically bred us. But for at least three millennia we have
been engaged in a cumulative and ambitious race to modify and
gain control of our environment, and in the process we have
come close to domesticating ourselves. Not many people are
likely, any more, to look upon what we call "progress" as an
50 unmixed blessing. Just as surely as it has brought us increased
comfort and more material goods, it has brought us spiritual
losses, and it threatens now to become the Frankenstein that will
destroy us. One means of sanity is to retain a hold on the
natural world, to remain, insofar as we can, good animals.
Americans still have that chance, more than many peoples; for
while we were demonstrating ourselves the most efficient and
ruthless environment-busters in history, and slashing and
burning and cutting our way through a wilderness continent, the
wilderness was working on us. It remains in us as surely as
60 Indian names remain on the land. If the abstract dream of
human liberty and human dignity became, in America, something

B PRIMARY SOURCES
What does Stegner's
description suggest about
life in the United States at
the time he wrote this?

---

1. **Brave New World:** a reference to Aldous Huxley's 1932 science fiction novel,
Brave New World, depicting a society in which happiness and the most basic
natural life functions are controlled by technology.

more than an abstract dream, mark it down at least partially to the fact that we were in subtle ways subdued by what we conquered. . . . **C**

The American experience has been the confrontation by old peoples and cultures of a world as new as if it had just risen from the sea. That gave us our hope and our excitement, and the hope and excitement can be passed on to newer Americans, Americans who never saw any phase of the frontier. But only so long as we keep the remainder of our wild as a reserve and a promise—a sort of wilderness bank. . . .

We need to demonstrate our acceptance of the natural world, including ourselves; we need the spiritual refreshment that being natural can produce. And one of the best places for us to get that is in the wilderness where the fun houses, the bulldozers, and the pavements of our civilization are shut out.

Sherwood Anderson, in a letter to Waldo Frank in the 1920's, said it better than I can. "Is it not likely that when the country was new and men were often alone in the fields and the forest they got a sense of bigness outside themselves that has now in some way been lost . . . Mystery whispered in the grass, played in the branches of trees overhead, was caught up and blown across the American line in clouds of dust at evening on the prairies . . . I am old enough to remember tales that strengthen my belief in a deep semi-religious influence that was formerly at work among our people. The flavor of it hangs over the best work of Mark Twain . . . I can remember old fellows in my home town speaking feelingly of an evening spent on the big empty plains. It had taken the shrillness out of them. They had learned the trick of quiet . . ."

We could learn it too, even yet; even our children and grand-children could learn it. But only if we save, for just such absolutely non-recreational, impractical, and mystical uses as this, all the wild that still remains to us. . . .

For myself, I grew up on the empty plains of Saskatchewan and Montana and in the mountains of Utah, and I put a very high valuation on what those places gave me. And if I had not been able periodically to renew myself in the mountains and deserts of western America I would be very near bughouse. Even when I can't get to the back country, the thought of the colored deserts of southern Utah, or the reassurance that there are still stretches of prairie where the world can be instantaneously perceived as disk and bowl, and where the little but intensely important human being is exposed to the five directions and the thirty-six winds, is a positive consolation. The idea alone can

C **PRIMARY SOURCES**
What does Stegner say is one potential cost of "progress"?

sustain me. But as the wilderness areas are progressively exploited or "improved," as the jeeps and bulldozers of uranium prospectors scar up the deserts and the roads are cut into the alpine timberlands, and as the remnants of the unspoiled and
110 natural world are progressively eroded, every such loss is a little death in me. In us. . . . **D**

Let me say something on the subject of the kinds of wilderness worth preserving. Most of those areas contemplated are in the national forests and in high mountain country. For all the usual recreational purposes, the alpine and forest wildernesses are obviously the most important, both as genetic banks and as beauty spots. But for the spiritual renewal, the recognition of identity, the birth of awe, other kinds will serve every bit as well. Perhaps, because they are less friendly to life, more abstractly
120 nonhuman, they will serve even better. On our Saskatchewan prairie, the nearest neighbor was four miles away, and at night we saw only two lights on all the dark rounding earth. The earth was full of animals—field mice, ground squirrels, weasels, ferrets, badgers, coyotes, burrowing owls, snakes. I knew them as my little brothers, as fellow creatures, and I have never been able to look upon animals in any other way since. The sky in that country came clear down to the ground on every side, and it was full of great weathers, and clouds, and winds, and hawks. I hope I learned something from knowing intimately the creatures of the
130 earth; I hope I learned something from looking a long way, from looking up, from being much alone. A prairie like that, one big enough to carry the eye clear to the sinking, rounding horizon, can be as lonely and grand and simple in its forms as the sea. It is as good a place as any for the wilderness experience to happen; the vanishing prairie is as worth preserving for the wilderness idea as the alpine forests.

So are great reaches of our western deserts, scarred somewhat by prospectors but otherwise open, beautiful, waiting. . . .

These are some of the things wilderness can do for us. That is
140 the reason we need to put into effect, for its preservation, some other principle than the principles of exploitation or "usefulness" or even recreation. We simply need that wild country available to us, even if we never do more than drive to its edge and look in. For it can be a means of reassuring ourselves of our sanity as creatures, a part of the geography of hope. **E**

Very sincerely yours,

Wallace Stegner

D PRIMARY SOURCES
Reread this paragraph. **Paraphrase** what Stegner is saying about the benefits of wilderness to his own life.

E PRIMARY SOURCES
Reread Stegner's closing paragraph. In a sentence, **summarize** his conclusion.

Comprehension

1. **Summarize** In Stegner's view, what is the danger for humans in losing touch with nature?

Critical Analysis

2. **Identify Author's Purpose** What does Stegner want Pesonen to understand?

3. **Analyze Primary Source** Review the chart you developed as you read Stegner's letter. What was being done to wilderness areas at that time? Explain.

4. **Evaluate Author's Message** Stegner makes a point of distinguishing between the recreational value of the wilderness and its value as a source of spiritual renewal. Do you agree that this is an important difference? Include specific references to the text in your answer.

Read for Information: Cite Evidence

PENNSYLVANIA STANDARDS

WRITING STANDARDS
1.4.11.B.5 Use primary and secondary sources
1.4.11.C.2 Include cited evidence

WRITING PROMPT

Bill Bryson and Wallace Stegner, each in his own way, have written in favor of wilderness areas. How are the pieces similar in this regard? How are they different? Support your response with specific quotations, ideas, and facts from Stegner's letter and Bryson's account.

The following steps will help you respond to the prompt:

1. Reread Bryson's narrative and Stegner's letter, looking for direct statements, facts, and anecdotes about wilderness areas.

2. Record direct quotations and summarize longer passages that seem relevant to your comparison. Note the author, source, and page numbers.

3. Review your notes and evaluate each item's usefulness in writing your comparison.

4. As you write your comparison, support your statements with direct quotations and citations of facts or anecdotes from these two sources. Always credit your sources and be sure to use quotation marks around direct quotations.

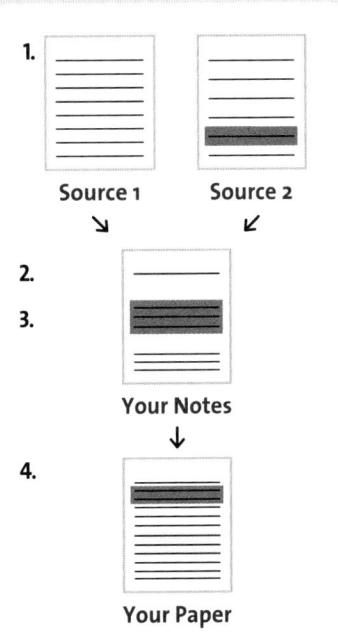

The Sharks
Poem by Denise Levertov

The Peace of Wild Things
Poem by Wendell Berry

What are the different faces of NATURE?

PENNSYLVANIA STANDARDS

READING STANDARDS
B.1.2.1 Evaluate connections
B.2.1.1 Identify and analyze imagery

KEY IDEA What do you think of when you hear the word *nature?* Storms? Flowers? Insects? Nature can have a variety of associations, such as peace, beauty, danger, and destruction. In the poems "The Sharks" and "The Peace of Wild Things," two poets describe sharply different **faces of nature.**

DISCUSS List eight elements of nature, four that you view as unsettling or frightening and four that you view as peaceful or soothing. After you have completed your list, get together with one or two classmates and compare notes.

● LITERARY ANALYSIS: IMAGERY AND MOOD

To create **mood** in poetry, writers rely on **imagery**—words and phrases that appeal to the reader's senses.

Dark fins appear, innocent
as if in fair warning.

In the above example from "The Sharks," note how the visual image of "dark fins" helps establish a mood of sinister foreboding.

As you read each poem in this lesson, use a chart to keep track of words and phrases that evoke a particular mood.

Imagery	Mood Created
"Dark fins appear, innocent as if in fair warning."	foreboding, threatening

● READING STRATEGY: CONNECT

Reading poetry can be a meaningful experience when you **connect** your own experiences and knowledge with the thoughts and feelings expressed in a poem. For example, you might have enjoyed the peaceful surroundings of a park or lake, like the speaker in "The Peace of Wild Things."

By allowing yourself to connect with the experience revealed in a poem, you enhance your understanding of the speaker and the ideas conveyed. As you read, make use of the "connect" strategy whenever appropriate.

Author Online

Denise Levertov 1923–1997

Denise Levertov: Destined for Poetry
Born in England, Denise Levertov (lĕv'ər-tôv') grew up in a home full of books, reading, and lively conversation. She began writing when she was five, and once said that she knew "from an early age—perhaps by 7 . . . that I was an artist-person and had a destiny." She wrote all of her life, publishing more than 30 volumes of poetry and prose. In commenting on her work, she emphasized the need for "precision in poetry." Levertov immigrated to the United States in 1948 and, in addition to her writing, was passionately committed to causes of peace and social justice.

Wendell Berry born 1934

Wendell Berry: A Love for the Land
A novelist, essayist, and poet, Wendell Berry grew up on a farm in Kentucky. After starting a promising career as a writer and college professor in California and then New York City, Berry chose to return to Kentucky. There he has combined farming and writing in a life committed to conserving the land and preserving the values of small farms and communities. Berry's novels, essays, and poems reflect his love of nature, the richness of farm and family life, and his concerns about the world and its problems. He writes in a direct style that evokes the rural world he knows so well.

 MORE ABOUT THE AUTHOR
For more on these poets, visit the **Literature Center** at ClassZone.com.

THE
SHARKS

Denise Levertov

Well then, the last day the sharks appeared.
Dark fins appear, innocent
as if in fair warning. The sea becomes
sinister, are they everywhere? **A**
5 I tell you, they break six feet of water.[1]
Isn't it the same sea, and won't we
play in it any more?
I liked it clear and not
too calm, enough waves
10 to fly in on. For the first time
I dared to swim out of my depth.
It was sundown when they came, the time
when a sheen of copper stills the sea,
not dark enough for moonlight, clear enough
15 to see them easily. Dark
the sharp lift of the fins.

A **IMAGERY AND MOOD**
Reread lines 1–4. What
is the mood at the
beginning of this poem?
Which words and images
help establish this mood?

ANALYZE VISUALS
How does the photograph
reflect the mood of the
poem?

---

1. **they break . . . water:** Sharks often show their dorsal fin if water is
shallow enough.

The Peace of Wild Things

Wendell Berry

When despair for the world grows in me
and I wake in the night at the least sound
in fear of what my life and my children's lives may be,
I go and lie down where the wood drake[1]
5 rests in his beauty on the water, and the great heron feeds.
I come into the peace of wild things
who do not tax their lives with forethought
of grief. I come into the presence of still water.
And I feel above me the day-blind stars
10 waiting with their light. For a time
I rest in the grace of the world, and am free. **B**

---

1. **wood drake:** a type of male duck.

B CONNECT
Think about how you feel when you walk in the woods, alongside a lake, or through a scenic park. In what ways does your experience connect with the speaker's ideas?

Comprehension

1. **Recall** What situation is presented in "The Sharks"?

2. **Summarize** What problem does the speaker in "The Peace of Wild Things" experience, and what does he do about it?

Literary Analysis

3. **Connect** As you read the poems, what connections were you able to make? Which of these had the strongest impact? Explain why.

4. **Identify Speaker** In "The Sharks," whom do you imagine the speaker to be? Consider the evidence in the poem about the speaker's age and situation. Remember that the speaker and the poet are not necessarily the same person.

5. **Analyze Speaker** Reread line 1 of "The Peace of Wild Things." Considering the speaker's "despair for the world," how would you describe the speaker?

6. **Compare and Contrast** Describe the **faces of nature** presented in each poem. What differences do you see in the comfort level each speaker has with his or her natural surroundings? Are there any similarities in their attitudes toward nature? Support your conclusions.

7. **Evaluate Mood** Review the charts you filled in as you read the poems. What overall mood is created by each poem? How effective are the **images** in creating each mood? Explain your opinion.

8. **Compare Literary Works** Reread Wallace Stegner's "Wilderness Letter" on pages 373–376. Which of Stegner's ideas does "The Peace of Wild Things" support?

Literary Criticism

9. **Historical Perspective** Reread "The Peace of Wild Things." Is Berry's perspective strictly a modern one? Might a person living 200 years ago, for example, have felt this same "despair for the world"? Give reasons for your opinions.

Writing Workshop

Short Story

The power of storytelling is evident in the literature you have read in this unit and in the stories you encounter in everyday life. Now you have a chance to invent a story of your own. The story you write can entertain, teach a lesson, or express your observations and feelings. To begin creating your fictional world, consult the **Writer's Road Map.**

WRITER'S ROAD MAP

Short Story

WRITING PROMPT 1

Writing from the Real World You have probably read many stories that were inspired by real-world events, issues, or people. Write your own short story based on a conflict, person, or setting that you find intriguing.

Places to Find Ideas
- news articles on events, scientific discoveries, or weather disasters
- magazine features that profile interesting people
- situations that you have seen or experienced, such as a conflict between siblings

WRITING PROMPT 2

Writing from Literature The best stories are often the ones that spring from life's big questions. From this unit, choose a prereading question that intrigues you. Then write a short story inspired by that question.

Questions to Inspire You
- When is a risk worth taking? ("Through the Tunnel")
- Is revenge ever justified? ("The Cask of Amontillado")
- Where do you find adventure? (*A Walk in the Woods*)

WRITING TOOLS
For prewriting, revision, and editing tools, visit the **Writing Center** at ClassZone.com.

KEY TRAITS

1. IDEAS
- Focuses on a well-developed **plot** and compelling **characters**
- Introduces, develops, and resolves a **central conflict**
- Includes **descriptive details** that reveal the setting and characters
- Uses **dialogue** to show characters' personalities

2. ORGANIZATION
- Sets the stage by **introducing** the characters, setting, or action
- Presents a clear and engaging **sequence of events**
- Resolves the conflict in a convincing **conclusion**

3. VOICE
- Maintains a consistent **point of view**

4. WORD CHOICE
- Uses **sensory language** to help readers imagine the fictional world

5. SENTENCE FLUENCY
- Uses the **active voice**

6. CONVENTIONS
- Employs **correct grammar and usage**

Part 1: Analyze a Student Model

Sarah Yovovich
Evanston Township High School

Like a Flower

"Just lend me ten bucks, John," Jessica begged. "Come on!"

"I'm sure the shirt is very cute and pink and perfect, Sis, but I don't have the ten. Now move—I gotta mow the lawn."

"In this heat?" she asked, fanning herself with manicured nails.

5   "You know, Mom and Dad pay me ten bucks to mow," John said.

"Oh! So you can lend it to me after you finish?"

He snorted. "Yeah, right. I'll let you mow the lawn, though."

"No way! That mower's heavy!" Jessica said, her mouth open.

"You know, a little physical labor wouldn't kill you."

10   "It *might*," she insisted.

"Okay, fine, wear something else." He paused. "What's that I hear? Oh—it's the sound of a thousand cute tops crying!"

"Shut up and show me how the thing works," she snapped. They went to the garage, and John pulled out the mower for her.

15   "So I just pull this cord?" She pulled tentatively, and the mower let out a brief, disgruntled growl. Jessica jumped back and let out an "Eep!"

"It's fine, Jess. Pull as hard as you can," John said. Jessica braced herself and pulled. The mower roared to life. She looked at John with terror.

20   "Good job!" he hollered. "Go to it!"

"Wait!" she squeaked, but he was gone. She took a deep breath and nudged the mower forward a few inches. It made a hideous *crrrunch* as it chewed up some twigs and spat out their remains. She shrieked, thinking of how *not* cute she would look with missing toes. The mower

25 kept roaring, and she realized that she didn't know how to turn it off.

KEY TRAITS IN ACTION

Uses **dialogue** and **descriptive details** (manicured nails) to reveal the characters' personalities.

Maintains a consistent third-person **point of view.**

Lively **sensory language** shows the reader how it felt to mow the lawn. The writer uses the **active voice.**

"John!" she shouted, but there was no way he could hear her. She nudged the evil machine forward and watched grass spew out the side. It was kind of cool. Terrifying, but cool.

She kept pushing, all the way to the other side of the lawn. The
30 mower was heavy, but she was strong enough. Turning around was another issue. She'd seen John tilt the machine and turn it a hundred and eighty degrees, but he was a foot taller and two years older. Still, she was tough, even if she liked pink. She pushed down on the handle, and the mower tilted up surprisingly easily. The sound was much louder,
35 but she didn't flinch. Slowly, she turned, then pushed forward to mow the next strip of grass. By the time she got to the end of the lawn, she had perfected her turning technique so that it was one fluid motion— push-swivel-drop-mow! The grass cringed at her approach, and she left no survivors.

40 No longer afraid of the mower, she moved her sweaty face closer to examine the controls. She found the off switch and cut the engine.

John emerged from inside and surveyed the lawn. "Nice job, Jess."

"Thank you. Excuse me, but I have money to collect, a shower to take, and a top to buy," she said as she walked past him.

45 That night she looked amazing in her new silk top. Her friend Alice said, "You look beautiful! Like a flower or something!"

"Thank you!" Jessica replied, thinking about how much fun it would be to mow right through a field of flowers, petals flying everywhere.

Develops a **plot** and a **central conflict** (Jessica versus the lawn mower) that make the piece a story, not just a description.

Sequence of events is clear. The writer **resolves** the conflict in a believable way.

Lighthearted **conclusion** shows how Jessica's attitude has changed.

2

WRITING STANDARD
1.4.11.A.1 Apply varying organizational methods

Part 2: Apply the Writing Process

PREWRITING

| *What Should I Do?* | *What Does It Look Like?* |

1. Think of a story you want to tell.
Brainstorm ideas for **plots, characters, settings,** or **themes** you want to get across. Use a graphic organizer to keep track of the possibilities. Highlight the idea that seems most promising.

TIP Can't think of anything? Choose a picture, a print advertisement, or another visual and start writing about the person or place shown.

▶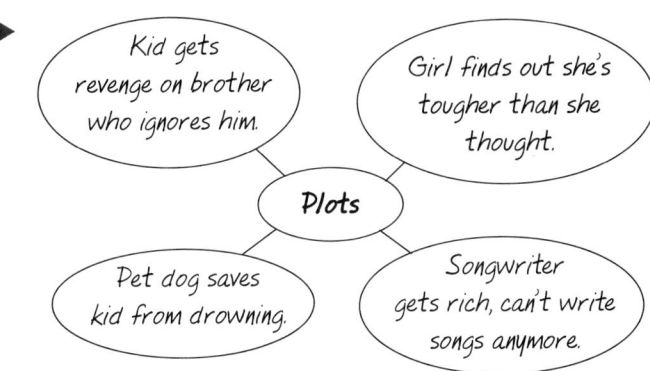

2. Flesh out your characters.
What do they look like? How do they speak and act? How do other characters treat them? What **conflicts** do they face? Create a chart to help you keep track of your characters and to make each of them distinct.

▶

Characters	Details
Jessica	has manicure, likes to look good, favorite color is pink, goes to lots of parties, doesn't like to be seen as weak
John	older, teases his sister but thinks she's OK, is willing to help her

3. Map your story.
Create a story graph, story map, list, or flow chart showing what happens to your characters. Ask yourself "what if" questions about problems or experiences they might have.

TIP Think about the rising action, climax, and falling action of your story, as shown in this story graph.

See page 172 for an example of a story map.

STORY GRAPH

▶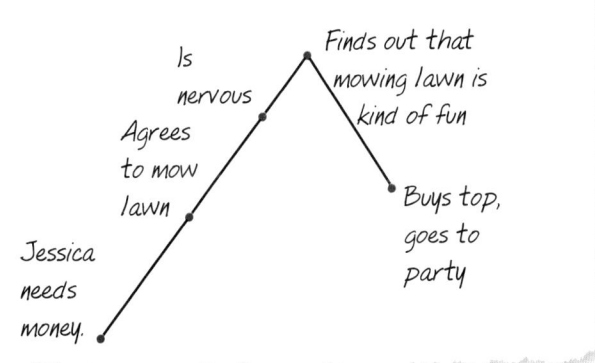

What Should I Do?	What Does It Look Like?
1. Start out strong. Consider beginning with some **dialogue** or a description of the scene or of a character. **TIP** If you can't come up with a great beginning right away, just start writing. You can revise later.	**Dialogue** "Just lend me ten bucks, John," Jessica begged. **Sensory language/descriptive details** The spiky, overgrown grass wilted in the blazing heat.
2. Choose a point of view. Decide who will tell your story. Use a **first-person narrator** if your main goal is to draw readers into the story; use a **third-person narrator** to give a broad view of characters and events.	**First-person point of view** We went to the garage, and John pulled out the mower for me. **Third-person point of view** They went to the garage, and John pulled out the mower for her.
3. Use dialogue to reveal characters' personalities. By carefully choosing characters' words, you can show what kind of people they are, including their ages, thoughts, and feelings.	"You know, a little physical labor wouldn't kill you." "It <u>might</u>," she insisted. "Okay, fine, wear something else." He paused. "What's that I hear? Oh—it's the sound of a thousand cute tops crying!" "Shut up and show me how the thing works," she snapped.
4. Develop a conclusion. Your conclusion might resolve the conflict, tie up loose ends, reveal something surprising, or give your reader something to think about. **TIP** Some writers decide how they want a story to end and work backwards from there.	That night she looked amazing in her new silk top. Her friend Alice said, "You look beautiful! Like a flower or something!" "Thank you!" Jessica replied, thinking about how much fun it would be to mow right through a field of flowers, petals flying everywhere.

REVISING AND EDITING

What Should I Do?	What Does It Look Like?

1. Evaluate how you start.
- Ask a peer reader to read the first two or three paragraphs.
- Discuss whether your beginning is clear or confusing, tired or attention grabbing.

See page 390: Ask a Peer Reader

▶ Reviewer's question: Are Jessica and John related?

"~~I'm~~ sure the shirt is very cute and pink and perfect, but I don't have the ten." *Sis,*

2. Make dialogue believable.
- Read aloud any dialogue in your story. Underline parts that seem phony or unnatural.
- Revise your dialogue to include contractions, slang, pauses, jargon, or exclamations that match the characters' ages and personalities.

▶ ~~"I will let you mow the lawn," he said.~~
~~"I do not want to. The lawnmower is very heavy."~~
He snorted. "Yeah, right. I'll let you mow the lawn, though."
"No way! That mower's heavy!"

3. Use active voice.
- The passive voice can make writing dull and lifeless. When the subject performs the action, the verb is in the active voice: *Jessica mowed the lawn.* In the passive voice, the subject is acted upon: *The lawn was mowed by Jessica.*
- (Circle) passive-voice verbs and change them to the active voice.

▶ **Passive voice**
The mower (was pulled) out of the garage by John.
Active voice
John pulled the mower out of the garage.

4. Brainstorm a title that fits.
Jot down titles that are appropriate for your story and that might capture a reader's interest. You might use a character's name or a bit of dialogue. This writer chose a title that refers to the conclusion of her story.

▶ ~~Mowing the Lawn~~
~~Jessica, John, and the Lawnmower~~
~~The Party's Tonight~~
Like a Flower *

Apply the Rubric

A strong short story . . .

- ☑ begins in a way that will interest the reader

- ☑ has a well-developed plot and intriguing characters

- ☑ develops an interesting and clearly presented central conflict

- ☑ includes descriptive details, sensory language, and dialogue

- ☑ makes the sequence of events clear and engaging

- ☑ maintains a consistent point of view

- ☑ uses the active voice

- ☑ resolves the conflict in a convincing conclusion

Ask a Peer Reader

- What could I do to make the beginning of my story clearer or more interesting?

- How would you describe the central conflict in my story?

- Which characters or actions would you like to know more about?

Use Descriptive Details

Use words like these to help your reader see and hear the action.

Sensory Verbs	Sensory Adjectives
flinch	delicate
holler	glittery
nudge	heavy
roar	pink
shiver	rough
snort	silky
squeak	sour

Check Your Grammar

- Use prepositional phrases to add important details to your story.

> She shrieked, thinking of how <u>not</u> cute she would look with missing toes.
>
> She pushed down on the handle.
>
> The grass cringed at her approach.

See page R48: The Sentence and Its Parts

Writing Onine

PUBLISHING OPTIONS
For publishing options, visit the **Writing Center** at ClassZone.com.

ASSESSMENT PREPARATION
For writing and grammar assessment practice, go to the **Assessment Center** at ClassZone.com.

Creating a Video Presentation

Have you ever wanted to direct a movie? Videotaping a scene from your short story can bring its characters, setting, and action to life.

Planning the Video

1. **Focus on a scene.** Think about the action you want to portray. Choose a scene that makes sense without extra explanation.
2. **Cast the characters and settle on a setting.** Ask classmates to take on the roles of your characters. Find a location that matches the setting. If you have set your story in another country or time period, you may need to use painted backdrops.
3. **Create a script.** Map out dialogue and action in a **rough script.** In addition to the characters' own words, consider using **voice-overs,** an offscreen person's descriptions of characters or actions. Include notes on **visual effects** and **sound effects** if applicable.
4. **Storyboard your scene.** Use sketches to show what shots you will need. Include a variety of perspectives, such as **establishing shots, medium shots,** and **close-ups.**

(Close-up) John: Good job! Go to it!

(Medium shot) Jessica: Wait!

Producing the Video

1. **Roll camera!** Follow your script and storyboard in shooting your video. You may want to have a classmate help you.
2. **Edit your masterpiece.** Use an editing software program to assemble your best footage. Then record voice-overs if needed, add music if you wish, and create a title screen and credits.

Reading Comprehension

ASSESS
The practice test items on the next few pages match skills listed on the Unit Goals page (page 301) and addressed throughout this unit. Taking this practice test will help you assess your knowledge of these skills and determine your readiness for the Unit Test.

REVIEW
After you take the practice test, your teacher can help you identify any skills you need to review.

• Setting
• Mood
• Imagery
• Analyze Details
• Make Inferences
• Paraphrase
• Connotation and Denotation
• Context Clues
• Present Tense
• Compound Predicates

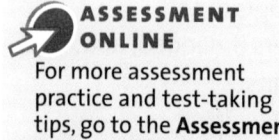

ASSESSMENT ONLINE
For more assessment practice and test-taking tips, go to the **Assessment Center** at ClassZone.com.

DIRECTIONS *Read the following selection and then answer the questions.*

from The Hobbit
Chapter VIII: Flies and Spiders

J. R. R. Tolkien

They walked in single file. The entrance to the path was like a sort of arch leading into a gloomy tunnel made by two great trees that leaned together, too old and strangled with ivy and hung with lichen to bear more than a few blackened leaves. The path itself was narrow and wound in and out among the trunks. Soon the light at the gate was like a little bright hole far behind, and the quiet was so deep that their feet seemed to thump along while all the trees leaned over them and listened.

As their eyes became used to the dimness they could see a little way to either side in a sort of darkened green glimmer. Occasionally a slender beam of sun
10 that had the luck to slip in through some opening in the leaves far above, and still more luck in not being caught in the tangled boughs and matted twigs beneath, stabbed down thin and bright before them. But this was seldom, and it soon ceased altogether.

There were black squirrels in the wood. As Bilbo's sharp inquisitive eyes got used to seeing things he could catch glimpses of them whisking off the path and scuttling behind tree-trunks. There were queer noises too, grunts, scufflings, and hurryings in the undergrowth, and among the leaves that lay piled endlessly thick in places on the forest-floor; but what made the noises he could not see. The nastiest things they saw were the cobwebs: dark dense
20 cobwebs with threads extraordinarily thick, often stretched from tree to tree, or tangled in the lower branches on either side of them. There were none stretched across the path, but whether because some magic kept it clear, or for what other reason they could not guess.

It was not long before they grew to hate the forest as heartily as they had hated the tunnels of the goblins, and it seemed to offer even less hope of any ending. But they had to go on and on, long after they were sick for a sight of the sun and of the sky, and longed for the feel of wind on their faces. There was no movement of air down under the forest-roof, and it was everlastingly still and dark and stuffy. Even the dwarves felt it, who were used to tunneling,
30 and lived at times for long whiles without the light of the sun; but the hobbit, who liked holes to make a house in but not to spend summer days in, felt that he was being slowly suffocated.

The nights were the worst. It then became pitch-dark—not what you call pitch-dark, but really pitch: so black that you really could see nothing. Bilbo tried flapping his hand in front of his nose, but he could not see it at all. Well, perhaps it is not true to say that they could see nothing: they could see eyes. They slept all closely huddled together, and took it in turns to watch; and when it was Bilbo's turn he would see gleams in the darkness round them, and sometimes pairs of yellow or red or green eyes would stare at him from a little
40 distance, and then slowly fade and disappear and slowly shine out again in another place. And sometimes they would gleam down from the branches just above him; and that was most terrifying. But the eyes that he liked the least were horrible pale bulbous sort of eyes. "Insect eyes," he thought, "not animal eyes, only they are much too big."

Although it was not yet very cold, they tried lighting watch-fires at night, but they soon gave that up. It seemed to bring hundreds and hundreds of eyes all round them, though the creatures, whatever they were, were careful never to let their bodies show in the little flicker of the flames. Worse still it brought thousands of dark-grey and black moths, some nearly as big as your hand,
50 flapping and whirring round their ears. They could not stand that, nor the huge bats, black as a top-hat, either; so they gave up fires and sat at night and dozed in the enormous uncanny darkness.

All this went on for what seemed to the hobbit ages upon ages; and he was always hungry, for they were extremely careful with their provisions. Even so, as days followed days, and still the forests seemed just the same, they began to get anxious. The food would not last for ever: it was in fact already beginning to get low. They tried shooting at the squirrels, and they wasted many arrows before they managed to bring one down on the path. But when they roasted it, it proved horrible to taste, and they shot no more squirrels.

60 They were thirsty too, for they had none too much water, and in all the time they had seen neither spring nor stream. This was their state when one day they found their path blocked by a running water. It flowed fast and strong but not very wide right across the way, and it was black, or looked it in the gloom. It was well that Beorn had warned them against it, or they would have drunk from it, whatever its color, and filled some of their emptied skins at its bank.

Comprehension

DIRECTIONS *Answer these questions about the excerpt from* The Hobbit.

1. Which of the following is the setting of "Flies and Spiders"?

   A   a gloomy tunnel

   B   a large, dense forest

   C   a squirrel-filled park

   D   a waterless desert

2. In lines 1–13 imagery is used to describe the path. What kind of mood does that imagery create?

   A   The mood is creepy because "strangled" and "blackened" suggest dead things.

   B   The mood is happy because the travelers are going for a walk.

   C   The mood is quiet because the leaves muffle footsteps.

   D   The mood makes the travelers feel crowded because the path is so narrow.

3. How does the description of the sunlight in lines 9–13 reflect the travelers' conflict?

   A   The sun shows sneakiness by slipping through the leaves.

   B   The sun is lucky to reach the ground, just as the travelers are lucky.

   C   The sun seems as threatening as the travelers when it stabs down through the leaves.

   D   The sun is soon defeated by the darkness, which hints at what will happen to the travelers.

4. From the way the characters react to the setting, you can tell that they are

   A   excited by the prospect of an adventure

   B   confident that they will get through the forest

   C   comfortable with the closeness of their surroundings

   D   disturbed by the dark stuffiness of the forest

5. The phrase "grunts, scufflings, and hurryings" appeals to which sense?

   A   sight

   B   smell

   C   touch

   D   hearing

6. Which is the best way to paraphrase the sentence that starts in line 16 and ends in line 19?

   A   Bilbo heard the scuffling noises the squirrels made.

   B   The leaves were piled so thick that they muffled all sounds.

   C   Bilbo heard strange noises but couldn't see what made them.

   D   Strange animals rushed through the undergrowth, grunting and scuffling.

7. The image of cobwebs in lines 19–21 suggests

   A   ropes hanging from trees

   B   a trap about to spring

   C   woven fabric

   D   a work of art

8. Which is the best way to paraphrase the sentence that starts in line 37 and ends in line 41?

   A They slept crowded together, and when it was Bilbo's turn to watch, he could see pairs of yellow or red or green eyes staring at him.

   B They slept crowded together, and yellow or red or green eyes stared at Bilbo, then faded and shone out again elsewhere.

   C When it was Bilbo's turn, pairs of yellow or red or green eyes stared at him.

   D When they slept crowded together, pairs of yellow or red or green eyes stared at Bilbo.

9. The image of the eyes in lines 38–44 creates a mood of

   A eager expectation

   B admiration for their beauty

   C curiosity and interest

   D fear and anxiety

10. From the details about strange noises, extraordinarily thick cobwebs, and watching eyes, you can infer that

    A the travelers are looking for trouble

    B other travelers are lost in the forest

    C strange creatures are watching the travelers

    D the forest is a very noisy place

11. Which image in lines 45–52 best describes the bats?

    A dark-grey and black

    B flapping and whirring

    C black as a top-hat

    D as big as your hand

12. Which is the best way to paraphrase lines 60–63?

    A When they were nearly out of drinking water, their path was blocked by a stream that looked black.

    B A stream that flowed fast and looked dark reminded the travelers of how thirsty they were.

    C Fast-running water blocked their path when they were nearly out of drinking water.

    D The thirsty travelers were nearly out of water when a fast-running black stream blocked their path.

Open-Ended Items

13. Identify four sensory details in lines 45–59 and tell what sense each appeals to.

14. Why was night the most difficult time for the travelers? Support your response with details from the story.

15. Describe some problems the characters face in this passage. Explain how the setting causes each problem.

Vocabulary

DIRECTIONS *Use your knowledge of connotation and denotation to answer the following questions. The line numbers will help you find the words in the excerpt from* The Hobbit.

1. The denotation of *scuttling* in line 16 is "running hastily." Which word below best describes its connotation?

   A jumping with joy

   B sneaking

   C celebrating

   D escaping

2. What connotation does *extraordinarily* have in line 20?

   A typically

   B surprisingly

   C usefully

   D hopefully

3. The author used the word *huddled* in line 37 with a connotation of

   A coziness

   B privacy

   C fear

   D warmth

4. What connotation does *enormous* have in line 52?

   A irritating

   B overwhelming

   C generous

   D ordinary

DIRECTIONS *Use context clues to answer the following questions. The line numbers will help you find the words in the excerpt from* The Hobbit.

5. Use context clues in lines 14–23 to decide what *inquisitive* means.

   A curious

   B far-seeing

   C pale

   D fearful

6. Which words give you a clue to the meaning of *bulbous* in line 43?

   A horrible pale

   B insect eyes

   C animal eyes

   D much too big

7. Which context clues help you figure out the meaning of *provisions* in line 54?

   A hungry, food

   B ages, days

   C always, same

   D shooting, arrows

8. Use context clues to figure out the meaning of *skins* in line 65.

   A fur coats

   B hands

   C containers

   D membranes

Writing & Grammar

DIRECTIONS *Read the passage and answer the questions that follow.*

(1) It was crowded at the 54th Street park. (2) Many different activities were in progress. (3) People are racing models. (4) People are playing chess. (5) People are jogging. (6) A group was playing bocce, a game brought over from Italy many years ago. (7) Grace brings her collie, Jake, to the park. (8) She throws sticks for him to fetch. (9) The dog ran circles around Grace. (10) Jake runs over to the bocce game. (11) He grabs the ball in his mouth. (12) He takes off.

1. To change sentences 1 and 2 to the present tense, which words need to be replaced?

   A crowded, kinds

   B It, were

   C was, were

   D park, activities

2. Choose the correct way to rewrite sentences 3–5, using a compound predicate.

   A People are racing models. They are playing chess. People are jogging.

   B People are racing models. People are playing chess. Some are jogging.

   C People are racing models, playing chess, and jogging.

   D People are racing models; people are playing chess; people are jogging.

3. How would you change sentence 6 to the present tense?

   A Change "was" to "is."

   B Change "was playing" to "played."

   C Change "brought" to "that was brought."

   D Change "many years ago" to "recently."

4. Choose the correct way to rewrite sentences 7 and 8, using a compound predicate.

   A Grace brings her collie, Jake, to the park; she throws sticks for him to fetch.

   B Grace brings her collie, Jake, to the park and throws sticks for him to fetch.

   C Grace brings her collie, Jake, to the park, where she throws sticks for him to fetch.

   D Grace brings her collie, Jake, to throw sticks for him to fetch.

5. Choose the correct way to write sentence 9 in the present tense.

   A The dog has run circles around Grace.

   B The dog runs circles around Grace.

   C The dog will run circles around Grace.

   D The dog was running circles around Grace.

6. Choose the correct way to rewrite sentences 10–12, using a compound predicate.

   A Jake runs over to the bocce game. Jake grabs the ball in his mouth. He takes off.

   B Jake runs over to the bocce game, grabs the ball in his mouth, and takes off.

   C Jake runs over to the bocce game. Grabbing the ball in his mouth, he takes off.

   D Jake runs over to the bocce game. He grabs the ball in his mouth before taking off.

STOP

Ideas for Independent Reading

Are there different kinds of adventure? Does seeking revenge lead to justice? Consider these questions when you read these works.

What do you look for in a friend?

The Moves Make the Man
by Bruce Brooks

"Jayfox," the only black student in his school, loves basketball. Bix, a white student, worships baseball. The two meet in a home ec class where each is learning to cook because his mother is ill.

The Friends
by Rosa Guy

When Phyllisia arrives in New York City from the West Indies, her classmates ridicule her. Only Edith tries to befriend her, but Phyllisia is not interested. Eventually, tragedies in her family change Phyllisia's mind about the meaning of friendship.

Sula
by Toni Morrison

Sula and Nel, both black and poor, meet as young girls in an Ohio town. For years they share everything, until life separates them. They meet years later to renew their friendship and heal old wounds.

Is revenge ever justified?

In the Middle of the Night
by Robert Cormier

Denny's father was the usher when a theater tragedy killed many children. His family endures hate mail and threats. When Denny answers the phone one night, a survivor initiates a plot for revenge, using Denny himself.

Hamlet
by William Shakespeare

Shakespeare's dramatic classic describes the agony of Hamlet, the prince of Denmark, as he determines how best to revenge his father's murder at the hands of his uncle.

One Flew over the Cuckoo's Nest
by Ken Kesey

McMurphy never intends to end up in a mental health ward. Once there, he organizes the inmates to resist the cruel Nurse Ratched. His plan for revenge against her humiliations has tragic consequences.

Where do you find adventure?

The Call of the Wild
by Jack London

London's classic novel tells the story of Buck, a domesticated dog stolen from his home and made to work as a sled dog during the Alaskan gold rush.

The Last Unicorn
by Peter Beagle

Beagle's classic fantasy tells of a lonely unicorn who searches for more of her own kind. She's aided in her thrilling and dangerous adventure by the totally incompetent magician Schmendrick, along with Molly Grue, a human girl.

The Birthday Boys
by Beryl Bainbridge

This historical novel is based on the diaries of five explorers, led by Robert Falcon Scott, who tried to be the first to reach the South Pole. They were beaten to the pole, and bad weather and poor planning led to their deaths on their way back to base camp.

UNIT 4

Getting the Message

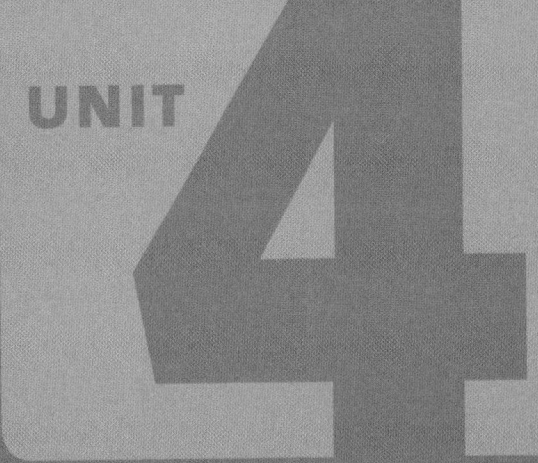

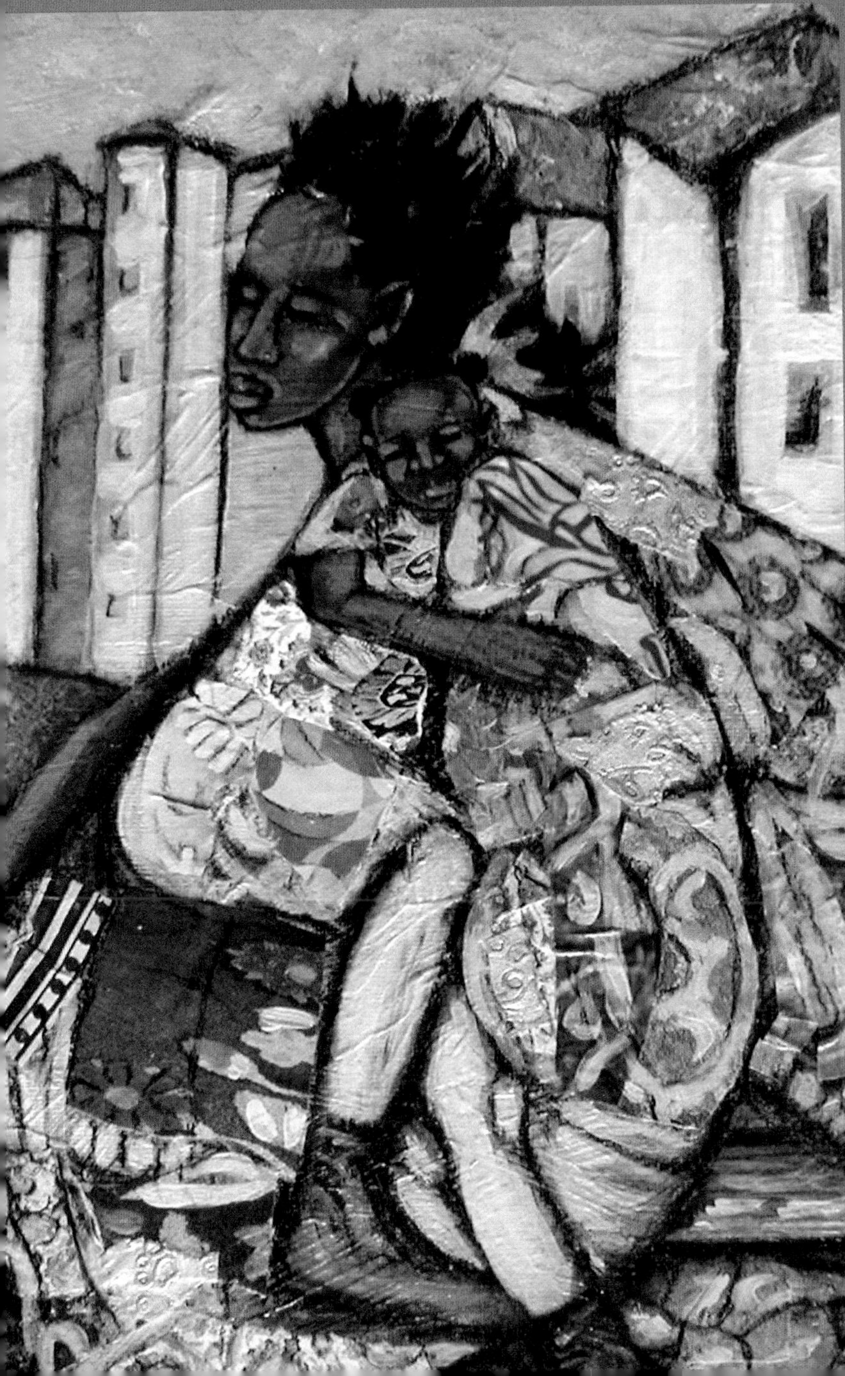

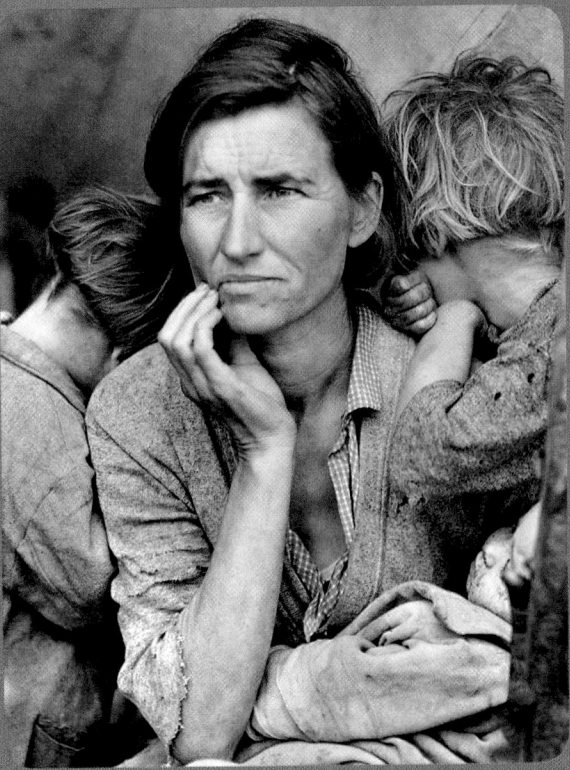

THEME AND SYMBOL

- In Fiction
- In Nonfiction
- In Poetry
- Across Genres

What MESSAGES *are timeless?*

"Beauty is in the eye of the beholder." "Love conquers all." These statements may have been communicated to you by family, friends, teachers, or others who wanted to send you messages about life and human nature. Those messages, called **themes** when they appear in works of fiction or movies, are often expressed in similar ways by writers across different cultures or time periods.

ACTIVITY Think about three or four of your favorite books or movies. For each, write down the theme that you think the author or director was trying to express. Consider the following questions:

- Does the book or movie have something to say about the way people behave under particular circumstances?

- Does the book or movie teach something about an abstract concept, such as war, love, or friendship?

- Does the book or movie try to convince you to act in a specific way?

Get together with your classmates to see how many of your listed items have similar themes. Make a group list of titles that are good examples of a particular theme.

PENNSYLVANIA STANDARDS

Preview Unit Goals

LITERARY ANALYSIS
- Identify and analyze a theme; analyze a theme across genres
- Compare and contrast universal themes
- Identify and interpret a symbol and how it conveys meaning
- Identify an author's perspective

READING
- Use reading strategies, including monitoring
- Make inferences and draw conclusions
- Identify an implied main idea
- Outline a text and analyze key ideas

WRITING AND GRAMMAR
- Write a literary analysis
- Develop ideas logically and support them with evidence
- Use rhetorical questions for effect
- Use independent clauses and subordinate clauses

SPEAKING, LISTENING, AND VIEWING
- Participate in a panel discussion

VOCABULARY
- Use context clues to unlock meaning
- Use suffixes to understand the meanings of words
- Understand and use the connotative meanings of words

ACADEMIC VOCABULARY
- context clues
- compare and contrast
- outline and analyze ideas
- symbol
- theme

Theme and Symbol

A dramatic plot, heart-pounding action, intriguing characters—one or all of these elements may play a part in capturing, and holding, your interest in a story. Often, though, stories resonate most when they provide insights into life or human nature. The meaning behind a story is the **theme,** the underlying message or big idea that the writer wants you to remember. Understanding this message and the writer's view of the world is the payoff you'll earn for reading carefully.

PENNSYLVANIA STANDARDS

READING STANDARDS
B.1.1.1.D.2 Evaluate the relationship between theme and other components

B.1.1.1.F.2 Evaluate the relationship between symbolism and other components

Part 1: Big Ideas in Literature

Many themes deal with emotions and experiences that are common across virtually all time periods and cultures. These **universal themes** show up again and again in literature—from ancient stories to today's bestsellers.

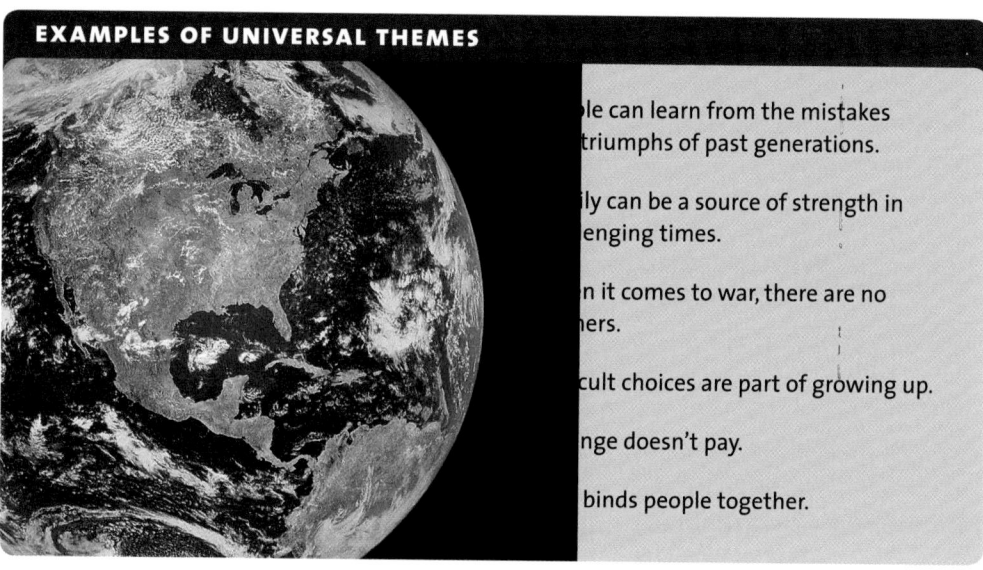

EXAMPLES OF UNIVERSAL THEMES

...le can learn from the mistakes ...triumphs of past generations.

...ly can be a source of strength in ...enging times.

...n it comes to war, there are no ...ers.

...cult choices are part of growing up.

...nge doesn't pay.

...binds people together.

A writer can use virtually every element of a story—characters, plot, and setting—to develop a theme. To convey a theme about the challenges of growing up, for example, a writer might craft a story about an insecure teenager who is plagued by difficult choices. As the character struggles to resolve the conflicts, he or she may learn a lesson about life.

A writer may also reinforce theme through the use of symbols. A **symbol** is a person, place, object, or activity that stands for something beyond itself. In the same story about the doubt-ridden teenager, a writer may use the following symbols to communicate the theme without having to directly state it:

- a fork in the road (an important decision)
- the color red (a character's anger at the world)
- a torrential rainstorm (an emotional upheaval)

MODEL: THEME AND SYMBOL

Some symbols, like the ivy leaf in this story, are hard *not* to notice.
The story is about Johnsy and Sue, two artists who become friends while
living in New York City. When Johnsy becomes sick with pneumonia,
she sinks into a deep depression. How does the symbol help you to
understand Johnsy's emotions?

from The Last Leaf

Short story by **O. Henry**

"Couldn't you draw in the other room?" asked Johnsy, coldly.

"I'd rather be here by you," said Sue. "Besides, I don't want you to keep
looking at those silly ivy leaves."

"Tell me as soon as you have finished," said Johnsy, closing her eyes, and
5   lying white and still as a fallen statue, "because I want to see the last one fall.
I'm tired of waiting. I'm tired of thinking. I want to turn loose my hold on
everything, and go sailing down, down, just like one of those poor,
tired leaves." . . .

When Sue awoke from an hour's sleep the next morning she found Johnsy
10   with dull, wide-open eyes staring at the drawn green shade.

"Pull it up; I want to see," she ordered, in a whisper.

Wearily Sue obeyed.

But, lo! after the beating rain and fierce gusts of wind that had endured
through the livelong night, there yet stood out against the brick wall one ivy
15   leaf. It was the last on the vine. Still dark green near its stem, but with its
serrated edges tinted with the yellow of dissolution and decay, it hung bravely
from a branch some twenty feet above the ground.

"It is the last one," said Johnsy. "I thought it would surely fall during the
night. I heard the wind. It will fall to-day, and I shall die at the same time." . . .

20   The day wore away, and even through the twilight they could see the lone
ivy leaf clinging to its stem against the wall. And then, with the coming of
the night the north wind was again loosed, while the rain still beat against the
windows and pattered down from the low Dutch eaves.

When it was light enough Johnsy, the merciless, commanded that the shade
25   be raised.

The ivy leaf was still there.

Johnsy lay for a long time looking at it. And then she called to Sue, who was
stirring her chicken broth over the gas stove.

"I've been a bad girl, Sudie," said Johnsy. "Something has made that last leaf
30   stay there to show me how wicked I was. It is a sin to want to die."

Close Read

1. Reread lines 4–8. How do
the ivy leaves symbolize
Johnsy and her feelings
about life?

2. Examine the boxed
description of the last leaf.
Which words or phrases
might also be used to
describe Johnsy? Explain.

3. The theme is revealed in
lines 29–30. Explain what
the writer is saying about
how people should view
life. How does the symbol
help to convey the theme?

Part 2: Identify Theme

Writers rarely state a story's theme directly. More often, the theme is implied. You have to analyze the layers of clues—for example, the characters and the conflicts—to see what they reveal about the theme. As you try to uncover the theme of a story, keep these guidelines in mind:

- The theme is not the subject of a story; it is what a story means. Love is a subject or topic. A theme is the writer's insight or idea about love, such as "Love may come when you least expect it."

- You can summarize a story's message by writing a theme statement. Use one or two complete sentences, not single words or phrases.

- Some works of literature have more than one theme, but in short stories, usually one theme stands out.

CLUES TO THEME

TITLE

The title may reflect a story's subject or a significant idea. Ask

- What in the story does the title refer to?
- Does the title have more than one meaning?
- What ideas does the title highlight?

CHARACTERS

Characters can reflect theme by what they do or say. Ask

- What do the main character's thoughts and actions reveal about him or her?
- How does the main character change?
- What lessons does the character learn?

PLOT AND CONFLICT

A story revolves around conflicts that are central to the theme. Ask

- What conflicts do the characters face?
- How are the conflicts resolved?
- Is the resolution portrayed positively or negatively?

SETTING

Setting can convey theme because of what it means to the characters and readers. Ask

- How does the setting affect the characters and the plot?
- What might the setting represent?

IMPORTANT STATEMENTS

The narrator or the characters may make statements that hint at the theme. Ask

- What key statements are made by the characters or the narrator?
- What ideas do these statements emphasize?

SYMBOLS

Characters, conflicts, and settings can serve as symbols that support the theme. Ask

- What might the characters, conflicts, and setting represent?
- What ideas do these symbols communicate?

Part 3: Analyze the Literature

This story takes place in Dublin, Ireland, during a civil war that erupted in 1922. Hidden by darkness, a sniper waits for his next target. As you read, track the clues to the theme. What message about war is the writer communicating?

 **The Sniper** Short story
by **Liam O'Flaherty**

The long June twilight faded into night. Dublin lay enveloped in darkness, but for the dim light of the moon, that shone through fleecy clouds, casting a pale light as of approaching dawn over the streets and the dark waters of the Liffey. Around the beleaguered Four Courts the heavy guns roared. Here and
5 there through the city machine guns and rifles broke the silence of the night, spasmodically, like dogs barking on lone farms. Republicans and Free Staters[1] were waging civil war.

On a roof-top near O'Connel Bridge, a Republican sniper lay watching. Beside him lay his rifle and over his shoulders were slung a pair of field-glasses.
10 His face was the face of a student—thin and ascetic, but his eyes had the cold gleam of the fanatic. They were deep and thoughtful, the eyes of a man who is used to looking at death.

He was eating a sandwich hungrily. He had eaten nothing since morning. He had been too excited to eat. He finished the sandwich, and taking a flask
15 of whiskey from his pocket, he took a short draught. Then he returned the flask to his pocket. He paused for a moment, considering whether he should risk a smoke. It was dangerous. The flash might be seen in the darkness and there were enemies watching. He decided to take the risk. Placing a cigarette between his lips, he struck a match, inhaled the smoke hurriedly and put out
20 the light. Almost immediately, a bullet flattened itself against the parapet[2] of the roof. The sniper took another whiff and put out the cigarette. Then he swore softly and crawled away to the left.

Cautiously he raised himself and peered over the parapet. There was a flash and a bullet whizzed over his head. He dropped immediately. He had
25 seen the flash. It came from the opposite side of the street.

He rolled over the roof to a chimney stack in the rear, and slowly drew himself up behind it, until his eyes were level with the top of the parapet. There was nothing to be seen—just the dim outline of the opposite housetop against the blue sky. His enemy was under cover.
30 Just then an armored car came across the bridge and advanced slowly up the street. It stopped on the opposite side of the street fifty yards ahead. The sniper could hear the dull panting of the motor. His heart beat faster. It was an enemy car. He wanted to fire, but he knew it was useless. His bullets would never pierce the steel that covered the grey monster.

---

1. **Republicans and Free Staters:** The Irish Republican Army (Republicans) wanted complete independence from England. The Irish Free Staters wanted Ireland to govern itself but still remain part of the British Empire.

2. **parapet:** a low wall along the edge of a roof or balcony.

Close Read

1. Which setting details in the first paragraph help convey a grim, dangerous picture of war? One detail has been boxed.

2. Reread the description of the sniper in lines 8–18. Through the character of the sniper, what might the writer be saying about soldiers who fight in wars?

35 Then round the corner of a side street came an old woman, her head
covered by a tattered shawl. She began to talk to the man in the turret of the
car. She was pointing to the roof where the sniper lay. An informer.

The turret opened. A man's head and shoulders appeared, looking towards
the sniper. The sniper raised his rifle and fired. The head fell heavily on the
40 turret wall. The woman darted toward the side street. The sniper fired again.
The woman whirled round and fell with a shriek into the gutter.

Suddenly from the opposite roof a shot rang out and the sniper dropped his
rifle with a curse. The rifle clattered to the roof. The sniper thought the noise
would wake the dead. He stopped to pick the rifle up. He couldn't lift it. His
45 forearm was dead. . . . He muttered, "I'm hit."

Dropping flat on to the roof, he crawled back to the parapet. With his left
hand he felt the injured right forearm. The blood was oozing through the
sleeve of his coat. There was no pain—just a deadened sensation, as if the arm
had been cut off.

50 Quickly he drew his knife from his pocket, opened it on the breastwork of
the parapet and ripped open the sleeve. There was a small hole where the bullet
had entered. On the other side there was no hole. The bullet had lodged in the
bone. It must have fractured it. He bent the arm below the wound. The arm
bent back easily. He ground his teeth to overcome the pain.

55 Then, taking out his field dressing, he ripped open the packet with his
knife. He broke the neck of the iodine bottle and let the bitter fluid drip into
the wound. A paroxysm of pain swept through him. He placed the cotton
wadding over the wound and wrapped the dressing over it. He tied the end
with his teeth.

60 Then he lay still against the parapet, and closing his eyes, he made an effort
of will to overcome the pain.

On the street beneath all was still. The armored car had retired speedily over
the bridge, with the machine gunner's head hanging lifeless over the turret.
The woman's corpse lay still in the gutter.
65 The sniper lay for a long time nursing his wounded arm and planning
escape. Morning must not find him wounded on the roof. The enemy on the
opposite roof covered his escape. He must kill that enemy and he could not use
his rifle. He had only a revolver to do it. Then he thought of a plan.

Taking off his cap, he placed it over the muzzle of his rifle. Then he pushed
70 the rifle slowly upwards over the parapet, until the cap was visible from the
opposite side of the street. Almost immediately there was a report, and a
bullet pierced the center of the cap. The sniper slanted the rifle forward. The
cap slipped down into the street. Then, catching the rifle in the middle, the
sniper dropped his left hand over the roof and let it hang, lifelessly. After a few
75 moments he let the rifle drop to the street. Then he sank to the roof, dragging
his hand with him.

Crawling quickly to the left, he peered up at the corner of the roof. His
ruse had succeeded. The other sniper seeing the cap and rifle fall, thought that

Close Read

3. Why does the sniper shoot the man in the armored car and the woman? Explain how you think the writer wants you to feel about the sniper's actions.

4. What conflicts are created by the presence of the enemy sniper?

5. Notice how the sniper refers to the other sniper only as "the enemy" in lines 65–68. In what ways might this help the sniper be effective in war?

he had killed his man. He was now standing before a row of chimney pots,
80 looking across, with his head clearly silhouetted against the western sky.

The Republican sniper smiled and lifted his revolver above the edge of the
parapet. The distance was about fifty yards—a hard shot in the dim light, and
his right arm was paining him. . . . He took a steady aim. His hand trembled
with eagerness. Pressing his lips together, he took a deep breath through his
85 nostrils and fired. He was almost deafened with the report and his arm shook
with the recoil.

Then, when the smoke cleared, he peered across and uttered a cry of joy.
His enemy had been hit. He was reeling over the parapet in his death
agony. He struggled to keep his feet, but he was slowly falling forward,
90 as if in a dream. The rifle fell from his grasp, hit the parapet, fell over, bounded
off the pole of a barber's shop beneath and then clattered on to the pavement.

Then the dying man on the roof crumpled up and fell forward. The body
turned over and over in space and hit the ground with a dull thud. Then it
lay still.

95 The sniper looked at his enemy falling and he shuddered. The lust of battle
died in him. He became bitten by remorse. The sweat stood out in beads on
his forehead. Weakened by his wound and the long summer day of fasting and
watching on the roof, he revolted from the sight of the shattered mass of his
dead enemy. His teeth chattered. He began to gibber to himself, cursing the
100 war, cursing himself, cursing everybody.

He looked at the smoking revolver in his hand and with an oath he hurled
it to the roof at his feet. The revolver went off with the concussion, and the
bullet whizzed past the sniper's head. He was frightened back to his senses by
the shock. His nerves steadied. The cloud of fear scattered from his mind and
105 he laughed.

Taking the whiskey flask from his pocket, he emptied it at a draught.
He felt reckless under the influence of the spirits. He decided to leave the roof
and look for his company commander to report. Everywhere around was quiet.
There was not much danger in going through the streets. He picked up his
110 revolver and put it in his pocket. Then he crawled down through the sky-light
to the house underneath.

When the sniper reached the laneway on the street level, he felt a sudden
curiosity as to the identity of the enemy sniper whom he had killed. He
decided that he was a good shot whoever he was. He wondered if he knew
115 him. Perhaps he had been in his own company before the split in the army.
He decided to risk going over to have a look at him. He peered around the
corner into O'Connell Street. In the upper part of the street there was heavy
firing, but around here all was quiet.

The sniper darted across the street. A machine gun tore up the
120 ground around him with a hail of bullets, but he escaped. He threw
himself face downwards beside the corpse. The machine gun stopped.

Then the sniper turned over the dead body and looked into his
brother's face.

Close Read

6. How does the Republican sniper resolve his conflict with the second sniper?

7. Reread the boxed text. How does the sniper change after seeing his enemy fall?

8. Which details in lines 112–116 tell you that the sniper starts to realize his fallen enemy is a human being? Explain.

9. Consider the last line of the story and the clues you noticed while reading. What is the writer saying about war? State the theme and cite details that helped you understand it.

Marigolds
Short Story by Eugenia Collier

What if life had a RESET *button?*

PENNSYLVANIA STANDARDS

READING STANDARDS
A.1.3.1 Make inferences and/or draw conclusions
B.1.1.1.D.2 Evaluate the relationship between theme and other components

KEY IDEA It's a terrible thing to drop your grandmother's prized china vase on the kitchen floor or to put your foot in your mouth in front of the cute new girl or boy in your class. And did you really have to be so mean to your little brother yesterday? At one time or another, we've all done or said something that makes us cringe with **regret.** We wish we could turn back the clock by a minute or a day and just do the whole thing over.

QUICKWRITE Think of something you wish you'd said or done differently. Write a paragraph describing the event and explain what you'd do if you were given the chance to try again.

● LITERARY ANALYSIS: THEME AND SETTING

"Marigolds" takes place in a rural African-American community during the 1930s—a time of racial segregation, poverty, and limited opportunity. This **setting** offers important clues to the story's **theme,** or underlying message about life and human nature. For example, the description of the setting as "arid" and "sterile" hints at the hopelessness of the narrator's situation. As you read "Marigolds," think about how the details of the setting contribute to the story's meaning. How does the setting influence the narrator's childhood experiences and the conflicts she faces? What message do those experiences teach us about life?

● READING SKILL: DRAW CONCLUSIONS

You remember that a **conclusion** is a logical judgment based on information in the text and on your own experience and prior knowledge. As you read "Marigolds," create a graphic organizer like the one shown. Include information from the text and your thoughts about the information. Then record your conclusions.

Text Information	+	Prior Knowledge	=	Conclusion
All the narrator remembers about her hometown is the dust.	+	Most people recall pleasant memories of their past.	=	She must not have many pleasant memories, or she would have remembered them.

Review: **Paraphrase**

▲ VOCABULARY IN CONTEXT

Collier creates a story based on her heritage with the help of the following words. See which ones you already know. Place each word in the appropriate column. Then write a brief definition of each word you are familiar with.

WORD LIST		
bravado	impotent	poignantly
degradation	nostalgia	retribution
exuberance	ostensibly	squalor
futile	perverse	stoicism

Know Well	Think I Know	Don't Know

Author Online

**Eugenia Collier
born 1928**

Respect for Education
Eugenia Collier grew up in the segregated part of Baltimore, Maryland, the city where she still lives today. From her parents, a doctor and a teacher, Collier learned the value of education at a young age. This led her to graduate with high honors from Howard University. She then received a master of arts from Columbia University.

Award-Winning Teacher and Writer
After working for five years as a caseworker for the Baltimore Department of Public Welfare, Collier became a college professor and started her writing career. She credits her African-American heritage as her inspiration. "The fact of my blackness is the core and center of my creativity." "Marigolds," one of her first stories, won the Gwendolyn Brooks Award for fiction in 1969. Since then, her stories, poems, and essays have appeared in many anthologies and magazines. She was selected as an outstanding educator from 1972–75 and won a Distinguished Writers Award in 1984.

 MORE ABOUT THE AUTHOR
For more on Eugenia Collier, visit the **Literature Center** at ClassZone.com.

Background

Hard Times During the Great Depression of the 1930s, millions of Americans suffered from unemployment. Government programs, such as the unemployment insurance available today, did not yet exist to help people get through the tough times. Although many Americans suffered, African Americans were particularly hard hit. In an age of racial segregation and prejudice, black people generally had fewer job opportunities and experienced higher unemployment rates.

Marigolds

Eugenia Collier

When I think of the home town of my youth, all that I seem to remember is dust—the brown, crumbly dust of late summer—arid, sterile dust that gets into the eyes and makes them water, gets into the throat and between the toes of bare brown feet. I don't know why I should remember only the dust. Surely there must have been lush green lawns and paved streets under leafy shade trees somewhere in town; but memory is an abstract painting—it does not present things as they are, but rather as they *feel*. And so, when I think of that time and that place, I remember only the dry September of the dirt roads and grassless yards of the shanty-town where I lived. And one other thing I

10 remember, another incongruency of memory—a brilliant splash of sunny yellow against the dust—Miss Lottie's marigolds. **Ⓐ**

Whenever the memory of those marigolds flashes across my mind, a strange **nostalgia** comes with it and remains long after the picture has faded. I feel again the chaotic emotions of adolescence, illusive as smoke, yet as real as the potted geranium before me now. Joy and rage and wild animal gladness and shame become tangled together in the multicolored skein of 14-going-on-15 as I recall that devastating moment when I was suddenly more woman than child, years ago in Miss Lottie's yard. I think of those marigolds at the strangest times; I remember them vividly now as I desperately pass away the time

20 waiting for you, who will not come.

I suppose that **futile** waiting was the sorrowful background music of our impoverished little community when I was young. The Depression that gripped the nation was no new thing to us, for the black workers of rural Maryland had always been depressed. I don't know what it was that we were waiting for; certainly not for the prosperity that was "just around the corner," for those were white folks' words, which we never believed. Nor did we wait for hard work and thrift to pay off in shining success as the American Dream[1] promised, for we knew better than that, too. Perhaps we waited for a miracle,

ANALYZE VISUALS
How would you describe the **mood** created by this painting?

Ⓐ THEME AND SETTING
Identify details that help you **visualize** the setting. What contrasts are presented?

nostalgia (nŏ-stăl′jə) *n.* bittersweet longing for things from the past

futile (fyo͞ot′l) *adj.* having no useful result

---

1. **American Dream:** the belief that through hard work one will achieve a comfortable and prosperous life.

amorphous in concept but necessary if one were to have the grit to rise before
30 dawn each day and labor in the white man's vineyard until after dark, or to
wander about in the September dust, offering one's sweat in return for some
meager share of bread. But God was chary[2] with miracles in those days, and so
we waited—and waited.

We children, of course, were only vaguely aware of the extent of our poverty.
Having no radios, few newspapers, and no magazines, we were somewhat
unaware of the world outside our community. Nowadays we would be called
"culturally deprived" and people would write books and hold conferences
about us. In those days everybody we knew was just as hungry and ill-clad as
we were. Poverty was the cage in which we all were trapped, and our hatred
40 of it was still the vague, undirected restlessness of the zoo-bred flamingo who
knows that nature created him to fly free. **B**

As I think of those days I feel most **poignantly** the tag-end of summer, the
bright dry times when we began to have a sense of shortening days and the
imminence of the cold.

By the time I was 14 my brother Joey and I were the only children left at our
house, the older ones having left home for early marriage or the lure of the city,
and the two babies having been sent to relatives who might care for them better
than we. Joey was three years younger than I, and a boy, and therefore vastly
inferior. Each morning our mother and father trudged wearily down the dirt
50 road and around the bend, she to her domestic job, he to his daily unsuccessful
quest for work. After our few chores around the tumbledown shanty, Joey and I
were free to run wild in the sun with other children similarly situated.

For the most part, those days are ill-defined in my memory, running
together and combining like a fresh water-color painting left out in the rain.
I remember squatting in the road drawing a picture in the dust, a picture that
Joey gleefully erased with one sweep of his dirty foot. I remember fishing for
minnows in a muddy creek and watching sadly as they eluded my cupped
hands, while Joey laughed uproariously. And I remember, that year, a strange
restlessness of body and of spirit, a feeling that something old and familiar was
60 ending, and something unknown and therefore terrifying was beginning. **C**

One day returns to me with special clarity for some reason, perhaps because
it was the beginning of the experience that in some inexplicable way marked
the end of innocence. I was loafing under the great oak tree in our yard, deep
in some reverie which I have now forgotten except that it involved some secret,
secret thoughts of one of the Harris boys across the yard. Joey and a bunch of
kids were bored now with the old tire suspended from an oak limb which had
kept them entertained for a while.

"Hey, Lizabeth," Joey yelled. He never talked when he could yell. "Hey,
Lizabeth, let's us go somewhere."

B DRAW CONCLUSIONS
Based on what you've
read so far, what
conclusions can you draw
about the narrator's life?
Cite details to support
your answer.

poignantly
(poin′yənt-lē) *adv.*
in a profoundly
moving manner

C DRAW CONCLUSIONS
Reread lines 58–60.
Lizabeth, the narrator,
is almost 15 at this point
in the story. What
changes are taking place
in her life?

---

2. **chary** (châr′ē): sparing or stingy.

70　　I came reluctantly from my private world. "Where you want to go? What you want to do?"

The truth was that we were becoming tired of the formlessness of our summer days. The idleness whose prospect had seemed so beautiful during the busy days of spring now had degenerated to an almost desperate effort to fill up the empty midday hours.

"Let's go see can we find some locusts on the hill," someone suggested.

Joey was scornful. "Ain't no more locusts there. Y'all got 'em all while they was still green."

The argument that followed was brief and not really worth the effort. 80 Hunting locust trees wasn't fun any more by now.

"Tell you what," said Joey finally, his eyes sparkling. "Let's go over to Miss Lottie's."

The idea caught on at once, for annoying Miss Lottie was always fun. I was still child enough to scamper along with the group over rickety fences and through bushes that tore our already raggedy clothes, back to where Miss Lottie lived. I think now that we must have made a tragicomic spectacle, five or six kids of different ages, each of us clad in only one garment—the girls in faded dresses that were too long or too short, the boys in patchy pants, their sweaty brown chests gleaming in the hot sun. A little cloud of dust followed 90 our thin legs and bare feet as we tramped over the barren land.

When Miss Lottie's house came into view we stopped, **ostensibly** to plan our strategy, but actually to reinforce our courage. Miss Lottie's house was the most ramshackle of all our ramshackle homes. The sun and rain had long since faded its rickety frame siding from white to a sullen gray. The boards themselves seemed to remain upright not from being nailed together but rather from leaning together like a house that a child might have constructed from cards. A brisk wind might have blown it down, and the fact that it was still standing implied a kind of enchantment that was stronger than the elements. There it stood, and as far as I know is standing yet—a gray rotting thing with 100 no porch, no shutters, no steps, set on a cramped lot with no grass, not even any weeds—a monument to decay. **D**

In front of the house in a squeaky rocking chair sat Miss Lottie's son, John Burke, completing the impression of decay. John Burke was what was known as "queer-headed." Black and ageless, he sat, rocking day in and day out in a mindless stupor, lulled by the monotonous squeak-squawk of the chair. A battered hat atop his shaggy head shaded him from the sun. Usually John Burke was totally unaware of everything outside his quiet dream world. But if you disturbed him, if you intruded upon his fantasies, he would become enraged, strike out at you, and curse at you in some strange enchanted 110 language which only he could understand. We children made a game of thinking of ways to disturb John Burke and then to elude his violent **retribution.**

ostensibly (ŏ-stĕn′sə-blē) *adv.* seemingly; to all outward appearances

D DRAW CONCLUSIONS
Reread lines 91–101. What does this description of Miss Lottie's home add to your understanding of her and her social and financial standing?

retribution (rĕt′rə-byōō′shən) *n.* something given in repayment, usually as a punishment

But our real fun and our real fear lay in Miss Lottie herself. Miss Lottie seemed to be at least a hundred years old. Her big frame still held traces of the tall, powerful woman she must have been in youth, although it was now bent and drawn. Her smooth skin was a dark reddish-brown, and her face had Indian-like features and the stern **stoicism** that one associates with Indian faces. Miss Lottie didn't like intruders either, especially children. She never left her yard, and nobody ever visited her. We never knew how she managed those
120 necessities that depend on human interaction—how she ate, for example, or even whether she ate. When we were tiny children, we thought Miss Lottie was a witch and we made up tales, that we half believed ourselves, about her exploits. We were far too sophisticated now, of course, to believe the witch-nonsense. But old fears have a way of clinging like cobwebs, and so when we sighted the tumble-down shack, we had to stop to reinforce our nerves.

"Look, there she is," I whispered, forgetting that Miss Lottie could not possibly have heard me from that distance. "She's fooling with them crazy flowers."

"Yeh, look at 'er."

Miss Lottie's marigolds were perhaps the strangest part of the picture.
130 Certainly they did not fit in with the crumbling decay of the rest of her yard. Beyond the dusty brown yard, in front of the sorry gray house, rose suddenly and shockingly a dazzling strip of bright blossoms, clumped together in enormous mounds, warm and passionate and sun-golden. The old black witch-woman worked on them all summer, every summer, down on her creaky knees, weeding and cultivating and arranging, while the house crumbled and John Burke rocked. For some **perverse** reason, we children hated those marigolds. They interfered with the perfect ugliness of the place; they were too beautiful; they said too much that we could not understand; they did not make sense. There was something in the vigor with which the old woman destroyed
140 the weeds that intimidated us. It should have been a comical sight—the old woman with the man's hat on her cropped white head, leaning over the bright mounds, her big backside in the air—but it wasn't comical, it was something we could not name. We had to annoy her by whizzing a pebble into her flowers or by yelling a dirty word, then dancing away from her rage, reveling in our youth and mocking her age. Actually, I think it was the flowers we wanted to destroy, but nobody had the nerve to try it, not even Joey, who was usually fool enough to try anything. **E**

"Y'all git some stones," commanded Joey now, and was met with instant giggling obedience as everyone except me began to gather pebbles from the
150 dusty ground. "Come on, Lizabeth."

I just stood there peering through the bushes, torn between wanting to join the fun and feeling that it was all a bit silly.

"You scared, Lizabeth?"

I cursed and spat on the ground—my favorite gesture of phony **bravado.** "Y'all children get the stones; I'll show you how to use 'em."

stoicism (stō'ĭ-sĭz'əm) *n.* indifference to pleasure or pain; a lack of visible emotion

perverse (pər-vûrs') *adj.* stubbornly contrary; wrong; harmful

E THEME AND SETTING
What do the marigolds represent to Miss Lottie? to the children?

bravado (brə-vä'dō) *n.* a false show of courage or defiance

Field of Hope, Charly Palmer. Mixed media collage on canvas, 24″ × 18″. © Charly Palmer.

ANALYZE VISUALS
How does this image compare with the narrator's description of the setting and Miss Lottie?

I said before that we children were not consciously aware of how thick were the bars of our cage. I wonder now, though, whether we were not more aware of it than I thought. Perhaps we had some dim notion of what we were, and how little chance we had of being anything else. Otherwise, why would we have been so preoccupied with destruction? Anyway, the pebbles were collected quickly, and everybody looked at me to begin the fun. **F**

"Come on, y'all."

We crept to the edge of the bushes that bordered the narrow road in front of Miss Lottie's place. She was working placidly, kneeling over the flowers, her

160

F THEME AND SETTING
What connection is made between poverty and destruction in lines 156–161?

dark hand plunged into the golden mound. Suddenly "zing"—an expertly-aimed stone cut the head off one of the blossoms.

"Who out there?" Miss Lottie's backside came down and her head came up as her sharp eyes searched the bushes. "You better git!"

We had crouched down out of sight in the bushes, where we stifled the
170 giggles that insisted on coming. Miss Lottie gazed warily across the road for a moment, then cautiously returned to her weeding. "Zing"—Joey sent a pebble into the blooms, and another marigold was beheaded.

Miss Lottie was enraged now. She began struggling to her feet, leaning on a rickety cane and shouting, "Y'all git! Go on home!" Then the rest of the kids let loose with their pebbles, storming the flowers and laughing wildly and senselessly at Miss Lottie's **impotent** rage. She shook her stick at us and started shakily toward the road crying, "Git 'long! John Burke! John Burke, come help!"

Then I lost my head entirely, mad with the power of inciting such rage,
180 and ran out of the bushes in the storm of pebbles, straight toward Miss Lottie chanting madly, "Old witch, fell in a ditch, picked up a penny and thought she was rich!" The children screamed with delight, dropped their pebbles and joined the crazy dance, swarming around Miss Lottie like bees and chanting, "Old lady witch!" while she screamed curses at us. The madness lasted only a moment, for John Burke, startled at last, lurched out of his chair, and we dashed for the bushes just as Miss Lottie's cane went whizzing at my head.

I did not join the merriment when the kids gathered again under the oak in our bare yard. Suddenly I was ashamed, and I did not like being ashamed. The child in me sulked and said it was all in fun, but the woman in me flinched
190 at the thought of the malicious attack that I had led. The mood lasted all afternoon. When we ate the beans and rice that was supper that night, I did not notice my father's silence, for he was always silent these days, nor did I notice my mother's absence, for she always worked until well into evening. Joey and I had a particularly bitter argument after supper; his **exuberance** got on my nerves. Finally I stretched out upon the palette in the room we shared and fell into a fitful doze. **G**

When I awoke, somewhere in the middle of the night, my mother had returned, and I vaguely listened to the conversation that was audible through the thin walls that separated our rooms. At first I heard no words, only voices.
200 My mother's voice was like a cool, dark room in summer—peaceful, soothing, quiet. I loved to listen to it; it made things seem all right somehow. But my father's voice cut through hers, shattering the peace.

"Twenty-two years, Maybelle, twenty-two years," he was saying, "and I got nothing for you, nothing, nothing."

"It's all right, honey, you'll get something. Everybody's out of work now, you know that."

"It ain't right. Ain't no man ought to eat his woman's food year in and year out, and see his children running wild. Ain't nothing right about that."

impotent (ĭm′pə-tənt)
adj. powerless; lacking strength or vigor

exuberance
(ĭg-zoo′bər-əns)
n. condition of unrestrained joy

G DRAW CONCLUSIONS
Reread lines 187–196. Why is the narrator torn between conflicting feelings?

"Honey, you took good care of us when you had it. Ain't nobody got
210 nothing nowadays."

"I ain't talking about nobody else, I'm talking about me. God knows I try."
My mother said something I could not hear, and my father cried out louder,
"What must a man do, tell me that?" Ⓗ

"Look, we ain't starving. I git paid every week, and Mrs. Ellis is real nice
about giving me things. She gonna let me have Mr. Ellis' old coat for you
this winter—"

"Damn Mr. Ellis' coat! And damn his money! You think I want white folks'
leavings? Damn, Maybelle"—and suddenly he sobbed, loudly and painfully,
and cried helplessly and hopelessly in the dark night. I had never heard a man
220 cry before. I did not know men ever cried. I covered my ears with my hands
but could not cut off the sound of my father's harsh, painful, despairing sobs.
My father was a strong man who would whisk a child upon his shoulders and
go singing through the house. My father whittled toys for us and laughed so
loud that the great oak seemed to laugh with him, and taught us how to fish
and hunt rabbits. How could it be that my father was crying? But the sobs
went on, unstifled, finally quieting until I could hear my mother's voice, deep
and rich, humming softly as she used to hum to a frightened child.

The world had lost its boundary lines. My mother, who was small and soft,
was now the strength of the family; my father, who was the rock on which
230 the family had been built, was sobbing like the tiniest child. Everything
was suddenly out of tune, like a broken accordion. Where did I fit into this
crazy picture? I do not now remember my thoughts, only a feeling of great
bewilderment and fear. Ⓘ

Long after the sobbing and the humming had stopped, I lay on the palette,
still as stone with my hands over my ears, wishing that I too could cry and
be comforted. The night was silent now except for the sound of the crickets
and of Joey's soft breathing. But the room was too crowded with fear to allow
me to sleep, and finally, feeling the terrible aloneness of 4 A.M., I decided to
awaken Joey.

240 "Ouch! What's the matter with you? What you want?" he demanded
disagreeably when I had pinched and slapped him awake.

"Come on, wake up."

"What for? Go 'way."

I was lost for a reasonable reply. I could not say, "I'm scared, and I don't want
to be alone," so I merely said, "I'm going out. If you want to come, come on."

The promise of adventure awoke him. "Going out now? Where to,
Lizabeth? What you going to do?"

I was pulling my dress over my head. Until now I had not thought of going
out. "Just come on," I replied tersely.

250 I was out the window and halfway down the road before Joey caught
up with me.

Ⓗ **DRAW CONCLUSIONS**
From the dialogue in lines 203–213, what can you conclude is bothering Lizabeth's father?

Ⓘ **THEME AND SETTING**
How does the conversation between Lizabeth's parents affect her? Cite details to support your answer.

New Dreams (2002), Ernest Crichlow. Litograph (Edition 150), 24¾″ × 16¾″. Photo by Maureen Turci, Mojo Portfolio. Courtesy of the Ernest Crichlow Estate.

"Wait, Lizabeth, where you going?"

I was running as if the Furies[3] were after me, as perhaps they were—running silently and furiously until I came to where I had half-known I was headed: to Miss Lottie's yard.

The half-dawn light was more eerie than complete darkness, and in it the old house was like the ruin that my world had become—foul and crumbling, a grotesque caricature.[4] It looked haunted, but I was not afraid because I was haunted too.

260   "Lizabeth, you lost your mind?" panted Joey.

I had indeed lost my mind, for all the smoldering emotions of that summer swelled in me and burst—the great need for my mother who was never there, the hopelessness of our poverty and **degradation,** the bewilderment of being neither child nor woman and yet both at once, the fear unleashed by my father's tears. And these feelings combined in one great impulse toward destruction. ◗

degradation
(dĕg′rə-dā′shən) *n.*
condition of being brought to a lower level; humiliation

◗ **THEME AND SETTING**
Reread lines 261–265. Why do the narrator's emotions produce an urge to destroy?

---

3. **Furies:** In Greek and Roman mythology, the Furies were three goddesses of vengeance, or revenge.

4. **a grotesque caricature** (grō-tĕsk′ kăr′ĭ-kə-choŏr′): a bizarre and absurdly exaggerated representation of something.

"Lizabeth!"

I leaped furiously into the mounds of marigolds and pulled madly, trampling and pulling and destroying the perfect yellow blooms. The fresh smell of early morning and of dew-soaked marigolds spurred me on as I went tearing and mangling and sobbing while Joey tugged my dress or my waist crying, "Lizabeth stop, please stop!"

And then I was sitting in the ruined little garden among the uprooted and ruined flowers, crying and crying, and it was too late to undo what I had done. Joey was sitting beside me, silent and frightened, not knowing what to say. Then, "Lizabeth, look."

I opened my swollen eyes and saw in front of me a pair of large calloused feet; my gaze lifted to the swollen legs, the age-distorted body clad in a tight cotton night dress, and then the shadowed Indian face surrounded by stubby white hair. And there was no rage in the face now, now that the garden was destroyed and there was nothing any longer to be protected.

"M-miss Lottie!" I scrambled to my feet and just stood there and stared at her, and that was the moment when childhood faded and womanhood began. That violent, crazy act was the last act of childhood. For as I gazed at the immobile face with the sad, weary eyes, I gazed upon a kind of reality that is hidden to childhood. The witch was no longer a witch but only a broken old woman who had dared to create beauty in the midst of ugliness and sterility. She had been born in **squalor** and lived in it all her life. Now at the end of that life she had nothing except a falling-down hut, a wrecked body, and John Burke, the mindless son of her passion. Whatever verve there was left in her, whatever was of love and beauty and joy that had not been squeezed out by life, had been there in the marigolds she had so tenderly cared for. **K**

Of course I could not express the things that I knew about Miss Lottie as I stood there awkward and ashamed. The years have put words to the things I knew in that moment, and as I look back upon it, I know that that moment marked the end of innocence. People think of the loss of innocence as meaning the loss of virginity, but this is far from true. Innocence involves an unseeing acceptance of things at face value, an ignorance of the area below the surface. In that humiliating moment I looked beyond myself and into the depths of another person. This was the beginning of compassion, and one cannot have both compassion and innocence. **L**

The years have taken me worlds away from that time and that place, from the dust and squalor of our lives and from the bright thing that I destroyed in a blind childish striking out at God-knows-what. Miss Lottie died long ago and many years have passed since I last saw her hut, completely barren at last, for despite my wild contrition she never planted marigolds again. Yet, there are times when the image of those passionate yellow mounds returns with a painful poignancy. For one does not have to be ignorant and poor to find that one's life is barren as the dusty yards of one's town. And I too have planted marigolds. ❧

squalor (skwŏl'ər) n. a filthy, shabby, and wretched condition, as from poverty

K DRAW CONCLUSIONS
A change has taken place in Lizabeth. Why is she suddenly able to see Miss Lottie as she really is?

L PARAPHRASE
Paraphrase the narrator's thoughts about innocence and compassion in lines 295–300.

Comprehension

1. **Recall** How old is the narrator in the story?

2. **Recall** What is unusual about Miss Lottie's marigolds?

3. **Summarize** What does the narrator do that she later **regrets?**

Literary Analysis

4. **Understand the Influence of Setting** Note the most prominent features of the story's setting. How do they affect the narrator's outlook on life?

5. **Draw Conclusions** Review the chart you made as you read. What leads the young Lizabeth to destroy Miss Lottie's marigolds? Support your conclusions with evidence from the story.

6. **Analyze Climax** Identify the climax of the story. What change does this turning point initiate in the narrator? in Miss Lottie? Cite evidence to support your answers.

7. **Analyze Symbolism** Miss Lottie's marigolds are central to the story. What do they symbolize? To help you interpret their meaning, create a chart like the one shown to record descriptions of the marigolds and the ideas you associate with them.

Description of Marigolds	Associations
"a brilliant splash of sunny yellow" (lines 10–11)	"sunny yellow," like the sun, gives energy and life

8. **Interpret Theme and Setting** The narrator and Miss Lottie respond to their impoverished surroundings in very different ways. What message does the story convey about the impact of poverty on people's lives? What other themes does the story impart?

9. **Evaluate Ideas** Reread the next-to-last paragraph (lines 292–300). Do you agree with what the narrator says about innocence and compassion? Use evidence from the story as well as your own experiences to explore your answer.

Literary Criticism

10. **Social Context** Can "Marigolds" be considered social commentary on racial segregation? Cite evidence to support your opinion.

PENNSYLVANIA STANDARDS

READING STANDARD
B.1.1.1.D.2 Evaluate the relationship between theme and other components

Vocabulary in Context

VOCABULARY PRACTICE

Decide whether the words in each pair are similar or different in meaning.

1. perverse/agreeable
2. squalor/splendor
3. exuberance/enthusiasm
4. retribution/retaliation
5. nostalgia/homesickness
6. futile/effective
7. poignantly/indifferently
8. bravado/timidity
9. degradation/humiliation
10. ostensibly/apparently
11. impotent/powerless
12. stoicism/emotionalism

WORD LIST

bravado

degradation

exuberance

futile

impotent

nostalgia

ostensibly

perverse

poignantly

retribution

squalor

stoicism

VOCABULARY IN WRITING

Pretend you are Lizabeth's 12-year-old brother Joey, and write a paragraph describing your feelings about your childhood and the events in this story. Use four or more vocabulary words. You might start this way.

> **EXAMPLE SENTENCE**
>
> When I think of my childhood, I feel no **nostalgia**.

VOCABULARY STRATEGY: THE SUFFIX *-or*

Many words have endings called **suffixes** that can help you determine a word's meaning. For example, the word *squalor* ends with *-or*, a noun suffix meaning "state or condition of." You may recognize it as similar to the word *squalid*, meaning "very dirty or filthy." These two insights can help you conclude that *squalor* means "a filthy condition." Recognizing this suffix in other unfamiliar words can provide clues to the meanings of those words.

PRACTICE Use each numbered word in a sentence. Then use your knowledge of the suffix *-or* to figure out the meaning of each word. Use a dictionary to check your work.

1. terror
2. furor
3. candor
4. stupor
5. fervor
6. pallor

PENNSYLVANIA STANDARDS

READING STANDARD
A.1.2.1 Identify word meaning using affixes

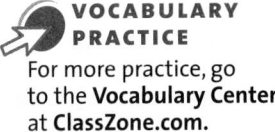

VOCABULARY PRACTICE
For more practice, go to the **Vocabulary Center** at **ClassZone.com**.

Sowing Change
Newspaper Article

Use with "Marigolds,"
page 410.

PENNSYLVANIA STANDARDS

READING & WRITING STANDARDS
A.2.4.1 Identify main ideas and supporting details

1.5.11.B.1 Analyze and organize information

What's the Connection?

In "Marigolds," Miss Lottie's garden is the only bright spot in her difficult life. In the North Lawndale neighborhood of Chicago, Illinois, a garden has also become a bright spot for residents. To find out more about this garden and its impact on the community, read "Sowing Change."

Skill Focus: Outline

When you need to thoroughly understand and absorb a great many ideas and facts, outlining can help. An **outline** is a way of organizing a text's main ideas and supporting details according to their levels of importance. Since the main ideas and supporting details are written in the form of brief phrases, an outline can be considered a text's skeleton. You can take notes in outline form by following these steps:

• Skim the text to figure out its main topic, subtopics, and pattern of organization.

• Draft a basic outline by recording the main topics (numbered with Roman numerals) and the subtopics (lettered with capital letters) in the order presented by the writer. Use sentences or phrases as outline headings.

• Then, as you read the text closely, find and add supporting details to your outline at the appropriate levels of importance. Use Arabic numerals and lower-case letters to show further levels of detail.

Follow the steps above to take notes on "Sowing Change" in outline form. You can use the outline begun here as your starting point or create a new one. (For more information on outlining, see the **Reading Handbook,** page R4.)

> *The African Heritage Garden in North Lawndale*
>   I. *What the Garden Looks Like*
>   A. *Covers a large corner lot*
>   B. *Contains many plants and special features*
>   *1.*
>   *a.*
>   *b.*
>   *2.*
>   II. *What It Took to Create the Garden*

Sowing Change

DONNA FREEDMAN

Many hands join to transform a barren city lot into a thriving green space for plants—and people in North Lawndale **A**

The 20-by-32-foot bed of marigolds is not just a sea of orange blooms, but a Rorschach blot. Back up a few feet, look again and the shape of the African continent emerges on a North Lawndale street corner.

A pair of doorway-like arbors invite passersby off the sidewalk and into a garden where raised beds are a glory of
10 lilies, daisies, hibiscus, nicotiana, shrub roses and other plants. In some places, flowers fight for space among broccoli, sweet potatoes and purple kale that are almost treelike in their vigor.

Three low, bark-covered mounds, plus a limestone-terraced hill at the rear of the site, give a sense of terrain. Shrubs, ornamental grasses and young hackberry, black locust, crab apple and magnolia trees
20 also provide vertical uplift on this city lot.

"This is what we need: open space, a place to sit and talk, to think a while," says North Lawndale resident Gerald Earles, sitting in the garden at 12th Place

and Central Park Avenue. The 130-by-100-foot garden seemed to spring up in a single day in late April. **B**

In reality, it took more than two years, about 400 volunteers and $200,000 in
30 donated materials and expertise to create the African Heritage Garden.

"I've always known that the community [was] capable of a project of this magnitude. We just needed a focus," says Valerie Leonard, executive director of the non-profit North Lawndale Small Grants Human Development Corp.

The corporation's attempts to garden on the site withered and died due to lack
40 of water. But things finally came together this year after the Chicago Botanic Garden NeighborSpace, a non-profit land trust, and The Enterprise Companies, a residential real estate development firm, provided financial and design support.

About 200 people, including about 25 people from the community, attended a design session in March to determine

A OUTLINE
Before you begin taking notes, **skim** the entire article to see what its main topics and subtopics are.

B OUTLINE
What important information in this paragraph is not covered in the draft outline on page 422? Add it to your own outline.

what the garden would become. All
50 agreed that the site should have a bed
shaped like the African continent and
incorporate a number of plants that grow
in Africa. Both ideas were part of Leonard's
original plan, which was inspired by
Unity Park, another Lawndale project.

That park was created five years ago by
residents fed up with crime near 19th
Street and Kostner Avenue. Gladys
Woodson, who spearheaded that project,
60 says that once the site became a well-used
and neatly maintained park, the criminal
element left.

"If you get enough good people to
come out, the bad people are going to
leave," Woodson says. She and other
Unity Park organizers are helping at the
African Heritage Garden as well. **C**

In fact, the heritage garden is thriving
under the care and nurturing of a variety
70 of groups, including the North Lawndale
Greening Committee, the Combined
Block Club, and Slumbusters. Neighbor-
Space, which purchased the land from
the city and leases it to North Lawndale,
also paid to install a water hookup.

The plants and landscape materials,
design, and onsite supervision were paid
for by a grant from the Chicago Botanic
Garden's   Neighborhood   Gardens
80 program. Each year, the Chicago Botanic
Garden awards money to community
groups interested in greening their
neighborhoods.

It all came together on April 26 when
about five dozen volunteers of varying
ages, mostly neighborhood residents,
planted hundreds of flowers and vegetable
seedlings under the supervision of the
Chicago Botanic Garden's Community
90 Gardens division. The Safer Foundation,
which helps men make the transition
from prison to the outside world, sent
clients to build arbors and a half-dozen
large raised beds.

With regular watering, the garden has
thrived—as have the weeds. Scheduled
work parties and neighborhood residents
keep the weeds at bay. **D**

In late June, the Chicago Botanic
100 Garden brought more trees and flowers,
which were planted by about 30 volunteers,
including 9-year-old Nikky Pierce. Nikky,
who lives down the street from the garden,
is pleased with the results.

"Before, it was just dirty and trashy,"
she says. "It looks pretty when there are
flowers in it."

Elder plantswoman and neighborhood
resident Annie Lott lends a hand as well as
110 her expertise. At 92, she is an avid gardener
who grows numerous flowers and 16
kinds of vegetables. It was her suggestion
to put "some food, something that's
healthy" in the flower beds.

"I love this garden because it brings
back memories of how I was raised," says
Lott, who is from Mississippi. "I was
raised on a farm and our father taught us
to do things for others and share."

120 The African Heritage Garden is a work
in progress. Areas among the beds and
mounds still need to be covered with
stones. A shelter symbolizing a tribal hut,
made with thatch and other materials
from Africa, is in the works. Park benches
also are likely.

But the progress has been huge, says
Leonard, even though some of the
volunteers had no gardening experience.
130 "They were involved, and now they're
asking, 'When can we do it again?'

"That's music to my ears," Leonard
says. "When you see how it was being
used before and how it's being used now,
that's an awesome feeling. It belongs to
the community now."

C OUTLINE
What do lines 63–67
add to your understanding
of the purpose of this
garden?

D OUTLINE
What new topic is
introduced in lines 95–98?

Comprehension

1. **Summarize** How has the African Heritage Garden changed the North Lawndale community?

Critical Analysis

2. **Analyze Your Outline** Review the outline you created as you read. What main ideas did you identify?

3. **Make Inferences** What are some of the values held by the North Lawndale community? How does the garden represent these values? Cite details from the article to support your answer.

4. **Make Judgments** Consider what you know about crime as well as what the article tells you about this particular community garden. Why would something as simple as a garden reduce crime in an area?

PENNSYLVANIA STANDARDS

READING & WRITING STANDARDS
A.2.4.1 Identify main ideas and supporting details

1.5.11.B.1 Analyze and organize information

Read for Information: Analyze Ideas

WRITING PROMPT
Both "Marigolds" and "Sowing Change" feature gardeners and their work. Write a brief analysis of the benefits of gardens. Use details from the short story and the article to support your ideas.

Writing an **analysis** involves identifying and explaining the parts of a subject and, finally, arriving at a conclusion. For help, follow these steps:

1. To analyze the benefits of gardens, review the benefits and consider how you might break them down. For example, the benefits might split naturally into "benefits to gardeners" and "benefits to the community."

2. Reread the selections to take notes on the particular benefits you want to address.

3. Review your notes. Identify any conclusions you can draw about gardening and its benefits.

As you write your analysis, be systematic. Introduce each main idea, identify its parts, and then elaborate on those parts before arriving at your conclusion.

Introduce Subject → Examine Part of Subject → Draw a Conclusion

The Scarlet Ibis

Short Story by James Hurst

Why do we HURT *the ones we* LOVE?

PENNSYLVANIA STANDARDS

READING STANDARDS
A.1.3.1 Make inferences
B.1.1.1.F.1 Analyze symbolism

KEY IDEA Cruelty can intrude on the most loving relationship, often in moments of anger or disappointment. How do you deal with **mixed emotions** like these? Adults usually control such urges, but children are more likely to act on their immediate feelings. What harm can come from a thoughtless word or action?

DISCUSS Sometimes we are harder on loved ones than on anyone else. Why do you think this is? Discuss this question with a small group of your classmates.

LITERARY ANALYSIS: SYMBOL

A **symbol** is a person, animal, place, object, or activity that stands for something beyond itself. A dove, for instance, often serves as a symbol for peace. Writers use symbols to emphasize important ideas in a story, which can act as clues to the theme. In "The Scarlet Ibis," for example, a swamp comes to symbolize the love between two brothers. To identify other symbols in this story, use these strategies as you read:

- Look for ideas that the writer emphasizes.
- Note striking images and character descriptions.
- Ask yourself what associations each one brings to mind.

Review: **Mood, Theme**

READING SKILL: MAKE INFERENCES ABOUT CHARACTERS

When you make an **inference,** you make a logical guess based on observations or information in a text and on your own knowledge and experience. Sometimes called "reading between the lines," making inferences is an essential step in understanding the characters and, ultimately, the story itself. As you read, use a chart like the one shown to record inferences about the relationship between the narrator and his brother.

Quotations	Inferences About Relationship
"Doodle ... was a nice crazy, like someone you meet in your dreams".	Narrator basically liked his brother, but thought he was odd.

VOCABULARY IN CONTEXT

The following boldfaced words are important to understanding this story of two brothers. To see how many of these words you already know, restate each phrase, using a different word for the boldfaced word.

1. **exotic** flowers from the tropics
2. **reiterate** your idea for emphasis
3. **evanesce,** like smoke into thin air
4. in **imminent** danger of falling
5. claimed **infallibility** in his deeply-held beliefs
6. worked hard and with **doggedness**
7. balanced **precariously** on the edge
8. dangerous beliefs that bordered on **heresy**

Author Online

A Man of Many Talents
James Hurst lives near the North Carolina coast, not far from the farm where he was born. After attending college and serving in the U.S. Army during World War II, he studied singing at New York's famous Juilliard School. Hoping for an operatic career, he also studied in Rome, Italy, but soon gave up on this goal. Then, in 1951, he settled into a long career at a large New York bank.

**James Hurst
born 1922**

A Tribute to the Human Spirit During his early years at the bank, Hurst published short stories and a play. "The Scarlet Ibis" received national attention after appearing in the *Atlantic Monthly* in July 1960 and winning the Atlantic First award that same year. When asked about the meaning of the story, Hurst once replied, "I hesitate to respond, since authors often do not understand what they write. That is why we have critics. I venture to say, however, that it comments on the tenacity and the splendor of the human spirit."

 MORE ABOUT THE AUTHOR
For more on James Hurst, visit the **Literature Center** at ClassZone.com.

Background
Drawn from Nature "The Scarlet Ibis" takes its title from a tropical bird rarely found in coastal North Carolina, where the story takes place. The lush natural environment of this setting is prominent in the story. In addition to the ibis, Hurst uses the local names of plants for the power of their symbolic associations. For example, the exotic ibis lands in a "bleeding tree," a type of pine that oozes a white sap when cut. "Graveyard flowers" are fragrant white gardenias often planted in cemeteries because they bloom year after year.

The *Scarlet* Ibis

James Hurst

It was in the clove of seasons,[1] summer was dead but autumn had not yet been born, that the ibis lit in the bleeding tree. The flower garden was stained with rotting brown magnolia petals and ironweeds grew rank amid the purple phlox. The five o'clocks by the chimney still marked time, but the oriole nest in the elm was untenanted and rocked back and forth like an empty cradle. The last graveyard flowers were blooming, and their smell drifted across the cotton field and through every room of our house, speaking softly the names of our dead. **Ⓐ**

It's strange that all this is still so clear to me, now that that summer has long since fled and time has had its way. A grindstone stands where the bleeding
10 tree stood, just outside the kitchen door, and now if an oriole sings in the elm, its song seems to die up in the leaves, a silvery dust. The flower garden is prim, the house a gleaming white, and the pale fence across the yard stands straight and spruce. But sometimes (like right now), as I sit in the cool, green-draped parlor, the grindstone begins to turn, and time with all its changes is ground away—and I remember Doodle.

Doodle was just about the craziest brother a boy ever had. Of course, he wasn't a crazy crazy like old Miss Leedie, who was in love with President Wilson and wrote him a letter every day, but was a nice crazy, like someone you meet in your dreams. He was born when I was six and was, from the
20 outset, a disappointment. He seemed all head, with a tiny body which was red and shriveled like an old man's. Everybody thought he was going to die— everybody except Aunt Nicey, who had delivered him. She said he would live because he was born in a caul,[2] and cauls were made from Jesus' nightgown. Daddy had Mr. Heath, the carpenter, build a little mahogany coffin for him. But he didn't die, and when he was three months old, Mama and Daddy decided they might as well name him. They named him William Armstrong, which was like tying a big tail on a small kite. Such a name sounds good only on a tombstone. **Ⓑ**

Ⓐ MOOD
What words or images contribute to the mood of sadness and longing in lines 1–7?

ANALYZE VISUALS
What qualities does the boy in the painting seem to have? Point to details of color, line, shape, and texture to support your answer.

Ⓑ MAKE INFERENCES
What inferences can you make about Doodle from the **details** offered in this paragraph? Explain your thought process.

---

1. **the clove of seasons:** a time between two seasons, in this case, summer and autumn.
2. **born in a caul:** born with a thin membrane covering the head.

Richard at Age Five (1944), Alice Neel. Oil on canvas, 26″ × 14″. © Estate of Alice Neel. Courtesy Robert Miller Gallery, New York.

I thought myself pretty smart at many things, like holding my breath,
30 running, jumping, or climbing the vines in Old Woman Swamp, and I wanted
more than anything else someone to race to Horsehead Landing, someone to
box with, and someone to perch with in the top fork of the great pine behind
the barn, where across the fields and swamps you could see the sea. I wanted a
brother. But Mama, crying, told me that even if William Armstrong lived, he
would never do these things with me. He might not, she sobbed, even be "all
there." He might, as long as he lived, lie on the rubber sheet in the center of
the bed in the front bedroom where the white marquisette curtains billowed
out in the afternoon sea breeze, rustling like palmetto fronds.[3]

It was bad enough having an invalid brother, but having one who possibly
40 was not all there was unbearable, so I began to make plans to kill him by
smothering him with a pillow. However, one afternoon as I watched him, my
head poked between the iron posts of the foot of the bed, he looked straight
at me and grinned. I skipped through the rooms, down the echoing halls,
shouting, "Mama, he smiled. He's all there! He's all there!" and he was. **C**

When he was two, if you laid him on his stomach, he began to move
himself, straining terribly. The doctor said that with his weak heart this strain
would probably kill him, but it didn't. Trembling, he'd push himself up,
turning first red, then a soft purple, and finally collapse back onto the bed
like an old worn-out doll. I can still see Mama watching him, her hand
50 pressed tight across her mouth, her eyes wide and unblinking. But he learned
to crawl (it was his third winter), and we brought him out of the front
bedroom, putting him on the rug before the fireplace. For the first time he
became one of us.

As long as he lay all the time in bed, we called him William Armstrong,
even though it was formal and sounded as if we were referring to one of our
ancestors, but with his creeping around on the deerskin rug and beginning to
talk, something had to be done about his name. It was I who renamed him.
When he crawled, he crawled backward, as if he were in reverse and couldn't
change gears. If you called him, he'd turn around as if he were going in the
60 other direction, then he'd back right up to you to be picked up. Crawling
backward made him look like a doodlebug, so I began to call him Doodle, and
in time even Mama and Daddy thought it was a better name than William
Armstrong. Only Aunt Nicey disagreed. She said caul babies should be treated
with special respect since they might turn out to be saints. Renaming my
brother was perhaps the kindest thing I ever did for him, because nobody
expects much from someone called Doodle. **D**

Although Doodle learned to crawl, he showed no signs of walking, but he
wasn't idle. He talked so much that we all quit listening to what he said. It was
about this time that Daddy built him a go-cart and I had to pull him around.

C MAKE INFERENCES
Compare the narrator's
initial reaction to Doodle
with his response to
Doodle's grin. What
can you infer about the
change in the narrator's
attitude?

D SYMBOL
Reread lines 60–66. A
nickname can sometimes
be a kind of symbol.
What does Doodle's
nickname tell you
about the feelings and
expectations others have
for him?

---

3. **palmetto fronds:** the fanlike leaves of a kind of palm tree.

Cypress Swamp, Texas (1940), Florence McClung. Oil on masonite, 24″ × 30″. Gift of the Roger H. Ogden Collection. The Ogden Museum of Southern Art.

70 At first I just paraded him up and down the piazza, but then he started crying to be taken out into the yard, and it ended up by my having to lug him wherever I went. If I so much as picked up my cap, he'd start crying to go with me, and Mama would call from wherever she was, "Take Doodle with you."

He was a burden in many ways. The doctor had said that he mustn't get too excited, too hot, too cold, or too tired and that he must always be treated gently. A long list of don'ts went with him, all of which I ignored once we got out of the house. To discourage his coming with me, I'd run with him across the ends of the cotton rows and careen him around corners on two wheels. Sometimes I accidentally turned him over, but he never told Mama. His skin
80 was very sensitive, and he had to wear a big straw hat whenever he went out. When the going got rough and he had to cling to the sides of the go-cart, the hat slipped all the way down over his ears. He was a sight. Finally, I could see I was licked. Doodle was my brother and he was going to cling to me forever, no matter what I did, so I dragged him across the burning cotton field to share with him the only beauty I knew, Old Woman Swamp. I pulled the go-cart through the sawtooth fern, down into the green dimness where the palmetto

fronds whispered by the stream. I lifted him out and set him down in the soft
rubber grass beside a tall pine. His eyes were round with wonder as he gazed
about him, and his little hands began to stroke the rubber grass. Then he
90 began to cry.

"For heaven's sake, what's the matter?" I asked, annoyed.

"It's so pretty," he said. "So pretty, pretty, pretty."

After that day Doodle and I often went down into Old Woman Swamp.
I would gather wildflowers, wild violets, honeysuckle, yellow jasmine,
snakeflowers, and water lilies, and with wire grass we'd weave them into
necklaces and crowns. We'd bedeck ourselves with our handiwork and loll
about thus beautified, beyond the touch of the everyday world. Then when the
slanted rays of the sun burned orange in the tops of the pines, we'd drop our
jewels into the stream and watch them float away toward the sea. **E**

100 There is within me (and with sadness I have watched it in others) a knot of
cruelty borne by the stream of love, much as our blood sometimes bears the
seed of our destruction, and at times I was mean to Doodle. One day I took **F**
him up to the barn loft and showed him his casket, telling him how we all had
believed he would die. It was covered with a film of Paris green[4] sprinkled to
kill the rats, and screech owls had built a nest inside it.

Doodle studied the mahogany box for a long time, then said, "It's not mine."

"It is," I said. "And before I'll help you down from the loft, you're going to
have to touch it."

"I won't touch it," he said sullenly.

110 "Then I'll leave you here by yourself," I threatened, and made as if I were
going down.

Doodle was frightened of being left. "Don't go leave me, Brother," he cried,
and he leaned toward the coffin. His hand, trembling, reached out, and when
he touched the casket he screamed. A screech owl flapped out of the box into
our faces, scaring us and covering us with Paris green. Doodle was paralyzed,
so I put him on my shoulder and carried him down the ladder, and even when
we were outside in the bright sunshine, he clung to me, crying, "Don't leave
me. Don't leave me."

When Doodle was five years old, I was embarrassed at having a brother of
120 that age who couldn't walk, so I set out to teach him. We were down in Old
Woman Swamp and it was spring and the sick-sweet smell of bay flowers hung
everywhere like a mournful song. "I'm going to teach you to walk, Doodle,"
I said.

He was sitting comfortably on the soft grass, leaning back against the pine.
"Why?" he asked.

I hadn't expected such an answer. "So I won't have to haul you around all
the time."

"I can't walk, Brother," he said.

E MAKE INFERENCES
Describe the relationship
that develops between
the brothers. What do
you think is the reason
that Doodle wins the
narrator over?

F THEME
In lines 100–102, the
narrator makes a direct
statement that offers
clues to the theme.
Paraphrase the message
he expresses.

---

4. **Paris green:** a poisonous green powder used to kill pests.

"Who says so?" I demanded.

130 "Mama, the doctor—everybody."

"Oh, you can walk," I said, and I took him by the arms and stood him up. He collapsed onto the grass like a half-empty flour sack. It was as if he had no bones in his little legs.

"Don't hurt me, Brother," he warned.

"Shut up. I'm not going to hurt you. I'm going to teach you to walk." I heaved him up again, and again he collapsed.

This time he did not lift his face up out of the rubber grass. "I just can't do it. Let's make honeysuckle wreaths."

"Oh yes you can, Doodle," I said. "All you got to do is try. Now come on,"
140 and I hauled him up once more.

It seemed so hopeless from the beginning that it's a miracle I didn't give up. But all of us must have something or someone to be proud of, and Doodle had become mine. I did not know then that pride is a wonderful, terrible thing, a seed that bears two vines, life and death. Every day that summer we went to the pine beside the stream of Old Woman Swamp, and I put him on his feet at least a hundred times each afternoon. Occasionally I too became discouraged because it didn't seem as if he was trying, and I would say, "Doodle, don't you *want* to learn to walk?" **G**

He'd nod his head, and I'd say, "Well, if you don't keep trying, you'll never
150 learn." Then I'd paint for him a picture of us as old men, white-haired, him with a long white beard and me still pulling him around in the go-cart. This never failed to make him try again.

Finally one day, after many weeks of practicing, he stood alone for a few seconds. When he fell, I grabbed him in my arms and hugged him, our laughter pealing through the swamp like a ringing bell. Now we knew it could be done. Hope no longer hid in the dark palmetto thicket but perched like a cardinal in the lacy toothbrush tree, brilliantly visible.

"Yes, yes," I cried, and he cried it too, and the grass beneath us was soft and the smell of the swamp was sweet.

160 With success so **imminent,** we decided not to tell anyone until he could actually walk. Each day, barring rain, we sneaked into Old Woman Swamp, and by cotton-picking time Doodle was ready to show what he could do. He still wasn't able to walk far, but we could wait no longer. Keeping a nice secret is very hard to do, like holding your breath. We chose to reveal all on October eighth, Doodle's sixth birthday, and for weeks ahead we mooned around the house, promising everybody a most spectacular surprise. Aunt Nicey said that, after so much talk, if we produced anything less tremendous than the Resurrection,[5] she was going to be disappointed.

At breakfast on our chosen day, when Mama, Daddy, and Aunt Nicey were
170 in the dining room, I brought Doodle to the door in the go-cart just as usual and had them turn their backs, making them cross their hearts and hope to

G MAKE INFERENCES
Why does the narrator try so hard to teach Doodle to walk? Point out statements in lines 141–148 that support your answer.

imminent (ĭm′ə-nənt) *adj.* about to occur

---

5. **the Resurrection:** the rising of Jesus Christ from the dead after his burial.

die if they peeked. I helped Doodle up, and when he was standing alone I let them look. There wasn't a sound as Doodle walked slowly across the room and sat down at his place at the table. Then Mama began to cry and ran over to him, hugging him and kissing him. Daddy hugged him too, so I went to Aunt Nicey, who was thanks praying in the doorway, and began to waltz her around. We danced together quite well until she came down on my big toe with her brogans,[6] hurting me so badly I thought I was crippled for life.

180 Doodle told them it was I who had taught him to walk, so everyone wanted to hug me, and I began to cry.

"What are you crying for?" asked Daddy, but I couldn't answer. They did not know that I did it for myself; that pride, whose slave I was, spoke to me louder than all their voices, and that Doodle walked only because I was ashamed of having a crippled brother. **H**

Within a few months Doodle had learned to walk well and his go-cart was put up in the barn loft (it's still there) beside his little mahogany coffin. Now, when we roamed off together, resting often, we never turned back until our destination had been reached, and to help pass the time, we took up lying. From the beginning Doodle was a terrible liar and he got me in the habit. Had 190 anyone stopped to listen to us, we would have been sent off to Dix Hill.[7]

My lies were scary, involved, and usually pointless, but Doodle's were twice as crazy. People in his stories all had wings and flew wherever they wanted to go. His favorite lie was about a boy named Peter who had a pet peacock with a ten-foot tail. Peter wore a golden robe that glittered so brightly that when he walked through the sunflowers they turned away from the sun to face him. When Peter was ready to go to sleep, the peacock spread his magnificent tail, enfolding the boy gently like a closing go-to-sleep flower, burying him in the gloriously iridescent, rustling vortex.[8] Yes, I must admit it. Doodle could beat me lying. **I**

200 Doodle and I spent lots of time thinking about our future. We decided that when we were grown we'd live in Old Woman Swamp and pick dog-tongue for a living. Beside the stream, he planned, we'd build us a house of whispering leaves and the swamp birds would be our chickens. All day long (when we weren't gathering dog-tongue) we'd swing through the cypresses on the rope vines, and if it rained we'd huddle beneath an umbrella tree and play stickfrog. Mama and Daddy could come and live with us if they wanted to. He even came up with the idea that he could marry Mama and I could marry Daddy. Of course, I was old enough to know this wouldn't work out, but the picture he painted was so beautiful and serene that all I could do was whisper Yes, yes.

H MAKE INFERENCES
Reread lines 181–184. Why is the narrator ashamed of himself?

I GRAMMAR AND STYLE
Reread lines 194–199. Hurst uses a variety of sentence structures, containing **independent** and **subordinate clauses**, to add rhythm and interest to his writing.

---

6. **brogans** (brō′gənz): heavy, ankle-high work shoes.

7. **Dix Hill:** common name for a mental hospital in Raleigh, North Carolina.

8. **iridescent rustling vortex:** the shimmering, rainbow-colored peacock feathers are in a funnel shape, like a whirlpool or whirlwind (vortex).

210   Once I had succeeded in teaching Doodle to walk, I began to believe in my own **infallibility,** and I prepared a terrific development program for him, unknown to Mama and Daddy, of course. I would teach him to run, to swim, to climb trees, and to fight. He, too, now believed in my infallibility, so we set the deadline for these accomplishments less than a year away, when, it had been decided, Doodle could start to school.

    That winter we didn't make much progress, for I was in school and Doodle suffered from one bad cold after another. But when spring came, rich and warm, we raised our sights again. Success lay at the end of summer like a pot of gold, and our campaign got off to a good start. On hot days, Doodle

220 and I went down to Horsehead Landing, and I gave him swimming lessons or showed him how to row a boat. Sometimes we descended into the cool greenness of Old Woman Swamp and climbed the rope vines or boxed

infallibility
(ĭn-făl′ə-bĭl′ĭ-tē) *n.* an inability to make errors

Autumn Embers (Frosted Scarlet Sage) (1944), Charles Burchfield. © Kennedy Galleries, New York.

ANALYZE VISUALS
How do the color, brush strokes, and subject matter of this painting create a **mood** of sorrow and despair?

scientifically beneath the pine where he had learned to walk. Promise hung about us like the leaves, and wherever we looked, ferns unfurled and birds broke into song.

That summer, the summer of 1918, was blighted. In May and June there was no rain and the crops withered, curled up, then died under the thirsty sun. One morning in July a hurricane came out of the east, tipping over the oaks in the yard and splitting the limbs of the elm trees. That afternoon it roared

230 back out of the west, blew the fallen oaks around, snapping their roots and tearing them out of the earth like a hawk at the entrails of a chicken. Cotton bolls were wrenched from the stalks and lay like green walnuts in the valleys between the rows, while the cornfield leaned over uniformly so that the tassels touched the ground. Doodle and I followed Daddy out into the cotton field, where he stood, shoulders sagging, surveying the ruin. When his chin sank down onto his chest, we were frightened, and Doodle slipped his hand into mine. Suddenly Daddy straightened his shoulders, raised a giant knuckly fist, and with a voice that seemed to rumble out of the earth itself began cursing heaven, hell, the weather, and the Republican Party.[9] Doodle and I, prodding

240 each other and giggling, went back to the house, knowing that everything would be all right.

---

9. **Republican Party:** In 1918, most Southerners were Democrats.

And during that summer, strange names were heard through the house: Château-Thierry, Amiens, Soissons, and in her blessing at the supper table, Mama once said, "And bless the Pearsons, whose boy Joe was lost at Belleau Wood."[10]

So we came to that clove of seasons. School was only a few weeks away, and Doodle was far behind schedule. He could barely clear the ground when climbing up the rope vines, and his swimming was certainly not passable. We decided to double our efforts, to make that last drive and reach our pot of gold. I made him swim until he turned blue and row until he couldn't lift an oar. Wherever we went, I purposely walked fast, and although he kept up, his face turned red and his eyes became glazed. Once, he could go no further, so he collapsed on the ground and began to cry.

"Aw, come on, Doodle," I urged. "You can do it. Do you want to be different from everybody else when you start school?"

"Does it make any difference?"

"It certainly does," I said. "Now, come on," and I helped him up.

As we slipped through dog days,[11] Doodle began to look feverish, and Mama felt his forehead, asking him if he felt ill. At night he didn't sleep well, and sometimes he had nightmares, crying out until I touched him and said, "Wake up, Doodle. Wake up." **J**

It was Saturday noon, just a few days before school was to start. I should have already admitted defeat, but my pride wouldn't let me. The excitement of our program had now been gone for weeks, but still we kept on with a tired **doggedness.** It was too late to turn back, for we had both wandered too far into a net of expectations and had left no crumbs behind.

Daddy, Mama, Doodle, and I were seated at the dining-room table having lunch. It was a hot day, with all the windows and doors open in case a breeze should come. In the kitchen Aunt Nicey was humming softly. After a long silence, Daddy spoke. "It's so calm, I wouldn't be surprised if we had a storm this afternoon."

"I haven't heard a rain frog," said Mama, who believed in signs, as she served the bread around the table.

"I did," declared Doodle. "Down in the swamp."

"He didn't," I said contrarily.

"You did, eh?" said Daddy, ignoring my denial.

"I certainly did," Doodle **reiterated,** scowling at me over the top of his iced-tea glass, and we were quiet again.

Suddenly, from out in the yard, came a strange croaking noise. Doodle stopped eating, with a piece of bread poised ready for his mouth, his eyes popped round like two blue buttons. "What's that?" he whispered.

J MAKE INFERENCES
What is happening to Doodle?

doggedness
(dô′gĭd-nĭs)
n. persistence; stubbornness

reiterate (rē-ĭt′ə-rāt′)
v. to repeat

---

10. **Château-Thierry** (shä-tō-tyĕ-rē′), **Amiens** (ä-myăn′), **Soissons** (swä-sōn′), . . . **Belleau** (bel′ō) **Wood:** places in France where famous battles were fought near the end of World War I (1914–1918).

11. **dog days:** the hot, uncomfortable days between early July and early September (named after the Dog Star, Sirius, which rises and sets with the sun at this time).

I jumped up, knocking over my chair, and had reached the door when Mama called, "Pick up the chair, sit down again, and say excuse me."

By the time I had done this, Doodle had excused himself and had slipped out into the yard. He was looking up into the bleeding tree. "It's a great big red bird!" he called. **K**

The bird croaked loudly again, and Mama and Daddy came out into the yard. We shaded our eyes with our hands against the hazy glare of the sun and peered up through the still leaves. On the topmost branch a bird the size of a chicken, with scarlet feathers and long legs, was perched **precariously.**
Its wings hung down loosely, and as we watched, a feather dropped away and floated slowly down through the green leaves.

"It's not even frightened of us," Mama said.

"It looks tired," Daddy added. "Or maybe sick."

Doodle's hands were clasped at his throat, and I had never seen him stand still so long. "What is it?" he asked.

Daddy shook his head. "I don't know, maybe it's—"

At that moment the bird began to flutter, but the wings were uncoordinated, and amid much flapping and a spray of flying feathers, it tumbled down, bumping through the limbs of the bleeding tree and landing at our feet with a thud. Its long, graceful neck jerked twice into an S, then straightened out, and the bird was still. A white veil came over the eyes and the long white beak unhinged. Its legs were crossed and its clawlike feet were delicately curved at rest. Even death did not mar its grace, for it lay on the earth like a broken vase of red flowers, and we stood around it, awed by its **exotic** beauty. **L**

"It's dead," Mama said.

"What is it?" Doodle repeated.

"Go bring me the bird book," said Daddy.

I ran into the house and brought back the bird book. As we watched, Daddy thumbed through its pages. "It's a scarlet ibis," he said, pointing to a picture. "It lives in the tropics—South America to Florida. A storm must have brought it here."

Sadly, we all looked back at the bird. A scarlet ibis! How many miles it had traveled to die like this, in *our* yard, beneath the bleeding tree.

"Let's finish lunch," Mama said, nudging us back toward the dining room.

"I'm not hungry," said Doodle, and he knelt down beside the ibis.

"We've got peach cobbler for dessert," Mama tempted from the doorway.

Doodle remained kneeling. "I'm going to bury him."

"Don't you dare touch him," Mama warned. "There's no telling what disease he might have had."

"All right," said Doodle. "I won't."

Daddy, Mama, and I went back to the dining-room table, but we watched Doodle through the open door. He took out a piece of string from his pocket

SYMBOL
What clues suggest that the appearance of the bird might be important?

precariously
(prĭ-kâr′ē-əs-lē) *adv.*
insecurely; in a dangerous or unstable way

exotic (ĭg-zŏt′ĭk) *adj.*
excitingly strange

SYMBOL
What characteristics of the scarlet ibis are emphasized in lines 298–306?

and, without touching the ibis, looped one end around its neck. Slowly, while singing softly "Shall We Gather at the River," he carried the bird around to the front yard and dug a hole in the flower garden, next to the petunia bed. Now we were watching him through the front window, but he didn't know it. His awkwardness at digging the hole with a shovel whose handle was twice as long
330 as he was made us laugh, and we covered our mouths with our hands so he wouldn't hear.

When Doodle came into the dining room, he found us seriously eating our cobbler. He was pale and lingered just inside the screen door. "Did you get the scarlet ibis buried?" asked Daddy.

Doodle didn't speak but nodded his head.

"Go wash your hands, and then you can have some peach cobbler," said Mama.

"I'm not hungry," he said.

"Dead birds is bad luck," said Aunt Nicey, poking her head from the
340 kitchen door. "Specially *red* dead birds!" Ⓜ

As soon as I had finished eating, Doodle and I hurried off to Horsehead Landing. Time was short, and Doodle still had a long way to go if he was going to keep up with the other boys when he started school. The sun, gilded with the yellow cast of autumn, still burned fiercely, but the dark green woods through which we passed were shady and cool. When we reached the landing, Doodle said he was too tired to swim, so we got into a skiff and floated down the creek with the tide. Far off in the marsh a rail was scolding, and over on the beach locusts were singing in the myrtle trees. Doodle did not speak and kept his head turned away, letting one hand trail limply in the water.

350 After we had drifted a long way, I put the oars in place and made Doodle row back against the tide. Black clouds began to gather in the southwest, and he kept watching them, trying to pull the oars a little faster. When we reached Horsehead Landing, lightning was playing across half the sky and thunder roared out, hiding even the sound of the sea. The sun disappeared and darkness descended, almost like night. Flocks of marsh crows flew by, heading inland to their roosting trees; and two egrets, squawking, arose from the oyster-rock shallows and careened away.

Doodle was both tired and frightened, and when he stepped from the skiff he collapsed onto the mud, sending an armada of fiddler crabs rustling off into
360 the marsh grass. I helped him up, and as he wiped the mud off his trousers, he smiled at me ashamedly. He had failed and we both knew it, so we started back home, racing the storm. We never spoke (What are the words that can solder[12] cracked pride?), but I knew he was watching me, watching for a sign of mercy. The lightning was near now, and from fear he walked so close behind me he kept stepping on my heels. The faster I walked, the faster he walked, so

Ⓜ **SYMBOL**
What is the connection between Doodle and the scarlet ibis?

---

12. **solder** (sŏd´ər): to join or bond together.

I began to run. The rain was coming, roaring through the pines, and then, like a bursting Roman candle, a gum tree ahead of us was shattered by a bolt of lightning. When the deafening peal of thunder had died, and in the moment before the rain arrived, I heard Doodle, who had fallen behind, cry out,
370 "Brother, Brother, don't leave me! Don't leave me!"

The knowledge that Doodle's and my plans had come to naught[13] was bitter, and that streak of cruelty within me awakened. I ran as fast as I could, leaving him far behind with a wall of rain dividing us. The drops stung my face like nettles, and the wind flared the wet glistening leaves of the bordering trees. Soon I could hear his voice no more. **N**

I hadn't run too far before I became tired, and the flood of childish spite **evanesced** as well. I stopped and waited for Doodle. The sound of rain was everywhere, but the wind had died and it fell straight down in parallel paths like ropes hanging from the sky. As I waited, I peered through the downpour, but no
380 one came. Finally I went back and found him huddled beneath a red nightshade bush beside the road. He was sitting on the ground, his face buried in his arms, which were resting on his drawn-up knees. "Let's go, Doodle," I said.

He didn't answer, so I placed my hand on his forehead and lifted his head. Limply, he fell backward onto the earth. He had been bleeding from the mouth, and his neck and the front of his shirt were stained a brilliant red.

"Doodle! Doodle!" I cried, shaking him, but there was no answer but the ropy rain. He lay very awkwardly, with his head thrown far back, making his vermilion[14] neck appear unusually long and slim. His little legs, bent sharply at the knees, had never before seemed so fragile, so thin.
390 I began to weep, and the tear-blurred vision in red before me looked very familiar. "Doodle!" I screamed above the pounding storm and threw my body to the earth above his. For a long long time, it seemed forever, I lay there crying, sheltering my fallen scarlet ibis from the **heresy** of rain. ❧

N MAKE INFERENCES
Why does the narrator continue to run when he knows Doodle has fallen behind him?

evanesce (ĕv′ə-nĕs′) v. to disappear; vanish

heresy (hĕr′ĭ-sē) n. an action or opinion contrary to what is generally thought of as right

---

13. **had come to naught:** had resulted in nothing.

14. **vermilion** (vər-mĭl′yən): bright red to reddish orange.

W O M A N
with *Flower*

Naomi Long Madgett

I wouldn't coax the plant if I were you.
Such watchful nurturing may do it harm.
Let the soil rest from so much digging
And wait until it's dry before you water it.
5 The leaf's inclined to find its own direction;
Give it a chance to seek the sunlight for itself.

Much growth is stunted by too careful prodding,
Too eager tenderness.
The things we love we have to learn to leave alone.

After Reading

Comprehension

1. **Clarify** How is Doodle different from other children?

2. **Recall** What are the narrator's motives for teaching Doodle?

3. **Summarize** What happens to Doodle, and why?

READING STANDARD
A.1.3.1 Make inferences

Literary Analysis

4. **Make Inferences** Look back at the chart you made as you read. Review the inferences you made about the relationship between Doodle and the narrator. How would you describe their relationship over the course of the story?

5. **Analyze Character** The narrator has **mixed emotions** about Doodle. How might he answer the big question on page 426?

6. **Interpret Symbol** The narrator sees Doodle as the scarlet ibis at the end, but Doodle identifies with the exotic bird immediately. To explore this symbolic connection, identify as many similarities between the ibis and Doodle as you can. Record your comparison in a chart like the one shown.

> *Scarlet Ibis and Doodle*
>
> *Both are unusual and don't fit in their surroundings.*

7. **Analyze Theme and Symbol** Which of the following themes does the **symbolism** of the ibis support? Find details to support your answer.

   a. Selfish pride generally causes more harm than good.

   b. Delicate creatures need to be protected and cared for.

   c. Spiteful cruelty toward a loved one often stems from wounded pride.

8. **Examine Foreshadowing and Mood** Reread lines 298–306. The dramatic death of the ibis foreshadows Doodle's death. Find at least three other examples of such foreshadowing. What mood do they create?

9. **Compare Literary Works** What advice does the speaker in "Woman with Flower" seem to offer the narrator of "The Scarlet Ibis"? In what ways are the themes of these works similar? In what ways are they different?

Literary Criticism

10. **Author's Style** "The Scarlet Ibis" can be viewed as an example of Southern literature, which is characterized in part by its emphasis on details of time and place, the importance of family and community, an exploration of the past, and a sense of moral dilemma. How are these characteristics evident in this story? Cite details from the story to support your answer.

THE SCARLET IBIS **443**

Vocabulary in Context

VOCABULARY PRACTICE

Identify the word that is not related in meaning to the other words in the set.

1. (a) exotic, (b) ordinary, (c) unusual, (d) foreign
2. (a) impending, (b) imminent, (c) approaching, (d) remote
3. (a) fidelity, (b) heresy, (c) conformity, (d) compliance
4. (a) echo, (b) repeat, (c) originate, (d) reiterate
5. (a) errancy, (b) infallibility, (c) inaccuracy, (d) imperfection
6. (a) insecurely, (b) cleverly, (c) precariously, (d) dangerously
7. (a) disappear, (b) float, (c) vanish, (d) evanesce
8. (a) doggedness, (b) perseverance, (c) tenacity, (d) casualness

WORD LIST

doggedness

evanesce

exotic

heresy

imminent

infallibility

precariously

reiterate

VOCABULARY IN WRITING

Use at least four vocabulary words in a paragraph that describes Doodle. Make sure that your paragraph creates a vivid image of him. Here is an example.

> **EXAMPLE SENTENCE**
>
> *From the very beginning, Doodle was like an **exotic** bird, staring at everyone with his arms flapping about.*

VOCABULARY STRATEGY: CONNOTATION

PENNSYLVANIA STANDARDS

READING STANDARD
A.1.1 Apply the meaning of vocabulary

The term **connotation** refers to the attitudes or feelings associated with a word. For example, *doggedness* and *stubbornness* could both be defined as "the quality of not giving in readily," but Hurst's choice of the word *doggedness* to describe Doodle's efforts conveys positive connotations not associated with *stubbornness*. Writers use connotation to communicate certain feelings and to evoke a mood. Being aware of these connotations can enrich your understanding of what you read.

PRACTICE Place the words in each group on a continuum like the one shown to show the positive or negative associations each word connotes. Then compare your answers with those of a classmate.

highly negative ← ————————————— → *highly positive*

1. talk, vent, articulate
2. new, fresh, original
3. choosy, finicky, particular
4. smile, smirk, grin
5. responsibility, obligation, duty

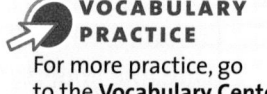

VOCABULARY PRACTICE
For more practice, go to the **Vocabulary Center** at ClassZone.com.

Reading-Writing Connection

Add to your understanding of "The Scarlet Ibis" by responding to these prompts. Then use **Revision: Grammar and Style** to improve your writing.

WRITING PROMPTS	SELF-CHECK
A. Short Response: Analyze Character What is your opinion of Doodle's character? Write a **one- or two-paragraph response** that discusses his strengths and weaknesses, his fears, his imagination, and his relationship with his brother.	*A successful explanation will . . .* • identify at least one strength and one weakness • include details or examples that support your opinion
B. Extended Response: Analyze Actions Do you blame the narrator for what happens to Doodle? Consider his age, his **mixed emotions,** and what he says about himself. Write a **three-to-five-paragraph response** analyzing his role in Doodle's death.	*A strong analysis will . . .* • explain your judgment of the narrator's actions • provide examples and quotations from the story

REVISION: GRAMMAR AND STYLE

WRITING STANDARD
1.5.11.D.1 Use different types and lengths of sentences

VARY SENTENCE STRUCTURE Review the **Grammar and Style** note on page 434. Hurst uses a variety of sentence structures in his writing. Using only one type of sentence can make your writing sound dull.

All complete sentences contain at least one **independent clause,** which can stand on its own (*Doodle went to sleep.*) Some combine the independent clause or clauses with one or more **subordinate clauses,** which cannot stand alone. (*Doodle went to sleep <u>while the family ate dinner.</u>*) This kind of variety, as found in this passage from Hurst's story, makes for better-sounding prose:

> *I lifted him out and set him down in the soft rubber grass beside a tall pine. His eyes were round with wonder as he gazed about him, and his little hands began to stroke the rubber grass.* (lines 87–89)

Notice how the revisions in red improve the rhythm of this first draft. Revise your responses to the prompts by incorporating a variety of sentence structures.

STUDENT MODEL

The narrator sometimes shows he cares for Doodle. ^but^ He also seems to enjoy
making his brother feel trapped and alone. ^as if^ ~~He treats~~ Doodle ~~like~~ ^were^ an animal.
In reality, Doodle is just a child. ^who^ /He does his best to overcome a serious illness.

WRITING TOOLS
For prewriting, revision, and editing tools, visit the **Writing Center** at ClassZone.com.

Math and After Math
Essay by Lensey Namioka

What are you really GOOD *at?*

PENNSYLVANIA STANDARDS

READING STANDARDS
A.2.4.1 Identify and/or explain stated or implied main ideas
B.3.3.4 Analyze the sequence

KEY IDEA Knowing what you're good at can take you a long way toward finding work and activities that you enjoy. In "Math and After Math," Lensey Namioka describes how she first embarked on one career path and then later discovered her true **talent.**

DISCUSS Make a list of activities you particularly enjoy. For each one, list the skills that help you succeed at the activity. With a partner, brainstorm career possibilities that could make use of those skills.

> Cooking
> • ability to follow recipes
> • knack for combining ingredients

● ELEMENTS OF NONFICTION: IMPLIED MAIN IDEA

In nonfiction, the writer's central idea or message is called the **main idea.** The main idea may be stated directly, or it may be implied or suggested through details or anecdotes.

In "Math and After Math," Lensey Namioka develops the main idea primarily through a series of anecdotes. To identify the implied main idea as you read, ask yourself, What important idea is conveyed by the anecdotes? How does this idea relate to the author's conclusion?

● READING SKILL: ANALYZE SEQUENCE OF EVENTS

The events in a memoir are not always described in the same sequence in which they occurred. When relating events, a writer may move back and forth in time to make a point. This skipping around in time can be confusing, however, so it's important for the reader to keep track of the real **sequence of events.** Signal words, such as *when, by the time,* or *for years,* help to clarify this sequence.

As you read "Math and After Math," use a chart to jot down the important events in each stage of Namioka's life. Then number them in the order they occurred in time.

Stage in Life	Order	Event
Second grade		Namioka suffers "abacus anxiety."
Years later		Family emigrates to America. Math is best subject.

▲ VOCABULARY IN CONTEXT

Lensey Namioka uses the following boldfaced words to tell her tale of personal discovery. Use context clues to determine the meaning of each one.

1. The speaker's **dialect** revealed that he was not a native of the area.
2. The movie's **scenario** included no plot twists or surprises.
3. Her ability to act is **intuitive;** she has never had a lesson.
4. The detective's **analytic** approach to solving problems led him to the killer.
5. Your **hypothesis** will not stand up to further testing.

Author Online

Always an Outsider
Lensey Namioka was born in China and moved to the United States when she was nine years old. She has lived in many places and, consequently, has felt herself to be something of an outsider wherever she has lived. It's not surprising, then, that the protagonists in her stories for young adults are usually outsiders too.

Lensey Namioka born 1929

Multicultural Author Namioka's writing draws on both her Chinese heritage and her husband's Japanese heritage. She has written humorous novels about young Chinese immigrants in America, as well as a series of adventure-mystery books about two 16th-century Japanese samurai.

MORE ABOUT THE AUTHOR
For more on Lensey Namioka, visit the **Literature Center** at **ClassZone.com.**

Background

Girls and Math In "Math and After Math," Namioka describes how she stood out in her American classrooms as a girl who was good at math. Researchers have long sought to determine whether the differences in math performance between girls and boys stem from biology or culture. In elementary school, girls tend to outperform boys in many subjects, including math. In high school, however, the situation changes. Statistics show that, as a group, boys score slightly higher than girls on math aptitude tests. Also, boys tend to choose math-related college majors and careers more often than girls do, although this is changing. Researchers continue to debate various hypotheses that explain these gender differences.

Math

and After Math

LENSEY NAMIOKA

ANALYZE VISUALS
What elements of the photograph reflect the writer's attitude toward math?

"Seven!" shouted the teacher.

Or did he shout "Four"?

I shrank down in my seat. Math class was an absolute nightmare. The teacher scared me so much that my hands got sweaty, and my fingers slipped on the abacus[1] beads.

I was in the second grade when I discovered that I suffered from abacus anxiety. The trouble was that I was going to a school where the teacher spoke a different **dialect.** I grew up with Mandarin, the dialect spoken by the majority of the Chinese. When the eastern part of China was occupied by the Japanese, 10 our family moved inland, to a region where I could barely understand the local dialect.

Writing was pretty much the same in any dialect, so in language and history classes I didn't have trouble with what was on the blackboard. My problems started in the math class, where we had to learn the abacus. Before the days of the calculator, the abacus was the main tool for adding and multiplying. It still is, in many parts of China (as well as in countries like Japan and Russia).

The abacus teacher would shout out the numbers he wanted us to add or multiply. My ears didn't always understand what he said, so *seven,* for instance, sounded a lot like *four.*

dialect (dī′ə-lĕkt′) *n.* a variety of a standard language unique to a certain region or social group

---

1. **abacus** (ăb′ə-kəs): a manual computing device consisting of rods hung within a frame and strung with movable counters.

20 Until that class, math was one of my better subjects, especially when it came to multiplication. Years later, when we emigrated to America, I was astounded to hear one of my American friends recite the multiplication table:

"Two times one is two. Two times two is four. Two times three is six . . ." It seemed to take forever. 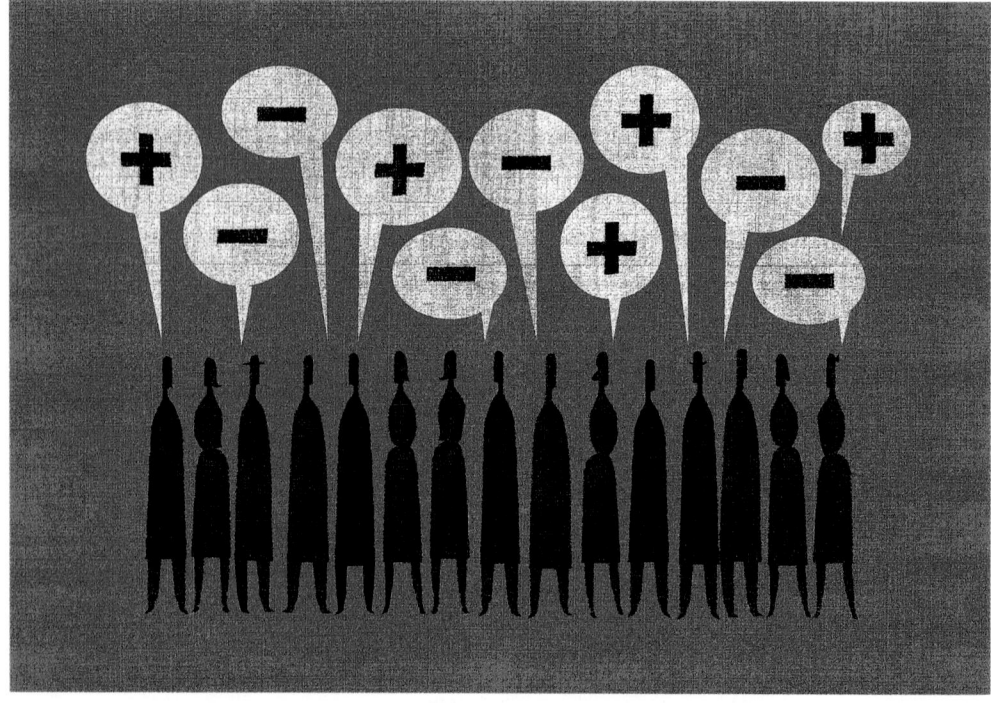 A

The multiplication table is much shorter in Chinese. One reason is that the Chinese names for numbers are all one-syllable. We don't have numbers like *seven*.

Also, we omit words like *times* and *equals* while reciting. Instead of "Seven times two equals fourteen," we say, *Er qi shi si,* or literally, *two seven fourteen.* So we do it in four syllables instead of eight.

30 The best trick is that we memorize only half as many entries, because we know that seven times two is the same as two times seven. (I learned later this was called the Commutative Law.)

This meant I could rattle off the multiplication table about three times faster than my American classmates. But I learned the table even faster than my *Chinese* classmates. The reason was that I sang it.

"You can remember a tune better than a string of numbers," my father told me. "So I want you to sing the multiplication table."

The standard way to teach musical notation in Chinese schools was to give numbers to the diatonic scale:[2] *do* was one (not a female deer), *re* was two (not

40 a ray of sunshine), *mi* was three, and so on. When I had to remember that two times seven was fourteen, my father told me to hum the little tune *re ti do fa.* This was not a pretty tune, but it certainly stuck in my mind.

---

2. **diatonic** (dī′ə-tŏn′ĭk) **scale:** the standard musical scale of seven tones, often referred to as *do, re, mi, fa, sol, la,* and *ti.*

A SEQUENCE OF EVENTS
Reread lines 20–24. Which words indicate the passage of time?

© Images.com/Corbis

Following Father's suggestion, I learned the multiplication table very quickly, and even now I still hum. The other day, when I was in the store buying candy bars, I noticed another customer staring at me. I was trying to figure out if my fistful of change was enough for four candy bars, and I must have been humming as I multiplied.

When I entered American schools, my best subject was math. I didn't need to know much English to manage the Arabic numbers,[3] and my Chinese
50 school had been a year ahead of American schools in math (because of shorter multiplication tables, maybe). **Ⓑ**

After a while I realized that my classmates found me weird. During our early years in America, my family lived in towns where there weren't too many Asians, and I looked different from everybody else in class. It turned out that my weirdness wasn't just because I looked different, or because I hummed funny tunes.

"How come you're so good at math?" asked one of my classmates.

"Why shouldn't I be?" I asked.

"You're a girl!"
60 In America, apparently, it was unusual for a girl to be good at math. It was different in China, where women were good at figures. They regularly kept the household accounts and managed the family budget.

A few years ago, I saw a movie about Chinese-Americans called *Dim Sum.*[4] A Chinese man who ran a restaurant in Chinatown brought his receipts to a woman friend, who figured out his accounts for him.

My American friends found the situation strange. "It's not unusual at all," I told them. "In my family, for instance, my mother made the major financial decisions."

In fact, my mother made a financial killing when we were living in Berkeley,
70 California. A neighbor took her to a land auction. A piece of land near our house was offered for sale, and Mother thought it would be fun to bid on it. Someone was bound to top her bid, she thought.

She was stunned when nobody else made a bid, and Mother found herself the owner of a large plot of land.

As she and her friend prepared to leave the auction room, a man rushed up to them. He was a realtor who had planned to bid for the land, but had arrived at the auction too late.

"I'll give you whatever you paid, plus something extra!" he told Mother.

"No, thank you," said Mother. "I'm quite happy with the purchase."
80 The realtor raised his offer, but Mother still turned him down. He became frantic. "Look, I'll go as high as two thousand dollars above your bid!"

This just made Mother more stubborn. "No, I want to keep the land."

The realtor obtained our address and phone number, and immediately called our house.

Ⓑ IMPLIED MAIN IDEA
Consider Namioka's childhood success with math. What is she implying about Chinese math education?

---

3. **Arabic numbers:** the numerical symbols *1, 2, 3, 4, 5, 6, 7, 8, 9,* and *0.*

4. ***Dim Sum:*** the movie title refers to a Chinese cuisine in which small portions of a variety of foods, including an assortment of dumplings, are served.

When Father answered the phone, the realtor shouted, "Do you know what your wife just did? She threw away a chance to make two thousand dollars!"

"I'm sure she had her reasons," Father answered calmly. Nothing that the realtor said could disturb him.

90 The land turned out to be an excellent investment, and helped to provide a tidy nest egg for my parents in their old age. **C**

In many other Asian countries, too, the housewife is the one who manages money. It's normal for the husband to hand over his paycheck to his wife, and out of it she gives him an allowance. Perhaps it's the result of Confucius's teaching[5] that a gentleman is above money, so it's the woman's duty to be concerned with such petty matters.

Things were very different in America. An American husband would hit the roof if his wife did what my mother had done. Women here were supposed to be hopeless when it came to money matters and figures.

100 Many girls got good math grades in elementary school, but their grades began to slip when they entered middle school. By then they were getting interested in boys, and they didn't want the boys to think they were weird.

I was weird in elementary and middle school because I was a real whiz at multiplication. In high school, I continued to be a whiz in my geometry and algebra classes. I was lucky to have a geometry teacher who addressed us by last name and didn't care whether you were a boy or a girl, as long as you agreed with Euclid.[6]

My high school geometry class was also the first place where the word *argument* meant something good. My parents complained that I was always arguing. In geometry class, making an argument meant presenting something 110 in an orderly, logical manner.

I also liked the story or word problems in my algebra class. Years later, when I was teaching math, I couldn't understand why many students complained bitterly about them. To me, story problems meant fiction, romance. The most **D** exciting one involved an army column marching forward at a certain speed. A messenger at the head of the column was sent back to the rear. If the column was so many miles long, would he be able to deliver his message in time? I pictured the following **scenario:**

"We expect to engage the enemy in half an hour," the commander told the messenger. "You have to get word to the men in the rear of the column!"
120 The mud-splashed rider desperately lashed his horse, while arrows fell on him from ambushers. How fast did he have to ride so that he would reach the rear guard in time to deliver his message?

Attacking these story problems with relish, I was usually one of the first in the class to finish, and I was often sent to the board to write out the solution.

C **IMPLIED MAIN IDEA**
Reread Namioka's anecdote about her mother's real estate purchase. What is the main idea of this anecdote?

D **SEQUENCE OF EVENTS**
In this paragraph Namioka flashes forward to her adulthood. What is she able to reveal by doing this?

scenario (sǐ-nâr′ē-ō′) *n.* a description of a possible course of action or events

---

5. **Confucius's** (kən-fyoō′shəs-ĭz) **teaching:** the Chinese philosopher Confucius (551–479 B.C.) taught ideas about practical moral values that are still widely followed in China today.

6. **Euclid** (yoō′klĭd): a third-century-B.C. Greek mathematician upon whose ideas much of the study of geometry in schools is based.

A math lecture in a university lecture hall

By the time I started college, I began to realize that it was unusual, unnatural—maybe even unhealthy—for girls to be good at math. I entered Radcliffe College, which was connected with Harvard. Some of my laboratory courses were taken together with the Harvard students, but classes such as English and math were taught separately on the small Radcliffe campus.

130 The English classes usually had around twenty students, but my beginning calculus class had only five of us. According to rumor, new instructors at Harvard were assigned to teach Radcliffe math classes as a test.

"If they manage to get through the year without breaking down, they're allowed to go on to higher things," we heard.

On the first day of our math class, the instructor (who later became a famous mathematician) crept into the room without looking at us, and spent the whole period mumbling into the blackboard. In fact, he spent the whole year mumbling into the blackboard.

"He's awfully shy, isn't he?" I remarked to a friend.

140 "Maybe he's just scared of girls who study math," she said.

Things got better when I entered the University of California, which was co-ed. The math classes were larger, and five girls in a class of forty boys weren't enough to scare the instructors.

By this time I knew that in America a girl who was good at math was not only unusual, unnatural, unhealthy, but—worst of all—unattractive.

"Boys don't date you if you're a math whiz," I was told. **E**

The situation was different for me. First of all, racial cross-dating was still rare when I was in college, so I dated only Chinese-American boys, who were hardened to the sight of their mothers or sisters doing math.

150 I got very good grades in math throughout my school years and majored in mathematics in college. I had a head start in the multiplication table, and I loved arguing and proving things. By the time I learned that I wasn't supposed to do well in math, it was too late.

A hot topic when I was in graduate school was the right-brain, left-brain debate. Scientists decided that men tended to use their left brain, which was the reasoning part, while women used their right brain, the **intuitive** part.

"That's why we're good at hard sciences and math," the boys in my classes assured us. "You girls should stick with poetry, history, art, and things like that. It's a matter of genes or hormones."

160 Then, later studies showed that the Japanese listened to insect sounds with their left (**analytic**) brain, while Westerners listened to insects with their right brain. Still other studies showed that professional musicians (both male and female) listened to music with the analytic side of their brain, while the general public listened with their intuitive side.

It began to seem that training and social pressure, not genes and hormones, influenced which side of the brain was used. I eagerly followed the debate and could hardly wait for the day when it was okay for women to study science and math in America. **F**

Today, attitudes are finally beginning to change. My daughters tell me that
170 girls in high school math classes are less afraid to do well, and many women go into science and math in college. (One of my daughters is a computer scientist, and the other is an engineer.)

For years, I seemed to be doing well in math because of my Chinese background, because I wasn't afraid to get good math grades in school. I did all the assigned problems without much trouble. But it wasn't enough to do all the problems assigned by the teacher. To be a creative mathematician, you also have to make up problems. I finally learned that I would never do really original work in mathematics.

I found that, for math at least, I lacked what the Chinese call *huo qi,*[7]
180 literally "fiery breath," in other words, ambition and drive. In English the

E IMPLIED MAIN IDEA
What do Namioka's anecdotes about college suggest is the main reason that American girls do poorly in math?

intuitive (ĭn-tōō'ĭ-tĭv) *adj.* based on what seems to be true without conscious reasoning; instinctive

analytic (ăn'ə-lĭt'ĭk) *adj.* using logical reasoning or analysis

F IMPLIED MAIN IDEA
Reread lines 160–168. How do these later studies on the brain support Namioka's main idea?

---

7. *huo qi* (hwō chē).

expression "fire in the belly" comes close. I didn't think I was creative enough in mathematics to do good research, nor did I have the drive. **G**

My immediate excuse for getting out of math was the difficulty of arranging for childcare. To be completely honest, I have to admit that I left mathematics because I wasn't all that good, despite my early impressive grades.

I made the transition from mathematics to freelance writing through translation work. For a brief period, I translated mathematical papers from Chinese into English.

190 My work dried up, however, when the Cultural Revolution[8] swept over China. Mathematicians, like other scholars, were ordered to stop research and write papers confessing their political shortcomings. (These were the lucky ones. The unlucky ones spent their time cleaning latrines.) With no mathematical papers to translate, I eventually took up freelance writing.

My parents reproached me. "How can you give up a beautiful subject like mathematics?"

"We can admire beautiful pictures or music," I told them. "But we don't all have the gift to paint or compose."

"You spent so many years studying math," some people say. "Does it help you at all in your writing?"

200 Math has taught me the useful lesson of thrift. I've met hundreds of mathematicians, and not one of them was a spendthrift. In math you're taught to squeeze the strongest possible result out of the weakest possible **hypothesis**—in other words, you try to get the most value for your money.

This thrifty habit stayed with me after I became a writer. When I put people or events into a book, I squeeze the most out of them. Very few things are thrown in and then forgotten later. As a result my plots seem to be carefully worked out in advance, instead of being made up as I go along.

Years ago, I enjoyed story problems because the stories fired my imagination. In fact, writing fiction was where I finally found my "fiery breath." Instead 210 of story problems, I can write problem stories. And that's what I'm still doing today. ✎

G IMPLIED MAIN IDEA
What does Namioka suggest is needed in order for a person to express a true talent?

hypothesis (hī-pŏth′ĭ-sĭs) *n.* an assumption made in order to test its possible consequences

---

8. **Cultural Revolution:** a political upheaval in China in the 1960s that resulted in many attacks on intellectuals.

Comprehension

1. **Recall** Why did Namioka do so well in math as a young child?

2. **Recall** In the United States, how did Namioka's classmates regard her talent for math? Why?

3. **Summarize** According to Namioka, what is the typical Chinese attitude about girls' and women's abilities in the area of math?

4. **Clarify** Why did Namioka finally give up her work in mathematics?

Critical Analysis

5. **Compare and Contrast Cultures** What is the main cultural difference discussed in this selection? Support your answer with details from the selection.

6. **Analyze Conflict** In this essay, Namioka traces her struggle to determine her true **talent.** What part of this conflict is **internal?** What part is **external?** Give reasons for your responses.

7. **Identify Implied Main Idea** In your own words, state the main idea of this selection. Cite evidence from the selection to support your answer.

8. **Evaluate Sequence** On your sequence chart, review the parts of the essay where Namioka describes events out of chronological order. In each case, evaluate the effect of this change of sequence. Do you think this is a good technique? Cite evidence to explain your opinion.

9. **Make Judgments** How do contemporary views on women's talent in math compare with those discussed in this selection? Cite evidence to support your claim.

PENNSYLVANIA STANDARDS

READING STANDARD
A.2.4.1 Identify and/or explain stated or implied main ideas

Vocabulary in Context

VOCABULARY PRACTICE

Decide whether these statements are true or false.

1. If you have an **intuitive** understanding of a procedure, you will probably check each step as you go.
2. Spanish is a **dialect** of English.
3. A student asking for more homework is an unlikely **scenario.**
4. A **hypothesis** is often the first step in an investigation.
5. A person with an **analytic** mind could probably be a successful mathematician.

WORD LIST

analytic

dialect

hypothesis

intuitive

scenario

VOCABULARY IN WRITING

Write a summary of this memoir using at least three of the vocabulary words. Here is a sample opening.

> **EXAMPLE SENTENCE**
>
> *The teacher's **dialect** confused young Namioka and stopped her from doing her best in math.*

VOCABULARY STRATEGY: USING CONTEXT CLUES

Dialect refers to a variety of speech that differs from the standard speech patterns of a given culture. Vocabulary is one element of dialect. For example, a person might refer to a sweet, carbonated beverage as a soda, a pop, or a soft drink, depending on where he or she lives in the United States. You can often infer the meaning of a word in dialect by noting **context clues** in the sentences and paragraphs that surround the word.

PRACTICE Identify the meaning of the underlined term in each sentence. Use context clues and your own knowledge to determine its meaning. Work with other students to try to identify where or by whom the term is mostly used.

1. Put a <u>schmeer</u> of cream cheese on that bagel.
2. The <u>gumbands</u> holding the papers together were old and frayed.
3. You can pack your lunch in that little <u>poke</u>.
4. My grandparents lived on the top floor of the <u>two-flat</u> where I grew up.
5. That <u>plug</u> ought to be put out to pasture.
6. After drinking the chocolate <u>frappé</u>, he wasn't hungry for dinner.
7. Leon is getting together with his <u>homeboys</u>.
8. You can get some water from the <u>bubbler</u> in the hallway.

PENNSYLVANIA STANDARDS

READING STANDARD
A.1.2.2 Use context clues

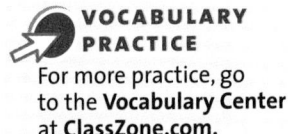

VOCABULARY PRACTICE
For more practice, go to the **Vocabulary Center** at **ClassZone.com.**

The Future in My Arms
Essay by Edwidge Danticat

What does a community OWE *its* CHILDREN?

PENNSYLVANIA STANDARDS

READING STANDARDS
A.2.4.1 Identify and/or explain main ideas and relevant details

A.2.6.1 Describe the author's purpose

KEY IDEA Parents, of course, have a huge commitment to their children. But what is the **responsibility** of a community to its young? A familiar African proverb states, "It takes a village to raise a child." Do you agree?

QUICKWRITE In a small group, discuss how people in your community have influenced your life. Did someone teach you to play soccer or baseball? What about the person who always made a point of asking how you were doing? Create a concept web, as shown, with people who have helped you. Then choose one person and write a paragraph describing how he or she has made a difference in your life.

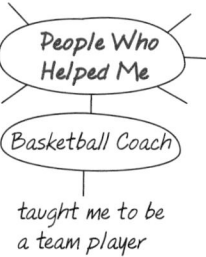

People Who Helped Me

Basketball Coach

taught me to be a team player

LITERARY ANALYSIS: AUTHOR'S PERSPECTIVE

An **author's perspective** is the lens through which a writer views a subject. This lens is made up of the writer's ideas, values, feelings, and beliefs—products of the writer's life experiences and cultural upbringing. For example, in "Math and After Math" (page 448), Lensey Namioka writes from the perspective of a Chinese–American female who has a talent for math and was raised to believe that it is "not unusual at all" for a woman to excel at mathematics. Readers learn her perspective from direct statements as well as anecdotes that illustrate her views.

As you read "The Future in My Arms," determine Edwidge Danticat's perspective by examining the following:

- statements of opinion
- tone, or attitude
- diction, or word choice
- repeated words or ideas
- the descriptions of cultural customs
- the portrayal of her niece

READING STRATEGY: MONITOR

Monitoring is the strategy of checking your comprehension as you read and intentionally using other strategies to improve it. For example, if as you read you realize that you are not understanding the text very well, you might decide you need to slow down your reading pace, reread, or skim the next section before reading it. With "The Future in My Arms," the following strategies may be especially helpful:

- **Predict** what will happen later in the selection.
- **Question** the events described and their significance.
- **Reread** passages that you find confusing.

As you read, keep track of your thoughts, ideas, and questions by jotting them down.

Author Online

An Early Start
When Edwidge Danticat came to the United States from Haiti at the age of 12, she had a hard time fitting in at school. She sought refuge in writing and began a story that would develop into her first novel, *Breath, Eyes, Memory.* She published the novel in 1994, when she was in her mid-20s, after earning a Master of Fine Arts degree in creative writing from Brown University. Other major works include *Krik? Krak!, The Farming of Bones,* and *The Dew Breaker.*

**Edwidge Danticat
born 1969**

One Voice in a Million Critics have acclaimed Danticat as "the voice of Haitian Americans," but she resists the title. Danticat says, "There are millions and millions of Haitian voices. Mine is only one. My greatest hope is that mine becomes one voice in a giant chorus that is trying to understand and express artistically what it's like to be a Haitian immigrant in the United States."

 MORE ABOUT THE AUTHOR
For more on Edwidge Danticat, visit the **Literature Center** at ClassZone.com.

Background

The Haitian Diaspora Danticat's transition into a new country and culture was eased by the support of her family and of the Haitian community in Brooklyn, New York. Many Haitians emigrate to the United States and other countries to escape the extreme poverty and political instability of their native country. This emigration of hundreds of thousands of Haitians to other countries has been called the Haitian Diaspora.

THE FUTURE in My Arms. Ⓐ

Edwidge Danticat

I had never held any living thing so tiny in my hands. Six pounds and one ounce, lighter than my smallest dumbbell was my newborn niece, her face bright pink, her eyes tightly shut, her body coiled around itself in a fetal position, still defiantly resisting the world into which she'd just been thrust. I had been awaiting her birth with feverish anticipation; I was going away for the summer, and I didn't want to leave before she was born, only to come back eight weeks later and find that she had grown accustomed to most things in the world except her only auntie on her father's side, the sole woman child in a family of men, who all her life had dreamed of having a sister. Ⓑ

10   She arrived the day before I was to leave. I was at the Brooklyn Public Library researching an article when I called to check my messages. In a breathless voice, my brother Andre announced, "You are now the proud aunt of Nadira Amahs Danticat.[1] Her name means, 'She whom God has chosen.'"

I ran out of the library and headed toward a flower shop on Flatbush Avenue. As I approached, I heard someone call out my name. It was my brother Karl and Mia, who were expecting their own child in a few months. They, too, were heading to the hospital to see Nadira.

On the way there, I remembered a message that a girlfriend of mine, a new mother, had sent me for my thirtieth birthday a few months before. "May 20 your arms always be a repozwa, a place where a child can rest her head," it said. I had told her that two of my brothers were becoming fathers, and she wanted me to share those words with them. But I'd decided to wait until both my niece and nephew were born to share this with their parents—that we had each become a *repozwa,*[2] the Haitian Creole[3] term for "sacred place," in whose shelter children would now seek rest.

---

1. **Nadira Amahs Danticat** (nä-dîr'ä ä-mäs' dăn-tĭ-kä').
2. *repozwa* (râ-pōz-wä').
3. **Haitian Creole:** the French-based language spoken in Haiti.

Ⓐ **MONITOR**
Based on the essay title and the painting, what do you **predict** this essay will be about?

Ⓑ **AUTHOR'S PERSPECTIVE**
What do lines 1–9 reveal about Danticat's attitude toward children, especially her niece? Cite details.

ANALYZE VISUALS
What elements of this painting suggest the idea of *repozwa* mentioned and defined in lines 22–25?

Mama's Cradle, April Harrison. Mixed media collage on canvas board, 14″ × 18″. © April Harrison.

By the time we got to the hospital, my sister-in-law, Carol, had already had a few visitors. She appeared exhausted but in good spirits as she and Andre took us down the corridor to the maternity-ward window. Which one was Nadira? Andrew wanted us to guess, to pick her out of the rows of infants
30 like a long-lost relative in a crowd of strangers. We were aided in our task by the small pink name tag glued to her bassinet. Carol asked if we wanted to have a closer look. We went back to the room and waited for the nurse to bring her in.

We all stood up when she was carried in. I knew I was getting ahead of myself, but this made me think of a wedding where everyone immediately— and almost instinctively—rises to greet the bride. She was passed from loving hand to loving hand, but I kept her longer. I would soon have to leave, so I wanted to hold her, to cradle her in my arms, let her tiny head rest in the crook of my elbow. I wanted to watch her ever so slightly open her eyes and
40 tighten her mouth as she battled to make sense of all the new sounds around her, all the laughter, the wild comparisons with relatives living and gone, all so very present in her face. I wanted to read her lines from Sonia Sanchez's "Poem at Thirty": "i am here waiting / remembering that / once as a child / i walked two / miles in my sleep. / did i know / then where i / was going? / traveling. i'm always traveling. / i want to tell / you about me . . . / here is my hand." **C**

Nadira's presence had already transformed the room. Her opening her eyes was like a Hollywood press conference, with all the video and picture cameras going off, trying to capture something that perhaps none of us knew how to express, that we had suddenly been allowed a closer view of one of life's great
50 wonders, and by being there, were an extension of a miracle that happened every second of every day in every part of the world, but had generously now granted us a turn.

That day, when we lined up for a glance, a touch, a picture, and tried to imagine a life for Nadira in a new country, we each made our own silent promises not to let her face that new world alone. We were telling her and her parents that we were her village with our offers of baby-sitting favors, our giant teddy bears, our handfuls of flowers, and the crooks of our arms and necks and laps, which we hoped that she would run to if she ever needed a refuge. **D**

Looking back on my own thirty years, having crossed many borders, loved
60 and lost many family and friends, young and old, to time, migrations, illnesses, I couldn't help but worry for Nadira, and for my nephew yet to be born. Are there ahead for them wars, a depression, a holocaust, a new civil-rights struggle as there were for those children born at the dawn of the last century? Will they have to face the colonization of new planets, genetic cloning, new forms of slavery, and other nightmares we have yet to imagine? Will we, their tiny village, give them enough love and assurance to help them survive, thrive, and even want to challenge those things? **E**

Before handing Nadira back to her parents, I felt torn between wanting her to grow up quickly so that her body might match the wits she'd need to face
70 her future and at the same time wanting her to stay small so that she might be

C MONITOR
Reread lines 42–45. What significance might these lines of poetry have for Danticat?

D AUTHOR'S PERSPECTIVE
What do Danticat's promises suggest about her beliefs concerning the responsibility adults have toward children?

E GRAMMAR AND STYLE
Reread lines 62–67. Notice how Danticat poses a series of **rhetorical questions** about the future to prompt readers to share her concern.

Circle of Joy, Keith Mallett. © Keith Mallett Studio, Inc./www.keithmallett.com.

easier to shield and carry along the length of our elbows to the reach of our palms. I wanted to tell her parents that though I had never held any living thing so tiny in my hands, I had never held anything so grand either, a bundle so elaborately complex and yet fragile, encompassing both our past and our future.

    Though Nadira and my soon-to-arrive nephew were not created specifically with me in mind, I felt as though they were the most magical gifts that could ever have blessed my thirtieth year of life. Humbled by my responsibility to them, I silently promised their parents that for the next thirty years and the thirty after that, my heart and soul would be their children's *repozwa*, a sacred place where they would always find rest. ↜

Comprehension

1. **Recall** What is Danticat's relationship to the baby she holds?

2. **Recall** How does Danticat regard the baby and her birth?

3. **Clarify** Why is the baby so special to her?

4. **Summarize** What role does she hope to play in the baby's life?

PENNSYLVANIA STANDARDS

READING STANDARD
A.2.4.1 Identify and/or explain main ideas and relevant details

Literary Analysis

5. **Identify Main Idea** Review the questions, thoughts, and ideas you noted as you **monitored** your reading. Then, using this information as a guide, state the main idea, or **thesis,** of "The Future in My Arms."

6. **Make Inferences About Author's Perspective** What can you infer about Danticat's values, feelings, and beliefs concerning the role of adults in children's lives? Support your inferences with details from the text.

7. **Analyze Concept** Complete a concept chart like the one shown for the word *repozwa*. What is the significance of the word in this essay? Give evidence to support your answer.

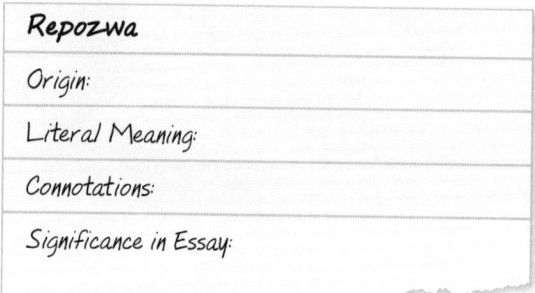

Repozwa

Origin:

Literal Meaning:

Connotations:

Significance in Essay:

8. **Interpret Text** Reread lines 72–75. What does Danticat mean when she states that the baby Nadira encompasses "both our past and our future"? Support your answer with details from the essay.

Literary Criticism

9. **Social Context** How do your community's views on the **responsibility** of adults toward children compare with those in this selection? Consider the role of institutions such as parks, schools, daycare facilities, and neighborhood-watch programs in your area. What role do neighbors and extended families have in the care of children? Cite evidence to support your evaluation.

Reading-Writing Connection

Increase your understanding of "The Future in My Arms" by responding to these prompts. Then use **Revision: Grammar and Style** to improve your writing.

WRITING PROMPTS	SELF-CHECK

A. Short Response: Analyze a Text

Danticat has many concerns about the world her niece and nephew will encounter. Are her fears valid, or is she overreacting? Write a **one- or two-paragraph response** explaining your thoughts.

A strong analysis will . . .
- state an opinion and give reasons to support it
- provide examples from the text as support

B. Extended Response: Write a Letter

How might Danticat encourage a community to become a *repozwa* for its children? Drawing on ideas in her essay, write a **three-to-five-paragraph letter** that Danticat might send to a local newspaper encouraging that community to examine its **responsibilities** to its children.

A successful response will . . .
- clearly state the writer's views
- include rhetorical questions to motivate readers

REVISION: GRAMMAR AND STYLE

ADD RHETORICAL QUESTIONS Review the **Grammar and Style** note on page 462. Here, the author uses **interrogative sentences** to ask rhetorical questions that not only express her own concerns but also prompt similar concerns in her readers. Unlike other questions, **rhetorical questions** do not require answers; they are used for effect. For example, notice how the following rhetorical questions make this paragraph more powerful than it would be with only declarative statements:

> *A community is only as strong as its members. Our community needs to reach out to all children who live in our town. What are their needs? What will help them grow strong? How can we help them become responsible citizens who will, in turn, make this a better community?*

Now study the following model. Notice how the revisions in red make this first draft more powerful and effective.

> **STUDENT MODEL**
>
> *What is my responsibility to this child? What is our responsibility to all children in the community?*
>
> Recently, I became an aunt to a beautiful baby girl. This joyous occasion caused me to reflect upon my role in her life. ~~I started to consider my responsibilities to her and the other children in our community.~~

PENNSYLVANIA STANDARDS

WRITING STANDARD
1.5.11.D.1 Use different types and lengths of sentences

WRITING TOOLS

For prewriting, revision, and editing tools, visit the **Writing Center** at ClassZone.com.

Poem on Returning to Dwell in the Country
Poem by T'ao Ch'ien

My Heart Leaps Up
Poem by William Wordsworth

The Sun
Poem by Mary Oliver

Where do you go to GET AWAY *from it all?*

PENNSYLVANIA STANDARDS

READING STANDARDS
B.1.1.1.D.2 Evaluate the relationship between theme and other components

B.1.2.1 Analyze, and/or evaluate connections between texts

KEY IDEA What does **nature** do for you? Whether it's staring at a fishbowl, escaping to the mountains, or simply taking a walk in the park, many people look to nature for beauty, serenity, or rejuvenation. The poems that follow reflect on the experience of basking in the natural world.

QUICKWRITE Make a concept web like the one shown, identifying a part of nature you enjoy and how it makes you feel. Then write a paragraph explaining your thoughts.

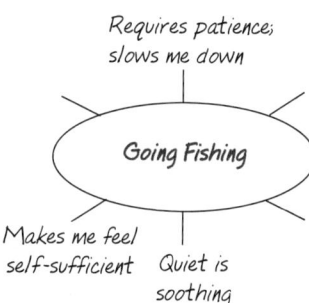

Requires patience; slows me down

Going Fishing

Makes me feel self-sufficient

Quiet is soothing

LITERARY ANALYSIS: UNIVERSAL THEME

Some poems have a **universal theme;** they express ideas that people from many cultures and times have found to be true. The poems you are about to read all describe a love of nature. Although written by poets who lived centuries apart and in very different cultures, all three poems touch upon the same universal theme. As you read each poem, use these strategies to identify their shared message:

- Think about the idea each poem is expressing about nature. What theme does each poem convey?
- Examine each poet's approach to the subject and look for similarities and differences.

READING STRATEGY: READING POETRY FOR THEME

The words in a poem are carefully chosen and arranged to convey the poet's message. As a result, to understand **theme** in poetry, you need to look at details differently than you would when reading prose. The strategies that follow can help you discover the theme in each poem in this lesson:

- Identify the **speaker,** or voice, that "talks" to the reader. What attitude does the speaker have toward the subject of the poem?
- Notice key **images** and think about their meanings.
- Identify words and phrases that are emphasized or repeated or that strike you as important. Consider what ideas and feelings the words and phrases convey.

As you read, keep a list of significant words, images, and phrases from each poem.

> "Poem on Returning to Dwell in the Country"
>
> "For my nature always/loved the hills and mountains." (lines 3–4)

Author Online

T'ao Ch'ien: Grandfather of Chinese Wilderness Poetry T'ao Ch'ien worked for the government before he returned to his family farm to live as a farmer—a radical decision at the time. His poetry reflects Taoist philosophy, which emphasizes living simply and close to nature. Both his life and his natural, conversational style of poetry inspired many later Chinese writers.

T'ao Ch'ien
365–427

William Wordsworth: England's Poet of Nature William Wordsworth grew up in the Lake District of northern England. As a boy, he loved being outdoors and appreciated the natural beauty of the region; this love of nature never left him. His poetry introduced a new view of the relationship between people and nature. Wordsworth became one of the leaders of the Romantic movement in English literature.

William Wordsworth
1770–1850

Mary Oliver: American Celebrant of Nature Mary Oliver became a distinguished poet and professor without ever having finished college. Her poetry, which links the worlds of people, animals, and plants, has won the Pulitzer Prize and the National Book Award.

Mary Oliver
born 1935

 MORE ABOUT THE AUTHOR
For more on these poets, visit the **Literature Center** at ClassZone.com.

Plum Blossoms by Moonlight, Ma Yuan, Southern Sung. John M. Crawford, Jr. Collection. Photo © Wan-go H. C. Weng/Metropolitan Museum of Art, New York.

Poem on Returning to Dwell in the Country

T'ao Ch'ien

In youth I had nothing
    that matched the vulgar tone,[1]
For my nature always
    loved the hills and mountains.
5 Inadvertently I fell
    into the Dusty Net,[2]
Once having gone
    it was more than thirteen years.
The tame bird
10   longs for his old forest—
The fish in the house-pond
    thinks of his ancient pool. **A**
I too will break the soil
    at the edge of the southern moor,
15 I will guard simplicity
    and return to my fields and garden.
My land and house—
    a little more than ten acres,
In the thatched cottage—
20   only eight or nine rooms.
Elms and willows
    shade the back verandah,
Peach and plum trees
    in rows before the hall.

A **READING POETRY**
Consider the **images** in lines 9–12. Why does the speaker mention the tame bird and the fish in the house-pond?

---

1. **matched the vulgar tone:** The speaker is saying that he was never coarse or raucous in his youth.

2. **Dusty Net:** a term that refers to being caught up in professional ambition and materialism.

<pre>
25 Hazy and dimly seen
      a village in the distance,
   Close in the foreground
      the smoke of neighbors' houses.
   A dog barks
30   amidst the deep lanes,
   A cock is crowing
      atop a mulberry tree.
   No dust and confusion
      within my doors and courtyard;
35 In the empty rooms
      more than sufficient leisure.
   Too long I was held
      within the barred cage.
   Now I am able
40   to return again to Nature. ⓑ
              Translated by William Acker
</pre>

ⓑ UNIVERSAL THEME
Reread the last four lines.
What is the "barred cage"?

My Heart Leaps Up

WILLIAM WORDSWORTH

<pre>
   My heart leaps up when I behold
      A rainbow in the sky:
   So was it when my life began;
   So is it now I am a man;
 5 So be it when I shall grow old,
      Or let me die! ⓒ
   The Child is father of the Man;
   And I could wish my days to be
   Bound each to each by natural piety.¹
</pre>

ⓒ UNIVERSAL THEME
Paraphrase what the
speaker reveals in lines
1–6 about his feelings
toward nature.

---

1. **piety** (pī′ĭ-tē): the quality of showing devotion or
   being reverent.

The SUN

Mary Oliver

Have you ever seen
anything
in your life
more wonderful

5 than the way the sun,
every evening,
relaxed and easy,
floats toward the horizon

and into the clouds or the hills,
10 or the rumpled sea,
and is gone—
and how it slides again

out of the blackness,
every morning,
15 on the other side of the world,
like a red flower

streaming upward on its heavenly oils,
say, on a morning in early summer,
at its perfect imperial distance—
20 and have you ever felt for anything **D**

such wild love—
do you think there is anywhere, in any language,
a word billowing enough
for the pleasure

25 that fills you,
as the sun
reaches out,
as it warms you

as you stand there,
30 empty-handed—
or have you too
turned from this world—

or have you too
gone crazy
35 for power,
for things? **E**

D READING POETRY
Note the **imagery** in
lines 5–20. What can you
infer about the speaker's
attitude toward nature
from this description of
the sun?

E UNIVERSAL THEME
Notice that the speaker
asks several questions in
this poem. What clues do
these questions give you
for identifying the theme?

After Reading

READING STANDARD
B.1.1.1.D.2 Evaluate the relationship between theme and other components

Comprehension

1. **Recall** In "Poem on Returning to Dwell in the Country," what change does the speaker make in his life?

2. **Recall** In "My Heart Leaps Up," what does the speaker wish for?

3. **Summarize** In "The Sun," what does the speaker regard as the most wonderful thing in life?

Literary Analysis

4. **Compare and Contrast** In "Poem on Returning to Dwell in the Country," contrast the speaker's feelings about his former life in the city and his new life in the country. Why does the speaker prefer the country life? Provide evidence from the poem to support your answer.

5. **Interpret Meaning** "My Heart Leaps Up" includes the famous line "The Child is father of the Man." Think about how childhood experiences influence the person one becomes as an adult. What do you think the speaker means?

6. **Make Inferences** In "The Sun," who is the **speaker** addressing? Pay particular attention to the last stanza of the poem.

7. **Analyze Universal Theme** Use a chart like the one shown to record the theme reflected in each poem. Then come up with a single universal theme that all three poems share.

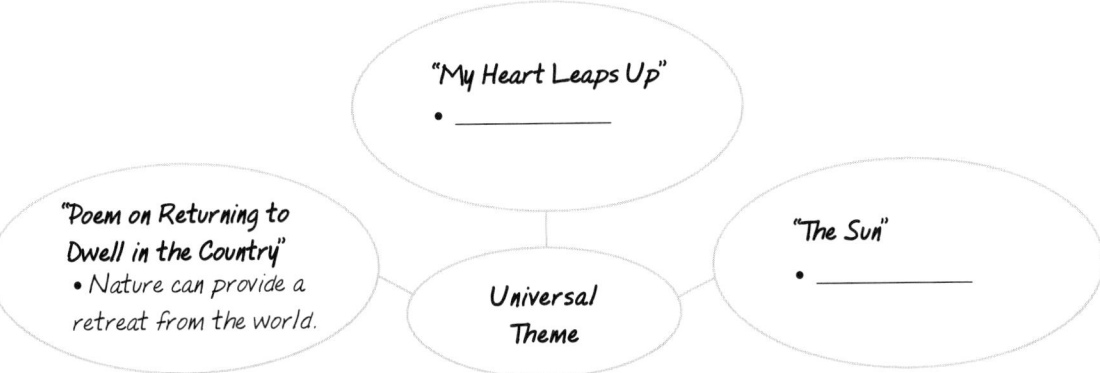

8. **Evaluate** In your opinion, which poem makes the strongest statement about the power of **nature?** Cite evidence to support your choice.

Literary Criticism

9. **Historical Context** England's Romantic poets had a deep reverence for nature. Their work shows an emphasis on imagination, the expression of emotions, and wonder at the world around them. How does Wordsworth's poem reflect this tradition? To what extent do these traits appear in T'ao Ch'ien's and Mary Oliver's poems? Cite evidence to support your answer.

Two Kinds
Short Story by Amy Tan

Rice and Rose Bowl Blues
Poem by Diane Mei Lin Mark

How do EXPECTATIONS *affect performance?*

PENNSYLVANIA STANDARDS

READING STANDARDS
B.1.1.1.D.1 Evaluate the theme
B.1.2.1 Analyze, and/or evaluate connections between texts

KEY IDEA Think of a time when someone in authority set a very high goal for you. Perhaps a coach expected you to be the team's top scorer, or a parent expected you to get straight A's. How did you respond to these **expectations?** Were you motivated to work harder? Did you inwardly rebel?

DISCUSS With a small group of classmates, discuss why parents in particular might have high expectations of their children. Record three or more reasons from your discussion and then share them with other groups.

LITERARY ANALYSIS: THEME ACROSS GENRES

The short story and the poem you are about to read are literary works about young people struggling to be themselves in the face of parental expectations. Each has a specific **theme,** or message, about that topic. The fiction writer and the poet use different techniques to express the theme of the work. The chart shows the techniques each writer uses.

As you read, try to identify the theme of each work by paying attention to the following.

In the Short Story	In the Poem
• details about the main character's traits, motivations, and values	• words and phrases describing the speaker's thoughts and feelings
• details about how the characters change and the lessons they learn	• key images
• the major internal and external conflicts	• stanzas and lines that present an idea or compare images
• information about the setting	• sound devices, such as alliteration and repetition, that may emphasize an idea
• the story's title	• the poem's title

READING STRATEGY: SET A PURPOSE FOR READING

When you **set a purpose for reading,** you establish specific reasons to read a work. For example, your purpose for reading "Two Kinds" and "Rice and Rose Bowl Blues" is to identify the theme of each so that you can compare and contrast them. As you read, think about the important struggles each main character faces. After you read, you will use the **Points of Comparison** chart on page 487 to help you analyze and compare the two selections.

Review: **Draw Conclusions**

▲ VOCABULARY IN CONTEXT

Decide whether each word in the list has a positive or a negative connotation.

WORD LIST			
	debut	fiasco	prodigy
	discordant	lament	reproach
	encore	mesmerizing	

Author On|ine

Amy Tan born 1952

Amy Tan: Late Bloomer
Like the narrator in "Two Kinds," Amy Tan is the daughter of Chinese immigrants. Raised in the San Francisco Bay area, she spent most of her high school years traveling through Europe with her family after the death of her father and brother. Although she had studied literature and worked as a business writer, Tan did not turn to fiction writing until age 33 when her analyst fell asleep during a session for the third time. At that point, she abandoned therapy in favor of fiction.

Overnight Success After publishing a handful of short stories, Tan came out with *The Joy Luck Club,* a collection of related short stories about four Chinese women friends and their daughters. Critically acclaimed, the book became a bestseller and was made into a movie. Her work has been translated into more than 20 languages, including Chinese.

Diane Mei Lin Mark: Maker of Images
A fifth-generation Chinese American, Diane Mark is a successful writer and filmmaker. She co-produced the film *Picture Bride,* a lyrical depiction of Hawaii's plantation culture in the early 20th century. The film won

Diane Mei Lin Mark

the Audience Award for Best Dramatic Film at the 1995 Sundance Film Festival.

MORE ABOUT THE AUTHOR
For more on Amy Tan and Diane Mei Lin Mark, visit the **Literature Center** at **ClassZone.com.**

Two **Kinds**

Amy Tan

My mother believed you could be anything you wanted to be in America. You could open a restaurant. You could work for the government and get good retirement. You could buy a house with almost no money down. You could become rich. You could become instantly famous.

"Of course you can be **prodigy,** too," my mother told me when I was nine. "You can be best anything. What does Auntie Lindo know? Her daughter, she is only best tricky."

America was where all my mother's hopes lay. She had come here in 1949 after losing everything in China: her mother and father, her family home, her
10 first husband, and two daughters, twin baby girls. But she never looked back with regret. There were so many ways for things to get better. **Ⓐ**

We didn't immediately pick the right kind of prodigy. At first my mother thought I could be a Chinese Shirley Temple.[1] We'd watch Shirley's old movies on TV as though they were training films. My mother would poke my arm and say, *"Ni kan"*—You watch. And I would see Shirley tapping her feet, or singing a sailor song, or pursing her lips into a very round O while saying, "Oh my goodness."

"Ni kan," said my mother as Shirley's eyes flooded with tears. "You already know how. Don't need talent for crying!"

20 Soon after my mother got this idea about Shirley Temple, she took me to a beauty training school in the Mission district[2] and put me in the hands of a student who could barely hold the scissors without shaking. Instead of getting big fat curls, I emerged with an uneven mass of crinkly black fuzz. My mother dragged me off to the bathroom and tried to wet down my hair.

"You look like Negro Chinese," she lamented, as if I had done this on purpose.

The instructor of the beauty training school had to lop off these soggy clumps to make my hair even again. "Peter Pan is very popular these days,"

prodigy (prŏd′ə-jē)
n. a person who is exceptionally talented or intelligent

Ⓐ THEME
Reread lines 1–11. What does the narrator's mother want for her daughter? Consider what this suggests about the mother's **character.**

ANALYZE VISUALS
What do the posture, facial expressions, dress, and printed background suggest about the mother and daughter in this picture? Explain.

---

1. **Shirley Temple:** a popular child movie star of the 1930s.

2. **Mission district:** a residential neighborhood in San Francisco.

the instructor assured my mother. I now had hair the length of a boy's, with
30 straight-across bangs that hung at a slant two inches above my eyebrows. I
liked the haircut, and it made me actually look forward to my future fame.

In fact, in the beginning, I was just as excited as my mother, maybe even
more so. I pictured this prodigy part of me as many different images, trying
each one on for size. I was a dainty ballerina girl standing by the curtains,
waiting to hear the right music that would send me floating on my tiptoes.
I was like the Christ child lifted out of the straw manger, crying with holy
indignity. I was Cinderella stepping from her pumpkin carriage with sparkly
cartoon music filling the air.

In all of my imaginings, I was filled with a sense that I would soon become
40 *perfect.* My mother and father would adore me. I would be beyond **reproach.** I
would never feel the need to sulk for anything.

But sometimes the prodigy in me became impatient. "If you don't hurry
up and get me out of here, I'm disappearing for good," it warned. "And then
you'll always be nothing." **B**

Every night after dinner, my mother and I would sit at the Formica[3]
kitchen table. She would present new tests, taking her examples from stories
of amazing children she had read in *Ripley's Believe It or Not,* or *Good
Housekeeping, Reader's Digest,* and a dozen other magazines she kept in a pile
in our bathroom. My mother got these magazines from people whose houses
50 she cleaned. And since she cleaned many houses each week, we had a great
assortment. She would look through them all, searching for stories about
remarkable children.

The first night she brought out a story about a three-year-old boy who knew
the capitals of all the states and even most of the European countries. A teacher
was quoted as saying the little boy could also pronounce the names of the
foreign cities correctly.

"What's the capital of Finland?" my mother asked me, looking at the
magazine story.

All I knew was the capital of California, because Sacramento was the name
60 of the street we lived on in Chinatown. "Nairobi!"[4] I guessed, saying the most
foreign word I could think of. She checked to see if that was possibly one way
to pronounce "Helsinki" before showing me the answer.

The tests got harder—multiplying numbers in my head, finding the queen
of hearts in a deck of cards, trying to stand on my head without using my
hands, predicting the daily temperatures in Los Angeles, New York, and
London.

One night I had to look at a page from the Bible for three minutes and then
report everything I could remember. "Now Jehoshaphat[5] had riches and honor
in abundance and . . . that's all I remember, Ma," I said. **C**

---

3. **Formica** (fôr-mī′kə): a heat-resistant material used on kitchen counters, table tops, and similar surfaces.

4. **Nairobi** (nī-rō′bē): the capital of the African nation of Kenya.

5. **Jehoshaphat** (jə-hŏsh′ə-făt′): a king of the ancient Biblical land of Judah in the ninth century B.C.

reproach (rĭ-prōch′) *n.*
blame; criticism

B THEME
Reread lines 32–44.
What are the narrator's
conflicting feelings about
being a prodigy?

C THEME
Reread lines 45–69.
How successfully does
the narrator perform
the tests given by her
mother?

70   And after seeing my mother's disappointed face once again, something inside of me began to die. I hated the tests, the raised hopes and failed expectations. Before going to bed that night, I looked in the mirror above the bathroom sink and when I saw only my face staring back—and that it would always be this ordinary face—I began to cry. Such a sad, ugly girl! I made high-pitched noises like a crazed animal, trying to scratch out the face in the mirror.

    And then I saw what seemed to be the prodigy side of me—because I had never seen that face before. I looked at my reflection, blinking so I could see more clearly. The girl staring back at me was angry, powerful. This girl and I
80 were the same. I had new thoughts, willful thoughts, or rather thoughts filled with lots of won'ts. I won't let her change me, I promised myself. I won't be what I'm not. **D**

    So now on nights when my mother presented her tests, I performed listlessly, my head propped on one arm. I pretended to be bored. And I was. I got so bored I started counting the bellows of the foghorns out on the bay while my mother drilled me in other areas. The sound was comforting and reminded me of the cow jumping over the moon. And the next day, I played a game with myself, seeing if my mother would give up on me before eight bellows. After a while I usually counted only one, maybe two bellows at most.
90 At last she was beginning to give up hope.

    Two or three months had gone by without any mention of my being a prodigy again. And then one day my mother was watching The *Ed Sullivan Show*[6] on TV. The TV was old and the sound kept shorting out. Every time my mother got halfway up from the sofa to adjust the set, the sound would go back on and Ed would be talking. As soon as she sat down, Ed would go silent again. She got up, the TV broke into loud piano music. She sat down. Silence. Up and down, back and forth, quiet and loud. It was like a stiff, embraceless dance between her and the TV set. Finally she stood by the set with her hand on the sound dial.
100   She seemed entranced by the music, a little frenzied piano piece with this **mesmerizing** quality, sort of quick passages and then teasing lilting ones before it returned to the quick playful parts.

    "*Ni kan,*" my mother said, calling me over with hurried hand gestures, "Look here."

    I could see why my mother was fascinated by the music. It was being pounded out by a little Chinese girl, about nine years old, with a Peter Pan haircut. The girl had the sauciness of a Shirley Temple. She was proudly modest like a proper Chinese child. And she also did this fancy sweep of a curtsy, so that the fluffy skirt of her white dress cascaded slowly to the floor
110 like the petals of a large carnation.

D THEME
Reread lines 70–82. What causes the narrator to rebel against her mother? Point out statements that reveal her new insights and provide clues to the theme.

mesmerizing
(mĕz′mə-rīz′ĭng) *adj.* holding one's attention in an almost hypnotic manner **mesmerize** *v.*

---

6. **The *Ed Sullivan Show*:** a popular television variety show in the 1950s and 1960s.

In spite of these warning signs, I wasn't worried. Our family had no piano and we couldn't afford to buy one, let alone reams of sheet music and piano lessons. So I could be generous in my comments when my mother bad-mouthed the little girl on TV.

120 "Play note right, but doesn't sound good! No singing sound," complained my mother.

"What are you picking on her for?" I said carelessly. "She's pretty good. Maybe she's not the best, but she's trying hard." I knew almost immediately I would be sorry I said that.

"Just like you," she said. "Not the best. Because you not trying."
130 She gave a little huff as she let go of the sound dial and sat down on the sofa.

The little Chinese girl sat down also to play an **encore** of "Anitra's Dance" by Grieg.[7] I remember the song, because later on I had to learn how to play it.

encore (ŏn′kōr′) *n.* a repeated or additional performance

Three days after watching *The Ed Sullivan Show,* my mother told me what my schedule would be for piano lessons and piano practice. She had talked to Mr. Chong, who lived on the first floor of our apartment building. Mr. Chong
140 was a retired piano teacher and my mother had traded housecleaning services for weekly lessons and a piano for me to practice on every day, two hours a day, from four until six.

When my mother told me this, I felt as though I had been sent to hell. I whined and then kicked my foot a little when I couldn't stand it anymore.

"Why don't you like me the way I am? I'm *not* a genius! I can't play the piano. And even if I could, I wouldn't go on TV if you paid me a million dollars!" I cried.

My mother slapped me. "Who ask you be genius?" she shouted. "Only ask you be your best. For you sake. You think I want you be genius? Hnnh! What
150 for! Who ask you!"

"So ungrateful," I heard her mutter in Chinese. "If she had as much talent as she has temper, she would be famous now." **E**

E THEME
Examine the **conflict** between the characters as revealed in lines 128–132 and lines 145–152. Why does the mother continue to push her daughter?

---

7. **Grieg** (grēg): Norwegian composer Edvard Grieg (1843–1907).

Mr. Chong, whom I secretly nicknamed Old Chong, was very strange, always tapping his fingers to the silent music of an invisible orchestra. He looked ancient in my eyes. He had lost most of the hair on top of his head and he wore thick glasses and had eyes that always looked tired and sleepy. But he must have been younger than I thought, since he lived with his mother and was not yet married.

160 I met Old Lady Chong once and that was enough. She had this peculiar smell like a baby that had done something in its pants. And her fingers felt like a dead person's, like an old peach I once found in the back of the refrigerator; the skin just slid off the meat when I picked it up.

I soon found out why Old Chong had retired from teaching piano. He was deaf. "Like Beethoven!" he shouted to me. "We're both listening only in our head!"[8] And he would start to conduct his frantic silent sonatas.

Our lessons went like this. He would open the book and point to different things, explaining their purpose: "Key! Treble! Bass! No sharps or flats! So this is C major! Listen now and play after me!"

And then he would play the C scale a few times, a simple chord, and then,
170 as if inspired by an old, unreachable itch, he gradually added more notes and running trills and a pounding bass until the music was really something quite grand.

I would play after him, the simple scale, the simple chord, and then I just played some nonsense that sounded like a cat running up and down on top of garbage cans. Old Chong smiled and applauded and then said, "Very good! But now you must learn to keep time!"

So that's how I discovered that Old Chong's eyes were too slow to keep up with the wrong notes I was playing. He went through the motions in half-time. To help me keep rhythm, he stood behind me, pushing down on my
180 right shoulder for every beat. He balanced pennies on top of my wrists so I would keep them still as I slowly played scales and arpeggios.[9] He had me curve my hand around an apple and keep that shape when playing chords. He marched stiffly to show me how to make each finger dance up and down, staccato[10] like an obedient little soldier.

He taught me all these things, and that was how I also learned I could be lazy and get away with mistakes, lots of mistakes. If I hit the wrong notes because I hadn't practiced enough, I never corrected myself. I just kept playing in rhythm. And Old Chong kept conducting his own private reverie.

So maybe I never really gave myself a fair chance. I did pick up the basics
190 pretty quickly, and I might have become a good pianist at that young age.

---

8. **Beethoven ... in our head!** (bā′tō′vən): Ludwig van Beethoven (1770–1827) continued to compose great music even after becoming totally deaf during the last years of his life.

9. **arpeggios** (är-pĕj′ē-ōz′): chords in which the notes are played separately in quick sequence rather than at the same time.

10. **staccato** (stə-kä′tō): producing distinct, abrupt breaks between successive tones.

But I was so determined not to try, not to be anybody different, that I learned to play only the most ear-splitting preludes,[11] the most **discordant** hymns. **F**

Over the next year, I practiced like this, dutifully in my own way. And then one day I heard my mother and her friend Lindo Jong both talking in a loud, bragging tone of voice so others could hear. It was after church, and I was leaning against the brick wall wearing a dress with stiff white petticoats. Auntie Lindo's daughter, Waverly, who was about my age, was standing farther down the wall about five feet away. We had grown up together and shared all the closeness of two sisters squabbling over crayons and dolls. In other words, for the most part, we hated each other. I thought she was snotty. Waverly Jong had gained a certain amount of fame as "Chinatown's Littlest Chinese Chess Champion."

"She bring home too many trophy," **lamented** Auntie Lindo that Sunday. "All day she play chess. All day I have no time do nothing but dust off her winnings." She threw a scolding look at Waverly, who pretended not to see her.

"You lucky you don't have this problem," said Auntie Lindo with a sigh to my mother.

And my mother squared her shoulders and bragged: "Our problem worser than yours. If we ask Jing-mei[12] wash dish, she hear nothing but music. It's like you can't stop this natural talent."

And right then, I was determined to put a stop to her foolish pride. **G**

A few weeks later, Old Chong and my mother conspired to have me play in a talent show which would be held in the church hall. By then, my parents had saved up enough to buy me a secondhand piano, a black Wurlitzer spinet[13] with a scarred bench. It was the showpiece of our living room.

For the talent show, I was to play a piece called "Pleading Child" from Schumann's[14] *Scenes from Childhood.* It was a simple, moody piece that sounded more difficult than it was. I was supposed to memorize the whole thing, playing the repeat parts twice to make the piece sound longer. But I dawdled over it, playing a few bars and then cheating, looking up to see what notes followed. I never really listened to what I was playing. I daydreamed about being somewhere else, about being someone else.

The part I liked to practice best was the fancy curtsy: right foot out, touch the rose on the carpet with a pointed foot, sweep to the side, left leg bends, look up and smile.

F THEME
Why does the narrator intentionally do poorly in her piano lessons?

discordant (dĭ-skôr'dnt) *adj.* having a disagreeable or clashing sound

lament (lə-mĕnt') *v.* to express grief or deep regret

G DRAW CONCLUSIONS
After overhearing her mother's conversation with Auntie Lindo in lines 203–211, the narrator concludes that "foolish pride" motivates her mother. Based on what you know about the mother so far, do you agree? Explain your answer.

---

11. **preludes** (prĕl'yōōdz'): short piano compositions, each usually based on a single musical theme.

12. **Jing-mei** (jĭng'mā').

13. **Wurlitzer spinet:** Wurlitzer was a well-known manuracturer of organs and pianos, including the small upright piano known as a spinet.

14. **Schumann's** (shōō'mänz'): composed by Robert Schumann (1810–1856), a German composer famous for his piano works.

My parents invited all the couples from the Joy Luck Club[15] to witness my **debut.** Auntie Lindo and Uncle Tin were there. Waverly and her two older brothers had also come. The first two rows were filled with children both
230 younger and older than I was. The littlest ones got to go first. They recited simple nursery rhymes, squawked out tunes on miniature violins, twirled Hula-Hoops,[16] pranced in pink ballet tutus, and when they bowed or curtsied, the audience would sigh in unison, "Awww," and then clap enthusiastically.

When my turn came, I was very confident. I remember my childish excitement. It was as if I knew, without a doubt, that the prodigy side of me really did exist. I had no fear whatsoever, no nervousness. I remember thinking to myself, This is it! This is it! I looked out over the audience, at my mother's blank face, my father's yawn, Auntie Lindo's stiff-lipped smile, Waverly's sulky expression. I had on a white dress layered with sheets of lace, and a pink bow
240 in my Peter Pan haircut. As I sat down I envisioned people jumping to their feet and Ed Sullivan rushing up to introduce me to everyone on TV. **H**

And I started to play. It was so beautiful. I was so caught up in how lovely I looked that at first I didn't worry how I would sound. So it was a surprise to me when I hit the first wrong note and I realized something didn't sound quite right. And then I hit another and another followed that. A chill started at the top of my head and began to trickle down. Yet I couldn't stop playing, as though my hands were bewitched. I kept thinking my fingers would adjust themselves back, like a train switching to the right track. I played this strange jumble through two repeats, the sour notes staying with me all the way
250 to the end.

debut (dā-byo͞o′) *n.* first public performance or showing

H THEME
Reread lines 234–241. What **internal conflict** is revealed by the narrator's expectations of her own performance?

---

15. **Joy Luck Club:** the social group to which the family in this story belongs.

16. **Hula-Hoops:** plastic hoops that are whirled around the body by means of hip movements.

When I stood up, I discovered my legs were shaking. Maybe I had just been nervous and the audience, like Old Chong, had seen me go through the right motions and had not heard anything wrong at all. I swept my right foot out, went down on my knee, looked up and smiled. The room was quiet, except for Old Chong, who was beaming and shouting, "Bravo! Bravo! Well done!" But then I saw my mother's face, her stricken face. The audience clapped weakly, and as I walked back to my chair, with my whole face quivering as I tried not to cry, I heard a little boy whisper loudly to his mother, "That was awful," and the mother whispered back, "Well, she certainly tried."

260   And now I realized how many people were in the audience, the whole world it seemed. I was aware of eyes burning into my back. I felt the shame of my mother and father as they sat stiffly throughout the rest of the show.

We could have escaped during intermission. Pride and some strange sense of honor must have anchored my parents to their chairs. And so we watched it all: the eighteen-year-old boy with a fake mustache who did a magic show and juggled flaming hoops while riding a unicycle. The breasted girl with white makeup who sang from *Madama Butterfly*[17] and got honorable mention. And the eleven-year-old boy who won first prize playing a tricky violin song that sounded like a busy bee.

270   After the show, the Hsus,[18] the Jongs, and the St. Clairs from the Joy Luck Club came up to my mother and father.

"Lots of talented kids," Auntie Lindo said vaguely, smiling broadly.

"That was somethin' else," said my father, and I wondered if he was referring to me in a humorous way, or whether he even remembered what I had done.

Waverly looked at me and shrugged her shoulders. "You aren't a genius like me," she said matter-of-factly. And if I hadn't felt so bad, I would have pulled her braids and punched her stomach.

But my mother's expression was what devastated me: a quiet, blank look
280 that said she had lost everything. I felt the same way, and it seemed as if everybody were now coming up, like gawkers at the scene of an accident, to see what parts were actually missing. When we got on the bus to go home, my father was humming the busy-bee tune and my mother was silent. I kept thinking she wanted to wait until we got home before shouting at me. But when my father unlocked the door to our apartment, my mother walked in and then went to the back, into the bedroom. No accusations. No blame. And in a way, I felt disappointed. I had been waiting for her to start shouting, so I could shout back and cry and blame her for all my misery.

I assumed my talent-show **fiasco** meant I never had to play the piano again.
290 But two days later, after school, my mother came out of the kitchen and saw me watching TV.

fiasco (fē-ăs′kō) *n.* a complete failure

---

17. *Madama Butterfly:* a famous opera by the Italian composer Giacomo Puccini.

18. **Hsus** (shüz).

"Four clock," she reminded me as if it were any other day. I was stunned, as though she were asking me to go through the talent-show torture again. I wedged myself more tightly in front of the TV.

"Turn off TV," she called from the kitchen five minutes later.

I didn't budge. And then I decided. I didn't have to do what my mother said anymore. I wasn't her slave. This wasn't China. I had listened to her before and look what happened. She was the stupid one.

She came out from the kitchen and stood in the arched entryway of the 300 living room. "Four clock," she said once again, louder.

"I'm not going to play anymore," I said nonchalantly. "Why should I? I'm not a genius."

She walked over and stood in front of the TV. I saw her chest was heaving up and down in an angry way.

"No!" I said, and I now felt stronger, as if my true self had finally emerged. So this was what had been inside me all along.

"No! I won't!" I screamed.

She yanked me by the arm, pulled me off the floor, snapped off the TV. She was frighteningly strong, half pulling, half carrying me toward the piano 310 as I kicked the throw rugs under my feet. She lifted me up and onto the hard bench. I was sobbing by now, looking at her bitterly. Her chest was heaving even more and her mouth was open, smiling crazily as if she were pleased I was crying.

"You want me to be someone that I'm not!" I sobbed. "I'll never be the kind of daughter you want me to be!"

"Only two kinds of daughters," she shouted in Chinese. "Those who are obedient and those who follow their own mind! Only one kind of daughter can live in this house. Obedient daughter!" ❶

"Then I wish I wasn't your daughter. I wish you weren't my mother," I 320 shouted. As I said these things I got scared. It felt like worms and toads and slimy things crawling out of my chest, but it also felt good, as if this awful side of me had surfaced, at last.

"Too late change this," said my mother shrilly.

And I could sense her anger rising to its breaking point. I wanted to see it spill over. And that's when I remembered the babies she had lost in China, the ones we never talked about. "Then I wish I'd never been born!" I shouted. "I wish I were dead! Like them."

It was as if I had said the magic words. Alakazam!—and her face went blank, her mouth closed, her arms went slack, and she backed out of the 330 room, stunned, as if she were blowing away like a small brown leaf, thin, brittle, lifeless.

❶ **THEME**
The **title** of a story is often a clue to its theme. The title of this story comes from the exchange between mother and daughter in lines 314–318. How do the narrator's values differ from her mother's? Cite examples in your answer.

It was not the only disappointment my mother felt in me. In the years that followed, I failed her so many times, each time asserting my own will, my right to fall short of expectations. I didn't get straight A's. I didn't become class president. I didn't get into Stanford. I dropped out of college.

For unlike my mother, I did not believe I could be anything I wanted to be. I could only be me.

And for all those years, we never talked about the disaster at the recital or my terrible accusations afterward at the piano bench. All that remained 340 unchecked, like a betrayal that was now unspeakable. So I never found a way to ask her why she had hoped for something so large that failure was inevitable.

And even worse, I never asked her what frightened me the most: Why had she given up hope?

For after our struggle at the piano, she never mentioned my playing again. The lessons stopped. The lid to the piano was closed, shutting out the dust, my misery, and her dreams.

So she surprised me. A few years ago, she offered to give me the piano, for my thirtieth birthday. I had not played in all those years. I saw the offer as a sign of forgiveness, a tremendous burden removed.

"Are you sure?" I asked shyly. "I mean, won't you and Dad miss it?"

"No, this your piano," she said firmly. "Always your piano. You only one can play."

"Well, I probably can't play anymore," I said. "It's been years."

"You pick up fast," said my mother, as if she knew this was certain. "You have natural talent. You could been genius if you want to."

"No I couldn't."

"You just not trying," said my mother. And she was neither angry nor sad. She said it as if to announce a fact that could never be disproved. "Take it," she said. **J**

But I didn't at first. It was enough that she had offered it to me. And after that, every time I saw it in my parents' living room, standing in front of the bay windows, it made me feel proud, as if it were a shiny trophy I had won back.

Last week I sent a tuner over to my parents' apartment and had the piano reconditioned, for purely sentimental reasons. My mother had died a few months before and I had been getting things in order for my father, a little bit at a time. I put the jewelry in special silk pouches. The sweaters she had knitted in yellow, pink, bright orange—all the colors I hated—I put those in mothproof boxes. I found some old Chinese silk dresses, the kind with little slits up the sides. I rubbed the old silk against my skin, then wrapped them in tissue and decided to take them home with me.

After I had the piano tuned, I opened the lid and touched the keys. It sounded even richer than I remembered. Really, it was a very good piano. Inside the bench were the same exercise notes with handwritten scales, the same secondhand music books with their covers held together with yellow tape.

I opened up the Schumann book to the dark little piece I had played at the recital. It was on the left-hand side of the page, "Pleading Child." It looked more difficult than I remembered. I played a few bars, surprised at how easily the notes came back to me.

And for the first time, or so it seemed, I noticed the piece on the right-hand side. It was called "Perfectly Contented." I tried to play this one as well. It had a lighter melody but the same flowing rhythm and turned out to be quite easy. "Pleading Child" was shorter but slower; "Perfectly Contented" was longer, but faster. And after I played them both a few times, I realized they were two halves of the same song. 🙣

J DRAW CONCLUSIONS
Reread lines 354–359. Has the mother changed during the course of the story or not? Explain your answer.

RICE
and
ROSE BOWL BLUES

Diane Mei Lin Mark

I remember the day
Mama called me in from
the football game with brothers
and neighbor boys
5 in our front yard

said it was time
I learned to
wash rice for dinner

glancing out the window
10 I watched a pass interception
setting the other team up
on our 20
    Pour some water
    into the pot,
15   she said pleasantly,
    turning on the tap
    Rub the rice
    between your hands,
    pour out the clouds,
20   *fill it again*
    (I secretly traced
    an end run through
    the grains in
    between pourings) **K**
25 with the rice
settled into a simmer
I started out the door
but was called back

the next day
30 Roland from across the street
sneeringly said he heard
I couldn't play football
anymore

I laughed loudly,
35 asking him
where
he'd heard
such a thing **L**

K THEME
Reread lines 21–24. What does the text in parentheses tell you about the speaker's feelings and interests? Why do you think the poet used parentheses here?

L THEME
What can you tell about the speaker's feelings from her reaction to Roland?

Comprehension

PENNSYLVANIA STANDARDS

READING STANDARD
B.1.1.1.D.1 Evaluate the theme

1. **Recall** In "Two Kinds," what does the narrator's mother want her to become?

2. **Recall** What does the narrator's mother offer her on her 30th birthday?

3. **Recall** How does the narrator feel after the talent show?

4. **Summarize** What can you tell about the character of the speaker in "Rice and Rose Bowl Blues"?

Literary Analysis

5. **Analyze Conflict** In "Two Kinds," why does the narrator's conflict with her mother last so long and become so bitter? Is it ever resolved? Cite evidence from the story to support your answer.

6. **Make Judgments** The narrator in "Two Kinds" insists that her mother wants to change her. Is it possible that her mother only wants to help her discover who she really is? Support your opinion with evidence.

7. **Interpret Text** The story ends with the narrator at the piano, playing with enjoyment for the first time and at peace with the music and herself. What might the narrator mean by saying that "Pleading Child" and "Perfectly Contented" are "two halves of the same song"?

8. **Analyze Gender Roles** In "Rice and Rose Bowl Blues," how does gender play a role in the tension between the speaker and her mother? Use evidence from the poem to support your answer.

Comparing Across Genres

Now that you have read both selections about parental **expectations,** you are ready to identify each writer's **theme,** or message. The **Points of Comparison** chart will help you get started.

Points of Comparison	In the Short Story	In the Poem
How would you describe the main conflict?		
What lesson does the narrator or the speaker learn?		
What images strike you as important?		
What idea does the title emphasize?		
Write a sentence stating the theme as you interpret it.		
Which techniques are important in conveying the theme?		

Vocabulary in Context

VOCABULARY PRACTICE

Answer the questions to show your understanding of the vocabulary words.

1. Is a **prodigy** considered a late bloomer?
2. Which would you be more likely to **lament**—your dog's death or an A on a test?
3. Which might be a **fiasco**—enjoying a vacation or knocking over a bookcase?
4. Would a **reproach** cause someone to rejoice or feel bad?
5. If a television show is an **encore** presentation, is it a new program or a rerun?
6. Which are **discordant** sounds—blaring car horns or softly rippling waves?
7. Which might be **mesmerizing** to a child—a newspaper or a shiny toy?
8. If someone is making a **debut,** is he or she likely to be excited or bored?

WORD LIST

debut

discordant

encore

fiasco

lament

mesmerizing

prodigy

reproach

VOCABULARY IN WRITING

Write a short review of the narrator's piano performance for a local newspaper. Use four or more vocabulary words. You might begin like this.

> **EXAMPLE SENTENCE**
>
> Usually we like to say kind things about a young performer's **debut**.

VOCABULARY STRATEGY: WORD ORIGINS

Words that derive from the names of people or places are called **eponyms.** For example, the vocabulary word *mesmerizing* (the present participle of *mesmerize*) comes from the name Franz Mesmer, an Austrian doctor who popularized hypnotism. The etymology in the dictionary entry of an eponym will help you understand the term's origin.

> **mes•mer•ize** (mĕz′mə-rīz′) *tr.v.* **-ized, -iz•ing, -iz•es 1.** To spellbind; enthrall.
> **2.** To hypnotize. [After Franz Mesmer, Austrian physician, 1734–1815.]

PRACTICE Use an unabridged dictionary to identify the person or place from which each word derives. Then write a brief explanation of the connection.

1. saxophone
2. boycott
3. poinsettia
4. frankfurter
5. bedlam
6. shrapnel
7. tangerine
8. Ferris wheel

PENNSYLVANIA STANDARDS

READING STANDARD
A.1.1 Apply the meaning of vocabulary

VOCABULARY PRACTICE
For more practice, go to the **Vocabulary Center** at **ClassZone.com.**

Writing for Assessment

1. READ THE PROMPT

In writing assessments, you will often be asked to **compare and contrast** two works of literature that contain a similar conflict. You are now going to practice writing an essay that requires this type of focus.

PROMPT

The conflict between parents and children is an age-old problem, explored here by Amy Tan and Diane Mei Lin Mark. In Tan's story "Two Kinds," what is the theme expressed by the mother-daughter struggle? What is the theme of Mark's poem "Rice and Rose Bowl Blues"? In a three- or four-paragraph essay, explore how their messages are similar or different. Do you think the similarities have anything to do with culture? Support your analysis with evidence.

◀ **STRATEGIES IN ACTION**

1. I have to state the **theme** of each work
2. I need to **compare and contrast** the themes.
3. I need to include **details and quotations** from each work.

2. PLAN YOUR WRITING

- Review the **Points of Comparison** chart you created on page 487.
- Decide whether the themes are basically similar or markedly different.
- Using your chart, find examples to use as evidence for the points you develop in your essay. If necessary, review the selections again to identify more examples.
- Create an outline to organize your ideas. You may want to discuss each selection separately and then compare them, or you may choose to discuss each point of comparison in its own paragraph.

I. Conflict
  A. Tan piece
  B. Mark piece

II. Lesson learned
  A. Tan piece
  B. Mark piece

3. DRAFT YOUR RESPONSE

Introduction Introduce the topic—parental expectations—and then explain that you will discuss what the two works say about it. Include the titles and authors of the selections.

Body State and explain Amy Tan's theme in the second paragraph and Diane Mei Lin Mark's in the third. In a fourth paragraph, compare the two themes.

Conclusion Wrap up your essay with a final thought about parental expectations.

Revision Check your use of transitional words and phrases to connect ideas within and between paragraphs. Words and phrases such as *likewise, both,* and *in the same way* signal similarities. *On the other hand, however, in contrast,* and *nevertheless* signal differences.

Writing Workshop

Literary Analysis

The selections in this unit and other works of literature can surprise you, enlighten you, or even change your life. A good way to enhance your understanding of a story and to share what you have learned from it is to write a literary analysis. Begin your writing process by carefully examining the **Writer's Road Map.**

WRITER'S ROAD MAP

Literary Analysis

WRITING PROMPT 1

Writing from Literature Write an essay analyzing the meaning of a literary work. Your essay should focus on one or more literary elements and explain how they contribute to the work's meaning.

Literary Elements to Analyze

- symbols and character in "The Scarlet Ibis"
- setting and theme in "Marigolds"
- character and dialogue in "Two Kinds"

WRITING PROMPT 2

Writing from the Real World Stories are everywhere—not just in your literature anthology. Write an analysis of a memorable story you recently viewed or read. Make sure you go beyond a summary of the story to analyze the elements that make it meaningful and interesting.

Sources of Stories

- television shows that use conflict, suspense, or surprise endings
- movies that have compelling main characters
- graphic novels with a strong sense of setting and mood

 WRITING TOOLS
For prewriting, revision, and editing tools, visit the **Writing Center** at **ClassZone.com.**

KEY TRAITS

1. **IDEAS**
   - Presents a **thesis statement** that clearly identifies key points of the discussion
   - Uses **evidence** from the text to support each key point

2. **ORGANIZATION**
   - Has an engaging **introduction** that identifies the literary work being analyzed
   - Includes a clear **organizational pattern**
   - Summarizes ideas and makes broader judgments about the work in a strong **conclusion**

3. **VOICE**
   - Uses a **tone** that is appropriate for the audience and purpose

4. **WORD CHOICE**
   - Uses precise **adjectives** and **adverbs** to convey ideas clearly

5. **SENTENCE FLUENCY**
   - Varies **sentence structures**

6. **CONVENTIONS**
   - Employs **correct grammar and usage**

Part 1: Analyze a Student Model

WRITING STANDARD
1.4.11.B Write complex informational pieces

Jason Bernales
Escalante High School

"The Scarlet Ibis" and the Theme of Pride

"All of us must have something or someone to be proud of, and Doodle had become mine. I did not know then that pride is a wonderful, terrible thing, a seed that bears two vines, life and death." In these words from "The Scarlet Ibis," James Hurst states one of the
5 story's main themes: that pride is both wonderful and terrible. Because of his feelings of pride, the narrator forces his brother Doodle to become stronger. He also rejects Doodle for showing signs of weakness.

As a child, the narrator is full of pride: "I thought myself pretty smart at many things, like holding my breath, running, jumping, or
10 climbing." When he is six, his mother gives birth to a baby who is disabled, physically and perhaps mentally. "It was bad enough having an invalid brother, but having one who possibly was not all there was unbearable," the narrator explains. Shockingly, he plans to kill his brother—until the baby smiles at him.

15 The child, nicknamed Doodle, learns to crawl but not to walk. The narrator is too proud to allow such an unusual situation to continue: "When Doodle was five years old, I was embarrassed at having a brother of that age who couldn't walk, so I set out to teach him."

Doodle is content to accept what his mother and the doctor have
20 told him—that he will never walk. But the narrator is determined. He and Doodle spend weeks practicing, the narrator hauling Doodle to a standing position again and again. When Doodle does learn to walk, the family is delighted. "Everyone wanted to hug me," says the narrator, "and I began to cry. . . . They did not know that I did it for myself; that

KEY TRAITS IN ACTION

Introduction captures reader's attention with a powerful quotation, identifies the literary work being analyzed, and makes a strong **thesis statement.**

Follows a clear **organizational pattern,** concentrating on one element (theme) and proceeding chronologically. Uses precise **adjectives** (*unusual*) and **adverbs** (*shockingly*).

Includes quotations and other **evidence** from "The Scarlet Ibis" to support the thesis.

25 pride, whose slave I was, spoke to me louder than all their voices, and
that Doodle walked only because I was ashamed of having a crippled
brother."

Success makes the narrator's pride even stronger: "I began to believe
in my own infallibility, and I prepared a terrific development program
30 for him." Doodle doesn't see why being different is bad, but his brother
stubbornly expects him to run, swim, climb, and fight by the time
school starts. The training leaves Doodle weak and feverish. "I should
have already admitted defeat, but my pride wouldn't let me," the
narrator explains.

35 Days before school begins, a scarlet ibis dies in the family's yard. The
bird was weak and unsure of itself, much like Doodle. That day the
narrator makes his brother practice rowing, but Doodle is tired and sad
after burying the ibis. The boys are far from home when a storm begins:
"We never spoke (What are the words that can solder cracked pride?),
40 but I knew he was watching me . . . for a sign of mercy." Instead, the
narrator runs too fast for Doodle, leaving him to collapse and die.

Serious, sincere **tone**
is formal enough for its
audience (a teacher and
perhaps classmates)
and purpose (to analyze
literature).

Devastated and heartbroken, the narrator weeps. He loved his brother
but also resented and punished him, feelings that he describes as "a knot
of cruelty borne by the stream of love." The narrator's pride leads to a
45 wonderful event, Doodle's learning to walk. It also leads to a terrible
event, Doodle's death. The contrast between these two types of pride is a
powerful theme that makes "The Scarlet Ibis" a compelling story.

Conclusion goes beyond
summary to explain why
the theme of pride is
crucial to the story.
Writer varies **sentence
structures** to make the
essay more interesting
and sophisticated.

2

WRITING STANDARD
1.5.11.A.2 Establish and maintain a single point of view

Part 2: Apply the Writing Process

PREWRITING

What Should I Do?

What Does It Look Like?

1. **Explore the elements of the story.**
   Use a graphic organizer to list observations or questions you have about story elements such as characters, plot, symbols, and theme. (Circle) the element or elements that intrigue you most.

   ▶

Characters	Doodle, narrator, ibis (?)
Plot	Narrator teaches Doodle to walk. Narrator makes Doodle do too much, helps cause his death.
Symbols	What does ibis stand for— Doodle, death?
Theme	*Narrator's pride helps and hurts his brother.*

2. **Choose a focus for your analysis.**
   Decide which story element you want to write about. Then jot down a **working thesis statement** that identifies the literary element you've chosen and lists the key points you want to make about it.

   ▶

   Working Thesis Statement:

   The theme of "The Scarlet Ibis" is that "pride is a wonderful, terrible thing." Because of his pride, the narrator helps his brother Doodle to become stronger. However, the narrator rejects Doodle for showing signs of weakness.

3. **Collect evidence from the story.**
   Read through the story again carefully. List quotations, details, and ideas that support the key points you noted in your **working thesis statement.**

   ▶

Evidence	What It Means
"I was embarrassed at having a brother . . . who couldn't walk"	Narrator decides to teach brother to walk.
Narrator cries when Doodle learns to walk.	Narrator is proud of what he did but ashamed of why he did it.
"My pride wouldn't let me" stop training Doodle.	Narrator wants Doodle to be like other kids, no matter what.

DRAFTING

What Should I Do?	What Does It Look Like?

1. Organize your ideas.
Consider different ways of presenting your material. Do you want to start with your most important, complex, or interesting idea—or end with it? This writer developed ideas in the order they're discussed in the story (Pattern 1).

Review your key points to be sure that each one directly relates to your thesis statement.

PATTERN 1

Introduction and Thesis
1. Doodle is born.
2. Doodle crawls.
3. Doodle learns to walk.
4. Narrator trains Doodle harder.
5. Narrator abandons Doodle.
Conclusion

PATTERN 2

Introduction and Thesis
A. Pride is wonderful.
  1. Narrator teaches Doodle to walk.
B. Pride is terrible.
  1. Narrator plans to kill Doodle.
  2. Narrator is ashamed of Doodle.
  3. Narrator abandons Doodle.
Conclusion

2. Support each key point with details from the text.
Every statement that you make should be backed up with evidence from the story. You also should explain how and why each detail supports your ideas.

As a child, the narrator is full of pride: — Key point

"I thought myself pretty smart at many things, like holding my breath, running, jumping, or climbing." — Support

3. Create a satisfying and memorable conclusion.
Summarize your key ideas and give your reader something new to think about. This could be an overall statement about the literary work or its effect on readers.

TIP Before revising, consult the **key traits** on page 490 and the **rubric** and **peer-reader questions** on page 496.

The narrator's pride leads to a wonderful event, Doodle's learning to walk. It also leads to a terrible event, Doodle's death. — Summary

The contrast between these two types of pride is a powerful theme that makes "The Scarlet Ibis" a compelling story. — Why it matters

REVISING AND EDITING

What Should I Do?

What Does It Look Like?

1. Strengthen your introduction.
- Draw a box around the first two or three sentences of your essay.
- Ask yourself: Would this beginning capture my attention?
- Consider starting with a powerful quotation, a question, or an unexpected idea.

▶

An unexpected idea
Pride can motivate us to do great things, but it can also cause us to hurt the people we love.

A quotation
"All of us must have something or someone to be proud of, and Doodle had become mine. I did not know then that pride is a wonderful, terrible thing, a seed that bears two vines, life and death."

2. Tune your tone.
- Ask a peer reader to [bracket] vocabulary that is too slangy or casual.
- Revise your essay so that it is formal throughout.

See page 496: Ask a Peer Reader

▶

[The narrator is disgusting. He's ready to kill his own little brother just for not being perfect. But then the kid smiles at him and he changes his mind.]
Shockingly, he plans to kill his brother—until the baby smiles at him.

3. Choose adjectives and adverbs carefully and wisely.
- Circle adjectives and adverbs in your essay.
- If you don't have many circles, think of modifiers to add.
- Ask yourself: Could I use sharper modifiers to express myself more accurately?

▶

Doodle doesn't see why being different is (bad) but
stubbornly
his brother expects him to run, swim, climb, and fight by the time school starts. The training leaves Doodle (tired,) weak and feverish.

4. Vary the types and structures of your sentences.
- Read your essay aloud. Highlight repeated sentence types or structures.
- Rewrite some of these sentences to give your writing fluency and a pleasing rhythm.

▶

The narrator weeps. He loved his brother. He also resented and punished him.
Devastated and heartbroken, the narrator weeps. He loved his brother but also resented and punished him.

Literary Analysis

Apply the Rubric

A strong literary analysis . . .

- ☑ opens by identifying the author and the literary work

- ☑ includes a strong, clear thesis statement

- ☑ develops ideas in a logical organizational scheme

- ☑ supports ideas with specific evidence from the text

- ☑ has a tone appropriate to the audience and purpose

- ☑ maintains interest with strong modifiers and varied sentence structures

- ☑ concludes with a statement addressing the work or its effect as a whole

Ask a Peer Reader

- How would you restate my thesis in your own words?

- Is the tone right for a literary analysis, or should some parts be more formal?

- Which parts of my analysis do you most strongly agree or disagree with? Why?

Check Your Grammar

- A literary analysis contains many quotations. Make sure that you punctuate them correctly. Periods and commas go inside quotation marks.

> *"I should have already admitted defeat, but, my pride wouldn't let me," the narrator explains.*

- If you choose to omit words from within a quotation, use ellipses (three spaced periods).

> *"I knew he was watching me . . . for a sign of mercy."*

- If you quote a word or phrase within a sentence of your own, do not capitalize the first letter of the word or phrase.

> *He loved his brother but also resented and punished him, feelings he described as "a knot of cruelty borne by the steam of love."*

- You can use a colon to introduce a long quotation.

> *Success makes the narrator's pride even stronger: "I began to believe in my own infallibility, and I prepared a terrific development program for him."*

See pages R49–R51: Quick Reference: Punctuation and Capitalization

Writing Online

PUBLISHING OPTIONS
For publishing options, visit the **Writing Center** at **ClassZone.com.**

ASSESSMENT PREPARATION
For writing and grammar assessment practice, go to the **Assessment Center** at **ClassZone.com.**

Participating in a Panel Discussion

Taking part in a panel discussion can deepen your understanding of a literary work, improve your public-speaking skills, and give you practice in "thinking on your feet."

Planning the Discussion

1. **Identify panel members.** The teacher may choose participants, or students interested in a specific story may form a panel.

2. **Appoint a moderator.** Panel members should ask for a volunteer or appoint one student to moderate the discussion.

3. **Agree on rules for the discussion.** Participants should agree to speak clearly and concisely, listen respectfully without interrupting, and ask thoughtful questions.

4. **Review the story and your thoughts about it.** Reread both the literary work and your written analysis of it. Jot down your main thoughts about the story.

Holding the Discussion

1. **Get started.** The moderator should identify the story, introduce the panelists, and ask a question such as, "What literary element contributes most to the meaning of this story?"

2. **State your ideas.** Respond to the question posed by the moderator. Make any related points that support your answer.

3. **Give others a chance to respond.** Listen while another speaker summarizes your ideas and adds his or her own thoughts.

> *"So you're saying that the setting of "The Scarlet Ibis" is the most important literary element in the story? I agree that it is a sad place filled with death and that this contributes to the story's mood and theme. But I think the dialogue in the story is more important. Here's why."*

4. **Be respectful.** Give everyone a chance to talk.

5. **Wrap it up.** The moderator should summarize the ideas and thank the panelists for participating.

Reading Comprehension

DIRECTIONS *Read the following selection and answer the questions.*

The Apple-Tree

Katherine Mansfield

There were two orchards belonging to the old house. One, that we called the "wild" orchard, lay beyond the vegetable garden; it was planted with bitter cherries and damsons and transparent yellow plums. For some reason it lay under a cloud; we never played there, we did not even trouble to pick up the fallen fruit; and there, every Monday morning, to the round open space in the middle, the servant girl and the washerwoman carried the wet linen— Grandmother's nightdresses, Father's striped shirts, the hired man's cotton trousers and the servant girl's "dreadfully vulgar" salmon-pink flannelette drawers jigged and slapped in horrid familiarity.

10   But the other orchard, far away and hidden from the house, lay at the foot of a little hill and stretched right over to the edge of the paddocks—to the clumps of wattles bobbing yellow in the bright sun and the blue gums with their streaming sickle-shaped leaves. There, under the fruit trees, the grass grew so thick and coarse that it tangled and knotted in your shoes as you walked, and even on the hottest day it was damp to touch when you stopped and parted it this way and that, looking for windfalls—the apples marked with a bird's beak, the big bruised pears, the quinces, so good to eat with a pinch of salt, but so delicious to smell that you could not bite for sniffing. . . .

One year the orchard had its Forbidden Tree. It was an apple-tree discovered
20   by Father and a friend during an after-dinner prowl one Sunday afternoon.

"Great Scott!" said the friend, lighting upon it with every appearance of admiring astonishment: "Isn't that a ——?" And a rich, splendid name settled like an unknown bird on the tree.

"Yes, I believe it is," said Father lightly. He knew nothing whatever about the names of fruit trees.

"Great Scott!" said the friend again. "They're wonderful apples. Nothing like 'em—and you're going to have a tip-top crop. Marvellous apples! You can't beat 'em!"

"No, they're very fine—very fine," said Father carelessly, but looking upon
30   the tree with new and lively interest.

"They're rare—they're very rare. Hardly ever see 'em in England nowadays," said the visitor and set a seal on Father's delight. For Father was a self-made

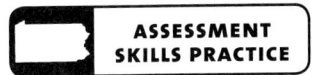

man and the price he had to pay for everything was so huge and so painful that nothing rang so sweet to him as to hear his purchase praised. He was young and sensitive still. He still wondered whether in the deepest sense he got his money's worth. He still had hours when he walked up and down in the moonlight half deciding to "chuck this confounded rushing to the office every day—and clear out—clear out once and for all." And now to discover that he'd a valuable apple-tree thrown in with the orchard—an apple-tree that this
40 Johnny from England positively envied!

"Don't touch that tree! Do you hear me, children!" said he, bland and firm; and when the guest had gone, with quite another voice and manner:

"If I catch either of you touching those apples you shall not only go to bed—you shall each have a good sound whipping." Which merely added to its magnificence.

Every Sunday morning after church Father, with Bogey and me tailing after, walked through the flower garden, down the violet path, past the lace-bark tree, past the white rose and syringa bushes, and down the hill to the orchard. The apple-tree—like the Virgin Mary—seemed to have been miraculously
50 warned of its high honour, standing apart from its fellows, bending a little under its rich clusters, fluttering its polished leaves, important and exquisite before Father's awful eye. His heart swelled to the sight—we knew his heart swelled. He put his hands behind his back and screwed up his eyes in the way he had. There it stood—the accidental thing—the thing that no one had been aware of when the hard bargain was driven. It hadn't been counted in, hadn't in a way been paid for. If the house had been burned to the ground at that time it would have meant less to him than the destruction of his tree. And how we played up to him, Bogey and I,—Bogey with his scratched knees pressed together, his hands behind his back, too, and a round cap on his head with
60 "H.M.S. Thunderbolt" printed across it.

The apples turned from pale green to yellow; then they had deep pink stripes painted on them, and then the pink melted all over the yellow, reddened, and spread into a fine clear crimson.

At last the day came when Father took out of his waistcoat pocket a little pearl pen-knife. He reached up. Very slowly and very carefully he picked two apples growing on a bough.

"By Jove! They're warm," cried Father in amazement. "They're wonderful apples! Tip-top! Marvellous!" he echoed. He rolled them over in his hands.

"Look at that!" he said. "Not a spot—not a blemish!" And he walked
70 through the orchard with Bogey and me stumbling after, to a tree-stump
under the wattles. We sat, one on either side of Father. He laid one apple
down, opened the pearl pen-knife and neatly and beautifully cut the other
in half.

"By Jove! Look at that!" he exclaimed.

"Father!" we cried, dutiful but really enthusiastic, too. For the lovely red
colour had bitten right through the white flesh of the apple; it was pink to
the shiny black pips lying so justly in their scaly pods. It looked as though the
apple had been dipped in wine.

"Never seen *that* before," said Father. "You won't find an apple like that in a
80 hurry!" He put it to his nose and pronounced an unfamiliar word. "Bouquet!
What a bouquet!" And then he handed to Bogey one half, to me the other.

"Don't *bolt* it!" said he. It was agony to give even so much away. I knew it,
while I took mine humbly and humbly Bogey took his.

Then he divided the second with the same neat beautiful little cut of the
pearl knife.

I kept my eyes on Bogey. Together we took a bite. Our mouths were full of a
floury stuff, a hard, faintly bitter skin—a horrible taste of something dry. . . .

"Well?" asked Father, very jovial. He had cut his two halves into quarters
and was taking out the little pods. "Well?"
90 Bogey and I stared at each other, chewing desperately. In that second of
chewing and swallowing a long silent conversation passed between us—and
a strange meaning smile. We swallowed. We edged near Father, just touching
him.

"Perfect!" we lied. "Perfect—Father! Simply lovely!"

But it was no use. Father spat his out and never went near the apple-tree again.

Comprehension

DIRECTIONS *Answer these questions about "The Apple-Tree."*

1. What makes the apple tree seem valuable to the father?

   A His children love the tree.

   B He has never seen a tree like it before.

   C He has always wanted an apple tree.

   D His friend tells him that it is rare.

2. As the apples on the tree ripen, the father

   A becomes more and more proud of owning the apple tree

   B begins to lose interest in the apple tree

   C worries that his children will somehow harm the apple tree

   D knows that the tree is worth more than his house

3. What is the main theme of the story?

   A If your expectations are too high, you may end up disappointed.

   B Beautiful apple trees often produce bitter fruit.

   C Telling the truth is always the best policy.

   D When you own something, you must constantly take care of it.

4. How are the ripe apples different from what the characters expect?

   A They are small instead of large.

   B The apples are pale pink instead of red.

   C They taste bitter instead of sweet.

   D The apples smell like flowers instead of fruit.

5. Why do the children lie to their father about how the apple tastes?

   A They are afraid of being punished.

   B They don't want him to be disappointed.

   C They want to trick him into liking the apple.

   D They don't care what he thinks.

6. What does the apple tree symbolize after the visitor praises it?

   A the father's power

   B the children's obedience

   C the visitor's wisdom

   D the fruit's sweetness

Open–Ended Items

7. Give one reason why the author calls the apple tree the Forbidden Tree. Support your idea about why the author uses this symbol with an example from the text or from your own knowledge.

8. Explain why the father believes his friend's statement that the apples are rare and will be marvelous. Support your answer with three details from the story.

Vocabulary

DIRECTIONS *Use context clues to answer the following questions.*

1. Which is the most likely meaning of *damson* from line 3?

   A a type of cloud

   B a kind of fruit

   C an orchard

   D a vegetable garden

2. Which nearby words give a clue to the meaning of *damson?*

   A *cherries* and *plums*

   B *transparent yellow*

   C *vegetable garden*

   D *under a cloud*

3. Which is the most likely meaning of *gums* from line 12?

   A strong colors

   B a certain type of tree

   C a structure in the mouth

   D chewy substances

4. Which nearby word gives the best clue to the meaning of *gums?*

   A *blue*

   B *streaming*

   C *sickle*

   D *leaves*

5. Use context clues to figure out what *windfalls* refers to in line 16.

   A broken branches

   B clumps of thick grass

   C fallen fruit

   D injured birds

DIRECTIONS *Use context clues and your knowledge of suffixes to answer the following questions.*

6. What is the most likely meaning of the word *magnificence* as it appears in the following quotation from lines 43–45?

   "If I catch either of you touching those apples you shall not only go to bed—you shall each have a good sound whipping." Which merely added to its <u>magnificence</u>.

   A hugeness

   B bright light

   C grand quality

   D lack of power

7. What is the meaning of *humbly* as it appears in the following quotation from lines 82–83?

   "Don't *bolt* it!" said he. It was agony to give even so much away. I knew it, while I took mine <u>humbly</u> and <u>humbly</u> Bogey took his.

   A full of joy

   B in a respectful manner

   C under pressure

   D out of a sense of kindness

8. Read the following two excerpts from the selection. Which word means nearly the same as the word *jovial* in line 88?

   "Never seen *that* before," said Father. "You won't find an apple like that in a hurry!" He put it to his nose and pronounced an unfamiliar word. "Bouquet! What a bouquet!" And then he handed to Bogey one half, to me the other.

   "Well?" asked Father, very <u>jovial</u>. He had cut his two halves into quarters and was taking out the little pods. "Well?"

   A smug   C bitter

   B cheerful   D triumphant

Grammar & Style

DIRECTIONS *Read the passage and answer the questions that follow.*

> (1) Nadia walked down the street. (2) She heard a noise behind her. (3) She considered her options. (4) She decided to run. (5) But it was dark now. (6) She was in an unfamiliar part of town. (7) Suddenly, she felt hot breath on the back of her leg. (8) She poised herself to kick. (9) Then she realized it was just a dog. (10) Had she really been so afraid of a friendly little beagle? (11) Or had something else been behind her too?

1. Choose the correct way to rewrite sentences 1 and 2 as one sentence containing one independent clause and one subordinate clause. Choose D if no other answer choice is correct.

   A Nadia walked down the street, hearing a noise behind her.

   B Nadia walked down the street, she heard a noise behind her.

   C As Nadia walked down the street, she heard a noise behind her.

   D None of the above

2. Choose the correct way to rewrite sentences 3 and 4 as one sentence containing one independent clause. Choose D if no other answer choice is correct.

   A She considered her options and decided to run.

   B She considered her options, and then she decided to run.

   C She considered her options; she decided to run.

   D None of the above

3. Choose the correct way to rewrite sentences 5 and 6 as one sentence containing two independent clauses. Choose D if no other answer choice is correct.

   A Since it was dark now, this part of town was unfamiliar.

   B But it was dark now, and she was in an unfamiliar part of town.

   C Because it was dark now, she realized she was in an unfamiliar part of town.

   D None of the above

4. Choose the correct way to rewrite sentences 7–9 as one sentence containing one subordinate clause and two independent clauses. Choose D if no other answer choice is correct.

   A Suddenly, she felt hot breath on the back of her leg, and as she poised herself to kick, she realized it was just a dog.

   B Suddenly, she felt hot breath on the back of her leg, poised herself to kick, and realized it was just a dog.

   C Suddenly, she felt hot breath on the back of her leg, then she poised herself to kick, and then she realized it was just a dog.

   D None of the above

STOP

Great Reads

Ideas for Independent Reading

Which of the themes in this unit has the most importance in your life? Discover how these themes affect others in the following books.

How do expectations affect performance?

Music of the Heart
by Roberta Gaspari

No one expected Gaspari's students to succeed at the violin. But she and her kids—more than one thousand over the years—proved that expectations and talent can lead to good music.

Gifted Hands
by Ben Carson, M.D. with Cecil Murphy

Carson's mother expected him to do something worthwhile with his life. He did not disappoint her. In 1987, the surgeon helped complete the first successful separation of Siamese twins joined at the head.

Lanterns: A Memoir of Mentors
by Marian Wright Edelman

The lawyer, civil rights activist, and founder of the Children's Defense Fund honors the famous and not-so-famous people in her life who kept her expectations high while she struggled to make a difference.

Why do we hurt the ones we love?

The Kite Runner
by Khaled Hosseini

Amir and Hassan grow up together in Afghanistan. Amir fails his friend Hassan before leaving for America. He returns years later to try to make up for his betrayal.

The Once and Future King
by T. H. White

In this retelling of the legend of King Arthur, Queen Guinevere loves both her husband Arthur and the knight Lancelot, Arthur's best friend. Though each one loves the other two, all three suffer terribly.

This Boy's Life
by Tobias Wolff

Divorce may be necessary for adults, but the children in the family often get hurt. The award-winning author remembers his struggle to grow up and find himself while frequently separated from his father.

What are you really good at?

One Writer's Beginnings
by Eudora Welty

In this memoir, Welty brings to life her family, her younger self, and the American South in the early 1900s. She also conveys her love for stories—those she found in books as well as those she heard on long, hot summer afternoons.

I'd Rather Teach Peace
by Colman McCarthy

As a *Washington Post* columnist, McCarthy has written for many years on nonviolence as a way of life. Here he talks about teaching peace to students, prisoners, and others.

The Other Side of the Mountain
by Evans G. Valens

Valens tells the inspiring true story of skier Jill Kinmont, who found a way to reshape her life after a crippling accident.

UNIT 5

Ideas Made Visible

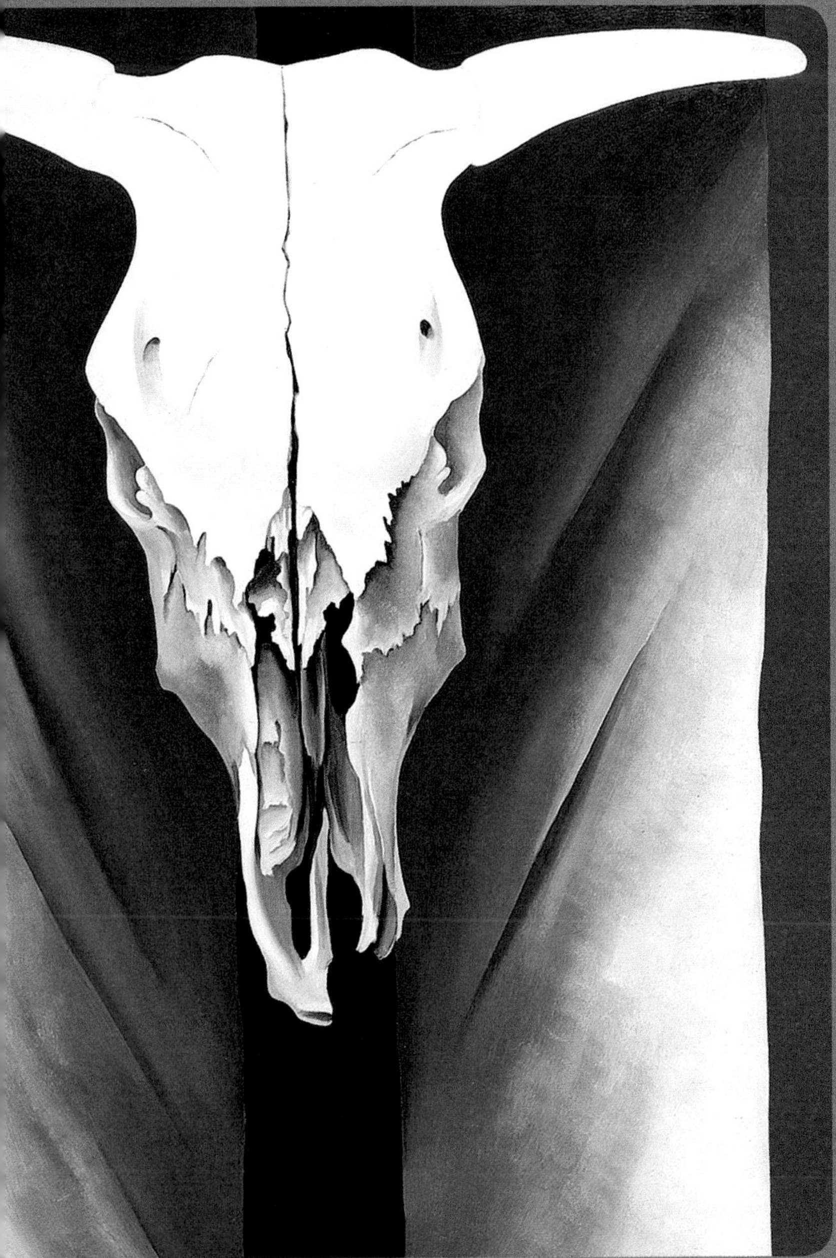

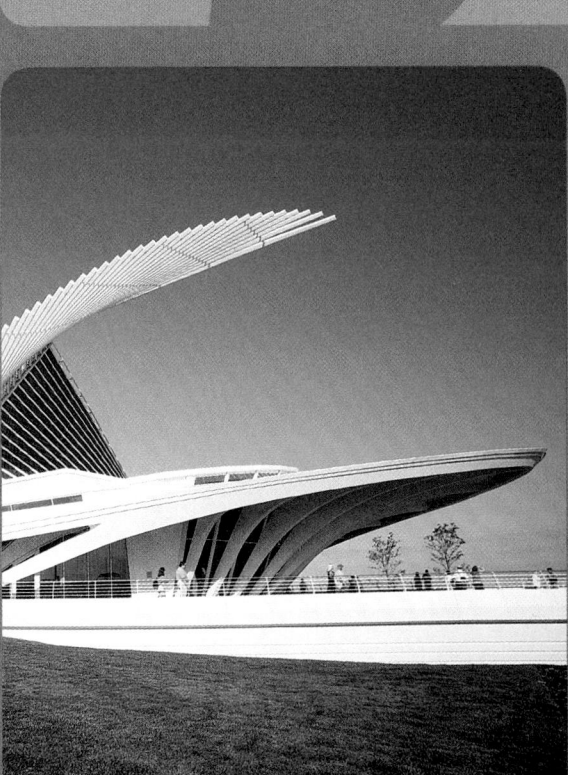

AUTHOR'S PURPOSE

- In Nonfiction
- In Media
- In Fiction

Share What You Know

Why do writers WRITE?

A letter to the editor. A research paper. An e-mail to a friend. Any of these writing products might come from your pen or computer and be shared with others or kept to yourself. The reasons that any individual writes are as varied as the personality and goals of the writer. But the writer always has a **purpose** for crafting words in a particular form and in a particular way.

ACTIVITY List five things you have read and five things you have written in the last month. Answer the following:

- Which did you read to get information? Which did you write to provide information?

- Which tried to persuade you? Which did you write to persuade someone else?

- Which did you write to express how you felt?

Think about your answers. For which purpose did you most often read? For which purpose did you most often write? Are you surprised?

PENNSYLVANIA
STANDARDS

Preview Unit Goals

LITERARY ANALYSIS
- Identify and analyze tone and diction
- Recognize and analyze an author's perspective

READING
- Use reading strategies, including predicting
- Make inferences
- Analyze patterns of organization, including chronological order and comparison and contrast
- Use text features to locate and comprehend information
- Identify and analyze an author's purpose
- Interpret graphic aids
- Identify an implied main idea

WRITING AND GRAMMAR
- Write a problem-solution essay
- Use nouns, adverbs, and conjunctions correctly

SPEAKING, LISTENING, AND VIEWING
- Interpret and evaluate how events and information are presented in nonprint sources
- Create a news segment
- Produce a video documentary

VOCABULARY
- Use word roots to understand the meaning of words
- Use Greek suffixes to understand specialized vocabulary

ACADEMIC VOCABULARY
- tone
- author's perspective
- text features
- diction
- author's purpose
- patterns of organization

Author's Purpose

Before architects draft their blueprints, they need to understand the purpose of the proposed building. Are they designing a stadium to seat screaming spectators or a library for quiet study? This purpose drives every decision that architects make, from the layout of their buildings to the design. Like architects, writers carefully construct their stories and essays with a specific purpose in mind. Recognizing this purpose is essential to understanding everything you read.

PENNSYLVANIA STANDARDS

READING STANDARDS
A.2.6.1 Describe the author's purpose
B.3.3.1 Interpret and analyze text organization

Part 1: Author's Purpose and Perspective

An **author's purpose** is what the writer hopes to achieve by crafting a particular work. Although a writer may have more than one purpose, usually one purpose stands out. A writer's purpose could be any of the following:

- to inform or explain
- to persuade
- to express thoughts or feelings
- to entertain

You can uncover an author's purpose by looking at the choices the writer made. Every choice—from the subject and the tone to the particular words and details—is a clue that can reveal the purpose. Another clue is your reaction to what you read. For instance, if you are convinced by an argument to fight for a cause, then the author's primary purpose is probably to persuade.

AUTHOR'S PURPOSE	CLUES IN THE WRITING
TO INFORM OR EXPLAIN **Examples: encyclopedia or magazine articles, documentaries, instruction manuals, Web sites**	• facts and statistics • directions • steps in a process • diagrams or illustrated explanations
TO PERSUADE **Examples: editorials, TV ads, political speeches**	• a statement of opinion • supporting evidence • appeals to emotion • a call to action
TO ENTERTAIN **Examples: short stories, novels, plays, humorous essays, movies**	• suspenseful or exciting situations • humorous or fascinating details • intriguing characters
TO EXPRESS THOUGHTS OR FEELINGS **Examples: personal essays, poems, diaries, journals**	• thoughtful descriptions • insightful observations • the writer's personal feelings

MODEL 1: TO INFORM OR EXPLAIN

Writing that informs or explains typically leaves you feeling more knowledgeable. As you read this article, look for clues that suggest its purpose.

from WEB MASTERS

Nonfiction article by **Joe Bower**

Spiderwebs are flexible yet strong, ultrasensitive, adaptable to different settings, and able to span great distances (compared with the size of their makers). They perform a variety of impressive functions, the most obvious of which is capturing prey.

5   Not all of the world's estimated 37,000 known spider species make webs. In fact, arachnologists categorize spiders based on this ability. Tarantulas and jumping spiders belong to the large group that doesn't make webs. Instead, these arachnids, which are sometimes referred to as wandering spiders, stalk or ambush their prey.

Close Read

1. Which words and phrases suggest that this is an informative article? One word has been boxed.

2. Identify one other clue that suggests the author's purpose is to inform or explain.

MODEL 2: TO EXPRESS THOUGHTS OR FEELINGS

This essay also focuses on spiders, but the writer does not include a single fact or statistic. How do the details, the language, and the writer's tone help you understand her feelings about spiders?

from Weaving THE WORLD

Personal essay by **Janisse Ray**

Every night the spiders weave the world back together. This morning I see webs whole again, shining freshly gossamer in the new sun, webs we tore down last night accidentally, setting up the tent on the platform. All day paddling, we have been watching for them—zippers and bananas and crabs, colorful and intriguing.

5   They are everywhere, stitching leaves to trees, and trees to shrubs, and shrubs to ground. . . .

The spiders have adapted to their fragility, their vulnerability; when we humans bungle into their webs, they scurry off, up a single thread into a sweet bay. They have no new technologies, no new economies. Across the

10   prairies they spin and spin, as they have done for thousands of years, holding this outrageously glorious world together.

Close Read

1. Examine the boxed details that the writer uses to describe spiders and their webs. How do these details differ from those in "Web Masters"?

2. Is the writer's attitude toward spiders admiring or matter-of-fact? Support your answer.

RECOGNIZING AUTHOR'S PERSPECTIVE

Even if they have similar purposes, no two writers will approach a topic in the same way. Their perspectives influence what they write and how they write it. An **author's perspective** is the lens through which a writer looks at a topic. This lens is colored by the writer's experiences, values, and feelings.

Consider the two excerpts on the previous page. Factual articles, such as "Web Masters," usually don't reveal a writer's viewpoint. However, essays, such as "Weaving the World," include clues that convey an author's perspective. Notice how the following clues reveal a writer who appreciates nature.

- **Focus of Essay** Instead of focusing on spiders' creepy qualities, the writer marvels at their ability to create webs from nothing.

- **Word Choice** Words and phrases such as "colorful and intriguing" and "vulnerability" reveal the writer's fascination with the wonders of nature.

- **Tone** A writer's **tone** is his or her attitude toward a subject. The words and details in "Weaving the World" reflect an admiring tone—not a fearful one.

Part 2: Organization and Format

To achieve their purpose, writers choose particular patterns of organization, such as **cause-effect** and **classification**. Recognizing these patterns can help you determine an author's purpose, locate information, and understand relationships between ideas. Here are two common patterns.

CHRONOLOGICAL	COMPARISON-CONTRAST
What It Does	***What It Does***
• Describes events in time order	• Highlights similarities and differences between two or more subjects
Why Writers Use It	***Why Writers Use It***
• To explain a sequence of events in an easy-to-follow way	• To show the benefits of one subject over another
• To tell a suspenseful or exciting story	• To compare an unfamiliar subject with a familiar one
How to Recognize It	***How to Recognize It***
• Look for signal words such as *before, finally, first, next,* and *then.*	• Look for signal words such as *also, and, but, in contrast, unlike,* and *while.*

In addition to these patterns, writers of nonfiction use **text features** to help you understand a topic. Imagine a scientific article without **subheadings, captions,** and **boldfaced type** to guide you. Who wouldn't be confused?

MODEL: CLASSIFICATION ORGANIZATION

In this scientific article, the writer uses classification organization to group information by common characteristics. As you read, think about how this organization, with the help of the text features, helps you digest the information.

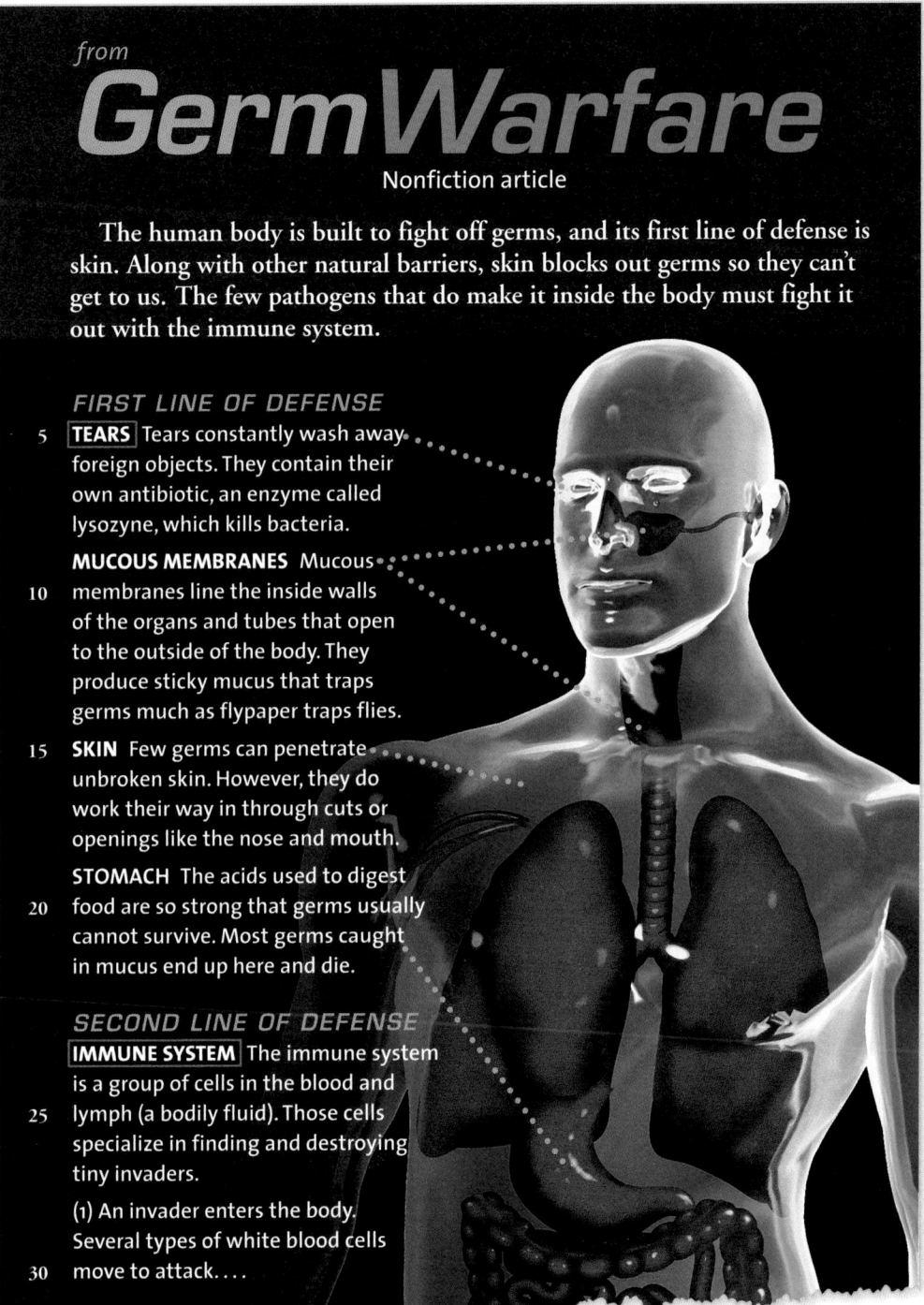

from

GermWarfare
Nonfiction article

The human body is built to fight off germs, and its first line of defense is skin. Along with other natural barriers, skin blocks out germs so they can't get to us. The few pathogens that do make it inside the body must fight it out with the immune system.

FIRST LINE OF DEFENSE

5 **TEARS** Tears constantly wash away foreign objects. They contain their own antibiotic, an enzyme called lysozyne, which kills bacteria.

MUCOUS MEMBRANES Mucous
10 membranes line the inside walls of the organs and tubes that open to the outside of the body. They produce sticky mucus that traps germs much as flypaper traps flies.

15 **SKIN** Few germs can penetrate unbroken skin. However, they do work their way in through cuts or openings like the nose and mouth.

STOMACH The acids used to digest
20 food are so strong that germs usually cannot survive. Most germs caught in mucus end up here and die.

SECOND LINE OF DEFENSE

IMMUNE SYSTEM The immune system is a group of cells in the blood and
25 lymph (a bodily fluid). Those cells specialize in finding and destroying tiny invaders.

(1) An invader enters the body. Several types of white blood cells
30 move to attack....

Close Read

1. Into what two main categories is the information grouped? Explain how you can tell.

2. Notice the boldfaced words used throughout the article. Two have been boxed. What purpose do they serve?

3. What does the information in the annotated diagram add to your understanding of mucous membranes?

Part 3: Compare Texts

What happens when lightning strikes an airplane? Both of the following excerpts answer this question, but their similarities end there. As you read, use what you have just learned about clues—details, tone, and choice of words—to determine each author's purpose and perspective.

from
Aha Moment

Essay by **Julia Alvarez**

I was in the tiny bathroom in the back of the plane when I felt the slamming jolt, then the horrible swerve that threw me against the door. Oh Lord, I thought, this is it! Somehow I managed to unbolt the door and scramble out. The flight attendants, already strapped in, waved wildly for me
5 to sit down. As I lunged ahead toward my seat, passengers looked up at me with the stricken expression of creatures who know they are about to die.
    "I think we got hit by lightning," the girl in the seat next to mine said. She was from a small town in east Texas, and this was only her second time on an airplane. She had won a trip to England by competing in a high school
10 geography bee and was supposed to make a connecting flight when we landed in Newark.
    In the next seat, at the window, sat a young businessman who had been confidently working. Now he looked worried—something that really worries me: when confident-looking businessmen look worried. The laptop was put
15 away. "Something's not right," he said.
    The pilot's voice came over the speaker. I heard vaguely through my fear, "Engine number two . . . hit . . . emergency landing . . . New Orleans." When he was done, the voice of a flight attendant came on, reminding us of the emergency procedures she had reviewed before takeoff. Of course I never paid
20 attention to this drill, always figuring that if we ever got to the point where we needed to use life jackets, I would have already died of terror.
    Now we began a roller-coaster ride through the thunderclouds. I was ready to faint, but when I saw the face of the girl next to me I pulled myself together. I reached for her hand and reassured her that we were going to make it. "What a
25 story you're going to tell when you get home!" I said. "After this, London's going to seem like small potatoes."

Close Read

1. Reread the boxed details. Is Alvarez reporting "just the facts" or is she sharing personal impressions? Explain the intended effect of these details.

2. Although Alvarez describes a frightening experience, her tone is not fearful. Identify the tone and three details that convey it.

3. Do you think Alvarez's primary purpose is to persuade, to entertain, to inform, or to express thoughts and feelings? Support your answer.

4. Consider the descriptions in lines 1–3 and 19–21, as well as Alvarez's tone. What can you infer about her perspective?

Now read this article, and compare it to Alvarez's dramatic account.
Use the clues in the text to identify the author's purpose and perspective.

Aircraft Built to Shrug Off Lightning Strike

Newspaper article by **Tom McNamee**

Lightning strikes airplanes now and again, but seldom with tragic results.

In a typical year, lightning
5   causes only a handful of aircraft accidents in the United States, and occasionally none at all. From 1983 through 1995, 29 accidents resulted in 37 deaths. But a 30th
10 accident proved the exception. On Aug. 2, 1985, lightning struck a Lockheed L-1011 as it came in for a landing at Dallas-Fort Worth International Airport, slamming
15 the jet to the ground and killing 137 passengers.

One witness on the ground, an aviation weather expert, recalled seeing "lightning from cloud to
20 cloud." Another witness said the plane exploded even before crashing into "just a big ball of fire."

A Plane's Built-in Protection

As a rule, however, the laws of nature favor aircraft in a collision
25 with lightning. Lightning's electrical charge usually spreads across the entire outer skin of the craft, robbing it of its concentrated power, before it is shed like rainwater.
30 The metallic skin of some aircraft is ideal for conducting and diluting an electrical charge. And planes with skins made of lighter-weight composite materials, such as

The most common areas for lightning to strike a plane include the wing tips and the fuselage nose.

35 graphite, are commonly fitted with an underlying metal mesh to collect and route the charge. . . .

Aircraft Size and Condition

As a rule, larger planes are least threatened by lightning, said Donald
40 Kemp, retired chief of accident investigations for the Federal Aviation Administration. Larger aircraft have more surface area to absorb lightning's electrical charge,
45 and they are fitted with pencil-like "shedders" on the back of the wings to collect and "bleed off" electricity.

"If a plane is in proper condition, you shouldn't have a problem,"
50 Kemp said.

Close Read

1. How do the boxed details in this article differ from those in "Aha Moment"?

2. Identify two text features that the writer uses. What information do these features convey?

3. What is the author's purpose? Describe two clues that helped you determine that purpose.

4. Consider the writer's tone and the details in this article. Do they tell you anything about the writer's perspective? Explain your answer.

Island Morning
Descriptive Essay by Jamaica Kincaid

What place do you call HOME?

PENNSYLVANIA STANDARDS

READING STANDARDS
A.2.6.1 Describe the author's purpose
B.3.3.2 Interpret and/or analyze purpose for text organization

KEY IDEA The word *home* can mean many different things. When you think about your home, you might envision the building you live in or your own familiar neighborhood. You may picture the streets of your hometown or the landscape of your home country. *Home* can include the people you care about and your memories of growing up. It can even be a place where you no longer live that still feels more like home than where you live today.

QUICKWRITE What does the word *home* bring to mind? In a short paragraph, describe the first image—be it person, place, or thing— you picture when you think of *home*. If you'd like, attach a sketch to accompany your description.

LITERARY ANALYSIS: DICTION

Diction includes both a writer's choice of words as well as syntax, or the way those words are arranged into sentences. Jamaica Kincaid arranges words in unique ways, often using repetition to create rhythmic sounds. Describing her neighbors' morning routine, she writes,

All of these different people doing all these different things did this one thing: they were all up and about by half past five in the morning.

As you read, look for other passages in which Kincaid creates unusual sentences or chooses words to establish rhythm as well as imagery.

Review: **Tone**

READING SKILL: ANALYZE PATTERNS OF ORGANIZATION

To show relationships between ideas, writers arrange their information in an order that emphasizes those relationships. In this essay, Kincaid uses both **comparison and contrast** and **chronological order.**

- When organizing according to comparison and contrast, Kincaid presents all of the details about one subject or place and then all of the details about another.

- When Kincaid uses chronological order, she presents events in the order in which they typically occur.

As you read, record **signal words** that help you identify both patterns of organization that Kincaid uses in this essay.

Signal Words	Pattern of Organization
"by six o'clock" (line 29)	chronological order
"I now live in ..." (line 93)	comparison and contrast

Author Online

Jamaica Kincaid
born 1949

Leaving the Island
Jamaica Kincaid is the name Elaine Potter Richardson chose for herself when she began writing. Born on Antigua, a small Caribbean island that was then a British colony, Kincaid was educated in British schools. Although she was often at the top of her class, her mother removed her from school at age 17 against her wishes and sent her to America to support the family.

Musical Musings When she arrived in America, Kincaid explains, "I didn't know there was such a world as the literary world. I didn't know anything, except maybe how to put one foot in front of the other." She broke ties with her family and took a number of different jobs—and was fired from each one. In 1976, Kincaid landed a job at the *New Yorker*, a literary magazine, where her unique and resilient writing voice emerged. Much of Kincaid's writing expresses her anger at colonialism and the British disregard for her identity as an African-Caribbean woman. Her prose is celebrated for its lyrical beauty. "My work," she says, "is a chord that develops in many different ways."

 MORE ABOUT THE AUTHOR
For more on Jamaica Kincaid, visit the
Literature Center at **ClassZone.com.**

Background

History of Antigua Kincaid's birthplace, a small island in the eastern Caribbean, was a British colony for over 300 years. In 1981, Antigua united with a small neighboring island to become Antigua and Barbuda, an independent state. Most Antiguans have African heritage, as they are descendants of slaves brought to the island centuries ago to work in the tobacco and sugarcane fields.

Island MORNING

Jamaica Kincaid

I grew up on an island in the West Indies which has an area of a hundred and eight square miles. On the island were many sugarcane fields and a sugar-making factory and a factory where both white and dark rum were made. There were cotton fields, but there were not as many cotton fields as there were sugarcane fields. There were arrowroot[1] fields and tobacco fields, too, but there were not as many arrowroot fields and tobacco fields as there were cotton fields. Some of the fifty-four thousand people who lived on the island grew bananas and mangoes and eddoes and dasheen and christophine[2] and sweet potatoes and white potatoes and plums and guavas and papaws and
10 limes and lemons and oranges and grapefruits, and every Saturday they would bring them to the market, which was on Market Street, and they would sell the things they had grown. This was the only way many of them could make **Ⓐ** a living, and, though it sounds like farming, they weren't farmers in the way a Midwestern wheatgrower is a farmer, and they don't think of the plots of land on which they grew these things as The Farm. Instead, the plots of land were called The Ground. They might say, "Today, me a go up ground." The Ground was often many miles away from where they lived, and they got there not by taking a truck or some other kind of automotive transportation but by riding a donkey or by walking. A small number—a very small number—of the fifty-
20 four thousand people worked in banks or in offices. The rest of them—the ones who didn't grow things that were sold in the market on Saturday or work in the factories or in the fields, the banks or the offices—were carpenters or

ANALYZE VISUALS
Examine the painting on page 517. What **mood** do the bright colors, busy people, and whimsical animals create? Explain your answer.

Ⓐ DICTION
Reread lines 7–12 aloud. What is the effect of listing each fruit and vegetable separately instead of simply referring to the crops as a group?

---

1. **arrowroot:** a West Indian plant from which a starch is derived, for use in cooking and medicine.
2. **eddoes and dasheen and christophine:** eddoes and dasheen are plants with edible corms, or small bulblike growths. Christophine is a fruit-growing plant.

Detail of *Harvest Scene with Twelve People,*
R. Mervilus. Oil on canvas.
Private collection. © SuperStock.

masons or servants in the new hotels for tourists which were appearing suddenly all over the island, or servants in private homes, or seamstresses, or tailors, or shopkeepers, or fishermen, or dockworkers, or schoolchildren. All of these different people doing all these different things did this one thing: they were all up and about by half past five in the morning, and they did this without the help of an alarm clock or an automatic clock radio. Every morning—workday, Saturday, or Sunday—the whole island was alive by six o'clock. People got up
30 early on weekdays to go to work or to school; they got up early on Saturday to go to market; and they got up early on Sunday to go to church. **B**

It is true that the early morning is the most beautiful time of day on the island. The sun has just come up and is immediately big and bright, the way the sun always is on the island, but the air is still cool from the night; the sky is deep, cool blue (like the sea, it gets lighter as the day wears on, and then it gets darker, until by midnight it looks black); the red in the hibiscus and the flamboyant³ flowers seems redder; the green of the trees and grass seems greener. If it is December, there is dew everywhere: dew on the painted red galvanized rooftops;⁴ dew on my mother's upside-down washtubs; dew on the stones that
40 make up her stone heap (a round mound of big and little stones in the middle of our yard; my mother spreads out soapy white laundry on these stones, so that the hot sun will bleach them even whiter); dew on the vegetables in my mother's treasured (to her, horrible to me) vegetable garden. But it wasn't to admire any of these things that people got up so early. I had never, in all the time I lived there, heard anyone say, "What a beautiful morning." Once, just the way I had read it in a book, I stretched and said to my mother, "Oh, isn't it a really lovely morning?" She didn't reply to that at all, but she pulled my eyelids this way and that and then said that my sluggish liver was getting even more sluggish. I don't know why people got up so early, but I do know that they took great pride in
50 this. It wasn't unusual at all to hear one woman say to another, "Me up since **C** way 'fore day mornin'," and for the other woman to say back to her, with a laugh, "Yes, my dear, you know de early bird ketch de early worm."

In our house, we got up every day at half past five. This is what got us up: every morning, Mr. Jarvis—a dockworker who lived with his wife (she sold sweets she made herself to schoolchildren at the bus depot just before they boarded buses that would take them back to their homes in the country) and their eight children in a house at the very end of our street—would take his herd of goats to pasture. At exactly half past five, he and his goats reached our house. We heard the cries of the goats and the sound the stake at the end of the chain tied around their
60 necks made as it dragged along the street. Above the sound of what my mother called "the early morning racket," we could hear Mr. Jarvis whistling. Mostly, he whistled the refrain of an old but popular calypso⁵ tune. The words in the refrain were "Come le' we go, Soukie, Come le' we go." If we heard only the crying of

B DICTION
Reread lines 28–31. What effect is created by the **repetition** of the phrase "got up early"?

C GRAMMAR AND STYLE
Reread lines 32–50. Kincaid creates long, fluid sentences by using the **coordinating conjunctions** *and* and *but*.

---

3. **flamboyant:** another name for the royal poinciana (poin′sē-ăn′ə) tree, known for its huge red flowers.

4. **galvanized rooftops:** metal roofs coated with a layer of zinc to prevent rust.

5. **calypso** (kə-lĭp′sō): a type of West Indian music based on African rhythms, often with lyrics about local events or personalities.

Farm in Haiti, Roosevelt. Oil on canvas. Private collection. © SuperStock.

the goats and the sound of their chain, we knew it was Mr. Jarvis's son Nigel, a rude wharf-rat boy, who was taking the goats to pasture. **D**

   We weren't the only ones who got up to the sound of Mr. Jarvis and his goats. Mr. Gordon, a man who grew lettuce and sold most of it to the new hotels and who lived right next to us, would get up soon after Mr. Jarvis passed. He would throw open all the windows and all the doors in his house, and he would turn on
70 his radio and tune it to a station in St. Croix,[6] a station which at that hour played American country-and-Western music. It may have been from this that my mother developed her devotion to the music of Hank Williams.[7] Mr. Gordon was very nice to my family, but that didn't prevent me from deciding that he resembled a monkey, and so I nicknamed him Monkey Lettuce. I called him this only behind his and my parents' back, of course. We never tuned our radio to the station in St. Croix. Instead, at exactly seven o'clock, my parents turned on our radio and tuned it to the station on our island. A man's voice would say, "It is seven o'clock." Then another voice, a completely different voice, would say, "This is BBC London."[8] Then we would listen to the news being broadcast. At
80 around that time, we sat down to eat breakfast. **E**

---

6. **St. Croix** (kroi): an island in the Caribbean Sea, one of the U.S. Virgin Islands.

7. **Hank Williams:** American songwriter, known for many country-and-Western hits, who died at the age of 29.

8. **BBC London:** the British Broadcasting Corporation, based in London, broadcasts in many areas that are part of the Commonwealth of Nations.

D DICTION
Reread lines 61–65. Compare the dialect in the song Kincaid quotes with Kincaid's own words, such as "a rude wharf-rat boy." Describe how they differ.

E PATTERNS OF ORGANIZATION
Identify the pattern of organization used in lines 75–80, and cite the specific words that signal this pattern. How does the organization help you to follow the events Kincaid describes?

Between the time I got up and eight o'clock, I would have helped my mother fill her washtubs with water, swept up the yard, fed the chickens, taken a bath in cold water, polished my shoes, pressed my school uniform (gray pleated-linen tunic, pink poplin blouse), gone to the grocer (Mr. Richards) to buy fresh bread (two fourpence loaves, one each for my mother and father; a twopence loaf for me; and three penny loaves, one each for my little brothers) and also to buy butter and cheese (made in New Zealand), gone to Miss Roma to have my hair freshly braided, and eaten a breakfast of porridge, eggs, bread and butter, cheese, and hot Ovaltine.[9] By that time, it was no longer early morning on our island, and half an hour later, together with two hundred and ninety-nine other girls and three hundred boys, I would be in my school auditorium singing, "All things bright and beautiful, All creatures great and small."

I now live in Manhattan. The only thing it has in common with the island where I grew up is a geographical definition. Certainly no one I know gets up at half past five, at six o'clock, at seven o'clock, at half past seven, at eight o'clock. I know one person who sleeps all day and stays up all night. I know another person who has to take a nap if he gets up before noon. And how easy it is, I have noticed, to put a great distance between you and a close friend if you should call that friend before ten in the morning. **F**

I wake up, still, without an alarm, at half past five. In the neighborhood in which I live, it is very quiet at that hour. It is not romantic at all to hear nothing in the city. At around six o'clock, I begin to hear the sound of moving vehicles. Trucks. I know they are trucks because the sound I hear is a rumbling sound that only trucks make. The sound sometimes comes from streets far away. If I get up and look out, I might not see anyone. If I see anyone, it is always two or three men together, dressed identically, in tight black leather pants, a black leather jacket, a black leather cap, and black leather boots. They will walk very quickly down my street as if they are in a great hurry. When I look out, I never notice the early light playing on the street or on the brownstone houses across the street from me. In Manhattan, I notice only whether it is sunny or bright or cloudy and gray or raining or snowing. I never notice things like gradations of light,[10] but my friends tell me that they are there.

Between six and seven, I sit and read women's magazines. I read articles about Elizabeth Taylor's new, simple life, articles about Mary Tyler Moore, articles about Jane Pauley, articles about members of the Carter family, articles about Candice Bergen, articles about Doris Day, articles about Phyllis Diller, and excerpts from Lana Turner's autobiography.[11] I know many things about these people—things that they may have forgotten themselves and things that, should we ever meet, they might wish I would forget also. At seven o'clock, I **G**

F PATTERNS OF ORGANIZATION
Reread lines 93–99. Which pattern of organization does the author use to highlight the differences between Antigua and Manhattan? Identify the word or phrase that signals a shift in subject.

G TONE
How would you describe Kincaid's tone, or attitude, in lines 113–119? Explain your answer.

---

9. **Ovaltine:** a nutritious chocolate drink.

10. **gradations of light:** shades of light; light that changes by very small degrees from lighter to darker.

11. **Elizabeth Taylor's . . . Turner's autobiography:** The people named are actors, journalists, musicians, and other celebrities of the time, whose exploits would have made it into the pages of popular magazines.

Brownstones, Patti Mollica. © Patti Mollica/SuperStock.

ANALYZE VISUALS
Compare this painting with the one on page 519. How well does each capture the **setting** Kincaid describes? Consider the colors and lines in both paintings, as well as each artist's depiction of light.

120 watch the morning news for one whole hour. I watch the morning news for two reasons: it makes me feel as if I am living in Chicago, and on the morning news I see and hear the best reports on anything having to do with pigs. I don't know why the morning news makes me feel as if I am living in Chicago and not, say, Cleveland, but there it is. I love Chicago and would like to live there, but only for an hour. Some days, after watching the morning news, my head is filled with useless (to me) but interesting information about pigs. Some of the information, though, is good only for a day. Then, for half an hour, I watch Captain Kangaroo. I love Captain Kangaroo and have forgiven him for saying to Chastity Bono, when they were both guests on her parents' television
130 show,[12] "Now, let me lay this on you, Chastity."[13] Surely a grown man, even if he is a children's hero (perhaps because he is a children's hero), shouldn't talk like that.

Then it is half past eight and no longer early morning in Manhattan, either. ❧

October 17, 1977

---

12. **Captain Kangaroo . . . television show:** Captain Kangaroo, a.k.a. Bob Keeshan, was the host of a long-running television program for children. Chastity Bono is the daughter of Sonny Bono and Cher, pop singers who hosted a variety TV show in the 1970s.

13. **"Now, let me . . . Chastity":** Captain Kangaroo was using a slang expression of the time. Used mostly by young people, it meant, "Now, let me tell you something."

Comprehension

1. **Recall** What does Kincaid compare and contrast in this essay?

2. **Recall** What time did most people in Kincaid's home country start their day?

3. **Clarify** Explain why the author feels that the only thing Manhattan and Antigua share is "a geographical definition" of being an island.

PENNSYLVANIA STANDARDS

READING STANDARD
B.3.3.2 Interpret and/or analyze purpose for text organization

Literary Analysis

4. **Analyze Patterns of Organization** To **compare and contrast** Antigua and Manhattan, Kincaid includes many of the same kinds of details in her description of each place. Use the chart you created as you read to find examples of these points of comparison. In your opinion, which one highlights similarities and differences between the two islands most effectively? Support your opinion with evidence.

5. **Analyze Author's Perspective** An author's perspective is the way he or she looks at a topic. How might Kincaid's childhood experiences in Antigua have influenced her perspective on living in New York? If she had grown up in a big city, would her new home seem less foreign to her? Use evidence from the text to support your answer.

6. **Draw Conclusions** Reread lines 100–112. Why do the author's friends in Manhattan notice the gradations of light, while she herself does not? What might this tell you about her feelings toward Manhattan as her **home?** Explain your answer.

7. **Evaluate Diction** Kincaid frequently uses lists and repetition to achieve her unique style. In a chart like the one shown, record three examples of such usage. Then complete your chart by briefly explaining the effect created by each example.

Example of Kincaid's Diction	Effect Created
"Certainly no one I know gets up at <u>half past five</u>, at <u>six o'clock</u>, at <u>seven o'clock</u>, at <u>half past seven</u>, at <u>eight o'clock</u>." (lines 94–96)	Kincaid's use of repetition here helps emphasize how solitary her mornings in New York are. It gives the paragraph a reflective, lonely tone.

Literary Criticism

8. **Critical Interpretations** The literary critic Suzanne Freeman has said that Kincaid's "singsong style" produces "images that are as sweet and mysterious as the secrets that children whisper in your ear." In your opinion, does this comment apply to Kincaid's depiction of her island birthplace? Cite details and description from the selection to support your opinion.

Reading-Writing Connection

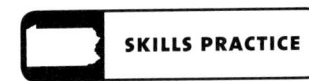

Expand your knowledge of "Island Morning" by responding to these prompts.
Then use **Revision: Grammar and Style** to improve your writing.

WRITING PROMPTS

A. Short Response: Support an Opinion
Which place do you think Jamaica Kincaid calls **home?**
In your opinion, does she seem more attached to her
island birthplace or to her new city? Write a **one- or
two-paragraph response,** citing evidence from the text
to support your opinion.

B. Extended Response: Compare and Contrast
Choose one of the two mornings Kincaid describes and
compare it with your own daily routine. Use the rich
details presented in the selection to write a **three-to-
five-paragraph comparison.**

SELF-CHECK

A strong response will . . .
- clearly state an opinion about
  which place Kincaid prefers
- offer specific words and
  phrases from the selection
  to support your opinion

A successful comparison will . . .
- discuss at least three features
  of Kincaid's morning, citing
  details from the text
- explain how Kincaid's routine
  is similar to or different from
  your own

REVISION: GRAMMAR AND STYLE

IMPROVE SENTENCE FLOW Review the **Grammar and Style** note on page 518.
Jamaica Kincaid uses **coordinating conjunctions** to join independent clauses and
connect ideas. She creates long sentences and achieves a conversational style.

Like Kincaid, use the coordinating conjunctions *and, but, for, nor, or, so,* and *yet*
when you want to combine shorter sentences or connect ideas. In the following
excerpt, notice how the author uses *and* to join two independent clauses and
but to connect ideas:

> *The Ground was often many miles away from where they lived, and they got
> there not by taking a truck or some other kind of automotive transportation but
> by riding a donkey or by walking.* (lines 16–19)

Notice how the revisions in red help to improve the flow of this first draft. Revise
your responses to the prompts by using similar techniques.

**PENNSYLVANIA
STANDARDS**

WRITING STANDARD
1.5.11.E Revise writing to improve
style, word choice, sentence variety

STUDENT MODEL

My house is home to a family of seven. *but* There is only one bathroom. *so* All five
of us kids race crazily down the hall every weekday morning. My older sister
almost always gets there first. *so* The rest of us stand blinking and yawning in
the hallway. *or* We drift slowly downstairs to the kitchen.

**WRITING
TOOLS**
For prewriting, revision,
and editing tools, visit
the **Writing Center** at
ClassZone.com.

Georgia O'Keeffe

Biographical Essay by Joan Didion

What is the source of INSPIRATION?

PENNSYLVANIA STANDARDS

READING STANDARDS

A.2.4.1 Identify and/or explain stated or implied main ideas

B.1.1.1.E.1 Interpret and evaluate the tone, style, and/or mood

KEY IDEA What drives painters to create vibrant pictures? What compels movie directors to invent alien worlds or makes songwriters dream up meaningful lyrics? Artists find **inspiration** in their daily lives, in nature, or even in the work of other artists.

QUICKWRITE Think of the most powerful work by your favorite artist, be it a painter, a dancer, an actor, an author, or a musician. What do you think inspired the artist to create this work? Whether it's a song about the person who broke his heart or a huge mural of her neighborhood, try to imagine the inspiration behind the art. Describe your artist's source of inspiration in a short paragraph.

LITERARY ANALYSIS: TONE

Tone is a writer's attitude toward his or her subject. Just as people often speak in a particular tone of voice, such as sarcastic or amused, writers create a tone with their choice of words. As you read "Georgia O'Keeffe," record details that help you identify Joan Didion's tone. Look for the following:

- unusual words Didion uses to describe O'Keeffe
- emphasized or repeated words and phrases
- details about O'Keeffe's life Didion chooses to include

Details from the Text	Tone Established
Didion describes O'Keeffe as "this angelic rattlesnake." (lines 63–64)	

READING SKILL: IDENTIFY IMPLIED MAIN IDEAS

The **main idea** is the most important idea in a paragraph or essay. Often, the main idea is not directly stated but **implied** by supporting details. As you read, use these strategies to identify and understand Didion's main ideas:

- Identify the specific topic of each paragraph or section.
- Examine all the details the author includes in that section.
- Ask what idea or message the details convey about the topic.
- State the idea or message in a sentence.

▲ VOCABULARY IN CONTEXT

Didion's vibrant portrait of Georgia O'Keeffe is enhanced by her use of the words shown in bold. To see how many words you already know, restate each phrase, using a different word or words for each boldfaced term.

1. a **condescending** attitude toward teenagers
2. witness the **genesis** of an idea
3. scorned with a **derisive** laugh
4. bitter **rancor** between enemies
5. painted with bright, **immutable** colors

Author Online

A Sharp Eye
Joan Didion's keen observations of American society have earned her popularity and critical acclaim. Whether on the antiwar movement of the 1960s or American politics in the aftermath of September 11, Didion's insights have earned her a prominent place in American literature. They have also served a more personal purpose. "I write," she says, "entirely to find out what I'm thinking."

**Joan Didion
born 1934**

Speak for Yourself Didion's work, which includes essays, novels, and screenplays, spans four decades. The author is a firm believer in the power of language. She warns young people not to "settle for other people's words" but rather to voice their own opinions. "I am still committed," Didion declares, "to the idea that the ability to think for one's self depends on one's mastery of the language."

MORE ABOUT THE AUTHOR
For more on Joan Didion, visit the **Literature Center** at ClassZone.com.

Background

Artistic Flair Georgia O'Keeffe (1887–1986) was a significant 20th-century American painter intrigued by the idea of "filling space in a beautiful way." Although she was born in Wisconsin, she is most closely associated with New Mexico, where she spent much of her life. In the Southwest, O'Keeffe painted what she saw: clouds, desert flowers, bones, and rocks. Some of O'Keeffe's most famous paintings are dramatic close-ups of flowers.

Georgia O'Keeffe

JOAN DIDION

"Where I was born and where and how I have lived is unimportant," Georgia O'Keeffe told us in the book of paintings and words published in her ninetieth year on earth. She seemed to be advising us to forget the beautiful face in the Stieglitz photographs.[1] She appeared to be dismissing the rather **condescending** romance that had attached to her by then, the romance of extreme good looks and advanced age and deliberate isolation. "It is what I have done with where I have been that should be of interest." I recall an August afternoon in Chicago in 1973 when I took my daughter, then seven, to see what Georgia O'Keeffe had done with where she had been. One of the vast O'Keeffe "Sky Above Clouds"

10 canvases floated over the back stairs in the Chicago Art Institute that day, dominating what seemed to be several stories of empty light, and my daughter looked at it once, ran to the landing, and kept on looking. "Who drew it," she whispered after a while. I told her. "I need to talk to her," she said finally.

My daughter was making, that day in Chicago, an entirely unconscious, but quite basic assumption about people and the work they do. She was assuming that the glory she saw in the work reflected a glory in its maker, that the painting was the painter as the poem is the poet, that every choice one made alone—every word chosen or rejected, every brush stroke laid or not laid down—betrayed one's character. *Style is character.* It seemed to me that afternoon that I had rarely

20 seen so instinctive an application of this familiar principle, and I recall being pleased not only that my daughter responded to style as character but that it was Georgia O'Keeffe's particular style to which she responded: this was a hard woman who had imposed her 192 square feet of clouds on Chicago. **A**

---

condescending
(kŏn′dĭ-sĕn′dĭng) *adj.* assuming an air of superiority

ANALYZE VISUALS
Examine this 1932 Stieglitz photograph of O'Keeffe. List three **traits** you would attribute to O'Keeffe based solely on this photograph.

A IMPLIED MAIN IDEAS
Reread lines 14–23 and think about the details Didion includes about her daughter's reaction to O'Keeffe's work. What is the main idea of the paragraph?

---

1. **Stieglitz** (stĕg′lĭts) **photographs:** American photographer Alfred Stieglitz, O'Keeffe's husband, took and exhibited many photographs of O'Keeffe.

"Hardness" has not been in our century a quality much admired in women, nor in the past twenty years has it even been in official favor for men. When hardness surfaces in the very old we tend to transform it into "crustiness" or eccentricity, some tonic pepperiness to be indulged at a distance. On the evidence of her work and what she has said about it, Georgia O'Keeffe is neither "crusty" nor eccentric. She is simply hard, a straight shooter, a woman clean of received wisdom and open to what she sees. This is a woman who could early on dismiss most of her contemporaries as "dreamy," and would later single out one she liked as "a very poor painter." (And then add, apparently by way of softening the judgment: "I guess he wasn't a painter at all. He had no courage and I believe that to create one's own world in any of the arts takes courage.") This is a woman who in 1939 could advise her admirers that they were missing her point, that their appreciation of her famous flowers was merely sentimental. "When I paint a red hill," she observed coolly in the catalogue for an exhibition that year, "you say it is too bad that I don't always paint flowers. A flower touches almost everyone's heart. A red hill doesn't touch everyone's heart." This is a woman who could describe the **genesis** of one of her most well-known paintings—the "Cow's Skull: Red, White and Blue" owned by the Metropolitan—as an act of quite deliberate and **derisive** orneriness. "I thought of the city men I had been seeing in the East," she wrote. "They talked so often of writing the Great American Novel—the Great American Play—the Great American Poetry. . . . So as I was painting my cow's head on blue I thought to myself, 'I'll make it an American painting. They will not think it great with the red stripes down the sides—Red, White and Blue—but they will notice it.'"

The city men. The men. They. The words crop up again and again as this astonishingly aggressive woman tells us what was on her mind when she was making her astonishingly aggressive paintings. It was those city men who stood accused of sentimentalizing her flowers: "I made you take time to look at what I saw and when you took time to really notice my flower you hung all your associations with flowers on my flower and you write about my flower as if I think and see what you think and see—and I don't." *And I don't.* Imagine those words spoken, and the sound you hear is *don't tread on me.* "The men" believed it impossible to paint New York, so Georgia O'Keeffe painted New York. "The men" didn't think much of her bright color, so she made it brighter. The men yearned toward Europe so she went to Texas, and then New Mexico. The men talked about Cézanne,[2] "long involved remarks about the 'plastic quality' of his form and color," and took one another's long involved remarks, in the view of this angelic rattlesnake in their midst, altogether too seriously. "I can paint one of those

---

2. **Cézanne** (sā-zăn'): Paul Cézanne, late-19th-century French painter whose style and study of shapes influenced new art movements in the early 20th century.

B GRAMMAR AND STYLE
Reread lines 30–31. Didion uses both **concrete nouns,** such as *woman,* and **abstract nouns,** such as *wisdom,* to discuss O'Keeffe. Concrete nouns add substance to abstract ideas.

genesis (jĕn'ĭ-sĭs) *n.* the origin or coming into being (of something)

derisive (dĭ-rī'sĭv) *adj.* expressing contempt or ridicule

C TONE
Think about the words and phrases that Didion italicizes or repeats in lines 50–64. How would you describe her tone? Explain your answer.

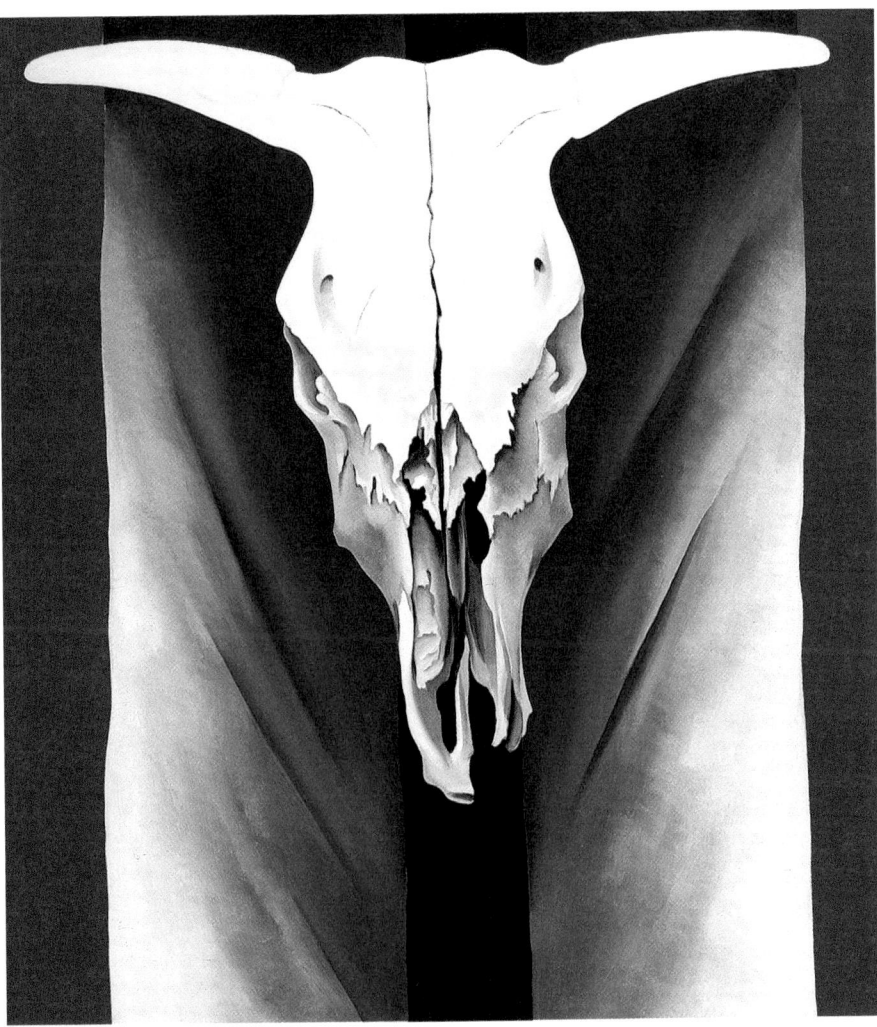

Cow's Skull: Red, White, and Blue (1931), Georgia O'Keeffe. Oil on canvas, 39⅞" × 35⅞". The Metropolitan Museum of Art, Alfred Stieglitz Collection, 1952. © 2007 Georgia O'Keeffe Museum/Artists Rights Society (ARS), New York. Photo © Georgia O'Keeffe/Metropolitan Museum of Art (52.203).

ANALYZE VISUALS
Reread lines 41–49. What message do you think O'Keeffe was sending to the "city men" when she painted this piece? Explain your answer, citing details from the text as well as the painting.

dismal-colored paintings like the men," the woman who regarded herself always as an outsider remembers thinking one day in 1922, and she did: a painting of a shed "all low-toned and dreary with the tree beside the door." She called the act of **rancor** "The Shanty" and hung it in her next show. "The men seemed to approve of it," she reported fifty-four years later, her contempt
70 undimmed. "They seemed to think that maybe I was beginning to paint. That was my only low-toned dismal-colored painting."

   Some women fight and others do not. Like so many successful guerrillas[3] in the war between the sexes, Georgia O'Keeffe seems to have been equipped early with an **immutable** sense of who she was and a fairly clear understanding that she would be required to prove it. On the surface her upbringing was conventional. She was a child on the Wisconsin prairie who played with china dolls and painted watercolors with cloudy skies because sunlight was too hard to paint and, with her brother and sisters, listened every night to her mother read stories of the Wild West, of Texas, of Kit Carson and Billy the Kid.[4] She

rancor (răng'kər) *n.* bitter and deep ill will

immutable (ĭ-myōō'tə-bəl) *adj.* unchanging

---

3. **guerrillas** (gə-rĭl'əz): members of irregular military units who work to undermine the enemy using tactics such as surprise raids.
4. **Kit Carson and Billy the Kid:** Carson was a scout in the American West; Billy the Kid was an outlaw.

80 told adults that she wanted to be an artist and was embarrassed when they asked what kind of artist she wanted to be: she had no idea "what kind." She had no idea what artists did. She had never seen a picture that interested her, other than a pen-and-ink Maid of Athens[5] in one of her mother's books, some Mother Goose illustrations printed on cloth, a tablet cover that showed a little girl with pink roses, and the painting of Arabs on horseback that hung in her grandmother's parlor.

90 At thirteen, in a Dominican convent, she was mortified when the sister corrected her drawing. At Chatham Episcopal Institute in Virginia she painted lilacs and sneaked time alone to walk out to where she could see the line of the Blue Ridge Mountains on the horizon. At the Art Institute in Chicago she was shocked by the presence of live models and wanted to abandon anatomy lessons. At the Art Students League in New York one of her fellow students advised her that, since he 100 would be a great painter and she would end up teaching painting in a girls' school, any work of hers was less important than modeling for him. Another painted over her work to show her how the Impressionists[6] did trees. She had not before heard how the Impressionists did trees and she did not much care.

At twenty-four she left all those opinions behind and went for the first time to live in Texas, where there were no trees to paint and no one to tell her how not to paint them. In Texas there was only the horizon she craved. In Texas 110 she had her sister Claudia with her for a while, and in the late afternoons they would walk away from town and toward the horizon and watch the evening star come out. "That evening star fascinated me," she wrote. "It was in some way very exciting to me. My sister had a gun, and as we walked she would throw bottles in the air and shoot as many as she could before they hit the ground. I had nothing but to walk into nowhere and the wide sunset space with the star. Ten watercolors were made from that star." In a way one's interest is compelled as much by the sister Claudia with the gun as by the painter Georgia with the star, but only the painter left us this shining record. Ten watercolors were made from that star. ೲ **D**

Jimson Weed (1932), Georgia O'Keeffe. The Georgia O'Keeffe Museum, Santa Fe, New Mexico. © 2007 Georgia O'Keeffe Museum/Artists Rights Society (ARS), New York. Photo © Art Resource, New York.

ANALYZE VISUALS
O'Keeffe is celebrated for her ability to make even flowers look strong and imposing. Explain how she creates this air of strength, considering elements such as the flower's size, position, and color.

D TONE
Reread lines 107–119. What is the "shining record" Didion refers to? Describe the tone conveyed by the writer's **word choice**.

---

5. **Maid of Athens:** the subject of a love poem by 19th-century English writer George Gordon, Lord Byron.

6. **Impressionists:** members of an influential 19th-century French school of painting who focused on depicting quick visual impressions and conveying how light influenced the scenes they painted.

After Reading

Comprehension

PENNSYLVANIA STANDARDS

READING STANDARD
A.2.4.1 Identify and/or explain stated or implied main ideas

1. **Recall** What anecdote, or short personal story, does Didion tell at the beginning of this essay?

2. **Clarify** What did O'Keeffe's critics tend to think of her work?

Literary Analysis

3. **Paraphrase** O'Keeffe asserts, "Where I was born and where and how I have lived is unimportant. It is what I have done with where I have been that should be of interest." Paraphrase this quotation. Then explain what O'Keeffe meant.

4. **Understand Motives** What inspired O'Keeffe to act the way she did? For each action described in the chart, identify O'Keeffe's motive, or **inspiration.** Use a graphic organizer like the one shown to record your answers.

Motive ⟶	Action
	O'Keeffe paints "Cow's Skull: Red, White, and Blue" (line 42).
	O'Keeffe uses even brighter colors in her paintings (line 60).
	O'Keeffe moves to the Southwest (line 108).

5. **Identify Implied Main Idea** Reread lines 72–106. Examine the details in this paragraph. What is the implied main idea conveyed by these details? Use evidence from the text to support your answer.

6. **Analyze Characterization** Didion reveals her subject's traits using the same methods of characterization used by fiction writers. Identify at least two methods of characterization Didion uses in this selection. Then explain which of O'Keeffe's traits are revealed in each case, citing evidence from the text.

7. **Analyze Tone** Review the chart you filled in as you read. How does Didion's tone help convey the ideas she wants to express about O'Keeffe?

Literary Criticism

8. **Author's Style** Joan Didion has remarked that "writing is hostile in that you're trying to make somebody see something the way you see it, trying to impose your idea, your picture." In what ways might this essay be considered "hostile"? Did Didion achieve her goal of making you see Georgia O'Keeffe the same way she does? Explain your answer.

Vocabulary in Context

VOCABULARY PRACTICE

Determine the relationship between the first pair of words in each analogy.
Then write the vocabulary word that best completes the second pair.

1. *Tolerant* is to *easygoing* as *smug* is to _____.
2. *Contemptuous* is to *speech* as _____ is to *remark*.
3. *Filth* is to *squalor* as _____ is to *permanent*.
4. *Embrace* is to *affection* as *insult* is to _____.
5. *Birth* is to *death* as _____ is to *termination*.

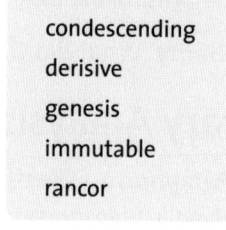

WORD LIST

condescending

derisive

genesis

immutable

rancor

VOCABULARY IN WRITING

Imagine you had gotten the chance to interview Georgia O'Keeffe while she
was still alive. Write three questions that you would have liked to ask the artist
about her life and work. Use at least three vocabulary words in your questions.

PENNSYLVANIA STANDARDS

READING STANDARD
A.2.2 Apply word recognition skills

> **EXAMPLE SENTENCE**
>
> How did you respond to people who expressed **derisive** attitudes
> about your paintings?

VOCABULARY STRATEGY: THE WORD ROOT *gen*

The vocabulary word *genesis* contains the
Greek root *gen*, which means "birth, race, or
origin." *Gen* is also a Latin root with a similar
meaning. The root *gen* is found in a number
of English words. To understand the meaning
of words with *gen*, use context clues as well
as your knowledge of the root.

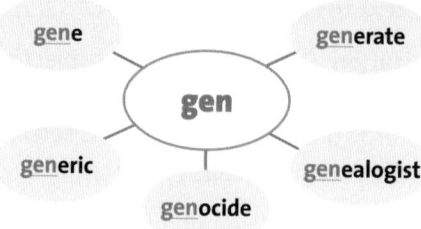

gene   generate

gen

generic   genealogist

genocide

PRACTICE Choose the word from the word web that best completes each
sentence. Use context clues to help you or, if necessary, consult a dictionary.

1. They hired a _____ to trace their family tree.
2. _____ products are usually less expensive than those with brand names.
3. The defective _____ that he inherited led to a serious blood disease.
4. _____ is the attempt to destroy a race of people.
5. They could not _____ enough interest in their project to get financial
   backing for it.

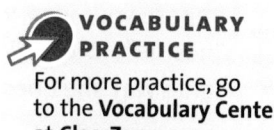

VOCABULARY PRACTICE
For more practice, go
to the **Vocabulary Center**
at **ClassZone.com**.

Reading-Writing Connection

Improve your understanding of "Georgia O'Keeffe" by responding to these prompts. Then use **Revision: Grammar and Style** to improve your writing.

WRITING PROMPTS

A. Short Response: Evaluate Characterization

What character trait does Didion highlight in her essay on Georgia O'Keeffe? How effective are the details the author includes to illustrate this trait? Write a **one- or two-paragraph response,** citing evidence from the text.

B. Extended Response: Describe Inspiration

In your opinion, what was O'Keeffe's main source of **inspiration?** Write **three to five paragraphs** discussing the objects or ideas that compelled O'Keeffe to paint. Use details from the text as well as the paintings featured in this selection to support your analysis.

SELF-CHECK

A strong evaluation will . . .

- explain which character trait Didion emphasizes
- establish criteria for judging the effectiveness of the details Didion uses

A successful discussion will . . .

- consider different possible inspirations, such as the natural world and the artist's relationship with her critics
- explain how O'Keeffe's inspiration drove her to create

REVISION: GRAMMAR AND STYLE

USE DESCRIPTIVE LANGUAGE Review the **Grammar and Style** note on page 528. A **concrete noun** names an object that can be seen, heard, smelled, touched, or tasted and is useful for conveying tangible information. An **abstract noun** names an idea or quality, making it useful for conveying feelings and traits. Didion uses both types of nouns to form a complete picture of Georgia O'Keeffe.

PENNSYLVANIA STANDARDS

WRITING STANDARD
1.5.11.F.4 Use nouns properly

Concrete Nouns: *She was a child on the Wisconsin prairie who played with china dolls and painted watercolors. . . .* (lines 76–77)

Abstract Nouns: *She appeared to be dismissing the rather condescending romance that had attached to her by then, the romance of extreme good looks and advanced age and deliberate isolation.* (lines 4–6)

The revisions in red incorporate a mix of concrete and abstract nouns to enhance the description. Use similar techniques to revise your responses to the prompts.

STUDENT MODEL

One source of O'Keeffe's inspiration was her conflict with her male critics.
asserted her independence through her paintings. ~~conform to her critics' expectations.~~
O'Keeffe ~~was very independent.~~ She refused to ~~listen to her critics.~~ Though

critics praised her painting "The Shanty," O'Keeffe would not paint others

    just to earn their praise.
like it.

WRITING TOOLS
For prewriting, revision, and editing tools, visit the **Writing Center** at ClassZone.com.

Who Killed the Iceman?
Magazine Article

Skeletal Sculptures
Process Description by Donna M. Jackson

How do scientists UNLOCK *the past?*

PENNSYLVANIA STANDARDS

READING & WRITING STANDARDS
B.3.3.1 Analyze the effect of text organization
1.6.11.A.3 Take notes

KEY IDEA Everyone knows bones and corpses can't talk. Or can they? As you may know from true-crime shows or sci-fi thrillers, human remains often have their own stories to tell. As police detectives unravel intricate cases and scientists **investigate** unexplained phenomena, these remains often tell stories that help piece the past together.

DISCUSS What types of criminal or scientific investigation do you know about? With a partner, choose one to discuss. List the methods investigators use to track down the truth. Then briefly explain the purpose of each method.

Criminal Investigation

Method	Purpose
1. Finger-printing	Identify suspect
2.	
3.	

534

ELEMENTS OF NONFICTION: TEXT FEATURES

Text features are design elements that highlight the organization and key information of a text. They can help you preview what you'll read and recognize key ideas.

- **Subheadings** signal the beginning of a new topic or section. They often identify the focus of the text that follows them.
- **Graphic aids,** such as maps and photographs, present information visually. They are frequently accompanied by **captions,** which describe or clarify the information.
- **Numbered lists** often consist of steps in a process that should be followed in order.

As you read, use the text features mentioned to help you find and comprehend the important information in each article.

READING STRATEGY: TAKE NOTES

When you **take notes,** your goal should be to record a text's main ideas and key information in a way that is easy to understand and remember. Since text features highlight main ideas and key information, including them in your notes can help.

As you read each section of "Who Killed the Iceman?" jot down its subheading. Then record the important details included in the section.

As you read "Skeletal Sculptures," note the key information in each step.

Review: **Monitor**

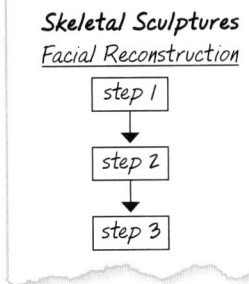

> **Who Killed the Iceman?**
> *Background*
> • He was frozen for 5,000 years.
> • Hikers found him in 1991 on the border between Austria and Italy.

> **Skeletal Sculptures**
> *Facial Reconstruction*
>
> | step 1 |
> ↓
> | step 2 |
> ↓
> | step 3 |

▲ VOCABULARY IN CONTEXT

Find a word that could be used in each newspaper headline.

WORD LIST	anthropology	compile	refute
	artifact	presumed	

1. Woman **Thought** Guilty of Murder
2. New Study to **Pull Together** Years of Research
3. Unusual **Object** Found in Archaeological Dig
4. **Science** Spotlight: Ancient Tribes
5. Scholar to **Deny Accuracy of** Theory

Background

Stumbling onto a Mummy
"Who Killed the Iceman?" chronicles some of the theories surrounding the death of a man who met his demise around 3000 B.C. The "Iceman," the oldest frozen mummy ever found, was discovered by German hikers vacationing in the Alps. When they spied a body embedded in the ice, the hikers assumed they had found the remains of a mountain climber who'd met a dismal fate. They had no idea they'd stumbled onto a 5,000-year-old relic. The Iceman now resides at the South Tyrol Museum of Archaeology in Bolzano, Italy.

Rescue workers and forensic experts examine the Iceman.

Crime-Fighting Scientists "Skeletal Sculptures" describes how forensic anthropologists help police track down the truth. Anthropology is the scientific study of humans—our origins, behavior, environment, and physical features. Forensics is the use of science to solve crimes. Forensic anthropologists use their knowledge of human characteristics to assist in cracking tough cases involving human remains. The scientists identify the victim's age, sex, race, and physical characteristics. They also determine the likely cause of death, which makes them an integral part of many murder investigations.

BUILDING BACKGROUND
To learn more about the Iceman and forensics, visit the **Literature Center** at **ClassZone.com.**

FROM NATIONAL GEOGRAPHIC MAGAZINE

WHO KILLED THE ICEMAN?

A TEXT FEATURES
Examine this **photograph** and its accompanying **caption.** Does the 5,000-year-old mummy look as you expected him to, or does his appearance surprise you? Explain your answer.

Among the first to reach the scene, these mountaineers used makeshift tools to help free the mummy.

Background

He spent some 5,000 years frozen in a mountain glacier on the Austro-Italian border before passing hikers discovered him, sprawled in the melting snow, in 1991. He now resides in a refrigerated room at a museum in Italy. Over the 11 years since his discovery the Iceman mummy has been examined from every possible angle. But not until this past summer did those studying his still frozen body notice a crucial piece of evidence that dramatically rewrites his story: "Ötzi," nicknamed for the Ötztal Alps where he was found, didn't freeze to death in a sudden snow storm while tending sheep as some had suggested. Instead he was killed, a victim of warfare, murder, or human sacrifice. **B**

B TAKE NOTES
What is the most important information provided in the section labeled "Background"? Be sure to record each section's essential details in your notes.

Clues Discovered

10 X-rays reveal an arrowhead buried deep in the Iceman's left shoulder—an injury that could not possibly have been self-inflicted. This discovery consequently led archaeologists to believe that the Iceman had been killed. The wound, visible as a small dark smudge beneath the mummy's leathery skin, had been overlooked in all previous examinations. Though no arrow shaft protrudes from the wound and no blood marks the arrow's entrance, it's now clear that the Iceman was shot in the back. But who did it? And why?

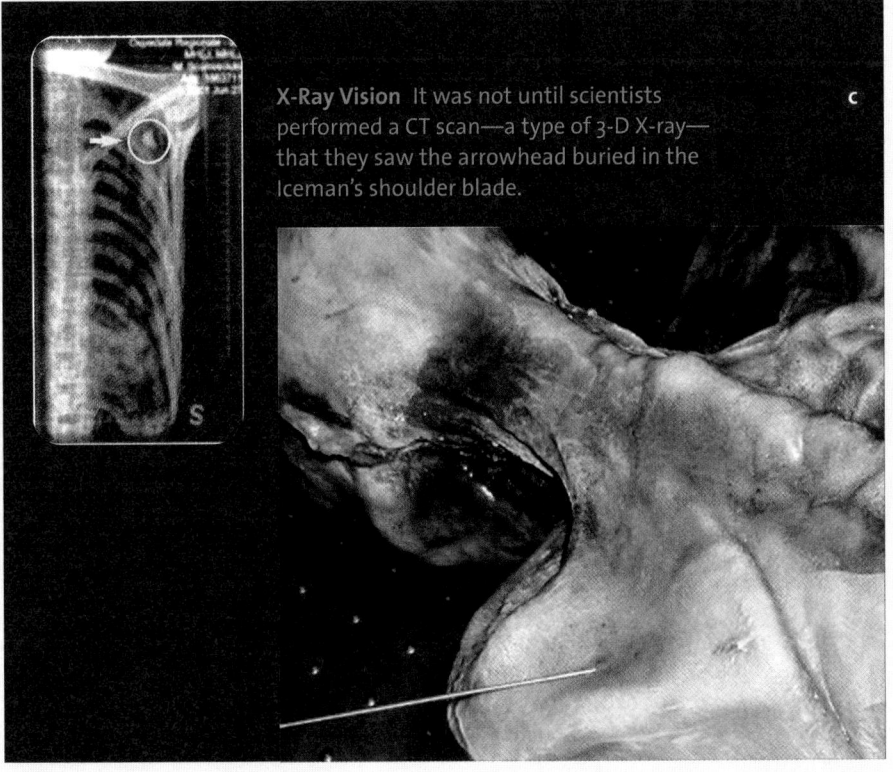

X-Ray Vision It was not until scientists performed a CT scan—a type of 3-D X-ray—that they saw the arrowhead buried in the Iceman's shoulder blade.

C

C TEXT FEATURES
How do these photographs support the **main idea** of the "Clues Discovered" section? Explain, citing details from the text and the photos.

Differing Theories **D**

"There's no way anyone can ever really know," says archaeologist Johan Reinhard, a National Geographic Society explorer-in-residence. "It might have been murder. Or it might have been ritual sacrifice."[1]

20 Reinhard knows mummies. Among the many he has discovered is the Inca "ice maiden," a victim of sacrifice, on the frozen slopes of Peru's Nevado Ampato[2] in 1995. His experience studying mountain cultures in the Andes, the Himalayas, and elsewhere has convinced him that the Iceman's death was not a random killing.

D TAKE NOTES
As you begin reading the section about the controversy surrounding Ötzi's death, take careful notes to keep track of the differing theories.

---

1. **ritual sacrifice:** a sacrifice that is part of a religious ceremony.
2. **Nevado Ampato** (nə-vä'dō äm-pä'tō): a volcano in the Central Andes.

artifact (är′tə-făkt′) *n.*
something created by
humans, usually for a
practical purpose

"Look at where he died," Reinhard says. "It's a prominent pass, between two of the highest peaks in the Ötztal Alps. This is the kind of place where people from mountain cultures have traditionally made offerings to their mountain gods. We know that mountain worship was important in prehistoric Europe during the Bronze Age," he says. "And there is good
30 evidence that it may also have played a role earlier, in the Copper Age."[3]

Reinhard's interpretation seems to answer questions about **artifacts** found with the mummy that have long puzzled experts. For example, breaking objects was a ceremonial practice in Neolithic[4] Europe. This might explain the broken arrows lying near the mummy. The Iceman's copper ax—the oldest prehistoric ax in Europe with its bindings and handle intact—is also significant. Its copper had to have been mined, and mountains, as the source of valuable metals used to make tools, "were worshiped by miners throughout the world," says Reinhard. "This helps explain why the ax was left with the body after the killing." Murderers would likely have taken something so
40 useful with them. But people performing a ritual might have left it for the Iceman's use in the afterlife or as a tribute to the gods.

ⓔ TEXT FEATURES
Examine the **map** that accompanies this article. What information does it convey? List two details you can learn from this graphic aid.

ⓔ Where Ötzi Died

AUSTRIA
SWITZERLAND
• Innsbruck
Ötztal Alps

Venice •

ITALY

Ötzi was found at approximately 10, 500 feet in the Ötztal Alps on the border between Austria and Italy. After closely examining Ötzi's clothing and possessions—including a sheath and dagger (shown at right)—archaeologists realized they had uncovered a 5, 300-year-old find.

3. **Bronze Age . . . Copper Age:** The Bronze Age in Europe, when bronze tools began to be used, lasted roughly from 3500 B.C. to 1000 B.C. The Copper Age overlaps with the earliest part of the Bronze Age.

4. **Neolithic** (nē′ə-lĭth′ĭk): having to do with the prehistoric period when food growing began, but before metal tools were used—about 4000 B.C. in Europe.

Another clue: The Iceman's body was found in a naturally formed trench along the pass. Prior explanations had him taking shelter there from sudden bad weather. "But the trench is not deep and is at a high point of the pass. It 50 would have been a poor place to sit out a storm," explains Reinhard. Perhaps, instead, the Iceman was buried there by whoever killed him, which would account for the body's being so well preserved. **F**

Reinhard's ideas have not been met with enthusiasm by European experts. In contrast 60 with his beliefs, the mummy's caretaker, pathologist Eduard Egarter Vigl of South Tyrol Museum of Archaeology, believes that Ötzi may have been fleeing from an attacker, saying, "The Iceman was hit by an arrow from behind." Others maintain that arrows aren't efficient means of ritual killing and that no clear evidence of any other Copper Age sacrifice exists.

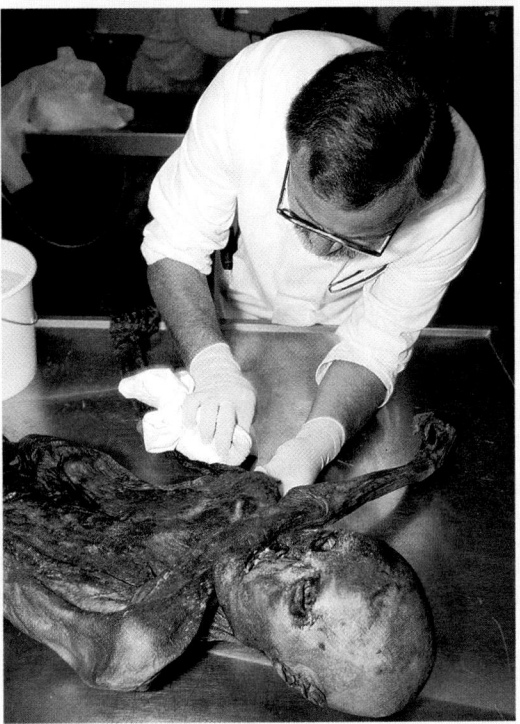

A scientist examines the skeletal remains of the Iceman.

So Who Killed the Iceman?

"They view the idea of human sacrifice as too sensational," says Reinhard. "But they can't **refute** what I've pointed out, and I believe my theory better explains the known facts.

"I know it's controversial," he admits. "But it's time to **compile** all the 70 evidence and reexamine it from a different perspective. Let's look at these artifacts not only relative to each other but also within social, sacred, and geographical contexts."

F MONITOR
One important part of monitoring your reading is **evaluating** the information that's provided. Do you find Reinhard's theory convincing? Why or why not?

refute (rĭ-fyo͞ot′) v. to prove false by argument or evidence

compile (kəm-pīl′) v. to put together by gathering from many sources

Skeletal SCULPTURES

anthropology
(ăn'thrə-pŏl'ə-jē) *n.* the science or study of human beings, including their physical characteristics and cultures

Dr. Michael Charney is an expert in forensic[1] **anthropology.** His expertise has enabled him to take a few pieces of a skeleton found in Missouri and compile a portrait of a five-foot, 120-pound Asian woman in her mid-twenties. Still, that isn't enough to identify her.

10 The dead woman's "face" needs to be brought back to life.

Reconstructing the likeness of a person in clay, using the skull as a guide, is a last resort at identification, Dr. Charney says. It gives police a new lead to follow, a visual clue that can be photographed and displayed in the media.

Facial reconstruction is not
20 an identifying tool, he warns. The goal is to trigger someone to recognize the model and to identify the person through scientific means.

"All that's needed is a general recognition that it looks like so-and-so," he says. **G**

Before re-creating a face, Dr. Charney and forensic sculptor
30 Nita Bitner search the skull for signs of disease, injury, and structural defects.

"We look for things that shouldn't be there," Bitner says. "Sometimes we find broken noses, cuts, or dentures." These

Dr. Michael Charney measures a skull with spreading calipers.

affect the face's appearance and aid in the identification process. If the nose bone is curved to one
40 side, for example, it's important to show it in the face because it's a distinguishing feature.

"We have to be careful, however, not to include anything that happened at the time of death," Bitner notes, "because it wouldn't be recognizable to others."

Age also influences how a face is built. Wrinkled skin, which
50 might help illustrate an older person, is often incorporated into a sculpture for accuracy.

After studying the Missouri woman's skull, Bitner makes a latex mold and pours a plaster cast. Now she's ready to sculpt the face.

G MONITOR
As you read, stop to **clarify:** why does Dr. Charney call facial reconstruction "a last resort at identification"?

---

1. **forensic:** having to do with applying scientific methods to crime investigation.

1. Forensic sculptor Nita Bitner begins a facial restoration by cutting round rubber pegs into different lengths. The pegs, called landmarks, represent the thickness of the soft tissue (muscle, fat, and skin) at different points on the face. These tissue depths, which vary for men and women of varying ages, were first calculated from corpses by nineteenth-century scientists and later updated. **H**

H **TAKE NOTES**
As you read the numbered items in this section, record the steps of the process in your notes. For each step, include only the **details** that are most important.

2. She then glues the rubber pegs to the skull cast.

3. Bitner "connects the dots" with strips of modeling clay. When attaching the strips of clay, she begins at the forehead and works her way down to the cheekbones, nasal area, chin, and mouth.

4. Once the dots are connected, Bitner fills in the spaces with clay and fleshes out the face. Now the prominent cheekbones of the Missouri woman become strikingly clear. Suddenly her broad face and delicate nose emerge.

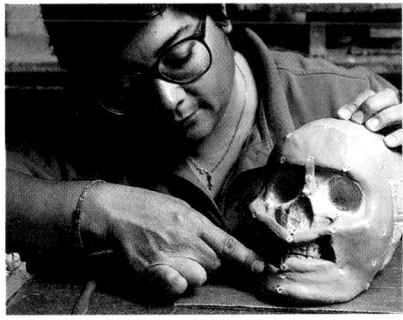

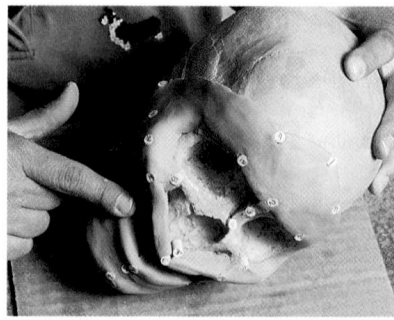

5. As Bitner smooths the clay with her thumb and fingers, the face develops like a photograph.

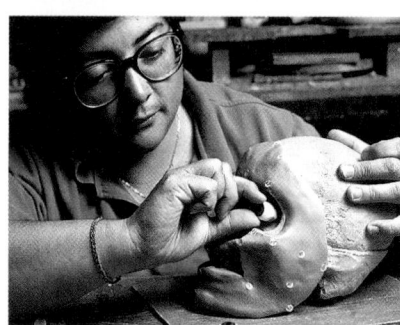

6. Bitner sets the plastic brown eyes in their sockets.

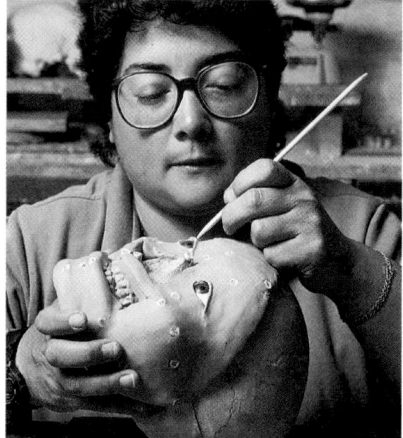

7. Next come the eyelids.

8. Bitner then sculpts the sides of the nose.

9. She measures the nose with a ruler to ensure it is the correct width.

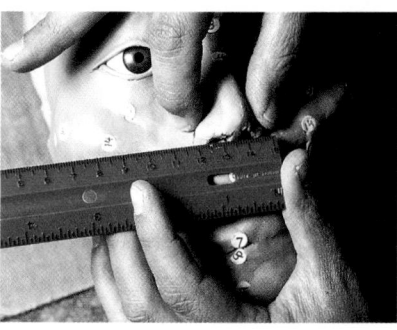

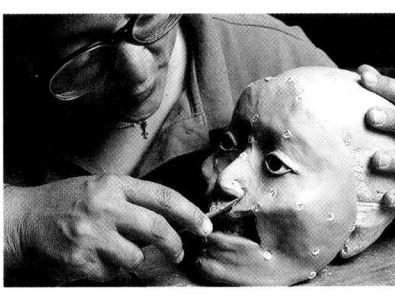

10. Now it's time to mold the upper lip.

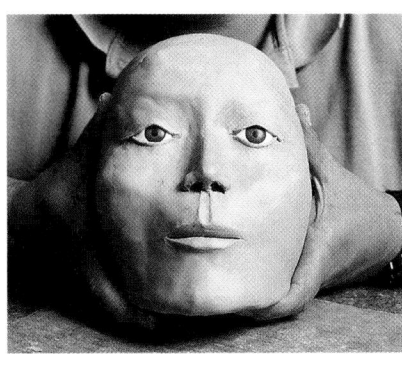

11. The face is nearly complete. Because the Missouri woman is **presumed** to be Asian, Bitner will add a black wig. She will then add a scarf for a finishing touch.

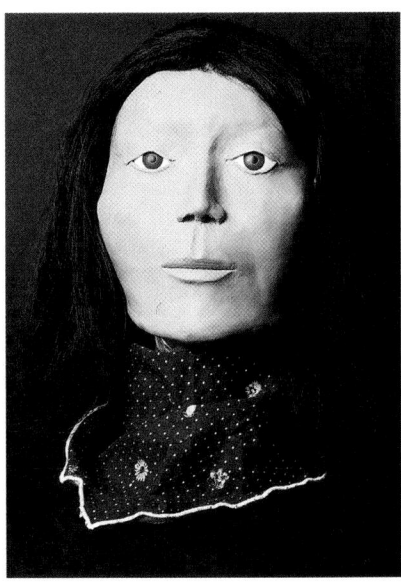

12. The model is now ready to be photographed and publicized in the media so that millions of amateur detectives can help solve the riddle of her identity. ❶

presumed (prĭ-zōōmd′) *adj.* thought to be true **presume** *v.*

❶ **TEXT FEATURES**
Review the **photographs** illustrating the process. Which step do you think is the most critical for transforming a skull into a recognizable human face? Explain your answer.

Comprehension

1. **Recall** Why is the Iceman nicknamed Ötzi?

2. **Summarize** What is Johan Reinhard's theory about how the Iceman died?

3. **Clarify** What is facial reconstruction, and for what is it used?

Critical Analysis

4. **Summarize Notes** Review the notes you took as you read "Skeletal Sculptures." Using your notes, write one or two paragraphs summarizing the process of facial reconstruction.

5. **Draw Conclusions** In your opinion, is disagreement between scientists helpful or harmful to further investigation? Use evidence from "Who Killed the Iceman?" to support your conclusion.

6. **Analyze Text Features** Think about the information communicated by the text features in "Who Killed the Iceman?" If you had simply scanned the title, subheads, and graphic aids, would you have had an accurate idea of what the article was about? What information would you have missed? Explain.

7. **Evaluate** Examine the methods of **investigation** listed in the chart shown. Complete the chart, noting the information each method provided to the scientists studying the Iceman. In your opinion, which method yielded the most crucial information? Cite details to support your answer.

Method of Investigation	Information Provided
X-rays of Ötzi's shoulder	
Analysis of where the body was found	
Evaluation of artifacts found with the Iceman's body	

Reading-Writing Connection

WRITING PROMPT	SELF-CHECK
Short Response: Compare and Contrast How do Reinhard's theories about the mummy's death differ from those of the other scientists mentioned in "Who Killed the Iceman?" Using your notes and examples from the text, write **one or two paragraphs** comparing and contrasting Reinhard's theories with the other scientists' beliefs.	*A successful comparison will . . .* • clearly explain each of the differing theories • offer specific details from the text to support your comparison

Vocabulary in Context

VOCABULARY PRACTICE

WORD LIST
anthropology
artifact
compile
presumed
refute

Decide whether these statements are true or false.

1. A wildflower originally identified centuries ago is an ancient **artifact.**
2. If I **refute** an argument, I make a convincing case against it.
3. To write a good report, you should **compile** information from several sources.
4. A person interested in animal behavior might want to study **anthropology.**
5. Someone **presumed** to be at fault has already been proved wrong.

VOCABULARY IN WRITING

Imagine you were the first scientist to reach the scene when the Iceman was discovered. Write four sentences you might have used if you had had to file a report about the discovery. Use at least three vocabulary words in your sentences.

EXAMPLE SENTENCE

*The Iceman's copper axe is an **artifact** that will help me determine just how old this mummy is.*

VOCABULARY STRATEGY: SPECIALIZED FIELDS, OR "OLOGIES"

The words for many fields of study, such as *anthropology,* end with the Greek suffix *-ology,* meaning "study of." The word for the person doing the studying often ends in *-ologist,* as in *anthropologist.* Many of these words, such as *toxicology* (the study of poisons), are recognizable because they have a familiar root. Others, like *penology* (the study of prisons), have a Greek or Latin root you may have to learn.

PENNSYLVANIA STANDARDS

READING STANDARD
A.2.1.2 Identify and/or apply meaning of content-specific words

PRACTICE Choose the word in parentheses that fits each sentence. Use context clues, your knowledge of roots, or, if necessary, a dictionary.

1. Because his grandfather had Alzheimer's disease, Jeremy decided to specialize in (gerontology, geology).
2. A (cosmetologist, criminologist) was brought in to examine the murder scene.
3. If you study (ornithology, psychology), you will become an expert on birds.
4. Please have your hearing checked by an (audiologist, ecologist).
5. Ed, an amateur (cytologist, herpetologist), viewed lizards, snakes, and turtles near the beach.
6. Learning a little about (meteorology, oncology) helped me anticipate thunderstorms.

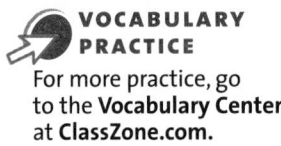

VOCABULARY PRACTICE
For more practice, go to the **Vocabulary Center** at **ClassZone.com.**

The Lost Boys

Magazine Article by Sara Corbett

How far would you go to find FREEDOM?

PENNSYLVANIA STANDARDS

READING STANDARDS
A.2.6.1 Describe the author's purpose
B.3.3.3 Interpret and/or analyze graphics and charts

KEY IDEA It's impossible for most of us to imagine what it would be like to be a **refugee**—someone who faces terrible danger in his or her home country and flees in search of freedom and protection. What would you do if you were imprisoned for your religious or political beliefs or harassed about the color of your skin? What would it take to make you leave your home and seek refuge in a strange, new place?

DISCUSS With a partner, discuss what it might be like to be forced to leave your home, your friends, your family, and everything familiar to you. Describe the one thing you would take with you if you had to leave quickly, and explain what you think you would miss most.

● ELEMENTS OF NONFICTION: AUTHOR'S PURPOSE

An **author's purpose** is what he or she hopes to achieve by writing a particular work. An author might write for any of several purposes:

- to persuade
- to inform or explain
- to entertain
- to express thoughts and feelings

In fact, an author may have more than one purpose for writing a given piece. For example, an author could be attempting to persuade you to register to vote while also expressing feelings about democracy. Understanding the purpose of a text is essential to getting the most out of what you read. As you read "The Lost Boys," use a chart to identify the purpose of key passages in the text.

Passage	Purpose
"According to U.S. State Department estimates, some 17,000 boys were separated from their families...." (lines 27–29)	inform

● READING SKILL: INTERPRET GRAPHIC AIDS

Magazine articles like "The Lost Boys" often include **graphic aids**—such as charts, maps, and photographs—that present key information.

- As you read, examine the **photographs** in this article. Consider the subjects' body language and facial expressions. What do they tell you about the subjects' feelings or experiences?
- As you study the **map** in this article, note details about Sudan. Where is this country? What features appear on the map? What else does the map communicate?

Review: **Connect**

▲ VOCABULARY IN CONTEXT

The words listed here are crucial to understanding the Lost Boys' journey to freedom. Place each word in the column where it belongs. Define each word you know.

WORD LIST	boon	fractious	posse
	exodus	marauding	subsist

Know Well	Think I Know	Don't Know

Background

A Devastating Division
The young refugees profiled in this article are from Sudan, the largest country in Africa. Sudan has been torn apart by Africa's longest-running civil war. Their country devastated by war and ravaged by

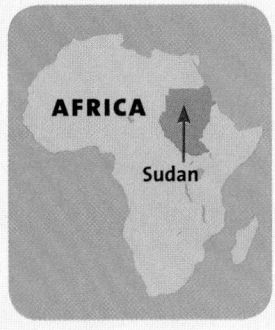

AFRICA

Sudan

religious conflicts, over 4 million Sudanese people have been driven from their homes, 2 million have died, and thousands more have been forced into slavery. Since 1955, Sudan's Islamic fundamentalist government has fought against groups of rebels from southern Sudan. The government is intent on imposing Islamic law on the people of Sudan, while the southern Sudanese groups demand religious freedom and economic power. Peace talks aimed at ending the war have produced glimmers of hope, and on May 26, 2004, a power-sharing agreement was signed by both sides. However, further crisis broke out in western Sudan shortly thereafter, plunging the country back into chaos and creating more orphans and refugees.

BUILDING BACKGROUND
To learn more about the Lost Boys of Sudan, visit the **Literature Center** at **ClassZone.com.**

The Lost Boys

SARA CORBETT

THESE YOUNG AFRICAN REFUGEES SURVIVED LIONS, CROCODILES, AND STARVATION. NOW THEY'RE STARTING LIFE OVER IN AMERICA.

One evening in late January, Peter Dut, 21, leads his two teenage brothers through the brightly lit corridors of the Minneapolis airport, trying to mask his confusion. Two days earlier, the brothers, refugees from Africa, had encountered their first light switch and their first set of stairs. An aid worker in Nairobi[1] had demonstrated the flush toilet to them—also the seat belt, the shoelace, the fork. And now they find themselves alone in Minneapolis, three bone-thin African boys confronted by a swirling river of white faces and rolling suitcases.

Finally, a traveling businessman recognizes their uncertainty. "Where are you flying to?" he asks kindly, and the eldest brother tells him in halting, 10 bookish English. A few days earlier, they left a small mud hut in a blistering-hot Kenyan refugee camp, where they had lived as orphans for nine years after walking for hundreds of miles across Sudan.[2] They are now headed to a new home in the U.S.A. "Where?" the man asks in disbelief when Peter Dut says the city's name. "Fargo? North Dakota? You gotta be kidding me. It's too cold there. You'll never survive it!"

And then he laughs. Peter Dut has no idea why. **B**

In the meantime, the temperature in Fargo has dropped to 15 below. The boys tell me that, until now, all they have ever known about cold is what they felt grasping a bottle of frozen water. An aid worker handed it to them one day 20 during a "cultural orientation" session at the Kakuma[3] Refugee Camp, a place where the temperature hovers around 100 degrees.

Peter Dut and his two brothers belong to an unusual group of refugees referred to by aid organizations as the Lost Boys of Sudan, a group of roughly 10,000 boys who arrived in Kenya in 1992 seeking refuge from their country's

---

A GRAPHIC AIDS
This **photograph** was taken shortly after the Dut brothers arrived in North Dakota. What do their facial expressions and body language suggest about their comfort level in their new surroundings?

B AUTHOR'S PURPOSE
The writer begins this article with an **anecdote** instead of immediately presenting statistics about Sudan. How does this choice affect your perception of the subject matter?

---

1. **Nairobi** (nī-rō′bē): the capital city of Kenya, a country in Africa.
2. **Sudan:** a country in eastern Africa northwest of Kenya.
3. **Kakuma** (kə-kōō′mä).

fractious civil war. The fighting pits a northern Islamic government against rebels in the south who practice Christianity and tribal religions.

The Lost Boys were named after Peter Pan's **posse** of orphans. According to U.S. State Department estimates, some 17,000 boys were separated from their families and fled southern Sudan in an **exodus** of biblical proportions after
30 fighting intensified in 1987. They arrived in throngs, homeless and parentless, having trekked about 1,000 miles from Sudan to Ethiopia, back to Sudan, and finally to Kenya. The majority of the boys belonged to the Dinka or Nuer tribes, and most were between the ages of 8 and 18. (Most of the boys don't know for sure how old they are; aid workers assigned them approximate ages after they arrived in 1992.)

Along the way, the boys endured attacks from the northern army and **marauding** bandits, as well as lions who preyed on the slowest and weakest among them. Many died from starvation or thirst. Others drowned or were eaten by crocodiles as they tried to cross a swollen Ethiopian river. By the time
40 the Lost Boys reached the Kakuma Refugee Camp, their numbers had been cut nearly in half.

fractious (frăk′shəs) *adj.* hard to manage or hold together; unruly

posse (pŏs′ē) *n.* a band

exodus (ĕk′sə-dəs) *n.* a mass departure

marauding (mə-rô′dĭng) *adj.* roaming about in search of plunder **maraud** *v.*

THE LOST BOYS' PERILOUS JOURNEY TO FREEDOM

C GRAPHIC AIDS
List two details included on the **map** that are not provided in the article. What do you think is the most important piece of information communicated by this map?

In 1992, roughly 10,000 boys from Sudan poured into a refugee camp in Kenya.

Now, after nine years of **subsisting** on rationed corn mush and lentils and living largely ungoverned by adults, the Lost Boys of Sudan are coming to America. In 1999, the United Nations High Commissioner for Refugees, which handles refugee cases around the world, and the U.S. government agreed to send 3,600 of the boys to the U.S.—since going back to Sudan was out of the question. About 500 of the Lost Boys still under the age of 18 will be living in apartments or foster homes across the U.S. by the end of this year. The boys will start school at a grade level normal for their age, thanks to a
50 tough English-language program at their refugee camp. The remaining 3,100 Lost Boys will be resettled as adults. After five years, each boy will be eligible for citizenship, provided he has turned 21.

NIGHTTIME IN AMERICA?

On the night that I stand waiting for Peter Dut and his brothers to land in Fargo, tendrils of snow are snaking across the tarmac. The three boys file through the gate without money or coats or luggage beyond their small backpacks. The younger brothers, Maduk, 17, and Riak, 15, appear petrified. As a social worker passes out coats, Peter Dut studies the black night through the airport window. "Excuse me," he says worriedly. "Can you tell me, please, is it now night or day?"
60   This is a stove burner. This is a can opener. This is a brush for your teeth. The new things come in a tumble. The brothers' home is a sparsely furnished, two-bedroom apartment in a complex on Fargo's south side. Rent is $445 a month. It has been stocked with donations from area churches and businesses: toothpaste, bread, beans, bananas.

subsist (səb-sĭst′) *v.* to support oneself at a minimal level

A caseworker empties a garbage bag full of donated clothing, which looks to have come straight from the closet of an elderly man. I know how lucky the boys are: The State Department estimates that war, famine, and disease in southern Sudan have killed more than 2 million people and displaced another 4 million. Still I cringe to think of the boys showing up for school in these clothes.

70   The next day, when I return to the apartment at noon, the boys have been up since 5 and are terribly hungry. "What about your food?" I ask, gesturing to the bread and bananas and the box of cereal sitting on the counter.

Peter grins sheepishly. I suddenly realize that the boys, in a lifetime of cooking maize and beans over a fire pit, have never opened a box. I am placed in the role of teacher. And so begins an opening spree. We open potato chips. We open a can of beans. We untwist the tie on the bagged loaf of bread. Soon, the boys are seated and eating a hot meal. **D**

LIVING ON LEAVES AND BERRIES

The three brothers have come a long way since they fled their village in Sudan with their parents and three sisters—all of whom were later killed by Sudanese 80 army soldiers. The Lost Boys first survived a 6- to 10-week walk to Ethiopia, often subsisting on leaves and berries and the occasional **boon** of a warthog carcass. Some boys staved off dehydration by drinking their own urine. Many fell behind; some were devoured by lions or trampled by buffalo.

The Lost Boys lived for three years in Ethiopia, in UN-supported camps, before they were forced back into Sudan by a new Ethiopian government no longer sympathetic to their plight. Somehow, more than 10,000 of the boys miraculously trailed into Kenya's UN camps in the summer of 1992—as Sudanese government planes bombed the rear of their procession.

For the Lost Boys, then, a new life in America might easily seem to be the 90 answer to every dream. But the real world has been more complicated than that. Within weeks of arriving, Riak is placed in a local junior high; Maduk starts high school classes; and Peter begins adult-education classes.

REFUGEE BLUES

Five weeks later, Riak listens quietly through a lesson on Elizabethan history at school, all but ignored by white students around him.

Nearby at Fargo South High School, Maduk is frequently alone as well, copying passages from his geography textbook, trying not to look at the short skirts worn by many of the girls.

Peter Dut worries about money. The three brothers say they receive just $107 in food stamps each month and spend most of their $510 monthly cash 100 assistance on rent and utilities.

Resettlement workers say the brothers are just undergoing the normal transition. Scott Burtsfield, who coordinates resettlement efforts in Fargo through Lutheran Social Services, says: "The first three months are always the toughest. It really does get better."

D AUTHOR'S PURPOSE
What is Corbett's purpose in lines 70–77? Explain, citing specific details from the passage.

boon (bōōn) *n.* a benefit; blessing

Riak Dut, shown here in his school lunch line, eats alone most days.

The Lost Boys can only hope so; they have few other options. A return to southern Sudan could be fatal. "There is nothing left for the Lost Boys to go home to—it's a war zone," says Mary Anne Fitzgerald, a Nairobi-based relief consultant.

Some Sudanese elders have criticized sending boys to the U.S. They worry
110 their children will lose their African identity. One afternoon, an 18-year-old Lost Boy translated a part of a tape an elder had sent along with many boys: "He is saying: 'Don't drink. Don't smoke. Don't kill. Go to school every day, and remember, America is not your home.'" **F**

But if adjustment is hard, the boys also experience consoling moments.

One of these comes on a quiet Friday night last winter. As the boys make a dinner of rice and lentils, Peter changes into an African outfit, a finely woven green tunic, with a skullcap to match, bought with precious food rations at Kakuma.

Just then, the doorbell rings unexpectedly. And out of the cold tumble four
120 Sudanese boys—all of whom have resettled as refugees over the last several years. I watch one, an 18-year-old named Sunday, wrap his arms encouragingly around Peter Dut. "It's a hard life here," Sunday whispers to the older boy, "but it's a free life, too." ∾

E **GRAPHIC AIDS**
What can you **infer** about Riak's experiences at his junior high in North Dakota based on this photograph? Explain your answer.

F **CONNECT**
Think about what it's like to receive instructions from a parent or other adult. Do you think these taped messages will influence the boys? Explain.

Comprehension

PENNSYLVANIA STANDARDS

READING STANDARD
B.3.3.3 Interpret and/or analyze graphics and charts

1. **Recall** Why did the Lost Boys leave Sudan?

2. **Summarize** What hardships did the boys endure as they fled from their homes in Sudan to the refugee camp in Kenya?

3. **Clarify** How did Peter Dut's friend comfort him at the end of the article?

Critical Analysis

4. **Connect** Think back to the discussion you had about what it might be like to be forced from your home. Did reading about these young **refugees** change your feelings at all? Explain why or why not, citing details from the selection.

5. **Analyze Characterization** How would you describe the Dut brothers? What details caused you to form this impression? Use a spider map like the one shown to record the details—such as the boys' words, or statements about them—that influenced your opinion. Then describe the brothers in one or two sentences.

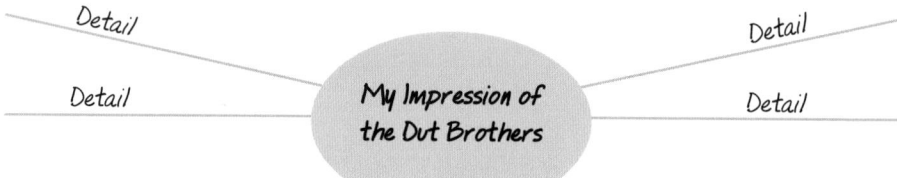

Detail

Detail

Detail

Detail

My Impression of the Dut Brothers

6. **Interpret Graphic Aids** Examine the **map** on page 550 and the **photographs** on pages 549, 551, and 553. Which was most effective at helping you understand the Lost Boys' experiences? Which had the strongest effect on you? Explain, describing the type of information conveyed by each graphic aid.

7. **Evaluate Author's Purpose** Review the chart you filled in as you read. What do you think is Corbett's primary purpose? Which purpose does she achieve most effectively? Explain your answers, citing evidence from the text.

Reading-Writing Connection

WRITING PROMPT

Short Response: Analyze a Problem
Of all the struggles these **refugees** faced in America, which do you think must have been the most difficult? Consider the alienation caused by culture shock, financial hardship, loneliness, and the new climate. Write **one or two paragraphs** explaining your view, citing evidence.

SELF-CHECK

A strong analysis will . . .
- demonstrate a thorough understanding of the boys' ordeal
- incorporate relevant and convincing examples from the text to support your opinion

Vocabulary in Context

VOCABULARY PRACTICE

Choose the word that is not related in meaning to the other words.

1. migration, exodus, consolation, flight
2. boon, building, structure, edifice
3. conspiring, ravaging, plundering, marauding
4. amusement, posse, recreation, entertainment
5. subsist, survive, manage, reconsider
6. irritable, divisive, fractious, connected

WORD LIST

boon

exodus

fractious

marauding

posse

subsisting

VOCABULARY IN WRITING

Imagine you are a journalist writing about the conflict in Sudan. Write headlines that could appear above your story, using each vocabulary word at least once.

> **EXAMPLE HEADLINE**
>
> *Civil War Causes Exodus as Refugees Flee for Their Lives*

VOCABULARY STRATEGY: THE LATIN ROOT *fract*

The vocabulary word *fractious* contains the Latin root *fract,* which means "to break." This root may also appear as *frag* and *fring.* To understand the meaning of words with these root forms, use context clues and your knowledge of the root.

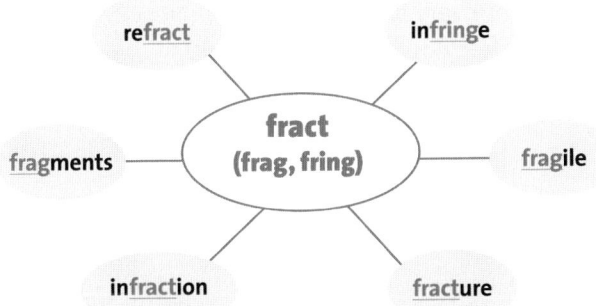

PRACTICE Choose the word from the word web that best completes each sentence. Use context clues to help you or, if necessary, check a dictionary.

1. Don't put _____ objects where children can reach them.
2. _____ of the shattered glass still lay on the floor.
3. The protesters feared that the police would _____ on their rights.
4. Because water will _____ light, a pencil in a glass of water will look broken.
5. Any serious _____ of the rules will be punished by a two-day suspension.
6. He suffered a hairline _____ of his collarbone.

PENNSYLVANIA STANDARDS

READING STANDARD
A.2.2 Apply word recognition skills

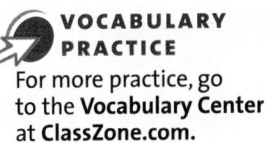

VOCABULARY PRACTICE
For more practice, go to the **Vocabulary Center** at **ClassZone.com.**

News Reports

TV Newscast Clip / Web News Report on *MediaSmart* DVD

How do you get the NEWS?

PENNSYLVANIA STANDARDS

SPEAKING/LISTENING STANDARD
1.6.11.F.2 Evaluate the role of media in focusing attention and forming opinions

KEY IDEA When you need to know the latest **news,** where do you turn? To the nearest TV or radio? To the Internet? To the nearest friend? Some people get their news through brief summaries, while others seek forms that are chock-full of details. The two news formats you'll explore, a segment of a TV newscast and an article from a news Web site, will shed light on the different ways the news media can cover the same event and the advantages and disadvantages of news formats.

Background

Digging for News The news event you'll investigate took place in Somerset, Pennsylvania, in 2002. Nine coal miners were trapped nearly 240 feet underground in a mineshaft that was filling up rapidly with icy water. Mining crews worked frantically to drill a rescue shaft and construct a basket of steel-wire mesh to transport each miner. During four very tense days, new developments about the rescue effort flowed from a variety of news sources, including TV- and radio-network newscasts, newspaper reports, and Internet news services.

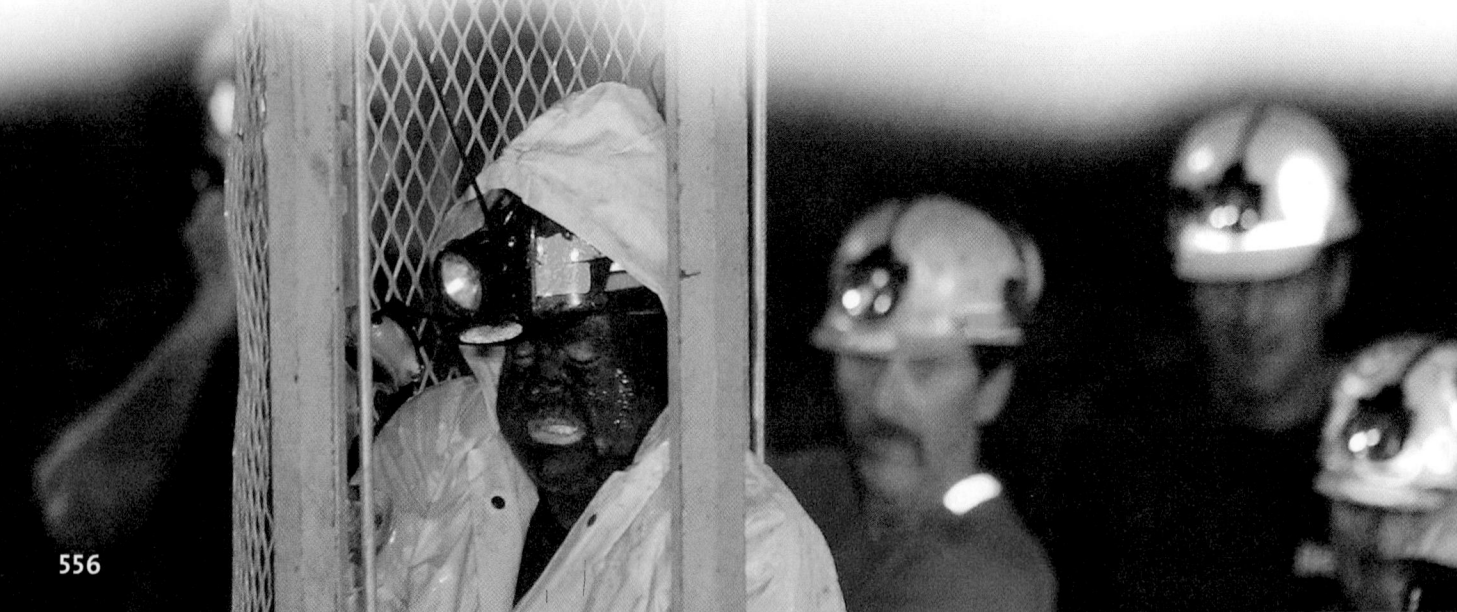

Media Literacy: News Formats

News formats are packaged in a variety of ways, not only to deliver information but to get and keep an audience's attention. Shown below are features of two electronic news sources.

FEATURES OF A TV NEWSCAST

1 The **anchor** introduces the news story with a **lead-in.**

2 Then the scene cuts to **video footage,** which is shot and edited to illustrate the events of the news story. As the footage plays, the anchor or a **field reporter** describes the details.

3 The **voice-over** is the unseen reporter's voice that plays over the images. A voice-over makes a news story easy to follow.

4 **Sound bites,** brief statements from interviews with experts or witnesses, can provide details and stir emotions.

Advantages

- TV news stories can be aired as soon as the event is known.
- A typical news segment lasts 30 seconds to 2 minutes. This allows more news stories to be reported in a short period of time.
- Video and audio give a story immediacy and drama.

Disadvantages

- Because a news segment is short, it may not cover an event thoroughly enough.
- Sometimes stations "go live," or air a story, before all the facts are gathered.

FEATURES OF A WEB NEWS REPORT

1 **Menus** on the page help users to navigate the site.

2 The **lead,** the first sentence (or first few sentences), starts the report.

3 **Captions** explain the photographs or other visuals.

4 **Hyperlinks**—typically, highlighted words, phrases, or images—allow users to jump directly to updates or more information.

   Quotations from those involved add human interest.

Advantages

- Breaking stories can be posted and updated at any time.
- Space is usually not a limitation. A Web news report can run for an indefinite length.
- **Streaming video** or **animations** bring the scene to life.

Disadvantages

- Web articles may not be accessible to everyone.
- Sometimes stories are posted so quickly that the facts may be inaccurate.

STRATEGIES FOR VIEWING

- In any news format, look for answers to the **5 W's** and the **H** questions: Who? What? Where? When? Why? and How?
- Be sure you can spot the **lead.** Try restating the lead in your own words to be sure it covers all the essential details.

SOMERSET, Pennsylvania (CNN) -- One by one, nine soggy and exhausted miners, their faces blackened with coal dust, were pulled early Sunday from a flooded Pennsylvania coal mine after being trapped underground for more than three days.

The last one pulled from the 240-foot deep shaft was 41-year-old Mark Popernack, who emerged at 2:45 a.m. and gave his rescuers a thumbs-up.

John Phillippi was the fifth miner to be pulled from the Pennsylvania mine on Sunday.

All nine men were taken to hospitals where they will remain under observation for at least 24 hours, officials said. They will be reunited with their families at the medical facilities.

SAVE THIS   EMAIL THIS
PRINT THIS   MOST POPULAR

The first miner, Randy Fogle, who had complained of chest pains, was taken by helicopter to Conemaugh Hospital.

Dr. Richard Saluzzo said Fogle was hypothermic, meaning his temperature was

Viewing Guide for
News Reports

Both the NBC video clip and the CNN.com news report were originally presented the day after the rescue. The video clip, as an in-depth news feature, lasts longer than a typical news segment.

View the clip several times and take as much time as you need to look over the Web report. As you explore these two news formats, consider how each delivers the facts and take note of the specific techniques each uses to capture attention.

NOW VIEW

FIRST VIEWING: Comprehension

1. **Summarize** In a brief statement, describe how the coal miners were rescued. Base the statement on the TV newscast.

2. **Clarify** In using the Web news site, what would you need to do to find additional information about Randy Fogle?

CLOSE VIEWING: Media Literacy

3. **Draw Conclusions** By TV news standards, the newscast you've viewed is much longer than a typical news story. Basic news stories range in length from 30 seconds to 2 minutes. Why do you think so much time is devoted to this story?

4. **Analyze Techniques** The TV newscast includes **sound bites** from two rescued miners and from certain officials. The Web news report includes **quotations** from similar sources. Why do you think both news formats included such information?

5. **Compare Formats** You've examined how two news formats covered the same event. Use a Venn diagram to compare how the TV news segment and the Web news report are alike and different.

TV News Segment   Web News Report

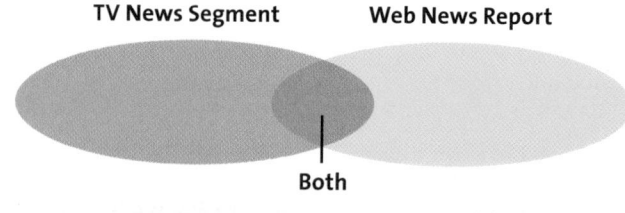

Both

Write or Discuss

Compare the News Formats Which news format—the TV news segment or the Web news report—is more effective at covering the rescue? Explain your opinion. Keep the following criteria in mind:

- the effectiveness of the lead in each format in delivering the important facts about the rescue
- the techniques used to capture and keep your interest
- the time or space limitations of each format

Produce Your Own Media

Create a News Segment Select an article from your school newspaper or from a community newspaper. Determine how you would create an update to the article in the form of a TV news segment. Then divide into teams to draft a script, conduct interviews, and plan to shoot the video footage of the segment.

HERE'S HOW Work in the assigned planning groups to address these questions:

- Who would be the anchor and the on-camera reporter?
- Whom would you interview for sound bites?
- What lead-in would your anchor provide?
- What voice-over would you need to include to structure the story?
- What video footage would you shoot?

MEDIA TOOLS

For help with creating a news segment, visit the **Media Center** at **ClassZone.com.**

STUDENT MODEL

WHAT VIEWERS SEE	WHAT VIEWERS HEAR	SHOT KEY		
ON-CAMERA REPORTER BIANCA EXT—DAY 1. LS of reporter standing with a group of student protesters in a parking lot.	BIANCA: Since the start of the school year, a growing group of students at Optima High believe the school parking lot to be in need of a makeover. . . .	**LS**	Long Shot	
		MS	Medium Shot	
		VWS	Very Wide Shot	
		EXT	Exterior	
CUT TO: MS of BIANCA 2. Quickly zoom out to a VWS that reveals the potholes—some rather deep—dotting the lot.	BIANCA: . . . an extreme makeover.			

Tech Tip

You might use a design program to create a graphic for the report.

A LOT OF TROUBLE

The Open Window

Short Story by Saki

How should you treat a GUEST?

PENNSYLVANIA STANDARDS

READING STANDARDS
A.1.3.1 Make inferences and/or draw conclusions
B.1.1.1.E.1 Evaluate the tone, style, and/or mood

KEY IDEA You're sitting at home when the doorbell rings. Instead of the pizza-delivery guy you were expecting, it's an uninvited **guest.** If that guest happens to be your best friend, you now have someone fun to share your pizza with. If, however, that guest is someone you would rather not hang out with, what should you do?

DISCUSS In your opinion, do you have an obligation to treat a guest, invited or not, with hospitality? Discuss your opinion with a small group of classmates. Talk about the obligations you have as a host—especially to a guest you would rather not spend time with. Are there minimum standards you have to meet in order not to be rude? After you've discussed these questions, think about whether or not your opinion has changed and, if so, why.

LITERARY ANALYSIS: TONE AND AUTHOR'S PURPOSE

A writer's **tone,** or attitude toward a subject, can often reveal his or her **purpose.** Just as you might use one tone of voice to make a joke and another to criticize someone, writers use different tones to accomplish different purposes. A writer's tone may be playful or solemn, sarcastic or admiring. Figuring out the writer's tone can help you decide what his or her purpose might be. As you read Saki's famous short story "The Open Window," ask yourself

• Does the narrator's description of other characters reveal whether Saki is portraying them in a favorable or an unfavorable light?

• Does Saki use formal or informal language? What effect does this create?

Review: **Point of View**

READING STRATEGY: PREDICT

To make **predictions** about characters, try the following strategies:

• Think about each character's personality. How might someone with these traits respond to conflict or to new situations?

• Consider different characters' actions. What might happen as a result of these actions?

• Use your own experience. If you were ever in a situation similar to the one in the story, how did it turn out?

As you read "The Open Window," stop occasionally to predict what might happen next. Record text clues that help you make reasonable guesses, and check your predictions against what actually happens.

Text Clues	My Prediction	Actual Outcome
Mrs. Sappleton has had a "great tragedy." (line 26)	She will still be very sad, even though it happened years ago.	

Author Online

Saki
1870–1916

Also Known As . . .
"Saki" is the pen name of Hector Hugo Munro, a British author best known for his satirical short stories. Munro was born in Burma, a country in Asia then controlled by the British. When he was very young, his mother was killed in an accident. His father sent Munro and his siblings to England to be raised by their aunts, two old women who believed in old-fashioned discipline.

Saki's Saga When he was 23, Munro returned to Burma to join the military police. Stricken with malaria a year later, he gave up his badge and his pet tiger cub and returned to England to try his hand at writing. As he embarked on his literary career, he picked up the name Saki from the *Rubáiyát,* a long poem by 12th-century Persian writer Omar Khayyám. Although he wrote nonfiction, political cartoons, novels, and plays, Saki is most famous for his short stories, which are praised for their whimsical humor and shrewd social criticism. When World War I began, the writer rushed to enlist. During a night march through France in 1916, he was shot and killed by a German sniper.

MORE ABOUT THE AUTHOR
For more on Saki, visit the **Literature Center** at **ClassZone.com.**

Background

Ridiculing the Rich "The Open Window" depicts the world of the British upper class in the early 1900s. Saki, himself a member of the upper class, often ridiculed the customs of high society. For instance, he made fun of the fact that people were expected to present formal letters of introduction when visiting strangers and poked fun at the "nerve cure," a trip to the countryside to treat anxiety.

The Open Window

SAKI

"My aunt will be down presently, Mr. Nuttel," said a very self-possessed young lady of fifteen; "in the mean-time you must try and put up with me."

Framton Nuttel endeavored to say the correct something that should duly flatter the niece of the moment without unduly discounting the aunt that was to come. Privately he doubted more than ever whether these formal visits on a succession of total strangers would do much toward helping the nerve cure[1] which he was supposed to be undergoing. **A**

"I know how it will be," his sister had said when he was preparing to migrate to this rural retreat; "you will bury yourself down there and not speak 10 to a living soul, and your nerves will be worse than ever from moping. I shall just give you letters of introduction to all the people I know there. Some of them, as far as I can remember, were quite nice."

Framton wondered whether Mrs. Sappleton, the lady to whom he was presenting one of the letters of introduction, came into the nice division.

"Do you know many of the people round here?" asked the niece, when she judged that they had had sufficient silent communion.

"Hardly a soul," said Framton. "My sister was staying here, at the rectory,[2] you know, some four years ago, and she gave me letters of introduction to some of the people here."

20 He made the last statement in a tone of distinct regret.

"Then you know practically nothing about my aunt?" pursued the self-possessed young lady.

"Only her name and address," admitted the caller. He was wondering whether Mrs. Sappleton was in the married or widowed state. An undefinable something about the room seemed to suggest masculine habitation.[3]

A TONE AND AUTHOR'S PURPOSE
Paraphrase lines 3–7. So far, how would you describe Saki's tone, or his attitude toward this character? Explain your answer, citing evidence.

ANALYZE VISUALS
The narrator describes the niece as "self-possessed," or confident and in control. In your opinion, does the young woman in this painting look self-possessed? Explain, citing the **details** that influenced your opinion.

---

1. **nerve cure:** a treatment for nervousness or anxiety.

2. **the rectory** (rĕk′tə-rē): the parish priest's house.

3. **masculine habitation:** that men lived there.

"Her great tragedy happened just three years ago," said the child; "that would be since your sister's time."

"Her tragedy?" asked Framton; somehow in this restful country spot tragedies seemed out of place.

"You may wonder why we keep that window wide open on an October afternoon," said the niece, indicating a large French window[4] that opened on to a lawn.

"It is quite warm for the time of the year," said Framton; "but has that window got anything to do with the tragedy?" **B**

"Out through that window, three years ago to a day, her husband and her two young brothers went off for their day's shooting. They never came back. In crossing the moor to their favorite snipe-shooting ground they were all three engulfed by a treacherous piece of bog. It had been that dreadful wet summer, you know, and places that were safe in other years gave way suddenly without warning. Their bodies were never recovered. That was the dreadful part of it." Here the child's voice lost its self-possessed note and became falteringly human. "Poor aunt always thinks that they will come back some day, they and the little brown spaniel that was lost with them, and walk in that window just as they used to do. That is why the window is kept open every evening till it is quite dusk. Poor dear aunt, she has often told me how they went out, her husband with his white waterproof coat over his arm, and Ronnie, her youngest brother, singing 'Bertie, why do you bound?' as he always did to tease her, because she said it got on her nerves. Do you know, sometimes on still, quiet evenings like this, I almost get a creepy feeling that they will all walk in through that window—"

She broke off with a little shudder. It was a relief to Framton when the aunt bustled into the room with a whirl of apologies for being late in making her appearance.

"I hope Vera has been amusing you?" she said.

"She has been very interesting," said Framton. **C**

"I hope you don't mind the open window," said Mrs. Sappleton briskly; "my husband and brothers will be home directly from shooting, and they always come in this way. They've been out for snipe in the marshes today, so they'll make a fine mess over my poor carpets. So like you menfolk, isn't it?"

She rattled on cheerfully about the shooting and the scarcity of birds, and the prospects for duck in the winter. To Framton it was all purely horrible. He made a desperate but only partially successful effort to turn the talk on to a less ghastly topic; he was conscious that his hostess was giving him only a fragment of her attention, and her eyes were constantly straying past him to the open window and the lawn beyond. It was certainly an unfortunate coincidence that he should have paid his visit on this tragic anniversary.

B POINT OF VIEW
Is this story told from the **first-person** or the **third-person** point of view? Explain how you determined this, citing evidence.

C PREDICT
Will Nuttel say anything to Mrs. Sappleton about her "great tragedy"? Give reasons for your prediction.

---

4. **French window:** a pair of windows that extend to the floor and open like doors.

"The doctors agree in ordering me complete rest, an absence of mental excitement, and avoidance of anything in the nature of violent physical exercise," announced Framton, who labored under the tolerably widespread delusion that total strangers and chance acquaintances are hungry for the least detail of one's ailments and infirmities, their cause and cure. "On the matter of diet they are not so much in agreement," he continued. **D**

"No?" said Mrs. Sappleton, in a voice which only replaced a yawn at the last moment. Then she suddenly brightened into alert attention—but not to what Framton was saying.

"Here they are at last!" she cried. "Just in time for tea, and don't they look as if they were muddy up to the eyes!"

Framton shivered slightly, and turned toward the niece with a look intended to convey sympathetic comprehension. The child was staring out through the open window with dazed horror in her eyes. In a chill shock of nameless fear Framton swung round in his seat and looked in the same direction.

In the deepening twilight three figures were walking across the lawn toward the window; they all carried guns under their arms, and one of them was additionally burdened with a white coat hung over his shoulders. A tired brown spaniel kept close at their heels. Noiselessly they neared the house, and then a hoarse young voice chanted out of the dusk:

"I said, Bertie, why do you bound?"

Framton grabbed wildly at his stick and hat; the hall door, the gravel drive, and the front gate were dimly noted stages in his headlong retreat. A cyclist coming along the road had to run into the hedge to avoid imminent collision. **E**

"Here we are, my dear," said the bearer of the white mackintosh, coming in through the window; "fairly muddy, but most of it's dry. Who was that who bolted out as we came up?"

"A most extraordinary man, a Mr. Nuttel," said Mrs. Sappleton; "could only talk about his illnesses, and dashed off without a word of goodbye or apology when you arrived. One would think he had seen a ghost."

"I expect it was the spaniel," said the niece calmly; "he told me he had a horror of dogs. He was once hunted into a cemetery somewhere on the banks of the Ganges[5] by a pack of pariah dogs[6], and had to spend the night in a newly dug grave with the creatures snarling and grinning and foaming just above him. Enough to make anyone lose his nerve."

Romance[7] at short notice was her specialty. ❧

D TONE AND AUTHOR'S PURPOSE
Is the language Saki uses to describe Nuttel's endless discussion of his health formal or informal? Explain the tone this language helps convey.

E GRAMMAR AND STYLE
Reread lines 89–91. Saki uses the **adverbs** *wildly* and *dimly* to emphasize Nuttel's desperate flight from the house.

---

5. **Ganges** (găn'jēz'): a large river in northern India.

6. **pariah** (pə-rī'ə) **dogs:** dogs that have escaped from their owners and become wild.

7. **romance:** highly imaginative fiction.

After Reading

Comprehension

1. **Recall** Describe the "great tragedy" that Vera relates to Mr. Nuttel. According to Vera, why does her aunt keep the window open?

2. **Recall** Why does Nuttel leave so abruptly, and how does Vera explain his frantic departure?

3. **Paraphrase** Reread the story's final line. Then restate it in your own words.

Literary Analysis

4. **Draw Conclusions** A **surprise ending** is an unexpected twist at the end of a story. Reread lines 15–25 and think about Vera's behavior. Now that you know how "The Open Window" ends, what would you say was Vera's **motive** for asking Nuttel each question listed in the chart shown?

Vera's Question	Motive
"Do you know many of the people round here?" (line 15)	
"Then you know practically nothing about my aunt?" (line 21)	

5. **Evaluate Predictions** Review the chart you created as you read. How accurate were your predictions? If they were very accurate, describe the clues that allowed you to make such on-target guesses. If your predictions were off, explain how Saki caught you by surprise.

6. **Analyze Point of View** Saki uses a **third-person omniscient narrator** in "The Open Window." The narrator is an outside voice that gives you access to the thoughts and feelings of all the characters and relates events that may be happening simultaneously. How would the end of this story be different if it were told exclusively from Nuttel's point of view? Explain your answer.

7. **Analyze Tone and Author's Purpose** Think about Saki's use of formal language to describe silly situations, as well as his depiction of Mr. Nuttel. From Saki's tone, what can you infer about his purpose? Explain what he might be trying to tell his readers about people like Mr. Nuttel. Cite evidence from the text to support your analysis.

Literary Criticism

8. **Critical Interpretations** According to critic Rena Corb, the "successful ending" of this story depends on "the reader's belief, along with Nuttel's, that Vera is telling the truth." Whether you, like Nuttel, fell for Vera's story or you knew she was lying to her **guest** all along, explain why you agree or disagree with Corb's assertion. Support your opinion with evidence from the selection.

PENNSYLVANIA STANDARDS

READING STANDARD
A.1.3.1 Make inferences and/or draw conclusions

Reading-Writing Connection

Extend your interaction with "The Open Window" by responding to these prompts. Then use **Revision: Grammar and Style** to improve your writing.

WRITING PROMPTS

A. Short Response: Predict Nuttel's Reaction

Imagine that Framton Nuttel learned the truth about the Sappleton "tragedy." How might he respond to the news? Write **one or two paragraphs** describing how Nuttel might feel and act upon learning that he had been tricked.

B. Extended Response: Analyze Characters

How would you describe the characters of Vera and her **guest**, Framton Nuttel? Is Vera deceitful or just imaginative? Is Nuttel stupidly gullible, or is he simply a trusting person? Write a **three-to-five-paragraph response**, citing evidence.

SELF-CHECK

A successful response will . . .

- describe in clear detail how Nuttel might act when he learns Vera has tricked him
- convey what Nuttel might be thinking, based on the traits he exhibits in the story

A strong analysis will . . .

- discuss three features of each character's personality
- use examples from the story to support your ideas

REVISION: GRAMMAR AND STYLE

ADD DESCRIPTIVE DETAILS Review the **Grammar and Style** note on page 565. Through his use of descriptive **adverbs**, Saki gives the reader a greater sense of the urgency with which Nuttel flees the scene.

Adverbs are used to modify verbs, adjectives, and other adverbs. Adverbs should accurately and descriptively convey where, when, how, or to what extent something is happening. In the following excerpts, notice how the adverbs Saki uses reveal important details about Vera's character:

> *"That was the dreadful part of it." Here the child's voice lost its self-possessed note and became falteringly human.* (lines 40–42)

> *"I expect it was the spaniel," said the niece calmly; "he told me he had a horror of dogs."* (lines 98–99)

Notice how the revisions in red make this first draft more descriptive. Revise your responses to the prompts by using similar techniques.

 PENNSYLVANIA STANDARDS

WRITING STANDARD
1.4.11.B.2 Use precise language and specific detail

STUDENT MODEL

cunningly
Vera is ^clever. She knows she will have a few minutes alone with Mr. Nuttel,
spontaneously   *clearly*
so she ^decides to toy with him. She has ^made up stories like this before, since
                          elaborately
it takes her very little time to ^describe the events to Mr. Nuttel.

 **WRITING TOOLS**
For prewriting, revision, and editing tools, visit the **Writing Center** at ClassZone.com.

from **The House on Mango Street**
Fiction by Sandra Cisneros

What STORIES
will you tell your children?

PENNSYLVANIA STANDARDS

READING STANDARDS
A.1.6.1 Identify and/or analyze intended purpose of text

B.1.1.1.A.1 Evaluate character

KEY IDEA Whether it's a tale about the sweet taste of victory or a description of a devastating loss, you have important stories to tell. These stories, if you choose to tell them, will someday be the next generation's **legacy**—stories, beliefs, and traditions passed on from one generation to the next.

PRESENT With a classmate, share a few stories you might want to tell your kids someday. Then pick your favorite—maybe it's the funniest, or the most outrageous, or the one that says the most about you. With a small group, take turns telling your chosen tales. Explain why these are the stories you would pass on to the next generation.

LITERARY ANALYSIS: AUTHOR'S PERSPECTIVE

Just as your own experiences influence the way you think about different issues, a writer's personal experiences affect the way he or she approaches a topic. When you analyze an **author's perspective,** you work to figure out how the writer looks at his or her subject. As you read this excerpt from *The House on Mango Street*, think about Sandra Cisneros's perspective on the narrator's circumstances.

- Pay attention to the writer's choice of details. In these vignettes, Cisneros describes a rundown house in vivid detail. What do her descriptions of its small windows, crumbling bricks, and tiny yard help emphasize?

- Consider direct statements of the narrator's thoughts or feelings. What kind of person is she?

As you read, consider what these details and statements reveal about Cisneros's ideas, as well as her feelings about what it's like to grow up in a place like the house on Mango Street.

Review: **Tone**

READING SKILL: MAKE INFERENCES ABOUT CHARACTER

Writers don't usually spell out every single thing their characters are thinking and feeling. They often leave it up to the reader to **make inferences** about what isn't directly stated. As you read the following vignettes, keep track of significant details that tell you something about the narrator's background, personality, and feelings. Then record what you can infer from these details.

Details from the Text	My Inferences
Esperanza's family has moved around a lot, and she doesn't sound very happy about that. (lines 1–3)	Esperanza probably wishes her family could just stay in one place and not move around so much.
When the family moves to Mango Street, they finally get their own house. But Esperanza says that "it's not the house we'd thought we'd get." (line 9)	

Author On|ine

**Sandra Cisneros
born 1954**

Defining Her Destiny
Sandra Cisneros grew up in a male-dominated household where her father and six brothers were the authority figures. She quietly rebelled against the traditional role she was expected to play as a Mexican-American female, writing in secret until she went away to college. The author now uses her work to give voice to the experiences of Mexican-American women. "I'm trying to write the stories that haven't been written," Cisneros explains. "I'm determined to fill a literary void."

Latina Power Much of Cisneros's writing deals with the shame of poverty and the guilt that comes with rejecting certain aspects of one's culture. Her poetry and prose have received critical acclaim. "I am a woman and I am a Latina," the author says proudly. "Those are the things that make my writing distinctive. Those are the things that give my writing power."

 MORE ABOUT THE AUTHOR
For more on Sandra Cisneros, visit the **Literature Center** at **ClassZone.com.**

Background

No Place Like Home When Cisneros was young, her family moved frequently from Chicago to Mexico City and back again. She never remained in one place long enough to make close friends, and she longed for a "perfect" house like the ones she read about and saw on TV. When she was 11, Cisneros and her family finally moved into a shabby house in a poor Chicago neighborhood. The rundown house was not the dream home she had longed for. Esperanza Cordero, the narrator of *The House on Mango Street*, faces similar issues.

The House on
Mango *Street*

Sandra Cisneros

The House on Mango Street

We didn't always live on Mango Street. Before that we lived on Loomis on the third floor, and before that we lived on Keeler. Before Keeler it was Paulina, and before that I can't remember. But what I remember most is moving a lot. Each time it seemed there'd be one more of us. By the time we got to Mango Street we were six—Mama, Papa, Carlos, Kiki, my sister Nenny and me.

The house on Mango Street is ours, and we don't have to pay rent to anybody, or share the yard with the people downstairs, or be careful not to make too much noise, and there isn't a landlord banging on the ceiling with a broom. But even so, it's not the house we'd thought we'd get.

10 We had to leave the flat[1] on Loomis quick. The water pipes broke and the landlord wouldn't fix them because the house was too old. We had to leave fast. We were using the washroom next door and carrying water over in empty milk gallons. That's why Mama and Papa looked for a house, and that's why we moved into the house on Mango Street, far away, on the other side of town. **A**

They always told us that one day we would move into a house, a real house that would be ours for always so we wouldn't have to move each year. And our house would have running water and pipes that worked. And inside it would have real stairs, not hallway stairs, but stairs inside like the houses on TV. And

ANALYZE VISUALS
What effect is created by the heightened colors and blurred lines in this image? Explain your answer.

A **MAKE INFERENCES ABOUT CHARACTER**
Reread lines 6–14. What can you infer about the family's economic circumstances? Explain your answer.

---

1. **flat:** an apartment on one floor of a building.

we'd have a basement and at least three washrooms so when we took a bath we
20 wouldn't have to tell everybody. Our house would be white with trees around
it, a great big yard and grass growing without a fence. This was the house
Papa talked about when he held a lottery ticket and this was the house Mama
dreamed up in the stories she told us before we went to bed.

But the house on Mango Street is not the way they told it at all. It's small
and red with tight steps in front and windows so small you'd think they were
holding their breath. Bricks are crumbling in places, and the front door is so
swollen you have to push hard to get in. There is no front yard, only four little
elms the city planted by the curb. Out back is a small garage for the car we
don't own yet and a small yard that looks smaller between the two buildings
30 on either side. There are stairs in our house, but they're ordinary hallway stairs,
and the house has only one washroom. Everybody has to share a bedroom—
Mama and Papa, Carlos and Kiki, me and Nenny.

Once when we were living on Loomis, a nun from my school passed by and
saw me playing out front. The laundromat downstairs had been boarded up
because it had been robbed two days before and the owner had painted on the
wood YES WE'RE OPEN so as not to lose business.

Where do you live? she asked.

There, I said pointing up to the third floor.

You live *there*?

40   *There.* I had to look to where she pointed—the third floor, the paint
peeling, wooden bars Papa had nailed on the windows so we wouldn't fall out.
You live *there?* The way she said it made me feel like nothing. *There.* I lived
there. I nodded. **B**

I knew then I had to have a house. A real house. One I could point to. But
this isn't it. The house on Mango Street isn't it. For the time being, Mama says.
Temporary, says Papa. But I know how those things go.

My Name

In English my name means hope. In Spanish it means too many letters. It
means sadness, it means waiting. It is like the number nine. A muddy color.
It is the Mexican records my father plays on Sunday mornings when he is
50 shaving, songs like sobbing. **C**

It was my great-grandmother's name and now it is mine. She was a horse
woman too, born like me in the Chinese year of the horse[2]—which is
supposed to be bad luck if you're born female—but I think this is a Chinese
lie because the Chinese, like the Mexicans, don't like their women strong.

My great-grandmother. I would've liked to have known her, a wild horse
of a woman, so wild she wouldn't marry. Until my great-grandfather threw
a sack over her head and carried her off. Just like that, as if she were a fancy
chandelier. That's the way he did it.

**B MAKE INFERENCES
ABOUT CHARACTER**
Reread lines 33–43.
Consider the narrator's
reaction to the nun's
remark. What do these
lines reveal about the
narrator's feelings?

C TONE
Reread lines 47–50.
Identify striking words or
phrases in this paragraph.
What tone does Cisneros's
word choice convey?
Explain your answer.

---

2. **Chinese year of the horse:** In the traditional Chinese calendar, each succeeding year is named after 1
of 12 animals. People born in the year of the horse are thought to be energetic and quick-witted.

And the story goes she never forgave him. She looked out the window her
60 whole life, the way so many women sit their sadness on an elbow. I wonder if
she made the best with what she got or was she sorry because she couldn't be
all the things she wanted to be. Esperanza. I have inherited her name, but I
don't want to inherit her place by the window.

D **AUTHOR'S PERSPECTIVE**
Reread lines 51–63.
What cultural expectations and values does Cisneros reveal in these paragraphs?

At school they say my name funny as if the syllables were made out of tin and hurt the roof of your mouth. But in Spanish my name is made out of a softer something, like silver, not quite as thick as sister's name—Magdalena— which is uglier than mine. Magdalena who at least can come home and become Nenny. But I am always Esperanza.

70   I would like to baptize myself under a new name, a name more like the real me, the one nobody sees. Esperanza as Lisandra or Maritza or Zeze the X. Yes. Something like Zeze the X will do.

Mango Says Goodbye Sometimes

I like to tell stories. I tell them inside my head. I tell them after the mailman says, Here's your mail. Here's your mail he said.

I make a story for my life, for each step my brown shoe takes. I say, "And so she trudged up the wooden stairs, her sad brown shoes taking her to the house she never liked."

I like to tell stories. I am going to tell you a story about a girl who didn't want to belong.

We didn't always live on Mango Street. Before that we lived on Loomis on 80 the third floor, and before that we lived on Keeler. Before Keeler it was Paulina, but what I remember most is Mango Street, sad red house, the house I belong but do not belong to.

I put it down on paper and then the ghost does not ache so much. I write it down and Mango says goodbye sometimes. She does not hold me with both arms. She sets me free. **E**

One day I will pack my bags of books and paper. One day I will say goodbye to Mango. I am too strong for her to keep me here forever. One day I will go away.

Friends and neighbors will say, What happened to that Esperanza? Where 90 did she go with all those books and paper? Why did she march so far away?

They will not know I have gone away to come back. For the ones I left behind. For the ones who cannot out. ❧

E AUTHOR'S PERSPECTIVE
Reread lines 83–85. What might the author be saying about the power of writing? Explain your answer.

Comprehension

1. **Recall** Describe Esperanza's house on Mango Street.

2. **Recall** What does Esperanza's name mean in English?

3. **Clarify** What does Esperanza mean when she refers to her home as "the house I belong but do not belong to"?

PENNSYLVANIA STANDARDS

READING STANDARD
B.1.1.1.A.1 Evaluate character

Literary Analysis

4. **Make Inferences About Character** Review the inferences you made about Esperanza as you read. Based on your inferences, what **conclusions** can you draw about this character? List the adjectives you would use to describe Esperanza, and then explain why you chose each. Cite evidence to support your conclusions.

5. **Understand Tone** How would you describe Cisneros's tone in these vignettes? Jot down words and phrases that stood out to you, and think about the tone they help create. Describe Cisneros's tone in a sentence or two.

6. **Interpret Text** Reread lines 51–63 and consider Esperanza's feelings about her **legacy.** She says she doesn't want to inherit her great-grandmother's "place by the window." What does she mean? What else doesn't she want to inherit? Explain your answer.

7. **Draw Conclusions** Consider Cisneros's statement on page 569 that she strives to "write the stories that haven't been written." On the basis of what you know about her, why do you think Cisneros chose to tell Esperanza's story? Explain your answer, citing evidence.

8. **Analyze Author's Perspective** Think about the details Cisneros includes in these vignettes, as well as Esperanza's feelings about her life. Then consider what you learned about Cisneros in the biography and background on page 569. What do you think is Cisneros's perspective on growing up poor? Use evidence from the selection as well as details from the biography to support your answer.

Literary Criticism

9. **Author's Style** Cisneros says that in writing *The House on Mango Street* she "was trying to write something that was a cross between fiction and poetry." In your opinion, are these vignettes more like verse or more like fiction? Consider the author's choice of words and details as well as what she communicates with each vignette. Defend your answer with evidence from the selection.

Writing Workshop

Problem-Solution Essay

What problems have you encountered in your life? How did you solve them? Writing about a problem can help you clarify possible solutions and persuade others to take action. To learn how to write about problems and solutions that matter to you, consult the **Writer's Road Map.**

WRITER'S ROAD MAP

Problem-Solution Essay

WRITING PROMPT 1

Writing for the Real World Problems exist at school, at home, in your community, and in the world at-large. Sometimes writing about a problem can help you find a solution. Choose a problem that deeply interests you, and write an essay in which you define the problem, examine its causes, and explore possible solutions.

Problems to Explore
- environmental issues, such as acid rain or noise pollution
- issues at school, such as video cameras in the hallways, locker searches, or metal detectors

WRITING PROMPT 2

Writing from Literature Sometimes, something you read makes you think about a problem in a new way. Choose a problem you found in a literary work that you want to explore. Write an essay in which you describe the problem and identify a possible solution.

Selections to Explore
- "Island Morning" (homesickness)
- "The Lost Boys" (adjusting to a new life)

 WRITING TOOLS
For prewriting, revision, and editing tools, visit the **Writing Center** at **ClassZone.com.**

KEY TRAITS

1. IDEAS
- States the problem in a clearly worded **thesis statement**
- Explores the **causes and effects** of the problem
- Addresses different **solutions**
- Chooses the **best solution** and supports it with relevant **details**

2. ORGANIZATION
- Shows the **significance** of the problem in the **introduction**
- Uses **transitions** to connect ideas
- Follows a consistent **organizational pattern**
- Concludes with a strongly stated **call to action**

3. VOICE
- **Tone** is suited to topic, audience, and purpose

4. WORD CHOICE
- Uses **precise words** to convey the problem and solution

5. SENTENCE FLUENCY
- Uses a variety of **sentence types**

6. CONVENTIONS
- Employs **correct grammar and usage**

Part 1: Analyze a Student Model

WRITING STANDARD
1.4.11.B Write complex informational pieces

Karen Conboy
Belleplaine Academy

The Disappearing Arts

Walking down the halls at Belleplaine Academy isn't like it used to be. No new artwork decorates our school, and the paintings and sculptures from years past are becoming dusty. Instead of the sweet sounds of the swing choir or the sharps and flats of an orchestra tuning
5 up, there are only slamming doors and shuffling feet. Why? After the state legislature reduced funding for education, our local school board eliminated arts classes. Students must have a chance to learn about and practice fine arts, or we will miss out on a vital part of our education.

The two major causes of eliminating arts classes are money and
10 priorities. Our state has serious budget problems, and the first programs to get cut are so-called nonessential subjects, such as the arts and physical education. Many administrators and teachers believe that schools have to concentrate on traditional subjects, such as reading, history, math, and writing, so that students can get into college
15 and compete for jobs. As a result, the arts are a low priority; they're considered "extras."

However, the arts deserve to be a higher priority. Participating in the arts can help motivate and focus students. A Stanford University study showed that young people who participate in the arts are four times as
20 likely as nonparticipants to be recognized for academic achievement and more than four times as likely to perform community service. Learning to draw, paint, act, dance, sing, or play an instrument can build confidence. A chance to create or perform can encourage a reluctant student to keep attending school. Also, learning about the arts can give

---

KEY TRAITS IN ACTION

Vivid description in the introduction "hooks" the reader. **Thesis statement** explains the problem and its **significance.**

The writer explores the **causes and effects** of the problem.

Transitions connect ideas.

The writer provides relevant **statistics and reasons** to explain why her position is valid. **Tone** is appropriate to her audience—anyone who cares about education.

25 us new ideas about what careers to pursue after graduation.

How can we solve this problem? Some people want to pressure the state legislature to increase the amount of money it provides for education. They suggest letter-writing campaigns and even marching to the capitol. With more money, they argue, local school boards could
30 restore the programs and classes they've had to cut. The legislature has made it clear, however, that it can't provide money that it doesn't have.

We can't count on financial help from the state, so the best solution is to start thinking creatively and provide our own arts education. For example, students could start our own after-school and weekend arts
35 activities. We could plan visits to local art museums and galleries. We might also start student-run arts clubs, such as a photography club for students interested in learning how to shoot and print photos, or a theater club for those who want to see locally produced plays. Teachers can also get involved, sponsoring clubs and using online resources from
40 organizations such as Americans for the Arts to bring arts education into their classes. Furthermore, community members can be a valuable resource. Local artists, actors, and musicians might be persuaded to donate some time to teach young people about their particular crafts.

Budget cuts do not have to signal the end of arts education. We can
45 do for ourselves what the state is unable to do. With determination, passion, and creativity, we can fill the halls of Belleplaine with art and music once again.

> The writer **varies sentence types,** using an occasional question to add interest to her writing. She addresses **different solutions** to the problem.

> She offers what she considers **the best solution** and supports it with **relevant details.**

> A strong **conclusion** uses **precise words** (*determination, passion, creativity*) to **call** audience members **to action.**

2

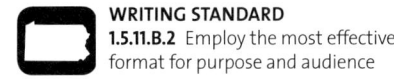

WRITING STANDARD
1.5.11.B.2 Employ the most effective
format for purpose and audience

Part 2: Apply the Writing Process

PREWRITING

| **What Should I Do?** | **What Does It Look Like?** |

1. Analyze the prompt.
Look closely at the prompt you chose on page 576. (Circle) the words that tell you what to do. Think about how you will choose a problem and how you will structure your essay.

▶ **WRITING PROMPT** Problems exist at school, at home, in your community, and in the world. Sometimes writing about a problem can help you find a solution. (Choose a problem) that deeply interests you, and (write an essay) in which you (define the problem, examine its causes,) and (explore possible solutions.)

It's clear from the prompt that my essay will be organized into three parts—the problem, its causes, and its solutions.

2. Consider possible problems.
Think of some general categories of problems to explore. List each category on a sheet of paper and under each write whatever specific problems come to mind. Put a star next to the problem you want to write about.

▶

Environment	Privacy	School
• the West Side landfill	• no lockers at school	✱ • no fine arts classes
• summer ozone alerts	• cameras in the mall's food court	• security guards

3. Brainstorm possible solutions.
Now that you've selected a problem to write about, you need to consider possible solutions. Create a graphic organizer, such as a cluster diagram, to write down all the ways the problem might be solved.

TIP Don't edit as you brainstorm. Write down every possible solution you can think of.

▶

Protest at state capitol

Letters to representatives

More money from state

Get teachers involved

Bring in local artists

No fine arts classes

After-school activities

4. Collect supporting details.
Find details that support your solution. You might interview people, do research in newspapers or magazines, or check out relevant Internet sites.

▶

Ideas for Sources	Questions to Ask
• local newspaper	• What arts programs exist in our community?
• school librarian	
• the Internet	• What sources outside of school can help?

DRAFTING

What Should I Do?	What Does It Look Like?

1. Identify the problem and its significance. Early on in your essay, let your readers know what problem you are addressing. Also, give them some sense of why the problem is important to you.

▶

> Students must have a chance to learn — Problem
> about and practice fine arts, or we will — Significance
> miss out on a vital part of our education.

2. Decide where to state your solution. Some writers choose to state the solution right after they identify the problem. Other writers prefer to state the problem, discuss its causes, and then propose a solution.

▶

> (Paragraph 1) Local school board eliminated arts
>   classes ... Problem
> (Paragraph 2) The two major causes ... Causes
> (Paragraph 4) How can we solve this problem? ... Solution

3. Explain causes and effects. Every problem has at least one cause. Likewise, an important problem has significant effects. Be sure to provide details, such as facts, statistics, examples, and quotations, to make causes and effects clear.

▶

> Causes: Effects on Students:
> no money → arts classes cut
> in budget
>
> arts not   money put toward more
> a priority ↘ traditional subjects

4. Address different solutions. People see problems and solutions from different points of view. Discussing a variety of solutions lets your reader know that you've looked at the issue from all sides.

TIP For more advice as you draft, consult the **key traits** on page 576 and the **rubric and peer-reader questions** on page 582.

▶

> How can we solve this problem? Some people want to
> pressure the state legislature to increase the amount
> of money it provides for education. They suggest letter-
> writing campaigns and even marching to the capitol.
> With more money, they argue, local school boards could
> restore the programs and classes they've had to cut.
> The legislature has made it clear, however, that it can't
> provide money that it doesn't have.

REVISING AND EDITING

What Should I Do?	What Does It Look Like?

1. Provide a "hook."
- Draw a box around the first two or three sentences of your essay. Do they capture your reader's attention?
- If not, add a vivid description, a bit of dialogue, or an interesting fact or statistic.

▶ Walking down the halls at Belleplaine Academy isn't like it used to be. No new artwork decorates our school. Instead of the sweet sounds of the swing choir, there are only slamming doors and shuffling feet. Why? After the state legislature reduced funding for education, our local school board eliminated arts classes.

2. Add supporting details.
- Underline supporting details in your essay.
- If you have few words or phrases underlined, add interesting facts, statistics, examples, or quotations to make your writing more informative.

▶ Many administrators and teachers believe that schools have to concentrate on traditional subjects so that students can get into college and compete for jobs.
, such as reading, history, math, and writing,

3. Address different solutions thoroughly.
- Number the parts of your essay where you discuss different solutions.
- Add additional solutions or details to further clarify your argument.

▶ For example, students could start our own ① after-school and weekend arts activities. We could plan visits to local art museums and galleries.
We might also start student-run arts clubs, such as ② a photography club or a theater club.

4. Strengthen the conclusion.
- Ask a peer reader to draw a wavy line under parts of your conclusion that seem weak or vague.
- How well does the conclusion sum up your ideas? Strengthen your conclusion so that it reinforces what has gone before.

See page 582: Ask a Peer Reader

▶ Budget cuts do not have to signal the end of arts education. We can do for ourselves what the state is unable to do. With determination, passion, and creativity, we can fill the halls of Belleplaine with art and music once again.

Problem-Solution Essay

Apply the Rubric

A strong problem-solution essay . . .

- ☑ clearly identifies the problem
- ☑ helps the reader understand the issues involved
- ☑ analyzes the causes and effects of the problem
- ☑ includes relevant facts, statistics, examples, or quotations
- ☑ explores more than one possible solution
- ☑ persuasively supports the most suitable solution
- ☑ uses language and a tone that are appropriate to the audience
- ☑ uses a variety of sentence types

Ask a Peer Reader

- How would you describe the problem I wrote about?
- How could I explain the causes and effects more clearly?
- What could I add or subtract to improve my conclusion?

Add Transition Words

For Introducing Causes and Effects	
after	for this reason
as a result	if . . . then
because	since
before	so
consequently	therefore

Check Your Grammar

- Use a comma before the conjunction that joins the two main clauses of a compound sentence.

> Our state has serious budget problems, and the first programs to get cut are so-called nonessential subjects, such as the arts and physical education.

- Use a semicolon to join the parts of a compound sentence if no coordinating conjunction is used.

> As a result, the arts are a low priority; they're considered "extras."

See page R63: Compound Sentences

Writing Online

PUBLISHING OPTIONS
For publishing options, visit the **Writing Center** at **ClassZone.com.**

ASSESSMENT PREPARATION
For writing and grammar assessment practice, go to the **Assessment Center** at **ClassZone.com.**

PUBLISHING WITH TECHNOLOGY

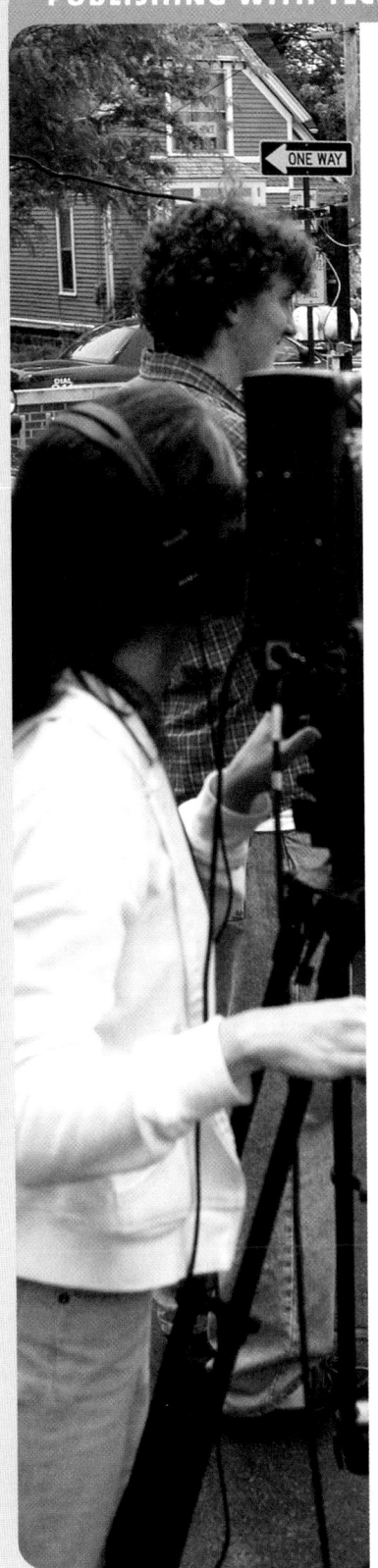

Producing a Video Documentary

A video documentary can dramatize the problem you explored and the solution you proposed. Follow these guidelines.

Planning the Documentary

1. **Create a script.** Use your essay as the basis for the **script** of your documentary. Your script will contain narration, stage directions, camera directions, and directions for inserting interviews.

2. **Create a storyboard.** Use sketches to illustrate, shot by shot, what viewers will see. Think about including various shots: **close-ups, medium shots,** and **establishing shots.**

Voice-over:
Students are missing out on an important part of a well-rounded education.

Voice-over:
Some people want to pressure the state legislature to increase education funding.

Voice-over:
But without financial help from the state, the best solution is to start thinking creatively.

Producing the Documentary

1. **Shoot the footage and record the voice-over.** Using your completed script and a digital camcorder, shoot the scenes that will make up your finished documentary. Get help from students and teachers who are willing to appear in your video. Record the voice-over—the narrative the viewers will hear.

2. **Wrap it up.** Using video-editing software, edit your documentary until you're satisfied with the sequence of scenes. Add a title screen, credits, and music if appropriate.

Reading Comprehension

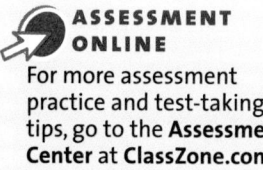
DIRECTIONS *Read the following selections and then answer the questions.*

His Name Was Pete

William Faulkner

His name was Pete. He was just a dog, a fifteen-months-old pointer, still almost a puppy even though he had spent one hunting season learning to be the dog he would have been in another two or three if he had lived that long.

But he was just a dog. He expected little of the world into which he came without past and nothing of immortality either:—food (he didn't care what nor how little just so it was given with affection—a touch of a hand, a voice he knew even if he could not understand and answer the words it spoke); the earth to run on; air to breathe, sun and rain in their seasons and the covied quail which were his heritage long before he knew the earth and felt the sun, whose scent he knew already from his staunch and faithful ancestry before he himself ever winded it. That was all he wanted. But that would have been enough to fill the eight or ten or twelve years of his natural life because twelve years are not very many and it doesn't take much to fill them.

Yet short as twelve years are, he should normally have outlived four of the kind of motorcars which killed him—cars capable of climbing hills too fast to avoid a grown pointer dog. But Pete didn't outlive the first of his four. He wasn't chasing it; he had learned not to do that before he was allowed on highways. He was standing on the road waiting for his little mistress on the horse to catch up, to squire her safely home. He shouldn't have been in the road. He paid no road tax, held no driver's license, didn't vote. Perhaps his trouble was that the motorcar which lived in the same yard he lived in had a horn and brakes on it and he thought they all did. To say he didn't see the car because the car was between him and the late afternoon sun is a bad excuse because that brings the question of vision into it and certainly no one unable with the sun at his back to see a grown pointer dog on a curveless two-lane highway would think of permitting himself to drive a car at all, let alone one without either horn or brakes because next time Pete might be a human child and killing human children with motorcars is against the law.

No, the driver was in a hurry: that was the reason. Perhaps he had several miles to go yet and was already late for supper. That was why he didn't have time to slow or stop or drive around Pete. And since he didn't have time to do that, naturally he didn't have time to stop afterward; besides Pete was only a dog flung broken and crying into a roadside ditch and anyway the car had passed him by then and the sun was at Pete's back now, so how could the driver be expected to hear his crying?

But Pete has forgiven him. In his year and a quarter of life he never had anything but kindness from human beings; he would gladly give the other six or eight or ten of it rather than make one late for supper.

Dog Proves As Smart As Average Toddler

Margaret Munro

A nine-year-old border collie with a 200-word "vocabulary" has provided scientific proof that dogs understand what their masters are saying, according to new research.

Knows Word Meanings

Rico knows the meaning of about 200 words and can infer and remember the meaning of new ones with the same ability as very young children, according to a report published in the journal *Science* yesterday.

Rico, who lives in Germany, can retrieve randomly chosen items from a collection of balls and toys. He understands requests to put toys in boxes and
10 bring them to certain people.

He can also fetch, by name, objects that he has never seen before.

A month after seeing them just once, he still remembered and fetched the new objects on demand, reported Julia Fischer and her colleagues with the Max Planck Institute for Evolutionary Anthropology.

Makes Inferences

The scientists say Rico's abilities provide evidence that dogs are capable of a type of learning and inference that has long been considered the domain of humans.

"There are some things that some people believe are uniquely human, such
20 as language acquisition," said Ms. Fischer. "Maybe it's not so special after all."

She said dogs appear to have innate and superior word-learning skills, which could help explain why they are such popular pets.

One of Canada's leading dog experts is impressed.

"It doesn't surprise me, but it's wonderful someone actually set out and spent all the time to plug that stuff into [Rico's] mind," said Dr. Stanley Coren, a psychologist at the University of British Columbia who has written extensively about the intelligence of dogs.

1 2 Next

BACK FORWARD STOP REFRESH HOME PRINT

news*leader*.com
Serving the Central Shenandoah Valley

Home   News   Entertainment   Communities   Classifieds   Shopping   Cars   Jobs   Customer Service

Archive (1999-)   Local News - Monday, September 13, 2004

SEARCH   ☑ SUBSCRIBE TO THE NEWS LEADER

Home
News
  Local News
  Archives
  Local Sports
  Elections
  Nation/World
  Obituaries
  Family Tributes
  Engagement
  Announcements
  Opinion
  Technology
  Space & Science
  Weather

Entertainment
Communities
Classifieds
Cars
Jobs
Customer Service

Heroic pooch helps save elderly neighbor
Oakley alerted owner to need

classiter@newsleader.com

STAUNTON -- Valerie Locklear knew her black labradoodle, Oakley, was a great companion.

On Sunday morning, she learned he was a rescue dog, too.

The poodle-Labrador retriever mix alerted his owner to an elderly neighbor who needed medical attention.

1 **2** Next

Chris Lassiter/News Leader

Oakley, a black Labradoodle, alerted his owner Valerie Locklear that an elderly neighbor had fallen.

✉ Email this story

Originally published Monday, September 13, 2004

Comprehension

DIRECTIONS *Answer these questions about the essay "His Name Was Pete."*

1. Which word best describes the author's tone throughout this essay?

  A superior

  B nostalgic

  C sarcastic

  D straightforward

2. What is the main idea of lines 14–28?

  A Pete didn't chase cars.

  B Pete shouldn't have been on the road.

  C Running over children is illegal.

  D There is no excuse for running over a dog.

3. In lines 34–35, the phrase "how could the driver" reveals the author's

  A sympathy with the driver

  B anger at the driver

  C feelings about cars

  D impatience with Pete

4. The author's two purposes in writing this essay were to

  A inform and entertain

  B inform and express feelings

  C persuade and express feelings

  D persuade and entertain

DIRECTIONS *Answer these questions about the article "Dog Proves As Smart As Average Toddler."*

5. The subheadings "Knows Word Meanings" and "Makes Inferences" are clues that the author's primary purpose is to

A inform or explain

B persuade

C entertain

D express feelings

6. One way the author organizes the article is by comparing and contrasting

A words and toys

B dogs and children

C scientists and research projects

D pets and language acquisition

DIRECTIONS *Answer this question about both selections.*

7. Which one of the following statements would most likely be supported by both authors?

A Most dogs are not as smart as Rico.

B A dog should always be on a leash.

C Dogs can interact with people.

D Dogs are patient animals.

DIRECTIONS *Answer these questions about the news Web site.*

8. From the information in the photograph and the caption, you can identify that the hero of the story is

A an elderly woman who fell down

B someone who needed medical attention

C a large black dog called a labradoodle

D Valerie Locklear, a dog owner who lives in Staunton

9. Which of the following could you find by selecting a hyperlink from the menu on this Web site?

A the lead to this story

B a video clip of Oakley's rescue

C more local news

D more pictures of Oakley

Open-Ended Items

10. What was Faulkner's attitude toward the dog's death in "His Name Was Pete"? Support your answer with details from the essay.

11. Compare and contrast the main ideas of "His Name Was Pete" and "Dog Proves As Smart As Average Toddler." Name one way in which the selections are alike and one way in which they are different. Support your answer with two details from each of the selections.

Vocabulary

DIRECTIONS *Use context clues and the word-root definitions to answer the following questions.*

1. The Latin word root *mort* means "death." What does *immortality* mean in line 5 of "His Name Was Pete"?

   A eternal life

   B great fame

   C good behavior

   D a promising future

2. The Latin word root *nat* means "born." What does *innate* mean in line 21 of "Dog Proves As Smart As Average Toddler"?

   A taught by humans

   B learned over time

   C present from birth

   D taken from memory

3. The Latin word root *scient* means "knowing." What does *scientific* mean in line 2 of "Dog Proves As Smart As Average Toddler"?

   A from animals

   B from imagination

   C based on theory

   D based on facts

4. The Latin word root *uni* means "one." What does *uniquely* mean in line 19 of "Dog Proves As Smart As Average Toddler"?

   A superficially

   B exclusively

   C partially

   D lonely

DIRECTIONS *Use context clues in the article "Dog Proves As Smart As Average Toddler" to help you answer the following questions about words in specialized fields.*

5. Anthropologists research the origins, behavior, and development of humans. If anthropologists studied dogs instead of people, they would most likely

   A groom dogs daily

   B dissect dogs who have died from an illness

   C increase the protein in dogs' diets

   D look at the actions and reactions of dogs

6. The word *psychologist* in line 26 refers to a person who studies

   A obedience in dogs

   B vocabulary words

   C word-learning skills

   D mental processes and behavior

7. In line 7 of the article, the term *journal* means

   A a ship's log

   B a personal diary

   C a magazine published periodically

   D an accounting ledger that lists transactions

8. The word *Institute* in line 14 most likely refers to

   A a pattern of behavior

   B an authoritative rule

   C an organization

   D a workshop

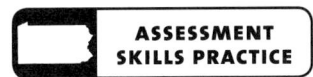

Writing & Grammar

DIRECTIONS *Read the passage and answer the questions that follow.*

(1) For years, many people claimed that animals were not emotional. (2) Recently, scientists have documented what every pet owner already knows. (3) Animals can, indeed, feel emotions. (4) The author and former psychoanalyst Jeffrey Masson studies animal emotions in his book *When Elephants Weep.* (5) Masson describes an elephant that feels happy when drawing pictures. (6) He tells of a chimp that nursed its sick owner back to health. (7) Some scientists resist Masson's conclusions, but many believe that animals do feel emotions.

1. Choose the correct coordinating conjunction that can be used to combine sentences 1 and 2.

   A   and   C   or
   B   but   D   so

2. Identify the abstract noun in sentence 4.

   A   psychoanalyst
   B   Jeffrey Masson
   C   emotions
   D   book

3. Choose the correct way to rewrite sentence 5 by using an adverb.

   A   Masson describes an elephant that feels happy when playfully drawing pictures.
   B   Masson describes an elephant that feels happy when drawing fanciful pictures.
   C   Masson describes a talented elephant that feels happy when drawing pictures.
   D   Masson describes an elephant that draws happy pictures.

4. Choose the correct coordinating conjunction that can be used to combine sentences 5 and 6.

   A   or   C   yet
   B   for   D   and

5. Identify the two concrete nouns in sentence 7.

   A   conclusions, emotions
   B   scientists, animals
   C   emotions, scientists
   D   animals, conclusions

6. Choose the correct way to rewrite sentence 7 by using an adverb.

   A   Some stubborn scientists resist Masson's conclusions, but many believe that animals do feel emotions.
   B   Some scientists resist Masson's conclusions, and many believe that animals do feel emotions.
   C   Some scientists resist Masson's conclusions, but many believe that animals do feel something.
   D   Some scientists resist Masson's conclusions, but many strongly believe that animals do feel emotions.

STOP

UNIT 5
Great Reads

Ideas for Independent Reading

What ideas does each writer communicate in the following works?

What place do you call home?

Desert Solitaire
by Edward Abbey

Abbey's love song to the deserts of the southwestern United States has become a touchstone for writing about a place. This volume shows readers why the desert was Abbey's spiritual home.

Barrio Boy
by Ernesto Galarza

In this autobiography, Galarza describes his early years in western Mexico and his childhood in a barrio in Sacramento, California.

My Place
by Sally Morgan

Morgan was not told of her aboriginal heritage until she was 15. She wrote this highly personal memoir to show readers what Australian aboriginal people have endured as outsiders in their own land.

Why would people leave their homelands?

Picture Bride
By Yoshiko Uchida

In this novel, Hana Omiya journeys from Japan to the United States to escape a more restricted life in Japan. She finds that life in America has its own barriers to happiness and freedom.

Of Beetles and Angels: A Boy's Remarkable Journey from a Refugee Camp to Harvard
by Mawi Asgedom

Asgedom and his family fled civil war in Ethiopia in 1983. In 1999, he graduated from Harvard. His father's words, "Treat all people—even the most unsightly beetles—as though they were angels from heaven," have guided him.

How the García Girls Lost Their Accents
by Julia Alvarez

After the four García girls leave the Dominican Republic, they eagerly embrace American culture, often to the dismay of their old-world parents.

What stories will you tell your children?

The Kitchen God's Wife
by Amy Tan

In this contemporary novel, a woman tries to communicate with her daughter by telling of her struggle for survival in the harsh world of China before and during World War II.

A Yellow Raft in Blue Water
by Michael Dorris

Three generations of Native American women share their lives and their secrets in three interwoven fictional narratives.

Fahrenheit 451
by Ray Bradbury

Four hundred fifty-one degrees Fahrenheit is the temperature at which books burn. Bradbury's classic novel considers an unnamed society in which ideas are so dangerous that people must be "protected" from the stories of the past.

UNIT 6

Taking Sides

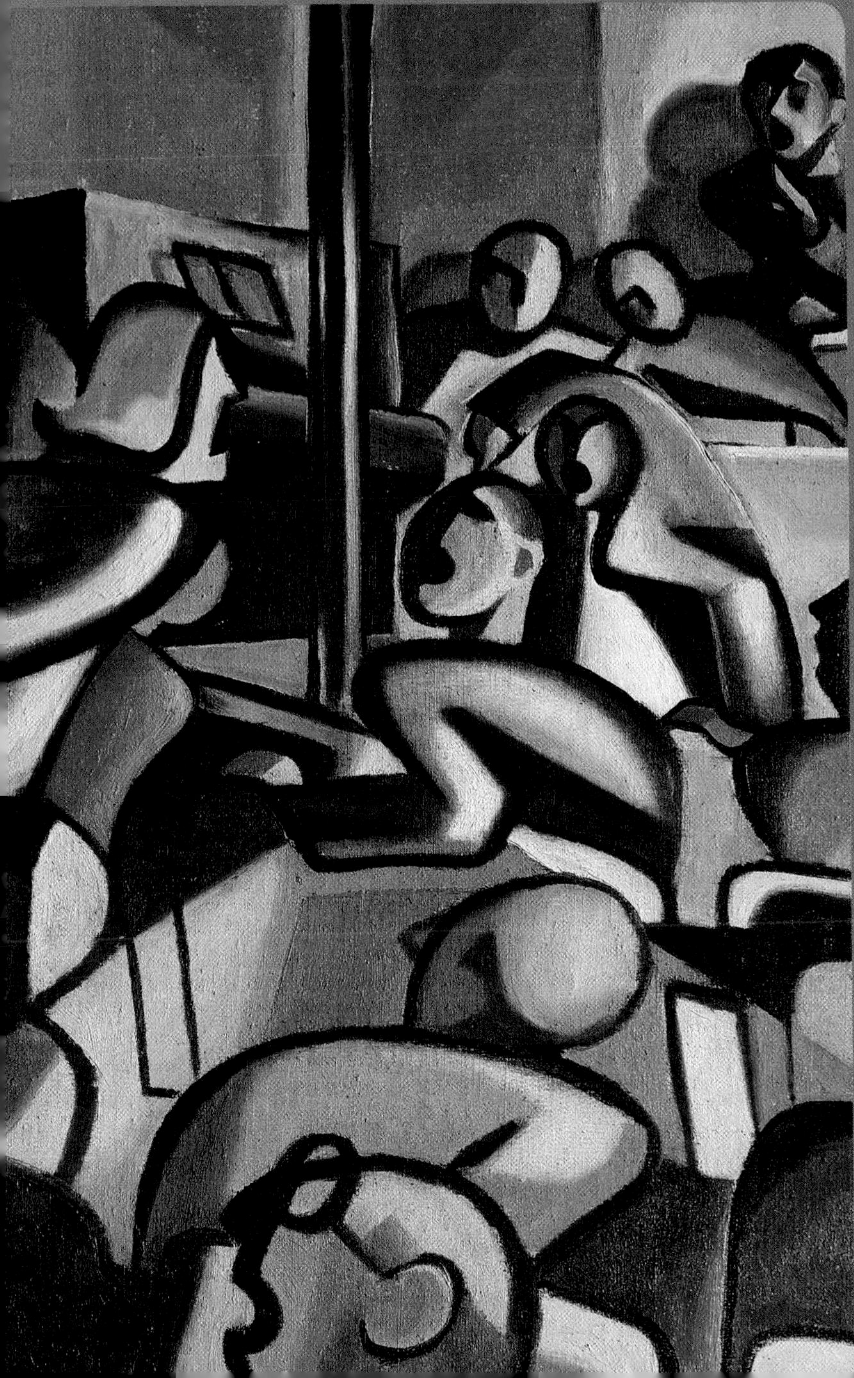

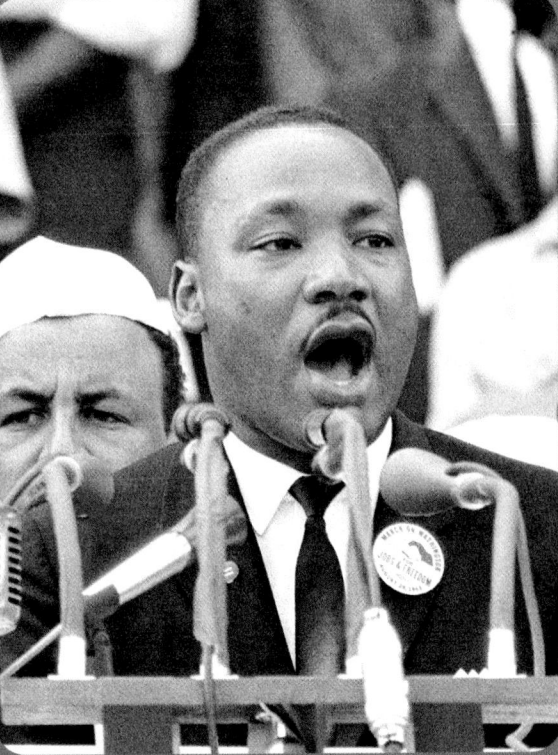

ARGUMENT AND PERSUASION

- In Nonfiction
- In Media
- Across Genres

UNIT 6

Share What You Know

How can we INFLUENCE *others?*

You convince your friend to see your side in an argument. You get your teacher to give you an extension on an assignment. You influence your classmates to vote for you in a school election. Each time you succeed in getting someone to side with you on an idea, a plan, or an action, you have practiced the art of **persuasion.** Similarly, whenever you purchase a product you saw advertised or go see a movie after viewing its trailer, the art of persuasion has influenced you.

ACTIVITY Recall a time when you were determined to get your way. Then fill in a chart like the one shown. Think about

- what worked to help you get your point across
- what information you supplied and how you organized it
- what techniques you used to convince your audience
- what you would have done differently if you were less successful than you had hoped

What Worked	What Didn't Work
• *a logical argument*	• *whining*

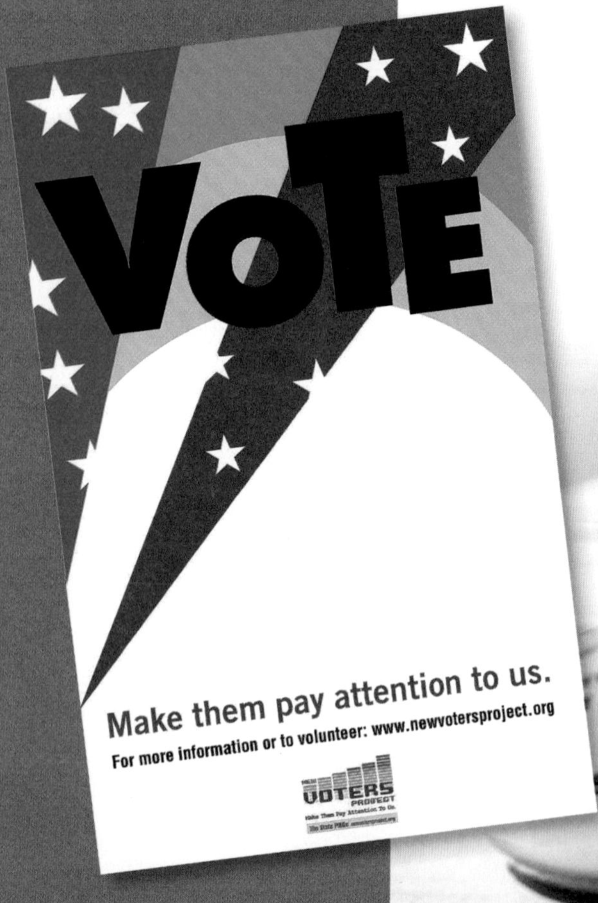

VOTE
Make them pay attention to us.
For more information or to volunteer: www.newvotersproject.org
VOTERS PROJECT

End Homelessness
VOTE

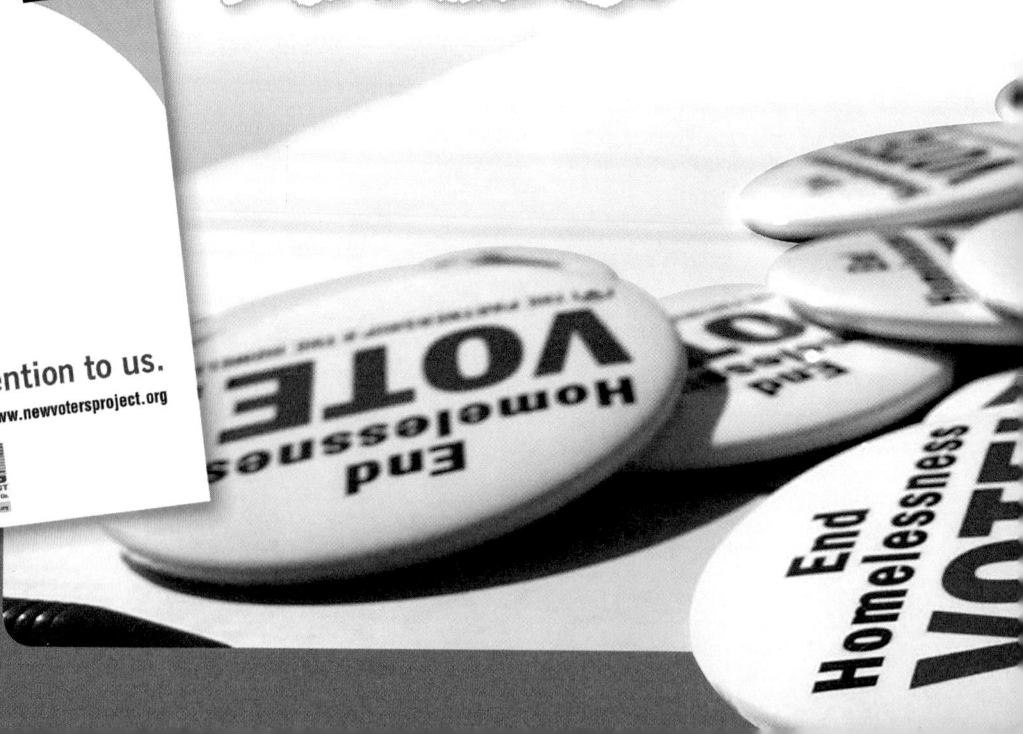

PENNSYLVANIA STANDARDS

Preview Unit Goals

LITERARY ANALYSIS	• Compare and contrast the author's message across genres
READING	• Summarize
	• Distinguish fact from opinion
	• Recognize and analyze bias
	• Identify and analyze the elements of an argument—claim, support, reasons, evidence, and counterarguments
	• Analyze rhetorical devices—repetition, parallelism, and analogy
	• Analyze persuasive techniques, including emotional appeals
WRITING AND GRAMMAR	• Write a persuasive speech
	• Support a position and answer opposing views
	• Use persuasive language effectively
	• Understand and use appropriate sentence types
	• Understand and use parallelism
SPEAKING, LISTENING, AND VIEWING	• Present a persuasive speech
	• Create a persuasive print ad
VOCABULARY	• Understand and use specialized and technical vocabulary
	• Understand foreign words and phrases in English
	• Use a dictionary
ACADEMIC VOCABULARY	• argument • bias
	• persuasive techniques • fact and opinion
	• rhetorical devices • summarize

Argument and Persuasion

You encounter arguments and opinions everywhere. Friends share their views on controversial issues. Politicians explain why they deserve your vote. Ads claim that products can fix your problems. Which arguments have merit, and which are just cleverly persuasive? So many decisions you make depend on your ability to analyze arguments and recognize the techniques that are being used to persuade you.

PENNSYLVANIA STANDARDS

READING STANDARDS
B.3.1.1 Analyze the use of facts and opinions to construct an argument
B.3.2.1 Identify and/or interpret bias and propaganda techniques

Part 1: The Elements of an Argument

You've heard the word *argument* all your life. It suggests heated fights characterized by strong feelings and loud voices. In formal speaking and writing, however, an argument is not emotional. An **argument** expresses a position on an issue and supports the position with reasons and evidence. Sound arguments appeal strictly to reason, not emotions. They include these elements:

• the **claim**—the writer's or speaker's position on an issue

• the **support**—the reasons and evidence that support the claim

In addition to supporting the claim, strong arguments anticipate objections that opponents might raise and counter those objections with evidence.

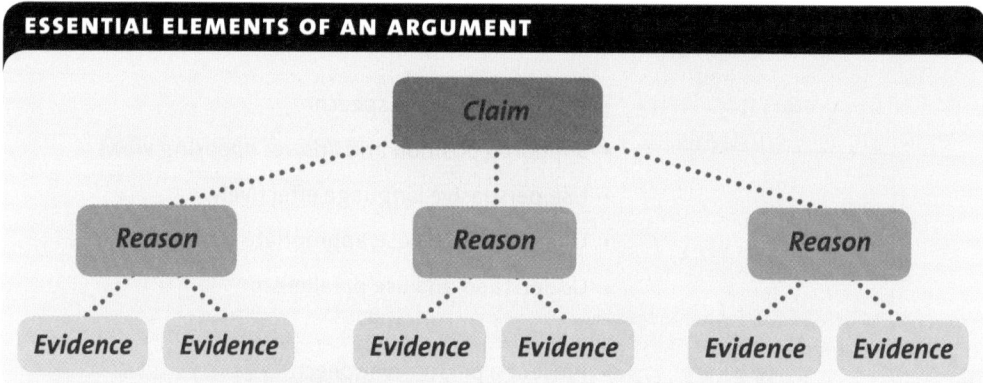

ESSENTIAL ELEMENTS OF AN ARGUMENT

STRATEGIES FOR READING AN ARGUMENT

• **Look for the claim.** Often, the claim is stated in the introduction or the conclusion of an argument. Make sure you look for clues in the title too. When the claim is not stated directly, ask yourself: What does the evidence tell me about the writer's or speaker's position?

• **Track the evidence.** Convincing arguments include a great deal of support. As a result, most arguments are not short. To keep track of the ideas, jot down the evidence that the writer or speaker uses to support his or her position. Look for facts, statistics, examples, anecdotes, and quotations from experts.

MODEL: THE ELEMENTS OF AN ARGUMENT

In this testimony given before the Maryland Senate, the speaker makes a strong claim about the state's motorcycle helmet law. As you read, look for the elements that she uses to effectively prove her position.

from MOTORCYCLE HELMET BILL

Testimony before the Maryland Senate by **Janice Golec**

I respectfully urge you to oppose any legislation that weakens Maryland's current "all riders" motorcycle helmet law.

Motorcycle helmets help save lives and reduce critical head injuries, and laws requiring helmet use have a dramatic life-saving effect. This has been

5   proven in Maryland and every other state where all riders are required to wear helmets. In such states, death rates from head injuries are half what they are among cyclists in states with no helmet laws or laws which only apply to minors. Where helmet [laws] have been enacted, then repealed, death rates for motorcyclists rise in the absence of a helmet law.

10   This is hardly a fluke; the General Accounting Office, a non-partisan research agency of the U.S. Government, reviewed 46 studies of motorcycle helmets and helmet laws, and reported that every study comparing helmeted with non-helmeted crash victims found that helmeted riders had lower fatality rates, ranging from 28 percent to 73 percent lower. . . .

15   Helmet laws save taxpayers money, too. Studies in six states show that public funds pay up to 82 percent of the costs to treat orthopedic injuries sustained by motorcyclists. A Maryland study showed that acute care costs to non-helmeted riders averaged three times those of helmeted riders. . . .

A partial law is almost as bad as no law at all. Statistically speaking, there is

20   negligible difference in death and injury rates between states with no helmet law and states with partial laws. Because partial helmet laws are difficult for police to enforce, helmet-use rates for all riders remain low in states with restricted helmet laws.

Helmet law opponents love to talk about motorcyclists' right to decide whether

25   or not they will wear helmets, but some rights are not worth having. . . . To weaken Maryland's helmet law is to condemn 28—or more—Maryland motorcyclists to death. That's a right nobody should have.

Close Read

1. What is the speaker's claim, or position?

2. One reason that the speaker uses to prove her claim is boxed. Cite two pieces of evidence that support this reason.

3. Find another reason that the speaker uses to support her claim. What evidence supports this reason?

4. The speaker anticipates opponents' arguments in lines 19–27. How does she counter these viewpoints?

Part 2: The Craft of Persuasion

Never underestimate the power of **persuasion**—that is, the art of swaying people's feelings, opinions, and actions. With compelling language, writers and speakers can enhance strong arguments or disguise the flaws in weak ones. To evaluate the real strength of an argument, you first need to recognize the persuasive techniques and rhetorical devices that are being used to sway you. Then you can objectively examine the evidence and determine your position.

PERSUASIVE TECHNIQUES

Consider where you have encountered the following persuasive techniques. What are their intended effects on readers, listeners, and viewers?

TECHNIQUES	EXAMPLES
Appeals by Association	
Bandwagon Appeal Taps into people's desire to belong	▶ You have to come to the concert. Everyone's going to be there.
"Plain Folks" Appeal Implies that ordinary people are on "our side" or that a candidate is like an ordinary person	▶ Senator Jacobs knows what it's like to struggle to make ends meet.
Testimonial Relies on endorsements from well-known people or satisfied customers	▶ As an Olympic athlete, I need all the energy I can get. That's why I start my day with Grain Puffs.
Transfer Connects a product, a candidate, or a cause with a positive image or idea	▶ Freedom is in your hands the minute you hit the road in a Mountainback XRV.
Emotional Appeals	
Appeals to Pity, Fear, or Vanity Uses words that evoke strong feelings, rather than facts and evidence, to persuade	**Appeal to Pity** ▶ For just one dollar a day, you can give a stray pet a second chance.
Appeal to Values	
Ethical Appeal Taps into people's values or moral standards	▶ Volunteer today—because it's the right thing to do.
Word Choice	
Loaded Language Uses words with strongly positive or negative connotations to stir people's emotions	▶ For the safety of our innocent children, we must protect our community from rampant crime.

MODEL 1: PERSUASION IN SPEECHES

In this speech, a government official pledges his commitment to promoting organ donation. What techniques does he use to win you over?

from The Gift of Life

Speech by **Tommy Thompson**

This month in Fresno, California, members of the Hispanic community gathered . . . to remember 19-year-old Maribel Cordova. Maribel had received an identification card this year and told her mother she wanted to become a donor.
    Two weeks later, a damaged blood vessel in her head tragically cut her
5 life short.
    Because of Maribel's selfless act, others lived. A 35-year-old man from Northern California received her lungs. A 66-year-old Southern California woman got her liver. . . .
    These are the human experiences of hope out of loss, of life out of death,
10 that touch and motivate us, that drive us to do everything within our power to promote organ and tissue donation. Through education, outreach, science and the vitally important work of people like you, we will reach that future when organ donation is, quite simply, a fact of life.

Close Read

1. Find two examples of loaded language. One has been boxed.

2. Identify one other persuasive technique used in this speech. Cite details that helped you find it.

MODEL 2: PERSUASION IN THE MEDIA

Persuasive techniques are also at work in TV and magazine ads. How do the words and the visual in this print ad help convey a powerful message?

Make your home defensible against wildfires. Visit Firewise.org, where you can discover some simple things you can do to help protect your home and your loved ones. What have you got to lose, except everything.

Close Read

1. What persuasive technique is used in this ad? Cite specific details to support your answer.

2. Describe the intended effect of the ad on viewers.

RHETORICAL DEVICES

In addition to employing persuasive techniques, writers and speakers use **rhetorical devices** to emphasize their ideas. In these examples, notice how the wording makes the message memorable.

RHETORICAL DEVICE	EXAMPLE
REPETITION Uses the same word or words more than once for emphasis	Let there be justice for all. Let there be peace for all. Let there be work, bread, water and salt for all. —from "Glory and Hope" by Nelson Mandela
PARALLELISM Uses similar grammatical constructions to express ideas that are related or equal in importance. Often creates a rhythm.	We cannot, we must not, refuse to protect the right of every American to vote in every election. . . . And we ought not, and we cannot, and we must not wait another eight months before we get a bill. —from "We Shall Overcome" by Lyndon Baines Johnson
ANALOGY Makes a comparison between two subjects that are alike in some ways	Have you heard the canned, frozen and processed product being dished up to the world as American popular music today? —from a commencement address by Billy Joel

Sojourner Truth, a 19th-century leader in the antislavery and women's rights movements, made many powerful speeches. Here, Truth responds to men who had spoken against women's rights. How does her use of rhetorical devices enhance her message?

from And Ain't I a *Woman?*

Speech by **Sojourner Truth**

That man over there say that women needs to be helped into carriages, and lifted over ditches, and to have the best place everywhere. Nobody ever helps me into carriages, or over mud-puddles, or give me any best place! And ain't I a woman? Look at me! Look at my arm! I have ploughed, and planted, and
5 gathered into barns, and no man could head me! And ain't I a woman? I could work as much and eat as much as a man—when I could get it—and bear the lash as well! And ain't I a woman? I have borne thirteen children, and seen 'em mos' all sold off to slavery, and when I cried out with my mother's grief, none but Jesus heard me! And ain't I a woman?

Close Read

1. Notice the boxed question that the speaker repeats. What is the effect of the repetition?

2. Find an example of parallelism. Identify the words, phrases, or sentences that are parallel.

Part 3: Analyze the Text

In 1962, when President John F. Kennedy gave this stirring speech about space exploration, people were feeling threatened by the possibility of war with the Soviet Union. Using what you've just learned, analyze Kennedy's argument. What techniques does he use to persuade his audience?

from ## The New *Frontier*

Speech by **John F. Kennedy**

No man can fully grasp how far and how fast we have come, but condense, if you will, the 50,000 years of man's recorded history in a time span of but a half century. Stated in these terms, we know very little about the first 40 years, except at the end of them advanced man had learned to use the skins
5 of animals to cover them. Then about 10 years ago, under this standard, man emerged from his caves to construct other kinds of shelter. Only five years ago man learned to write and use a cart with wheels. Christianity began less than two years ago. The printing press came this year, and then less than 2 months ago, during this whole 50-year span of human history, the steam engine
10 provided a new source of power.

Newton explored the meaning of gravity. Last month electric lights and telephones and automobiles and airplanes became available. Only last week did we develop penicillin and television and nuclear power, and now if America's new spacecraft succeeds in reaching Venus, we will have literally reached the
15 stars before midnight tonight.

This is a breathtaking pace, and such a pace cannot help but create new ills as it dispels old, new ignorance, new problems, new dangers. Surely the opening vistas of space promise high costs and hardships, as well as high reward. . . .

If this capsule history of our progress teaches us anything, it is that man, in
20 his quest for knowledge and progress, is determined and cannot be deterred. The exploration of space will go ahead, whether we join in it or not, and it is one of the great adventures of all time, and no nation which expects to be the leader of other nations can expect to stay behind in this race for space.

Those who came before us made certain that this country rode the first
25 waves of the industrial revolutions, the first waves of modern invention, and the first wave of nuclear power, and this generation does not intend to founder in the backwash of the coming age of space. We mean to be a part of it—we mean to lead it. For the eyes of the world now look into space, to the moon and to the planets beyond, and we have vowed that we shall not see it governed
30 by a hostile flag of conquest, but by a banner of freedom and peace. We have vowed that we shall not see space filled with weapons of mass destruction, but with instruments of knowledge and understanding.

Close Read

1. Summarize Kennedy's claim.

2. Does this speech mostly appeal to reason or to emotion? Explain your answer.

3. In lines 1–15, Kennedy uses a "capsule history" to describe a span of 50,000 years. Why might he begin with this analogy?

4. Identify one persuasive technique that Kennedy uses. Cite evidence to support your answer.

5. One example of parallelism has been boxed. What is its effect? Identify another example.

I Have a Dream

Speech by Dr. Martin Luther King Jr.

Can a DREAM change the world?

PENNSYLVANIA
STANDARDS

READING STANDARDS
A.2.6.2 Analyze examples that support the author's purpose
B.3.1.1 Analyze the use of facts and opinions to construct an argument

KEY IDEA Time and again someone has a dream, or **vision,** of how to make the world a better place. That vision finds expression in powerful words—words that stir others to find ways to improve our lives. In the speech you are about to read, Dr. Martin Luther King Jr. eloquently sets forth the vision he had for the future.

QUICKWRITE What is your vision for a better world? Does it involve better schools? safer communities? cleaner air? Write a paragraph describing your vision of how to change one aspect of the world.

● ELEMENTS OF NONFICTION: ARGUMENT

In an **argument,** a writer or speaker takes a position on an issue and provides support for the position by appealing strictly to reason. The position is referred to as the **claim.** The **support** for the claim may be reasons, evidence, or both. In "I Have a Dream," King makes the following claim about the status of African Americans in American society:

But one hundred years later [after the Emancipation Proclamation], *the Negro still is not free. . . .*

As you read the speech, look for this claim and the reasons and evidence King provides to support it.

● READING SKILL: UNDERSTAND RHETORICAL DEVICES

Since arguments appeal only to reason, writers and speakers typically use more than just arguments to persuade. They also use rhetorical devices such as the following:

- **Repetition** is the repeated use of the same word or phrase. It is used primarily for emphasis.

- **Parallelism** is the repetition of similar grammatical structures, words, phrases, or sentences. It is used to show that ideas are related or equal in importance.

- An **analogy** is a point-by-point comparison of two subjects. It can help convey ideas that are hard to grasp.

As you read, write down examples of these devices and describe their effects, using a chart like the one shown.

Word, Phrase, or Sentence	Type of Device	Effect
"one hundred years later"	repetition	emphasizes how long African Americans have been denied their rights

▲ VOCABULARY IN CONTEXT

Martin Luther King Jr. chose the words shown in boldface to inspire his audience. Use the context to figure out the meaning of each word.

1. a **momentous** occasion
2. miss payments and **default** on a loan
3. felt **exalted** listening to great music
4. turned from protest to **militancy**
5. two evils **inextricably** joined
6. a **legitimate** excuse

Author On|ine

Crusader for Justice
Preaching a philosophy of nonviolence, Dr. Martin Luther King Jr. became a catalyst for social change in the 1950s and 1960s. He galvanized people of all races to participate in boycotts, marches, and demonstrations against racial injustice. His moral

Dr. Martin Luther King Jr.
1929–1968

leadership stirred the conscience of the nation and helped bring about the passage of the Civil Rights Act of 1964. In that same year he was awarded the Nobel Peace Prize. King continued his work for justice and equality until he was assassinated in 1968.

Inspirational Speaker An eloquent Baptist minister from Atlanta, King often used religious references in his speeches. On the night before his death, he told an audience in Memphis, Tennessee: "I've seen the Promised Land. I may not get there with you, but I want you to know tonight, that we as a people will get to the Promised Land."

 MORE ABOUT THE AUTHOR
For more on Dr. Martin Luther King Jr., visit the **Literature Center** at **ClassZone.com.**

Background

March on Washington In August 1963, thousands of Americans marched on Washington, D.C., to urge Congress to pass a civil rights bill. King delivered his "I Have a Dream" speech on the steps of the Lincoln Memorial before more than 200,000 people.

I HAVE A DREAM

DR. MARTIN LUTHER KING JR.

I am happy to join with you today in what will go down in history as the greatest demonstration for freedom in the history of our nation.

Five score[1] years ago, a great American, in whose symbolic shadow we stand today, signed the Emancipation Proclamation.[2] This **momentous** decree came as a great beacon light of hope to millions of Negro slaves who had been seared in the flames of withering injustice. It came as a joyous daybreak to end the long night of their captivity.

But one hundred years later, the Negro still is not free; one hundred years later, the life of the Negro is still sadly crippled by the manacles of segregation and the chains of discrimination; one hundred years later, the Negro lives on a lonely island of poverty in the midst of a vast ocean of material prosperity; one hundred years later, the Negro is still languishing in the corners of American society and finds himself in exile in his own land. **Ⓐ**

So we've come here today to dramatize a shameful condition. In a sense we've come to our nation's capital to cash a check. When the architects of our republic wrote the magnificent words of the Constitution and the Declaration of Independence, they were signing a promissory note[3] to which every American was to fall heir. This note was the promise that all men, yes, black men as well as white men, would be guaranteed the unalienable rights of life, liberty, and the pursuit of happiness.

It is obvious today that America has **defaulted** on this promissory note insofar as her citizens of color are concerned. Instead of honoring this sacred obligation, America has given the Negro people a bad check, a check which has come back marked "insufficient funds." But we refuse to believe that the bank of justice is bankrupt. We refuse to believe that there are insufficient funds in

---

1. **five score:** 100; *score* means "twenty." (This phrasing recalls the beginning of Abraham Lincoln's Gettysburg Address: "Four score and seven years ago . . .")

2. **Emancipation Proclamation:** a document signed by President Lincoln in 1863, during the Civil War, declaring that all slaves in states still at war with the Union were free.

3. **promissory** (prŏm′ĭ-sôr′ē) **note:** a written promise to repay a loan.

ANALYZE VISUALS
What impression do you get of Martin Luther King Jr. from this photograph?

momentous
(mō-mĕn′təs) *adj.*
of great importance

Ⓐ ARGUMENT
Reread lines 8–13. What evidence does King provide to **support** the **claim** that "the Negro still is not free"?

default (dĭ-fôlt′) *v.* to fail to keep a promise, especially a promise to repay a loan

August 28, 1963: Dr. Martin Luther King Jr. delivers his speech at the Lincoln Memorial during the March on Washington, D.C.

More than 200,000 marchers gather on the mall between the Washington Monument and the Lincoln Memorial. To the right, civil rights leaders march with King.

the great vaults of opportunity of this nation. And so we've come to cash this check, a check that will give us upon demand the riches of freedom and the security of justice.

We have also come to this hallowed spot to remind America of the fierce
30 urgency of now. This is no time to engage in the luxury of cooling off or to take the tranquilizing drug of gradualism.[4] Now is the time to make real the promises of democracy; now is the time to rise from the dark and desolate valley of segregation to the sunlit path of racial justice; now is the time to lift our nation from the quicksands of racial injustice to the solid rock of brotherhood; now is the time to make justice a reality for all of God's children. It would be fatal for the nation to overlook the urgency of the moment. This sweltering summer of the Negro's **legitimate** discontent will not pass until there is an invigorating autumn of freedom and equality. **B**

Nineteen sixty-three is not an end, but a beginning. And those who hope
40 that the Negro needed to blow off steam and will now be content will have a rude awakening if the nation returns to business as usual. There will be neither rest nor tranquility in America until the Negro is granted his citizenship rights. The whirlwinds of revolt will continue to shake the foundations of our nation until the bright day of justice emerges.

legitimate (lə-jĭt′ə-mĭt)
adj. justifiable; reasonable

B RHETORICAL DEVICES
Reread lines 29–38. What rhetorical device does King use, and what is the effect of using it?

---

4. **gradualism:** a policy of seeking to reach a goal slowly, in gradual stages.

A young woman participates in the demonstration.

But there is something that I must say to my people, who stand on the worn threshold which leads into the palace of justice. In the process of gaining our rightful place we must not be guilty of wrongful deeds. Let us not seek to satisfy our thirst for freedom by drinking from the cup of bitterness and hatred. We must forever conduct our struggle on the high plain of dignity
50 and discipline. We must not allow our creative protests to degenerate into physical violence. Again and again we must rise to the majestic heights of meeting physical force with soul force. The marvelous new **militancy,** which has engulfed the Negro community, must not lead us to a distrust of all white people. For many of our white brothers, as evidenced by their presence here today, have come to realize that their destiny is tied up with our destiny. And they have come to realize that their freedom is **inextricably** bound to our freedom. We cannot walk alone. And as we walk, we must make the pledge that we shall always march ahead. We cannot turn back.

There are those who are asking the devotees of civil rights, "When will you
60 be satisfied?" We can never be satisfied as long as the Negro is the victim of the unspeakable horrors of police brutality; we can never be satisfied as long as our bodies, heavy with the fatigue of travel, cannot gain lodging in the motels of the highways and the hotels of the cities; we cannot be satisfied as long as the Negro's basic mobility is from a smaller ghetto to a larger one; we can never be satisfied as long as our children are stripped of their selfhood and robbed of

ANALYZE VISUALS
What do these photographs suggest about King's effectiveness as an orator and a leader? Explain.

militancy (mĭl'ĭ-tənt-sē) *n.* the act of aggressively supporting a political or social cause

inextricably (ĭn-ĕk'strĭ-kə-blē) *adv.* in a way impossible to untangle

their dignity by signs stating For Whites Only; we cannot be satisfied as long as the Negro in Mississippi cannot vote and a Negro in New York believes he has nothing for which to vote. No! No, we are not satisfied, and we will not be satisfied until "justice rolls down like waters and righteousness like a
70 mighty stream." **C**

I am not unmindful that some of you have come here out of great trials and tribulations. Some of you have come fresh from narrow jail cells. Some of you have come from areas where your quest for freedom left you battered by the storms of persecution and staggered by the winds of police brutality. You have been the veterans of creative suffering. Continue to work with the faith that unearned suffering is redemptive.[5] Go back to Mississippi. Go back to Alabama. Go back to South Carolina. Go back to Georgia. Go back to Louisiana. Go back to the slums and ghettos of our Northern cities, knowing that somehow this situation can and will be changed. Let us not wallow in the
80 valley of despair.

I say to you today, my friends, even though we face the difficulties of today and tomorrow, I still have a dream. It is a dream deeply rooted in the American dream. I have a dream that one day this nation will rise up and live out the true meaning of its creed, "We hold these truths to be self-evident; that all men are created equal." I have a dream that one day on the red hills of Georgia, sons of former slaves and the sons of former slave owners will be able to sit down together at the table of brotherhood. I have a dream that one day even the state of Mississippi, a state sweltering with the heat of injustice, sweltering with the heat of oppression, will be transformed into an oasis of freedom and
90 justice. I have a dream that my four little children will one day live in a nation where they will not be judged by the color of their skin, but by the content of their character. **D**

I have a dream today!

I have a dream that one day down in Alabama—with its vicious racists, with its Governor having his lips dripping with the words of interposition and nullification[6]—one day right there in Alabama, little black boys and black girls will be able to join hands with little white boys and white girls as sisters and brothers.

I have a dream today!

I have a dream that one day every valley shall be **exalted,** and every hill and
100 mountain shall be made low. The rough places will be plain and the crooked places will be made straight, "and the glory of the Lord shall be revealed, and all flesh shall see it together."

This is our hope. This is the faith that I go back to the South with. With this faith we will be able to hew out of the mountain of despair a stone of hope. With this faith we will be able to transform the jangling discords of our nation into a beautiful symphony of brotherhood. With this faith we will

C ARGUMENT
Identify the examples of racial injustice that King provides as **evidence** to convince his audience to share his views.

D RHETORICAL DEVICES
Reread lines 71–92. What examples of **parallelism** help make the expression of ideas concise and memorable?

exalted (ĭg-zôl′tĭd) *adj.* raised up **exalt** *v.*

---

5. **unearned suffering is redemptive:** undeserved suffering is a way of earning freedom or salvation.

6. **Governor . . . nullification:** Rejecting a federal order to desegregate the University of Alabama, Governor George Wallace claimed that the principle of nullification (a state's alleged right to refuse a federal law) allowed him to resist federal "interposition," or interference, in state affairs.

be able to work together, to pray together, to struggle together, to go to jail together, to stand up for
110 freedom together, knowing that we will be free one day. And this will be the day. This will be the day when all of God's children will be able to sing with new meaning, "My country 'tis of thee, sweet land of liberty, of thee I sing. Land where my fathers died, land of the pilgrims' pride, from every mountainside, let freedom ring."
120 And if America is to be a great nation, this must become true.

So let freedom ring from the prodigious hilltops of New Hampshire; let freedom ring from the mighty mountains of New York; let freedom ring from the heightening Alleghenies of Pennsylvania; let freedom ring from the snowcapped Rockies of
130 Colorado; let freedom ring from the curvaceous slopes of California. But not only that. Let freedom ring from Stone Mountain of Georgia; let freedom ring from Lookout Mountain of Tennessee; let freedom ring from every hill and molehill of Mississippi. "From every mountainside, let freedom ring."

And when this happens, and
140 when we allow freedom to ring, when we let it ring from every village and every hamlet, from every state and every city, we will be able to speed up that day when all of God's children— black men and white men, Jews and Gentiles, Protestants and Catholics—will be able to join hands and sing in the words of the old Negro spiritual, "Free at last. Free at last. Thank God Almighty, we are free at last." ❧

January 20, 2003: Marchers in St. Louis celebrate King's birthday, a national holiday.

Comprehension

1. **Recall** What examples of racial injustice does King describe?

2. **Clarify** What does King predict will happen if justice is denied African Americans?

3. **Summarize** What is King's dream, or **vision?**

PENNSYLVANIA STANDARDS

READING STANDARD
B.3.1.1 Analyze the use of facts and opinions to construct an argument

Critical Analysis

4. **Analyze the Argument** On a graphic organizer like the one shown, list at least three examples of racial injustice that King uses as **support** for his **claim** that African Americans are not free.

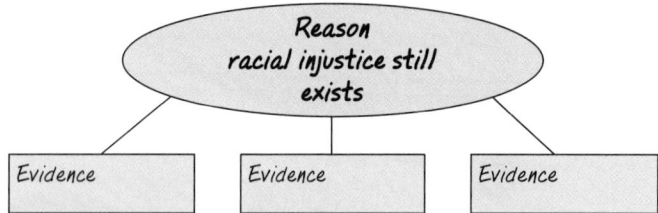

Reason racial injustice still exists

Evidence | Evidence | Evidence

5. **Understand Rhetorical Devices** Review the chart you created as you read. Then identify an example of **repetition** or **parallelism** and explain the effect it creates.

6. **Understand an Analogy** Reread lines 14–28. In these paragraphs, King uses an analogy to compare a familiar object—a promissory note—to something abstract—the promise of equal rights. What does King mean when he says that America has given African Americans a "bad check"? Explain your answer.

7. **Evaluate an Allusion** Reread lines 81–85. An allusion is an indirect reference, within a work, to something that the audience or reader is expected to know. As King begins to explain his **vision,** he alludes to the Declaration of Independence, quoting its famous lines. How effective is this allusion? Support your evaluation.

Reading-Writing Connection

WRITING PROMPT

Extended Response: Write an Analysis
How would you account for the extraordinary acclaim King's speech has received, not only when it was first delivered but many years later? Write a **three-to-five-paragraph analysis** of the effectiveness of King's address. Consider both the strength of its logic and its emotional power.

SELF-CHECK

A strong analysis will . . .
• state the qualities that make the speech memorable
• provide examples from the speech

Vocabulary in Context

WORD LIST
default
exalted
inextricably
legitimate
militancy
momentous

VOCABULARY PRACTICE

Answer the questions to show your understanding of the vocabulary words.

1. Which would be more **momentous**—the birth of a baby or the first snow of the season in upstate New York?

2. If you **default** on a loan, do you sign up to borrow money or fail to make a payment?

3. If your teacher judges your doctor's note to be **legitimate,** would you be sent to the principal's office or allowed to miss gym?

4. Who would be more likely to support a course of **militancy**—a person starting a new job or a person unfairly denied an opportunity to work?

5. Which items are more likely to be **inextricably** linked—the products on a shelf at a grocery store, or the necklaces kept in a dresser drawer?

6. Would a high priestess or a herder be the more **exalted** member of a tribe?

VOCABULARY IN WRITING

Assume that you had had the chance to interview King after he delivered his impassioned speech. Write several questions you might have asked him about his life and vision, using three or more vocabulary words. Here is an example.

> **EXAMPLE SENTENCE**
> Can you describe a **momentous** event in your childhood?

VOCABULARY STRATEGY: POLITICAL WORDS

Specialized vocabulary terms, such as *militancy,* often appear in political texts and articles. You will better understand world events if you know the exact meaning of such terms.

PRACTICE Use a dictionary to help you write the definition of each word listed. Then use each word in a sentence.

1. despot   4. nationalism
2. geopolitics   5. theocracy
3. imperialism

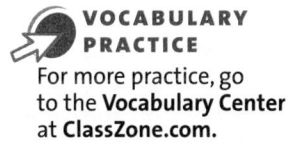

VOCABULARY PRACTICE
For more practice, go to the **Vocabulary Center** at **ClassZone.com.**

Testimony Before the Senate

Speech by Michael J. Fox

How do you
SELL AN IDEA?

PENNSYLVANIA
STANDARDS

READING STANDARDS
A.2.5.1 Summarize
A.2.6.2 Analyze examples that
support the author's purpose

KEY IDEA Teenagers are a hot market—companies are always trying to convince them to buy something. You're familiar with commercials and ads that try to sell you a product. But are you aware that a great deal of energy and money is spent trying to sell you on people and ideas? People in almost every business work hard at crafting their **pitch.**

DISCUSS With a partner, brainstorm a list of times when you realized someone was trying to sell you an idea, an image, or a person's expertise. What techniques were used? Which ones worked?

Idea	Pitch Used
Say "no" to drugs.	Commercial about saving a friend who's drowning; features the slogan "Friends, the anti-drug."

● ELEMENTS OF NONFICTION: PERSUASIVE TECHNIQUES

Writers and speakers typically use more than just arguments to persuade. They use rhetorical devices and **persuasive techniques**—that is, messages and descriptions that appeal to people's emotions, values, and desires to belong to a particular group or be like a particular person.

In "Testimony Before the Senate," Michael J. Fox often uses the persuasive techniques that are classified as emotional appeals. **Emotional appeals** are descriptions designed to win support by appealing to people's feelings of compassion or, sometimes, fear. Here Fox appeals to our sense of pity:

There are doctors, teachers, policemen, nurses, and parents who are no longer able to work, to provide for their families, and live out their dreams.

As you read his testimony, look for other examples of emotional appeals.

● READING SKILL: SUMMARIZE

A **summary** is a brief retelling of the main ideas of a written or spoken text. When you summarize, use your own words to restate the main ideas. As you read Fox's speech, prepare to summarize it by jotting down main ideas and important details on a chart like the one shown.

> **Paragraph/Section 1**
>
> | Main Idea: |
> | Important Details: |
>
>
>
> **Paragraph/Section 2**
>
> | Main Idea: |
> | Important Details: |
>
> ↓

▲ VOCABULARY IN CONTEXT

The following boldfaced words are key to understanding Michael J. Fox's persuasive plea. Restate each phrase, using a different word or words for the boldfaced term.

1. rejecting the **status quo**
2. a **meager** salary, which doesn't allow for luxuries
3. a **neurological** disorder causing tremors
4. **eradicate** poverty and other social problems

Background

Parkinson's Disease Parkinson's disease results from a loss of brain cells that produce dopamine, a chemical that transmits brain signals. The disease's many symptoms include tremors, slowness of movement, and problems with balance. Over time, walking and other ordinary activities become more and more difficult. The cause of Parkinson's is still unknown, and as yet no cure has been found. Unfortunately, the medications used to treat the disease often have serious side effects.

PARKINSON'S DISEASE RESEARCH AND TREATMENT

HEARING

BEFORE A
SUBCOMMITTEE OF THE
COMMITTEE ON APPROPRIATIONS
UNITED STATES SENATE

ONE HUNDRED SIXTH CONGRESS

FIRST SESSION

SPECIAL HEARING

Printed for the use of the Committee on Appropriations

Senator SPECTER. We have with us today Mr. Michael J. Fox, a successful actor for many years. First, as Alex P. Keaton, on the television series "Family Ties." You always work with a middle initial, do you not, Mr. Fox? Later in many movies, including "Back to the Future," and, most recently, on television again in the highly acclaimed "Spin City." Michael was diagnosed with Parkinson's in 1991, at the age of 30.

He has become very, very active in Parkinson's advocacy. One of the facts of life is that when someone like Michael J. Fox steps forward, it very heavily personalizes the problem, focuses a lot of public attention on it,
10 and has the public understanding of the need for doing whatever we can as a country to conquer this disease and many, many others. So we thank you for being here, Michael J. Fox, and look forward to your testimony.

Again, we will put the lights on, for 5 minutes, on testimony.

Mr. FOX. Mr. Chairman, Senator Harkin, and members of the Subcommittee—thank you for inviting me to testify today about the need for a greater federal investment in Parkinson's research. I would like to thank you, in particular, for your tremendous leadership in the fight to double funding for the National Institutes of Health.[1] **Ⓐ**

Ⓐ **PERSUASIVE TECHNIQUES**
What persuasive technique mentioned on page 596 in the Critical Reading Workshop is Fox using in lines 14–18?

---

1. **National Institutes of Health:** a government organization that conducts and supports research designed to improve the health of the nation.

Michael J. Fox testifies before the U.S. Senate.

ANALYZE VISUALS
Think about your reaction to seeing a famous actor linked with a cause or product. Are you more willing to read this speech and consider its message because the author is a celebrity? Explain your answer.

   Some, or perhaps most of you are familiar with me from 20 years of
20 work in film and television. What I wish to speak to you about today has
little or nothing to do with celebrity—save for this brief reference.

   When I first spoke publicly about my 8 years of experience as a person
with Parkinson's, many were surprised, in part because of my age (although
30 percent of all Parkinson's patients are under 50, and 20 percent are
under 40, and that number is growing). I had hidden my symptoms and
struggles very well, through increasing amounts of medication, through
surgery, and by employing the hundreds of little tricks and techniques a
person with Parkinson's learns to mask his or her condition for as long
as possible.

30   While the changes in my life were profound and progressive, I kept
them to myself for a number of reasons: fear, denial for sure, but I also
felt that it was important for me to just quietly "soldier on." **B**

   When I did share my story, the response was overwhelming, humbling,
and deeply inspiring. I heard from thousands of Americans affected by
Parkinson's, writing and calling to offer encouragement and to tell me
of their experience. They spoke of pain, frustration, fear and hope.
Always hope.

B **SUMMARIZE**
Reread lines 22–32, and record the passage's important details in your chart. Then restate the main idea of the passage in your own words.

What I understood very clearly is that the time for quietly "soldiering on" is through. The war against Parkinson's is a winnable war, and I am resolved to play a role in that victory.

What celebrity has given me is the opportunity to raise the visibility of Parkinson's disease and focus more attention on the desperate need for more research dollars. While I am able, for the time being, to continue to do what I love best, others are not so fortunate. There are doctors, teachers, policemen, nurses, and parents who are no longer able to work, to provide for their families, and live out their dreams. **C**

Fox starred in the sitcom *Spin City* from 1996 to 2000, when he retired from acting.

The one million Americans living with Parkinson's want to beat this disease. So do millions more Americans who have family members suffering from Parkinson's. But it won't happen until Congress adequately funds Parkinson's research.

For many people with Parkinson's, managing their disease is a full-time job. It is a constant balancing act. Too little medicine causes tremors and stiffness. Too much medicine produces uncontrollable movement and slurring. And far too often, Parkinson's patients wait and wait for the medicines to "kick-in." New investigational therapies have helped some people like me control my symptoms, but in the end, we all face the same reality: the medicines stop working. **D**

For people living with Parkinson's, the **status quo** isn't good enough.

As I began to understand what research might promise for the future, I became hopeful I would not face the terrible suffering so many with Parkinson's endure. But I was shocked and frustrated to learn that the amount of funding for Parkinson's research is so **meager.** Compared with the amount of federal funding going to other diseases, research funding for Parkinson's lags far behind.

In a country with a $15 billion investment in medical research we can and we must do better.

At present, Parkinson's is inadequately funded, no matter how one cares to spin it. Meager funding means a continued lack of effective treatments, slow progress in understanding the cause of the disease, and little chance
70 that a cure will come in time. I applaud the steps we are taking to fulfill the promise of the Udall Parkinson's Research Act, but we must be clear—we aren't there yet.

If, however, an adequate investment is made, there is much to be hopeful for. We have a tremendous opportunity to close the gap for Parkinson's. We are learning more and more about this disease. The scientific community
80 believes that with a significant investment in Parkinson's research, new discoveries and improved treatments strategies are close-at-hand. Many have called Parkinson's the most curable **neurological** disorder and the one expected to produce a breakthrough first. Scientists tell me that a cure is possible, some say even by the end
90 of the next decade—if the research dollars match the research opportunity.

Fox is greeted by Senators Paul Wellstone and Arlen Specter.

Mr. Chairman, you and the members of the Subcommittee have done so much to increase the investment in medical research in this country. I thank you for your vision. Most people don't know just how important this research is until they or someone in their family faces a serious illness. I know I didn't.

The Parkinson's community strongly supports your efforts to double medical research funding. At the same time, I implore you to do more for people with Parkinson's. Take up Parkinson's as if your life depended on it.
100 Increase funding for Parkinson's research by $75 million over current levels for the coming fiscal year.[2] Make this a down payment for a fully funded

meager (mē′gər) *adj.* lacking in quantity or quality

neurological (nŏŏr′ə-lŏj′ĭ-kəl) *adj.* having to do with the nervous system

---

2. **fiscal year:** a 12-month period—which may or may not coincide with the calendar year—during which a company or organization keeps accounting records.

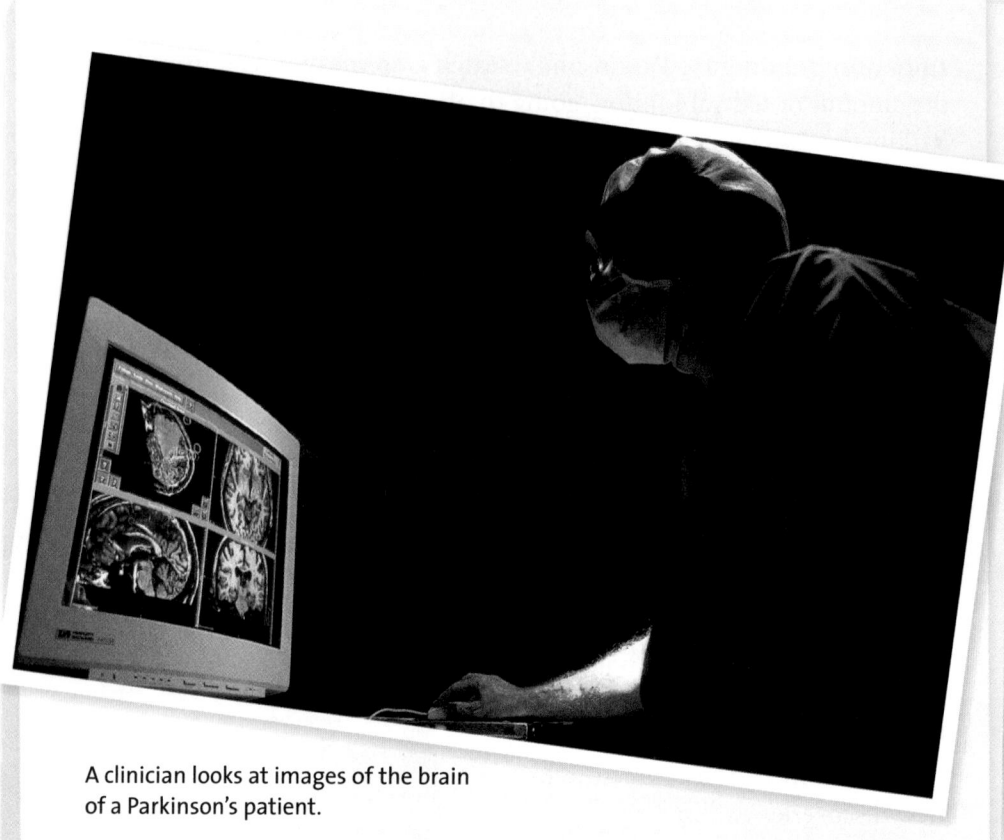

A clinician looks at images of the brain of a Parkinson's patient.

E GRAMMAR AND STYLE
Reread lines 97–103. Fox uses **imperative sentences** to urge Congress to increase research funding.

Parkinson's research agenda that will make Parkinson's nothing more than a footnote in medical textbooks. **E**

I would like to close on a personal note. Today you will hear from, or have already heard from, more than a few experts, in the fields of science, book-keeping and other areas. I am an expert in only one—what it is like to be a young man, husband, and father with Parkinson's disease. With the help of daily medication and selective exertion, I can still perform my job, in my case in a very public arena. I can still help out with the daily 110 tasks and rituals involved in home life. But I don't kid myself . . . that will change. Physical and mental exhaustion will become more and more of a factor, as will increased rigidity, tremor and dyskinesia.[3] I can expect in my 40s to face challenges most wouldn't expect until their 70s and 80s—if ever. But with your help, if we all do everything we can to **eradicate** this disease, in my 50s I'll be dancing at my children's weddings. And mine will be just one of millions of happy stories.

Thank you again for your time and attention.

Senator SPECTER. Thank you very much, Mr. Fox, for those very profound and moving words.

eradicate (ĭ-răd′ĭ-kāt′) *v.* to do away with completely

---

3. **dyskinesia** (dĭs′kə-nē′zhə): inability to control bodily movements.

Comprehension

PENNSYLVANIA STANDARDS

READING STANDARD
A.2.5.1 Summarize

1. **Recall** How did other people with Parkinson's disease respond to Fox when he made his condition known?

2. **Recall** What did Fox resolve to do after he shared his situation with the public?

3. **Clarify** Why is managing the disease a full-time job for people with Parkinson's?

Critical Analysis

4. **Summarize** Review the notes you took as you read. Then summarize what you learned about Parkinson's disease from reading Fox's testimony.

5. **Draw Conclusions** How does Fox's personal experience with Parkinson's help him make his **pitch** to his audience? Explain your answer.

6. **Analyze the Argument** Fox's **claim** is that Congress should increase federal spending for Parkinson's research. What reasons and evidence does he provide as **support** for his claim? Write them on a graphic organizer like the one shown.

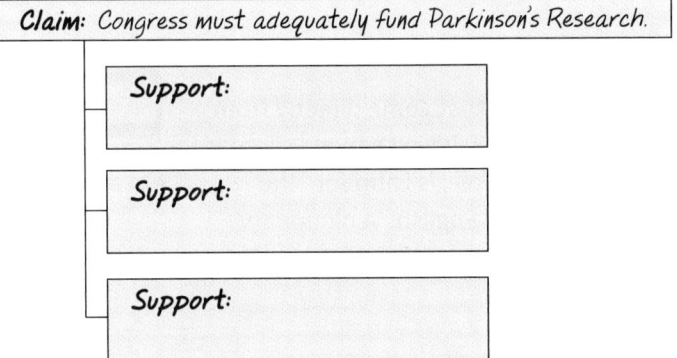

Claim: Congress must adequately fund Parkinson's Research.

Support:

Support:

Support:

7. **Analyze the Counterargument** What potential objection is Fox countering in lines 90–101?

8. **Evaluate Persuasive Techniques** Reread lines 102–114. Fox concludes his testimony by describing two contrasting visions of his future. What emotion does each vision create? What is the effect of concluding his speech with this **emotional appeal?**

9. **Synthesize** Does it strengthen or weaken a cause to have a celebrity associated with it? Would a plea from an ordinary person carry as much weight as one from a celebrity? Consider Michael J. Fox's association with Parkinson's research and think of other celebrities who support particular causes.

Vocabulary in Context

VOCABULARY PRACTICE

Write the word from the Word List that best completes each sentence.

1. _____ diseases can damage the brain.

2. The goal of medical research is to _____ these diseases.

3. A _____ increase in funding might slow progress toward finding a cure.

4. Clearly, it is important to progress instead of maintaining the _____.

WORD LIST

eradicate

meager

neurological

status quo

VOCABULARY IN WRITING

If you were given the chance, what important issue would you publicly support? Write a short paragraph identifying an issue and explaining its importance. Use at least two vocabulary words. You might start like this.

> **EXAMPLE SENTENCE**
>
> We need to **_eradicate_** air pollution, especially in our big cities. . . .

VOCABULARY STRATEGY: USING A DICTIONARY

A dictionary is an important tool for understanding terms that come directly from another language. The meaning of some foreign terms may have changed slightly since they were brought into English. _Status quo,_ for example, is Latin for "the state in which" but means "the existing state of affairs" in English. A dictionary will have the definitions of many foreign terms commonly used in English, and some will include the term's etymology, or history.

PENNSYLVANIA STANDARDS

READING STANDARD
A.2.1 Apply the meaning of vocabulary

PRACTICE Create a four-column chart with these headings: "Foreign Term," "Original Language," "Original Meaning," and "Meaning in English." Then, using a dictionary, fill in the chart for each term.

1. à la carte   **5.** faux pas

2. al dente   **6.** ad hoc

3. quid pro quo   **7.** caveat emptor

4. piñata   **8.** alfresco

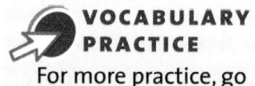

VOCABULARY PRACTICE
For more practice, go to the **Vocabulary Center** at **ClassZone.com.**

Reading-Writing Connection

Broaden your understanding of "Testimony Before the Senate" by responding to these prompts. Then use **Revision: Grammar and Style** to improve your writing.

WRITING PROMPTS	SELF-CHECK

A. Short Response: Prepare a Radio Message

How would you persuade others to donate money for Parkinson's research? Using what you learned from "Testimony Before the Senate," write **a one- or two-paragraph message** for a radio broadcast that makes a **pitch** for raising money.

A strong message will . . .
- clearly state the action you wish people to take
- provide at least two reasons for taking the action

B. Extended Response: Write a Memo

Imagine you are a senator who has just heard Fox's testimony. How would you respond? Write **a three-to-five-paragraph memo** to a fellow senator, describing your reaction and identifying the most convincing parts of Fox's testimony.

A successful memo will . . .
- describe your reaction to the testimony
- identify convincing parts of Fox's testimony

REVISION: GRAMMAR AND STYLE

PENNSYLVANIA STANDARDS

WRITING STANDARD
1.5.11.D.1 Use different types and lengths of sentences

SET THE TONE Review the **Grammar and Style** note on page 616. Fox uses **imperative sentences**—sentences that express a command or request—in his testimony. By using imperative sentences, rather than other sentence types, Fox creates a sense of directness and urgency. (The subject of imperative sentences is usually *you*, often understood rather than stated.)

Here is an example of one student's use of imperative sentences:

> *Take up the cause with me. Give full support to the Parkinson's community by increasing research funding.*

Now study the model. Notice how the revisions in red make the tone stronger and more urgent. Revise your responses to the prompts by employing similar techniques.

WRITING TOOLS
For prewriting, revision, and editing tools, visit the **Writing Center** at ClassZone.com.

STUDENT MODEL

~~You can~~ make a difference in the war against Parkinson's disease. *Send in* ~~Your~~ donation~~will go to research for a cure~~.

How Private Is Your Private Life?
Magazine Article by Andrea Rock

The Privacy Debate:
One Size Doesn't Fit All
Newspaper Editorial by Arthur M. Ahalt

Is PRIVACY
an illusion?

PENNSYLVANIA STANDARDS

READING STANDARDS
B.3.1.1 Analyze the use of facts and opinions

B.3.2.1 Identify and/or interpret bias and propaganda

KEY IDEA Your phone number appears in a hundred databases. Your favorite Web site keeps track of your every click. Do these advances in technology pose a threat to your **privacy?** Big Brother (along with 30 of his closest friends) may be watching you.

DEBATE With a small group, break into two teams and stage a debate over the question of personal privacy in today's society. Is your privacy at risk, or isn't it? Be prepared to back up your opinions with examples and other evidence.

PRIVATE PROPERTY
KEEP OUT
TRESPASSERS WILL BE PROSECUTED

● ELEMENTS OF NONFICTION: FACT AND OPINION

Most persuasive writers use facts and opinions to support their claims. A **fact** is a statement that can be proved, or verified. An **opinion** is a statement that cannot be proved because it expresses a person's beliefs, feelings, or thoughts. It's important to distinguish facts from opinions because facts tend to be less disputable than opinions—unless the opinions come from experts. Can you distinguish the fact from opinion here?

The constant invasion of our privacy is an outrage.

According to a 1999 Wall Street Journal *poll, loss of privacy is the number-one concern of Americans.*

The first statement is an opinion. The second is a fact; it can be proved by consulting the 1999 *Wall Street Journal* poll.

As you read each of the following selections, identify the significant facts and opinions in a chart like the one shown.

Location	Example	Fact/Opinion
lines 2–3	A 1999 poll found that loss of privacy is the number-one concern of Americans.	Fact

● READING SKILL: RECOGNIZE BIAS

Bias is an unfair preference for or against a particular topic or issue. To detect bias, be on the lookout for the following:

- an argument in which the evidence is unbalanced, giving one side stronger or more adequate support than the other
- the presence of **loaded language**—words with intensely positive or negative connotations
- opinions stated as if they were facts
- the use of overgeneralizations, such as **stereotyping,** and other faulty reasoning (See **Reading Handbook,** page R24.)

▲ VOCABULARY IN CONTEXT

Which of the following words can be used to discuss

- the promotion of a cause?
- something unsettling?
- an unbiased discussion?
- a skilled talker?

WORD LIST		
advocacy	articulate	disconcerting
affiliate	awry	nonpartisan
anonymity	browser	pervasive
		surveillance

Background

Technology and Privacy Many Americans are becoming increasingly concerned that the miracles of technology have come at a high cost—namely, the loss of personal privacy. Internet companies, for example, can monitor Web sites to gather information about their visitors—information that can be sold to other companies for marketing purposes. In many large corporations, computer software can screen workers' e-mail messages. Some Americans want Congress to pass stronger privacy laws like those that have been established in other countries. In the United States, however, corporate opponents have lobbied successfully against such legislation.

"Meet the new head of security."

© Mike Baldwin/www.CartoonStock.com

BUILDING BACKGROUND
To learn more about technology and privacy, visit the **Literature Center** at **ClassZone.com.**

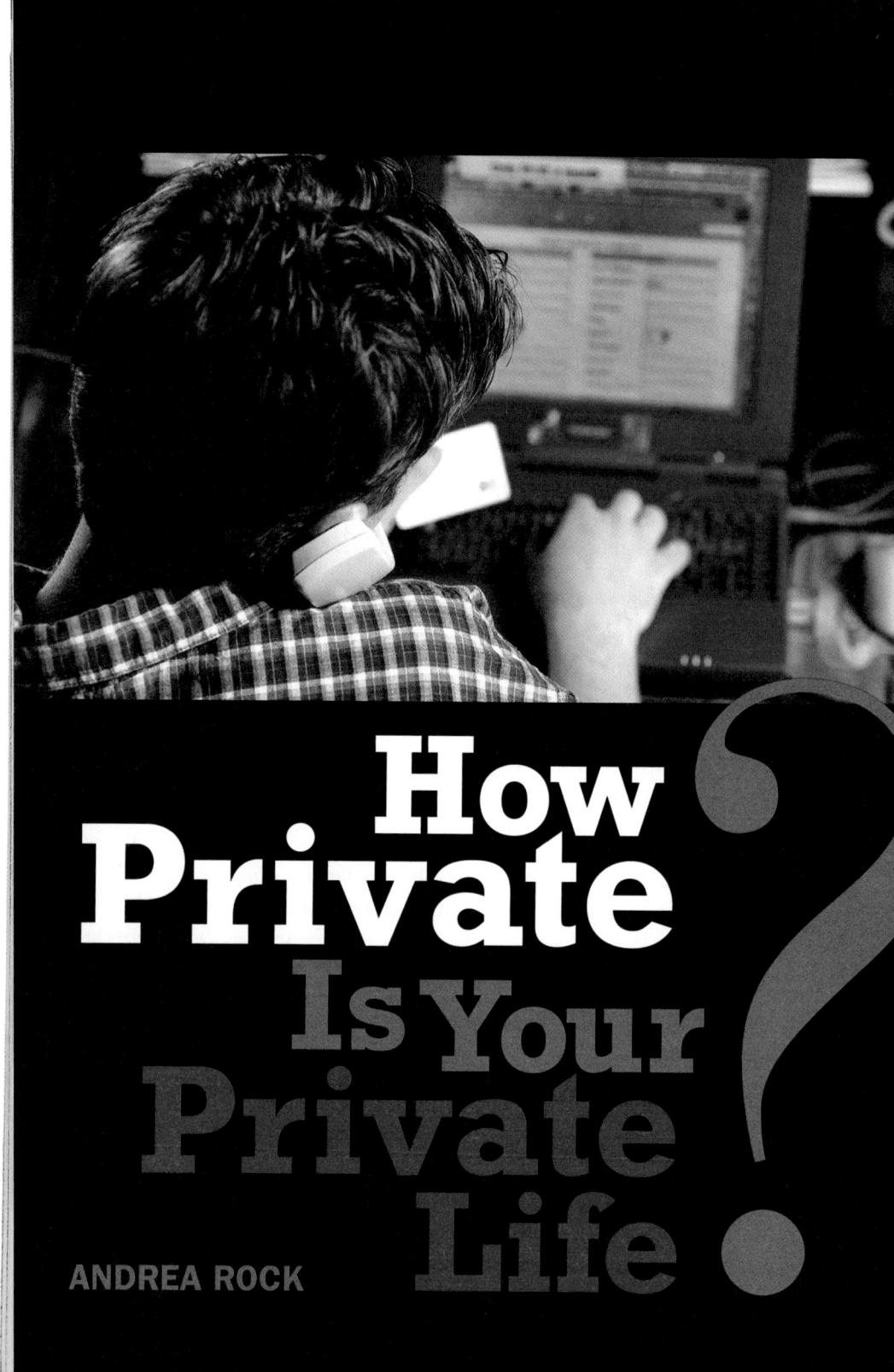

How Private
Is Your Private Life
?

ANDREA ROCK

When you go online, file an insurance claim or even eat out, you reveal personal information to strangers. Here's what you need to know about who's watching you—and how to protect yourself.

Rapid advances in technology have fostered an ever-growing assault on our private lives. A 1999 *Wall Street Journal* poll found that loss of privacy **Ⓐ** ranked as Americans' number-one concern for the new century—ahead of depression, war and terrorism.

Regulators and lawmakers alike have proposed measures to safeguard privacy, but they face strong opposition from businesses whose aim is to collect as much information as possible about consumers' financial and medical histories, their shopping habits and other personal details. Companies profit by selling this information to advertisers and other
10 businesses, or simply by using it to tailor their own advertising.

To find out how **pervasive** the system really is, the editors of LHJ[1] asked me to see how often in a single day my activities resulted in a legal invasion of privacy. I was surprised by what I learned:

9:00 A.M.
After sending my two sons off to school, I go to the grocery store. At the register, I hand the cashier my supermarket discount card. Later, I discover that this card allows retailers to track exactly what I've purchased, how much I spend and how often I shop. These details can then be shared with product manufacturers so that coupons and other offers can be targeted to me. "People should be aware that when they use these cards, they are
20 literally selling their privacy," says Ari Schwartz, senior policy analyst at the Center for Democracy and Technology, an **advocacy** organization in Washington, D.C. Schwartz adds that his group has already seen cases where these records have been used in lawsuits. **Ⓑ**

9:25 A.M.
After returning a video, I stop at the post office to mail an insurance claim form. Amazingly, the privacy of my video-rental records is protected by federal law, but not the data in my medical records. By signing the claim form, I authorize doctors to release sensitive information about myself to insurers and other third parties,[2] such as the Medical Information Bureau, which keeps records of health problems reported on some
30 insurance applications and informs insurers (on request) about pre-existing conditions.

---

1. **editors of LHJ:** The author was given this assignment by the editors of *Ladies' Home Journal.*
2. **release sensitive information . . . other third parties:** Congress attempted to address this problem by passing the Health Insurance Portability and Accountability Act, which makes the unauthorized release of medical information a crime.

Ⓐ RECOGNIZE BIAS
Notice the phrase "ever-growing assault on our private lives." Does this **loaded language** portray technology as positive or negative? Explain.

pervasive (pər-vā′sĭv) *adj.* spreading widely through an area or group of people

advocacy (ăd′və-kə-sē) *adj.* involving public support for an idea or policy

Ⓑ FACT AND OPINION
Reread lines 14–23. What facts are included here? Cite examples from the text.

Although my medical records can be shared with people I don't know, in about half the states in the U.S., I don't have the legal right to see them myself.

10:00 A.M.

I call the car dealer about the 1997 Subaru I just purchased. When I register a car or apply for a driver's license in New York, my name, address, date of birth and the model of my car may be sold to marketers, private investigators and others who access the state's database. Policies may vary by state, with some selling Social Security numbers, too.

40   The federal Driver's Privacy Protection Act of 1994 requires application forms to inform consumers that personal information may be disclosed to third parties and that they must be given an opportunity to prohibit such disclosures. **C**

C FACT AND OPINION
How could the statement in lines 41–43 be verified?

10:20 A.M.

On my way into New York City to meet a friend for lunch, I save time by paying the toll with my E-Z Pass, a radio tag that deducts the toll from my account. But using the pass means that a record of my travels is being kept. While it can help track criminals, the data could also be used to legally obtain personal information about law-abiding citizens.

11:30 A.M.

50 As I'm waiting to cross the corner of 45th Street and Fifth Avenue, I'm being filmed by a hidden video camera. At twenty-second intervals, the device transmits the images onto an Internet site. The camera is operated by a private company simply for the use of promotional purposes and entertainment on its Web site, but **surveillance** cameras are increasingly being used by police and merchants to fight crime, as well.

"By the end of the decade, I imagine most public places will have surveillance cameras connected to a computer that spontaneously compares faces shown on a monitor with mug shots of people wanted by the police," says John Pike, a security analyst at the Federation of American Scientists, a private policy group in Washington D.C.

NOON

60 My friend Diane joins me at Daniel, a lovely French restaurant. In my research, I found out that tiny cameras strategically positioned in the

disconcerting
(dĭs'kən-sûr'tĭng) *adj.*
causing one to feel
confused or embarrassed
disconcert *v.*

D FACT AND OPINION
Identify at least one fact
and one opinion in
lines 60–64.

ceiling allow the chefs to watch diners eating so that they can time their
delivery of the courses. The food is delicious, but it's **disconcerting** to
know that every bite I take is being filmed. **D**

Diane tells me that a friend of hers just received a ticket by mail for
running a red light six months earlier in Los Angeles. A police surveillance
camera caught the license plate of the rental car, which the authorities used
to track down his name and address.

1:30 P.M.

I use Diane's cell phone to leave a message for a friend, aware that my
70 conversation could be intercepted by someone with a radio receiver. Says
Pike: "If you are discussing something highly sensitive that you wouldn't
want your prying neighbor or worst enemy to know, don't have that
conversation on a cell or portable phone."

4:00 P.M.

After I check my e-mail on my home-office computer, my older son,
Adam, visits a site that provides all the research he needs for his fifth-grade
science project. I feel much more comfortable about his use of the Internet

now that a new federal law prohibits commercial Web sites from collecting personal information from children under thirteen without parental consent.

6:11 P.M.

80 I use online banking services to see if a recent deposit has been credited to my account. When I first signed up for this service, I was instructed to use my Social Security number as my customer access code. I avoid giving out that number when possible, but in this case, I had no choice. The bank protects my account information from hackers and other unauthorized third parties, but it does share that data with inside **affiliates,** such as brokerage partners.[3]

Consumer advocates say financial privacy has been further endangered by a federal law that made it easier for banks to merge with other financial firms, such as brokerages and insurance companies. Though the law
90 includes provisions to protect consumer privacy, critics say there are loopholes that could lead, for example, to a bank denying a loan to a customer because its health-insurance affiliate's data reveals that he or she is being treated for a life-threatening illness.

9:35 P.M.

When I visit *Amazon.com* to check out a book, a message on my computer screen says that the Web site is trying to place a "cookie," a tag that identifies me to an Internet company whenever I visit its site, on my hard drive. Normally, consumers don't receive this alert, but I've learned how to activate a feature on my computer's **browser** that will warn me every time a cookie is about to be placed, giving me the option of accepting it or not.
100 Adam and I have visited eleven Web sites today, accumulating forty-nine cookies in all.

Cookies can give you more than you bargained for. A Web site may share its data with an ad network, such as DoubleClick, which places banner ads on more than 1,800 Web sites. An online profile of you is created, which associates your computer with any sites you visit on that ad network, noting what you look at or buy. Your profile continues to expand and can be sold to anyone without your knowledge or consent. Visiting a gardening Web site just to learn about varieties of roses might trigger a deluge of seed catalogs in your mailbox later. **E**

10:45 P.M.

110 To wrap up, I return to my Excite home page to read my horoscope. "Your home is your castle," it says, "and you are the supreme ruler within its walls." After today, I'm not so sure.

affiliate (ə-fĭl′ē-ĭt) *n.* a person or an organization officially connected to a larger body

browser (brou′zər) *n.* a program used to navigate the Internet

E RECOGNIZE BIAS
Reread lines 102–109. Loaded language can sometimes take the form of **hyperbole,** or exaggeration. Find an example of hyperbole in this paragraph. How might this influence a reader?

---

3. **brokerage partners:** individuals or companies that buy and sell stocks or other assets for others.

The Privacy Debate

Arthur M. Ahalt

One Size Doesn't Fit All

"One man's justice is another man's injustice," said Ralph Waldo Emerson, neatly summarizing the complexity of most debates.

Unfortunately, the current debate over privacy issues rarely illuminates both sides of this complex issue. Instead, we are told there should be no debate over the
10 need for privacy.

This article will explore the other side of the privacy debate and demonstrate the benefit of access and openness, particularly in the area of public records.

As a retired state circuit court judge with 17 years on the bench, I've observed firsthand the benefits to our judicial, government and
20 economic systems of open access to public records. Unfortunately, too many Americans seem willing to reduce such access in the name of privacy.

Why is the siren call[1] of privacy so strong?

Maybe it stems from the impersonal nature of modern society, lack of community and
30 the rise of the global economy, all of which makes us wish for more **anonymity**. There now are 280 million Americans, and we're long past doing business at the corner store where everybody knew your name. **F**

Maybe technology is to blame, with credit cards and consumer information automated to move
40 consumers from the practical obscurity of paper records to huge computer databases.

Maybe it's some politicians, the media and any number of self-styled advocates and experts who traffic in scare headlines, breathless press releases and emotional soapbox speeches. It's no mystery—privacy concerns affect **articulate** middle
50 class citizens who buy papers and vote—creating a "squeaky" wheel that gets the grease.

---

1. **siren call:** alluring but possibly dangerous appeal (after the Sirens, mythological creatures whose irresistible songs lured sailors into danger).

anonymity
(ăn′ə-nĭm′ĭ-tē) *n.*
the condition of being unknown

F FACT AND OPINION
Identify a fact and an opinion in lines 27–36.

articulate (är-tĭk′yə-lĭt)
adj. able to speak clearly and coherently; well-spoken

Privacy is also a **nonpartisan** concern which neither political party owns, and represents an issue where conservatives and liberals often meet in unison. Media stories about privacy issues often are human-interest heart-tuggers that
60 sell and gather an audience. Think tanks, clearinghouses² and "experts" flock to issue press releases, hold seminars, appear on television and generally stoke the fires of paranoia³ and emotionalism. **G**

In this atmosphere, confusion, fear and concern replace a balanced view of the privacy issue.

Politicians and the media quote
70 polls—"93 percent of people are concerned about privacy." Well, no doubt. (I would like to know about the 7 percent who are not concerned about privacy, but that is another matter.) Those polls, however, don't appear to probe the trade-offs, such as "would you prefer a bank loan in three days or three months?" Most Americans
80 not only prefer to obtain immediate credit and debt, they demand it.

But instant credit and debt is more than a convenience; it's also the very basis of the underlying strength and power of our economic system, which moves at the speed of light as a direct result of the transparency of information available to economic decision
90 makers. Car, home and bank loans and the issuance of credit and debit cards can be made quickly because information about most of us is available. It's the source of our

nonpartisan
(nŏn-pär′tĭ-zən) *adj.* not supporting or controlled by any political group

G RECOGNIZE BIAS
Reread lines 53–65. Identify the **loaded language** in lines 53–58. What does the writer's language suggest about the people who raise concerns about invasions of privacy?

---

2. **think tanks, clearinghouses:** A think tank is a research institute organized to investigate social problems; a clearinghouse is an organization that collects and distributes information.

3. **stoke the fires of paranoia:** increase fear and suspicion.

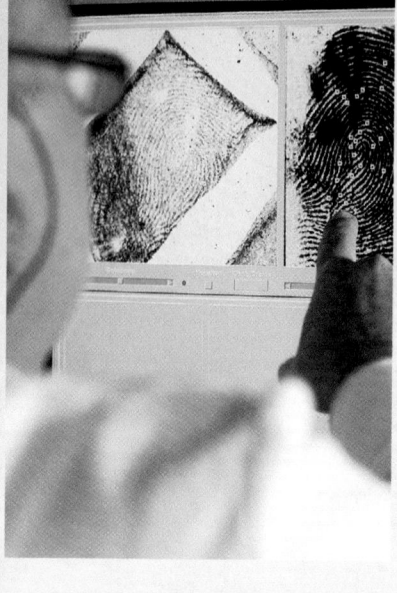

retail sector's[7] strength. It's the reason we can buy and sell property in weeks; not months or years. Federal Trade Commission Chairman Tim Muris calls this system, which we all take for granted, "the miracle of instant credit."

Economist Walter Kitchenman says that our consumer credit system is the "secret ingredient of the U.S. economy's resilience."

Aside from economic benefits, transparency also provides other specific benefits. It makes it possible to find absent spouses and enforce child support payments; to screen day care workers and school bus drivers to keep our kids safe from substance abusers and child molesters; to check the background of bank tellers to avoid embezzlement; to connect heirs with fortunes; and to help prevent identity theft, and make it easier to fix if it occurs. **H**

There are real problems that affect real people in the privacy arena, but it's the classic case of bad news always selling, and good news remaining invisible.

Each day, billions of financial transactions occur in our economy. Do some go **awry?** Of course, but it is a small percentage. Unfortunately, no one wants to read a headline "Today 299,999,033 Americans Did Not Suffer Privacy-Related Problems."

There is also a need to segment privacy from one huge ball of confusion into separate, more manageable and different issues, which require different approaches. **I**

Tracking Internet surfing and purchases is different from identity theft, which is different from telemarketing calls, which is different from access to public records, which is also different from the use of Social Security numbers as a unique identifier.

Privacy supporters would have us believe that "one size fits all" when it comes to addressing matters of privacy.

I hold no portfolio on some of these issues, but as one who now is working directly in the area of public records accessibility, I am vitally concerned about access to these records and their contents.

Remember the old adage when you hear self-styled privacy experts expound on the need to keep information hidden: "for every problem, there is a simple solution, which is usually wrong."

---

7. **retail sector's:** of the branch of the nation's economy that deals with products people buy and use.

Comprehension

PENNSYLVANIA STANDARDS

READING STANDARD
B.3.2.1 Identify and/or interpret bias and propaganda

1. **Recall** According to the author of "How Private Is Your Private Life?" what happens when a driver uses an E-Z Pass to pay a toll?

2. **Clarify** In the context of the Internet, what is a **cookie?**

3. **Summarize** According to the author of "The Privacy Debate: One Size Doesn't Fit All," how do we benefit from sacrificing some part of our **privacy?**

Critical Analysis

4. **Distinguish Fact from Opinion** Review the chart you filled in as you read. Does Andrea Rock rely more on fact or opinion in making her case? What about Arthur M. Ahalt? Cite evidence from the selections to support your answers.

5. **Analyze Argument** What question does Andrea Rock set out to explore? What conclusions does the bulk of her evidence support? How does she let readers know what she thinks by the end of her research day?

6. **Analyze Bias** Any piece of persuasive writing is likely to reflect the bias of its author. Which of the two articles do you think reflects a stronger bias? Support your answer with evidence from the texts.

7. **Identify Modes of Reasoning** The process of piecing together facts and other evidence to arrive at a logical conclusion or generalization is called **inductive reasoning.** Which of the two arguments you just read reaches its conclusion using inductive reasoning? Explain. (To learn more about inductive reasoning, see **Reading Handbook,** pages R22–R23.)

8. **Compare Texts** Which article do you find more convincing, and why?

9. **Make Judgments** How have these articles helped shape your thinking on the privacy issue? What does your reading experience suggest about the role that magazine articles and newspaper editorials can serve in civic life? Explain your answer.

Vocabulary in Context

VOCABULARY PRACTICE

Choose the word that is not related in meaning to the other words.

1. awry, amiss, assemble, astray
2. namelessness, disguise, anonymity, fretfulness
3. distressing, embarrassing, disconcerting, inspiring
4. electrician, browser, plumber, carpenter
5. pervasive, widespread, arrogant, extensive
6. enemy, associate, affiliate, partner
7. broadcasting, spying, observing, surveillance
8. impartial, uneasy, nonpartisan, unbiased
9. articulate, illogical, eloquent, expressive
10. rejection, advocacy, rebuff, disdain

WORD LIST
advocacy
affiliate
anonymity
articulate
awry
browser
disconcerting
nonpartisan
pervasive
surveillance

VOCABULARY IN WRITING

In a paragraph, describe an invasion of privacy that someone you know has experienced. Use four or more vocabulary words. Here is a way to start.

> **EXAMPLE SENTENCE**
>
> _Anonymity_ seems to be impossible in the world today.

VOCABULARY STRATEGY: INTERNET WORDS

You often hear Internet terms, but do you know what they actually mean? Some terms, like the vocabulary word _browser,_ are common words used in specialized ways; other terms are unique to discussion of the Internet. To be Web literate, you need a working knowledge of basic Internet terms.

PRACTICE With a partner, write definitions for each term, and check them in a current dictionary or Web site glossary. Then list three other Internet terms you think your classmates should know, and define them.

1. server
2. portal
3. hyperlink
4. Webcast
5. site map
6. wireless fidelity

PENNSYLVANIA STANDARDS

READING STANDARD
A.2.1.2 Identify and/or apply meaning of content-specific words

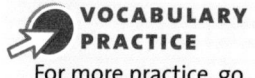

VOCABULARY PRACTICE
For more practice, go to the **Vocabulary Center** at **ClassZone.com.**

Reading-Writing Connection

Explore the arguments presented in "How Private is Your Private Life?" and "The Privacy Debate: One Size Doesn't Fit All" by responding to these prompts. Then use **Revision: Grammar and Style** to improve your writing.

WRITING PROMPTS	SELF-CHECK

A. Short Response: Write a Critique

Write a letter to one of the authors in which you explain how his or her piece could be made more convincing. In your critique, write **one or two paragraphs** describing your reaction to the article and your suggestions for improvement.

A successful critique will . . .
- offer specific suggestions about what information to add or remove
- contain well-supported advice about how to make the language more balanced or more powerful

B. Extended Response: Write an Argument

Do you regard technology as a threat to your **privacy**? Why or why not? Write **three to five paragraphs** in which you argue your point.

A strong argument will . . .
- clearly state a position
- provide at least two supporting reasons

REVISION: GRAMMAR AND STYLE

USE RHETORICAL DEVICES Review the **Grammar and Style** note on page 630. **Parallelism**—the use of similar grammatical constructions to express ideas that are related or equal in importance—can add rhythm or emphasis to speech or writing. In the following example from "The Privacy Debate: One Size Doesn't Fit All," notice how the author uses a series of adjective clauses, all beginning with "which is," to emphasize how privacy needs differ:

> *Tracking Internet surfing and purchases is different from identity theft, which is different from telemarketing calls, which is different from access to public records, which is also different from the use of Social Security numbers as a unique identifier.* (lines 138–145)

Now study the model. Notice how the revisions in red add emphasis to the writer's ideas. Revise your response to Prompt B by using parallel structures.

PENNSYLVANIA STANDARDS

WRITING STANDARD
1.5.11.E Revise writing to improve sentence variety

STUDENT MODEL

The great privacy debate includes some pretty minor issues. *Why do we care if someone knows that we buy dog food?* ∧ ~~Some people don't consider their grocery purchases to be so~~ *Why do we* ~~private. Others don't~~ *someone knows that we drove down Fremont Highway on Tuesday?* ∧ care ~~if their comings and goings are tracked.~~

WRITING TOOLS
For prewriting, revision, and editing tools, visit the **Writing Center** at ClassZone.com.

Billy Thomas
Life Is Calling

Public Service Announcements on *MediaSmart* DVD

How do you
PROMOTE *a cause?*

**PENNSYLVANIA
STANDARDS**

SPEAKING/LISTENING STANDARD
1.6.11.F.2 Evaluate the role of the
media in focusing attention and
forming opinions

KEY IDEA Have you ever wondered how you can get involved in
your community? Perhaps you'd like to volunteer at a local soup
kitchen, help restore a rundown building, or donate blood. The
two public service announcements (PSAs) in this lesson **promote**
worthy causes by inspiring viewers to get involved. See if they
motivate you to take action.

Background

Making a Difference The PSAs you will view promote two well-
known organizations. The first PSA, "Billy Thomas," is from the
Boys and Girls Clubs of America, an organization that provides
afterschool and weekend activities for boys and girls. The second
PSA, "Life Is Calling," is part of a campaign for the Peace Corps,
a government agency whose volunteers work in developing
countries to help advance world peace.

**WHAT'S GOING TO STOP YOUR KID
FROM NOT WEARING A SEAT BELT?**

BUCKLE UP. *Kansas Clicks*

A public service message from the Kansas Department of Transportation

Media Literacy: Persuasion in PSAs

Whether they're asking an audience to help end homelessness or to help save the environment, PSAs draw on many of the same techniques that are used in commercial advertising. Images, words, and music can attract an audience, but in order to raise awareness of important issues and get people to act, PSAs depend on **persuasive techniques.**

PERSUASIVE TECHNIQUES IN PUBLIC SERVICE ANNOUNCEMENTS

A **celebrity spokesperson** who possesses admirable qualities may appeal to a particular audience.

By giving a **testimonial,** or a personal recommendation, an individual directly associates himself or herself with the cause. For example,

Voice-over: Does it work? It did for me.

Images may represent ideas and values that appeal to a particular audience. Notice how this image conveys the idea of unity.

A **slogan** is a memorable phrase that helps an audience remember an organization's message. For example,

Life is calling.
How far will you go?

STRATEGIES FOR ANALYZING PUBLIC SERVICE ANNOUNCEMENTS

- Make note of any words, images, and persuasive techniques that help you define the **target audience.** Ask yourself: Who might be interested in this cause?
- Pay attention to the delivery of the **message.** Ask yourself: Do the people, images, and words spoken help deliver a clear message? Is the information helpful to the viewer or listener?
- Be conscious of **emotional appeals**—messages that persuade an audience by creating strong feelings. Ask yourself: How do the words, images, symbols, and music create emotional appeal?
- Consider who the spokesperson is. Ask yourself: What qualities does this person possess? How might viewers identify with this person?
- Look for a logo to help you determine what group is behind the message. A **logo** is a unique symbol, name, or trademark that is associated with an organization. Ask yourself: When and where does the logo appear?

MediaSmart DVD

- **PSA 1:** "Billy Thomas" from the Boys and Girls Clubs of America
- **PSA 2:** "Life Is Calling" from Peace Corps
- **Genre:** Public Service Announcements

Viewing Guide for

Public Service Announcements

In "Billy Thomas," Denzel Washington, a highly regarded actor who won an Academy Award in 2001, recalls a childhood experience. The second PSA, "Life Is Calling," poses a number of rhetorical questions designed to persuade viewers to volunteer and help those in need.

The questions that follow will help you critically analyze these PSAs. Make sure to view each PSA several times.

NOW VIEW

FIRST VIEWING: Comprehension

1. **Clarify** Who exactly is Billy Thomas?

2. **Recall** Describe an image in "Life Is Calling" that creates a positive impression of the Peace Corps.

CLOSE VIEWING: Media Literacy

3. **Make Inferences** What impressions might viewers have of the Boys and Girls Clubs of America on the basis of Denzel Washington's testimonial? Use evidence from the PSA to support your views.

4. **Analyze Message** In "Life Is Calling," many of the images support the idea of going on a journey. Why might this idea appeal to the target audience?

5. **Compare and Contrast Audience** Describe the target audience for "Billy Thomas" and for "Life Is Calling." How are these audiences similar? How are they different? Think about the following characteristics: age, values, and background.

Write or Discuss

Evaluate Emotional Appeal The PSAs in this lesson use emotional appeal to persuade viewers. Choose one of the PSAs and make a list of the techniques that are used to create emotional appeal. In your opinion, which of these elements is most effective? As part of your evaluation, consider the following:

- the use of celebrity endorsement or voice-over to deliver the message
- the target audience and techniques used to appeal to this audience
- your reaction to the PSA and how you think the intended audience might react

Produce Your Own Media

Create a PSA The PSA shown in the professional model is from the National Crime Prevention Council. It is part of a campaign that encourages teens to get involved by taking an activity they enjoy and using it to help others in their community. Your job is to create a PSA like the one shown.

HERE'S HOW Think of a well-known organization or charity that supports an issue you care about. For example, if you're interested in helping cancer patients, you might want to create a PSA for the American Cancer Society.

- Consider the layout of your PSA, including the size and placement of visuals, text, and a slogan.
- Use catchy words and images that grab your audience's attention.

MEDIA TOOLS

For help with creating a PSA, visit the **Media Center** at **ClassZone.com.**

Tech Tip

Use your own photographs and photo-editing software to give your PSA a professional quality.

PROFESSIONAL MODEL

❶ "Before" and "after" images show how an activity can be used to help others.

❷ A catchy slogan describes the message.

❸ A sign identifies the volunteer activity.

❹ The logo identifies the organization.

Primal Screen
Essay by Ellen Goodman

The Pedestrian
Short Story by Ray Bradbury

Could we live without TELEVISION?

PENNSYLVANIA STANDARDS

READING STANDARDS
A.1.6.1 Identify and/or analyze intended purpose

B.1.2.1 Evaluate connections between texts

KEY IDEA Some of us spend a lot of our time watching television. According to research, the average American family is glued to the screen for more than seven hours a day. Is this **television habit** helping us or hurting us?

SURVEY How much time do you and your friends spend watching TV? Survey a small group of your classmates, tally their responses, and then discuss the results.

> **TV Viewing Habits**
> 1. How many hours do you watch TV each day?
> 2. How many hours do you watch TV each week?
> 3. How many TV sets does your family own?

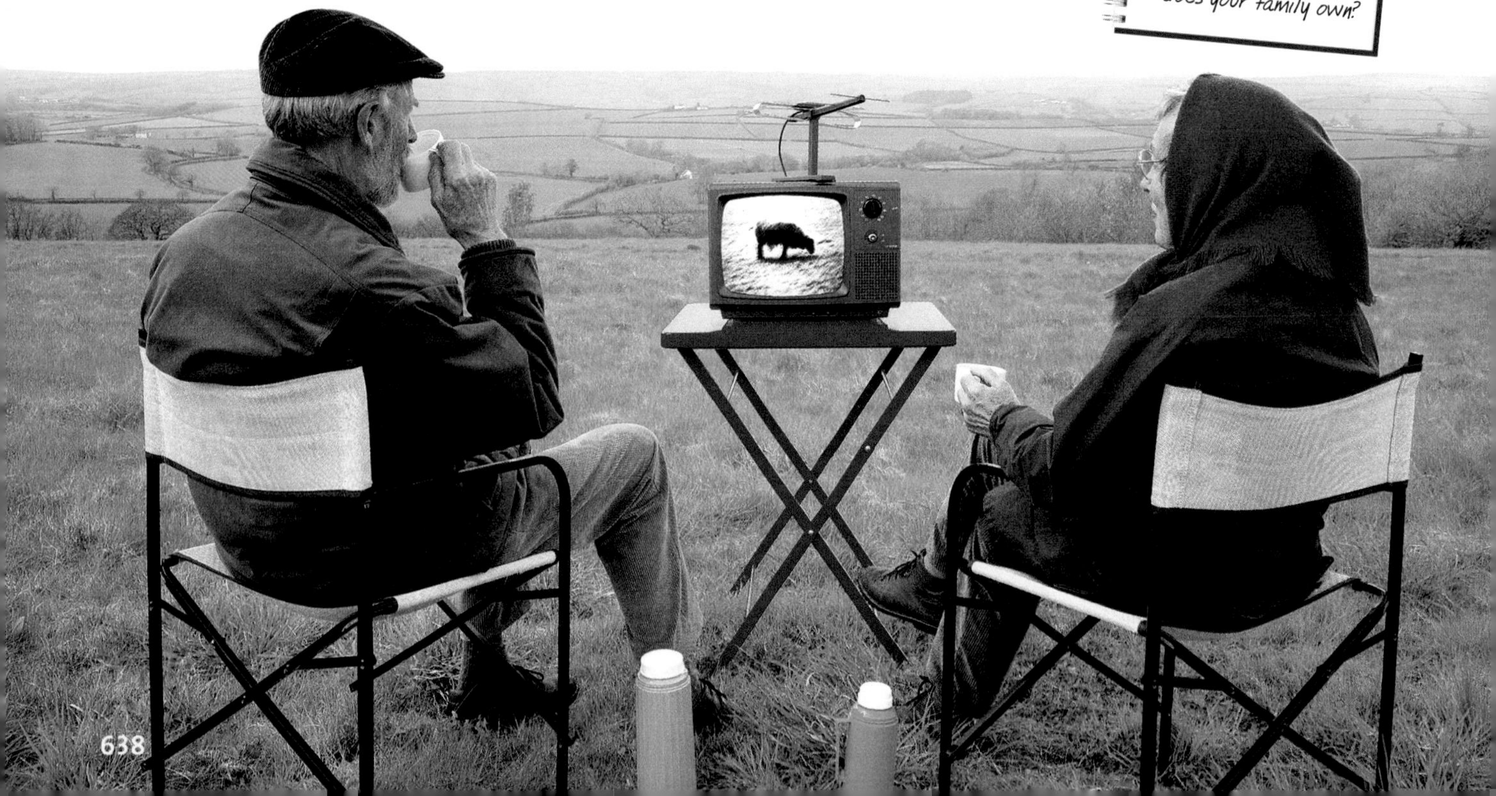

LITERARY ANALYSIS: WRITER'S MESSAGE ACROSS GENRES

The essay and short story you are about to read are works of **social criticism,** or literature that addresses real-life issues—political, religious, economic, or social. However, while both selections comment on the same topic, the impact of television viewing, each has a different message, or main point, and conveys it through different methods. As you read, try to determine each **writer's message** by paying attention to the following:

In the Essay	In the Short Story
• direct statements	• setting and imagery
• facts, statistics, and other evidence, such as descriptions of people's behavior and interactions	• mood, sensory details, and word choice
• explanations of causes and effects	• characters
• word choice	• dialogue
• tone	• plot—especially the nature of the conflict and its resolution
• the writer's call to action at the end	• the lesson you take from the story

READING SKILL: SET A PURPOSE FOR READING

When you **set a purpose for reading,** you identify specific goals to accomplish as you read. For example, after reading these next two selections, you'll be asked to write an essay comparing each writer's message. To prepare for this essay, you'll want to read with the following goals in mind:

- to determine each writer's message
- to identify the similarities and differences in the two messages

Take a moment now to consider how you will accomplish these goals. Will you try to keep track of similarities and differences in the writers' messages as you read? Or do you need to determine each writer's message first and then review the selections to discover ways in which the messages differ?

Author Online

Ellen Goodman: Pioneering Newswoman
After beginning her career as a research trainee at *Newsweek* in the early 1960s, Ellen Goodman broke into reporting and eventually became a columnist for the *Boston Globe*. Today her columns cover a wide range of topics— from politics to parenting—and appear in more than 450 newspapers across the country. Goodman rewards her readers with both good laughs and something to think about.

Ellen Goodman
born 1941

Ray Bradbury: Social Prognosticator
Ray Bradbury is one of the best-known and most highly regarded writers of science fiction. His stories have been termed "warning fictions" because they often explore the dire consequences of society's dependence on technology. Though his stories are serious, Bradbury relishes writing them. "I write for fun," he has said. "I have fun with ideas."

Ray Bradbury
born 1920

MORE ABOUT THE AUTHOR
For more on Ellen Goodman and Ray Bradbury, visit the **Literature Center** at **ClassZone.com.**

Primal Screen

Ellen Goodman

Someday, I would like to see a television series about a family that sits around the set watching a series about a family that sits around the set.

It might not make the Nielsen top ten,[1] but it isn't such a strange idea. Especially when you think about what's going on right now.

Night after night, inside the tube, warm and wiggly families spend their prime time "communicating" like crazy and "solving problems" together like mad. Meanwhile, outside the tube, real families sit and wait for a commercial break just to talk to each other. **A**

About the only subject that never comes up before our glazed eyes
10 is what the medium does to our family life. But, I suppose we already know that.

According to a recent Gallup Poll, television comes out as a major heavy in our family lives. On the scale of problems, TV didn't rate as bad as inflation, but it ran neck-and-neck with unemployment.

According to a recent Roper Poll, it even causes fights. When people were asked what husbands and wives argued about, money was the champion. But television was a strong contender. Considering how much more time we spend in front of the tube, that may not be such a shock.

To a certain extent, we blame the programs. In the Gallup Poll, for
20 example, people worried most about the overemphasis on sex and violence. But surely half of those fights between husbands and wives must be about the more fundamental issue of turning it off.

Deep down below our poll-taking consciousness, we know that the worst aspect of our addiction isn't what's on TV, but how long the TV is on. We can't help but be aware of what happens when we spend more time facing the screen than facing each other.

In that same Gallup Poll, a large number of us said that the way to improve family life is by sharing—sharing family needs, recreational activities and chores. But when you are watching, you aren't doing.
30 The only experience you are sharing is a vicarious one.

I am absolutely convinced that the average wife feels tuned out by the twelfth consecutive weekend sports event because she *is* being tuned out.

---

1. **Nielsen top ten:** the ten most-watched television shows, as determined by the Nielsen rating service.

The average kid develops that distant, slack-jawed, hypnotic, hooked stare because he or she *is* hooked.

In the same way, the people who spend night after night in front of the tube should worry about it. They've become an audience and not a family. Television simply presents us with one model of family life. Watching it makes us fit another model.

But the striking thing in all of this research about how we feel and 40 behave is the role of choice. On the one hand, we have real anxiety about what TV's doing to us. On the other hand, we allow it to happen. **B**

B WRITER'S MESSAGE
What is Goodman's message about excessive TV viewing?

ANALYZE VISUALS
What are your impressions of the family in this photograph?

We choose to turn it on and each other off. We choose peace and quiet when we let the kids watch TV instead of running around the living room. We choose to "relax" in the semi-comatose slump.

The average viewing time of the American child between six and sixteen years of age is twenty to twenty-four hours a week. A large percentage of parents place no restrictions on either the number of hours watched or the type of program viewed.

At the very least, we behave as if we were powerless to wrench each 50 other away.

I grant you that there are a lot of things that touch on our families that are totally out of our individual control. We can't regulate foreign affairs. We can't set the price for oil.

But a television set has a dial and a plug. And we have hands. It is absurd to let our feelings of impotence in the world start creeping into our private lives.

Just once, we ought to create a private show about a real-life family that kicked the habit.

THE PEDESTRIAN

Ray Bradbury

ANALYZE VISUALS
What details in the
painting help create
a somber mood?

To enter out into that silence that was the city at eight o'clock of a misty
evening in November, to put your feet upon that buckling concrete walk,
to step over grassy seams and make your way, hands in pockets, through the
silences, that was what Mr. Leonard Mead most dearly loved to do. He would
stand upon the corner of an intersection and peer down long moonlit avenues
of sidewalk in four directions, deciding which way to go, but it really made
no difference; he was alone in this world of A.D. 2053, or as good as alone,
and with a final decision made, a path selected, he would stride off, sending
patterns of frosty air before him like the smoke of a cigar.

10   Sometimes he would walk for hours and miles and return only at midnight
to his house. And on his way he would see the cottages and homes with their
dark windows, and it was not unlike walking through a graveyard where only
the faintest glimmers of firefly light appeared in flickers behind the windows.
Sudden gray phantoms seemed to manifest upon inner room walls where a
curtain was still undrawn against the night, or there were whisperings and
murmurs where a window in a tomblike building was still open. **C**

Mr. Leonard Mead would pause, cock his head, listen, look, and march
on, his feet making no noise on the lumpy walk. For long ago he had wisely
changed to sneakers when strolling at night, because the dogs in intermittent
20   squads would parallel his journey with barkings if he wore hard heels, and
lights might click on and faces appear and an entire street be startled by the
passing of a lone figure, himself, in the early November evening.

C WRITER'S MESSAGE
Reread lines 10–16. What
do the **imagery** and the
figurative language in
this passage suggest
about Bradbury's position
on TV viewing?

Detail of *Tourists Beware: New Buffalo Speed Trap* (1985), Roger Brown.
Oil on canvas, 48″ × 48″. © The School of the
Art Institute of Chicago and the Brown family.

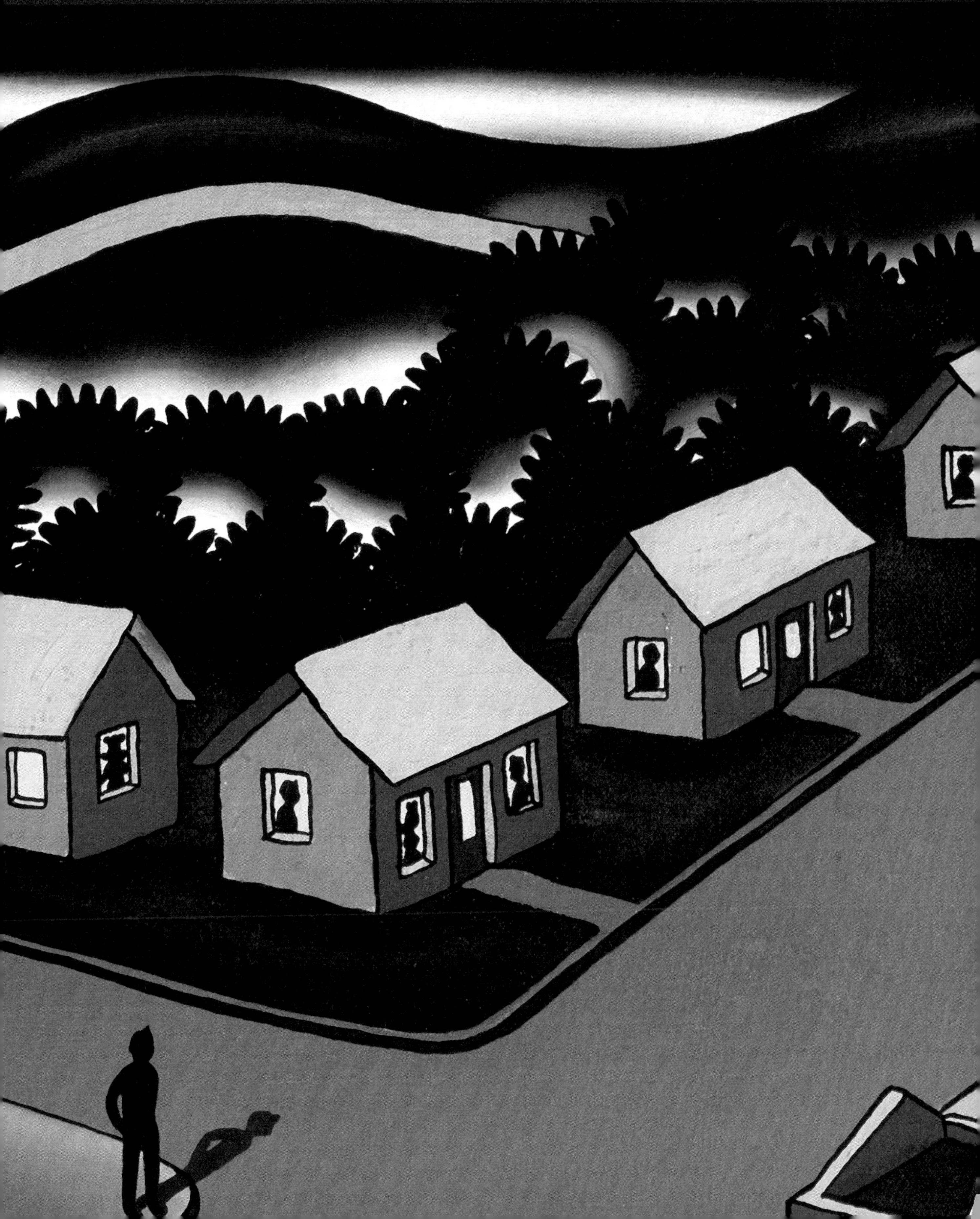

Clouds Over Alabama or Midnight in Alabama (1994), Roger Brown. Oil on canvas, 48″ × 72″.
© The School of the Art Institute of Chicago and the Brown family.

On this particular evening he began his journey in a westerly direction, toward the hidden sea. There was a good crystal frost in the air; it cut the nose and made the lungs blaze like a Christmas tree inside; you could feel the cold light going on and off, all the branches filled with invisible snow. He listened to the faint push of his soft shoes through autumn leaves with satisfaction, and whistled a cold quiet whistle between his teeth, occasionally picking up a leaf as he passed, examining its skeletal pattern in the infrequent lamplights as he
30 went on, smelling its rusty smell.

"Hello, in there," he whispered to every house on every side as he moved. "What's up tonight on Channel 4, Channel 7, Channel 9? Where are the cowboys rushing, and do I see the United States Cavalry over the next hill to the rescue?"

The street was silent and long and empty, with only his shadow moving like the shadow of a hawk in midcountry. If he closed his eyes and stood very still, frozen, he could imagine himself upon the center of a plain, a wintry, windless Arizona desert with no house in a thousand miles, and only dry river beds, the streets, for company.

40 "What is it now?" he asked the houses, noticing his wrist watch. "Eight-thirty P.M.? Time for a dozen assorted murders? A quiz? A revue? A comedian falling off the stage?"

Was that a murmur of laughter from within a moon-white house? He hesitated, but went on when nothing more happened. He stumbled over a particularly uneven section of sidewalk. The cement was vanishing under flowers and grass. In ten years of walking by night or day, for thousands of miles, he had never met another person walking, not one in all that time. **D**

D WRITER'S MESSAGE
Consider the reason why Mead never encounters anyone on his nightly walks. How does this detail help you determine Bradbury's message?

He came to a cloverleaf intersection which stood silent where two main highways crossed the town. During the day it was a thunderous surge of cars, the gas stations open, a great insect rustling and a ceaseless jockeying for position as the scarab-beetles,[1] a faint incense puttering from their exhausts, skimmed homeward to the far directions. But now these highways, too, were like streams in a dry season, all stone and bed and moon radiance.

He turned back on a side street, circling around toward his home. He was within a block of his destination when the lone car turned a corner quite suddenly and flashed a fierce white cone of light upon him. He stood entranced, not unlike a night moth, stunned by the illumination, and then drawn toward it.

A metallic voice called to him:

"Stand still. Stay where you are! Don't move!"

He halted.

"Put up your hands!"

"But—" he said.

"Your hands up! Or we'll shoot!"

The police, of course, but what a rare, incredible thing; in a city of three million, there was only one police car left, wasn't that correct? Ever since a year ago, 2052, the election year, the force had been cut down from three cars to one. Crime was ebbing; there was no need now for the police, save for this one lone car wandering and wandering the empty streets.

"Your name?" said the police car in a metallic whisper. He couldn't see the men in it for the bright light in his eyes.

"Leonard Mead," he said.

"Speak up!"

"Leonard Mead!"

"Business or profession?"

"I guess you'd call me a writer."

"No profession," said the police car, as if talking to itself. The light held him **E** fixed, like a museum specimen, needle thrust through chest.

"You might say that," said Mr. Mead. He hadn't written in years. Magazines and books didn't sell any more. Everything went on in the tomblike houses at night now, he thought, continuing his fancy. The tombs, ill-lit by television light, where the people sat like the dead, the grey or multicolored lights touching their faces, but never really touching *them*.

"No profession," said the phonograph voice, hissing. "What are you doing out?"

"Walking," said Leonard Mead.

"Walking!"

"Just walking," he said simply, but his face felt cold.

"Walking, just walking, walking?"

"Yes, sir."

E WRITER'S MESSAGE
Why does the voice reply "No profession" when Mead says he is a writer?

---

1. **scarab-beetles:** large beetles considered to be sacred in ancient Egypt.

Detail of *Tourists Beware: New Buffalo Speed Trap* (1985), Roger Brown. Oil on canvas, 48″ × 48″.
© The School of the Art Institute of Chicago and the Brown family.

"Walking where? For what?"

"Walking for air. Walking to see."

"Your address!"

"Eleven South Saint James Street."

"And there is air in your house, you have an air *conditioner,* Mr. Mead?"

"Yes."

"And you have a viewing screen in your house to see with?"

"No."

"No?" There was a crackling quiet that in itself was an accusation. **F**

100   "Are you married, Mr. Mead?"

"No."

"Not married," said the police voice behind the fiery beam. The moon was high and clear among the stars and the houses were gray and silent.

"Nobody wanted me," said Leonard Mead with a smile.

"Don't speak unless you're spoken to!"

Leonard Mead waited in the cold night.

F WRITER'S MESSAGE
Notice the voice's reaction when Mead admits to not having a viewing screen. How important is TV viewing to the people of the future?

"Just *walking*, Mr. Mead?"

"Yes."

"But you haven't explained for what purpose."

110 "I explained; for air, and to see, and just to walk."

"Have you done this often?"

"Every night for years."

The police car sat in the center of the street with its radio throat faintly humming.

"Well, Mr. Mead," it said.

"Is that all?" he asked politely.

"Yes," said the voice. "Here." There was a sigh, a pop. The back door of the police car sprang wide. "Get in."

"Wait a minute, I haven't done anything!"

120 "Get in."

"I protest!"

"Mr. Mead."

He walked like a man suddenly drunk. As he passed the front window of the car he looked in. As he had expected, there was no one in the front seat, no one in the car at all.

"Get in."

He put his hand to the door and peered into the back seat, which was a little cell, a little black jail with bars. It smelled of riveted steel. It smelled of harsh antiseptic; it smelled too clean and hard and metallic. There was nothing

130 soft there.

"Now if you had a wife to give you an alibi," said the iron voice. "But—"

"Where are you taking me?"

The car hesitated, or rather gave a faint whirring click, as if information, somewhere, was dripping card by punch-slotted card[2] under electric eyes. "To the Psychiatric Center for Research on Regressive Tendencies."[3] **G**

He got in. The door shut with a soft thud. The police car rolled through the night avenues, flashing its dim lights ahead.

They passed one house on one street a moment later, one house in an entire city of houses that were dark, but this one particular house had all of its

140 electric lights brightly lit, every window a loud yellow illumination, square and warm in the cool darkness.

"That's *my* house," said Leonard Mead.

No one answered him.

The car moved down the empty river-bed streets and off away, leaving the empty streets with the empty sidewalks, and no sound and no motion all the rest of the chill November night. ∾

G WRITER'S MESSAGE
What "crime" has Leonard Mead committed?

---

2. **punch-slotted card:** At the time this story was written, cards punched with coded holes were used to feed data into computers.

3. **Regressive Tendencies:** habits of acting in ways that belong to an earlier stage of human development, such as childhood.

Comprehension

1. **Recall** Describe the city where Leonard Mead walks in "The Pedestrian."

2. **Clarify** Why does Mead seem especially suspicious to the police car?

3. **Clarify** In "Primal Screen," what does Goodman urge Americans to do?

PENNSYLVANIA
STANDARDS

READING STANDARD
A.1.6.1 Identify and/or analyze
intended purpose

Literary Analysis

4. **Analyze Support** In "Primal Screen," Goodman claims that the **habit** of television watching is a more serious problem than the content of the programs. What evidence does she use to support this claim?

5. **Synthesize** The title of Goodman's essay, "Primal Screen," is a **pun,** or a play on words. It refers to primal scream therapy, a type of treatment in which patients scream to vent frustrations. Why do you think Goodman titled her column "Primal Screen"?

6. **Make Judgments** Of Leonard Mead's several responses to the police car, which do you think gets him into the most trouble? Why?

7. **Draw Conclusions About Writer's Message** Reread lines 79–83 in "The Pedestrian." Bradbury uses **imagery** and **figurative language** to describe the people of the future. In describing the future, what does he imply about the people of today?

Comparing Across Genres

Reflect on Your Purpose Now that you have read each selection, consider whether you have discovered enough similarities and differences in the writers' messages to compare and contrast them. If so, write your observations on a chart like the one shown. If not, reread the selections to gather more evidence and then fill in the chart.

Points of Comparison	In the Essay	In the Short Story
What is the writer's focus?	what television watching is doing to family life	what television is doing to American society in general
What problems are identified or portrayed?		
What solutions are recommended or suggested?		
What methods are used to convey the message?		

Writing for Assessment

1. READ THE PROMPT

In writing assessments, you will often be asked to compare and contrast two works that are similar in some way, such as the two examples of social criticism that you have just read. You are now going to practice writing an essay that involves this type of comparison.

PROMPT

Writers sometimes use literature to target faults or alarming trends in society. Consider Goodman's "Primal Screen" and Bradbury's "The Pedestrian." In a four- or five-paragraph essay, compare and contrast these works as examples of social criticism, identifying each writer's message and the techniques used to convey it. In your opinion, which work makes a stronger case? Support your analysis with details from the two works.

◀ **STRATEGIES IN ACTION**

1. I need to summarize each **writer's message**.
2. I have to identify the **methods** each writer uses to convey his or her message.
3. I need to determine the **similarities and differences** between the messages and methods.
4. I need to **evaluate** which message is more powerful or persuasive and **explain why**.

2. PLAN YOUR WRITING

- Review the chart you filled out for "Primal Screen" and "The Pedestrian" on page 648.
- Using your chart, find examples for the points you wish to develop in your essay. If necessary, review the selections again to look for more examples.
- Create an outline to organize your ideas.

3. DRAFT YOUR RESPONSE

Introduction Introduce the topic—literature as a tool of social criticism—and then explain that you will be comparing an essay and a short story, both on the subject of television viewing. Be sure to include the title and author of each work.

Body Use your outline to develop the key points of your essay. In one paragraph, for example, you might compare and contrast the solution each writer offers. Within each paragraph you write, give specific details to back up your points.

Conclusion Wrap up your essay with a restatement of your main idea and a brief summary of your main points.

Revision Check your use of signal words—such as *similarly, also, like, but,* and *while*—to make sure that your comparisons and contrasts are clear.

Writing Workshop

Persuasive Speech

As you have seen in this unit, persuasive words can be powerful. They can change people's minds, convince people to take action, or even make a difference in the world. A good way to give your words this power is to write and deliver a heartfelt and well-reasoned speech about a topic that's important to you. To take the first steps to your personal podium, follow the **Writer's Road Map.**

WRITER'S ROAD MAP

Persuasive Speech

WRITING PROMPT 1

Writing from the Real World Sometimes an issue in your life or your community affects you so deeply that you must speak out to persuade others to see your point of view. Write a persuasive speech in which you attempt to convince your listeners to adopt your opinion or to take the action you propose.

Issues to Explore
- health issues, such as the link between obesity and fast food
- social problems, such as stereotyping
- problems in your community or school

WRITING PROMPT 2

Writing from Literature Choose an issue that was covered in a selection in this unit—an issue that matters to you. Write a persuasive speech in which you respond to the ideas expressed by the writer.

Selections to Explore
- "Primal Screen" (negative effects of television)
- "Testimony Before the Senate" (funding for medical research)

 WRITING TOOLS
For prewriting, revision, and editing tools, visit the **Writing Center** at ClassZone.com.

KEY TRAITS

1. IDEAS
- Clearly identifies the **issue**
- Presents a clear, logical, and forceful **claim,** or position, in a **thesis statement**
- Uses relevant and convincing details to **support** the position
- Anticipates and answers **opposing viewpoints** and counterclaims

2. ORGANIZATION
- Provides a memorable **introduction** to the issue
- Uses a consistent **organizational pattern**
- Concludes with a **summary** or a **call to action**

3. VOICE
- Uses a **tone** that is appropriate for the audience and purpose

4. WORD CHOICE
- Addresses the **audience** directly and uses **rhetorical devices** such as repetition and parallelism

5. SENTENCE FLUENCY
- Uses effective **sentence types and structures,** such as imperative sentences

6. CONVENTIONS
- Employs **correct grammar and usage**

Part 1: Analyze a Student Model

WRITING STANDARD
1.4.11.C Write persuasive pieces

Sara Jenkins
Danford High School

Bring Back Our Snacks

Superintendent Klein and other administrators, imagine how it would feel to arrive at your office and find the desk missing. You would probably be surprised and try to get it back. That's how I felt when I discovered that our school's three vending machines were removed
5 recently without warning. Let me explain why I believe the vending machines are important to students and should be brought back.

For **S**tarters—**S**—We need **S**nacks during **S**chool. High school students are growing rapidly and burn up enormous numbers of calories. Our half-hour lunch period is barely enough time to buy a hot lunch or
10 gulp down a sandwich, and we're hungry again before the next bell. We need quick energy to keep going and doing our best. As a result, we often go to the snack machines between classes. I did an informal survey of my homeroom and found that 67 percent of those students buy snacks or drinks from the vending machines at least once a day.

15 You might argue that the salty, fatty foods and sweet drinks available in the vending machines provide only empty calories—no real nutrition. It's hard to disagree with that point when reports of obesity in young people fill the media. There's a better solution, though: make nuts, dried fruit, or trail mix available instead of chips and candy; and fruit juice,
20 milk, or water instead of soft drinks. I'm not a junk-food junkie, and I don't think other students are either. When the munchies hit, we'd be happy to eat whatever came out of the machines.

Next—**N**—We **N**eed them **N**earby. In fact, snacks have to be available inside the school, since students aren't allowed to leave the
25 building during the day. You might say that students have to provide for

KEY TRAITS IN ACTION

Addresses the **audience** directly in an effective **introduction.** Presents the **claim** in a clear **thesis statement.**

Uses the letters of *snack* as a memorable **organizational pattern.**

Uses facts and a statistic as relevant and convincing **support.**

Anticipates and answers **opposing viewpoints** and counterclaims. Varied and sophisticated **sentence structures** help hold reader interest.

The writer introduces each of her points in a similar way. This parallelism is an effective **rhetorical device.**

their own nutritional needs. My response is that there's barely room in our lockers for our books, gym clothes, and jackets. Many of us have even started buying our lunches rather than eating the squashed remains of something brought from home.

30   **A**nd now—**A**—We can **A**ct like responsible **A**dults. I know that there have been some concerns about students using the vending-machine area as a hangout between classes. This loitering has led to congestion in the hallways and an increase in tardiness. If the machines were reinstalled, I'm sure students would agree to stop using the
35   snack center as a meeting place. We would remind each other of this condition and make a special effort to not be late to class.

> Direct, serious **tone** shows awareness of and respect for the audience.

There also have been several instances of vandalism to the machines. Only a small number of students are responsible for these acts, and it's unfair for the rest of us to be punished on their account. One solution
40   to this problem would be to assign a hall monitor to the snack center. Since monitors are on duty throughout the building, one could easily be reassigned.

> Includes specific details and logic to **support** the statement.

Coming to—**C**—We **C**are and deserve to be **C**onsulted. The removal of the vending machines affects students directly, and we
45   should have been asked to take part in the decision-making process. How can we develop good judgment and learn to accept responsibility for our decisions if we aren't given the opportunity to practice those skills? People tend to live up to others' expectations of them, and if we aren't trusted, we may never become trustworthy. Bringing back the
50   vending machines would show your confidence in students and, at the same time, help us build self-confidence.

And finally—**K**—We **K**now you respect us and will **K**eep our best interests in mind. All spelled out, that means: Bring back our **SNACK**s.

> Effective **summary** makes a clear **call to action** and echoes the title. Imperative sentence at the end makes the message more forceful.

2

Part 2: Apply the Writing Process

WRITING STANDARD
1.5.11.A.1 Identify topic, task and audience

PREWRITING

What Should I Do?	**What Does It Look Like?**

1. Analyze the prompt.
Look back at the two prompts on page 650. Choose the one that appeals to you more. (Circle) words that tell you what kind of writing you will be doing. Underline details that help you focus your topic. Think about your **purpose** and **audience.** Who are you writing for, and why?

▶ **WRITING PROMPT** Sometimes an issue in your life or your community affects you so deeply that you must speak out to persuade others to see your point of view. Write a persuasive speech in which you attempt to convince your listeners to adopt your opinion or to take the action you propose.

I'm supposed to write a speech convincing listeners to agree with me about an issue that's important to me.

2. Zero in on your topic and purpose.
Make a list of situations that you feel strongly about. It's not enough to come up with a meaningful topic. You need to decide what change you want to advocate and what person or group you want to convince.

▶ *Issues:*
• Drivers talking on cell phones
• Proposed skate-park
• Removal of school vending machines

Goal: Return of vending machines
Audience: Superintendent and school administrators

3. Determine your supporting points.
List as many reasons for your position as you can. Ask yourself: What makes this issue worth debating? What are some possible solutions?

TIP Don't forget to consider opposing views. List arguments against your position and possible answers to those arguments.

▶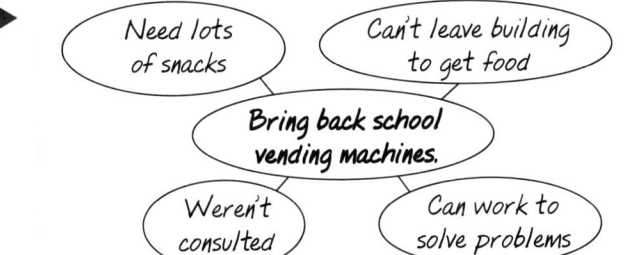

4. Gather support for your position.
Look for facts, statistics, expert opinions, anecdotes, and logical arguments to lend weight to each supporting point. Think about how much audience members already know about the issue and what information they will need.

▶ *Supporting point: Students need lots of snacks.*
Details:
1. Students growing rapidly, burn calories
2. Lunch period only 30 minutes
3. Lots of students used machines. (How many students used them? Survey homeroom to find out.)

What Should I Do?	What Does It Look Like?
1. Craft a strong, clear thesis statement. Explain the issue, your position on it (in other words, your **claim**), and what you want your listeners to do about it. Be as clear and as forceful as you can. The working thesis statement will help guide your writing, but feel free to modify it as you go along.	▶ **Working thesis:** I was surprised that our school's three vending machines were removed recently without warning. Let me explain why I believe the vending machines are important to students and should be brought back.

2. Anticipate objections by others. Don't leave your listeners with unanswered questions. By anticipating and clearly answering opposing viewpoints, you have a much greater chance of persuading others to agree with you. Use a chart to think through opposing arguments and your answers.

▶

Who might object?	Possible objections	My arguments
School administrators	1. Snack foods lack nutrition.	1. Nuts, dried fruit, juice are fine.
	2. Students can bring snacks from home.	2. Lockers are too small.
	3. Students loiter near snack machines.	3. Students agree to avoid using that area as a meeting place.
	4. Machines have been vandalized.	4. Assign a hall monitor.

3. Make your points memorable. Because this is a speech, listeners hear your ideas only once. This writer began with an analogy (a point-by-point comparison of two things) directed at her target audience. Then she organized her essay in a way that makes each point easy to remember.

TIP Words with repeated sounds at the beginning (alliteration) or at the end (rhyme) can help make your message memorable.

▶ **Analogy**

Superintendent Klein and other administrators, imagine how it would feel to arrive at your office and find the desk missing. You would probably be surprised and try to get it back. That's how I felt when I discovered that our school's three vending machines were removed recently without warning.

Parallelism

For Starters—S—We need Snacks during School.

Next—N—We Need them Nearby.

REVISING AND EDITING

What Should I Do?	*What Does It Look Like?*

1. Use emotional appeals wisely.

- Ask a peer reader which of your reasons are strongest and which are weakest.

- <u>Underline</u> words or phrases that are so emotionally charged or extreme that they may cause audience members to dismiss your entire message.

- Replace extreme statements with appeals supported by sound reasoning and evidence.

See page 656: Emotional Appeals

▶ ~~If you don't bring back the vending machines, we will continue to go hungry, day after day. How can you treat us so <u>cruelly</u>?~~ You might say that students have to provide for their own nutritional needs. My response is that there's barely room in our lockers for our books, gym clothes, and jackets. Many of us have even started buying our lunches rather than eating the squashed remains of something brought from home.

2. Shore up your support.

- Put [brackets] around statements of your ideas.

- Review each statement. Is it supported with explanations and details? If not, add facts, statistics, expert opinions, or reasons.

▶ [We need quick energy to keep going and doing our best. As a result, we often go to the snack machines between classes.]

I did an informal survey of my homeroom and found that 67 percent of those students buy snacks or drinks from the vending machines at least once a day.

3. Make it clear, so they will hear.

- Read your speech aloud to identify sentences that are boring or bland.

- Use rhyme, repetition, parallelism, or other devices to help listeners remember your main points.

▶ For Starters—**S**—We need **S**nacks during **S**chool. ~~The snacks have to be where we can buy them when we get hungry.~~

Next—**N**—We **N**eed them **N**earby.

4. Sharpen your conclusion.

- Highlight your conclusion. Reread it, asking yourself: Does it summarize what has come before? Is it concise? Does it suggest a course of action?

- Edit your sentences so they summarize your points forcefully and call for action.

▶ And finally—**K**—We **K**now you respect us and will **K**eep our best interests in mind. ~~Students (not administrators, staff, or teachers) use the vending machines, and you removed them when we weren't looking.~~

All spelled out, that means: Bring back our **SNACK**s.

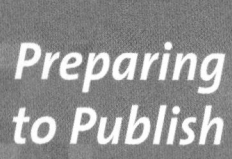

Preparing to Publish

Persuasive Speech

Apply the Rubric

A strong persuasive speech . . .

☑ has a strong introduction that identifies the issue and grabs listeners' attention

☑ explains the writer's claim in a clear, logical thesis statement

☑ addresses the audience directly in an appropriate tone

☑ supports ideas with convincing details, and answers opposing viewpoints

☑ uses persuasive techniques and rhetorical devices

☑ has a consistent organizational pattern

☑ concludes with a concise summary of ideas and a memorable call for action

☑ uses effective sentence types and structures

Ask a Peer Reader

- How would you restate my position on this issue?

- What details are needed to make my case stronger?

- Which of my persuasive techniques are best? Why?

Emotional Appeals

It's fine to try to create strong feelings when you deliver your speech. However, make sure your appeals don't make audience members feel manipulated.

- *Overemotional appeal to pity:* Do you want us to starve?

- *Effective appeal to pity:* Our half-hour lunch period is barely enough time to gulp down a sandwich, and we're hungry again before the next bell.

See page 596 for information on persuasive techniques.

Check Your Grammar

- Make sure that modifiers are placed near the words they modify. Misplaced modifiers confuse listeners and lessen the impact of your message.

> *I know that there have been some concerns (between classes) about students using the vending-machine area as a hangout. This loitering has led to congestion (and an increase in tardiness (in the hallways).*

See page R59: Misplaced Modfiers

Writing Online

PUBLISHING OPTIONS
For publishing options, visit the **Writing Center** at ClassZone.com.

ASSESSMENT PREPARATION
For writing and grammar assessment practice, go to the **Assessment Center** at ClassZone.com.

SPEAKING AND LISTENING

Presenting a Persuasive Speech

The hard part is over: you've already written a persuasive speech on an issue you feel strongly about. Now put your words into action by presenting them to an audience.

Planning the Speech

1. **Review your audience and purpose.** Remind yourself why you wrote your speech. Put yourself in the place of the audience members as you consider what information should be stressed and how.

2. **Support your argument with visuals.** Sara Jenkins used a poster like the one shown when she presented her speech. She also could have used a photograph of crowded lockers or a graph showing students' use of vending machines. Consider using posters, charts, graphs, or photographs to enhance your message. Mark your speech so you know when to refer to them.

> **S** — We need **S**nacks during **S**chool.
>
> **N** — We **N**eed them **N**earby.
>
> **A** — We can **A**ct like responsible **A**dults.
>
> **C** — We deserve to be **C**onsulted.
>
> **K** — We **K**now you respect us.

3. **Take the time to rehearse.** Practice your speech alone and with friends and family. In the first case, stand in front of a mirror to see yourself as your audience will see you. In the second case, ask your audience for feedback.

Delivering the Speech

1. **Be deliberate in your delivery.** Speak slowly and pause after key ideas to allow the audience time to take in the information. Sara Jenkins paused after each of the main points shown in the poster.

2. **Connect with your audience.** When you address objections and counterclaims, make eye contact with audience members who may not agree with your ideas.

3. **Pay attention to audience reactions.** Make a mental note of techniques that do—or don't—go over well. Use what you learn this time to improve your next persuasive speech.

See page R79: Evaluate a Persuasive Speech

Reading Comprehension

ASSESS
The practice test items on the next few pages match skills listed on the Unit Goals page (page 593) and addressed throughout this unit. Taking this practice test will help you assess your knowledge of these skills and determine your readiness for the Unit Test.

REVIEW
After you take the practice test, your teacher can help you identify any skills you need to review.

• Elements of Argument
• Persuasive Techniques
• Rhetorical Devices
• Fact and Opinion
• Summarize Main Idea
• Specialized and Technical Vocabulary
• Dictionary
• Imperative Sentences
• Parallelism

ASSESSMENT ONLINE
For more assessment practice and test-taking tips, go to the **Assessment Center** at **ClassZone.com**.

DIRECTIONS *Read the following selection and then answer the questions.*

Appearances Are Destructive

Mark Mathabane

As public schools reopen for the new year, strategies to curb school violence will once again be hotly debated. Installing metal detectors and hiring security guards will help, but the experience of my two sisters makes a compelling case for greater use of dress codes as a way to protect students and promote learning.

Shortly after my sisters arrived here from South Africa I enrolled them at the local public school. I had great expectations for their educational experience. Compared with black schools under apartheid, American schools are Shangri-Las, with modern textbooks, school buses, computers, libraries, lunch programs and dedicated teachers.

10 But despite these benefits, which students in many parts of the world only dream about, my sisters' efforts at learning were almost derailed. They were constantly taunted for their homely outfits. A couple of times they came home in tears. In South Africa students were required to wear uniforms, so my sisters had never been preoccupied with clothes and jewelry.

They became so distraught that they insisted on transferring to different schools, despite my reassurances that there was nothing wrong with them because of what they wore.

I have visited enough public schools around the country to know that my sisters' experiences are not unique. In schools in many areas, brand names are
20 more familiar names to students than Zora Neale Hurston, Shakespeare and Faulkner. Many students seem to pay more attention to what's on their bodies than in their minds.

Teachers have shared their frustrations with me at being unable to teach those students willing to learn because classes are frequently disrupted by other students ogling themselves in mirrors, painting their fingernails, combing their hair, shining their gigantic shoes, or comparing designer labels on jackets, caps and jewelry.

The fiercest competition among students is often not over academic achievements, but over who dresses most expensively. And many students now
30 measure parental love by how willing their mothers and fathers are to pamper them with money for the latest fads in clothes, sneakers and jewelry.

Those parents without the money to waste on such meretricious extravagances are considered uncaring and cruel. They often watch in dismay and helplessness as their children become involved with gangs and peddle drugs to raise the money.

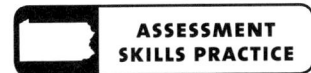

When students are asked why they attach so much importance to clothing, they frequently reply that it's the cool thing to do, that it gives them status and earns them respect. And clothes are also used to send other messages, with girls thinking that the only things that make them attractive to boys are skimpy
40 dresses and gaudy looks, rather than intelligence and academic excellence.

The argument by civil libertarians that dress codes infringe on freedom of expression is misleading. We observe dress codes in nearly every aspect of our lives without any diminution of our freedoms—as demonstrated by flight attendants, bus drivers, postal employees, high school bands, military personnel, sports teams, Girl and Boy Scouts, employees of fast-food chains, restaurants and hotels.

In many countries where students outperform their American counterparts academically, school dress codes are observed as part of creating the proper learning environment. Their students tend to be neater, less disruptive in
50 class and more disciplined, mainly because their minds are focused more on learning and less on materialism.

It's time Americans realized that the benefits of safe and effective schools far outweigh any perceived curtailment of freedom of expression brought on by dress codes.

Comprehension

DIRECTIONS *Answer these questions about the selection.*

1. What is the author's main claim in this selection?

   A Teens demand too much money from their parents.

   B Schools need metal detectors and guards to curb school violence.

   C Dress codes will help protect students and promote learning.

   D American schools offer more advantages than South African schools.

2. In lines 10–19, the author supports his claim by

   A stating personal experience and observation

   B citing statistics about transfer students

   C using logical reasoning and deductions

   D countering the opposition's objections

3. Which of the following statements is an opinion?

   A "Shortly after my sisters arrived here from South Africa, I enrolled them at the local public school."

   B "A couple of times they came home in tears."

   C "I have visited enough public schools around the country. . . ."

   D "Many students seem to pay more attention to what's on their bodies than in their minds."

4. Which rhetorical device is used in the following sentence from lines 21–22?

   Many students seem to pay more attention to what's on their bodies than in their minds.

   A repetition

   B parallelism

   C analogy

   D rhetorical question

5. Which sentence summarizes lines 10–17?

   A The sisters often came home in tears from their new American school.

   B In South Africa, wearing uniforms improves the educational experience.

   C Being teased about their clothes ruined the sisters' experience.

   D There was nothing wrong with the sisters' clothing.

6. In lines 23–27, what new source of evidence does the author introduce to support his claim?

   A teachers

   B students

   C parents

   D polls

7. Parallelism is used in lines 23–27 to emphasize the

   A differences in the clothing students wear to school

   B relationship between the teachers and the students

   C disruption caused by the students' behavior

   D items with designer labels worn by the students

8. Which word in lines 28–29 gives strong emotional meaning to the author's opinion?

   A fiercest

   B academic

   C competition

   D expensively

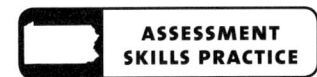

9. Which sentence summarizes the relationship between students and their parents, according to the author in lines 28–31?

   A Students and their parents care more about clothes than about grades.

   B Parents will do anything to help their children become popular.

   C Parents reward their children when they do well in school.

   D Students judge their parents by how much money the parents give them.

10. What persuasive technique does the author use in lines 32–35?

   A emotional (vanity)

   B emotional (fear)

   C association (bandwagon)

   D association ("plain folks")

11. What opposing argument does the author anticipate in lines 41–46?

   A Our opinions affect how we view wearing uniforms.

   B Our freedoms are not affected by dress codes.

   C Dress codes reduce our freedom of expression.

   D Many people observe dress codes for their jobs.

12. What evidence does the author present to counter the opposing argument in lines 41–46?

   A Too many people are forced to follow dress codes for their jobs.

   B People throughout our society follow dress codes without losing their freedom of expression.

   C Civil libertarians have a fundamental misunderstanding of what freedom of expression means.

   D Dress codes diminish our freedoms not just in school but also in sports and business.

13. Which of the following ideas from lines 47–51 is the author's opinion?

   A In many countries, students perform better than Americans in school subjects.

   B Schools in many countries of the world have dress codes.

   C American students have academic counterparts in other countries.

   D Students in other countries learn well because their minds are focused less on materialism.

Open-Ended Items

14. List three facts that the author uses in the essay to support his claim. List two opinions that the author uses to support his claim.

15. Give two examples of loaded language from the essay. Then replace each one with a neutral word or phrase.

16. Summarize the essay in your own words. Be sure to identify the claim, or main idea. Include reasons and evidence the author gives to support his claim.

GO ON

Vocabulary

DIRECTIONS *Use context clues and your knowledge of specialized vocabularies to answer the following questions.*

> Compared with black schools under apartheid, American schools are <u>Shangri-Las</u>, with modern textbooks, school buses, computers, libraries, lunch programs and dedicated teachers.

1. What is the most likely meaning of *Shangri-Las* in lines 7–8 of the essay?

   A flawed institutions

   B average schools

   C ideal places

   D suitable locales

> The argument by <u>civil libertarians</u> that dress codes infringe on <u>freedom of expression</u> is misleading.

2. What does the term *civil libertarians* mean in line 41 of the essay?

   A writers and artists who express themselves

   B designers of casual and professional clothing

   C enforcers of school safety requirements

   D protectors of individuals' rights

3. There are many ways of defining the term *freedom of expression.* Choose the definition that best defines *freedom of expression* as it is used in lines 41–42.

   A freedom to dress as one pleases

   B freedom to speak or write anything

   C freedom from spending money on outfits

   D freedom from popularity contests

DIRECTIONS *Read this dictionary entry and answer the questions that follow.*

> **benefit** (bĕn´ə-fĭt) *noun* **1.** An advantage. **2.** A payment made or an entitlement available in accordance with a wage agreement, an insurance policy, or a public assistance program. **3.** A fund-raising public entertainment. **4.** *Archaic* A kindly deed. *verb* **1.** To be helpful or advantageous to. **2.** To derive benefit; profit. [From Latin *benefactum,* good deed.] **Synonyms:** *noun:* advantage, subsidy, assistance; *verb:* capitalize, profit, help, gain

4. Which definition best matches the meaning of the word *benefits* as it is used in line 10 of the essay?

   A noun definition 1

   B noun definition 2

   C noun definition 3

   D noun definition 4

5. Which word is a synonym for the word *benefits* in the following sentence?

   They bought groceries with the emergency government <u>benefits</u>.

   A gains   C profit

   B assistance   D advantage

6. In which sentence is the word *benefits* used as a verb?

   A We are organizing three benefits to raise money for the zoo.

   B Everyone benefits when students love learning and are focused on academic success.

   C The benefits of good health should be taught to children at a young age.

   D The company's profits boosted the benefits that all of the employees received.

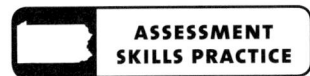
ASSESSMENT
SKILLS PRACTICE

Grammar & Style

DIRECTIONS *Read this passage and answer the questions that follow.*

(1) Why are people so afraid of stepping outside their social circles? (2) Every day in class, I notice how students congregate in separate groups. (3) Cheerleaders are in one corner. (4) There are art students who are in another corner. (5) Even though we might have different interests, that doesn't mean we can't try to find some common ground. (6) Breaking out of your mold can be good for you. (7) I recommend that you try speaking to someone you don't usually speak to. (8) Just go up to someone and start a conversation. (9) You might find that it's not so bad. (10) It's even possible that the two of you might like each other.

1. Choose how to rewrite sentence 4 so that its structure is parallel to that of sentence 3.
   A Art students, who are in another group, also stand in a corner.
   B Art students are in another corner.
   C In another corner are art students.
   D Art students, who are in another corner, are in a different group.

2. Choose how to rewrite sentence 6 as an imperative sentence.
   A Sometimes it's good to break out of your mold.
   B Why not break out of your mold?
   C Molds are meant to be broken.
   D Break out of your mold.

3. Choose how to rewrite sentence 7 as an imperative sentence.
   A Speaking to someone you don't usually speak to is a good idea.
   B What's wrong with speaking to someone you don't usually speak to?
   C Try speaking to someone you don't usually speak to.
   D Why don't you try speaking to someone you don't usually speak to?

4. Choose how to rewrite sentence 10 so that its structure is parallel to that of sentence 9.
   A You might even find that the two of you like each other!
   B That the two of you might like each other is a possibility.
   C How could you not like each other?
   D It would be impossible that the two of you wouldn't like each other.

STOP

UNIT 6
Great Reads

Ideas for Independent Reading

How do you persuade others that your ideas have value? Read the following works to see how various individuals made their case.

Can a dream change the world?

Mountains Beyond Mountains
by Tracy Kidder

Kidder writes about Dr. Paul Farmer, whose dream of medical care as a human right—untied to financial status—has taken root in places such as Haiti, Russian and Peruvian prisons, and inner-city Boston.

Eco-Heroes: Twelve Tales of Environmental Victory
by Aubrey Wallace

These 12 crusaders had dreams of saving forests, cleaning up toxic waste, and preventing the slaughter of dolphins. All 12 have motivated others to dream and to work for change.

Eyes on the Prize: America's Civil Rights Years, 1954–1965
by Juan Williams

The dream to end Jim Crow segregation has deep roots. This book chronicles *Brown v. Board of Education,* the Montgomery bus boycott, sit-ins and freedom rides, and the courage of those engaged in the struggle.

How do you sell an idea?

Silent Spring
by Rachel Carson

In this groundbreaking book, Carson brought to the world's attention the fragility of our modern-day environment.

Still Me
by Christopher Reeve

Severely paralyzed in an accident, popular actor Reeve wrote and spoke eloquently about his condition. His activism led to increased research and breakthroughs in treating spinal cord injuries.

How the Other Half Lives
by Jacob Riis

Riis's writings and photographs of the poor in New York tenements of the late 19th century led to social reforms in the areas of housing and fire prevention.

Is privacy an illusion?

The Right to Privacy
by Ellen Alderman and Caroline Kennedy

The authors present an overview of the ways in which our privacy has been invaded over the years, including the recent threats to privacy posed by cyberspace.

The Firm
by John Grisham

In this contemporary thriller, Mitch McDeere begins his legal career with a firm that seems to offer him everything—until he and his wife learn that their every move is under surveillance.

1984
by George Orwell

This novel portrays a chilling vision of a totalitarian society, a world in which the government can control individual thought and even reality itself.

7

Special Effects

**THE LANGUAGE
OF POETRY**

What POEMS *do you remember?*

Snippets of a nursery rhyme, verses from a favorite bedtime story, lines from an old favorite song or commercial jingle—chances are that the words from these **poems** linger in your memory because you have heard them over and over again.

ACTIVITY Write down the words to one of your favorite poems. Choose from poems you have read, heard, or memorized. Answer the following questions:

- What is your poem about?
- Has it been set to music?
- Are there any words that rhyme or repeat?
- Do you picture anything when you read or hear the poem?
- What is your favorite part of the poem?

Discuss with your classmates the qualities your favorites have in common.

MOTHER GOOSE
NURSERY RHYMES

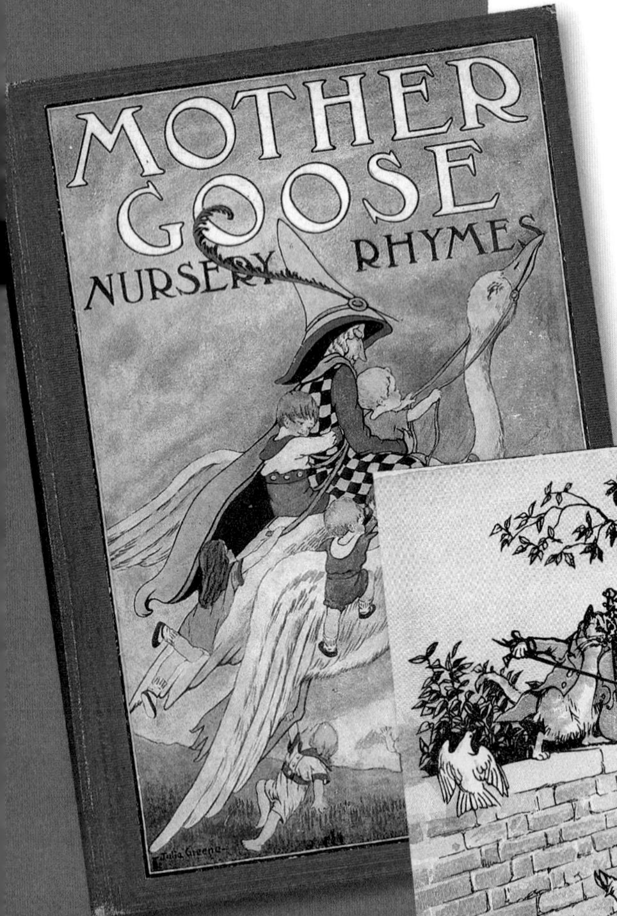

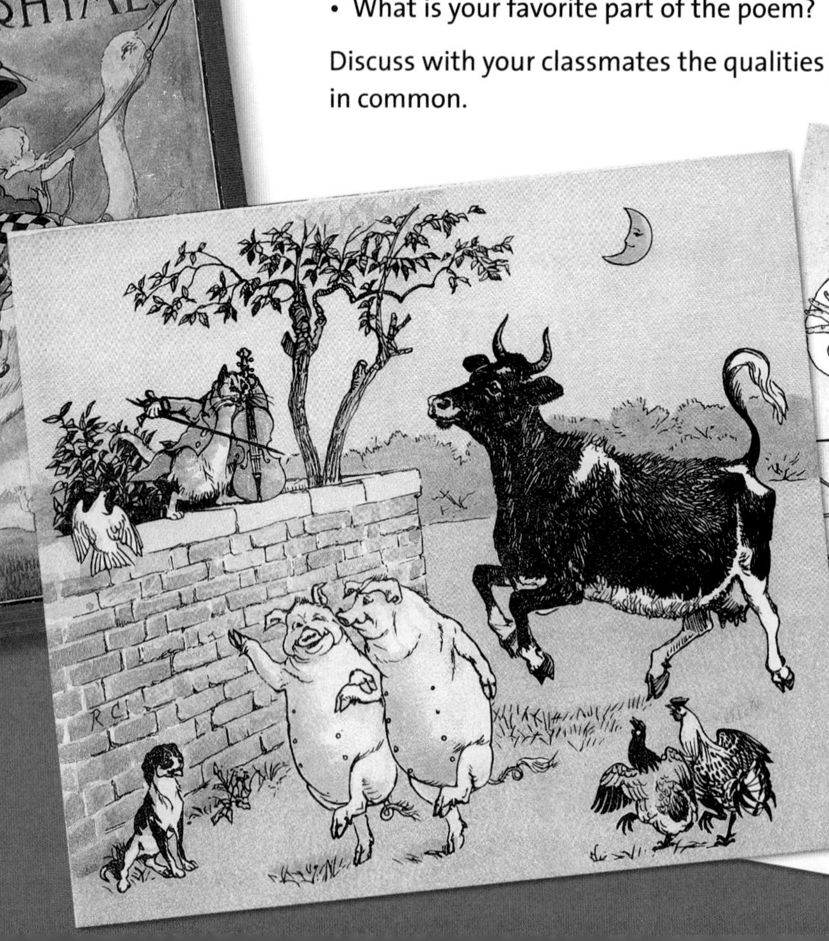

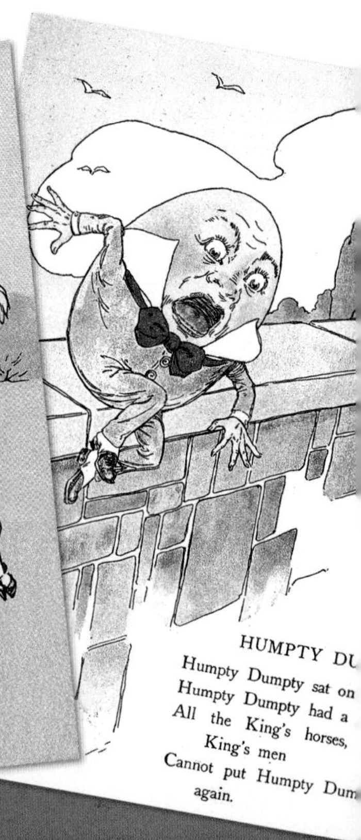

HUMPTY DU
Humpty Dumpty sat on
Humpty Dumpty had a
All the King's horses,
King's men
Cannot put Humpty Dum
again.

Online **LITERATURE** CLASSZONE.COM

Literature and Reading Center
Writing Center
Vocabulary Center

PENNSYLVANIA STANDARDS

Preview Unit Goals

LITERARY ANALYSIS
- Recognize characteristics of a variety of forms of poetry, including lyric poetry, elegy, concrete poetry, ode, ballad, dramatic monologue, sonnet, free verse
- Analyze form, including line and stanza
- Analyze figurative language, including metaphor, simile, and personification; analyze imagery
- Analyze sound devices, including repetition, alliteration, assonance, onomatopoeia, rhyme, rhythm, and meter
- Analyze speaker

READING
- Use reading strategies, including visualizing and connecting
- Make inferences
- Synthesize ideas from multiple sources; paraphrase

WRITING AND GRAMMAR
- Write a personal response
- Support key ideas with details and quotations
- Use descriptive language effectively; write concisely
- Use participles and participial phrases
- Use infinitives and infinitive phrases

SPEAKING, LISTENING, AND VIEWING
- Create a multimedia presentation

ACADEMIC VOCABULARY
- line
- stanza
- figurative language
- sound devices
- speaker
- imagery
- visualize
- synthesize
- paraphrase

The Language of Poetry

The poet Samuel Taylor Coleridge once described poetry as "the best words in their best order." Poets sear images into readers' minds, create unforgettable rhythms, and experiment with poetic forms. Whether they embrace the traditional rules of poetry, play with them, or break them altogether, poets use the techniques of their craft to inspire readers and communicate ideas. Experience these techniques in action by immersing yourself in the poetry of this unit.

PENNSYLVANIA STANDARDS

READING STANDARDS
B.1.1.1.D.2 Evaluate the relationship between theme and other components
B.2.1.2 Analyze figurative language
B.3.3.2 Interpret and/or analyze purpose for text organization and content

Part 1: Form

Poetry is as much about form as it is about language and sound. *Form* refers to a poem's structure, or the way the words are arranged on the page. All poems are made up of series of **lines.** The length of the lines, where they break, and how they are punctuated all contribute to a poem's rhythm and meaning. In many poems, the lines are grouped into **stanzas,** which function like paragraphs in prose. Each stanza plays a part in conveying the overall message of a poem.

Poems come in a variety of forms, but they are usually talked about in terms of two categories—traditional and organic.

TRADITIONAL

Characteristics
- follows fixed rules, such as a specified number of lines
- has a regular pattern of rhythm and/or rhyme

▼

Forms
epic, ode, ballad, sonnet, haiku, limerick

▼

Example
Surgeons must be very careful
When they take the knife!
Underneath their fine incisions
Stirs the Culprit—*Life!*

—by Emily Dickinson

ORGANIC

Characteristics
- does not follow established rules for form
- does not have a regular pattern of rhythm and may not rhyme at all
- may use unconventional spelling, punctuation, and grammar

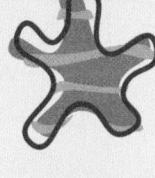

▼

Forms
free verse, concrete poetry

▼

Example
we're everyanything more than believe
(with a spin
leap
alive we're alive)
we're wonderful one times one

—from "If Everything Happens That Can't Be Done" by E. E. Cummings

---

MODEL 1: TRADITIONAL FORM

For centuries, poets have written sonnets that explore everything from unrequited love to the mysteries of nature. There are several types of sonnets, but all of them have 14 lines and are written in a strict pattern of rhythm and rhyme. Read this poem, which is a **Petrarchan sonnet,** to determine the characteristics of this particular form.

Pretty Words

Poem by **Elinor Wylie**

Poets make pets of pretty, docile words:
I love smooth words, like gold-enamelled fish
Which circle slowly with a silken swish,
And tender ones, like downy-feathered birds:
5 Words shy and dappled, deep-eyed deer in herds,
Come to my hand, and playful if I wish,
Or purring softly at a silver dish,
Blue Persian kittens, fed on cream and curds.

I love bright words, words up and singing early;
10 Words that are luminous in the dark, and sing;
Warm lazy words, white cattle under trees;
I love words opalescent, cool, and pearly,
Like midsummer moths, and honied words like bees,
Gilded and sticky, with a little sting.

Close Read

1. How many lines make up the first stanza? How many are in the second stanza?

2. In the first stanza, each group of end-rhyming words is highlighted in the same color. Identify the end-rhyming words in the second stanza.

3. Compare the ideas expressed in the first stanza with those in the second one.

MODEL 2: ORGANIC FORM

Poems written in **free verse,** like the one shown, do not adhere to a regular pattern of rhythm and rhyme.

from **Beware: *Do Not Read This Poem***

Poem by **Ishmael Reed**

the hunger of this poem is legendary
it has taken in many victims
back off from this poem
it has drawn in yr feet
5 back off from this poem
it has drawn in yr legs
back off from this poem

Close Read

1. Identify three characteristics that make this poem unconventional.

2. Even though the poet does not use punctuation, this poem has a natural rhythm. Read the poem aloud, using the rhythm you think is appropriate.

Part 2: Poetic Elements

For a poet, deciding on a subject and form is just the beginning. Will the poem hum along at a steady beat or charge ahead with a bold rhythm? What images or sounds will convey a mood? Using sound devices and language, poets can convey meaning, make music, and tap into the senses.

SOUND DEVICES

Like music, language has rhythm. In poetry, the pattern of stressed and unstressed syllables in each line is what creates the **rhythm. Rhyme** also enhances the musical quality of a poem. It can occur at the ends of lines as **end rhyme** or within lines as **internal rhyme.**

A regular pattern of rhythm is called a **meter.** A regular pattern of rhyme is called a **rhyme scheme.** Meter is charted in a process called **scansion,** where stressed syllables are marked with a ´ and unstressed syllables with a ˘. A rhyme scheme is charted by assigning a letter of the alphabet to matching end rhymes. Notice how the meter and rhyme scheme are marked in these lines from "A Birthday" by Christina Rossetti:

My̆ hért / ĭs lı́ke / ă sı́ng / ĭng bı́rd	a
Whŏse nést / ĭs ı́n / ă wá/ tĕred shóot:	b
My̆ hért / ĭs lı́ke / ăn áp / plĕ-trée	c
Whŏse bóughs / ăre bént/ wĭth thı́ck / sĕt frúit;	b

Here are some other techniques that poets use to create sound effects.

SOUND DEVICE	EXAMPLE
REPETITION a sound, word, phrase, or line that is repeated for emphasis and unity ▶	back off from this poem it has drawn in yr feet back off from this poem —from "Beware: Do Not Read This Poem"
ALLITERATION repetition of consonant sounds at the beginnings of words ▶	Which circle slowly with a silken swish —from "Pretty Words"
ASSONANCE repetition of vowel sounds in words that don't end with the same consonant ▶	Words shy and dappled, deep-eyed deer in herds —from "Pretty Words"
CONSONANCE repetition of consonant sounds within and at the ends of words ▶	Whose nest is in a watered shoot —from "A Birthday"

MODEL 1: METER

To identify a poem's meter, you have to break each line into smaller units, called feet. A **foot** consists of one stressed syllable and one or two unstressed ones. Look at the type and the number of feet in each line. Then combine the terms listed on the side—for example, **trochaic trimeter** or **iambic pentameter**—to describe what you find. Scan this poem to determine its meter.

METER

TYPES OF FEET
iamb (reSIST)
trochee (ABsent)
spondee (GOAL LINE)

NUMBER OF FEET
trimeter (3)
tetrameter (4)
pentameter (5)

FIRE AND ICE
Poem by **Robert Frost**

Some say the world will end in fire,
Some say in ice.
From what I've tasted of desire
I hold with those who favor fire.
5 But if it had to perish twice,
I think I know enough of hate
To say that for destruction ice
Is also great
And would suffice.

Close Read

1. What is the metrical pattern of the lines in the box?

2. What is the poem's rhyme scheme?

MODEL 2: OTHER SOUND DEVICES

Edgar Allan Poe wrote "The Bells" to experiment with the musical qualities of language. Read this excerpt aloud to get the full impact.

from The Bells
Poem by **Edgar Allan Poe**

Hear the sledges with the bells—
    Silver bells!
What a world of merriment their melody foretells!
    How they tinkle, tinkle, tinkle,
5   In the icy air of night!
    While the stars that oversprinkle
    All the Heavens, seem to twinkle
        With a crystalline delight;
    Keeping time, time, time,
10   In a sort of Runic rhyme, . . .

Close Read

1. Identify four examples of sound devices used in this poem.

2. What effects do these sound devices create? Explain how they add to Poe's description of the bells.

IMAGERY AND FIGURATIVE LANGUAGE

Unlike prose, poetry is very concise: a limited number of words must carry a great deal of meaning. One of the ways poets expand their ability to make meaning is by using imagery and figurative language.

You've already learned how **imagery** in fiction evokes sensory experiences for readers by appealing to the five senses. Poets also use sensory details to illustrate and elaborate on their ideas and feelings. For example, look again at "Fire and Ice" on the preceding page. Robert Frost uses two powerful sensory details—fire and ice—to help you picture the end of the world. Not only can you probably visualize the world engulfed in flames or numbed by ice, but you can also probably imagine what each type of destruction would feel like. These details are enough to spark unsettling images in your mind.

Like imagery, **figurative language** opens up the mind to more than the literal meanings of words. In this example, notice how the figurative expression not only is more descriptive but also conveys a stronger emotion:

Literal: He was angry.

Figurative: He burned with anger.

FIGURATIVE LANGUAGE	EXAMPLE
SIMILE a comparison between two unlike things, containing the words *like*, *as*, or *as if*	My heart is like a singing bird —from "A Birthday"
METAPHOR a comparison between two unlike things without the word *like* or *as*	Poets make pets of pretty, docile words —from "Pretty Words"
PERSONIFICATION a description of an object, an animal, a place, or an idea in human terms	it [this poem] has taken in many victims —from "Beware: Do Not Read This Poem"
HYPERBOLE an exaggeration for emphasis or humorous effect	the hunger of this poem is legendary —from "Beware: Do Not Read This Poem"

MODEL 3: IMAGERY AND FIGURATIVE LANGUAGE

In this poem, the writer uses sensory details and figurative language to acquaint you with a vivid character. As you read, notice the contrasting images of Miss Rosie—what she was and what she has become. Also, pay attention to the poem's **speaker,** the voice that describes the character. How does the speaker's impression of Miss Rosie affect your perception of her?

miss rosie

Poem by **Lucille Clifton**

when i watch you
wrapped up like garbage
sitting, surrounded by the smell
of too old potato peels
5   or
when i watch you
in your old man's shoes
with the little toe cut out
sitting, waiting for your mind
10 like next week's grocery
i say
when i watch you
you wet brown bag of a woman
who used to be the best looking gal in georgia
15 used to be called the Georgia Rose
i stand up
through your destruction
i stand up

Close Read

1. Point out three unusual comparisons and identify them as similes or metaphors. What image of Miss Rosie does this figurative language convey?

2. Find the hyperbole and explain its effect.

3. Reread the boxed lines. What is the speaker's attitude toward Miss Rosie? Explain how it affects your impression of Miss Rosie.

Part 3: Analyze the Literature

Now that you've learned about poetic forms and techniques, you're ready to see how everything works together in two distinctly different love poems.

The first poem is a Shakespearean sonnet, which has a rhyme scheme and organization different from those of the Petrarchan sonnet on page 669. A **Shakespearean sonnet** consists of three **quatrains,** or four-line units, and a final **couplet,** or pair of rhyming lines. Read the sonnet aloud first to understand what it is saying. Then read it again to analyze its poetic elements. What techniques are used to complement and extend the poem's meaning?

NOT IN A SILVER CASKET...

Poem by **Edna St. Vincent Millay**

Not in a silver casket cool with pearls
Or rich with red corundum[1] or with blue,
Locked, and the key withheld, as other girls
Have given their loves, I give my love to you;
5 Not in a lovers'-knot, not in a ring
Worked in such fashion, and the legend plain—
Semper fidelis,[2] where a secret spring
Kennels a drop of mischief for the brain:
Love in the open hand, no thing but that,
10 Ungemmed, unhidden, wishing not to hurt,
As one should bring you cowslips[3] in a hat
Swung from the hand, or apples in her skirt,
I bring you, calling out as children do:
"Look what I have!—And these are all for you."

---

1. **corundum:** an extremely hard mineral, red and blue forms of which are rubies and sapphires.

2. *Semper fidelis Latin:* always faithful.

3. **cowslips:** plants that have fragrant yellow flowers.

Close Read

1. Identify the rhyme scheme of the poem.

2. This poem is written in iambic pentameter. Find and scan two lines that reflect this meter. Then find two lines that vary from the pattern. What is the effect of the change in rhythm?

3. How do the images in lines 1–8 contrast with those in lines 9–12?

Now read this poem, which offers another perspective on love. As you read, notice how the sound devices, figurative language, and form help convey a heartfelt and sincere message.

I AM OFFERING THIS POEM

Poem by **Jimmy Santiago Baca**

I am offering this poem to you,
since I have nothing else to give.
Keep it like a warm coat
when winter comes to cover you,
5 or like a pair of thick socks
the cold cannot bite through,

      I love you,

I have nothing else to give you,
so it is a pot full of yellow corn
10 to warm your belly in winter,
it is a scarf for your head, to wear
over your hair, to tie up around your face,

      I love you,

Keep it, treasure this as you would
15 if you were lost, needing direction,
in the wilderness life becomes when mature;
and in the corner of your drawer,
tucked away like a cabin or hogan[1]
in dense trees, come knocking,
20 and I will answer, give you directions,
and let you warm yourself by this fire,
rest by this fire, and make you feel safe,

      I love you,

It's all I have to give,
25 and all anyone needs to live,
and to go on living inside,
when the world outside
no longer cares if you live or die;
remember,
30   I love you.

---

1. **hogan:** a one-room Navajo building that is used as a dwelling or for ceremonial purposes.

Close Read

1. Is this poem traditional or organic in form? Explain how you can tell.

2. Find four specific sound devices in the poem that give it unity and rhythm.

3. Identify the similes and metaphors in lines 1–12. A simile has been boxed. What qualities of the love poem do these comparisons help to emphasize?

4. Compare what these poems say about love. Cite similarities as well as differences.

My Papa's Waltz
Poem by Theodore Roethke

I Ask My Mother to Sing
Poem by Li-Young Lee

Grape Sherbet
Poem by Rita Dove

Who lives in your MEMORY?

KEY IDEA What are some of your most vivid family **memories?** They might include a raucous pillow fight with your sister or a rained-out picnic with your cousins. These memories can take a special shape in your mind; some might linger as stories to tell, but others might remain simply a series of images. The following poems contain such images, boiled down to their essential qualities.

QUICKWRITE Choose a memory involving someone close to you and write a brief sketch of your recollection. Include sensory details as well as events that present a clear picture of your subject.

● POETIC FORM: LYRIC POETRY

These three poems are all examples of **lyric poetry,** brief poems in which the speakers share personal thoughts and feelings on a subject. In ancient Greek, the word *lyric* referred to a type of poetry that expressed the feelings of a single singer, accompanied by a lyre, a small harplike instrument. Though no longer sung, lyric poems have a lot in common with songs, including

- a sense of rhythm and melody
- imaginative language
- the creation of a single, unified impression

Reading the following poems aloud will help you experience the imagery and the sounds of the language as the poets intended.

● LITERARY ANALYSIS: IMAGERY

One of the most important elements of any poem is its **imagery**—the words and phrases that appeal to one or more of the five senses. In addition to re-creating sensory experiences, however, imagery calls up particular ideas and emotions. In the following lines from "My Papa's Waltz," the imagery appeals to sight and hearing but also suggests certain feelings:

We romped until the pans
Slid from the kitchen shelf

These lines call up a sense of rowdy, out-of-control playtime. As you read, look for other images that evoke strong feelings.

● READING SKILL: MAKE INFERENCES

Lyric poems tend to be very condensed; in many cases, more is suggested than directly stated. It's particularly important, then, to make inferences about their meanings. When you encounter a puzzling line or stanza, think about the ideas and emotions suggested by the images. As you read each poem, write down the images and your inferences on a chart like the one shown.

"Grape Sherbet"		
Image	My Associations	Inference
"[Memorial Day] morning we galloped / through the grassed-over mounds / and named each stone / for a lost milk tooth."	• Memorial Day commemorates the dead. • Grassy mounds and stones are found in cemeteries	They are running through a cemetery.

Author Online

Theodore Roethke: Self-Taught Poet

Theodore Roethke learned to write verse by imitating other poets; he sought inspiration from his notebooks, where he had recorded his thoughts, feelings, and observations. He went on to earn a Pulitzer

Theodore Roethke
1908–1963

Prize and two National Book Awards. He once advised his readers to "listen" to his poems, "for they are written to be heard."

Li-Young Lee: Son of Chinese Exiles

After his parents fled China to escape political persecution, Li-Young Lee's family lived in several Asian countries before arriving in the United States in 1964. After college, Lee began to write poetry—about

Li-Young Lee
born 1957

love, family, and ordinary experiences.

Rita Dove: Poet Laureate

Rita Dove's first attempts as a writer came early: in third or fourth grade, she composed a science-fiction novel based on her classroom spelling lists. Her poetry collections have won many awards, including

Rita Dove
born 1952

a Pulitzer Prize in 1987. From 1993 to 1995, she served as U.S. poet laureate. Asked to name the most important quality for success, Dove replied, "I think that without imagination, we can go nowhere."

 MORE ABOUT THE AUTHOR
For more on these poets, visit the
Literature Center at ClassZone.com.

My Papa's Waltz

THEODORE ROETHKE

The whiskey on your breath
Could make a small boy dizzy;
But I hung on like death:
Such waltzing was not easy.

5 We romped until the pans
Slid from the kitchen shelf;
My mother's countenance[1]
Could not unfrown itself.

The hand that held my wrist
10 Was battered on one knuckle;
At every step you missed
My right ear scraped a buckle.

You beat time on my head
With a palm caked hard by dirt,
15 Then waltzed me off to bed
Still clinging to your shirt. **A**

ANALYZE VISUALS
What are your impressions of the characters depicted in the painting? Cite the details that create this impression.

A LYRIC POETRY
How does the **speaker** feel about his bedtime waltz with his father? Explain why you think as you do.

---

1. **countenance:** face or facial expression.

Detail of *Tender Moments* (2000),
Francks Deceus. Mixed media.
© Francks Deceus/The Bridgeman Art Library.

I Ask My Mother to Sing

LI-YOUNG LEE

Mother and Child by Grand Canal (2000), Hung Liu.
Oil on canvas, 80″ × 80″. Courtesy Rena Bransten Gallery.

She begins, and my grandmother joins her.
Mother and daughter sing like young girls.
If my father were alive, he would play
his accordion and sway like a boat.

5 I've never been in Peking, or the Summer Palace,
nor stood on the great Stone Boat to watch
the rain begin on Kuen Ming Lake, the picnickers
running away in the grass. **B**

But I love to hear it sung;
10 how the waterlilies fill with rain until
they overturn, spilling water into water,
then rock back, and fill with more.

Both women have begun to cry.
But neither stops her song. **C**

B IMAGERY
Reread lines 5–9. How is the **speaker** able to describe images of a place he's never seen? Describe the feelings evoked by the images.

C MAKE INFERENCES
Why do the speaker's mother and grandmother start to cry during their song?

Grape Sherbet

RITA DOVE

The day? Memorial.
After the grill
Dad appears with his masterpiece—
swirled snow, gelled light.
5 We cheer. The recipe's
a secret and he fights
a smile, his cap turned up
so the bib resembles a duck.

That morning we galloped
10 through the grassed-over mounds
and named each stone
for a lost milk tooth. Each dollop
of sherbet, later,
is a miracle,
15 like salt on a melon that makes it sweeter.

Everyone agrees—it's wonderful!
It's just how we imagined lavender
would taste. The diabetic grandmother
stares from the porch,
20 a torch
of pure refusal. **D**

We thought no one was lying
there under our feet,
we thought it
25 was a joke. I've been trying
to remember the taste,
but it doesn't exist.
Now I see why
you bothered,
30 father. **E**

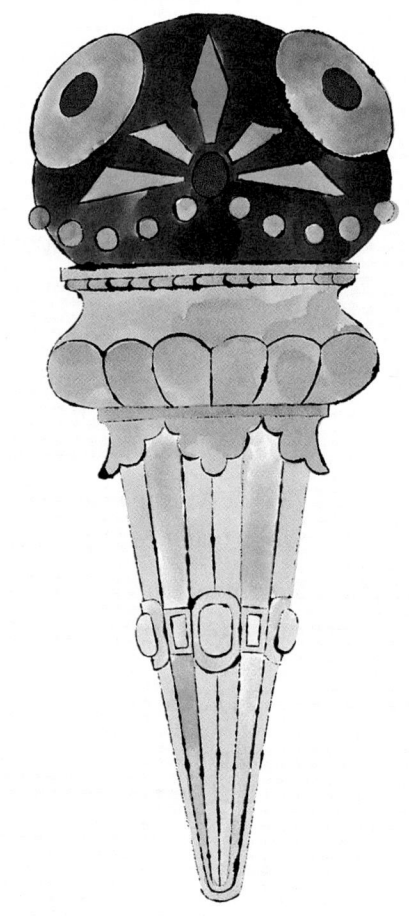

Ice Cream Dessert (1959), Andy Warhol © 2007 Andy
Warhol Foundation for the Visual Arts/Artists Rights
Society (ARS), New York. Photo © Corbis.

D MAKE INFERENCES
Reread lines 18–21. What
does the image of the
grandmother suggest
about her actions?

E LYRIC POETRY
What feeling is the
speaker expressing in
this poem?

Comprehension

1. **Recall** In "My Papa's Waltz," why is the speaker's mother frowning?

2. **Clarify** In "I Ask My Mother to Sing," what is the mother's song about?

3. **Summarize** Describe the setting of "Grape Sherbet" as you visualize it.

PENNSYLVANIA STANDARDS

READING STANDARD
B.2.1.1 Analyze examples of imagery

Literary Analysis

4. **Make Inferences** Review the charts you made as you read. What key inferences helped you understand each poem? What clues did you use to make these inferences?

5. **Compare and Contrast** In "My Papa's Waltz" and "Grape Sherbet," the speakers recall childhood **memories.** How are their experiences with their fathers alike? How are they different?

6. **Interpret Imagery** Reread lines 9–12 in "I Ask My Mother to Sing." What idea is suggested by the image of the water lilies filling with water, spilling it into the lake, and filling up again? Consider the event described in the final stanza.

7. **Analyze Lyric Poetry** Review the definition of lyric poetry on page 677. Then identify the qualities of a lyric poem found in "I Ask My Mother to Sing."

8. **Make Judgments** In "My Papa's Waltz," how do you judge the father's behavior toward the **speaker?** Cite evidence to support your answer.

Literary Criticism

9. **Critical Interpretations** In writing about "My Papa's Waltz," one critic remarked that Roethke reveals "something of his own joy, and bafflement, as the victim of his father's exuberant energy." Do you consider *victim* too harsh a word to describe the boy's part in the evening waltz? Why or why not?

Reading-Writing Connection

Increase your understanding of the family poems by responding to these prompts. Then use **Revision: Grammar and Style** to improve your writing.

WRITING PROMPTS

A. Short Response: Write a Diary Entry

The speaker in "My Papa's Waltz" notices his mother frowning during his waltz with his father. Write **one or two paragraphs** of a diary entry by the mother, recording her reaction to this dance.

B. Extended Response: Analyze Relationships

What message does each poem convey about the relationship between parents and children? Write **three to five paragraphs** discussing the ways this relationship is depicted in the three poems.

SELF-CHECK

A meaningful entry will . . .

• provide images and details about the dance

• describe the mother's thoughts and feelings

A successful analysis will . . .

• clearly state the theme that each poet shares about parents and children

• use quotations and details from the three poems as supporting evidence

REVISION: GRAMMAR AND STYLE

USE DESCRIPTIVE LANGUAGE One way to add interesting details to your writing is by using **participles** and **participial phrases.** A participle is a verb form that acts as an adjective. Present participles, as in "the *crying* baby," end in *-ing*, and past participles, as in "the freshly *washed* car," often end in *-ed*. A participial phrase consists of a participle and its modifiers and complements.

Here is an example of Rita Dove's use of participles in "Grape Sherbet":

> *Dad appears with his masterpiece—*
> *swirled snow, gelled light.* (lines 3–4)

Theodore Roethke uses a participial phrase in his poem "My Papa's Waltz":

> *You beat time on my head*
> *With a palm caked hard by dirt* (lines 13–14)

Notice how the revisions in red use participles to make this first draft more descriptive. Revise your responses to the prompts by using a similar technique.

PENNSYLVANIA STANDARDS

WRITING STANDARD
1.5.11.E Revise writing to improve style, word choice, sentence variety

STUDENT MODEL

Li-Young Lee describes a ~~sweet~~ *touching* scene between mother and son. The son shows an appreciation for his mother's past and the memory of his father *, deceased but not forgotten.*

WRITING TOOLS
For prewriting, revision, and editing tools, visit the **Writing Center** at ClassZone.com.

Spring is like a perhaps hand
Poem by E. E. Cummings

Elegy for the Giant Tortoises
Poem by Margaret Atwood

Today
Poem by Billy Collins

Can you think
OUT OF THE BOX?

PENNSYLVANIA STANDARDS

READING STANDARDS
A.1.6.1 Identify and/or analyze intended purpose
A.1.5.1 Summarize

KEY IDEA Some of the best things in life are those unlike anything ever thought of before. Whether it's a brilliant invention (light bulb), a playful game (lizard boat), or an entertaining story (dog bites man), a new idea makes life more interesting and worthwhile. **Creativity** is a poet's bread and butter; a good poet always looks at things in a new way.

PRESENT With a small group, draw up a design for a new tool. Then share your invention with other groups and explain how it works.

POETIC FORM: ELEGY

An **elegy** is a specific type of lyric poem. In an elegy, the speaker meditates about death, usually as a tribute to one who has recently died. Generally the tone is serious and the diction is formal. The second poem in this lesson is an elegy.

LITERARY ANALYSIS: DICTION

Poetry is known for its concise and exact use of language. When reading poetry, notice the **diction** (the choice of words) and the syntax (the order in which the words appear). For example, in "Today," Billy Collins describes his reaction to a spring day:

> . . . *it made you want to throw*
> *open all the windows in the house*

This particular use of words creates a sense of joy, freedom, and movement—more so than if he had simply said he felt like opening a window. Like any good poet, Collins has chosen his words carefully to create an intended effect. As you read these poems, notice the diction and the effects it creates.

READING STRATEGY: PARAPHRASE

Sometimes poems can be difficult to understand because of an unusual sentence structure. When you **paraphrase** a line or stanza in a poem, you rephrase the poet's words with your own words. Unlike a summary, a paraphrase is not necessarily shorter than the original text; it is simply a recasting of the same ideas. To paraphrase, you should

- find the main ideas and important details
- think of simpler or more familiar ways of saying what the writer has written
- rewrite sentences in standard, subject-verb order

As you read each of the poems that follow, create a chart in which you paraphrase difficult passages.

"Elegy for the Giant Tortoises"

Original Wording	Paraphrase
"on the road where I stand they will materialize, / plodding past me in a straggling line / awkward without water"	They [the tortoises] will appear on the road where I stand, walking slowly by in a scattered line, looking clumsy because they are not in the water.

Author Online

E. E. Cummings: Innovative and Popular Critics who praise Cummings rank him among the most innovative 20th-century poets. Believing in individuality and free expression, Cummings played with language, shaping it to fit his ideas. Though one of the most experimental of poets, he was enormously popular with the general public.

E. E. Cummings
1894–1962

Margaret Atwood: Canada's Treasure Margaret Atwood, a poet, novelist, essayist, and short story writer, has been called "a national heroine of the arts" in her native Canada. Her novels feature female characters searching for identity in a confusing and often threatening world. She is especially popular in Canada, where she has gained the status usually accorded only to movie stars and musicians.

Margaret Atwood
born 1939

Billy Collins: "Most Popular Poet in America" Billy Collins's poetry appeals to a wide and ever-growing audience: high school students, fellow poets, literary critics, and general readers. According to one critic, "With his books selling briskly and his readings packing them in, Mr. Collins is the most popular poet in America."

Billy Collins
born 1941

MORE ABOUT THE AUTHOR
For more on these poets, visit the
Literature Center at ClassZone.com.

Spring is like a perhaps hand

E. E. Cummings

Spring is like a perhaps hand
(which comes carefully
out of Nowhere) arranging
a window, into which people look (while
5 people stare
arranging and changing placing
carefully there a strange
thing and a known thing here) and

changing everything carefully

10 spring is like a perhaps
Hand in a window
(carefully to
and fro moving New and
Old things, while
15 people stare carefully
moving a perhaps
fraction of flower here placing
an inch of air there) and **A**

without breaking anything.

ANALYZE VISUALS
What springlike elements do you find in this image? State your answer in terms of subject matter, color, shape, and texture.

A DICTION
Reread lines 16–18. What do the words *fraction* and *inch* suggest about the concept of spring presented in the poem?

Untitled (2001), Laura Owens. Watercolor, color pencil, and photo on paper, 14″ × 10″. Courtesy Gavin Brown's enterprise, New York (LO 185d).

Elegy for the GIANT TORTOISES

MARGARET ATWOOD

Let others pray for the passenger pigeon
the dodo, the whooping crane,[1] the eskimo:
everyone must specialize

I will confine myself to a meditation
5 upon the giant tortoises
withering finally on a remote island.

I concentrate in subway stations,
in parks, I can't quite see them,
they move to the peripheries of my eyes

10 but on the last day they will be there;
already the event
like a wave travelling shapes vision: **B**

on the road where I stand they will materialize,
plodding past me in a straggling line
15 awkward without water

their small heads pondering
from side to side, their useless armour
sadder than tanks and history,

in their closed gaze ocean and sunlight paralysed,
20 lumbering up the steps, under the archways
toward the square glass altars

where the brittle gods are kept,
the relics of what we have destroyed,
our holy and obsolete symbols. **C**

Sea Turtle (about 1985), Andy Warhol. Synthetic polymer paint and silkscreen ink on canvas, 42″ × 50″. © Art Resource, New York/2007 Andy Warhol Foundation for the Visual Arts/Artists Rights Society (ARS), New York.

B **PARAPHRASE**
Paraphrase lines 7–12. What does "the last day" refer to?

C **ELEGY**
Reread lines 20–24. Notice the religious language—*altars, gods, relics,* and *holy.* Why is such language appropriate in an elegy?

---

1. **the passenger pigeon / the dodo, the whooping crane:** extinct or extremely endangered birds.

TODAY

BILLY COLLINS

If ever there were a spring day so perfect,
so uplifted by a warm intermittent breeze

that it made you want to throw
open all the windows in the house

5 and unlatch the door to the canary's cage,
indeed, rip the little door from its jamb,

a day when the cool brick paths
and the garden bursting with peonies

seemed so etched in sunlight
10 that you felt like taking

a hammer to the glass paperweight
on the living room end table,

releasing the inhabitants
from their snow-covered cottage

15 so they could walk out,
holding hands and squinting

into this larger dome of blue and white, **D**
well, today is just that kind of day.

Flower (1964), Andy Warhol. Screenprint printed on white paper, 23″ × 23″.
© 2007 Andy Warhol Foundation for the Visual Arts/Artists Rights Society
(ARS), New York. © Art Resource, New York.

D DICTION
Reread lines 13–17. What
words does the speaker
use to characterize the
inhabitants of the glass
paperweight? What
sense or feeling is evoked
by this language?

MAGAZINE ARTICLE Several poets in this unit have served as U.S. poet laureate. Read the following article to learn about this honorable and worthwhile position.

U.S. POET LAUREATES

Getting the Word Out

What should be the job of a national poet? Many readers suspect poets of being deliberately mysterious—of placing a hidden meaning behind a smokescreen of random line breaks and cryptic symbols. If that were true, then wouldn't a national poet keep these secrets under lock and key?

Not so. Every year since 1937, the U.S. Library of Congress has appointed a poet laureate to serve as the national poet. Apart from a few official duties, the poet is encouraged to continue to develop his or her own projects as well as promote the general appreciation of poetry. Some poet laureates have taken seriously their mission to dispel the poetry mystique.

Rita Dove, Poet Laureate from 1993–1995, visited schools and gave readings, presenting her complex poems in a down-to-earth manner.

"I really began to think about how poetry can reach every person. . . . If I can reduce the anxiety level of the audience out there and just read the poem as if it's an everyday thing . . . people would come up and say, 'I didn't realize poetry could be like that!' They [are] just terrified, that's all."

Billy Collins, Poet Laureate from 2001–2003, developed "Poetry 180," a website (www.loc.gov/poetry/180) featuring one poem for each day of the school year. He encourages students and teachers to read aloud a poem a day, with the strict rule that the poems are to be simply enjoyed—not analyzed or interpreted. Collins even helped establish a poetry channel for Delta Airlines.

"Well, there is always a temptation just to go to Washington and sit in this office and blow smoke rings for a year while I look out at the Capitol. But because of the excessive activism of my predecessors, it seems that an obligation falls my way to get out and light poetry bonfires and to spread the word of poetry."

After Reading

Comprehension

1. **Recall** When does the speaker of "Elegy for the Giant Tortoises" expect to actually see these reptiles?

2. **Clarify** In "Today," what does "this larger dome" refer to?

3. **Clarify** What is the hand in "Spring is like a perhaps hand" doing?

400-Meter Free Style
Poem by Maxine Kumin

Bodybuilders' Contest
Poem by Wislawa Szymborska

What makes a great COMPETITOR?

PENNSYLVANIA STANDARDS

READING STANDARDS
B.1.2.1 Evaluate connections
B.3.3.2 Analyze text organization and content

KEY IDEA Does a great **competitor's** success mainly rely on natural talent? hard work? luck? The next two poems describe the experiences of two athletes pursuing athletic achievement.

DISCUSS With a partner, discuss your favorite kinds of competition. Then generate a list of qualities you think great competitors have in common. Present your list to other pairs to compare your ideas.

Qualities of a Great Competitor
1.
2.
3.
4.
5.

POETIC FORM: CONCRETE POETRY

Some poets go beyond the usual structural elements of line and stanza to write concrete poems. A **concrete poem** is one in which the poet uses visible shape to create a picture related to the poem's subject. For example, a concrete poem about stars might be written in the shape of a star. One of the poems you're about to read, "400-Meter Free Style," is a concrete poem.

LITERARY ANALYSIS: FORM

In poetry, **form** is the arrangement of words on a page. Poets use form deliberately to organize their thoughts, to help create rhythm, and to emphasize ideas and images. The two basic elements of form in poetry are **lines** and **stanzas.**

- **Lines:** The lines of a poem may be long or short. Poets manipulate line length to emphasize words and ideas and to establish rhythm.
- **Stanzas:** The lines of a poem may be grouped together in clusters known as stanzas. Poets use stanzas to organize important ideas and, in some cases, to develop rhyme schemes.

To understand how form can create a sense of rhythm in a poem, ask yourself the following questions:

- How long are the lines?
- Do the lines rhyme?
- Do the sentences always end at the end of a line?
- How many lines are in each stanza?

The two poems you are about to read have very different forms. "Bodybuilders' Contest" contains **couplets,** rhyming pairs of lines of equal length. "400-Meter Free Style," on the other hand, contains no rhyme but still has a strong rhythm. In each case, the form supports the poet's ideas.

As you read the poems in this lesson, notice the elements of form and how they affect the meaning.

READING STRATEGY: CONNECT

The poems you read will be more meaningful if you **connect** your own experiences to the ideas and feelings they express. For example, you might be on a swim team, or perhaps you have watched a swim meet like the one described in "400-Meter Free Style." Your own experience can help you understand the ideas expressed. As you read the following poems, make use of this strategy whenever appropriate.

Author Online

Maxine Kumin: Late Bloomer
Maxine Kumin didn't truly begin to write poetry until she was in her 30s. She did, however, have a few false starts before this. As a college freshman, she gave some of her poems to an instructor for comments. He returned the poems

Maxine Kumin
born 1925

with a note that read, "Say it with flowers, but ... don't try to write poems." Kumin didn't write poetry again for six years.

Despite Bad Advice Kumin published her first poetry collection in 1961. Since then, she has published 14 volumes of poetry, as well as novels, essays, and children's books. She received a Pulitzer Prize in 1973 and was U.S. poet laureate from 1981 to 1982.

Wislawa Szymborska: Poland's Quiet Poet
Wislawa Szymborska was a renowned poet in her native Poland for many years before she became known in other countries. She was awarded the Nobel Prize in literature in 1996, which brought her international fame. Being thrust

Wislawa Szymborska
born 1923

into the spotlight made the shy poet very uncomfortable. Today she lives quietly in Poland, where she continues to write and publish her poetry.

 MORE ABOUT THE AUTHOR
For more on these poets, visit the **Literature Center** at ClassZone.com.

400-Meter
Free Style

Maxine Kumin

THE GUN full swing the swimmer catapults[1] and cracks
    s
    i
    x

5 feet away onto that perfect glass he catches at **Ⓐ**
a
n
d
throws behind him scoop after scoop cunningly moving

10   t
                                         h
                                       e
water back to move him forward. Thrift is his wonderful
s

15 e
c
ret; he has schooled out all extravagance. No muscle **Ⓑ**
                                         r
                                       i
                                       p

20 ples without compensation wrist cock to heel snap to
h
i
s
25 mobile mouth that siphons[2] in the air that nurtures
                                       h
                                       i
                                       m
at half an inch above sea level so to speak.

---

1. **catapults** (kăt′ə-pŭlts′): springs.
2. **siphons** (sī′fənz): draws in, as if with a tube.

Ⓐ FORM
Would you say that the **lines** in this poem have endings, or does the poem consist of one long line? Explain.

Ⓑ CONNECT
The swimmer is completely focused on moving through the water as quickly and efficiently as possible. Think about a time when all your attention was focused on a single goal. Did it help you attain the goal?

30 T
h
e
astonishing whites of the soles of his feet rise
a
35   n
d
salute us on the turns. He flips, converts, and is gone
a
l
40 l
in one. We watch him for signs. His arms are steady at
t
h
e
45 catch, his cadent[3] feet tick in the stretch, they know
t
h
e
lesson well. Lungs know, too; he does not list for
50   a
i
r
he drives along on little sips carefully expended
b
55 u
t
that plum red heart pumps hard cries hurt how soon
i
t
s
60
near one more and makes its final surge Time: 4:25:9 **C**

C **CONCRETE POETRY**
Describe the movement created by the arrangement of the poem's lines.

---

3. **cadent** (kād'nt): moving in a rhythmic pattern, or cadence.

BODYBUILDERS' CONTEST

Wislawa Szymborska

Municipal Bonds (2004), Byron Spicer. Mixed media, 45″ × 45″. © Byron Spicer.

From scalp to sole, all muscles in slow motion.
The ocean of his torso drips with lotion.
The king of all is he who preens[1] and wrestles
with sinews twisted into monstrous pretzels.

5 Onstage, he grapples with a grizzly bear
the deadlier for not really being there.
Three unseen panthers are in turn laid low,
each with one smoothly choreographed[2] blow.

He grunts while showing his poses and paces.
10 His back alone has twenty different faces.
The mammoth fist he raises as he wins
is tribute to the force of vitamins. **D**

Translated by Stanislaw Baranczak and Clare Cavanagh

---

1. **preens:** makes himself attractive and then shows off his appearance.
2. **choreographed** (kôr′ē-ə-grăft′): with the movements planned and arranged, as in a dance.

ANALYZE VISUALS
What qualities of a bodybuilder are reflected in the painting? Cite details.

D FORM
Notice the form of this poem. How has the poet used **stanzas** to organize her ideas?

Comprehension

1. **Recall** In "Bodybuilders' Contest," what does the bodybuilder look like he is doing onstage?

2. **Recall** What is the very first thing that happens in "400-Meter Free Style"?

3. **Clarify** What "signs" has the speaker been watching for in "400-Meter Free Style"?

PENNSYLVANIA STANDARDS

READING STANDARD
B.3.3.2 Analyze text organization and content

Literary Analysis

4. **Connect** What connections were you able to make to these two poems? Which athlete did you think was the better **competitor?** Explain.

5. **Analyze a Concrete Poem** In what ways does the shape of "400-Meter Free Style" reflect the poem's subject? Would the poem have as much impact if it were written in **stanzas** with clear line breaks? Explain.

6. **Interpret Imagery** Reread lines 30–41 in "400-Meter Free Style." How is the "salute" by the soles of the swimmer's feet in keeping with his other movements?

7. **Examine Sound Devices** In Kumin's poem, there are a number of sound devices, including **alliteration,** the repetition of consonant sounds at the beginning of words. Identify at least five examples of alliteration. What effect do they have when the poem is read aloud?

8. **Analyze Rhyme** "Bodybuilders' Contest" uses rhyming **couplets** to call attention to certain images in each stanza and to create humor. What humorous images are emphasized in the poem?

9. **Examine Form** The form of "Bodybuilders' Contest" is very controlled. In what ways does this form fit the subject of the poem?

Reading-Writing Connection

WRITING PROMPT

Extended Response: Write a Concrete Poem
Write your own **concrete poem** by first choosing a topic that suggests an object or an action, such as a bird or someone jumping. Then think of a simple **shape** that reflects that object or action. Draw an outline of the object, and write a poem to fit into the shape.

SELF-CHECK

A successful concrete poem will . . .
- focus on a single object or action
- have a shape that closely connects to the subject
- use precise, sensory words in a fresh and interesting way

The Night Poetry Rocked the House

Magazine Article

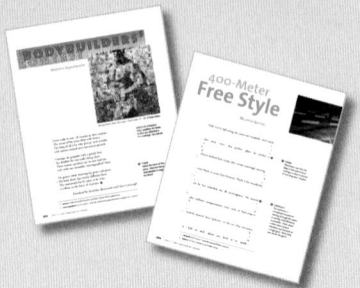

Use with "400-Meter Free Style" and "Bodybuilders' Contest," pages 694 and 696.

PENNSYLVANIA STANDARDS

READING & WRITING STANDARDS

A.2.4.1 Identify main ideas and supporting details

1.4.11.C.2 Include convincing and properly cited evidence

What's the Connection?

The last two poems brought to life two athletic competitions: a swim meet and a bodybuilders' contest. The article you are about to read will give you an idea of what it feels like to compete at a very different sort of event—a poetry slam.

Skill Focus: Synthesize

Magazine articles often include **sidebars**—news items or short features inserted near the main text. When you read a magazine article that has a sidebar, you need to **synthesize** the information from both the article and its sidebar. By putting together the facts, ideas, and details from each, you'll get a fuller understanding of the topic.

How do you do that? What do you read first? Do you interrupt your reading of one piece to read the other? Here's how you can synthesize the ideas and details from "The Night Poetry Rocked the House" and the accompanying sidebar, "Not Your Father's Poetry."

- **Skim** both the main article and the sidebar to get a basic idea of what each is about and how each is organized.
- **Read** the main article from start to finish; then **summarize** its main ideas and details for yourself.
- **Note** any questions you have after reading the main article.
- **Read** the sidebar. As you read, ask yourself: What am I learning here that I did not learn from the main article?

After reading the sidebar, think about why the information in it was given separately from the main article. The answers you come up with may help you recognize the focus and strengths of the main article. For more help synthesizing the article and sidebar that follow, complete a chart like the one started here.

Source	Main Ideas & Information	Questions & New Information
1. "The Night Poetry Rocked the House"	Rachel Shapiro's last performance in the National Youth Poetry Slam in San Francisco is amazing.	What exactly is a poetry slam?

The NIGHT POETRY ROCKED the HOUSE

Rachel Shapiro

We may not have won the national poetry slam—but that wasn't the point. **A**

We were brimming and overflowing with excitement. We had made it to the finals of the National Youth Poetry Slam in San Francisco, where more than 100 of the top teenage poets from across the country gathered to perform. It was 1 A.M., the last performance of the third and final round, and my team, representing
10 New York City, was about to go on, ending the entire weekend of inspiring words.

Onome, Casey, and I planned to perform a group piece that the three of us had written about women. *A girl thinks rich, thorough thoughts . . . Why doesn't she speak up in class?* We knew we would have points deducted because our piece was well over the
20 three-minute limit. But it didn't matter. We had something to say. We had a message to leave with San Francisco.

ELOQUENT WORDS

The three of us walked out on the stage gazing at the chandeliers and the 1,200 faces who cheered, who came to hear the voices of the young poets of the country. We performed on a stage blessed with the eloquent words of
30 skinny girls with proud, deep voices,

13-year-olds who roused the entire crowd, round women from Atlanta who sang amid their poetry; it was a stage ridden with confusion, rebirth, inspiration, talent, and pride.

Many words that night had shocked us with their brilliance. Now it was our turn. *Does she learn to dismiss her anger when/ he says he's sick of male-*
40 *bashing poems/ did she dump him when he bashed her?*

We had an open stage, a free forum to share the plight of the young girl who doesn't speak up in class—*who could never realize she was brilliant*—to speak of the silencing and submission of women—*Was she always this numb? Was she always this quiet?*—the abuse, the sellouts, and the lack of respect—
50 *Did her tears fall like raindrops/ outside a soundproof window?*

The words poured out with emotion and house-rocking force. We traded solos like a jazz trio; we jammed in counterpoint, in unison, in rhythm. *She was brilliant. Was she always this?* **B**

The second after we released the last word, the crowd was frozen, stunned. And then the room started to
60 shake with energy—in an instant my coach was onstage, people whom I had never met were hugging me, someone

A SYNTHESIZE
What do the title and the statement below it suggest the **main idea** of the article will be?

B SYNTHESIZE
Based on what you've read so far, how would you describe this poetry slam?

Not Your Father's Poetry
By Bruce Weber/*The New York Times*

C **SYNTHESIZE**
Skim the title and topic sentences of the sidebar. What do you think you will learn from it?

C Poetry slams have come of age. As poetry in general has surged in popularity in the United States, this offshoot has emerged as a way for passionate, mostly young people—representing a wide ethnic and racial range—to air their voices and for an evidently eager audience to hear and embrace them.

10   Slamming is a weird and lively amalgam of performance art, hip-hop concert, and—with its judges holding up numerical score cards—Olympic figure skating. It's a national grassroots movement, which began when a Chicago poet named Marc Smith held the first competitions in a bar in 1984.

The 11th annual National Poetry Slam was held in August, and the 3rd annual
20 National Youth Poetry Slam was held last spring.

Slam poetry has been boosted by, among other things, the popularity of rap music, the boom in stand-up comedy, and the proliferation of stage monologuists. At the same time, sales of poetry books have soared 30 percent in the last three years.

Watching others perform, says
30 Danny Solis, who has competed out of Albuquerque, New Mexico, "showed me that poetry could be something that lifts an audience to another place, like jazz, salsa or dance."

D **SYNTHESIZE**
What element of Shapiro's experience is emphasized in this paragraph?

came up to us crying, saying, "Thank you. As a woman, I knew that had to be said, and you all said it so beautifully."

ARENAS OF SUPPORT
I knew then that it was real, and that it was necessary to find creative ways to express yourself, so that people,
70 especially adults, will take you seriously and realize that you have some monumental things to say as well. Poetry slams give poets arenas full of excitement and support that

encourage us, urge us to tell them what we have to say. **D**

We didn't win, but it couldn't have mattered less to me. When I think of the young men and women with
80 whom I shared the stage, and especially of my team, I think of an Adrienne Rich poem:

> *No one has imagined us. We want to*
> *live like trees,*
> *Sycamores blazing through the*
> *sulfuric air,*
> *dappled with scars still exuberantly*
> *budding.*

Comprehension

1. **Recall** Why have these young poets gathered as described in "The Night Poetry Rocked the House"?

2. **Summarize** How was the National Youth Poetry Slam a rewarding experience for the author?

Critical Analysis

3. **Synthesize** Review the chart you filled in as you read the main article and the sidebar. What does the sidebar add to your understanding of Shapiro's poetry slam experience? Explain.

4. **Analyze Tone** Describe the tone of the main article and the tone of the sidebar. Why do you suppose their tones differ?

Read for Information: Support an Opinion

PENNSYLVANIA STANDARDS

READING & WRITING STANDARDS
A.2.4.1 Identify main ideas and supporting details
1.4.11.C.2 Include convincing and properly cited evidence

WRITING PROMPT

You have just read three very different portrayals of three very different forms of competition—a swim meet, a bodybuilders' contest, and a poetry slam. Which portrayal do you find the most compelling? What elements of that piece make it more interesting to you than the others?

To answer this prompt, follow these steps:

1. Decide which piece you find yourself caring the most about. Write a brief statement explaining why. This statement will be your **claim.**

2. Write down the elements of this piece that make it the most compelling of the three. These will be the **reasons** for your choice.

3. Find details in the selection that illustrate each of your reasons. These will be your **evidence.**

4. State your opinion and support it with your reasons and evidence. You may want to mention any strengths of the other selections, but also point out the reasons why—despite these strengths—they don't match up to your favorite.

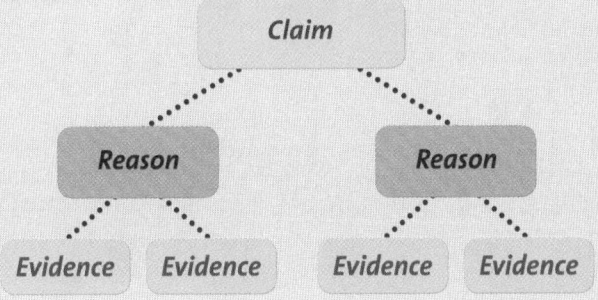

For Poets
Poem by Al Young

Ode to My Socks
Poem by Pablo Neruda

egg horror poem
Poem by Laurel Winter

What makes your IMAGINATION *soar?*

PENNSYLVANIA STANDARDS

READING STANDARDS
A.1.6.1 Identify and/or analyze intended purpose of text

B.2.1.2 Analyze figurative language

KEY IDEA It's easy to see why people might be inspired to creativity by something grand, like love or mountains, but **imagination** is not limited to the grand. A poet might see something as simple as a shoelace in a completely new way.

QUICKWRITE Write a short description of a familiar object as though you'd never seen it before. What does it make you think of? Use your imagination.

POETIC FORM: ODE

A traditional **ode** is a poem that highly praises something—usually a person, an event, or an idea. Traditional odes are about serious subjects, and they have a formal tone. In this lesson, you'll read an ode by Pablo Neruda, who broke with tradition by writing odes about everyday objects—in this case a pair of cozy socks.

LITERARY ANALYSIS: FIGURATIVE LANGUAGE

Figurative language goes beyond the literal meaning of words, creating a comparison between two things not usually associated with one another. Such **figures of speech** allow the writer to characterize one of the two items in a particular, often unusual, way. Figurative language has three basic types, all found in Pablo Neruda's "Ode to My Socks."

- A **simile** compares two unlike things that have something in common, using the word *like* or *as*.

  two socks soft / as rabbits

- A **metaphor** directly compares two unlike things by saying that one thing actually *is* the other.

  my feet became / two woolen / fish

- **Personification** lends human qualities to an object, animal, or idea.

  my feet seemed / unacceptable to me, / two tired old / fire fighters

As you read, identify the figurative language used, and think of the qualities the comparision gives to the subject being described.

Poem	Passage	Figure of Speech	Meaning of Comparision
"For Poets"	"Breathe in trees"	metaphor	

READING STRATEGY: VISUALIZE

The process of forming a mental picture from a written description is called **visualizing.** Good readers visualize the images and comparisons in a poem to help them understand the poet's ideas. As you read the next three poems, pause frequently to visualize the images and comparisons you find.

Author Online

Al Young: A Man of Many Talents
In his varied life, Al Young has written screenplays, essays, and novels, but poetry is his first love. "Poetry sweetens the tongue, deepens the heart, and expands the mind," he once said. "Even a writer of annual reports may draw richly from the conventions and techniques of poetry."

Al Young
born 1939

Pablo Neruda: Poetry and Politics Acclaimed both in his native Chile and internationally, Pablo Neruda's life was a mix of poetry and politics. After writing love poetry early in his career, Neruda turned to more political verse in the 1930s and 1940s. In the 1950s he began writing about everyday objects in a simple style that many people could understand and enjoy. Neruda was awarded the Nobel Prize in literature in 1971.

Pablo Neruda
1904–1973

Laurel Winter: Sci-Fi/ Fantasy Poet "I grew up as an odd kid in the mountains of Montana," writes Laurel Winter. "I was klutzy and bookwormish and didn't always fit in." Today Winter is an award-winning writer. On writing science fiction and fantasy, she said, "To me as a writer, in fantasy everything is available. If you can think of it, you can write it."

Laurel Winter
born 1959

MORE ABOUT THE AUTHOR
For more on these poets, visit the **Literature Center** at **ClassZone.com.**

For Poets

AL YOUNG

Stay beautiful
but dont stay down underground too long
Dont turn into a mole
or a worm
5 or a root
or a stone

Come on out into the sunlight
Breathe in trees
Knock out mountains
10 Commune[1] with snakes
& be the very hero of birds **Ⓐ**

Dont forget to poke your head up
& blink
think
15 Walk all around
Swim upstream **Ⓑ**

Dont forget to fly

---

1. **commune** (kə-myo͞on′): communicate intimately.

ANALYZE VISUALS
What elements of this image express the sentiments of this poem? Be specific.

Ⓐ FIGURATIVE LANGUAGE
In lines 7–11, the speaker is not offering literal advice. What is he really suggesting?

Ⓑ VISUALIZE
Reread lines 12–16. What mental pictures do these lines create?

From *Wings* (2000), Christopher Myers © 2000 Christopher Meyers. Reprinted by permission of Scholastic, Inc.

ODE TO MY SOCKS

PABLO NERUDA

Maru Mori brought me
a pair
of socks
knitted with her own
5 shepherd's hands,
two socks soft
as rabbits.
I slipped
my feet into them
10 as if
into
jewel cases
woven
with threads of
15 dusk
and sheep's wool. **C**

Me trajo Maru Mori
un par
de calcentines
que tejió con sus manos
de pastora,
dos calcentines suaves
como liebres.
En ellos
metí los pies
como en
dos
estuches
tejidos
con hebras del
crepúsculo
y pellejo de ovejas.

C **FIGURATIVE LANGUAGE**
Identify the two **similes** in lines 1–16. What qualities of the socks is suggested by each simile?

Audacious[1] socks,
my feet became
two woolen
20 fish,
two long sharks
of lapis[2] blue
shot
with a golden thread,
25 two mammoth blackbirds,
two cannons,
thus honored
were
my feet
30 by
these
celestial[3]
socks. **D**
They were
35 so beautiful
that for the first time
my feet seemed
unacceptable to me,
two tired old
40 fire fighters

Violentos calcentines,
mis pies fueron
dos pescados
de lana,
dos largos tiburones
de azul ultramarino
atravesados
por una trenza de oro,
dos gigantescos mirlos,
dos cañones:
mis pies
fueron honrados
de este modo
por
estos
celestiales
calcentines.
Eran
tan hermosos
que por primera vez
mis pies me parecieron
inaceptables
como dos decrépitos
bomberos, bomberos

D FIGURATIVE
LANGUAGE
Reread lines 17–33. What
unusual **metaphors**
does the speaker use to
emphasize the amazing
nature of the socks?

---

1. **audacious** (ô-dā′shəs): bold or original.

2. **lapis:** the color of the stone lapis lazuli (lăp′ĭs lăz′ə-lē); bright blue.

3. **celestial** (sə-lĕs′chəl): heavenly.

not worthy	indignos
of the woven	de aquel fuego
fire	bordado,
of those luminous	de aquellos luminosos
45 socks.	calcetines.
Nonetheless,	Sin embargo
I resisted	resistí
the strong temptation	la tentación aguda
to save them	de guardarlos
50 the way schoolboys	como los colegiales
bottle	preservan
fireflies,	las luciérnagas,
the way scholars	como los cruditos
hoard	coleccionan
55 sacred documents.	documentos sagrados,
I resisted	resistí
the wild impulse	el impulso furioso
to place them	de ponerlos
in a cage	en una jaula
60 of gold	de oro
and daily feed them	y darles cada día
birdseed	alpiste
and rosy melon flesh. **E**	y pulpa de melón rosado.
Like explorers	Como descubridores
65 who in the forest	que en la selva
surrender a rare	entregan el rarísimo
and tender deer	venado verde
to the spit	al asador
and eat it	y se lo comen
70 with remorse,	con remordimiento,
I stuck out	estiré
my feet	los pies
and pulled on	y me enfundé
the	los
75 handsome	bellos
socks,	calcetines
and	y
then my shoes.	luego los zapatos.

E VISUALIZE
Reread lines 46–63. As you visualize the images in these lines, think about what they have in common. What is the speaker saying about his socks?

So this is
80 the moral of my ode:
twice beautiful
is beauty
and what is good doubly
good
85 when it is a case of two
woolen socks
in wintertime. **F**

Y es ésta
la moral de mi oda:
dos veces es belleza
la belleza
y lo que es bueno es doblemente
bueno
cuando se trata de dos calcentines
de lana
en el invierno.

F ODE
Traditional odes have a
serious **tone,** or attitude
toward the subject. What
is the tone of this ode?

Translated by Margaret Sayers Peden

egg
horror
poem

LAUREL WINTER

small
white
afraid of heights
whispering
5 in the cold, dark carton
to the rest of the dozen. **G**
They are ten now.
Any meal is dangerous,
but they fear breakfast most.
10 They jostle in their compartments
trying for tiny, dark-veined cracks—
not enough to hurt much,
just anything to make them unattractive
to the big hands that reach in
15 from time to random time.
They tell horror stories
that their mothers,
the chickens,
clucked to them—
20 meringues,
omelettes,
egg salad sandwiches,
that destroyer of dozens,
the homemade angel food cake. **H**
25 The door opens.
Light filters into the carton,
"Let it be the milk,"
they pray.

G FIGURATIVE
LANGUAGE
In lines 1–6, what object
is being **personified?**
Identify the words that
convey human qualities.

H FIGURATIVE
LANGUAGE
Reread lines 16–24.
Why might meringues,
omelettes, and the other
foods mentioned in these
lines seem horrifying to
an egg?

But the carton opens,
30 a hand reaches in—
once,
twice.
Before they can even jiggle,
they are alone again,
35 in the cold,
in the dark,
new spaces hollow
where the two were.
Through the heavy door
40 they hear the sound of the mixer,
deadly blades whirring. ◻

They huddle,
the eight,
in the cold,
45 in the dark,
and wait.

◻ **VISUALIZE**
Reread lines 29–41. What
events do you picture
happening inside and
outside the refrigerator?

After Reading

Comprehension

1. **Recall** According to the speaker in "For Poets," what is the danger of staying underground too long?

2. **Recall** What two comparisons in "Ode to My Socks" involve the speaker's feet rather than his socks?

3. **Clarify** What is the eggs' great fear in "egg horror poem"?

Literary Analysis

4. **Visualize** Which poem creates the most vivid pictures in your mind? What specific images and comparisons in the poem create these pictures?

5. **Interpret Metaphor** What does the speaker in "For Poets" mean by telling poets, "Dont forget to fly"? What activity does flying represent?

6. **Interpret Personification** What is life like for the eggs described in "egg horror poem"? Describe your impressions and support your ideas with details from the poem.

7. **Identify Onomatopoeia** When words have sounds that echo their own meaning, as in *buzz* and *gargle*, it is known as onomatopoeia. Reread "egg horror poem" and identify the onomatopoetic words.

8. **Analyze an Ode** Reread the description of an ode on page 703. In what ways is "Ode to My Socks" like a traditional ode? In what ways is it different? What do you think Neruda's intent was in writing an ode to a pair of socks?

9. **Evaluate Figurative Language** Review the examples of figurative language you recorded in your chart. Which figures of speech do you find the most effective or compelling? Explain your preferences.

10. **Evaluate Ideas** Skim "Ode to My Socks" and "egg horror poem." Which poet shows more **imagination** in making an everyday object seem new or unusual? Support your opinion with details from the poems.

Literary Criticism

11. **Critical Interpretations** The critic Dean Rader wrote that "'Ode to My Socks' is a poem about poetry." He believes that Neruda's ode is commenting on "what poetry is and what it should be." If this is true, what is Neruda saying about poetry? Explain your ideas.

PENNSYLVANIA STANDARDS

READING STANDARD
B.2.1.2 Analyze figurative language

Reading-Writing Connection

Add to your understanding of the poems by responding to these prompts.
Then use **Revision: Grammar and Style** to improve your writing.

WRITING PROMPTS	SELF-CHECK

A. Short Response: Write a Poem

Using "egg horror poem" as a model, write a **five-to-ten-line poem** using an extended example of personification.

An effective poem will . . .
- show the human qualities of a recognizable place, object, or animal
- give insight into the subject that is not immediately obvious

B. Extended Response: Give Advice

Think about the advice Al Young gives in "For Poets." What have you learned that you could pass along to someone younger or less experienced? You may even have your own advice for poets. Write **three to five paragraphs** explaining your advice.

Good written advice will . . .
- respectfully explain what it takes to succeed
- mention mistakes to avoid
- give examples to support and clarify your points

REVISION: GRAMMAR AND STYLE

WRITE CONCISELY Because poetry typically consists of a compact, carefully chosen group of words, it benefits from the use of concise language. Other types of writing can also be improved when made concise. By incorporating **infinitives** and **infinitive phrases** into your writing, you can avoid unnecessary words. An infinitive is a verb form that begins with *to* and functions as a noun, an adjective, or an adverb. An infinitive phrase consists of an infinitive plus its modifiers and complements. Note the following examples:

> *Dont forget to fly* ("For Poets," line 17)

> *I resisted / the wild impulse / to place them / in a cage / of gold*
> ("Ode to My Socks," lines 56–60)

In the revisions in red, infinitives and infinitive phrases are used to combine sentences, making the writing more concise. Revise your responses to the prompts by making similar changes.

PENNSYLVANIA STANDARDS

WRITING STANDARD
1.5.11.D.2 Use precise language

STUDENT MODEL

The kitchen at last settles down. ~~It wants~~ to nap.

The refrigerator hums softly in slumber.

It is happy. ~~It wishes~~ to do nothing for a while.

WRITING TOOLS
For prewriting, revision, and editing tools, visit the **Writing Center** at ClassZone.com.

O What Is That Sound
Poem by W. H. Auden

What triggers a sense of ALARM?

PENNSYLVANIA STANDARDS

READING STANDARDS
A.1.6.1 Identify and/or analyze intended purpose of text
B.2.2.1 Identify and analyze point of view

KEY IDEA Strange noises, flashing lights, the smell of something burning—any of these things would catch your attention. But would they set your heart pounding? At what point does something unusual become threatening? The following poem describes someone reacting to an approaching threat with a growing sense of **alarm.**

QUICKWRITE Imagine a situation that might cause you to panic. It could be something as dangerous as getting lost in the woods or as mild as forgetting to study for a quiz. Write a short paragraph describing your physical and mental reaction.

POETIC FORM: BALLAD

W. H. Auden was a modern poet, but he used a traditional ballad form for "O What Is That Sound." A **ballad** is a narrative poem that is meant to be sung or recited. Typically, a traditional ballad focuses on a single tragic event and usually implies more than it tells explicitly. A ballad typically includes

- a setting, plot, and characters
- dialogue and repetition
- a regular and simple rhyme scheme (commonly *abab*, *abcb*, or *aabb*)

LITERARY ANALYSIS: SOUND DEVICES

Originally meant to be spoken or sung, poetry has a musical quality you won't always find in prose. This is no accident; poets use various **sound devices** to create rhythm and mood and to emphasize ideas in their poems. In "O What Is That Sound," W. H. Auden uses the following sound devices to help create suspense and meaning, as well as melody:

- **Rhyme:** similar sounds at the ends of lines (**end rhyme**) or within lines (**internal rhyme**)
- **Repetition:** words or phrases that are repeated (*drumming, drumming*)
- **Assonance:** repetition of vowel sounds within words that don't rhyme (*only soldiers*)

As you read this poem, look for examples of sound devices, and notice how they help create a feeling of anxiety.

READING SKILL: ANALYZE SPEAKERS

In this poem, everything you learn about the story and the characters' feelings comes from the dialogue between the two speakers. As you read, use the reactions of the speakers to imagine what is happening; also look for changes in either speaker's attitude. In a chart like the one shown, record what you infer about the speakers, including who they are and how they react to events—both early and then later on.

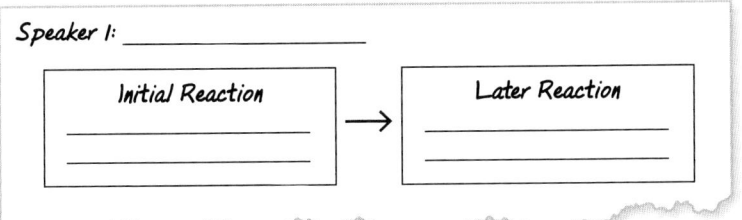

Speaker 1: _____

Initial Reaction → Later Reaction

Author Online

Admiration and Controversy

**W. H. Auden
1907–1973**

W. H. Auden is one of the giants of 20th-century poetry. Born in northern England, he first intended to study science but soon realized his talent for poetry. His early poems, among them "O What Is That Sound," attracted both admiration and controversy. Perhaps Auden's most controversial act was moving to New York in 1939; he ultimately became a U.S. citizen. Some Englishmen never forgave him for leaving his country on the eve of World War II.

An Enduring Legacy In his poetry, Auden confronted the tumultuous ideas and events that rocked his age—Freudian psychology, Marxism, fascism, civil war, and world war. In winning the National Medal for Literature in 1967 he was praised for illuminating "our lives and times with grace, wit and vitality." After the terrorist attacks of September 11, 2001, Web sites and New York subway walls displayed two of his finest poems, "Musée des Beaux Arts" and "September 1, 1939."

MORE ABOUT THE AUTHOR
For more on W. H. Auden, visit the **Literature Center** at ClassZone.com.

Background

Long Ago and Far Away? The references to drums, horses, and the red uniforms of soldiers in "O What Is That Sound" suggest a faraway time, perhaps around the time of the American Revolution. However, the poem was written in the 1930s, a decade that Auden called "the age of anxiety." Frightened by worldwide economic depression and the rise of fascism in Italy and Germany, ordinary citizens felt vulnerable to events beyond their control.

O What Is That Sound

W. H. AUDEN

O what is that sound which so thrills the ear
    Down in the valley drumming, drumming?
Only the scarlet soldiers,[1] dear,
    The soldiers coming.

5 O what is that light I see flashing so clear
    Over the distance brightly, brightly?
Only the sun on their weapons, dear,
    As they step lightly.

O what are they doing with all that gear,
10   What are they doing this morning, this morning?
Only their usual maneuvers,[2] dear,
    Or perhaps a warning. **A**

O why have they left the road down there,
    Why are they suddenly wheeling, wheeling?[3]
15 Perhaps a change in their orders, dear.
    Why are you kneeling? **B**

ANALYZE VISUALS
What is the **mood** created by this painting? Identify the elements of subject matter, shape, and color that contribute to this mood.

A **SOUND DEVICES**
Reread lines 9–12 aloud. Which of the lines in this stanza contains **assonance?** Identify the assonance, and explain its effect.

B **ANALYZE SPEAKERS**
Do the two speakers seem to feel the same way about the approaching soldiers? Explain.

---

1. **scarlet soldiers:** a reference suggesting British soldiers, who wore bright red coats.
2. **maneuvers:** training exercises carried out by troops.
3. **wheeling:** turning around quickly so as to face in the opposite direction.

Returning to the Trenches (1914), C. R. W. Nevinson. Oil on canvas, 51.2 cm × 76.8 cm. Gift of the Massey Collection of English Painting, 1946. © National Gallery of Canada, Ottawa/The Nevinson Estate/Bridgeman Art Library.

Detail of *Returning to the Trenches.* © National Gallery of Canada, Ottawa.

O haven't they stopped for the doctor's care,
    Haven't they reined their horses, their horses?
Why, they are none of them wounded, dear.
20   None of these forces. **C**

O is it the parson they want, with white hair,
    Is it the parson, is it, is it?
No, they are passing his gateway, dear,
    Without a visit.

25 O it must be the farmer who lives so near.
    It must be the farmer so cunning, so cunning?
They have passed the farmyard already, dear,
    And now they are running. **D**

O where are you going? Stay with me here!
30   Were the vows you swore deceiving, deceiving?
No, I promised to love you, dear,
    But I must be leaving.

O it's broken the lock and splintered the door,
    O it's the gate where they're turning, turning;
35 Their boots are heavy on the floor
    And their eyes are burning. **E**

C SOUND DEVICES
Slant rhyme refers to end rhymes that are not exact, as in "chair" and "cheer." Which two lines in this stanza create slant rhyme?

D BALLAD
What characteristics of a ballad do you find in this poem?

E SOUND DEVICES
Reread lines 33–36 aloud. What words in this stanza are emphasized by **rhyme** and **repetition?**

After Reading

Comprehension

1. **Recall** Whom do the speakers observe in the distance?

2. **Clarify** Which speaker seems calmer?

3. **Clarify** Reread the last stanza. What happens to the second speaker?

Literary Analysis

4. **Understand Poetry** What is happening in this poem? Briefly describe the actions that take place. Give possible reasons for these actions.

5. **Analyze Speakers** Review the chart you completed as you read. Who are the two speakers in the poem? What is their relationship? Describe what you inferred about the speakers' identities and their reactions to events. Be sure to support your **inferences** with details from the poem.

6. **Analyze Sound Devices** Reread the poem, looking for examples of **rhyme, repetition,** and **assonance.** Use a chart like the one shown to record two examples of each sound device. Which sound device is most effective in conveying a sense of anxiety and drama in the poem? Explain your thinking.

Sound Devices	Examples
Rhyme (internal or end)	
Repetition	
Assonance	

7. **Interpret Imagery** Reread lines 33–36 and note the words and phrases that describe the soldiers and their actions. On the basis of this imagery, what is your impression of the soldiers? Will they defend the speakers or attack them? Explain your answer.

8. **Evaluate a Ballad** In this ballad, one speaker asks a series of questions, and a second speaker gives answers. How does this pattern of **repetitive dialogue** affect the level of tension throughout the poem? What is the point of greatest tension? Cite evidence to support your answer.

Literary Criticism

9. **Historical Context** Auden wrote "O What Is That Sound" in the 1930s. During this decade, many European countries, including Germany and Italy, were being taken over by fascist dictators. These tyrannical leaders exercised complete control over every aspect of public and private life and used force, such as police or military terror, to crush opposition. In what ways does the poem reflect these political realities of the 1930s?

PENNSYLVANIA STANDARDS

READING STANDARD
B.2.2.1 Identify and analyze point of view

The Seven Ages of Man
Poem by William Shakespeare

The Road Not Taken
Poem by Robert Frost

Do you set your own COURSE?

PENNSYLVANIA STANDARDS

READING STANDARDS
A.1.4.1 Identify and explain main ideas and relevant details
B.3.3.2 Analyze text organization and content

KEY IDEA If life is a **journey,** then who's driving? Some people feel that they make their own choices about where to turn and how far to drive, while others feel they are simply following a course set by someone else. The poems that follow suggest two very different views of this question.

ROLE-PLAY Imagine you are applying for a job or preparing for a college interview. With a partner, take turns interviewing one another about your life goals. Where do you see yourself in 5 years? in 10 years? in 15 years? When answering these questions, explain what choices you may have to make in order to achieve these goals.

POETIC FORM: DRAMATIC MONOLOGUE

A **dramatic monologue** is a poem in which the speaker addresses a silent or absent listener, as if engaged in a private conversation. The speaker often reveals his or her own feelings, attitudes, motivations, and character traits in a moment of high intensity or deep emotion. "The Seven Ages of Man" is an example of a dramatic monologue; it is delivered by a character in Shakespeare's play *As You Like It*.

LITERARY ANALYSIS: METER

Rhythm is the pattern of stressed and unstressed syllables in a line of poetry. Rhythm that follows a regular pattern from line to line is called **meter**. The following lines from Shakespeare use a very even meter:

Thĕy háve thĕir éxits ănd thĕir éntrăncĕs;

Ănd óne măn ín hĭs tíme plăys mány párts.

In the next example, from Frost, notice that the number of accents is the same in each line, but the rhythm varies slightly:

Í shăll bĕ télling thĭs wĭth ă sígh

Sómewhĕre ágĕs ănd ágĕs hénce

Why bother to use meter? For the same reasons that a songwriter bothers to use music: it sounds nice, it's easy to remember, and it allows for extra emphasis of words or phrases. Read the following poems aloud and tap your foot as you go. Then ask yourself these questions:

- Is the meter obvious or subtle? Is it close to normal speech?
- Where does the emphasis fall in each line?

Review: **Rhyme Scheme**

READING SKILL: ANALYZE IDEAS IN POETRY

You can better understand poems by looking for the **main idea** in each section. "The Seven Ages of Man" can be divided into seven sections—one for each "age." "The Road Not Taken" is already divided into four stanzas. As you read each poem, record the main idea of each "age" or stanza.

"The Seven Ages of Man"	
Age	Main Idea
1. infancy	
2. school-boy days	

Author Online

William Shakespeare: Timeless Greatness
Shakespeare is certainly the most famous writer in the world and arguably the greatest writer who ever lived. He wrote 37 plays, ranging from comedies to tragedies. He also published some of the most beautiful

**William Shakespeare
1564–1616**

lyric poetry in the English language, including 154 sonnets, before he died at age 52. In his own time, theater audiences loved him and critics praised his incredible talent. But his contemporary Ben Jonson foresaw Shakespeare's indelible mark on the future: "He was not of an age, but for all time!"

Robert Frost: Beloved American Poet
Declared America's poet laureate before the official creation of such a position, Robert Frost had become a beloved public figure by the time he died. The U.S. Senate passed a resolution honoring him, the state of Vermont named a

**Robert Frost
1874–1963**

mountain after him, and he was the first poet ever invited to recite his work at a presidential inauguration. Still, Frost is something of a puzzle. He was a modern poet who often used traditional rhyme and meter, a New England farmer whose folksy manner concealed an inner torment, and a man of ideas who valued both objectivity and a "tantalizing vagueness" in poetry.

MORE ABOUT THE AUTHOR
For more on William Shakespeare and Robert Frost, visit the **Literature Center** at ClassZone.com.

THE SEVEN AGES OF MAN

William Shakespeare

JAQUES:
All the world's a stage,
And all the men and women merely players:
They have their exits and their entrances;
And one man in his time plays many parts,
5 His acts being seven ages. At first the infant,
Mewling[1] and puking in the nurse's arms.
And then the whining school-boy, with his satchel,
And shining morning face, creeping like snail
Unwillingly to school. And then the lover, **Ⓐ**
10 Sighing like furnace, with a woeful ballad[2]
Made to his mistress' eyebrow. Then a soldier,
Full of strange oaths, and bearded like the pard,[3]
Jealous in honor, sudden and quick in quarrel,
Seeking the bubble reputation[4]
15 Even in the cannon's mouth. And then the justice,
In fair round belly with good capon lin'd,[5]
With eyes severe, and beard of formal cut,
Full of wise saws and modern instances;[6]
And so he plays his part. The sixth age shifts
20 Into the lean and slipper'd pantaloon,[7]
With spectacles on nose and pouch on side,
His youthful hose well sav'd, a world too wide **Ⓑ**

Ⓐ DRAMATIC MONOLOGUE
Reread lines 5–9. Notice how Jaques describes the infant and the schoolboy. What do these descriptions reveal about his attitude toward childhood?

Ⓑ RHYME SCHEME
Does Shakespeare employ a rhyme scheme for this poem? Support your answer.

---

1. **mewling:** crying or whimpering.
2. **woeful ballad:** sad, sentimental song.
3. **pard:** leopard.
4. **bubble reputation:** reputation, which disintegrates as quickly as a bubble.
5. **with good capon** (kā′pŏn′) **lin'd:** full of chicken.
6. **saws...instances:** old sayings and examples showing how they still apply.
7. **pantaloon** (păn′tə-lōōn′): a foolish old man.

The First and the Last Steps, Emilio Longoni. Private Collection. © Alinari/Art Resource, New York.

ANALYZE VISUALS
After reading the poem, what connection can you see between the poem and this image?

For his shrunk shank;[8] and his big manly voice,
Turning again toward childish treble,[9] pipes
25 And whistles in his sound. Last scene of all, **C**
That ends this strange eventful history,
Is second childishness and mere oblivion,[10]
Sans[11] teeth, sans eyes, sans taste, sans everything.

C METER
Read aloud lines 20–25, tapping your foot at each stressed syllable. How many stressed syllables are in each line?

8. **youthful hose . . . shank:** The stockings of his youth are too large for his shrunken calves.

9. **treble:** a high-pitched voice.

10. **oblivion** (ə-blĭv′ē-ən): complete forgetfulness.

11. **sans** (sän) *French:* without.

The Road Not Taken

In the Beechwoods, William Samuel Jay. Oil on canvas, 91.4 × 122 cm. Private collection. © Bourne Gallery, Reigate, Surrey/The Bridgeman Art Library.

ROBERT FROST

Two roads diverged[1] in a yellow wood,
And sorry I could not travel both
And be one traveler, long I stood
And looked down one as far as I could
5 To where it bent in the undergrowth; **D**

Then took the other, as just as fair,
And having perhaps the better claim,
Because it was grassy and wanted wear;
Though as for that the passing there
10 Had worn them really about the same, **E**

And both that morning equally lay
In leaves no step had trodden[2] black.
Oh, I kept the first for another day!
Yet knowing how way leads on to way,
15 I doubted if I should ever come back.

I shall be telling this with a sigh
Somewhere ages and ages hence:
Two roads diverged in a wood, and I—
I took the one less traveled by,
20 And that has made all the difference. **F**

D ANALYZE IDEAS
Reread lines 1–5. What main idea is the poet expressing here?

E METER
Read aloud lines 1-10, tapping your foot with each stressed syllable. How many pulses are in each line? Which words in the second stanza are emphasized by the pulses?

F RHYME SCHEME
What rhyme scheme does Frost use in this poem?

---

1. **diverged:** branched out; went in different directions.

2. **trodden:** walked on or trampled.

Comprehension

1. **Recall** In "The Seven Ages of Man," which two stages follow infancy and childhood?

2. **Paraphrase** According to Jaques, what happens to people in the last stage of life?

3. **Recall** In "The Road Not Taken," where do Frost's roads diverge?

4. **Clarify** Which road does the speaker choose?

PENNSYLVANIA STANDARDS

READING STANDARD
A.1.4.1 Identify and explain main ideas and relevant details

Literary Analysis

5. **Analyze Ideas** Look at the chart of main ideas that you filled out for each poem as you read. On the basis of these ideas taken together, what do you think is the **theme** of each poem?

6. **Interpret Extended Metaphor** An extended metaphor compares two unlike things at length and in a number of ways, sometimes throughout an entire work. In "The Seven Ages of Man," the speaker compares the world to a stage. What does this comparison imply about the speaker's view of life?

7. **Analyze Dramatic Monologue** "The Seven Ages of Man" comes from Shakespeare's play *As You Like It*. Other characters in this play refer to Jaques as "the melancholy Jaques." Do you agree that Jaques has a gloomy outlook on life? Support your answer with details from his **dramatic monologue.** What else can you **infer** about Jaques from his speech?

8. **Interpret Symbol** In "The Road Not Taken," both roads lead into the woods, so the speaker cannot see where they go. What do the woods symbolize?

9. **Compare Themes** How would Frost's speaker respond to Jaques' statement "All the world's a stage, / And all the men and women merely players"? Cite evidence to support your answer.

10. **Evaluate Meter** "The Seven Ages of Man" is written in **iambic pentameter,** which has five stressed syllables alternating with five unstressed syllables per line. It is said to be the closest meter to human speech in English. "The Road Not Taken" is written loosely in **iambic tetrameter,** which has only four stresses instead of five. Do you find one poem easier to read aloud than the other? Explain your answer.

Literary Criticism

11. **Author's Style** In many of Shakespeare's plays, there is a character who comments philosophically on the world of the characters and on the world at large. It is sometimes thought that this character is speaking for Shakespeare himself. Could Jaques's monologue be seen as giving voice to the playwright? Explain your answer, giving evidence from the text.

Personal Response to a Poem

As you may have learned from the poems in this unit, it's hard to read a poem without reacting to it—positively or negatively. Just as you may want to share your reactions to a movie you've seen or a concert you've heard, you can share your reactions to a poem by writing a personal response. The **Writer's Road Map** can show you the way.

WRITER'S ROAD MAP

Personal Response to a Poem

WRITING PROMPT 1

Writing from Literature Choose a poem or group of poems that caused a strong emotional response in you. Write a personal response that helps you figure out the meaning of the poem or poems. If you wish, include information about how your own memories or experiences affected your reaction.

Poems to Explore

- "My Papa's Waltz"
- "Grape Sherbet"
- "The Road Not Taken"

WRITING PROMPT 2

Writing for the Real World Song lyrics are poems set to music. Write an essay for a music magazine in which you describe your response to a song or a type of music. Give readers specific examples of lyrics to show why the song or type of music matters to you.

Types of Music to Explore

- rap
- country and western

WRITING TOOLS
For prewriting, revision, and editing tools, visit the **Writing Center** at ClassZone.com.

KEY TRAITS

1. **IDEAS**
   - Clearly presents an **overall response** to the poem or poems
   - Provides specific **details** and **quotations** to support the key ideas
   - **Elaborates** on the examples

2. **ORGANIZATION**
   - Begins by **identifying** the poem or group of poems
   - Includes an engaging **introduction** and a **conclusion** that summarizes the response

3. **VOICE**
   - **Tone** reflects the writer's personal reaction

4. **WORD CHOICE**
   - Uses **precise language** to convey the personal response

5. **SENTENCE FLUENCY**
   - Varies **sentence beginnings** to add interest and energy

6. **CONVENTIONS**
   - Employs **correct grammar and usage**

Part 1: Analyze a Student Model

WRITING STANDARD
1.4.11.B Write complex informational pieces

Leshon Reynolds
Wells High School

Two Views of Competition

When I play basketball, I play to win; but I also love to hear a cheering, shouting, stomping crowd of fans. The poems "400-Meter Free Style" by Maxine Kumin and "Bodybuilders' Contest" by Wislawa Szymborska are about athletes, and because I am an athlete, they caught
5 my attention. Both poems have to do with sports, and both are told from a spectator's point of view. However, because they portray athletes so differently, the poems made me think about the positive and negative aspects of competition.

Maxine Kumin's poem has a positive view of competition. "400-
10 Meter Free Style" is full of action: "full swing the swimmer catapults and cracks." The lines of the poem rush back and forth across the page like a swimmer in a race. The poem describes a talented swimmer. According to the speaker, "he has schooled out all extravagance," which means that he doesn't waste energy. His muscles, mouth, arms, feet, and lungs all know
15 exactly what to do as he surges forward. The speaker comments, "We watch him for signs." This could mean that the spectators are looking for indications that he is getting tired, or it could mean that the spectators admire him and look up to him. The poet seems to respect the swimmer for focusing all his energy and talent on one goal—to be as fast as
20 possible when competing. I respect the swimmer, too. He isn't interested in what the spectators think of him. All he cares about is the time on the clock. Similarly, in basketball, all that really matters is the final score.

In contrast, Wislawa Szymborska's poem has a negative view of

---

KEY TRAITS IN ACTION

Engaging **introduction identifies** the poems and states the writer's **overall response.**

Provides specific **details** and **quotations** from the poem so readers can understand the response.

Elaborates on the examples to explain his response. Thoughtful, sincere **tone** expresses the writer's personal reaction.

competition. "Bodybuilders' Contest" seems admiring at first. The
25 bodybuilder is "all muscles. . . . The king of all is he. . . ." However, the
speaker mocks the bodybuilder, saying that he "preens" and that his
sinews are "twisted into monstrous pretzels." He is someone to make
fun of, not someone to admire or fear. In the second stanza, the speaker
mentions that the bodybuilder's routine is "smoothly choreographed,"
30 but he doesn't actually do anything. The bear and panthers he fights
are imaginary. I believe the poet is saying that bodybuilding is vain
and pointless, no matter how much the bodybuilder practices or how
many prizes he wins. At first I agreed with this point of view, but I have
changed my mind. Posing *is* the bodybuilder's sport. Maybe battling the
35 imaginary animals is an expected part of the routine. Instead of a clock
or a final score, a group of judges decides who wins.

> Uses **precise language**
> (*vain, pointless, battling*).
> Varied **sentence
> beginnings** create rhythm
> and flow.

    Reading these poems made me think about how I act on the
basketball court and how I view other players. Flashy moves and dunks
impress fans and teammates, much as the "poses and paces" do in
40 "Bodybuilders' Contest." But there's something to be said for efficiency,
for channeling every bit of energy into getting the job done, like the
swimmer in "400-Meter Free Style." Each poem gives a spectator's view
of a highly competitive athlete. Even though I love the cheers of the
crowd, I would rather be like the swimmer than the bodybuilder.

> **Conclusion** summarizes
> the response and explains
> what the writer learned.

2

Part 2: Apply the Writing Process

WRITING STANDARD
1.4.11.B.1 Develop the main idea

PREWRITING

What Should I Do?

1. Note words or lines that puzzle or move you.
Use a reading log to jot down lines and your understanding of them. (Circle) the quotations, questions, and comments that seem most important.

TIP If the poem reminds you of an experience from your own life, think about including that information in your response.

What Does It Look Like?

Quotations	My Interpretations
"the swimmer catapults and cracks"	He's rushing back and forth like the lines in the poem.
"he has schooled out all extravagance"	He's a good swimmer because he doesn't waste energy.
"The (king) of all is he who preens and wrestles"	He's strong, but is the poet making fun of him?

2. Freewrite about the poem(s) and your reactions.
Look at the quotations and interpretations you circled in step 1. What do they have in common? How are they different? Jot down your thoughts and feelings.

▶ 2 poems, both about athletes, I'm an athlete so that's why they interest me
how are they different? is one poem positive & the other negative?

3. Draft a working thesis statement.
Think about your interpretation of the poem(s). Draft a statement that explains your overall response.

▶ *Working thesis statement:*

I'm an athlete, so the poems got my attention. Both are about athletes, but from the spectator's point of view. One shows a positive view of an athlete and the other is negative.

4. Look for more evidence.
Reread the poems. Look for ideas, quotations, or devices (such as repetition) that support your thesis statement. For easy reference during drafting, use a chart or other graphic device to record these elements.

▶ *Kumin poem: positive view*

1. Powerful: "catapults and cracks"
2. Efficient: "schooled out all extravagance"
3. "We watch him for signs": we admire him, want to be like him?

DRAFTING

What Should I Do?	**What Does It Look Like?**

1. Create a powerful introduction.
Grab readers' attention with an introduction that identifies the poem or poems you are responding to and outlines your response.

TIP Consider opening with a quotation from the poem(s), a question to readers, or a vivid description from the poem(s) or your own life.

▶

A question

Have you ever won a game in front of a cheering crowd? If so, you may enjoy the two views of athletes presented in the poems "400-Meter Free Style" by Maxine Kumin and "Bodybuilders' Contest" by Wislawa Szymborska.

A vivid description

When I play basketball, I play to win; but I also love to hear a cheering, shouting, stomping crowd of fans. . . .

2. Organize your response.
Two ways of organizing your response are (1) to discuss the poem(s) using quotations and ideas in the order in which they appear in the poem, and (2) to discuss the most important quotation or idea first, then the second most important, and so on, ending with the least important quotation or idea in the poem(s).

Because this writer included two poems in his response, he decided to discuss one poem at a time to avoid confusing his reader. Each idea or quotation is discussed in the order in which it appears in the poem.

▶

Introduction: Poems present two views of competition.

Positive view: Kumin
1. Powerful: "catapults and cracks"
2. Efficient: "schooled out all extravagance"
3. "We watch him for signs": We admire him, want to be like him?
4. My thoughts: I respect the swimmer.

Negative view: Szymborska
1. Powerful: "all muscles"
2. Ridiculous: "preens," "monstrous"
3. Fights imaginary monsters
4. My thoughts: Poet is too harsh.

Conclusion: Poems made me think about how I compete.

3. Go beyond the evidence.
Don't just cite words and lines from the poem(s) that affected you. Explain how you reacted and why.

TIP Stay focused on your response to the poem(s). Give readers only the information that supports your ideas.

▶

The speaker mentioned that the bodybuilder's routine is "smoothly choreographed," but the animals he fights are imaginary. ⎤ Quotation

I believe the poet is saying that bodybuilding is ridiculous. At first I agreed, but I have changed my mind. Posing _is_ the bodybuilder's sport. Maybe battling the imaginary animals is part of the routine. ⎤ Personal response

REVISING AND EDITING

What Should I Do?

1. Strengthen your support.
- Number the reasons, examples, or explanations you provided.
- If you don't have many numbers, add supporting evidence and elaboration.

2. Vary sentence beginnings.
- Read aloud what you have written. Do many of your sentences have the same beginning?
- Highlight sentences that begin the same way.
- Rewrite the beginnings of some sentences to create interest and fluency.

3. Eliminate vague vocabulary.
- Ask a peer reader to point out words and phrases in your response that lack detail.
- [Bracket] vocabulary that is weak and imprecise.
- Replace these words or phrases with strong, specific ones.

   See page 732: Ask a Peer Reader

4. Include appropriate transitions.
- Look at the beginning and end of each paragraph. Have you included transitional words, phrases , or sentences that help the reader understand your message?
- Draw a box around sentences that are not connected logically.
- Insert transitions that show the relationship between ideas.

What Does It Look Like?

▶ Maxine Kumin's poem has a positive view of competition. It is full of action: "the swimmer catapults and cracks." ①

The swimmer is talented. "He has schooled out all extravagance," which means that he doesn't waste energy. ②

His muscles, mouth, arms, feet, and lungs all know what to do as he surges forward. ③

▶ ~~He has to pose because it's part of his sport.~~
~~He has to battle the imaginary animals.~~

Posing is the bodybuilder's sport. Maybe battling the imaginary animals is an expected part of the routine.

▶   respect
I [like] the swimmer, too. He isn't interested in
       the spectators
what [people] think of him.

▶ Similarly, in basketball, all that really matters is the final score.

   Wislawa Szymborska's poem has a negative view of competition.
In contrast,

Personal Response to a Poem

Apply the Rubric

An effective personal response to a poem . . .

☑ begins by identifying the poem and stating an overall response

☑ provides information and specific details from the poem to support statements

☑ explains how and why lines from the poem elicited the personal response

☑ expresses ideas clearly in strong, precise language

☑ has a tone that reflects the writer's feelings

☑ creates fluency and interest with varied sentence beginnings

☑ concludes by effectively summarizing the response

Ask a Peer Reader

• How would you describe my reaction to the poem or poems?

• What evidence could I have included to make my statements more convincing?

• Which parts of my response could be more specific?

Check Your Grammar

• Use complete sentences. Correct any fragments—words or phrases that are punctuated as sentences but are missing a subject, a predicate, or both.

> He isn't interested in what the spectators think of him. ~~Just the time on the clock. In basketball too.~~
>
> He isn't interested in what the spectators think of him. All he cares about is the time on the clock. Similarly, in basketball, all that really matters is the final score.

See page R64: Correcting Fragments

• Keep verbs in the active voice. Active verbs help make your response forceful and convincing.

> Teammates and fans <u>are impressed by</u> flashy moves and dunks.
>
> Flashy moves and dunks impress fans and teammates.

See page R57: Active and Passive Voice

Writing Online

PUBLISHING OPTIONS
For publishing options, visit the **Writing Center** at **ClassZone.com.**

ASSESSMENT PREPARATION
For writing and grammar assessment practice, go to the **Assessment Center** at **ClassZone.com.**

PUBLISHING WITH TECHNOLOGY

Creating a Multimedia Presentation

Expand and strengthen your personal response to a poem by turning it into a multimedia presentation.

Planning the Presentation

1. **Know your technology.** Ask your teacher or your school's media specialist what authoring programs are available. An authoring program is a tool that lets you combine word processing with different types of media. Depending on the program, you might create a slide-show presentation or an interactive project with multiple links.

2. **Focus on your response.** Identify your main point about the poem(s). List quotations that illustrate that point.

3. **Gather media elements.** Find or create pictures, video clips, sound effects, words, and music that convey a mood or message similar to your response.

4. **Chart it out.** Make a flow chart that shows how your presentation will be organized. A slide-show presentation is usually linear, with one screen leading to another. An interactive presentation has branches like a tree, with each branch being a different choice that the user can make. See page 1231 for an example of this type of chart.

5. **Create a storyboard.** Sketch out, frame by frame, what your audience will see and hear. Specify the images, text, buttons, links, and sounds you will use. Think about whether you want to read lines from the poem as voice-overs or use them as onscreen text. See page 391 for an explanation of storyboarding.

Producing the Presentation

1. **Author the project.** Scan, download, or record the elements and use the authoring program to combine them.

2. **Test and revise.** Make sure that all information is correct and that all links work. Ask a few classmates to review your presentation before you give it.

3. **Present and reflect.** Present your project to an audience, or have small groups explore it on their own. Ask for feedback about small details and about the "big picture." What message did audience members take away from your presentation? Was that the message you wanted to send?

Reading Comprehension

DIRECTIONS *Read the following poems and then answer the questions.*

The Sower

Victor Hugo

Peaceful and cool, the twilight grey
Draws a dim curtain o'er the day,
While in my cottage-porch I lurk
And watch the last lone hour of work.

5 The fields around are bathed in dew,
And, with emotion filled, I view
An old man clothed in rags, who throws
The seed amid the channeled rows.

His shadowy form is looming now
10 High o'er the furrows of the plough;
Each motion of his arm betrays
A boundless faith in future days.

He stalks along the ample plain,
Comes, goes, and flings abroad the grain;
15 Unnoted, through the dreamy haze
With meditative soul I gaze.

At last, the vapours of the night
Dilate to heav'n the old man's height,
Till every gesture of his hand
20 Seems to my eyes sublimely grand!

Translated by George Murray

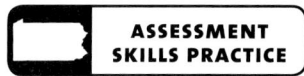
To Be of Use

Marge Piercy

The people I love the best
jump into work head first
without dallying in the shallows
and swim off with sure strokes almost out of sight.
5 They seem to become natives of that element,
the black sleek heads of seals
bouncing like half-submerged balls.

I love people who harness themselves, an ox to a heavy cart,
who pull like water buffalo, with massive patience,
10 who strain in the mud and the muck to move things forward,
who do what has to be done, again and again.

I want to be with people who submerge
in the task, who go into the fields to harvest
and work in a row and pass the bags along,
15 who are not parlor generals and field deserters
but move in a common rhythm
when the food must come in or the fire be put out.

The work of the world is common as mud.
Botched, it smears the hands, crumbles to dust.
20 But the thing worth doing well done
has a shape that satisfies, clean and evident.
Greek amphoras for wine or oil,
Hopi vases that held corn, are put in museums
but you know they were made to be used.
25 The pitcher cries for water to carry
and a person for work that is real.

GO ON

Comprehension

DIRECTIONS *Answer these questions about "The Sower."*

1. The speaker uses a metaphor in lines 1–4 to compare the twilight to

    A a peaceful workplace

    B a dim curtain

    C a cottage-porch

    D a lonely job

2. Each stanza in "The Sower" is made up of

    A four lines that are incomplete sentences

    B four complete sentences that rhyme with each other

    C one complete sentence with rhyming parts

    D one part of a sentence that concludes in the last stanza

3. The rhyme scheme in every stanza of "The Sower" is

    A *abab*   C *abba*

    B *aabb*   D *abcd*

4. Which pair of words is an example of alliteration in the poem?

    A form, arm (lines 9, 11)

    B haze, gaze (lines 15, 16)

    C draws, dim (line 2)

    D furrows, plough (line 10)

5. From the image in lines 17–20, you can infer that the speaker

    A thinks that the old man is an amazing person

    B is frightened by the shadows that are on the field

    C hopes that he is not just dreaming about the farm

    D believes that the work of planting grain is noble

6. Which pair of words is an example of assonance in the poem?

    A old, clothed (line 7)

    B seed, amid (line 8)

    C stalks, ample (line 13)

    D seems, eyes (line 20)

7. Which group of words in lines 13–16 helps you visualize what the old man is doing in the field?

    A stalks, comes, goes, flings

    B along, ample, abroad, unnoted

    C plain, grain, dreamy, soul

    D he, through, haze, meditative

DIRECTIONS *Answer these questions about "To Be of Use."*

8. What is the most likely meaning of the metaphor in lines 1–7?

    A Seals and people like to swim long distances instead of wading in shallow water.

    B Some people immerse themselves in work in the way that seals immerse themselves in water.

    C Seals and people dive right into their work and have the same good work habits.

    D Some people have as much fun at work as seals do when they play around in the water.

9. Which of the following is an example of a simile in the poem?

    A "I love people who harness themselves"

    B "The work of the world is common as mud."

    C "I want to be with people who submerge / in the task"

    D "But the thing worth doing well done / has a shape that satisfies"

10. In lines 8–11, the speaker uses the repetition of "who" and "again" to emphasize an image of

A people who diligently struggle to do their work

B sturdy animals that are trained to haul heavy loads

C the type of work that the speaker prefers to do

D people who are required to be physically strong to do their work

11. The assonance and alliteration used in line 10 help to create an image of

A people who are clumsy when they perform physical labor

B people who struggle against obstacles to accomplish their work

C animals that are forced to perform dangerous tasks

D animals that work alongside people on farms

12. The alliteration in "But the thing worth doing well done" (line 20) emphasizes the

A importance of rewarding people who do a good job

B different ways that people perform their jobs

C connection between working and doing a good job

D necessity of carrying out a job from the beginning to the end

13. The phrase "work that is real" in line 26 most likely refers to work that

A has a meaningful purpose

B is physically challenging

C includes making objects

D takes place outdoors

14. Which one of the following objects is personified in lines 22–26?

A corn   C vase

B amphoras   D pitcher

DIRECTIONS *Answer the following questions about both poems.*

15. Which type of work can you visualize from images in both poems?

A fishing   C farming

B logging   D building

16. The speakers of both poems would most likely agree with which one of the following statements?

A Outdoor occupations are dangerous.

B Workers' relationships are important.

C The best workers love their work.

D Work is something to be valued.

Open-Ended Items

17. List five words or phrases that help you visualize the time of day at which "The Sower" takes place. Why is visualizing that particular time of day important to this poem?

18. Compare the form of the poem "The Sower" with that of "To Be of Use." Explain how the line length, meter, and rhyme help convey the ideas and images of each poem.

Writing and Grammar

DIRECTIONS *Read this passage and answer the questions that follow.*

(1) In her poem "For the Young Who Want To," Marge Piercy encourages young people who are in pursuit of their passion. (2) As is the case with many of Piercy's poems, the structure of this poem is organic. (3) Since it has no meter or end rhymes, it is difficult to memorize. (4) But its six stanzas are filled with strong statements that grab the reader's attention. (5) "Talent is what they say / you have after the novel / is published and favorably / reviewed," the poet states. (6) This assertion reflects Piercy's belief that artists receive praise from the public only after they have received the admiration of critics. (7) During the countless years that artists sacrifice so much time working on their art, their friends think it's just a hobby. (8) They keep asking artists when they are going to search for a real job. (9) As a result of this indirect form of criticism, artists sometimes seek to prove the legitimacy of their craft. (10) Piercy suggests that even though artists don't have licenses, they are still experts in their field. (11) She then points out that the real writer is the one who practices the craft of writing. (12) Finally, Piercy concludes that what drives an artist is loving the work, with or without recognition.

1. How would you change sentence 1 to include an infinitive?

   A Change "encourages" to "convinces."

   B Change "who are in pursuit of" to "pursuing."

   C Change "who are in pursuit of" to "to pursue."

   D No change is needed.

2. Choose the correct way to rewrite sentence 3 using a participial phrase.

   A Lacking meter or end rhymes, it is difficult to memorize.

   B Since it lacks both meter and end rhymes, it is difficult to memorize.

   C The lack of meter or end rhymes makes it difficult to memorize.

   D No change is needed.

3. How would you change sentence 4 to include a participle?

   A Change "grab" to "demand."

   B Change "strong" to "vivid."

   C Change "strong" to "arresting."

   D No change is needed.

4. How would you change sentence 6 to include a participle?

   A Change "of critics" to "of newspaper critics."

   B Change "the admiration of critics" to "compliments from admiring critics."

   C Change "receive praise from the public" to "are praised by the public."

   D No change is needed.

5. How would you change sentence 7 to include an infinitive?

A Change "working" to "to work."

B Change "sacrifice" to "are sacrificing."

C Change "During the countless years" to "For the years."

D No change is needed.

6. How would you change sentence 8 to include an infinitive?

A Change "They keep asking artists" to "They wonder."

B Change "going to search" to "searching."

C Change "going to search" to "looking."

D No change is needed.

7. Choose the correct way to rewrite sentence 9 using a participle.

A As a result of this implied criticism, artists sometimes seek to prove the legitimacy of their craft.

B As a result of this indirect form of criticism, artists sometimes seek to prove that their craft is legitimate.

C As a result of this indirect form of criticism, artists sometimes are forced to prove the legitimacy of their craft.

D No change is needed.

8. Choose the correct way to rewrite sentence 10 using a participial phrase.

A Piercy suggests that although artists don't have licenses, they are still experts in their field.

B Piercy suggests that even though artists don't have licenses, it doesn't mean they lack talent.

C Piercy suggests that even though artists don't have licenses hanging on their walls, they are still experts in their field.

D No change is needed.

9. Choose the correct way to rewrite sentence 12 using an infinitive phrase.

A Finally, Piercy draws the conclusion that what drives an artist is loving the work, with or without recognition.

B Finally, Piercy concludes that what drives an artist is the ability to love the work, with or without recognition.

C Finally, Piercy concludes that what drives an artist is loving the work, whether or not the art is recognized.

D No change is needed.

STOP

Great Reads

Ideas for Independent Reading

Writers use poetic language in both the poetry and prose of the following selections.

What makes a strong competitor?

The Old Man and the Sea
by Ernest Hemingway

Hemingway's concise style depicts Santiago, a Cuban fisherman, as he battles a giant marlin. The competition does not end when Santiago lands the huge creature.

The Hot Zone
by Richard Preston

This suspenseful true account of dealing with an outbreak of Ebola virus serves as a warning to humankind. The struggle between viruses and humans is likely to intensify in the future.

The Big Year: A Tale of Man, Nature, and Fowl Obsession
by Mark Obmascik

A birding marathon in 1998 lasted for 365 days, during which bird watchers tried to set a new record for number of species seen worldwide. The author describes the marathon and three of the passionate competitors.

Where can your imagination take you?

About This Life
by Barry Lopez

The author's ability to see the natural world in fresh and startling ways makes him one of the nation's most valued naturalists and writers.

19 Varieties of Gazelle
by Naomi Shihab Nye

A Palestinian-American poet, Nye writes of animals, people, food, war and peace, and how life has changed in painful ways for Palestinians living in the occupied West Bank.

Spoon River Anthology
by Edgar Lee Masters

Under the sod of a Midwestern cemetery lie 244 souls. In this poetic classic, they speak to readers about their lives—full of disappointment and loss—and their inevitable deaths, some peaceful and some violent.

Do you set your own course?

We Die Alone: A WWII Epic of Escape and Endurance
by David Howarth

Norwegian commandos race for the Swedish border to escape from Nazi pursuers. This true account demonstrates the strength and endurance of the human spirit.

Great Expectations
by Charles Dickens

Set in 19th-century England, this novel depicts the rags-to-riches story of the orphan Pip. Pip dreams of becoming a gentleman, and a secret patron arranges for this to happen. When Pip moves to London to fulfill his "great expectations," he learns the true meaning of nobility and love.

In the Shadow of Man
by Jane Goodall

From her memoir we learn that when Goodall began chimpanzee research in 1960, women didn't do primate studies. Her scientific discoveries paved the way for other women to do similar work.

UNIT 8

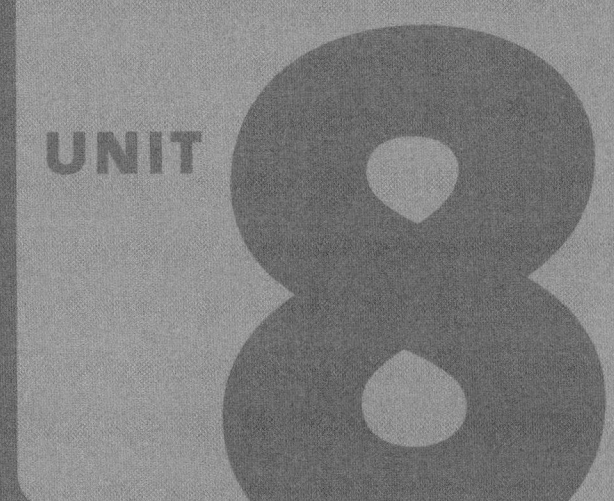

A Way with Words

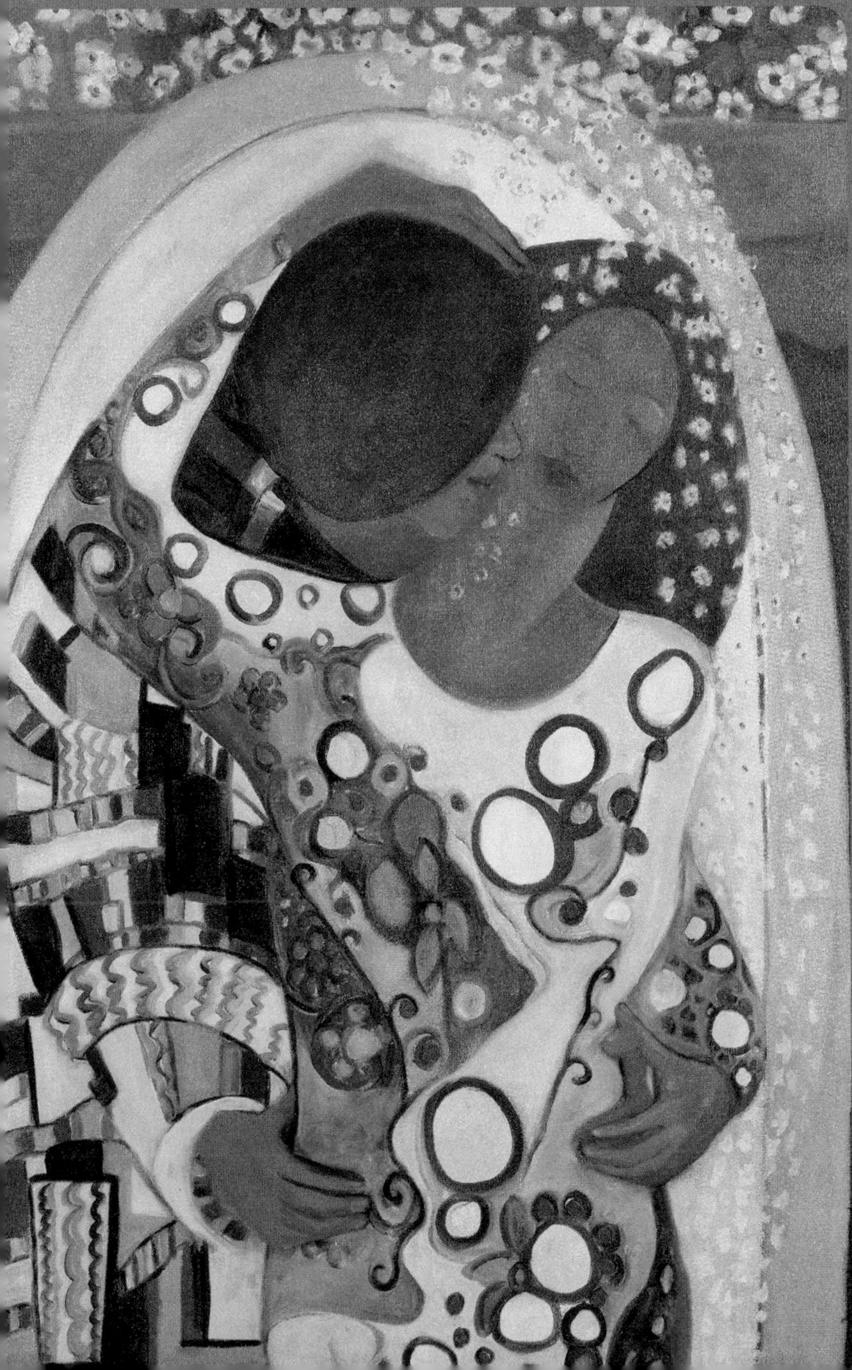

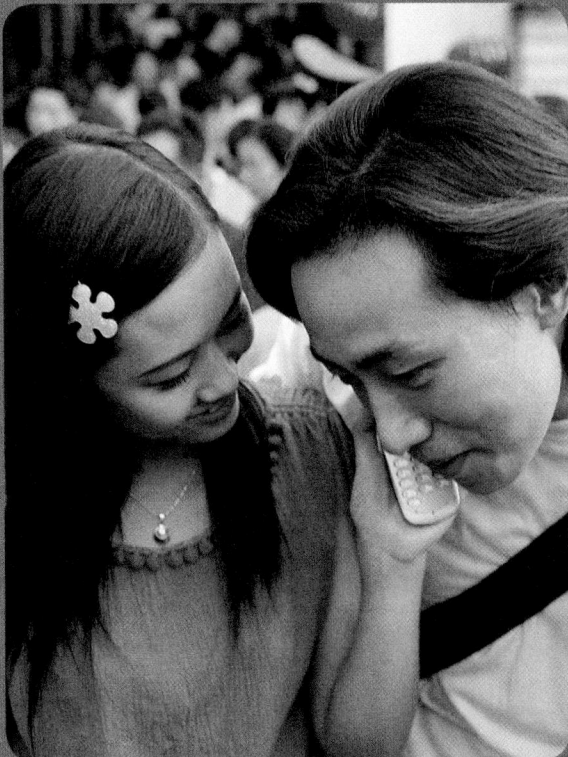

AUTHOR'S STYLE AND VOICE

- In Fiction
- In Media
- In Nonfiction
- In Poetry
- In Drama

What is STYLE?

What draws you to a certain band's songs, a specific director's movies, or a particular writer's work? The answer to these questions can often be attributed to **style.** Style is what makes the work of writers and other creative people distinctive.

ACTIVITY With a small group, list artists—actors, songwriters, painters, authors, or directors—who have unique styles. Then pick one of these people and answer the following questions:

• What about the artist's work is distinctive? Are there characteristics that make his or her work immediately recognizable?

• What ties all of the artist's work together? For example, maybe your favorite songwriter uses the same imagery in all of his or her lyrics.

• What three words would you use to describe your artist's style?

PENNSYLVANIA
STANDARDS

Preview Unit Goals

LITERARY ANALYSIS
- Identify and analyze elements of style, including word choice, tone, sentence structure, and figurative language
- Analyze the impact of style on meaning
- Analyze writers' styles
- Analyze humor, parody, and farce

READING
- Use reading strategies, including visualizing and predicting
- Summarize and paraphrase
- Interpret ideas in poetry

WRITING AND GRAMMAR
- Write an analysis of an author's style
- Support main points with examples from the text
- Vary sentence types

SPEAKING, LISTENING, AND VIEWING
- Analyze Alfred Hitchcock's style in film
- Analyze visual elements in film
- Create a production still
- Deliver a dramatic reading

VOCABULARY
- Use prefixes to help unlock meaning
- Understand and use homonyms

ACADEMIC VOCABULARY
- elements of style
- realism
- irony
- humor
- parody
- visual elements in film
- homonym

Author's Style and Voice

What makes classical music different from rap? How can you tell the difference between a spine-tingling Edgar Allan Poe story and a Stephen King thriller? The answer is style, or the unique elements that make everything—from music to writing—distinctive. Style is what helps you tell *Newsweek* from the *National Enquirer* or a Shakespearean sonnet from a poem by E. E. Cummings. Often, the style of what you read can affect you just as much as the substance.

 PENNSYLVANIA STANDARDS

READING STANDARDS
B.1.1.1.E.1 Analyze and/or evaluate tone and style
B.2.1.2 Analyze the author's use of figurative language in text

Part 1: What Is Style?

In literature, **style** is the way a particular work is written—not what is said, but *how* it's said. A writer's style depends on many elements, including his or her choice of words, tone, and sentence structures. Does the writer use long sentences packed with flowery details or ones that are short and to the point? Is the tone laced with sarcasm, or is it sincere?

COMMON STYLE	EXAMPLE
FORMAL • uses sophisticated, abstract language • may use complex sentence structures • carefully observes rules of grammar	And was Mr. Rochester now ugly in my eyes? No, reader: gratitude and many associations, all pleasurable and genial, made his face the object I best liked to see. . . . —from *Jane Eyre* by Charlotte Brontë
Informal • sounds like everyday conversation • may use contractions and slang • may use simple sentences and fragments	Remember that boy you thought you could not live without? What was his name? Randy. You don't remember? —from *The Kitchen God's Wife* by Amy Tan
Journalistic • uses neutral words to report facts • often includes simple sentences • reader notices what's said, not who's talking	A lightning flash can happen in half a second. In that instant, the lightning flash superheats the surrounding air to a temperature five times hotter than that on the surface of the sun. —from *nationalgeographic.com*
Literary • may use imagery to convey a mood • often includes long, elaborate sentences • reader often gets to know the narrator—the voice that tells the story	The lightning quivered about the pinnacles of the ancient Hôtel de Ville, and shed flickering gleams over the open space in front. —from "The Adventure of the German Student" by Washington Irving

MODEL 1: STYLE

This excerpt comes from a famous novel about life on the Nebraska prairie. As you read, consider the common styles listed on the preceding page. Which style or styles do you think characterize the writing?

from
My Ántonia
Novel by **Willa Cather**

While the train flashed through never-ending miles of ripe wheat, by country towns and bright-flowered pastures and oak groves wilting in the sun, we sat in the observation car, where the woodwork was hot to the touch and red dust lay deep over everything. The dust and heat, the burning wind, reminded us of many things. We were talking about what it is like to spend one's childhood in little towns like these, buried in wheat and corn, under stimulating extremes of climate: burning summers when the world lies green and billowy beneath a brilliant sky, when one is fairly stifled in vegetation, in the color and smell of strong weeds and heavy harvests; blustery winters with little snow, when the whole country is stripped bare and gray as sheet-iron.

5

10

Close Read

1. Notice the sentence length and the use of imagery in the boxed text. On the basis of these details, how would you describe the style of this excerpt?

2. Identify another detail that helped you determine the style.

MODEL 2: STYLE

Here, another writer offers a different description of a prairie. As you read, consider how the writer's style compares with Willa Cather's in the excerpt from *My Ántonia*.

from
PRAIRYERTH
Nonfiction by **William Least Heat-Moon**

The Flint Hills are the last remaining grand expanse of tallgrass prairie in America. On a geologic map, their shape something like a stone spear point, they cover most of the two-hundred-mile longitude of Kansas from Nebraska to Oklahoma, a stony upland twenty to eighty miles wide. At their western edge, the mixed-grass prairie begins and spreads a hundred or so miles to the shortgrass country of the high plains.

5

Close Read

1. Is this excerpt literary or journalistic? Support your answer.

2. Contrast Heat-Moon's style with Cather's. Identify at least two specific differences.

Part 2: Style and Voice

Almost every choice a writer makes contributes to the style of his or her work. These choices also help to create a **voice,** the personality that comes across on the page. The voice may be the writer's, or it may belong to a fictional character in a story.

Here, two writers express feelings about their craft. A close look at three key elements—word choice, sentence structure, and tone—in these passages can help you better understand each writer's unique style.

COMPARING STYLES

It is [the writer's] privilege to help man endure by lifting his heart, by reminding him of the courage and honor and hope and pride and compassion and pity and sacrifice which have been the glory of his past.

—William Faulkner, Nobel Prize acceptance speech, 1950

The very first thing I tell my new students on the first day of a workshop is that good writing is about telling the truth. We are a species that needs and wants to understand who we are. Sheep lice do not seem to share this longing, which is one reason they write so very little.

—Anne Lamott, *Bird by Bird*

WORD CHOICE

If you've ever struggled to find the perfect words to describe something, then you know how important **word choice** can be. A short boy can be *compact, shrimpy,* even *Lilliputian*—or just *short.* The **denotation** (literal meaning) is the same, but the **connotations** (emotional associations) are quite different.

In his speech, Faulkner uses formal, dramatic words and phrases—for example, "the glory of his past"—to emphasize the serious responsibility of writers. Lamott's writing, however, is more conversational. Her use of *I* and *we,* as well as phrases like "the very first thing," contributes to her personable style.

SENTENCE STRUCTURE

Sentences can be short and to the point (like Lamott's) or long and complex (like Faulkner's). In fact, the Faulkner excerpt is one long sentence that strings together *hope, courage,* and other weighty words with a series of *and*'s. This structure adds to the dramatic impact of the writing and helps to create its formal style.

TONE

Tone is a writer's attitude toward a subject, as expressed through choice of words and details. Faulkner's focus on the writer's "privilege" conveys a formal tone. Lamott, however, scampers playfully from truth to sheep lice. Such incongruous details help to create a humorous tone.

MODEL 1: ELEMENTS OF STYLE

Sandra Cisneros has a unique and recognizable style of writing. As you read this excerpt, pay attention to her word choice and the structure of the sentences. To get the full effect of Cisneros's style, read the excerpt aloud. Does it sound like someone writing or like someone talking?

from **Geraldo**
No Last Name

Vignette by **Sandra Cisneros**

She met him at a dance. Pretty too, and young. Said he worked in a restaurant, but she can't remember which one. Geraldo. That's all. Green pants and Saturday shirt. Geraldo. That's what he told her.

And how was she to know she'd be the last one to see him alive. An accident, don't you know. Hit-and-run. Marin, she goes to all those dances. Uptown.
Logan. Embassy. Palmer. Aragon. Fontana. The Manor. She likes to dance.
She knows how to do cumbias and salsas and rancheras even. And he was just someone she danced with. Somebody she met that night. That's right.

That's the story. That's what she said again and again. Once to the hospital people and twice to the police. No address. No name. Nothing in his pockets.

Close Read

1. Describe the structure of the sentences in the box. What effect do these sentences have on the style of the excerpt and the narrator's voice?

2. Find an example of word choice that would not belong in a story written in a formal style.

MODEL 2: ELEMENTS OF STYLE

Jane Austen is known for her "novels of manners," in which she recorded the details of 19th-century middle-class British life with irony and humor. How does her style of writing differ from Cisneros's?

from *Pride* and *Prejudice*

Novel by **Jane Austen**

Elizabeth Bennet had been obliged by the scarcity of gentlemen to sit down for two dances; and during part of that time, Mr. Darcy had been standing near enough for her to overhear a conversation between him and Mr. Bingley, who came from the dance for a few minutes to press his friend to join it.

"Come, Darcy," said he, "I must have you dance. I hate to see you standing about by yourself in this stupid manner. You had much better dance."

"I certainly shall not. You know how I detest it, unless I am particularly acquainted with my partner. At such an assembly as this, it would be insupportable. Your sisters are engaged, and there is not another woman in the room whom it would not be a punishment to me to stand up with."

Close Read

1. What specific words and details in this excerpt help to convey a prim and proper tone?

2. Reread lines 1–4. What sentence structure does the writer use for the narrator's voice?

3. Rewrite the boxed text in a conversational style.

Part 3: Analyze the Literature

Apply what you've just learned about style as you analyze these two excerpts. Though both writers take on the subject of outer space, they have distinctly different styles.

The first excerpt comes from a classic science fiction novel first published in 1898. As you read, pay attention to the elements—word choice, sentence structure, and tone—that reveal the writer's style.

from THE **WAR** OF THE **WORLDS**

Novel by **H. G. Wells**

A big, grayish rounded bulk, the size, perhaps, of a bear, was rising slowly and painfully out of the cylinder. As it bulged up and caught the light, it glistened like wet leather.

Two large dark-colored eyes were regarding me steadfastly. The mass that
5   framed them, the head of the thing, was rounded, and had, one might say, a face. There was a mouth under the eyes, the lipless brim of which quivered and panted, and dropped saliva. The whole creature heaved and pulsated convulsively. A lank tentacular appendage gripped the edge of the cylinder, another swayed in the air.

Those who have never seen a living Martian can scarcely imagine the strange
10 horror of its appearance. The peculiar V-shaped mouth with its pointed upper lip, the absence of brow ridges, the absence of a chin beneath the wedgelike lower lip, the incessant quivering of this mouth, the Gorgon groups of tentacles, the tumultuous breathing of the lungs in a strange atmosphere, the evident heaviness and painfulness of movement due to the greater gravitational energy
15 of the earth—above all, the extraordinary intensity of the immense eyes—were at once vital, intense, inhuman, crippled and monstrous. There was something fungoid in the oily brown skin, something in the clumsy deliberation of the tedious movements unspeakably nasty.

Close Read

1. One aspect of Wells's style is his use of vivid images to help you visualize the Martian. Three examples are boxed. Identify three additional examples.

2. Reread the sentence in lines 10–16. What do its structure and length help to emphasize?

3. Review the styles of writing on page 744. Which style or styles does Wells's writing display? Support your answer.

In the next excerpt, the astronaut Sally Ride describes her feelings and impressions as she looked down on her home planet from space. How does her style compare with the one Wells used in *The War of the Worlds*?

from

Single Room, Earth View

Essay by **Sally Ride**

Everyone I've met has a glittering, if vague, mental image of space travel. And naturally enough, people want to hear about it from an astronaut: "How did it feel . . . ?" "What did it look like . . . ?" "Were you scared?" Sometimes, the questions come from reporters, their pens poised and their tape recorders
5 silently reeling in the words; sometimes, it's wide-eyed, ten-year-old girls who want answers. I find a way to answer all of them, but it's not easy.

Imagine trying to describe an airplane ride to someone who has never flown. An articulate traveler could describe the sights but would find it much harder to explain the difference in perspective provided by the new view from
10 a greater distance, along with the feelings, impressions, and insights that go with that new perspective. And the difference is enormous: Space flight moves the traveler another giant step farther away. Eight and one-half thunderous minutes after launch, an astronaut is orbiting high above the Earth, suddenly able to watch typhoons form, volcanos smolder, and meteors streak through
15 the atmosphere below.

While flying over the Hawaiian Islands, several astronauts have marveled that the islands look just like they do on a map. When people first hear that, they wonder what should be so surprising about Hawaii looking the way it does in the atlas. Yet, to the astronauts it is an absolutely startling sensation:
20 The islands really *do* look as if that part of the world has been carpeted with a big page torn out of Rand-McNally, and all we can do is try to convey the surreal quality of that scene.

In orbit, racing along at five miles per second, the space shuttle circles the Earth once every 90 minutes. I found that at this speed, unless I kept my nose
25 pressed to the window, it was almost impossible to keep track of where we were at any given moment—the world below simply changes too fast. If I turned my concentration away for too long, even just to change film in a camera, I could miss an entire land mass. It's embarrassing to float up to a window, glance outside, and then have to ask a crewmate, "What continent is this?"

Close Read

1. Reread the boxed sentence. What do you notice about its structure and Ride's choice of words? Explain whether these elements indicate a conversational style or a formal, academic one.

2. Consider the tone that Ride takes toward her subject. Is it enthusiastic or detached? Cite evidence to support your answer.

3. How would you characterize Ride's voice—the personality revealed through her writing? Explain.

4. Using examples from both excerpts, contrast Ride's and Wells's styles. Find three differences.

Where Have You Gone, Charming Billy?

Short Story by Tim O'Brien

Is **FEAR** *our worst enemy?*

PENNSYLVANIA STANDARDS

READING STANDARDS
A.1.6.1 Analyze intended purpose of text

B.1.1.C.1 Evaluate elements of the plot

KEY IDEA Your heart pounds. Your hands shake. Your stomach churns. Adrenaline floods your body. You are gripped by **fear,** and the way you react to it is as unique as your fingerprints. In "Where Have You Gone, Charming Billy?" a young soldier struggling through his first night in Vietnam tries desperately to combat his growing terror.

DISCUSS With a partner, discuss the different ways people respond to fear. Talk about negative reactions, like blind panic, as well as positive ones, such as increased concentration or sudden bursts of strength. Then decide whether you think fear elicits primarily positive reactions or mostly negative ones.

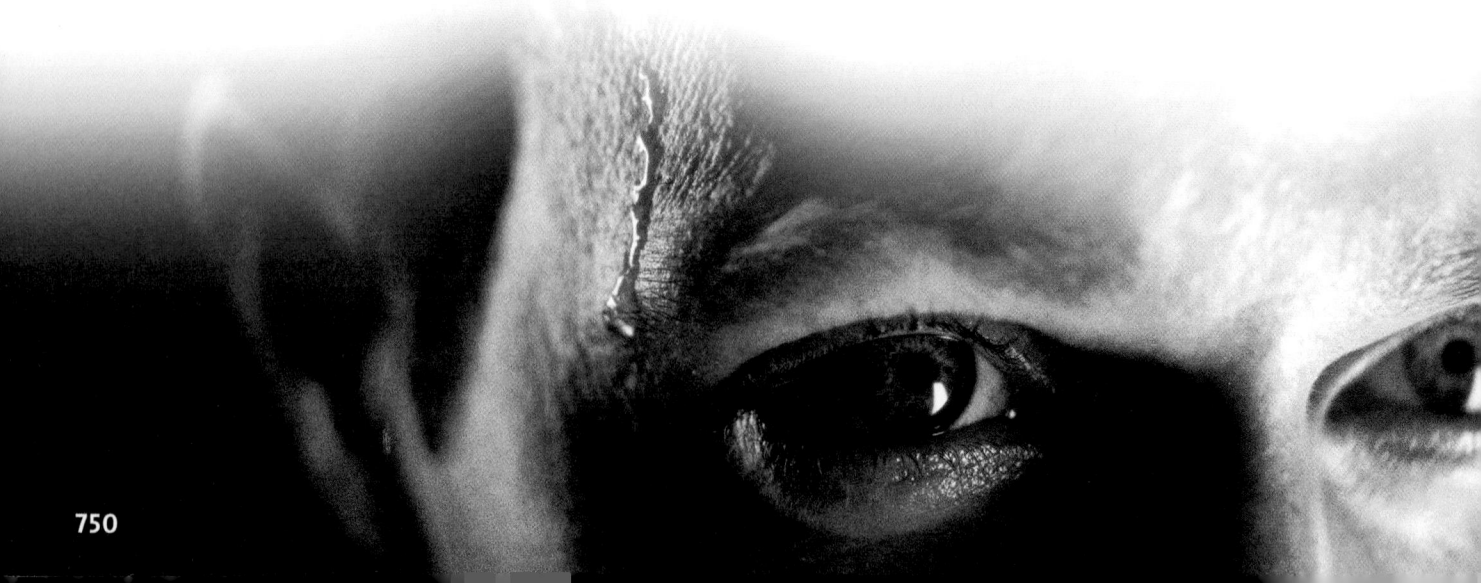

LITERARY ANALYSIS: REALISM

You know that just as you and your friends have a style all your own, so do writers. A writer's style is the unique way he or she communicates ideas. This style is reflected in the dialogue, word choice, and sentence structure of every piece of writing. In this story, Tim O'Brien uses the style of **realism** to depict the horrors of combat as seen through the eyes of a young soldier. To make the story seem real to the reader, he uses

- dialogue that sounds natural, like actual speech
- vivid, realistic descriptions of what the soldier sees
- a mix of long and short sentences to communicate the soldier's thoughts and feelings

As you read, think about the way the characters talk to each other, and consider O'Brien's word choice and sentence structure. Note passages that seem particularly realistic to you.

Review: **Point of View**

READING SKILL: ANALYZE SEQUENCE

The **sequence** of a story is the order in which events occur. Sometimes a writer interrupts this order with a **flashback,** the account of an event that happened before the beginning of the story's action. A flashback provides more background information about the current situation and helps the reader understand the story's events. To identify a flashback, look for sudden changes in scene. As you read this story, keep track of its sequence of events by filling in a sequence chain like the one shown.

Event 1	Event 2	Event 3
The soldiers march in single file.		

VOCABULARY IN CONTEXT

Restate each phrase, using a different word or words for the boldfaced term.

1. a secret mission depending on **stealth**
2. huge stalks of corn in the rich, **fecund** field
3. an argument too **diffuse** to understand
4. lying around in a state of **inertia**

Author Online

From Dull to Dangerous
"If you look in a dictionary under the word *boring*," Tim O'Brien says sarcastically, "you will find a little pen-and-ink illustration of Worthington, Minnesota, where I grew up." As a kid, O'Brien escaped from the quiet predictability of his

**Tim O'Brien
born 1946**

hometown by burying himself in books. Just after he graduated from a small Minnesota college, O'Brien's life got more exciting—but not in a way he ever would have chosen. He was drafted and sent to Vietnam.

Combat Zone O'Brien was strongly opposed to the Vietnam War and considered fleeing to Canada to avoid serving in the army. He knew, however, that failing to enlist would make him an outcast in his hometown. "That's a tough thing to do when you're that old," O'Brien says, "to decide to walk away from your whole history." He was shipped to Vietnam in 1969, and though some of his experiences there were gruesome, they inspired him to write. In 1973, O'Brien published his first book, an account of his time in Vietnam. The war has been the main subject of his writing ever since.

 MORE ABOUT THE AUTHOR
For more on Tim O'Brien, visit the **Literature Center** at **ClassZone.com.**

Background

Vietnam War This story takes place in the Southeast Asian country of Vietnam during a war in which over 58,000 Americans died. Rebels backed by Communist-ruled North Vietnam tried to take over South Vietnam in 1957. The U.S. entered the war as a South Vietnamese ally in 1964. Between 1965 and 1973, over 2 million Americans were sent to Vietnam. Few were prepared for the fear and anxiety that would overcome them.

WHERE HAVE YOU GONE,
Charming Billy?

TIM O'BRIEN

The platoon of twenty-six soldiers moved slowly in the dark, single file, not talking.

One by one, like sheep in a dream, they passed through the hedgerow, crossed quietly over a meadow and came down to the rice paddy.[1] There they stopped. Their leader knelt down, motioning with his hand, and one by one the other soldiers squatted in the shadows, vanishing in the primitive **stealth** of warfare. For a long time they did not move. Except for the sounds of their breathing, . . . the twenty-six men were very quiet: some of them excited by the adventure, some of them afraid, some of them exhausted from the long night
10 march, some of them looking forward to reaching the sea where they would be safe. At the rear of the column, Private First Class Paul Berlin lay quietly with his forehead resting on the black plastic stock of his rifle, his eyes closed. He was pretending he was not in the war, pretending he had not watched Billy Boy Watkins die of a heart attack that afternoon. He was pretending he was a boy again, camping with his father in the midnight summer along the Des Moines River. In the dark, with his eyes pinched shut, he pretended. He pretended that when he opened his eyes, his father would be there by the campfire and they would talk softly about whatever came to mind and then roll into their sleeping bags, and that later they'd wake up and it would be morning and there would
20 not be a war, and that Billy Boy Watkins had not died of a heart attack that afternoon. He pretended he was not a soldier. **A**

---

1. **hedgerow . . . rice paddy:** A hedgerow is a thick hedge separating fields or farms; a rice paddy is a flooded field in which rice is grown.

Infantry (1997), James E. Faulkner. Oil on canvas. Collection of Nature's Nest Gallery, Golden, Colorado. Photo courtesy of the artist.

ANALYZE VISUALS
Would you describe this painting as **realistic** or **abstract**? Cite details about the painting's subject, setting, and mood, as well as the artist's use of light and color.

stealth (stělth) *n.* cautious or secret action or movement

A REALISM
Reread lines 11–21, and consider O'Brien's use of both long and short sentences to convey Paul Berlin's thoughts. What effect does this stylistic choice create?

In the morning, when they reached the sea, it would be better. The hot afternoon would be over, he would bathe in the sea and he would forget how frightened he had been on his first day at the war. The second day would not be so bad. He would learn.

There was a sound beside him, a movement and then a breathed: "Hey!"
He opened his eyes, shivering as if emerging from a deep nightmare.
"Hey!" a shadow whispered. "We're *moving*. . . . Get up."
"Okay."
30 "You sleepin', or something?"
"No." He could not make out the soldier's face. With clumsy, concrete hands he clawed for his rifle, found it, found his helmet.

The soldier-shadow grunted. "You got a lot to learn, buddy. I'd shoot you if I thought you was sleepin'. Let's go." **B**

Private First Class Paul Berlin blinked.

Ahead of him, silhouetted against the sky, he saw the string of soldiers wading into the flat paddy, the black outline of their shoulders and packs and weapons. He was comfortable. He did not want to move. But he was afraid, for it was his first night at the war, so he hurried to catch up, stumbling once,
40 scraping his knee, groping as though blind; his boots sank into the thick paddy water and he smelled it all around him. He would tell his mother how it smelled: mud and algae and cattle manure and chlorophyll, decay, breeding mosquitoes and leeches as big as mice, the **fecund** warmth of the paddy waters rising up to his cut knee. But he would not tell how frightened he had been.

Once they reached the sea, things would be better. They would have their rear guarded by three thousand miles of ocean, and they would swim and dive into the breakers and hunt crayfish and smell the salt, and they would be safe.

He followed the shadow of the man in front of him. It was a clear night. Already the Southern Cross[2] was out. And other stars he could not yet name—
50 soon, he thought, he would learn their names. And puffy night clouds. There was not yet a moon. Wading through the paddy, his boots made sleepy, sloshing sounds, like a lullaby, and he tried not to think. Though he was afraid, he now knew that fear came in many degrees and types and peculiar categories, and he knew that his fear now was not so bad as it had been in the hot afternoon, when poor Billy Boy Watkins got killed by a heart attack. His fear now was **diffuse** and unformed: ghosts in the tree line, nighttime fears of a child, a boogieman in the closet that his father would open to show empty, saying "See? Nothing there, champ. Now you can sleep." In the afternoon it had been worse: the fear had been bundled and tight and he'd been on his hands and knees, crawling like an insect,
60 an ant escaping a giant's footsteps and thinking nothing, brain flopping like wet cement in a mixer, not thinking at all, watching while Billy Boy Watkins died.

Now as he stepped out of the paddy onto a narrow dirt path, now the fear was mostly the fear of being so terribly afraid again.

He tried not to think.

B REALISM
Reread lines 26–34. What specific features of the characters' speech make this **dialogue** sound realistic? Explain, citing evidence to support your answer.

fecund (fē′kənd) *adj.* producing much growth; fertile

diffuse (dĭ-fyōōs′) *adj.* unfocused

---
2. **Southern Cross:** a cross-shaped group of stars visible in the Southern Hemisphere.

There were tricks he'd learned to keep from thinking. Counting: He counted his steps, concentrating on the numbers, pretending that the steps were dollar bills and that each step through the night made him richer and richer, so that soon he would become a wealthy man, and he kept counting and considered the ways he might spend the money after the war and what he would do. He would look his father in the eye and shrug and say, "It was pretty bad at first, but I learned a lot and I got used to it." Then he would tell his father the story of Billy Boy Watkins. But he would never let on how frightened he had been. "Not so bad," he would say instead, making his father feel proud. **C**

Songs, another trick to stop from thinking: *Where have you gone, Billy Boy, Billy Boy, Oh, where have you gone, charming Billy? I have gone to seek a wife, she's the joy of my life, but she's a young thing and cannot leave her mother,* and other songs that he sang in his thoughts as he walked toward the sea. And when he reached the sea he would dig a deep hole in the sand and he would sleep like the high clouds, and he would not be afraid any more.

The moon came out. Pale and shrunken to the size of a dime.

The helmet was heavy on his head. In the morning he would adjust the leather binding. He would clean his rifle, too. Even though he had been frightened to shoot it during the hot afternoon, he would carefully clean the breech and the muzzle and the ammunition so that next time he would be ready and not so afraid. In the morning, when they reached the sea, he would begin to make friends with some of the other soldiers. He would learn their names and laugh at their jokes. Then when the war was over he would have war buddies, and he would write to them once in a while and exchange memories. **D**

Walking, sleeping in his walking, he felt better. He watched the moon come higher.

Once they skirted a sleeping village. The smells again—straw, cattle, mildew. The men were quiet. On the far side of the village, buried in the dark smells, a dog barked. The column stopped until the barking died away; then they marched fast away from the village, through a graveyard filled with conical-shaped burial mounds and tiny altars made of clay and stone. The graveyard had a perfumy smell. A nice place to spend the night, he thought. The mounds would make fine battlements, and the smell was nice and the place was quiet. But they went on, passing through a hedgerow and across another paddy and east toward the sea. **E**

He walked carefully. He remembered what he'd been taught: Stay off the center of the path, for that was where the land mines and booby traps were planted, where stupid and lazy soldiers like to walk. Stay alert, he'd been taught. Better alert than inert. Ag-ile, mo-bile, hos-tile.[3] He wished he'd paid better attention to the training. He could not remember what they'd said about how to stop being afraid; they hadn't given any lessons in courage—not that he could remember—and they hadn't mentioned how Billy Boy Watkins would die of a heart attack, his face turning pale and the veins popping out.

C SEQUENCE
Summarize the story's events up to this point. Which events take place in Vietnam? Which are scenes the narrator imagines will happen in the future or remembers from his past?

D GRAMMAR AND STYLE
Reread lines 81–88. Notice O'Brien's repetition of "he would," which reflects Paul's way of coping with his current situation.

E REALISM
Reread lines 91–98. Identify the **sensory details**—details that appeal to the five senses—O'Brien includes. How do these details contribute to the vivid, realistic style of this story?

---

3. **Better alert . . . hos-tile:** sayings and chants reminding soldiers to pay attention rather than be lifeless (inert), and to be light on their feet (agile), ready to move (mobile), and aggressive (hostile).

Private First Class Paul Berlin walked carefully.

Stretching ahead of him like dark beads on an invisible chain, the string of shadow-soldiers whose names he did not yet know moved with the silence and
110 slow grace of smoke. Now and again moonlight was reflected off a machine gun or a wrist watch. But mostly the soldiers were quiet and hidden and far-away-seeming in a peaceful night, strangers on a long street, and he felt quite separate from them, as if trailing behind like the caboose on a night train, pulled along by **inertia,** sleepwalking, an afterthought to the war.

So he walked carefully, counting his steps. When he had counted to three thousand, four hundred and eighty-five, the column stopped.

One by one the soldiers knelt or squatted down.

The grass along the path was wet. Private First Class Paul Berlin lay back and turned his head so that he could lick at the dew with his eyes closed,
120 another trick to forget the war. He might have slept. "I *wasn't* afraid," he was screaming or dreaming, facing his father's stern eyes. "I wasn't afraid," he was saying. When he opened his eyes, a soldier was sitting beside him, quietly chewing a stick of Doublemint gum. **F**

"You sleepin' again?" the soldier whispered.

"No," said Private First Class Paul Berlin. . . .

The soldier grunted, chewing his gum. Then he twisted the cap off his canteen, took a swallow and handed it through the dark.

"Take some," he whispered.

"Thanks."
130 "You're the new guy?"

"Yes." He did not want to admit it, being new to the war.

The soldier grunted and handed him a stick of gum. "Chew it quiet—okay? Don't blow no bubbles or nothing."

"Thanks. I won't." He could not make out the man's face in the shadows.

They sat still and Private First Class Paul Berlin chewed the gum until all the sugars were gone; then the soldier said, "Bad day today, buddy."

Private First Class Paul Berlin nodded wisely, but he did not speak.

"Don't think it's always so bad," the soldier whispered. "I don't wanna scare you. You'll get used to it soon enough. . . . They been fighting wars a long
140 time, and you get used to it."

"Yeah."

"You will."

They were quiet awhile. And the night was quiet, no crickets or birds, and it was hard to imagine it was truly a war. He searched for the soldier's face but could not find it. It did not matter much. Even if he saw the fellow's face, he would not know the name; and even if he knew the name, it would not matter much.

"Haven't got the time?" the soldier whispered.

"No."

"Rats. . . . Don't matter, really. Goes faster if you don't know the time,
150 anyhow."

"Sure."

inertia (ĭ-nûr'shə) *n.* tendency to continue to do what one has been doing

F **POINT OF VIEW**
Identify the point of view from which this story is told. How might your impression of Paul be different if you didn't receive such detailed descriptions of his thoughts and feelings?

"What's your name, buddy?"

"Paul."

"Nice to meet ya," he said, and in the dark beside the path they shook hands. "Mine's Toby. Everybody calls me Buffalo, though." The soldier's hand was strangely warm and soft. But it was a very big hand. "Sometimes they just call me Buff," he said.

And again they were quiet. They lay in the grass and waited. The moon was very high now and very bright, and they were waiting for cloud cover.

160   The soldier suddenly snorted.

"What is it?"

"Nothin'," he said, but then he snorted again. "A bloody *heart attack!*" the soldier said. "Can't get over it—old Billy Boy croaking from a lousy heart attack. . . . A heart attack—can you believe it?"

The idea of it made Private First Class Paul Berlin smile. He couldn't help it.

"Ever hear of such a thing?"

"Not till now," said Private First Class Paul Berlin, still smiling.

"Me neither," said the soldier in the dark.

". . . Dying of a heart attack. Didn't know him, did you."

170   "No."

"Tough as nails."

Class of '67 (1987), Charlie Shobe. Oil on canvas. © Michael Tropea/National Vietnam Veterans Art Museum.

ANALYZE VISUALS
In this painting, the prone soldiers' boots take up the **foreground,** or front of the painting, while the standing soldiers are relegated to the **background.** What does this suggest about the message of the painting?

"Yeah."

"And what happens? A heart attack. Can you imagine it?"

"Yes," said Private First Class Paul Berlin. He wanted to laugh. "I can imagine it." And he imagined it clearly. He giggled—he couldn't help it. He imagined Billy's father opening the telegram: SORRY TO INFORM YOU THAT YOUR SON BILLY BOY WAS YESTERDAY SCARED TO DEATH IN ACTION IN THE REPUBLIC OF VIETNAM, VALIANTLY SUCCUMBING TO[4] A HEART ATTACK SUFFERED WHILE UNDER
180 ENORMOUS STRESS, AND IT IS WITH GREATEST SYMPATHY THAT . . . He giggled again. He rolled onto his belly and pressed his face into his arms. His body was shaking with giggles.

The big soldier hissed at him to shut up, but he could not stop giggling and remembering the hot afternoon, and poor Billy Boy, and how they'd been drinking Coca-Cola from bright-red aluminum cans, and how they'd started on the day's march, and how a little while later poor Billy Boy stepped on the mine, and how it made a tiny little sound—*poof*—and how Billy Boy stood there with his mouth wide-open, looking down at where his foot had been blown off, and how finally Billy Boy sat down very casually, not saying a word,
190 with his foot lying behind him, most of it still in the boot.

He giggled louder—he could not stop. He bit his arm, trying to stifle it, but remembering: "War's over, Billy," the men had said in consolation, but Billy Boy got scared and started crying and said he was about to die. "Nonsense," the medic said, Doc Peret, but Billy Boy kept bawling, tightening up, his face going pale and transparent and his veins popping out. Scared stiff. Even when Doc Peret stuck him with morphine,[5] Billy Boy kept crying. **G**

"Shut up!" the big soldier hissed, but Private First Class Paul Berlin could not stop. Giggling and remembering, he covered his mouth. His eyes stung, remembering how it was when Billy Boy died of fright.

200 "Shut up!"

But he could not stop giggling, the same way Billy Boy could not stop bawling that afternoon.

Afterward Doc Peret had explained: "You see, Billy Boy really died of a heart attack. He was scared he was gonna die—so scared, he had himself a heart attack—and that's what really killed him. I seen it before."

So they wrapped Billy in a plastic poncho, his eyes still wide-open and scared stiff, and they carried him over the meadow to a rice paddy, and then when the Medevac helicopter[6] arrived they carried him through the paddy and put him aboard, and the mortar rounds[7] were falling everywhere, and the
210 helicopter pulled up and Billy Boy came tumbling out, falling slowly and then faster, and the paddy water sprayed up as if Billy Boy had just executed a long

G SEQUENCE
Reread lines 183–196. What happens to the story's sequence in these lines? Identify the clues that helped you form your answer.

---

4. **valiantly succumbing** (sə-kŭm'ĭng) **to:** bravely dying from.

5. **morphine** (môr'fēn'): a powerful drug used as a painkiller.

6. **Medevac** (mĕd'ĭ-văk') **helicopter:** a helicopter used for transporting injured people to places where they can receive medical care. "Medevac" is a contraction of "medical evacuation."

7. **mortar rounds:** shells fired from small, portable cannons.

and dangerous dive, as if trying to escape Graves Registration, where he would be tagged and sent home under a flag, dead of a heart attack.

"Shut up, . . . !" the soldier hissed, but Paul Berlin could not stop giggling, remembering: scared to death.

220 Later they waded in after him, probing for Billy Boy with their rifle butts, elegantly and delicately probing for Billy Boy in the stinking paddy, singing—some of them— *Where have you gone, Billy Boy, Billy Boy, Oh, where have you gone, charming Billy?* Then they found him. Green and covered with algae, his eyes still wide-open and scared

230 stiff, dead of a heart attack suffered while—

Chopper Lift-Out (1967), Ken McFadyen. Oil on canvas on hardboard, 30.6 cm × 48.2 cm. © The Australian War Memorial Collection.

"Shut up, . . . !" the soldier said loudly, shaking him.

But Private First Class Paul Berlin could not stop. The giggles were caught in his throat, drowning him in his own laughter: scared to death like Billy Boy.

Giggling, lying on his back, he saw the moon move, or the clouds moving across the moon. Wounded in action, dead of fright. A fine war story. He would tell it to his father, how Billy Boy had been scared to death, never letting on . . . He could not stop.

The soldier smothered him. He tried to fight back, but he was weak from the giggles.

240 The moon was under the clouds and the column was moving. The soldier helped him up. "You okay now, buddy?"

"Sure."

"What was so bloody funny?"

"Nothing."

"You can get killed, laughing that way."

"I know. I know that."

"You got to stay calm, buddy." The soldier handed him his rifle. "Half the battle, just staying calm. You'll get better at it," he said. "Come on, now."

He turned away and Private First Class Paul Berlin hurried after him. He

250 was still shivering.

He would do better once he reached the sea, he thought, still smiling a little. A funny war story that he would tell to his father, how Billy Boy Watkins was scared to death. A good joke. But even when he smelled salt and heard the sea, he could not stop being afraid. ⚬

H SEQUENCE
What information has been communicated to the reader in this **flashback?** Explain, citing details from the text.

INTERVIEW In this revealing interview, Tim O'Brien talks about two kinds of bravery and discusses the courage it took to make one frightening choice.

Tim O'Brien: *The Naked Soldier*

Douglas Novielli, Christopher Connal, and Jackson Ellis, Verbicide Magazine

Verbicide Do you think you would have pursued writing if you hadn't gone to Vietnam?

O'Brien Probably. It probably would've been something different. If I'd gone to Canada I'd be writing about that. Life provides you plenty of material, with girlfriends or whatever.

V Do you think you romanticize Vietnam at all?

O No. I think a lot of veterans think I haven't done that enough, but I refuse to do it.

V Is there a reason they think it should be romanticized?

O Yeah, they look back on it as more heroic, and with nostalgia, and they talk about the fellowship or fraternity among men, and there's some truth to that. But it's an artificial one; it's borne of necessity. Even if you don't like someone, you've got to trust them at night when they're on guard and you're sleeping. And you learn who to trust and who not to trust, and you bond that way. But I never found it very heroic, I just found it stone-man, gotta stay alive stuff. And that's all there was to it.

V Are soldiers heroes?

O In some ways. It's heroic just not to stop. Physically, there are always alternatives, I mean, just stop walking. What can they do? Court martial you, but they're not gonna kill you. It looks pretty attractive, especially in bad days when guys have been dropping like flies. . . .

You just keep humping. There's a weird heroism in that. Unglamorous kind of valor to just keep going, knowing you might die with every step, and just keep walking.

V Is the heroism there in your books to be interpreted if the reader wants it, or is it directly implied?

O I remember one part in *The Things They Carried* when I was talking about humping and just taking one step after the next, and at one point I called it a kind of courage, which it is, just to keep your legs moving. I'm kind of explicit about that kind of courage, but there are other kinds of courage just like there are kinds of truth. It took a lot of guts, for example, to go to Canada. Your whole hometown is going to think of you as a sissy or a coward, even though it's totally conscientious. So I admire the heroism and courage it took. I didn't have the guts to do it, to cross over the border.

V Do you still regret that?

O Yeah, you can't live your life over, but it would have been the right thing to do. I mean, think how hard it would be, even now it would be hard and I'm grown up. It was the thing that was worse than anything about the war, just going to it. Once you're in the war, it's pretty much what you'd expect. But, boy, making that decision, because you're in control of things. You can go in the army, or you can go to Canada. I never actually made that drive and went to the Rainy River.[1] That's invented. But it did happen in my head all summer long. I thought about driving to Canada.

---

1. **Rainy River:** a river on the U.S.–Canadian border. In O'Brien's short story "On the Rainy River," the main character drives to the river and considers whether he should cross the border into Canada and dodge the draft.

Comprehension

1. **Recall** According to Doc Peret, what causes the death of Billy Boy Watkins?

2. **Clarify** Why does Toby want to keep Paul quiet?

3. **Summarize** How does the story end?

PENNSYLVANIA STANDARDS

READING STANDARD
B.1.1.1.C.1 Evaluate elements of the plot

Literary Analysis

4. **Draw Conclusions** Think back to the discussion you had about the different ways people respond to **fear**. Describe how Paul Berlin tries to combat his fear in this story. How successful is he? Cite evidence to support your conclusion.

5. **Identify Conflict** Is the main conflict in this story **internal** or **external?** Explain, citing details from the text to support your answer.

6. **Analyze Sequence** Review the chart you made as you read, and think about the **flashback** in lines 183–196, in which Paul recalls the death of Billy Boy Watkins in vivid detail. Why might O'Brien have used the flashback at this point in the story? What did it help you, the reader, understand?

7. **Analyze Realism** Find examples in the text that illustrate each element of **style** shown on the chart. Use your completed chart to explain how O'Brien's use of realism contributes to the reader's perceptions of Paul and his situation.

Element of Style	Examples from Text
Realistic dialogue	
Description featuring sensory details	
Passages made up of both long and short sentences	
Use of flashback	

8. **Synthesize** In "The Naked Soldier" on page 760, O'Brien talks about two different kinds of courage—the courage it took to serve in Vietnam and the courage it took to defy the draft and flee to Canada. In your opinion, which act was more courageous? Use evidence from both the story and the interview to support your opinion.

Literary Criticism

9. **Author's Style** In describing what he strives for when creating stories, O'Brien stated, "You aim for tension and suspense, a sense of drama, displaying in concrete terms the actions and reactions of human beings contesting problems of the heart." How successfully did O'Brien fulfill the above criteria in this story? Cite evidence from the selection to support your opinion.

Vocabulary in Context

VOCABULARY PRACTICE

Write the word from the Word List that best completes each sentence.

1. The soldiers moved with _____ across the countryside so that they would not be spotted by the enemy.

2. In spite of all the bombing it had suffered, the land they traveled through was still _____.

3. In their nervousness, it was hard to bring their _____ thoughts back into clear focus.

4. They relied on _____ and force of habit to keep them on the path.

VOCABULARY IN WRITING

Pretend that you are Paul Berlin's commanding officer, and write a paragraph describing the problems facing your platoon. Use at least two vocabulary words. You might start like this:

EXAMPLE SENTENCE

The **diffuse** attention of my soldiers is starting to worry me. . . .

VOCABULARY STRATEGY: WORDS THAT START WITH *in-*

The forms of certain words beginning with *in-* can sometimes cause confusion. When you see a word like *inertia,* for example, in which *in-* means "unable to" or "not," you might make the assumption that you can remove the prefix to form a word with an opposite, "positive" meaning. However, there is no such English word as *ertia.* To avoid writing incorrect antonyms for words with *in-*, always check a dictionary.

PRACTICE Create a two-column chart with these headings: "No Positive Form" and "Positive Form Not Often Used." Use a dictionary to place each word in the correct column. Then write a brief definition of each word.

1. incorrigible
2. inclement
3. insomnia
4. indolent
5. insuperable
6. insipid
7. incognito
8. incongruous

PENNSYLVANIA STANDARDS

READING STANDARD
A.1.2.1 Identify word meaning using affixes

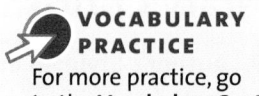

VOCABULARY PRACTICE
For more practice, go to the **Vocabulary Center** at **ClassZone.com.**

Reading-Writing Connection

Demonstrate your knowledge of "Where Have You Gone, Charming Billy?" by responding to these prompts. Then use **Revision: Grammar and Style** to improve your writing.

WRITING PROMPTS

A. Short Response: Write a Letter

Think about Paul Berlin's deep desire to please his father and the **fear** he grapples with in this story. Using details from the text, pretend you are Paul and write a **one- or two-paragraph letter** home.

B. Extended Response: Analyze Realism

O'Brien served in the Vietnam War for over a year, until an injury sustained in a grenade attack ended his enlistment. In your opinion, which details in this story could have been written only by someone who actually served in Vietnam? Which details seem to be products of the writer's artistic imagination? Citing evidence to support your opinion, write a **three-to-five-paragraph response.**

SELF-CHECK

A compelling letter will . . .

- describe Paul's experiences and how he's coping with being a soldier
- sound as if it were written by Paul, on the basis of the traits he exhibits in the story

A strong analysis will . . .

- consider the different details O'Brien includes in this story, such as sensory images and descriptions of the soldiers' feelings
- cite relevant and convincing examples of both realistic and imaginative details

REVISION: GRAMMAR AND STYLE

ADD SUPPORTING DETAILS Review the **Grammar and Style** note on page 755. O'Brien depicts Paul as a frightened and inexperienced soldier by using details to provide a window into Paul's mental state. The **repetition** that marks Paul's thoughts reflects his continuing fear, anxiety, and denial. Here is an example from the story. Note that O'Brien repeats the verb *pretending:*

> *He was pretending he was not in the war, pretending he had not watched Billy Boy Watkins die of a heart attack that afternoon. He was pretending he was a boy again, camping with his father in the midnight summer along the Des Moines River.* (lines 12–16)

Notice how the revisions in red use repetition to reflect Paul's feelings of denial and anxiety. Revise your response to Prompt A by using similar techniques.

STUDENT MODEL

I'm exhausted and hungry, but I'm not afraid. Don't worry about me,
—*I don't worry about me.*
Dad∧ I know I'll be home soon. ∧*I'll be home sooner than you think.*

PENNSYLVANIA STANDARDS

WRITING STANDARD
1.4.11.A.7 Use literary devices

WRITING TOOLS
For prewriting, revision, and editing tools, visit the **Writing Center** at ClassZone.com.

The Princess and the Tin Box
Fable by James Thurber

Are DIAMONDS
really a girl's best friend?

PENNSYLVANIA STANDARDS

READING STANDARDS
A.1.3.1 Make inferences and/or draw conclusions

B.1.1.1.E.1 Analyze and/or evaluate tone and style

KEY IDEA For that matter, do clothes really make the man? We all know people who are **superficial** or shallow, concerned only with appearance rather than substance. In this takeoff on a fairy tale, James Thurber presents just such a person: a rich, spoiled princess.

PRESENT With a partner, create a "portrait" of a superficial person, using both words and images. Make your portrait as serious or as comically exaggerated as you like, but be sure to communicate how your subject thinks and acts. You can even outfit him or her in whatever clothes and accessories you think appropriate. After you've finished, pair up with another group and take turns presenting your portraits.

LITERARY ANALYSIS: PARODY

Humorist James Thurber is known for his sly, skillful way of making fun of society. "The Princess and the Tin Box" begins in a very familiar way:

Once upon a time, in a far country, there lived a king whose daughter was the prettiest princess in the world.

With that opening sentence, readers immediately recognize that they have been whisked into a fairy tale. This particular tale, however, is a **parody**—a literary work that imitates another piece of literature in order to poke fun at it. To analyze this imitation fairy tale, be on the lookout for the following stylistic techniques:

- **Word Choice:** Notice how Thurber imitates the language used in fairy tales, as in the opening lines above.

- **Exaggeration:** Look for characters or situations exaggerated by the author for comic effect.

- **Irony:** Identify ironic plot twists, or moments when things happen very differently from the way you would expect.

As you read, look for evidence of these techniques. Think about the ways in which this parody resembles a typical fairy tale and the ways in which it does not.

READING STRATEGY: PREDICT

Fairy tales are usually pretty predictable. As you read this selection, jot down your impressions of the princess. Use these notes about the princess's character to make **predictions** about what will happen next in the story. After the last events have unfolded, ask yourself if this is the "happily ever after" you anticipated.

Early Years One of the great humorists of American literature, James Thurber made a career out of poking fun at society. Despite a childhood eye injury that left him with lifelong vision problems, Thurber attended college and got early jobs as a clerk and then as a journalist.

James Thurber
1894–1961

In 1927, the *New Yorker,* a literary magazine, published one of his stories. He would write for the magazine for the rest of his life.

The *New Yorker* Years The *New Yorker* gave Thurber his fame, and he gave the magazine much of the sophisticated style it has today. Thurber often provided his own illustrations to accompany his writing. Although he did not consider himself an artist, his cartoons had a distinctive style and became as popular as his stories. Readers loved him for being so funny, but Thurber took humor seriously. "I write humor the way a surgeon operates," he said, "because it is a livelihood, because I have a great urge to do it, because many interesting challenges are set up, and because I have the hope it may do some good."

Last Years By the age of 57, Thurber's childhood eye injury had degenerated to almost total blindness. When his vision began to fail completely, Thurber started dictating stories to his secretary. His memory was so sharp that he could easily compose a 2,000-word story in his mind, remember it overnight, and dictate it to his secretary the next day. His friend and fellow-writer E. B. White described him this way: "During his happiest years, Thurber did not write the way a surgeon operates, he wrote the way a child skips rope, the way a mouse waltzes."

MORE ABOUT THE AUTHOR
For more on James Thurber, visit the **Literature Center** at ClassZone.com.

THE *Princess* AND THE *Tin Box*

JAMES THURBER

Once upon a time, in a far country, there lived a king whose daughter was the prettiest princess in the world. Her eyes were like the cornflower, her hair was sweeter than the hyacinth, and her throat made the swan look dusty.

From the time she was a year old, the princess had been showered with presents. Her nursery looked like Cartier's window.[1] Her toys were all made of gold or platinum or diamonds or emeralds. She was not permitted to have wooden blocks or china dolls or rubber dogs or linen books, because such materials were considered cheap for the daughter of a king.

When she was seven, she was allowed to attend the wedding of her brother
10 and throw real pearls at the bride instead of rice. Only the nightingale, with his lyre of gold, was permitted to sing for the princess. The common blackbird, with his boxwood flute,[2] was kept out of the palace grounds. She walked in silver-and-samite slippers to a sapphire-and-topaz bathroom and slept in an ivory bed inlaid with rubies. **Ⓐ**

On the day the princess was eighteen, the king sent a royal ambassador to the courts of five neighboring kingdoms to announce that he would give his daughter's hand in marriage to the prince who brought her the gift she liked the most.

The first prince to arrive at the palace rode a swift white stallion and laid
20 at the feet of the princess an enormous apple made of solid gold which he had taken from a dragon who had guarded it for a thousand years. It was placed on a long ebony table set up to hold the gifts of the princess's suitors. The second prince, who came on a gray charger,[3] brought her a nightingale made

1. **Cartier's** (kär-tyāz′) **window:** the show window of a well-known jewelry store.
2. **lyre** (līr) **of gold . . . boxwood flute:** The nightingale's voice is likened to a golden harp; the blackbird's voice is likened to a cheap wooden flute.
3. **charger:** warhorse.

ANALYZE VISUALS
Thurber often sketched childlike line drawings like this one to accompany his stories. What basic ideas about love or courtship does he present in this sketch?

Ⓐ PARODY
Reread lines 1–14 and identify at least two examples of **exaggeration**. What is the effect of this stylistic technique? Explain your answer.

The Princess and the Tin Box (1948), © James Thurber. © renewed 1976 by Rosemary A. Thurber. Reprinted by arrangement with Rosemary A. Thurber and the Barbara Hogenson Agency

of a thousand diamonds, and it was placed beside the golden apple. The third prince, riding on a black horse, carried a great jewel box made of platinum and sapphires, and it was placed next to the diamond nightingale. The fourth prince, astride a fiery yellow horse, gave the princess a gigantic heart made of rubies and pierced by an emerald arrow. It was placed next to the platinum-and-sapphire jewel box.

30   Now the fifth prince was the strongest and handsomest of all the five suitors, but he was the son of a poor king whose realm had been overrun by mice and locusts and wizards and mining engineers so that there was nothing much of value left in it. He came plodding up to the palace of the princess on a plow horse and he brought her a small tin box filled with mica and feldspar and hornblende[4] which he had picked up on the way. **B**

The other princes roared with disdainful laughter when they saw the tawdry[5] gift the fifth prince had brought to the princess. But she examined it with great interest and squealed with delight, for all her life she had been glutted with precious stones and priceless metals, but she had never seen tin
40 before or mica or feldspar or hornblende. The tin box was placed next to the ruby heart pierced with an emerald arrow. **C**

"Now," the king said to his daughter, "you must select the gift you like best and marry the prince that brought it."

The princess smiled and walked up to the table and picked up the present she liked the most. It was the platinum-and-sapphire jewel box, the gift of the third prince.

"The way I figure it," she said, "is this. It is a very large and expensive box, and when I am married, I will meet many admirers who will give me precious gems with which to fill it to the top. Therefore, it is the most valuable of all the
50 gifts my suitors have brought me and I like it the best."

The princess married the third prince that very day in the midst of great merriment and high revelry.[6] More than a hundred thousand pearls were thrown at her and she loved it.

Moral: All those who thought the princess was going to select the tin box filled with worthless stones instead of one of the other gifts will kindly stay after class and write one hundred times on the blackboard "I would rather have a hunk of aluminum silicate[7] than a diamond necklace." ❧

B PARODY
Think about the typical plot, setting, and characters of a fairy tale. Find three places where Thurber mimics these conventions in this story.

C PREDICT
Consider your impression of the princess and her reactions to her suitors' gifts. Do you think she will choose to marry the poor but handsome prince or one of the rich, snobby ones? Give reasons for your prediction.

---

4. **mica** (mī′kə) **and feldspar and hornblende** (hôrn′blĕnd′): three common minerals.

5. **tawdry** (tô′drē): flashy but cheap.

6. **revelry** (rĕv′əl-rē): noisy celebrating.

7. **aluminum silicate** (sĭl′ĭ-kāt′): a basically worthless chemical compound; refers to the mica, feldspar, and hornblende in the prince's box.

Comprehension

1. **Recall** What does the king do on his daughter's 18th birthday?

2. **Summarize** Describe the five gifts the suitors bring, which one the princess chooses to accept, and why.

3. **Paraphrase** Restate the moral of the story in your own words.

PENNSYLVANIA STANDARDS

READING STANDARD
B.1.1.1.E.1 Analyze and/or evaluate tone and style

Literary Analysis

4. **Interpret Irony** Reread lines 54–58. How does the end of this story play against the reader's normal expectations of a fairy tale? Explain how the ending is ironic, citing evidence from the text.

5. **Analyze Parody** In a chart like the one shown, record examples of the **stylistic techniques** Thurber uses to parody a fairy tale. Use your completed chart to explain what human trait or quality Thurber is poking fun at in this story.

Stylistic Technique	Examples from the Text
Imitation of standard fairy tale language	
Exaggeration	
Irony	

6. **Evaluate Predictions** How accurately did you predict what would happen at the end of the story? Explain whether or not you think Thurber intended to take his readers by surprise, and why.

7. **Make Judgments** A **parody** is an imitation of a writer's style, a type of literature, or a specific work, and is usually designed to make fun of something. In your opinion, is humor an effective tool for social criticism? Can making a joke or commenting on something in a comic way ever help bring about change? Explain your answer.

Reading-Writing Connection

WRITING PROMPT

Short Response: Rewrite the Ending
What would have happened if the princess had made a different choice? How else could this story have ended? In **one or two paragraphs,** imagine an alternate ending to the story and create a new moral to go with it. Try to mimic Thurber's dry, comic style.

SELF-CHECK

An entertaining ending will . . .
- clearly convey what the princess's new choice is and explain why she chose as she did
- include a humorous moral written in a style similar to Thurber's

from **The Birds**

Film Clip on  *MediaSmart* DVD

What makes a director a master of S T Y L E ?

PENNSYLVANIA STANDARDS

SPEAKING/LISTENING STANDARD
1.6.11.F.2 Evaluate the role of media

KEY IDEA Long before there was a Steven Spielberg or a Peter Jackson, there was a world-class director known for creating spellbinding films. By viewing a clip from one of Alfred Hitchcock's most famous movies, you'll experience the **stylistic touches** that made this director a movie legend.

Background

Fear Factor Born in England in 1899, Alfred Hitchcock learned moviemaking from the ground up, beginning in the 1920s. In 1939, as a full-fledged director, he moved to the United States. Over the next three decades, the director crafted movies, and later produced two TV series, that earned him the titles of "master of suspense" and "master of the thriller." Hitchcock was known for engaging the minds and emotions of his audiences. The director once said, "They [fans of the thriller genre] want to put their toe in the cold waters of fear."

The Birds (1963)—considered Hitchcock's last great movie—portrays a California coastal town in which the bird population suddenly turns vicious. The movie is loosely based on the short story by suspense writer Daphne du Maurier.

Media Literacy: Style in Movies

A writer conveys his or her style primarily through carefully crafted words. A filmmaker achieves style through carefully selected images that can create specific meanings and trigger specific emotions. Director Alfred Hitchcock was often asked for insights into his craft. He once said, "Self-plagiarism is style." By this he meant that directors who consistently use and refine certain techniques from movie to movie can develop features recognizable as their own. To explore Hitchcock's style, it helps to have a sense of a director's basic techniques.

ELEMENTS OF STYLE	STRATEGIES FOR VIEWING	
Expressing Themes A director's stylistic techniques can be used to express particular themes or viewpoints that are characteristic of the director's work.	Become familiar with some common characteristics of Hitchcock's works. • Presentation of misfortune or evil as a fact of life • Ordinary, innocent people caught up in frightening circumstances • Threat of danger from unlikely settings, such as in a public place in full daylight • Fast-paced scenes in which tension builds • Probing exploration of a character's emotional or psychological state • Strong suspense mixed with humorous touches	**North by Northwest**  **The Birds** 
Creating Atmosphere A director can become known for trademark film techniques that he or she uses to convey meaning and to create an atmosphere.	Discover a few of Hitchcock's filming techniques. • Interpret **point of view** (POV) **shots,** which show what a character sees, and **reaction shots,** which show a character's response to whatever he or she faces. Hitchcock's POV shots allow viewers to slip into the role of a character and to identify with the character's predicament. • Watch for **camera placement.** For example, a camera placed at odd angles might portray a very confined setting or a confused state of mind. • Think about what the director is trying to achieve through the **pace** of the **editing.** Hitchcock was known for using **long takes** to promote reflection and **quick cuts** to increase tension.	**Rear Window**  **Vertigo** 

MediaSmart DVD

- **Film Clip:** from *The Birds*
- **Director:** Alfred Hitchcock
- **Genre:** Thriller
- **Running Time:** 2 minutes

Viewing Guide for
The Birds

Just before the start of the clip, main character Melanie Daniels is in a restaurant, overhearing anxious townspeople discussing the increasing threat of bird attacks. Then, through the windows, Melanie spots another attack in progress, which leads to a fiery explosion at a gasoline station.

    View the clip several times, and take as much time as you need to observe the events that take place. Keep the following questions in mind as you view.

NOW VIEW

FIRST VIEWING: Comprehension

1. **Summarize** What happens from the point at which the man crashes his car until the end of the clip?

2. **Recall** Where is Melanie in most of this scene?

CLOSE VIEWING: Media Literacy

3. **Make Inferences** Describe what you think are Melanie's thoughts and feelings as she witnesses the unfolding events.

4. **Analyze Techniques** What types of shots does Hitchcock use to convey the tense nature of Melanie's situation?

5. **Analyze Mood** In terms of mood and atmosphere, how is the very beginning of the clip different from the ending?

6. **Draw Conclusions** In folklore and other works of literature, the sighting of a bird often signals the coming of chaos. Why do you think a familiar device like the sighting of a bird would appeal to a director known for suspenseful thrillers?

7. **Evaluate Style** A **set piece** is a scene staged so skillfully that it serves as a textbook example of a filmmaking technique or style. The phone booth scene you've viewed is a famous set piece. Review the details about Hitchcock's work on page 771. Explain what examples of Hitchcock's style you think are effectively represented in this scene.

Write or Discuss

Analyzing Hitchcock's Style Here are more quotes from Alfred Hitchcock about his approach to moviemaking. Choose one that you think comes closest to the stylistic techniques used in the scene. Support your opinion with evidence.

- "Give them [the audience] pleasure—the same pleasure they have when they wake up from a nightmare."
- "If it's a good movie, the sound could go off and the audience would still have a perfectly clear idea of what was going on."
- "Always make the audience suffer as much as possible."

Produce Your Own Media

Create a Production Still Imagine you're part of a team promoting a new, Hitchcock-styled version of a fairy tale or folktale. Create a production still for the movie in the style of Hitchcock. A **production** or **promotional still** is a photograph taken during the making of a film. Sometimes a still shows an actual scene from the movie or an image that represents the highlights.

HERE'S HOW Here are a few suggestions for making the production still:

- Choose a familiar tale on which to base the production still.
- To add Hitchcock-flavored twists, think about how to take any familiar element of the tale to a thrilling extreme. Draw a sketch of a daytime setting that is ordinarily a safe public place. Then draw a sketch that includes elements of danger in the same setting.

MEDIA TOOLS

For help with creating a production still, visit the **Media Center** at ClassZone.com.

Tech Tip

Search the Internet for more images of Hitchcock's threatening settings.

PROFESSIONAL MODELS

These images are production stills from *North by Northwest*.

Going to Japan

Essay by Barbara Kingsolver

Have you ever felt OUT OF PLACE?

PENNSYLVANIA STANDARDS

READING STANDARDS
A.2.5.1 Summarize

B.2.1.1 Analyze examples of hyperbole, satire, and irony in text

KEY IDEA You know the feeling—that sinking sense of not quite fitting in. Pretty much everybody feels **out of place** at some point, whether it's at a party where you don't know anyone or on your first day at a new school in a new town. In "Going to Japan," Barbara Kingsolver describes a time when she felt totally out of her element. She relates the blunders she made as she tried to blend in.

QUICKWRITE In a paragraph, describe a situation in which you felt out of place. Include all the details you can remember—even the embarrassing ones! What about the situation made you feel self-conscious? Did you eventually relax and feel better, or were you uncomfortable the whole time?

LITERARY ANALYSIS: HUMOR

Have you ever used a joke to get your point across? Writers often use **humor** to convey a perspective on a topic. Humor is expressed through description and word choice that create surprise and amusement. The following techniques are common devices of humor:

- **Hyperbole:** exaggeration of the truth
- **Irony:** a contrast between what you expect to happen and what actually happens
- **Wordplay:** verbal wit, when a writer plays with words and word sounds

In this essay, Kingsolver presents an exaggerated account of how she felt out of place in Japan. "When I stepped on a streetcar," she writes, "a full head taller than all the other passengers, I became an awkward giant." As you read, consider how the writer felt Japanese people perceived her. Note passages that you find humorous.

READING SKILL: SUMMARIZE

When you **summarize,** you use your own words to restate the main points and important details of what you've read. As you read, use a chart like the one shown to record the important details presented in each of the essay's three parts. In your own words, sum up the main point of each part.

Part	Details Included	Main Point
Part I: lines 1–15		
Part II: lines 16–59		
Part III: lines 60–91		

▲ VOCABULARY IN CONTEXT

The boldfaced words help Kingsolver turn her embarrassing experiences into funny anecdotes. Write sentences showing the meaning of each boldfaced word as you understand it.

1. showed defiance by speaking **brazenly**
2. felt **mortified** when her father sang in public
3. **cede** control to the new student council president
4. accepted his **abject** apology
5. a **baleful** and frightening threat

Author Online

Barbara Kingsolver
born 1955

A Scientific Leaning Though Barbara Kingsolver began writing stories and essays as a child, she never dreamed she'd someday become a professional author. The writers she read, she explains, "were mostly old, dead men from England. It was inconceivable that I might grow up to be one of those myself." Kingsolver majored in biology in college, but also took one creative writing class—and found she loved it.

Writing for Change Kingsolver wrote her first novel holed up in a closet, typing while her husband slept. Her dedication paid off, and *The Bean Trees* was a critical and popular success. Kingsolver is now an award-winning author of essays, novels, and short stories. She believes that literature can be a force for social change. "I'm extremely interested in cultural difference," Kingsolver says, "in social and political history, and [in] the sparks that fly when people with different ways of looking at the world come together."

MORE ABOUT THE AUTHOR
For more on Barbara Kingsolver, visit the **Literature Center** at ClassZone.com.

Background

Hiroshima On August 6, 1945, at a crucial moment in World War II, the U.S. dropped the first atomic bomb on the Japanese city of Hiroshima. The bomb destroyed the city and killed 80,000 people almost instantly; thousands more died later from radiation illness and other injuries. The city of Hiroshima has been rebuilt and is now at the center of a movement to abolish atomic weapons. Ground Zero, where the bomb fell, is now home to Peace Memorial Park.

Going to Japan

Barbara Kingsolver

My great-aunt Zelda went to Japan and took an abacus, a bathysphere, a conundrum, a diatribe, an eggplant. That was a game we used to play. All you had to do was remember everything in alphabetical order. Right up to Aunt Zelda.

Then I grew up and was actually invited to go to Japan, not with the fantastic Aunt Zelda but as myself. As such, I had no idea what to take. I knew what I planned to be doing: researching a story about the memorial at Hiroshima;[1] visiting friends; trying not to get lost in a place where I couldn't even read the street signs. Times being what they were—*any* times—I intended to do my very best to respect the cultural differences, avoid sensitive topics I might not comprehend, and, in short, be anything but an Ugly American. When I travel, I like to try to blend in. I've generally found it helps to be prepared. So I asked around, and was warned to expect a surprisingly modern place.

My great-aunt Zelda went to Japan and took Appliances, Battery packs, Cellular technology. . . . That seemed to be the idea. Ⓐ

And so it came to pass that I arrived in Kyoto[2] an utter foreigner, unprepared. It's true that there are electric streetcars there, and space-age gas stations with uniformed attendants who rush to help you from all directions at once. There are also golden pagodas[3] on shimmering lakes, and Shinto shrines[4]

ANALYZE VISUALS
Examine the collage on page 777. Name three elements that contribute to how out of place the photograph on top looks against the background images.

Ⓐ **HUMOR**
What clues in lines 1–15 hint that this will be a humorous essay? Explain your answer, citing evidence.

---

1. **the memorial at Hiroshima** (hĭ-rō′shə-mə): The Hiroshima Peace Memorial Park commemorates the deaths and destruction caused by the U.S. bombing of Hiroshima near the end of World War II.

2. **Kyoto** (kē-ō′tō): A Japanese city rich in history and culture, Kyoto was the nation's capital from 794 until 1868.

3. **pagodas** (pə-gō′dəz): sacred buildings of the Buddhist religion, typically towers with many levels.

4. **Shinto shrines**: shrines from the Shinto religion, one of the main religions of Japan.

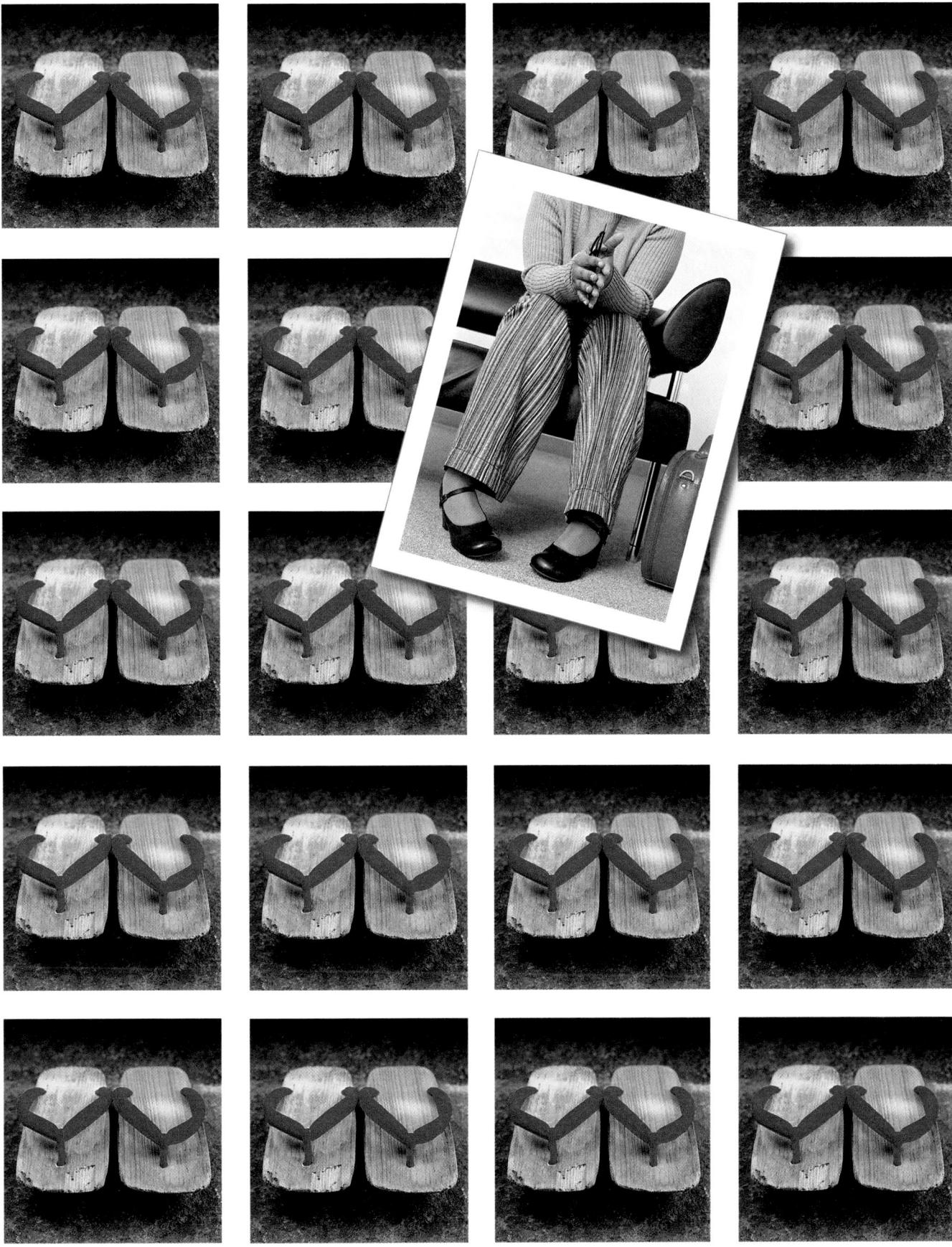

20 in the forests. There are bamboo groves and nightingales. And finally there are more invisible guidelines for politeness than I could fathom. When I stepped on a streetcar, a full head taller than all the other passengers, I became an awkward giant. I took up too much space. I blended in like Igor would blend in with the corps de ballet in *Swan Lake.*[5] I bumped into people. I crossed my arms when I listened, which turns out to be, in Japanese body language, the sign for indicating **brazenly** that one is bored.

But I wasn't! I was struggling through my days and nights in the grip of boredom's opposite—i.e., panic. I didn't know how to eat noodle soup with chopsticks, and I did it most picturesquely *wrong.* I didn't know how to order, 30 so I politely deferred to my hosts and more than once was served a cuisine with heads, including eyeballs. I managed to wrestle these creatures to my lips with chopsticks, but it was already too late by the time I got the message that *one does not spit out anything.*

I undertook this trip in high summer, when it is surprisingly humid and warm in southern Japan. I never imagined that in such sweltering heat women would be expected to wear stockings, but every woman in Kyoto wore nylon stockings. Coeds in shorts *on the tennis court* wore nylon stockings. I had packed only skirts and sandals; people averted their eyes.

When I went to Japan I took my Altitude, my Bare-naked legs, my Callous 40 foreign ways. I was **mortified.** Ⓑ

My hosts explained to me that the Japanese language does not accommodate insults, only infinite degrees of apology. I quickly memorized an urgent one, *"Sumimasen,"* and another for especially extreme cases, *"Moshi wake gozaimasen."*[6] This translates approximately to mean, "If you please, my transgression is so inexcusable that I wish I were dead."

I needed these words. When I touched the outside surface of a palace wall, curious to know what it was made of, I set off screeching alarms and a police car came scooting up the lawn's discreet gravel path. *"Moshi wake gozaimasen,*

brazenly
(brā′zən-lē′) *adv.* boldly and without shame

mortified (môr′tə-fīd′) *adj.* very embarrassed; humiliated **mortify** *v.*

Ⓑ **HUMOR**
Kingsolver repeats this alphabetical **word play** throughout the essay. How does this contribute to the humor of the piece? Explain your answer.

---

5. **Igor . . . corps de ballet** (kôr′də bă-lā′) **in *Swan Lake:*** Igor is the clumsy assistant in many Frankenstein movies. *Swan Lake* is a Russian ballet composed by Peter Ilich Tchaikovsky (chī-kôf′skē).

6. *Sumimasen* (soō-mē-mä-sĕn) . . . *Moshi wake gozaimasen* (mō-shē wä-kĕ gō-zī-mä-sĕn).

Officer! Wish I were dead!" And in the public bath, try as I might, I couldn't
50 get the hang of showering with a hand-held nozzle while sitting fourteen inches
from a stranger. I sprayed my elderly neighbor with cold water. In the face.

"Moshi wake gozaimasen," I declared, with feeling.

She merely stared, dismayed by the foreign menace. **C**

I visited a Japanese friend, and in her small, perfect house I spewed out
my misery. "Everything I do is wrong!" I wailed like a child. "I'm a blight
on your country."

"Oh, no," she said calmly. "To forgive, for us, is the highest satisfaction.
To forgive a foreigner, ah! Even better." She smiled. "You have probably made
many people happy here."

60 To stomp about the world ignoring cultural differences is arrogant, to
be sure, but perhaps there is another kind of arrogance in the presumption
that we may ever really build a faultless bridge from one shore to another,
or even know where the mist has **ceded** to landfall. When I finally arrived
at Ground Zero in Hiroshima, I stood speechless. What I found there was
a vast and exquisitely silent monument to forgiveness. I was moved beyond
words, even beyond tears, to think of all that can be lost or gained in the gulf
between any act of will and its consequences. In the course of every failure of
understanding, we have so much to learn.

I remembered my Japanese friend's insistence on forgiveness as the highest
70 satisfaction, and I understood it really for the first time: What a rich wisdom
it would be, and how much more bountiful a harvest, to gain pleasure not
from achieving personal perfection but from understanding the inevitability
of imperfection and pardoning those who also fall short of it. **D**

I have walked among men and made mistakes without number. When I
went to Japan I took my **Abject** goodwill, my **Baleful** excuses, my Cringing
remorse. I couldn't remember everything, could not even recite the proper
alphabet. So I gave myself away instead, evidently as a kind of public service.
I prepared to return home feeling empty-handed.

At the Osaka[7] Airport I sat in my plane on the runway, waiting to leave for
80 terra cognita,[8] as the aircraft's steel walls were buffeted by the sleet and winds
of a typhoon. We waited for an hour, then longer, with no official word from
the cockpit, and then suddenly our flight was canceled. Air traffic control in
Tokyo had been struck by lightning; no flights possible until the following day.

"We are so sorry," the pilot told us. "You will be taken to a hotel, fed, and
brought back here for your flight tomorrow."

As we passengers rose slowly and disembarked, we were met by an airline
official who had been posted in the exit port for the sole purpose of saying
to each and every one of us, "Terrible, terrible. *Sumimasen.*" Other travelers
nodded indifferently, but not me. I took the startled gentleman by the hands
90 and practically kissed him.

"You have no idea," I told him, "how thoroughly I forgive you." ❧

---

7. **Osaka** (ō-sä'kə).

8. **terra cognita** (tĕr'ə kŏg-nē'tə): Latin for "a familiar land or country."

Comprehension

1. **Recall** Why did the author go to Japan?

2. **Recall** List three examples Kingsolver gives to illustrate her inability to blend in on her trip to Japan.

PENNSYLVANIA
STANDARDS

READING STANDARD
B.2.1.1 Analyze examples of hyperbole, satire, and irony in text.

Literary Analysis

3. **Draw Conclusions** Why did Kingsolver react so strongly to the airline official's apology while her fellow travelers simply "nodded indifferently"? Explain, citing evidence from the selection to support your conclusion.

4. **Identify Irony** This essay is filled with examples of **situational irony,** the contrast between what a reader or character expects and what actually exists or happens. Identify three examples of situational irony and explain what is ironic about each.

5. **Summarize** Review the chart you filled in as you read. Taken together, what do the details you recorded reveal about Kingsolver's overall message? Summarize the author's **main point** in your own words.

6. **Analyze Tone** How would you describe Kingsolver's tone in this essay? Use a graphic like the one shown to record striking or unusual words and phrases from the essay. Then describe the tone Kingsolver's **word choice** helps create.

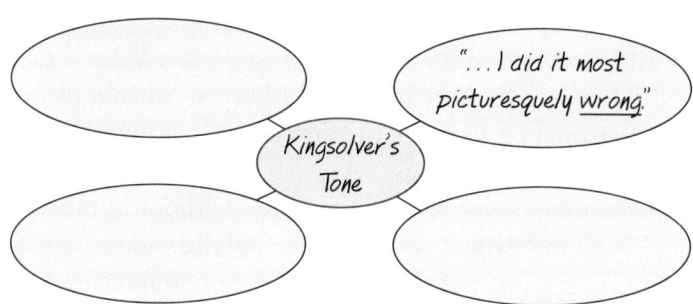

Kingsolver's Tone

"...I did it most picturesquely wrong."

7. **Evaluate Humor** Review the bulleted list of humorous techniques on page 775, and think about how Kingsolver uses humor to communicate her perspective. In your opinion, which technique best helps Kingsolver to convey her thoughts and feelings in a funny way? Give examples from the essay to support your answer.

Literary Criticism

8. **Different Perspectives** Kingsolver is a writer who has long been fascinated by cultural differences and who works to make others see these differences as unique and positive. Would someone less attuned to cultural differences have felt as **out of place** as Kingsolver did? Explain, citing evidence from "Going to Japan" to support your opinion.

Vocabulary in Context

VOCABULARY PRACTICE

Decide whether these statements are true or false.

1. You might be **mortified** if you get the lowest test score in the class.
2. Hearing a **baleful** speech is likely to frighten or anger many people.
3. If you speak **brazenly,** your parents will probably compliment you on your politeness.
4. Mornings usually **cede** to afternoons.
5. **Abject** flattery has to do with praising someone's choice of clothing.

VOCABULARY IN WRITING

Write sentences describing the author's embarrassing mishaps in Japan. Use three or more vocabulary words.

> **EXAMPLE SENTENCE**
>
> *Kingsolver was **mortified** by how clumsily she wielded her chopsticks.*

VOCABULARY STRATEGY: APPROPRIATE WORD CHOICE

To communicate effectively, you should consider several factors when choosing your words. One is a word's **denotation**—its surface meaning or definition. The other is the word's **connotation,** or the overtone of meaning it carries beyond its surface definition. Saying that "Jake spoke *brazenly*," for example, has a stronger negative connotation than saying he spoke *boldly.* Another factor to consider is the formality of the situation. A word like *cede* is rather formal and might sound inappropriate in casual speech or writing.

PENNSYLVANIA STANDARDS

READING STANDARD
A.2.2.2 Use context clues

PRACTICE Choose the word or phrase that is more appropriate in each situation.

1. In a negative review of a singer: Her voice was (shrill, high-pitched).
2. In a letter to a friend: We were (taken in by a con artist, duped by a charlatan).
3. In a formal report: Dr. White was (uptight, apprehensive) about the decision.
4. In a letter of recommendation: He has a (reserved, tight-lipped) but friendly manner.

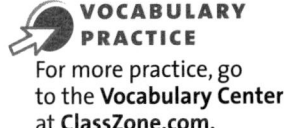

VOCABULARY PRACTICE
For more practice, go to the **Vocabulary Center** at **ClassZone.com.**

A Few Words

Essay by Mary Oliver

Is "CUTE" *a compliment?*

PENNSYLVANIA STANDARDS

READING STANDARD
A.2.5.1 Summarize
B.1.1.1.E.1 Analyze and/or evaluate tone and style

KEY IDEA Before you answer, think about it: What does *cute* really mean? Can you be cute and still be taken seriously? still be strong? still be respected? In this essay, Mary Oliver has a few words to say about what happens when we label something *cute*.

DEBATE With a group of classmates, jot down what comes to mind when you think of something cute. Would you want to be described this way? Form two teams and square off to settle the question of whether or not *cute* is a compliment.

LITERARY ANALYSIS: TONE

A writer's **tone,** or attitude toward a subject, can subtly sneak up on you as you read or boldly hit you over the head in the first paragraph. By noticing a writer's choice of words and details, you can detect and analyze his or her tone. Mary Oliver begins this essay by declaring, "Nothing in the forest is charming." Her blunt statement immediately challenges a common perception of the forest and establishes her tone. As you read "A Few Words," note striking words, details, and images that Oliver uses, and consider the tone they convey.

READING STRATEGY: PARAPHRASE

To understand difficult passages or sentences, it is sometimes helpful to **paraphrase,** or restate the writer's ideas in your own words. When you paraphrase, be sure to

- restate both the main idea and any important details
- use simpler words than those in the original text

As you read, paraphrase this essay's difficult passages in a chart like the one shown.

Passage	My Paraphrase
"Gardens are charming, and man-made grottos, and there is a tranquility about some scenes of husbandry and agriculture that is charming—orderly rows of vegetation, or lazy herds, or the stalks of harvest lashed and leaning together." (lines 1–4)	Man-made elements of nature, like gardens and grottos, are pleasant. Some farm scenes, like orderly rows of crops, tame animals, and harvested produce, look peaceful and calm.

▲ VOCABULARY IN CONTEXT

Mary Oliver uses these words to make her case about the perils of cuteness. To see how many you already know, choose the word that makes sense in each phrase.

WORD LIST	deftness	stalk
	diminutive	valorous

1. a _____ of wheat standing tall in the field
2. the _____ of a quarterback eluding tacklers
3. a _____ teddy bear among larger toys
4. _____ action in the face of danger

Author Online

A Natural Writer
Mary Oliver has been mesmerized by the natural world ever since she was a child growing up in Ohio. She has also always been enthralled by poetry. "I decided very early that I wanted to write," she says. "It was the most exciting thing, the most powerful

**Mary Oliver
born 1935**

thing, the most wonderful thing to do with my life." So she did it. Many years and countless awards later, Oliver still loves writing. "I feel writing is work, and I feel it's also play—bound together," she explains.

Perfecting a Gift Oliver has been described as an "indefatigable guide to the natural world." An ardent observer of nature, she writes about the mysteries and wisdom that it reveals to us. For inspiration, she takes solitary walks in the fields and woods, which she calls part of her writing process. "Walks work for me," she explains. Critics and readers agree with her: Oliver is the winner of numerous awards, including the Pulitzer Prize and a National Book Award. Despite her success, Oliver confesses, "I never have felt yet that I've done it right. This is the marvelous thing about language. It can always be done better."

 MORE ABOUT THE AUTHOR
For more on Mary Oliver, visit the **Literature Center** at **ClassZone.com.**

A Few Words

Mary Oliver

Nothing in the forest is charming. Gardens are charming, and man-made grottos,[1] and there is a tranquility about some scenes of husbandry[2] and agriculture that is charming—orderly rows of vegetation, or lazy herds, or the **stalks** of harvest lashed and leaning together.

And nothing in the forest is cute. The dog fox is not cute, nor the little foxes. I watch them as they run up and down the dune. One is carrying the soiled wing of a gull; the others grab onto it and pull. They fly in and out of the blond grasses, their small teeth snapping. They are not adorable, or charming, or cute.

10 The owl is not cute. The milk snake is not cute, nor the spider in its web, nor the striped bass. Neither is the skunk cute, and its name is not "Flower." Nor is there a rabbit in the forest whose name is "Thumper," who is cute.

Toys are cute. But animals are not toys. Neither are trees, rivers, oceans, swamps, the Alps, the mockingbird singing all night in the bowers of thorn, the snapping turtle, or the purple-fleshed mushroom. **Ⓐ**

Such words—"cute," "charming," "adorable"—miss the mark, for what is perceived of in this way is stripped of dignity, and authority. What is cute is entertainment, and replaceable. The words lead us and we follow: what is cute is **diminutive,** it is powerless, it is capturable, it is trainable, it is ours. It is all a
20 mistake. At our feet are the ferns—savage and resolute they rose, when the race of man was *nowhere* and altogether unlikely ever to be at all, in the terrifying shallows of the first unnamed and unnameable oceans. We find them pretty, delicate, and charming, and carry them home to our gardens.

Thus we manage to put ourselves in the masterly way—if nature is full of a hundred thousand things adorable and charming, diminutive and powerless, then who is in the position of power? We are! We are the parents, and the

---

stalk (stôk) *n.* a stem or main axis of a plant

Ⓐ TONE
Reread lines 1–15. How would you describe Oliver's tone? Identify the words and images the author uses to create this tone.

diminutive (dǐ-mǐn′yə-tǐv) *adj.* very small

---

1. **man-made grottos** (grŏt′ōz): artificial caves created for coolness and pleasure.

2. **husbandry** (hŭz′bən-drē): farming.

784 UNIT 8: AUTHOR'S STYLE AND VOICE

governors. The notion facilitates a view of the world as playground and laboratory, which is a meager view surely. And it is disingenuous, for it seems so harmless, so responsible. But it is neither. **B**

30　　For it makes impossible the other view of nature, which is of a realm both sacred and intricate, as well as powerful, of which we are no more than a single part. Nature, the total of all of us, is the wheel that drives our world; those who ride it willingly might yet catch a glimpse of a dazzling, even a spiritual restfulness, while those who are unwilling simply to hang on, who insist that the world must be piloted by man for his own benefit, will be dragged around and around all the same, gathering dust but no joy. **C**

　　Humans or tigers, tigers or tiger lilies—note their differences and still how alike they are! Don't we all, a few summers, stand here, and face the sea and, with whatever physical and intellectual **deftness** we can muster, improve our
40 state—and then, silently, fall back into the grass, death's green cloud? What is cute or charming as it rises, as it swoons? Life is Niagara, or nothing. I would not be the overlord of a single blade of grass, that I might be its sister. I put my face close to the lily, where it stands just above the grass, and give it a good greeting from the stem of my heart. We live, I am sure of this, in the same country, in the same household, and our burning comes from the same lamp. We are all wild, **valorous,** amazing. We are, none of us, cute. ❧

B **GRAMMAR AND STYLE**
Reread lines 24–29. Notice how Oliver uses a variety of **interrogative, exclamatory,** and **declarative sentences** to express her views on human arrogance.

C **PARAPHRASE**
What is Oliver saying about human attitudes toward nature in lines 32–36? Paraphrase this sentence, breaking it down into several shorter sentences if necessary.

deftness (dĕft'nĭs) *n.* the quality of quickness and skillfulness

valorous (văl'ər-əs) *adj.* brave

ANALYZE VISUALS
Compare your reaction to these photographs with your reaction to the one on page 785. In your opinion, do these photos illustrate Oliver's message better than the one on the preceding page? Explain your answer.

Comprehension

1. **Recall** How does Oliver describe the foxes at the beginning of the essay?

2. **Recall** List three other animals or plants the author discusses.

3. **Clarify** In Oliver's view, if we see nature as made up of cute, powerless animals, then who is in a position of power?

PENNSYLVANIA
STANDARDS

READING STANDARD
B.1.1.1.E.1 Analyze and/or evaluate
tone and style

Literary Analysis

4. **Draw Conclusions** Reread the essay's last line on page 786. Has "A Few Words" changed your opinion about what it means to label something *cute?* Do you think *cute* can ever be a compliment? Explain, citing lines from the essay you agree or disagree with.

5. **Analyze Tone** Describe Oliver's overall tone in this essay. As a reader, what can you tell about her attitude toward nature? Explain, citing evidence from the essay to support your analysis.

6. **Paraphrase** Review the paraphrasing chart you created as you read. Using your chart, summarize the main idea of this essay in your own words.

7. **Examine Author's Style** Oliver is most widely known for her poetry. In what way might this selection be described as poetic? In a chart like the one shown, record examples of the poetic elements Oliver uses in this essay. Use your completed chart to explain whether you think "A Few Words" is more like poetry or more like prose.

Poetic Element	Examples from the Text
Alliteration	• "At our feet are the ferns ..." (line 20) • •
Metaphor	
Imagery	
Repetition	

Literary Criticism

8. **Critical Interpretations** Critics have praised Oliver's quest to, in the words of Holly Prado of the *L.A. Times Book Review,* "understand both the wonder and pain of nature." In your opinion, how well does Oliver explain both the beautiful and the not-so-beautiful aspects of the natural world? Support your answer with evidence from the selection.

Vocabulary in Context

VOCABULARY PRACTICE

In which situation might you use each vocabulary word?

1. **diminutive:** (a) describing a miniature poodle, (b) listing the pros and cons of a school committee's proposal, (c) explaining how to draw trees

2. **stalk:** (a) explaining how to apply paint, (b) describing a field of corn, (c) listing the reasons you like bungee jumping

3. **valorous:** (a) telling about a peaceful day in the country, (b) describing how the hero of a movie saved the day, (c) detailing how to lay a brick sidewalk

4. **deftness:** (a) watching leaves fall in a windstorm, (b) describing how a runner broke away from the pack to win, (c) choosing a birthday card for your brother

WORD LIST

deftness

diminutive

stalk

valorous

VOCABULARY IN WRITING

Do you agree with Mary Oliver? Write a paragraph explaining why or why not. Use two or more vocabulary words. Here is a sample first sentence.

EXAMPLE SENTENCE

Like Mary Oliver, I believe that thinking about animals as **diminutive,** *helpless creatures is unjust. . . .*

VOCABULARY STRATEGY: HOMONYMS

Homonyms are words that have the same pronunciation and often the same spelling but different meanings. For example, the vocabulary word *stalk*, which means "a stem or main axis of a plant," looks and sounds just like the word *stalk*, meaning "to move threateningly or menacingly." Because they are pronounced and spelled the same way, homonyms can be confusing. The context of the sentence or passage can usually help you determine which of a set of homonyms is being used. However, sometimes it's difficult to figure out the meaning of a homonym from its context. In such cases, check a dictionary.

PRACTICE Identify the homonyms described by each pair of definitions. If you're stumped, figure out which word just one of the definitions describes. Then use a dictionary to find out if that word has any homonyms.

1. to move a boat forward with oars/a line of people or objects
2. place where a dead person is buried/very serious or solemn
3. a type of something/friendly and considerate
4. the skin of an animal/to conceal or keep secret
5. to intend to do something/unkind
6. belonging to me/an underground cavern from which gold is extracted

PENNSYLVANIA STANDARDS

READING STANDARD
A.2.1.1 Apply meaning of multiple-meaning words

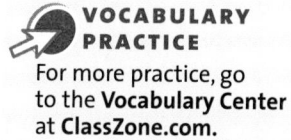

VOCABULARY PRACTICE
For more practice, go to the **Vocabulary Center** at **ClassZone.com.**

Reading-Writing Connection

Increase your understanding of "A Few Words" by responding to these prompts. Then use **Revision: Grammar and Style** to improve your writing.

WRITING PROMPTS

A. Short Response: Analyze Tone

Did the tone of Oliver's essay make you more or less receptive to her ideas? Would you have agreed with her more if she'd tried to sweet-talk you into seeing things her way? In **one or two paragraphs,** describe how the author's tone affected your response to her message.

B. Extended Response: Express an Opinion

Oliver makes the case that we do nature a disservice when we label it *cute*. Can this apply to calling a person *cute*, as well? Write a **three-to-five-paragraph response** explaining whether or not you think this label can be harmful to humans.

SELF-CHECK

An effective analysis will . . .

- describe Oliver's tone in "A Few Words," using evidence from the selection to support your description
- reveal whether or not Oliver's tone affected how you feel about her views

A strong response will . . .

- clearly state whether labeling a person *cute* can have negative repercussions
- use evidence from the text to support your opinion

REVISION: GRAMMAR AND STYLE

VARY SENTENCE TYPES Reread the **Grammar and Style** note on page 786. Oliver believes that some people have a very condescending view of nature. To express her outrage at this perception, she uses a variety of sentence types that allow her emotions to shine through. Here, Oliver enlists **imperative, interrogative,** and **declarative sentences** to get her point across:

> *Humans or tigers, tigers or tiger lilies—note their differences and still how alike they are! Don't we all, a few summers, stand here, and face the sea and, with whatever physical and intellectual deftness we can muster, improve our state— and then, silently, fall back into the grass, death's green cloud? What is cute or charming as it rises, as it swoons? Life is Niagara, or nothing.* (lines 37–41)

Notice how the revisions in red employ sentence types that more accurately reflect the emotions of the writer, making the statements more powerful. Revise your responses to the prompts by varying your sentence types.

PENNSYLVANIA STANDARDS

WRITING STANDARD
1.5.11.D.1 Use different types and lengths of sentences

STUDENT MODEL

I don't ~~think we should~~ refer to people as "cute." It belittles them,

Why not
~~and it doesn't~~ take into account their achievements. ~~I think~~ we should give

people credit for something more worthwhile, like hard work.

WRITING TOOLS
For prewriting, revision, and editing tools, visit the **Writing Center** at ClassZone.com.

A narrow Fellow in the Grass
"Hope" is the thing with feathers—

Poems by Emily Dickinson

What is a poet's JOB?

PENNSYLVANIA STANDARDS

READING/SPEAKING STANDARDS
B.1.1.1.E.1 Analyze and/or evaluate tone and style
1.6.11.C.3 Adjust stress, volume and inflection to provide emphasis to ideas

KEY IDEA Have you ever tried to describe something important, only to find yourself at a total loss for words? Some things are hard to explain, but certain people seem able to explain them anyway. Poets use their skill with language to communicate **insights,** or perceptive comments, about everything from emotions and adventure to animals and art.

PRESENT Write a want ad seeking a poet to communicate an insight you think is worth sharing. Include a description of what you want explained, the skills your poet should possess, and the kind of poetry you're looking for. Then pair up with a classmate and take turns presenting your ads.

Wanted:
Wild words to explain
why in the world . . .

LITERARY ANALYSIS: DICKINSON'S STYLE

Emily Dickinson's style is unmistakable. One of the originators of modern American poetry, she broke with tradition, creating a unique style all her own. Dickinson's poems are usually short—no more than 20 lines—but they often convey stunning insights in spite of their brevity. Distinct elements of Dickinson's style include

- dense stanzas that echo the **rhythms** of church hymns
- **slant rhymes,** or words that do not rhyme exactly
- unconventional capitalization that adds emphasis to certain words or phrases
- frequent use of dashes to highlight important words and break up the singsong rhythm of her poems
- original **figurative language,** including similes, metaphors, and personification

As you read, notice the poet's use of these elements, and consider the insights she communicates by using them.

READING STRATEGY: READING POETRY

The following suggestions can help you increase both your understanding and your enjoyment of Dickinson's poetry:

- Read the poems aloud to appreciate Dickinson's unique rhythm and imagery.
- Pay close attention to words that are capitalized for emphasis.
- Analyze the poet's use of figurative language.
- Pause when you encounter dashes, just as you would for a comma or a period in a more conventional poem.

Author On|ine

Emily Dickinson
1830–1886

Close to Home Except for a year she spent away at school, Emily Dickinson lived her entire life in the small community of Amherst, Massachusetts, with her family. She was very close to her older brother and younger sister. Though she adored her stern and principled father, she had a complicated relationship with her mother. By her 40s, Dickinson began to dress only in white and refused to leave her family's house. Except for the many letters she wrote and received, she withdrew from the world, living in isolation until her death.

A Private Poet After Dickinson's death, her sister Lavinia carried out the poet's wishes, burning all of her letters from family and friends. However, Lavinia rescued a little box filled with poems. Since her late teens or early 20s, Emily Dickinson had been writing poetry. She'd jot down her thoughts during the day—on scraps of paper, old recipes, and the backs of envelopes—and write all night by candlelight. Though she wrote 1,775 poems, Dickinson published only 7, anonymously, during her lifetime. The private poet left the world pondering her untold secrets.

A Rich Life The first volume of Emily Dickinson's poetry was published in 1890, four years after her death. Today, she is known as one of the most popular and influential U.S. poets. Even though Dickinson lived in isolation, her poems, according to 20th-century poet Allen Tate, reveal a life that was "one of the richest and deepest ever lived on this continent."

 MORE ABOUT THE AUTHOR
For more on Emily Dickinson, visit the **Literature Center** at **ClassZone.com.**

A narrow Fellow IN THE Grass

EMILY DICKINSON

A narrow Fellow in the Grass
Occasionally rides—
You may have met Him—did you not
His notice sudden is—

5 The Grass divides as with a Comb—
A spotted shaft is seen—
And then it closes at your feet
And opens further on— Ⓐ

He likes a Boggy Acre
10 A Floor too cool for Corn—
Yet when a Boy, and Barefoot—
I more than once at Noon
Have passed, I thought, a Whip lash
Unbraiding in the Sun
15 When stopping to secure it
It wrinkled, and was gone— Ⓑ

Several of Nature's People
I know, and they know me—
I feel for them a transport
20 Of cordiality—[1]

But never met this Fellow
Attended, or alone
Without a tighter breathing
And Zero at the Bone—

Ⓐ **DICKINSON'S STYLE**
What is the "narrow Fellow" Dickinson describes? Explain why you think the poet chose to capitalize certain words in the first two stanzas.

Ⓑ **DICKINSON'S STYLE**
Identify one example of **slant rhyme** in this stanza. What other distinctive features of Dickinson's style can you see in this poem? Support your answer with evidence.

---

1. **a transport of cordiality:** a very strong feeling of warmth and friendliness.

"Hope" is the thing with feathers—

EMILY DICKINSON

"Hope" is the thing with feathers—
That perches in the soul—
And sings the tune without the words—
And never stops—at all— **C**

5 And sweetest—in the Gale—is heard—
And sore[1] must be the storm—
That could abash[2] the little Bird
That kept so many warm—

I've heard it in the chillest land—
10 And on the strangest Sea—
Yet, never, in Extremity,[3]
It asked a crumb—of Me. **D**

C DICKINSON'S STYLE
What **metaphor** does Dickinson present in the first stanza? Explain your answer.

D READING POETRY
Reread lines 11–12 aloud. What is the effect of Dickinson's unusual punctuation and capitalization in these lines?

---

1. **sore:** severe
2. **abash:** cause to be upset or embarrassed.
3. **Extremity:** greatest need or danger.

JOURNAL ARTICLE Intrigued by the mysterious Ms. Dickinson? Read on to learn why some scholars think the poet was anything but solitary.

Unraveling the Mystery of Emily Dickinson

"I'm Nobody! Who are you?
Are you—Nobody—too?"

These lines come from one of Emily Dickinson's famous poems. Imagine that a friend sent those words to you. Would you think your friend was feeling witty? contemplative? sad? Like the faceless e-mail and text messages sent between friends today, Dickinson's letters and poetry could be interpreted numerous ways by her friends. Scholars still debate Dickinson's mysterious words and life.

Many theories exist about her reasons for withdrawing from the world and her seclusion at the family home for the last 20 years of her life. Some say that it was an opportunity to concentrate her energies on her writing. Others believe it was a case of agoraphobia (fear of crowds). No one can prove which, if any, is correct, but the best available evidence is found in her correspondence. Some people even believe her letters indicate her life was far from antisocial. They suggest that it was her editors, who hoped to persuade the public that Dickinson was an upstanding single lady in accordance with her time, who perpetuated the notion of Dickinson as a recluse.

The sheer volume of her writing indicates she often wrote a few letters or poems each day, keeping in frequent touch with family and friends. Scholars also note the Dickinson house was an active gathering place, so Dickinson did not have to leave to socialize. Her best friend, Susan, lived next door for 30 years. Famous writers of Dickinson's time came to visit, as did some of her mentors. In addition, the household library contained nearly 1,000 books, and the grounds offered gardens and woods—some of her favorite spots to spend time when she wasn't helping with the household, working on her writing, or caring for her brother's children.

Although popularly characterized as a shy adult, as a child Dickinson was known for her sense of humor. An account of her meeting with literary critic Thomas Wentworth Higginson in 1870 shows her to be a talkative woman— Higginson found her draining. Of course, it could be that she was simply so excited to finally meet the famous mentor she had corresponded with for eight years. One friend commented that Dickinson was so surrounded by friends at a party that she couldn't even talk to her.

Despite their long correspondence—over 20 years—Higginson didn't know what to make of the mysterious poet. "She was much too enigmatical a being for me to solve in an hour's interview," he wrote in an article for the *Atlantic* after her death.

Was Emily Dickinson a shy, troubled woman; a fulfilled, solitary soul; or someone in between? Study her writing closely, and perhaps you will discover a clue.

Comprehension

1. **Recall** What are two places where the "narrow Fellow" can be found?

2. **Recall** List three ways Dickinson compares hope to a bird.

Literary Analysis

3. **Interpret Theme in Poetry** In one or two sentences, state the theme of each poem. Then explain which poem you think offers a more interesting or perceptive **insight.**

4. **Analyze Mood** Reread lines 17–24 of "A narrow Fellow in the Grass." How does the mood of the fourth stanza differ from that of the fifth? Explain which words or phrases contribute to the change in mood.

5. **Identify Symbol** A symbol is something that stands for more than itself. In "'Hope' is the thing with feathers—" what do "the Gale," "the chillest land," and "the strangest Sea" represent? Cite evidence to support your answer.

6. **Analyze Extended Metaphor** An extended metaphor compares two things at some length and in several ways. In "'Hope' is the thing with feathers—" Dickinson compares hope to a bird. How does she develop this metaphor throughout the poem? Use a graphic like the one shown to help organize your evidence.

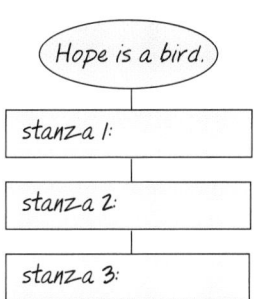

Hope is a bird.

stanza 1:

stanza 2:

stanza 3:

7. **Examine Emily Dickinson's Style** Review the bulleted list of Dickinson's stylistic hallmarks on page 791. Pick two elements of the poet's style and find examples of them in "A narrow Fellow in the Grass" and "'Hope' is the thing with feathers—." Then explain the effect created by each example.

Literary Criticism

8. **Author's Style** Dickinson's first volume of poetry, and each collection after that until 1955, consisted of "corrected" versions of her poems. In other words, editors "fixed" Dickinson's punctuation and capitalization. Acting as a 19th-century editor, rewrite one of Dickinson's poems using standard punctuation and capitalization. Read your finished product. Is there something missing? Do you prefer the poem Dickinson's way? Explain your answer.

PENNSYLVANIA STANDARDS

READING STANDARD
B.1.1.1.E.1 Analyze and/or evaluate tone and style

Luxury
Kidnap Poem
Poems by Nikki Giovanni

What would win your HEART?

PENNSYLVANIA STANDARDS

READING STANDARDS
A.1.4.1 Identify and explain main ideas and relevant details
B.1.1.1.E.1 Analyze and/or evaluate tone and style

KEY IDEA What would it take to win you over? Candy and flowers? A pretty face? A sense of humor? What about **love poems**—could they ever help someone win your heart? The following poems are so passionate that if you answered no, you might change your mind after reading them.

QUICKWRITE What is the one thing someone could do to make you totally fall for him or her? In a paragraph, describe the act or gesture—be it grand and thrilling or small and ordinary—that would win your heart.

LITERARY ANALYSIS: GIOVANNI'S STYLE

Nikki Giovanni is a poet who goes by her own rules. "I want my writing to sound like I talk," she says. To that end, Giovanni employs a conversational style that breaks with convention. Most of her work consists of lyric poetry written in **free verse,** which lacks a regular rhyme and meter and often sounds like natural speech. Giovanni's unique style also includes

- a deliberate lack of punctuation and capitalization

- stanzas and lines of varying length

- simple language and clear metaphors

- the use of sound devices such as **alliteration** and **repetition** to create a distinct rhythm

As you read, look for evidence of these techniques, and think about how Giovanni's style helps her communicate her message.

READING SKILL: INTERPRET IDEAS IN POETRY

The key to understanding and interpreting poetry is often digesting little chunks at a time. Working through a poem slowly can help you extract its meaning and its message. As you read "Luxury" and "Kidnap Poem," write down interesting stanzas and unusual phrases. Then record what you think each means.

Phrase or Stanza	Meaning
i suppose living in a materialistic society luxury to some would be having more than what you need ("Luxury," lines 1–5)	People in money-centered societies think excess equals luxury.

Author Online

Nikki Giovanni born 1943

Family Ties Yolande Cornelia Giovanni Jr. was nicknamed Nikki by her older sister. Giovanni's close-knit family moved from Tennessee to Ohio just after she was born, but they often returned to visit her dynamic, outspoken grandmother, who was a huge influence on the poet. Giovanni says her grandmother, a great storyteller, was also "the only person I know for sure whose love I did not have to earn."

Young and Driven Giovanni always suspected she'd be famous one day. Her drive led her to Fisk University, but her independent spirit got her kicked out after just one semester. Giovanni eventually returned to Fisk, where she became active in the civil rights movement. A year after graduating with honors, Giovanni published *Black Feeling, Black Talk,* her first book of poetry. The book was inspired both by the death of her grandmother and by the poet's increasing outrage at the way African Americans were treated in the U.S. Giovanni was determined to change society through her poetry. Writing, according to Giovanni, is the easy part. "Then," she says, "comes the hard part: you have to find someone to read it."

The Journey Much of Giovanni's early work consisted of militant calls to action and angry demands for racial equality. While she hasn't lost her political edge, Giovanni's later poetry also explores more personal territory, delving into family, love, and loneliness. Giovanni battled cancer in the 1990s, but after successful surgery, she resumed her work. Writing poetry, Giovanni says, "is a journey without end."

 MORE ABOUT THE AUTHOR
For more on Nikki Giovanni, visit the **Literature Center** at ClassZone.com.

Luxury

Nikki Giovanni

i suppose living
in a materialistic society
luxury
to some would be having
5 more than what you need

living in an electronic age seeing
the whole world by
   pushing a button
the *nth* degree[1] might
10   perhaps be
adequately represented
   by having
someone there to push
the buttons for you **A**

15 i have thought if only
i could become rich and famous
   i would
live luxuriously in new york
   knowing
20 famous people eating
in expensive restaurants calling
long distance anytime i want

but you held me
one evening and now i know
25 the ultimate luxury
of your love **B**

ANALYZE VISUALS
Does this painting
seem **luxurious** to you?
Consider its colors, shapes,
and textures, as well as
the figures it depicts.
Explain your opinion,
citing details.

A **GIOVANNI'S STYLE**
What elements of
Giovanni's distinctive
style are apparent so far
in this poem? Explain
your answer, referring to
specific lines for evidence.

B **INTERPRET IDEAS
IN POETRY**
Reread lines 23–26. How
does the idea expressed
in this stanza compare
with the ideas in previous
stanzas of the poem?

---

1. **the *nth* degree:** the ultimate degree of something;
   as much or as far as possible.

Tumbling Flowers (1954), Hyacinth Manning-Carner.
© Hyacinth Manning-Carner/SuperStock.

Kidnap POEM

NIKKI GIOVANNI

Sleeping Couple I (2000), Hyacinth Manning-Carner.
© Hyacinth Manning-Carner/SuperStock.

ever been kidnapped
by a poet
if i were a poet
i'd kidnap you
5 put you in my phrases and meter
you to jones beach
or maybe coney island[1]
or maybe just to my house
lyric you in lilacs
10 dash you in the rain
blend into the beach
to complement my see[2] **C**
play the lyre[3] for you
ode you with my love song
15 anything to win you
wrap you in the red Black green
show you off to mama
yeah if i were a poet i'd kid
nap you

C **GIOVANNI'S STYLE**
Read lines 9–12 aloud.
Describe the **rhythm**
created by Giovanni's use
of short phrases like "lyric
you in lilacs" and "dash
you in the rain." How
does the rhythm help
communicate her ideas
in this poem?

---

1. **jones beach . . . coney island:** beach and
   amusement areas on the outskirts of
   New York City.

2. **complement my see:** complete or perfect
   my kingdom.

3. **lyre** (līr): stringed instrument like a small,
   U-shaped harp.

Comprehension

1. **Recall** What is the "ultimate luxury" described toward the end of the first poem?

2. **Recall** List three things the speaker of "Kidnap Poem" says she would do if she were a poet.

Literary Analysis

3. **Interpret Ideas in Poetry** Review the chart you filled in as you read. Using the interpretations you recorded, summarize the main message, or **theme,** of each poem.

4. **Analyze Voice** Voice refers to a writer's unique use of language that allows you to "hear" a personality in his or her writing. How would you characterize the voice of the speaker in "Luxury"? Consider the point of view from which the poem is told and the language it uses, as well as the poem's rhythm and message.

5. **Analyze Diction** Reread lines 5–14 of "Kidnap Poem." Consider Giovanni's unconventional use of words like *meter, lyric,* and *ode.* How does Giovanni's unusual word usage help her communicate her message about the power of poetry? Support your answer with evidence from the poem.

6. **Examine Giovanni's Style** Think about the poet's description of her own writing on page 797, and review the bulleted list of Giovanni's trademarks. Which stylistic elements help create Giovanni's loose, conversational style in "Kidnap Poem"? Explain your answer, citing evidence.

7. **Compare and Contrast** In terms of **style,** how are "Luxury" and "Kidnap Poem" similar? In what ways do they differ? Think about the form and rhythm of each poem, as well as the language Giovanni uses in each. Cite specific examples from both poems to support your comparison.

Literary Criticism

8. **Critical Interpretations** Rapper, singer, and actress Queen Latifah discovered Giovanni's poetry at age 14. "Nikki's poems struck me," Latifah explains. "I could feel her. I liked how some of the things she wrote were so clever and cool. I liked how she threw a little bit of rhythm around. All her poetry seemed to be real and to have love in it." After reading "Luxury" and "Kidnap Poem," do you agree or disagree with this description? Explain, citing evidence from both poems.

PENNSYLVANIA STANDARDS

READING STANDARD
A.1.4.1 Identify and explain main ideas and relevant details

The Sneeze

Drama by Neil Simon

Based on a story by Anton Chekhov

Who makes you LAUGH?

PENNSYLVANIA STANDARDS

READING STANDARDS
A.1.3.1 Make inferences and/or draw conclusions
A.1.6.1 Analyze intended purpose of text

KEY IDEA Whether it's your best friend or a professional comedian, who makes you laugh—*really* **laugh?** What does this person do that you find so funny? If you get a kick out of ridiculous characters bumbling into trouble because of their out-of-control bodily functions, you'll love "The Sneeze."

QUICKWRITE Think about the last time you succumbed to helpless laughter—the kind that makes you gasp for breath and clutch your stomach. What set you off? Create your own top-ten list describing the things and the people you find funniest.

LITERARY ANALYSIS: FARCE

A **farce** is a humorous play that prompts laughter by presenting ridiculous situations, comic dialogue, and physical humor—in this case, an enormous sneeze. Often, the purpose of a farce is simply to keep the audience laughing. However, sometimes the writer of a farce has the goal of poking fun at someone or something in particular. To spot a farce, look for

- absurd plots driven by humorous conflicts
- exaggerated behavior and language
- characters who often exhibit just one comic trait or quality
- clever wordplay, including puns and double meanings
- physical comedy

As you read "The Sneeze," think about how it exhibits these features. Note situations or characters that you find especially funny.

READING STRATEGY: VISUALIZE

When you **visualize,** you use details, description, and dialogue to create mental pictures of what you read. Visualizing the hilarity of this play can help you interpret and enjoy it. Try the following:

- Read the stage directions to get a mental picture of the setting and actions taking place.
- Pay attention to the narrator's description of the other characters. Do you get an image of how they might look and behave?
- To help you picture the characters, try mentally casting your favorite comedic actor in the lead role.
- Use your own imagination and sense of humor.

As you read, keep track of the details that help you visualize different aspects of the play.

Details from the Text	My Visualization
"He is in his mid-thirties, mild-mannered and unassuming." (lines 4–5)	I picture a timid-looking, boring man with a pale, slightly anxious face.

Author Online

Popular Playwright
Neil Simon, one of America's most popular dramatists, was born on the 4th of July in New York City. He began writing comedy sketches for radio during the 1940s, then migrated to television and finally to the theater. Most of Simon's plays are set in his hometown

**Neil Simon
born 1927**

of New York City and deal with the domestic problems of middle-class Americans.

Russian Master
One of his country's greatest authors, Anton Chekhov was born to a poor family in Russia. He enrolled in medical school as a young man, but his family needed his financial support, so he began writing comical sketches and selling them to magazines.

**Anton Chekhov
1860–1904**

Writing, not medicine, became his career. Chekhov wrote short stories and one-act farces before turning to the full-length plays that made him a legend.

Background

A Team . . . Sort of Neil Simon's *The Good Doctor* is a series of dramatic sketches based on Chekhov's stories. The sketches are tied together through the character of the Writer, who reveals his ideas for stories to the audience. "The Sneeze" is one of those sketches. Simon has jokingly referred to Chekhov as "my non-consenting collaborator."

MORE ABOUT THE AUTHOR
For more on the authors, visit the **Literature Center** at ClassZone.com.

THE SNEEZE

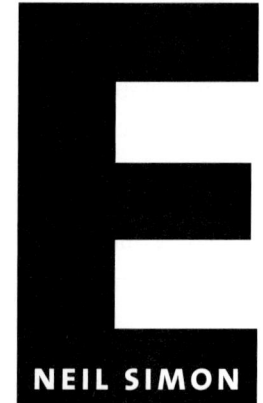

NEIL SIMON

FROM *THE GOOD DOCTOR*

BASED ON A STORY BY ANTON CHEKHOV

Writer. If Ivan Ilyitch Cherdyakov,[1] a civil servant, a clerk in the Ministry of Public Parks, had any passion in life at all, it was the theater. (*Enter* Ivan Cherdyakov *and his* Wife. *He is in his mid-thirties, mild-mannered and unassuming. He and his* Wife *are dressed in their best, but are certainly no match for the grandeur around them. They are clearly out of their element here. They move into their seats. As his* Wife *peruses her program,* Cherdyakov *is*
10 *beaming with happiness as he looks around and in back at the theater and its esteemed audience. He is a happy man tonight.*) He certainly had hopes and ambitions for higher office and had dedicated his life to hard work, zeal and patience. Still, he would not deny himself his one great pleasure. So he purchased two tickets in the very best section of the theater for the opening night performance of Rostov's *The Bearded Countess.*[2] (*A splendidly uniformed* General *and his* Wife *enter, looking for*
20 *their seats.*) As fortune would have it, into the theater that night came His Respected Superior, General Mikhail Brassilhov,[3] the Minister of Public Parks himself.

(*The* General *and his* Wife *take their seats in the first row, the* General *directly in front of* Cherdyakov.)

Cherdyakov (*leans over to the* General). Good evening, General.

General (*turns, looks at* Cherdyakov *coldly*).
30 Hmm? . . . What? Oh, yes. Yes. Good evening.

(*The* General *turns front again, looks at his program.*)

Cherdyakov. Permit me, sir. I am Cherdyakov . . . Ivan Ilyitch. This is a great honor for me, sir.

General (*turns; coldly*). Yes.

Cherdyakov. Like yourself, dear General, I too serve the Ministry of Public Parks . . . That is to say, I serve *you,* who is indeed *himself* the Minister of Public Parks. I am the Assistant Chief Clerk in
40 the Department of Trees and Bushes.

General. Ahh, yes. Keep up the good work . . . Lovely trees and bushes this year. Very nice.

---

1. **Ivan Ilyitch Cherdyakov** (ē-vän′ ĭl-yēch′ chĕrd′yə-kəv).
2. **Rostov's *The Bearded Countess:*** a made-up author and play.
3. **Mikhail Brassilhov** (mē′kä-ēl′ bräs′ĭl-əv).

(*The* General *turns back.* Cherdyakov *sits back, happy, grinning like a cat. The* General's Wife *whispers to him and he shrugs back. Suddenly the unseen curtain rises on the play and they all applaud.* Cherdyakov *leans forward again.*)

Cherdyakov. My wife would like very much to say hello, General. This is she. My wife, Madame
50 Cherdyakov.

Wife (*smiles*). How do you do?

General. My pleasure.

Wife. *My* pleasure, General.

General. How do you do?

(*He turns front, flustered.* Cherdyakov *beams at his* Wife; *then*)

Cherdyakov (*to the* General's Wife). Madame Brassilhov—my wife, Madame Cherdyakov.

Wife. How do you do, Madame Brassilhov?

60 **Madame Brassilhov** (*coldly*). How do you do?

Wife. I just had the pleasuse of meeting your husband.

Cherdyakov (*to* Madame Brassilhov). And I am my wife's husband. How do you do, Madame Brassilhov?

(*The* Writer *"shushes" them.*)

General (*to the* Writer). Sorry. Terribly sorry.

(*The* General *tries to control his anger as they all go back to watching the play.*)

70 **Cherdyakov.** I hope you enjoy the play, sir.

General. I will if I can watch it.

(*He is getting hot under the collar. They all go back to watching the performance.*)

Writer. Feeling quite pleased with himself for having made the most of this golden opportunity, Ivan Ilyitch Cherdyakov sat back to enjoy *The Bearded Countess.* He was no longer a stranger to the Minister of Public Parks. They had become, if one wanted to be generous about the matter,

80 familiar with each other . . . And then, quite suddenly, without any warning, like a bolt from a gray thundering sky, Ivan Ilyitch Cherdyakov reared his head back, and—

Cherdyakov. AHHHHHHHH— CHOOOOOOOO!!! (Cherdyakov *unleashes a monstrous sneeze, his head snapping forward. The main blow of the sneeze discharges on the back of the* General's *completely bald head. The* General *winces and his hand immediately goes to his now-*
90 *dampened head.*) Ohhh, my goodness, I'm *sorry,* your Excellency! I'm so terribly sorry!

(*The* General *takes out his handkerchief and wipes his head.*)

General. Never mind. It's all right.

Cherdyakov. *All right?* . . . It certainly is *not* all right! It's unpardonable. It was monstrous of me—

General. You make too much of the matter. Let it rest.

100 (*He puts away his handkerchief.*)

Cherdyakov (*quickly takes out his own handkerchief*). How can I let it rest? It was inexcusable. Permit me to wipe your neck, General. It's the least I can do.

(*He starts to wipe the* General's *head. The* General *pushes his hand away.*)

General. Leave it be! It's all right, I say.

Cherdyakov. But I splattered you, sir. Your complete head is splattered. It was an accident,
110 I assure you—but it's *disgusting!*

Writer. Shhhh!

General. I'm sorry. My apologies.

Cherdyakov. The thing is, your Excellency, it came completely without warning. It was out of my nose before I could stifle it.

Madame Brassilhov. Shhh!

Cherdyakov. Shhh, yes, certainly. I'm sorry . . . (*He sits back, nervously. He blows his nose with his handkerchief. Then* Cherdyakov *leans forward.*) It's not a cold, if that's what you were worrying about, sir. Probably a particle of dust in the nostril—

General. Shhh!

(*They watch the play in silence, and* Cherdyakov *sits back, unhappy with himself.*)

Writer. But try as he might, Cherdyakov could not put the incident out of his mind. The sneeze, no more than an innocent anatomical accident,[4] grew out of all proportion in his mind, until it resembled the angry roar of a cannon aimed squarely at the enemy camp. He played the incident back in his mind, slowing the procedure down so he could view again in horror the infamous deed.

(Cherdyakov, *in slow motion, repeats the sneeze again, but slowed down so that it appears to us as one frame at a time. It also seems to be three times as great in intensity as the original sneeze. The* General, *also in slow motion, reacts as though he has just taken a fifty-pound hammer blow at the base of his skull. They all go with the slow motion of the "sneeze" until it is completed, when the unseen curtain falls and they applaud. They all rise and begin to file out of the theater, chattering about the lovely evening they have just spent.*)

General. Charming . . . Charming.

Madame Brassilhov. Yes, charming.

General. Charming . . . Simply charming. Wasn't it charming, my dear?

Madame Brassilhov. I found it utterly charming.

(Cherdyakov *stands behind them tapping the* General.)

Writer. I was completely charmed by it.

Cherdyakov (*still tapping away at the* General). Excuse me, Excellency—

General. Who's tapping? Somebody's tapping me. Who's that tapping?

Cherdyakov. I'm tapping, sir. I'm the tapper . . . Cherdyakov.

Madame Brassilhov (*quickly pulls the* General *back*). Stand back, dear, it's the sneezer.

Cherdyakov. No, no, it's all right. I'm all sneezed out . . . I was just concerned about your going out into the night air with a damp head.

General. Oh, that. It was a trifle. A mere faux pas. Forget it, young man. Amusing play, don't you think? Did you find it amusing?

Cherdyakov. Amusing? Oh, my goodness, yes. Ha, ha. So true. Ha, ha. I haven't laughed as much in years. Ha, ha, ha . . .

General. Which part interested you the most?

Cherdyakov. The sneeze. When I sneezed on you. It was unforgivable, sir.

General. Forget it, young man. Come, my dear. It looks like rain. I don't want to get my head wet again.

Madame Brassilhov. You shouldn't let people sneeze on you, dear. You're not to be sneezed at.

(*They are gone.*)

Cherdyakov. I'm ruined! Ruined! He'll have me fired from Trees and Bushes. They'll send me down to Branches and Twigs.

Wife. Come, Ivan.

Cherdyakov. What?

Wife. You mustn't let it concern you. It was just a harmless little sneeze. The General's probably forgotten it already.

Cherdyakov. Do you really think so?

Wife. No! I'm scared, Ivan.

---

4. **innocent anatomical accident:** A biological act over which Cherdyakov had no control.

Writer. And so they walked home in despair.

190 **Cherdyakov.** Perhaps I should send him a nice gift. Maybe some Turkish towels.

Writer. Cherdyakov's once-promising career had literally been blown away.

Cherdyakov (*as they arrive home*). Why did this happen to me? Why did I go to the theater at all? Why didn't I sit in the balcony with people of our own class? They love sneezing on each other.

Wife. Come to bed, Ivan.

Cherdyakov. Perhaps if I were to call on the
200 General and explain matters again, but in such a charming, honest and self-effacing manner, he would have no choice but to forgive me . . .

Wife. Maybe it's best not to remind him, Ivan.

Cherdyakov. No, no. If I ever expect to become a gentleman, I must behave like one.

Writer. And so the morning came. It so happened this was the day the General listened to petitions, and since there were fifty or sixty petitions ahead of Cherdyakov, he waited from morning till late,
210 late afternoon . . .

(Cherdyakov *moves into the office set.*)

General. Next! . . . NEXT!

Cherdyakov. I'm not next, your Excellency . . . I'm last.

General. Very well, then . . . Last!

Cherdyakov. That's me, sir.

General. Well, what is your petition?

Cherdyakov. I have no petition, sir. I'm not a petitioner.

220 **General.** Then you waste my time.

Cherdyakov. Do you not recognize me, sir? We met last night under rather "explosive" circumstances . . . I am the splatterer.

---

5. **Gesundheit** (gə-zŏont′hīt′): German for "good health," this term is often used after someone sneezes.

General. The what?

Cherdyakov. The sneezer. The one who sneezed. The sneezing splatterer.

General. Indeed? And what is it you want now? A *Gesundheit?*[5]

Cherdyakov. No, Excellency . . . Your forgiveness.
230 I just wanted to point out there was no political or antisocial motivation behind my sneeze. It was a nonpartisan, nonviolent act of God. I curse the day the protuberance formed itself on my face. It's a hateful nose, sir, and I am not responsible for its indiscretions . . . (*grabbing his own nose*) Punish that which committed the crime, but absolve the innocent body behind it. Exile my nose, but forgive me, your kindship. Forgive me.

General. My dear young man, I'm not angry with
240 your nose. I'm too busy to have time for your nasal problems. I suggest you go home and take a hot bath—or a cold one—take *something*, but don't bother me with this silly business again . . . Gibber, gibber gibber, that's all I've heard all day. (*going offstage*) Gibber, gibber, gibber, gibber . . . (Cherdyakov *stands alone in the office sobbing.*)

Cherdyakov. Thank you, sir. God bless you and your wife and your household. May your days be sweet and may your nights be better than your days.

250 **Writer.** The feeling of relief that came over Cherdyakov was enormous . . .

Cherdyakov. May the birds sing in the morning at your window and may the coffee in your cup be strong and hot . . .

Writer. The weight of the burden that was lifted was inestimable . . .

Cherdyakov. I worship the chair you sit on and the uniform you wear that sits on the chair that I worship . . .

260 **Writer.** He walked home, singing and whistling like a lark. Life was surely a marvel, a joy, a heavenly paradise . . .

Cherdyakov. Oh, God, I am happy!

Writer. And yet—

Cherdyakov. And yet—

Writer. When he arrived home, he began to think . . .

Cherdyakov. Have I been the butt of a cruel and thoughtless joke?

270 **Writer.** Had the Minister toyed with him?

Cherdyakov. If he had no intention of punishing me, why did he torment me so unmercifully?

Writer. If the sneeze meant so little to the Minister, why did he deliberately cause Cherdyakov to writhe in his bed?

Cherdyakov. . . . to twist in agony the entire night?

Writer. Cherdyakov was furious!

Cherdyakov. I AM FURIOUS!

280 **Writer.** He foamed and fumed and paced the night through, and in the morning he called out to his wife, "SONYA!"

Cherdyakov. SONYA! (*She rushes in.*) I have been humiliated.

Wife. *You*, Ivan? Who would humiliate *you?* You're such a kind and generous person.

Cherdyakov. Who? I'll tell you who! General Brassilhov, the Minister of Public Parks.

Wife. What did he do?

290 **Cherdyakov.** The swine! I was humiliated in such subtle fashion, it was almost indiscernible. The man's cunning is equal only to his cruelty. He practically forced me to come to his office to grovel and beg on my knees. I was reduced to a gibbering idiot.

Wife. You were that reduced?

---

6. **humiliated by I . . . humiliate he:** Cherdyakov uses an incorrect pronoun, and the Writer mimics him.

Cherdyakov. I must go back and tell him what I think of him. The lower classes must speak up . . . (*He is at the door.*) The world must be made 300 safe so that men of all nations and creeds, regardless of color or religion, will be free to sneeze on their superiors! It is *he* who will be humiliated by *I!*

Writer. And so, the next morning, Cherdyakov came to humiliate *he.*[6]

(*Lights up on the* General *at his desk.*)

General. Last! (Cherdyakov *goes to the* General's *desk. He stands there glaring down at the* General *with a faint trace of a smile on his lips. The* General *looks up.*) Well?

310 **Cherdyakov** (*smiles*). Well? Well, you say? . . . Do you not recognize me, your Excellency? Look at my face . . . Yes. You're quite correct. It is I once again.

General (*looks at him, puzzled*). It is you once again who?

Cherdyakov (*confidentially*). Cherdyakov, Excellency. I have returned, having taken neither a hot bath nor a cold one.

General. Who let this filthy man in? What is it?

320 **Cherdyakov** (*on top of the situation now*). What is it? . . . What is it, you ask? You sit there behind your desk and ask, What is it? You sit there in your lofty position as General and Minister of Public Parks, a member in high standing among the upper class and ask me, a lowly civil servant, What is it? You sit there with full knowledge that there is no equality in this life, that there are those of us who serve and those that are served, those of us that obey and those that are obeyed, those of us who bow and those that 330 are bowed to, that in this life certain events take place that cause some of us to be humiliated and those that are the cause of that humiliation . . . and still you ask, "WHAT IS IT?"!

General (*angrily*). *What is it?* Don't stand there gibbering like an idiot! What is it you want?

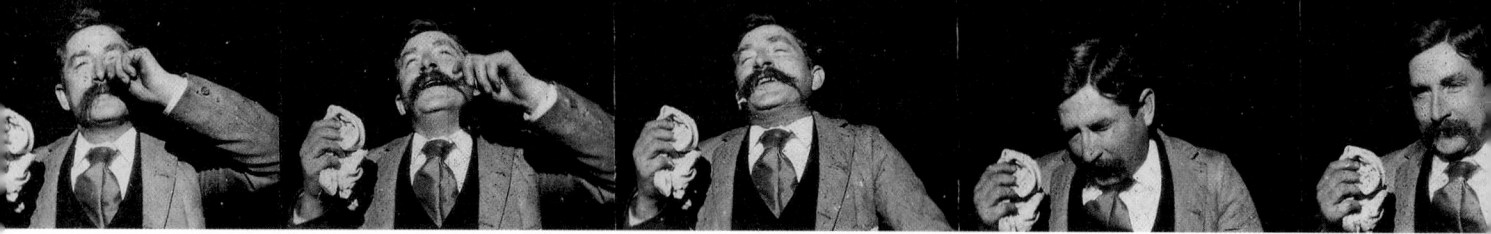

Cherdyakov. *I'll tell you what I want!* . . . I wanted to apologize again for sneezing on you . . . I wasn't sure I made it clear. It was an accident, an accident, I assure you . . .

340 **General** (*stands and screams out*). *Out! Out, you idiot!* Fool! Imbecile! Get out of my sight! I never want to see you again. If you ever cross my line of vision I'll have you exiled forever . . . WHAT'S YOUR NAME?

Cherdyakov. Ch—Cherdyakov!

(*It comes out as a sneeze in the* General's *face.*)

General (*wiping himself*). You germ spreader! You maggot! You insect! You are lower than an insect. You are the second cousin to a cockroach! The

350 son-in-law of a bed bug! You are the nephew of a *ringworm!* You are nothing, nothing, do you hear me? . . . *NOTHING!*

(Cherdyakov *backs away, and returns home.*)

Writer. At that moment, something broke loose inside of Cherdyakov . . . Something so deep and vital, so organic, that the damage that was done seemed irreparable . . . Something drained from him that can only be described as the very life force itself . . . (Cherdyakov *takes off his coat. He*

360 *sits on the sofa, head in hands.*) The matter was over, for once, for all, forever. What happened next was quite simple . . . (Cherdyakov *lies back on the sofa.*) Ivan Ilyitch Cherdyakov arrived at home . . . removed his coat . . . lay down on the sofa—and died! (Cherdyakov's *head drops and his hand falls to the floor.*)

Blackout

After Reading

Comprehension

1. **Recall** Where does the opening scene of the play take place?

2. **Summarize** How does the General react when Cherdyakov sneezes?

3. **Recall** Why does Cherdyakov go to see the General in his office the next morning?

4. **Clarify** How does the play end?

Literary Analysis

5. **Visualize** Review the chart you filled in as you read. Which scene or situation in the play were you able to picture most vividly? Write a short paragraph describing the details. If you'd like, create a sketch to accompany your paragraph.

6. **Draw Conclusions** What is the role of the Writer in "The Sneeze"? Explain the function he performs, citing evidence to support your answer.

7. **Analyze Farce** Which element of farce made you **laugh** the most? Using a chart like the one shown, record examples of ridiculous situations, exaggerated behavior or language, and physical comedy that appear in "The Sneeze." What in particular does Neil Simon seem to be mocking?

Ridiculous Situations	Exaggerated Behavior/Language	Physical Comedy
• •	• •	• •

8. **Identify Dramatic Irony** Dramatic irony occurs when the audience (or the reader) knows more information about a character or a situation than the characters themselves know. Find an example of dramatic irony in the play, and explain what makes it ironic.

Literary Criticism

9. **Author's Style** Neil Simon has said, "My idea of the ultimate achievement in a comedy is to make a whole audience fall onto the floor, writhing and laughing so hard that some of them pass out." Did he accomplish this goal with "The Sneeze"? Cite evidence from the play to support your opinion.

PENNSYLVANIA STANDARDS

READING STANDARD
A.1.3.1 Make inferences and/or draw conclusions

Writing Workshop

Analysis of an Author's Style

Every writer—and human being—has a unique way of experiencing life and sharing his or her experience. As you've learned in this unit, exploring the elements that make up this uniqueness can help you understand and appreciate literary works. Use the **Writer's Road Map** to get started writing an analysis of an author's style.

WRITER'S ROAD MAP

Analysis of an Author's Style

WRITING PROMPT 1

Writing from Literature Choose a piece of literature and write an analysis of the author's style. If you can, read several pieces by the same author. Your analysis should help readers understand important elements of that author's style, such as word choice, sentence structure, tone, figurative language, and imagery.

Authors to Explore

- Tim O'Brien, "Where Have You Gone, Charming Billy?"
- Barbara Kingsolver, "Going to Japan"
- Emily Dickinson, "A narrow Fellow in the Grass"

WRITING PROMPT 2

Writing for the Real World Style isn't limited to writing. Choose a creative person you know about and write an analysis of his or her distinctive style. Explain how that style communicates the individual's personality, values, or message.

People to Consider

- artists
- musicians
- actors or film directors

 WRITING TOOLS
For prewriting, revision, and editing tools, visit the **Writing Center** at ClassZone.com.

KEY TRAITS

1. IDEAS
- Presents a **thesis statement** that identifies the main points of the analysis
- Uses relevant **details** to support the main points
- **Elaborates** on the details to explain the style

2. ORGANIZATION
- Identifies the author and literary work (or the person being analyzed) in an engaging **introduction**
- Provides enough **information** about the literary work (or the person) for readers to follow the analysis
- **Concludes** with a summary of the ideas and offers insights into the author's (or person's) style

3. VOICE
- Speaks directly to the reader in an active, engaging **voice**

4. WORD CHOICE
- Uses precise **terms** to describe and analyze the style

5. SENTENCE FLUENCY
- Uses a variety of **sentence structures**

6. CONVENTIONS
- Employs **correct grammar and usage**

Part 1: Analyze a Student Model

WRITING STANDARD
1.4.11.B Write complex informational pieces

Leslie Wu
Reagan High School

Nikki Giovanni's Notable Style

Have you ever been kidnapped by a poet? Nikki Giovanni asks this surprising question in "Kidnap Poem." In that poem and in "Luxury," Giovanni uses an informal, personal, playful style of writing to explore the importance of love.

5   Giovanni's informal tone creates a sense of closeness and familiarity. Both poems are free verse rather than a more structured style, with line breaks in the middle of a thought or even in the middle of a word ("i'd kid / nap you"). There is no punctuation in either poem except for contractions, which make the writing sound more like spoken language.

10 Simple, direct language adds to the conversational tone. Words and phrases such as "rich and famous" and "maybe coney island / or maybe just to my house" are straightforward and fairly easy to understand. The poems' loosely structured, casual style makes sense because in each poem the speaker is addressing a loved one. "Kidnap Poem" is a love poem, or

15 maybe even a love song. The main message of "Luxury" is that love is more important than power, wealth, and fame.

Another important aspect of this poet's style has to do with point of view. Giovanni uses the first-person point of view in both poems. The speaker addresses the loved one as "you" rather than using a name or

20 giving any details about the person. This technique makes both poems sound like a close, personal conversation. "Luxury" and "Kidnap Poem" make the reader feel as if he or she is eavesdropping on two people who know each other very well. These are extremely personal poems about love and relationships.

KEY TRAITS IN ACTION

Introduction includes an intriguing question and identifies the author and literary works. **Thesis statement** presents the elements of the author's style.

Supports a main point about the author's style with relevant **details** from the poems, and **elaborates** on the details to explain the effect on readers.

Writer uses precise **terms** in her analysis.

25   A third stylistic similarity the poems share is playful imagery. For
example, in "Kidnap Poem," Giovanni uses poetry terms in unusual
ways: "put you in my phrases and meter / you to jones beach," "lyric
you in lilacs / dash you in the rain," "ode you with my love song."
Giovanni *is* a poet, so the speaker's repeated comment "if i were a poet"
30   shows a teasing and flirtatious attitude. The speaker seems to be saying
that she will use all the techniques that poets have perfected throughout
the centuries to write a love song. Playful, thought-provoking images
in "Luxury" have to do with modern life: "living in an electronic age
seeing / the whole world by / pushing a button." In "materialistic
35   society," the speaker suggests, true luxury might be having pushbutton
gadgets to do everything—and also having someone to push the
buttons for you. Although the middle two stanzas are playful, "Luxury"
ends with a more serious message. The speaker concludes that even
though luxuries are appealing, love means far more.

40   An author's style helps to bring out the meaning of the work. By
analyzing the different elements of Nikki Giovanni's style, a reader
can better understand why she constructed her poems in this way and
what meaning she is conveying to her audience. In "Kidnap Poem"
and "Luxury," Nikki Giovanni uses tone, point of view, and imagery to
45   deliver her message that love is "the ultimate luxury."

The variety of **sentence structures** creates interest and flow. Writer provides enough **information** about the poems for reader to understand the analysis.

Writer's **voice** is straightforward and confident as she analyzes imagery and meaning.

Concludes with an insightful summary of the author's style.

2

Part 2: Apply the Writing Process

WRITING STANDARD
1.5.11.A.2 Establish and maintain a single point of view

PREWRITING

What Should I Do?

1. Choose and examine a subject for analysis.
If you are responding to Prompt 1, keep an ongoing reader's log, listing elements of the work that catch your attention, along with your questions or comments. Indicate in your log how your understanding of the work developed or changed with each reading.

If you are responding to Prompt 2, freewrite about a person whose style interests you. What makes that person's style interesting or significant?

2. Focus on the aspects of style you want to analyze.
For Prompt 1, review the elements of literary style and their definitions in the Literary Analysis Workshop on pages 744–747. Think about other elements of literary style you have learned about this year. Use a graphic organizer to list style elements and examples from the literary work.

For Prompt 2, make some notes about how specific aspects of the person's style reflect his or her personality or values. For example, how do a singer's lyrics reflect his or her beliefs?

See page 818: Terms for Writing About Literary Style

3. Develop a working thesis statement.
Your thesis should identify the main points that you plan to analyze. Continue refining or modifying this statement as you draft.

What Does It Look Like?

Details about Nikki Giovanni's Poems	Comments
• no punctuation	• makes poems hard to read but got used to it
• "if i were a poet"	• but Giovanni <u>is</u> a poet— is she making a joke?
• "ode you with my love song"	• uses poetry terms in unusual ways
• "the ultimate luxury / of your love"	• Oh, "Luxury" is about love.

Style Element	"Kidnap Poem"	"Luxury"
Tone	• informal, simple words, loose structure	• mostly simple words, loose structure has four stanzas
Point of view	• first person, talking directly to a loved one	• first person, talking directly to a loved one
Imagery	• fun, teasing, "lyric you in lilacs"	• about modern technology, but message is that love is more important

Working thesis statement:

Nikki Giovanni's "Kidnap Poem" and "Luxury" are both about love. Each poem uses a relaxed, fun style to get the author's message across.

What Should I Do?	What Does It Look Like?

1. Organize your ideas.
Think about how you can present your ideas to make your analysis clear to readers. You could discuss style elements in the order of their importance. If you are comparing two or more works by one writer, you could proceed one work at a time.

▶

ORDER OF IMPORTANCE (LEAST TO MOST)

1. **Tone in both poems**
   • *loosely structured*
   • *mostly simple language*
   • *affects meaning: Both are about love.*
2. **Point of view in both**
   • *first person*
   • *affects meaning: extremely personal*
3. **Imagery in both**
   • *playful, creative*
   • *affects meaning: Love is important.*

COMPARING TWO OR MORE WORKS

1. **"Kidnap Poem"**
   • *tone: informal, flirtatious*
   • *point of view: first person*
   • *imagery: playful*
   • *message: The speaker will use poets' techniques to write a love song.*
2. **"Luxury"**
   • *tone: informal*
   • *point of view: first person*
   • *imagery: playful, about a pushbutton society*
   • *message: Love is the ultimate luxury.*

2. Back up each statement with examples.
Every point you make about the author's style should be supported with examples and details. Be sure to explain exactly how and why each detail supports your analysis.

▶

A third stylistic similarity the poems share is playful imagery. ⎤ Identifies element of style

For example, in "Kidnap Poem," Giovanni uses poetry terms in unusual ways: "meter / you to jones beach," "lyric you in lilacs." ⎤ Gives example of imagery

The speaker seems to be saying that she will use all the techniques that poets have perfected throughout the centuries to write a love song. ⎤ Explains how style affects meaning

3. End with a strong conclusion.
Summarize your analysis and offer an overall insight about style and meaning.

TIP Before revising, consult the key traits on page 812 and the rubric and peer-reader questions on page 818.

▶

By analyzing the different elements of Nikki Giovanni's style, a reader can better understand the meaning she is conveying. In "Kidnap Poem" and "Luxury," Nikki Giovanni uses tone, point of view, and imagery to deliver her message that love is "the ultimate luxury."

REVISING AND EDITING

What Should I Do?	What Does It Look Like?

1. **Make your introduction engaging.**
   - [Bracket] the first few sentences of your introduction.
   - Review the bracketed text. If you are just stating the obvious, insert some details to make your analysis more interesting.

   TIP Consider beginning with a powerful quotation or a question to readers.

   ▶ [~~"Luxury" and "Kidnap Poem" are the poems I read. They're both about love and have a similar style.~~] Have you ever been kidnapped by a poet? Nikki Giovanni asks this surprising question in "Kidnap Poem."

2. **Add appropriate transitions.**
   - Highlight the transitional words and phrases that signal a new topic.
   - If you have few or no highlights, add transitions that clarify how ideas are connected.

   ▶ Another important aspect of this poet's style has to do with point of view. ⌄Giovanni uses the first-person point of view in both poems.

   A third stylistic similarity the poems share is playful imagery. For example, ⌄In "Kidnap Poem," Giovanni uses poetry terms in unusual ways.

3. **Include enough information about the literary work.**
   - Ask a peer reader to <u>underline</u> confusing passages that need more explanation.
   - Add details to help readers understand your points.

   See page 818: Ask a Peer Reader

   ▶ <u>"Luxury" ends with a more serious message.</u> ⌄The speaker concludes that even though luxuries are appealing, love means far more.

4. **Vary the structures of your sentences.**
   - Draw a box around consecutive sentences that all begin the same way.
   - Rewrite some of these sentences to make your writing more rhythmic and interesting.

   ▶ ~~The speaker describes a "materialistic society." The speaker suggests that true luxury might be having pushbutton gadgets to do everything. Also, having someone to push the buttons for you would be even better.~~ In "materialistic society," the speaker suggests, true luxury might be having pushbutton gadgets to do everything—and also having someone to push the buttons for you.

Analysis of an Author's Style

Apply the Rubric

A strong analysis of style . . .

☑ identifies the author and literary work (or the person being analyzed) in the introduction

☑ clarifies the main points of the analysis in a strong thesis statement

☑ supports ideas with relevant details and information

☑ uses precise terms to define and analyze style

☑ has a confident, engaging voice

☑ varies sentence structures for rhythm

☑ concludes by summarizing the analysis and offering insight into the individual's style

Ask a Peer Reader

- What are the main points of my analysis?

- Which statements need to be supported with more information?

Terms for Writing About Literary Style

Term	Definition
Diction	choice of words
Imagery	sensory and figurative language
Point of view	angle from which the story is told
Sentence structure	type and length of sentences
Tone	writer's attitude toward the subject

Check Your Grammar

- Run-on sentences make your analysis confusing.

  > Giovanni's informal tone creates a sense of closeness and familiarity, ~~both~~ ₒBoth poems are free verse.

- Eliminate unnecessary words. If your analysis is too short, add more quotations and examples.

  > ~~What I am trying to say is that~~ the main message of ~~the poem~~ "Luxury" is that love is more important than ~~other things such as~~ power, wealth, and fame.

See page R64–R65: Writing Complete Sentences

Writing On|ine

PUBLISHING OPTIONS
For publishing options, visit the **Writing Center** at ClassZone.com.

ASSESSMENT PREPARATION
For writing and grammar assessment practice, go to the **Assessment Center** at ClassZone.com.

Delivering an Oral Interpretation

Delivering a reading of a literary work can make an author's style come alive for your audience.

Planning the Oral Interpretation

1. **Choose passages that clearly illustrate the style.** Find material that includes several style elements and that your audience can understand without explanation or background information.
2. **Mark up the selection.** Highlight words to stress, and indicate places where you would like to change your pacing and emphasis. Add punctuation marks if you need to.

> play the lyre for you,
> ode you with my love song,
> anything to win you! ← smile
> wrap you in the red Black green
> show you off to mama ← pause
> yeah if i were a poet i'd kid
> nap you
>
> Yellow = Use emphasis.
> Blue = Pick up the pace.

3. **Read into a tape recorder.** Practice your delivery by speaking into a tape recorder.
4. **Rehearse in front of a mirror.** See and hear yourself as your audience will. Go over any difficult words, and practice your pacing, tone, emphasis, and gestures until they come naturally.

Delivering the Oral Interpretation

1. **Maintain eye contact with your listeners.** If you are using notes, hold them in front of you so that you can glance at them while keeping your head and body directed at your audience.
2. **Reveal the author's style by using your voice, facial expressions, and gestures.** Depending on the content of your reading, you might smile, frown, or point during part of your presentation.

   See page R80: Evaluate an Oral Interpretation

Reading Comprehension

DIRECTIONS *Read the following selections and then answer the questions.*

The two characters in this excerpt from The Sea Wolf *have escaped from the cruel captain of the* Ghost, *a seal-hunting schooner. They are adrift in a small sailing boat hundreds of miles off the coast of Japan.*

from The Sea Wolf

Jack London

Maud's condition was pitiable. She sat crouched in the bottom of the boat, her lips blue, her face gray and plainly showing the pain she suffered. But ever her eyes looked bravely at me, and ever her lips uttered brave words.

The worst of the storm must have blown that night, though little I noticed it. I had succumbed and slept where I sat in the stern-sheets. The morning of the fourth day found the wind diminished to a gentle whisper, the sea dying down and the sun shining upon us. Oh, the blessed sun! How we bathed our poor bodies in its delicious warmth, reviving like bugs and crawling things after a storm. We smiled again, said amusing things, and waxed optimistic
10 over our situation. Yet it was, if anything, worse than ever. We were farther from Japan than the night we left the *Ghost*. Nor could I more than roughly guess our latitude and longitude. At a calculation of a two-mile drift per hour, during the seventy and odd hours of the storm, we had been driven at least one hundred and fifty miles to the northeast. But was such calculated drift correct? For all I knew, it might have been four miles per hour instead of two. In which case we were another hundred and fifty miles to the bad.

Where we were I did not know, though there was quite a likelihood that we were in the vicinity of the *Ghost*. There were seals about us, and I was prepared to sight a sealing schooner at any time. We did sight one, in the afternoon,
20 when the northwest breeze had sprung up freshly once more. But the strange schooner lost itself on the sky-line and we alone occupied the circle of the sea.

Came days of fog, when even Maud's spirit drooped and there were no merry words upon her lips; days of calm, when we floated on the lonely immensity of sea, oppressed by its greatness and yet marveling at the miracle of tiny life, for we still lived and struggled to live; days of sleet and wind and snow-squalls, when nothing could keep us warm; or days of drizzling rain, when we filled our water-breakers from the drip of the wet sail.

from Pilgrim at Tinker Creek

Annie Dillard

It was just this time last year that we had the flood. It was Hurricane Agnes, really, but by the time it got here, the weather bureau had demoted it to a tropical storm. I see by a clipping I saved that the date was June twenty-first, the solstice, midsummer's night, the longest daylight of the year; but I didn't notice it at the time. Everything was so exciting, and so very dark.

All it did was rain. It rained, and the creek started to rise. The creek, naturally, rises every time it rains; this didn't seem any different. But it kept raining, and, that morning of the twenty-first, the creek kept rising.

That morning I'm standing at my kitchen window. Tinker Creek is out of
10 its four-foot banks, way out, and it's still coming. The high creek doesn't look like our creek. Our creek splashes transparently over a jumble of rocks; the high creek obliterates everything in flat opacity. It looks like somebody else's creek that has usurped or eaten our creek and is roving frantically to escape, big and ugly, like a blacksnake caught in a kitchen drawer. The color is foul, a rusty cream. Water that has picked up clay soils looks worse than other muddy waters, because the particles of clay are so fine; they spread out and cloud the water so that you can't see light through even an inch of it in a drinking glass.

Everything looks different. Where my eye is used to depth, I see the flat water, near, too near. I see trees I never noticed before, the black verticals of
20 their rain-soaked trunks standing out of the pale water like pilings for a rotted dock. The stillness of grassy banks and stony ledges is gone; I see rushing, a wild sweep and hurry in one direction, as swift and compelling as a waterfall. The Atkins kids are out in their tiny rain gear, staring at the monster creek. It's risen up to their gates; the neighbors are gathering; I go out.

I hear a roar, a high windy sound more like air than like water, like the run-together whaps of a helicopter's propeller after the engine is off, a high million rushings. The air smells damp and acrid, like fuel oil, or insecticide. It's raining.

GO ON ➡

Comprehension

DIRECTIONS *Answer these questions about the excerpt from* The Sea Wolf.

1. The author's style in *The Sea Wolf* can be characterized by his use of

A all long sentences

B all short sentences

C a mix of long and short sentences

D mostly very short sentences

2. Which word best describes the tone of lines 5–9?

A hopeful   C frenzied

B suspicious   D gloomy

3. In which of the following sentences from lines 9–12 does the tone shift to reveal the narrator's doubts?

A "We smiled again, said amusing things, and waxed optimistic over our situation."

B "Yet it was, if anything, worse than ever."

C "We were farther from Japan than the night we left the *Ghost*."

D "Nor could I more than roughly guess our latitude and longitude."

4. Notice the verbs *drooped, oppressed, marveling,* and *struggled* in lines 22–27. What tone do these words convey?

A serious   C playful

B sentimental   D confident

DIRECTIONS *Answer these questions about the excerpt from* Pilgrim at Tinker Creek.

5. The author's sentences and word choices in lines 12–14 help you

   A look at the flood objectively, like a scientist

   B experience the flood with the author

   C imagine what the author's kitchen looks like

   D see a snake that crawled out of the creek

6. Which word best describes the tone of the sentence in lines 15–17?

   A melodramatic   C informative

   B humorous   D sarcastic

7. The author's style can best be characterized by her use of

   A descriptive language and a conversational tone

   B long explanations and words that convey despair

   C flowery language and a sarcastic tone

   D neutral words and simple sentences

DIRECTIONS *Answer this question about both selections.*

8. Which of the following elements of style is found in both selections?

   A flashbacks   C realistic dialogue

   B vivid language   D contractions

DIRECTIONS *Answer these questions about the photograph.*

9. Notice the visual elements in this photograph. What story does the photo tell?

   A A man thinks he can run down a tornado.

   B After his friend is hurt, a man runs for help.

   C A newly formed tornado is moving away from the man.

   D A man is running toward his car to get out of the tornado's path.

10. What is the effect of the blurred figure in the photograph?

    A It helps highlight the landscape surrounding the tornado.

    B It focuses the viewer's attention on the power of nature.

    C It conveys a sense of motion, urgency, and fear.

    D It puts less emphasis on the car, the fence, and the person.

Open–Ended Items

11. Both authors chose to repeat words or phrases in their selections. Identify one word or phrase from each selection that is repeated. Why are these words repeated?

12. Compare how each author uses these elements of style: word choice, sentences, tone. How are the authors' styles different or alike? Use examples from the selections to support your answer.

GO ON ➤

Vocabulary

DIRECTIONS *Use context clues and your knowledge of homonyms to answer the following questions.*

> That morning I'm standing at my kitchen window. Tinker Creek is out of its four-foot <u>banks</u>, way out, and it's still coming.

1. Which sentence uses *banks* as it is used in line 10 of *Pilgrim at Tinker Creek?*

A   A number of colorful houseboats are moored along the banks of the channel.

B   Luis banks the plane toward the south to give us a clear view of the canyon.

C   Sonia heads the finance ethics division for all of our North American banks.

D   The two banks of elevators are on the north and west sides of the building.

> Water that has picked up clay soils looks worse than other muddy waters, because the particles of clay are so <u>fine</u>; they spread out and cloud the water so that you can't see <u>light</u> through even an inch of it in a drinking glass.

2. Which sentence uses *fine* as it is used in line 16 of *Pilgrim at Tinker Creek?*

A   Solana paid her library fine yesterday.

B   It was such a fine day that we decided to walk to town.

C   The recipe called for fresh cinnamon, ground as fine as powder.

D   "We are fine!" they yelled from the boat.

3. Which sentence uses *light* as it is used in line 17 of *Pilgrim at Tinker Creek?*

A   The menu called for a light supper.

B   I heard him yell, "Light the fire!"

C   She gave him a light tap on the shoulder.

D   We searched by the light of the moon.

DIRECTIONS *Use context clues and your knowledge of prefixes to answer the following questions.*

> How we bathed our poor bodies in its delicious warmth, <u>reviving</u> like bugs and crawling things after a storm.

4. The prefix *re-* means "again," and the root *viv* means "to live." What does the word *reviving* mean in line 8 of *The Sea Wolf?*

A   coming back to life

B   no longer living

C   having lived before

D   unable to live

> Came days of fog, when even Maud's spirit drooped and there were no merry words upon her lips; days of calm, when we floated on the lonely <u>immensity</u> of sea, oppressed by its greatness and yet marveling at the miracle of tiny life . . .

5. The prefix *im-* means "not" or "unable," and the Latin root *mens* means "to measure." What does the word *immensity* mean in line 24 from *The Sea Wolf?*

A   waves too rough to navigate

B   awesome character

C   hollowed-out shape

D   area too vast to determine

> Our creek splashes transparently over a jumble of rocks; the high creek <u>obliterates</u> everything in flat opacity.

6. The prefix *ob-* means "against," and the Latin root *liter* means "letter." What does *obliterates* mean in line 12 of *Pilgrim at Tinker Creek?*

A   erases   C   opposes

B   writes   D   drowns

Writing & Grammar

DIRECTIONS *Read this passage and answer the questions that follow.*

> (1) I wasn't prepared for the massive destruction of Hurricane Ivan. (2) What began as a tropical depression eventually caused billions of dollars in damage and the deaths of 130 people. (3) The hurricane swept across the Caribbean, slamming into St. Vincent, Barbados, and Jamaica! (4) Another hard-hit place was my country, Grenada. (5) By the time it reached the capital, St. George's, Ivan was traveling at 140 miles per hour. (6) Virtually every major building in St. George's suffered structural damage. (7) I saw trees ripped from the ground and people displaced from their homes. (8) People wonder how they can avoid this kind of destruction. (9) The best thing to do is never find yourself in the path of a hurricane.

1. How might the writer revise sentence 2 to make it interrogative?

   A What began as a tropical depression eventually caused billions of dollars in damage and the deaths of 130 people!

   B Imagine that what began as a tropical depression eventually caused billions of dollars in damage and the deaths of 130 people.

   C How could I foresee that what began as a tropical depression would eventually cause billions of dollars in damage and the deaths of 130 people?

   D No change is needed.

2. How might the writer revise sentence 5 to make it exclamatory?

   A Was Ivan traveling at 140 miles per hour when it reached the capital, St. George's?

   B Traveling at 140 miles per hour, Ivan reached the capital, St. George's.

   C By the time it reached the capital, St. George's, Ivan was traveling at 140 miles per hour!

   D No change is needed.

3. How might the writer revise sentence 6 to make it declarative?

   A Did you know that virtually every major building in St. George's suffered structural damage?

   B Virtually every major building in St. George's suffered structural damage!

   C Take note that every major building in St. George's suffered structural damage.

   D No change is needed.

4. How might the writer revise sentence 9 to make it imperative?

   A Never find yourself in the path of a hurricane.

   B I recommend that you never find yourself in the path of a hurricane!

   C Have you ever found yourself in the path of a hurricane?

   D No change is needed.

STOP

Ideas for Independent Reading

Highly individualistic writing styles are apparent in the following works.

Is fear our worst enemy?

One Day in the Life of Ivan Denisovich
by Alexandr Solzhenitsyn

The author's indictment of the Soviet gulags, in which he was once a prisoner, shows that hunger, cold, and humiliation are just as powerful as fear.

Things Fall Apart
by Chinua Achebe

Okonkwo, the main character in Achebe's novel of the effects of colonialism on Nigeria, fears the dissolution of his world and his own powerlessness to resist it.

Ethan Frome
by Edith Wharton

Ethan Frome is locked into a sterile marriage that keeps him from finding love with Mattie. This famous novel suggests that isolation and loneliness are the enemies of human fulfillment.

Have you ever felt out of place?

All Creatures Great and Small
by James Herriot

In the well-known veterinarian's first collection, he lands a position in the Yorkshire Dales. He can't understand the dialect, the farmers think he's crazy, and he makes a mess of the first dates with his eventual wife. But his patients love him.

Brave New World
by Aldous Huxley

In this classic novel's vision of the future, Bernard Marx feels out of place in the World State, in which everything— feelings, childbirth, human experience—is artificial. Can he escape?

Red Scarf Girl: A Memoir of the Cultural Revolution
by Ji-li Jiang

The author's world was turned upside down during China's Cultural Revolution. At first she accepted the spying, humiliation, and fear. Then, as dangerous as it was, she determined that she would think for herself.

Who makes you laugh?

I'm a Stranger Here Myself
by Bill Bryson

After living in Britain for 20 years, Bryson returned to the United States with a fresh eye for the absurdities of U.S. life.

Funny Letters from Famous People
by Charles Osgood

Popular broadcaster Charles Osgood offers us the witty remarks of notable people from Abraham Lincoln to Andy Rooney.

The Wit and Wisdom of Mark Twain
edited by Alex Ayres

This anthology compiles the most humorous excerpts of Twain's fiction, speeches, and letters.

UNIT 9

Putting It in Context

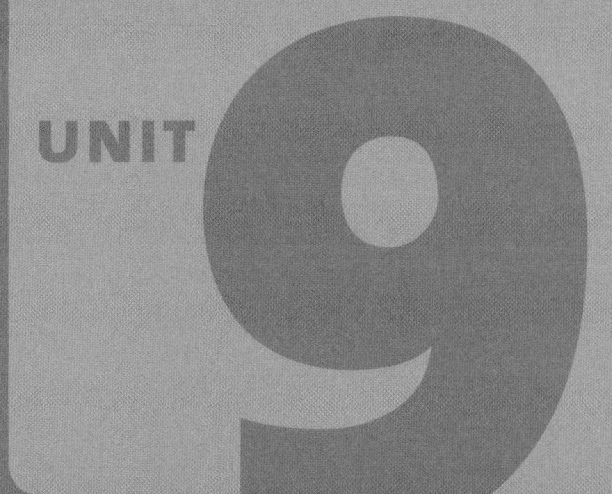

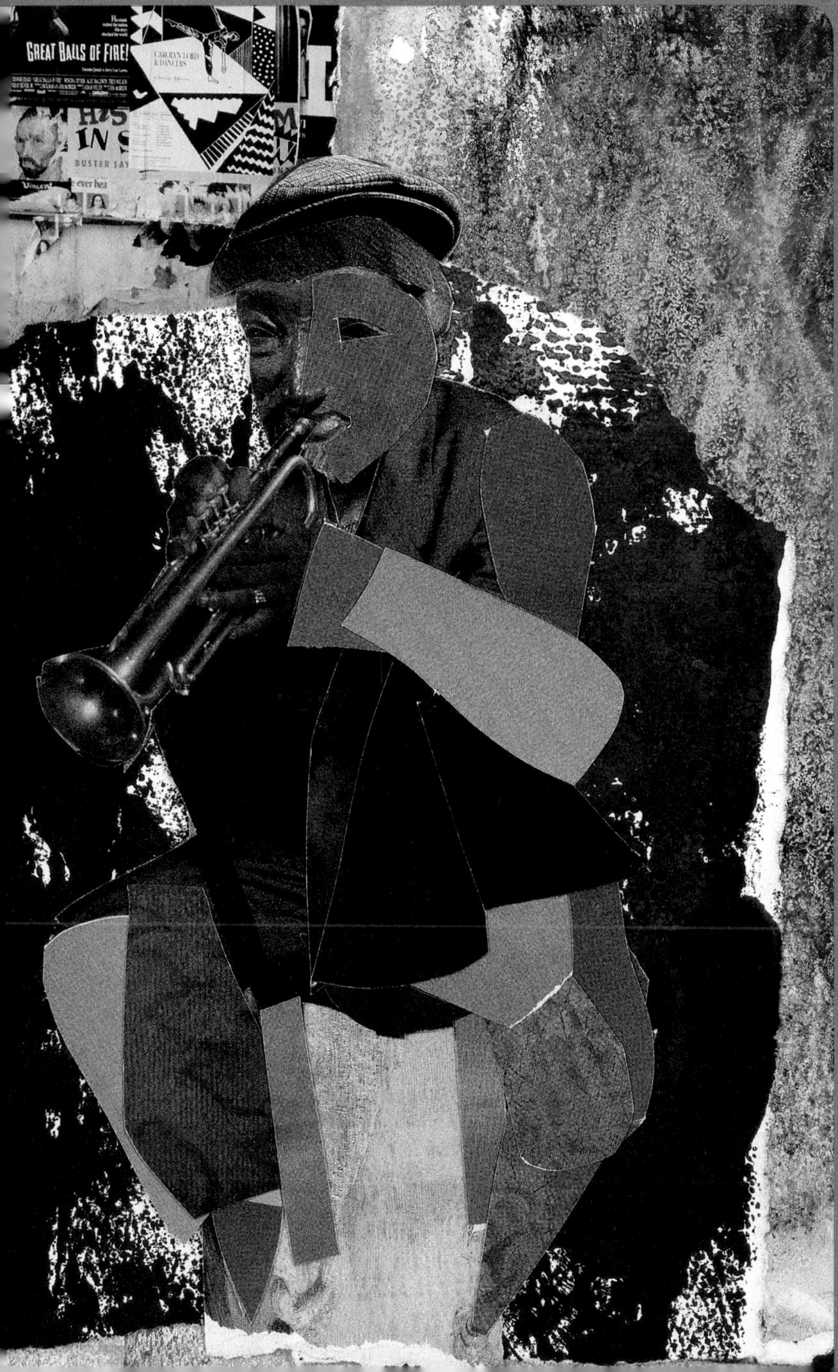

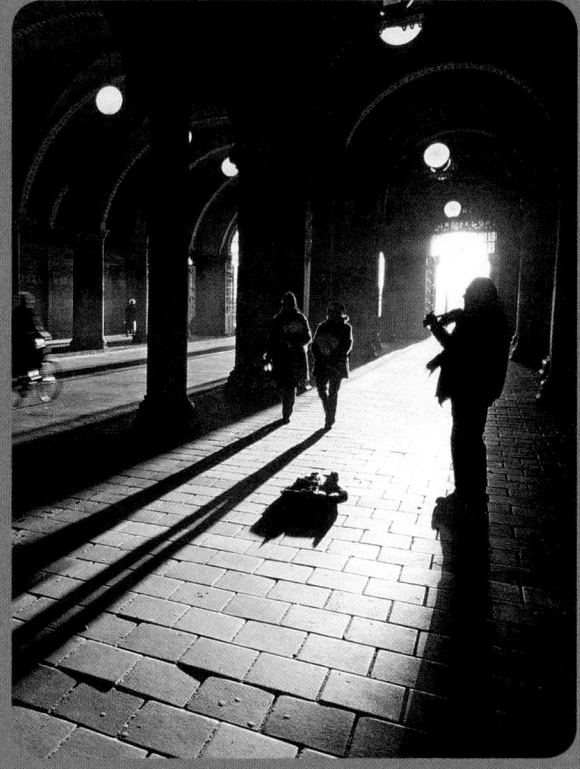

HISTORY, CULTURE, AND THE AUTHOR

- In Nonfiction
- In Fiction
- In Poetry

What SHAPES
who you are?

What helped make you the individual you are today? Your family, friends, and personal experiences probably played key roles. But broader factors—like the neighborhood you grew up in and the decade you were born into—have also influenced who you are.

ACTIVITY Think of someone who has made a strong impression on you—either a historical figure, a fictional character, or someone you know. Consider how the following factors may have shaped that person:

- **When he or she grew up.** How would his or her daily life have been different from our lives today?

- **Where he or she is from.** Was the person from a bustling city or a tiny town? a peaceful island or a war-torn nation?

- **What happened during his or her lifetime.** Maybe the person grew up during the Great Depression, fled Europe during the Holocaust, or turned 18 in the midst of the Vietnam War.

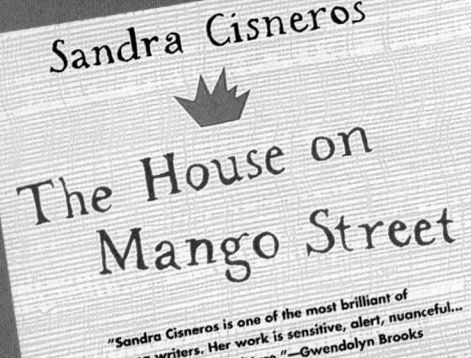

Sandra Cisneros

The House on Mango Street

"Sandra Cisneros is one of the most brilliant of today's young writers. Her work is sensitive, alert, nuanceful... rich with music and picture."—Gwendolyn Brooks

PENNSYLVANIA STANDARDS

Preview Unit Goals

LITERARY ANALYSIS	• Analyze influence of author's background
	• Analyze influence of historical and cultural context
	• Recognize how cultures and time periods are represented in literature
	• Identify and interpret cultural symbols
	• Identify and analyze allusions, voice, and dialect
READING	• Make inferences and draw conclusions
	• Synthesize
WRITING AND GRAMMAR	• Write a persuasive essay
	• Use gerunds and gerund phrases to write concisely
	• Use vivid verbs
SPEAKING, LISTENING, AND VIEWING	• Debate an issue
VOCABULARY	• Use knowledge of word roots to help unlock word meanings
	• Use context clues to determine meanings of idioms
ACADEMIC VOCABULARY	• author's background
	• historical and cultural context
	• cultural symbol
	• allusion
	• voice
	• dialect
	• summarize and synthesize
	• gerund and gerund phrase
	• word root
	• idiom

History, Culture, and the Author

You are a product of your time. In other words, who you are depends on the year you were born, the places you've lived, and the people—both family and friends—who surround you. Similarly, writers are influenced by the experiences and events they themselves live through. By examining clues within the literature you read, you can learn about a culture or time period, or about how both may have affected the writer. Armed with more knowledge, such as information about the events that inspired a story, you can often see literature in a new light.

PENNSYLVANIA STANDARDS

READING STANDARDS
A.1.6.1 Identify and/or analyze intended purpose of text

B.1.1.1.D.2 Evaluate the relationship between the theme and other components

Part 1: Context Within the Literature

Think about stories that have introduced you to other times and places, such as Harper Lee's *To Kill a Mockingbird,* set in the South in the 1930s. Unless you had researched small Southern towns in the early 20th century, you probably would have little understanding of that time and place. Yet by analyzing details in the novel, you can learn about the world the writer created.

In nonfiction, writers often provide these details directly. Fiction writers, however, use details of setting and plot and vivid language to acquaint you with the times and places they describe. Notice how Bret Harte brings the Old West to life in his short story "The Outcasts of Poker Flat."

"THE OUTCASTS OF POKER FLAT"

From this single sentence, you begin to get a sense of a small Western town in the 1850s and can start to question the values of the time. (Is gambling a common pastime?)

As Mr. John Oakhurst, gambler, stepped into the main street of Poker Flat on the morning of the twenty-third of November, 1850, he was conscious of a change in its moral atmosphere. . . .

The dialect lets you hear how people in Poker Flat sounded.

"It's agin justice," said Jim Wheeler, "to let this yer young man from Roaring Camp—an entire stranger—carry away our money."

Imagery helps you imagine what the Old West was like at this time.

The road . . . lay over a steep mountain range. It was distant a day's severe travel. In that advanced season, the party soon passed out of the moist, temperate regions of the foot-hills into the dry, cold, bracing air of the Sierras.

MODEL 1: READING NONFICTION

As you read this excerpt, notice the writer's descriptions of people and places, as well as details about historical events and cultural traditions.

---

from THE NAMES
of Women

Biographical essay by **Louise Erdrich**

Ikwe is the word for woman in the language of the Anishinabe, my mother's people, whose descendants, mixed with and married to French trappers and farmers, are the Michifs of the Turtle Mountain reservation in North Dakota. Every Anishinabe *Ikwe,* every mixed-blood descendant like me, who can trace
5 her way back a generation or two, is the daughter of a mystery. The history of the woodland Anishinabe—decimated by disease, fighting Plains Indian tribes to the west and squeezed by European settlers to the east—is much like most other Native American stories, a confusion of loss, a tale of absences, of a culture that was blown apart and changed so radically in such a short time that
10 only the names survive.

Close Read

1. Review the boxed text. What does it tell you about what life was like for the Anishinabe people?

2. What does the writer's choice of words (such as *decimated* and *loss*) reveal about her feelings toward her subject?

MODEL 2: READING FICTION

As you read this excerpt, ask yourself: What do the details tell me about the time and place? What can I infer about the characters' values?

---

from
The Son from AMERICA

Short story by **Isaac Bashevis Singer**

The village of Lentshin was tiny—a sandy marketplace where the peasants of the area met once a week. It was surrounded by little huts with thatched roofs or shingles green with moss. The chimneys looked like pots. Between the huts there were fields, where the owners planted vegetables or pastured their goats.
5 In the smallest of these huts lived old Berl, a man in his eighties, and his wife, who was called Berlcha (wife of Berl). Old Berl was one of the Jews who had been driven from their villages in Russia and had settled in Poland. In Lentshin, they mocked the mistakes he made while praying aloud. He spoke with a sharp "r." He was short, broad-shouldered, and had a small white beard,
10 and summer and winter he wore a sheepskin hat, a padded cotton jacket, and stout boots. He walked slowly, shuffling his feet. He had a half acre of field, a cow, a goat, and chickens.
The couple had a son, Samuel, who had gone to America forty years ago.

Close Read

1. How would you describe the village of Lentshin?

2. What does the description of old Berl tell you about the people of Lentshin and their culture?

3. The boxed text is a clue to the historical period. Many Jews left Russia following persecution in the 1880s. Find another clue that helps identify the time.

Part 2: Context Outside the Literature

Consider a story about a soldier who grapples with the horrors of World War II. By looking within the text, you can probably learn some details about the war. But what happens when you discover that the writer himself was a soldier in that war? With a little background, you can often uncover new levels of meaning.

HISTORICAL AND CULTURAL INFLUENCES

Writers respond to the world around them: events, such as the first landing of humans on the moon; places, such as the battlefield at Gettysburg; and social conditions, such as racial discrimination. For this reason, it can be helpful to think about a work's **historical** and **cultural contexts**—that is, the social and cultural conditions that may have influenced the work. For instance, consider Dr. Martin Luther King's "I have a dream" speech, which he delivered to a crowd of around 250,000 at the March on Washington on August 28, 1963. King's message of peace and hope becomes more impressive when you discover that he spoke just months after the assassination of another civil rights leader.

CONTEXT	LITERATURE
Two months before the March on Washington, the civil rights leader Medgar Evers was assassinated. Concerned about violence, President John F. Kennedy considered canceling the march.	 "We must forever conduct our struggle on the high plain of dignity. . . ."

As you read any text, ask

- What significant events were taking place at the time this text was written?
- What were the predominant values in the society of the time?

THE WRITER'S BACKGROUND

Personal factors can also affect a writer's work. A writer who grew up poor in the rural South will have been influenced by his or her experiences, as will a writer who spent years working on a nature preserve in Africa. Gender, ethnicity, national identity, family—all these factors help shape a writer's view of the world.

CONSIDERING A WRITER'S BACKGROUND

First analyze the clues within the text. Ask
- What values are conveyed? (Look for direct commentary as well as characters' actions.)
- What is the tone? (Notice characters and ideas that are respected or criticized.)

Then consider how a writer's background may be mirrored in his or her work. Ask
- What do I know about the writer's personal history?
- How does this information shed light on my reading?

MODEL 1: INTERPRETING POETRY

As you read this poem, look at details such as imagery and setting to help you interpret its meaning.

The *Butterfly*

Poem by **Pavel Friedmann**

The last, the very last,
So richly, brightly, dazzlingly yellow.
    Perhaps if the sun's tears would sing
    against a white stone . . .

5 Such, such a yellow
Is carried lightly 'way up high.
It went away I'm sure because it wished to
    kiss the world goodbye.

For seven weeks I've lived in here,
10 Penned up inside this ghetto
But I have found my people here.
The dandelions call to me
And the white chestnut candles in the court.
Only I never saw another butterfly.

15 That butterfly was the last one.
Butterflies don't live in here,
    In the ghetto.

Close Read

1. Look at the boxed text. How does it help you understand the speaker's description of the butterfly in lines 1–8?

2. What might the butterfly symbolize in the poem?

MODEL 2: UNDERSTANDING THE CONTEXT

Now read this background information about the era in which "The Butterfly" was written.

BACKGROUND Beginning in 1941 when the Holocaust was sweeping across Europe, Adolf Hitler rounded up Jews from Czechoslovakia and many other countries and moved them to the small Czech town of Terezin—the "ghetto" Pavel Friedmann describes in his poem. Originally home to about 7,000
5 people, Terezin eventually held more than 550,000 Jews at one time. Under such conditions, thousands died from starvation and disease. Thousands more were shipped to the Auschwitz death camp. Friedmann was 21 years old when he arrived in the town of Terezin. He died two years later at Auschwitz.

Close Read

1. How does this information change your interpretation of the poem?

2. What is the theme of the poem? Support your answer with information from the background as well as details from the poem.

Part 3: Analyze the Literature

From the title of this poem, you know it is about the "Vietnam Wall." Think about what you may already know about the wall and read through the poem a first time. Then read the background information on the next page. How does the background information change or enhance your understanding of the poem? Read the poem again before answering the **Close Read** questions.

THE VIETNAM WALL

Poem by **Alberto Ríos**

I
Have seen it
And I like it: The magic,
The way like cutting onions
5 It brings water out of nowhere.
Invisible from one side, a scar
Into the skin of the ground
From the other, a black winding
Appendix line.
10   A dig.
      An archaeologist can explain.
The walk is slow at first
Easy, a little black marble wall
Of a dollhouse,
15 A smoothness, a shine
The boys in the street want to give.
One name. And then more
Names, long lines, lines of names until
They are the shape of the U.N. building
20 Taller than I am: I have walked
Into a grave.
And everything I expect has been taken away, like that, quick:
      The names are not alphabetized.
      They are in the order of dying,
25   An alphabet of—somewhere—screaming.
I start to walk out. I almost leave
But stop to look up names of friends,
My own name. There is somebody
Severiano Ríos.
30 Little kids do not make the same noise
Here, junior high school boys don't run
Or hold each other in headlocks.

No rules, something just persists
Like pinching on St. Patrick's Day
35 Every year for no green.
      No one knows why.
Flowers are forced
Into the cracks
Between sections.
40 Men have cried
At this wall.
I have
Seen them.

BACKGROUND

Vietnam: THE WAR AND THE WALL

The Vietnam War was one of the most controversial and divisive wars in U.S. history. During the major years of combat, 1964–1972, more
5   than 58,000 Americans were killed or missing in action. The United States spent about $200 billion to support the South Vietnamese government against soldiers from
10 both North and South Vietnam fighting to unite the country under Communist rule. Two years after the withdrawal of U.S. troops, North Vietnamese forces overran the south
15 and united the country. Many in the United States questioned the worth of our involvement in the war.

In 1979, a group was organized to create the Vietnam Veterans
20 Memorial to honor the U.S. soldiers who died in the war. Some hoped that the construction of a memorial would help to heal the wounds at home caused by the war.

25 A young Yale University student named Maya Ying Lin won a nationwide competition to design the memorial. Lin's abstract design consisted of two walls of polished
30 black granite plunging on a slant into the ground to meet at a 125° angle. The names of the soldiers were carved into the granite in the order that they died, highlighting
35 the individual sacrifices that made up the war. A walkway running the length of each 246-foot wall allows visitors not only to read the names but to touch them and leave
40 messages and other mementos.

When U.S. involvement in the Vietnam War ended in 1973, the poet Alberto Ríos was 21 years old— the same age as the young Severiano
45 Ríos whose name the speaker notices on the wall. Corporal Ríos died from small-arms fire on April 2, 1970, in Tay Ninh, South Vietnam.

Close Read

1. Reread the boxed lines of the poem. What information in the background helped you to understand the imagery in these lines?

2. According to the background, why were soldiers' names placed in their particular order on the wall? Explain the effect their arrangement has on the speaker of the poem.

3. Why might the speaker of the poem be moved by the sight of the name Severiano Ríos on the wall?

4. According to the background, what was the purpose of the Vietnam Veterans Memorial? After reading Ríos's poem, do you think the wall accomplishes that purpose? Support your answer.

from **Angela's Ashes**
Memoir by Frank McCourt

How does FRIENDSHIP *begin?*

PENNSYLVANIA STANDARDS

READING STANDARDS
A.2.6.1 Identify and/or analyze intended purpose
A.2.3.1 Make inferences

KEY IDEA Old friends, new friends, close friends, best friends—what makes two people connect? Whether it's a simple act of kindness or the discovery of a shared interest, something special happens to turn a mere acquaintance into a friend. In his memoir *Angela's Ashes,* writer Frank McCourt describes two **friendships** that develop under unusual circumstances.

QUICKWRITE Have you ever formed an unlikely friendship? Perhaps it was with someone much older or much younger than you—or simply with someone very different from you. Write a paragraph about the circumstances under which your friendship formed.

LITERARY ANALYSIS: MEMOIR

Frank McCourt was born in New York, but he grew up in Limerick, Ireland, as he describes in his memoir *Angela's Ashes*. A **memoir** is a form of autobiographical writing in which a writer shares his or her personal experiences and observations of significant events and people. Often informal or even intimate in tone, memoirs usually give readers insights into the influence of history on people's lives.

In this selection, McCourt recalls being hospitalized with typhoid, a highly infectious, life-threatening illness. As you read, think about the impact of this event on his life. In addition, note what you learn about Irish history and culture, especially the influence of the Roman Catholic Church.

READING SKILL: USE ALLUSIONS TO MAKE INFERENCES

One way Frank McCourt adds meaning to his writing is through allusions. An **allusion** is a reference to a well-known person, place, event, or literary work. It depends on shared knowledge of both the writer and the reader. For example, a writer might refer to a character as having the patience of Job—a biblical figure who endured great suffering without losing his faith in God. Writers use allusions

- to help characterize people or situations
- to evoke ideas or feelings in the reader's mind
- to clarify or highlight important ideas, including the theme

As you read, look for allusions. What can you infer from them? Develop a chart like the one shown.

Allusion	Significance	Inference
"Oh, yes, he knows Roddy McCorley. He'll sing it for me...." (line 134)	Refers to a folk song about Roddy McCorley, a famous Irish labor leader of the late 1700s	Seamus loves music and is very patriotic.

Review: **Draw Conclusions**

▲ VOCABULARY IN CONTEXT

Use context clues to figure out the meanings of the words in bold.

1. The **relapse** of his illness put him back in the hospital.
2. Her persuasive speech **induced** me to support her cause.
3. **Torrents** of rain caused the roads to flood.
4. The officer's **perfidy** led him to be charged with treason.

Author Online

Frank McCourt born 1930

A Spellbinding Storyteller Frank McCourt worked as a messenger, a barkeeper, a laborer, and an actor, but it was as a high school writing teacher that he gained his reputation as a consummate storyteller. Columnist Dennis Dugan noted that McCourt "has a way of finding incredible humor in the worst situations"—a trait that has helped him throughout his life. McCourt's advice to students to "write what you know" eventually led him to tell his own story.

Late-Blooming Writer Frank McCourt was 60 years old when he completed his first book, the Pulitzer Prize–winning *Angela's Ashes*. He waited so long to write this memoir of childhood because he needed time to come to terms with his early, poverty-stricken years with an alcoholic father. "I had attitudes and these attitudes had to be softened. I had to get rid of them, I had to become, as it says in the Bible, as a child. The child started to speak in this book. And that was the only way to do it, without judging." The success of *Angela's Ashes* led him to continue his memoir in *'Tis*.

MORE ABOUT THE AUTHOR
For more on Frank McCourt, visit the **Literature Center** at ClassZone.com.

Background

Catholic Ireland in the Mid-1900s When Frank McCourt was growing up in Ireland, the Roman Catholic Church held a firm grip on Irish society. Recognized by Ireland's constitution as the "guardian of the faith," the church operated the schools and hospitals; it had such pervasive influence on society that Irish law did not permit divorce, and censorship of books and films was common.

Angela's Ashes

FRANK McCOURT

Mam comes with Dr. Troy. He feels my forehead, rolls up my eyelids, turns me over to see my back, picks me up and runs to his motor car. Mam runs after him and he tells her I have typhoid fever. Mam cries, . . . am I to lose the whole family? Will it ever end? She gets into the car, holds me in her lap and moans all the way to the Fever Hospital at the City Home.[1]

The bed has cool white sheets. The nurses have clean white uniforms and the nun, Sister Rita, is all in white. Dr. Humphrey and Dr. Campbell have white coats and things hanging from their necks which they stick against my chest and all over. I sleep and sleep but I'm awake when they bring in jars of
10 bright red stuff that hang from tall poles above my bed and they stick tubes into my ankles and the back of my right hand. Sister Rita says, You're getting blood, Francis. Soldier's blood from the Sarsfield Barracks.

Mam is sitting by the bed and the nurse is saying, You know, missus, this is very unusual. No one is ever allowed into the Fever Hospital for fear they'd catch something but they made an exception for you with his crisis coming. If he gets over this he'll surely recover. **Ⓐ**

I fall asleep. Mam is gone when I wake but there's movement in the room and it's the priest, Father Gorey, from the Confraternity[2] saying Mass at a table in the corner. I drift off again and now they're waking me and pulling down the
20 bedclothes. Father Gorey is touching me with oil and praying in Latin. I know it's Extreme Unction[3] and that means I'm going to die and I don't care. They wake me again to receive Communion. I don't want it, I'm afraid I might get sick. I keep the wafer on my tongue and fall asleep and when I wake up again it's gone.

It's dark and Dr. Campbell is sitting by my bed. He's holding my wrist and looking at his watch. He has red hair and glasses and he always smiles when he talks to me. He sits now and hums and looks out the window. His eyes close and he snores a little. . . .

---

1. **Mam cries, . . . City Home:** The Fever Hospital was a special section of the Limerick City Home Hospital where patients who had fever-related illnesses like typhoid were treated. The McCourt family had already lost a baby daughter and twin boys to childhood disease.

2. **Confraternity** (kŏn'frə-tûr'nĭ-tē): a religious society or association.

3. **Extreme Unction** (ŭngk'shən): a Roman Catholic sacrament given to a person thought to be near death.

ANALYZE VISUALS
What does this class photograph tell you about the time period and subject of this memoir?

Ⓐ MEMOIR
Reread lines 1–16. What **inferences** can you make about economic conditions in Ireland at this time?

Frank McCourt (right front) in the playground of Leamy's school in Limerick, Ireland, about 1938.

ister Rita's white habit is bright in the sun that comes in the
window. She's holding my wrist, looking at her watch, smiling.
Oh, she says, we're awake, are we? Well, Francis, I think we've come
through the worst. Our prayers are answered and all the prayers of
those hundreds of little boys at the Confraternity. Can you imagine
that? Hundreds of boys saying the rosary[4] for you and offering up
their communion. **B**

My ankles and the back of my hand are throbbing from the tubes bringing
in the blood and I don't care about boys praying for me. I can hear the swish of
Sister Rita's habit and the click of her rosary beads when she leaves the room.
I fall asleep and when I wake it's dark and Dad is sitting by the bed with his
hand on mine.

Son, are you awake?

I try to talk but I'm dry, nothing will come out and I point to my mouth.
He holds a glass of water to my lips and it's sweet and cool. He presses my
hand and says I'm a great old soldier and why wouldn't I? Don't I have the
soldier's blood in me?

The tubes are not in me anymore and the glass jars are gone.

Sister Rita comes in and tells Dad he has to go. I don't want him to go
because he looks sad. When he looks sad it's the worst thing in the world and
I start crying. Now what's this? says Sister Rita. Crying with all that soldier
blood in you? There's a big surprise for you tomorrow, Francis. You'll never
guess. Well, I'll tell you, we're bringing you a nice biscuit[5] with your tea in the
morning. Isn't that a treat? And your father will be back in a day or two, won't
you, Mr. McCourt?

Dad nods and puts his hand on mine again. He looks at me, steps away,
stops, comes back, kisses me on the forehead for the first time in my life and
I'm so happy I feel like floating out of the bed. **C**

The other two beds in my room are empty. The nurse says I'm the only
typhoid patient and I'm a miracle for getting over the crisis.

The room next to me is empty till one morning a girl's voice says, Yoo hoo,
who's there?

I'm not sure if she's talking to me or someone in the room beyond.

Yoo hoo, boy with the typhoid, are you awake?

I am.

Are you better?

I am.

Well, why are you here?

I don't know. I'm still in the bed. They stick needles in me and give me
medicine.

What do you look like?

I wonder, What kind of a question is that? I don't know what to tell her.

---

4. **rosary** (rō′zə-rē): a series of prayers repeated by Roman Catholics as a form of devotion
to the Virgin Mary—usually counted off on a string of beads as they are said.

5. **biscuit**: cookie.

B MEMOIR
Reread lines 28–34.
What do you learn
about the Catholic
Church's influence over
Irish children and their
education at this time?

C DRAW CONCLUSIONS
How would you describe
Frank's relationship with
his father? Cite details to
support your answer.

Yoo hoo, are you there, typhoid boy?

I am.

What's your name?

Frank.

That's a good name. My name is Patricia Madigan. How old are you?

Ten.

Oh. She sounds disappointed.

But I'll be eleven in August, next month.

Well, that's better than ten. I'll be fourteen in September. Do you want to know why I'm in the Fever Hospital?

I do.

I have diphtheria[6] and something else.

What's something else?

They don't know. They think I have a disease from foreign parts because my father used to be in Africa. I nearly died. Are you going to tell me what you look like?

I have black hair.

You and millions.

I have brown eyes with bits of green that's called hazel.

You and thousands.

I have stitches on the back of my right hand and my two feet where they put in the soldier's blood.

Oh, . . . did they?

They did.

You won't be able to stop marching and saluting.

There's a swish of habit and click of beads and then Sister Rita's voice. Now, now, what's this? There's to be no talking between two rooms especially when it's a boy and a girl. Do you hear me, Patricia?

I do, Sister.

Do you hear me, Francis?

I do, Sister.

You could be giving thanks for your two remarkable recoveries. You could be saying the rosary. You could be reading *The Little Messenger of the Sacred Heart*[7] that's beside your beds. Don't let me come back and find you talking. She comes into my room and wags her finger at me. Especially you, Francis, after thousands of boys prayed for you at the Confraternity. Give thanks, Francis, give thanks. She leaves and there's silence for awhile. Then Patricia whispers, Give thanks, Francis, give thanks, and say your rosary, Francis, and I laugh so hard a nurse runs in to see if I'm all right. She's a very stern nurse from the County Kerry[8] and she frightens me. What's this, Francis? Laughing? What is
there to laugh about? Are you and that Madigan girl talking? I'll report you to

---

6. **diphtheria** (dĭf-thîr′ē-ə): a highly infectious disease caused by the bacterium *Corynebacterium diphtheriae.* It is spread by infected secretions from the nose and throat and can create toxins that destroy the heart and nervous system.

7. *The Little . . . Heart:* a Roman Catholic magazine.

8. **County Kerry:** a largely rural county to the west of Limerick.

A Limerick hospital in the early part of the 20th century

Sister Rita. There's to be no laughing for you could be doing serious damage to your internal apparatus.[9]

She plods out and Patricia whispers again in a heavy Kerry accent, No laughing, Francis, you could be doin' serious damage to your internal apparatus. Say your rosary, Francis, and pray for your internal apparatus.

Mam visits me on Thursdays, I'd like to see my father, too, but I'm out of danger, crisis time is over, and I'm allowed only one visitor. Besides, she says, he's back at work at Rank's Flour Mills and please God this job will last a while with the war on and the English desperate for flour. She brings me a chocolate
120 bar and that proves Dad is working. She could never afford it on the dole.[10] He sends me notes. He tells me my brothers are all praying for me, that I should be a good boy, obey the doctors, the nuns, the nurses, and don't forget to say my prayers. He's sure St. Jude pulled me through the crisis because he's the patron saint of desperate cases and I was indeed a desperate case. **D**

Patricia says she has two books by her bed. One is a poetry book and that's the one she loves. The other is a short history of England and do I want it? She gives it to Seamus,[11] the man who mops the floors every day, and he brings it to me. He says, I'm not supposed to be bringing anything from a diphtheria room to a typhoid room with all the germs flying around and hiding between
130 the pages and if you ever catch diphtheria on top of the typhoid they'll know and I'll lose my good job and be out on the street singing patriotic songs with a tin cup in my hand, which I could easily do because there isn't a song ever written about Ireland's sufferings I don't know. . . .

Oh, yes, he knows Roddy McCorley.[12] He'll sing it for me right enough but he's barely into the first verse when the Kerry nurse rushes in. What's this,

D MEMOIR
Reread lines 116–124.
What details describe
Frank's family and the role
of religion in their lives?

---

9. **internal apparatus:** the internal organs of the body.

10. **on the dole:** living on government unemployment payments.

11. **Seamus** (shā′məs).

12. **Roddy McCorley:** a song about Roddy McCorley, a local leader during an Irish uprising. McCorley was hanged by the English in 1798.

Seamus? Singing? Of all the people in this hospital you should know the rules against singing. I have a good mind to report you to Sister Rita.

Ah, . . . don't do that, nurse.

Very well, Seamus. I'll let it go this one time. You know the singing could
140 lead to a **relapse** in these patients.

When she leaves he whispers he'll teach me a few songs because singing is good for passing the time when you're by yourself in a typhoid room. He ⓔ says Patricia is a lovely girl the way she often gives him sweets from the parcel her mother sends every fortnight.[13] He stops mopping the floor and calls to Patricia in the next room, I was telling Frankie you're a lovely girl, Patricia, and she says, You're a lovely man, Seamus. He smiles because he's an old man of forty and he never had children but the ones he can talk to here in the Fever Hospital. He says, Here's the book, Frankie. Isn't it a great pity you have to be reading all about England after all they did to us, that there isn't a history of
150 Ireland to be had in this hospital. ⓕ

The book tells me all about King Alfred and William the Conqueror and all the kings and queens down to Edward, who had to wait forever for his mother, Victoria, to die before he could be king. The book has the first bit of Shakespeare I ever read.

> *I do believe, __induced__ by potent circumstances*
> *That thou art mine enemy.*

The history writer says this is what Catherine, who is a wife of Henry the Eighth, says to Cardinal Wolsey, who is trying to have her head cut off. I don't know what it means and I don't care because it's Shakespeare and it's like
160 having jewels in my mouth when I say the words. If I had a whole book of Shakespeare they could keep me in the hospital for a year. ⓖ

Patricia says she doesn't know what induced means or potent circumstances and she doesn't care about Shakespeare, she has her poetry book and she reads to me from beyond the wall a poem about an owl and a pussycat that went to sea in a green boat with honey and money[14] and it makes no sense and when I say that Patricia gets huffy and says that's the last poem she'll ever read to me. She says I'm always reciting the lines from Shakespeare and they make no sense either. Seamus stops mopping again and tells us we shouldn't be fighting over poetry because we'll have enough to fight about when we grow up and
170 get married. Patricia says she's sorry and I'm sorry too so she reads me part of another poem which I have to remember so I can say it back to her early in the morning or late at night when there are no nuns or nurses about,

> *The wind was a __torrent__ of darkness among the gusty trees,*
> *The moon was a ghostly galleon tossed upon cloudy seas,*
> *The road was a ribbon of moonlight over the purple moor,*

relapse (rē'lăps) *n.* a worsening of an illness after a partial recovery

ⓔ **GRAMMAR AND STYLE**
Reread lines 139–142. Notice McCourt's use of the **gerund** *singing*. A gerund is a verb form that ends in *–ing* and is used as a noun.

ⓕ **ALLUSIONS**
Here Seamus refers to the troubled relationship between England and Ireland. What does this reveal about him? about Irish culture?

induced (ĭn-do͞ost') *adj.* led on; persuaded **induce** *v.*

ⓖ **MEMOIR**
What does this first encounter with Shakespeare reveal about Frank?

torrent (tôr'ənt) *n.* a heavy, uncontrolled outpouring

---

13. **fortnight:** two weeks.

14. **a poem . . . money:** "The Owl and the Pussycat," a humorous poem by the 19th-century British poet and artist Edward Lear.

And the highwayman came riding
Riding riding
The highwayman came riding, up to the old inn-door.
He'd a French cocked-hat on his forehead,
180 *a bunch of lace at his chin,*
A coat of the claret velvet, and breeches of brown doe-skin,
They fitted with never a wrinkle, his boots were up to the thigh.
And he rode with a jeweled twinkle,
His pistol butts a-twinkle,
His rapier hilt a-twinkle, under the jeweled sky.[15]

Every day I can't wait for the doctors and nurses to leave me alone so I can learn a new verse from Patricia and find out what's happening to the highwayman and the landlord's red-lipped daughter. I love the poem because it's exciting and almost as good as my two lines of Shakespeare. The redcoats 190 are after the highwayman because they know he told her, I'll come to thee by moonlight. . . . ⓗ

I'd love to do that myself, come by moonlight for Patricia in the next room. . . . She's ready to read the last few verses when in comes the nurse from Kerry shouting at her, shouting at me, I told ye there was to be no talking between rooms. Diphtheria is never allowed to talk to typhoid and visa versa. I warned ye. And she calls out, Seamus, take this one. Take the by.[16] Sister Rita said one more word out of him and upstairs with him. We gave ye a warning to stop the blathering but ye wouldn't. Take the by, Seamus, take him.

Ah, now, nurse, sure isn't he harmless. 'Tis only a bit o' poetry.

200 Take that by, Seamus, take him at once. ⓘ

He bends over me and whispers, Ah, . . . I'm sorry, Frankie. Here's your English history book. He slips the book under my shirt and lifts me from the bed. He whispers that I'm a feather. I try to see Patricia when we pass through her room but all I can make out is a blur of dark head on a pillow.

Sister Rita stops us in the hall to tell me I'm a great disappointment to her, that she expected me to be a good boy after what God had done for me, after all the prayers said by hundreds of boys at the Confraternity, after all the care from the nuns and nurses of the Fever Hospital, after the way they let my mother and father in to see me, a thing rarely allowed, and this is how I 210 repaid them lying in the bed reciting silly poetry back and forth with Patricia Madigan knowing very well there was a ban on all talk between typhoid and diphtheria. She says I'll have plenty of time to reflect on my sins in the big ward upstairs and I should beg forgiveness for my disobedience reciting a pagan English poem about a thief on a horse and a maiden with red lips who commits a terrible sin when I could have been praying or reading the life of a saint. She made it her business to read that poem so she did and I'd be well advised to tell the priest in confession.

ⓗ **MEMOIR**
In what ways is Frank and Patricia's situation like that of the characters in "The Highwayman"?

ⓘ **MEMOIR**
Reread lines 193–200. McCourt uses **dialect** to provide a realistic portrayal of the nurse. How does this influence your reaction to her?

---

15. **The wind . . . jeweled sky:** the opening lines of "The Highwayman," a romantic, action-packed narrative poem by the 20th-century British writer Alfred Noyes.

16. **by:** boy (spelled to indicate the nurse's dialectal pronunciation).

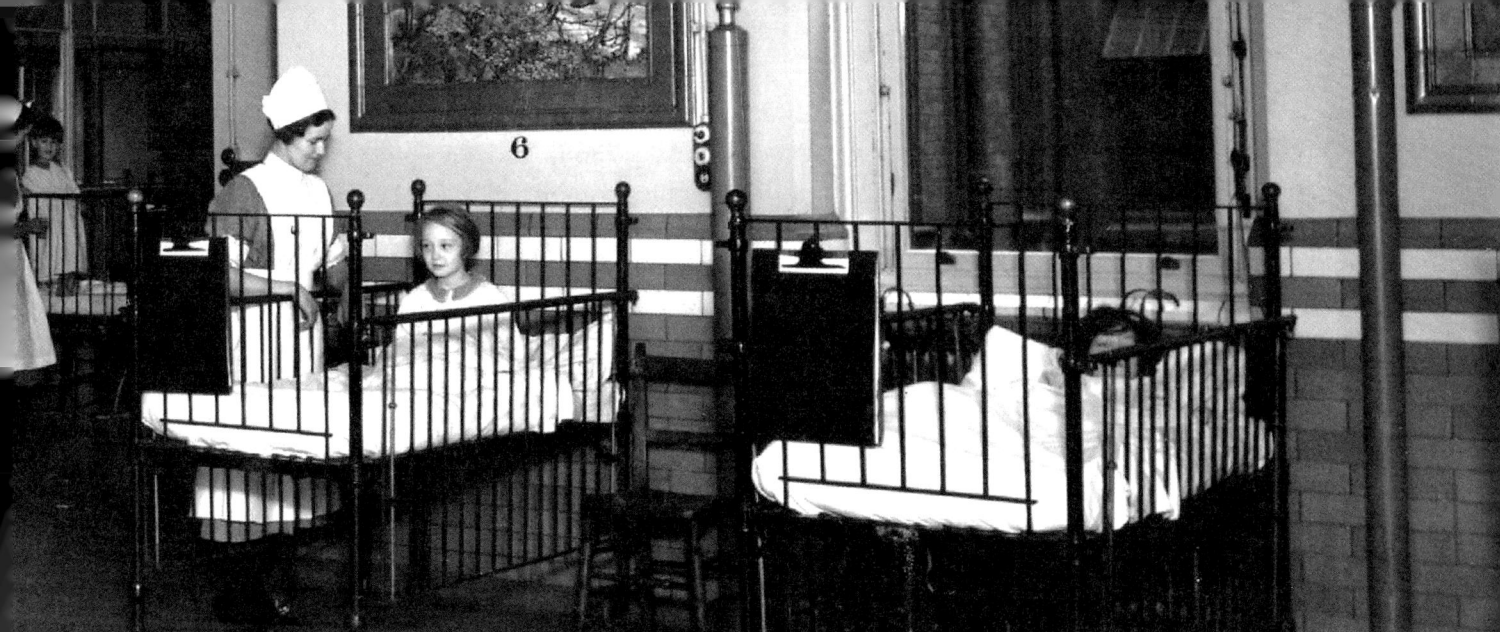

A children's ward typical of British and Irish hospitals in the 1940s

The Kerry nurse follows us upstairs gasping and holding on to the banister. She tells me I better not get the notion she'll be running up to this part of the 220 world every time I have a little pain or a twinge.

There are twenty beds in the ward, all white, all empty. The nurse tells Seamus put me at the far end of the ward against the wall to make sure I don't talk to anyone who might be passing the door, which is very unlikely since there isn't another soul on this whole floor. She tells Seamus this was the fever ward during the Great Famine[17] long ago and only God knows how many died here brought in too late for anything but a wash before they were buried and there are stories of cries and moans in the far reaches of the night. She says 'twould break your heart to think of what the English did to us, that if they didn't put the blight[18] on the potato they didn't do much to take it off. 230 No pity. No feeling at all for the people that died in this very ward, children suffering and dying here while the English feasted on roast beef and guzzled the best of wine in their big houses, little children with their mouths all green from trying to eat the grass in the fields beyond, God bless us and save us and guard us from future famines. **J**

Seamus says 'twas a terrible thing indeed and he wouldn't want to be walking these halls in the dark with all the little green mouths gaping at him. The nurse takes my temperature, 'Tis up a bit, have a good sleep for yourself now that you're away from the chatter with Patricia Madigan below who will never know a gray hair.[19]

240 She shakes her head at Seamus and he gives her a sad shake back.

J MEMOIR
Reread lines 221–234. What insights do you get about the sufferings the Irish endured during the famine and its lasting effect on their culture?

---

17. **Great Famine** (făm´ĭn): a devastating food shortage in Ireland in the late 1840s, caused by a failure of the potato crop. Over a million Irish people died of starvation during the famine, and about 1.5 million emigrated, mainly to the United States.

18. **blight**: a plant disease—in this case, the one that destroyed the Irish potato crop.

19. **never know a gray hair**: won't live to be old.

Nurses and nuns never think you know what they're talking about. If you're ten going on eleven you're supposed to be simple like my uncle Pat Sheehan who was dropped on his head. You can't ask questions. You can't show you understand what the nurse said about Patricia Madigan, that she's going to die, and you can't show you want to cry over this girl who taught you a lovely poem which the nun says is bad.

The nurse tells Seamus she has to go and he's to sweep the lint from under my bed and mop up a bit around the ward. Seamus tells me . . . that you can't catch a disease from a poem. . . . He never heard the likes of it, a little
250 fella shifted upstairs for saying a poem and he has a good mind to go to the Limerick Leader[20] and tell them print the whole thing except he has this job and he'd lose it if ever Sister Rita found out. Anyway, Frankie, you'll be outa here one of these fine days and you can read all the poetry you want though I don't know about Patricia below, I don't know about Patricia. . . .

He knows about Patricia in two days because she got out of the bed to go to the lavatory when she was supposed to use a bedpan and collapsed and died in the lavatory. Seamus is mopping the floor and there are tears on his cheeks and he's saying, 'Tis a dirty rotten thing to die in a lavatory when you're lovely in yourself. She told me she was sorry she had you reciting that poem and getting
260 you shifted from the room, Frankie. She said 'twas all her fault.

It wasn't, Seamus.

I know and didn't I tell her that.

Patricia is gone and I'll never know what happened to the highwayman and Bess, the landlord's daughter. I ask Seamus but he doesn't know any poetry at all especially English poetry. He knew an Irish poem once but it was about fairies and had no sign of a highwayman in it. Still he'll ask the men in his local pub where there's always someone reciting something and he'll bring it back to me. Won't I be busy meanwhile reading my short history of England
270 and finding out all about their **perfidy**. That's what Seamus says, perfidy, and I don't know what it means and he doesn't know what it means but if it's something the English do it must be terrible.

He comes three times a week to mop the floor and the nurse is there every morning to take my temperature and pulse. The doctor listens to my chest with the thing hanging from his neck. They all say, And how's our little soldier today? A girl with a blue dress brings meals three times a day and never talks to me. Seamus says she's not right in the head so don't say a word to her.

The July days are long and I fear the dark. There are only two ceiling lights in the ward and they're switched off when the tea tray is taken away
280 and the nurse gives me pills. The nurse tells me go to sleep but I can't because I see people in the nineteen beds in the ward all dying and green around their mouths where they tried to eat grass and moaning for soup

perfidy (pûr´fĭ-dē) n. treachery; betrayal of trust

---

20. *Limerick Leader:* a newspaper published in Limerick.

Protestant soup[21] any soup and I cover my face with the pillow hoping they won't come and stand around the bed clawing at me and howling for bits of the chocolate bar my mother brought last week. **K**

K ALLUSIONS
Reread lines 280–285 and identify the allusions McCourt makes to tragic events that occurred during the Great Famine. Why do you think McCourt includes these references?

No, she didn't bring it. She had to send it in because I can't have any more visitors. Sister Rita tells me a visit to the Fever Hospital is a privilege and after my bad behavior with Patricia Madigan and that poem I can't have the privilege anymore. She says I'll be going home in a few weeks and my job is
290 to concentrate on getting better and learn to walk again after being in bed for six weeks and I can get out of bed tomorrow after breakfast. I don't know why she says I have to learn how to walk when I've been walking since I was a baby but when the nurse stands me by the side of the bed I fall to the floor and the nurse laughs, See, you're a baby again.

I practice walking from bed to bed back and forth back and forth. I don't want to be a baby. I don't want to be in this empty ward with no Patricia and no highwayman and no red-lipped landlord's daughter. I don't want the ghosts of children with green mouths pointing bony fingers at me and clamoring for bits of my chocolate bar.
300 Seamus says a man in his pub knew all the verses of the highwayman poem and it has a very sad end. Would I like him to say it because he never learned how to read and he had to carry the poem in his head? He stands in the middle of the ward leaning on his mop and recites,

Tlot-tlot, in the frosty silence! Tlot-tlot in the echoing night!
Nearer he came and nearer! Her face was like a light!
Her eyes grew wide for a moment, she drew one last deep breath,
Then her finger moved in the moonlight,
Her musket shattered the moonlight,
Shattered her breast in the moonlight and warned him—with her death.

310 He hears the shot and escapes but when he learns at dawn how Bess died he goes into a rage and returns for revenge only to be shot down by the redcoats.

Blood-red were his spurs in the golden noon; wine-red was his velvet coat,
When they shot him down on the highway,
Down like a dog on the highway,
And he lay in his blood on the highway, with a bunch of lace at his throat.

Seamus wipes his sleeve across his face and sniffles. He says, There was no call at all to shift you up here away from Patricia when you didn't even know what happened to the highwayman and Bess. 'Tis a very sad story and when I said it to my wife she wouldn't stop crying the whole night till we went to bed.
320 She said there was no call for them redcoats to shoot that highwayman, they are responsible for half the troubles of the world and they never had any pity on the Irish, either. Now if you want to know any more poems, Frankie, tell me and I'll get them from the pub and bring 'em back in my head. ✍

---

21. **Protestant soup:** soup provided by the English to the starving Irish during the famine, often in return for renouncing Catholicism and joining the Protestant faith.

MAGAZINE ARTICLE As a high school teacher, Frank McCourt encouraged his students to write from their experiences. Years later, he recalled the honesty and bravery of their writing and found the inspiration to write his own memoir.

THE EDUCATION of Frank McCourt

By Barbara Sande Dimmitt

The bell rang in the faculty lounge at Stuyvesant High School in Manhattan. When McCourt began teaching at the prestigious public high school in 1972, he joked that he'd finally made it to paradise. . . .

The bits and pieces that bubbled into his consciousness enlivened the stories he told in class. "Everyone has a story to tell," he said. "Write about what you know with conviction, from the heart. Dig deep," he urged. "Find your own voice and dance your own dance!"

On Fridays the students read their compositions aloud. To draw them out, McCourt would read excerpts from his duffel bag full of notebooks. "You had such an interesting childhood, Mr. McCourt," they said. "Why don't you write a book?" They threw his own words back at him: "It sounds like there's more to that story; dig deeper . . ."

McCourt was past 50 and painfully aware of the passage of time. But despite his growing frustration at his [own memoir begun six years earlier], he never tired of his students' work.

Over the years some talented writers passed through McCourt's popular classes. Laurie Gwen Shapiro was one of them. He decided she was coasting along on her technical skills. "You're capable of much more," McCourt told her. "Try writing something that's meaningful to you for a change."

Near the end of the semester, McCourt laid an essay—graded 100—on Laurie's desk. "If Laurie is willing to read her essay," he announced to the class, "I think we'll all benefit."

Laurie began to read a portrait of love clouded by anger and shame. She told of her father, partially paralyzed, and of resenting his inability to play with her or help her ride a bicycle. The paper shook in her trembling hands, and McCourt understood all too well what it cost her to continue. She also admitted she was embarrassed by her father's limp. The words, McCourt knew, were torn straight from her soul.

When Laurie finished, with tears streaming down her face, the students broke into applause. McCourt looked around the room, his own vision blurred.

These young people have been giving you lessons in courage, he thought. When will you dare as mightily as they?

It was October 1994. Frank McCourt, now retired, sat down and read his book's new opening, which he had written a few days before and still found satisfying. But many blank pages lay before him. *What if I never get it right?* he wondered grimly.

He stared at the logs glowing in the fireplace and could almost hear students' voices from years past, some angry, some defeated, others confused and seeking guidance. "It's no good, Mr. McCourt. I don't have what it takes."

Then Frank McCourt, author, heard the steadying tones of Frank McCourt, teacher:

Of course you do. Dig deeper. Find your own voice and dance your own dance.

He scribbled a few lines. "I'm in a playground on Classon Avenue in Brooklyn with my brother Malachy. He's two, I'm three. We're on the seesaw." In the innocent voice of an unprotected child who could neither comprehend nor control the world around him, Frank McCourt told his tale of poverty and abandonment.

After Reading

Comprehension

1. **Recall** Why is Frank in the hospital?

2. **Recall** What rules does Frank break?

3. **Clarify** What happens to Patricia Madigan?

4. **Clarify** According to "The Education of Frank McCourt," who or what finally prompted McCourt to complete *Angela's Ashes*?

PENNSYLVANIA STANDARDS

READING STANDARD
A.2.6.1 Identify and/or analyze intended purpose

Literary Analysis

5. **Understand Memoir** Frank develops two **friendships** in the hospital. What is the basis for each friendship? Give reasons to support your response.

6. **Draw Conclusions About Character** What kind of a man is Seamus? Support your answer with examples of his actions and his words.

7. **Analyze Character Motives** What motivates Sister Rita to forbid Frank to talk to Patricia? Considering Patricia's fate, were Sister Rita's actions justified? Cite details to support your response.

8. **Use Allusions to Make Inferences** Review the allusions and inferences you recorded in your chart as you read. What would your reading experience have been like if McCourt had not included these allusions?

9. **Identify Author's Perspective** On the basis of the numerous **allusions** to Catholic clergy, rituals, practices, and beliefs in this selection, what do you think is McCourt's view of the Catholic Church and its influence on Irish culture and society in the 1940s? Explain your answer.

10. **Evaluate Voice** A writer's unique style of expression is called voice. In *Angela's Ashes*, McCourt writes in the "innocent voice of an unprotected child." How effective is this voice in relating not only events from McCourt's childhood but also his adult feelings about these events?

Literary Criticism

11. **Critical Interpretations** One critic has said that while reading *Angela's Ashes* "you never know whether to weep or roar—and find yourself doing both at once." Did you think any of the incidents described in this selection were at the same time sad and humorous? Cite examples to support your answer.

Vocabulary in Context

VOCABULARY PRACTICE

Write the letter of the phrase that best clarifies the meaning of the boldfaced word.

1. Experiencing a **relapse** of the flu usually means that (a) one will be sick for a little longer, (b) it is time for a flu shot, (c) it is time to go back to school or work.

2. A **torrent** of water could most likely be produced by (a) a leaky hose, (b) a large rain cloud, (c) a spray bottle.

3. Experiencing an act of **perfidy** might make you (a) get interested in mountain climbing, (b) feel angry and betrayed, (c) decide to read historical fiction.

4. If you have **induced** a friend to join you on a boring errand, you are probably good at (a) persuading others, (b) staying on schedule, (c) working alone.

WORD LIST
induced
perfidy
relapse
torrent

VOCABULARY IN WRITING

Imagine what Seamus might say to Patricia's parents about her time in the hospital. What anecdotes or words of comfort might he share? Write a paragraph that expresses his sentiments, using at least two vocabulary words. Here is an example.

PENNSYLVANIA STANDARDS

READING STANDARD
A.2.2 Apply word recognition skills

> **EXAMPLE SENTENCE**
>
> *Well, Missus, your Patricia was a lovely girl. I cried a **torrent** of tears over her passing.*

VOCABULARY STRATEGY: THE LATIN ROOT *fid*

The word *perfidy* contains the Latin root *fid*, which means "faith; trust; belief." This root is found in a number of English words. To understand the meaning of words with *fid*, use context clues as well as your knowledge of the root.

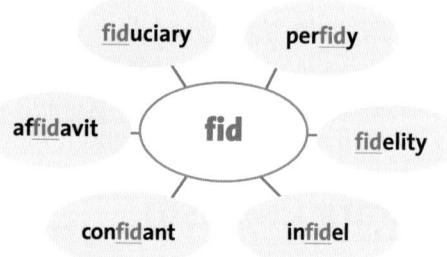

PRACTICE Write the word from the word web that best completes each sentence. Use context clues to help you or, if necessary, consult a dictionary.

1. The _____ of the sound from those speakers is amazing; the music sounds like a live concert.

2. Everyone needs a trusted _____, someone to rely on.

3. A (An) _____ is usually sworn to in front of a public official.

4. In a (an) _____ agreement, one party holds money or property in trust for another.

5. You shouldn't call Leo a (an) _____ just because he doesn't believe in your religion.

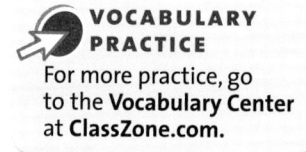

VOCABULARY PRACTICE
For more practice, go to the **Vocabulary Center** at **ClassZone.com**.

Reading-Writing Connection

Increase your understanding of the people portrayed in *Angela's Ashes* by responding to these prompts. Then use **Revision: Grammar and Style** to improve your writing.

WRITING PROMPTS

A. Short Response: Write an Argument
Sister Rita is in charge of patient care, while Seamus takes care of the building. Who is the more caring person? Write **one or two paragraphs** in which you explain why Sister Rita or Seamus is the more compassionate person.

B. Extended Response: Write a Dialogue
Imagine the conversation in which Sister Rita tells Mam that she can no longer visit her son because he was reciting a poem with a girl. Write **one page of dialogue** that includes Mam's reaction.

SELF-CHECK

A successful argument will . . .
- identify the person who is more compassionate
- provide examples of his or her behavior to support the choice

A strong dialogue will . . .
- portray a likely exchange between the two people
- reflect the speech characteristics of the two people

REVISION: GRAMMAR AND STYLE

WRITE CONCISELY Review the **Grammar and Style** note on page 843. A gerund is a verb form that ends in *-ing* and acts as a noun. A **gerund phrase** consists of a gerund plus its modifiers and complements. Because gerunds can be used to replace entire groups of words, they often help to make writing more concise.

Here are two examples of McCourt's use of gerund phrases:

> *I practice walking from bed to bed back and forth back and forth.*
> (line 295)

> *He stops mopping the floor and calls to Patricia. . . .* (lines 144–145)

Notice how the revisions in red insert gerunds and a gerund phrase to make the writing more concise. Revise your responses to the prompts by employing similar techniques.

 PENNSYLVANIA STANDARDS

WRITING STANDARD
1.5.11.D.2 Use precise language

STUDENT MODEL

Seamus thinks that Patricia and Frank ~~should be able to recite~~ *reciting poetry is good for*

~~poetry to each other~~ while Sister Rita believes that patients *refrain from talking or laughing.* ~~shouldn't talk with each other or laugh with each other.~~

WRITING TOOLS
For prewriting, revision, and editing tools, visit the **Writing Center** at ClassZone.com.

Revisiting Sacred Ground
Essay by N. Scott Momaday

What makes something SACRED?

PENNSYLVANIA STANDARDS

READING STANDARDS
A.2.4.1 Identify main ideas and supporting details

B.1.1.1.F.1 Evaluate the use of symbolism

KEY IDEA The word *sacred* means "holy" or "associated with divine power." Different religions and cultures hold different objects and places sacred. In "Revisiting Sacred Ground," Native American author N. Scott Momaday describes a journey to a sacred place that has spiritual significance for his people, the Kiowa.

QUICKWRITE Imagine that you have been invited into a sacred place. What do you need to know? How should you behave? List your ideas on how to act in this special location.

> Being in a Sacred Place
> 1. Be silent, or speak softly, to allow people to think or to absorb the feeling of the place.
> 2.
> 3.

You already know that a symbol is an object, a place, or a person that has meaning beyond itself. A **cultural symbol** is one that has shared meaning for an entire culture. In "Revisiting Sacred Ground," N. Scott Momaday incorporates many cultural symbols that are important to the Kiowa and other Plains tribes. These cultural symbols include

- places, such as the Black Hills and the Bighorn Mountains
- animals, such as the deer and the coyote
- concepts, such as the four directions
- objects, such as prayer bundles

As you read, note the significance of these cultural symbols. What do these symbols tell you about Momaday's heritage and the way he feels about it?

When you read, you can increase your comprehension by pausing occasionally to check, or **monitor,** how well you understand the text. As you read "Revisiting Sacred Ground," use the following strategies to monitor your comprehension:

- Reread difficult passages.
- Write down questions you may have about the content.

Make a chart like the one shown to record your questions, and answer them, when possible, from information found in the text.

Questions	Answers
Why is the Medicine Wheel significant to the author?	

Restate each phrase, using a different word or words for the boldfaced term.

1. ill will and **alienation** within the family
2. suggest **cosmetic** changes to the plan
3. **sauntering** lazily through the park
4. a fender-bender causing **negligible** damage
5. visited an ancient **petrified** forest
6. the **inherent** sweetness of honey
7. a **monolith** standing alone in the desert
8. **engender** goodwill by his kindness

Poet with a Native Voice
N. Scott Momaday was born in Oklahoma and raised on Southwestern Indian reservations. His mother was a teacher and writer of children's stories, and his father was an art teacher. Even though Momaday won a Pulitzer Prize for his novel *House Made of Dawn,* he thinks of himself primarily as a poet—and as a Native American.

N. Scott Momaday born 1934

Harmony with Nature Momaday's Kiowa heritage inspires both his poetry and his prose, which often portray the Native American view that people need to live in harmony with nature. "I believe that the Indian has a [unique] understanding of the physical world and of the earth as a spiritual entity," says Momaday. "The whole world view of the Indian is predicated upon the principle of harmony in the universe."

MORE ABOUT THE AUTHOR
For more on N. Scott Momaday, visit the **Literature Center** at **ClassZone.com.**

Background

The Nomadic Kiowa As of the 1600s, the Kiowa were living as nomadic hunters in what is now western Montana. Around 1700, they moved to the Black Hills of present-day eastern Wyoming and southwestern South Dakota and then migrated to the southern Great Plains. When the U.S. government moved Native Americans onto reservations by the late 1800s, the Kiowa settled in reservations in Oklahoma. However, many sites in their former homelands, where traditions originated or important tribal events occurred, still have spiritual significance to the Kiowa.

Revisiting SACRED GROUND

N. Scott Momaday

There is great good in returning to a landscape that had extraordinary meaning in one's life. It happens that we return to such places in our minds irresistibly. There are certain villages and towns, mountains and plains that, having seen them, walked in them, lived in them, even for a day, we keep forever in the mind's eye. They become indispensable to our well-being; they define us, and we say, I am who I am because I have been there, or there. There is good, too, in actual, physical return.

Some years ago I made a pilgrimage into the heart of North America. I began the journey proper in western Montana. From there I traveled across the
10 high plains of Wyoming into the Black Hills, then southward to the southern plains, to a cemetery at Rainy Mountain, in Oklahoma. It was a journey made by my Kiowa[1] ancestors long before. In the course of their migration they became the people of the Great Plains, and theirs was the last culture to evolve in North America. They had been for untold generations a mountain tribe of hunters. Their ancient nomadism, which had determined their way of life even before they set foot on this continent, perhaps thirty thousand years ago, was raised to its highest level of expression when they entered upon the Great Plains and acquired horses. Their migration brought them to a golden age. At the beginning of their journey they were a people of hard circumstances,
20 often hungry and cold, fighting always for sheer survival. At its end, and for a hundred years, they were the lords of the land, a daring race of centaurs[2] and buffalo hunters whose love of freedom and space was profound.

Recently I returned to the old migration route of the Kiowas. I had in me a need to behold again some of the principle landmarks of that long, prehistoric quest, to descend again from the mountain to the plain. **A**

With my close friend Chuck I drove north to the Montana-Wyoming border. I wanted to intersect the Kiowa migration route at the Bighorn Medicine Wheel, high in the Bighorn Mountains. We gradually ascended

---

1. **Kiowa** (kī′ə-wô′).

2. **centaurs** (sĕn′tôrz′): in Greek mythology, creatures that were half man and half horse.

to eight thousand feet on a well-maintained but winding highway. Then we
30 climbed sharply, bearing upon timberline. It was early October, and although
the plain below had been comfortable, even warm at midday, the mountain
air was cold, and much of the ground was covered with snow. We turned off
the pavement, on a dirt road that led three miles to the Medicine Wheel. The
road was forbidding; it was narrow and winding, and the grades were steep
and slippery; here and there the shoulders fell away into deep ravines. But at
the same time something wonderful happened: we crossed the line between
civilization and wilderness. Suddenly the earth persisted in its original being.
Directly in front of us a huge white-tailed buck crossed our path, ambling
without haste into a thicket of pines. As we drove over his tracks we saw four
40 does above on the opposite bank, looking down at us, their great black eyes
bright and benign, curious. There seemed no wariness, nothing of fear or
alienation. Their presence was a good omen, we thought; somehow in their
attitude they bade us welcome to their sphere of wilderness. **B**

There was a fork in the road, and we took the wrong branch. At a steep,
hairpin curve we got out of the car and climbed to the top of a peak. An icy
wind whipped at us; we were among the bald summits of the Bighorns. Great
flumes of sunlit snow erupted on the ridges and dissolved in spangles on
the sky. Across a deep saddle we caught sight of the Medicine Wheel. It was
perhaps two miles away.

50 When we returned to the car we saw another vehicle approaching. It was
a very old Volkswagen bus, in much need of repair, **cosmetic** repair at least.
Out stepped a thin, bearded young man in thick glasses. He wore a wool cap,
a down parka, and well-worn hiking boots. "I am looking for the Medicine
Wheel," he said, having nodded to us. He spoke softly, with a pronounced
accent. His name was Jurg, and he was from Switzerland; he had been traveling
for some months in Canada and the United States. Chuck and I shook his
hand and told him to follow us, and we drove down into the saddle. From
there we climbed on foot to the Medicine Wheel.

The Medicine Wheel is a ring of stones, some fifty feet in diameter. Stone
60 spokes radiate from the center to the circumference. Cairns[3] are placed at
certain points on the circumference, one in the center, and one just outside
the ring to the southwest. We do not know as a matter of fact who made the
wheel or to what purpose. It had been proposed that it is an astronomical
observatory, a solar calendar, and the ground design of a Kiowa Sun Dance
lodge.[4] What we know without doubt is that it is a sacred expression, an
equation of man's relation to the cosmos.

There was a great calm upon that place. The hard, snow-bearing wind that
had burned our eyes and skin only minutes before had died away altogether.
The sun was warm and bright, and there was a profound silence. On the wire

alienation (āl′yə-nā′shən)
n. a feeling of separation
or isolation

B CULTURAL SYMBOL
Native Americans
believe animals are
representatives of higher
powers who impart
wisdom to humans. What
might the appearance of
the deer represent to the
author in this setting?

cosmetic (kŏz-mĕt′ĭk)
adj. decorative rather
than functional

---

3. **cairns** (kârnz): mounds of rough stones built as memorials or landmarks.

4. **Kiowa Sun Dance lodge:** For the annual Sun Dance ceremony, the most important
   Kiowa religious rite through much of the 19th century, Kiowa members built a sweat
   lodge for their purification and self-renewal.

Reaching 80 feet across, the Medicine Wheel sits atop a ridge of Medicine Mountain in north-central Wyoming.

70 fence which had been erected to enclose and protect the wheel were fixed offerings, small prayer bundles. Chuck and Jurg and I walked about slowly, standing for long moments here and there, looking into the wheel or out across the great distances. We did not say much; there was little to be said. But we were deeply moved by the spirit of that place. The silence was such that it must be observed. To the north we could see down to timberline, to the snowfields and draws that marked the black planes of forest among the peaks of the Bighorns. To the south and west the mountains fell abruptly to the plains. We could see thousands of feet down and a hundred miles across the dim expanse.

80   When we were about to leave, I took from my pocket an eagle-bone whistle that my father had given me, and I blew it in the four directions. The sound was very high and shrill, and it did not break the essential silence. As we were walking down we saw far below, crossing our path, a coyote **sauntering** across the snow into a wall of trees. It was just there, a wild being to catch sight of, and then it was gone. The wilderness, which had admitted us with benediction let us go. **C**

saunter (sôn′tər)
v. to walk in a slow, relaxed manner

C **CULTURAL SYMBOL**
Many ceremonies of the Plains Indians begin with a call to the four directions, which represent different powers or ways of perceiving. Why does the narrator call to the four directions?

When we came within a stone's throw of the highway, Chuck and I said goodbye to Jurg, but not before he had got out his camp stove and boiled water for tea. There in the dusk we enjoyed a small ceremonial feast of tea and crackers. The three of us had become friends. Only later did I begin to understand the extraordinary character of that friendship. It was the friendship of those who come together in recognition of the sacred. If we never meet again, I thought, we shall not forget this day.

On the plains the fences and roads and windmills and houses seemed almost **negligible,** all but overwhelmed by the earth and sky. It is a landscape of great clarity; its vastness is that of the ocean. It is the near revelation of infinity. Antelope were everywhere in the grassy folds, grazing side by side with horses and cattle. Hawks sailed above, and crows scattered before us. The place names were American—Tensleep, Buffalo, Dull Knife, Crazy Woman, Spotted Horse. **D**

The Black Hills are an isolated group of mountains in South Dakota and Wyoming. They lie very close to both the geographic center of the United States, if you include Alaska and Hawaii, and the geographic center of the North American continent. They form an island, an elliptical area of nearly six thousand square miles, in the vast sea of grasses that is the northern Great Plains. The Black Hills are a calendar of geologic time[5] that is truly remarkable. Their foundation rocks are much older than the sedimentary layers[6] of which the Americas are primarily formed. An analysis of this foundation, made in 1964, indicates an age of between two and three billion years.

A documented record of exploration in this region is found in the Lewis and Clark journals, 1804–1806. The first white party known definitely to have entered the Black Hills proper was led by Jedidiah Smith in 1823. The diary of this expedition, kept by one James Clyman, is notable. Clyman reports a confrontation between Jedidiah Smith and a grizzly bear, in which Smith lost one of his ears. There is also reported the discovery of a **petrified** ("putrified," as Clyman has it) forest in which petrified birds sing petrified songs.

The Lakotas, or Teton Sioux, called these mountains *Paha Sapa,* "hills that are black." Other tribes, beside the Kiowas and the Sioux, thought of the Black Hills as sacred ground, a place that is crucial in their past. The Arapahos[7] lived here. So did the Cheyennes. Bear Butte, near Sturgis, South Dakota, on the northeast edge of the Black Hills, is the Cheyennes' sacred mountain. It remains, like the Medicine Wheel, a place of the greatest spiritual intensity. So great was thought to be the power **inherent** in the Black Hills that the Indians did not camp there. It was a place of rendezvous, a hunting ground, but above all an inviolate, sacred ground. It was a place of thunder and lightning, a dwelling place of the gods.

On the edge of the Black Hills nearest the Bighorn Mountain is Devil's Tower, the first of our national monuments. The Lakotas called it *Mateo*

negligible (nĕg'lĭ-jə-bəl) *adj.* not large or important enough to merit attention

D MONITOR
Reread lines 94–99 and note how the writer describes man-made objects in relation to nature.

petrified (pĕt'rə-fīd') *adj.* turned into stone
petrify *v.*

inherent (ĭn-hîr'ənt) *adj.* forming part of the essential nature of something; built-in

---

5. **geologic time:** the period of time defined by the formation and development of the earth.

6. **sedimentary layers:** layers of earth and stone deposited by wind, water, and ice.

7. **Arapahos** (ə-răp'ə-hōz').

Tepee, "Grizzly Bear Lodge." The Kiowas called it *Tsoai*, "Rock Tree." Devil's Tower is a great **monolith** that rises high above the timber of the Black Hills.
130 In conformation it closely resembles the stump of a tree. It is a cluster of rock columns of phonolite porphyry[8] 1,000 feet across at the base and 275 feet across at the top. It rises 865 feet above the high ground upon which it stands and 1,280 feet above the Belle Fourche River, which runs in the valley below.

It has to be seen to be believed. "There are things in nature that **engender** an awful quiet in the heart of man; Devil's Tower is one of them." I wrote these words almost twenty years ago. They remain true to my experience. Each time I behold this *Tsoai* anew I am more than ever in awe of it.

Two hundred years ago, more or less, the Kiowas came upon this place. They were moved to tell a story about it:

140 *Eight children were there at play, seven sisters and their brother. Suddenly the boy was struck dumb; he trembled and began to run upon his hands and feet. His fingers became claws, and his body was covered with fur. Directly there was a bear where the boy had been. The sisters were terrified; they ran, and the bear after them. They came to the stump of a great tree, and the tree spoke to them. It bade them climb upon it, and as they did so it began to rise into the air. The bear came to kill them, but they were just beyond its reach. It reared against the tree and scored the bark all around with its claws. The seven sisters were borne into the sky, and they became the stars of the Big Dipper.* **E**

This story, which I have known from the time I could first understand
150 language, exemplifies the sacred for me. The storyteller, that anonymous man who told the story for the first time, succeeded in raising the human condition to the level of universal significance. Not only did he account for the existence of the rock tree, but in the process he related his people to the stars.

When Chuck and I had journeyed over this ground together, when we were about to go our separate ways, I reminded him of our friend Jurg, knowing well enough that I needn't have; Jurg was on our minds. I can't account for it. He had touched us deeply with his trust, not unlike that of the wild animals we had seen, and with his generosity of spirit, his concern to see beneath the surface of things, his attitude of free, clear, direct, disinterested kindness.
160 "Did he tell us what he does?" I asked. "Does he have a profession?"

"I don't think he said." Chuck replied. "I think he's a pilgrim."

"Yes."

"Yes." ❧

monolith (mŏn′ə-lĭth′) *n.* something, such as a monument, made from a single large stone

engender (ĕn-jĕn′dər) *v.* to bring into existence

E CULTURAL SYMBOL
How does the story of the origin of *Tsoai* reflect the Kiowa belief in people's kinship with nature?

---

8. **phonolite porphyry** (fō′nə-līt′ pôr′fə-rē): a type of hard volcanic rock with fairly large crystals, set in a fine-grained groundmass.

Comprehension

1. **Recall** What journey does Momaday describe?

2. **Recall** Why does he want to make this journey?

3. **Recall** Whom do Momaday and Chuck meet at the Medicine Wheel?

4. **Clarify** Why is the friendship between the three men significant to Momaday?

PENNSYLVANIA STANDARDS

READING STANDARD
B.1.1.1.F.1 Evaluate the use of symbolism

Literary Analysis

5. **Monitor** Review the questions and answers you listed as you read. How many questions were you able to answer from further reading in the text? For questions without answers, how would you go about finding the answers?

6. **Interpret Cultural Symbols** Momaday mentions a number of places, animals, and objects that are considered **sacred** to the Kiowa. Explain what these symbols represent to Momaday's heritage. Cite evidence from the text.

7. **Draw Conclusions** Momaday describes seeing deer upon entering the site of the Medicine Wheel and a coyote upon leaving. Why is the appearance of the animals meaningful to Momaday at those particular points in his journey?

8. **Analyze Cultural Context** In many Native American traditions, quests helped people define their relationship with the world around them. How does Momaday's journey fit within this tradition?

9. **Analyze Author's Perspective** An author's perspective is the unique combination of ideas, values, and beliefs that influences the way he or she looks at a topic. After reading this essay, how would you define Momaday's perspective on the relationship between people and the natural world? Cite evidence from the text to support your answers.

10. **Evaluate Word Choice** At the end of the selection, Chuck says he thinks Jurg is a "pilgrim." What does he mean by this? Why is this description appropriate?

Literary Criticism

11. **Different Perspectives** Momaday describes the land and its creatures as being responsive to him. For example, he says the "wilderness, which had admitted us with benediction let us go" and the deer "bade us welcome." How does this viewpoint differ from the typical Anglo-American perspective?

Vocabulary in Context

VOCABULARY PRACTICE

Determine whether these statements are true or false.

1. If I'm experiencing **alienation** from a friend, it's likely I'm not getting along with him.
2. A woman who **saunters** down the street is probably in a hurry.
3. A large car is a good example of a **monolith.**
4. An **inherent** quality of granite is its hardness.
5. If a committee submits a **cosmetic** reform proposal, it is suggesting major changes.
6. One small critical comment on a long essay would be considered **negligible.**
7. If I **engender** something, I build it with brick and mortar.
8. You would not expect a **petrified** bird to fly.

WORD LIST

alienation

cosmetic

engender

inherent

monolith

negligible

petrified

saunter

VOCABULARY IN WRITING

Write a paragraph about the feelings Momaday experienced during his journey. Use three or more vocabulary words. You might start this way.

> **EXAMPLE SENTENCE**
>
> The **_inherent_** nobility of the Medicine Wheel made a great impression on Momaday. . . .

PENNSYLVANIA STANDARDS

READING STANDARD
A.1.2.2 Use context clues to determine meaning

VOCABULARY STRATEGY: THE GREEK WORD ROOT *cosmo*

The vocabulary word *cosmetic* stems from the Greek word root *cosm*, from the Greek word *kosmos*, meaning "order." This root is found in a number of English words. To understand the meaning of words with *cosm*, use context clues as well as your knowledge of the root.

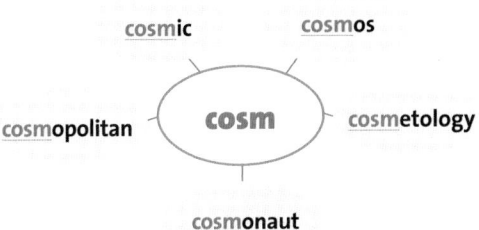

PRACTICE Write the word from the word web that best completes each sentence. Use word structure and context clues to help you. If necessary, consult a dictionary.

1. Astronomers make an academic study of the _____ .
2. After leaving the space station, the _____ had to spend several weeks being reconditioned for life on Earth.
3. My cousin wants to study _____ and become a hairstylist.
4. New York is a very _____ city; people come there from all over the world.
5. _____ dust covered the ground near the fallen meteorite.

VOCABULARY PRACTICE
For more practice, go to the **Vocabulary Center** at **ClassZone.com.**

Blues Ain't No Mockin Bird

Short Story by Toni Cade Bambara

How important is SELF-RESPECT?

PENNSYLVANIA STANDARDS

READING STANDARDS
A.1.3.1 Make inferences and/or draw conclusions

B.1.1.1.E.1 Analyze and/or evaluate tone and style

KEY IDEA When you treat someone with respect, you treat him or her with regard and esteem. When you have **self-respect,** you treat yourself with regard and esteem, and you can often gain others' respect in return. In "Blues Ain't No Mockin Bird," Toni Cade Bambara explores how an African-American family respond with self-respect when their privacy is invaded.

DISCUSS Think of a situation you have seen or read about in which someone showed self-respect in the face of ridicule or embarrassment. What did that person do? With a small group of classmates, discuss the situation and the way the person behaved. Then generate a word web detailing actions or behaviors that show self-respect. What is gained by displaying these behaviors?

Acts of Self-Respect

speaking up for yourself

remaining calm

BELIEVE IN YO[U]
A Guide to Self Re[...]

The **3** Pillars of Self-Esteem
Suraiya Nathani

J.D. H[...]
The Power of YOU
by Erik Koelle
[T]HE SELF-ESTEEM HANDBOOK
[T]he Power of Self-Esteem

I'm Terrific!
Learning Self-Respect
Kurt Devlaeminck

LITERARY ANALYSIS: VOICE AND DIALECT

When you pick up the telephone, you probably recognize the voice of your best friend immediately; no one else sounds exactly like him or her. Similarly, writers have a distinct voice in their writing. **Voice** is a writer's unique style of expression.

In "Blues Ain't No Mockin Bird," the narrator seems to be talking personally to the reader. Bambara creates the narrator's voice through the use of **dialect**—a form of language as it is spoken in a particular geographic area or by a particular social or ethnic group. In writing, dialect can be reflected in specific pronunciations, vocabulary, idioms or expressions, and grammatical constructions.

For example, in "Blues Ain't No Mockin Bird," Bambara captures the cadence, or rhythm, of rural Southern black speech in the 1960s.

. . . and Granny was onto the steps, the screen door bammin soft and scratchy against her palms.

As you read the story, notice how the author uses dialect to create the narrator's distinctive voice.

READING SKILL: DRAW CONCLUSIONS

Many of Bambara's stories feature strong African-American female characters and reflect social issues of concern to African Americans. This story was published in 1971—a time when issues of racial equality and civil rights influenced many writers.

As you read "Blues Ain't No Mockin Bird," record details that give you clues about social issues. Then use those details to help you draw conclusions about the writer's beliefs regarding the issues she presents. Ask yourself the following questions:

- Who are the characters? Do they represent stereotypes, real people, or the writer's ideals?

- What do the characters say to each other? What types of issues are at the heart of their dialogue?

- What is the conflict? Does the conflict reflect a social issue unique to the time when the writer lived?

Author Online

Wide-Ranging Career Toni Cade Bambara's lifework spanned many arenas. As a social activist, she became a respected leader in the civil rights and feminist movements of the 1960s and 1970s. She was a social worker, teacher, theater director, and filmmaker as

**Toni Cade Bambara
1939–1995**

well as a writer of short stories, novels, and scripts. Her writing reflects the wide range of her experiences as well as her deep commitment to the welfare of African Americans. In 1981, she won the American Book Award for her novel *The Salt Eaters*.

Supportive Parenting Born Miltona Mirkin Cade in 1939, Toni Cade Bambara adopted the African name Bambara in 1970. She was raised by her mother in New York City, and after attending Queens College there, she studied in Europe and lived in the Harlem and Brooklyn sections of New York. Bambara credited her mother as her main inspiration in life.

 MORE ABOUT THE AUTHOR
For more on Toni Cade Bambara, visit the **Literature Center** at **ClassZone.com.**

Background

Racism in the South The civil rights movement of the 1950s and 1960s sought to end decades of racial discrimination against African Americans in the South. This discrimination took many forms, including segregation in education, housing, and public places. Although laws and court rulings from the 1940s through the 1960s made such discrimination illegal, African Americans still faced prejudice, restrictions, and physical and verbal intimidation.

BLUES AIN'T NO MOCKIN BIRD

Toni Cade Bambara

ANALYZE VISUALS
Consider the **setting** depicted in this painting, as well as the subject's posture and expression. What feelings do these elements convey? Explain.

The puddle had frozen over, and me and Cathy went stompin in it. The twins from next door, Tyrone and Terry, were swingin so high out of sight we forgot we were waitin our turn on the tire. Cathy jumped up and came down hard on her heels and started tap-dancin. And the frozen patch splintered every which way underneath kinda spooky. "Looks like a plastic spider web," she said. "A sort of weird spider, I guess, with many mental problems." But really it looked like the crystal paperweight Granny kept in the parlor. She was on the back porch, Granny was, making the cakes drunk. The old ladle dripping rum into the Christmas tins, like it used to drip maple syrup into the pails when we
10 lived in the Judson's woods, like it poured cider into the vats when we were on the Cooper place, like it used to scoop buttermilk and soft cheese when we lived at the dairy.

"Go tell that man we ain't a bunch of trees."

"Ma'am?"

"I said to tell that man to get away from here with that camera." Me and Cathy look over toward the meadow where the men with the station wagon'd been roamin around all mornin. The tall man with a huge camera lassoed to his shoulder was buzzin our way. **Ⓐ**

"They're makin movie pictures," yelled Tyrone, stiffenin his legs and twistin
20 so the tire'd come down slow so they could see.

"They're makin movie pictures," sang out Terry.

"That boy don't never have anything original to say," say Cathy grown-up.

By the time the man with the camera had cut across our neighbor's yard, the twins were out of the trees swingin low and Granny was onto the steps, the screen door bammin soft and scratchy against her palms. "We thought we'd get a shot or two of the house and everything and then—"

Ⓐ VOICE AND DIALECT
Reread lines 1–18. Identify the distinctive vocabulary and grammar that characterize the narrator's dialect.

Detail of *Cotton Choppers* (1965), Benny Andrews. Oil on canvas, 25" × 35". © ACA Galleries, New York.

"Good mornin," Granny cut him off. And smiled that smile.

"Good mornin," he said, head all down the way Bingo does when you yell
at him about the bones on the kitchen floor. "Nice place you got here, aunty.
30 We thought we'd take a—"

"Did you?" said Granny with her eyebrows. Cathy pulled up her socks
and giggled.

"Nice things here," said the man, buzzin his camera over the yard. The
pecan barrels, the sled, me and Cathy, the flowers, the printed stones along
the driveway, the trees, the twins, the toolshed.

"I don't know about the thing, the it, and the stuff," said Granny, still talkin
with her eyebrows. "Just people here is what I tend to consider."

Camera man stopped buzzin. Cathy giggled into her collar.

"Mornin, ladies," a new man said. He had come up behind us when we
40 weren't lookin. "And gents," discoverin the twins givin him a nasty look.
"We're filmin for the county," he said with a smile. "Mind if we shoot a bit
around here?"

"I do indeed," said Granny with no smile. Smilin man was smiling up a
storm. So was Cathy. But he didn't seem to have another word to say, so he
and the camera man backed on out the yard, but you could hear the camera
buzzin still. "Suppose you just shut that machine off," said Granny real low
through her teeth, and took a step down off the porch and then another.

"Now, aunty,"[1] Camera said, pointin the thing straight at her.

"Your mama and I are not related."

50 Smilin man got his notebook out and a chewed-up pencil. "Listen," he said
movin back into our yard, "we'd like to have a statement from you . . . for the
film. We're filmin for the county, see. Part of the food stamp campaign. You
know about the food stamps?"

Granny said nuthin.

"Maybe there's somethin you want to say for the film. I see you grow your
own vegetables," he smiled real nice. "If more folks did that, see, there'd be
no need—" **B**

Granny wasn't sayin nuthin. So they backed on out, buzzin at our
clothesline and the twins' bicycles, then back on down to the meadow. The
60 twins were danglin in the tire, lookin at Granny. Me and Cathy were waitin,
too, cause Granny always got somethin to say. She teaches steady with no let-
up. "I was on this bridge one time," she started off. "Was a crowd cause this
man was goin to jump, you understand. And a minister was there and the
police and some other folks. His woman was there, too."

"What was they doin?" asked Tyrone.

"Tryin to talk him out of it was what they was doin. The minister talkin
about how it was a mortal sin,[2] suicide. His woman takin bites out of her own
hand and not even knowin it, so nervous and cryin and talkin fast."

B DRAW CONCLUSIONS
What is the men's
purpose for making the
film? What evidence in
the text helped you draw
that conclusion?

---

1. **aunty:** a derogatory term of address once commonly used for black women in the South.

2. **mortal sin:** in many religions, an extremely serious offense against the laws of God.

Brothers (1934), Malvin Gray Johnson. Smithsonian American Art Museum, Washington, D.C. Photo © Smithsonian American Art Museum, Washington, D.C./Art Resource, New York.

ANALYZE VISUALS
Look at the way the artist mixes colors in this painting—for example, on the boys' sleeves and overalls, as well as on the fence. What effect does this create? How well, in your opinion, does this technique fit the subject matter of the painting? Explain.

"So what happened?" asked Tyrone.

70   "So here comes . . . this person . . . with a camera, takin pictures of the man and the minister and the woman. Takin pictures of the man in his misery about to jump, cause life so bad and people been messin with him so bad. This person takin up the whole roll of film practically. But savin a few, of course."

"Of course," said Cathy, hatin the person. Me standin there wonderin how Cathy knew it was "of course" when I didn't know and it was *my* grandmother.

After a while Tyrone said, "Did he jump?"

"Yeh, did he jump?" say Terry all eager.

And Granny just stared at the twins till their faces swallow up the eager and they don't even care any more about the man jumpin. Then she goes back onto the porch and lets the screen door go for itself. I'm lookin to Cathy to finish the story cause she knows Granny's whole story before me even. Like she knew about how come we move so much and Cathy ain't nothin but a third cousin we picked up on the way last Thanksgivin visitin. But she knew it was on account of people drivin Granny crazy till she'd get up in the night and start packin. Mumblin and packin and wakin everybody up sayin, "Let's get on away from here before I kill me somebody." Like people wouldn't pay her for things like they said they would. Or Mr. Judson bringin us boxes of old clothes and raggedy magazines. Or Mrs. Cooper comin in our kitchen and touchin everything and sayin how clean it all was. Granny goin crazy, and Granddaddy Cain pullin her off people sayin, "Now, now, Cora." But next day loadin up the truck, with rocks all in his jaw, madder than Granny in the first place. **C**

"I read a story once," said Cathy soundin like Granny teacher. "About this lady Goldilocks who barged into a house that wasn't even hers. And not invited, you understand. Messed over the people's groceries and broke up the people's furniture. Had the nerve to sleep in the folks' bed."

"Then what happened?" asked Tyrone. "What they do, the folks, when they come in to all this mess?"

"Did they make her pay for it?" asked Terry, makin a fist. "I'd've made her pay me."

I didn't even ask. I could see Cathy actress was very likely to just walk away and leave us in mystery about this story which I heard was about some bears.

"Did they throw her out?" asked Tyrone, like his father sounds when he's bein extra nasty-plus to the washin-machine man.

"Woulda," said Terry. "I woulda gone upside her head with my fist and—"

"You woulda done whatcha always do—go cry to Mama, you big baby," said Tyrone. So naturally Terry starts hittin on Tyrone, and next thing you know they tumblin out the tire and rollin on the ground. But Granny didn'y say a thing or send the twins home or step out on the steps to tell us about how we can't afford to be fightin amongst ourselves. She didn't say nuthin. So I get into the tire to take my turn. And I could see her leanin up against the pantry table, starin at the cakes she was puttin up for the Christmas sale, mumblin real low and grumpy and holdin her forehead like it wanted to fall off and mess up the rum cakes.

Behind me I hear before I can see Granddaddy Cain comin through the woods in his field boots. Then I twist around to see the shiny black oilskin cuttin through what little left there was of yellows, reds, and oranges. His great white head not quite round cause of this bloody thing high on his shoulder, like he was wearin a cap on sideways. He takes the shortcut through the pecan grove, and the sound of twigs snapping overhead and underfoot travels clear and cold all the way up to us. And here comes Smilin and Camera up behind

C VOICE AND DIALECT
An **idiom** is a common phrase whose meaning is different from the meaning of its individual words. On the basis of the context, identify the meaning of the idiom "with rocks all in his jaw."

him like they was goin to do somethin. Folks like to go for him sometimes. Cathy say it's because he's so tall and quiet and like a king. And people just can't stand it. But Smilin and Camera don't hit him in the head or nuthin. **D** They just buzz on him as he stalks by with the chicken hawk slung over his shoulder, squawkin, drippin red down the back of the oilskin. He passes the porch and stops a second for Granny to see he's caught the hawk at last, but she's just starin and mumblin, and not at the hawk. So he nails the bird to the toolshed door, the hammerin crackin through the eardrums. And the bird flappin himself to death and droolin down the door to paint the gravel in the
130   driveway red, then brown, then black. And the two men movin up on tiptoe like they was invisible or we were blind, one. **E**

    "Get them persons out of my flower bed, Mister Cain," say Granny moanin real low like at a funeral.

    "How come your grandmother calls her husband 'Mister Cain' all the time?" Tyrone whispers loud and noisy and from the city and don't know no better. Like his mama, Miss Myrtle, tell us never mind the formality as if we had no better breeding than to call her Myrtle, plain. And then this awful thing—a giant hawk—come wailin up over the meadow, flyin low and tilted and screamin, zigzaggin through the pecan grove, breakin branches and hollerin,
140   snappin past the clothesline, flyin every which way, flyin into things reckless with crazy.

Woodshed (1944), Andrew Wyeth. Collection of the Brandywine River Museum. Bequest of C. Porter Schutt, 1995. © Andrew Wyeth.

"He's come to claim his mate," say Cathy fast, and ducks down. We all fall quick and flat on the gravel driveway, stones scrapin my face. I squinch my eyes open again at the hawk on the door, tryin to fly up out of her death like it was just a sack flown into by mistake. Her body holdin her there on that nail, though. The mate beatin the air overhead and clutchin for hair, for heads, for landin space.

The camera man duckin and bendin and runnin and fallin, jigglin the camera and scared. And Smilin jumpin up and down swipin at the huge bird,
150 tryin to bring the hawk down with just his raggedy ole cap. Granddaddy Cain straight up and silent, watchin the circles of the hawk, then aimin the hammer off his wrist. The giant bird fallin, silent and slow. Then here comes Camera and Smilin all big and bad now that the awful screechin thing is on its back and broken, here they come. And Granddaddy Cain looks up at them like it was the first time noticin, but not payin them too much mind[3] cause he's listenin, we all listening, to that low groanin music comin from the porch. And we figure any minute, somethin in my back tells me any minute now, Granny gonna bust through that screen with somethin in her hand and murder on her mind. So Granddaddy say above the buzzin, but quiet, "Good day,
160 gentlemen." Just like that. Like he'd invited them in to play cards and they'd stayed too long and all the sandwiches were gone and Reverend Webb was droppin by and it was time to go. ⓕ

They didn't know what to do. But like Cathy say, folks can't stand Grandaddy tall and silent and like a king. They can't neither. The smile the men smilin is pullin the mouth back and showin the teeth. Lookin like the wolf man, both of them. Then Granddaddy holds his hand out—this huge hand I used to sit in when I was a baby and he'd carry me through the house to my mother like I was a gift on a tray. Like he used to on the trains. They called the other men just waiters. But they spoke of Granddaddy separate and said,
170 The Waiter. And said he had engines in his feet and motors in his hands and couldn't no train throw him off and couldn't nobody turn him around. They were big enough for motors, his hands were. He held that one hand out all still and it gettin to be not at all a hand but a person in itself.

"He wants you to hand him the camera," Smilin whispers to Camera, tiltin his head to talk secret like they was in the jungle or somethin and come upon a native that don't speak the language. The men start untyin the straps, and they put the camera into that great hand speckled with the hawk's blood all black and crackly now. And the hand don't even drop with the weight, just the fingers move, curl up around the machine. But Granddaddy lookin straight at
180 the men. They lookin at each other and everywhere but at Granddaddy's face.

"We filmin for the county, see," say Smilin. "We puttin together a movie for the food stamp program . . . filmin all around these parts. Uhh, filmin for the county."

ⓕ **VOICE AND DIALECT**
Reread lines 160–162. Notice the grammatical construction of this sentence. What effect does the use of a long chain of clauses have on the voice of the narrator?

---

3. **not payin them too much mind:** barely noticing them; ignoring them.

"Can I have my camera back?" say the tall man with no machine on his shoulder, but still keepin it high like the camera was still there or needed to be. "Please, sir." **G**

Then Granddaddy's other hand flies up like a sudden and gentle bird, slaps down fast on top of the camera and lifts off half like it was a calabash[4] cut for sharing.

190 "Hey," Camera jumps forward. He gathers up the parts into his chest and everything unrollin and fallin all over. "Whata tryin to do? You'll ruin the film." He looks down into his chest of metal reels and things like he's protectin a kitten from the cold.

"You standin in the misses' flower bed," say Granddaddy. "This is our own place."

The two men look at him, then at each other, then back at the mess in the camera man's chest, and they just back off. One sayin over and over all the way down to the meadow, "Watch it, Bruno. Keep ya fingers off the film." Then Granddaddy picks up the hammer and jams it into the oilskin pocket, scrapes 200 his boots, and goes into the house. And you can hear the squish of his boots headin through the house. And you can see the funny shadow he throws from the parlor window onto the ground by the string-bean patch. The hammer draggin the pocket of the oilskin out so Granddaddy looked even wider. Granny was hummin now—high, not low and grumbly. And she was doin the cakes again, you could smell the molasses from the rum.

"There's this story I'm goin to write one day," say Cathy dreamer. "About the proper use of the hammer."

"Can I be in it?" Tyrone say with his hand up like it was a matter of first come, first served.

210 "Perhaps," say Cathy, climbin onto the tire to pump us up. "If you there and ready." ❧

G **DRAW CONCLUSIONS**
Why does the camera man add "Please, sir" to his request for the camera?

---

4. **calabash** (kăl′ə-băsh′): a fruit whose dried shell is used to make things like bottles, bowls, and rattles.

Comprehension

1. **Recall** Who are Smilin man and Camera man?

2. **Recall** What do they do that offends Granny?

3. **Recall** What does Granddaddy Cain do to their camera?

PENNSYLVANIA STANDARDS

READING STANDARD
A.1.3.1 Make inferences and/or draw conclusions

Literary Analysis

4. **Predict** What might have happened if Granddaddy Cain had not come home when he did?

5. **Interpret Text** Reread lines 62–95. How do the anecdotes about the suicide attempt and Goldilocks relate to the events in the story?

6. **Make Inferences** What does Cathy mean at the end when she says she is going to write a story about "the proper use of the hammer"?

7. **Analyze Voice and Dialect** Create a chart with examples of the distinctive vocabulary, pronunciation, grammar, and idioms that characterize the narrator's dialect. How would you describe the narrator's voice?

Distinctive Characteristics of Narrator's Dialect			
Vocabulary	Pronunciation	Grammar	Idioms
bammin	stompin kinda	me and Cathy went	smiling up a storm

8. **Draw Conclusions About Values and Beliefs** Review the conclusions you drew about social issues presented in the story. What conclusions can you draw about Bambara's values and beliefs concerning those social issues? Cite evidence from the story to support your conclusions.

9. **Evaluate Characters** How do Granny and Granddaddy Cain demonstrate their **self-respect**? Cite evidence from the text to support your response.

Literary Criticism

10. **Critical Interpretations** One critic stated that Bambara "presents black culture as embattled but unbowed" in her stories. How does that comment apply to "Blues Ain't No Mockin Bird"? Support your interpretation with evidence from the text.

Reading-Writing Connection

Demonstrate your understanding of the characters portrayed in "Blues Ain't No Mockin Bird" by responding to these prompts. Then use **Revision: Grammar and Style** to improve your writing.

WRITING PROMPTS	SELF-CHECK
A. Short Response: Analyze Action Why do you think Granddaddy smashes the man's camera? Do you think his action is justifiable, or do you think he is overreacting? Write **one or two paragraphs** in which you argue your point.	**A successful analysis will . . .** • clearly state your opinion of Granddaddy's behavior • discuss the concept of **self-respect** • use examples from the story to support your opinion
B. Extended Response: Describe Granny How would you describe Granny's attitude and behavior? Identify two of her character traits in a **three-to-five-paragraph response.** Be sure to include examples from the story to support your characterization.	**A strong characterization will . . .** • include descriptive language that accurately conveys Granny's personality • use at least two examples from the story to illustrate each of the traits

REVISION: GRAMMAR AND STYLE

CHOOSE EFFECTIVE WORDS Review the **Grammar and Style** note on page 869. Bambara brings life to her story by peppering it with a series of **vivid verbs.** Follow Bambara's example by choosing words that add liveliness and depth to your writing; avoid words that are too bland or generic. Both you and your reader will find the end result far more satisfying. Here is another example of how Bambara effectively uses vivid verbs in her descriptions:

> *Then Granddaddy's other hand flies up like a sudden and gentle bird, slaps down fast on top of the camera and lifts off half like it was a calabash cut for sharing.* (lines 187–189)

Notice how the revisions in red enhance the description in this first draft. Revise your responses to the prompts by similarly incorporating vivid verbs.

PENNSYLVANIA STANDARDS

WRITING STANDARD
1.5.11.D.2 Use precise language

STUDENT MODEL

Granny seems like a grumpy person. She ~~talks under her breath~~ *mumbles* all the time and refuses to smile. She doesn't hide her dislike for the two men who come to film them and ~~tells~~ *commands* Granddaddy to get them out of her flower bed.

WRITING TOOLS
For prewriting, revision, and editing tools, visit the **Writing Center** at ClassZone.com.

American History
Short Story by Judith Ortiz Cofer

When do WORLD EVENTS *hit home?*

PENNSYLVANIA STANDARDS

READING STANDARDS
A.1.6.1 Analyze intended purpose of text

B.1.2.1 Evaluate connections

KEY IDEA Once in a while, large numbers of people feel such a **connection** to a news event that they stop everything. The selection you are about to read takes place on November 22, 1963, when the assassination of President John F. Kennedy stunned and distressed an entire nation.

QUICKWRITE List world events that have captured your attention. Then choose one that really "hit home" and write about where you were, what you were doing, and what your reactions were when you first learned about the event.

> **World Events That Caught Our Attention**
> 1. Terrorist attacks of September 11, 2001
> 2. Russian school hostage crisis in September 2004
> 3.

RUCTION FIRM. U.N. SECRETARY-GENERAL KOFI ANNAN TE

ch "Fantasy" RANDY JOHNSON GOT HIS 4,137TH STRIKE

LITERARY ANALYSIS: INFLUENCE OF AUTHOR'S BACKGROUND

An **author's background**—that is, the writer's life experiences and cultural heritage—shapes his or her perspective on the world and inevitably influences what he or she writes, whether it is fiction or nonfiction. For example, Judith Ortiz Cofer was born in Puerto Rico but moved at a young age to Paterson, New Jersey. She sets many of her stories in Paterson, featuring Puerto Rican–born Americans.

Before you read "American History," learn more about Cofer from the biography on this page. Then, as you read the story, look for the following:

- references to places you know Cofer has lived or visited
- characters whose beliefs, values, or heritage echo Cofer's
- events and circumstances that are similar to Cofer's own

Review: **Character**

READING STRATEGY: CONNECT

Good readers **connect** what they know about a person, place, or situation to what they are reading in order to understand it better. As you read "American History," connect your own life experiences to what you find in the story—the characters' circumstances, actions, and feelings. Record your connections on a chart such as the one begun here.

Detail from Story	Connection	Better Understanding
tenement	I read about tenements in social studies—large, rundown apartment buildings with poor tenants.	El Building must be big and rundown.

VOCABULARY IN CONTEXT

Try to guess the meaning of each boldfaced word from its context.

1. soft music and **muted** conversation
2. **hierarchy** of command
3. **maneuvering** the car
4. **infatuated** and in love
5. **vigilant** protection
6. **enthralled** by the movie
7. **distraught** at losing her job
8. **resigned** to failing
9. a **dilapidated** shack
10. seeking **solace** in prayer

Author Online

A Child of Two Cultures
It's no wonder that Judith Ortiz Cofer writes about what it's like to be a Puerto Rican girl growing up in a mainland U.S. city. "I write about the things I have known," she says. Cofer was born in Puerto Rico but moved at a young age to Paterson, New Jersey, where she lived in a large apartment building known by its residents as *El Building*. Whenever her father, a navy man, was on active duty, however, her mother would take the family back to Puerto Rico to live with their grandmother. Her father pushed her to adopt American ways, while her mother counseled her to hold on to Puerto Rican customs.

**Judith Ortiz Cofer
born 1952**

The Power of Words Cofer first became aware of the power of storytelling during visits with her grandmother, who Cofer says "could silence an entire room when she said 'Tengo un cuento' ('I have a story to tell')." Cofer especially loves writing poetry, because in a poem "every word weighs a ton."

Background

A Great Loss "American History" takes place on the day of President John F. Kennedy's assassination. The president's death deeply saddened the Puerto Rican–American community because, as Cofer points out, "President Kennedy was a saint to these people." Not only was he a charming young father and husband, but his goals were their dreams. He pledged to fight racial discrimination in the United States, raise the standard of living, and wipe out communism in Latin American countries.

MORE ABOUT THE AUTHOR AND BACKGROUND
For more on Judith Ortiz Cofer and John F. Kennedy, visit the **Literature Center** at ClassZone.com.

American History

JUDITH ORTIZ COFER

I once read in a "Ripley's Believe It or Not" column that Paterson, New Jersey, is the place where the Straight and Narrow (streets) intersect. The Puerto Rican tenement known as *El Building* was one block up from Straight. It was, in fact, the corner of Straight and Market; not "at" the corner, but *the* corner. At almost any hour of the day, El Building was like a monstrous jukebox, blasting out *salsas*[1] from open windows as the residents, mostly new immigrants just up from the island,[2] tried to drown out whatever they were currently enduring with loud music. But the day President Kennedy was shot there was a profound silence in El Building; even the abusive tongues of viragoes,[3] the
10 cursing of the unemployed, and the screeching of small children had been somehow **muted.** President Kennedy was a saint to these people. In fact, soon his photograph would be hung alongside the Sacred Heart and over the spiritist altars[4] that many women kept in their apartments. He would become part of the **hierarchy** of martyrs they prayed to for favors that only one who had died for a cause would understand. **A**

On the day that President Kennedy was shot, my ninth grade class had been out in the fenced playground of Public School Number 13. We had been given "free" exercise time and had been ordered by our P.E. teacher, Mr. DePalma, to "keep moving." That meant that the girls should jump rope and the boys
20 toss basketballs through a hoop at the far end of the yard. He in the meantime would "keep an eye" on us from just inside the building.

---

1. *salsas* (säl'säs): Latin-American dance tunes.

2. **the island:** Puerto Rico.

3. **abusive tongues of viragoes** (və-rä'gōz): hurtful comments of noisy, scolding women.

4. **alongside the Sacred Heart . . . spiritist altars:** The Sacred Heart, an image showing the physical heart of Jesus Christ, symbolizes Christ's love to some Roman Catholics. Spiritist altars are places of worship set up to observe spiritism, a set of religious beliefs based on the idea that spirits of the dead communicate with the living.

ANALYZE VISUALS
Consider the images on page 877. Why might the artist have chosen to place the photographs on a filmstrip background? Describe the effect created by this technique.

muted (myōō'tĭd) *adj.* softened or muffled

hierarchy (hī'ə-rär'kē) *n.* a body of persons having authority

A AUTHOR'S BACKGROUND
Reread lines 1–15. What story elements appear to come from the author's background? Explain.

It was a cold gray day in Paterson. The kind that warns of early snow. I was miserable, since I had forgotten my gloves, and my knuckles were turning red and raw from the jump rope. I was also taking a lot of abuse from the black girls for not turning the rope hard and fast enough for them.

"Hey, Skinny Bones, pump it, girl. Ain't you got no energy today?" Gail, the biggest of the black girls had the other end of the rope, yelled, "Didn't you eat your rice and beans and pork chops for breakfast today?"

The other girls picked up the "pork chop" and made it into a refrain: "pork
30 chop, pork chop, did you eat your pork chop?" They entered the double ropes in pairs and exited without tripping or missing a beat. I felt a burning on my cheeks and then my glasses fogged up so that I could not manage to coordinate the jump rope with Gail. The chill was doing to me what it always did; entering my bones, making me cry, humiliating me. I hated the city, especially in winter. I hated Public School Number 13. I hated my skinny flat-chested body, and I envied the black girls who could jump rope so fast that their legs became a blur. They always seemed to be warm while I froze. **B**

There was only one source of beauty and light for me that school year. The only thing I had anticipated at the start of the semester. That was seeing
40 Eugene. In August, Eugene and his family had moved into the only house on the block that had a yard and trees. I could see his place from my window in El Building. In fact, if I sat on the fire escape I was literally suspended above Eugene's backyard. It was my favorite spot to read my library books in the summer. Until that August the house had been occupied by an old Jewish couple. Over the years I had become part of their family, without their knowing it, of course. I had a view of their kitchen and their backyard, and though I could not hear what they said, I knew when they were arguing, when one of them was sick, and many other things. I knew all this by watching them at mealtimes. I could see their kitchen table, the sink, and the stove. During
50 good times, he sat at the table and read his newspapers while she fixed the meals. If they argued, he would leave and the old woman would sit and stare at nothing for a long time. When one of them was sick, the other would come and get things from the kitchen and carry them out on a tray. The old man had died in June. The last week of school I had not seen him at the table at all. Then one day I saw that there was a crowd in the kitchen. The old woman had finally emerged from the house on the arm of a stocky, middle-aged woman, whom I had seen there a few times before, maybe her daughter. Then a man had carried out suitcases. The house had stood empty for weeks. I had had to resist the temptation to climb down into the yard and water the flowers the old
60 lady had taken such good care of.

By the time Eugene's family moved in, the yard was a tangled mass of weeds. The father had spent several days mowing, and when he finished, from where I sat, I didn't see the red, yellow, and purple clusters that meant flowers to me. I didn't see this family sit down at the kitchen table together. It was just the mother, a red-headed tall woman who wore a white uniform—a nurse's,

B CONNECT
Think about a time when you continued to do something even though you were miserable doing it. Why might the narrator continue to turn the jump rope?

I guessed it was; the father was gone before I got up in the morning and was never there at dinner time. I only saw him on weekends when they sometimes sat on lawn chairs under the oak tree, each hidden behind a section of the newspaper; and there was Eugene. He was tall and blond, and he wore glasses. I liked him right away because he sat at the kitchen table and read books for hours. That summer, before we had even spoken one word to each other, I kept him company on my fire escape.

Once school started I looked for him in all my classes, but P.S. 13 was a huge, overpopulated place and it took me days and many discreet questions to discover that Eugene was in honors classes for all his subjects; classes that were not open to me because English was not my first language, though I was a straight A student. After much **maneuvering,** I managed "to run into him" in the hallway where his locker was—on the other side of the building from mine—and in study hall at the library where he first seemed to notice me, but did not speak; and finally, on the way home after school one day when I decided to approach him directly, though my stomach was doing somersaults. **C**

I was ready for rejection, snobbery, the worst. But when I came up to him, practically panting in my nervousness, and blurted out: "You're Eugene. Right?" he smiled, pushed his glasses up on his nose, and nodded. I saw then that he was blushing deeply. Eugene liked me, but he was shy. I did most of the talking that day. He nodded and smiled a lot. In the weeks that followed, we walked home together. He would linger at the corner of El Building for a few minutes then walk down to his two-story house. It was not until Eugene moved into that house that I noticed that El Building blocked most of the sun, and that the only spot that got a little sunlight during the day was the tiny square of earth the old woman had planted with flowers.

I did not tell Eugene that I could see inside his kitchen from my bedroom. I felt dishonest, but I liked my secret sharing of his evenings, especially now that I knew what he was reading since we chose our books together at the school library.

One day my mother came into my room as I was sitting on the window-sill staring out. In her abrupt way she said: "Elena, you are acting 'moony.'" *Enamorada*[5] was what she really said, that is—like a girl stupidly **infatuated.** Since I had turned fourteen . . . , my mother had been more **vigilant** than ever. She acted as if I was going to go crazy or explode or something if she didn't watch me and nag me all the time about being a *señorita*[6] now. She kept talking about virtue, morality, and other subjects that did not interest me in the least. My mother was unhappy in Paterson, but my father had a good job at the bluejeans factory in Passaic[7] and soon, he kept assuring us, we would be moving to our own house there. Every Sunday we drove out to the suburbs of Paterson, Clifton, and Passaic, out to where people mowed grass on Sundays

line numbers: 70, 80, 90, 100

maneuvering
(mə-nōo′vər-ĭng) *n.* an action skillfully designed to achieve a goal
maneuver *v.*

C CHARACTER
In what ways are the narrator and Eugene similar? In what ways do they differ? Explain.

infatuated
(ĭn-făch′ōo-ā′tĭd) *adj.* possessed by an unreasoning love or attraction

vigilant (vĭj′ə-lənt) *adj.* on the alert; watchful

---

5. *enamorada* (ĕ-nä′mô-rä′dä) *Spanish:* in love.

6. *señorita* (sĕ′nyō-rē′tä) *Spanish:* young lady.

7. **Passaic** (pə-sā′ĭk).

Little Girl Reading #3 (1973), Simon Samsonian. Oil on canvas, 42″ × 32″. Private collection, New York.

in the summer, and where children made snowmen in the winter from pure white snow, not like the gray slush of Paterson which seemed to fall from the sky in that hue. I had learned to listen to my parents' dreams, which were spoken in Spanish, as fairy tales, like the stories about life in the island paradise of Puerto Rico before I was born. I had been to the island once as a little girl, to grandmother's funeral, and all I remembered was wailing women in black, my mother becoming hysterical and being given a pill that made her sleep two days, and me feeling lost in a crowd of strangers all claiming to be my aunts, uncles, and cousins. I had actually been glad to return to the city. We had not been back there since then, though my parents talked constantly about buying a house on the beach someday, retiring on the island—that was a common topic among the residents of El Building. As for me, I was going to go to college and become a teacher. **D**

But after meeting Eugene I began to think of the present more than of the future. What I wanted now was to enter that house I had watched for so many years. I wanted to see the other rooms where the old people had lived, and where the boy spent his time. Most of all, I wanted to sit at the kitchen table with Eugene like two adults, like the old man and his wife had done, maybe drink some coffee and talk about books. I had started reading *Gone with the Wind*.[8] I was **enthralled** by it, with the daring and the passion of the beautiful girl living in a mansion, and with her devoted parents and the slaves who did everything for them. I didn't believe such a world had ever really existed, and I wanted to ask Eugene some questions since he and his parents, he had told me, had come up from Georgia, the same place where the novel was set. His father worked for a company that had transferred him to Paterson. His mother was very unhappy, Eugene said, in his beautiful voice that rose and fell over words in a strange, lilting way. The kids at school called him "the hick" and made fun of the way he talked. I knew I was his only friend so far, and I liked that, though I felt sad for him sometimes. "Skinny Bones" and the "Hick" was what they called us at school when we were seen together.

The day Mr. DePalma came out into the cold and asked us to line up in front of him was the day that President Kennedy was shot. Mr. DePalma, a short, muscular man with slicked-down black hair, was the science teacher, P.E. coach, and disciplinarian at P.S. 13. He was the teacher to whose homeroom you got assigned if you were a troublemaker, and the man called out to break up playground fights, and to escort violently angry teen-agers to the office. And Mr. DePalma was the man who called your parents in for "a conference."

That day, he stood in front of two rows of mostly black and Puerto Rican kids, brittle from their efforts to "keep moving" on a November day that was turning bitter cold. Mr. DePalma, to our complete shock, was crying. Not just silent adult tears, but really sobbing. There were a few titters from the back of the line where I stood shivering.

D AUTHOR'S BACKGROUND
Reread lines 103–119. Think back to what you learned about Cofer in the biography on page 875. What experiences and circumstances from Cofer's life are echoed in Elena's life? Explain.

enthralled (ĕn-thrôld′) *adj.* charmed greatly **enthrall** *v.*

---

8. *Gone with the Wind:* a 1936 novel, written by Margaret Mitchell and set in the South during and immediately after the Civil War.

"Listen," Mr. DePalma raised his arms over his head as if he were about
to conduct an orchestra. His voice broke, and he covered his face with his
hands. His barrel chest was heaving. Someone giggled behind me.

"Listen," he repeated, "something awful has happened." A strange
gurgling came from his throat, and he turned around and spat on the
cement behind him.

"Gross," someone said, and there was a lot of laughter. **E**

"The President is dead, you idiots. I should have known that wouldn't mean
anything to a bunch of losers like you kids. Go home." He was shrieking now.
No one moved for a minute or two, but then a big girl let out a "Yeah!" and
ran to get her books piled up with the others against the brick wall of the
school building. The others followed in a mad scramble to get to their things
before somebody caught on. It was still an hour to the dismissal bell.

A little scared, I headed for El Building. There was an eerie feeling on the
streets. I looked into Mario's drugstore, a favorite hangout for the high school
crowd, but there were only a couple of old Jewish men at the soda-bar talking
with the short order cook in tones that sounded almost angry, but they were
keeping their voices low. Even the traffic on one of the busiest intersections
in Paterson—Straight Street and Park Avenue—seemed to be moving slower.
There were no horns blasting that day. At El Building, the usual little group of
unemployed men were not hanging out on the front stoop making it difficult
for women to enter the front door. No music spilled out from open doors in
the hallway. When I walked into our apartment, I found my mother sitting in
front of the grainy picture of the television set.

She looked up at me with a tear-streaked face and just said: "*Dios mio,*"[9]
turning back to the set as if it were pulling at her eyes. I went into my room.

Though I wanted to feel the right thing about President Kennedy's death,
I could not fight the feeling of elation that stirred in my chest. Today was the
day I was to visit Eugene in his house. He had asked me to come over after
school to study for an American history test with him. We had also planned to
walk to the public library together. I looked down into his yard. The oak tree
was bare of leaves and the ground looked gray with ice. The light through the
large kitchen window of his house told me that El Building blocked the sun
to such an extent that they had to turn lights on in the middle of the day. I
felt ashamed about it. But the white kitchen table with the lamp hanging just
above it looked cozy and inviting. I would soon sit there, across from Eugene,
and I would tell him about my perch just above his house. Maybe I should.

In the next thirty minutes I changed clothes, put on a little pink lipstick,
and got my books together. Then I went in to tell my mother that I was going
to a friend's house to study. I did not expect her reaction.

"You are going out *today?*" The way she said "today" sounded as if a storm
warning had been issued. It was said in utter disbelief. Before I could answer,
she came toward me and held my elbows as I clutched my books.

E CONNECT
Reread lines 144–155 and
think about how different
people receive bad news.
Why do you think the
students are reacting this
way to Mr. DePalma?

---

9. *Dios mio* (dyôs mē'ō) *Spanish:* my God.

Rag in Window (1959), Alice Neel. 33″ × 24″. Gift of the Estate of Arthur M. Bullowa 1993.
Courtesy of the Philadelphia Museum of Art.

"*Hija*,[10] the President has been killed. We must show respect. He was a great man. Come to church with me tonight."

She tried to embrace me, but my books were in the way. My first impulse was to comfort her, she seemed so **distraught**, but I had to meet Eugene in fifteen minutes.

"I have a test to study for, Mama. I will be home by eight."

distraught (dĭ-strôt′) *adj.* deeply upset

10. *hija* (ē′hä) *Spanish:* daughter.

"You are forgetting who you are, *Niña*.[11] I have seen you staring down at that boy's house. You are heading for humiliation and pain." My mother said this in Spanish and in a **resigned** tone that surprised me, as if she had no intention of stopping me from "heading for humiliation and pain." I started for the door. She sat in front of the TV holding a white handkerchief to her face.

I walked out to the street and around the chainlink fence that separated El Building from Eugene's house. The yard was neatly edged around the little walk that led to the door. It always amazed me how Paterson, the inner core of the city, had no apparent logic to its architecture. Small, neat, single residences like this one could be found right next to huge, **dilapidated** apartment buildings like El Building. My guess was that the little houses had been there first, then the immigrants had come in droves, and the monstrosities had been raised for them—the Italians, the Irish, the Jews, and now us, the Puerto Ricans and the blacks. The door was painted a deep green: *verde,* the color of hope, I had heard my mother say it: *Verde-Esperanza.* I knocked softly. A few suspenseful moments later the door opened just a crack. The red, swollen face of a woman appeared. She had a halo of red hair floating over a delicate ivory face—the face of a doll—with freckles on the nose. Her smudged eye make-up made her look unreal to me, like a mannequin seen through a warped store window.

"What do you want?" Her voice was tiny and sweet-sounding, like a little girl's, but her tone was not friendly.

"I'm Eugene's friend. He asked me over. To study." I thrust out my books, a silly gesture that embarrassed me almost immediately.

"You live there?" She pointed up to El Building, which looked particularly ugly, like a gray prison with its many dirty windows and rusty fire escapes. The woman had stepped halfway out and I could see that she wore a white nurse's uniform with St. Joseph's Hospital on the name tag.

"Yes. I do."

She looked intently at me for a couple of heartbeats, then said as if to herself, "I don't know how you people do it." Then directly to me: "Listen. Honey. Eugene doesn't want to study with you. He is a smart boy. Doesn't need help. You understand me. I am truly sorry if he told you you could come over. He cannot study with you. It's nothing personal. You understand? We won't be in this place much longer, no need for him to get close to people— it'll just make it harder for him later. Run back home now."

I couldn't move. I just stood there in shock at hearing these things said to me in such a honey-drenched voice. I had never heard an accent like hers, except for Eugene's softer version. It was as if she were singing me a little song.

"What's wrong? Didn't you hear what I said?" She seemed very angry, and I finally snapped out of my trance. I turned away from the green door, and heard her close it gently. **F**

---

11. *Niña* (nē'nyä) *Spanish:* little girl.

resigned (rĭ-zīnd') *adj.* marked by acceptance of a condition or action as unavoidable

dilapidated (dĭ-lăp'ĭ-dā'tĭd) *adj.* broken down and shabby

F CONNECT
Reread lines 228–240. Think about how you and people you know react to confrontation. Why does Elena become so entranced with Eugene's mother's voice?

Detail of *Loneliness* (1970), Alice Neel. Oil on canvas, 80" x 38". Gift of Arthur M. Bullowa, in honor of the 50th Anniversary of the National Gallery of Art. Photo by Lyle Peterzell. Image © 2005 Board of Trustees, National Gallery of Art, Washington, D.C.

Our apartment was empty when I got home. My mother was in someone else's kitchen, seeking the **solace** she needed. Father would come in from his late shift at midnight. I would hear them talking softly in the kitchen for hours that night. They would not discuss their dreams for the future, or life in Puerto Rico, as they often did; that night they would talk sadly about the young widow and her two children, as if they were family. For the next few days, we would observe *luto* in our apartment; that is, we would practice restraint and silence—no loud music or laughter. Some of the women of El Building would wear black for weeks. **G**

250   That night, I lay in my bed trying to feel the right thing for our dead President. But the tears that came up from a deep source inside me were strictly for me. When my mother came to the door, I pretended to be sleeping. Sometime during the night, I saw from my bed the streetlight come on. It had a pink halo around it. I went to my window and pressed my face to the cool glass. Looking up at the light I could see the white snow falling like a lace veil over its face. I did not look down to see it turning gray as it touched the ground below. ∾

solace (sŏl′ĭs) *n.* comfort from sorrow or misfortune

G AUTHOR'S BACKGROUND
What **inferences** can you make about Puerto Rican culture from the description of mourning in lines 241–249?

Comprehension

1. **Recall** What attracts Elena to Eugene? How does he respond to her?

2. **Recall** What world event happens on November 22, 1963?

3. **Summarize** What is Elena's greatest personal concern on this day?

PENNSYLVANIA STANDARDS

READING STANDARD
B.1.2.1 Evaluate connections

Literary Analysis

4. **Draw Conclusions** What do you think is the real reason that Eugene's mother turns Elena away? Explain why you think as you do.

5. **Understand a Character's Social Context** Elena faces a variety of social barriers. What are these barriers and how are they demonstrated or enforced? Record your answers in a chart like the one shown.

WHO	Is Separated HOW	from WHOM
Elena	• • •	the black girls

6. **Analyze the Influence of the Author's Background** Reread Cofer's biography and Background on page 875. Identify three descriptive passages in the story that refer to events or circumstances that actually occurred in Cofer's life.

7. **Connect Literature to Life Experiences** Refer to the chart you created as you read. Did the connections you made while reading improve your understanding of Elena and her situation? Explain.

8. **Make Judgments** Elena is far more preoccupied with her private loss than with the loss affecting the entire nation. Do you think this is reasonable? Explain why or why not.

Literary Criticism

9. **Historical Context** When President Kennedy died, many Americans felt that their chance to realize the dreams and hopes he had championed, such as racial equality, died with him. Why might Cofer have chosen to set Elena's story on the day of the president's assassination?

Vocabulary in Context

WORD LIST

dilapidated

distraught

enthralled

hierarchy

infatuated

maneuvering

muted

resigned

solace

vigilant

VOCABULARY PRACTICE

Write the letter of the word that is most different in meaning from the others.

1. (a) spellbound, (b) enthralled, (c) considerate, (d) thrilled
2. (a) cowardly, (b) watchful, (c) observant, (d) vigilant
3. (a) muted, (b) noisy, (c) deafening, (d) boisterous
4. (a) consolation, (b) solace, (c) depression, (d) sympathy
5. (a) rejecting, (b) jockeying, (c) maneuvering, (d) strategizing
6. (a) hierarchy, (b) order, (c) religion, (d) classification
7. (a) perplexed, (b) infatuated, (c) surprised, (d) confounded
8. (a) fired, (b) accepting, (c) resigned, (d) submissive
9. (a) enlivened, (b) entertained, (c) amused, (d) distraught
10. (a) dilapidated, (b) antique, (c) decaying, (d) neglected

VOCABULARY IN WRITING

Two different responses to Kennedy's death are described in this story. Using three or more vocabulary words, write a paragraph describing these responses.

> **EXAMPLE SENTENCE**
>
> Many in Elena's community were **distraught** at the president's death. . . .

VOCABULARY STRATEGY: IDIOMS

An idiom is a phrase whose overall meaning is different from the grammatical or logical meaning of its individual parts. For example, the narrator of this story says, "That summer, . . . I kept him company on my fire escape." "Kept him company" is an idiomatic expression.

If you run into an unfamiliar idiom, you can often use context clues to figure out its meaning. Otherwise, consult a dictionary. Many dictionaries list idioms at the end of the entry for the main word in the idiom. So *kept him company* would be explained under *keep*, as part of a list like this:

—*idioms:* **for keeps** To hold indefinitely: *He gave me the book for keeps.* **keep an eye on** To watch over attentively. **keep (someone) company** To accompany or stay with.

PRACTICE Identify the idiom in each sentence and write a definition of it. Use context clues or a dictionary.

1. Your advice flies in the face of good sense.
2. Her shoe fell off, so she finished her dance routine on a wing and a prayer.
3. No one will follow those rules unless you put some teeth into them.
4. Winning this contract will really put him on the map in our community.

PENNSYLVANIA STANDARDS

READING STANDARD
A.2.2.2 Use context clues

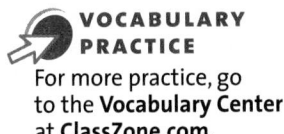

VOCABULARY PRACTICE
For more practice, go to the **Vocabulary Center** at **ClassZone.com**.

Four Days in November

- Newspaper Article, page 889
- Diary Entry, page 890
- Magazine Article, page 891
- Political Cartoon, page 892

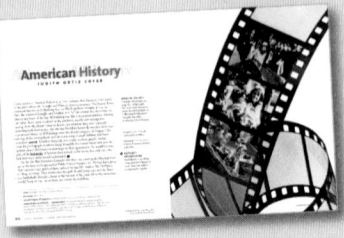

Use with
"American History,"
page 876.

What's the Connection?

"American History" takes place on the day that President John F. Kennedy was killed. The nonfiction selections you are about to read will add to your sense of how that tragic event affected those close to the president and the nation at large.

Skill Focus: Synthesize

When you read different texts on the same topic, you **synthesize** information—that is, you put together the facts, ideas, and details you get from each of them. As a result, you gain a fuller understanding of the topic than you would get if you relied on only one text.

Here's how to synthesize the information from the pieces about President Kennedy's assassination:

- Summarize the main ideas in each selection.
- Jot down any questions that occur to you as you read a selection; look for answers to those questions in other selections.
- Ask yourself why certain information might appear in one selection but not another.
- Reread the selections to answer your questions and fill in gaps in your understanding.

For more help synthesizing, complete a chart like the one started here as you read the selections that follow. Begin by writing down any questions "American History" raised for you.

Source	Main Ideas	Questions & New Information
"American History"	Everybody is sad that the president is dead, but Elena winds up feeling bad for her own personal reasons.	Did students really get dismissed early from school? Did teachers cry?
"President Dead"	The president was killed by a sniper on the afternoon of November 22, 1963. Governor Connally was also shot.	Did Gov. Connally live? Did the president get to say anything to his wife before he died?

THE DALLAS TIMES HERALD FINAL EDITION

CONTINUOUSLY PUBLISHED FOR 87 YEARS   THE TIMES 1876   THE HERALD 1886   CONSOLIDATED 1898

87th year—No. 292   ★★ DALLAS, TEXAS, FRIDAY EVENING, NOVEMBER 22, 1963   3 PARTS   PRICE FIVE CENTS

PRESIDENT DEAD

Connally Also Hit by Sniper

President Kennedy greets supporters upon his arrival in Forth Worth.

BY GEORGE CARTER

President Kennedy died of assassin's bullets in Dallas Friday afternoon.

The President and Gov. John Connally were ambushed as they drove in the President's open convertible in a downtown motorcade.

Two priests announced shortly before 1:30 that the President was dead.

Bullets apparently came from a
10 high-powered rifle in a building at Houston and Elm.

A man was arrested and taken to the sheriff's office. **B**

The President immediately clutched his chest and slumped into the arms of his wife. Gov. Connally, apparently shot in the chest, fell to the floor under his wife's feet.

Secret service agents immediately
20 dispatched the motorcade at high speed to Parkland Hospital.

Gov. Connally was reported in critical condition.

Witnesses standing on a balcony at the courthouse gave this account of what they saw:

The motorcade had just turned into Houston Street from Main Street when a shot rang out. Pigeons flew up from
30 the street. Then, two more shots rang out and Mr. Kennedy fell to the floor of the car.

B **SYNTHESIZE**
News articles often begin by answering the questions *who, what, where, when,* and *how.* Which of those questions are answered at the start of this article? Record any unanswered questions on your chart.

C SYNTHESIZE
This diary entry was written by the wife of Vice-President Lyndon Johnson. She had accompanied her husband to Dallas on November 22, 1963. As you read, combine information she provides with what you learned from the newspaper account on page 889.

D SYNTHESIZE
What sort of information does this account provide that the **news article** does not?

A
White House
Diary
by Lady Bird Johnson **C**

DALLAS Friday, November 22, 1963

It all began so beautifully. After a drizzle in the morning, the sun came out bright and clear. We were driving into Dallas. In the lead car were President and Mrs. Kennedy, John and Nellie Connally, a Secret Service car full of men, and then our car with Lyndon and me and Senator Ralph Yarborough.

The streets were lined with people—
10 lots and lots of people—the children all smiling, placards, confetti, people waving from windows. . . .

Then, almost at the edge of town, on our way to the Trade Mart for the Presidential luncheon, we were rounding a curve, going down a hill, and suddenly there was a sharp, loud report. It sounded like a shot. The sound seemed to me to come from a
20 building on the right above my shoulder. A moment passed, and then two more shots rang out in rapid succession. There had been such a gala air about the day that I thought the noise must come from firecrackers—part of the celebration. Then the Secret Service men were suddenly down in the lead car. Over the car radio system, I heard "Let's get out of here!" and our
30 Secret Service man, Rufus Youngblood, vaulted over the front seat on top of Lyndon, threw him to the floor, and said, "Get down."

Senator Yarborough and I ducked our heads. The car accelerated

terrifically—faster and faster. Then, suddenly, the brakes were put on so hard that I wondered if we were going to make it as we wheeled left and went
40 around the corner. We pulled up to a building. I looked up and saw a sign, "HOSPITAL." Only then did I believe that this might be what it was. Senator Yarborough kept saying in an excited voice, "Have they shot the President? Have they shot the President?" I said something like, "No, it can't be."

As we ground to a halt—we were still the third car—Secret Service men
50 began to pull, lead, guide, and hustle us out. I cast one look over my shoulder and saw in the President's car a bundle of pink, just like a drift of blossoms, lying on the back seat. It was Mrs. Kennedy lying over the President's body. **D**

The Secret Service men rushed us to the right, then to the left, and then onward into a quiet room in the
60 hospital—a very small room. It was lined with white sheets, I believe. . . .

[The Secret Service] began to lead me up one corridor and down another. Suddenly I found myself face to face with Jackie in a small hallway. . . . I don't think I ever saw anyone so much alone in my life. I went up to her, put my arms around her, and said . . . something like "God, help us all.". . .
70 I turned and went back to the small white room where Lyndon was. Mac Kilduff, the President's press man on this trip, and Kenny O'Donnell were coming and going. I think it was from Kenny's face that I first knew the truth and from Kenny's voice that I first heard the words "The President is dead." Mr. Kilduff entered and said to Lyndon, "Mr. President."

Special Report

BY KENNETH T. WALSH **E**

NOVEMBER 24, 2003

In the days immediately after 9/11, Americans in large numbers showed up at the John F. Kennedy Library and Museum in Boston, apparently looking for strength and hope at a time of national peril and sorrow. They were drawn in particular to a film recounting the Cuban missile crisis, when Kennedy guided the nation
10 through a confrontation with the Soviet Union that could easily have led to nuclear war. Many visitors seemed comforted by the idea that prudent leadership and common sense could make all the difference, even in the worst of times. **F**

The fact that Kennedy still has such a hold on America's imagination comes as no surprise to historians and other
20 observers of popular culture. This connection will become even more apparent in the coming weeks as the nation marks the 40th anniversary of his assassination, on Nov. 22, 1963.

Yet the reasons for his mystique are less clear. The fact that he was assassinated in the prime of life goes only so far in explaining it. President William McKinley, another popular
30 leader, was murdered in 1901, but his death generated no vast outpouring of emotion and no enduring sense of a lost legacy. In contrast, millions of Americans still recall where they were when they heard that Kennedy had

been shot. (I was attending history class at St. Rose High School in Belmar, N.J., when the principal came on the public-address system and,
40 choking back tears, told us what had happened. Everyone marched to our nearby church, and we spent the next few hours praying for the president's survival and, a bit later, his soul.) **G**

We all seem to have vivid memories of his funeral, carried on live television, with those unforgettable images of his grieving widow and his young son saluting smartly when his father's
50 cortege passed by.

"Kennedy is frozen in our memory at age 46," says historian Robert Dallek, author of *An Unfinished Life: John F. Kennedy 1917–1963*. "People don't realize that this past May 29 he would have been 86 years of age."

Some deft PR by the White House helped to create his charismatic aura in the first place. He and his advisers
60 quickly grasped the power of the new medium of television, and the handsome, eloquent young leader quickly mastered it and went on to convey an image of optimism and charm that still surrounds him today. His performances at live press conferences are remembered as tours de force. His speeches are used as brilliant examples of political
70 communication. And if his legislative

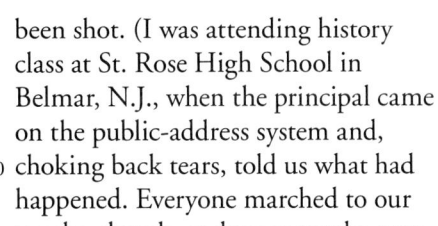

E SYNTHESIZE
On the 40th anniversary of Kennedy's assassination, *U.S. News & World Report* featured this special report. As you read, consider what this perspective adds to your understanding of Kennedy and his tragic death.

F SYNTHESIZE
Summarize the main ideas and details in lines 1–16.

G SYNTHESIZE
Reread the first sentence of the third paragraph. What does this **topic sentence** suggest about Walsh's focus for the rest of the article? Turn that sentence into a question and read on to find an answer.

record fell short, his ideas about ending the Cold War and achieving racial equality at home, at least under the law, eventually took root and became reality.

Further, his glamorous wife, Jacqueline, reinforced the exciting image of Camelot, especially in contrast to his solid but dull
80 predecessor, Dwight Eisenhower. Ike had been the oldest man to serve as president up until that time; Kennedy was the youngest ever elected to the office. The White House never let anyone forget it.

"One of the things President Kennedy did was instill in the American people the idea they could make a difference," says Deborah Leff,
90 director of the Kennedy Library and Museum. ". . . It was a time when you saw America striving to be its best."

For his part, Kennedy said in one of his famous speeches, at American University on June 10, 1963: "No problem of human destiny is beyond human beings. Man's reason and spirit have often solved the seemingly unsolvable—and we believe they can
100 do it again."

The tragic Kennedy mythology was reinforced when his brother Robert was assassinated in 1968 and, later, when his son, John F. Kennedy Jr., died in a plane crash in 1999. All of this perpetuated the idea that the Kennedys, despite all their advantages, were not immune from life's calamities. This deepened their connection to the
110 rest of us.

Yet Kennedy governed prior to the age of cynicism brought on by the Vietnam War, the Watergate scandal, and the wrenching social changes of the past four decades (including, of course, his own assassination). Perhaps not even Kennedy could have emerged from this era unscathed had he lived and remained in public life.

120 "The sudden end to Kennedy's life and presidency has left us with tantalizing 'might have beens,'" Dallek writes. "Yet even setting these aside and acknowledging some missed opportunities and false steps, it must be acknowledged that the Kennedy thousand days spoke to the country's better angels, inspired visions of a less divisive nation and world, and
130 demonstrated that America was still the last best hope of mankind." It is a legacy any president would be proud of.

H

This famous cartoon by Bill Mauldin appeared in the *Chicago Sun-Times* the day after Kennedy was assassinated.

H SYNTHESIZE
What is the cartoonist suggesting about the connection between Presidents Lincoln and Kennedy? If you can't answer the question, record it in your chart and consider reading further to find an answer.

Comprehension

1. **Recall** What facts do you learn from "President Dead" that you did not learn from the short story "American History"?

2. **Recall** What was Mrs. Johnson's reaction to these events?

3. **Summarize** According to Kenneth Walsh, why did so many Americans show up at the John F. Kennedy Library and Museum in Boston in the days immediately after September 11, 2001?

Critical Analysis

4. **Synthesize** What does the political cartoon add to your understanding of how Kennedy's loss affected the nation? Explain.

5. **Evaluate** Which of the selections you just read do you think is the best source of information about the assassination of President Kennedy? Explain.

PENNSYLVANIA STANDARDS

READING STANDARDS
A.2.4.1 Identify main ideas and supporting details

B.1.2.1 Evaluate connections between texts

Read for Information: Summarize Information from Multiple Sources

WRITING PROMPT

On the basis of the information in the selections you just read, describe the emotional impact of John F. Kennedy's assassination on the people of the United States.

To answer this prompt, you will first need to synthesize information on this topic. Then you will need to summarize that information. Following these steps can help:

1. Review your chart to identify any main ideas that have to do with people's emotional reactions to the assassination.

2. Reread the selections with the prompt in mind. Record any direct statements or facts that add to your understanding of the topic.

3. Study the information you have compiled, looking for similarities in people's reactions as well as the range of those reactions.

4. Summarize the emotional impact of this event on the nation.

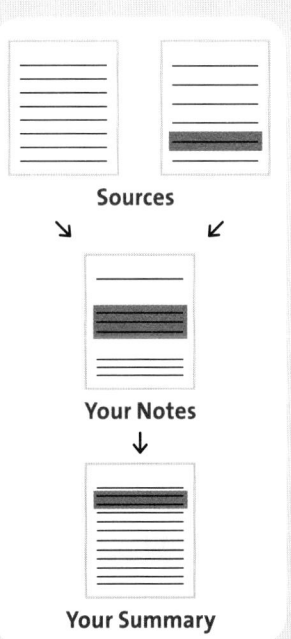

Sources

Your Notes

Your Summary

The Tropics in New York
Poem by Claude McKay

Theme for English B
Poem by Langston Hughes

How does **HERITAGE** *shape identity?*

PENNSYLVANIA STANDARDS

READING STANDARDS
A.1.3.1 Make inferences and/or draw conclusions
A.1.6.1 Analyze intended purpose of text

KEY IDEA Your identity is certainly shaped by your personal experiences, but your **heritage** also has something to do with it. No matter who you are, your family and the culture in which you grew up shaped the person you are today, as well as the person you will be in the future. In the poems "The Tropics in New York" and "Theme for English B," two African-American writers explore and celebrate the importance of their heritage.

QUICKWRITE What is your heritage, and how important has it been in shaping your identity? Jot down your thoughts, and then write a paragraph describing how your heritage has influenced who you are.

LITERARY ANALYSIS: HARLEM RENAISSANCE LITERATURE

In the early 1920s, a literary movement known as the **Harlem Renaissance** took root in the New York City neighborhood known as Harlem. African-American writers, artists, and musicians created works that expressed their own heritage, style, and voice rather than mimicking the style and voice of white culture.

Claude McKay and Langston Hughes were key writers in this movement. Both poets were concerned with the social issues facing African Americans. McKay, who grew up on the tropical island of Jamaica, wrote poetry that reflected the lush landscape and the rhythms of life on the island. Langston Hughes experimented with bringing the rhythms of blues and jazz music into his poetry. As you read these poems, note the following:

- images that are unique to the cultural background of the writer
- ideas or cultural experiences that are expressed through the speaker
- words or cultural ideas that are unique to the time period

READING STRATEGY: READING POETRY

Rhythm and melody play an important role in most poetry, including the poetry of the Harlem Renaissance. In fact, you can find in these poems sounds and rhythms that continue to occur in contemporary African-American poetic forms. After reading each poem silently, read the poems aloud. Notice the rhythms created by the words as well as the sounds of the words in combination. Jot down examples of **sound devices,** such as alliteration, assonance, repetition, and rhyme.

"The Tropics in New York"	
Example	Type of Sound Device
"dewy dawns"	alliteration

Author Online

Claude McKay: From Rural Jamaican to World Traveler The 11th child of peasant farmers, Claude McKay was born and raised in Jamaica. By the time he came to the United States in 1912 to attend college, he had published two volumes of verse in Jamaican dialect. He moved to New York in 1914, and by the early 1920s he had emerged as one of the first inspirational voices of the Harlem Renaissance movement. McKay lived and traveled widely as a poet, novelist, and journalist.

Claude McKay
1889–1948

Langston Hughes: Spokesman for the Common People Born in Joplin, Missouri, Langston Hughes moved often during his youth and grew up in various Midwestern cities. Like Claude McKay, Hughes became a world traveler, but he lived in New York's Harlem neighborhood at several points in his life. He was deeply influenced by the sights and sounds of Harlem and played a key role in the Harlem Renaissance. Hughes's poetry focuses on the experiences of ordinary black people in America and reflects his love of blues and jazz music.

Langston Hughes
1902–1967

MORE ABOUT THE AUTHOR
For more on Claude McKay and Langston Hughes, visit the **Literature Center** at ClassZone.com.

The Tropics in New York

CLAUDE McKAY

Bananas ripe and green, and ginger-root,
    Cocoa in pods and alligator pears,
And tangerines and mangoes and grape fruit,
    Fit for the highest prize at parish fairs, Ⓐ

5 Set in the window, bringing memories
    Of fruit-trees laden by low-singing rills,
And dewy dawns, and mystical blue skies
    In benediction over nun-like hills.

My eyes grow dim, and I could no more gaze;
10   A wave of longing through my body swept,
And, hungry for the old, familiar ways,
    I turned aside and bowed my head and wept.

Ⓐ **READING POETRY**
Reread lines 1–4 aloud.
What word is repeated in
a way that emphasizes
the rhythm?

Theme for
English B
Langston Hughes

The instructor said,

　　Go home and write
　　a page tonight.
　　And let that page come out of you—
5　Then, it will be true.

I wonder if it's that simple?
I am twenty-two, colored, born in Winston-Salem.
I went to school there, then Durham,[1] then here
to this college on the hill above Harlem.[2]
10 I am the only colored student in my class.
The steps from the hill lead down into Harlem,
through a park, then I cross St. Nicholas,
Eighth Avenue, Seventh, and I come to the Y,
the Harlem Branch Y, where I take the elevator
15 up to my room, sit down, and write this page: **B**

It's not easy to know what is true for you or me
at twenty-two, my age. But I guess I'm what
I feel and see and hear. Harlem, I hear you:
hear you, hear me—we two—you, me talk on this page.
20 (I hear New York, too.) Me—who?

B HARLEM RENAISSANCE
Reread lines 6–15. What
do you learn about the
speaker in these lines?

---

1. **Winston-Salem . . . Durham:** cities in North Carolina.
2. **this college on the hill above Harlem:** Columbia University in New York City.

Young Man Studying (Portrait of Langston Hughes) (1932), Hilda Wilkinson Brown. Oil on canvas.
Photo by Gregory R. Staley © Lilian T. Burwell/Howard University.

Well, I like to eat, sleep, drink, and be in love.
I like to work, read, learn, and understand life.
I like a pipe for a Christmas present,
or records—Bessie, bop, or Bach.[3]
25 I guess being colored doesn't make me not like
the same things other folks like who are other races.
So will my page be colored that I write?
Being me, it will not be white. **C**
But it will be
30 a part of you, instructor.
You are white—
yet a part of me, as I am a part of you.
That's American.
Sometimes perhaps you don't want to be a part of me.
35 Nor do I often want to be a part of you.
But we are, that's true!
As I learn from you,
I guess you learn from me—
although you're older—and white—
40 and somewhat more free.

This is my page for English B.

C READING POETRY
Reread lines 16–28.
What sound devices
do you recognize
in these lines?

---

3. **Bessie, bop, or Bach:** Bessie Smith was a leading jazz and blues singer of the
1920s and early 1930s. Bop is a style of jazz that became popular in the 1940s.
Johann Sebastian Bach was an 18th-century German composer.

THE HARLEM RENAISSANCE:

A Cultural Explosion

From the "stompin'" jazz performances at the Savoy Ballroom to the lavish, racially-integrated literary events at the Dark Tower, 1920s Harlem in New York City hosted a vibrant cultural scene known as the Harlem Renaissance.

Scholars disagree about the exact dates of the Harlem Renaissance but generally place this cultural revolution between 1919 and the mid-1930s. The Harlem Renaissance represented a movement that was occurring throughout the country, as African Americans explored artistic, political, and social acts to raise race consciousness. Black people experiencing poverty and racial tension, particularly in the rural South, flocked to Harlem in the hopes of creating a more unified, self-determined community.

Harlem's population quickly exploded, despite high rents there. The "city within a city" drew residents from as far as Africa and the West Indies, as its influence spread throughout the world. The result was a strong community of African-American businesses, churches, schools, and civic and entertainment centers. Although Harlemites had problems and differences, residents drew together to enjoy "strolling" (a pastime that involved dressing up to walk the neighborhood and meet neighbors), parades (which could occur a few times in one day and involve the whole crowd), and rent parties (hosted by tenants hoping to earn enough money from a cover charge to pay the month's rent).

During the Harlem Renaissance, African Americans from all walks of life, as well as other audiences, developed greater appreciation for both the folk and more sophisticated aspects of black culture. Musical forms such as jazz and the blues swelled in popularity. Plays by African Americans appeared on Broadway, black artists gained prominence, and black writers published more books than during any previous era.

Some of the Harlem Renaissance's most prominent figures, such as poet Langston Hughes, drew inspiration from "the low-down folks," a term he used to describe the masses. Hughes, who experimented with dialect and music in his writing, believed African Americans needed to be proud of their individuality and blackness. Others, such as the scholar W. E. B. DuBois, felt that African-American art should serve the political purpose of portraying its people in the best possible light, in order to show equality with whites and to defy stereotypes. Despite these differences, writers of the movement found enough in common to support one another.

The Harlem Renaissance suffered when the stock market crashed in 1929 and wealthy white patrons from New York City's uptown neighborhoods no longer frequented Harlem's clubs. Other factors, such as race riots, the repeal of Prohibition, and growing dissent affected the movement as well. Today the Harlem Renaissance remains a powerful influence among artists such as Nobel Prize winner Toni Morrison, Pulitzer Prize winner Alice Walker, Poet Laureate Rita Dove, and many others.

Comprehension

PENNSYLVANIA STANDARDS

SPEAKING STANDARD
A.1.3.1 Make inferences and/or draw conclusions

1. **Recall** In "The Tropics in New York," what do the fruits in the window remind the speaker of?

2. **Recall** What causes him to weep?

3. **Recall** In "Theme for English B," what instructions are given to the speaker?

4. **Summarize** What aspect of his identity does he discuss?

Literary Analysis

5. **Examine Title** Consider the title of "The Tropics in New York." How does it affect your understanding of the poem?

6. **Draw Conclusions** In "Theme for English B," the speaker says that he and the instructor are part of each other. What does he mean? Explain.

7. **Analyze Theme** In your own words, explain the theme of the poem "Theme for English B." What is the message the poet wants to convey? Support your answer with evidence from the text.

8. **Identify Tone** A poet's choice of words and details conveys a certain tone, or attitude toward the subject. Identify the tone of each poem by completing a chart like the one shown.

"The Tropics in New York"	
Tone of Poem	Words/Details That Convey Tone
sad, nostalgic	

9. **Understand Sound in Poetry**
Review the sound devices you recorded as you read the two poems. How does noticing these sound devices affect the way you perceive these poems?

10. **Interpret Harlem Renaissance Literature** Writers of the Harlem Renaissance explored and celebrated their African-American **heritage.** What does the article "The Harlem Renaissance: A Cultural Exlplosion" add to your understanding of these two poems? Be specific.

Literary Criticism

11. **Biographical Context** Claude McKay grew up in a Jamaican town populated mainly by blacks. When he went to work in the city of Kingston, with a greater proportion of whites, he was shocked by the racism he encountered. He later went to the United States with great optimism about the opportunity he might find "even for a Negro," but he was quickly disillusioned about the conditions for black Americans: "It was the first time I had ever come face to face with such manifest, implacable hate of my race." What does this knowledge about his life add to your perception of the homesickness described in "The Tropics in New York"? Explain.

Haiku
Poems by Matsuo Bashō

Haiku
Poems by Richard Wright

Honku
Poems by Aaron Naparstek

How many WORDS *do you need?*

PENNSYLVANIA STANDARDS

READING STANDARDS
A.1.6.1 Identify and/or analyze intended purpose of text
B.2.1.1 Analyze imagery

KEY IDEA Sometimes a few words can leave a big impression. Even three short lines can contain a thoughtful observation about life. Poets of haiku are masters of being **concise** in this way. In this lesson, you'll read the works of three poets from very different places and time periods who use the tiny three-line haiku to create unforgettable images and express powerful ideas.

QUICKWRITE Can you create a vivid or unusual image from only three or four words? Choose a few of the words pictured here, and arrange them to create a striking image or idea.

POETIC FORM: HAIKU

Haiku originated in Japan hundreds of years ago. Over time, many poets in many cultures have used and adapted the form. But the haiku still presents a challenge with its strict rules about form and content. It requires

- three unrhymed lines of five, seven, and five syllables
- two common images, usually from nature, that are juxtaposed to suggest a greater meaning
- an allusion to a season, as in the phrase "Heat waves shimmering," which suggests summer

As you read, note how each poet uses and experiments with each of these characteristics.

LITERARY ANALYSIS: HISTORICAL AND CULTURAL CONTEXT

The poets Matsuo Bashō and Richard Wright lived in vastly different times and places, and Aaron Naparstek's world is vastly different from theirs. The varied social conditions that inspired these poets to write their poems is the **historical** or **cultural context** of their work.

Before you read each group of poems, read about the author to learn historical and cultural details that will help you interpret the poetry. Then read the poems, focusing on their imagery, symbolism, word choice, and themes. Notice how these elements reflect the life, times, and culture of the poet.

READING SKILL: INTERPRET IMAGERY

Imagery consists of words and phrases that appeal to a reader's sense of sight, hearing, touch, smell, or taste. In haiku, the imagery has added weight because the form is so brief; each word and phrase is critical to the meaning. As you read, follow these steps to find deeper meaning in each poem.

1. Record the images in the poem.
2. Identify the mood, idea, or feeling the images evoke.
3. Explain the meaning of the images.

Record details in a chart as shown.

First Haiku by Bashō: "Harvest Moon"		
Imagery	Mood, Idea, or Feeling	Meaning
the moon walking around the pond all night	mood—quiet or serene; idea—moon stays all night	Nature is abundant and constant.

Author Online

Matsuo Bashō: Japanese Haiku Master
A samurai before he was a poet, Matsuo Bashō elevated haiku from a popular social pastime into a literary art form. Bashō brought the gentle spirit of Zen Buddhism to both his writing and his life. He spent his later life writing poetry as he journeyed through Japan.

Matsuo Bashō
1644–1694

Richard Wright: African-American Novelist
Considered one of the most important black authors of the 1900s, Richard Wright is best known for his novel *Native Son* and his autobiography *Black Boy.* He also wrote short stories, essays, and poetry about life in Northern ghettos and racial oppression of blacks.

Richard Wright
1908–1960

Aaron Naparstek: Activism Meets Poetry
Fed up with the noise created by motorists in his Brooklyn neighborhood, Aaron Naparstek began writing "honku"— haiku about honking cars—and taping them to lampposts. Others began posting their own honkus, and a movement was born. In 2003 Naparstek published *Honku: The Zen Antidote to Road Rage.*

Aaron Naparstek
born 1970

 MORE ABOUT THE AUTHOR
For more on these poets, visit the **Literature Center** at ClassZone.com.

Millet Fields with the Sun and the Moon (Early Edo period, 1600s), Anonymous. Pair of six-fold screens, painted, 150.5 cm. × 348.8 cm. Restricted gift of the Rice Foundation, 1989. Reproduction, The Art Institute of Chicago.

H A I K U

Matsuo Bashō

Harvest moon—
walking around the pond
all night long.

Heat waves shimmering
one or two inches
above the dead grass.

You could turn this way,
I'm also lonely
this autumn evening.

A HISTORICAL AND CULTURAL CONTEXT
Author: Matsuo Bashō
Time: mid- to late 1600s
Place: Japan
Development of haiku: Bashō established the tradition of focusing the content of haiku on nature. The haiku on this page do not reflect the five-seven-five syllable pattern because they are translations from Japanese.

Jazz Player III (1991), Louise Freshman Brown. Collage. © SuperStock

Haiku

RICHARD WRIGHT

From a tenement,
The blue jazz of a trumpet
Weaving autumn mists. **B**

B HISTORICAL AND
CULTURAL CONTEXT
Author: Richard Wright
Time: mid-1900s
Place: United States
Evolution of haiku:
Wright uses the
traditional form but
adapts the content to
reflect on urban life
rather than nature.

Twisting violently,
A lost kite seeks its freedom
From telegraph wires.

Standing in the crowd
In a cold drizzling rain,—
How lonely it is.

HONKU AARON NAPARSTEK

clinton street autos
honk, guzzle and burn away
our crisp, clean spring days **C**

C HISTORICAL AND
CULTURAL CONTEXT
Author: Aaron Naparstek
Time: early 2000s
Place: New York City
Evolution of haiku:
Naparstek modifies the
form by eliminating
end punctuation and,
sometimes, capitalization
and adapts its contents
to reflect concerns
about modern life and
technology.

Morning commuters
follow measured lines, honking—
how like geese we are

When the light turns green
like a leaf on a spring wind
the horn blows quickly

Comprehension

READING STANDARD
B.2.1.1 Analyze imagery

1. **Recall** What subject is common to all three of the "honku" by Aaron Naparstek?

2. **Recall** What kind of music is mentioned in the first haiku by Richard Wright?

3. **Clarify** What season is suggested in the first poem by Matsuo Bashō?

Literary Analysis

4. **Interpret Imagery** Review the chart in which you analyzed the imagery in the haiku. How do the three poets differ in the kinds of imagery they use and the moods they create?

5. **Compare and Contrast Word Choice** Notice the use of verbs in all three sets of poems. Which two sets are the most similar? different? How do the verbs affect the messages of the poems? Explain your answer.

6. **Evaluate Figurative Language** In **personification,** an animal, object, or idea is given human attributes. Identify three examples of personification in these poems, and explain how each strengthens or weakens the writer's message.

7. **Recognize Cultural and Historical Context** For each poet, write a brief summary of how his cultural and historical background may have influenced the images and themes in the haiku.

8. **Analyze Poetic Form** In **haiku,** the image presented is often symbolic of a greater truth or meaning. In the second haiku by Richard Wright, what does the kite trapped in the wires symbolize? Explain your answer, citing evidence from the text.

9. **Interpret Ambiguity** When a situation can be interpreted in more than one way, it has the quality of ambiguity. In the first haiku by Bashō, note the ambiguity in the first two lines. Who is walking around the pond—the moon, the speaker, or both? Explain your answer.

10. **Evaluate** Matsuo Bashō wrote his haiku in the 1600s. Do the poems seem dated, or are they timeless? Explain your answer.

Literary Criticism

11. **Critical Interpretations** Author Aaron Naparstek says that "haiku poems are sort of the perfect little sound bytes. They fit our culture." Using what you know about the haiku and about American culture, explain what Naparstek might mean by that statement. How do the characteristics of the haiku seem well suited to contemporary American culture?

Writing Workshop

Persuasive Essay

"We must clean up toxic waste now!" "Vote for me!" "My client is innocent!" When an issue affects you deeply, you want to convince others to agree with you. Expressing your thoughts on a topic that is significant to you, as writers in this unit have done, can change your life and your community. To learn how to persuade others effectively, take a look at the **Writer's Road Map.**

WRITER'S ROAD MAP

Persuasive Essay

WRITING PROMPT 1

Writing for the Real World Choose an issue you feel strongly about. Write a persuasive essay in which you explain the issue and attempt to convince readers to support your position.

Issues to Explore
- new restrictions on teenage drivers
- discrimination in various forms
- censorship of student newspapers

WRITING PROMPT 2

Writing from Literature Sometimes reading a work of literature can give you a whole new perspective on an issue. Using something you have read as a springboard, write a persuasive essay about an issue that is meaningful to you.

Issues to Explore
- medical treatment of children (*Angela's Ashes*)
- racial discrimination ("Blues Ain't No Mockin Bird" and "American History")
- preserving the sacred places of different cultures ("Revisiting Sacred Ground")

 WRITING TOOLS
For prewriting, revision, and editing tools, visit the **Writing Center** at ClassZone.com.

KEY TRAITS

1. IDEAS
- Presents a **thesis statement** that makes a **claim,** or takes a position, on a clearly identified issue
- Uses **relevant and convincing reasons and evidence** to support the position
- Anticipates and addresses **opposing arguments** and objections

2. ORGANIZATION
- Describes the issue in a **strong introduction**
- Uses **transitions** to create a **consistent organizational pattern**
- Concludes by **summarizing** the position or issuing a **call to action**

3. VOICE
- Reflects the **writer's commitment** to his or her opinion
- Addresses the **audience** directly

4. WORD CHOICE
- Uses **persuasive language** effectively

5. SENTENCE FLUENCY
- Varies **sentence beginnings**

6. CONVENTIONS
- Employs **correct grammar and usage**

Part 1: Analyze a Student Model

WRITING STANDARD
1.4.11.C Write persuasive pieces

Daniel Carpenter
Concord West High School

Curfews: Fairness and the Facts

Two weeks ago, the Concord City supervisors proposed a new law that discriminates against young people who have done nothing wrong. The new law would establish a curfew for anyone under age 18. The weekday curfew would be 10:00 P.M. to 5:00 A.M., and the weekend

5   curfew would last from 11:00 P.M. until 5:00 A.M. Anyone violating curfew would be fined $50. The proposed law has two serious flaws: it is based on feelings instead of facts, and it violates the rights of Concord's young people and their parents.

According to Supervisor Ellen Baxter, the main reason for the law is

10   to prevent juvenile crime. This includes crimes committed by juveniles and crimes committed against juveniles. If minors are off the streets at night, she says, Concord's crime rate would drop.

Her argument sounds good, but unfortunately, the facts do not support it. A study by two university professors, William Ruefle and

15   Kenneth Mike Reynolds, showed there is almost no evidence that curfews lowered crime rates. In fact, the FBI reported recently that most juvenile crimes take place between 3:00 P.M. and 6:00 P.M.—not at night.

Supervisor Frank Angelo says that there are no reasons for youth to be outside late at night. They should be home studying, he says, and

20   spending time with their families. Supervisor Angelo was quoted in the *Concord Clarion* saying, "Anything kids want to do at 11:30 at night can just as easily be done at 8:30."

Supervisor Angelo's argument also ignores the facts. Teenagers have many good reasons to be out at night. Some have part-time jobs that

KEY TRAITS IN ACTION

Strong **introduction** is tailored to the interest of **audience** members (Daniel Carpenter's classmates and teacher).

Thesis statement makes a clear, detailed **claim**.

Throughout the essay, the writer clearly explains **opposing arguments** and rebuts them with relevant **facts, statistics, and expert opinions.**

Organization is easy to follow—opposing argument followed by answer to that argument.

25 don't end until 9:00 or 10:00. Some participate in activities sponsored
by youth groups or church groups. Some may be responding to family
emergencies. Why should teens have to risk being arrested and fined
just for living their lives?

Finally, Mayor Erika Snow said that she supported the proposed law
30 because it was "just good government." Providing a safe place to live is
the city government's most important task, she said.

It is true, as Mayor Snow says, that the city has a responsibility to
keep its citizens safe. However, that doesn't mean the city can violate
parental or constitutional rights. The city government has no business
35 telling parents when their children must be home. That's a decision for
parents to make. Also, the U.S. Constitution says that citizens' private
lives should be free from unnecessary government interference. It makes
no sense to punish teenagers for problems they haven't caused.

Juvenile crime is a problem in many places, including Concord, but
40 curfews are not the solution. The proper response to juvenile crime is to
arrest the criminals, not to put law-abiding young people under house
arrest. I encourage those of you who believe the curfew law is unfair
and distorts the facts to write to your city supervisors and make your
opinions known.

Transitions connect ideas. **Varied sentence beginnings** help keep the essay interesting.

The writer uses **persuasive language** to make an effective appeal based on ethical belief. The essay is forceful but not bullying.

Conclusion **summarizes** the writer's position, suggests a more effective response to the problem, and issues a **call to action** that addresses the **audience** directly.

2

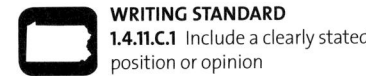

WRITING STANDARD
1.4.11.C.1 Include a clearly stated position or opinion

Part 2: Apply the Writing Process

PREWRITING

What Should I Do?

What Does It Look Like?

1. Analyze the prompt.
Study the prompt you chose on page 908. (Circle) the part of the prompt that tells you what you will be writing. Then <u>underline</u> words and phrases in the prompt that help you focus your thoughts.

▶ **WRITING PROMPT** Choose an issue you feel strongly about. (Write a persuasive essay) in which you <u>explain the issue</u> and attempt to <u>convince readers to support your position.</u>

The key here is to find an issue I really care about so that my passion for my position comes through loud and clear.

2. Think about what really matters to you.
List some questions that explore your current state of mind. Think of issues in your school, neighborhood, community, state, or region. Place a star next to any issue that might make a suitable topic for your persuasive essay.

TIP Remember, to be effective, your argument must have two sides to it.

▶ *1. What's bothering me at school?*
geometry class, Richie Franklin, * backpack searches, rising cafeteria prices
2. What's been happening in the community lately?
vandalism, * proposed curfew law, new community center

3. Develop a working thesis statement.
Spend some time crafting a thesis that includes a **claim**—a forceful statement of your position. Your thesis should reflect the tone and point of view of the rest of the essay. The writer of the student model wanted to concentrate on two main points, so he built his thesis around them.

▶ *The proposed curfew law is a terrible idea.*
1. The people proposing the law are basing it on their feelings about young people and crime, not the facts.
2. The law would violate our rights and our parents' rights.

4. Gather support material.
You're going to need strong reasons and solid evidence to support your position. If you need facts and statistics, you might try using an Internet search engine.

▶ *Possible Sources*
• *Article in Concord Clarion*
• *Ask school librarian for research tips.*
• *Internet search keywords: "curfew," "teen curfew," "juvenile crime," "Constitutional rights of juveniles"*

DRAFTING

What Should I Do?	What Does It Look Like?

1. Plan your organization.

Two common ways to organize the body of a persuasive essay are shown here. In both cases, the writer places his strongest argument last.

- **Pattern 1** Present all opposing arguments, then refute them with counterarguments.
- **Pattern 2** Raise one opposing argument and immediately counter it, then raise another opposing argument and counter it.

PATTERN 1

Introduction and Thesis
Opposing Arguments:
- *Deters juvenile crime*
- *No need for teens to be out*
- *Government must keep citizens safe.*

Counterarguments:
- *Facts show curfews don't deter juvenile crime.*
- *Many good reasons for teens to be out*
- *Curfews violate citizens' rights.*

Conclusion

PATTERN 2

Introduction and Thesis
Opposing Argument 1: *Deters juvenile crime*
Counterargument 1: *Facts say otherwise.*
Opposing Argument 2: *No need for teens to be out*
Counterargument 2: *Many good reasons*
Opposing Argument 3: *Government must keep citizens safe.*
Counterargument 3: *Curfews violate citizens' rights.*
Conclusion

2. Use persuasive language.

Don't be hesitant or vague. Use language that shows your commitment to and strong feelings about your argument.

See page 596: Persuasive Techniques

The city government has no business telling parents when their children must be home. That's a decision for parents to make.

3. Support key ideas.

If you want your audience to be truly persuaded, you must offer convincing support for what you say. Back up your arguments with strong reasons and convincing facts, statistics, and expert opinions.

TIP Before revising, consult the **key traits** on page 908 and the **rubric** and **peer-reader questions** on page 914.

Her argument sounds good, but unfortunately, the facts do not support it. — Key idea
A study by two university professors, William Ruefle and Kenneth Mike Reynolds, showed there is almost no evidence that curfews lowered crime rates. — Supporting evidence (expert opinion)

REVISING AND EDITING

What Should I Do?	*What Does It Look Like?*

1. Be alert for errors in reasoning.

- Put [brackets] around statements that are not based on sound reasoning. Watch out for statements that are too broad to prove. These often include words and phrases such as *everyone, every time, no one,* and *none.*

See page 914: Errors in Reasoning

▶

Juvenile crime is a problem in many areas, including Concord, but curfews are not the solution.
[Everyone knows that curfews are a bad idea.]
The proper response to juvenile crime is to arrest the criminals, not to put law-abiding young people under house arrest.

2. Fully develop supporting material.

- <u>Underline</u> the key idea in each paragraph.
- Reread the material supporting each key idea. **Add reasons, facts, or statistics** if needed. This writer supported his idea with three specific reasons.

▶

<u>Teenagers have many good reasons to be out at night.</u> Why should teens have to risk being arrested and fined just for living their lives?
Some have part-time jobs that don't end until 9:00 or 10:00. Some participate in activities sponsored by youth groups or church groups. Some may be responding to family emergencies.

3. Use precise vocabulary.

- Read your essay aloud. (Circle) words and phrases that seem vague or overused.
- Replace circled words and phrases with language that is **precise** and **reflects your strong feelings** about the subject.

▶

arrest the criminals,
The proper response to juvenile crime is to (look)
law-abiding young people
(for the bad ones) not to put (the rest of us) under house arrest.

4. Write a strong conclusion.

- Have a peer reader draw a <u>wavy line</u> under parts of your conclusion that are weak or that need details.
- Revise the conclusion to make sure it **includes a call to action.** Most conclusions also include a **concise restatement** of the position.

See page 914: Ask a Peer Reader

▶

including Concord, but curfews are not the solution.
<u>Juvenile crime is a problem in many places.</u> The proper response to juvenile crime is to arrest the criminals, not to put law-abiding young people under house arrest. I encourage those of you who believe the curfew law is unfair and distorts the facts to write to your city supervisors and make your opinions known.

Preparing to Publish

Persuasive Essay

Apply the Rubric

A strong persuasive essay . . .

- ☑ has an attention-getting introduction
- ☑ states the issue and the writer's opinion in a thesis statement
- ☑ is sensibly organized
- ☑ supports opinions with reasons and evidence
- ☑ raises and refutes opposing arguments and objections
- ☑ addresses the audience directly
- ☑ uses persuasive language that shows the writer's commitment
- ☑ concludes with a summary or a call to action

Ask a Peer Reader

- Did my argument convince you? Why or why not?
- Which point is strongest? Did I use it in the right place?
- Does my essay seem biased? If so, could you explain how and why?
- How can I improve my conclusion?

Errors in Reasoning

Circular Reasoning trying to prove a statement by repeating it using different words ("Curfew laws are unnecessary because we don't need them.")

Overgeneralization a statement that is too broad or general to prove ("Nobody supports curfews.")

Either/Or Fallacy claiming there is one possible outcome to an action when there may be several ("Either this law passes or there will be no safety.")

False Cause assuming that one event led to another just because the second event followed the first ("Merrillville passed a curfew law, and there hasn't been a burglary there in months.")

See page R24: Identifying Faulty Reasoning

Check Your Grammar

- Use *who* as the subject of a sentence.

  > *Who is responsible for making laws?*

  Who is the subject of the verb *is*.

- Use *whom* as an object in a sentence.

  > *For whom is this law intended?*

  Whom is the object of the preposition *for*.

  See page R54: Interrogative Pronouns

Writing Online

PUBLISHING OPTIONS
For publishing options, visit the **Writing Center** at ClassZone.com.

ASSESSMENT PREPARATION
For writing and grammar assessment practice, go to the **Assessment Center** at ClassZone.com.

SPEAKING/LISTENING STANDARD
1.6.11.E.5 Participate in informal
debate around a specific topic

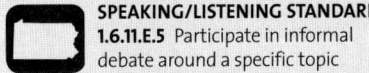

SPEAKING AND LISTENING

Debating an Issue

Further explore your feelings about your topic by debating the issue.

Planning the Debate

1. **Set up teams.** A traditional debate requires two two-person teams and a moderator. Debate participants are usually assigned to a team without regard for how each member feels about the issue.
2. **Write a clear resolution.** A resolution is a statement of the issue to be debated. Example: *The city of Concord should establish a curfew for residents under age 18.*
3. **Decide who will take the affirmative and negative positions.** The affirmative team argues in favor of the resolution. This team needs to present two to four reasons backed by strong supporting evidence. The negative team argues that the resolution should be rejected. This team must present two to four reasons backed by strong evidence to show that a problem does not exist or that a solution is already in place.
4. **Appoint a moderator.** The moderator states the resolution, introduces the debate participants, and sets and enforces time limits for speakers.
5. **Plan your position and rebuttal speeches carefully.** Do research to identify the main differences between your position and that of the opposing team. Use your research to develop specific reasons and to identify evidence to support your position. A position speech explains your argument, and a rebuttal speech rebuilds that argument after the opposing team has attacked it. When planning your rebuttal speech, think of ways that the opposition may attack your argument and decide on the best ways to respond.

Presenting the Debate

1. **Maintain eye contact.** Don't look at just one audience member— let your gaze shift from one person to another.
2. **Vary your pace and your facial expressions.** Expressions showing surprise, sadness, or disbelief can make your presentation more effective.

See page R79: Evaluate a Team in a Debate

Reading Comprehension

DIRECTIONS *Read the excerpt from the novel* All Quiet on the Western Front *and the two supplementary background selections. The Historical Background material will help you understand what was happening in Europe when the story takes place. The Author's Background material will help you understand what life experiences might have influenced the author to write this novel. Use this supplementary material to help you answer the questions.*

In All Quiet on the Western Front, *Erich Maria Remarque brings to life the horrors of combat and the tragic effects of World War I on his generation. The following excerpt from the novel recounts a conversation among young soldiers stationed along the front.*

from All Quiet on the Western Front
Erich Maria Remarque

Albert cleans his nails with a knife. We are surprised at this delicacy. But it is merely pensiveness. He puts the knife away and continues: "That's just it. Kat and Detering and Haie will go back to their jobs because they had them already. Himmelstoss too. But we never had any. How will we ever get used to one after this, here?"—he makes a gesture toward the front.

"What we'll want is a private income, and then we'll be able to live by ourselves in a wood," I say, but at once feel ashamed of this absurd idea.

"But what will really happen when we go back?" wonders Müller, and even he is troubled.

10   Kropp gives a shrug, "I don't know. Let's get back first, then we'll find out."
We are all utterly at a loss. "What could we do?" I ask.

"I don't want to do anything," replies Kropp wearily. "You'll be dead one day, so what does it matter? I don't think we'll ever go back."

"When I think about it, Albert," I say after a while rolling over on my back, "when I hear the word 'peace-time,' it goes to my head: and if it really came, I think I would do some unimaginable thing—something, you know, that it's worth having lain here in the muck for. But I can't even imagine anything. All I do know is that this business about professions and studies and salaries and so on—it makes me sick, it is and always was disgusting. I don't see anything

20   at all, Albert."

All at once everything seems to me confused and hopeless.

Kropp feels it too. "It will go pretty hard with us all. But nobody at home seems to worry much about it. Two years of shells and bombs—a man won't peel that off as easy as a sock."

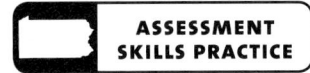
We agree that it's the same for everyone; not only for us here, but everywhere, for everyone who is of our age; to some more, and to others less. It is the common fate of our generation.

Albert expresses it: "The war has ruined us for everything."

30 He is right. We are not youth any longer. We don't want to take the world by storm. We are fleeing. We fly from ourselves. From our life. We were eighteen and had begun to love life and the world; and we had to shoot it to pieces. The first bomb, the first explosion, burst in our hearts. We are cut off from activity, from striving, from progress. We believe in such things no longer, we believe in the war.

Historical Background

World War I erupted in Europe in 1914. It was fueled by the nationalism and militarism that were rampant on the European continent. Millions of young soldiers entered a war that would not be fought as earlier wars had been. New technologies—machine guns and advanced artillery—forced troops from both sides into an elaborate system of trenches. On the western front, these trenches stretched for hundreds of miles through France and Belgium and were the bloody battlefields where the Central Powers and the Allies fought each other. Craters and barbed-wire marked the barren no man's land between the lines of trenches. Troops lived in and fought from these muddy, rat-infested trenches for months at a time. They suffered from the ravages of the seasons as well as from diseases such as trench fever, a debilitating illness spread by lice. Surprise charges from the trenches to engage the enemy in hand-to-hand battle were met by bursts of machine-gun fire and clouds of poison gas. By the end of the war, about 8.5 million soldiers had lost their lives; millions more were missing.

Those soldiers who survived the war became a generation that felt it had been robbed of its youth. The discontented German soldiers found it difficult to settle back into mainstream civilian life, especially given the economic troubles that beset Germany after its defeat. Many returning soldiers on both sides were disillusioned by the war and by their elders, who had not prepared them for its grim realities.

Author's Background

Erich Maria Remarque was born in Germany in 1898. His family was poor, but Remarque was a bright student with a keen interest in music, literature, and art. He decided to pursue a teaching career, but his college studies were interrupted in 1916, when he was drafted into the German army for service in World War I.

The 18-year-old Remarque was assigned to a trench unit near the western front, the region in northern France where the bloody fighting was deadlocked. He saw many of his friends killed or wounded in battle, and he himself was severely injured. After the war, Remarque had trouble finding a career. He took on odd jobs, including substitute teaching, writing advertising copy, and working as associate editor of a sports magazine. He faltered when he took his first steps as a novelist in 1920, but he surprised everyone with the publication of *All Quiet on the Western Front* in 1929. In this book, Remarque brought to life the horrors of combat and the tragic effects the war had on his generation. The novel made a deep impression on readers around the world.

Comprehension

DIRECTIONS *Use the Historical Background and Author's Background information to help you answer these questions about the excerpt from* All Quiet on the Western Front.

1. Which of the following quotations from the excerpt indicates that the soldiers were engaged in trench warfare?

   A "'But what will really happen when we go back?' wonders Müller, and even he is troubled." (lines 8–9)

   B . . . "I think I would do some unimaginable thing—something, you know, that it's worth having lain here in the muck for." (lines 16–17)

   C "We don't want to take the world by storm. We are fleeing. We fly from ourselves. From our life." (lines 29–30)

   D "We were eighteen and had begun to love life and the world; and we had to shoot it to pieces." (lines 30–32)

2. Which fact from the author's life probably had the greatest influence on what he wrote in lines 17–20?

   "But I can't even imagine anything. All I do know is that this business about professions and studies and salaries and so on—it makes me sick, it is and always was disgusting. I don't see anything at all, Albert."

   A his birth into a poor family at the turn of the century

   B his decision to go to college to become a teacher

   C the artillery injury he got during the war

   D the difficult time he had finding a career after the war

3. Which of the following facts from the Historical Background material best reflects what Kropp means in lines 23–24?

   "Two years of shells and bombs—a man won't peel that off as easy as a sock."

   A World War I was fueled by nationalism and militarism.

   B New types of weapons were used in World War I.

   C Returning soldiers had trouble adjusting to civilian life.

   D Millions of soldiers were killed or wounded in combat.

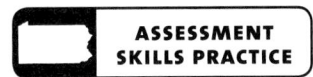

4. Which conclusion might you draw about the soldiers who fought in World War I from Albert's statement in line 28?

"The war has ruined us for everything."

A They lost their enthusiasm for life.

B They could not find work after the war.

C They were not interested in anything but the war.

D They enjoyed their wartime experiences.

5. In line 34, what does the narrator most likely mean by "we believe in the war"?

A The soldiers support Germany and the Central Powers in the war.

B The soldiers can't see beyond their immediate experience in the war.

C The soldiers really don't believe in the issues being fought over in the war.

D The soldiers are proud of their part in the war.

6. Which consequence of the war is the author most likely referring to in lines 29–33?

A that the war robbed his generation of their youth

B that some nations suffered severely from the effects of the war

C that new technology changed warfare

D that the war had serious economic effects on the modern world

Open-Ended Items

7. Reread lines 6–7. What does the narrator most likely mean when he says, "What we'll want is a private income, and then we'll be able to live by ourselves in a wood"? Cite one fact from the Historical Background material and one fact from the Author Background material to support your interpretation of this statement.

8. Describe three characters' views that reflect the author's life and times. Give specific examples from *All Quiet on the Western Front* and use the Historical Background and Author's Background evidence to support your answer.

GO ON ▶

Vocabulary

DIRECTIONS *Use context clues and your knowledge of idioms to answer the following questions.*

1. In line 11, the soldiers are described as being "utterly at a loss." Which of the following words best defines that idiom?

   A vanished

   B deprived

   C perplexed

   D injured

2. In line 15, the narrator says that the word *peace-time* "goes to my head." Which of the following phrases best defines that idiom?

   A makes me overjoyed

   B confuses me

   C angers me

   D causes me pain

3. In lines 29–30, the narrator says, "We don't want to take the world by storm." The idiom "take the world by storm" means

   A cause trouble violently

   B look for happiness

   C live in anger

   D achieve success quickly

DIRECTIONS *Use the Greek and Latin word definitions to answer the following questions.*

4. The Greek word *bombos* means "a deep and hollow sound." Which of the following words from the excerpt most likely comes from the Greek word *bombos?*

   A explosion

   B bomb

   C burst

   D absurd

5. The Greek word *genos* means "birth." Which of the following words from the excerpt most likely comes from the Greek word *genos?*

   A generation

   B disgusting

   C gesture

   D imagine

6. The Latin word *pensare* means "to consider." Which of the following words from the excerpt most likely comes from the Latin word *pensare?*

   A pensiveness

   B private

   C peace-time

   D professions

Writing & Grammar

DIRECTIONS *Read the passage and answer the questions that follow.*

(1) Wars are fought and won not just on the battlefield but on the home front as well. (2) In addition to requiring military forces, wars need to be financed and need supplies. (3) So it was with the entry of the United States into World War I. (4) The government decided that to sell Liberty Bonds was a good way to raise money. (5) Throughout cities and towns, colorful posters <u>asked</u> citizens to contribute to the war effort. (6) Many people <u>took</u> the opportunity to become involved. (7) Young men enlisted, and women knit socks for soldiers. (8) Children <u>collected</u> tin and paper. (9) In addition, many families took steps to cut out expensive purchases and to plant "victory gardens."

1. Choose the correct way to rewrite sentence 2 by adding a gerund.

   A In addition to requiring military forces, wars need financing and supplies.

   B Wars require military forces and need to be financed and supplied.

   C In addition to requiring military forces, wars have to be financed and need supplies.

   D In addition to requiring military forces, wars need to be financed and need to be supplied.

2. Choose the correct way to rewrite sentence 4 by using a gerund phrase.

   A The government decided that to sell Liberty Bonds was a good solution to raise money.

   B The government decided that selling Liberty Bonds was a good way to raise money.

   C The government was deciding to sell Liberty Bonds as a good way to raise money.

   D The government was going out to sell Liberty Bonds as a good way to raise money.

3. Choose a more vivid verb to replace the underlined word in sentence 5.

   A told   C requested

   B urged   D invited

4. Choose a more vivid verb to replace the underlined word in sentence 6.

   A accepted   C seized

   B sought   D liked

5. Choose a more vivid verb to replace the underlined word in sentence 8.

   A obtained   C carried

   B gathered   D scavenged

6. Choose the correct way to rewrite sentence 9 by using two gerund phrases.

   A In addition, many families cut out purchases that were expensive and planted victory gardens.

   B To cut out purchases that were expensive and to plant victory gardens were additional steps taken by many families.

   C In addition, many families participated by cutting out expensive purchases and planting victory gardens.

   D In addition, many families were taking steps to cut out purchases that were expensive and to plant victory gardens.

STOP

Great Reads

Ideas for Independent Reading

Which of the questions in Unit 9 intrigued you the most?
Continue exploring them with these additional works.

How does friendship begin?

Watership Down
by Richard Adams

Adams's unusual novel describes how rabbits Fiver, Hazel, and Bigwig form a friendship in the face of danger. They must flee human encroachment and warlike rabbits to find a new and safe homeland.

A Separate Peace
by John Knowles

A New England boarding school is the setting for the developing friendship between studious Gene and athletic Phineas. This is a novel of personal growth and the loss of innocence.

The Beekeeper's Apprentice
by Laurie R. King

Mary, a 15-year-old orphan, stumbles across Sherlock Holmes as he is watching bees. They become friends, and she helps the famous detective solve mysteries.

When do world events hit home?

Refuge: An Unnatural History of Family and Place
by Terry Tempest Williams

Williams chronicles the seasons around the Great Salt Lake near her Utah home. She also sees a connection between the high number of family members with cancer—herself included—and their proximity to 1950s atom bomb testing.

Small Wonder
by Barbara Kingsolver

In the wake of the events of September 11, 2001, the author writes about reasons to have hope. She considers children, conservation projects, gardening, and a new definition of the word *patriotism*.

A World of Hurt: Between Innocence and Arrogance in Vietnam
by Mary Reynolds Powell

The author, an army nurse in Vietnam, recalls the steps that led her to becoming an anti-war activist. She describes several friends who were with her in Vietnam and who have taken the same journey.

How does heritage shape identity?

Dust Tracks on a Road: An Autobiography
by Zora Neale Hurston

Hurston, a writer born in poverty in the American South, wrote during the Harlem Renaissance. She helped preserve African-American heritage as a novelist, a folklorist, and an anthropologist.

The Names: A Memoir
by N. Scott Momaday

Momaday, a Kiowa Indian, comes from a family of storytellers. His memoir extols the value of words and the voice of the speaker. He writes in many voices to tell of his childhood and youth.

Lest Innocent Blood be Shed
by Philip Hallie

The people of Le Chambon, France, were descended from Huguenots. They had suffered persecution themselves and during World War II chose to protect the Jews in their midst. They saved over 4,500 people from the Nazi concentration camps.

UNIT 10

Shakespearean Drama

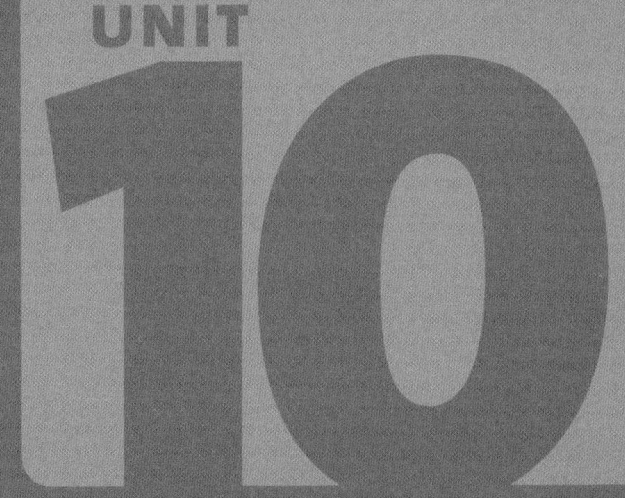

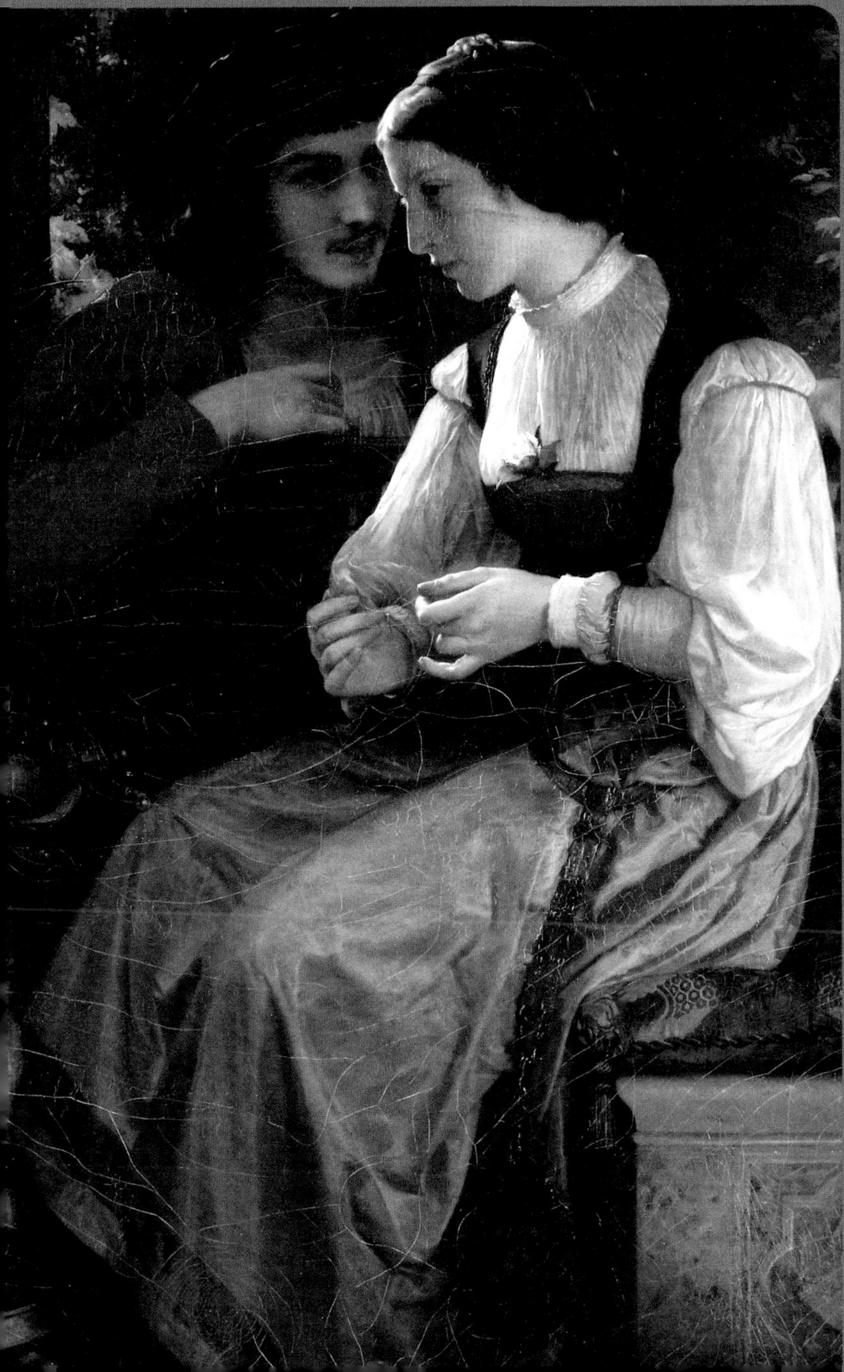

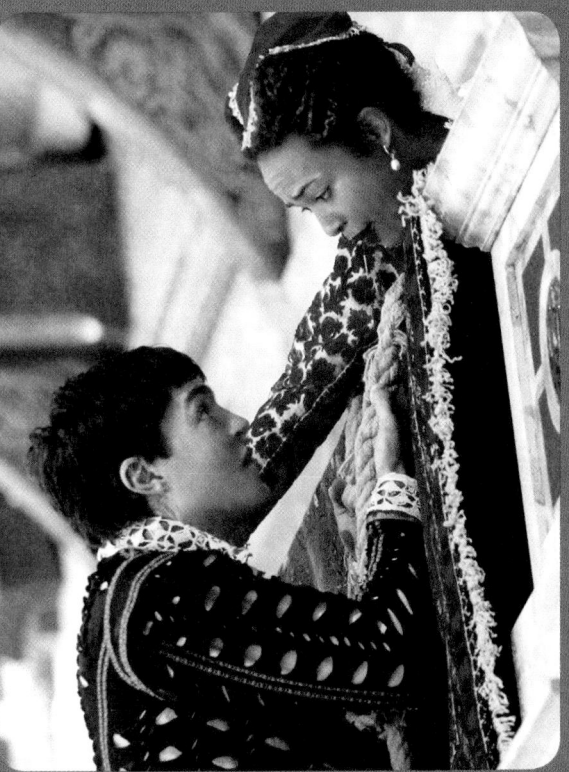

THE TRAGEDY OF ROMEO AND JULIET

- In Drama
- In Media
- In Poetry

UNIT 10

Share What You Know

What is the ultimate LOVE STORY?

From cynics to sentimentalists, almost everyone can appreciate a good **love story.** These stories are everywhere, from great literary masterpieces to last week's made-for-TV movie. One of the most famous love stories ever written is William Shakespeare's *Romeo and Juliet,* the tale of two reckless teenagers who fall in love at first sight. It is a story that has captivated readers and audiences for over 400 years.

ACTIVITY With a partner, think of a few love stories you remember reading or watching. Whether it's an old-fashioned fairy tale or a modern romantic comedy, a tear-jerker novel or a film featuring the couple you love to hate, which story do you remember most vividly? Working together, make a list of titles and then settle on the tale *you* consider the ultimate love story.

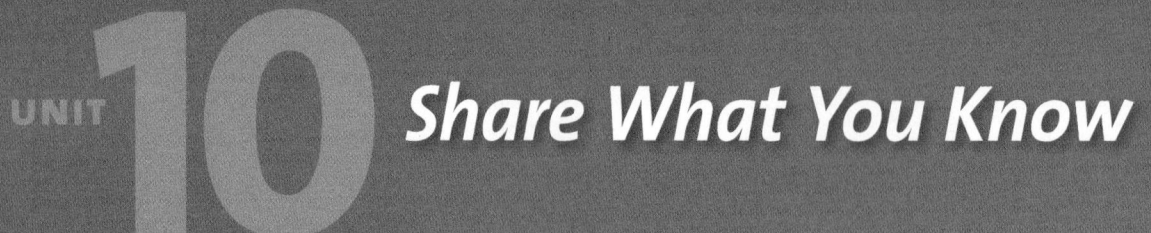

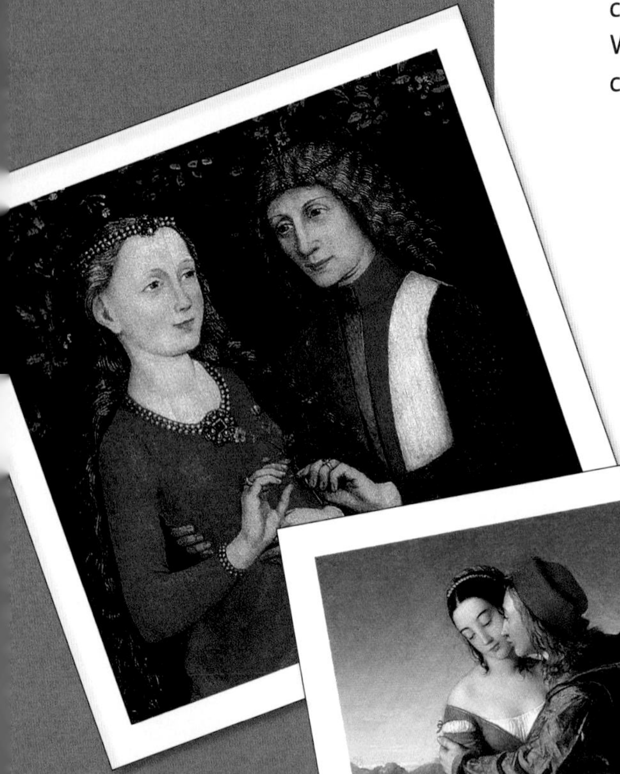

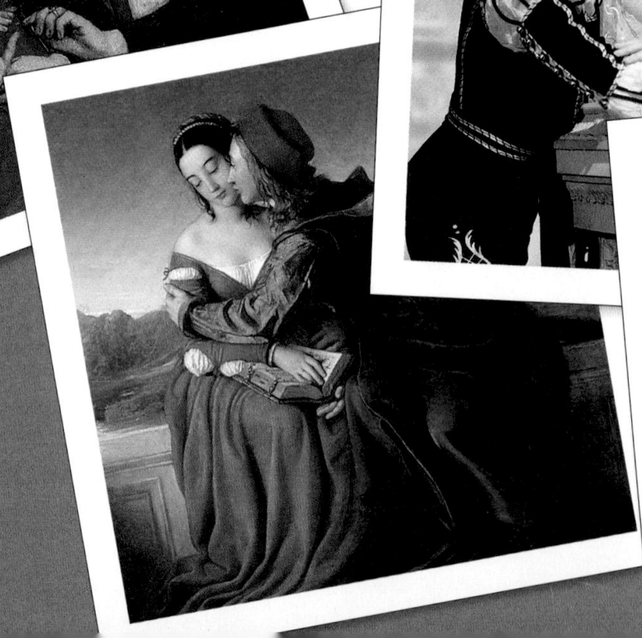

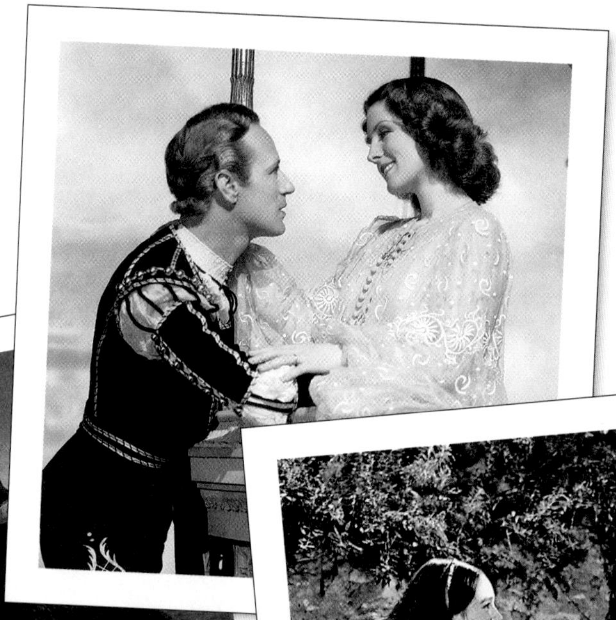

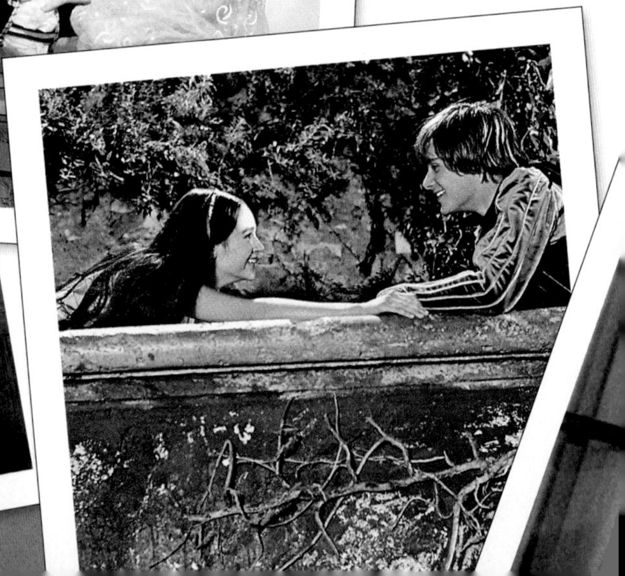

PENNSYLVANIA STANDARDS

Preview Unit Goals

LITERARY ANALYSIS
- Identify the characteristics of Shakespearean drama and tragedy
- Identify and analyze Shakespearean language, including word play and blank verse
- Identify and analyze character foils and the tragic hero
- Identify and analyze soliloquies, asides, and allusions
- Analyze influence of historical and cultural context
- Interpret literature in relation to its literary period

READING
- Use strategies for reading Shakespearean drama, including keeping track of events and character relationships
- Paraphrase passages as an aid to comprehension
- Identify and analyze a critical review
- Compare and contrast a critical review with your own response

WRITING AND GRAMMAR
- Compare a film with a play
- Understand and use parallel structure

SPEAKING, LISTENING, AND VIEWING
- Identify, analyze, and evaluate mise en scène
- Create a visual treatment
- Stage a scene

ACADEMIC VOCABULARY
- tragedy
- tragic hero
- character foil
- word play and blank verse
- soliloquy and aside
- allusion
- paraphrase
- critical review

Shakespeare's World

England in Shakespeare's Day

Renaissance Man
William Shakespeare is widely considered to be the greatest writer in the English language and the greatest playwright of all time. His plays have been produced more often and in more countries than those of any other

**William Shakespeare
1564–1616**

author. Shakespeare lived in England during the flowering of intellectual activity known as the Renaissance. The European Renaissance was marked by a renewed interest in science, commerce, philosophy, and the arts. Basic to Renaissance thinking was a new emphasis on the individual and on freedom of choice. The Renaissance movement began in 14th-century Italy and gradually moved north and west toward England, where it reached its peak during the reign of Queen Elizabeth I. Shakespeare started his literary career during Elizabeth's reign, a period that lasted from 1558 to 1603 and is often called the Elizabethan Age.

All Hail the Queen Elizabeth was the last member of England's royal house of Tudor. Her grandfather, King Henry VII, brought stability and prosperity to his kingdom, and it was during his

reign that Renaissance ideas began taking hold in England. However, political and religious problems surfaced during the reign of Elizabeth's father, Henry VIII, and continued into the early years of Elizabeth's own reign. Luckily, Elizabeth proved to be a strong monarch, able to guide England along a more moderate and prosperous course. It was a course that most Elizabethans, including Shakespeare, seem to have appreciated.

Like her grandfather and father before her, Elizabeth I was a strong supporter of English culture. As a result, artists of all types—including playwrights, poets, painters, sculptors, musicians, and architects—were held in high esteem. Taking the cue from their monarch, members of England's upper class often became patrons, or financial sponsors, of the arts. In the early 1590s, Shakespeare began acting in and writing plays for a theater company sponsored by two men who had both held the office of lord chamberlain, a high-ranking position in Elizabeth's court. The company was called the Lord Chamberlain's Men, and Elizabeth herself attended some of its productions.

**Queen Elizabeth I
1533–1603**

Theater in Shakespeare's Day

A Writer for All Time Though acting companies toured throughout England, London was the center of the Elizabethan stage. In 1576, well before Shakespeare became affiliated with the Lord Chamberlain's Men, the company built England's first theater in the suburbs of London; by the end of the 1590s, London boasted more theaters than any other European capital. One reason the London theaters did so well was that they attracted an audience of rich and poor alike. In fact, the Elizabethan theater was one of the few forms of entertainment available to working-class people of the day, and one of the few places where the working class and the educated upper class could mix. Shakespeare appealed to English audience members of all classes by including a great deal of variety in his plays: poetic speeches, exciting action, fast-paced humor, vivid character portrayals, and wise observations about human nature. Thus, while he was respected by the rich and powerful people of his day, he also became very popular with the common people.

Around the Globe In 1599, Shakespeare and the other shareholders of the Lord Chamberlain's Men became joint owners of the company's new home, the Globe Theatre. The Globe was a three-story wooden structure with an open-air courtyard in the center. Actors performed on a raised platform stage. The theater could hold 3,000 spectators, many of whom stood in the part of the courtyard near the stage, known as the pit. These customers paid the lowest admission charge, usually just a penny. Richer theatergoers paid more and sat in the inner balconies, which surrounded most of the courtyard. Audiences became emotionally involved in performances, openly showing their pleasure or their disappointment. They cheered, booed, hissed, and even threw rotten vegetables. They applauded agile sword fighting and dramatic sound effects, such as blares of trumpets, drum rolls, and claps of thunder.

THE GLOBE

This illustration shows what scholars believe the Globe Theatre looked like.

1 raised platform stage

2 pit

3 courtyard

4 inner balconies

Impact on Language

Elizabethan theater relied heavily on the audience's imagination. Most theaters had no curtains, no artificial lighting, and very little scenery. Instead, props, sound effects, and sometimes lines of dialogue let the audience know when and where a scene took place. However, while the staging was simple, it was hardly dull. Swords, shields, brightly colored banners, and elegant costumes often added to the spectacle. The costumes also helped audiences imagine that women were playing the female roles, which in fact were played by young male actors. In Shakespeare's day, no women belonged to English acting companies—it was considered improper for women to appear on stage. The boys who played female roles underwent rigorous training in acting, singing, and dancing. Before one could play a role such as Juliet in a first-rate company, he had to learn to move gracefully and speak convincingly.

HIS WORDS LIVE ON
Shakespeare continues to influence modern culture, as the following images demonstrate.

Word Master Shakespeare was a master of dramatic language and a great experimenter with spoken English. He was clever and imaginative, playing with words and their meanings and creating striking images that, once heard or read, are rarely forgotten.

Shakespeare contributed more words, phrases, and expressions to the English language than any other writer. Some of these words were his own invention, including *assassination, bump,* and *lonely.* Other expressions might have been part of the everyday speech of Elizabethan England, but Shakespeare was the first to use them in writing, and their inclusion in his plays gave them a permanent place in the language.

Many of these phrases and expressions have become so common that people use them without realizing that they are quoting Shakespeare. In fact, the expressions have become "household words"— a term first used in Shakespeare's historical play *Henry V.* Other expressions that have become part of the language include "dead as a doornail" (*Henry VI, Part 2*), "laughingstock" (*The Merry Wives of Windsor*), and "for goodness' sake" (*Henry VIII*). Shakespeare's fine ear for the English language prompted the British writer George Orwell to call him a "word musician."

Actors from a popular 1993 film based on Shakespeare's *Much Ado About Nothing*

"He's, like, 'To be or not to be,' and I'm, like, 'Get a life.'"

A cartoon from the *New Yorker* magazine does a takeoff on *Hamlet.*

More About the Man

The Bard of Avon Although Shakespeare is probably the most famous writer who ever lived, it is largely through his plays and poetry that we know him. The known facts about his personal life are surprisingly few. We know that he came from Stratford-on-Avon, a small town on the river Avon about 90 miles northwest of London. His father was a glove maker who later became the town's mayor; his mother was a distant relative of a wealthy family who lived just outside town. Church records indicate that Shakespeare was baptized on April 26, 1564, which suggests that he was born a few days earlier. He probably went to the local grammar school, although school records no longer exist. There he would have studied Latin and read works by ancient Roman writers, such as Virgil and Seneca.

Making His Way At 18, Shakespeare married Anne Hathaway, a local farmer's daughter. The couple had a daughter named Susanna in 1583 and boy and girl twins named Hamnet and Judith two years later. There are no records of what Shakespeare did in the next seven years, which some scholars call the "lost years" of his life. During that time he apparently left his family back in Stratford, where they could live comfortably, and made his way to London, center of the theater world. He probably joined a theater company and traveled with it as an actor. When next we hear of Shakespeare, it is as a successful playwright and sometime actor in London. His earliest plays include *Richard III* and *The Comedy of Errors;* he also was writing lyric and narrative poetry. In 1593 he published his long poem *Venus and Adonis,* apparently written during the 1592–1593 season, when London's theaters were shut because of an outbreak of the plague.

Fame and Fortune By 1596, the year *Romeo and Juliet* was probably first performed, ten of Shakespeare's plays had already been produced in London, and he was a shareholder in the Lord Chamberlain's Men. Shakespeare's plays helped make the theater company the most successful of its day. In 1599, he became part owner of London's popular new Globe Theatre. In 1603, when James I succeeded Elizabeth I on the throne of England, the new king himself became the patron of Shakespeare's theater company, which became known as the King's Men. Shakespeare's business interests and revenues from plays brought him a good deal of money, enough to purchase a beautiful home for his family in Stratford. He also may have purchased a coat of arms for his father, an important symbol that allowed his father to move officially into the ranks of gentlemen.

The End In 1609, Shakespeare took advantage of his fame by publishing his sonnets, a series of poems about love and friendship that most scholars feel he wrote in the 1590s. Shakespeare also began spending more time in Stratford, retiring there permanently in 1613. He wrote no plays after that year; his last complete plays are believed to be *Cymbeline, The Tempest, The Winter's Tale,* and *Henry VIII.* While there are no documentary records of the date of his death, the monument that marks his grave indicates that he died on April 23, 1616.

MORE ABOUT THE AUTHOR
For more on William Shakespeare, visit the **Literature Center** at **ClassZone.com.**

OTHER PLAYS BY WILLIAM SHAKESPEARE

- *Hamlet*
- *Julius Caesar*
- *King Lear*
- *Macbeth*
- *A Midsummer Night's Dream*
- *Much Ado About Nothing*
- *Othello*
- *Richard II*
- *Twelfth Night*

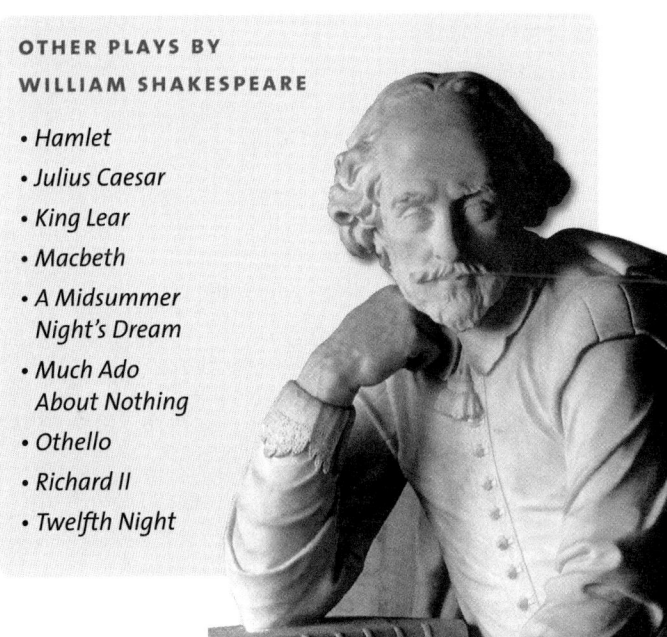

Shakespearean Drama

"If we wish to know the force of human genius," the writer William Hazlitt once proclaimed, "we should read Shakespeare." Though he wrote them over 400 years ago, Shakespeare's 37 plays are arguably as popular today as they were in Elizabethan times; they still draw avid fans to packed theaters. Shakespeare's comedies and histories remain crowd-pleasing classics, but his tragedies are perhaps his most powerful plays. One of Shakespeare's most famous tragedies is *The Tragedy of Romeo and Juliet*, the story of two lovestruck teenagers from feuding families.

PENNSYLVANIA STANDARDS

READING STANDARDS
B.1.1.1.A.1 Evaluate character
B.1.1.1.C.1 Evaluate elements of the plot
B.1.1.1.D.2 Evaluate the relationship between theme and other components

Part 1: Characteristics of Shakespearean Tragedy

A **tragedy** is a drama that ends in catastrophe—most often death—for the main characters. Shakespearean tragedies, however, offer more than just despair; they also include comic moments that counter the overall seriousness of the plot. Familiarize yourself with the characters and dramatic conventions of Shakespearean tragedy before you begin reading *Romeo and Juliet*.

CHARACTERS

Tragic Hero
- is the **protagonist,** or central character—the one with whom audiences identify
- usually fails or dies because of a character flaw or a cruel twist of fate
- often has a high rank or status; shows strength while facing his or her destiny

Antagonist
- is the force working against the protagonist
- can be another character, a group of characters, or something nonhuman, such as nature or society

Foil
- is a character whose personality and attitude contrast sharply with those of another character
- highlights both characters' traits—for example, a timid character can make a talkative one seem even chattier

DRAMATIC CONVENTIONS

Soliloquy
- is a speech given by a character alone on stage
- lets the audience know what the character is thinking or feeling

Aside
- is a character's remark, either to the audience or to another character, that others on stage do not hear
- reveals the character's private thoughts

Dramatic Irony
- is when the audience knows more than the characters—for example, the audience is aware of Romeo and Juliet's tragic demise long before the characters themselves face it
- helps build suspense

Comic Relief
- is a humorous scene or speech intended to lighten the mood
- serves to heighten the seriousness of the main action by contrast

MODEL 1: CHARACTER IN TRAGEDY

In this excerpt, Romeo—the young protagonist of the play and a member of the Montague family—complains to his cousin, Benvolio, about a problem that is plaguing him. What do you learn about Romeo's personality?

from Act One, SCENE 1

Lines 153–161

Benvolio. Good morrow, cousin.

Romeo.   Is the day so young?

Benvolio. But new struck nine.

Romeo.   Ay me! sad hours seem long.
155 Was that my father that went hence so fast?

Benvolio. It was. What sadness lengthens Romeo's hours?

Romeo. Not having that which having makes them short.

Benvolio. In love?

Romeo. Out—

160 **Benvolio.** Of love?

Romeo. Out of her favor where I am in love.

Close Read

1. What is Romeo experiencing that most readers could relate to?

2. What possible weakness or flaw does Romeo's attitude hint at?

MODEL 2: SOLILOQUY

Through this soliloquy, readers gain access to the thoughts and feelings of Juliet, a Capulet and therefore a hated enemy of any Montague.

from Act Three, SCENE 2

Lines 20–31

20 **Juliet.** . . . Come, gentle night; come, loving, black-browed night;
Give me my Romeo; and, when he shall die,
Take him and cut him out in little stars,
And he will make the face of heaven so fine
That all the world will be in love with night
25 And pay no worship to the garish sun.
O, I have bought the mansion of a love,
But not possessed it; and though I am sold,
Not yet enjoyed. So tedious is this day
As is the night before some festival
30 To an impatient child that hath new robes
And may not wear them. . . .

Close Read

1. What does the imagery in lines 20–25 reveal about Juliet's feelings for Romeo?

2. Reread the boxed text. What is Juliet's mood as she waits for Romeo? Point out specific words and details that reveal her state of mind.

Part 2: The Language of Shakespeare

Shakespeare's plays deal with experiences and emotions that are easy to relate to, but his language can be challenging for modern readers to decipher. However, once you get past the play's unfamiliar language, learn the rhythm of its poetry, and discover how to decode Shakespeare's allusions and puns, you will come to appreciate the romance, drama, and humor that await you.

BLANK VERSE

Shakespeare wrote his plays primarily in **blank verse,** the form of poetry that most resembles natural speech. Blank verse is made up of unrhymed lines of **iambic pentameter,** a type of meter that has five unstressed syllables (˘), each followed by a stressed syllable (´). Read the following lines aloud, making sure to emphasize each stressed syllable:

> ˘ ´ ˘ ´ ˘ ´ ˘ ´ ˘ ´
> Yet tell me not, for I have heard it all.
>
> ˘ ´ ˘ ´ ˘ ´ ˘ ´ ˘ ´
> Here's much to do with hate but more with love.

While this pattern is the general rule, it is often broken. Variations in the rhythm prevent the play from sounding monotonous. Breaks in the pattern also help to emphasize important ideas or dramatic moments. As you read, pay close attention to places where characters speak in rhyming poetry instead of unrhymed prose.

ALLUSION AND WORD PLAY

An **allusion** is a reference, within a work, to something that the audience is expected to know. Shakespeare's audience was familiar with Greek and Roman mythology as well as the Bible, so he sprinkled references to these works throughout his plays. In this romantic tragedy, Shakespeare included allusions to Venus, the Roman goddess of love.

Shakespeare was also a master of clever **puns,** or jokes that result from multiple word meanings or rhyming sounds. In Act One, a depressed Romeo puns on two meanings of the word *light* when he offers to carry a torch: "Being but heavy, I will bear the light."

MODEL 1: BLANK VERSE

The fact that Shakespeare wrote in verse should not intimidate you.
Since iambic pentameter is fairly close to English speech patterns, it can
be spoken naturally, without much awkwardness. Read the following
excerpt aloud to get a feel for its rhythm.

from Act Two, SCENE 2

Lines 2–6

But soft! What light through yonder window breaks?
It is the East, and Juliet is the sun!
Arise, fair sun, and kill the envious moon,
5 Who is already sick and pale with grief
That thou her maid art far more fair than she.

Close Read

1. Reread the excerpt, tapping your foot at each stressed syllable. How many stressed syllables are in each line?

2. Point out a place where the pattern breaks. One example has been boxed. What ideas are emphasized by these variations in rhythm?

MODEL 2: ALLUSION AND WORD PLAY

For a tragedy, *Romeo and Juliet* contains quite a bit of humor. In the first
two acts, much of the comedy comes courtesy of Mercutio, who clowns
around, trying to make his friend Romeo laugh. Look for several puns and
an allusion in this comic conversation.

from Act One, SCENE 4

Lines 13–22

Mercutio. Nay, gentle Romeo, we must have you dance.

Romeo. Not I, believe me. You have dancing shoes
15 With nimble soles; I have a soul of lead
So stakes me to the ground I cannot move.

Mercutio. You are a lover. Borrow Cupid's wings
And soar with them above a common bound.

Romeo. I am too sore enpierced with his shaft
20 To soar with his light feathers, and so bound
I cannot bound a pitch above dull woe.
Under love's heavy burden do I sink.

Close Read

1. Identify the allusion in this excerpt, and describe the mental image it conjures up for you. Why do you think Shakespeare included this reference?

2. One example of a pun has been boxed. Find one other example and explain the play on words.

Part 3: Reading Shakespearean Drama

As you read *Romeo and Juliet,* you will encounter tools and strategies on every page. The following tips will show you how to make the most of them:

READING DRAMA

- Study the opening **cast of characters** to see who's in the play.

- Read the **stage directions** to find out where a scene takes place as well as who's on stage and what they're doing. Stage directions in *Romeo and Juliet* are minimal, so you'll sometimes have to infer what's happening from the dialogue.

- Visualize the setting and the action by noting key details in the stage directions and the **synopsis** at the beginning of every scene.

READING SHAKESPEAREAN TRAGEDY

- Keep track of the characters' relationships, such as whether they are friends, relatives, or enemies. Also think about what role a character has—tragic hero, antagonist, foil, or comic relief. This will help you interpret his or her speech and actions.

- Note important character traits revealed through **dialogue, soliloquies,** and **asides** as well as the action. Consider whether the characters exhibit any flaws or weaknesses.

- Look for cause-and-effect relationships between events, especially those events that lead to the tragic outcome. Track them in a graphic like the one shown.

Cause	Effect
As part of a plan to cheer up Romeo, Benvolio and other Montagues bring him to a party that the Capulets are throwing.	At the party, Romeo sees Juliet for the first time and falls madly in love.

READING SHAKESPEARE'S LANGUAGE

- Use the **marginal notes** to help you figure out unfamiliar words and unusual sentence structures. In a chart like this one, record difficult lines and then rephrase them to read like modern speech.

- **Paraphrase** passages to help clarify their meaning. Remember, when you paraphrase something, you restate the main ideas using your own words.

- Just as when you read poetry, don't automatically stop reading when you come to the end of a line. Look carefully at each line's punctuation and consider the meaning of the complete sentence or phrase.

Text	What It Really Says	What It Means
"O Romeo, Romeo! wherefore art thou Romeo?" Juliet, Act Two, Scene 2, line 33	"Why are you Romeo?"	Why do you have to be a Montague, an enemy of my family?

MODEL: READING SHAKESPEAREAN DRAMA

This fight scene takes place in a public square in Verona, the city in which the play is set. Sampson and Gregory, servants of the Capulets, have gotten into a heated argument with Abram and Balthasar, servants of the Montagues. Use the strategies you learned on the preceding page and what you already know about tragedy to analyze this episode.

from Act One, SCENE 1

Lines 51–67

[*Enter* Benvolio, *nephew of Montague and first cousin of Romeo.*]

Gregory [*aside to* Sampson]. Say "better." Here comes one of my master's kinsmen.

Sampson. Yes, better, sir.

Abram. You lie.

55 **Sampson.** Draw, if you be men. Gregory, remember thy swashing blow.

[*They fight.*]

Benvolio. Part, fools! [*beats down their swords*] Put up your swords. You know not what you do.

[*Enter* Tybalt, *hot-headed nephew of Lady Capulet and first cousin of Juliet.*]

Tybalt. What, art thou drawn among these heartless hinds?

60 Turn thee, Benvolio! look upon thy death.

Benvolio. I do but keep the peace. Put up thy sword, Or manage it to part these men with me.

Tybalt. What, drawn, and talk of peace? I hate the word
As I hate hell, all Montagues, and thee.
65 Have at thee, coward!

[*They fight.*]

[*Enter several of both houses, who join the fray; then enter* Citizens *and* Peace Officers, *with clubs.*]

Officer. Clubs, bills, and partisans! Strike! beat them down!

Citizens. Down with the Capulets! Down with the Montagues!

51–52 Gregory notices that Tybalt, a Capulet, is arriving.

59–65 Tybalt does not understand that Benvolio is trying to stop the fight. He challenges Benvolio.

59 heartless hinds: cowardly servants.

63 drawn: with your sword out.

65 Have at thee: Defend yourself.

66 bills, and partisans: spears.

Close Read

1. First, read through this excerpt. Then describe the setting, characters, and action you visualized as you read. Cite details from the dialogue and stage directions that helped you form a mental image.

2. What is Benvolio trying to do when Tybalt enters? Support your answer.

3. Using the marginal notes as necessary, paraphrase Tybalt's speech in the boxed lines. Why does Tybalt hate Benvolio so much?

4. How would you characterize Tybalt on the basis of this excerpt? In what way is he different from Benvolio? Cite details from the text to support your answer.

Part 4: Analyze the Literature

Apply the skills you've learned in this workshop as you analyze a longer excerpt from the beginning of the tragedy. This scene takes place at a costume party hosted by the Capulets. Disguised by their masks, Romeo and other Montagues have crashed the party. The important moment that follows—when Romeo notices Juliet from across the room and falls in love at first sight—sets the course of tragic events in motion.

from Act One, SCENE 5

Lines 14–62

[Maskers *appear with* Capulet, Lady Capulet, Juliet, *all the* Guests, *and* Servants.]

Capulet. Welcome, gentlemen! Ladies that have their toes

15 Unplagued with corns will have a bout with you.
Ah ha, my mistresses! which of you all
Will now deny to dance? She that makes dainty,
She I'll swear hath corns. Am I come near ye now?
Welcome, gentlemen! I have seen the day

20 That I have worn a visor and could tell
A whispering tale in a fair lady's ear,
Such as would please. 'Tis gone, 'tis gone, 'tis gone!
You are welcome, gentlemen! Come, musicians, play.
A hall, a hall! give room! and foot it, girls.

[*Music plays and they dance.*]

25 More light, you knaves! and turn the tables up,
And quench the fire, the room is grown too hot.
Ah, sirrah, this unlooked-for sport comes well.
Nay, sit, nay, sit, good cousin Capulet,
For you and I are past our dancing days.

30 How long is't now since last yourself and I
Were in a mask?

Second Capulet. By'r Lady, thirty years.

Capulet. What, man? 'Tis not so much, 'tis not so much!

14–27 Capulet welcomes his guests and invites them all to dance. At the same time, like a good host, he is trying to get the party going. He alternates talking with his guests and telling the servants what to do.

17–18 She that . . . corns: Any woman too shy to dance will be assumed to have corns, ugly and painful growths on the toes.

20 visor: mask.

28–38 Capulet and his relative watch the dancing as they talk of days gone by.

Close Read

1. Choose a passage with several unfamiliar or Elizabethan words. Paraphrase the passage, using the marginal notes and the word list on page 932 as necessary.

2. Consider Capulet's behavior toward his guests and his treatment of his servants. How would you describe Capulet? Support your answer with details from the text.

'Tis since the nuptial of Lucentio,
Come Pentecost as quickly as it will,
35 Some five-and-twenty years, and then we masked.
     Second Capulet. 'Tis more, 'tis more! His son is elder,
       sir;
His son is thirty.
     Capulet.   Will you tell me that?
His son was but a ward two years ago.
     Romeo [*to a* Servingman]. What lady's that, which
       doth enrich the hand
40 Of yonder knight?
     Servant. I know not, sir.

     Romeo. O, she doth teach the torches to burn
       bright!
It seems she hangs upon the cheek of night
Like a rich jewel in an Ethiop's ear—
45 Beauty too rich for use, for earth too dear!
So shows a snowy dove trooping with crows
As yonder lady o'er her fellows shows.
The measure done, I'll watch her place of stand
And, touching hers, make blessed my rude hand.
50 Did my heart love till now? Forswear it, sight!
For I ne'er saw true beauty till this night.

     Tybalt. This, by his voice, should be a Montague.
Fetch me my rapier, boy. What, dares the slave
Come hither, covered with an antic face,
55 To fleer and scorn at our solemnity?
Now, by the stock and honor of my kin,
To strike him dead I hold it not a sin.
     Capulet. Why, how now, kinsman? Wherefore storm
       you so?
     Tybalt. Uncle, this is a Montague, our foe;
60 A villain, that is hither come in spite,
To scorn at our solemnity this night.
     Capulet. Young Romeo is it?
     Tybalt.   'Tis he, that villain Romeo.

33 nuptial: marriage.

39–40 Romeo has spotted Juliet across the dance floor and is immediately entranced by her beauty.

44–45 Ethiop's ear: the ear of an Ethiopian (African); **for earth too dear:** too precious for this world.

52–57 Tybalt recognizes Romeo's voice and tells his servant to get his sword (**rapier**). He thinks Romeo has come to make fun of (**fleer**) their party.

Close Read

3. Reread the boxed text. How is the pattern of Romeo's smitten speech different from the pattern of earlier lines in this scene?

4. Reread lines 52–57. What does Tybalt want to do to Romeo? Explain what has made Tybalt so enraged.

5. Tybalt is just one of many antagonists working against Romeo and Juliet. Cite details that reveal Tybalt's searing hatred of Romeo.

6. Given what you know about the characters' personalities, what do you think might happen next between Romeo and Tybalt? Support your prediction with evidence.

The Tragedy of Romeo and Juliet
Drama by William Shakespeare

Is LOVE *stronger than* HATE?

PENNSYLVANIA STANDARDS

READING STANDARDS
B.1.1.1.A.1 Evaluate character
B.1.1.1.C.1 Evaluate elements of the plot

KEY IDEA It sounds like a story ripped from the tabloids. Two teenagers fall in **love** at a party. Then they learn that their parents **hate** each other. The teenagers' love is forbidden, so not surprisingly, they cling to each other even more tightly. Murder and suffering ensue, and by the end, a whole town is in mourning. What love can—and cannot—overcome is at the heart of *Romeo and Juliet*, considered by many to be the greatest love story of all time.

DEBATE People say that love conquers all. Is this statement true, or is it just a cliché? How powerful *is* love? Discuss this topic in a small group. Talk about instances in which love has brought people together as well as times when hate has driven them apart. Then form two teams and debate the age-old question, Is love stronger than hate?

LITERARY ANALYSIS: SHAKESPEAREAN DRAMA

You can probably guess that a **tragedy** isn't going to end with the words "and they all lived happily ever after." Shakespearean tragedies are dramas that end in disaster—most often death—for the main characters. The conflicts in a tragedy are usually set in motion by the main characters' actions, but fate can also play a part in the catastrophic course of events. As you read *Romeo and Juliet,* pay attention to specific characteristics of Shakespearean drama.

- Notice what **soliloquies** and **asides** reveal about the characters. Reading these is like being around when someone is "thinking out loud"—you may learn valuable information about characters' private thoughts.

- Watch for and analyze **allusions.** Once you decode them, they add an extra layer of meaning to certain passages.

- Consider Shakespeare's use of **comic relief** to ease the tension of certain scenes. Think of the comic episodes as brief breaks that allow you to absorb earlier events in the plot and get ready for new developments.

- Pay attention to the rhythm of each line. Shakespeare wrote his plays in **blank verse,** a poetic form that resembles the rhythm of natural speech.

READING STRATEGY: READING SHAKESPEAREAN DRAMA

Though his plays can sweep you away, Shakespeare's English is sometimes hard for modern readers to understand. These strategies can help:

- Read the synopsis, or summary, of each scene to get an idea of what happens in that part of the play.

- Use the marginal notes to figure out the meanings of unfamiliar words, unusual grammatical structures, and allusions.

- Keep track of events to make the plot easier to follow. All the events in *Romeo and Juliet* take place in six days. As you read, use a chart to record plot developments and interactions between characters.

Sunday	Monday	Tuesday	Wednesday	Thursday	Friday
street brawl					

Overview

Act One We meet the Montagues and the Capulets, two long-feuding families in the Italian city of Verona. At the beginning of the play, Romeo, a Montague, is in love with Rosaline. Juliet, a Capulet, is asked by her parents to consider marrying Paris. Romeo and Juliet meet at a masked ball and fall in love, each later realizing that the other is from the enemy family.

Act Two Forced to meet in secret, Romeo and Juliet declare their love to each other and decide to get married. Romeo visits Friar Laurence, a priest, and asks him to perform the wedding. Aided by Juliet's nurse, Romeo and Juliet meet and marry in secret.

Act Three During a street fight, Juliet's cousin Tybalt kills Romeo's friend Mercutio. Romeo loses his temper and kills Tybalt; he then flees, realizing with horror what he has done. Romeo is banished from Verona under pain of death. Juliet grieves the double loss of her cousin and her husband. With the help of Friar Laurence and the nurse, Romeo and Juliet make plans to flee to Mantua, another city. Her parents, not knowing she is already married to Romeo, order her to marry Paris.

Act Four A distraught Juliet visits Friar Laurence for help and threatens to kill herself. He gives her a potion that will not kill her but put her into a deathlike sleep for two days, with the plan that Romeo will rescue her from the family tomb when she awakens. Friar Laurence sends a letter to Romeo in Mantua, describing this plan. Juliet takes the potion. Her family finds her and prepares her burial, believing her dead.

Act Five Romeo does not get Friar Laurence's letter before he hears of Juliet's death and believes it is real. Grief stricken, he returns to Verona. He finds Juliet in her deathlike sleep, takes real poison, and dies. Juliet awakens and, finding Romeo dead, kills herself with his dagger. When the families realize what has happened, Lord Capulet and Lord Montague agree to end their feud.

THE TRAGEDY OF
Romeo & Juliet

WILLIAM SHAKESPEARE

**GO BEHIND
THE CURTAIN**

One Play, Many Productions
The images at the top
of page 941 capture five
different interpretations of
Romeo and Juliet. Though
the productions were
staged at different times
in different countries, each
director had the same goal:
to thrill audiences with
Shakespeare's timeless tale
of two reckless, lovesick
teenagers. As you read
the play, you will discover
many more images from
a variety of productions.
You'll also encounter **Behind
the Curtain** feature pages
that will help you explore
the stagecraft used to
create moving theatrical
productions of this
famous play.

TIME
The 14th century

CAST

THE MONTAGUES

Lord Montague (mŏn'tə-gyōō')

Lady Montague

Romeo, son of Montague

Benvolio (bĕn-vō'lē-ō), nephew
of Montague and friend of Romeo

Balthasar (bäl'thə-sär'), servant
to Romeo

Abram, servant to Montague

THE CAPULETS

Lord Capulet (kăp'yōō-lĕt')

Lady Capulet

Juliet, daughter of Capulet

Tybalt (tĭb'əlt), nephew of Lady
Capulet

Nurse to Juliet

Peter, servant to Juliet's nurse

Sampson, servant to Capulet

Gregory, servant to Capulet

An Old Man of the Capulet family

PLACE
Verona (və-rō'nə) and Mantua
(măn'chōō-ə) in northern Italy

OTHERS

Prince Escalus (ĕs'kə-ləs), ruler of
Verona

Mercutio (mĕr-kyōō'shē-ō), kinsman
of the prince and friend of Romeo

Friar Laurence, a Franciscan priest

Friar John, another Franciscan priest

Count Paris, a young nobleman,
kinsman of the prince

Apothecary (ə-pŏth'ĭ-kĕr'ē)

Page to Paris

Chief Watchman

Three Musicians

An Officer

Chorus

Citizens of Verona, **Gentlemen**
and **Gentlewomen** of both houses,
**Maskers, Torchbearers, Pages,
Guards, Watchmen, Servants,** and
Attendants

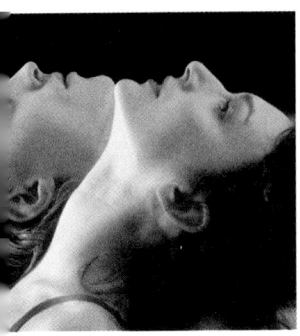

Prologue

The Chorus is one actor who serves as a narrator. He enters from the back of the stage to introduce and explain the theme of the play. His job is to "hook" the audience's interest by telling them just enough to quiet them down and make them eager for more. In this prologue, or preview, the narrator explains that the play will be about a feud between two families (the Capulets and the Montagues). In addition, the narrator says that the feud will end in tragedy. As you read the prologue, determine what the tragedy will be.

[*Enter* Chorus.]

Chorus. Two households, both alike in dignity,
In fair Verona, where we lay our scene,
From ancient grudge break to new mutiny,
Where civil blood makes civil hands unclean.
5 From forth the fatal loins of these two foes,
A pair of star-crossed lovers take their life,
Whose misadventured piteous overthrows
Doth with their death bury their parents' strife.
The fearful passage of their death-marked love,
10 And the continuance of their parents' rage,
Which, but their children's end, naught could remove,
Is now the two hours' traffic of our stage,
The which if you with patient ears attend,
What here shall miss, our toil shall strive to mend.

[*Exit.*]

3–4 ancient . . . unclean: A new outbreak of fighting (**mutiny**) between families has caused the citizens of Verona to have one another's blood on their hands.

6 star-crossed: doomed. The position of the stars when the lovers were born was not favorable. In Shakespeare's day, people took astrology very seriously.

7 misadventured: unlucky.

11 but: except for; **naught:** nothing.

12 the two hours' . . . stage: what will be shown on the stage in the next two hours.

14 what . . . mend: The play will fill in the details not mentioned in the prologue.

Act One

SCENE 1   *A public square in Verona.*

As the scene opens, two young Capulet servants swagger across the stage, joking and bragging. When they happen to meet servants from the rival house of Montague, a quarrel begins that grows into an ugly street fight. Finally the ruler of Verona, Prince Escalus, appears. He is angry about the violence in his city and warns that the next offenders will receive the death penalty. The crowd fades away, and the stage is set for the entrance of Romeo, heir of the Montague family. Romeo, infatuated and miserable, can talk of nothing but his love for Rosaline and her cruelty in refusing to love him back.

[*Enter* Sampson *and* Gregory, *servants of the house of Capulet, armed with swords and bucklers (shields).*]

Sampson. Gregory, on my word, we'll not carry coals.

Gregory. No, for then we should be colliers.

Sampson. I mean, an we be in choler, we'll draw.

Gregory. Ay, while you live, draw your neck out of collar.

5 **Sampson.** I strike quickly, being moved.

Gregory. But thou art not quickly moved to strike.

Sampson. A dog of that house of Montague moves me.

Gregory. To move is to stir, and to be valiant is to stand. Therefore, if thou art moved, thou runnest away.

10 **Sampson.** A dog of that house shall move me to stand. I will take the wall of any man or maid of Montague's.

Gregory. That shows thee a weak slave, for the weakest goes to the wall.

Sampson. 'Tis true; and therefore women, being the weaker
15 vessels, are ever thrust to the wall. Therefore push I will Montague's men from the wall and thrust his maids to the wall.

Gregory. The quarrel is between our masters and us their men.

Sampson. 'Tis all one. I will show myself a tyrant. When I have fought with the men, I will be cruel with the maids: I will cut
20 off their heads.

Gregory. The heads of the maids?

Sampson. Ay, the heads of the maids, or their maidenheads. Take it in what sense thou wilt.

Gregory. They must take it in sense that feel it.

1–2 we'll not carry coals: we won't stand to be insulted. **Colliers,** those involved in the dirty work of hauling coal, were often the butt of jokes.

3–4 in choler: angry; **collar:** a hangman's noose.

11 take the wall: walk nearest to the wall. People of higher rank had the privilege of walking closer to the wall, to avoid any water or garbage in the street. *What claim is Sampson making about himself and anyone from the rival house of Montague?*

14–24 Sampson's tough talk includes boasts about his ability to overpower women.

Romeo and Juliet in the Anželika Cholina Dance Theatre's 2003 production

25 **Sampson.** Me they shall feel while I am able to stand; and 'tis known I am a pretty piece of flesh.

Gregory. 'Tis well thou art not fish; if thou hadst, thou hadst been poor-John. Draw thy tool! Here comes two of the house of Montagues.

[*Enter* Abram *and* Balthasar, *servants to the Montagues.*]

30 **Sampson.** My naked weapon is out. Quarrel! I will back thee.

Gregory. How? turn thy back and run?

Sampson. Fear me not.

Gregory. No, marry. I fear thee!

Sampson. Let us take the law of our sides; let them begin.

35 **Gregory.** I will frown as I pass by, and let them take it as they list.

Sampson. Nay, as they dare. I will bite my thumb at them; which is disgrace to them, if they bear it.

Abram. Do you bite your thumb at us, sir?

Sampson. I do bite my thumb, sir.

40 **Abram.** Do you bite your thumb at us, sir?

Sampson [*aside to* Gregory]. Is the law of our side if I say ay?

Gregory [*aside to* Sampson]. No.

Sampson. No, sir, I do not bite my thumb at you, sir; but I bite my thumb, sir.

45 **Gregory.** Do you quarrel, sir?

Abram. Quarrel, sir? No, sir.

Sampson. But if you do, sir, I am for you. I serve as good a man as you.

Abram. No better.

50 **Sampson.** Well, sir.

[*Enter* Benvolio, *nephew of Montague and first cousin of Romeo.*]

Gregory [*aside to* Sampson]. Say "better." Here comes one of my master's kinsmen.

Sampson. Yes, better, sir.

Abram. You lie.

55 **Sampson.** Draw, if you be men. Gregory, remember thy swashing blow. ➊

[*They fight.*]

Benvolio. Part, fools! [*beats down their swords*] Put up your swords. You know not what you do.

---

28 poor-John: a salted fish, considered fit only for poor people to eat.

33 marry: a short form of "by the Virgin Mary" and so a mild exclamation.

34–44 Gregory and Sampson decide to pick a fight by insulting the Montague servants with a rude gesture (**bite my thumb**).

51–52 Gregory notices that Tybalt, a Capulet, is arriving. *Why do you think Gregory and Sampson behave more aggressively as soon as they realize that Tybalt is approaching?*

➊ ASIDE
Contrast what the servants say openly in lines 35–56 with what they say in **asides,** or whispers to each other. What does this contrast reveal about Sampson and Gregory?

[*Enter* Tybalt, *hot-headed nephew of Lady Capulet and first cousin of Juliet.*]

Tybalt. What, art thou drawn among these heartless hinds?
60 Turn thee, Benvolio! look upon thy death.

Benvolio. I do but keep the peace. Put up thy sword,
Or manage it to part these men with me.

Tybalt. What, drawn, and talk of peace? I hate the word
As I hate hell, all Montagues, and thee.
65 Have at thee, coward!

[*They fight.*]

[*Enter several of both houses, who join the fray; then enter*
Citizens *and* Peace Officers, *with clubs.*]

Officer. Clubs, bills, and partisans! Strike! beat them down!

Citizens. Down with the Capulets! Down with the Montagues!

[*Enter old* Capulet *and* Lady Capulet.]

Capulet. What noise is this? Give me my long sword, ho!

Lady Capulet. A crutch, a crutch! Why call you for a sword?

70 **Capulet.** My sword, I say! Old Montague is come
And flourishes his blade in spite of me.

[*Enter old* Montague *and* Lady Montague.]

Montague. Thou villain Capulet!—Hold me not, let me go.

Lady Montague. Thou shalt not stir one foot to seek a foe.

[*Enter* Prince Escalus, *with attendants. At first no one hears him.*]

Prince. Rebellious subjects, enemies to peace,
75 Profaners of this neighbor-stained steel—
Will they not hear? What, ho! you men, you beasts,
That quench the fire of your pernicious rage
With purple fountains issuing from your veins!
On pain of torture, from those bloody hands
80 Throw your mistempered weapons to the ground
And hear the sentence of your moved prince.
Three civil brawls, bred of an airy word
By thee, old Capulet, and Montague,
Have thrice disturbed the quiet of our streets
85 And made Verona's ancient citizens
Cast by their grave beseeming ornaments
To wield old partisans, in hands as old,
Cankered with peace, to part your cankered hate.
If ever you disturb our streets again,
90 Your lives shall pay the forfeit of the peace.

59–65 Tybalt does not understand that Benvolio is trying to stop the fight. He challenges Benvolio.

59 heartless hinds: cowardly servants.

63 drawn: with your sword out.

65 Have at thee: Defend yourself.

66 bills, and partisans: spears.

69 A crutch ... sword: You need a crutch more than a sword.

74–81 The prince is furious about the street fighting caused by the feud. He orders the men to drop their weapons and pay attention.

77 pernicious: destructive.

82–90 Three ... peace: The prince holds Capulet and Montague responsible for three recent street fights, each probably started by an offhand remark or insult (**airy word**). He warns that they will be put to death if any more fights occur.

For this time all the rest depart away.
You, Capulet, shall go along with me;
And, Montague, come you this afternoon,
To know our farther pleasure in this case,
95 To old Freetown, our common judgment place.
Once more, on pain of death, all men depart.

[*Exeunt all but* Montague, Lady Montague, *and* Benvolio.]

Montague. Who set this ancient quarrel new abroach?
Speak, nephew, were you by when it began?

Benvolio. Here were the servants of your adversary
100 And yours, close fighting ere I did approach.
I drew to part them. In the instant came
The fiery Tybalt, with his sword prepared;
Which, as he breathed defiance to my ears,
He swung about his head and cut the winds,
105 Who, nothing hurt withal, hissed him in scorn. **B**
While we were interchanging thrusts and blows,
Came more and more, and fought on part and part,
Till the Prince came, who parted either part.

Lady Montague. O, where is Romeo? Saw you him today?
110 Right glad I am he was not at this fray.

Benvolio. Madam, an hour before the worshiped sun
Peered forth the golden window of the East,
A troubled mind drave me to walk abroad,
Where, underneath the grove of sycamore
115 That westward rooteth from the city's side,
So early walking did I see your son.
Towards him I made, but he was ware of me
And stole into the covert of the wood.
I—measuring his affections by my own,
120 Which then most sought where most might not be found,
Being one too many by my weary self—
Pursued my humor, not pursuing his,
And gladly shunned who gladly fled from me.

Montague. Many a morning hath he there been seen,
125 With tears augmenting the fresh morning's dew,
Adding to clouds more clouds with his deep sighs;
But all so soon as the all-cheering sun
Should in the farthest East begin to draw
The shady curtains from Aurora's bed,
130 Away from light steals home my heavy son
And private in his chamber pens himself,
Shuts up his windows, locks fair daylight out,

exeunt: the plural form of *exit*, indicating that more than one person is leaving the stage.

97 Who . . . abroach: Who reopened this old argument?

99 adversary: enemy.

100 ere: before.

B CHARACTER
According to Benvolio, what kind of person is Tybalt? **Predict** how Tybalt might act if he runs into Benvolio—or any other Montague—again.

107 on part and part: some on one side, some on the other.

110 fray: fight.

113 drave: drove.

115 rooteth: grows.

117–123 made: moved; **covert:** covering. Romeo saw Benvolio coming and hid in the woods. Since Benvolio himself was seeking solitude, he decided to respect Romeo's privacy and did not go after him. *What does this action tell you about Benvolio?*

124–135 Romeo has been seen wandering through the woods at night, crying. At dawn he returns home and locks himself in his darkened room. Montague feels that this behavior is a bad sign and that his son needs guidance.

129 Aurora's bed: Aurora was the goddess of the dawn.

And makes himself an artificial night.
Black and portentous must this humor prove
135 Unless good counsel may the cause remove.

Benvolio. My noble uncle, do you know the cause?

Montague. I neither know it nor can learn of him.

Benvolio. Have you importuned him by any means?

Montague. Both by myself and many other friends;
140 But he, his own affections' counselor,
Is to himself—I will not say how true—
But to himself so secret and so close,
So far from sounding and discovery,
As is the bud bit with an envious worm
145 Ere he can spread his sweet leaves to the air
Or dedicate his beauty to the sun.
Could we but learn from whence his sorrows grow,
We would as willingly give cure as know.

[*Enter* Romeo *lost in thought.*]

Benvolio. See, where he comes. So please you step aside,
150 I'll know his grievance, or be much denied.

Montague. I would thou wert so happy by thy stay
To hear true shrift. Come, madam, let's away.

[*Exeunt* Montague *and* Lady.]

Benvolio. Good morrow, cousin.

Romeo.   Is the day so young?

Benvolio. But new struck nine.

Romeo.   Ay me! sad hours seem long.
155 Was that my father that went hence so fast?

Benvolio. It was. What sadness lengthens Romeo's hours?

Romeo. Not having that which having makes them short.

Benvolio. In love?

Romeo. Out—

160 **Benvolio.** Of love?

Romeo. Out of her favor where I am in love.

Benvolio. Alas that love, so gentle in his view,
Should be so tyrannous and rough in proof!

Romeo. Alas that love, whose view is muffled still,
165 Should without eyes see pathways to his will!
Where shall we dine?—O me! What fray was here?—
Yet tell me not, for I have heard it all.

134 portentous: indicating evil to come; threatening.

138 importuned: asked in an urgent way.

140 his own affections' counselor: Romeo keeps to himself.

143–148 so far from . . . know: Finding out what Romeo is thinking is almost impossible. Montague compares his son to a young bud destroyed by the bite of a worm before it has a chance to open its leaves. Montague wants to find out what is bothering Romeo so he can help him.

152 shrift: confession.

153 cousin: any relative or close friend. The informal version is *coz*.

157–163 *Why has Romeo been so depressed?*

162–164 love: references to Cupid, the god of love, typically pictured as a blind boy with wings and a bow and arrow. Anyone hit by one of his arrows falls in love instantly. Cupid looks sweet and gentle, but in reality he can be a harsh master.

Here's much to do with hate, but more with love.
Why then, O brawling love! O loving hate!
170 O anything, of nothing first create!
O heavy lightness! serious vanity!
Misshapen chaos of well-seeming forms!
Feather of lead, bright smoke, cold fire, sick health!
Still-waking sleep, that is not what it is!
175 This love feel I, that feel no love in this.
Dost thou not laugh?

Benvolio.   No, coz, I rather weep.

Romeo. Good heart, at what?

Benvolio.   At thy good heart's oppression.

Romeo. Why, such is love's transgression.
Griefs of mine own lie heavy in my breast,
180 Which thou wilt propagate, to have it prest
With more of thine. This love that thou hast shown
Doth add more grief to too much of mine own.
Love is a smoke raised with the fume of sighs;
Being purged, a fire sparkling in lovers' eyes;
185 Being vexed, a sea nourished with lovers' tears.
What is it else? A madness most discreet,
A choking gall, and a preserving sweet.
Farewell, my coz.

Benvolio.   Soft! I will go along.
An if you leave me so, you do me wrong.

190 **Romeo.** Tut! I have lost myself; I am not here:
This is not Romeo, he's some other where.

Benvolio. Tell me in sadness, who is that you love?

Romeo. What, shall I groan and tell thee?

Benvolio.   Groan? Why, no;
But sadly tell me who.

195 **Romeo.** Bid a sick man in sadness make his will.
Ah, word ill urged to one that is so ill!
In sadness, cousin, I do love a woman.

Benvolio. I aimed so near when I supposed you loved.

Romeo. A right good markman! And she's fair I love.

200 **Benvolio.** A right fair mark, fair coz, is soonest hit.

Romeo. Well, in that hit you miss. She'll not be hit
With Cupid's arrow. She hath Dian's wit,
And, in strong proof of chastity well armed,
From Love's weak childish bow she lives unharmed.

168–176 Romeo, confused and upset, tries to describe his feelings about love. He uses phrases like "loving hate" and other contradictory expressions.

176–182 Benvolio expresses his sympathy for Romeo. Romeo replies that this is one more problem caused by love. He now feels worse than before because he must carry the weight of Benvolio's sympathy along with his own grief.

184 purged: cleansed (of the smoke).

185 vexed: troubled.

187 gall: something causing bitterness or hate.

188 Soft: Wait a minute.

192 sadness: seriousness.

201–204 She'll . . . unharmed: The girl isn't interested in falling in love. She is like Diana, the goddess of chastity, who fended off Cupid's arrows.

Casting

Even plays as timeless as Shakespearean dramas need powerful performances to bring them to life. Examine these photographs, and think about the choices the directors made when **casting,** or selecting, the pairs of actors for the roles of Juliet and Romeo. If you were in charge of casting a production of *Romeo and Juliet*, which pair would you choose, and why?

The Royal Shakespeare Company's 1992 production

A 2004 coproduction of the Chicago Shakespeare Theater and Second City

The Cottesloe Theatre's 2000 production

205 She will not stay the siege of loving terms,
Nor bide the encounter of assailing eyes,
Nor ope her lap to saint-seducing gold.
O, she is rich in beauty; only poor
That, when she dies, with beauty dies her store.

210 **Benvolio.** Then she hath sworn that she will still live chaste?

Romeo. She hath, and in that sparing makes huge waste;
For beauty, starved with her severity,
Cuts beauty off from all posterity.
She is too fair, too wise, wisely too fair,
215 To merit bliss by making me despair.
She hath forsworn to love, and in that vow
Do I live dead that live to tell it now.

Benvolio. Be ruled by me: forget to think of her.

Romeo. O, teach me how I should forget to think!

220 **Benvolio.** By giving liberty unto thine eyes:
Examine other beauties.

Romeo.   'Tis the way
To call hers (exquisite) in question more.
These happy masks that kiss fair ladies' brows,
Being black, puts us in mind they hide the fair.
225 He that is strucken blind cannot forget
The precious treasure of his eyesight lost.
Show me a mistress that is passing fair,
What doth her beauty serve but as a note
Where I may read who passed that passing fair?
230 Farewell. Thou canst not teach me to forget.

Benvolio. I'll pay that doctrine, or else die in debt.

[*Exeunt.*]

SCENE 2 *A street near the Capulet house.*

This scene opens with Count Paris, a young nobleman, asking Capulet for permission to marry his daughter, Juliet. Capulet says that Juliet is too young but gives Paris permission to court her and try to win her heart. He also invites Paris to a party he is giving that night.

Romeo finds out about the party and discovers that Rosaline, the girl who rejected him, will be present. Benvolio urges Romeo to go to the party to see how Rosaline compares with the other women.

[*Enter* Capulet *with* Paris, *a kinsman of the Prince, and* Servant.]

Capulet. But Montague is bound as well as I,
In penalty alike; and 'tis not hard, I think,
For men so old as we to keep the peace.

205–207 **She will not . . . saint-seducing gold:** She is not swayed by Romeo's declaration of love, his adoring looks, or his wealth.

212–213 **For beauty . . . posterity:** By denying herself love and marriage, she wastes her beauty, which will not be passed on to future generations.

215–216 **to merit . . . despair:** The girl will reach heaven (**bliss**) by being so virtuous, which causes Romeo to feel hopelessness or despair; **forsworn to:** sworn not to.

220–221 *What is Benvolio's advice?*

221–222 **'Tis . . . more:** That would only make me appreciate my own love's beauty more.

223 Masks were worn by Elizabethan women to protect their complexions from the sun.

227–229 **Show me . . . that passing fair:** A woman who is exceedingly (**passing**) beautiful will only remind me of my love, who is even prettier.

231 **I'll pay . . . debt:** I'll convince you you're wrong, or die trying.

1 **bound:** obligated.

Paris. Of honorable reckoning are you both,

5 And pity 'tis you lived at odds so long.
But now, my lord, what say you to my suit?

Capulet. But saying o'er what I have said before:
My child is yet a stranger in the world,
She hath not seen the change of fourteen years;

10 Let two more summers wither in their pride
Ere we may think her ripe to be a bride.

Paris. Younger than she are happy mothers made.

Capulet. And too soon marred are those so early made.
The earth hath swallowed all my hopes but she;

15 She is the hopeful lady of my earth.
But woo her, gentle Paris, get her heart;
My will to her consent is but a part.
An she agree, within her scope of choice
Lies my consent and fair according voice. **C**

20 This night I hold an old accustomed feast,
Whereto I have invited many a guest,
Such as I love, and you among the store,
One more, most welcome, makes my number more.
At my poor house look to behold this night

25 Earth-treading stars that make dark heaven light.
Such comfort as do lusty young men feel
When well-appareled April on the heel
Of limping Winter treads, even such delight
Among fresh female buds shall you this night

30 Inherit at my house. Hear all, all see,
And like her most whose merit most shall be;
Which, on more view of many, mine, being one,
May stand in number, though in reck'ning none.
Come, go with me. [*to Servant, giving him a paper*]
                    Go, sirrah, trudge about

35 Through fair Verona; find those persons out
Whose names are written there, and to them say,
My house and welcome on their pleasure stay.

[*Exeunt* Capulet *and* Paris.]

Servant. Find them out whose names are written here! It is
written that the shoemaker should meddle with his yard and the

40 tailor with his last, the fisher with his pencil and the painter
with his nets; but I am sent to find those persons whose names
are here writ, and can never find what names the writing person
hath here writ. I must to the learned. In good time!

---

4 reckoning: reputation.

6 what say ... suit: Paris is asking for Capulet's response to his proposal to marry Juliet.

10 let two more summers ... pride: let two more years pass.

14 The earth ... she: All my children are dead except Juliet.

16 woo her: try to win her heart.

18–19 An ... voice: I will give my approval to the one she chooses.

20 old accustomed feast: a traditional or annual party.

C BLANK VERSE
Reread lines 16–19 aloud, tapping your foot at each stressed syllable. How many stressed syllables are in each line?

29–33 among ... none: Tonight at the party you will witness the loveliest young girls in Verona, including Juliet. When you see all of them together, your opinion of Juliet may change.

34 sirrah: a term used to address a servant.

38–43 The servant cannot seek out the people on the list because he cannot read. In his remarks he confuses the craftsmen and their tools, tapping a typical source of humor for Elizabethan comic characters.

43 In good time: What luck (a reference to the arrival of Romeo and Benvolio, who will be able to help the servant read the list).

[*Enter* Benvolio *and* Romeo.]

Benvolio. Tut, man, one fire burns out another's burning;
45 One pain is lessened by another's anguish;
Turn giddy, and be holp by backward turning;
One desperate grief cures with another's languish.
Take thou some new infection to thy eye,
And the rank poison of the old will die.

50 **Romeo.** Your plantain leaf is excellent for that.

Benvolio. For what, I pray thee?

Romeo. For your broken shin.

Benvolio. Why, Romeo, art thou mad?

Romeo. Not mad, but bound more than a madman is;
Shut up in prison, kept without my food,
55 Whipped and tormented and—God-den, good fellow.

Servant. God gi' go-den. I pray, sir, can you read?

Romeo. Ay, mine own fortune in my misery.

Servant. Perhaps you have learned it without book. But
I pray, can you read anything you see?

60 **Romeo.** Ay, if I know the letters and the language.

Servant. Ye say honestly. Rest you merry!

[Romeo*'s joking goes over the clown's head. He concludes that*
Romeo *cannot read and prepares to seek someone who can.*]

Romeo. Stay, fellow; I can read. [*He reads.*]
"Signior Martino and his wife and daughters;
County Anselmo and his beauteous sisters;
65 The lady widow of Vitruvio;
Signior Placentio and his lovely nieces;
Mercutio and his brother Valentine;
Mine uncle Capulet, his wife, and daughters;
My fair niece Rosaline and Livia;
70 Signior Valentio and his cousin Tybalt;
Lucio and the lively Helena."
[*gives back the paper*]
A fair assembly. Whither should they come?

Servant. Up.

Romeo. Whither?

75 **Servant.** To supper, to our house.

Romeo. Whose house?

Servant. My master's.

Romeo. Indeed I should have asked you that before.

44–49 Tut, man . . . die: Romeo and Benvolio are still discussing Romeo's love problems. Benvolio says Romeo should find a new love—that a "new infection" will cure the old one.

55 god-den: good evening. Romeo interrupts his lament to talk to the servant.

56 God gi' go-den: God give you a good evening.

69 Rosaline: This is the woman that Romeo is in love with. Mercutio, a friend of both Romeo and the Capulets, is also invited to the party.

72 whither: where.

Servant. Now I'll tell you without asking. My master is the great
80 rich Capulet; and if you be not of the house of Montagues, I
pray come and crush a cup of wine. Rest you merry!

[*Exit.*]

Benvolio. At this same ancient feast of Capulet's
Sups the fair Rosaline whom thou so lovest,
With all the admired beauties of Verona.
85 Go thither, and with unattainted eye
Compare her face with some that I shall show,
And I will make thee think thy swan a crow.

Romeo. When the devout religion of mine eye
Maintains such falsehood, then turn tears to fires;
90 And these, who, often drowned, could never die,
Transparent heretics, be burnt for liars!
One fairer than my love? The all-seeing sun
Ne'er saw her match since first the world begun.

Benvolio. Tut! you saw her fair, none else being by,
95 Herself poised with herself in either eye;
But in that crystal scales let there be weighed
Your lady's love against some other maid
That I will show you shining at this feast,
And she shall scant show well that now shows best.

100 **Romeo.** I'll go along, no such sight to be shown,
But to rejoice in splendor of mine own.

[*Exeunt.*]

81 crush a cup of wine: slang for "drink some wine."

85 unattainted: unbiased; unprejudiced.

88–91 When . . . liars: If the love I have for Rosaline, which is like a religion, changes because of such a lie (that others may be more beautiful), let my tears be turned to fire and my eyes be burned.

94–99 Tut . . . best: You've seen Rosaline alone; now compare her with some other women. *How does Benvolio think Rosaline will measure up against the other girls?*

100–101 Romeo agrees to go to the party, but only to see Rosaline.

SCENE 3 *Capulet's house.*

In this scene, you will meet Juliet, her mother, and her nurse. The nurse, a merry and slightly crude servant, has been in charge of Juliet since her birth. Once she starts talking, she can't stop. Just before the party, Juliet's mother asks if Juliet has thought about getting married. Lady Capulet is matchmaking, trying to convince her daughter that Paris would make a good husband. Juliet responds just as you might if your parents set up a blind date for you—without much enthusiasm.

[*Enter* Lady Capulet *and* Nurse.]

Lady Capulet. Nurse, where's my daughter? Call her forth to me.

Nurse. Now, by my maidenhead at twelve year old,
I bade her come. What, lamb! what, ladybird!
God forbid! Where's this girl? What, Juliet!

[*Enter* Juliet.]

5 **Juliet.** How now? Who calls?

3–4 what: a call like "Hey, where are you?"

Nurse. Your mother.

Juliet. Madam, I am here. What is your will?

Lady Capulet. This is the matter—Nurse, give leave awhile,
We must talk in secret. Nurse, come back again;
10 I have remembered me, thou's hear our counsel.
Thou knowest my daughter's of a pretty age.

Nurse. Faith, I can tell her age unto an hour.

Lady Capulet. She's not fourteen.

Nurse.   I'll lay fourteen of my teeth—
And yet, to my teen be it spoken, I have but four—
15 She's not fourteen. How long is it now
To Lammastide?

Lady Capulet.   A fortnight and odd days.

8–11 **give leave . . . counsel:** Lady Capulet seems flustered or nervous, not sure whether she wants the nurse to stay or leave; **of a pretty age:** of an attractive age, ready for marriage.

14 **teen:** sorrow.

16 **Lammastide:** August 1, a religious feast day. It is two weeks (**a fortnight**) away.

Juliet and her nurse in the 1994 production of the Shakespeare Theatre in Washington, D.C.

Nurse. Even or odd, of all days in the year,
Come Lammas Eve at night shall she be fourteen.
Susan and she (God rest all Christian souls!)
20 Were of an age. Well, Susan is with God;
She was too good for me. But, as I said,
On Lammas Eve at night shall she be fourteen;
That shall she, marry; I remember it well.
'Tis since the earthquake now eleven years;
25 And she was weaned (I never shall forget it),
Of all the days of the year, upon that day.
For I had then laid wormwood to my dug,
Sitting in the sun under the dovehouse wall.
My lord and you were then at Mantua—
30 Nay, I do bear a brain—But, as I said,
When it did taste the wormwood on the nipple
Of my dug and felt it bitter, pretty fool,
To see it tetchy and fall out with the dug!
Shake, quoth the dovehouse! 'Twas no need, I trow,
35 To bid me trudge.
And since that time it is eleven years,
For then she could stand alone; nay, by the rood,
She could have run and waddled all about;
For even the day before, she broke her brow;
40 And then my husband (God be with his soul!
'A was a merry man) took up the child.
"Yea," quoth he, "dost thou fall upon thy face?
Thou wilt fall backward when thou has more wit,
Wilt thou not, Jule?" And, by my holidam,
45 The pretty wretch left crying, and said "Ay."
To see now how a jest shall come about!
I warrant, an I should live a thousand years,
I never should forget it. "Wilt thou not, Jule?" quoth he,
And, pretty fool, it stinted, and said "Ay." **D**
50 **Lady Capulet.** Enough of this. I pray thee hold thy peace.

Nurse. Yes, madam. Yet I cannot choose but laugh
To think it should leave crying and say "Ay."
And yet, I warrant, it had upon its brow
A bump as big as a young cock'rel's stone;
55 A perilous knock; and it cried bitterly.
"Yea," quoth my husband, "fallst upon thy face?
Thou wilt fall backward when thou comest to age,
Wilt thou not, Jule?" It stinted, and said "Ay."

17–49 The nurse begins to babble about various memories of Juliet's childhood. She talks of her own dead daughter, Susan, who was the same age as Juliet. Susan probably died in infancy, leaving the nurse available to become a wet nurse to (that is, breastfeed) Juliet. She remembers an earthquake that happened on the day she stopped breast-feeding Juliet (**she was weaned**).

27 laid wormwood to my dug: applied wormwood, a plant with a bitter taste, to her breast in order to discourage the child from breastfeeding.

33 tetchy: touchy; cranky.
34–35 Shake … trudge: When the dove house shook, I knew enough to leave.

37 by the rood: by the cross of Christ (a mild oath).

39 broke her brow: cut her forehead.

42–49 "Yea" … "Ay": To quiet Juliet after her fall, the nurse's husband made a crude joke, asking the baby whether she'd fall the other way (on her back) when she was older. Although at three Juliet didn't understand the question, she stopped crying (**stinted**) and innocently answered "Yes." The nurse finds the story so funny that she can't stop retelling it.

D CHARACTER
So far, how would you describe the nurse? List three **traits** this character exhibits.

55 perilous: hazardous; dangerous.

Juliet. And stint thou too, I pray thee, nurse, say I.

60 **Nurse.** Peace, I have done. God mark thee to his grace!
Thou wast the prettiest babe that e'er I nursed.
An I might live to see thee married once,
I have my wish.

Lady Capulet. Marry, that "marry" is the very theme
65 I came to talk of. Tell me, daughter Juliet,
How stands your disposition to be married?

Juliet. It is an honor that I dream not of.

Nurse. An honor? Were not I thine only nurse,
I would say thou hadst sucked wisdom from thy teat.

70 **Lady Capulet.** Well, think of marriage now. Younger than you,
Here in Verona, ladies of esteem,
Are made already mothers. By my count,
I was your mother much upon these years
That you are now a maid. Thus then in brief:
75 The valiant Paris seeks you for his love.

Nurse. A man, young lady! lady, such a man
As all the world—why he's a man of wax.

Lady Capulet. Verona's summer hath not such a flower.

Nurse. Nay, he's a flower, in faith—a very flower.

80 **Lady Capulet.** What say you? Can you love the gentleman?
This night you shall behold him at our feast.
Read o'er the volume of young Paris' face,
And find delight writ there with beauty's pen;
Examine every several lineament,
85 And see how one another lends content;
And what obscured in this fair volume lies
Find written in the margent of his eyes.
This precious book of love, this unbound lover,
To beautify him only lacks a cover.
90 The fish lives in the sea, and 'tis much pride
For fair without the fair within to hide.
That book in many's eyes doth share the glory,
That in gold clasps locks in the golden story;
So shall you share all that he doth possess,
95 By having him making yourself no less.

Nurse. No less? Nay, bigger! Women grow by men.

Lady Capulet. Speak briefly, can you like of Paris' love?

Juliet. I'll look to like, if looking liking move;
But no more deep will I endart mine eye

64 Marry ... "marry": two different usages of the same word—the first meaning "by the Virgin Mary" and the second meaning "to wed."

73–74 I was ... maid: I was your mother at about your age, yet you are still unmarried.

77 a man of wax: a man so perfect he could be a wax statue, of the type sculptors once used as models for their works.

82–89 Read ... cover: Lady Capulet uses an extended metaphor that compares Paris to a book that Juliet should read.

84 every several lineament: each separate feature (of Paris' face).

87 margent ... eyes: She compares Paris' eyes to the margin of a page, where notes are written to explain the content.

88–91 This ... hide: This beautiful book (Paris) needs only a cover (wife) to become even better. He may be hiding even more wonderful qualities inside.

96 The nurse can't resist commenting that women get bigger (pregnant) when they marry.

98 I'll look ... move: I'll look at him with the intention of liking him, if simply looking can make me like him.

99 endart: look deeply, as if penetrating with a dart.

100 Than your consent gives strength to make it fly. **E**

[*Enter a* Servingman.]

Servingman. Madam, the guests are come, supper served up, you
called, my young lady asked for, the nurse cursed in the pantry,
and everything in extremity. I must hence to wait. I beseech you
follow straight.

105 **Lady Capulet.** We follow thee. [*Exit* Servingman.] Juliet, the County
     stays.

Nurse. Go, girl, seek happy nights to happy days.

[*Exeunt.*]

E **TRAGEDY**
How might Lady Capulet's desire for
Juliet to marry Paris lead to **conflict**
later in the play? Explain your
answer.

103–104 **extremity:** great confusion;
straight: immediately.

105 **the County stays:** Count Paris is
waiting for you.

SCENE 4   *A street near the Capulet house.*

*It is the evening of the Capulet masque, or costume ball. Imagine the guests
proceeding through the darkened streets with torches to light the way.*

*Romeo and his friends Mercutio and Benvolio join the procession. Their masks
will prevent Romeo's and Benvolio's being recognized as Montagues. Mercutio
and Benvolio are in a playful, partying mood, but Romeo is still depressed by
his unanswered love for Rosaline. Romeo has also had a dream that warned
him of the harmful consequences of this party. He senses trouble.*

[*Enter* Romeo, Mercutio, Benvolio, *with five or six other* Maskers;
Torchbearers.]

Romeo. What, shall this speech be spoke for our excuse?
Or shall we on without apology?

Benvolio. The date is out of such prolixity.
We'll have no Cupid hoodwinked with a scarf,
5 Bearing a Tartar's painted bow of lath,
Scaring the ladies like a crowkeeper;
Nor no without-book prologue, faintly spoke
After the prompter, for our entrance;
But let them measure us by what they will,
10 We'll measure them a measure, and be gone.

Romeo. Give me a torch. I am not for this ambling;
Being but heavy, I will bear the light.

Mercutio. Nay, gentle Romeo, we must have you dance.

Romeo. Not I, believe me. You have dancing shoes
15 With nimble soles; I have a soul of lead
So stakes me to the ground I cannot move.

Mercutio. You are a lover. Borrow Cupid's wings
And soar with them above a common bound.

Romeo. I am too sore enpierced with his shaft
20 To soar with his light feathers, and so bound

1–10 **What, shall this . . . be gone:**
Romeo asks whether they should send
a messenger announcing their arrival
at the party. Benvolio replies that this
custom is out of date. He says that they'll
dance one dance with the partygoers
(**measure them a measure**) and
then leave.

12 **heavy:** sad. Romeo makes a joke based
on the meanings of *heavy* and *light*.

14–32 Romeo continues to talk about his
sadness, while Mercutio jokingly makes
fun of him to try to cheer him up.

I cannot bound a pitch above dull woe.
Under love's heavy burden do I sink. **F**

Mercutio. And, to sink in it, should you burden love—
Too great oppression for a tender thing.

25 **Romeo.** Is love a tender thing? It is too rough,
Too rude, too boist'rous, and it pricks like thorn.

Mercutio. If love be rough with you, be rough with love.
Prick love for pricking, and you beat love down.
Give me a case to put my visage in.
30 A visor for a visor! What care I
What curious eye doth quote deformities?
Here are the beetle brows shall blush for me.

Benvolio. Come, knock and enter, and no sooner in
But every man betake him to his legs.

35 **Romeo.** A torch for me! Let wantons light of heart
Tickle the senseless rushes with their heels;
For I am proverbed with a grandsire phrase,
I'll be a candle-holder and look on;
The game was ne'er so fair, and I am done.

40 **Mercutio.** Tut, dun's the mouse, the constable's own word!
If thou art Dun, we'll draw thee from the mire
Of, save your reverence, love, wherein thou stickst
Up to the ears. Come, we burn daylight, ho!

Romeo. Nay, that's not so.

Mercutio.   I mean, sir, in delay
45 We waste our lights in vain, like lamps by day.
Take our good meaning, for our judgment sits
Five times in that ere once in our five wits.

Romeo. And we mean well in going to this masque;
But 'tis no wit to go.

Mercutio.   Why, may one ask?

50 **Romeo.** I dreamt a dream tonight.

Mercutio.   And so did I.

Romeo. Well, what was yours?

Mercutio.   That dreamers often lie.

Romeo. In bed asleep, while they do dream things true.

Mercutio. O, then I see Queen Mab hath been with you.
She is the fairies' midwife, and she comes
55 In shape no bigger than an agate stone
On the forefinger of an alderman,
Drawn with a team of little atomies

F PUN
Identify two puns in lines 11–22.
What effect do they have on the
mood of this scene?

29–32 Give . . . for me: Give me a mask
for an ugly face. I don't care if people
notice my appearance. Here, look at
my bushy eyebrows.

34 betake . . . legs: dance.

35–38 Let . . . look on: Let playful people
tickle the grass (**rushes**) on the floor
with their dancing. I'll follow the old
saying (**grandsire phrase**) and just be
a spectator.

40–43 Tut . . . daylight: Mercutio jokes,
using various meanings of the word
dun, which sounds like Romeo's last
word, *done*. He concludes by saying they
should not waste time (**burn daylight**).

53–95 This famous speech is yet one
more attempt by Mercutio to cheer up
Romeo. He talks of Mab, queen of the
fairies, a folktale character well-known
to Shakespeare's audience. His language
includes vivid descriptions, puns, and
satires of people; and ultimately he gets
caught up in his own wild imaginings. It
is not necessary to understand everything
Mercutio says to recognize the beauty of
this born storyteller's tale.

55 agate stone: jewel for a ring.

57 atomies: tiny creatures.

Romeo and Juliet in the Globe Theatre's 2004 production

Costume Design

Classic dramas such as *Romeo and Juliet* can be staged in many different ways. **Costumes** are one means of making a production distinctive. Think about the interpretations of the play pictured here. (Note: The middle shot is of Romeo and Juliet in the midst of the famous balcony scene, coming up in Act Two—and the ladder serves as the balcony!) How are the different costume choices in these photographs appropriate for the different productions?

Romeo and Juliet in the Globe Theatre's 2000 production

Romeo and Juliet in the Royal Ballet's 2003 production

Athwart men's noses as they lie asleep;
Her wagon spokes made of long spinners' legs,
60 The cover, of the wings of grasshoppers;
Her traces, of the smallest spider's web;
Her collars, of the moonshine's wat'ry beams;
Her whip, of cricket's bone; the lash, of film;
Her wagoner, a small grey-coated gnat,
65 Not half so big as a round little worm
Pricked from the lazy finger of a maid;
Her chariot is an empty hazelnut,
Made by the joiner squirrel or old grub,
Time out o' mind the fairies' coachmakers.
70 And in this state she gallops night by night
Through lovers' brains, and then they dream of love;
O'er courtiers' knees, that dream on curtsies straight;
O'er lawyers' fingers, who straight dream on fees;
O'er ladies' lips, who straight on kisses dream,
75 Which oft the angry Mab with blisters plagues,
Because their breaths with sweetmeats tainted are.
Sometime she gallops o'er a courtier's nose,
And then dreams he of smelling out a suit,
And sometime comes she with a tithe-pig's tail
80 Tickling a parson's nose as 'a lies asleep,
Then dreams he of another benefice.
Sometime she driveth o'er a soldier's neck,
And then dreams he of cutting foreign throats,
Of breaches, ambuscadoes, Spanish blades,
85 Of healths five fathom deep; and then anon
Drums in his ear, at which he starts and wakes,
And being thus frighted, swears a prayer or two
And sleeps again. This is that very Mab
That plaits the manes of horses in the night
90 And bakes the elflocks in foul sluttish hairs,
Which once untangled much misfortune bodes.
This is the hag, when maids lie on their backs,
That presses them and learns them first to bear,
Making them women of good carriage.
95 This is she—

Romeo.   Peace, peace, Mercutio, peace!
Thou talkst of nothing.

Mercutio.   True, I talk of dreams;
Which are the children of an idle brain,
Begot of nothing but vain fantasy;
Which is as thin of substance as the air,
100 And more inconstant than the wind, who woos

---

59 spinners' legs: spiders' legs.

61 traces: harness.

68 joiner: carpenter.

77–78 Sometimes she . . . suit: Sometimes Mab makes a member of the king's court dream of receiving special favors.

81 benefice: a well-paying position for a clergyman.

84 ambuscadoes: ambushes; **Spanish blades:** high-quality Spanish swords.

89 plaits: braids.

96–103 True . . . South: Mercutio is trying to keep Romeo from taking his dreams too seriously.

Even now the frozen bosom of the North
And, being angered, puffs away from thence,
Turning his face to the dew-dropping South.

Benvolio. This wind you talk of blows us from ourselves.
105 Supper is done, and we shall come too late.

Romeo. I fear, too early; for my mind misgives
Some consequence, yet hanging in the stars,
Shall bitterly begin his fearful date
With this night's revels and expire the term
110 Of a despised life, closed in my breast,
By some vile forfeit of untimely death.
But he that hath the steerage of my course
Direct my sail! On, lusty gentlemen!

Benvolio. Strike, drum.

[*Exeunt.*]

106–111 Romeo, still depressed, fears that some terrible event caused by the stars will begin at the party. Remember the phrase "star-crossed lovers" from the prologue on page 941.

SCENE 5   *A hall in Capulet's house; the scene of the party.*

This is the scene of the party at which Romeo and Juliet finally meet. Romeo and his friends, disguised in their masks, arrive as uninvited guests. As he watches the dancers, Romeo suddenly sees Juliet and falls in love at first sight. At the same time, Tybalt recognizes Romeo's voice and knows he is a Montague. Tybalt alerts Capulet and threatens to kill Romeo. Capulet, however, insists that Tybalt behave himself and act like a gentleman. Promising revenge, Tybalt leaves. Romeo and Juliet meet and kiss in the middle of the dance floor. Only after they part do they learn each other's identity.

[Servingmen *come forth with napkins.*]

First Servingman. Where's Potpan, that he helps not to take away? He shift a trencher! he scrape a trencher!

Second Servingman. When good manners shall lie all in one or two men's hands, and they unwashed too, 'tis a foul thing.

5 **First Servingman.** Away with the joint-stools, remove the court-cupboard, look to the plate. Good thou, save me a piece of marchpane and, as thou lovest me, let the porter let in Susan Grindstone and Nell. Anthony, and Potpan!

Second Servingman. Ay, boy, ready.

10 **First Servingman.** You are looked for and called for, asked for and sought for, in the great chamber.

Third Servingman. We cannot be here and there too. Cheerly, boys! Be brisk awhile, and the longer liver take all.

[*Exeunt.*]

1–13 These opening lines are a comic conversation among three servants as they work.

2 trencher: wooden plate.

6–7 plate: silverware and silver plates; **marchpane:** marzipan, a sweet made from almond paste.

[Maskers *appear with* Capulet, Lady Capulet, Juliet, *all the* Guests, *and* Servants.]

Capulet. Welcome, gentlemen! Ladies that have their toes
15 Unplagued with corns will have a bout with you.
Ah ha, my mistresses! which of you all
Will now deny to dance? She that makes dainty,
She I'll swear hath corns. Am I come near ye now?
Welcome, gentlemen! I have seen the day
20 That I have worn a visor and could tell
A whispering tale in a fair lady's ear,
Such as would please. 'Tis gone, 'tis gone, 'tis gone!
You are welcome, gentlemen! Come, musicians, play.
A hall, a hall! give room! and foot it, girls.

[*Music plays and they dance.*]

25 More light, you knaves! and turn the tables up,
And quench the fire, the room is grown too hot.
Ah, sirrah, this unlooked-for sport comes well.
Nay, sit, nay, sit, good cousin Capulet,
For you and I are past our dancing days.
30 How long is't now since last yourself and I
Were in a mask?

Second Capulet. By'r Lady, thirty years.

Capulet. What, man? 'Tis not so much, 'tis not so much!

14–27 Capulet welcomes his guests and invites them all to dance. At the same time, like a good host, he is trying to get the party going. He alternates talking with his guests and telling the servants what to do.

17–18 **She that . . . corns:** Any woman too shy to dance will be assumed to have corns, ugly and painful growths on the toes.

20 **visor:** mask.

28–38 Capulet and his relative watch the dancing as they talk of days gone by.

Guests dance at the Capulets' ball in the Royal Ballet's 1996 production.

'Tis since the nuptial of Lucentio,
Come Pentecost as quickly as it will,
35 Some five-and-twenty years, and then we masked.

Second Capulet. 'Tis more, 'tis more! His son is elder, sir;
His son is thirty.

Capulet.   Will you tell me that?
His son was but a ward two years ago.

Romeo [*to a* Servingman]. What lady's that, which doth enrich
   the hand
40 Of yonder knight?

Servant. I know not, sir.

Romeo. O, she doth teach the torches to burn bright!
It seems she hangs upon the cheek of night
Like a rich jewel in an Ethiop's ear—
45 Beauty too rich for use, for earth too dear!
So shows a snowy dove trooping with crows
As yonder lady o'er her fellows shows.
The measure done, I'll watch her place of stand
And, touching hers, make blessed my rude hand.
50 Did my heart love till now? Forswear it, sight!
For I ne'er saw true beauty till this night. **G**

Tybalt. This, by his voice, should be a Montague.
Fetch me my rapier, boy. What, dares the slave
Come hither, covered with an antic face,
55 To fleer and scorn at our solemnity?
Now, by the stock and honor of my kin,
To strike him dead I hold it not a sin.

Capulet. Why, how now, kinsman? Wherefore storm you so?

Tybalt. Uncle, this is a Montague, our foe;
60 A villain, that is hither come in spite
To scorn at our solemnity this night.

Capulet. Young Romeo is it?

Tybalt.   'Tis he, that villain Romeo.

Capulet. Content thee, gentle coz, let him alone.
'A bears him like a portly gentleman,
65 And, to say truth, Verona brags of him
To be a virtuous and well-governed youth.
I would not for the wealth of all this town
Here in my house do him disparagement.
Therefore be patient, take no note of him.
70 It is my will; the which if thou respect,

33 nuptial: marriage.

39–40 Romeo has spotted Juliet across the dance floor and is immediately entranced by her beauty.

44–45 Ethiop's ear: the ear of an Ethiopian (African); **for earth too dear:** too precious for this world.

G **BLANK VERSE**
Romeo's awestruck speech is in rhymed couplets, not blank verse. Why do you think Shakespeare chose to use rhymed verse here? Explain your answer.

52–57 Tybalt recognizes Romeo's voice and tells his servant to get his sword (**rapier**). He thinks Romeo has come to make fun of (**fleer**) their party. *What does Tybalt want to do to Romeo?*

64 portly: dignified.

68 do him disparagement: speak critically or insultingly to him.

Show a fair presence and put off these frowns,
An ill-beseeming semblance for a feast.

Tybalt. It fits when such a villain is a guest.
I'll not endure him.

Capulet. He shall be endured.
75 What, goodman boy? I say he shall. Go to!
Am I the master here, or you? Go to!
You'll not endure him? God shall mend my soul!
You'll make a mutiny among my guests!
You will set cock-a-hoop! You'll be the man.

80 **Tybalt.** Why, uncle, 'tis a shame.

Capulet. Go to, go to!
You are a saucy boy. Is't so, indeed?
This trick may chance to scathe you. I know what.
You must contrary me! Marry, 'tis time.—
Well said, my hearts!—You are a princox—go!
85 Be quiet, or—More light, more light!—For shame!
I'll make you quiet; what!—Cheerly, my hearts!

Tybalt. Patience perforce with willful choler meeting
Makes my flesh tremble in their different greeting.
I will withdraw; but this intrusion shall,
90 Now seeming sweet, convert to bitter gall.

[*Exit.*]

Romeo. If I profane with my unworthiest hand
This holy shrine, the gentle fine is this:
My lips, two blushing pilgrims, ready stand
To smooth that rough touch with a tender kiss.

95 **Juliet.** Good pilgrim, you do wrong your hand too much,
Which mannerly devotion shows in this;
For saints have hands that pilgrims' hands do touch,
And palm to palm is holy palmers' kiss.

Romeo. Have not saints lips, and holy palmers too?

100 **Juliet.** Ay, pilgrim, lips that they must use in prayer.

Romeo. O, then, dear saint, let lips do what hands do!
They pray; grant thou, lest faith turn to despair.

Juliet. Saints do not move, though grant for prayers' sake.

Romeo. Then move not while my prayer's effect I take.
105 Thus from my lips, by thine my sin is purged.

[*kisses her*]

Juliet. Then have my lips the sin that they have took.

72 **semblance:** outward appearance.

75 **goodman boy:** a term used to address an inferior; **Go to:** Stop, that's enough!

79 **set cock-a-hoop:** cause everything to be upset.

82–83 **scathe:** harm; **I know . . . contrary me:** I know what I'm doing! Don't you dare challenge my authority.

84–86 Capulet intersperses his angry speech to Tybalt with comments to his guests and servants.

87–90 **Patience . . . gall:** Tybalt says he will restrain himself, but his suppressed anger (**choler**) makes his body shake. *What do you think he will do about his anger?*

91–108 Romeo and Juliet are in the middle of the dance floor, with eyes only for each other. They touch the palms of their hands together. Their conversation revolves around Romeo's comparison of his lips to pilgrims who have traveled to a holy shrine. Juliet goes along with the comparison.

105 **purged:** washed away.

Romeo and Juliet in the Shakespeare & Company's 2004 Spring Tour Production

Romeo. Sin from my lips? O trespass sweetly urged!
Give me my sin again.

[*kisses her*]

Juliet.   You kiss by the book.

Nurse. Madam, your mother craves a word with you.

110 **Romeo.** What is her mother?

Nurse.   Marry, bachelor,
Her mother is the lady of the house.
And a good lady, and a wise and virtuous.
I nursed her daughter that you talked withal.
I tell you, he that can lay hold of her
115 Shall have the chinks.

Romeo.   Is she a Capulet?
O dear account! my life is my foe's debt.

108 kiss by the book: Juliet could mean "You kiss like an expert, someone who has studied and practiced." Or she could be teasing Romeo, meaning "You kiss coldly, as though you had learned how by reading a book."

109 At the nurse's message, Juliet walks to her mother.

115 shall have the chinks: shall become rich.

116 my life ... debt: my life belongs to my enemy.

Benvolio. Away, be gone, the sport is at the best.

Romeo. Ay, so I fear; the more is my unrest.

Capulet. Nay, gentlemen, prepare not to be gone;
120 We have a trifling foolish banquet towards.

[*They whisper in his ear.*]

Is it e'en so? Why then, I thank you all.
I thank you, honest gentlemen. Good night.
More torches here! [*Exeunt* Maskers.] Come on then, let's to bed.
Ah, sirrah, by my fay, it waxes late;
125 I'll to my rest.

[*Exeunt all but* Juliet *and* Nurse.]

Juliet. Come hither, nurse. What is yond gentleman?

Nurse. The son and heir of old Tiberio.

Juliet. What's he that now is going out of door?

Nurse. Marry, that, I think, be young Petruchio.

130 **Juliet.** What's he that follows there, that would not dance?

Nurse. I know not.

Juliet. Go ask his name.—If he be married,
My grave is like to be my wedding bed.

Nurse. His name is Romeo, and a Montague,
135 The only son of your great enemy.

Juliet. My only love, sprung from my only hate!
Too early seen unknown, and known too late!
Prodigious birth of love it is to me
That I must love a loathed enemy.

140 **Nurse.** What's this? what's this?

Juliet.   A rhyme I learnt even now
Of one I danced withal.

[*One calls within, "Juliet."*]

Nurse.   Anon, anon!
Come, let's away; the strangers all are gone.

[*Exeunt.*]

120 **towards:** coming up.

126–130 Juliet asks the nurse to identify various guests as they leave. *What does she really want to know?*

137–138 **Too early . . . too late:** I fell in love with him before I learned who he is; **prodigious:** abnormal; unlucky. *How does Juliet feel about the fact that she's fallen in love with the son of her father's enemy?*

Comprehension

PENNSYLVANIA
STANDARDS

READING STANDARD
B.1.1.1.A.1 Evaluate character

1. **Recall** What warning does Prince Escalus give the Capulets and the Montagues?

2. **Recall** What agreement do Paris and Lord Capulet reach?

3. **Recall** Why does Romeo go to the Capulets' party?

4. **Clarify** What is the chief obstacle to Romeo and Juliet's love?

Literary Analysis

5. **Reading Shakespearean Drama** Review the chart you created. Which events in Act One seem most important in setting up **conflicts** in the plot?

6. **Identify Character Foils** A foil is a character who highlights, through sharp contrast, the qualities of another character. Identify two characters in Act One who are foils for each other. What do you learn about the characters by seeing them in contrast to one another?

7. **Analyze Foreshadowing** Examine the examples of foreshadowing listed in the chart. To clarify your understanding of the examples, try paraphrasing them. Then explain what event each ominous passage foreshadows.

Foreshadowing	Paraphrase	What It Hints At
I fear, too early; for my mind misgives Some consequence, yet hanging in the stars, Shall bitterly begin his fearful date With this night's revels and expire the term Of a despised life, closed in my breast, By some vile forfeit of untimely death. - Romeo (Act One, Scene 4, lines 106–111)		
My grave is like to be my wedding bed. - Juliet (Act One, Scene 5, line 133)		

8. **Evaluate Blank Verse** Find and copy a group of four lines of blank verse in Act One, marking the unstressed (˘) and the stressed (´) syllables in each line. Then explain whether the lines show the typical **iambic pentameter** pattern or contain rhythmic variations. In your opinion, does the passage accurately capture the sound of spoken English? Explain.

Literary Criticism

9. **Critical Interpretations** Works with tremendous critical acclaim can sometimes fail to live up to our expectations. Who hasn't been disappointed after hype? According to critic Robert Graves, the "remarkable thing about Shakespeare is that he is really very good—in spite of all the people who say he is very good." Is *Romeo and Juliet* living up to your expectations? Explain.

Prologue

In a sonnet the Chorus summarizes what has happened so far in the play. He reviews how Romeo and Juliet have fallen in love and suggests both the problems and the delights they now face. He also includes hints about what will result from the events of Act One.

[*Enter* Chorus.]

Chorus. Now old desire doth in his deathbed lie,
And young affection gapes to be his heir.
That fair for which love groaned for and would die,
With tender Juliet matched, is now not fair.
5 Now Romeo is beloved, and loves again,
Alike bewitched by the charm of looks;
But to his foe supposed he must complain,
And she steal love's sweet bait from fearful hooks.
Being held a foe, he may not have access
10 To breathe such vows as lovers use to swear,
And she as much in love, her means much less
To meet her new beloved anywhere;
But passion lends them power, time means, to meet,
Temp'ring extremities with extreme sweet.

[*Exit.*]

1–4 Now . . . fair: Romeo's love for Rosaline (**old desire**) is now dead. His new love (**young affection**) replaces the old. Compared to Juliet, Rosaline no longer seems so beautiful.

6 *What attracted Romeo and Juliet to each other?*

7 but . . . complain: Juliet, a Capulet, is Romeo's supposed enemy, yet she is the one to whom he must plead (**complain**) his love.

14 temp'ring . . . sweet: moderating great difficulties with extreme delights.

Act Two

SCENE 1   *A lane by the wall of Capulet's orchard.*

Later in the evening of the party, Romeo returns alone to the Capulet home, hoping for another glimpse of Juliet. He climbs the wall and hides outside, in the orchard. Meanwhile, Benvolio and Mercutio come looking for him, but he remains hidden behind the wall. Mercutio makes fun of Romeo and his lovesick condition. Keep in mind that Mercutio and Benvolio think Romeo is still in love with Rosaline, since they know nothing about his meeting with Juliet.

[*Enter* Romeo *alone.*]

Romeo. Can I go forward when my heart is here?
Turn back, dull earth, and find thy center out.

[*climbs the wall and leaps down within it*]

[*Enter* Benvolio *with* Mercutio.]

Benvolio. Romeo! my cousin Romeo! Romeo!

1–2 Can . . . out: How can I leave when Juliet is still here? My body (**dull earth**) has to find its heart (**center**).

Balcony scene from the Globe Theatre's 2004 production

Mercutio.   He is wise,
And, on my life, hath stol'n him home to bed.

5 **Benvolio.** He ran this way, and leapt this orchard wall.
Call, good Mercutio.

Mercutio.   Nay, I'll conjure too.
Romeo! humors! madman! passion! lover!
Appear thou in the likeness of a sigh;
Speak but one rhyme, and I am satisfied!
10 Cry but "Ay me!" pronounce but "love" and "dove";
Speak to my gossip Venus one fair word, Ⓐ
One nickname for her purblind son and heir,
Young Adam Cupid, he that shot so trim
When King Cophetua loved the beggar maid!
15 He heareth not, he stirreth not, he moveth not;
The ape is dead, and I must conjure him.
I conjure thee by Rosaline's bright eyes,
By her high forehead and her scarlet lip,
By her fine foot, straight leg, and quivering thigh,
20 And the demesnes that there adjacent lie,
That in thy likeness thou appear to us!

Benvolio. An if he hear thee, thou wilt anger him.

Mercutio. This cannot anger him. 'Twould anger him
To raise a spirit in his mistress' circle
25 Of some strange nature, letting it there stand
Till she had laid it and conjured it down.
That were some spite; my invocation
Is fair and honest and in his mistress' name
I conjure only but to raise up him.

30 **Benvolio.** Come, he hath hid himself among these trees
To be consorted with the humorous night.
Blind is his love, and best befits the dark.

Mercutio. If love be blind, love cannot hit the mark.
Now will he sit under a medlar tree
35 And wish his mistress were that kind of fruit
As maids call medlars when they laugh alone.
Oh, Romeo, that she were, O, that she were
An open et cetera, thou a pop'rin pear!
Romeo, good night. I'll to my truckle bed;
40 This field-bed is too cold for me to sleep.
Come, shall we go?

Benvolio.   Go then, for 'tis in vain
To seek him here that means not to be found.

[*Exeunt.*]

6 conjure: use magic to call him.

8–21 Appear . . . us: Mercutio jokes about Romeo's lovesickness. He tries to make Romeo appear by suggestively naming parts of Rosaline's body.

Ⓐ **GRAMMAR AND STYLE**
In lines 8–11, Shakespeare creates rhythm through **parallelism,** or the use of similar grammatical structures to express related ideas. Notice how each of these lines begins with a verb in the imperative mood.

20 demesnes: areas; **adjacent:** next to.

23–29 'Twould . . . raise up him: It would anger him if I called a stranger to join his beloved (**mistress**), but I'm only calling Romeo to join her.

31 to be . . . night: to keep company with the night, which is as gloomy as Romeo is.

34 medlar: a fruit that looks like a small brown apple.

39 truckle bed: trundle bed, a small bed that fits in beneath a bigger one.

SCENE 2 *Capulet's orchard.*

The following is one of the most famous scenes in all literature. The speeches contain some of the most beautiful poetry Shakespeare ever wrote.

Juliet appears on the balcony outside her room. She cannot see Romeo, who stands in the garden just below. At the beginning of the scene, both characters are speaking private thoughts to themselves. Romeo, however, can hear Juliet as she expresses her love for him despite his family name. Eventually, he speaks directly to her, and they declare their love for each other. Just before dawn Romeo leaves to make plans for their wedding.

[*Enter* Romeo.]

Romeo. He jests at scars that never felt a wound.

[*Enter* Juliet *above at a window.*]

But soft! What light through yonder window breaks?
It is the East, and Juliet is the sun!
Arise, fair sun, and kill the envious moon,
5 Who is already sick and pale with grief
That thou her maid art far more fair than she.
Be not her maid, since she is envious;
Her vestal livery is but sick and green,
And none but fools do wear it; cast it off.
10 It is my lady; O, it is my love!
O that she knew she were!
She speaks, yet she says nothing. What of that?
Her eye discourses; I will answer it.
I am too bold; 'tis not to me she speaks.
15 Two of the fairest stars in all the heaven,
Having some business, do entreat her eyes
To twinkle in their spheres till they return.
What if her eyes were there, they in her head?
The brightness of her cheek would shame those stars
20 As daylight doth a lamp; her eyes in heaven
Would through the airy region stream so bright
That birds would sing and think it were not night.
See how she leans her cheek upon her hand!
O that I were a glove upon that hand,
25 That I might touch that cheek! **Ⓑ**

Juliet.   Ay me!

Romeo.   She speaks.
O, speak again, bright angel! for thou art
As glorious to this night, being o'er my head,
As is a winged messenger of heaven

---

1 **He jests...wound:** Romeo has overheard Mercutio and comments that Mercutio makes fun of love because he has never been wounded by it.

2–9 **But soft...cast it off:** Romeo sees Juliet at the window. For a moment he is speechless (**soft:** be still), but then he describes her beauty in glowing images.

13–14 **Her eye...speaks:** Romeo shifts back and forth between wanting to speak to Juliet and being afraid.

15–22 **Two of...not night:** Romeo compares Juliet's eyes to stars in the sky.

Ⓑ SOLILOQUY
To whom is Romeo speaking in lines 2–25? Explain what this soliloquy tells you about Romeo's thoughts.

25 Juliet begins to speak, not knowing that Romeo is nearby.

26–32 **thou art...of the air:** He compares Juliet to an angel (**winged messenger of heaven**) who stands on (**bestrides**) the clouds.

Unto the white-upturned wond'ring eyes
30 Of mortals that fall back to gaze on him
When he bestrides the lazy-pacing clouds
And sails upon the bosom of the air.

Juliet. O Romeo, Romeo! wherefore art thou Romeo?
Deny thy father and refuse thy name!
35 Or, if thou wilt not, be but sworn my love,
And I'll no longer be a Capulet.

Romeo [*aside*]. Shall I hear more, or shall I speak at this?

Juliet. 'Tis but thy name that is my enemy.
Thou art thyself, though not a Montague.
40 What's Montague? It is nor hand, nor foot,
Nor arm, nor face, nor any other part
Belonging to a man. O, be some other name!
What's in a name? That which we call a rose
By any other name would smell as sweet.
45 So Romeo would, were he not Romeo called,
Retain that dear perfection which he owes
Without that title. Romeo, doff thy name;
And for that name, which is no part of thee,
Take all myself.

Romeo.   I take thee at thy word.
50 Call me but love, and I'll be new baptized;
Henceforth I never will be Romeo.

Juliet. What man art thou that, thus bescreened in night,
So stumblest on my counsel?

Romeo.   By a name
I know not how to tell thee who I am.
55 My name, dear saint, is hateful to myself,
Because it is an enemy to thee.
Had I it written, I would tear the word.

Juliet. My ears have yet not drunk a hundred words
Of that tongue's utterance, yet I know the sound.
60 Art thou not Romeo, and a Montague?

Romeo. Neither, fair saint, if either thee dislike.

Juliet. How camest thou hither, tell me, and wherefore?
The orchard walls are high and hard to climb,
And the place death, considering who thou art,
65 If any of my kinsmen find thee here.

33 wherefore: why. Juliet asks why Romeo is who he is—someone from her enemy's family. *What does Juliet ask Romeo to do? What does she promise to do?*

43–47 Juliet tries to convince herself that a name is just a meaningless word that has nothing to do with the person. She asks Romeo to get rid of (**doff**) his name.

52–53 Juliet is startled that someone hiding (**bescreened**) nearby hears her private thoughts (**counsel**).

63–65 *What warning does Juliet give Romeo?*

Romeo. With love's light wings did I o'erperch these walls;
For stony limits cannot hold love out,
And what love can do, that dares love attempt.
Therefore thy kinsmen are no let to me.

70 **Juliet.** If they do see thee, they will murder thee.

Romeo. Alack, there lies more peril in thine eye
Than twenty of their swords! Look thou but sweet,
And I am proof against their enmity.

Juliet. I would not for the world they saw thee here.

75 **Romeo.** I have night's cloak to hide me from their sight;
And but thou love me, let them find me here.
My life were better ended by their hate
Than death prorogued, wanting of thy love. **C**

Juliet. By whose direction foundst thou out this place?

80 **Romeo.** By love, that first did prompt me to enquire.
He lent me counsel, and I lent him eyes.
I am no pilot, yet, wert thou as far
As that vast shore washed with the farthest sea,
I would adventure for such merchandise.

85 **Juliet.** Thou knowest the mask of night is on my face;
Else would a maiden blush bepaint my cheek
For that which thou hast heard me speak tonight.
Fain would I dwell on form—fain, fain deny
What I have spoke; but farewell compliment!

90 Dost thou love me? I know thou wilt say "Ay";
And I will take thy word. Yet, if thou swearst,
Thou mayst prove false. At lovers' perjuries,
They say Jove laughs. O gentle Romeo,
If thou dost love, pronounce it faithfully.

95 Or if thou thinkst I am too quickly won,
I'll frown, and be perverse, and say thee nay,
So thou wilt woo; but else, not for the world.
In truth, fair Montague, I am too fond,
And therefore thou mayst think my 'havior light;

100 But trust me, gentleman, I'll prove more true
Than those that have more cunning to be strange.
I should have been more strange, I must confess,
But that thou overheardst, ere I was ware,
My true love's passion. Therefore pardon me,

105 And not impute this yielding to light love,
Which the dark night hath so discovered.

66–69 **With . . . me:** Love helped me climb (**o'erperch**) the walls. Neither walls nor your relatives are a hindrance (**let**) to me.

72–73 **Look . . . enmity:** Smile on me, and I will be defended against my enemies' hatred (**enmity**).

78 **than death . . . love:** than my death postponed (**prorogued**) if you don't love me.

C **CHARACTER**
Reread lines 75–78, and explain what Romeo means. Do you think he is seriously thinking of death here, or is he just exaggerating because he's head over heels in love? Explain.

85–89 **Thou . . . compliment:** Had I known you were listening, I would have gladly (**fain**) behaved more properly, but now it's too late for good manners (**farewell compliment**). *Why is Juliet embarrassed that Romeo overheard her?*

92–93 **At . . . laughs:** Jove, the king of the gods, laughs at lovers who lie to each other.

95–101 **Or if . . . strange:** You might think I've fallen in love too easily and that I'm too outspoken. But I'll be truer to you than those who play games to hide their real feelings (**be strange**).

Romeo. Lady, by yonder blessed moon I swear,
That tips with silver all these fruit-tree tops—

Juliet. O, swear not by the moon, the inconstant moon,
110 That monthly changes in her circled orb,
Lest that thy love prove likewise variable.

Romeo. What shall I swear by?

Juliet.   Do not swear at all;
Or if thou wilt, swear by thy gracious self,
Which is the god of my idolatry,
115 And I'll believe thee.

109–111 *Why doesn't Juliet want Romeo to swear by the moon?*

Balcony scene from the Seattle Repertory Theatre's 2003 production

Romeo. If my heart's dear love—

Juliet. Well, do not swear. Although I joy in thee,
I have no joy of this contract tonight.
It is too rash, too unadvised, too sudden;
Too like the lightning, which doth cease to be
120 Ere one can say "It lightens." Sweet, good night!
This bud of love, by summer's ripening breath,
May prove a beauteous flow'r when next we meet.
Good night, good night! As sweet repose and rest
Come to thy heart as that within my breast! **D**

125 **Romeo.** O, wilt thou leave me so unsatisfied?

Juliet. What satisfaction canst thou have tonight?

Romeo. The exchange of thy love's faithful vow for mine.

Juliet. I gave thee mine before thou didst request it;
And yet I would it were to give again.

130 **Romeo.** Wouldst thou withdraw it? For what purpose, love?

Juliet. But to be frank and give it thee again.
And yet I wish but for the thing I have.
My bounty is as boundless as the sea,
My love as deep; the more I give to thee,
135 The more I have, for both are infinite.
I hear some noise within. Dear love, adieu!

[Nurse *calls within.*]

Anon, good nurse! Sweet Montague, be true.
Stay but a little, I will come again.
[*Exit.*]

Romeo. O blessed, blessed night! I am afeard,
140 Being in night, all this is but a dream,
Too flattering-sweet to be substantial.

[*Re-enter* Juliet, *above.*]

Juliet. Three words, dear Romeo, and good night indeed.
If that thy bent of love be honorable,
Thy purpose marriage, send me word tomorrow,
145 By one that I'll procure to come to thee,
Where and what time thou wilt perform the rite;
And all my fortunes at thy foot I'll lay
And follow thee my lord throughout the world.

Nurse [*within*]. Madam!

150 **Juliet.** I come, anon.—But if thou meanst not well,
I do beseech thee—

---

117 I have . . . contract: I am concerned about this declaration of love (**contract**).

D CHARACTER
Reread lines 116–124, and describe Juliet's attitude at this point. How does she feel about Romeo? Why does she seem uneasy about their relationship?

137–138 anon: right away. Juliet calls to her nurse but asks Romeo to wait, as she will come back soon.

143–146 If that . . . rite: I'll send a messenger to you tomorrow. If your intention is to marry me, tell the messenger where and when the ceremony will be.

150–151 But if . . . thee: Juliet is still worried that Romeo is not serious.

Nurse [*within*].   Madam!

Juliet.   By-and-by I come.—
To cease thy suit and leave me to my grief.
Tomorrow will I send.

Romeo.   So thrive my soul—

Juliet. A thousand times good night! [*Exit.*]

155 **Romeo.** A thousand times the worse, to want thy light!
Love goes toward love as schoolboys from their books;
But love from love, towards school with heavy looks.

[*Enter* Juliet *again, above.*]

Juliet. Hist! Romeo, hist! O for a falc'ner's voice
To lure this tassel-gentle back again!
160 Bondage is hoarse and may not speak aloud;
Else would I tear the cave where Echo lies,
And make her airy tongue more hoarse than mine
With repetition of my Romeo's name.
Romeo!

165 **Romeo.** It is my soul that calls upon my name.
How silver-sweet sound lovers' tongues by night,
Like softest music to attending ears!

Juliet. Romeo!

Romeo.   My sweet?

Juliet.   What o'clock tomorrow
Shall I send to thee?

Romeo.   By the hour of nine.

170 **Juliet.** I will not fail. 'Tis twenty years till then.
I have forgot why I did call thee back.

Romeo. Let me stand here till thou remember it.

Juliet. I shall forget, to have thee still stand there,
Rememb'ring how I love thy company.

175 **Romeo.** And I'll still stay, to have thee still forget,
Forgetting any other home but this.

Juliet. 'Tis almost morning. I would have thee gone—
And yet no farther than a wanton's bird,
That lets it hop a little from her hand,
180 Like a poor prisoner in his twisted gyves,
And with a silk thread plucks it back again,
So loving-jealous of his liberty.

Romeo. I would I were thy bird.

156–157 Love . . . looks: The simile means that lovers meet as eagerly as schoolboys leave their books; lovers separate with the sadness of boys going to school.

158–163 Hist . . . name: Listen, Romeo, I wish I could speak your name as loudly as a falconer calls his falcon (**tassel-gentle**), but because of my parents I must whisper. **Echo** was a nymph in Greek mythology whose unreturned love for Narcissus caused her to waste away till only her voice was left.

177–182 I would . . . liberty: I know you must go, but I want you close to me like a pet bird that a thoughtless child (**wanton**) keeps on a string.

Juliet.   Sweet, so would I.
Yet I should kill thee with much cherishing.
185 Good night, good night! Parting is such sweet sorrow,
That I shall say good night till it be morrow.

[*Exit.*]

Romeo. Sleep dwell upon thine eyes, peace in thy breast!
Would I were sleep and peace, so sweet to rest!
Hence will I to my ghostly father's cell,
190 His help to crave and my dear hap to tell.

[*Exit.*]

189–190 ghostly father: spiritual adviser or priest; **dear hap:** good fortune.

SCENE 3   *Friar Laurence's cell in the monastery.*

Romeo goes from Capulet's garden to the monastery where Friar Laurence lives. The friar knows Romeo well and often gives him advice. As the scene begins, Friar Laurence is gathering herbs in the early morning. He talks of good and bad uses for herbs. Keep this in mind, since Friar Laurence's skill at mixing herbs becomes important later in the play. Romeo tells the friar that he loves Juliet and wants to marry her. The friar is amazed that Romeo has forgotten about Rosaline so easily and suggests that Romeo might be acting in haste. Eventually, however, he agrees to marry Romeo and Juliet, hoping that the marriage will end the feud between their families.

[*Enter* Friar Laurence *alone, with a basket.*]

Friar Laurence. The grey-eyed morn smiles on the frowning night,
Chequ'ring the Eastern clouds with streaks of light;
And flecked darkness like a drunkard reels
5 From forth day's path and Titan's fiery wheels.
Now, ere the sun advance his burning eye
The day to cheer and night's dank dew to dry,
I must upfill this osier cage of ours
With baleful weeds and precious-juiced flowers.
10 The earth that's nature's mother is her tomb,
What is her burying grave, that is her womb;
And from her womb children of divers kind
We sucking on her natural bosom find;
Many for many virtues excellent,
15 None but for some, and yet all different.
O, mickle is the powerful grace that lies
In plants, herbs, stones, and their true qualities;
For naught so vile that on the earth doth live
But to the earth some special good doth give;

1–30 Friar Laurence begins his speech by describing how night changes into day. He then speaks of the herbs he is collecting. The friar is particularly fascinated with the idea that in herbs as well as man both good and evil can exist.

4 Titan is the god whose chariot pulls the sun into the sky each morning.

7 osier cage: willow basket.

9–12 The earth ... find: The same earth that acts as a tomb is also the womb, or birthplace, of various useful plants that people can harvest.

15–18 mickle: great. The friar says that nothing from the earth is so evil that it doesn't do some good.

Nor aught so good but, strained from that fair use,
20 Revolts from true birth, stumbling on abuse.
Virtue itself turns vice, being misapplied,
And vice sometime's by action dignified.
Within the infant rind of this small flower
Poison hath residence, and medicine power;
25 For this, being smelt, with that part cheers each part;
Being tasted, slays all senses with the heart.
Two such opposed kings encamp them still
In man as well as herbs—grace and rude will;
And where the worser is predominant,
30 Full soon the canker death eats up that plant.

[*Enter* Romeo.]

Romeo. Good morrow, father.

Friar Laurence.   Benedicite!
What early tongue so sweet saluteth me?
Young son, it argues a distempered head
So soon to bid good morrow to thy bed.
35 Care keeps his watch in every old man's eye,
And where care lodges sleep will never lie;
But where unbruised youth with unstuffed brain
Doth couch his limbs, there golden sleep doth reign.
Therefore thy earliness doth me assure
40 Thou art uproused with some distemp'rature;
Or if not so, then here I hit it right—
Our Romeo hath not been in bed tonight.

Romeo. That last is true, the sweeter rest was mine.

Friar Laurence. God pardon sin! Wast thou with Rosaline?

45 **Romeo.** With Rosaline, my ghostly father? No.
I have forgot that name, and that name's woe.

Friar Laurence. That's my good son! But where hast thou been
     then?

Romeo. I'll tell thee ere thou ask it me again.
I have been feasting with mine enemy,
50 Where on a sudden one hath wounded me
That's by me wounded. Both our remedies
Within thy help and holy physic lies.
I bear no hatred, blessed man, for, lo,
My intercession likewise steads my foe.

55 **Friar Laurence.** Be plain, good son, and homely in thy drift.
Riddling confession finds but riddling shrift.

23–26 Within . . . heart: He holds a flower that can be used either as a poison or as a medicine. If the flower is smelled, its fragrance can improve health in each part of the body; if it is eaten, it causes death.

28 grace and rude will: good and evil. Both exist in people as well as in plants.

31 Benedicite (bĕ′nĕ-dī′sĭ-tē′): God bless you.

33–42 it argues . . . tonight: Only a disturbed (**distempered**) mind could make you get up so early. Old people may have trouble sleeping, but it is not normal for someone as young as you. Or were you up all night?

44 God . . . Rosaline: The friar is shocked that Romeo has not been to bed yet. *Where does he think Romeo has been?*

49–56 Romeo tries to explain the situation, asking for help both for himself and his "foe" (Juliet). The friar does not understand Romeo's convoluted language and asks him to speak clearly so that he can help.

Romeo. Then plainly know my heart's dear love is set
On the fair daughter of rich Capulet;
As mine on hers, so hers is set on mine,
60 And all combined, save what thou must combine
By holy marriage. When, and where, and how
We met, we wooed, and made exchange of vow,
I'll tell thee as we pass; but this I pray,
That thou consent to marry us today.

65 **Friar Laurence.** Holy Saint Francis! What a change is here!
Is Rosaline, that thou didst love so dear,
So soon forsaken? Young men's love then lies
Not truly in their hearts, but in their eyes.

66–68 *What is Friar Laurence saying in these lines?*

Friar Laurence counsels Romeo in the University of Victoria's 1998 production.

Jesu Maria! What a deal of brine

70 Hath washed thy sallow cheeks for Rosaline!
How much salt water thrown away in waste,
To season love, that of it doth not taste!
The sun not yet thy sighs from heaven clears,
Thy old groans ring yet in mine ancient ears.

75 Lo, here upon thy cheek the stain doth sit
Of an old tear that is not washed off yet.
If e'er thou wast thyself, and these woes thine,
Thou and these woes were all for Rosaline.
And art thou changed? Pronounce this sentence then:

80 Women may fall when there's no strength in men.

Romeo. Thou chidst me oft for loving Rosaline.

Friar Laurence. For doting, not for loving, pupil mine.

Romeo. And badest me bury love.

Friar Laurence.   Not in a grave
To lay one in, another ought to have.

85 **Romeo.** I pray thee chide not. She whom I love now
Doth grace for grace and love for love allow.
The other did not so.

Friar Laurence.   O, she knew well
Thy love did read by rote, that could not spell.
But come, young waverer, come go with me.

90 In one respect I'll thy assistant be;
For this alliance may so happy prove
To turn your households' rancor to pure love. **E**

Romeo. O, let us hence! I stand on sudden haste.

Friar Laurence. Wisely, and slow. They stumble that run fast.

[*Exeunt.*]

69 brine: salt water—that is, the tears that Romeo has been shedding for Rosaline.

80 Women . . . men: If men are so weak, women may be forgiven for sinning.

81–82 chidst: scolded. The friar replies that he scolded Romeo for being lovesick, not for loving.

85–88 She whom . . . spell: Romeo says that the woman he loves feels the same way about him. That wasn't true of Rosaline. The friar replies that Rosaline knew that he didn't know what real love is.

91–92 For this . . . prove: this marriage may work out so well; **rancor:** bitter hate.

E CHARACTER
Why does Friar Laurence agree to help Romeo marry Juliet, despite his worry that Romeo falls in love too easily? Explain the friar's **motives.**

SCENE 4 *A street.*

Several hours after his meeting with Friar Laurence, Romeo meets Benvolio and Mercutio in the street. He is excited and happy; his mood is key to the comic nature of this scene, which includes much talk of swordplay and many suggestive jokes. Mercutio makes fun of Tybalt and teases Romeo. The nurse comes to carry a message from Romeo to Juliet. Romeo tells her that Juliet should meet him at Friar Laurence's cell for their secret marriage ceremony.

[*Enter* Benvolio *and* Mercutio.]

Mercutio. Where the devil should this Romeo be?
Came he not home tonight?

Benvolio. Not to his father's. I spoke with his man.

Mercutio. Why, that same pale hard-hearted wench, that Rosaline,
5 Torments him so that he will sure run mad.

Benvolio. Tybalt, the kinsman to old Capulet,
Hath sent a letter to his father's house.

Mercutio. A challenge, on my life.

Benvolio. Romeo will answer it.

10 **Mercutio.** Any man that can write may answer a letter.

Benvolio. Nay, he will answer the letter's master, how he dares, being dared.

Mercutio. Alas, poor Romeo, he is already dead! stabbed with a white wench's black eye; shot through the ear with a love song;
15 the very pin of his heart cleft with the blind bow-boy's butt-shaft; and is he a man to encounter Tybalt?

Benvolio. Why, what is Tybalt?

Mercutio. More than Prince of Cats, I can tell you. O, he's the courageous captain of compliments. He fights as you sing
20 pricksong—keeps time, distance, and proportion; rests me his minim rest, one, two, and the third in your bosom! the very butcher of a silk button, a duelist, a duelist! a gentleman of the very first house, of the first and second cause. Ah, the immortal *passado!* the *punto reverso!* the *hay!*

25 **Benvolio.** The what?

Mercutio. The pox of such antic, lisping, affecting fantasticoes—these new tuners of accent! "By Jesu, a very good blade! a very tall man! a very good whore!" Why, is not this a lamentable thing, grandsire, that we should be thus afflicted with these strange flies,
30 these fashion-mongers, these perdona-mi's, who stand so much on the new form that they cannot sit at ease on the old bench? O, their bones, their bones!

[*Enter* Romeo, *no longer moody.*]

Benvolio. Here comes Romeo! here comes Romeo!

Mercutio. Without his roe, like a dried herring. O, flesh, flesh,
35 how art thou fishified! Now is he for the numbers that Petrarch flowed in. Laura, to his lady, was but a kitchen wench (marry, she had a better love to berhyme her), Dido a dowdy, Cleopatra a gypsy, Helen and Hero hildings and harlots, Thisbe a grey eye

3 man: servant.

6–12 Tybalt . . . dared: Tybalt, still angry about Romeo's crashing the Capulet party, has sent a letter challenging Romeo to a duel. Benvolio says that Romeo will do more than answer the letter; he will accept Tybalt's challenge and fight him.

15 blind bow-boy's butt-shaft: Cupid's dull practice arrow. Mercutio suggests that Romeo fell in love with very little work on Cupid's part.

18–24 More than . . . hay: Mercutio mocks Tybalt's name. **Prince of Cats** refers to a cat in a fable, named Tybalt, who was known for his slyness. Then Mercutio makes fun of Tybalt's fancy new style of dueling, comparing it to precision singing (**pricksong**). *Passado, punto reverso,* and *hay* were terms used in the new dueling style.

26–32 The pox . . . their bones: Mercutio continues to make fun of people who embrace new styles and new manners of speaking.

34–39 without his roe: only part of himself (Mercutio makes fun of Romeo's name and his lovesickness); **numbers:** verses. Mercutio mentions Petrarch, who wrote sonnets to his love, Laura. According to Mercutio, Romeo's feelings for Rosaline are so intense that great loves in literature—Laura, Dido, and others—could never measure up.

or so, but not to the purpose. Signior Romeo, *bon jour!* There's a French salutation to your French slop. You gave us the counterfeit fairly last night.

Romeo. Good morrow to you both. What counterfeit did I give you?

Mercutio. The slip, sir, the slip. Can you not conceive?

45 **Romeo.** Pardon, good Mercutio. My business was great, and in such a case as mine a man may strain courtesy.

Mercutio. That's as much as to say, such a case as yours constrains a man to bow in the hams.

Romeo. Meaning, to curtsy.

50 **Mercutio.** Thou hast most kindly hit it.

Romeo. A most courteous exposition.

Mercutio. Nay, I am the very pink of courtesy.

Romeo. Pink for flower.

Mercutio. Right.

55 **Romeo.** Why, then is my pump well-flowered.

Mercutio. Well said! Follow me this jest now till thou hast worn out thy pump, that, when the single sole of it is worn, the jest may remain, after the wearing, solely singular.

Romeo. Oh, single-soled jest, solely singular for the singleness!

60 **Mercutio.** Come between us, good Benvolio! My wits faint.

Romeo. Switch and spurs, switch and spurs! or I'll cry a match.

Mercutio. Nay, if our wits run the wild-goose chase, I am done; for thou hast more of the wild goose in one of thy wits than, I am sure, I have in my whole five. Was I with you there for the
65 goose?

Romeo. Thou wast never with me for anything when thou wast not there for the goose.

Mercutio. I will bite thee by the ear for that jest.

Romeo. Nay, good goose, bite not!

70 **Mercutio.** Thy wit is a very bitter sweeting; it is a most sharp sauce.

Romeo. And is it not, then, well served in to a sweet goose?

Mercutio. O, here's a wit of cheveril, that stretches from an inch narrow to an ell broad!

39–44 *bon jour:* "Good day" in French; **There's . . . last night:** Here's a greeting to match your fancy French trousers (**slop**). You did a good job of getting away from us last night. (A piece of counterfeit money was called a **slip**.)

44–81 In these lines, Romeo and Mercutio have a battle of wits. They keep trying to top each other with funnier comments and cleverer puns.

55 pump: shoe; **well-flowered:** Shoes were "pinked," or punched out in flowerlike designs.

61 Switch . . . match: Keep going, or I'll claim victory.

64–65 Was . . . goose: Have I proved that you are a foolish person?

73 cheveril: kidskin, which is flexible. Mercutio means that a little wit stretches a long way.

75 **Romeo.** I stretch it out for that word "broad," which, added to the goose, proves thee far and wide a broad goose.

Mercutio. Why, is not this better now than groaning for love? Now art thou sociable, now art thou Romeo; now art thou what thou art, by art as well as by nature. For this driveling love is like 80 a great natural that runs lolling up and down to hide his bauble in a hole.

Benvolio. Stop there, stop there!

Mercutio. Thou desirest me to stop in my tale against the hair.

Benvolio. Thou wouldst else have made thy tale large.

85 **Mercutio.** O, thou art deceived! I would have made it short; for I was come to the whole depth of my tale, and meant indeed to occupy the argument no longer.

[*Enter* Nurse *and* Peter, *her servant. He is carrying a large fan.*]

Romeo. Here's goodly gear!

Mercutio. A sail, a sail!

90 **Benvolio.** Two, two! a shirt and a smock.

Nurse. Peter!

Peter. Anon.

Nurse. My fan, Peter.

Mercutio. Good Peter, to hide her face; for her fan's the fairer of 95 the two.

Nurse. God ye good morrow, gentlemen.

Mercutio. God ye good-den, fair gentlewoman.

Nurse. Is it good-den?

Mercutio. 'Tis no less, I tell ye, for the bawdy hand of the dial is 100 now upon the prick of noon.

Nurse. Out upon you! What a man are you!

Romeo. One, gentlewoman, that God hath made himself to mar.

Nurse. By my troth, it is well said. "For himself to mar," quoth'a? Gentlemen, can any of you tell me where I may find the young 105 Romeo?

Romeo. I can tell you; but young Romeo will be older when you have found him than he was when you sought him. I am the youngest of that name, for fault of a worse.

80–81 **great natural:** an idiot, like a jester or clown who carries a fool's stick (**bauble**).

88–89 **goodly gear:** something fine to joke about; **a sail:** Mercutio likens the nurse in all her petticoats to a huge ship coming toward them.

93 Fans were usually carried only by fine ladies. The nurse is trying to pretend that she is more than a servant.

Nurse. You say well.

110 **Mercutio.** Yea, is the worst well? Very well took, i' faith! wisely, wisely.

Nurse. If you be he, sir, I desire some confidence with you.

Benvolio. She will endite him to some supper.

Mercutio. A bawd, a bawd, a bawd! So ho!

115 **Romeo.** What hast thou found?

Mercutio. No hare, sir; unless a hare, sir, in a lenten pie, that is something stale and hoar ere it be spent.

[*sings*]

> "An old hare hoar,
> And an old hare hoar,
120 > Is very good meat in Lent.
> But a hare that is hoar,
> Is too much for a score
> When it hoars ere it be spent."

Romeo, will you come to your father's? We'll to dinner thither.

125 **Romeo.** I will follow you.

Mercutio. Farewell, ancient lady. Farewell, [*sings*] lady, lady, lady.

[*Exeunt* Mercutio *and* Benvolio.]

Nurse. Marry, farewell! I pray you, sir, what saucy merchant was this that was so full of his ropery?

Romeo. A gentleman, nurse, that loves to hear himself talk and 130 will speak more in a minute than he will stand to in a month.

Nurse. An 'a speak anything against me, I'll take him down, an 'a were lustier than he is, and twenty such Jacks; and if I cannot, I'll find those that shall. Scurvy knave! I am none of his flirt-gills; I am none of his skainsmates. [*turning to* Peter] And thou must 135 stand by too, and suffer every knave to use me at his pleasure?

Peter. I saw no man use you at his pleasure. If I had, my weapon should quickly have been out, I warrant you. I dare draw as soon as another man, if I see occasion in a good quarrel, and the law on my side.

112–113 confidence: The nurse means *conference;* she uses big words without understanding their meaning; **endite:** Benvolio makes fun of the nurse by using this word rather than *invite.*

114–124 Mercutio calls the nurse a **bawd,** or woman who runs a house of prostitution. His song uses the insulting puns **hare,** a rabbit or prostitute, and **hoar,** old.

128 ropery: roguery, or jokes.

133–134 The nurse is angry that Mercutio treated her like one of his loose women (**flirt-gills**) or his gangsterlike friends (**skainsmates**).

Behind the Curtain

The Orlando-UCF Shakespeare Festival's 1992 production

The University of South Carolina's 1999 production

The Royal Shakespeare Company's 1992 production

Set Design

Often, set designers recreate the world of *Romeo and Juliet* in strikingly unique ways. Designers of the productions pictured here created radically different **sets** for the balcony scene. List three adjectives you would use to describe each set. What factors might make a designer choose to create one of these particular set styles?

140 **Nurse.** Now, afore God, I am so vexed that every part about me
quivers. Scurvy knave! Pray you, sir, a word; and as I told you,
my young lady bade me enquire you out. What she bid me say,
I will keep to myself; but first let me tell ye, if ye should lead her
into a fool's paradise, as they say, it were a very gross kind of
145 behavior, as they say; for the gentlewoman is young; and
therefore, if you should deal double with her, truly it were an ill
thing to be offered to any gentlewoman, and very weak dealing.

Romeo. Nurse, commend me to thy lady and mistress. I protest
unto thee—

150 **Nurse.** Good heart, and i' faith I will tell her as much. Lord,
Lord! she will be a joyful woman.

Romeo. What wilt thou tell her, nurse? Thou dost not mark me.

Nurse. I will tell her, sir, that you do protest, which, as I take it,
is a gentlemanlike offer.

155 **Romeo.** Bid her devise
Some means to come to shrift this afternoon;
And there she shall at Friar Laurence' cell
Be shrived and married. Here is for thy pains.

Nurse. No, truly, sir; not a penny.

160 **Romeo.** Go to! I say you shall.

Nurse. This afternoon, sir? Well, she shall be there.

Romeo. And stay, good nurse, behind the abbey wall.
Within this hour my man shall be with thee
And bring thee cords made like a tackled stair,
165 Which to the high topgallant of my joy
Must be my convoy in the secret night.
Farewell. Be trusty, and I'll quit thy pains.
Farewell. Commend me to thy mistress.

Nurse. Now God in heaven bless thee! Hark you, sir.

170 **Romeo.** What sayst thou, my dear nurse?

Nurse. Is your man secret? Did you ne'er hear say,
Two may keep counsel, putting one away?

Romeo. I warrant thee my man's as true as steel.

Nurse. Well, sir, my mistress is the sweetest lady. Lord, Lord!
175 when 'twas a little prating thing—O, there is a nobleman in
town, one Paris, that would fain lay knife aboard; but she, good
soul, had as lief see a toad, a very toad, as see him. I anger her

142–147 The nurse warns Romeo that he'd better mean what he said about marrying Juliet. She holds back her news while she tries to decide if Romeo's love is genuine.

148 commend me: give my respectful greetings.

155–159 Romeo tells the nurse to have Juliet come to Friar Laurence's cell this afternoon, using the excuse that she is going to confess her sins (**shrift**). There she will receive forgiveness for her sins (**be shrived**) and be married.

164–165 tackled stair: rope ladder; **topgallant:** highest point.

167–172 quit thy pains: reward you. The nurse then asks Romeo if his servant can be trusted, then quotes the saying that two can keep a secret but not three.

174–177 The nurse begins to babble about Paris' proposal but says that Juliet would rather look at a toad than at Paris.

sometimes, and tell her that Paris is the properer man; but I'll warrant you, when I say so, she looks as pale as any clout in the 180 versal world. Doth not rosemary and Romeo begin both with a letter?

Romeo. Ay, nurse, what of that? Both with an R.

Nurse. Ah, mocker! that's the dog's name. R is for the—No; I know it begins with some other letter; and she hath the prettiest 185 sententious of it, of you and rosemary, that it would do you good to hear it.

Romeo. Commend me to thy lady.

Nurse. Ay, a thousand times. [*Exit* Romeo.] Peter!

Peter. Anon.

190 **Nurse.** Peter, take my fan, and go before, and apace.

[*Exeunt.*]

179–186 **clout:** old cloth; **the versal world:** the entire world; **Doth not . . . hear it:** The nurse tries to recall a clever saying that Juliet made up about Romeo and rosemary, the herb for remembrance, but cannot remember it. She is sure that the two words couldn't begin with *R* because this letter sounds like a snarling dog; **sententious:** The nurse means *sentences*.

190 **apace:** quickly.

SCENE 5   *Capulet's orchard.*

Juliet is a nervous wreck, having waited for more than three hours for the nurse to return. When the nurse does arrive, she simply won't come to the point. Juliet gets more and more upset, until the nurse finally reveals the wedding arrangements.

[*Enter* Juliet.]

Juliet. The clock struck nine when I did send the nurse;
In half an hour she promised to return.
Perchance she cannot meet him. That's not so.
O, she is lame! Love's heralds should be thoughts,
5 Which ten times faster glide than the sun's beams
Driving back shadows over lowering hills.
Therefore do nimble-pinioned doves draw Love,
And therefore hath the wind-swift Cupid wings. **F**
Now is the sun upon the highmost hill
10 Of this day's journey, and from nine till twelve
Is three long hours; yet she is not come.
Had she affections and warm youthful blood,
She would be as swift in motion as a ball;
My words would bandy her to my sweet love,
15 And his to me.
But old folks, many feign as they were dead—
Unwieldy, slow, heavy, and pale as lead.
[*Enter* Nurse *and* Peter.] O God, she comes! O honey nurse,
   what news?

4–6 **Love's . . . hills:** Love's messengers should be thoughts, which travel ten times faster than sunbeams.

7 **nimble-pinioned . . . Love:** Swift-winged doves pull the chariot of Venus, goddess of love.

F **ALLUSION**
What do Juliet's allusions to Venus and to Cupid emphasize about her state of mind as she waits for the nurse to return?

14 **bandy:** toss.

16 **feign as:** act as if.

Hast thou met with him? Send thy man away.

20 **Nurse.** Peter, stay at the gate.

[*Exit* Peter.]

Juliet. Now, good sweet nurse—O Lord, why lookst thou sad?
Though news be sad, yet tell them merrily;
If good, thou shamest the music of sweet news
By playing it to me with so sour a face.

25 **Nurse.** I am aweary, give me leave awhile.
Fie, how my bones ache! What a jaunce have I had!

Juliet. I would thou hadst my bones, and I thy news.
Nay, come, I pray thee speak. Good, good nurse, speak.

Nurse. Jesu, what haste! Can you not stay awhile?

30 Do you not see that I am out of breath?

Juliet. How art thou out of breath when thou hast breath
To say to me that thou art out of breath?
The excuse that thou dost make in this delay
Is longer than the tale thou dost excuse.

35 Is thy news good or bad? Answer to that.
Say either, and I'll stay the circumstance.
Let me be satisfied, is't good or bad?

Nurse. Well, you have made a simple choice; you know not how
to choose a man. Romeo? No, not he. Though his face be better

40 than any man's, yet his leg excels all men's; and for a hand and a
foot, and a body, though they be not to be talked on, yet they are
past compare. He is not the flower of courtesy, but, I'll warrant
him, as gentle as a lamb. Go thy ways, wench; serve God. What,
have you dined at home?

45 **Juliet.** No, no. But all this did I know before.
What say he of our marriage? What of that?

Nurse. Lord, how my head aches! What a head have I!
It beats as it would fall in twenty pieces.
My back o' t'other side—ah, my back, my back!

50 Beshrew your heart for sending me about
To catch my death with jauncing up and down!

Juliet. I' faith, I am sorry that thou art not well.
Sweet, sweet, sweet nurse, tell me, what says my love?

21–22 The nurse teases Juliet by putting on a sad face as if the news were bad.

25–26 give me . . . I had: Leave me alone for a while. I ache all over because of the running back and forth I've been doing.

36 I'll . . . circumstance: I'll wait for the details.

38 simple: foolish.

50–51 Beshrew . . . down: Curse you for making me endanger my health by running around. *Considering the nurse's feelings for Juliet, do you think this is really an angry curse? Explain.*

Nurse. Your love says, like an honest gentleman, and a courteous,
55 and a kind, and a handsome, and, I warrant, a virtuous—Where
is your mother?

Juliet. Where is my mother? Why, she is within.
Where should she be? How oddly thou repliest!
"Your love says, like an honest gentleman,
60 'Where is your mother?'"

Nurse.   O God's Lady dear!
Are you so hot? Marry come up, I trow.
Is this the poultice for my aching bones?
Hence forward do your messages yourself.

Juliet. Here's such a coil! Come, what says Romeo?

65 **Nurse.** Have you got leave to go to shrift today?

Juliet. I have.

Nurse. Then hie you hence to Friar Laurence' cell;
There stays a husband to make you a wife.
Now comes the wanton blood up in your cheeks:
70 They'll be in scarlet straight at any news.
Hie you to church; I must another way,
To fetch a ladder, by the which your love
Must climb a bird's nest soon when it is dark.
I am the drudge, and toil in your delight;
75 But you shall bear the burden soon at night.
Go; I'll to dinner; hie you to the cell.

Juliet. Hie to high fortune! Honest nurse, farewell.

[*Exeunt.*]

61–62 Marry . . . bones: Control yourself! Is this the treatment I get for my pain?

64 coil: fuss.

67–68 Then hie . . . a wife: Then go quickly to Friar Laurence's cell, where Romeo is waiting to marry you.

71–73 The nurse will get the ladder that Romeo will use to climb to Juliet's room after they are married.

SCENE 6   *Friar Laurence's cell.*
Friar Laurence cautions Romeo to be more sensible in his love for Juliet. When she arrives, the two confess their love to each other and prepare to be married by Friar Laurence.

[*Enter* Friar Laurence *and* Romeo.]

Friar Laurence. So smile the heavens upon this holy act
That after-hours with sorrow chide us not!

Romeo. Amen, amen! But come what sorrow can,
It cannot countervail the exchange of joy
5 That one short minute gives me in her sight.
Do thou but close our hands with holy words,
Then love-devouring death do what he dare—
It is enough I may but call her mine.

1–2 So smile . . . us not: May heaven so bless this act that we won't regret it in the future (**after-hours**).

4 countervail: outweigh.

Friar Laurence. These violent delights have violent ends
10 And in their triumph die, like fire and powder,
Which, as they kiss, consume. The sweetest honey
Is loathsome in his own deliciousness
And in the taste confounds the appetite.
Therefore love moderately: long love doth so;
15 Too swift arrives as tardy as too slow. **Ⓖ**

[*Enter* Juliet.]

Here comes the lady. O, so light a foot
Will ne'er wear out the everlasting flint.
A lover may bestride the gossamer
That idles in the wanton summer air,
20 And yet not fall; so light is vanity.

Juliet. Good even to my ghostly confessor.

Friar Laurence. Romeo shall thank thee, daughter, for us both.

Juliet. As much to him, else is his thanks too much.

Romeo. Ah, Juliet, if the measure of thy joy
25 Be heaped like mine, and that thy skill be more
To blazon it, then sweeten with thy breath
This neighbor air, and let rich music's tongue
Unfold the imagined happiness that both
Receive in either by this dear encounter.

30 **Juliet.** Conceit, more rich in matter than in words,
Brags of his substance, not of ornament.
They are but beggars that can count their worth;
But my true love is grown to such excess
I cannot sum up sum of half my wealth.

35 **Friar Laurence.** Come, come with me, and we will make short work;
For, by your leaves, you shall not stay alone
Till Holy Church incorporate two in one.

[*Exeunt.*]

9–15 These . . . slow: The friar compares Romeo's passion to gunpowder and the fire that ignites it—both are destroyed—then to honey, whose sweetness can destroy the appetite. He reminds Romeo to practice moderation in love.

Ⓖ TRAGEDY
Consider what you know about Shakespearean tragedy. Do you think Romeo will take the advice Friar Laurence gives him in lines 9–15? Explain.

18–20 A lover . . . vanity: A lover can walk across a spider's web (**gossamer**) without falling.

23 as much to him: I give the same greeting to Romeo that he offers to me.

24–29 if the measure . . . encounter: If you are as happy as I am and have more skill to proclaim it, then sweeten the air by singing of our happiness to the world.

30–31 Conceit . . . ornament: True understanding (**conceit**) needs no words.

37 till Holy Church . . . one: till you are joined in marriage in a religious ceremony.

Comprehension

PENNSYLVANIA STANDARDS

READING STANDARD
B.1.1.1.A.1 Evaluate character

1. **Recall** Who challenges Romeo to a duel, and why?

2. **Recall** What important message from Romeo does the nurse bring to Juliet?

3. **Clarify** Why does Friar Laurence agree to marry Romeo and Juliet despite his reservations? Explain what he hopes this marriage will accomplish.

Literary Analysis

4. **Reading Shakespearean Drama** Examine the events you recorded in your chart as you read Act Two. Which events seem most crucial in escalating the **conflicts** in the plot? Explain your answer.

5. **Make Inferences About Character Motives** Why do Romeo and Juliet rush to get married after declaring their love? Support your inference with evidence from the text. Then explain whether you think the young lovers get married too soon, and why or why not.

6. **Analyze Soliloquy and Aside** Identify at least one soliloquy and one aside in Act Two and record them in a chart like the one shown. Complete the chart by explaining what each example reveals about the character speaking.

Scene and Lines	Character Who Speaks	Soliloquy or Aside?	What Is Revealed?
Scene 2, lines 1–25	Romeo		

7. **Analyze Character Development** Compare Romeo's behavior before he meets Juliet with his behavior after they declare their love for each other. What do you learn about Romeo from the change in his behavior?

Literary Criticism

8. **Author's Style** Shakespeare is often praised for his masterly use of **figurative language,** or language that communicates ideas beyond the ordinary, literal meaning of the words. Find two examples of particularly striking figurative language in Act Two and discuss what makes each example effective.

Act Three

SCENE 1 *A public place.*

Act Two ends with the joyful Romeo and Juliet secretly married. Their happiness, however, is about to end abruptly. In this scene, Mercutio, Benvolio, and Romeo meet Tybalt on the street. Tybalt insults Romeo, but Romeo, who has just returned from his wedding, remains calm. Mercutio, on the other hand, is furious with Tybalt, and they begin to fight. As Romeo tries to separate them, Tybalt stabs Mercutio, who later dies. Romeo then challenges Tybalt, kills him, and flees. The prince arrives and demands an explanation. He announces that Romeo will be killed if he does not leave Verona immediately.

[*Enter* Mercutio, Benvolio, Page, *and* Servants.]

Benvolio. I pray thee, good Mercutio, let's retire.
The day is hot, the Capulets abroad,
And if we meet, we shall not scape a brawl,
For now, these hot days, is the mad blood stirring.

5 **Mercutio.** Thou art like one of those fellows that, when he enters the confines of a tavern, claps me his sword upon the table and says "God send me no need of thee!" and by the operation of the second cup draws him on the drawer, when indeed there is no need.

10 **Benvolio.** Am I like such a fellow?

Mercutio. Come, come, thou art as hot a Jack in thy mood as any in Italy; and as soon moved to be moody, and as soon moody to be moved.

Benvolio. And what to?

15 **Mercutio.** Nay an there were two such, we should have none shortly, for one would kill the other. Thou! why, thou wilt quarrel with a man that hath a hair more or a hair less in his beard than thou hast. Thou wilt quarrel with a man for cracking nuts, having no other reason but because thou hast hazel eyes.

20 What eye but such an eye would spy out such a quarrel? Thy head is as full of quarrels as an egg is full of meat; and yet thy head hath been beaten as addle as an egg for quarreling. Thou hast quarreled with a man for coughing in the street, because he hath wakened thy dog that hath lain asleep in the sun. Didst

25 thou not fall out with a tailor for wearing his new doublet before Easter? with another for tying his new shoes with old riband? And yet thou wilt tutor me from quarreling!

3–4 we shall . . . stirring: We shall not avoid a fight, since the heat makes people ill-tempered.

7–8 by the . . . drawer: feeling the effects of a second drink, is ready to fight (**draw on**) the waiter who's pouring the drinks (**drawer**).

12–13 as soon moved . . . to be moved: as likely to get angry and start a fight.

15–27 Mercutio teases his friend by insisting that Benvolio is quick to pick a fight, though everyone knows that Benvolio is gentle and peace loving.

25 doublet: jacket.
26 riband: ribbon or laces.

Mercutio and Tybalt duel in the 2004 coproduction of the Chicago Shakespeare Theater and Second City.

Benvolio. An I were so apt to quarrel as thou art, any man should buy the fee simple of my life for an hour and a quarter.

30 **Mercutio.** The fee simple? O simple!

[*Enter* Tybalt *and others.*]

Benvolio. By my head, here come the Capulets. **A**

Mercutio. By my heel, I care not.

Tybalt. Follow me close, for I will speak to them. Gentlemen, good den. A word with one of you.

35 **Mercutio.** And but one word with one of us? Couple it with something; make it a word and a blow.

Tybalt. You shall find me apt enough to that, sir, an you will give me occasion.

Mercutio. Could you not take some occasion without giving?

40 **Tybalt.** Mercutio, thou consortest with Romeo.

Mercutio. Consort? What, dost thou make us minstrels? An thou make minstrels of us, look to hear nothing but discords. Here's my fiddlestick; here's that shall make you dance. Zounds, consort!

45 **Benvolio.** We talk here in the public haunt of men.
Either withdraw unto some private place
And reason coldly of your grievances,
Or else depart. Here all eyes gaze on us.

Mercutio. Men's eyes were made to look, and let them gaze.
50 I will not budge for no man's pleasure, I.

[*Enter* Romeo.]

Tybalt. Well, peace be with you, sir. Here comes my man.

Mercutio. But I'll be hanged, sir, if he wear your livery.
Marry, go before to field, he'll be your follower!
Your worship in that sense may call him man.

55 **Tybalt.** Romeo, the love I bear thee can afford
No better term than this: thou art a villain.

Romeo. Tybalt, the reason that I have to love thee
Doth much excuse the appertaining rage
To such a greeting. Villain am I none.
60 Therefore farewell. I see thou knowst me not. **B**

Tybalt. Boy, this shall not excuse the injuries
That thou hast done me; therefore turn and draw.

Romeo. I do protest I never injured thee,
But love thee better than thou canst devise

28–29 An I . . . quarter: If I picked fights as quickly as you do, anybody could own me for the smallest amount of money.

A TRAGEDY
As you read lines 31–79, think about the play's mounting **conflict.** Ask yourself: Who is responsible for starting this sword fight? Cite evidence to support your viewpoint.

40–44 consortest: keep company with. Tybalt means "You are friends with Romeo." Mercutio pretends to misunderstand him, assuming that Tybalt is insulting him by calling Romeo and him a **consort,** a group of traveling musicians. He then refers to his sword as his **fiddlestick,** the bow for a fiddle.

45–48 *What does Benvolio want Tybalt and Mercutio to do?*

51–54 When Romeo enters, Mercutio again pretends to misunderstand Tybalt. By **my man,** Tybalt means "the man I'm looking for." Mercutio takes it to mean "my servant." (**Livery** is a servant's uniform.) He assures Tybalt that the only place Romeo would follow him is to the dueling field.

57–59 I forgive your anger because I have reason to love you.

B CHARACTER
What **motive** does Romeo have for not wanting to fight Tybalt? Who else knows about this motive?

61 boy: an insulting term of address.

65 Till thou shalt know the reason of my love;
And so, good Capulet, which name I tender
As dearly as mine own, be satisfied.

Mercutio. O calm, dishonorable, vile submission!
Alla stoccata carries it away.

[*draws*]

70 Tybalt, you ratcatcher, will you walk?

Tybalt. What wouldst thou have with me?

Mercutio. Good King of Cats, nothing but one of your nine lives.
That I mean to make bold withal, and, as you shall use me
hereafter, dry-beat the rest of the eight. Will you pluck your
75 sword out of his pilcher by the ears? Make haste, lest mine be
about your ears ere it be out.

Tybalt. I am for you.

[*draws*]

Romeo. Gentle Mercutio, put thy rapier up.

Mercutio. Come, sir, your *passado!*

[*They fight.*]

80 **Romeo.** Draw, Benvolio; beat down their weapons.
Gentlemen, for shame! forbear this outrage!
Tybalt, Mercutio, the Prince expressly hath
Forbid this bandying in Verona streets.
Hold, Tybalt! Good Mercutio!

[Tybalt, *under* Romeo's *arm, thrusts* Mercutio *in, and flies with his* Men.]

Mercutio.   I am hurt.
85 A plague o' both your houses! I am sped.
Is he gone and hath nothing?

Benvolio.   What, art thou hurt?

Mercutio. Ay, ay, a scratch, a scratch. Marry, 'tis enough.
Where is my page? Go, villain, fetch a surgeon.

[*Exit* Page.]

Romeo. Courage, man. The hurt cannot be much.

90 **Mercutio.** No, 'tis not so deep as a well, nor so wide as a church
door; but 'tis enough, 'twill serve. Ask for me tomorrow, and you
shall find me a grave man. I am peppered, I warrant, for this
world. A plague o' both your houses! Zounds, a dog, a rat, a
mouse, a cat, to scratch a man to death! A braggart, a rogue, a

---

66 tender: cherish.

68–70 Mercutio assumes that Romeo is afraid to fight. **Alla stoccata** is a move used in sword fighting; Mercutio is suggesting that Tybalt has won the battle of words with Romeo. Mercutio then dares Tybalt to step aside and fight (**walk**).

72–74 nothing but . . . eight: I intend to take one of your nine lives (as a cat supposedly has) and give a beating to the other eight.

79 *passado*: a sword-fighting maneuver.

80–84 Romeo wants Benvolio to help him stop the fight. They are able to hold back Mercutio.

83 bandying: fighting.

85 A plague . . . sped: I curse both the Montagues and the Capulets. I am destroyed.

90–96 Even as he lies dying, Mercutio continues to joke and make nasty remarks about Tybalt. He makes a pun on the word *grave.*

95 villain, that fights by the book of arithmetic! Why the devil came
    you between us? I was hurt under your arm.

    Romeo. I thought all for the best.

    Mercutio. Help me into some house, Benvolio,
    Or I shall faint. A plague o' both your houses! **C**
100 They have made worms' meat of me. I have it,
    And soundly too. Your houses!

    [*Exit, supported by* Benvolio.]

    Romeo. This gentleman, the Prince's near ally,
    My very friend, hath got this mortal hurt
    In my behalf—my reputation stained
105 With Tybalt's slander—Tybalt, that an hour
    Hath been my kinsman, O sweet Juliet,
    Thy beauty hath made me effeminate
    And in my temper softened valor's steel!

    [*Reenter* Benvolio.]

    Benvolio. O Romeo, Romeo, brave Mercutio's dead!
110 That gallant spirit hath aspired the clouds,
    Which too untimely here did scorn the earth.

    Romeo. This day's black fate on mo days doth depend;
    This but begins the woe others must end.

    [*Reenter* Tybalt.]

    Benvolio. Here comes the furious Tybalt back again.

115 **Romeo.** Alive in triumph, and Mercutio slain?
    Away to heaven respective lenity,
    And fire-eyed fury be my conduct now!
    Now, Tybalt, take the "villain" back again
    That late thou gavest me, for Mercutio's soul
120 Is but a little way above our heads,
    Staying for thine to keep him company.
    Either thou or I, or both, must go with him. **D**

    Tybalt. Thou, wretched boy, that didst consort him here,
    Shalt with him hence.

    Romeo.   This shall determine that.

    [*They fight.* Tybalt *falls.*]

125 **Benvolio.** Romeo, away, be gone!
    The citizens are up, and Tybalt slain.
    Stand not amazed. The Prince will doom thee death
    If thou art taken. Hence, be gone, away!

C TRAGEDY
What curse does Mercutio repeat three times in this scene? Explain what this ominous curse might **foreshadow**.

102–108 This gentleman . . . valor's steel: My friend has died protecting my reputation against a man who has been my relative for only an hour. My love for Juliet has made me less manly and brave.

110 aspired: soared to.

112–113 This day's . . . must end: This awful day will be followed by more of the same.

116 respective lenity: considerate mildness.

D CHARACTER
What drives Romeo to challenge Tybalt to fight?

124 The sword fight probably goes on for several minutes, till Romeo runs his sword through Tybalt.

Romeo. O, I am fortune's fool!

Benvolio.   Why dost thou stay?

[*Exit* Romeo.]

[*Enter* Citizens.]

130 **Citizen.** Which way ran he that killed Mercutio?
Tybalt, that murderer, which way ran he?

Benvolio. There lies that Tybalt.

Citizen.   Up, sir, go with me.
I charge thee in the Prince's name obey.

[*Enter* Prince *with his* Attendants, Montague, Capulet, *their* Wives, *and others.*]

Prince. Where are the vile beginners of this fray?

135 **Benvolio.** O noble Prince, I can discover all
The unlucky manage of this fatal brawl.
There lies the man, slain by young Romeo,
That slew thy kinsman, brave Mercutio.

Lady Capulet. Tybalt, my cousin! O my brother's child!
140 O Prince! O cousin! O husband! O, the blood is spilled
Of my dear kinsman! Prince, as thou art true,
For blood of ours shed blood of Montague.
O cousin, cousin!

Prince. Benvolio, who began this bloody fray?

145 **Benvolio.** Tybalt, here slain, whom Romeo's hand did slay.
Romeo, that spoke him fair, bid him bethink
How nice the quarrel was, and urged withal
Your high displeasure. All this—uttered
With gentle breath, calm look, knees humbly bowed—
150 Could not take truce with the unruly spleen
Of Tybalt deaf to peace, but that he tilts
With piercing steel at bold Mercutio's breast;
Who, all as hot, turns deadly point to point,
And, with a martial scorn, with one hand beats
155 Cold death aside and with the other sends
It back to Tybalt, whose dexterity
Retorts it. Romeo he cries aloud,
"Hold, friends! friends, part!" and swifter than his tongue,
His agile arm beats down their fatal points,
160 And 'twixt them rushes; underneath whose arm
An envious thrust from Tybalt hit the life

---

129 I am fortune's fool: Fate has made a fool of me.

135–136 Benvolio says he can tell (**discover**) what happened.

141–142 as thou . . . Montague: If your word is good, you will sentence Romeo to death for killing a Capulet.

146–147 Romeo, that . . . was: Romeo talked calmly (**fair**) and told Tybalt to think how trivial (**nice**) the argument was.

150–151 could . . . peace: could not quiet the anger of Tybalt, who would not listen to pleas for peace.

156–157 whose dexterity retorts it: whose skill returns it.

159–160 his agile . . . rushes: He rushed between them and pushed down their swords.

Of stout Mercutio, and then Tybalt fled,
But by-and-by comes back to Romeo,
Who had but newly entertained revenge,
165 And to't they go like lightning; for, ere I
Could draw to part them, was stout Tybalt slain;
And, as he fell, did Romeo turn and fly.
This is the truth, or let Benvolio die.

Lady Capulet. He is a kinsman to the Montague;
170 Affection makes him false, he speaks not true.
Some twenty of them fought in this black strife,
And all those twenty could but kill one life.
I beg for justice, which thou, Prince, must give.
Romeo slew Tybalt; Romeo must not live. **E**

175 **Prince.** Romeo slew him; he slew Mercutio.
Who now the price of his dear blood doth owe?

Montague. Not Romeo, Prince; he was Mercutio's friend;
His fault concludes but what the law should end,
The life of Tybalt.

164 **entertained:** thought of.

E TRAGEDY
Why does Lady Capulet think Benvolio is lying? **Paraphrase** the accusation she makes, and explain what she begs the prince to do.

178–179 Romeo is guilty only of avenging Mercutio's death, which the law would have done anyway.

Lady Capulet mourns Tybalt in the Royal Shakespeare Company's 2004 production.

Prince.   And for that offense
180 Immediately we do exile him hence.
     I have an interest in your hate's proceeding,
     My blood for your rude brawls doth lie a-bleeding;
     But I'll amerce you with so strong a fine
     That you shall all repent the loss of mine.
185 I will be deaf to pleading and excuses;
     Nor tears nor prayers shall purchase out abuses.
     Therefore use none. Let Romeo hence in haste,
     Else, when he is found, that hour is his last.
     Bear hence this body, and attend our will.
190 Mercy but murders, pardoning those that kill.

     [*Exeunt.*]

179–190 The prince banishes Romeo from Verona. He angrily points out that one of his own relatives is dead because of the feud and declares that Romeo will be put to death unless he flees immediately.

SCENE 2 *Capulet's orchard.*

The scene begins with Juliet impatiently waiting for night to come so that Romeo can climb to her bedroom on the rope ladder. Suddenly the nurse enters with the terrible news of Tybalt's death and Romeo's banishment. Juliet mourns for the loss of her cousin and her husband and threatens to kill herself. To calm her, the nurse promises to find Romeo and bring him to Juliet before he leaves Verona.

[*Enter* Juliet *alone.*]

Juliet. Gallop apace, you fiery-footed steeds,
     Toward Phoebus' lodging! Such a wagoner
     As Phaëton would whip you to the West,
     And bring in cloudy night immediately.
5   Spread thy close curtain, love-performing night,
     That runaways' eyes may wink, and Romeo
     Leap to these arms, untalked of and unseen. ⓕ
     Lovers can see to do their amorous rites
     By their own beauties; or, if love be blind,
10 It best agrees with night. Come, civil night,
     Thou sober-suited matron, all in black,
     And learn me how to lose a winning match,
     Played for a pair of stainless maidenhoods.
     Hood my unmanned blood bating in my cheeks
15 With thy black mantle; till strange love, grown bold,
     Think true love acted simple modesty.
     Come, night; come, Romeo, come; thou day in night;
     For thou wilt lie upon the wings of night
     Whiter than new snow on a raven's back.
20 Come, gentle night; come, loving, black-browed night;
     Give me my Romeo; and, when he shall die,
     Take him and cut him out in little stars,

2–3 Phoebus: Apollo, the god of the sun; **Phaëton:** a mortal who lost control of the sun's chariot when he drove it too fast.

ⓕ **ALLUSION**
Paraphrase lines 1–7. Why does Juliet allude to Phoebus and Phaëton in this **soliloquy?**

14–16 Hood . . . modesty: Juliet asks that the darkness hide her blushing cheeks on her wedding night.

And he will make the face of heaven so fine
That all the world will be in love with night
25 And pay no worship to the garish sun.
O, I have bought the mansion of a love,
But not possessed it; and though I am sold,
Not yet enjoyed. So tedious is this day
As is the night before some festival
30 To an impatient child that hath new robes
And may not wear them. Oh, here comes my nurse,

[*Enter* Nurse, *wringing her hands, with the ladder of cords in her lap.*]

And she brings news; and every tongue that speaks
But Romeo's name speaks heavenly eloquence.
Now, nurse, what news? What hast thou there? the cords
35 That Romeo bid thee fetch?

Nurse.   Ay, ay, the cords.

Juliet. Ay me! what news? Why dost thou wring thy hands?

Nurse. Ah, well-a-day! he's dead, he's dead, he's dead!
We are undone, lady, we are undone!
Alack the day! he's gone, he's killed, he's dead!

40 **Juliet.** Can heaven be so envious? **G**

Nurse.   Romeo can,
Though heaven cannot. O Romeo, Romeo!
Who ever would have thought it? Romeo!

Juliet. What devil art thou that dost torment me thus?
This torture should be roared in dismal hell.
45 Hath Romeo slain himself? Say thou but "I,"
And that bare vowel "I" shall poison more
Than the death-darting eye of a cockatrice.
I am not I, if there be such an "I,"
Or those eyes shut, that make thee answer "I."
50 If he be slain, say "I," or if not, "no."
Brief sounds determine of my weal or woe.

Nurse. I saw the wound, I saw it with mine eyes,
(God save the mark!) here on his manly breast.
A piteous corse, a bloody piteous corse;
55 Pale, pale as ashes, all bedaubed in blood,
All in gore blood. I swounded at the sight.

Juliet. O, break, my heart! poor bankrout, break at once!
To prison, eyes; ne'er look on liberty!
Vile earth, to earth resign; end motion here,
60 And thou and Romeo press one heavy bier!

26–27 I have ... possessed it: Juliet protests that she has gone through the wedding ceremony (**bought the mansion**) but is still waiting to enjoy the rewards of marriage.

34 the cords: the rope ladder.

37–42 well-a-day: an expression used when someone has bad news. The nurse wails and moans without clearly explaining what has happened, leading Juliet to assume that Romeo is dead.

G DRAMATIC IRONY
How is Juliet's belief that her new husband is dead an example of dramatic irony?

45–50 Juliet's "I" means "aye," or "yes." A **cockatrice** is a mythological beast whose glance kills its victims.

51 my weal or woe: my happiness or sorrow.

53–56 God ... mark: an expression meant to scare off evil powers, similar to "Knock on wood"; **corse:** corpse; **swounded:** fainted.

57–60 Juliet say her heart is broken and bankrupt (**bankrout**). She wants to be buried with Romeo, sharing his burial platform (**bier**).

Nurse. O Tybalt, Tybalt, the best friend I had!
O courteous Tybalt! honest gentleman!
That ever I should live to see thee dead!

Juliet. What storm is this that blows so contrary?
65 Is Romeo slaughtered, and is Tybalt dead?
My dear-loved cousin, and my dearer lord?
Then, dreadful trumpet, sound the general doom!
For who is living, if those two are gone?

Nurse. Tybalt is gone, and Romeo banished;
70 Romeo that killed him, he is banished.

Juliet. O God! Did Romeo's hand shed Tybalt's blood?

Nurse. It did! it did! alas the day, it did!

Juliet. O serpent heart, hid with a flow'ring face!
Did ever dragon keep so fair a cave?
75 Beautiful tyrant! fiend angelical!
Dove-feathered raven! wolvish-ravening lamb!
Despised substance of divinest show!
Just opposite to what thou justly seemst,
A damned saint, an honorable villain!
80 O nature, what hadst thou to do in hell
When thou didst bower the spirit of a fiend
In mortal paradise of such sweet flesh?
Was ever book containing such vile matter
So fairly bound? O, that deceit should dwell
85 In such a gorgeous palace!

Nurse.   There's no trust,
No faith, no honesty in men; all perjured,
All forsworn, all naught, all dissemblers.
Ah, where's my man? Give me some aqua vitae.
These griefs, these woes, these sorrows make me old.
90 Shame come to Romeo!

Juliet.   Blistered be thy tongue
For such a wish! He was not born to shame.
Upon his brow shame is ashamed to sit;
For 'tis a throne where honor may be crowned
Sole monarch of the universal earth.
95 O, what a beast was I to chide at him! **H**

Nurse. Will you speak well of him that killed your cousin?

Juliet. Shall I speak ill of him that is my husband?
Ah, poor my lord, what tongue shall smooth thy name
When I, thy three-hours' wife, have mangled it?
100 But wherefore, villain, didst thou kill my cousin?
That villain cousin would have killed my husband.

73–85 Juliet's contradictory phrases here show her conflicting feelings about the events the nurse has described. *What is Juliet's first reaction to the news that Romeo has killed Tybalt?*

81 **bower...fiend:** give a home to the spirit of a demon.

87 **all...dissemblers:** All are liars and pretenders.

88 **aqua vitae:** brandy.

H TRAGEDY
Compare Juliet's initial reaction to the news of Tybalt's death with her response to the nurse in lines 90–95. What **internal conflict** is Juliet wrestling with in this scene?

Back, foolish tears, back to your native spring!
Your tributary drops belong to woe,
Which you, mistaking, offer up to joy.
105 My husband lives, that Tybalt would have slain;
And Tybalt's dead, that would have slain my husband.
All this is comfort; wherefore weep I then?
Some word there was, worser than Tybalt's death,
That murdered me. I would forget it fain;
110 But O, it presses to my memory
Like damned guilty deeds to sinners' minds!
"Tybalt is dead, and Romeo—banished."
That "banished," that one word "banished,"
Hath slain ten thousand Tybalts. Tybalt's death
115 Was woe enough, if it had ended there;
Or, if sour woe delights in fellowship
And needly will be ranked with other griefs,
Why followed not, when she said "Tybalt's dead,"
Thy father, or thy mother, nay, or both,
120 Which modern lamentation might have moved?
But with a rearward following Tybalt's death,
"Romeo is banished"—to speak that word
Is father, mother, Tybalt, Romeo, Juliet,
All slain, all dead. "Romeo is banished"—
125 There is no end, no limit, measure, bound,
In that word's death; no words can that woe sound.
Where is my father and my mother, nurse?

Nurse. Weeping and wailing over Tybalt's corse.
Will you go to them? I will bring you thither.

130 **Juliet.** Wash they his wounds with tears? Mine shall be spent,
When theirs are dry, for Romeo's banishment.
Take up those cords. Poor ropes, you are beguiled,
Both you and I, for Romeo is exiled.
He made you for a highway to my bed;
135 But I, a maid, die maiden-widowed.
Come, cords; come, nurse. I'll to my wedding bed;
And death, not Romeo, take my maidenhead!

Nurse. Hie to your chamber. I'll find Romeo
To comfort you. I wot well where he is.
140 Hark ye, your Romeo will be here at night.
I'll to him; he is hid at Laurence' cell.

Juliet. O, find him! give this ring to my true knight
And bid him come to take his last farewell.

[*Exeunt.*]

102–106 Juliet is uncertain whether her tears should be of joy or of sorrow.

114–127 Juliet says that if the news of Tybalt's death had been followed by the news of her parents' deaths, she would have felt normal (**modern**), or expected, grief. To follow the story of Tybalt's death with the terrible news of Romeo's banishment creates a sorrow so deep it cannot be expressed in words.

132 beguiled: cheated.

135–137 I…maidenhead: I will die a widow without ever really having been a wife. Death, not Romeo, will be my husband.

139 wot: know.

SCENE 3   *Friar Laurence's cell.*

Friar Laurence tells Romeo of his banishment, and Romeo collapses in grief. When he learns from the nurse that Juliet, too, is in despair, he threatens to stab himself. The friar reacts by suggesting a plan. Romeo is to spend a few hours with Juliet and then escape to Mantua. While he is away, the friar will announce the wedding and try to get a pardon from the prince.

[*Enter* Friar Laurence.]

Friar Laurence. Romeo, come forth; come forth, thou fearful man.
Affliction is enamored of thy parts,
And thou art wedded to calamity.

[*Enter* Romeo.]

Romeo. Father, what news? What is the Prince's doom?
5 What sorrow craves acquaintance at my hand
That I yet know not?

Friar Laurence.   Too familiar
Is my dear son with such sour company.
I bring thee tidings of the Prince's doom.

Romeo. What less than doomsday is the Prince's doom?

10 **Friar Laurence.** A gentler judgment vanished from his lips—
Not body's death, but body's banishment.

Romeo. Ha, banishment? Be merciful, say "death";
For exile hath more terror in his look,
Much more than death. Do not say "banishment."

15 **Friar Laurence.** Hence from Verona art thou banished.
Be patient, for the world is broad and wide.

Romeo. There is no world without Verona walls,
But purgatory, torture, hell itself.
Hence banished is banish'd from the world,
20 And world's exile is death. Then "banishment,"
Is death misterm'd. Calling death "banishment,"
Thou cuttst my head off with a golden axe
And smilest upon the stroke that murders me.

Friar Laurence. O deadly sin! O rude unthankfulness!
25 Thy fault our law calls death; but the kind Prince,
Taking thy part, hath rushed aside the law,
And turned that black word death to banishment.
This is dear mercy, and thou seest it not.

Romeo. 'Tis torture, and not mercy. Heaven is here,
30 Where Juliet lives; and every cat and dog
And little mouse, every unworthy thing,
Live here in heaven and may look on her;
But Romeo may not. More validity,

2 affliction . . . parts: Trouble loves you.

4 doom: sentence.

9 doomsday: death.

10 vanished: came.

17–23 There is . . . murders me: Being exiled outside Verona's walls is as bad as being dead. And yet you smile at my misfortune.

24–28 The angry friar reminds Romeo that by law he should have gotten the death penalty. The prince has shown Romeo mercy.

More honorable state, more courtship lives
35 In carrion flies than Romeo. They may seize
On the white wonder of dear Juliet's hand
And steal immortal blessing from her lips,
Who, even in pure and vestal modesty,
Still blush, as thinking their own kisses sin;
40 But Romeo may not—he is banished.
This may flies do, when I from this must fly;
They are free men, but I am banished.
And sayst thou yet that exile is not death?
Hadst thou no poison mixed, no sharp-ground knife,
45 No sudden mean of death, though ne'er so mean,
But "banished" to kill me—"banished"?
O friar, the damned use that word in hell;
Howling attends it! How hast thou the heart,
Being a divine, a ghostly confessor,
50 A sin-absolver, and my friend professed,
To mangle me with that word "banished"?

Friar Laurence. Thou fond mad man, hear me a little speak.

Romeo. O, thou wilt speak again of banishment.

Friar Laurence. I'll give thee armor to keep off that word;
55 Adversity's sweet milk, philosophy,
To comfort thee, though thou art banished.

Romeo. Yet "banished"? Hang up philosophy!
Unless philosophy can make a Juliet,
Displant a town, reverse a prince's doom,
60 It helps not, it prevails not. Talk no more.

Friar Laurence. O, then I see that madmen have no ears.

Romeo. How should they, when that wise men have no eyes?

Friar Laurence. Let me dispute with thee of thy estate.

Romeo. Thou canst not speak of that thou dost not feel.
65 Wert thou as young as I, Juliet thy love,
An hour but married, Tybalt murdered,
Doting like me, and like me banished,
Then mightst thou speak, then mightst thou tear thy hair,
And fall upon the ground, as I do now,
70 Taking the measure of an unmade grave.

[Nurse *knocks within.*]

Friar Laurence. Arise; one knocks. Good Romeo, hide thyself.

Romeo. Not I; unless the breath of heartsick groans
Mist-like infold me from the search of eyes.

[*knock*]

33–35 More validity . . . than Romeo: Even flies that live off the dead (**carrion**) will be able to get closer to Juliet than Romeo will.

44–46 Hadst . . . to kill me: Couldn't you have killed me with poison or a knife instead of with that awful word *banished? Why does Romeo think banishment is a worse punishment than death?*

52 fond: foolish.

54–56 The friar offers philosophical comfort and counseling (**adversity's sweet milk**) as a way to overcome hardship.

63 dispute: discuss; **estate:** situation.

72–73 Romeo will hide only if his sighs create a mist and shield him from sight.

Friar Laurence. Hark, how they knock! Who's there? Romeo, arise;
75 Thou wilt be taken.—Stay awhile!—Stand up;

[*knock*]

Run to my study.—By-and-by!—God's will,
What simpleness is this.—I come, I come!

[*knock*]

Who knocks so hard? Whence come you? What's your will?

Nurse [*within*]. Let me come in, and you shall know my errand.
80 I come from Lady Juliet.

Friar Laurence.   Welcome then.

[*Enter* Nurse.]

Nurse. O holy friar, O, tell me, holy friar,
Where is my lady's lord, where's Romeo?

Friar Laurence. There on the ground, with his own tears made
    drunk.

Nurse. O, he is even in my mistress' case,
85 Just in her case! O woeful sympathy!
Piteous predicament! Even so lies she,
Blubb'ring and weeping, weeping and blubbering.
Stand up, stand up! Stand, an you be a man.
For Juliet's sake, for her sake, rise and stand!
90 Why should you fall into so deep an O?

Romeo [*rises*]. Nurse—

Nurse. Ah sir! ah sir! Well, death's the end of all.

Romeo. Spakest thou of Juliet? How is it with her?
Doth not she think me an old murderer,
95 Now I have stained the childhood of our joy
With blood removed but little from her own?
Where is she? and how doth she? and what says
My concealed lady to our canceled love?

Nurse. O, she says nothing, sir, but weeps and weeps;
100 And now falls on her bed, and then starts up,
And Tybalt calls; and then on Romeo cries,
And then down falls again.

Romeo.   As if that name,
Shot from the deadly level of a gun,
Did murder her; as that name's cursed hand
105 Murdered her kinsman. O tell me, friar, tell me,
In what vile part of this anatomy
Doth my name lodge? Tell me, that I may sack
The hateful mansion.

[*draws his dagger*]

84–85 **he is even ... her case:** He is acting the same way that Juliet is.

90 **into so deep an O:** into such deep grief.

96 **blood ... from her own:** the blood of a close relative of hers.

98 **concealed lady:** secret bride.

102 **that name:** the name Romeo.

106–108 **in what vile part ... mansion:** Romeo asks where in his body (**anatomy**) his name can be found so that he can cut the name out. *What is Romeo about to do?*

Friar Laurence.   Hold thy desperate hand.
Art thou a man? Thy form cries out thou art;
110 Thy tears are womanish, thy wild acts denote
The unreasonable fury of a beast.
Unseemly woman in a seeming man!
Or ill-beseeming beast in seeming both!
Thou hast amazed me. By my holy order,
115 I thought thy disposition better tempered.
Hast thou slain Tybalt? Wilt thou slay thyself?
And slay thy lady too that lives in thee,
By doing damned hate upon thyself?
Why railst thou on thy birth, the heaven, and earth?
120 Since birth and heaven and earth, all three do meet
In thee at once; which thou at once wouldst lose.
Fie, fie, thou shamest thy shape, thy love, thy wit,
Which, like a usurer, aboundst in all,
And usest none in that true use indeed
125 Which should bedeck thy shape, thy love, thy wit.
Thy noble shape is but a form of wax,
Digressing from the valor of a man;
Thy dear love sworn but hollow perjury,
Killing that love which thou hast vowed to cherish;
130 Thy wit, that ornament to shape and love,
Misshapen in the conduct of them both,
Like powder in a skilless soldier's flask,
Is set afire by thine own ignorance,
And thou dismembered with thine own defense.
135 What, rouse thee, man! Thy Juliet is alive,
For whose dear sake thou wast but lately dead.
There art thou happy. Tybalt would kill thee,
But thou slewest Tybalt. There art thou happy.
The law, that threatened death, becomes thy friend
140 And turns it to exile. There art thou happy.
A pack of blessings light upon thy back;
Happiness courts thee in her best array;
But, like a misbehaved and sullen wench,
Thou poutst upon thy fortune and thy love.
145 Take heed, take heed, for such die miserable.
Go get thee to thy love, as was decreed,
Ascend her chamber, hence and comfort her.
But look thou stay not till the watch be set,
For then thou canst not pass to Mantua,
150 Where thou shalt live till we can find a time
To blaze your marriage, reconcile your friends,
Beg pardon of the Prince, and call thee back
With twenty hundred thousand times more joy

108–125 Hold thy . . . bedeck thy shape, thy love, thy wit: You're not acting like a man. Would you send your soul to hell by committing suicide (**doing damned hate upon thyself**)? Why do you curse your birth, heaven, and earth? You are refusing to make good use of your advantages, just as a miser refuses to spend his money.

126–134 The friar explains how by acting as he is, Romeo is misusing his shape (his outer form or body), his love, and his wit (his mind or intellect).

135–140 The friar tells Romeo to count his blessings instead of feeling sorry for himself. He lists the things Romeo has to be thankful for. *What three blessings does the friar mention?*

148–149 look . . . Mantua: Leave before the guards take their places at the city gates; otherwise you will not be able to escape to Mantua.

151 blaze . . . friends: announce your marriage and get the families (**friends**) to stop feuding.

Than thou wentst forth in lamentation.
155 Go before, nurse. Commend me to thy lady,
And bid her hasten all the house to bed,
Which heavy sorrow makes them apt unto.
Romeo is coming.

Nurse. O Lord, I could have stayed here all the night
160 To hear good counsel. O, what learning is!
My lord, I'll tell my lady you will come.

Romeo. Do so, and bid my sweet prepare to chide.

[Nurse *offers to go and turns again.*]

Nurse. Here is a ring she bid me give you, sir.
Hie you, make haste, for it grows very late.

[*Exit.*]

165 **Romeo.** How well my comfort is revived by this!

Friar Laurence. Go hence; good night; and here stands all your
    state:
Either be gone before the watch be set,
Or by the break of day disguised from hence.
Sojourn in Mantua. I'll find out your man,
170 And he shall signify from time to time
Every good hap to you that chances here.
Give me thy hand. 'Tis late. Farewell; good night.

Romeo. But that a joy past joy calls out on me,
It were a grief so brief to part with thee.
175 Farewell. ❶

[*Exeunt.*]

SCENE 4 *Capulet's house.*

*In this scene, Paris visits the Capulets, who are mourning the death of Tybalt.
He says he realizes that this is no time to talk of marriage. Capulet, however,
disagrees; he decides that Juliet should marry Paris on Thursday, three days
away. He tells Lady Capulet to inform Juliet immediately.*

[*Enter* Capulet, Lady Capulet, *and* Paris.]

Capulet. Things have fall'n out, sir, so unluckily
That we have had no time to move our daughter.
Look you, she loved her kinsman Tybalt dearly,
And so did I. Well, we were born to die.
5 'Tis very late; she'll not come down tonight.

162 bid ... chide: Tell Juliet to get ready
to scold me for the way I've behaved.

166–171 and here ... here: This is what
your fate depends on: either leave before
the night watchmen go on duty, or get
out at dawn in a disguise. Stay awhile in
Mantua. I'll find your servant and send
messages to you about what good things
are happening here.

❶ **TRAGEDY**
Despite Romeo and Juliet's
anguish, their problem at this point
seems solvable. **Summarize** the
plan that has been made to resolve
their dilemma.

1–2 Things have ... our daughter: Such
terrible things have happened that we
haven't had time to persuade (**move**)
Juliet to think about your marriage
proposal.

I promise you, but for your company,
I would have been abed an hour ago.

Paris. These times of woe afford no time to woo.
Madam, good night. Commend me to your daughter.

10 **Lady Capulet.** I will, and know her mind early tomorrow;
Tonight she's mewed up to her heaviness.

[Paris *offers to go and* Capulet *calls him again.*]

Capulet. Sir Paris, I will make a desperate tender
Of my child's love. I think she will be ruled
In all respects by me; nay more, I doubt it not.
15 Wife, go you to her ere you go to bed;
Acquaint her here of my son Paris' love
And bid her (mark you me?) on Wednesday next—
But, soft! what day is this?

Paris.   Monday, my lord.

Capulet. Monday! ha, ha! Well, Wednesday is too soon.
20 A Thursday let it be—a Thursday, tell her,
She shall be married to this noble earl.
Will you be ready? Do you like this haste?
We'll keep no great ado—a friend or two;
For hark you, Tybalt being slain so late,
25 It may be thought we held him carelessly,
Being our kinsman, if we revel much.
Therefore we'll have some half a dozen friends,
And there an end. But what say you to Thursday?

Paris. My lord, I would that Thursday were tomorrow.

30 **Capulet.** Well, get you gone. A Thursday be it then. ❶
Go you to Juliet ere you go to bed;
Prepare her, wife, against this wedding day.
Farewell, my lord.—Light to my chamber, ho!
Afore me, it is so very very late
35 That we may call it early by-and-by.
Good night.

[*Exeunt.*]

8 Sad times are not good times for talking of marriage.

11 Tonight she is locked up with her sorrow. *What do Juliet's parents think is causing this sorrow?*

12 desperate tender: bold offer.

16 Capulet is so sure that Juliet will accept Paris that he calls Paris "son" already.

23 no great ado: no big festivity.

❶ **TRAGEDY**
Predict how Juliet will react to the news that her parents have promised her to Paris. How might this turn of events add to the play's mounting **conflict**?

34–35 it is . . . by-and-by: It's so late at night that soon we'll be calling it early in the morning.

The Clarence Brown Theatre's 2003 production

The Seattle Repertory Theatre's 2003 production

The Bolshoi Ballet's 2004 production

Stage Combat

A character's movements can convey as much as his or her words. In fight scenes, **blocking** is used to decide exactly how the actors will move. From a stylistic point of view, how are the movements captured in these photographs different? Which fight looks most realistic, and why?

SCENE 5   *Capulet's orchard.*

Romeo and Juliet have spent the night together, but before daylight, Romeo leaves for Mantua. As soon as he leaves, Lady Capulet comes in to tell Juliet of her father's decision—that she will marry Count Paris on Thursday. Juliet is very upset and refuses to go along with the plan. Juliet's father goes into a rage at her disobedience and tells her that she will marry Paris or he will disown her.

The nurse advises Juliet to wed Paris, since her marriage to Romeo is over and Paris is a better man anyway. Juliet, now angry with the nurse, decides to go to Friar Laurence for help.

[*Enter* Romeo *and* Juliet *above, at the window.*]

Juliet. Wilt thou be gone? It is not yet near day.
It was the nightingale, and not the lark,
That pierced the fearful hollow of thine ear.
Nightly she sings on yond pomegranate tree.
5 Believe me, love, it was the nightingale.

Romeo. It was the lark, the herald of the morn;
No nightingale. Look, love, what envious streaks
Do lace the severing clouds in yonder East.
Night's candles are burnt out, and jocund day
10 Stands tiptoe on the misty mountain tops.
I must be gone and live, or stay and die.

Juliet. Yond light is not daylight; I know it, I.
It is some meteor that the sun exhales
To be to thee this night a torchbearer
15 And light thee on thy way to Mantua.
Therefore stay yet; thou needst not to be gone.

Romeo. Let me be ta'en, let me be put to death.
I am content, so thou wilt have it so.
I'll say yon grey is not the morning's eye,
20 'Tis but the pale reflex of Cynthia's brow;
Nor that is not the lark whose notes do beat
The vaulty heaven so high above our heads.
I have more care to stay than will to go.
Come, death, and welcome! Juliet wills it so.
25 How is't, my soul? Let's talk; it is not day.

Juliet. It is, it is! Hie hence, be gone, away!
It is the lark that sings so out of tune,
Straining harsh discords and unpleasing sharps.
Some say the lark makes sweet division;
30 This doth not so, for she divideth us.
Some say the lark and loathed toad changed eyes;
O, now I would they had changed voices too,

2 It was . . . lark: The nightingale sings at night; the lark sings in the morning. *What is Juliet trying to get Romeo to believe?*

9 night's candles: stars.

12–25 Juliet continues to pretend it is night to keep Romeo from leaving. Romeo gives in and says he'll stay if Juliet wishes it, even if staying means death.

20 reflex of Cynthia's brow: reflection of the moon. Cynthia is another name for Diana, the Roman goddess of the moon. She was often pictured with a crescent moon on her forehead.

26 Romeo's mention of death frightens Juliet, and she urges him to leave quickly.

29 division: melody.

31–34 I wish the lark had the voice of the hated (**loathed**) toad, since its voice is frightening us apart and acting as a morning song for hunters (**hunt's-up**).

Since arm from arm that voice doth us affray,
Hunting thee hence with hunt's-up to the day!
35 O, now be gone! More light and light it grows.

Romeo. More light and light—more dark and dark our woes!

[*Enter* Nurse, *hastily.*]

Nurse. Madam!

Juliet. Nurse?

Nurse. Your lady mother is coming to your chamber.
40 The day is broke; be wary, look about.

[*Exit.*]

Juliet. Then, window, let day in, and let life out.

Romeo. Farewell, farewell! One kiss, and I'll descend.

[*He starts down the ladder.*]

Juliet. Art thou gone so, my lord, my love, my friend?
I must hear from thee every day in the hour,
45 For in a minute there are many days.
O, by this count I shall be much in years
Ere I again behold my Romeo!

Romeo. Farewell!
I will omit no opportunity
50 That may convey my greetings, love, to thee.

Juliet. O, thinkst thou we shall ever meet again?

Romeo. I doubt it not; and all these woes shall serve
For sweet discourses in our time to come.

Juliet. O God, I have an ill-divining soul!
55 Methinks I see thee, now thou art below,
As one dead in the bottom of a tomb.
Either my eyesight fails, or thou lookst pale.

Romeo. And trust me, love, in my eye so do you.
Dry sorrow drinks our blood. Adieu! adieu!

[*Exit.*]

60 **Juliet.** O Fortune, Fortune! all men call thee fickle.
If thou art fickle, what dost thou with him
That is renowned for faith? Be fickle, Fortune,
For then I hope thou wilt not keep him long
But send him back.

Lady Capulet [*within*]. Ho, daughter! are you up?

65 **Juliet.** Who is't that calls? It is my lady mother.
Is she not down so late, or up so early?
What unaccustomed cause procures her hither?

46 much in years: very old.

54–56 I have . . . tomb: Juliet sees an evil vision of the future. *What is her vision?*

59 Dry . . . blood: People believed that sorrow drained the blood from the heart, causing a sad person to look pale.

60–62 fickle: changeable in loyalty or affection. Juliet asks fickle Fortune why it has anything to do with Romeo, who is the opposite of fickle.

67 What . . . hither: What unusual reason brings her here?

[*Enter* Lady Capulet.]

Lady Capulet. Why, how now, Juliet?

Juliet.   Madam, I am not well.

Lady Capulet. Evermore weeping for your cousin's death?
70 What, wilt thou wash him from his grave with tears?
An if thou couldst, thou couldst not make him live.
Therefore have done. Some grief shows much of love;
But much of grief shows still some want of wit.

Juliet. Yet let me weep for such a feeling loss.

75 **Lady Capulet.** So shall you feel the loss, but not the friend
Which you weep for.

Juliet.   Feeling so the loss,
I cannot choose but ever weep the friend.

Lady Capulet. Well, girl, thou weepst not so much for his death
As that the villain lives which slaughtered him.

80 **Juliet.** What villain, madam?

Lady Capulet.   That same villain Romeo.

Juliet [*aside*]. Villain and he be many miles asunder.—
God pardon him! I do, with all my heart;
And yet no man like he doth grieve my heart.

Lady Capulet. That is because the traitor murderer lives.

85 **Juliet.** Ay, madam, from the reach of these my hands.
Would none but I might venge my cousin's death!

Lady Capulet. We will have vengeance for it, fear thou not.
Then weep no more. I'll send to one in Mantua,
Where that same banished runagate doth live,
90 Shall give him such an unaccustomed dram
That he shall soon keep Tybalt company;
And then I hope thou wilt be satisfied.

Juliet. Indeed I never shall be satisfied
With Romeo till I behold him—dead—
95 Is my poor heart so for a kinsman vexed.
Madam, if you could find out but a man
To bear a poison, I would temper it;
That Romeo should, upon receipt thereof,
Soon sleep in quiet. O, how my heart abhors
100 To hear him named and cannot come to him,
To wreak the love I bore my cousin Tybalt
Upon his body that hath slaughtered him!

Lady Capulet. Find thou the means, and I'll find such a man.
But now I'll tell thee joyful tidings, girl.

69–70 *What does Lady Capulet think Juliet is crying about?*

72–73 have . . . wit: Stop crying (**have done**). A little grief is evidence of love, while too much grief shows a lack of good sense (**want of wit**).

81–102 In these lines Juliet's words have double meanings. To avoid lying to her mother, she chooses her words carefully. They can mean what her mother wants to hear—or what Juliet really has on her mind.

89 runagate: runaway.
90 unaccustomed dram: poison.

93–102 Dead could refer either to Romeo or to Juliet's heart. Juliet says that if her mother could find someone to carry a poison to Romeo, she would mix (**temper**) it herself.

105 **Juliet.** And joy comes well in such a needy time.
What are they, I beseech your ladyship?

Lady Capulet. Well, well, thou hast a careful father, child;
One who, to put thee from thy heaviness,
Hath sorted out a sudden day of joy
110 That thou expects not nor I looked not for.

Juliet. Madam, in happy time! What day is that?

Lady Capulet. Marry, my child, early next Thursday morn
The gallant, young, and noble gentleman,
The County Paris, at Saint Peter's Church,
115 Shall happily make thee there a joyful bride.

Juliet. Now by Saint Peter's Church, and Peter too,
He shall not make me there a joyful bride!
I wonder at this haste, that I must wed
Ere he that should be husband comes to woo.
120 I pray you tell my lord and father, madam,
I will not marry yet; and when I do, I swear
It shall be Romeo, whom you know I hate,
Rather than Paris. These are news indeed!

Lady Capulet. Here comes your father. Tell him so yourself,
125 And see how he will take it at your hands.

[*Enter* Capulet *and* Nurse.]

Capulet. When the sun sets the air doth drizzle dew,
But for the sunset of my brother's son
It rains downright.
How now? a conduit, girl? What, still in tears?
130 Evermore show'ring? In one little body
Thou counterfeitst a bark, a sea, a wind:
For still thy eyes, which I may call the sea,
Do ebb and flow with tears; the bark thy body is,
Sailing in this salt flood; the winds, thy sighs,
135 Who, raging with thy tears and they with them,
Without a sudden calm will overset
Thy tempest-tossed body. How now, wife?
Have you delivered to her our decree?

Lady Capulet. Ay, sir; but she will none, she gives you thanks.
140 I would the fool were married to her grave!

Capulet. Soft! take me with you, take me with you, wife.
How? Will she none? Doth she not give us thanks?
Is she not proud? Doth she not count her blest,
Unworthy as she is, that we have wrought
145 So worthy a gentleman to be her bridegroom?

121–123 Juliet mentions Romeo to show her mother how strongly opposed she is to marrying Paris, yet what she really means is that she loves Romeo.

127 the sunset . . . son: the death of Tybalt.

129–137 conduit: fountain. Capulet compares Juliet to a boat (**bark**), an ocean, and the wind because of her excessive crying.

141 take me with you: let me understand you.

Juliet. Not proud you have, but thankful that you have.
Proud can I never be of what I hate,
But thankful even for hate that is meant love.

Capulet. How, how, how, how, choplogic? What is this?
150 "Proud"—and "I thank you"—and "I thank you not"—
And yet "not proud"? Mistress minion you,
Thank me no thankings, nor proud me no prouds,
But fettle your fine joints 'gainst Thursday next
To go with Paris to Saint Peter's Church,
155 Or I will drag thee on a hurdle thither.
Out, you green-sickness carrion! out, you baggage!
You tallow-face!

Lady Capulet. Fie, fie; what, are you mad?

Juliet. Good father, I beseech you on my knees,

[*She kneels down.*]

Hear me with patience but to speak a word.

160 **Capulet.** Hang thee, young baggage! disobedient wretch!
I tell thee what—get thee to church a Thursday
Or never after look me in the face.
Speak not, reply not, do not answer me!
My fingers itch. Wife, we scarce thought us blest
165 That God had lent us but this only child;
But now I see this one is one too much,
And that we have a curse in having her.
Out on her, hilding!

Nurse.   God in heaven bless her!
You are to blame, my lord, to rate her so.

170 **Capulet.** And why, my Lady Wisdom? Hold your tongue,
Good Prudence. Smatter with your gossips, go!

Nurse. I speak no treason.

Capulet.   O, God-i-god-en!

Nurse. May not one speak?

Capulet.   Peace, you mumbling fool!
Utter your gravity o'er a gossip's bowl,
175 For here we need it not.

Lady Capulet.   You are too hot.

Capulet. God's bread! it makes me mad. Day, night, late, early,
At home, abroad, alone, in company,
Waking or sleeping, still my care hath been
To have her matched; and having now provided
180 A gentleman of princely parentage,

146–148 Not proud ... meant love: I'm not pleased, but I am grateful for your intentions.

149–157 In his rage, Capulet calls Juliet a person who argues unnecessarily over fine points (**choplogic**) and says she is a spoiled child (**minion**). He tells her to prepare herself (**fettle your fine joints**) for the wedding or he'll haul her there in a cart for criminals (**hurdle**). He calls her an anemic piece of dead flesh (**green-sickness carrion**) and a coward (**tallow-face**).

164 My fingers itch: I feel like hitting you.

168 hilding: a good-for-nothing person.

171 smatter: chatter.

174 Utter ... bowl: Save your words of wisdom for a gathering of gossips.

179 matched: married.

Of fair demesnes, youthful, and nobly trained,
Stuffed, as they say, with honorable parts,
Proportioned as one's thought would wish a man—
And then to have a wretched puling fool,
185 A whining mammet, in her fortunes tender,
To answer "I'll not wed, I cannot love;
I am too young, I pray you pardon me"!
But, an you will not wed, I'll pardon you.
Graze where you will, you shall not house with me.
190 Look to't, think on't; I do not use to jest.
Thursday is near; lay hand on heart, advise:
An you be mine, I'll give you to my friend;
An you be not, hang, beg, starve, die in the streets,
For, by my soul, I'll ne'er acknowledge thee,
195 Nor what is mine shall never do thee good.
Trust to't. Bethink you. I'll not be forsworn.

[*Exit.*]

Juliet. Is there no pity sitting in the clouds
That sees into the bottom of my grief?
O sweet my mother, cast me not away!
200 Delay this marriage for a month, a week;
Or if you do not, make the bridal bed
In that dim monument where Tybalt lies.

Lady Capulet. Talk not to me, for I'll not speak a word.
Do as thou wilt, for I have done with thee.

[*Exit.*]

205 **Juliet.** O God!—O nurse, how shall this be prevented?
My husband is on earth, my faith in heaven.
How shall that faith return again to earth
Unless that husband send it me from heaven
By leaving earth? Comfort me, counsel me.
210 Alack, alack, that heaven should practice stratagems
Upon so soft a subject as myself!
What sayst thou? Hast thou not a word of joy?
Some comfort, nurse.

Nurse.   Faith, here it is.
Romeo is banish'd; and all the world to nothing
215 That he dares ne'er come back to challenge you;
Or if he do, it needs must be by stealth.
Then, since the case so stands as now it doth,
I think it best you married with the County.
O, he's a lovely gentleman!
220 Romeo's a dishclout to him. An eagle, madam,

184 puling: crying.
185 mammet: doll.

189–195 Capulet swears that he'll kick Juliet out and cut her off financially if she refuses to marry.

196 I'll not be forsworn: I will not break my promise to Paris.

207–211 Juliet is worried about the sin of being married to two men. She asks how heaven can play such tricks (**practice stratagems**) on her.

213–222 The nurse gives Juliet advice. She says that since Romeo is banished, he's no good to her; Juliet should marry Paris. Romeo is a dishcloth (**dishclout**) compared to Paris.

Hath not so green, so quick, so fair an eye
As Paris hath. Beshrew my very heart,
I think you are happy in this second match,
For it excels your first; or if it did not,
225 Your first is dead—or 'twere as good he were
As living here and you no use of him.

Juliet. Speakst thou this from thy heart?

Nurse. And from my soul too; else beshrew them both.

Juliet. Amen!

230 **Nurse.** What?

Juliet. Well, thou hast comforted me marvelous much.
Go in; and tell my lady I am gone,
Having displeased my father, to Laurence' cell,
To make confession and to be absolved.

235 **Nurse.** Marry, I will; and this is wisely done.

[*Exit.*]

Juliet. Ancient damnation! O most wicked fiend!
Is it more sin to wish me thus forsworn,
Or to dispraise my lord with that same tongue
Which she hath praised him with above compare
240 So many thousand times? Go, counselor! **K**
Thou and my bosom henceforth shall be twain.
I'll to the friar to know his remedy.
If all else fail, myself have power to die.

[*Exit.*]

222 **beshrew:** curse.

223–225 This new marriage will be better than the first, which is as good as over.

229 **Amen:** I agree—that is, curse your heart and soul.

236–238 **ancient damnation:** old devil; **dispraise:** criticize.

241 **Thou . . . twain:** I'll no longer tell you my secrets.

K CHARACTER
How has Juliet's relationship with the nurse changed? Citing details from their **interactions,** explain the main reason for the change.

Comprehension

PENNSYLVANIA
STANDARDS

READING STANDARD
B.1.1.1.C.1 Evaluate elements of
the plot

1. **Recall** How is Romeo accidentally responsible for Mercutio's death?

2. **Recall** Why does Prince Escalus banish Romeo from Verona?

3. **Recall** What promise does Lord Capulet make to Paris?

4. **Clarify** Why does Lord Capulet become so enraged with Juliet?

Literary Analysis

5. **Reading Shakespearean Drama** Review your list detailing the events in Act
   Three. What event in this act causes the most problems for Romeo and Juliet?
   Cite evidence to support your answer.

6. **Analyze Character Motivation** What is Romeo's motivation for killing Tybalt?
   What are the consequences of this action? Citing evidence, explain whether you
   think Romeo's behavior is justified revenge or a disastrous mistake.

7. **Interpret Allusions** Find two allusions in Act Three, and record them in a chart
   like the one shown. Complete the chart by describing what each allusion is a
   reference to and explaining what each means.

Scene and Lines	Allusion	Meaning
Scene I, lines 70–72	**Mercutio.** . . . Tybalt, you ratcatcher, will you walk? **Tybalt.** What wouldst thou have with me? **Mercutio.** Good King of Cats, nothing but one of your nine lives.	In Act Two, Scene 4, there was an allusion to a cat named Tybalt in a common story of the time. Mercutio alludes to this story again here to taunt Tybalt and make him want to fight.

8. **Evaluate Characters** Compare and contrast the behaviors of the nurse and
   Friar Laurence in Act Three. On the basis of their actions and interactions with
   other characters, which of the two would you trust more if you were Romeo
   or Juliet? Explain, citing evidence from the play.

Literary Criticism

9. **Philosophical Context** In the first three acts of *Romeo and Juliet*, both the
   Chorus and the characters make frequent references to the role of fate in life.
   How does this notion of fate differ from contemporary views? Do people still
   think this way today? Explain your answer.

Act Four

SCENE 1   *Friar Laurence's cell.*

When Juliet arrives at Friar Laurence's cell, she is upset to find Paris there making arrangements for their wedding. When Paris leaves, the panicked Juliet tells the friar that if he has no solution to her problem, she will kill herself. The friar explains his plan. Juliet will drink a potion he has made from his herbs, which will put her in a deathlike coma. When she wakes up two days later in the family tomb, Romeo will be waiting for her, and they will escape to Mantua together.

[*Enter* Friar Laurence *and* Paris.]

Friar Laurence. On Thursday, sir? The time is very short.

Paris. My father Capulet will have it so,
And I am nothing slow to slack his haste.

Friar Laurence. You say you do not know the lady's mind.
5 Uneven is the course; I like it not. **Ⓐ**

Paris. Immoderately she weeps for Tybalt's death,
And therefore have I little talked of love;
For Venus smiles not in a house of tears.
Now, sir, her father counts it dangerous
10 That she do give her sorrow so much sway,
And in his wisdom hastes our marriage
To stop the inundation of her tears,
Which, too much minded by herself alone,
May be put from her by society.
15 Now do you know the reason of this haste.

Friar Laurence [*aside*]. I would I knew not why it should be
       slowed.—
Look, sir, here comes the lady toward my cell.

[*Enter* Juliet.]

Paris. Happily met, my lady and my wife!

Juliet. That may be, sir, when I may be a wife.

20 **Paris.** That may be must be, love, on Thursday next.

Juliet. What must be shall be.

Friar Laurence.   That's a certain text.

Paris. Come you to make confession to this father?

Juliet. To answer that, I should confess to you.

2–3 **My . . . haste:** Capulet is eager to have the wedding on Thursday and so am I.

4–5 **You . . . course:** You don't know how Juliet feels about this. It's a very uncertain (**uneven**) plan.

Ⓐ CHARACTER
What is the friar's real **motive** for wanting to slow down the wedding preparations?

13–14 **which . . . society:** which, thought about too much by her in privacy, may be put from her mind if she is forced to be with others. *According to Paris, why does Capulet want Juliet to marry so quickly?*

19–28 Juliet once again chooses her words carefully to avoid lying and to avoid telling her secret.

Friar Laurence mixes a potion in the Royal Shakespeare Company's 1995 production.

Paris. Do not deny to him that you love me.

25 **Juliet.** I will confess to you that I love him.

Paris. So will ye, I am sure, that you love me.

Juliet. If I do so, it will be of more price,
Being spoke behind your back, than to your face.

Paris. Poor soul, thy face is much abused with tears.

30 **Juliet.** The tears have got small victory by that,
For it was bad enough before their spite.

Paris. Thou wrongst it more than tears with that report.

Juliet. That is no slander, sir, which is a truth;
And what I spake, I spake it to my face.

35 **Paris.** Thy face is mine, and thou hast slandered it.

Juliet. It may be so, for it is not mine own.
Are you at leisure, holy father, now,
Or shall I come to you at evening mass?

Friar Laurence. My leisure serves me, pensive daughter, now.
40 My lord, we must entreat the time alone.

Paris. God shield I should disturb devotion!
Juliet, on Thursday early will I rouse ye.
Till then, adieu, and keep this holy kiss.

[*Exit.*]

Juliet. O, shut the door! and when thou hast done so,
45 Come weep with me—past hope, past cure, past help!

Friar Laurence. Ah, Juliet, I already know thy grief;
It strains me past the compass of my wits.
I hear thou must, and nothing may prorogue it,
On Thursday next be married to this County.

50 **Juliet.** Tell me not, friar, that thou hearst of this,
Unless thou tell me how I may prevent it.
If in thy wisdom thou canst give no help,
Do thou but call my resolution wise
And with this knife I'll help it presently.
55 God joined my heart and Romeo's, thou our hands;
And ere this hand, by thee to Romeo's sealed,
Shall be the label to another deed,
Or my true heart with treacherous revolt
Turn to another, this shall slay them both.
60 Therefore, out of thy long-experienced time,

25 *Whom does "him" refer to in this line?*

30–31 The tears . . . spite: The tears haven't ruined my face; it wasn't all that beautiful before they did their damage.

35 Paris says he owns Juliet's face (since she will soon marry him). Insulting her face, he says, insults him, its owner.

47–48 compass: limit; **prorogue:** postpone.

52–53 If in . . . wise: If you can't find a way to help me, at least agree that my plan is wise.

56–67 And ere this hand . . . of remedy: Before I sign another wedding agreement (**deed**), I will use this knife to kill myself. If you, with your years of experience (**long-experienced time**), can't help me, I'll end my sufferings (**extremes**) and solve the problem myself.

Give me some present counsel; or, behold,
'Twixt my extremes and me this bloody knife
Shall play the umpire, arbitrating that
Which the commission of thy years and art
65 Could to no issue of true honor bring.
Be not so long to speak. I long to die
If what thou speakst speak not of remedy.

Friar Laurence. Hold, daughter, I do spy a kind of hope,
Which craves as desperate an execution
70 As that is desperate which we would prevent.
If, rather than to marry County Paris,
Thou hast the strength of will to slay thyself,
Then is it likely thou wilt undertake
A thing like death to chide away this shame,
75 That copest with death himself to scape from it;
And, if thou darest, I'll give thee remedy.

Juliet. O, bid me leap, rather than marry Paris,
From off the battlements of yonder tower,
Or walk in thievish ways, or bid me lurk
80 Where serpents are; chain me with roaring bears,
Or shut me nightly in a charnel house,
O'ercovered quite with dead men's rattling bones,
With reeky shanks and yellow chapless skulls;
Or bid me go into a new-made grave
85 And hide me with a dead man in his shroud—
Things that, to hear them told, have made me tremble—
And I will do it without fear or doubt,
To live an unstained wife to my sweet love.

Friar Laurence. Hold, then. Go home, be merry, give consent
90 To marry Paris. Wednesday is tomorrow.
Tomorrow night look that thou lie alone:
Let not the nurse lie with thee in thy chamber.
Take thou this vial, being then in bed,
And this distilled liquor drink thou off;
95 When presently through all thy veins shall run
A cold and drowsy humor; for no pulse
Shall keep his native progress, but surcease;
No warmth, no breath, shall testify thou livest;
The roses in thy lips and cheeks shall fade
100 To paly ashes, thy eyes' windows fall

71–76 If, rather than . . . remedy: If you are desperate enough to kill yourself, then you'll be daring enough to try the deathlike solution that I propose.

77–88 Juliet gives a lengthy list of things she would do rather than marry Paris. **charnel house:** a storehouse for bones from old graves; **reeky shanks:** stinking bones; **chapless:** without jaws. The description in lines 84–88 comes closer to Juliet's future than she knows.

89–120 The friar explains his plan.

93 vial: small bottle.

96–106 humor: liquid; **no pulse . . . pleasant sleep:** Your pulse will stop (**surcease**), and you will turn cold, pale, and stiff, as if you were dead; this condition will last for 42 hours.

Like death when he shuts up the day of life;
Each part, deprived of supple government,
Shall, stiff and stark and cold, appear like death;
And in this borrowed likeness of shrunk death
105 Thou shalt continue two-and-forty hours,
And then awake as from a pleasant sleep.
Now, when the bridegroom in the morning comes
To rouse thee from thy bed, there art thou dead.
Then, as the manner of our country is,
110 In thy best robes uncovered on the bier
Thou shalt be borne to that same ancient vault
Where all the kindred of the Capulets lie.
In the meantime, against thou shalt awake,
Shall Romeo by my letters know our drift;
115 And hither shall he come; and he and I
Will watch thy waking, and that very night
Shall Romeo bear thee hence to Mantua.
And this shall free thee from this present shame,
If no inconstant toy nor womanish fear
120 Abate thy valor in the acting it.

Juliet. Give me, give me! O, tell me not of fear!

Friar Laurence. Hold! Get you gone, be strong and prosperous
In this resolve. I'll send a friar with speed
To Mantua, with my letters to thy lord.

125 **Juliet.** Love give me strength! and strength shall help afford.
Farewell, dear father.

[*Exeunt.*]

107–112 *According to the friar's plan, what will happen when Paris comes to wake Juliet?*

111–112 same ancient vault . . . lie: same ancient tomb where all members of the Capulet family are buried.

114 drift: plan.

119–120 inconstant toy: foolish whim; **abate thy valor:** weaken your courage.

SCENE 2 *Capulet's house.*
Capulet is making plans for the wedding on Thursday. Juliet arrives and apologizes to him, saying that she will marry Paris. Capulet is so relieved that he reschedules the wedding for the next day, Wednesday.

[*Enter* Capulet, Lady Capulet, Nurse, *and* Servingmen.]

Capulet. So many guests invite as here are writ.

[*Exit a* Servingman.]

Sirrah, go hire me twenty cunning cooks.

Servingman. You shall have none ill, sir; for I'll try if they can lick their fingers.

1–8 Capulet is having a cheerful conversation with his servants about the wedding preparations. One servant assures him that he will test (**try**) the cooks he hires by making them taste their own food (**lick their fingers**).

5 **Capulet.** How canst thou try them so?

Servingman. Marry, sir, 'tis an ill cook that cannot lick his own fingers. Therefore he that cannot lick his fingers goes not with me. **B**

Capulet. Go, begone.

[*Exit* Servingman.]

10 We shall be much unfurnished for this time.
What, is my daughter gone to Friar Laurence?

Nurse. Ay, forsooth.

Capulet. Well, he may chance to do some good on her.
A peevish self-willed harlotry it is.

[*Enter* Juliet.]

15 **Nurse.** See where she comes from shrift with merry look.

Capulet. How now, my headstrong? Where have you been gadding?

Juliet. Where I have learnt me to repent the sin
Of disobedient opposition
To you and your behests, and am enjoined
20 By holy Laurence to fall prostrate here
To beg your pardon. Pardon, I beseech you!
Henceforward I am ever ruled by you.

Capulet. Send for the County. Go tell him of this.
I'll have this knot knit up tomorrow morning.

25 **Juliet.** I met the youthful lord at Laurence' cell
And gave him what becomed love I might,
Not stepping o'er the bounds of modesty.

Capulet. Why, I am glad on't. This is well. Stand up.
This is as't should be. Let me see the County.
30 Ay, marry, go, I say, and fetch him hither.
Now, afore God, this reverend holy friar,
All our whole city is much bound to him. **C**

Juliet. Nurse, will you go with me into my closet
To help me sort such needful ornaments
35 As you think fit to furnish me tomorrow?

Lady Capulet. No, not till Thursday. There is time enough.

Capulet. Go, nurse, go with her. We'll to church tomorrow.

[*Exeunt* Juliet *and* Nurse.]

B COMIC RELIEF
Think about the purpose that comic relief serves. Why might Shakespeare have chosen to begin this scene with a light, humorous conversation?

10 unfurnished: unprepared.

14 A silly, stubborn girl she is.

19 behests: orders; **enjoined:** commanded.

24 I'll have this wedding scheduled for tomorrow morning.

C DRAMATIC IRONY
What is ironic about Capulet's praise of Friar Laurence?

36–39 Lady Capulet urges her husband to wait until Thursday as originally planned. She needs time to get food (**provision**) ready for the wedding party.

Lady Capulet. We shall be short in our provision.
'Tis now near night.

Capulet.   Tush, I will stir about,
40 And all things shall be well, I warrant thee, wife.
Go thou to Juliet, help to deck up her.
I'll not to bed tonight; let me alone.
I'll play the housewife for this once. What, ho!
They are all forth; well, I will walk myself
45 To County Paris, to prepare him up
Against tomorrow. My heart is wondrous light,
Since this same wayward girl is so reclaimed. **ⓓ**

[*Exeunt.*]

39–46 Capulet is so set on Wednesday that he promises to make the arrangements himself.

ⓓ TRAGEDY
Think about how the **plot** of this tragedy is unfolding. What does moving the wedding up by one day do to Friar Laurence's plan?

SCENE 3   *Juliet's bedroom.*

Juliet sends her mother and the nurse away and prepares to take the drug the friar has given her. She is confused and frightened but finally puts the vial to her lips and drinks.

[*Enter* Juliet *and* Nurse.]

Juliet. Ay, those attires are best; but, gentle nurse,
I pray thee leave me to myself tonight;
For I have need of many orisons
To move the heavens to smile upon my state,
5 Which, well thou knowest, is cross and full of sin.

[*Enter* Lady Capulet.]

3 orisons: prayers.

Lady Capulet. What, are you busy, ho? Need you my help?

Juliet. No madam; we have culled such necessaries
As are behooveful for our state tomorrow.
So please you, let me now be left alone,
10 And let the nurse this night sit up with you;
For I am sure you have your hands full all
In this so sudden business.

7–8 we have ... tomorrow: We have picked out (**culled**) everything appropriate for the wedding tomorrow.

Lady Capulet.   Good night.
Get thee to bed and rest, for thou hast need.

[*Exeunt* Lady Capulet *and* Nurse.]

Juliet. Farewell! God knows when we shall meet again.
15 I have a faint cold fear thrills through my veins
That almost freezes up the heat of life.
I'll call them back again to comfort me.
Nurse!—What should she do here?
My dismal scene I needs must act alone.

17–19 In her fear, Juliet starts to call the nurse back but realizes that she must be alone to drink the poison.

The Seattle Repertory Theatre, 2003

LOVE CONQUERS EVERYTHING.
EXCEPT STAB WOUNDS AND POISONING.

WILLIAM SHAKESPEARE

OMEO & JULIET

ROMEO Juliet

by William Shakespeare

The Arkansas Repertory Theatre, 2004

The National Theater of Poland, 1996

TEATR NARODOWY
Warszawa

SIERGIEJ
PROKOFIEW
ROMEO JULIA
Choreografia Emil

Promotion

Imagine that you knew nothing about the
story of the star-crossed lovers. What clues
about the play do each of these **promotional**
posters provide? Which poster would most
make you want to see the play? Explain
your answers.

20 Come, vial.
   What if this mixture do not work at all?
   Shall I be married then tomorrow morning?
   No, no! This shall forbid it. Lie thou there.

   [*lays down a dagger*]

   What if it be a poison which the friar
25 Subtly hath ministered to have me dead,
   Lest in this marriage he should be dishonored
   Because he married me before to Romeo?
   I fear it is; and yet methinks it should not,
   For he hath still been tried a holy man. **Ⓔ**
30 How if, when I am laid into the tomb,
   I wake before the time that Romeo
   Come to redeem me? There's a fearful point!
   Shall I not then be stifled in the vault,
   To whose foul mouth no healthsome air breathes in,
35 And there die strangled ere my Romeo comes?
   Or, if I live, is it not very like
   The horrible conceit of death and night,
   Together with the terror of the place—
   As in a vault, an ancient receptacle
40 Where for this many hundred years the bones
   Of all my buried ancestors are packed;
   Where bloody Tybalt, yet but green in earth,
   Lies fest'ring in his shroud; where, as they say,
   At some hours in the night spirits resort—
45 Alack, alack, is it not like that I,
   So early waking—what with loathsome smells,
   And shrieks like mandrakes torn out of the earth,
   That living mortals, hearing them, run mad—
   O, if I wake, shall I not be distraught,
50 Environed with all these hideous fears,
   And madly play with my forefathers' joints,
   And pluck the mangled Tybalt from his shroud,
   And, in this rage, with some great kinsman's bone
   As with a club dash out my desp'rate brains?
55 O, look! methinks I see my cousin's ghost
   Seeking out Romeo, that did spit his body
   Upon a rapier's point. Stay, Tybalt, stay!
   Romeo, I come! this do I drink to thee.

   [*She drinks and falls upon her bed within the curtains.*]

---

23 This shall forbid it: A dagger will be her alternative means of keeping from marrying Paris.

24–57 Juliet lists her various doubts and fears about what she is about to do.

Ⓔ CHARACTER
In her anxious state, what does Juliet suspect about Friar Laurence's **motives** for giving her the potion? Do you think she really believes this to be true? Explain.

36–43 Juliet fears the vision (**conceit**) she might have on waking in the family tomb and seeing the rotting body of Tybalt.

45–54 She fears that the smells together with the sounds of ghosts screaming might make her lose her mind and commit bizarre acts. Mandrake root was thought to look like the human form and to scream when pulled from the ground.

57 stay: stop.

SCENE 4 *Capulet's house.*

It is now the next morning, nearly time for the wedding. The household is happy and excited as everyone makes final preparations.

[*Enter* Lady Capulet *and* Nurse.]

Lady Capulet. Hold, take these keys and fetch more spices, nurse.

Nurse. They call for dates and quinces in the pastry.

[*Enter* Capulet.]

Capulet. Come, stir, stir, stir! The second cock hath crowed,
The curfew bell hath rung, 'tis three o'clock.
5 Look to the baked meats, good Angelica;
Spare not for cost.

Nurse.   Go, you cot-quean, go,
Get you to bed! Faith, you'll be sick tomorrow
For this night's watching.

Capulet. No, not a whit. What, I have watched ere now
10 All night for lesser cause, and ne'er been sick.

Lady Capulet. Ay, you have been a mouse-hunt in your time;
But I will watch you from such watching now.

[*Exeunt* Lady Capulet *and* Nurse.]

Capulet. A jealous hood, a jealous hood!

[*Enter three or four* Servants, *with spits and logs and baskets.*]

                    Now, fellow,
What is there?

15 **First Servant.** Things for the cook, sir; but I know not what.

Capulet. Make haste, make haste. [*Exit* Servant.] Sirrah, fetch
    drier logs.
Call Peter; he will show thee where they are.

Second Servant. I have a head, sir, that will find out logs
And never trouble Peter for the matter.

20 **Capulet.** Mass, and well said, merry whoreson, ha!
Thou shalt be loggerhead. [*Exit* Servant.] Good faith, 'tis day.
The County will be here with music straight,
For so he said he would. [*music within*] I hear him near.
Nurse! Wife! What, ho! What, nurse, I say!

2 pastry: the room where baking is done.

5 good Angelica: In his happy mood, Capulet even calls the nurse by her name.

6 cot-quean: The nurse playfully refers to Capulet as a "cottage quean," or housewife. This is a joke about his doing women's work (arranging the party).

11–13 Lord and Lady Capulet joke about his being a woman chaser (**mouse-hunt**) as a young man. He makes fun of her jealousy (**jealous hood**).

20–23 The joking between Capulet and his servants includes the mild oath **Mass,** short for "by the Mass," and **loggerhead,** a word for a stupid person as well as a pun, since the servant is searching for drier logs. **straight:** right away.

[*Reenter* Nurse.]

25 Go waken Juliet; go and trim her up.
I'll go and chat with Paris. Hie, make haste,
Make haste! The bridegroom he is come already:
Make haste, I say.

[*Exeunt.*]

SCENE 5 *Juliet's bedroom.*

The joyous preparations suddenly change into plans for a funeral when the nurse discovers Juliet on her bed, apparently dead. Lord and Lady Capulet, Paris, and the nurse are overcome with grief. Friar Laurence tries to comfort them and instructs them to bring Juliet's body to the Capulet family tomb. The scene abruptly switches to humor, in a foolish conversation between the servant Peter and the musicians hired to play at the wedding.

[*Enter* Nurse.]

Nurse. Mistress! what, mistress! Juliet! Fast, I warrant her, she.
Why, lamb! why, lady! Fie, you slugabed!
Why, love, I say! madam! sweetheart! Why, bride!
What, not a word? You take your pennyworths now,
5 Sleep for a week; for the next night, I warrant,
The County Paris hath set up his rest
That you shall rest but little. God forgive me,
Marry and amen, how sound is she asleep!
I needs must wake her. Madam, madam, madam!
10 Aye, let the County take you in your bed,
He'll fright you up, i' faith. Will it not be?

[*opens the curtains*]

What, dressed and in your clothes and down again?
I must needs wake you. Lady! lady! lady!
Alas, alas! Help, help! my lady's dead!
15 O well-a-day that ever I was born!
Some aqua vitae, ho! My lord! my lady!

[*Enter* Lady Capulet.]

Lady Capulet. What noise is here?

Nurse. O lamentable day!

Lady Capulet. What is the matter?

Nurse. Look, look! O heavy day!

Lady Capulet. O me, O me! My child, my only life!
20 Revive, look up, or I will die with thee!
Help! help! Call help.

1–11 The nurse chatters as she bustles around the room. She calls Juliet a **slugabed,** or sleepyhead, who is trying to get her **pennyworths,** or small portions, of rest now, since after the wedding Paris won't let her get much sleep. When Juliet doesn't answer, the nurse opens the curtains that enclose the bed.

17 **lamentable:** filled with grief.

[*Enter* Capulet.]

Capulet. For shame, bring Juliet forth; her lord is come.

Nurse. She's dead, deceased; she's dead! Alack the day!

Lady Capulet. Alack the day, she's dead, she's dead, she's dead!

25 **Capulet.** Ha! let me see her. Out alas! she's cold,
Her blood is settled, and her joints are stiff;
Life and these lips have long been separated.
Death lies on her like an untimely frost
Upon the sweetest flower of all the field.

30 **Nurse.** O lamentable day!

Lady Capulet.   O woeful time!

Capulet. Death, that hath ta'en her hence to make me wail,
Ties up my tongue and will not let me speak.

[*Enter* Friar Laurence *and* Paris, *with* Musicians.]

Friar Laurence. Come, is the bride ready to go to church?

28–29 What simile does Capulet use to describe what has happened to Juliet?

Friar Laurence and the Capulets mourn for Juliet in the University of Victoria's 1998 production.

Capulet. Ready to go, but never to return.
35 O son, the night before thy wedding day
Hath death lain with thy wife. See, there she lies,
Flower as she was, deflowered by him.
Death is my son-in-law, Death is my heir;
My daughter he hath wedded. I will die
40 And leave him all. Life, living, all is Death's.

    Paris. Have I thought long to see this morning's face,
And doth it give me such a sight as this?

    Lady Capulet. Accursed, unhappy, wretched, hateful day!
Most miserable hour that e'er time saw
45 In lasting labor of his pilgrimage!
But one, poor one, one poor and loving child,
But one thing to rejoice and solace in,
And cruel Death hath catched it from my sight!

    Nurse. O woe! O woeful, woeful, woeful day!
50 Most lamentable day, most woeful day
That ever, ever I did yet behold!
O day! O day! O day! O hateful day!
Never was seen so black a day as this.
O woeful day! O woeful day!

55 **Paris.** Beguiled, divorced, wronged, spited, slain!
Most detestable Death, by thee beguiled,
By cruel, cruel thee quite overthrown!
O love! O life! not life, but love in death!

    Capulet. Despised, distressed, hated, martyred, killed!
60 Uncomfortable time, why camest thou now
To murder, murder our solemnity?
O child! O child! my soul, and not my child!
Dead art thou, dead! alack, my child is dead,
And with my child my joys are buried!

65 **Friar Laurence.** Peace, ho, for shame! Confusion's cure lives not
In these confusions. Heaven and yourself
Had part in this fair maid! now heaven hath all,
And all the better is it for the maid.
Your part in her you could not keep from death,
70 But heaven keeps his part in eternal life.
The most you sought was her promotion,
For 'twas your heaven she should be advanced;
And weep ye now, seeing she is advanced
Above the clouds, as high as heaven itself?
75 O, in this love, you love your child so ill

40 Life . . . Death's: My life, my possessions, and everything else of mine belongs to Death.

44–48 Most miserable . . . my sight: This is the most miserable hour that time ever saw on its long journey. I had only one child to make me happy, and Death has taken (**catched**) her from me.

55 beguiled: tricked.

60–61 why . . . solemnity: Why did Death have to come to murder our celebration?

65–78 The friar comforts the family. He says that the cure for disaster (**confusion**) cannot be found in cries of grief. Juliet's family and heaven once shared her; now heaven has all of her. All the family ever wanted was the best for her; now she's in heaven—what could be better than that? It is best to die young, when the soul is still pure, without sin.

That you run mad, seeing that she is well.
She's not well married that lives married long,
But she's best married that dies married young.
Dry up your tears and stick your rosemary
80 On this fair corse, and, as the custom is,
In all her best array bear her to church;
For though fond nature bids us all lament,
Yet nature's tears are reason's merriment.

Capulet. All things that we ordained festival
85 Turn from their office to black funeral—
Our instruments to melancholy bells,
Our wedding cheer to a sad burial feast;
Our solemn hymns to sullen dirges change;
Our bridal flowers serve for a buried corse;
90 And all things change them to the contrary.

Friar Laurence. Sir, go you in; and, madam, go with him;
And go, Sir Paris. Every one prepare
To follow this fair corse unto her grave.
The heavens do lower upon you for some ill;
95 Move them no more by crossing their high will.

[*Exeunt* Capulet, Lady Capulet, Paris, *and* Friar.]

First Musician. Faith, we may put up our pipes, and be gone.

Nurse. Honest good fellows, ah, put up, put up,
For well you know this is a pitiful case.

[*Exit.*]

Second Musician. Aye, by my troth, the case may be amended. **F**

[*Enter* Peter.]

100 **Peter.** Musicians, oh, musicians, "Heart's ease, heart's ease." Oh,
an you will have me live, play "Heart's ease."

First Musician. Why "Heart's ease"?

Peter. Oh, musicians, because my heart itself plays "My heart is
full of woe." Oh, play me some merry dump, to comfort me.

105 **First Musician.** Not a dump we, 'tis no time to play now.

Peter. You will not, then?

First Musician. No.

Peter. I will then give it you soundly.

79–80 stick . . . corse: Put rosemary, an herb, on her corpse.

82–83 though . . . merriment: Though it's natural to cry, common sense tells us we should rejoice for the dead.

84 ordained festival: intended for the wedding.

88 sullen dirges: sad, mournful tunes.

94–95 The heavens . . . will: The fates (heavens) frown on you for some wrong you have done. Don't tempt them by refusing to accept their will (Juliet's death).

F PUN
Reread lines 96–99. The musician is talking about the case for his instrument. What "case" is the nurse referring to?

100–138 After the tragedy of Juliet's "death," Shakespeare injects a light and witty conversation between Peter and the musicians. Peter asks them to play "Heart's Ease," a popular song of the time, or a **dump,** a slow dance melody. They refuse to play, and insults and puns are traded. Peter says that instead of money he'll give them a jeering speech (**gleek**), and he insults them by calling them minstrels. In return they call him a servant. Then both make puns on notes of the musical scale, re and fa.

First Musician. What will you give us?

110 **Peter.** No money, on my faith, but the gleek. I will give you the minstrel.

First Musician. Then will I give you the serving creature.

Peter. Then will I lay the serving creature's dagger on your pate. I will carry no crotchets. I'll re you, I'll fa you, do you note me?

115 **First Musician.** An you re us and fa us, you note us.

Second Musician. Pray you put up your dagger, and put out your wit.

Peter. Then have at you with my wit! I will drybeat you with an iron wit, and put up my iron dagger. Answer me like men:

120   "When griping grief the heart doth wound
        And doleful dumps the mind oppress,
        Then music with her silver sound—"

Why "silver sound"? Why "music with her silver sound"?—What say you, Simon Catling?

125 **First Musician.** Marry, sir, because silver hath a sweet sound.

Peter. Pretty! What say you, Hugh Rebeck?

Second Musician. I say "silver sound" because musicians sound for silver.

Peter. Pretty too! What say you, James Soundpost?

130 **Third Musician.** Faith, I know not what to say.

Peter. Oh, I cry you mercy, you are the singer. I will say for you. It is "music with her silver sound" because musicians have no gold for sounding.

        "Then music with her silver sound
135   With speedy help doth lend redress."

[*Exit.*]

First Musician. What a pestilent knave is this same!

Second Musician. Hang him, Jack! Come, we'll in here. Tarry for the mourners, and stay dinner.

[*Exeunt.*]

Comprehension

1. **Recall** What reason does Paris give for Lord Capulet's decision to move up the wedding?

2. **Recall** At first, what does Juliet believe is the only solution to her problem?

3. **Summarize** What plan does Friar Laurence devise for Juliet, and what reservations does Juliet have about this plan?

PENNSYLVANIA STANDARDS

READING STANDARD
B.1.1.1.A.1 Evaluate character

Literary Analysis

4. **Reading Shakespearean Drama** Review the events you recorded as you read Act Four, and think about how the characters' interactions drive the plot forward. If the nurse had accompanied Juliet to Friar Laurence's cell, do you think Juliet would have made a different decision? Explain.

5. **Make Judgments** Do you feel sympathy for the Capulets, the nurse, and Paris when they express grief over Juliet's death? Why or why not?

6. **Identify Dramatic Irony** Dramatic irony exists when the reader or viewer knows something that one or more of the characters do not. Find three examples of dramatic irony in Act Four and record them in a chart like the one shown. Then explain how these ironic moments contribute to the building tension in the play.

Scene and Lines	Dramatic Irony
Scene 1, lines 24–28	Paris asks Juliet to confess to Friar Laurence that she loves him, and Juliet carefully avoids denying it. We know that Juliet loves Romeo, not Paris.

7. **Recognize Protagonist and Antagonist** If Romeo and Juliet are the protagonists of this play, who or what is the antagonist? Keep in mind that an antagonist can be a character, a group of characters, a set of circumstances, or even society as a whole. Use details from the play to support your answer.

8. **Evaluate Comic Relief** The humorous exchange between Peter and the musicians at the end of Act Four is an example of comic relief. It lightens the mood after the grief-filled speeches that follow the discovery of Juliet's body. If you were producing a stage or film version of *Romeo and Juliet,* would you cut this passage, or do you think it serves an important purpose? Explain.

Literary Criticism

9. **Different Perspectives** How might older and younger audiences differ in their assessment of Romeo's and Juliet's actions? Explain your opinion, citing specific actions and interactions in the play.

Act Five

SCENE 1 *A street in Mantua.*

Balthasar, Romeo's servant, comes from Verona to tell him that Juliet is dead and lies in the Capulets' tomb. Since Romeo has not yet received any word from the friar, he believes Balthasar. He immediately decides to return to Verona in order to die next to Juliet. He sends Balthasar away and sets out to find a pharmacist who will sell him poison.

[*Enter* Romeo.]

Romeo. If I may trust the flattering truth of sleep,
My dreams presage some joyful news at hand.
My bosom's lord sits lightly in his throne,
And all this day an unaccustomed spirit

5 Lifts me above the ground with cheerful thoughts.
I dreamt my lady came and found me dead
(Strange dream that gives a dead man leave to think!)
And breathed such life with kisses in my lips
That I revived and was an emperor.

10 Ah me! how sweet is love itself possessed,
When but love's shadows are so rich in joy! Ⓐ

[*Enter Romeo's servant,* Balthasar, *booted.*]

News from Verona! How now, Balthasar?
Dost thou not bring me letters from the friar?
How doth my lady? Is my father well?

15 How fares my Juliet? That I ask again,
For nothing can be ill if she be well.

Balthasar. Then she is well, and nothing can be ill.
Her body sleeps in Capels' monument,
And her immortal part with angels lives.

20 I saw her laid low in her kindred's vault
And presently took post to tell it you.
O, pardon me for bringing these ill news,
Since you did leave it for my office, sir.

Romeo. Is it e'en so? Then I defy you, stars!

25 Thou knowst my lodging. Get me ink and paper
And hire posthorses. I will hence tonight.

Balthasar. I do beseech you, sir, have patience.
Your looks are pale and wild and do import
Some misadventure.

1–5 **If I may . . . cheerful thoughts:** If I can trust my dreams, something joyful is about to happen. My heart (**bosom's lord**) is happy and I am content.

Ⓐ **TRAGEDY**
Paraphrase lines 1–11. What part of Romeo's seemingly happy dream **foreshadows** the tragic events to come?

17–19 Balthasar replies that Juliet is well, since although her body lies in the Capulets' (**Capels'**) burial vault, her soul (**her immortal part**) is with the angels.

21 **presently took post:** immediately rode (to Mantua).

23 **you did . . . office:** you gave me the duty of reporting important news to you.

24 **I . . . stars:** Romeo angrily challenges fate, which has caused him so much grief.

28–29 **import some misadventure:** suggest that something bad will happen.

Romeo and Juliet in the 1994 production of the Shakespeare Theatre in Washington, D.C.

Romeo.   Tush, thou art deceived.
30 Leave me and do the thing I bid thee do.
Hast thou no letters to me from the friar?

Balthasar. No, my good lord.

Romeo.   No matter. Get thee gone
And hire those horses. I'll be with thee straight.

[*Exit* Balthasar.]

Well, Juliet, I will lie with thee tonight. **B**
35 Let's see for means. O mischief, thou art swift
To enter in the thoughts of desperate men!
I do remember an apothecary,
And hereabouts he dwells, which late I noted
In tattered weeds, with overwhelming brows,
40 Culling of simples. Meager were his looks,
Sharp misery had worn him to the bones;
And in his needy shop a tortoise hung,
An alligator stuffed, and other skins
Of ill-shaped fishes; and about his shelves
45 A beggarly account of empty boxes,
Green earthen pots, bladders, and musty seeds,
Remnants of packthread, and old cakes of roses
Were thinly scattered, to make up a show.
Noting this penury, to myself I said,
50 "An if a man did need a poison now
Whose sale is present death in Mantua,
Here lives a caitiff wretch would sell it him."
O, this same thought did but forerun my need,
And this same needy man must sell it me.
55 As I remember, this should be the house.
Being holiday, the beggar's shop is shut.
What, ho! apothecary!

[*Enter* Apothecary.]

Apothecary.   Who calls so loud?

Romeo. Come hither, man. I see that thou art poor.
Hold, there is forty ducats. Let me have
60 A dram of poison, such soon-speeding gear
As will disperse itself through all the veins
That the life-weary taker may fall dead,
And that the trunk may be discharged of breath
As violently as hasty powder fired
65 Doth hurry from the fatal cannon's womb.

Apothecary. Such mortal drugs I have; but Mantua's law
Is death to any he that utters them.

B CHARACTER
What does Romeo mean in line 34? Explain whether he thoughtfully considers his options or plunges immediately into action.

35–40 Let's ... means: Let me find a way (to join Juliet in death); **apothecary:** pharmacist; **tattered weeds:** ragged clothes; **culling of simples:** selecting herbs.

47 cakes of roses: rose petals pressed together to create a perfume.

49 penury: poverty.

50–52 "An if a man ... sell it him": Though it is a crime to sell poison in Mantua, the apothecary is such a miserable (**caitiff**) wretch that he would probably do it for the money.

59 ducats: gold coins.

60–65 Romeo wants fast-acting (**soon-speeding**) poison that will work as quickly as gunpowder exploding in a cannon.

67 any ... them: any person who dispenses or sells them.

Romeo. Art thou so bare and full of wretchedness
And fearest to die? Famine is in thy cheeks,
70 Need and oppression starveth in thine eyes,
Contempt and beggary hangs upon thy back:
The world is not thy friend, nor the world's law;
The world affords no law to make thee rich;
Then be not poor, but break it and take this.

75 **Apothecary.** My poverty but not my will consents.

Romeo. I pay thy poverty and not thy will.

Apothecary. Put this in any liquid thing you will
And drink it off, and if you had the strength
Of twenty men, it would dispatch you straight.

80 **Romeo.** There is thy gold—worse poison to men's souls,
Doing more murder in this loathsome world,
Than these poor compounds that thou mayst not sell.
I sell thee poison; thou hast sold me none.
Farewell. Buy food and get thyself in flesh.
85 Come, cordial and not poison, go with me
To Juliet's grave; for there must I use thee.

[*Exeunt.*]

72–74 Romeo urges the apothecary to improve his situation by breaking the law and selling him the poison.

75 I'm doing this for the money, not because I think it's right.

79 dispatch you straight: kill you instantly.

85 Romeo refers to the poison as a **cordial,** a drink believed to be good for the heart. *Why does he refer to it in this way?*

SCENE 2 *Friar Laurence's cell in Verona.*

Friar Laurence's messenger arrives, saying that he was unable to deliver the letter to Romeo. Friar Laurence, his plans ruined, rushes to the Capulet vault before Juliet awakes. He intends to hide her in his room until Romeo can come to take her away.

[*Enter* Friar John.]

Friar John. Holy Franciscan friar, brother, ho!

[*Enter* Friar Laurence.]

Friar Laurence. This same should be the voice of Friar John.
Welcome from Mantua. What says Romeo?
Or, if his mind be writ, give me his letter.

5 **Friar John.** Going to find a barefoot brother out,
One of our order to associate me,
Here in this city visiting the sick,
And finding him, the searchers of the town,
Suspecting that we both were in a house
10 Where the infectious pestilence did reign,
Sealed up the doors, and would not let us forth,
So that my speed to Mantua there was stayed.

5–12 Friar John explains why he did not go to Mantua. He had asked another friar (**barefoot brother**), who had been caring for the sick, to go with him. The health officials of the town, believing that the friars had come into contact with a deadly plague (**infectious pestilence**), locked them up to keep them from infecting others.

Friar Laurence. Who bare my letter, then, to Romeo?

Friar John. I could not send it—here it is again—

15 Nor get a messenger to bring it thee,
So fearful were they of infection.

Friar Laurence. Unhappy fortune! By my brotherhood,
The letter was not nice, but full of charge,
Of dear import, and the neglecting it

20 May do much danger. Friar John, go hence,
Get me an iron crow and bring it straight
Unto my cell.

Friar John.   Brother, I'll go and bring it thee.

[*Exit.*]

Friar Laurence. Now must I to the monument alone.
Within this three hours will fair Juliet wake.

25 She will beshrew me much that Romeo
Hath had no notice of these accidents;
But I will write again to Mantua,
And keep her at my cell till Romeo come—
Poor living corse, closed in a dead man's tomb! **G**

[*Exit.*]

SCENE 3   *The cemetery that contains the Capulets' tomb.*

In the dark of night Paris comes to the cemetery to put flowers on Juliet's grave. At the same time Romeo arrives, and Paris hides. Paris assumes that Romeo is going to harm the bodies. He challenges Romeo, they fight, and Romeo kills Paris. When Romeo recognizes the dead Paris, he lays his body inside the tomb as Paris requested. Romeo declares his love for Juliet, drinks the poison, and dies. Shortly after, Friar Laurence arrives and discovers both bodies. When Juliet wakes up, the friar urges her to leave with him before the guard comes. Juliet refuses, and when the friar leaves, she kills herself with Romeo's dagger. The guards and the prince arrive, followed by the Capulets and Lord Montague, whose wife has just died of grief because of Romeo's exile. Friar Laurence explains what has happened. Capulet and Montague finally end their feud and promise to erect statues honoring Romeo and Juliet.

[*Enter* Paris *and his* Page *with flowers and a torch.*]

Paris. Give me thy torch, boy. Hence, and stand aloof.
Yet put it out, for I would not be seen.
Under yond yew tree lay thee all along,
Holding thine ear close to the hollow ground.

---

13 bare: carried (bore).

18–20 The letter wasn't trivial (**nice**) but contained a message of great importance (**dear import**). The fact that it wasn't sent (**neglecting it**) may cause great harm.

21 iron crow: crowbar.

25–26 She ... accidents: She will be furious with me when she learns that Romeo doesn't know what has happened.

G SOLILOQUY
Explain what you learn about the friar's new plan in this soliloquy. Why is it essential that the friar reach Juliet before Romeo does?

1 aloof: some distance away.

Behind the Curtain

The Royal Shakespeare Company's 2004 production

The Shakespeare Israeli Company's 1994 production

Lighting

Directors use a variety of techniques to make a play's **lighting** effective. For example, spotlights can illuminate one character while leaving others in semi-darkness, and effects such as candles or prominent shadows can help create specific moods. What is distinctive about the lighting in each of these shots? Explain the effect each technique produces.

The Royal Opera House's 2000 Covent Garden production

5 So shall no foot upon the churchyard tread
      (Being loose, unfirm, with digging up of graves)
      But thou shalt hear it. Whistle then to me,
      As signal that thou hearst something approach.
      Give me those flowers. Do as I bid thee, go.

10 **Page** [*aside*]. I am almost afraid to stand alone
      Here in the churchyard; yet I will adventure.

      [*withdraws*]

      Paris. Sweet flower, with flowers thy bridal bed I strew

      [*He strews the tomb with flowers.*]

      (O woe! thy canopy is dust and stones)
      Which with sweet water nightly I will dew;
15   Or, wanting that, with tears distilled by moans.
      The obsequies that I for thee will keep
      Nightly shall be to strew thy grave and weep.

      [*The* Page *whistles.*]

      The boy gives warning something doth approach.
      What cursed foot wanders this way tonight
20 To cross my obsequies and true love's rite?
      What, with a torch? Muffle me, night, awhile.

      [*withdraws*]

      [*Enter* Romeo *and* Balthasar *with a torch, a mattock, and a crow of iron.*]

      Romeo. Give me that mattock and the wrenching iron.
      Hold, take this letter. Early in the morning
      See thou deliver it to my lord and father.
25 Give me the light. Upon thy life I charge thee,
      Whate'er thou hearest or seest, stand all aloof
      And do not interrupt me in my course.
      Why I descend into this bed of death
      Is partly to behold my lady's face,
30 But chiefly to take thence from her dead finger
      A precious ring—a ring that I must use
      In dear employment. Therefore hence, be gone.
      But if thou, jealous, dost return to pry
      In what I farther shall intend to do,
35 By heaven, I will tear thee joint by joint
      And strew this hungry churchyard with thy limbs.
      The time and my intents are savage-wild,
      More fierce and more inexorable far
      Than empty tigers or the roaring sea. **D**

12–17 Paris promises to decorate Juliet's grave with flowers, as he does now, and sprinkle it with either perfume (**sweet water**) or his tears. He will perform these honoring rites (**obsequies**) every night.

20 cross: interfere with.

21 muffle: hide.

mattock . . . iron: an ax and a crowbar.

32 in dear employment: for an important purpose.

33 jealous: curious.

37–39 Romeo's intention is more unstoppable (**inexorable**) than hungry (**empty**) tigers or the waves of an ocean.

D TRAGEDY
Reread lines 25–39 and think about how tragedies usually end for the main characters. Paraphrase the two reasons Romeo gives for going into the tomb. What third reason does he hint at?

40 **Balthasar.** I will be gone, sir, and not trouble you.

Romeo. So shalt thou show me friendship. Take thou that.
Live, and be prosperous; and farewell, good fellow.

Balthasar [*aside*]. For all this same, I'll hide me hereabout.
His looks I fear, and his intents I doubt.

[*withdraws*]

45 **Romeo.** Thou detestable maw, thou womb of death,
Gorged with the dearest morsel of the earth,
Thus I enforce thy rotten jaws to open,
And in despite I'll cram thee with more food.

[Romeo *opens the tomb.*]

Paris. This is that banish'd haughty Montague
50 That murdered my love's cousin—with which grief
It is supposed the fair creature died—
And here is come to do some villainous shame
To the dead bodies. I will apprehend him.
Stop thy unhallowed toil, vile Montague!
55 Can vengeance be pursued further than death?
Condemned villain, I do apprehend thee.
Obey, and go with me; for thou must die.

Romeo. I must indeed; and therefore came I hither.
Good gentle youth, tempt not a desp'rate man.
60 Fly hence and leave me. Think upon these gone;
Let them affright thee. I beseech thee, youth,
Put not another sin upon my head
By urging me to fury. O, be gone!
By heaven, I love thee better than myself.
65 For I come hither armed against myself.
Stay not, be gone. Live, and hereafter say
A madman's mercy bid thee run away.

Paris. I do defy thy conjuration
And apprehend thee for a felon here.

70 **Romeo.** Wilt thou provoke me? Then have at thee, boy! **E**

[*They fight.*]

43 *Who else besides Balthasar is hiding in the cemetery at this point?*

45–49 Romeo addresses the tomb as though it were devouring people. He calls it a hateful stomach (**detestable maw**) that is filled (**gorged**) with Juliet, the **dearest morsel of the earth.** He uses his crowbar to open its **rotten jaws** and moves to enter the tomb.

49–53 Recognizing Romeo, Paris speaks these first few lines to himself. He is angry with Romeo, believing that Romeo's killing Tybalt caused Juliet to die of grief.

58–67 Romeo rejects Paris' challenge. He tells Paris to think of those already killed and to leave before Romeo is forced to kill him too. Romeo swears that he has come to harm himself, not Paris.

68 I reject your appeal.

E CHARACTER
Consider what you know about Romeo's **traits** and **flaws.** Is Romeo at fault for fighting Paris? Why or why not?

Page. O Lord, they fight! I will go call the watch.

[*Exit.*]

Paris. O, I am slain! [*falls*] If thou be merciful,
Open the tomb, lay me with Juliet.

[*dies*]

Romeo. In faith, I will. Let me peruse this face.
75 Mercutio's kinsman, noble County Paris!
What said my man when my betossed soul
Did not attend him as we rode? I think
He told me Paris should have married Juliet.
Said he not so? or did I dream it so?
80 Or am I mad, hearing him talk of Juliet,
To think it was so? O, give me thy hand,
One writ with me in sour misfortune's book!
I'll bury thee in a triumphant grave.
A grave? O, no, a lantern, slaughtered youth,
85 For here lies Juliet, and her beauty makes
This vault a feasting presence full of light.
Death, lie thou there, by a dead man interred.

[*lays* Paris *in the tomb*]

How oft when men are at the point of death
Have they been merry! which their keepers call
90 A lightning before death. O, how may I
Call this a lightning? O my love! my wife!
Death, that hath sucked the honey of thy breath,
Hath had no power yet upon thy beauty.
Thou art not conquered. Beauty's ensign yet
95 Is crimson in thy lips and in thy cheeks,
And death's pale flag is not advanced there.
Tybalt, liest thou there in thy bloody sheet?
O, what more favor can I do to thee
Than with that hand that cut thy youth in twain
100 To sunder his that was thine enemy?
Forgive me, cousin! Ah, dear Juliet,
Why art thou yet so fair? Shall I believe
That unsubstantial Death is amorous,
And that the lean abhorred monster keeps
105 Thee here in dark to be his paramour?
For fear of that I still will stay with thee
And never from this palace of dim night

74–78 Romeo discovers that the man he has just killed is Paris, who he vaguely remembers being told was supposed to marry Juliet.

82 Romeo notes that, like himself, Paris has been a victim of bad luck

84–87 Romeo will bury Paris with Juliet, whose beauty fills the tomb with light. Paris' corpse (**Death**) is being buried (**interred**) by a dead man in that Romeo expects to be dead soon.

94 ensign: sign.

98–100 O, what . . . enemy: I can best repay you (Tybalt) by killing your enemy (myself) with the same hand that cut your youth in two (**twain**).

102–105 Romeo can't get over how beautiful Juliet still looks. He asks whether Death is loving (**amorous**) and whether it has taken Juliet as its lover (**paramour**).

Depart again. Here, here will I remain
With worms that are thy chambermaids. O, here
110 Will I set up my everlasting rest
And shake the yoke of inauspicious stars
From this world-wearied flesh. Eyes, look your last!
Arms, take your last embrace! and, lips, O you
The doors of breath, seal with a righteous kiss
115 A dateless bargain to engrossing death!
Come, bitter conduct; come, unsavory guide!
Thou desperate pilot, now at once run on
The dashing rocks thy seasick weary bark!
Here's to my love! [*drinks*] O true apothecary!
120 Thy drugs are quick. Thus with a kiss I die.

[*falls*]

[*Enter* Friar Laurence, *with lantern, crow, and spade.*]

Friar Laurence. Saint Francis be my speed! how oft tonight
Have my old feet stumbled at graves! Who's there?

Balthasar. Here's one, a friend, and one that knows you well.

Friar Laurence. Bliss be upon you! Tell me, good my friend,
125 What torch is yond that vainly lends his light
To grubs and eyeless skulls? As I discern,
It burneth in the Capels' monument.

Balthasar. It doth so, holy sir; and there's my master,
One that you love.

Friar Laurence.   Who is it?

Balthasar.   Romeo.

130 **Friar Laurence.** How long hath he been there?

Balthasar.   Full half an hour.

Friar Laurence. Go with me to the vault.

Balthasar.   I dare not, sir.
My master knows not but I am gone hence,
And fearfully did menace me with death
If I did stay to look on his intents.

135 **Friar Laurence.** Stay then; I'll go alone. Fear comes upon me.
O, much I fear some ill unthrifty thing.

111–112 shake . . . flesh: rid myself of the burden of an unhappy fate (**inauspicious stars**). *On what does Romeo blame his imminent death?*

115 dateless: eternal; never-ending. Romeo means that what he is about to do can never be undone.

117–118 Romeo compares himself to the pilot of a ship (**bark**) who is going to crash on the rocks because he is so weary and sick.

132–134 My master . . . intents: My master told me to go away and threatened me with death if I watched what he did.

136 unthrifty: unlucky.

Balthasar. As I did sleep under this yew tree here,
I dreamt my master and another fought,
And that my master slew him.

Friar Laurence.   Romeo!

[*stoops and looks on the blood and weapons*]

140 Alack, alack, what blood is this which stains
The stony entrance of this sepulcher?
What mean these masterless and gory swords
To lie discolored by this place of peace?

[*enters the tomb*]

Romeo! O, pale! Who else? What, Paris too?
145 And steeped in blood? Ah, what an unkind hour
Is guilty of this lamentable chance!
The lady stirs.

[Juliet *rises.*]

Juliet. O comfortable friar! where is my lord?
I do remember well where I should be,
150 And there I am. Where is my Romeo?

Friar Laurence. I hear some noise. Lady, come from that nest

140–143 Alack . . . place of peace? Why
are these bloody swords lying here
at the tomb (**sepulcher**), a place that
should be peaceful? (The swords are also
masterless, or without their owners.)

148 comfortable: comforting.

Romeo and Juliet in the 2004
production of the Globe Theatre

Of death, contagion, and unnatural sleep.
A greater power than we can contradict
Hath thwarted our intents. Come, come away.
155 Thy husband in thy bosom there lies dead;
And Paris too. Come, I'll dispose of thee
Among a sisterhood of holy nuns.
Stay not to question, for the watch is coming.
Come, go, good Juliet. I dare no longer stay.

160 **Juliet.** Go, get thee hence, for I will not away.

[*Exit* Friar Laurence.]

What's here? A cup, closed in my true love's hand?
Poison, I see, hath been his timeless end.
O churl! drunk all, and left no friendly drop
To help me after? I will kiss thy lips.
165 Haply some poison yet doth hang on them
To make me die with a restorative.

[*kisses him*]

Thy lips are warm!

Chief Watchman [*within*]. Lead, boy. Which way?

Juliet. Yea, noise? Then I'll be brief. O happy dagger!

[*snatches Romeo's dagger*]

170 This is thy sheath; there rust, and let me die.

[*She stabs herself and falls.*]

[*Enter* Watchmen *with the* Page *of Paris.*]

Page. This is the place. There, where the torch doth burn.

Chief Watchman. The ground is bloody. Search about the
      churchyard.
Go, some of you; whoe'er you find attach.

[*Exeunt some of the* Watch.]

Pitiful sight! here lies the County slain;
175 And Juliet bleeding, warm, and newly dead,
Who here hath lain this two days buried.
Go, tell the Prince; run to the Capulets;
Raise up the Montagues; some others search.

[*Exeunt others of the* Watch.]

We see the ground whereon these woes do lie,
180 But the true ground of all these piteous woes
We cannot without circumstance descry.

[*Reenter some of the* Watch, *with* Balthasar.]

153–154 A greater . . . intents: A greater force than we can fight (**contradict**) has ruined our plans (**thwarted our intents**).

156–157 I'll dispose . . . nuns: I'll find a place for you in a convent of nuns.

158–159 *Why is the friar so anxious to leave?*

162 timeless: happening before its proper time.

163 churl: miser.

165 haply: perhaps.

173 attach: arrest.

178 raise up: awaken.

179–181 We see . . . descry: We see the earth (**ground**) these bodies lie on. But the real cause (**true ground**) of these deaths is yet for us to discover (**descry**).

Second Watchman. Here's Romeo's man. We found him in the
  churchyard.

Chief Watchman. Hold him in safety till the Prince come hither.

[*Reenter* Friar Laurence *and another* Watchman.]

Third Watchman. Here is a friar that trembles, sighs, and weeps.
185 We took this mattock and this spade from him
  As he was coming from this churchyard side.

Chief Watchman. A great suspicion! Stay the friar too.

[*Enter the* Prince *and* Attendants.]

Prince. What misadventure is so early up,
  That calls our person from our morning rest?

[*Enter* Capulet, Lady Capulet, *and others.*]

190 **Capulet.** What should it be, that they so shriek abroad?

Lady Capulet. The people in the street cry "Romeo,"
  Some "Juliet," and some "Paris"; and all run,
  With open outcry, toward our monument.

Prince. What fear is this which startles in our ears?

195 **Chief Watchman.** Sovereign, here lies the County Paris slain;
  And Romeo dead, and Juliet, dead before,
  Warm and new killed.

Prince. Search, seek, and know how this foul murder comes.

Chief Watchman. Here is a friar, and slaughtered Romeo's man,
200 With instruments upon them fit to open
  These dead men's tombs.

Capulet. O heavens! O wife, look how our daughter bleeds!
  This dagger hath mista'en, for, lo, his house
  Is empty on the back of Montague,
205 And it missheathed in my daughter's bosom!

Lady Capulet. O me! this sight of death is as a bell
  That warns my old age to a sepulcher.

[*Enter* Montague *and others.*]

Prince. Come, Montague; for thou art early up
  To see thy son and heir now early down.

210 **Montague.** Alas, my liege, my wife is dead tonight!
  Grief of my son's exile hath stopped her breath.
  What further woe conspires against mine age?

Prince. Look, and thou shalt see.

Montague. O thou untaught! what manners is in this,
215 To press before thy father to a grave?

182–187 The guards arrest Balthasar and Friar Laurence as suspicious characters.

194 startles: causes alarm.

203–205 This dagger . . . in my daughter's bosom: This dagger has missed its target. It should rest in the sheath (**house**) that Romeo wears. Instead it is in Juliet's chest.

210 liege: lord.

214–215 what manners . . . grave: What kind of behavior is this, for a son to die before his father?

Prince. Seal up the mouth of outrage for a while,
Till we can clear these ambiguities
And know their spring, their head, their true descent;
And then will I be general of your woes
220 And lead you even to death. Meantime forbear,
And let mischance be slave to patience.
Bring forth the parties of suspicion.

Friar Laurence. I am the greatest, able to do least,
Yet most suspected, as the time and place
225 Doth make against me, of this direful murder;
And here I stand, both to impeach and purge
Myself condemned and myself excused.

Prince. Then say at once what thou dost know in this.

Friar Laurence. I will be brief, for my short date of breath
230 Is not so long as is a tedious tale.
Romeo, there dead, was husband to that Juliet;
And she, there dead, that Romeo's faithful wife.
I married them; and their stol'n marriage day
Was Tybalt's doomsday, whose untimely death
235 Banish'd the new-made bridegroom from this city;
For whom, and not for Tybalt, Juliet pined.
You, to remove that siege of grief from her,
Betrothed and would have married her perforce
To County Paris. Then comes she to me
240 And with wild looks bid me devise some mean
To rid her from this second marriage,
Or in my cell there would she kill herself.
Then gave I her (so tutored by my art)
A sleeping potion; which so took effect
245 As I intended, for it wrought on her
The form of death. Meantime I writ to Romeo
That he should hither come as this dire night
To help to take her from her borrowed grave,
Being the time the potion's force should cease.
250 But he which bore my letter, Friar John,
Was stayed by accident, and yesternight
Returned my letter back. Then all alone
At the prefixed hour of her waking
Came I to take her from her kindred's vault;
255 Meaning to keep her closely at my cell
Till I conveniently could send to Romeo.
But when I came, some minute ere the time
Of her awaking, here untimely lay
The noble Paris and true Romeo dead.
260 She wakes; and I entreated her come forth

216–221 Seal...patience: Stop your emotional outbursts until we can find out the source (**spring**) of these confusing events (**ambiguities**). Wait (**forbear**) and be patient, and let's find out what happened.

223–227 Friar Laurence confesses that he is most responsible for these events. He will both accuse (**impeach**) himself and clear (**purge**) himself of guilt.

236 It was Romeo's banishment, not Tybalt's death, that made Juliet so sad.

248 borrowed: temporary.

254 kindred's: family's.

And bear this work of heaven with patience;
But then a noise did scare me from the tomb,
And she, too desperate, would not go with me,
But, as it seems, did violence on herself.
265 All this I know, and to the marriage
Her nurse is privy; and if aught in this
Miscarried by my fault, let my old life
Be sacrificed, some hour before his time,
Unto the rigor of severest law.

270 **Prince.** We still have known thee for a holy man.
Where's Romeo's man? What can he say in this?

Balthasar. I brought my master news of Juliet's death;
And then in post he came from Mantua
To this same place, to this same monument.
275 This letter he early bid me give his father,
And threatened me with death, going in the vault,
If I departed not and left him there.

Prince. Give me the letter. I will look on it.
Where is the County's page that raised the watch?
280 Sirrah, what made your master in this place?

Page. He came with flowers to strew his lady's grave;
And bid me stand aloof, and so I did.
Anon comes one with light to ope the tomb;
And by-and-by my master drew on him;
285 And then I ran away to call the watch.

Prince. This letter doth make good the friar's words,
Their course of love, the tidings of her death;
And here he writes that he did buy a poison
Of a poor 'pothecary, and therewithal
290 Came to this vault to die and lie with Juliet.
Where be these enemies? Capulet, Montague,
See what a scourge is laid upon your hate,
That heaven finds means to kill your joys with love!
And I, for winking at your discords too,
295 Have lost a brace of kinsmen. All are punished. **ⓕ**

Capulet. O brother Montague, give me thy hand.
This is my daughter's jointure, for no more
Can I demand.

265–269 and to . . . law: Her nurse can bear witness to this secret marriage. If I am responsible for any of this, let the law punish me with death.

270 *How does the Prince respond to the friar's acceptance of blame?*

273 in post: at full speed.

279–280 The Prince asks for Paris' servant, who notified the guards (**raised the watch**). Then he asks the servant why Paris was at the cemetery.

283–285 Anon . . . call the watch: Soon (**anon**) someone with a light came and opened the tomb. Paris drew his sword, and I ran to call the guards.

292–295 See what . . . punished: Look at the punishment your hatred has brought on you. Heaven has killed your children (**joys**) with love. For shutting my eyes to your arguments (**discords**), I have lost two relatives. We have all been punished.

ⓕ TRAGEDY
Reread lines 291–295. On what does the prince blame all the deaths? What **theme,** or message, might this passage suggest?

297–298 jointure: dowry, the payment a bride's father traditionally made to the groom. Capulet means that no one could demand more of a bride's father than he has already paid.

Montague.   But I can give thee more;
For I will raise her statue in pure gold,
300 That whiles Verona by that name is known,
There shall no figure at such rate be set
As that of true and faithful Juliet.

Capulet. As rich shall Romeo's by his lady's lie—
Poor sacrifices of our enmity!

305 **Prince.** A glooming peace this morning with it brings.
The sun for sorrow will not show his head.
Go hence, to have more talk of these sad things;
Some shall be pardoned, and some punished;
For never was a story of more woe
310 Than this of Juliet and her Romeo.

[*Exeunt.*]

301 at such rate be set: be valued so highly.

303–304 Capulet promises to do for Romeo what Montague will do for Juliet. Their children have become sacrifices to their hatred (**enmity**).

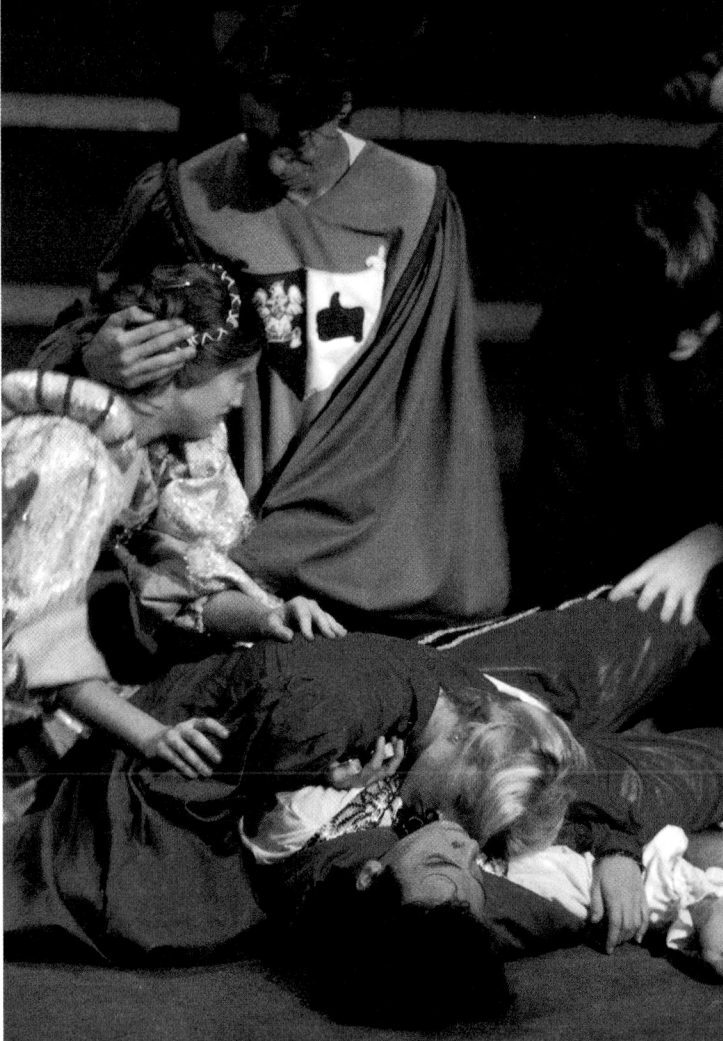

The Capulets and Lord Montague mourn their children's deaths in an Austin, Texas, high school production.

After Reading

Comprehension

1. **Recall** What prevents Friar John from delivering the letter to Romeo?

2. **Recall** Why does Paris attack Romeo at the Capulets' tomb?

3. **Summarize** How do the bodies of Paris, Romeo, and Juliet all end up in the Capulets' tomb? Explain how each character loses his or her life.

PENNSYLVANIA
STANDARDS

READING STANDARD
B.1.1.1.C.1 Evaluate elements of
the plot

Literary Analysis

4. **Reading Shakespearean Drama** In Shakespearean drama, the **resolution,** or final plot stage, occurs in the last act. Look back at the chart you completed as you read. Describe the events that make up the resolution of this tragedy. Do you think this sequence of events brings the play to a satisfying conclusion? Explain your answer.

5. **Make Judgments** In the play's final speech, Prince Escalus declares, "Some shall be pardoned, and some punished." If you were the ruler of Verona, whom would you pardon, and whom would you punish? Explain.

6. **Identify Soliloquy** Identify a soliloquy in Act Five. Citing specific lines of the play, explain what you learn about the character who is speaking.

7. **Analyze Tragedy** In a tragedy, the hero or heroine usually has a character flaw that leads to his or her downfall. Is this true of Romeo and Juliet? Cite evidence from the tragedy to support your explanation.

8. **Examine Universal Theme** Many of the themes in *Romeo and Juliet* are universal—they are as relevant today as they were in the 1590s. Examine the values and experiences shown, and think about how each is presented in *Romeo and Juliet*. Complete the chart by stating how each topic is conveyed as a theme in the play. Which theme do you find most relevant today?

Value or Experience	Statement of Theme
Fate	There are forces in life over which people have no control.
Family ties	
Friendship	
Love	

Literary Criticism

9. **Critical Interpretations** *Romeo and Juliet,* according to the critic F. M. Dickey, is "a drama of love and hate." Of these two feelings, the critic maintains, "love overshadows the other dramatically, since it is the passion of the protagonists and since Shakespeare has lavished his most moving poetry upon the love scenes." Do you agree that **love** overshadows **hate** in this play? Support your conclusion with evidence from the text.

1050 UNIT 10: SHAKESPEAREAN DRAMA

Reading-Writing Connection

Increase your understanding of *The Tragedy of Romeo and Juliet* by responding to these prompts. Then use **Revision: Grammar and Style** to improve your writing.

WRITING PROMPTS

A. Short Response: Write Blank Verse

What if Romeo had taken slower-acting poison? Imagine that Juliet wakes before the poison kills Romeo, so that he is able to utter his last words of love to her. Write **six to eight lines of blank verse** in which Romeo says goodbye to Juliet before dying.

B. Extended Response: Analyze Tragedy

How does Shakespeare portray both **love** and **hate** as causes of violence in *Romeo and Juliet*? Write a **three-to-five-paragraph response** describing how the writer presents each emotion as a cause of catastrophe.

SELF-CHECK

A successful verse will . . .

- be written in iambic pentameter (for help with this, turn back to page 932)
- mimic the lyric language of Shakespeare and sound like something Romeo would say

A strong analysis will . . .

- explore how each emotion contributes to the bloody resolution of the play
- include detailed evidence from the play as support

REVISION: GRAMMAR AND STYLE

CREATE RHYTHM Review the **Grammar and Style** note on page 970. **Parallelism** is the repetition of grammatical structures—phrases or clauses, for example. Shakespeare's use of parallelism creates cadence, or a balanced, rhythmic flow. Here are two examples from the play. The first contains a series of four past-tense verbs, each followed by the word *for*. In the second, Shakespeare uses the three parallel adjectives *stiff, stark* and *cold*. Think about how these passages might sound without the parallelism.

> **First Servingman.** *You are looked for and called for, asked for and sought for, in the great chamber.* (Act One, Scene 5, lines 10–11)

> **Friar Laurence.** *. . . Each part, deprived of supple government,*
>
> *Shall, stiff and stark and cold, appear like death;* (Act Four, Scene 1, lines 102–103)

Now consider how the revision in red makes use of parallelism to improve the rhythm of this first draft. Revise your responses to the prompts by using parallelism whenever possible.

PENNSYLVANIA STANDARDS

WRITING STANDARD
1.4.11.A.7 Use literary devices

STUDENT MODEL

All of the deaths in the play—the murders of Mercutio, Tybalt, and
~~Paris and the suicides~~—result largely from someone's acting out of love.
of Romeo and Juliet
Λ

WRITING TOOLS

For prewriting, revision, and editing tools, visit the **Writing Center** at ClassZone.com.

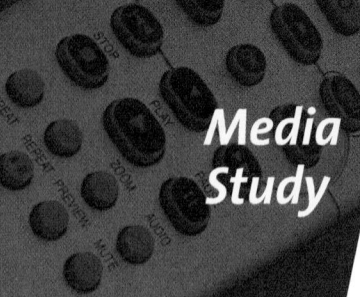

from **Romeo and Juliet**

Film Clip on  *MediaSmart* DVD

Why does HOLLYWOOD *love Shakespeare?*

PENNSYLVANIA STANDARDS

SPEAKING/LISTENING STANDARD
1.6.11.F.2 Evaluate the role of media in focusing attention and forming opinions

KEY IDEA Shakespeare's *Tragedy of Romeo and Juliet* has all the ingredients for a successful **Hollywood** adaptation: timeless, universal themes; vibrant characters; an exotic setting; and a string of misunderstandings that ultimately lead to tragedy. Now that you have read the play version of *Romeo and Juliet*, notice the choices the film director makes in bringing this play to the screen.

Background

Love at First Sight Some would argue that the true mark of a great movie is its ability to leave a long-lasting impression on its audience. When viewers and critics were first introduced to Franco Zeffirelli's *Romeo and Juliet* in 1968, the reaction was unanimous praise. Everything about the film—from the romantic setting to the playful yet sometimes somber music—captivated audiences. In addition, Zeffirelli did what no other director had done before. He cast as his leads two young, unknown actors who were 16 and 17 years old when filming began. By taking a risk on these young actors, Zeffirelli created an interpretation filled with innocence, liveliness, and passion.

Media Literacy: Shakespearean Drama in Movies

Long before a director can call out, "Lights, camera, action!" he or she must have a vision for the film. Together with a filmmaking crew, a director plans every detail of a movie, including the lighting, setting, props, costumes, and action. The arrangement and use of these filmmaking elements is known as **mise en scène** (mēz' än sĕn'). Notice how the following elements of mise en scène in the film clip shape our understanding of Shakespearean drama.

ELEMENTS OF MISE EN SCÈNE

❶ **Lighting** can be used to create a mood or a dramatic effect. It can also make a scene look realistic and can draw viewers' attention to an important object or person.

❷ The **setting** and **props** build certain expectations in viewers' minds and establish a location. For example, an exotic setting can help create an atmosphere of romance or love.

❸ A character's **facial expressions, body language,** and **actions** convey what he or she is thinking or feeling.

❹ A director deliberately positions characters within a **frame** to indicate the nature of the characters' relationship. For example, characters who don't trust each other may be placed at opposite ends of the frame.

❺ In a Shakespearean movie, **costumes** may provide clues about characters' social status and may also indicate a specific time period. A director can also experiment with costumes to reflect a character's personality.

MediaSmart DVD

- **Film Clip:** *Romeo and Juliet*
- **Director:** Franco Zeffirelli
- **Rating:** PG
- **Genre:** Drama
- **Running Time:** 11 minutes

Viewing Guide for
Romeo and Juliet

The scene you're about to view is perhaps the most well-known one in all of Shakespeare's plays—the balcony scene.

Because of the length of the clip, you may wish to view the scene once for the story. During any additional viewings, concentrate on such elements as mise en scène, camera shots, and sound. Keep the following questions in mind as you view.

NOW VIEW

FIRST VIEWING: Comprehension

1. **Summarize** Describe the setting of the clip in your own words.

2. **Clarify** What types of **shots** does the director use in the beginning of the clip to establish the scene?

CLOSE VIEWING: Media Literacy

3. **Interpret Mood** What kind of mood do you think the **lighting** creates?

4. **Analyze Setting** How does the setting compare with what you envisioned?

5. **Analyze Director's Techniques** How does the director show that time has passed from the beginning to the end of this scene? Consider how the director uses **lighting** and **sounds** to show the passing of time.

6. **Evaluate Music** Zeffirelli uses music throughout the movie to stir viewers' emotions. When is music used, and how effectively is it used, in this scene?

Write or Discuss

Evaluate Mise en Scène In your opinion, is Zeffirelli's film version of the balcony scene appealing and believable? Why or why not? Cite specific examples from the clip to support your view. Think about

- the actors' physical appearance, actions, and movements
- the details of the setting, costumes, and props
- the camera shots of the scene

Produce Your Own Media

Create a Visual Treatment Imagine you're filming a modern adaptation of *The Tragedy of Romeo and Juliet*. Before you begin filming, you'll want to create a **visual treatment,** a series of images that visually represent key scenes from the play. With a small group, determine who will be the costume designer, the set designer, and the cast of characters. Then choose six key scenes from the play that you want to photograph.

HERE'S HOW Use the professional model and the following tips to help you visualize the elements of **mise en scène:**

- **Characters:** What is the relationship between the characters, and how will you position them within the frame?
- **Setting:** What elements of the setting will convey a specific time or place?
- **Costumes:** What clues do the costumes reveal about the characters?
- **Lighting:** How does the lighting create a mood?

MEDIA TOOLS

For help with creating a visual treatment, visit the **Media Center** at **ClassZone.com.**

Tech Tip

If you have access to photo-editing software, use it to edit your pictures after the photo shoot.

PROFESSIONAL MODEL

Great Movies: *Romeo and Juliet*

Critical Review by Roger Ebert

Use with *Romeo and Juliet*, page 940.

PENNSYLVANIA STANDARDS

READING STANDARDS
A.2.5.1 Summarize the major points
A.2.6.1 Identify and describe intended purpose

What's the Connection?

You've just discovered why filmmakers love Shakespeare: plays like *Romeo and Juliet* present directors with terrific material to work with. You've also explored the choices one director, Franco Zeffirelli, made to transform Shakespeare's classic drama into a big-screen blockbuster. How do critics think Zeffirelli's movie measures up? Read to find out one movie reviewer's opinion.

Skill Focus: Analyze a Critical Review

A **critical review** is an essay in which the writer gives his or her opinions about a movie, a play, a book, a TV show, or another work. A critical review typically includes these elements:

- the name of the work and its creator
- a description of the work
- a clearly stated opinion of the work
- reasons that support the opinion
- examples or details that illustrate the reasons

A critical review may include other elements as well, like background information on the work's creator or descriptions of how audiences reacted when the work was released. The heart of a review, however, is the writer's opinion and the reasons and examples he or she uses to back it up.

As you read this critical review, use a chart like the one shown to record Roger Ebert's opinion and the main reasons he gives to support it. Keep track of the examples and details from the movie that Ebert uses to illustrate each reason.

Ebert's Opinion:	
Reason	**Examples or Details**
Reason 1:	
Reason 2:	

GREAT MOVIES

Romeo and Juliet

BY ROGER EBERT

"Romeo and Juliet" is always said to be the first romantic tragedy ever written, but it isn't really a tragedy at all. It's a tragic misunderstanding, scarcely fitting the ancient requirement of tragedy that the mighty fall through their own flaws. Romeo and Juliet have no flaws, and aren't old enough to be blamed if they did. They die because of the pigheaded
10 quarrel of their families, the Montagues and the Capulets. By writing the play, Shakespeare began the shaping of modern drama, in which the fates of ordinary people are as crucial as those of the great. The great tragedies of his time, including his own, involved kings, emperors, generals. Here, near the dawn of his career, perhaps remembering a sweet early romance before his forced marriage
20 to Anne Hathaway, he writes about teenagers in love.

   "Romeo and Juliet" has been filmed many times in many ways; Norma Shearer and Leslie Howard starred in the beloved 1936 Hollywood version, and modern transformations include Robert Wise's "West Side Story" (1961), which applies the plot to Manhattan gang warfare; Abel Ferrara's
30 "China Girl" (1987), about a forbidden romance between a girl of Chinatown and a boy of Little Italy; and Baz Luhrmann's "William Shakespeare's Romeo & Juliet" (1996), with California punk gangs on Verona Beach. But the favorite film version is likely to re-

Zeffirelli cast two young, unknown actors instead of more experienced stars in his 1968 film.

main, for many years, Franco Zeffirelli's 1968 production. **A**

   His crucial decision, in a film where
40 almost everything went well, was to cast actors who were about the right age to play the characters (as Howard and Shearer were obviously not). As the play opens, Juliet "hath not seen the change of 14 years," and Romeo is little older. This is first love for Juliet, and Romeo's crush on the unseen Rosalind is forgotten the moment he sees **B**

A CRITICAL REVIEW
In lines 1–38, Ebert introduces the play and provides information about other film versions of it. What opinion about Zeffirelli's film does Ebert state in lines 35–38?

B CRITICAL REVIEW
What was Zeffirelli's "crucial decision"? Paraphrase the first reason Ebert gives to support his opinion of the movie.

Olivia Hussey as Juliet proclaims her love in the balcony scene.

Juliet at the masked ball: "I ne'er saw
50 true beauty until this night." After a
well-publicized international search,
Zeffirelli cast Olivia Hussey, a 16-year-
old from Argentina, and Leonard
Whiting, a British 17-year-old.

They didn't merely look their parts,
they embodied them in the freshness of

Hussey and Whiting were so good because they didn't know any better.

---

their personalities, and although neither
was a trained actor, they were fully
equal to Shakespeare's dialogue for
60 them; Anthony Holden's new book
*William Shakespeare: The Man Behind
the Genius* contrasts "the beautiful simplicity with which the lovers speak at
their moments of uncomplicated happiness," with "the ornate rhetorical

flourishes which fuel so much else in
the play"—flourishes that Zeffirelli severely pruned, trimming about half the
play. He was roundly criticized for his
70 edits, but much that needs describing
on the stage can simply be shown onscreen, as when Benvolio is shown wit-
nessing Juliet's funeral and thus does
not need to evoke it in a description to
the exiled Romeo. Shakespeare, who
took such wholesale liberties with his
own sources, might have understood.

What is left is what people love the
play for—the purity of the young lovers'
80 passion, the earthiness of Juliet's nurse,
the well-intentioned plans of Friar Laurence, the hot-blooded feud between the
young men of the families, the cruel irony of the double deaths. And there is
time, too, for many of the great speeches, including Mercutio's poetic evoca-
tion of Mab, the queen of dreams.

Hussey and Whiting were so good
because they didn't know any better.
90 Another year or two of experience,
perhaps, and they would have been
too intimidated to play the roles. It
was my good fortune to visit the film

set, in a small hill town an hour or so outside Rome, on the night when the balcony scene was filmed. I remember Hussey and Whiting upstairs in the old hillside villa, waiting for their call, unaffected, uncomplicated. And when the balcony scene was shot, I remember the heedless energy that Hussey threw into it, take after take, hurling herself almost off the balcony for hungry kisses. (Whiting, balanced in a tree, needed to watch his footing.) **C**

Between shots, in the overgrown garden, Zeffirelli strolled with the composer Nino Rota, who had written the music for most of Fellini's films and now simply hummed the film's central theme, as the director nodded. Pasqualino De Santis, who was to win an Oscar for his cinematography, directed his crew quietly, urgently, trying to be ready for the freshness of the actors instead of making them wait for technical quibbles. At dawn, drinking strong coffee as cars pulled around to take his actors back to Rome, Zeffirelli said what was obvious: That the whole movie depended on the balcony and the crypt scenes, and he felt now that his casting decision had proven itself, and that the film would succeed.

It did, beyond any precedent for a film based on Shakespeare, even though Shakespeare is the most filmed writer in history. The movie opened in the tumultuous year of 1968, a time of political upheaval around the world, and somehow the story of the star-crossed lovers caught the mood of rebellious young people who had wearied of their elders' wars. "This of all works of literature eternizes the ardor of young love and youth's aggressive spirit," wrote Anthony Burgess. **D**

Zeffirelli, born in Florence in 1923, came early to the English language through prewar experiences hinted at in the loosely autobiographical "Tea with Mussolini" (1999). His crucial early artistic influence was Laurence Olivier's "Henry V" (1945), which inspired him to go into the theater; he has had parallel careers directing plays, films and operas. Before the great

C CRITICAL REVIEW
Reread lines 88–105. Why does Ebert think Hussey and Whiting were so successful at bringing the star-crossed lovers to life?

D CRITICAL REVIEW
Why does Ebert think audiences—particularly young people—were so taken with the movie when it premiered in 1968?

Leonard Whiting as Romeo gazes adoringly at his Juliet.

success of "Romeo and Juliet," he first visited Shakespeare for the shaky but high-spirited "Taming of the Shrew" (1967), with Burton and Taylor. Later he directed Placido Domingo in "Otello" (1986), Verdi's opera, and directed Mel Gibson in "Hamlet" (1990).

Something fundamental has changed in films about and for young people.

"Romeo and Juliet" remains the magical high point of his career. To see it again is to luxuriate. It is intriguing that Zeffirelli in 1968 focused on love, while Baz Luhrmann's popular version of 1996 focused on violence; something fundamental has changed in films about and for young people, and recent audiences seem shy of sex and love but eager for conflict and action. I wonder if a modern Friday night audience would snicker at the heart-baring sincerity of the lovers. . . .

The costumes by Danilo Donati won another Oscar for the film (it was also nominated for best picture and director), and they are crucial to its success; they are the avenue for color and richness to enter the frame, which is otherwise filled with gray and ochre stones and the colors of nature. The nurse (Pat Heywood) seems enveloped in a dry goods' sale of heavy fabrics, and Mercutio (John McEnery) comes flying a handkerchief that he uses as a banner, disguise and shroud. Hussey's dresses, with low bodices and simple patterns, set off her creamy skin and long hair; Whiting is able to inhabit his breeches, blouse and codpiece with the conviction that it is everyday clothing, not a costume. **E**

The costumes and everything else in the film—the photography, the music, above all Shakespeare's language—is so voluptuous, so sensuous. The stagecraft of the twinned death scenes is of course all contrivance; the friar's potion works with timing that is precisely wrong, and yet we forgive the manipulation because Shakespeare has been able to provide us with what is theoretically impossible, the experience of two young lovers each grieving the other's death. When the play was first staged in London, Holden writes, Shakespeare had the satisfaction "of seeing the groundlings moved to emotions far beyond anything before known in the theater." Why? Because of craft and art, yes, but also because Romeo and Juliet were not distant and august figures, not Caesars, Othellos or Macbeths, but a couple of kids in love, as everyone in the theater had known, and everyone in the theater had been.

Whiting and Hussey in Donati's sumptuous costumes

E CRITICAL REVIEW
Reread lines 168–186. What aspect of the film does Ebert praise in this paragraph? Explain why he found this element essential to the movie's success.

Comprehension

1. **Recall** What is Ebert's opinion of Franco Zeffirelli's film adaptation of *Romeo and Juliet*?

2. **Paraphrase** Reread lines 198–209. According to Ebert, why have audiences been so moved by the story of *Romeo and Juliet* ever since it was first staged?

Critical Analysis

3. **Analyze a Critical Review** Look at the chart you filled in as you read. What are the main reasons that Ebert gives to support his opinion of the film? Describe at least two examples or details that Ebert uses to illustrate each reason.

4. **Identify Author's Purpose** What do you think was Ebert's primary purpose in writing this critical review of a film that came out more than 35 years ago? Support your conclusion with evidence from the review.

5. **Evaluate an Opinion** Do you agree with Ebert that "Romeo and Juliet have no flaws" and that they die only "because of the pigheaded quarrel of their families"? Explain your answer.

Read for Information: Compare and Contrast

PENNSYLVANIA STANDARDS

READING STANDARDS
A.2.5.1 Summarize the major points
A.2.6.1 Identify and describe intended purpose

WRITING PROMPT

What did you think about the casting of Olivia Hussey and Leonard Whiting in Zeffirelli's film version of *Romeo and Juliet*, and how would you rate their performances in the balcony scene? How are your opinions similar to and different from Ebert's?

To answer this prompt, you will have to **compare and contrast,** or explain similarities and differences. To explore the similarities and differences between your views and those expressed by Ebert, follow these steps:

1. Consider your reactions to the movie's two main characters and their acting in the balcony scene. Sum up your opinion, and give at least two reasons for it. Identify details from the scene that support your opinion.

2. Review each of Ebert's main points and the evidence he gives to back them up. Which do you agree with? Which do you disagree with?

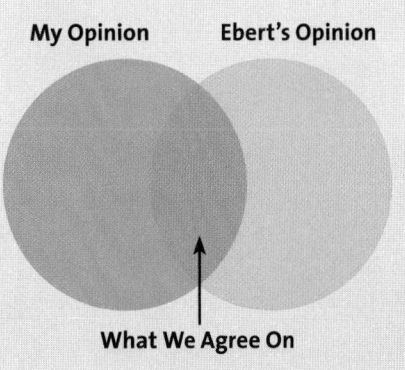

My Opinion   Ebert's Opinion

What We Agree On

Pyramus and Thisbe
Myth Retold by Ovid

What makes a CLASSIC STORY?

PENNSYLVANIA STANDARDS

READING STANDARDS
A.1.6.1 Identify and/or analyze intended purpose of text.
B.1.1.1.C.1 Analyze and/or evaluate elements of the plot

KEY IDEA Two teenagers fall madly in love, but their parents forbid them to see each other. Defying their families, they plan to run away together, but a series of misunderstandings leads to their disastrous demise. Sound familiar? Some stories are so universally appealing that they appear over and over, in everything from ancient myths to Shakespearean drama to modern soap operas. "Pyramus and Thisbe" is one of these **classic stories.**

DISCUSS What are some other examples of classic stories? In a small group, talk about situations that are replayed in fairy tales and bedtime stories, in movies and books, and on TV shows and Broadway stages. What do these stories share? Thrilling plots? Insurmountable conflicts? Happy endings? With your group, come up with a list detailing five characteristics of a classic story.

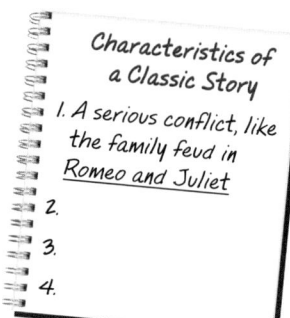

Characteristics of a Classic Story
1. A serious conflict, like the family feud in *Romeo and Juliet*
2.
3.
4.

LITERARY ANALYSIS: MYTH

Why does the sun rise in the east every morning? What makes thunderstorms strike so violently? Why do the seasons change? Different cultures throughout time have attempted to answer similar questions about the world. Frequently, these questions became the bases of myths. A **myth** is a traditional story usually created to explain why the world is the way it is or why things in nature happen as they do. Myths are also a form of entertainment that people have enjoyed since ancient times. The stories myths tell are filled with colorful characters, suspenseful plots, and daring adventures. Most myths share these basic characteristics:

• They explain how things connected with nature or humans came to be.

• They tell about supernatural beings or events.

• They present lessons or morals.

"Pyramis and Thisbe" is a classic myth, here retold in the form of a narrative poem. As you read this myth, notice what it attempts to explain. Also, consider the lesson the myth teaches about the value of love.

Review: **Narrative Poem**

READING SKILL: SEQUENCE

Timing is everything—especially when it comes to myths. The tragic action in "Pyramus and Thisbe" all takes place in two days. As you read this myth, look for signal words, such as *later*, *then*, and *after*, that make the sequence of events clear. Record the myth's main events in a sequence chain like this one.

Pyramus and Thisbe fall in love. → ☐ → ☐

Author Online

Ovid
43 B.C.–A.D. 17

A Bright Start Ovid is considered to be one of the greatest poets of antiquity. But if Ovid's father had had his way, his son would have followed a very different career path. Ovid's father was determined to see his son become a public official in the Roman Empire. He sent Ovid to Rome to study rhetoric and law under the best teachers. Instead of studying, Ovid followed his natural inclinations and focused on writing poetry. Luckily, he achieved success with his first work, the *Amores*, a series of short, witty poems about a love affair. The poet quickly became popular in fashionable Roman society.

A Lasting Legacy "Pyramus and Thisbe" is taken from the *Metamorphoses*, Ovid's masterpiece. A long narrative poem, the *Metamorphoses* retells many of the most important myths from ancient Greece and Rome. Ovid breathed new life into the old stories, shaping them in imaginative ways and strengthening their structure. Ovid's retellings have inspired writers for centuries—including Shakespeare.

A Grim End Before Ovid was able to publish the *Metamorphoses*, disaster struck. In A.D. 8, the emperor Augustus banished him from Rome and sent him to live in exile in Tomis, a desolate fishing village on the edge of the Roman Empire. The exact reason for this cruel punishment is unknown, but in many of the poems Ovid wrote while in exile, he begs for permission to return to Rome. His pleas fell on deaf ears. Ovid died in exile in A.D. 17.

MORE ABOUT THE AUTHOR
For more on Ovid, visit the **Literature Center** at **ClassZone.com**.

Pyramus and Thisbe

Ovid

The house of Pyramus[1] and that of Thisbe[2]
stood side by side within the mighty city
ringed by the tall brick walls Semíramis
had built[3]—so we are told. If you searched all
5 the East, you'd find no girl with greater charm
than Thisbe; and no boy in Babylon
was handsomer than Pyramus. They owed
their first encounters to their living close
beside each other—but with time, love grows.
10 Theirs did—indeed they wanted to be wed,
but marriage was forbidden by their parents:
yet there's one thing that parents can't prevent:
the flame of love that burned in both of them.
They had no confidant—and so used signs:
15 with these each lover read the other's mind:
when covered, fire acquires still more force.

The wall their houses shared had one thin crack,
which formed when they were built and then was left;
in all these years, no one had seen that cleft;
20 but lovers will discover every thing:
you were the first to find it, and you made
that cleft a passageway which speech could take. **Ⓐ**
For there the least of whispers was kept safe:
it crossed that cleft with words of tenderness.
25 And Pyramus and Thisbe often stood,
he on this side and she on that; and when
each heard the other sigh, the lovers said:
"O jealous wall, why do you block our path?
Oh wouldn't it be better if you let
30 our bodies join each other fully or,
if that is asking for too much, just stretched
your fissure wide enough to let us kiss!

ANALYZE VISUALS
Explain how this painting conveys a sense of Pyramus and Thisbe's separation and their longing to be together. Consider the painter's use of light and color, as well as Thisbe's expression and Pyramus' absence.

Ⓐ MYTH
What is keeping Pyramus and Thisbe apart, and what do they do to overcome these barriers? From what you've read so far, decide what lesson about love this myth might teach.

1. **Pyramus** (pĭr′ə-məs).
2. **Thisbe** (thĭz′bē).
3. **the mighty city . . . had built:** the walled city of Babylon (băb′ə-lən), the ruins of which are south of Baghdad, Iraq. In Greek mythology, it was founded by Semíramis (sə-mĭr′ə-məs), a powerful Assyrian queen.

Thisbe, John William Waterhouse.
Whitford and Hughes, London.
© The Bridgeman Art Library.

And we are not ungrateful: we admit
our words reach loving ears." And having talked
35 in vain, the lovers still remained apart.
Just so, one night, they wished each other well,
and each delivered kisses to the wall—
although those kisses could not reach their goal.
But on the morning after, when firstlight
40 had banished night's bright star-fires from the sky
and sun had left the brine-soaked[4] meadows dry,
again they took their places at the cleft.
Then, in low whispers—after their laments—
those two devised this plan: they'd circumvent
45 their guardians' watchful eyes[5] and, cloaked by night,
in silence, slip out from their homes and reach
a site outside the city. Lest each lose
the other as they wandered separately
across the open fields, they were to meet
50 at Ninus' tomb[6] and hide beneath a tree
in darkness; for beside that tomb there stood
a tall mulberry[7] close to a cool spring,
a tree well weighted down with snow-white berries. **B**
Delighted with their plan—impatiently—
55 they waited for the close of day. At last
the sun plunged down into the waves, and night
emerged from those same waves.

                Now Thisbe takes
great care, that none detect her as she makes
her way out from the house amid the dark;
60 her face is veiled; she finds the tomb; she sits
beneath the tree they'd chosen for their tryst.
Love made her bold. But now a lioness
just done with killing oxen—blood dripped down
her jaws, her mouth was frothing—comes to slake
65 her thirst at a cool spring close to the tree.
By moonlight, Thisbe sees the savage beast;
with trembling feet, the girl is quick to seek
a shadowed cave; but even as she flees,
her shawl slips from her shoulders. Thirst appeased,
70 the lioness is heading for the woods
when she, by chance, spies the abandoned shawl

B SEQUENCE
Explain the steps in the lovers' plan. Where and when do they decide to meet?

---

4. **brine-soaked:** dew-covered.

5. **they'd circumvent . . . eyes:** They would sneak past their parents.

6. **Ninus'** (nī'nəs) **tomb:** According to Greek legend, King Ninus was Semiramis' husband. When he died, she marked his burial place with a tall monument outside the walls of Babylon.

7. **mulberry:** a type of tree that produces small, sweet berries, which are usually deep red or purple in color.

upon the ground and, with her bloodstained jaws,
tears it to tatters.

                Pyramus had left
a little later than his Thisbe had,
75 and he could see what surely were the tracks
of a wild beast left clearly on deep dust.
His face grew ashen. And when he had found
the bloodstained shawl, he cried: "Now this same night
will see two lovers lose their lives: she was
80 the one more worthy of long life: it's I
who bear the guilt for this. O my poor girl,
it's I who led you to your death; I said
you were to reach this fearful place by night;
I let you be the first who would arrive.
85 O all you lions with your lairs beneath
this cliff, come now, and with your fierce jaws feast
upon my wretched guts! But cowards talk **C**
as I do—longing for their death but not
prepared to act." At this he gathered up
90 the bloody tatters of his Thisbe's shawl
and set them underneath the shady tree
where he and she had planned to meet. He wept
and cried out as he held that dear shawl fast:
"Now drink from my blood, too!" And then he drew
95 his dagger from his belt and thrust it hard
into his guts. And as he died, he wrenched
the dagger from his gushing wound. He fell,
supine, along the ground. The blood leaped high;
it spouted like a broken leaden pipe
100 that, through a slender hole where it is worn,
sends out a long and hissing stream as jets
of water cleave the air. And that tree's fruits,
snow-white before, are bloodstained now; the roots
are also drenched with Pyramus' dark blood,
105 and from those roots the hanging berries draw
a darker, purple color. **D**

                Now the girl
again seeks out the tree: though trembling still,
she would not fail his tryst;[8] with eyes and soul
she looks for Pyramus; she wants to tell
110 her lover how she had escaped such perils. **E**
She finds the place—the tree's familiar shape;
but seeing all the berries' color changed,

C SEQUENCE
Reread lines 73–87. What does Pyramus think has happened to Thisbe? Explain why Pyramus blames himself for this disaster.

D MYTH
Reread lines 96–106. Which events in this section seem supernatural?

E NARRATIVE POEM
Like fiction, narrative poetry often includes statements about the main characters. Describe the key traits of Pyramus and Thisbe, using specific words and phrases from the poem.

---

8. **fail his tryst:** neglect to meet him.

she is not sure. And as she hesitates,
she sights the writing body on the ground—
115 the bloody limbs—and, paler than boxwood,[9]
retreats; she trembles—even as the sea
when light wind stirs its surface. She is quick
to recognize her lover; with loud blows
she beats her arms—though they do not deserve
120 such punishment. She tears her hair, enfolds
her love's dear form; she fills his wounds with tears
that mingle with his blood; and while she plants
her kisses on his cold face, she laments:
"What struck you, Pyramus? Why have I lost
125 my love? It is your Thisbe—I—who call
your name! Respond! Lift up your fallen head!"
He heard her name; and lifting up his eyes
weighed down by death, he saw her face—and then
he closed his eyes again.

        She recognized
130 her own shawl and his dagger's ivory sheath.
She cried: "Dear boy, you died by your own hand:
your love has killed you. But I, too, command
the force to face at least this task: I can
claim love, and it will give me strength enough
135 to strike myself. I'll follow you in death;
and men will say that I—unfortunate—
was both the cause and comrade of your fate.
Nothing but death could sever you from me;
but now death has no power to prevent
140 my joining you. I call upon his parents
and mine; I plead for him and me—do not
deny to us—united by true love,
who share this fatal moment—one same tomb.
And may you, mulberry, whose boughs now shade
145 one wretched body and will soon shade two,
forever bear these darkly colored fruits
as signs of our sad end, that men remember
the death we met together." With these words, **F**
she placed the dagger's point beneath her breast,
150 then leaned against the blade still warm with her
dear lover's blood. The gods and parents heard
her prayer, and they were stirred. Her wish was granted.

Translated by Allen Mandelbaum

F MYTH
Why does the mulberry
tree produce deep red
berries?

---

9. **boxwood:** a white or light yellow type of wood.

Comprehension

1. **Recall** Describe how Pyramus and Thisbe communicate with each other at the beginning of the myth. Why can't they just talk face to face?

2. **Summarize** What secret plan do Pyramus and Thisbe make?

3. **Clarify** What happens to ruin the lovers' plan?

PENNSYLVANIA STANDARDS

READING STANDARD
B.1.1.1.C.1 Analyze and/or evaluate elements of the plot

Literary Analysis

4. **Make Judgments** As she decides to take her own life, Thisbe says, "I can / claim love, and it will give me strength enough / to strike myself." Both Pyramus and Thisbe seem to think that taking their own life is a strong or brave thing to do. If you had been with them that night, how could you have talked them into making a different decision? Explain.

5. **Analyze Sequence** Review the sequence chain you created as you read. How might the myth's ending have been different if Pyramus had left for the rendezvous at the same time Thisbe did? Cite evidence to support your answer.

6. **Analyze Myth** Use a chart like the following to explain how each characteristic of myth appears in "Pyramus and Thisbe."

Characteristic of Myth	In "Pyramus and Thisbe"
Explains how something connected to humans or nature came to be	
Tells about supernatural beings or events	
Presents a lesson or moral	

7. **Evaluate Theme** "Pyramus and Thisbe" is an ancient myth, passed down orally and in writing for generations before Ovid recorded it some 2,000 years ago. Explain whether you think the theme, or message, of this **classic story** is still relevant to contemporary audiences.

Reading-Writing Connection

WRITING PROMPT

Extended Response: Compare and Contrast
Many great writers have looked to myths for inspiration. "Pyramus and Thisbe" was retold by Ovid long before Shakespeare wrote *Romeo and Juliet*, and Ovid was one of Shakespeare's favorite authors. Compare and contrast *Romeo and Juliet* with "Pyramus and Thisbe" in terms of plot, conflict, characters, and theme.

SELF-CHECK

A strong comparison will . . .
- clearly present the selections' similarities and differences
- cite evidence from both myth and play
- state whether the selections are more alike or more different

Writing Workshop

Comparing a Play and a Film

Plays, novels, and short stories often provide inspiration for filmmakers. However, a film script is not the same as a literary source. In this workshop, you will compare and contrast part of a film with the literary work that inspired it. The **Writer's Road Map** will start you on your way.

WRITER'S ROAD MAP

Comparing a Play and a Film

WRITING PROMPT 1

Writing from Literature Write an essay in which you compare and contrast one scene from the Italian filmmaker Franco Zeffirelli's adaptation of *Romeo and Juliet* with the same scene in Shakespeare's play. Your comparison might discuss plot, setting, mood, characters, dialogue, lighting, costumes, or camera angles.

Scenes to Compare

- opening scene in the public square
- Romeo and Juliet's meeting
- balcony scene

WRITING PROMPT 2

Writing for the Real World Choose a book you have read and enjoyed. Compare and contrast it with a film it inspired. Your comparison might discuss plot, setting, mood, characters, dialogue, lighting, costumes, or camera angles.

Subjects to Consider

- *To Kill a Mockingbird*
- *The Lord of the Rings*
- *A Separate Peace*

 WRITING TOOLS
For prewriting, revision, and editing tools, visit the **Writing Center at ClassZone.com.**

KEY TRAITS

1. IDEAS

- Engaging **introduction** names the works being compared and clearly states the **focus** of the comparison
- Supports ideas with relevant **details** from the two works
- Presents a **thesis statement** that identifies important similarities and differences
- Provides **background information** for the reader where it is needed

2. ORGANIZATION

- Follows a consistent **organizational pattern**
- Uses **transitions** to connect ideas
- Ends with a summary and a broader **conclusion** about ideas or techniques in the two works

3. VOICE

- Uses a **tone** that is appropriate for the audience and purpose

4. WORD CHOICE

- Uses precise **literary and media terms** to discuss the written work and the film

5. SENTENCE FLUENCY

- Varies **sentence beginnings** for pacing and interest

6. CONVENTIONS

- Employs **correct grammar and usage**

Part 1: Analyze a Student Model

Lucas LaPaglia
Lakeview Academy of the Arts

A Night in Fair Verona

William Shakespeare's play *Romeo and Juliet* is a timeless and tragic tale of old grudges and young love. I recently read the play for my literature class, and then I watched a film version, directed in 1968 by the Italian filmmaker Franco Zeffirelli. I compared Act One, Scene 5, in
5   the play and the film and found differences in setting, plot, and dialogue that affect the meaning and the impact of the work. I learned that, while a filmmaker has to sacrifice some details to keep the running time reasonable, he or she can use scenery, music, and acting to create a vivid, fresh interpretation of what is on the page.

10   The setting is similar in the play and the film—a party at Capulet's house. However, what you have to imagine as you read the play is vividly presented onscreen. Colorfully costumed guests dance to traditional music in the film version. Blazing torches in the great hall are like Romeo's description of Juliet: "O, she doth teach the torches to
15   burn bright!" They symbolize the passion that will flare up this night.

Zeffirelli's camera also helps set the scene. The camera moves in rhythm to the music, swaying to the right and left while the dancers circle, drawing viewers into the scene as if they, too, are dancing in Capulet's house. During the dancing, the film cuts (jumps back and forth) from
20   Juliet's face to Romeo's, emphasizing their attraction to each other.

As for the plot, Zeffirelli remains mostly faithful to Shakespeare's design for Scene 5. However, there is one important exception. The filmmaker adds a song as a backdrop for the meeting and first kisses between Juliet and Romeo. A young man sings these words to the guests:
25   What is a youth? Impetuous fire.
        What is a maid? Ice and desire.

KEY TRAITS IN ACTION

Interesting **introduction** clearly states the **focus** of the essay. **Thesis statement** identifies what aspects of the play and the film are being compared.

Uses **point-by-point organization.** This paragraph covers the first point, comparison of setting. Varied **sentence beginnings** add interest.

Relevant **details** support the comparison.

Transitional words and phrases connect ideas. Formal **tone** is appropriate for audience (teacher and perhaps classmates).

WRITING STANDARD
1.4.11.B Write complex informational pieces

The youth, of course, is Romeo, and Juliet is the maid. The song reflects the feelings of Romeo and Juliet, and as it is sung, Zeffirelli's film cuts back and forth from the singer to the young lovers kissing and
30   proclaiming their desire for each other.

Perhaps the biggest difference between the play and the movie involves dialogue. Zeffirelli leaves out some of Shakespeare's text because a filmmaker is able to show what a playwright has to explain in dialogue or stage directions. For example, at the beginning of the scene,
35   Capulet encourages his guests to dance. Zeffirelli deletes this dialogue and simply shows people dancing. Another example involves Tybalt's outrage at Romeo's presence at the party. Instead of Shakespeare's many heated exchanges between Capulet and Tybalt, Zeffirelli demonstrates Tybalt's anger by showing his face in close-up shots, scowling with
40   rage. There is no need for dialogue; the actor's expression demonstrates Tybalt's hatred of Romeo. During the rest of the scene, the film cuts back again and again to Tybalt scowling directly into the camera—and, of course, directly at the viewer—reinforcing his ill feelings.

The rest of the movie follows the pattern evident in Scene 5. After
45   watching the movie, I understood that Shakespeare intended his play to be performed, not just read. Zeffirelli uses the tools of filmmaking to bring the setting, plot, and dialogue of *Romeo and Juliet* to life on the screen.

Provides helpful **background information** about the play.

Employs **precise terms** from the language of filmmaking.

Conclusion not only summarizes the comparison but also includes a broader judgment about techniques in the two works.

2

WRITING STANDARD
1.4.11.B.1 Include a variety of methods to develop the main idea

Part 2: Apply the Writing Process

PREWRITING

What Should I Do?	*What Does It Look Like?*

1. Choose a scene from the film.
Watch the film actively, taking notes as you do so. List those scenes that especially interest you or that seem the most different from those in the literary work. Draw a star next to the scene you decide to write about.

See page 1076: Techniques of Filmmaking

▶ ✸ *1. Act One, Scene 5: Romeo meets Juliet.*
- *replaces some of Shakespeare's dialogue with lively action*
- *includes a song*

2. Act Two, Scene 2: the balcony scene
- *mostly faithful to the play; some deletions*
- *scene lit with soft blue light*

3. Act Five, Scene 3: Romeo and Juliet die.
- *duel with Paris cut*
- *Friar's remarks moved to church steps*

2. Note differences between the film and the text.
Once you have chosen a scene to write about, reread that scene in the literary work. How are the setting, plot, and dialogue similar and different in the text and the movie? What techniques has the filmmaker used—lighting, music, and camera movements, for example—to bring the text to life on the screen?

TIP If you're watching the movie on DVD, turn on the English subtitles or the closed captioning. Then you can compare what the actors in the movie say with what the author wrote.

▶ *Similarities/differences:*
- *Setting is pretty much the same.*
- *A special dance is added; a song is added when Romeo and Juliet meet.*
- *Some dialogue is deleted; new dialogue is added at the beginning of the scene.*

Film techniques:
- *The hall is brightly lit by torches.*
- *The camera seems to dance with the dancers.*
- *Music plays throughout the scene.*
- *The film cuts back and forth to different characters.*

3. Write a thesis statement.
Now that you've analyzed the similarities and differences between the text and the movie, write a thesis statement that tells your reader the focus of your comparison. You can refine your thesis as you draft and revise your essay.

▶ *I compared Act One, Scene 5, in the play and the film and found differences in setting, plot, and dialogue. These differences affect the meaning and the impact of the work.*

What Should I Do?	What Does It Look Like?

1. Organize your ideas.

You can organize your comparison in many ways. Two common methods of organization are shown here.

- **Subject-by-Subject Organization**

  Discusses characteristics of the first subject before moving on to the next subject

- **Point-by-Point Organization**

  Compares or contrasts both subjects, one point at a time

SUBJECT BY SUBJECT

Subject A: Play
1. **Setting**: Capulet's house
2. **Plot**: Romeo meets Juliet.
3. **Dialogue**: original text

Subject B: Film
1. **Setting**: same as play, with lighting, music, costumes
2. **Plot**: same, but includes singer and song not in play
3. **Dialogue**: some deletions from play

POINT BY POINT

Point 1: Setting
   Play: Capulet's house
   Film: same as play, with lighting, music, costumes

Point 2: Plot
   Play: Romeo meets Juliet.
   Film: same, but includes singer and song not in play

Point 3: Dialogue
   Play: original text
   Film: some deletions

2. Include effective transitions.

Transitional words and phrases, such as *like, unlike, just as, while, in contrast, on the other hand,* and *however,* can signal comparisons and show the reader how ideas are connected.

However, there is one important exception.

Perhaps the biggest difference between the play and the movie involves dialogue.

3. Select evidence to support your comparison.

Whenever you tell your reader that something is similar to or different from something else, you have to provide supporting evidence, such as a quotation or an example.

TIP Before you begin revising, study the key traits on page 1070 and the rubric and peer-reader questions on page 1076.

Perhaps the biggest difference between the play and the movie involves dialogue. ⎤ Comparison

Instead of Shakespeare's many heated exchanges between Capulet and Tybalt, Zeffirelli demonstrates Tybalt's anger by showing his face in close-up shots, scowling with rage. There is no need for dialogue; the actor's expression demonstrates Tybalt's hatred of Romeo. ⎤ Supporting example

REVISING AND EDITING

What Should I Do?	What Does It Look Like?

1. Check the flow of your ideas.
- Draw boxes around the transitional words and phrases you have used to signal comparisons and connect ideas.
- If your essay lacks boxes, add transitions to make your ideas flow more smoothly.

▶

They symbolize the passion that will flare up this night.
Zeffirelli's camera ^(also) helps set the scene.

2. Keep your tone polite and formal.
- As you revise, keep in mind that your essay is a formal comparison. Read your essay aloud, highlighting slang expressions and language that is too casual or conversational.
- Replace highlighted words and phrases with language appropriate for your audience and purpose.

▶

~~Still, there's one pretty big change.~~
However, there is one important exception.

A young ~~guy~~ ^(man) sings these words to the guests:

3. Evaluate your evidence.
- Number each piece of supporting evidence you have used in your essay.
- If you don't have many numbers, add information to make your points clearer.

▶

Zeffirelli's camera also helps set the scene.

1. The camera moves in rhythm to the music.

2. During the dancing, the film cuts from Juliet's face to Romeo's, emphasizing their attraction to each other.

4. Define technical terms as necessary.
- Underline technical terms you have used to compare the literary work and the film.
- Have you defined terms that your audience might not know? Add definitions wherever needed to make your writing clear.

▶

During the dancing, the film cuts ^((jumps back and forth)) from Juliet's face to Romeo's, emphasizing their attraction to each other.

Preparing to Publish

Comparing a Play and a Film

Apply the Rubric

A strong essay comparing a play and a film . . .

☑ has a clear thesis statement that identifies the focus of the comparison

☑ includes relevant evidence and background information to support the writer's thesis

☑ follows a clear, logical organizational pattern

☑ connects ideas with transitions

☑ varies sentence beginnings

☑ maintains an appropriate tone

☑ uses literary and media terms correctly

☑ summarizes the writer's thesis and feelings in a satisfying conclusion

Ask a Peer Reader

- What makes my introduction either engaging or weak?

- Can you explain the focus of my comparison in your own words?

- Which evidence in my essay do you find most compelling?

Techniques of Filmmaking

Lighting: Soft lighting can make a scene more romantic; long shadows can make a scene mysterious or frightening.

Sound: Music and sound effects can establish mood. For example, lively music and laughing guests add to a party scene.

Camera Shots and Angles: Filmmakers use different camera shots (close-ups, pans, and long shots) and camera angles (from above, from below, or from the side).

Check Your Grammar

- When quoting a single line of verse, use quotation marks.

> Romeo describes Juliet this way: " O, she doth teach the torches to burn bright! "

- When quoting two or more lines of verse, indent the lines and don't use quotation marks.

> A young man sings these words to the guests:
> What is a youth? Impetuous fire.
> What is a maid? Ice and desire.

Writing Online

PUBLISHING OPTIONS
For publishing options, visit the **Writing Center** at ClassZone.com.

ASSESSMENT PREPARATION
For writing and grammar assessment practice, go to the **Assessment Center** at ClassZone.com.

Staging a Scene

When you and your classmates stage a scene, you learn firsthand the craft that goes into a play or a film. These guidelines will help you.

Planning to Stage the Scene

1. **Choose your cast.** Hold a "casting call," with your classmates as the aspiring actors.
2. **Decide what scenery and props you will need.** You don't need lots of scenery and props to stage your scene. A coat of arms on the wall and a table and chairs, for example, are all that's needed to suggest a room in a wealthy household.
3. **Prepare the script.** Create an annotated version of the script for your scene. The annotations should include stage directions, such as where the actors should stand and how they should speak. Make copies of the script for all the actors.
4. **Rehearse the scene.** Bring the actors together as often as needed to run through the scene. Each rehearsal is an opportunity to fine-tune the action and improve the quality of the acting. Rehearse until the scene achieves your vision of what it should look and sound like.

   TIP Shakespeare's dialogue can be difficult to understand and deliver. Ask your teacher or your school's drama teacher for help with pronunciation and rhythm.

Presenting the Scene

1. **Use a narrator.** A narrator can introduce the scene and provide background information.
2. **Speak clearly.** The actors should enunciate each word and speak loudly enough to be heard in the back of the room.
3. **Show emotion.** Emotions—happiness, sorrow, amazement, anger—are the core of an actor's performance. Laughter or tears can help actors connect with an audience.

   See page R80: Evaluate an Oral Interpretation

Reading Comprehension

DIRECTIONS *Read the following selection and then answer the questions.*

from The Tragedy of Romeo and Juliet

William Shakespeare

Friar Laurence's cell.
In Act Three, Scene 3, Friar Laurence tells Romeo of his banishment for the murder of Tybalt, and Romeo collapses in grief. Then he learns from the nurse that Juliet, too, is in despair.

[*Enter* Friar Laurence.]

Friar Laurence. Romeo, come forth; come forth, thou fearful man.
Affliction is enamored of thy parts,
And thou art wedded to calamity.

[*Enter* Romeo.]

Romeo. Father, what news? What is the Prince's doom?
5 What sorrow craves acquaintance at my hand
That I yet know not?

Friar Laurence.　　　　　Too familiar
Is my dear son with such sour company.
I bring thee tidings of the Prince's doom.

Romeo. What less than doomsday is the Prince's doom?

10 **Friar Laurence.** A gentler judgment vanished from his lips—
Not body's death, but body's banishment.

Romeo. Ha, banishment? Be merciful, say "death";
For exile hath more terror in his look,
Much more than death. Do not say "banishment."

15 **Friar Laurence.** Hence from Verona art thou banished.
Be patient, for the world is broad and wide.

Romeo. There is no world without Verona walls,
But purgatory, torture, hell itself.
Hence banished is banish'd from the world,
20 And world's exile is death. Then "banishment,"
Is death misterm'd. Calling death "banishment,"
Thou cuttst my head off with a golden axe
And smilest upon the stroke that murders me.

ASSESSMENT ONLINE
For more assessment practice and test-taking tips, go to the **Assessment Center** at ClassZone.com.

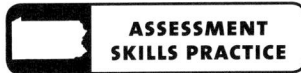

Friar Laurence. O deadly sin! O rude unthankfulness!
25   Thy fault our law calls death; but the kind Prince,
Taking thy part, hath rushed aside the law,
And turned that black word death to banishment.
This is dear mercy, and thou seest it not.

Romeo. 'Tis torture, and not mercy. Heaven is here,
30   Where Juliet lives; and every cat and dog
And little mouse, every unworthy thing,
Live here in heaven and may look on her;
But Romeo may not. More validity,
More honorable state, more courtship lives
35   In carrion flies than Romeo. They may seize
On the white wonder of dear Juliet's hand
And steal immortal blessing from her lips,
Who, even in pure and vestal modesty,
Still blush, as thinking their own kisses sin;
40   But Romeo may not—he is banished.
This may flies do, when I from this must fly;
They are free men, but I am banished.
And sayst thou yet that exile is not death?
Hadst thou no poison mixed, no sharp-ground knife,
45   No sudden mean of death, though ne'er so mean,
But "banished" to kill me—"banished"?
O friar, the damned use that word in hell;
Howling attends it! How hast thou the heart,
Being a divine, a ghostly confessor,
50   A sin-absolver, and my friend professed,
To mangle me with that word "banished"?

Friar Laurence. Thou fond mad man, hear me a little speak.

Romeo. O, thou wilt speak again of banishment.

Friar Laurence. I'll give thee armor to keep off that word;
55   Adversity's sweet milk, philosophy,
To comfort thee, though thou art banished.

Romeo. Yet "banished"? Hang up philosophy!
Unless philosophy can make a Juliet,
Displant a town, reverse a prince's doom,
60   It helps not, it prevails not. Talk no more.

Friar Laurence. O, then I see that madmen have no ears.

Romeo. How should they, when that wise men have no eyes?

Friar Laurence. Let me dispute with thee of thy estate.

Romeo. Thou canst not speak of that thou dost not feel.
65 Wert thou as young as I, Juliet thy love,
An hour but married, Tybalt murdered,
Doting like me, and like me banished,
Then mightst thou speak, then mightst thou tear thy hair,
And fall upon the ground, as I do now,
70 Taking the measure of an unmade grave.

[Nurse *knocks within.*]

Friar Laurence. Arise; one knocks. Good Romeo, hide thyself.

Romeo. Not I; unless the breath of heartsick groans
Mist-like infold me from the search of eyes.

[*knock*]

Friar Laurence. Hark, how they knock! Who's there? Romeo, arise;
75 Thou wilt be taken.—Stay awhile!—Stand up;

[*knock*]

Run to my study.—By-and-by!—God's will,
What simpleness is this.—I come, I come!

[*knock*]

Who knocks so hard? Whence come you? What's your will?

Nurse [*within*]. Let me come in, and you shall know my errand.
80 I come from Lady Juliet.

Friar Laurence.   Welcome then.

[*Enter* Nurse.]

Nurse. O holy friar, O, tell me, holy friar,
Where is my lady's lord, where's Romeo?

Friar Laurence. There on the ground, with his own tears made
  drunk.

Nurse. O, he is even in my mistress' case,
85 Just in her case! O woeful sympathy!
Piteous predicament! Even so lies she,
Blubb'ring and weeping, weeping and blubbering.
Stand up, stand up! Stand, an you be a man.
For Juliet's sake, for her sake, rise and stand!
90 Why should you fall into so deep an O?[1]

---

1. **into so deep an O:** into such deep grief.

Romeo [*rises*]. Nurse—

Nurse. Ah sir! ah sir! Well, death's the end of all.

Romeo. Spakest thou of Juliet? How is it with her?
Doth not she think me an old murderer,
95 Now I have stained the childhood of our joy
With blood removed but little from her own?
Where is she? and how doth she? and what says
My concealed lady to our canceled love?

Nurse. O, she says nothing, sir, but weeps and weeps;
100 And now falls on her bed, and then starts up,
And Tybalt calls; and then on Romeo cries,
And then down falls again.

Comprehension

DIRECTIONS *Answer these questions about the excerpt from* Romeo and Juliet.

1. Which line from the excerpt contains a play on words?

A "What less than doomsday is the Prince's doom?" (line 9)

B "There is no world without Verona walls. . . ." (line 17)

C "This is dear mercy, and thou seest it not." (line 28)

D "O, she says nothing, sir, but weeps and weeps; . . ."(line 99)

2. When Friar Laurence says "Thy fault our law calls death" (line 25), he means that

A the law says the punishment for Romeo's crime is death

B according to the law, death is a fault, not a crime

C Romeo's death would be Friar Laurence's fault

D it is Romeo's fault that he has been sentenced to death

3. The conflict in lines 17–28 presents two views of

A jealousy

B banishment

C murder

D the law

4. Which statement best describes why Friar Laurence disagrees with Romeo in lines 24–28?

A He hopes to keep Romeo from acting rashly or causing more harm.

B He blames Romeo for all that has gone wrong and wants to punish him.

C He thinks Romeo is ignorant of the law and needs to learn the facts.

D He thinks that Juliet deserves a better husband than Romeo.

GO ON ➤

5. In lines 29–36, which phrase breaks the pattern of blank verse?

A "But Romeo may not."

B "And little mouse, every unworthy thing . . ."

C "Where Juliet lives; . . ."

D "On the white wonder of dear Juliet's hand . . ."

6. What is Shakespeare contrasting in the pun in lines 41–42?

"This may flies do, when I from this must fly;
They are free men, but I am banished."

A insects and humans

B flies and free men

C Juliet and Romeo

D flies and Romeo

7. What does Friar Laurence mean by "madmen have no ears" (line 61)?

A An irrational person won't listen to advice.

B Deafness in a person is a sign of madness.

C Friar Laurence is angry at someone who doesn't listen.

D Romeo's anger is a sign of madness.

8. Which trait does Romeo exhibit most strongly in this excerpt?

A generosity

B dignity

C self-absorption

D coldness

9. Which statement best describes Friar Laurence's role as a foil to Romeo in this excerpt?

A Laurence is cynical; Romeo is hopeful.

B Laurence is reasonable; Romeo is emotional.

C Laurence is fearful; Romeo acts bravely.

D Laurence is comic; Romeo is tragic.

10. In lines 94–96, Romeo laments killing Tybalt. This murder intensifies Romeo's conflict between

A remaining loyal to Friar Laurence and upholding family responsibilities

B being in love with Juliet and feeling guilty for leaving Rosaline

C defending his personal honor and being worthy of Juliet

D performing religious duties and keeping his obligations to the Prince

Open-Ended Items

11. Paraphrase lines 54–56 and identify which character is speaking.

"I'll give thee armor to keep off that word;
Adversity's sweet milk, philosophy,
To comfort thee, though thou art banished."

12. What character flaw of Romeo's does the nurse call attention to in lines 84–90? Support your answer with details from the excerpt.

13. Why does Romeo disagree with Friar Laurence's advice in line 16: "Be patient, for the world is broad and wide"? Discuss Romeo's motivation for rejecting this advice and support your answer with details from the excerpt.

Writing & Grammar

DIRECTIONS *Read the passage and answer the questions that follow.*

> (1) The musical *West Side Story* is based on Shakespeare's play *Romeo and Juliet.*
> (2) Unlike the play, however, both *West Side Story*'s Broadway production and its
> Hollywood adaptation set the 14th-century tale of Italian lovers in 20th-century New
> York. (3) *Romeo and Juliet* features two wealthy and prominent families, while the
> depiction of working-class people is the focus of *West Side Story.* (4) In the musical,
> Romeo becomes "Tony," and filling the shoes of Juliet is "Maria." (5) Many aspects
> of *Romeo and Juliet* are updated in *West Side Story.* (6) An opulent house becomes
> a crowded tenement. (7) A duel becomes a street fight. (8) Maria uses a fire escape
> instead of a balcony. (9) In this way, *West Side Story* represents a modern urban tragedy.

1. Choose the best way to rewrite sentence 3 so
that its elements are parallel.

A *Romeo and Juliet* features wealthier and
more prominent families, while working-
class people are the focus of *West Side Story.*

B *Romeo and Juliet* features two families that
are wealthy and prominent, while working-
class people are focused on in *West Side
Story.*

C *Romeo and Juliet* features two wealthy and
prominent families, while *West Side Story*
focuses on working-class people.

D *Romeo and Juliet* features two wealthy and
prominent families; working-class people
are the focus of *West Side Story.*

2. Choose the best way to rewrite sentence 4 so
that its elements are parallel.

A In the musical, Romeo becomes "Tony," while
"Maria" is busy filling the shoes of Juliet.

B In the musical, Romeo becomes "Tony,"
and Juliet becomes "Maria."

C In the musical, Romeo becomes "Tony,"
with "Maria" trying to fill the shoes of Juliet.

D In the musical, Romeo becomes "Tony,"
and "Maria" and Juliet are each other.

3. Choose the best way to rewrite sentence 8
so that its structure is parallel to that of
sentences 6 and 7.

A A fire escape was a balcony in the play.

B A fire escape is a modern-day balcony in
West Side Story.

C A balcony becomes a fire escape.

D Balconies and fire escapes are the same
thing.

STOP

Ideas for Independent Reading

Find out who inspired Shakespeare and who Shakespeare inspired, and read more of his classic plays.

West Side Story
by Leonard Bernstein, Irving Schulman, and Stephen Sondheim

Sondheim, Schulman, and Bernstein move the story of *Romeo and Juliet* to 1950s New York City, where gang warfare dominates the West Side. Tony and Maria meet at a school dance and instantly fall in love. At first their happiness erases all else from their minds, but the harsh realities of their lives cannot be kept at bay. In some parts of the play, the authors are faithful to Shakespeare's plot; in others, they take greater liberty. In either case, the power of true love remains a resonant theme.

Metamorphoses
by Ovid

Metamorphoses is a collection of stories in which love causes physical transformation. One tale of thwarted love, "Pyramus and Thisbe," was an inspiration for *Romeo and Juliet*. The characters in the myths are sometimes brought closer together by their transformations, but sometimes they are pushed apart or separated forever. Ovid's tone, like Shakespeare's, changes suddenly from humorous to tragic and back again, allowing him to constantly surprise and entertain his readers.

A Midsummer Night's Dream
by William Shakespeare

In this play, Shakespeare takes a comic and magical approach to forbidden love. Four young people have run away from the Athenian court to escape an impending forced marriage. Far from their homes, they fall asleep in the forest on a summer evening. There they are visited by Puck, a devilish spirit who will use magic to change their passions and their lives. While their passions are as forceful as those of Romeo and Juliet, the results are both funnier and more hopeful.

Othello
by William Shakespeare

The mastermind in this Shakespearean tragedy is not Fate but a jilted assistant in the army. Othello, a military general, is choosing a new lieutenant; he passes over Iago in favor of another man in his battalion. Iago vows revenge on both of them. He tells Othello that the new lieutenant is romantically involved with Othello's beloved wife, Desdemona. Though both protest to the contrary, Othello's jealously blinds him to reason and reality, with devastating consequences.

The Wings of the Dove
by Henry Jame

Kate Croy is desperately in love with Merton Densher. Kate's family claims that Merton is too poor and will keep Kate from rising in the world, but the two have promised each other that they will somehow marry. When a wealthy, gravely ill young woman befriends Kate and falls in love with Merton, Kate plans to use the woman's feelings and friendship to meet her own needs. In *Romeo and Juliet,* overt tragedy and political strife change the lives of lovers. In *The Wings of the Dove,* subtle and intimate personal interactions cause love itself to change.

A Natural History of Love
by Diane Ackerman

In this book, Ackerman studies and explores the ways in which love has been portrayed through the ages. *A Natural History of Love* discusses the lessons that can be taken from tales of love throughout history, both from historical romances and from such fictional romances as Romeo and Juliet's, and examines how love has been treated throughout history. Both a poet and a journalist, Ackerman uses poetic language in writing this detailed and thorough history of a subject that has significance for every reader.

Epic Poetry

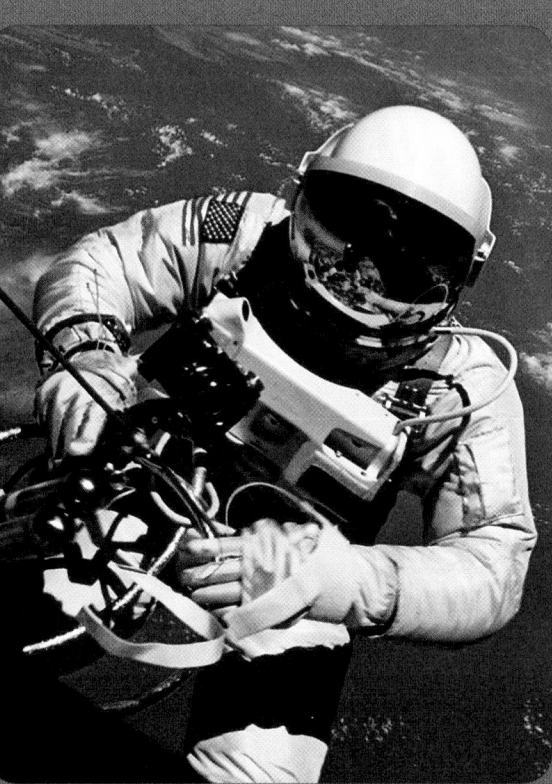

THE ODYSSEY

Is it the JOURNEY or the DESTINATION?

If attending high school is a journey, then the ultimate destination is graduation. As you strive to cross that finish line, you'll face new experiences, build friendships, and even run into some frustrating roadblocks. As you consider this journey, what do you think is more important—reaching your goal and clutching that diploma in your hand, or taking time to appreciate the many moments (both good and bad) that will lead up to graduation day?

ACTIVITY With a classmate, think of books, movies, or TV shows that depict a journey of some sort—whether it's a quest to find a long-lost family member, a struggle to make it safely back home, or a mission to fulfill an important dream. Which seems more important to the story, the destination the character strives to reach or the journey itself?

Preview Unit Goals

LITERARY ANALYSIS
- Identify and evaluate characteristics of an epic
- Identify and analyze epic hero and archetypes
- Identify and analyze epic similes, epithets, and allusions
- Identify and analyze plot, setting, and theme in an epic

READING
- Use strategies for reading an epic
- Summarize plot

WRITING AND GRAMMAR
- Write a subject analysis
- Use figurative language to add descriptive detail
- Use parallel construction
- Use correct subject-verb agreement

SPEAKING, LISTENING, AND VIEWING
- Deliver an oral report

VOCABULARY
- Use prefixes and word roots to help determine the meanings of unfamiliar words

ACADEMIC VOCABULARY
- epic
- epic hero
- archetypes
- epic simile
- epithet
- allusion
- subject analysis

HOMER'S WORLD

The acropolis of Athens, Greece, was the high point of the city and a place to worship the goddess Athena, the city's patroness.

Examining the Homeric Epics

Composed in Greece around 750–725 B.C., the *Iliad* and the *Odyssey* are perhaps the greatest masterpieces of the epic form, narrative poetry about a hero's adventures. Both stories were first told orally, perhaps even sung, and it may not have been until several generations later that they were set down in writing. The poems are traditionally credited to a blind poet named Homer. Although there have been many translations of the poems into English, Robert Fitzgerald's verse renderings are considered among the best at capturing the poems' high drama and intense emotions. Three important elements of the plot of each epic are the Trojan War, the heroism of Odysseus, and the interference of the gods.

The Trojan War This legendary war seems to have occurred sometime around 1200 B.C. The earliest literary accounts of it, found in the *Iliad* and the *Odyssey,* are elaborated in later classical literature.

According to legend, the Trojan War began after Paris, a Trojan prince, kidnapped the beautiful Helen from her husband, Menelaus (měn′ə-lā′əs), the king of Sparta. Menelaus recruited kings and soldiers from all over Greece to help him avenge his honor and recover his wife. The Greeks held Troy under siege for ten years.

The *Iliad* takes place during the tenth year of this war. It tells the story of the Greek warrior Achilles and his quarrel with Menelaus' brother Agamemnon, ending with the death and funeral of Paris' brother Hector.

After Hector's death, the Greeks brought the war to an end thanks to the cleverness of Odysseus, ruler of the island of Ithaca. To break the ten-year stalemate, Odysseus thought of a scheme to make the Trojans think that the Greeks had finally given up. He ordered a giant wooden horse to be built and left at the gates of Troy. The Trojans, waking to find it there—without a Greek in sight—assumed that the enemy had fled and left them a peace offering. They took the horse inside the city, only to discover, too late, that it was filled with Greek soldiers and that Troy was doomed.

Giovanni Domenico Tiepolo's *The Procession of the Trojan Horse into Troy*, painted in 1773

The Heroic Story of Odysseus The *Odyssey* deals with Odysseus' adventures as he makes his way home from Troy and with events that take place on Ithaca just before and after his return. The first excerpts that you will read depict some of the wanderings of Odysseus after his departure from Troy with a fleet of 12 ships carrying about 720 men. This time his opponents are not military ones. Instead, he encounters various monsters who try to devour him and enchanting women who try to keep him from his wife, Penelope. The final excerpts describe Odysseus' homecoming and his reunion with Penelope and his son, Telemachus. In addition to great strength and courage, what sets Odysseus apart from others is a special quality that has been called his craft or guile: the ingenious tricks he uses to get himself out of difficult situations.

The Intervention of the Gods and Goddesses
Adding another dimension to the human struggles recounted in Homer's epics are the conflicts among the gods and goddesses on Mount Olympus (ə-lĭm′pəs). In Homer's time, most Greeks believed that their gods not only took an active interest in human affairs but also behaved in recognizably human ways, often engaging in their own trivial quarrels and petty jealousies. For example, Athena, the goddess of war and practical wisdom, supported the Greek cause in the Trojan War and championed Odysseus, while Aphrodite (ăf′rə-dī′tē), the goddess of love, sided with Paris and his fellow Trojans. The story of Odysseus' return from Troy contains some notable instances of divine interference. Odysseus has Athena on his side, but he has displeased the gods who were on the side of Troy. Furthermore, as you will see, he angers another god during one of his first adventures and still another later on. As a result, he is forced to suffer many hardships before he manages to return home.

To Homer's audience, the *Odyssey,* with its interfering gods and goddesses and its strange lands and creatures, must have seemed as full of mystery and danger as science fiction and fantasy adventures seem to people today. Just as we can imagine aliens in the next galaxy or creatures created in a laboratory, the ancient Greeks could imagine monsters living just beyond the boundaries of their known world. It was not necessary for them to believe that creatures such as one-eyed giants did exist, but only that they might.

This detail of a late 18th-century frieze depicts several Greek gods and goddesses.

Eros	**Aphrodite**	**Apollo**	**Athena**	**Muses**
God of love (also known as Cupid)	Goddess of love and mother of Eros	God of music, poetry, and prophecy	Goddess of war, wisdom, and cleverness	Daughters of Zeus (three shown here), often viewed as sources of divine inspiration

Homer: The Epic Poet

Shadowy Figure Although the ancient Greeks credited a man named Homer with composing the *Iliad* and the *Odyssey,* scholars have long debated whether Homer really existed. There are many theories about who Homer may have been and when and where he may have lived. According to ancient accounts, he lived sometime between 900 and 700 B.C., possibly on the island of Chios in the eastern Aegean Sea, and he was blind. Most modern scholars agree that the Homeric poems are the work of one or two exceptionally talented bards—singers who made up their verses as they sang.

Oral History Homer's epics are all that remains of a series of poems that told the whole story of the Trojan War. In later centuries, the *Iliad* and the *Odyssey* were memorized by professional reciters, who performed them at religious festivals throughout Greece. They were also the first works read by Greek schoolchildren. By 300 B.C. many slightly different versions of the poems existed, and scholars began to work at restoring them to their original form.

Models for the Ages Homer's epics became models for many later writers, including the Roman poet Virgil, who wrote his own epic in Latin. Poets throughout English literature, from Chaucer in the Middle Ages to Shakespeare in the Renaissance to Keats in the Romantic era, have found inspiration in Homer's epics. Moreover, by helping to shape classical Greek culture, the epics contributed to the development of many later Western ideas and values.

A Living Tradition Artists of all kinds continue to be inspired by Homer's work. In 1922, the Irish writer James Joyce published his groundbreaking novel *Ulysses* ("Ulysses" is a Latin form of Odysseus' name), in which he turned a day in the life of an ordinary man into an Odyssean journey. In 2000, the Coen brothers' film *O Brother, Where Art Thou?* told the story of a Depression-era Ulysses, an escaped convict returning home to prevent his wife from marrying another man. The 2004 movie *Troy* is a more straightfoward adaptation of Homer's *Iliad*.

 MORE ABOUT THE AUTHOR
For more on Homer, visit the **Literature Center** at ClassZone.com.

A scene from the 2004 movie *Troy;* a bust of Homer

People and Places of the *Odyssey*

You will find it helpful to become familiar with important people and places in the *Odyssey* before you begin reading. The map identifies real places mentioned in the poem, such as Troy, Sparta, and Ithaca. It also shows where later readers have thought that some of the imaginary lands visited by Odysseus could have been located, after applying Mediterranean geography to Homer's descriptions. Following is a list of important characters. All Greek names used in Robert Fitzgerald's translation have been changed from their original spelling to a more familiar, Latinized spelling.

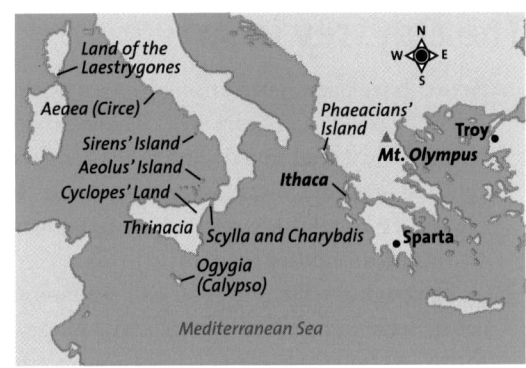

IMPORTANT CHARACTERS IN THE *ODYSSEY* (in order of mention)

BOOK 1
Helios (hē′lē-ŏs′)—the sun god, who raises his cattle on the island of Thrinacia (thrĭ-nā′shə)

Zeus (zo͞os)—the ruler of the Greek gods and goddesses; father of Athena and Apollo

Telemachus (tə-lĕm′ə-kəs)—Odysseus' son

Penelope (pə-nĕl′ə-pē)—Odysseus' wife

BOOK 5
Hermes (hûr′mēz)—the god of invention, commerce, and cunning; messenger of the gods

Calypso (kə-lĭp′sō)—a sea goddess who lives on the island of Ogygia (ō-gĭj′yə)

Laertes (lā-ûr′tēz)—Odysseus' father

BOOK 9
Alcinous (ăl-sĭn′ō-əs)—the king of the Phaeacians (fē-ā′shənz)

Circe (sûr′sē)—a goddess and enchantress who lives on the island of Aeaea (ē-ē′ə)

Cicones (sĭ-kō′nēz)—allies of the Trojans, who live at Ismarus (ĭs-măr′əs)

Lotus Eaters—inhabitants of a land Odysseus visits

Cyclopes (sī-klō′pēz)—a race of one-eyed giants; an individual member of the race is a Cyclops (sī′klŏps)

Apollo (ə-pŏl′ō)—the god of music, poetry, prophecy, and medicine

Poseidon (pō-sīd′n)—the god of the seas, earthquakes, and horses; father of the Cyclops who battles Odysseus

BOOK 10
Aeolus (ē′ə-ləs)—the guardian of the winds

Laestrygones (lĕs′trĭ-gō′nēz)—cannibal inhabitants of a distant land

Eurylochus (yo͞o-rĭl′ə-kəs)—a trusted officer of Odysseus'

Persephone (pər-sĕf′ə-nē)—the wife of Hades, ruler of the underworld

Tiresias (tī-rē′sē-əs) of Thebes (thēbz)—a blind prophet whose spirit Odysseus visits in the underworld

BOOK 11
Elpenor (ĕl-pē′nôr)—one of Odysseus' crew, killed in an accident

BOOK 12
Sirens (sī′rənz)—creatures, part woman and part bird, whose songs lure sailors to their death

Scylla (sĭl′ə)—a six-headed sea monster who devours sailors

Charybdis (kə-rĭb′dĭs)—a dangerous whirlpool personified as a female sea monster

BOOK 16
Athena (ə-thē′nə)—the goddess of war, wisdom, and cleverness; goddess of crafts

Eumaeus (yo͞o-mē′əs)—a servant in Odysseus' household

BOOK 17
Argos (är′gŏs)—Odysseus' dog

BOOKS 21—23
Antinous (ăn-tĭn′ō-əs)—a suitor of Penelope's

Eurymachus (yo͞o-rĭm′ə-kəs)—a suitor of Penelope's

Philoetius (fĭ-lē′shəs)—a servant in Odysseus' household

Amphinomus (ăm-fĭn′ə-məs)—a suitor of Penelope's

Eurynome (yo͞o-rĭn′ə-mē)—a female servant in Odysseus' household

Eurycleia (yo͞or′ĭ-klē′ə)—an old female servant, still loyal to Odysseus

The *Odyssey* in Art

Artists have been representing images from the *Odyssey* since the seventh century B.C., when Greek artists painted Odyssean images and scenes as decoration on ceramic urns and vases. Since then, artists have continued to tell Odysseus' story in painting, sculpture, and other media.

Throughout the unit, you will see how numerous artists have interpreted this epic in a range of styles and forms. As you look at the art illustrating each episode, ask yourself what the artists were trying to show about each part of the story and what their own attitudes toward characters and events may have been.

Looking at Art You've seen how understanding a writer's craft can help you appreciate the beauty and meaning of a literary text. In the same way, knowing about artists' techniques can help you understand and appreciate their work. The following list of terms and related questions may help you identify and think about the choices each artist made. Consider how these choices have contributed to the meaning and beauty of each piece.

Term	Questions
composition	What shape or space is emphasized?
material	Has the artist used paint, clay, pencil, ink, or some other material?
function	Is the piece useful, decorative, or both?
color	Does the piece have a broad palette (range of colors) or a limited one?
line	Are the lines clean, simple, rough, ornate, or jagged?
shape	Does the piece have large, bold shapes or smaller, more complex ones?
	Are they geometric or organic (free-form)?
texture	In painting, are the brush strokes distinct or smooth looking?
	In sculpture or ceramics, is the surface polished or rough?
scale	Does the piece show large things or small ones?
representation	Are the images realistic, stylized, or abstract?

Landscapes When you look at a Homeric landscape, ask questions like the ones that follow. See if the answers help you understand each artist's purpose.

- Which of the following two landscapes is more **realistic?** How so?
- What **material** has each artist used? Which do you prefer, and why?
- Look at the **composition** of each piece. What part of the scene is emphasized in the painting? What is emphasized in the collage?
- Describe the **mood** and **tone** of each piece. Which is more lush, and which is more spare? Consider the techniques that created these differences.

200s: *Ulysses and the Sirens*, Roman. Mosaic, 130 cm x 344 cm. Musée du Bardo, Tunis, Tunisia. © Bridgeman Art Library.

About 1650: *Ulysses Returns Chryseis to Her Father,* Claude Lorrain. Oil painting.

Portraiture As you look at a portrait, ask yourself what the image suggests about the character or characters being depicted. Try to identify the techniques that helped the artist create that impression.

- What does the **position** of the characters tell you about the scene rendered in terra cotta?
- Consider the difference in **dimension** between the two pieces; one is flat, while the other is in **relief.** How does that difference affect the feel of each piece?
- The pastel drawing is a highly **abstract** figure, as opposed to a realistic one. What do you think of it? Why might an artist choose such an abstract style?

Narrative Art Most of the artwork in this selection tells a story in one way or another. Consider how the artist's choices affect your sense of the events portrayed in each work.

- One of the following pieces is a decorative scene painted on a useful object, and the other is a book illustration. How does each piece's **function** affect its **style?**
- Compare the **backgrounds** on which the two scenes are painted. How does each background affect the way you view and understand the scene?
- Which scene makes more sense to you? Explain.

About 460–450 B.C.: Terra cotta plaque showing the return of Odysseus

About 450–440 B.C.: Clay urn showing Odysseus slaying Penelope's suitors

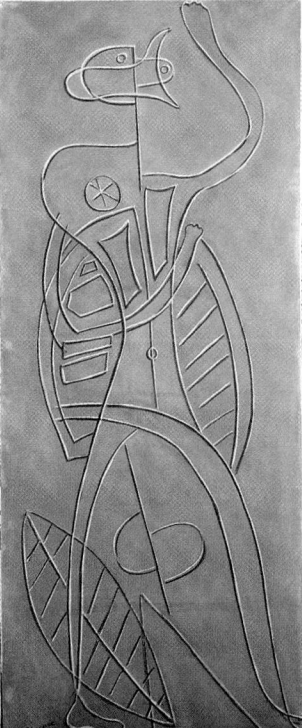

1931–1932: *Ulysses,* Georges Braque. Pastel drawing.

About 1915: Illustration from *Tales of the Gods and Heroes* by Sir G. W. Cox, Innes Fripp. Hermes, messenger of Zeus, urges the nymph Calypso to release Odysseus.

PENNSYLVANIA STANDARDS

READING STANDARDS
B.1.1.1.A.1 Evaluate character

B.1.1.1.C.1 Evaluate elements of the plot

B.2.1.2 Identify and analyze figurative language

The Epic

Extraordinary heroes and hideous monsters. Brutal battles and dangerous voyages. Spectacular triumphs and crushing defeats. The epic tradition, still very much alive in today's movies and novels, began thousands of years ago with the orally told epic poem. In ancient Greece, listeners crowded around poet-storytellers to hear about the daring exploits of a hero named Odysseus. With its storm-tossed seas, powerful evildoers, and narrow escapes, it's no wonder that Homer's *Odyssey* remains one of most famous epics in Western literature. It captivates us because it is a compelling narrative and a window into a time and place quite different from our own.

Part 1: Characteristics of the Epic

In literature, an **epic** is a long narrative poem. It recounts the adventures of an **epic hero,** a larger-than-life figure who undertakes great journeys and performs deeds requiring remarkable strength and cunning. As *you* journey through many episodes from the *Odyssey*, expect to encounter the following elements.

THE EPIC AT A GLANCE

EPIC HERO
- Possesses superhuman strength, craftiness, and confidence
- Is helped and harmed by interfering gods
- Embodies ideals and values that a culture considers admirable
- Emerges victorious from perilous situations

EPIC PLOT
Involves a long journey, full of complications, such as
- strange creatures
- divine intervention
- large-scale events
- treacherous weather

EPIC SETTING
- Includes fantastic or exotic lands
- Involves more than one nation

ARCHETYPES
All epics include **archetypes**—characters, situations, and images that are recognizable in many times and cultures:
- sea monster
- wicked temptress
- buried treasure
- suitors' contest
- epic hero
- loyal servant

EPIC THEMES
Reflect such universal concerns as
- courage
- the fate of a nation
- a homecoming
- beauty
- loyalty
- life and death

MODEL: CHARACTERISTICS OF THE EPIC

Here, the Greek (Achaean) king Menelaus is speaking to his wife, Helen. He recalls the moment when he and Odysseus hid with their fellow soldiers inside a giant wooden horse, waiting to attack the Trojans. Formerly a Trojan herself, Helen stood outside the horse and called to the soldiers inside, mimicking the voices of their wives. As you read, notice the characteristics of an epic that are revealed.

from BOOK 4: *The Red-Haired King and His Lady*

"In my life I have met, in many countries,
foresight and wit in many first rate men,
but never have I seen one like Odysseus
for steadiness and a stout heart. Here, for instance,
5 is what he did—had the cold nerve to do—
inside the hollow horse, where we were waiting,
picked men all of us, for the Trojan slaughter,
when all of a sudden, you came by—I dare say
drawn by some superhuman
10 power that planned an exploit for the Trojans;
and Deiphobus, that handsome man, came with you.
Three times you walked around it, patting it everywhere,
and called by name the flower of our fighters,
making your voice sound like their wives, calling.
15 Diomedes and I crouched in the center
along with Odysseus; we could hear you plainly;
and listening, we two were swept
by waves of longing—to reply, or go.
Odysseus fought us down, despite our craving,
20 and all the Achaeans kept their lips shut tight,
all but Anticlus. Desire moved his throat
to hail you, but Odysseus' great hands clamped
over his jaws, and held. So he saved us all,
till Pallas Athena led you away at last."

Close Read

1. King Menelaus mentions several heroic traits that Odysseus exhibited while carrying out his plan to defeat the Trojans. One trait has been boxed. Identify two more.

2. What archetype does Helen represent? Explain your answer.

3. Reread lines 8–10 and 23–24. Explain how the gods interfered in the episode that Menelaus is describing.

Part 2: The Language of Homer

Because the language of Homer was ancient Greek, what you will read is an English translation. The *Odyssey* has been translated many times, and each translator has interpreted it differently. Read these two versions of the opening of Book 2. The first is written in verse and has a more formal tone—closer to the original—while the second is written in prose and is less formal.

TRANSLATION 1	TRANSLATION 2
When primal Dawn spread on the eastern sky her fingers of pink light, Odysseus' true son stood up, drew on his tunic and his mantle, slung on a sword-belt and a new-edged sword, tied his smooth feet into good rawhide sandals, and left his room, a god's brilliance upon him. —translated by Robert Fitzgerald (1961)	Dawn came, showing her rosy fingers through the early mists, and Telemachus leapt out of bed. He dressed himself, slung a sharp sword over his shoulder, strapt a stout pair of boots on his lissom feet, and came forth from his chamber like a young god. —translated by W. H. D. Rouse (1937)

The Greeks who first experienced the *Odyssey* did not read a written version; they heard it as a live performance. Singing or reciting, a poet kept the audience enthralled with **epic similes, epithets,** and **allusions.**

- A **simile** is a comparison between two unlike things, using the word *like* or *as.* Homer often develops a simile at great length, so that it goes on for several lines. This is known as an **epic simile.** In this passage from Book 20, an angry Odysseus is compared to a sausage being roasted over a fire.

> His rage
> held hard in leash, submitted to his mind,
> while he himself rocked, rolling from side to side,
> as a cook turns a sausage, big with blood
> and fat, at a scorching blaze, without a pause,
> to broil it quick: so he rolled left and right, . . .

- An **epithet** is a brief descriptive phrase used to characterize a particular person or thing. When a poet needed to fill out a line, he'd add an epithet with the right meter and number of syllables. Odysseus is known by various epithets, including "son of Laertes" and "raider of cities."

- An **allusion** is a reference to a famous person, place, or event. To help his audience picture what he described, a poet might have made an allusion to something they already knew. For instance, when Odysseus' son first sees the palace of Menelaus, he says, "This is the way the court of Zeus must be." Every Greek would have understood this allusion to the ruler of the gods.

MODEL 1: EPIC SIMILE

In this excerpt, Odysseus is watching the performance of a bard (a poet like Homer himself). Suddenly he finds himself listening to the story of the fall of Troy and of his own part in it. Notice the epic simile that is developed over this entire passage.

from BOOK 8: *The Songs of the Harper*

And Odysseus
let the bright molten tears run down his cheeks,
weeping [like] the way a wife mourns for her lord
on the lost field where he has gone down fighting
5   the day of wrath that came upon his children.
At sight of the man panting and dying there,
she slips down to enfold him, crying out;
then feels the spears, prodding her back and shoulders,
and goes bound into slavery and grief.
10   Piteous weeping wears away her cheeks:
but no more piteous than Odysseus' tears,
cloaked as they were, now, from the company.

Close Read

1. What two things are being compared in this epic simile?

2. In the boxed lines, the wife cries first for her dying husband, then for herself. Consider what this might suggest about Odysseus' feelings. What might the epic hero be crying about?

MODEL 2: EPITHET

Here, the goddess Athena speaks to her father, Zeus, on behalf of Odysseus. Reminding Zeus of sacrifices made to him during the Trojan War, she begs him to let Odysseus return home. Athena has told Zeus that Odysseus is so homesick that he "longs to die."

from BOOK 1: *A Goddess Intervenes*

"Are you not moved by this, Lord of Olympus?
Had you no pleasure from Odysseus' offerings
beside the Argive ships, on Troy's wide seaboard?
O Zeus, what do you hold against him now?"

5   To this the summoner of cloud replied:

"My child, what strange remarks you let escape you.
Could I forget that kingly man, Odysseus?
There is no mortal half so wise; no mortal
gave so much to the lords of open sky."

Close Read

1. One epithet of Zeus is boxed. Find another.

2. What epithet does Zeus use to refer to Odysseus?

Part 3: Reading the Epic

Reading the *Odyssey* is a complex experience. On one level, the poem is an action-packed narrative that makes readers eagerly anticipate the hero's homecoming. On another level, it's a work of art to be appreciated and analyzed. Use the following strategies to help you make the most of your journey through the epic.

READING THE EPIC AS NARRATIVE

- Note the changing narrators. Who is telling the story at any given point? Consider how the different narrators deepen your understanding of characters and events.

- **Visualize** the action and the settings by using details in the text.

- Track the events and conflicts and try to **predict** the outcomes.

- Use a chart like the one shown to keep track of the characters, including gods and goddesses and Odysseus' friends and foes. What does each do to either help or harm him?

STRATEGIES IN ACTION

Characters Who Help Odysseus	Characters Who Harm Odysseus
Athena (goddess) • pleads with Zeus to help Odysseus escape Calypso's island	Poseidon (god) • stirs up nasty weather to create problems for Odysseus

READING THE EPIC AS POETRY

- Try reading the lines aloud, as the epic was originally performed.

- Read the lines for their sense, just as you would read prose. Follow the punctuation, and remember that the end of a line does not always mean the end of a thought.

- Listen for sound devices such as **alliteration, assonance, consonance,** and **rhyme** and notice how they reinforce meaning. (Although the sound devices in English aren't the same as those in the original Greek, they do reflect the translator's attempt to capture the spirit and technique of Homer's verse.)

- Consider how the **imagery** and **figurative language**—especially the **epic similes**—help you understand characters and events.

from **BOOK 4:** *The Red-Haired King and His Lady*

but never have I seen one like Odysseus for steadiness and a stout heart. . . .

Alliteration: The repeated "s" sound emphasizes the strength of the epic hero.

READING THE EPIC AS A REFLECTION OF ITS TIME

- Pay attention to the **character traits** of Odysseus, the epic hero, by looking closely at how he behaves and how he is described. What do these traits tell you about the values of the time?

- Think about what you've learned of Greek history. What events may have influenced Homer?

- Remember that in Homer's time most Greeks believed that the gods took an active interest in human affairs and themselves behaved much like humans. How are these religious beliefs apparent in the epic?

Odysseus' Traits	Evidence
strong, skilled, and swift	frequently referred to as "master mariner and soldier"
quick-witted; thinks on his feet	described as "strategist" when he responds to a difficult question posed by Calypso (Book 5)

MODEL: READING THE EPIC

Odysseus has been gone from his homeland for years, and all except
his family believe him dead. Young men make themselves at home in
Odysseus' castle while vying to marry his "widow," Penelope. Odysseus'
son, Telemachus, calls an assembly to discuss the situation. The following
excerpt is an exchange between Telemachus and one of Penelope's suitors.

from BOOK 2 : *A Hero's Son Awakens*

Telemachus addresses the crowd, complaining of the suitors' behavior.

"No; these men spend their days around our house
killing our beeves and sheep and fatted goats,
carousing, soaking up our good dark wine,
not caring what they do. They squander everything.
5   We have no strong Odysseus to defend us,
and as to putting up a fight ourselves—
we'd only show our incompetence in arms.
Expel them, yes, if I only had the power;
the whole thing's out of hand, insufferable."

A suitor responds to Telemachus' heated accusation.

10   "You want to shame us, and humiliate us,
but you should know the suitors are not to blame—
it is your own dear, incomparably cunning mother.
For three years now—and it will soon be four—
she has been breaking the hearts of the Achaeans,
15   holding out hope to all, and sending promises
to each man privately—but thinking otherwise.

Here is an instance of her trickery:
she had her great loom standing in the hall
and the fine warp of some vast fabric on it;
20   we were attending her, and she said to us:
'Young men, my suitors, now my lord is dead,
let me finish my weaving before I marry,
or else my thread will have been spun in vain.
It is a shroud I weave for Lord Laertes,
25   when cold death comes to lay him on his bier.
The country wives would hold me in dishonor
if he, with all his fortune, lay unshrouded.'
We have men's hearts; she touched them; we agreed.
So every day she wove on the great loom—
30   but every night by torchlight she unwove it;
and so for three years she deceived the Achaeans."

Close Read

1. Try to visualize the
   suitors at Odysseus'
   home by using details
   in lines 1–9. Describe
   the image that the lines
   conjured up in your mind.

2. Note the two speakers.
   What does Telemachus
   accuse the suitors of
   doing? How does one
   suitor defend his and the
   other suitors' actions?

3. Identify two examples
   of sound devices in the
   boxed text.

4. What do the accusations
   made in this excerpt tell
   you about Greek values?

5. How would you
   describe Penelope?
   Cite details that help
   you to understand the
   traits Greeks prized in
   a woman.

Part 4: Analyze the Literature

Here, Odysseus returns to his homeland at last, disguised as an old beggar. The first person he approaches is Eumaeus, his head swineherd. Welcoming the unknown beggar in the name of his missing lord, Eumaeus gives him a hot meal, a drink, and a place to sleep. To test the faithful swineherd and to try to keep warm in the frigid cold, the disguised Odysseus devises a story. Through the story, he hopes to encourage Eumaeus to give him—a supposed stranger—the cloak off his back. As you read this excerpt, use what you've learned to make sense of the episode.

from BOOK 14: *Hospitality in the Forest*

                                                    "Listen," he said,
"Eumaeus, and you others, here's a wishful
tale that I shall tell. The wine's behind it,
vaporing wine, that makes a serious man
5   break down and sing, kick up his heels and clown,
or tell some story that were best untold.
But now I'm launched, I can't stop now.
                                                    Would god I felt
the hot blood in me that I had at Troy!
Laying an ambush near the walls one time,
10 Odysseus and Menelaus were commanders
and I ranked third. I went at their request.
We worked in toward the bluffs and battlements
and, circling the town, got into canebrakes,
thick and high, a marsh where we took cover,
15 hunched under arms.
                                    The northwind dropped, and night
came black and wintry. A fine sleet descending
whitened the cane like hoarfrost, and clear ice
grew dense upon our shields. The other men,
all wrapt in blanket cloaks as well as tunics,
20 rested well, in shields up to their shoulders,
but I had left my cloak with friends in camp,
foolhardy as I was. No chance of freezing hard,
I thought, so I wore kilts and a shield only.
But in the small hours of the third watch, when stars
25 that rise at evening go down to their setting,
I nudged Odysseus, who lay close beside me;
he was alert then, listening, and I said:

'Son of Laertes and the gods of old,
Odysseus, master mariner and soldier,
30 I cannot hold on long among the living.

Close Read

1. Think about why Odysseus is telling Eumaeus this elaborate story. Through his plan of action, what traits does he display? Explain.

2. Reread the boxed text and visualize the imagery used to describe the setting. What does the imagery serve to emphasize?

3. What epithets does the soldier use to address Odysseus in the story?

The cold is making a corpse of me. Some god
inveigled me to come without a cloak.
No help for it now; too late.'

Next thing I knew

35   he had a scheme all ready in his mind—
and what a man he was for schemes and battles!
Speaking under his breath to me, he murmured:

'Quiet; none of the rest should hear you.'

Then,

propping his head on his forearm, he said:

'Listen, lads, I had an ominous dream,
40   the point being how far forward from our ships
and lines we've come. Someone should volunteer
to tell the corps commander, Agamemnon;
he may reinforce us from the base.'

At this,

Thoas jumped up, the young son of Andraemon,
45   put down his crimson cloak and headed off,
running shoreward.

Wrapped in that man's cloak

how gratefully I lay in the bitter dark
until the dawn came stitched in gold! I wish
I had that sap and fiber in me now!"

50   Then—O my swineherd!—you replied, Eumaeus:

"That was a fine story, and well told,
not a word out of place, not a pointless word.
No, you'll not sleep cold for lack of cover,
or any other comfort one should give
55   to a needy guest. However, in the morning,
you must go flapping in the same old clothes.
Shirts and cloaks are few here; every man
has one change only. When our prince arrives,
the son of Odysseus, he will make you gifts—
60   cloak, tunic, everything—and grant you passage
wherever you care to go."

On this he rose

and placed the bed of balsam near the fire,
strewing sheepskins on top, and skins of goats.
Odysseus lay down. His host threw over him
65   a heavy blanket cloak, his own reserve
against the winter wind when it came wild.

Close Read

4. What quality does Odysseus attribute to himself in telling this tale? Cite specific details to support your answer.

5. Reread lines 31–33 and 39–46. What do you learn about how the ancient Greeks perceived their gods and ominous dreams?

6. Think about where else you have encountered a character like Eumaeus. What archetype does he represent? Explain.

The Wanderings of Odysseus
from the Odyssey

Epic Poem by Homer

Translated by Robert Fitzgerald

What is a HERO?

PENNSYLVANIA STANDARDS

READING STANDARDS
B.1.1.1.A.1 Evaluate character
B.2.1.2 Identify and analyze figurative language

KEY IDEA When you hear the word *hero,* who comes to mind? Do you think of someone with unusual physical strength? great courage? a rare talent? In Homer's *Odyssey,* you'll meet one of the classic heroes of Western literature—Odysseus, a man with many heroic traits as well as human faults.

DISCUSS Work with a small group to make a list of people who are generally considered heroes. Discuss the heroic qualities of each. Which qualities seem essential to every hero?

LITERARY ANALYSIS: EPIC HERO

The **epic hero** is a larger-than-life character, traditionally a man, who pursues long and dangerous adventures. Alternately aided and blocked by the gods, he carries the fate of his people on his shoulders. The epic hero is an **archetypal** character—one found in works across time and cultures. Odysseus, one of the most famous heroes in Western culture, has shaped our ideas about the traits that a hero should have.

- extraordinary strength and courage
- cleverness and deceit, also known as guile
- extreme confidence and a tendency to dismiss warnings

Every epic hero embodies the values of his culture. As you read the *Odyssey,* consider how Odysseus faces various conflicts. What does this tell you about his character? What do his character traits tell you about what the ancient Greeks found admirable?

READING STRATEGY: READING AN EPIC POEM

The strategies for reading an epic are very similar to those for reading any narrative poem.

- Keep track of the events.
- Visualize the **imagery.**
- Notice how the **figurative language,** including **epic similes,** can make the story more vivid and interesting.
- Read difficult passages more than once. Use the side notes for help in comprehension.
- Read the poem aloud, as it was originally conveyed.

As you read, keep a list of major events and consider whether they lead Odysseus any closer to home.

▲ VOCABULARY IN CONTEXT

Place each of the following words in the appropriate column.

WORD LIST		
abominably	assuage	meditation
adversary	beguiling	ponderous
appalled	foreboding	profusion
ardor	harried	travail

Know Well	Think I Know	Don't Know

Overview

Book 1: A Goddess Intervenes The poet introduces Odysseus, a successful warrior who, after conquering the city of Troy, has wandered the seas for many years. Now he wants only to return safely to his home and family.

Book 5: Calypso, the Sweet Nymph Odysseus has been held captive for many years by the goddess Calypso on her island. Zeus sends the god Hermes to order her to release Odysseus; she offers her advice and helps him build a raft on which he can sail to Scheria, his next destination.

Book 9: New Coasts and Poseidon's Son Odysseus has met King Alcinous and begins telling him of his adventures since leaving Troy. He relates the tale of the Lotus Eaters and his encounter with the brutal Cyclops, a son of the sea-god Poseidon. Odysseus continues his tales in Books 10–12.

Book 10: Circe, the Grace of the Witch Eventually, Odysseus and his men arrive at the island home of Circe, a goddess and enchantress. She detains the men for a year, allowing them to go home only if they will visit the land of the dead and hear a prophecy from the ghost of Tiresias.

Book 11: The Land of the Dead Odysseus and his crew travel to the underworld, where Tiresias warns Odysseus against stealing the cattle of Helios, god of the sun. According to the prophecy, if Odysseus raids the cattle, he will lose his ship and crew and return home only after many years alone at sea.

Book 12: The Sirens; Scylla and Charybdis Odysseus and his men return to Circe's island, where she advises him on how to get past the bewitching Sirens and the horrible sea monsters Scylla and Charybdis. He successfully evades the Sirens but does not escape the monsters without losing some of his men.

BOOK 1:
A Goddess Intervenes

Sing in me, Muse, and through me tell the story
of that man skilled in all ways of contending,
the wanderer, **harried** for years on end,
after he plundered the stronghold
5 on the proud height of Troy.

                                    He saw the townlands
and learned the minds of many distant men,
and weathered many bitter nights and days
in his deep heart at sea, while he fought only
to save his life, to bring his shipmates home.
10 But not by will nor valor could he save them,
for their own recklessness destroyed them all—
children and fools, they killed and feasted on
the cattle of Lord Helios, the Sun,
and he who moves all day through heaven
15 took from their eyes the dawn of their return. Ⓐ

Of these adventures, Muse, daughter of Zeus,
tell us in our time, lift the great song again. . . .

*The story of Odysseus begins with the goddess Athena's appealing to Zeus
to help Odysseus, who has been wandering for ten years on the seas, to find
his way home to his family on Ithaca. While Odysseus has been gone, his son,
Telemachus, has grown to manhood and his wife, Penelope, has been besieged
by suitors wishing to marry her and gain Odysseus' wealth. The suitors have
taken up residence in her home and are constantly feasting on the family's cattle,
sheep, and goats. They dishonor Odysseus and his family. Taking Athena's
advice, Telemachus travels to Pylos for word of his father. Meanwhile, on
Ithaca, the evil suitors plot to kill Telemachus when he returns.*

1 Muse: a daughter of Zeus, credited with divine inspiration.

harried (hăr′ēd) *adj.* tormented; harassed **harry** *v.*

11–13 their own recklessness . . . the Sun: a reference to an event occurring later in the poem—an event that causes the death of Odysseus' entire crew.

Ⓐ EPIC HERO
This invocation (lines 1–15) introduces us to Odysseus, "that man skilled in all ways of contending." What **traits** is he shown to have?

ANALYZE VISUALS
This 1930s print, *The Ship of Odysseus*, is part of an *Odyssey* series by Francois-Louis Schmied. What qualities of this ship has Schmied emphasized with his use of color and shape? Explain.

The Ship of Odysseus, Francois-Louis Schmied. From *Homer the Odyssey*, published Paris (1930–1933). Color lithograph. The Stapleton Collection. © Bridgeman Art Library.
© 2007 Artists Rights Society (ARS), New York/ADAGP, Paris.

BOOK 5:
Calypso, the Sweet Nymph

For seven of the ten years Odysseus has spent wandering the Mediterranean Sea, he has been held captive by the goddess Calypso on her island. As Book 5 begins, Zeus sends the god Hermes to tell Calypso to release Odysseus. However, she is only to help him build a raft. He must sail for 20 days before landing on the island of Scheria, where he will be helped in his effort to return home.

No words were lost on Hermes the Wayfinder,
who bent to tie his beautiful sandals on,
ambrosial, golden, that carry him over water
or over endless land in a swish of the wind,
5 and took the wand with which he charms asleep—
or when he wills, awake—the eyes of men.
So wand in hand he paced into the air,
shot from Pieria down, down to sea level,
and veered to skim the swell. A gull patrolling
10 between the wave crests of the desolate sea
will dip to catch a fish, and douse his wings;
no higher above the whitecaps Hermes flew **B**
until the distant island lay ahead,
then rising shoreward from the violet ocean
15 he stepped up to the cave. Divine Calypso,
the mistress of the isle, was now at home.
Upon her hearthstone a great fire blazing
scented the farthest shores with cedar smoke
and smoke of thyme, and singing high and low
20 in her sweet voice, before her loom a-weaving,
she passed her golden shuttle to and fro.
A deep wood grew outside, with summer leaves
of alder and black poplar, pungent cypress.
Ornate birds here rested their stretched wings—
25 horned owls, falcons, cormorants—long-tongued
beachcombing birds, and followers of the sea.
Around the smoothwalled cave a crooking vine
held purple clusters under ply of green;
and four springs, bubbling up near one another
30 shallow and clear, took channels here and there
through beds of violets and tender parsley.

1–6 **Hermes** (hûr′mēz): the messenger of the gods, also known for his cleverness and trickery.

8 **Pieria** (pī-îr′ē-ə): an area next to Mount Olympus, home of the gods.

B EPIC SIMILE
Identify the epic simile in lines 9–12. What does this comparison tell you about Hermes?

ANALYZE VISUALS
How has the painter characterized Calypso in this 1906 portrait? Consider any relationship between her white dress and the white clouds.

28 **purple clusters:** grapes.

Calypso (about 1906), George Hitchcock. Oil on canvas, 111 cm × 89 cm. © Indianapolis Museum of Art, Indianapolis, Indiana/Bridgeman Art Library.

Even a god who found this place
would gaze, and feel his heart beat with delight:
so Hermes did; but when he had gazed his fill
35 he entered the wide cave. Now face to face
the magical Calypso recognized him,
as all immortal gods know one another
on sight—though seeming strangers, far from home.
But he saw nothing of the great Odysseus,
40 who sat apart, as a thousand times before,
and racked his own heart groaning, with eyes wet
scanning the bare horizon of the sea. . . .

Calypso invites Hermes to her table for food and drink, asking why he has come.
Hermes explains that he has brought with an order from Zeus that Calypso must
not detain Odysseus any longer but send him on his way home. She reluctantly
obeys, agreeing to offer Odysseus her advice about how to get home.

The strong god glittering left her as he spoke,
and now her ladyship, having given heed
45 to Zeus's mandate, went to find Odysseus
in his stone seat to seaward—tear on tear
brimming in his eyes. The sweet days of his life time
were running out in anguish over his exile,
for long ago the nymph had ceased to please.
50 Though he fought shy of her and her desire,
he lay with her each night, for she compelled him.
But when day came he sat on the rocky shore
and broke his own heart groaning, with eyes wet
scanning the bare horizon of the sea. **C**
55 Now she stood near him in her beauty, saying:

"O forlorn man, be still.
Here you need grieve no more; you need not feel
your life consumed here; I have pondered it,
and I shall help you go. . . ."

60 Swiftly she turned and led him to her cave,
and they went in, the mortal and immortal.
He took the chair left empty now by Hermes,
where the divine Calypso placed before him
victuals and drink of men; then she sat down
65 facing Odysseus, while her serving maids
brought nectar and ambrosia to her side.
Then each one's hands went out on each one's feast
until they had their pleasure; and she said:

C EPIC HERO
Reread lines 43–54. Which
of Odysseus' qualities is
emphasized here?

"Son of Laertes, versatile Odysseus,
70 after these years with me, you still desire
your old home? Even so, I wish you well.
If you could see it all, before you go—
all the adversity you face at sea—
you would stay here, and guard this house, and be
75 immortal—though you wanted her forever,
that bride for whom you pine each day.
Can I be less desirable than she is?
Less interesting? Less beautiful? Can mortals
compare with goddesses in grace and form?"

80 To this the strategist Odysseus answered:

"My lady goddess, here is no cause for anger.
My quiet Penelope—how well I know—
would seem a shade before your majesty,
death and old age being unknown to you,
85 while she must die. Yet, it is true, each day
I long for home, long for the sight of home. . . ." **D**

D EPITHET
Reread Odysseus' answer to Calypso
in lines 81–86. Why do you think
he is referred to in line 80 as "the
strategist Odysseus"? Explain.

With Calypso's help, Odysseus builds a raft and sets out to sea. For 17 days he sails until he is in sight of Scheria. For 3 more days he is pummeled by storms and finally swims for the island. He makes it safely ashore and crawls to rest under some bushes.

A man in a distant field, no hearthfires near,
will hide a fresh brand in his bed of embers
to keep a spark alive for the next day;
90 so in the leaves Odysseus hid himself,
while over him Athena showered sleep
that his distress should end, and soon, soon.
In quiet sleep she sealed his cherished eyes.

BOOK 9:
New Coasts and Poseidon's Son

In Books 6–8, Odysseus is welcomed by King Alcinous, who gives a banquet in his honor. That night the king begs Odysseus to tell who he is and what has happened to him. In Books 9–12, Odysseus relates to the king his adventures.

"I AM LAERTES' SON"

"What shall I
say first? What shall I keep until the end?
The gods have tried me in a thousand ways.
But first my name: let that be known to you,
5 and if I pull away from pitiless death,
friendship will bind us, though my land lies far.

I am Laertes' son, Odysseus.

Men hold me
formidable for guile in peace and war:
this fame has gone abroad to the sky's rim.
10 My home is on the peaked sea-mark of Ithaca
under Mount Neion's wind-blown robe of leaves,
in sight of other islands—Dulichium,
Same, wooded Zacynthus—Ithaca
being most lofty in that coastal sea,
15 and northwest, while the rest lie east and south.
A rocky isle, but good for a boy's training;
I shall not see on earth a place more dear,
though I have been detained long by Calypso,
loveliest among goddesses, who held me
20 in her smooth caves, to be her heart's delight,
as Circe of Aeaea, the enchantress,
desired me, and detained me in her hall.
But in my heart I never gave consent.
Where shall a man find sweetness to surpass
25 his own home and his parents? In far lands
he shall not, though he find a house of gold. **E**

ANALYZE VISUALS
This sculpture of Odysseus was produced in Rome sometime between A.D. 4 and 26. How would you describe the expression on his face?

7–8 hold me formidable for guile: consider me impressive for my cunning and craftiness.

11–13 Mount Neion's (nē′ŏnz′); **Dulichium** (dōō-lĭk′ē-əm); **Same** (sā′mē); **Zacynthus** (zə-sĭn′thəs).

18–26 Odysseus refers to two beautiful goddesses, Calypso and Circe, who have delayed him on their islands. (Details about Circe appear in Book 10.) At the same time, he seems nostalgic for his family and homeland, from which he has been separated for 18 years—10 of them spent fighting in Troy.

E **EPIC HERO**
Reread lines 24–26. What does Odysseus value most highly?

Detail of *Ulysses* from the *Polyphemos* group (second century B.C.), Hagesandros, Polydoros, and Athenodoros. Sperlonga, Italy. © Araldo de Luca/Corbis.

What of my sailing, then, from Troy?

What of those years

of rough adventure, weathered under Zeus? . . ."

Odysseus explains that soon after leaving Troy, he and his crew land near Ismarus, the city of the Cicones. The Cicones are allies of the Trojans and therefore enemies of Odysseus. Odysseus and his crew raid the Cicones, robbing and killing them, until the Ciconian army kills 72 of Odysseus' men and drives the rest out to sea. Delayed by a storm for two days, Odysseus and his remaining companions then continued their journey.

THE LOTUS EATERS

"I might have made it safely home, that time,

30 but as I came round Malea the current

took me out to sea, and from the north

a fresh gale drove me on, past Cythera.

Nine days I drifted on the teeming sea

before dangerous high winds. Upon the tenth

35 we came to the coastline of the Lotus Eaters,

who live upon that flower. We landed there

to take on water. All ships' companies

mustered alongside for the mid-day meal.

Then I sent out two picked men and a runner

40 to learn what race of men that land sustained.

They fell in, soon enough, with Lotus Eaters,

who showed no will to do us harm, only

offering the sweet Lotus to our friends—

but those who ate this honeyed plant, the Lotus,

45 never cared to report, nor to return:

they longed to stay forever, browsing on

that native bloom, forgetful of their homeland.

I drove them, all three wailing, to the ships,

tied them down under their rowing benches,

50 and called the rest: 'All hands aboard;

come, clear the beach and no one taste

the Lotus, or you lose your hope of home.'

Filing in to their places by the rowlocks

my oarsmen dipped their long oars in the surf,

55 and we moved out again on our sea faring.

THE CYCLOPS

In the next land we found were Cyclopes,

giants, louts, without a law to bless them.

In ignorance leaving the fruitage of the earth in mystery

to the immortal gods, they neither plow

30 Malea (mä-lē′ä).

32 Cythera (sĭ-thîr′ə).

38 mustered: assembled; gathered.

44–52 those who ate . . . hope of home.
How do the Lotus Eaters pose a threat to Odysseus and his men?

56 Cyclopes (sī-klō′pēz): refers to the creatures in plural; *Cyclops* is singular.

60 nor sow by hand, nor till the ground, though grain—
wild wheat and barley—grows untended, and
wine-grapes, in clusters, ripen in heaven's rain.
Cyclopes have no muster and no meeting,
no consultation or old tribal ways,
65 but each one dwells in his own mountain cave
dealing out rough justice to wife and child,
indifferent to what the others do. . . ."

58–67 *Why doesn't Odysseus respect the Cyclopes?*

Across the bay from the land of the Cyclopes was a lush, deserted island. Odysseus and his crew landed on the island in a dense fog and spent days feasting on wine and wild goats and observing the mainland, where the Cyclopes lived. On the third day, Odysseus and his company of men set out to learn if the Cyclopes were friends or foes.

"When the young Dawn with finger tips of rose ⓕ
came in the east, I called my men together
70 and made a speech to them:

'Old shipmates, friends,
the rest of you stand by; I'll make the crossing
in my own ship, with my own company,
and find out what the mainland natives are—
for they may be wild savages, and lawless,
75 or hospitable and god fearing men.'

ⓕ **EPITHET**
Notice the descriptive phrase used to characterize the dawn in line 68. What does this description tell you about the dawn?

At this I went aboard, and gave the word
to cast off by the stern. My oarsmen followed,
filing in to their benches by the rowlocks,
and all in line dipped oars in the gray sea.

77 stern: the rear end of a ship.

80 As we rowed on, and nearer to the mainland,
at one end of the bay, we saw a cavern
yawning above the water, screened with laurel,
and many rams and goats about the place
inside a sheepfold—made from slabs of stone
85 earthfast between tall trunks of pine and rugged
towering oak trees.

82 screened with laurel: partially hidden by laurel trees.

A prodigious man
slept in this cave alone, and took his flocks
to graze afield—remote from all companions,
knowing none but savage ways, a brute
90 so huge, he seemed no man at all of those
who eat good wheaten bread; but he seemed rather
a shaggy mountain reared in solitude.
We beached there, and I told the crew

91–92 *What does Odysseus' metaphor imply about the Cyclops?*

to stand by and keep watch over the ship;
95 as for myself I took my twelve best fighters
and went ahead. I had a goatskin full
of that sweet liquor that Euanthes' son,
Maron, had given me. He kept Apollo's
holy grove at Ismarus; for kindness
100 we showed him there, and showed his wife and child,
he gave me seven shining golden talents
perfectly formed, a solid silver winebowl,
and then this liquor—twelve two-handled jars
of brandy, pure and fiery. Not a slave
105 in Maron's household knew this drink; only
he, his wife and the storeroom mistress knew;
and they would put one cupful—ruby-colored,
honey-smooth—in twenty more of water,
but still the sweet scent hovered like a fume
110 over the winebowl. No man turned away
when cups of this came round.

                                    A wineskin full

I brought along, and victuals in a bag,
for in my bones I knew some towering brute
would be upon us soon—all outward power,
115 a wild man, ignorant of civility.

We climbed, then, briskly to the cave. But Cyclops
had gone afield, to pasture his fat sheep,
so we looked round at everything inside:
a drying rack that sagged with cheeses, pens
120 crowded with lambs and kids, each in its class:
firstlings apart from middlings, and the 'dewdrops,'
or newborn lambkins, penned apart from both.
And vessels full of whey were brimming there—
bowls of earthenware and pails for milking.
125 My men came pressing round me, pleading:

                                    'Why not

take these cheeses, get them stowed, come back,
throw open all the pens, and make a run for it?
We'll drive the kids and lambs aboard. We say
put out again on good salt water!'

                                    Ah,

130 how sound that was! Yet I refused. I wished
to see the caveman, what he had to offer—
no pretty sight, it turned out, for my friends.

97–98 Euanthes (yōō-ăn′thēz); **Maron** (mâr′ŏn′).

101 talents: bars of gold or silver of a specified weight, used as money in ancient Greece.

112 victuals (vĭt′lz): food.

121–122 The Cyclops has separated his lambs into three age groups.

123 whey: the watery part of milk, which separates from the curds, or solid part, during the making of cheese.

129 good salt water: the open sea.

130–132 *Why does Odysseus refuse his men's "sound" request?*

We lit a fire, burnt an offering,
and took some cheese to eat; then sat in silence
135 around the embers, waiting. When he came
he had a load of dry boughs on his shoulder
to stoke his fire at suppertime. He dumped it
with a great crash into that hollow cave,
and we all scattered fast to the far wall.
140 Then over the broad cavern floor he ushered
the ewes he meant to milk. He left his rams
and he-goats in the yard outside, and swung
high overhead a slab of solid rock
to close the cave. Two dozen four-wheeled wagons,
145 with heaving wagon teams, could not have stirred
the tonnage of that rock from where he wedged it
over the doorsill. Next he took his seat
and milked his bleating ewes. A practiced job
he made of it, giving each ewe her suckling;
150 thickened his milk, then, into curds and whey,
sieved out the curds to drip in withy baskets,
and poured the whey to stand in bowls
cooling until he drank it for his supper.
When all these chores were done, he poked the fire,
155 heaping on brushwood. In the glare he saw us.

'Strangers,' he said, 'who are you? And where from?
What brings you here by sea ways—a fair traffic?
Or are you wandering rogues, who cast your lives
like dice, and ravage other folk by sea?'

160 We felt a pressure on our hearts, in dread
of that deep rumble and that mighty man.
But all the same I spoke up in reply:

'We are from Troy, Achaeans, blown off course
by shifting gales on the Great South Sea;
165 homeward bound, but taking routes and ways
uncommon; so the will of Zeus would have it.
We served under Agamemnon, son of Atreus—
the whole world knows what city
he laid waste, what armies he destroyed. **G**
170 It was our luck to come here; here we stand,
beholden for your help, or any gifts
you give—as custom is to honor strangers.
We would entreat you, great Sir, have a care
for the gods' courtesy; Zeus will avenge
175 the unoffending guest.'

133 burnt an offering: burned a portion of the food as an offering to secure the gods' goodwill. (Such offerings were frequently performed by Greek sailors during difficult journeys.)

151 withy baskets: baskets made from twigs.

157 fair traffic: honest trading.

G ALLUSION
Reread lines 163–169. Agamemnon was the Greek king who led the war against the Trojans. Consider what Odysseus says about Agamemnon; what point is he making about himself by claiming this association?

172–175 It was a sacred Greek custom to honor strangers with food and gifts. Odysseus is warning the Cyclops that Zeus will punish anyone who mistreats a guest.

He answered this
from his brute chest, unmoved:

'You are a ninny,
or else you come from the other end of nowhere,
telling me, mind the gods! We Cyclopes
care not a whistle for your thundering Zeus
180 or all the gods in bliss; we have more force by far.
I would not let you go for fear of Zeus—
you or your friends—unless I had a whim to.
Tell me, where was it, now, you left your ship—
around the point, or down the shore, I wonder?'

185 He thought he'd find out, but I saw through this,
and answered with a ready lie:

'My ship?

Poseidon Lord, who sets the earth a-tremble,
broke it up on the rocks at your land's end.
A wind from seaward served him, drove us there.
190 We are survivors, these good men and I.' ●

Neither reply nor pity came from him,
but in one stride he clutched at my companions
and caught two in his hands like squirming puppies
to beat their brains out, spattering the floor.
195 Then he dismembered them and made his meal,
gaping and crunching like a mountain lion—
everything: innards, flesh, and marrow bones.
We cried aloud, lifting our hands to Zeus,
powerless, looking on at this, **appalled;**
200 but Cyclops went on filling up his belly
with manflesh and great gulps of whey,
then lay down like a mast among his sheep.
My heart beat high now at the chance of action,
and drawing the sharp sword from my hip I went
205 along his flank to stab him where the midriff
holds the liver. I had touched the spot
when sudden fear stayed me: if I killed him
we perished there as well, for we could never
move his **ponderous** doorway slab aside.
210 So we were left to groan and wait for morning.

When the young Dawn with fingertips of rose
lit up the world, the Cyclops built a fire ●
and milked his handsome ewes, all in due order,

Detail of *The Cyclops* (about 1914) Odilon Redon. Oil on canvas. Kroller-Muller Museum, Otterlo, Netherlands. © Peter Will/SuperStock.

178–182 *What is the Cyclopes' attitude toward the gods?*

● **EPIC HERO**
Reread lines 185–190. Why does Odysseus lie to the Cyclops about his ship?

appalled (ə-pôld') *adj.* filled with dismay; horrified **appall** *v.*

ponderous (pŏn'dər-əs) *adj.* heavy in a clumsy way; bulky

207–210 *Why doesn't Odysseus kill the Cyclops right now?*

● **EPITHET**
What **epithet** is repeated in lines 211–212? Look for more repetitions like this one.

putting the sucklings to the mothers. Then,
215 his chores being all dispatched, he caught
another brace of men to make his breakfast,
and whisked away his great door slab
to let his sheep go through—but he, behind,
reset the stone as one would cap a quiver.
220 There was a din of whistling as the Cyclops
rounded his flock to higher ground, then stillness.
And now I pondered how to hurt him worst,
if but Athena granted what I prayed for.
Here are the means I thought would serve my turn:

225 a club, or staff, lay there along the fold—
an olive tree, felled green and left to season
for Cyclops' hand. And it was like a mast
a lugger of twenty oars, broad in the beam—
a deep-sea-going craft—might carry:
230 so long, so big around, it seemed. Now I
chopped out a six foot section of this pole
and set it down before my men, who scraped it;
and when they had it smooth, I hewed again
to make a stake with pointed end. I held this
235 in the fire's heart and turned it, toughening it,
then hid it, well back in the cavern, under
one of the dung piles in **profusion** there.
Now came the time to toss for it: who ventured
along with me? whose hand could bear to thrust
240 and grind that spike in Cyclops' eye, when mild
sleep had mastered him? As luck would have it,
the men I would have chosen won the toss—
four strong men, and I made five as captain.

At evening came the shepherd with his flock,
245 his woolly flock. The rams as well, this time,
entered the cave: by some sheep-herding whim—
or a god's bidding—none were left outside.
He hefted his great boulder into place
and sat him down to milk the bleating ewes
250 in proper order, put the lambs to suck,
and swiftly ran through all his evening chores.
Then he caught two more men and feasted on them.
My moment was at hand, and I went forward
holding an ivy bowl of my dark drink,
255 looking up, saying:

216 brace: pair.

218–219 The Cyclops reseals the cave with the massive rock as easily as an ordinary human places the cap on a container of arrows.

226 left to season: left to dry out and harden.

228 lugger: a small, wide sailing ship.

profusion (prə-fyōō′zhən) *n.* abundance

238–243 *What does Odysseus plan to do to the Cyclops?*

'Cyclops, try some wine.
Here's liquor to wash down your scraps of men.
Taste it, and see the kind of drink we carried
under our planks. I meant it for an offering
if you would help us home. But you are mad,
260 unbearable, a bloody monster! After this,
will any other traveller come to see you?'

He seized and drained the bowl, and it went down
so fiery and smooth he called for more:

'Give me another, thank you kindly. Tell me,
265 how are you called? I'll make a gift will please you.
Even Cyclopes know the wine-grapes grow
out of grassland and loam in heaven's rain,
but here's a bit of nectar and ambrosia!'

Three bowls I brought him, and he poured them down.
270 I saw the fuddle and flush come over him,
then I sang out in cordial tones:

'Cyclops,
you ask my honorable name? Remember
the gift you promised me, and I shall tell you.
My name is Nohbdy: mother, father, and friends,
275 everyone calls me Nohbdy.'

And he said:
'Nohbdy's my meat, then, after I eat his friends.
Others come first. There's a noble gift, now.' **J**

Even as he spoke, he reeled and tumbled backward,
his great head lolling to one side: and sleep
280 took him like any creature. Drunk, hiccupping,
he dribbled streams of liquor and bits of men.

Now, by the gods, I drove my big hand spike
deep in the embers, charring it again,
and cheered my men along with battle talk
285 to keep their courage up: no quitting now.
The pike of olive, green though it had been,
reddened and glowed as if about to catch.
I drew it from the coals and my four fellows
gave me a hand, lugging it near the Cyclops
290 as more than natural force nerved them; straight
forward they sprinted, lifted it, and rammed it

255–261 *Why does Odysseus offer the Cyclops the liquor he brought from the ship?*

268 nectar (nĕk′tər) **and ambrosia** (ăm-brō′zhə): the drink and food of the gods.

270 fuddle and flush: the state of confusion and redness of the face caused by drinking alcohol.

J EPIC HERO
Say the name *Nohbdy* out loud and listen to what it sounds like. What might Odysseus be planning? Consider what this tells you about his **character.**

286 the pike: the pointed stake.

deep in his crater eye, and I leaned on it
turning it as a shipwright turns a drill
in planking, having men below to swing
295 the two-handled strap that spins it in the groove.
So with our brand we bored that great eye socket
while blood ran out around the red hot bar.
Eyelid and lash were seared; the pierced ball
hissed broiling, and the roots popped.

In a smithy

300 one sees a white-hot axehead or an adze
plunged and wrung in a cold tub, screeching steam—
the way they make soft iron hale and hard—:
just so that eyeball hissed around the spike. **K**
The Cyclops bellowed and the rock roared round him,
305 and we fell back in fear. Clawing his face
he tugged the bloody spike out of his eye,
threw it away, and his wild hands went groping;
then he set up a howl for Cyclopes
who lived in caves on windy peaks nearby.
310 Some heard him; and they came by divers ways
to clump around outside and call:

'What ails you,

Polyphemus? Why do you cry so sore
in the starry night? You will not let us sleep.
Sure no man's driving off your flock? No man
315 has tricked you, ruined you?'

Out of the cave

the mammoth Polyphemus roared in answer:

'Nohbdy, Nohbdy's tricked me, Nohbdy's ruined me!'

To this rough shout they made a sage reply:

'Ah well, if nobody has played you foul
320 there in your lonely bed, we are no use in pain
given by great Zeus. Let it be your father,
Poseidon Lord, to whom you pray.' **L**

So saying

they trailed away. And I was filled with laughter
to see how like a charm the name deceived them.
325 Now Cyclops, wheezing as the pain came on him,
fumbled to wrench away the great doorstone

---

299 smithy: blacksmith's shop.

300 adze (ădz): an axlike tool with a curved blade.

K EPIC SIMILE
Find the epic similes in lines 292–297 and lines 299–303. What two things are being compared in each case? What are the effects of this **figurative language?**

310 divers: various.

312 Polyphemus (pŏl'ə-fē'məs): the name of the Cyclops.

318 sage: wise.

319–322 Odysseus' lie about his name has paid off. *What do the other Cyclopes assume to be the source of Polyphemus' pain?*

L ALLUSION
What do you learn about Polyphemus from the allusion in lines 321–322?

and squatted in the breach with arms thrown wide
for any silly beast or man who bolted—
hoping somehow I might be such a fool.
330 But I kept thinking how to win the game:
death sat there huge; how could we slip away?
I drew on all my wits, and ran through tactics,
reasoning as a man will for dear life,
until a trick came—and it pleased me well.
335 The Cyclops' rams were handsome, fat, with heavy
fleeces, a dark violet.  Ⓜ

Three abreast

I tied them silently together, twining
cords of willow from the ogre's bed;
then slung a man under each middle one
340 to ride there safely, shielded left and right.
So three sheep could convey each man. I took
the woolliest ram, the choicest of the flock,
and hung myself under his kinky belly,
pulled up tight, with fingers twisted deep
345 in sheepskin ringlets for an iron grip.
So, breathing hard, we waited until morning.

When Dawn spread out her finger tips of rose
the rams began to stir, moving for pasture,
and peals of bleating echoed round the pens
350 where dams with udders full called for a milking.
Blinded, and sick with pain from his head wound,
the master stroked each ram, then let it pass,
but my men riding on the pectoral fleece
the giant's blind hands blundering never found.
355 Last of them all my ram, the leader, came,
weighted by wool and me with my **meditations.**
The Cyclops patted him, and then he said:

'Sweet cousin ram, why lag behind the rest
in the night cave? You never linger so,
360 but graze before them all, and go afar
to crop sweet grass, and take your stately way
leading along the streams, until at evening
you run to be the first one in the fold.
Why, now, so far behind? Can you be grieving
365 over your Master's eye? That carrion rogue
and his accurst companions burnt it out
when he had conquered all my wits with wine.
Nohbdy will not get out alive, I swear.

327 **breach:** opening.

Ⓜ **EPIC HERO**
Notice Odysseus' great mental struggle in lines 330–336. As you read on, note the clever plan he has managed to come up with on the spot.

353 **pectoral fleece:** the wool covering a sheep's chest.

meditation (mĕd'ĭ-tā'shən) *n.* the act of being in serious, reflective thought

This 1910 color print depicts Odysseus taunting Polyphemus as he and his men make their escape.

Detail of *Odysseus and Polyphem* (1910), after L. du Bois-Reymond. Color print. From *Sagen des klasseschen Altertums* by Karl Becker, Berlin. © akg-images.

Oh, had you brain and voice to tell
370 where he may be now, dodging all my fury!
Bashed by this hand and bashed on this rock wall
his brains would strew the floor, and I should have
rest from the outrage Nohbdy worked upon me.'

He sent us into the open, then. Close by,
375 I dropped and rolled clear of the ram's belly,
going this way and that to untie the men.
With many glances back, we rounded up
his fat, stiff-legged sheep to take aboard,
and drove them down to where the good ship lay. **N**
380 We saw, as we came near, our fellows' faces
shining; then we saw them turn to grief
tallying those who had not fled from death.
I hushed them, jerking head and eyebrows up,
and in a low voice told them: 'Load this herd;
385 move fast, and put the ship's head toward the breakers.'
They all pitched in at loading, then embarked
and struck their oars into the sea. Far out,
as far off shore as shouted words would carry,
I sent a few back to the **adversary:**

390 'O Cyclops! Would you feast on my companions?
Puny, am I, in a Caveman's hands?
How do you like the beating that we gave you,
you damned cannibal? Eater of guests
under your roof! Zeus and the gods have paid you!'

395 The blind thing in his doubled fury broke
a hilltop in his hands and heaved it after us.
Ahead of our black prow it struck and sank
whelmed in a spuming geyser, a giant wave
that washed the ship stern foremost back to shore.
400 I got the longest boathook out and stood
fending us off, with furious nods to all
to put their backs into a racing stroke—
row, row, or perish. So the long oars bent
kicking the foam sternward, making head
405 until we drew away, and twice as far.
Now when I cupped my hands I heard the crew
in low voices protesting:

'Godsake, Captain!
Why bait the beast again? Let him alone!'

N EPIC HERO
What **character traits** has Odysseus demonstrated in his dealings with Polyphemus?

385 put . . . the breakers: turn the ship around so that it is heading toward the open sea.

adversary (ăd'vər-sĕr'ē)
n. an opponent; enemy

390–394 Odysseus assumes that the gods are on his side.

395–403 The hilltop thrown by Polyphemus lands in front of the ship, causing a huge wave that carries the ship back to the shore. Odysseus uses a long pole to push the boat away from the land.

406 cupped my hands: put his hands on either side of his mouth in order to magnify his voice.

'That tidal wave he made on the first throw
410 all but beached us.'

'All but stove us in!'

'Give him our bearing with your trumpeting,
he'll get the range and lob a boulder.'

'Aye

He'll smash our timbers and our heads together!'

I would not heed them in my glorying spirit,
415 but let my anger flare and yelled:

'Cyclops,

if ever mortal man inquire
how you were put to shame and blinded, tell him
Odysseus, raider of cities, took your eye:
Laertes' son, whose home's on Ithaca!' ◉

420 At this he gave a mighty sob and rumbled:

'Now comes the weird upon me, spoken of old.
A wizard, grand and wondrous, lived here—Telemus,
a son of Eurymus; great length of days
he had in wizardry among the Cyclopes,
425 and these things he foretold for time to come:
my great eye lost, and at Odysseus' hands.
Always I had in mind some giant, armed
in giant force, would come against me here.
But this, but you—small, pitiful and twiggy—
430 you put me down with wine, you blinded me.
Come back, Odysseus, and I'll treat you well,
praying the god of earthquake to befriend you—
his son I am, for he by his avowal
fathered me, and, if he will, he may
435 heal me of this black wound—he and no other
of all the happy gods or mortal men.'

Few words I shouted in reply to him:
'If I could take your life I would and take
your time away, and hurl you down to hell!
440 The god of earthquake could not heal you there!'

At this he stretched his hands out in his darkness
toward the sky of stars, and prayed Poseidon:

◉ EPITHET
Notice that Odysseus uses the warlike **epithet** "raider of cities" in his second boast to the Cyclops. What **trait** does he display in revealing so much about himself?

421 Now comes . . . of old: Now I recall the destiny predicted long ago.

421–430 Now comes . . . you blinded me: Polyphemus tells of a prophecy made long ago by Telemus, a prophet who predicted that Polyphemus would lose his eye at the hands of Odysseus. *How have the actual events turned out differently from what Polyphemus expected?*

432 the god of earthquake: Poseidon.
433 avowal: honest admission.

'O hear me, lord, blue girdler of the islands,
if I am thine indeed, and thou art father:

445 grant that Odysseus, raider of cities, never
see his home: Laertes' son, I mean,
who kept his hall on Ithaca. Should destiny
intend that he shall see his roof again
among his family in his father land,

450 far be that day, and dark the years between.
Let him lose all companions, and return
under strange sail to bitter days at home.' ⓟ

In these words he prayed, and the god heard him.
Now he laid hands upon a bigger stone

455 and wheeled around, titanic for the cast,
to let it fly in the black-prowed vessel's track.
But it fell short, just aft the steering oar,
and whelming seas rose giant above the stone
to bear us onward toward the island.

There

460 as we ran in we saw the squadron waiting,
the trim ships drawn up side by side, and all
our troubled friends who waited, looking seaward.
We beached her, grinding keel in the soft sand,
and waded in, ourselves, on the sandy beach.

465 Then we unloaded all the Cyclops' flock
to make division, share and share alike,
only my fighters voted that my ram,
the prize of all, should go to me. I slew him
by the sea side and burnt his long thighbones

470 to Zeus beyond the stormcloud, Cronus' son,
who rules the world. But Zeus disdained my offering;
destruction for my ships he had in store
and death for those who sailed them, my companions.

Now all day long until the sun went down

475 we made our feast on mutton and sweet wine,
till after sunset in the gathering dark
we went to sleep above the wash of ripples.

When the young Dawn with finger tips of rose
touched the world, I roused the men, gave orders

480 to man the ships, cast off the mooring lines;
and filing in to sit beside the rowlocks
oarsmen in line dipped oars in the gray sea.
So we moved out, sad in the vast offing,
having our precious lives, but not our friends."

ⓟ **EPIC HERO**
Reread lines 437–452. Paraphrase
Polyphemus' curse. How has
Odysseus brought this curse upon
himself?

455 titanic for the cast: drawing on all his
enormous strength in preparing to throw.

457 aft: behind.

459 the island: the deserted island where
most of Odysseus' men had stayed behind.

470 Cronus' son: Zeus' father, Cronus,
was a Titan, one of an earlier race of gods.

483 offing: the part of the deep sea
visible from the shore.

BOOK 10:
Circe, the Grace of the Witch

Detail of *Tilla Durieux as Circe* (about 1912–1913), Franz von Struck. Oil on paper, 53.5 cm × 46.5 cm. Private collection. Photo © akg-images.

Odysseus and his men next land on the island of Aeolus, the wind king, and stay with him a month. To extend his hospitality, Aeolus gives Odysseus two parting gifts: a fair west wind that will blow the fleet of ships toward Ithaca, and a great bag holding all the unfavorable, stormy winds. Within sight of home, and while Odysseus is sleeping, the men open the bag, thinking it contains gold and silver. The bad winds thus escape and blow the ships back to Aeolus' island. The king refuses to help them again, believing now that their voyage has been cursed by the gods.

The discouraged mariners next stop briefly in the land of the Laestrygones, fierce cannibals who bombard the fleet of ships with boulders. Only Odysseus, his ship, and its crew of 45 survive the shower of boulders. The lone ship then sails to Aeaea, home of the goddess Circe, who is considered by many to be a witch. There, Odysseus divides his men into two groups. Eurylochus leads one platoon to explore the island, while Odysseus stays behind on the ship with the remaining crew.

"In the wild wood they found an open glade,
around a smooth stone house—the hall of Circe—
and wolves and mountain lions lay there, mild
in her soft spell, fed on her drug of evil.
5 None would attack—oh, it was strange, I tell you—
but switching their long tails they faced our men
like hounds, who look up when their master comes
with tidbits for them—as he will—from table.
Humbly those wolves and lions with mighty paws
10 fawned on our men—who met their yellow eyes
and feared them. ●

In the entrance way they stayed
to listen there: inside her quiet house
they heard the goddess Circe.

Low she sang

in her **beguiling** voice, while on her loom
15 she wove ambrosial fabric sheer and bright,

10 fawned on: showed affection for.

● **EPIC SIMILE**
In lines 6–11, notice the simile involving Circe's wolves and mountain lions. What is the point of this comparison? How does it affect your impression of Circe's hall?

beguiling (bǐ-gī′lǐng) *adj.* charming; pleasing **beguile** *v.*

15 ambrosial: fit for the gods.

by that craft known to the goddesses of heaven.
No one would speak, until Polites—most
faithful and likable of my officers, said:

17 **Polites** (pə-lī'tēz).

'Dear friends, no need for stealth: here's a young weaver
20 singing a pretty song to set the air
a-tingle on these lawns and paven courts.
Goddess she is, or lady. Shall we greet her?'

So reassured, they all cried out together,
and she came swiftly to the shining doors
25 to call them in. All but Eurylochus—
who feared a snare—the innocents went after her.
On thrones she seated them, and lounging chairs,
while she prepared a meal of cheese and barley
and amber honey mixed with Pramnian wine,
30 adding her own vile pinch, to make them lose
desire or thought of our dear father land.
Scarce had they drunk when she flew after them
with her long stick and shut them in a pigsty—
bodies, voices, heads, and bristles, all
35 swinish now, though minds were still unchanged.
So, squealing, in they went. And Circe tossed them
acorns, mast, and cornel berries—fodder
for hogs who rut and slumber on the earth.

23–26 If you were among this group, whom would you follow—Polites or Eurylochus? Why?

27–36 What happens to the men after they drink Circe's magic potion?

Down to the ship Eurylochus came running
40 to cry alarm, foul magic doomed his men!
But working with dry lips to speak a word
he could not, being so shaken; blinding tears
welled in his eyes; **foreboding** filled his heart.
When we were frantic questioning him, at last
45 we heard the tale: our friends were gone. . . ."

foreboding (fôr-bō'dĭng) *n.* a sense of approaching evil

Eurylochus tells Odysseus what has happened and begs him to sail away from Circe's island. Against this advice, however, Odysseus rushes to save his men from the enchantress. On the way, he meets the god Hermes, who gives him a magical plant called moly to protect him from Circe's power. Still, Hermes warns Odysseus that he must make the goddess swear she will play no "witches' tricks." Armed with the moly and Hermes' warning, Odysseus arrives at Circe's palace.

Circe gives Odysseus a magic drink, but it does not affect him and he threatens to kill her with his sword. Circe turns the pigs back into men but puts them all into a trance. They stay for one year, until Odysseus finally begs her to let them go home. She replies that they must first visit the land of the dead and hear a prophecy from the ghost of Tiresias.

BOOK 11:
The Land of the Dead

*Odysseus and his crew set out for the land of the dead. They arrive
and find the place to which Circe has directed them.*

"Then I addressed the blurred and breathless dead,
vowing to slaughter my best heifer for them
before she calved, at home in Ithaca,
and burn the choice bits on the altar fire;
5   as for Tiresias, I swore to sacrifice
a black lamb, handsomest of all our flock.
Thus to **assuage** the nations of the dead
I pledged these rites, then slashed the lamb and ewe,
letting their black blood stream into the wellpit.
10 Now the souls gathered, stirring out of Erebus,
brides and young men, and men grown old in pain,
and tender girls whose hearts were new to grief;
many were there, too, torn by brazen lanceheads,
battle-slain, bearing still their bloody gear.
15 From every side they came and sought the pit
with rustling cries; and I grew sick with fear.
But presently I gave command to my officers
to flay those sheep the bronze cut down, and make
burnt offerings of flesh to the gods below—
20 to sovereign Death, to pale Persephone. ®
Meanwhile I crouched with my drawn sword to keep
the surging phantoms from the bloody pit
till I should know the presence of Tiresias.

One shade came first—Elpenor, of our company,
25 who lay unburied still on the wide earth
as we had left him—dead in Circe's hall,
untouched, unmourned, when other cares compelled us.
Now when I saw him there I wept for pity
and called out to him:

assuage (ə-swāj′) *v.* to calm or pacify

10 Erebus (ĕr′ə-bəs): a region of the land of the dead, also known as the underworld or Hades. Hades is also the name of the god of the underworld.

18 flay: to strip off the outer skin of.

® ALLUSION
In lines 17–20, Odysseus makes a sacrifice to "sovereign Death," or Hades, and "pale Persephone" (pər-sĕf′ə-nē), his bride, who was kidnapped and forced to live with him for six months of every year. Her mother, goddess of the harvest, grieves during that time, causing winter to fall. What does this background information tell you about Hades? Consider how this information affects your impression of the underworld.

Ulysses Descending into the Underworld (16th century), Giovanni Stradano. Fresco. Palazzo Vecchio, Florence.
Photo © Scala/Art Resource, New York.

                         'How is this, Elpenor,

30 how could you journey to the western gloom
    swifter afoot than I in the black lugger?'

    He sighed, and answered:

                           'Son of great Laertes,
    Odysseus, master mariner and soldier,
    bad luck shadowed me, and no kindly power;
35 ignoble death I drank with so much wine.
    I slept on Circe's roof, then could not see
    the long steep backward ladder, coming down,
    and fell that height. My neck bone, buckled under,
    snapped, and my spirit found this well of dark.
40 Now hear the grace I pray for, in the name
    of those back in the world, not here—your wife
    and father, he who gave you bread in childhood,
    and your own child, your only son, Telemachus,
    long ago left at home.

ANALYZE VISUALS
This 16th-century painting illustrates the descent of Ulysses (Odysseus) into the underworld. How has the artist distinguished between Ulysses and the dead, also known as shades?

When you make sail

45 and put these lodgings of dim Death behind,
    you will moor ship, I know, upon Aeaea Island;
    there, O my lord, remember me, I pray,
    do not abandon me unwept, unburied,
    to tempt the gods' wrath, while you sail for home;
50 but fire my corpse, and all the gear I had,
    and build a cairn for me above the breakers—
    an unknown sailor's mark for men to come.
    Heap up the mound there, and implant upon it
    the oar I pulled in life with my companions.'

50–51 fire my corpse ... cairn: Elpenor wants Odysseus to hold a funeral for him.

55 He ceased, and I replied:

'Unhappy spirit,

    I promise you the barrow and the burial.'

So we conversed, and grimly, at a distance,
    with my long sword between, guarding the blood,
    while the faint image of the lad spoke on.
60 Now came the soul of Anticlea, dead,
    my mother, daughter of Autolycus,
    dead now, though living still when I took ship
    for holy Troy. Seeing this ghost I grieved,
    but held her off, through pang on pang of tears,
65 till I should know the presence of Tiresias.
    Soon from the dark that prince of Thebes came forward
    bearing a golden staff; and he addressed me:

58 with my long sword ... blood: the ghosts are attracted to the blood of the sacrifice; Odysseus must hold them at bay with his sword.

    'Son of Laertes and the gods of old,
    Odysseus, master of land ways and sea ways,
70 why leave the blazing sun, O man of woe,
    to see the cold dead and the joyless region?
    Stand clear, put up your sword;
    let me but taste of blood, I shall speak true.'

66 prince of Thebes: Tiresias, the blind seer, comes from the city of Thebes (thēbz).

At this I stepped aside, and in the scabbard
75 let my long sword ring home to the pommel silver,
    as he bent down to the sombre blood. Then spoke
    the prince of those with gift of speech:

'Great captain,

    a fair wind and the honey lights of home
    are all you seek. But anguish lies ahead;
80 the god who thunders on the land prepares it,
    not to be shaken from your track, implacable,

in rancor for the son whose eye you blinded.
One narrow strait may take you through his blows:
denial of yourself, restraint of shipmates.
85 When you make landfall on Thrinacia first
and quit the violet sea, dark on the land
you'll find the grazing herds of Helios
by whom all things are seen, all speech is known.
Avoid those kine, hold fast to your intent,
90 and hard seafaring brings you all to Ithaca.
But if you raid the beeves, I see destruction
for ship and crew. Though you survive alone,
bereft of all companions, lost for years,
under strange sail shall you come home, to find
95 your own house filled with trouble: insolent men
eating your livestock as they court your lady.
Aye, you shall make those men atone in blood!
But after you have dealt out death—in open
combat or by stealth—to all the suitors,
100 go overland on foot, and take an oar,
until one day you come where men have lived
with meat unsalted, never known the sea,
nor seen seagoing ships, with crimson bows
and oars that fledge light hulls for dipping flight.
105 The spot will soon be plain to you, and I
can tell you how: some passerby will say,
"What winnowing fan is that upon your shoulder?"
Halt, and implant your smooth oar in the turf
and make fair sacrifice to Lord Poseidon:
110 a ram, a bull, a great buck boar; turn back,
and carry out pure hekatombs at home
to all wide heaven's lords, the undying gods,
to each in order. Then a seaborne death
soft as this hand of mist will come upon you
115 when you are wearied out with rich old age,
your country folk in blessed peace around you.
And all this shall be just as I foretell.' . . ." **⑤**

*Odysseus speaks to the shade of his mother. She tells him that Penelope and
Telemachus are still grieving for him and that his father, Laertes, has moved
to the country, where he, too, mourns his son. Odysseus' mother explains that
she died from a broken heart. Odysseus also speaks with the spirits of many
great ladies and men who died, as well as those who were being punished
for their earthly sins. Filled with horror, Odysseus and his crew set sail.*

89–91 kine; beeves: two words for cattle.

101–102 where men have lived with meat unsalted: refers to an inland location where men do not eat salted (preserved) meat as sailors do aboard a ship.

⑤ EPIC HERO
An epic hero's fate is often a matter of great importance to the gods and to the hero's homeland. In lines 77–117, Odysseus' fate is the subject of a prophecy by Tiresias, a blind seer who now dwells among the dead. A prophecy such as this can serve as **foreshadowing** in an epic or other story. Do you think that Odysseus' fate will unfold exactly as Tiresias foretells it? Explain why you think as you do.

BOOK 12:
The Sirens; Scylla and Charybdis

Odysseus and his men return to Circe's island. While the men sleep, Circe takes Odysseus aside to hear about the underworld and to offer advice.

           "Then said the Lady Circe:
'So: all those trials are over.
               Listen with care
to this, now, and a god will arm your mind.
Square in your ship's path are Sirens, crying
5 beauty to bewitch men coasting by;
woe to the innocent who hears that sound!
He will not see his lady nor his children
in joy, crowding about him, home from sea;
the Sirens will sing his mind away
10 on their sweet meadow lolling. There are bones
of dead men rotting in a pile beside them
and flayed skins shrivel around the spot.

               Steer wide;
keep well to seaward; plug your oarsmen's ears
with beeswax kneaded soft; none of the rest
15 should hear that song.

               But if you wish to listen,
let the men tie you in the lugger, hand
and foot, back to the mast, lashed to the mast,
so you may hear those harpies' thrilling voices;
shout as you will, begging to be untied,
20 your crew must only twist more line around you
and keep their stroke up, till the singers fade.
What then? One of two courses you may take,
and you yourself must weigh them. I shall not
plan the whole action for you now, but only
25 tell you of both.

ANALYZE VISUALS
This detail from a 19th-century painting shows Odysseus tied to the mast of his ship to protect him from the Sirens' tempting song. Notice that his men have all covered their ears. How does the artist's depiction of the Sirens affect your understanding of the story? Explain.

2–3 In Circe, Odysseus has found a valuable ally. In the next hundred lines, she describes in detail each danger that he and his men will meet on their way home.

14 kneaded (nē′dĭd): squeezed and pressed.

18 those harpies' thrilling voices: the delightful voices of those horrible female creatures.

Detail of *Ulysses and the Sirens* (1891), John William Waterhouse. Oil on canvas, 100 cm × 201.7 cm. National Gallery of Victoria, Melbourne, Australia. Photo © Bridgeman Art Library.

Ahead are beetling rocks
and dark blue glancing Amphitrite, surging,
roars around them. Prowling Rocks, or Drifters,
the gods in bliss have named them—named them well.
Not even birds can pass them by. . . .

30   A second course
lies between headlands. One is a sharp mountain
piercing the sky, with stormcloud round the peak
dissolving never, not in the brightest summer,
to show heaven's azure there, nor in the fall.
35 No mortal man could scale it, nor so much
as land there, not with twenty hands and feet,
so sheer the cliffs are—as of polished stone.
Midway that height, a cavern full of mist
opens toward Erebus and evening. Skirting
40 this in the lugger, great Odysseus,
your master bowman, shooting from the deck,
would come short of the cavemouth with his shaft;
but that is the den of Scylla, where she yaps
abominably, a newborn whelp's cry,
45 though she is huge and monstrous. God or man,
no one could look on her in joy. Her legs—
and there are twelve—are like great tentacles,
unjointed, and upon her serpent necks
are borne six heads like nightmares of ferocity,
50 with triple serried rows of fangs and deep
gullets of black death. Half her length, she sways
her heads in air, outside her horrid cleft,
hunting the sea around that promontory
for dolphins, dogfish, or what bigger game
55 thundering Amphitrite feeds in thousands.
And no ship's company can claim
to have passed her without loss and grief; she takes,
from every ship, one man for every gullet.

The opposite point seems more a tongue of land
60 you'd touch with a good bowshot, at the narrows.
A great wild fig, a shaggy mass of leaves,
grows on it, and Charybdis lurks below
to swallow down the dark sea tide. Three times
from dawn to dusk she spews it up
65 and sucks it down again three times, a whirling
maelstrom; if you come upon her then
the god who makes earth tremble could not save you.

25 beetling: jutting or overhanging.

26 glancing Amphitrite (ăm′fĭ-trī′tē): sparkling seawater. (Amphitrite is the goddess of the sea and the wife of Poseidon. Here, Circe uses the name to refer to the sea itself.)

31 headlands: points of land jutting out into the sea; promontories.

34 heaven's azure (ăzh′ər): the blue sky.

abominably (ə-bŏm′ə-nə-blē) *adv.* in a hateful way; horribly

43–55 Circe presents a very unpleasant image of Scylla. *To get a better idea of what Odysseus and his crew will be up against, try using this detailed description to either visualize or draw a picture of Scylla.*

66 maelstrom (māl′strəm): a large, violent whirlpool.

No, hug the cliff of Scylla, take your ship
through on a racing stroke. Better to mourn
70 six men than lose them all, and the ship, too.'

So her advice ran; but I faced her, saying:

'Only instruct me, goddess, if you will,
how, if possible, can I pass Charybdis,
or fight off Scylla when she raids my crew?'

75 Swiftly that loveliest goddess answered me:

'Must you have battle in your heart forever?
The bloody toil of combat? Old contender,
will you not yield to the immortal gods?
That nightmare cannot die, being eternal
80 evil itself—horror, and pain, and chaos;
there is no fighting her, no power can fight her,
all that avails is flight.
                                Lose headway there
along that rockface while you break out arms,
and she'll swoop over you, I fear, once more,
85 taking one man again for every gullet. ❶
No, no, put all your backs into it, row on;
invoke Blind Force, that bore this scourge of men,
to keep her from a second strike against you.

Then you will coast Thrinacia, the island
90 where Helios' cattle graze, fine herds, and flocks
of goodly sheep. The herds and flocks are seven,
with fifty beasts in each.
                                No lambs are dropped,
or calves, and these fat cattle never die.
Immortal, too, their cowherds are—their shepherds—
95 Phaethusa and Lampetia, sweetly braided
nymphs that divine Neaera bore
to the overlord of high noon, Helios.
These nymphs their gentle mother bred and placed
upon Thrinacia, the distant land,
100 in care of flocks and cattle for their father.

Now give those kine a wide berth, keep your thoughts
intent upon your course for home,
and hard seafaring brings you all to Ithaca.
But if you raid the beeves, I see destruction
105 for ship and crew.

82 all . . . flight: all you can do is flee.

❶ EPIC HERO
Summarize the exchange between Odysseus and Circe in lines 68–85. What is Circe's advice to Odysseus? Do you think he will follow her advice? Explain.

87 invoke . . . men: pray to the goddess Blind Force, who gave birth to Scylla.

89 coast: sail along the coast of.

95–96 Phaethusa (fā'ə-thoo'sə); **Lampetia** (lăm-pē'shə); **Neaera** (nē-ē'rə).

101–105 Circe warns Odysseus not to steal Helios' fine cattle because Helios will take revenge.

Rough years then lie between
you and your homecoming, alone and old,
the one survivor, all companions lost.' . . ." **U**

*At dawn, Odysseus and his men continue their journey. Odysseus decides
to tell the men only of Circe's warnings about the Sirens, whom they will
soon encounter. He is fairly sure that they can survive this peril if he keeps
their spirits up. Suddenly, the wind stops.*

"The crew were on their feet
briskly, to furl the sail, and stow it; then,
110 each in place, they poised the smooth oar blades
and sent the white foam scudding by. I carved
a massive cake of beeswax into bits
and rolled them in my hands until they softened—
no long task, for a burning heat came down
115 from Helios, lord of high noon. Going forward
I carried wax along the line, and laid it
thick on their ears. They tied me up, then, plumb
amidships, back to the mast, lashed to the mast,
and took themselves again to rowing. Soon,
120 as we came smartly within hailing distance,
the two Sirens, noting our fast ship
off their point, made ready, and they sang. . . .

The lovely voices in **ardor** appealing over the water
made me crave to listen, and I tried to say
125 'Untie me!' to the crew, jerking my brows;
but they bent steady to the oars. Then Perimedes
got to his feet, he and Eurylochus,
and passed more line about, to hold me still.
So all rowed on, until the Sirens
130 dropped under the sea rim, and their singing
dwindled away.
                      My faithful company
rested on their oars now, peeling off
the wax that I had laid thick on their ears;
then set me free.
                      But scarcely had that island
135 faded in blue air than I saw smoke
and white water, with sound of waves in tumult—
a sound the men heard, and it terrified them.
Oars flew from their hands; the blades went knocking
wild alongside till the ship lost way,
140 with no oarblades to drive her through the water.

U EPIC HERO
Reread lines 104–107, and reconsider
your thoughts about Tiresias'
prophecy. Do you think Odysseus has
the power to steer his fate? Explain.

117–118 plumb amidships: exactly
in the center of the ship.

ardor (är′dər) *n.* passion

126 Perimedes (pĕr′ĭ-mē′dēz).

134–139 The men panic when they hear
the thundering surf.

Well, I walked up and down from bow to stern,
trying to put heart into them, standing over
every oarsman, saying gently,

                                     'Friends,
have we never been in danger before this?
145 More fearsome, is it now, than when the Cyclops
penned us in his cave? What power he had!
Did I not keep my nerve, and use my wits
to find a way out for us?

                                  Now I say
by hook or crook this peril too shall be
150 something that we remember.

                           Heads up, lads!
We must obey the orders as I give them.
Get the oarshafts in your hands, and lay back
hard on your benches; hit these breaking seas.
Zeus help us pull away before we founder.
155 You at the tiller, listen, and take in
all that I say—the rudders are your duty;
keep her out of the combers and the smoke;
steer for that headland; watch the drift, or we
fetch up in the smother, and you drown us.'

160 That was all, and it brought them round to action.
But as I sent them on toward Scylla, I
told them nothing, as they could do nothing.
They would have dropped their oars again, in panic,
to roll for cover under the decking. Circe's
165 bidding against arms had slipped my mind,
so I tied on my cuirass and took up
two heavy spears, then made my way along
to the foredeck—thinking to see her first from there,
the monster of the gray rock, harboring
170 torment for my friends. I strained my eyes
upon that cliffside veiled in cloud, but nowhere
could I catch sight of her.

                            And all this time,
in **travail,** sobbing, gaining on the current,
we rowed into the strait—Scylla to port
175 and on our starboard beam Charybdis, dire
gorge of the salt sea tide. By heaven! when she
vomited, all the sea was like a cauldron
seething over intense fire, when the mixture
suddenly heaves and rises. Ⓥ

154 founder: sink.

157 combers: breaking waves.

158–159 watch . . . smother: keep the ship on course, or it will be crushed in the rough water.

travail (trə-vāl´) *n.* painful effort

176 gorge: throat; gullet.

Ⓥ **EPIC HERO**
Consider Odysseus' behavior in lines 108–179. Do you think he is a good leader? Explain your opinion.

The shot spume
180 soared to the landside heights, and fell like rain.

But when she swallowed the sea water down
we saw the funnel of the maelstrom, heard
the rock bellowing all around, and dark
sand raged on the bottom far below.
185 My men all blanched against the gloom, our eyes
were fixed upon that yawning mouth in fear
of being devoured.
                            Then Scylla made her strike,
whisking six of my best men from the ship.
I happened to glance aft at ship and oarsmen
190 and caught sight of their arms and legs, dangling
high overhead. Voices came down to me
in anguish, calling my name for the last time.

A man surfcasting on a point of rock
for bass or mackerel, whipping his long rod
195 to drop the sinker and the bait far out,
will hook a fish and rip it from the surface
to dangle wriggling through the air:
                                            so these
were borne aloft in spasms toward the cliff.

She ate them as they shrieked there, in her den,
200 in the dire grapple, reaching still for me—
and deathly pity ran me through
at that sight—far the worst I ever suffered,
questing the passes of the strange sea.
                            We rowed on.

The Rocks were now behind; Charybdis, too,
205 and Scylla dropped astern. . . ."

*Odysseus tries to persuade his men to bypass Thrinacia, the island of the sun
god, Helios, but they insist on landing. Driven by hunger, they ignore Odysseus'
warning not to feast on Helios' cattle. This disobedience angers the sun god, who
threatens to stop shining if payment is not made for the loss of his cattle. To appease
Helios, Zeus sends down a thunderbolt to sink Odysseus' ship. Odysseus alone
survives. He eventually drifts to Ogygia, the home of Calypso, who keeps him
on her island for seven years. With this episode, Odysseus ends the telling of his
tale to King Alcinous.*

179 shot spume: flying foam.

185 blanched: became pale.

189 aft: toward the rear of the ship.

198 borne aloft in spasms: lifted
high while struggling violently.

200 grapple: grasp.

ANALYZE VISUALS
Apart from depicting a different
narrative moment, how does this
16th-century painting differ from
the one on page 1131? Be specific in
describing the differences in style
and mood.

Scylla and Charybdis from the *Ulysses Cycle* (1580), Alessandro Allori. Fresco. Banca
Toscana (Palazzo Salviati), Florence. Photo © Erich Lessing/Art Resource, New York.

Comprehension

1. **Recall** Why does Odysseus want to leave Calypso and her island?

2. **Recall** How does Odysseus escape from Polyphemus?

3. **Recall** What happens to Eurylochus' men after they drink Circe's wine?

4. **Recall** What does Tiresias predict will happen if Odysseus raids the herds of Helios?

5. **Summarize** How does Odysseus survive the dangers posed by the Sirens, Scylla, and Charybdis?

PENNSYLVANIA STANDARDS

READING STANDARD
B.1.1.1.A.1 Evaluate character

Literary Analysis

6. **Analyze Epic Hero** Create a two-column chart to analyze Odysseus' strengths and weaknesses. To what extent do the traits in each column seem fitting for an epic hero? Explain.

Strengths	Weaknesses
shows loyalty in his desire to reach home	pride

7. **Analyze Epithets** Identify at least five epithets used to describe Odysseus in Part 1. For each epithet, explain what it tells you about his **character.**

8. **Understand Character Motivation** After Odysseus escapes from Polyphemus, he makes sure that Polyphemus knows who outwitted him. Why does he care? What are the consequences of Odysseus' behavior?

9. **Interpret Epic Simile** Reread the epic simile on page 1136, lines 193–198, which describes the men being caught by Scylla. Explain what two items are being compared. What does the comparison help to emphasize?

10. **Interpret Allusions** In the opening lines of Book 1, the poet calls upon Muse, a daughter of Zeus often credited with inspiration. Why would he open the epic in this way? What does this allusion tell you about him as a poet?

11. **Examine Theme** One theme of the adventures described in Part 1 is that a hero must rely on clever deceit, or guile, to survive. Explain how this theme is conveyed. Can you identify any other themes in Part 1?

Literary Criticism

12. **Critical Interpretations** In discussing Homer's use of epic similes, the critic Eva Brann contends that "similes do much the same work in Homeric epic as do the gods, who also beautify and magnify human existence." Think about how the gods interact with humans in the *Odyssey.* Do you agree that they "beautify and magnify" human existence? Then consider the epic similes you have encountered so far; how might they be seen to do the same? Explain whether or not you think Brann is making a worthwhile comparison.

Vocabulary in Context

VOCABULARY PRACTICE

Decide whether the words in each pair are synonyms or antonyms.

1. harried/calmed
2. appalled/dismayed
3. profusion/shortage
4. ardor/indifference
5. assuage/soothe
6. adversary/friend
7. ponderous/awkward
8. travail/relaxation
9. beguiling/entrancing
10. foreboding/prediction
11. abominably/atrociously
12. meditation/contemplation

VOCABULARY IN WRITING

Write a paragraph describing one of the tricks Odysseus uses to escape from danger. Use four or more vocabulary words. Here is a sample beginning.

> **EXAMPLE SENTENCE**
>
> Odysseus had been warned about the Sirens' **beguiling** him.

VOCABULARY STRATEGY: WORDS WITH THE PREFIX *fore-*

The prefix *fore-*, which means "earlier," "in front of," or "beforehand," is used in forming numerous English words. In *foreboding*, it is combined with the verb *bode*, "to give signs of something." *Fore-* is also combined with many common words, as in *forehead* and *foretell*. Recognizing this prefix when it appears in words can help you determine their meanings.

PRACTICE Choose a word from the box to complete each sentence. Refer to a dictionary if you need help.

1. Our _____ came to this land looking for freedom.
2. Diandra tried to _____ Jack before he walked right into the trap.
3. In the _____ of the painting was a large house; behind the house was a barn.
4. Casual comments early in a story often _____ coming events.
5. The tennis star's strong _____ made her a formidable opponent.
6. To _____ a quick vote on the issue, the committee voted to study it further.
7. In what way was the horse and buggy the _____ of the automobile?

WORD LIST
abominably
adversary
appalled
ardor
assuage
beguiling
foreboding
harried
meditation
ponderous
profusion
travail

PENNSYLVANIA STANDARDS

READING STANDARD
A.1.2.1 Identify word meaning using affixes

WORDS WITH *fore-*
forefathers
foreground
forehand
forerunner
foreshadow
forestall
forewarn

VOCABULARY PRACTICE
For more practice, go to the **Vocabulary Center** at ClassZone.com.

The Homecoming
from the Odyssey

Epic Poem by Homer

Translated by Robert Fitzgerald

How does it feel to come HOME *again?*

PENNSYLVANIA STANDARDS

READING STANDARDS
A.1.5.1 Summarize the key details and events
B.1.1.1.D.2 Analyze and/or evaluate the relationship between the theme and other components

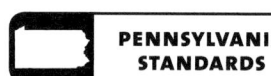

KEY IDEA If you spend enough time at any airport or bus station, you're bound to witness an emotional scene. A long-awaited **homecoming** can touch us more deeply than almost anything. Imagine a traveler who's been away for years, whose family thought he might never return. What kind of scene might you expect at his homecoming?

QUICKWRITE Recall a time when you or someone you know returned home after some time away. Write a brief description of the scene, and explain the emotions that went along with it.

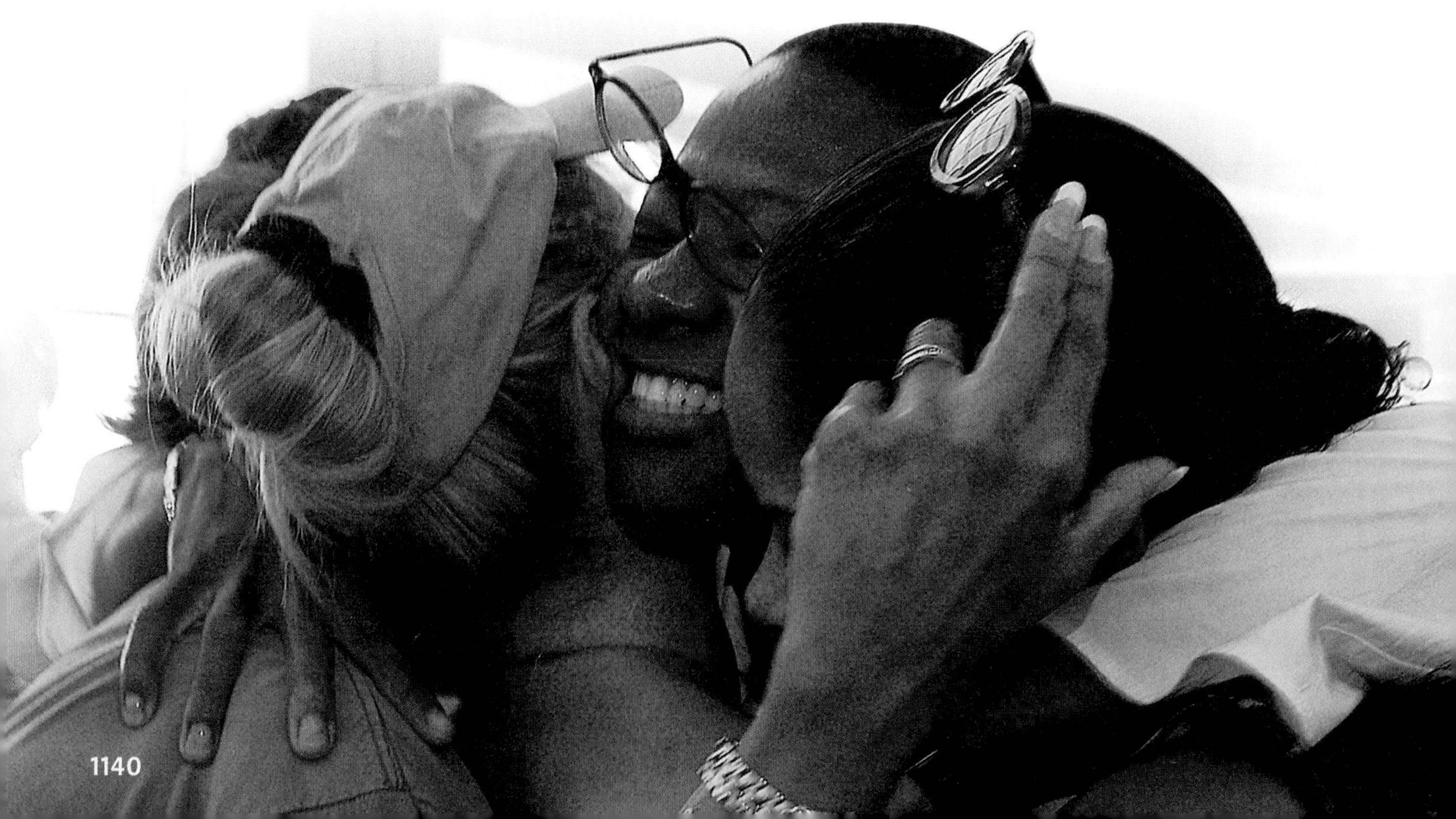

LITERARY ANALYSIS: CHARACTERISTICS OF AN EPIC

In the simplest terms, an epic is a long adventure story. An epic **plot** spans many years and involves a long journey. Often, the fate of an entire nation is at stake. An epic **setting** spans great distances and foreign lands. Epic **themes** reflect timeless concerns, such as courage, honor, life, and death.

Epics also contain **archetypes,** or patterns found in works across different cultures and time periods. As explained in Part 1, the epic hero is an archetype. So is the notion of a heroic journey. Other archetypes are also found in the *Odyssey*.

- intervention by gods
- descent into the underworld
- floods and storms
- heroic battles against monsters

As you read the second part of the *Odyssey*, look for these and other archetypes. Consider where else you might have encountered them in literature, art, or film.

READING STRATEGY: SUMMARIZING

Writing a **plot summary**—a brief retelling of a story—is a good way to make sure you're following the events of a narrative. An epic consists of many episodes, each with its own set of characters, conflicts, and resolution. As you read, record information that will help you summarize each episode.

Episode: Father and Son	
Characters: Odysseus, Eumaeus	**Setting**: Odysseus' homeland of Ithaca
Conflict:	**Resolution**:

▲ VOCABULARY IN CONTEXT

Replace the words in bold with synonyms from the word list.

WORD LIST	adversity	desolation	revulsion
	aloof	implacable	tremulous
	commandeer	restitution	
	contemptible	revelry	

1. It's **disgusting** to be **shaky** in the face of **hardship.**
2. He felt an **unforgiving hatred** for his captors.
3. Don't act **distant**; forget **sorrow** and join the **celebration!**
4. He could **seize** enemy ships as **repayment** for wrongs.

Overview

Book 16: Father and Son Sent safely on his way by King Alcinous, Odysseus reaches Ithaca. The goddess Athena disguises him as an old man so that he may surprise the evil suitors who are courting his wife, Penelope. Odysseus greets Eumaeus, his faithful swineherd, and Telemachus, his own son, returned home after many years abroad.

Book 17: The Beggar and the Manor Disguised as a beggar, Odysseus returns to his home.

Book 21: The Test of the Bow Not recognizing the beggar as her husband, and weary from grief and waiting, Penelope proposes an archery contest to the suitors, with marriage to her as the prize. Still disguised as an old man, Odysseus beats them all in the contest.

Book 22: Death in the Great Hall With Telemachus and Eumaeus at his side, Odysseus sheds his disguise and does battle with the suitors, showing them no mercy.

Book 23: The Trunk of the Olive Tree Hardened by years of waiting, Penelope is not convinced that this man is really her husband. She tests him, playing a trick that only Odysseus would recognize. Odysseus passes the test, and husband and wife are reunited.

Penelope weaving at her loom.

BOOK 16:
Father and Son

In Books 13–15, King Alcinous and his friends send Odysseus on his way home. Odysseus sleeps while the rowers bring him to Ithaca. When he awakens, he fails to recognize his homeland until Athena appears and tells him that he is indeed home. She disguises him as an old man, so that he can surprise the suitors, and then urges him to visit his faithful swineherd, Eumaeus. The swineherd welcomes the disguised Odysseus and tells him about what has been happening in Odysseus' home. Athena goes to Telemachus and tells him to return home. She warns him of the suitors' plot to kill him and advises him to stay with the swineherd for a night. Telemachus does as she bids.

But there were two men in the mountain hut—
Odysseus and the swineherd. At first light
blowing their fire up, they cooked their breakfast
and sent their lads out, driving herds to root
5 in the tall timber.

                     When Telemachus came,
the wolvish troop of watchdogs only fawned on him
as he advanced. Odysseus heard them go
and heard the light crunch of a man's footfall—
at which he turned quickly to say:

                              "Eumaeus,
10 here is one of your crew come back, or maybe
another friend: the dogs are out there snuffling
belly down; not one has even growled.
I can hear footsteps—"

                 But before he finished
his tall son stood at the door.

ANALYZE VISUALS
Review the information given in the summary at the top of this page. What do you think Marc Chagall wanted to capture in this painting?

Athene and Telemach, from *Odyssey II* (1975), Marc Chagall. Lithograph on Arches paper. 16.9″ × 13″. Photograph by George R. Staley. © 2007 Artists Rights Society (ARS), New York.

The swineherd

15 rose in surprise, letting a bowl and jug
   tumble from his fingers. Going forward,
   he kissed the young man's head, his shining eyes
   and both hands, while his own tears brimmed and fell.
   Think of a man whose dear and only son,
20 born to him in exile, reared with labor,
   has lived ten years abroad and now returns:
   how would that man embrace his son! Just so
   the herdsman clapped his arms around Telemachus **Ⓐ**
   and covered him with kisses—for he knew
25 the lad had got away from death. He said:

   "Light of my days, Telemachus,
   you made it back! When you took ship for Pylos
   I never thought to see you here again.
   Come in, dear child, and let me feast my eyes;
30 here you are, home from distant places! **Ⓑ**
   How rarely anyway, you visit us,
   your own men, and your own woods and pastures!
   Always in the town, a man would think
   you loved the suitors' company, those dogs!"

35 Telemachus with his clear candor said:

   "I am with you, Uncle. See now, I have come
   because I wanted to see you first, to hear from you
   if Mother stayed at home—or is she married
   off to someone and Odysseus' bed
40 left empty for some gloomy spider's weaving?"

   Gently the forester replied to this:

   "At home indeed your mother is, poor lady,
   still in the women's hall. Her nights and days
   are wearied out with grieving."

Stepping back

45 he took the bronze-shod lance, and the young prince
   entered the cabin over the worn door stone.
   Odysseus moved aside, yielding his couch,
   but from across the room Telemachus checked him:

   "Friend, sit down; we'll find another chair
50 in our own hut. Here is the man to make one!"

Ⓐ EPIC
Reread lines 19–23. What **theme** is being developed in this **epic simile**?

27 when you took ship for Pylos: Ten years earlier, Telemachus went to Pylos (pī′läs′) in search of knowledge about Odysseus' whereabouts.

Ⓑ EPIC
Reread lines 26–30. How do these lines indicate an epic **setting?**

The swineherd, when the quiet man sank down,
built a new pile of evergreens and fleeces—
a couch for the dear son of great Odysseus—
then gave them trenchers of good meat, left over
55 from the roast pork of yesterday, and heaped up
willow baskets full of bread, and mixed
an ivy bowl of honey-hearted wine.
Then he in turn sat down, facing Odysseus,
their hands went out upon the meat and drink
60 as they fell to, ridding themselves of hunger. . . .

Telemachus sends the swineherd to let his mother know he has returned safely.
Athena appears and urges Odysseus to let Telemachus know who he really is.

Saying no more,
she tipped her golden wand upon the man,
making his cloak pure white and the knit tunic
fresh around him. Lithe and young she made him,
65 ruddy with sun, his jawline clean, the beard
no longer grew upon his chin. And she
withdrew when she had done.

Detail of *Goddess Athena Disguises Ulysses as Beggar* (18th century), Giuseppe
Bottani. Civiche Racc d'Arte, Pavia, Italy. Photo © Dagli Orti /The Art Archive.

Then Lord Odysseus **C**
reappeared—and his son was thunderstruck.
Fear in his eyes, he looked down and away
70 as though it were a god, and whispered:

                                        "Stranger,

you are no longer what you were just now!
Your cloak is new; even your skin! You are
one of the gods who rule the sweep of heaven!
Be kind to us, we'll make you fair oblation
75 and gifts of hammered gold. Have mercy on us!"

The noble and enduring man replied:

"No god. Why take me for a god? No, no.
I am that father whom your boyhood lacked
and suffered pain for lack of. I am he."

80 Held back too long, the tears ran down his cheeks
as he embraced his son.

C EPIC
What supernatural event is
described in lines 61–67?

74 oblation: sacrifice

ANALYZE VISUALS
This detail of an ancient Roman
mosaic shows Odysseus (Ulysses)
and Telemachus. How does the
technique of clustering colored tiles
together affect the kind of image
that can be created? Be specific.

Ulysses and His Son Telemachus (A.D. first century). Mosaic.
Kunsthistorisches Museum, Vienna. © Erich Lessing/Art Resource, New York.

Only Telemachus,
uncomprehending, wild
with incredulity, cried out:

                              "You cannot
be my father Odysseus! Meddling spirits
85 conceived this trick to twist the knife in me!
    No man of woman born could work these wonders
    by his own craft, unless a god came into it
    with ease to turn him young or old at will.
    I swear you were in rags and old,
90 and here you stand like one of the immortals!" **D**

    Odysseus brought his ranging mind to bear
    and said:

                              "This is not princely, to be swept
    away by wonder at your father's presence.
    No other Odysseus will ever come,
95 for he and I are one, the same; his bitter
    fortune and his wanderings are mine.
    Twenty years gone, and I am back again
    on my own island. . . ."

                              Then, throwing
100 his arms around this marvel of a father
    Telemachus began to weep. Salt tears
    rose from the wells of longing in both men,
    and cries burst from both as keen and fluttering
    as those of the great taloned hawk,
105 whose nestlings farmers take before they fly.
    So helplessly they cried, pouring out tears,
    and might have gone on weeping so till sundown. . . . **E**

*Telemachus lets Odysseus know that they face more than 100 suitors. Odysseus
tells Telemachus to return home. He will follow—still disguised as an old man—
and Telemachus must pretend not to know him. He must also lock away
Odysseus' weapons and armor.*

D EPIC
Reread lines 61–90. What central
conflict is beginning to find
resolution in this scene? What
elements indicate the importance of
this moment?

91 brought his ranging mind to bear:
took control of his wandering thoughts.

E EPIC
Reread lines 99–107. What striking
character trait is emphasized in both
Odysseus and Telemachus? Why is
this unusual?

BOOK 17:
The Beggar at the Manor

Telemachus returns home, and Odysseus and the swineherd soon follow.
Odysseus is still diguised as a beggar.

ANALYZE VISUALS
This illustration of Odysseus and
his dog comes from the late 19th
or early 20th century. Compare it
with the scene depicted on the clay
urn shown on page 1093. What
elements do the two pieces have in
common?

                              While he spoke
an old hound, lying near, pricked up his ears
and lifted up his muzzle. This was Argos,
trained as a puppy by Odysseus,
5 but never taken on a hunt before
his master sailed for Troy. The young men, afterward,
hunted wild goats with him, and hare, and deer,
but he had grown old in his master's absence.
Treated as rubbish now, he lay at last
10 upon a mass of dung before the gates—
manure of mules and cows, piled there until
fieldhands could spread it on the king's estate.
Abandoned there, and half destroyed with flies,
old Argos lay.
                      But when he knew he heard
15 Odysseus' voice nearby, he did his best
to wag his tail, nose down, with flattened ears,
having no strength to move nearer his master.
And the man looked away,
wiping a salt tear from his cheek; but he
20 hid this from Eumaeus. Then he said:

"I marvel that they leave this hound to lie
here on the dung pile;
he would have been a fine dog, from the look of him,
though I can't say as to his power and speed
25 when he was young. You find the same good build
in house dogs, table dogs landowners keep
all for style."
                    And you replied, Eumaeus:

"A hunter owned him—but the man is dead
in some far place. If this old hound could show

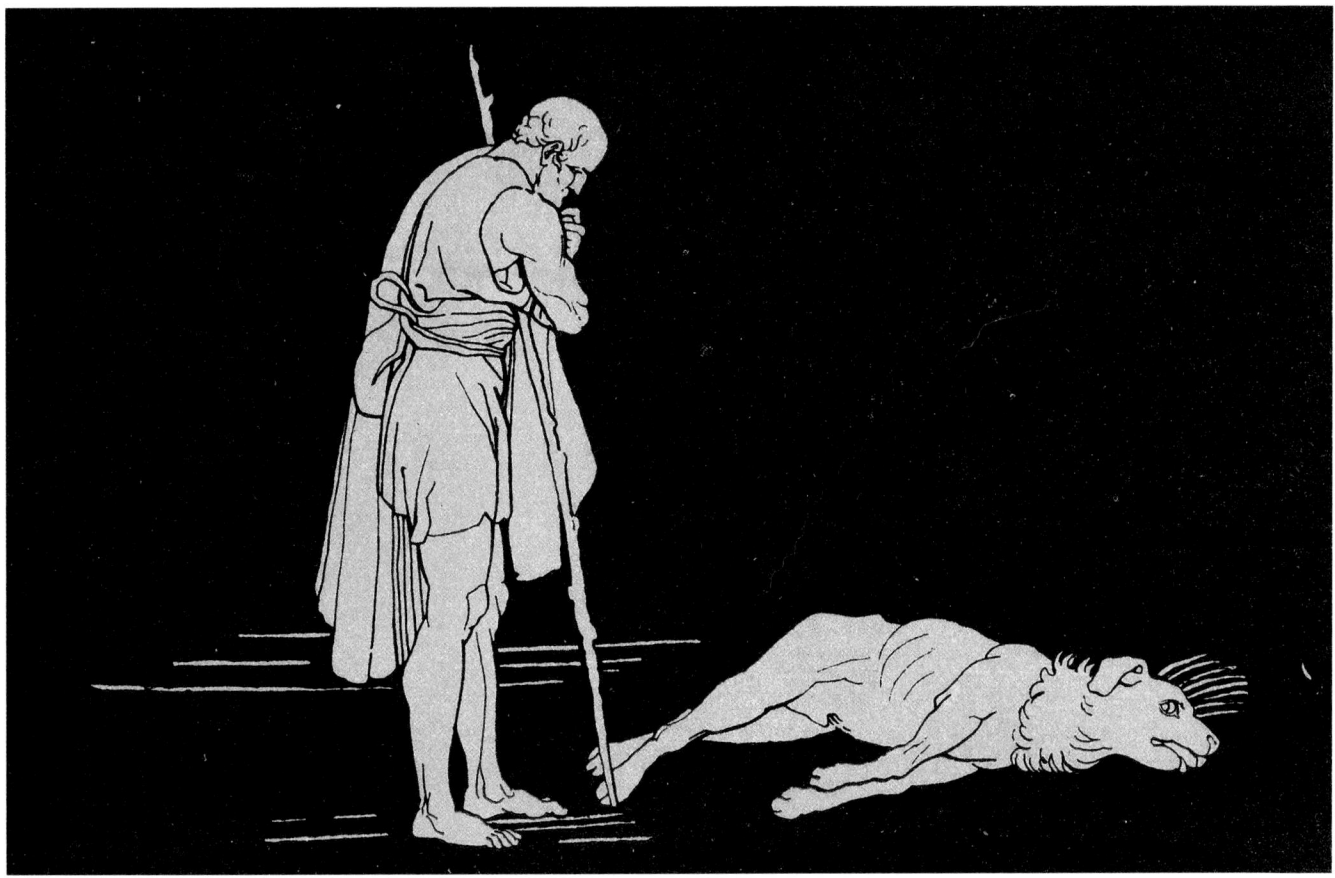

Ulysses and His Dog (about 1900). © Bettman/Corbis.

30 the form he had when Lord Odysseus left him,
    going to Troy, you'd see him swift and strong.
    He never shrank from any savage thing
    he'd brought to bay in the deep woods; on the scent
    no other dog kept up with him. Now misery
35 has him in leash. His owner died abroad,
    and here the women slaves will take no care of him.
    You know how servants are: without a master
    they have no will to labor, or excel.
    For Zeus who views the wide world takes away
40 half the manhood of a man, that day
    he goes into captivity and slavery." **F**

    Eumaeus crossed the court and went straight forward
    into the mégaron among the suitors;
    but death and darkness in that instant closed
45 the eyes of Argos, who had seen his master,
    Odysseus, after twenty years. . . .

Odysseus enters his home as a beggar, and the suitors mock and abuse him.
Penelope asks to speak with the beggar, but Odysseus puts her off until nightfall.

F EPIC
Reread lines 28–41. Eumaeus still does not know that he is speaking to Odysseus in disguise. This is known as **dramatic irony**—when the reader knows more than a character knows. What event does this speech cause you to anticipate?

43 mégaron: the main hall of a palace or house

BOOK 21:
The Test of the Bow

In Books 18–20, Odysseus observes the suitors and finds that two in particular, Antinous and Eurymachus, are rude and demanding. Penelope asks Odysseus the beggar for news of her husband. He says he has heard that Odysseus is on his way home. Penelope, however, has given up hope for Odysseus' return. She proposes an archery contest to the suitors, with marriage to her as the prize. She enters the storeroom and takes down the heavy bow that Odysseus left behind.

Now the queen reached the storeroom door and halted.
Here was an oaken sill, cut long ago
and sanded clean and bedded true. Foursquare
the doorjambs and the shining doors were set
5 by the careful builder. Penelope untied the strap
around the curving handle, pushed her hook
into the slit, aimed at the bolts inside
and shot them back. Then came a rasping sound
as those bright doors the key had sprung gave way—
10 a bellow like a bull's vaunt in a meadow— **G**
followed by her light footfall entering
over the plank floor. Herb-scented robes
lay there in chests, but the lady's milkwhite arms
went up to lift the bow down from a peg
15 in its own polished bowcase.

                           Now Penelope
sank down, holding the weapon on her knees,
and drew her husband's great bow out, and sobbed
and bit her lip and let the salt tears flow.
Then back she went to face the crowded hall,
20 tremendous bow in hand, and on her shoulder hung
the quiver spiked with coughing death. Behind her
maids bore a basket full of axeheads, bronze
and iron implements for the master's game.
Thus in her beauty she approached the suitors,
25 and near a pillar of the solid roof

ANALYZE VISUALS
This is a detail from an 18th-century portrait of Penelope. What qualities are emphasized in this portrait, and how do they compare with qualities emphasized in the text on this page? Explain.

G **ARCHETYPE**
Reread lines 8–10. What archetypal image do you recognize in these lines? Explain how this image helps to build **suspense.**

15–18 Notice that Penelope still grieves for Odysseus, even after 20 years.

21 quiver (kwĭv'ər): a case in which arrows are carried. *What is meant by "the quiver spiked with coughing death"?*

22–23 axeheads ... game: metal heads of axes (without handles) that Odysseus employs in a display of archery skill.

Detail of *Penelope Weeping Over the Bow of Ulysses* (about 1779), Angelica Kauffmann. Wolverhampton Art Gallery, Wolverhampton, United Kingdom (OP 531).

she paused, her shining veil across her cheeks,
her maids on either hand and still,
then spoke to the banqueters:

                              "My lords, hear me:
suitors indeed, you **commandeered** this house
30 to feast and drink in, day and night, my husband
being long gone, long out of mind. You found
no justification for yourselves—none
except your lust to marry me. Stand up, then:
we now declare a contest for that prize.
35 Here is my lord Odysseus' hunting bow.
Bend and string it if you can. Who sends an arrow
through iron axe-helve sockets, twelve in line?
I join my life with his, and leave this place, my home,
my rich and beautiful bridal house, forever
40 to be remembered, though I dream it only.". . .

Despite heating and greasing the bow, the lesser suitors prove unable to string it.
The most able suitors, Antinous and Eurymachus, hold off. While the suitors are
busy with the bow, Odysseus—still disguised as an old beggar—goes to enlist
the aid of two of his trusted servants, Eumaeus, the swineherd, and Philoetius,
the cowherd.

Two men had meanwhile left the hall:
swineherd and cowherd, in companionship,
one downcast as the other. But Odysseus
followed them outdoors, outside the court,
45 and coming up said gently:

                              "You, herdsman,
and you, too, swineherd, I could say a thing to you,
or should I keep it dark?
                              No, no; speak,
my heart tells me. Would you be men enough
to stand by Odysseus if he came back?
50 Suppose he dropped out of a clear sky, as I did?
Suppose some god should bring him?
Would you bear arms for him, or for the suitors?"

The cowherd said:

                              "Ah, let the master come!
Father Zeus, grant our old wish! Some courier
55 guide him back! Then judge what stuff is in me
and how I manage arms!"

commandeer (kŏm′ən-dîr′) *v.* to take
control of by force

35–37 Note that the contest has two
parts: first the suitor must bend the heavy
bow and string it—a task that requires
immense strength and skill—and then he
must shoot an arrow straight through the
holes in 12 axe heads set up in a row.

Likewise Eumaeus

fell to praying all heaven for his return,
so that Odysseus, sure at least of these,
told them:

"I am at home, for I am he.

60 I bore **adversities,** but in the twentieth year
I am ashore in my own land. I find
the two of you, alone among my people,
longed for my coming. Prayers I never heard
except your own that I might come again.
65 So now what is in store for you I'll tell you:
If Zeus brings down the suitors by my hand
I promise marriages to both, and cattle,
and houses built near mine. And you shall be
brothers-in-arms of my Telemachus. ⒣
70 Here, let me show you something else, a sign
that I am he, that you can trust me, look:
this old scar from the tusk wound that I got
boar hunting on Parnassus. . . ."

Shifting his rags

75 he bared the long gash. Both men looked, and knew,
and threw their arms around the old soldier, weeping,
kissing his head and shoulders. He as well
took each man's head and hands to kiss, then said—
to cut it short, else they might weep till dark—

80 "Break off, no more of this.
Anyone at the door could see and tell them.
Drift back in, but separately at intervals
after me.

Now listen to your orders:

when the time comes, those gentlemen, to a man,
85 will be dead against giving me bow or quiver.
Defy them. Eumaeus, bring the bow
and put it in my hands there at the door.
Tell the women to lock their own door tight.
Tell them if someone hears the shock of arms
90 or groans of men, in hall or court, not one
must show her face, but keep still at her weaving.
Philoetius, run to the outer gate and lock it.
Throw the cross bar and lash it.". . . ⒤

adversity (ăd-vûr′sĭ-tē) *n.* hardship; misfortune

⒣ **ARCHETYPE**
Identify the **trait** that Odysseus values so highly in these two servants. Where else in film or literature have you encountered these archetypal characters?

73 Parnassus (pär-năs′əs): a mountain in central Greece.

⒤ **EPIC**
Identify the **plot stage** in lines 84–93. What do you think is about to happen?

Odysseus the beggar asks the suitors if he might try the bow. Worried that the old man may show them up, they refuse, but Penelope urges them to let Odysseus try. At Telemachus' request, Penelope leaves the men to settle the question of the bow among themselves. Two trusted servants lock the doors of the room, and Telemachus orders the bow be given to Odysseus.

ANALYZE VISUALS
How does 20th-century-artist N. C. Wyeth show suspense in this detail from the painting *The Trial of the Bow?* Be specific.

And Odysseus took his time,
95 turning the bow, tapping it, every inch,
for borings that termites might have made
while the master of the weapon was abroad.
The suitors were now watching him, and some
jested among themselves:

"A bow lover!"

100 "Dealer in old bows!"

"Maybe he has one like it
at home!"

"Or has an itch to make one for himself."

"See how he handles it, the sly old buzzard!"

And one disdainful suitor added this:

"May his fortune grow an inch for every inch he bends it!" **J**

J EPIC
What is is the primary **conflict** in lines 94–104?

105 But the man skilled in all ways of contending,
satisfied by the great bow's look and heft,
like a musician, like a harper, when
with quiet hand upon his instrument
he draws between his thumb and forefinger

110 a sweet new string upon a peg: so effortlessly
Odysseus in one motion strung the bow.
Then slid his right hand down the cord and plucked it,
so the taut gut vibrating hummed and sang
a swallow's note.

                   In the hushed hall it smote the suitors
115 and all their faces changed. Then Zeus thundered
overhead, one loud crack for a sign.
And Odysseus laughed within him that the son
of crooked-minded Cronus had flung that omen down.
He picked one ready arrow from his table

120 where it lay bare: the rest were waiting still
in the quiver for the young men's turn to come.
He nocked it, let it rest across the handgrip,
and drew the string and grooved butt of the arrow,
aiming from where he sat upon the stool.

                           Now flashed
125 arrow from twanging bow clean as a whistle
through every socket ring, and grazed not one,
to thud with heavy brazen head beyond.

                      Then quietly
Odysseus said:

                 "Telemachus, the stranger
you welcomed in your hall has not disgraced you.
130 I did not miss, neither did I take all day
stringing the bow. My hand and eye are sound,
not so **contemptible** as the young men say.
The hour has come to cook their lordships' mutton—
supper by daylight. Other amusements later,
135 with song and harping that adorn a feast."

He dropped his eyes and nodded, and the prince
Telemachus, true son of King Odysseus,
belted his sword on, clapped hand to his spear,
and with a clink and glitter of keen bronze
140 stood by his chair, in the forefront near his father. **K**

---

106 heft: weight.

107–111 In this epic simile, Odysseus' stringing of the bow is compared to the stringing of a harp. *What qualities of Odysseus does this comparison emphasize?*

114 smote: struck; affected sharply.

115–116 The thunder, a sign from Zeus, indicates that the gods are on Odysseus' side.

118 Cronus (krō′nəs): Zeus' father.

122 nocked it: placed the arrow's feathered end against the bowstring.

127 brazen: made of brass.

contemptible (kən-tĕmp′tə-bəl) *adj.* deserving of scorn; despicable

K EPIC
Book 21 ends with the image of father and son standing side by side facing more than 100 enemies. How can this be considered an epic moment?

BOOK 22:
Death in the Great Hall

ANALYZE VISUALS
What stylistic elements of Wyeth's
The Slaughter of the Suitors
emphasize the conflict? Explain.

Now shrugging off his rags the wiliest fighter of the islands
leapt and stood on the broad door sill, his own bow in his hand.
He poured out at his feet a rain of arrows from the quiver 🅛
and spoke to the crowd:

  "So much for that. Your clean-cut game is over.
5 Now watch me hit a target that no man has hit before,
if I can make this shot. Help me, Apollo." 🅜

He drew to his fist the cruel head of an arrow for Antinous
just as the young man leaned to lift his beautiful drinking cup,
embossed, two-handled, golden: the cup was in his fingers:
10 the wine was even at his lips: and did he dream of death?
How could he? In that **revelry** amid his throng of friends
who would imagine a single foe—though a strong foe indeed—
could dare to bring death's pain on him and darkness on his
      eyes?
Odysseus' arrow hit him under the chin
15 and punched up to the feathers through his throat.

Backward and down he went, letting the winecup fall
from his shocked hand. Like pipes his nostrils jetted
crimson runnels, a river of mortal red,
and one last kick upset his table
20 knocking the bread and meat to soak in dusty blood.

Now as they craned to see their champion where he lay
the suitors jostled in uproar down the hall,
everyone on his feet. Wildly they turned and scanned
the walls in the long room for arms; but not a shield,
25 not a good ashen spear was there for a man to take and throw.
All they could do was yell in outrage at Odysseus:

🅛 GRAMMAR AND STYLE
Identify the **metaphor** in line 3.
What does this detail add to the
description of Odysseus as a warrior?

🅜 EPIC
Note that Odysseus calls upon the
help of the god Apollo, who was,
among other things, the supporter
and protector of archers. The bow
was his sacred weapon.

revelry (rĕv′əl-rē) *n.* noisy
merrymaking; festivity

18 **runnels:** streams.

7–20 *Why does Odysseus kill Antinous
first? Why does he do it in such a sudden,
terrible way?*

23–25 Earlier, in preparation for this
confrontation, Odysseus and Telemachus
removed all the weapons and shields
that were hanging on the walls.

The Slaughter of the Suitors (1929), N. C. Wyeth. Illustration from *The Odyssey of Homer,*
translated by George Herbert Palmer. © 1929 by Houghton Mifflin Company.

"Foul! to shoot at a man! That was your last shot!"

"Your own throat will be slit for this!"

"Our finest lad is down!
You killed the best on Ithaca."

"Buzzards will tear your eyes out!"

30 For they imagined as they wished—that it was a wild shot,
an unintended killing—fools, not to comprehend
they were already in the grip of death.
But glaring under his brows Odysseus answered:

"You yellow dogs, you thought I'd never make it
35 home from the land of Troy. You took my house to plunder,
twisted my maids to serve your beds. You dared
bid for my wife while I was still alive.
Contempt was all you had for the gods who rule wide heaven,
contempt for what men say of you hereafter.
40 Your last hour has come. You die in blood." **N**

As they all took this in, sickly green fear
pulled at their entrails, and their eyes flickered
looking for some hatch or hideaway from death.
Eurymachus alone could speak. He said:

45 "If you are Odysseus of Ithaca come back,
all that you say these men have done is true.
Rash actions, many here, more in the countryside.
But here he lies, the man who caused them all.
Antinous was the ringleader; he whipped us on
50 to do these things. He cared less for a marriage
than for the power Cronion has denied him
as king of Ithaca. For that
he tried to trap your son and would have killed him.
He is dead now and has his portion. Spare
55 your own people. As for ourselves, we'll make
restitution of wine and meat consumed,
and add, each one, a tithe of twenty oxen
with gifts of bronze and gold to warm your heart.
Meanwhile we cannot blame you for your anger." **O**

60 Odysseus glowered under his black brows
and said:

N EPIC
Paraphrase Odysseus' speech in lines
34–40. What reasons does he give
for killing the suitors?

42 entrails: internal organs.

47 rash: foolish; thoughtless.

51 Cronion (krō'nē-ŏn'): Zeus, the son
of Cronus.

restitution (rĕs'tĭ-tōo'shən) *n.* a
making good for loss or damage;
repayment
57 tithe: payment.

O EPIC
What is Eurymachus' **motivation** in
lines 45–59? What is his strategy
for achieving his goal?

"Not for the whole treasure of your fathers,
all you enjoy, lands, flocks, or any gold
put up by others, would I hold my hand.
There will be killing till the score is paid.
65 You forced yourselves upon this house. Fight your way out,
or run for it, if you think you'll escape death.
I doubt one man of you skins by."

They felt their knees fail, and their hearts—but heard
Eurymachus for the last time rallying them.

70 "Friends," he said, "the man is **implacable.**
Now that he's got his hands on bow and quiver
he'll shoot from the big door stone there
until he kills us to the last man.

                                          Fight, I say,
let's remember the joy of it. Swords out!
75 Hold up your tables to deflect his arrows.
After me, everyone: rush him where he stands.
If we can budge him from the door, if we can pass
into the town, we'll call out men to chase him.
This fellow with his bow will shoot no more."

80 He drew his own sword as he spoke, a broadsword of fine
      bronze,
honed like a razor on either edge. Then crying hoarse and loud
he hurled himself at Odysseus. But the kingly man let fly
an arrow at that instant, and the quivering feathered butt
sprang to the nipple of his breast as the barb stuck in his liver.
85 The bright broadsword clanged down. He lurched and fell
      aside,
pitching across his table. His cup, his bread and meat,
were spilt and scattered far and wide, and his head slammed
      on the ground.
Revulsion, anguish in his heart, with both feet kicking out,
he downed his chair, while the shrouding wave of mist closed
      on his eyes.

90 Amphinomus now came running at Odysseus,
broadsword naked in his hand. He thought to make
the great soldier give way at the door.
But with a spear throw from behind Telemachus hit him
between the shoulders, and the lancehead drove
95 clear through his chest. He left his feet and fell
forward, thudding, forehead against the ground. **P**

61–67 *Why do you think Odysseus rejects Eurymachus' explanation and offer of restitution?*

67 skins by: sneaks away.

implacable (ĭm-plăk′ə-bəl) *adj.* impossible to soothe; unforgiving

revulsion (rĭ-vŭl′shən) *n.* a sudden feeling of disgust or loathing

88–89 Eurymachus' death is physically painful, but he also has "revulsion, anguish in his heart." *What do you think causes this emotional pain?*

90 Amphinomus (ăm-fĭn′ə-məs): one of the suitors.

93–100 Telemachus proves to be a valuable help to his father.

P EPIC
How has the battle with the suitors taken on epic proportions?

Telemachus swerved around him, leaving the long dark spear
planted in Amphinomus. If he paused to yank it out
someone might jump him from behind or cut him down with
    a sword
100 at the moment he bent over. So he ran—ran from the tables
to his father's side and halted, panting, saying:

"Father let me bring you a shield and spear,
a pair of spears, a helmet.
I can arm on the run myself; I'll give
105 outfits to Eumaeus and this cowherd.
Better to have equipment."

ANALYZE VISUALS
Describe the **mood** of this 1944
chalk and ink drawing. How has the
artist's use of color and black line
contributed to this mood?

                  Said Odysseus:

"Run then, while I hold them off with arrows
as long as the arrows last. When all are gone
if I'm alone they can dislodge me."

                      Quick
110 upon his father's word Telemachus
ran to the room where spears and armor lay.
He caught up four light shields, four pairs of spears,
four helms of war high-plumed with flowing manes,
and ran back, loaded down, to his father's side.
115 He was the first to pull a helmet on
and slide his bare arm in a buckler strap.
The servants armed themselves, and all three took their stand
beside the master of battle. **Q**

113 **helms:** helmets.

               While he had arrows
he aimed and shot, and every shot brought down
120 one of his huddling enemies.
But when all barbs had flown from the bowman's fist,
he leaned his bow in the bright entry way
beside the door, and armed: a four-ply shield
hard on his shoulder, and a crested helm,
125 horsetailed, nodding stormy upon his head,
then took his tough and bronze-shod spears. . . .

Q EPIC
How does Telemachus conduct
himself in this **conflict** with
the suitors?

*The suitors make various unsuccessful attempts to expel Odysseus from his post at
the door. Athena urges Odysseus on to battle, yet holds back her fullest aid, waiting
for Odysseus and Telemachus to prove themselves. Six of the suitors attempt an
attack on Odysseus, but Athena deflects their arrows. Odysseus and his men seize
this opportunity to launch their own attack, and the suitors begin to fall. At last
Athena's presence becomes known to all, as the shape of her shield becomes visible*

*above the hall. The suitors, recognizing the intervention of the gods on Odysseus'
behalf, are frantic to escape but to no avail. Odysseus and his men are compared to
falcons who show no mercy to the flocks of birds they pursue and capture. Soon the
room is reeking with blood. Thus the battle with the suitors comes to an end, and
Odysseus prepares himself to meet Penelope.*

Death of the Suitors: The Odyssey (1944), Henry Spencer Moore. Black chalk, wash, and ink on paper, 13.3 cm ×
28.8 cm. Cecil Higgins Art Gallery, Bedford, Bedfordshire, United Kingdom. Photo © Bridgeman Art Library.
© The Henry Moore Foundation. This image may not be reproduced or altered without prior consent from the
Henry Moore Foundation.

BOOK 23:
The Trunk of the Olive Tree

ANALYZE VISUALS
This terracotta plaque from ancient Greece depicts Odysseus pleading with his wife. What can you tell about this moment in the story from looking at this image? Explain.

Greathearted Odysseus, home at last,
was being bathed now by Eurynome
and rubbed with golden oil, and clothed again
in a fresh tunic and a cloak. Athena
5 lent him beauty, head to foot. She made him
taller, and massive, too, with crisping hair
in curls like petals of wild hyacinth
but all red-golden. Think of gold infused
on silver by a craftsman, whose fine art
10 Hephaestus taught him, or Athena: one
whose work moves to delight: just so she lavished
beauty over Odysseus' head and shoulders.
He sat then in the same chair by the pillar,
facing his silent wife, and said:

                              "Strange woman,
15 the immortals of Olympus made you hard,
harder than any. Who else in the world
would keep **aloof** as you do from her husband
if he returned to her from years of trouble,
cast on his own land in the twentieth year?

20 Nurse, make up a bed for me to sleep on.
Her heart is iron in her breast."

                    Penelope

spoke to Odysseus now. She said:

                    "Strange man,
if man you are . . . This is no pride on my part
nor scorn for you—not even wonder, merely.
25 I know so well how you—how he—appeared
boarding the ship for Troy. But all the same . . . **R**

2 Eurynome (yŏo-rĭn′ə-mē): a female servant.

10 Hephaestus (hĭ-fĕs′təs): the god of metalworking.

11 lavished: showered.

15 immortals of Olympus: the gods, who live on Mount Olympus.

aloof (ə-lōōf′) *adj.* distant; remote; standoffish

R EPIC
Reread lines 22–26. What do you think is the **motivation** for Penelope's skepticism about this man who claims to be the husband she hasn't seen in 20 years? Consider her experiences in his absence.

Detail of plaque with the return of Odysseus (about 460–450 B.C.). Classical Greek. Melian. Terracotta, height 7 ³/₈″. Fletcher Fund, 1930. © The Metropolitan Museum of Art (30.11.9).

Make up his bed for him, Eurycleia.
Place it outside the bedchamber my lord
built with his own hands. Pile the big bed
30 with fleeces, rugs, and sheets of purest linen."

With this she tried him to the breaking point,
and he turned on her in a flash raging:

"Woman, by heaven you've stung me now!
Who dared to move my bed?
35 No builder had the skill for that—unless
a god came down to turn the trick. No mortal
in his best days could budge it with a crowbar.
There is our pact and pledge, our secret sign,
built into that bed—my handiwork
40 and no one else's!

                                An old trunk of olive
grew like a pillar on the building plot,
and I laid out our bedroom round that tree,
lined up the stone walls, built the walls and roof,
gave it a doorway and smooth-fitting doors.
45 Then I lopped off the silvery leaves and branches,
hewed and shaped that stump from the roots up
into a bedpost, drilled it, let it serve
as model for the rest. I planed them all,
inlaid them all with silver, gold and ivory,
50 and stretched a bed between—a pliant web
of oxhide thongs dyed crimson.
                                        There's our sign!
I know no more. Could someone else's hand
have sawn that trunk and dragged the frame away?"

Their secret! as she heard it told, her knees
55 grew **tremulous** and weak, her heart failed her.
With eyes brimming tears she ran to him,
throwing her arms around his neck, and kissed him, ❺
murmuring:

                        "Do not rage at me, Odysseus!
No one ever matched your caution! Think
60 what difficulty the gods gave: they denied us
life together in our prime and flowering years,
kept us from crossing into age together.
Forgive me, don't be angry. I could not
welcome you with love on sight! I armed myself

27–30 The bed, built from the trunk of an olive tree still rooted in the ground, is actually unmovable.

50–51 a pliant web . . . crimson: a network of ox-hide straps, dyed red, stretched between the sides of the bed to form a springy base for the bedding.

tremulous (trĕm′yə-ləs) *adj.* marked by trembling or shaking

❺ **ARCHETYPE**
How has Penelope tricked Odysseus into proving his identity? What do her actions suggest about archetypal characters?

65 long ago against the frauds of men,
impostors who might come—and all those many
whose underhanded ways bring evil on!
Helen of Argos, daughter of Zeus and Leda,
would she have joined the stranger, lain with him,
70 if she had known her destiny? known the Achaeans
in arms would bring her back to her own country?
Surely a goddess moved her to adultery,
her blood unchilled by war and evil coming,
the years, the **desolation**; ours, too.
75 But here and now, what sign could be so clear
as this of our own bed?
No other man has ever laid eyes on it—
only my own slave, Actoris, that my father
sent with me as a gift—she kept our door.
80 You make my stiff heart know that I am yours." **T**

Now from his breast into his eyes the ache
of longing mounted, and he wept at last,
his dear wife, clear and faithful, in his arms,
longed for
            as the sunwarmed earth is longed for by a swimmer
85 spent in rough water where his ship went down
under Poseidon's blows, gale winds and tons of sea.
Few men can keep alive through a big surf
to crawl, clotted with brine, on kindly beaches
in joy, in joy, knowing the abyss behind:
90 and so she too rejoiced, her gaze upon her husband,
her white arms round him pressed as though forever. . . . **U**

*Odysseus and Penelope tell each other about all that happened to them while
Odysseus was away. Then Odysseus visits his father, Laertes, to give him the
good news of his safe return. Meanwhile, the townspeople, angry about the
deaths of the young suitors, gather to fight Odysseus. In the end, Athena steps
in and makes peace among them all.*

68 **Argos** (är′gŏs); **Leda** (lē′də).

desolation (dĕs′ə-lā′shən) *n.* lonely
grief; misery

78 **Actoris** (ăk-tôr′ĭs).

T EPIC
Reread lines 58–80. What **traits** of
Penelope's does this speech reveal?

U EPIC SIMILE
What is Penelope compared
to in these final lines?

Dorothy Parker, an American writer of the early 20th century, wrote many poems offering a woman's perspective on life. In "Penelope," Parker imagines what Odysseus' wife might have thought about his journeys.

PENELOPE

DOROTHY PARKER

In the pathway of the sun,
  In the footsteps of a breeze,
Where the world and sky are one,
  He shall ride the silver seas,
5   He shall cut the glittering wave.
I shall sit at home, and rock;
Rise, to heed a neighbor's knock;
Brew my tea, and snip my thread;
Bleach the linen for my bed.
10   They will call him brave.

Comprehension

1. **Recall** Why is Telemachus fearful when his father first reveals his identity?

2. **Recall** How does Odysseus react when Argos recognizes him?

3. **Recall** Who helps Odysseus fight the suitors?

4. **Clarify** Why does Penelope test Odysseus?

PENNSYLVANIA STANDARDS

READING STANDARD
A.1.5.1 Summarize the key details and events

Literary Analysis

5. **Summarize the Plot** Review the chart you created as you read these episodes about Odysseus' homecoming. Use the chart to write a plot summary of Part 2; feel free to use the overview on page 1141 as a starter.

6. **Analyze Character** Why do you think Penelope devises the contest with the bow? What does this contest reveal about her character?

7. **Examine Archetypes** Think about other contests you have encountered in literature or film. Would you say that the contest of the bow is archetypal? Explain why or why not.

8. **Analyze Universal Theme** The *Odyssey* has themes reflecting timeless and universal concerns, such as courage and honor, good and evil, life and death, and the importance of home. Choose one of these topics. What message about this topic does Homer convey? Give evidence from the text to support your answer.

9. **Evaluate Epic Characteristics** One thing that all epics have in common is tremendous **scale.** Everything about an epic is big: an extended and complicated plot, a long journey over great distances, powerful gods and horrible monsters, and major universal themes. Identify one aspect each of epic **plot, setting, character,** and **theme** in the *Odyssey*. Which do you consider most impressive? Give reasons for your choice.

10. **Compare and Contrast Texts** In Dorothy Parker's poem "Penelope," is the attitude toward Odysseus similar to or different from Penelope's attitude in the *Odyssey* excerpts you have just read? Cite evidence to support your answer.

Literary Criticism

11. **Social Context** Assume that Odysseus represents the ancient Greeks' ideal of a man and that Penelope represents their ideal of a woman. In what ways are the characters similar to and different from the ideal man and woman of today?

Vocabulary in Context

VOCABULARY PRACTICE

Decide whether each item is true or false.

1. A person making **restitution** is trying to get revenge.
2. If I **commandeer** your boat, I have asked your permission before taking it.
3. A person who acts **aloof** often is unwilling to make friends.
4. One might feel **desolation** at the death of a close relative.
5. If I feel **revulsion** for you, I enjoy spending time with you.
6. **Adversity** is a serious skin condition.
7. A **tremulous** person tends to have very steady hands.
8. If my anger is **implacable,** I am not going to get over it soon.
9. New Year's Eve is a common night for **revelry.**
10. Being kind to a pet is **contemptible** behavior.

WORD LIST

adversity
aloof
commandeer
contemptible
desolation
implacable
restitution
revelry
revulsion
tremulous

VOCABULARY IN WRITING

Using four or more vocabulary words, write a paragraph to describe how Odysseus' old servants feel about events going on in the palace. You might start like this.

> **EXAMPLE SENTENCE**
>
> The servants felt a strong **revulsion** toward the suitors in the palace.

PENNSYLVANIA STANDARDS

READING STANDARD
A.1.2.1 Identify word meaning using affixes

VOCABULARY STRATEGY: THE LATIN WORD ROOT *solus*

The vocabulary word *desolation* contains a form of the Latin root *solus*, which means "alone." This root is found in numerous other English words. To understand the meaning of words formed from *solus*, use context clues as well as your knowledge of the root.

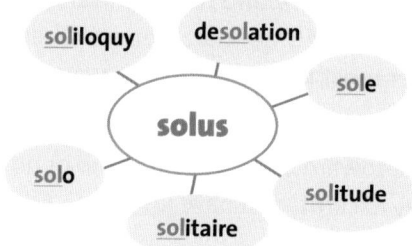

PRACTICE Insert the word from the word web that best completes each sentence. Use context clues to help you or, if necessary, consult a dictionary.

1. After months of training with an instructor, he was ready for his first _____ flight.
2. Jeannette often plays a game of _____ on her computer.
3. Rupert lived on a desert island because he wanted _____.
4. The _____ requirement for joining the club is that you are 13 or older.
5. An actor delivering a _____ generally stands on the stage alone.

VOCABULARY PRACTICE
For more practice, go to the **Vocabulary Center** at ClassZone.com.

Reading-Writing Connection

Engage with the main characters in the *Odyssey* by responding to these prompts.
Then use **Revision: Grammar and Style** to improve your writing.

WRITING PROMPTS

A. Short Response: Write a Monologue

What do you think Penelope's hopes for the future might be after Odysseus' **homecoming?** Write a **stanza** (at least ten lines) in the style of the *Odyssey* in which Penelope expresses her dreams for her future years with Odysseus.

B. Extended Response: Evaluate a Character

Is Odysseus someone who would be admired by young people today? Write a **three-to-five-paragraph response** in which you describe Odysseus' behavior and attitudes and explain why people would or would not look up to him today.

SELF-CHECK

An effective stanza will . . .
- mimic the style of Homer's writing
- express Penelope's likely hopes for the future

A successful response will . . .
- clearly introduce an opinion
- describe aspects of Odysseus' attitudes and actions
- give reasons why young people today would or would not admire him

REVISION: GRAMMAR AND STYLE

ADD DESCRIPTIVE DETAILS Review the **Grammar and Style** note on page 1156. Similes and metaphors are types of **figurative language**—they communicate ideas beyond their literal meaning. A **simile** is a comparison that uses the **prepositions** *like* or *as*. A **metaphor** directly compares two things by saying or suggesting that one thing *is* another. Using figurative language can make your readers see things in a new way. Here are two examples.

> "Like pipes his nostrils jetted
> crimson runnels, a river of mortal red. . . ." (simile, Book 22, lines 17–18)

> "'Her heart is iron in her breast.'" (metaphor, Book 23, line 21)

Notice how the revisions in red use figurative language to add interesting descriptive details to this first draft. Revise your response to prompt A by incorporating different types of figurative language.

WRITING STANDARD
1.4.11.B.2 Use precise language and specific detail

STUDENT MODEL

We have missed one another for many years.

Like two pieces of the same puzzle,

∧We have been separated

and then joined again.

 **WRITING TOOLS**
For prewriting, revision, and editing tools, visit the **Writing Center** at ClassZone.com.

Writing Workshop

Subject Analysis

Have you ever taken something apart and put it back together? When you write a subject analysis, you break a subject into different elements and draw a conclusion about what you found. Writing a subject analysis can deepen your understanding of a complex literary work such as the *Odyssey*. To get started, consult the **Writer's Road Map.**

WRITER'S ROAD MAP

Subject Analysis

WRITING PROMPT 1

Writing from Literature Choose a topic related to the *Odyssey* that you would like to understand better. Write a subject analysis in which you examine the parts of your topic in detail.

Subjects to Consider
- women in the *Odyssey*
- monsters in the *Odyssey*
- Odysseus' strengths and failings as a leader

WRITING PROMPT 2

Writing for the Real World Taking something apart and examining its separate parts is a good way to understand almost anything, from an electronic device to a political concept. Write an analysis of a subject you consider important. Be sure your analysis identifies and explores the significant parts of your subject.

Subjects to Consider
- scientific concepts, such as carbon dating
- medical issues, such as a flu epidemic
- social issues, such as voter turnout

 WRITING TOOLS
For prewriting, revision, and editing tools, visit the **Writing Center** at ClassZone.com.

KEY TRAITS

1. **IDEAS**
   - Presents a **thesis statement** that identifies the main points of the analysis
   - Uses **evidence** to support and explain the main points

2. **ORGANIZATION**
   - Identifies the subject of the analysis in an engaging **introduction**
   - Uses **transitions** to connect ideas
   - Follows a consistent **organizational pattern**
   - Concludes by **summarizing** and showing the **significance** of the analysis

3. **VOICE**
   - **Tone** adds interest and is appropriate for the purpose and audience

4. **WORD CHOICE**
   - Uses words that are **specific** and **accurate**

5. **SENTENCE FLUENCY**
   - Varies **sentence structure and length**

6. **CONVENTIONS**
   - Employs **correct grammar and usage**

Part 1: Analyze a Student Model

WRITING STANDARD

1.5.TL.8.1 Write topic-based informational piece.

**Ted Jorgenssen
Park West High School**

Are You a Hero?

Everyone has heroes. We read about them in books and see them on the news or in the movies. We might even live next door to one. What qualities do these people share? Some display great strength and courage. Some put others' lives ahead of their own. Some show honesty and
5 humility in difficult situations. I believe that only someone with all of these traits is truly a hero. This definition may seem obvious, but it can lead to surprising conclusions. Often, people considered to be heroes are not, while others who don't see themselves as special are truly heroic. Someday, you may even find out that you are someone's hero.

10 One individual who has always been considered a hero is Odysseus, the main character of Homer's *Odyssey*. When we examine him on the basis of the characteristics listed above, however, he falls short. Odysseus does have great strength and courage. He resists the Sirens, blinds and escapes from the Cyclops, survives Scylla and Charybdis, and returns
15 home after 20 years.

However, Odysseus survives by putting his own life above the lives of others. Because of his love of battle, he ignores advice from his men and the gods. Not one of the 720 men he left Ithaca with returns alive. In failing to fulfill the vow "to bring his shipmates home," which he makes
20 at the start of his journey, he fails to fulfill the second criterion of a hero.

Odysseus also shows little honesty or humility. He enjoys hiding and disguising himself—in the wooden horse during the Trojan War, under the Cyclops's sheep, and as a beggar on his return to Ithaca—and is proud of his deception. In his arrogance, he forgets that he survives

KEY TRAITS IN ACTION

Engaging **introduction** captures reader interest. **Thesis statement** presents the main points of analysis (the three qualities that make a person a hero).

Provides specific **evidence** to support the opinion that Odysseus is strong and brave.

Tone is straightforward and sincere. Varied **sentence structure and length** provide rhythm and interest.

25　many adventures because of help from the god Hermes and the
goddesses Athena and Circe. Odysseus is reunited with his wife, but
his return is achieved through selfishness and dishonesty. In the final
analysis, he is no hero.

　　In contrast to Odysseus, my brother Jerry has never commanded
30　a fleet of ships or wandered hundreds of miles from home. Jerry is a
teenager unknown outside of my community. However, he is heroic in a
way that Odysseus never could be.

　　Two years ago, Jerry was riding his bike when a car hit him. One
minute he was a regular 14-year-old, and the next he was in the
35　hospital, facing pain and fears that most of us can't even imagine. He
has shown a hero's strength and courage in undergoing three operations
and hundreds of hours of painful physical therapy.

　　Although Jerry has many problems to worry about, he turns his
attention to others. He talks with other accident victims on the phone
40　and sends them e-mails and instant messages. He gives advice about
how to deal with frustrating physical therapy sessions. He suggests
what to say to friends who don't know how to act around somebody
recovering from a major injury. Jerry thinks it is ridiculous that I
consider him to be a hero. "I went through something that most people
45　don't experience," he said. "It makes sense to try to help somebody else
who's going through the same thing."

　　That's what makes a hero—bravery, unselfishness, honesty, and
humility. Whether our heroes are famous or unknown, or from
literature or real life, they have qualities that we admire and try to
50　achieve. Whose hero are you?

> Writer uses a compare-contrast strategy as he continues to analyze the characteristics of a hero. **Transitions** make the organization clear.

> **Specific, accurate** words give the reader a precise understanding of the situation.

> Concludes by **summarizing** and explaining the **significance** of the analysis. Question refers back to the title of the essay.

2

WRITING STANDARD
1.4.11.B.2 Use precise language and specific detail

Part 2: Apply the Writing Process

PREWRITING

What Should I Do?	*What Does It Look Like?*

1. Brainstorm ideas for your analysis.
Use a graphic organizer to identify aspects of the *Odyssey* that intrigue you. Highlight the topics that you'd like to analyze further.

▶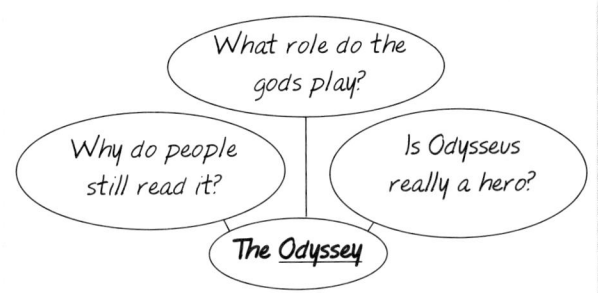

2. Focus on a topic and freewrite about it.
After choosing the subject you want to analyze, freewrite about it to examine the elements it is made up of.

▶ *Odysseus has a lot of exciting adventures, but he isn't a very nice person. He doesn't really take care of his men, and he is always using trickery to get his way. All he really seems to care about is himself. So what are the things that make someone a hero?*

3. Explore your topic.
Think about how your topic breaks down into parts. Creating a list or chart can help.

TIP You might list the distinguishing characteristics of your topic, as this writer has done. Other approaches include comparing and contrasting your topic with a related subject, breaking your topic into a series of steps or stages, or writing an extended definition of your topic.

▶ *Qualities of a Hero*
- *brave, honest, strong*
- *should not boast or be proud*
- *should care about others*

Heroes in Literature and in Real Life
- *Is Odysseus a hero?*
- *Is my brother Jerry a hero?*

4. Create a working thesis statement.
Review the information you have gathered, and condense your ideas into a statement that explains the main idea of your analysis. Your working thesis is a forecast of what points your essay will cover.

▶ *Working thesis statement:*

Everybody has heroes. Some have strength and courage. Some put others' lives ahead of their own. Some show honesty and humility in difficult situations. I believe that only someone with all of these traits is a hero.

What Should I Do?

1. Grab your reader's attention.
Draw your reader into your analysis from the first sentence. Make a statement or ask a question that provokes curiosity, surprise, or agreement.

TIP A catchy title can intrigue a reader.

2. Outline.
An informal outline can help you organize your analysis. Ask yourself: Which parts of my subject do I want to discuss? How do those parts work together?

3. Elaborate.
Don't just state the facts. Show readers how each idea relates to the topic as a whole by giving examples, comparing and contrasting, and evaluating each part of the analysis.

4. Go beyond a summary.
Your conclusion should show readers why they should care about and remember what you have written.

TIP Before revising, consult the key traits on page 1132 and the rubric and peer-reader questions on page 1138.

What Does It Look Like?

Are You a Hero?
Everyone has heroes. We read about them in books and see them on the news or in the movies. We might even live next door to one. What qualities do these people share?

Analysis of a hero

1. List characteristics.
2. Odysseus is not a hero.
• strong and brave
• not concerned about others
• not honest or humble

3. Jerry is a hero.
• brave
• helps others
• modest
4. Conclusion: Good qualities are more important than fame.

Odysseus survives by putting his own life above the lives of others. ⎱ Key point

He ignores advice from his men and the gods. Not one of the 720 men he left Ithaca with returns alive. In failing to fulfill the vow "to bring his shipmates home," which he makes at the start of his journey, he fails to fulfill the second criterion of a hero. ⎱ 2 examples + quotation

That's what makes a hero—bravery, unselfishness, honesty, and humility. ⎱ Summary

Whether our heroes are famous or unknown, they have qualities that we admire and try to achieve. Whose hero are you? ⎱ Significance + question for reader

REVISING AND EDITING

| *What Should I Do?* | *What Does It Look Like?* |

1. Eliminate irrelevant information.
- Ask a peer reader to <u>underline</u> statements that seem to be unnecessary or off the topic.
- Replace these sentences with examples, quotations, or other appropriate details.

See page 1176: Ask a Peer Reader

▶ One individual who has always been considered a hero is Odysseus, ~~He is also called Ulysses, and the American president Ulysses S. Grant was named after him.~~

    the main character of Homer's Odyssey.

2. Connect ideas with transitions.
- Highlight transitional words and phrases, such as *first, after, however,* and *in contrast to.*
- If your essay has few highlights, add transitional words or phrases to show how ideas are related.

▶ When we examine Odysseus on the basis of the characteristics listed above, however, he falls short.

Although
^Jerry has many problems to worry about, ^He turns his attention to others.

3. Be specific.
- ⃝Circle⃝ boring, general words and phrases, such as *a lot, some, very, really,* and *things.*
- Choose specific, accurate words that get your point across.

▶ ~~Odysseus is (very) strong and (really) brave. He has to (deal with) the Sirens, the Cyclops, and Scylla and Charybdis. It takes him a (long time) to get back home.~~

Odysseus does have great strength and courage. He resists the Sirens, blinds and escapes from the Cyclops, survives Scylla and Charybdis, and returns home after 20 years.

4. Fine-tune your tone.
- Read your essay aloud. [Bracket] words or phrases that are too slangy or that make you seem uncertain of your opinions.
- Substitute formal vocabulary that is appropriate for a subject analysis.

▶ ~~Jerry thinks I am [kind of a goof] for calling him a hero. [I guess] he went through something that is [sort of weird.]~~

Jerry thinks it is ridiculous that I consider him to be a hero. "I went through something that most people don't experience," he said.

Subject Analysis

Apply the Rubric

A strong subject analysis . . .

- ☑ presents the main points of the subject being analyzed in a clear thesis statement
- ☑ develops ideas logically, connecting them with appropriate transitions
- ☑ includes evidence to support ideas
- ☑ has a tone that is tailored to the audience and purpose
- ☑ maintains interest by using strong, specific vocabulary
- ☑ varies sentence structures and lengths
- ☑ goes beyond a mere summary of ideas to show the significance of the subject

Ask a Peer Reader

- What are my main points?
- Which part of my analysis has the strongest support? Which lacks convincing evidence?
- Does my analysis include unnecessary information?

Check Your Grammar

- Use parallel structure. Sentence parts that have the same function should have the same form.

> He resists the Sirens, blinds and escapes from the Cyclops, survives Scylla and Charybdis, and returns home after 20 years.

> Jerry talks with other accident victims. He gives advice about how to deal with physical therapy. He suggests what to say to friends who don't know how to act around somebody recovering from a major injury.

See page R64: Parallel Structure

- Make sure that indefinite-pronoun subjects have the correct verbs. Remember that the indefinite pronouns *all, any, more, most, none,* and *some* can take either singular or plural verbs depending on the noun they refer to.

> Everyone has heroes. What qualities do these people share? Some display great strength and courage. Most are not well known. All are worthy of respect.

See page R54: Indefinite Pronouns

Writing Online

PUBLISHING OPTIONS
For publishing options, visit the **Writing Center** at ClassZone.com.

ASSESSMENT PREPARATION
For writing and grammar assessment practice, go to the **Assessment Center** at ClassZone.com.

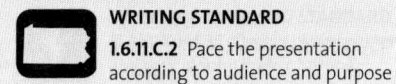
SPEAKING AND LISTENING

Delivering an Oral Report

To make your subject analysis even more interesting and to reach a broader audience than you can in writing, present it as an oral report.

Planning the Oral Report

1. **Decide what information to cover.** Find out who your audience will be and how long you will be expected to talk. Tailor your presentation to those guidelines. If your teacher expects you to answer questions afterwards, think of what the most likely questions will be and how you will answer them.

2. **Collect or create visuals to illustrate your points.** Consider creating a flip chart, poster, or slide presentation.

3. **Rehearse your report.** Run through your report several times in front of family or friends. Consider having someone time you. Be sure you can incorporate the visuals easily and naturally into your presentation.

Qualities of a Hero	Odysseus
Strong and brave	Yes
Puts others first	No
Honest and humble	No

Delivering the Oral Report

1. **Speak directly to your audience.** Don't talk to your shoes or to the ceiling. If possible, have a friend in the audience signal you if you begin rushing through what you have to say.

2. **Avoid "um" and "uh."** It's okay to pause for a moment and take a breath instead of filling every second of your presentation with speech.

3. **Use facial expressions for emphasis.** For example, if your topic is funny or entertaining, don't be afraid to smile.

4. **Ask for feedback.** Find out what a few audience members thought of your report. You may learn about weaknesses that you can correct the next time you speak before a group.

5. **Evaluate your performance.** Turn to page R78 to read about what qualities make an oral report effective.

Reading Comprehension

DIRECTIONS *Read the following excerpt from Book 9 of the* Odyssey *and then answer the questions.*

from The Odyssey
Homer

Blinded, and sick with pain from his head wound,
the master stroked each ram, then let it pass,
but my men riding on the pectoral fleece
the giant's blind hands blundering never found.
5 Last of them all my ram, the leader, came,
weighted by wool and me with my meditations.
The Cyclops patted him, and then he said:

'Sweet cousin ram, why lag behind the rest
in the night cave? You never linger so,
10 but graze before them all, and go afar
to crop sweet grass, and take your stately way
leading along the streams, until at evening
you run to be the first one in the fold.
Why, now, so far behind? Can you be grieving
15 over your Master's eye? That carrion rogue
and his accurst companions burnt it out
when he had conquered all my wits with wine.
Nohbdy will not get out alive, I swear.
Oh, had you brain and voice to tell
20 where he may be now, dodging all my fury!
Bashed by this hand and bashed on this rock wall
his brains would strew the floor, and I should have
rest from the outrage Nohbdy worked upon me.'

He sent us into the open, then. Close by,
25 I dropped and rolled clear of the ram's belly,
going this way and that to untie the men.
With many glances back, we rounded up
his fat, stiff-legged sheep to take aboard,
and drove them down to where the good ship lay.
30 We saw, as we came near, our fellows' faces
shining; then we saw them turn to grief
tallying those who had not fled from death.

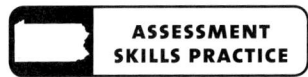

I hushed them, jerking head and eyebrows up,
and in a low voice told them: 'Load this herd;
35 move fast, and put the ship's head toward the breakers.'
They all pitched in at loading, then embarked
and struck their oars into the sea. Far out,
as far off shore as shouted words would carry,
I sent a few back to the adversary:

40 'O Cyclops! Would you feast on my companions?
Puny, am I, in a Caveman's hands?
How do you like the beating that we gave you,
you damned cannibal? Eater of guests
under your roof! Zeus and the gods have paid you!'

45 The blind thing in his doubled fury broke
a hilltop in his hands and heaved it after us.
Ahead of our black prow it struck and sank
whelmed in a spuming geyser, a giant wave
that washed the ship stern foremost back to shore.
50 I got the longest boathook out and stood
fending us off, with furious nods to all
to put their backs into a racing stroke—
row, row, or perish. So the long oars bent
kicking the foam sternward, making head
55 until we drew away, and twice as far.
Now when I cupped my hands I heard the crew
in low voices protesting:

                              'Godsake, Captain!
Why bait the beast again? Let him alone!'

'That tidal wave he made on the first throw
60 all but beached us.'

                              'All but stove us in!'

'Give him our bearing with your trumpeting,
he'll get the range and lob a boulder.'

                                        'Aye

He'll smash our timbers and our heads together!'
I would not heed them in my glorying spirit,
65 but let my anger flare and yelled:

'Cyclops,

if ever mortal man inquire
how you were put to shame and blinded, tell him
Odysseus, raider of cities, took your eye:
Laertes' son, whose home's on Ithaca!'

70 At this he gave a mighty sob and rumbled:

'Now comes the weird upon me, spoken of old.
A wizard, grand and wondrous, lived here—Telemus,
a son of Eurymus; great length of days
he had in wizardry among the Cyclopes,
75 and these things he foretold for time to come:
my great eye lost, and at Odysseus' hands.
Always I had in mind some giant, armed
in giant force, would come against me here.
But this, but you—small, pitiful and twiggy—
80 you put me down with wine, you blinded me.
Come back, Odysseus, and I'll treat you well,
praying the god of earthquake to befriend you—
his son I am, for he by his avowal
fathered me, and, if he will, he may
85 heal me of this black wound—he and no other
of all the happy gods or mortal men.'

Few words I shouted in reply to him:
'If I could take your life I would and take
your time away, and hurl you down to hell!

90 The god of earthquake could not heal you there!'

At this he stretched his hands out in his darkness
toward the sky of stars, and prayed Poseidon:

'O hear me, lord, blue girdler of the islands,
if I am thine indeed, and thou art father:
95 grant that Odysseus, raider of cities, never
see his home: Laertes' son, I mean,
who kept his hall on Ithaca. Should destiny
intend that he shall see his roof again
among his family in his father land,
100 far be that day, and dark the years between.

Let him lose all companions, and return
under strange sail to bitter days at home.'

Comprehension

DIRECTIONS *Answer these questions about the excerpt from the* Odyssey.

1. The cave mentioned in line 9 is an epic setting because it is
   A home to a fantastic, archetypal creature
   B a beautiful, hidden location
   C a rugged, barren land formation
   D an imaginary but believable place

2. Which statement summarizes the escape plan for Odysseus and his men?
   A They beg Poseidon to make the Cyclops free them.
   B They blind the Cyclops and then sneak away during the night.
   C They hide in the rams' wool and let the rams carry them past the Cyclops.
   D They roll boulders down a hill to distract the Cyclops, and then run.

3. Which quality of an epic hero does Odysseus display in lines 24–35?
   A strength in pursuit of adventure
   B honesty in the face of conflict
   C dependence on the gods
   D cunning in the face of danger

4. Which statement summarizes Odysseus' heroic actions in lines 45–55?
   A He blinds the Cyclops with a boathook.
   B He throws a boulder that causes a wave to flood the ship.
   C He single-handedly pushes the ship out to sea while urging his men to row.
   D He taunts the Cyclops from the shore while the ship is sinking.

5. What conflict develops between Odysseus and his men in lines 56–69?
   A They disagree about where to hide from the Cyclops.
   B The men beg Odysseus to stop taunting the Cyclops, but he continues.
   C They disagree about whether or not to kill the Cyclops.
   D The men want to steal the Cyclops' sheep without telling Odysseus.

6. Which character trait causes Odysseus to reveal his name to the Cyclops?
   A pride   C dishonesty
   B cowardice   D vengefulness

7. Which theme of the *Odyssey* is revealed in the Cyclops' speech in lines 75–80?
   A the rescue of a nation from invaders
   B a hero's loyalty to his friends
   C the victorious homecoming of a hero
   D a hero's triumph over a powerful opponent

Open-Ended Items

8. Briefly summarize the conflict between Odysseus and the Cyclops. Support your answer with details from the excerpt.

9. Explain the importance of the sea and the role of Poseidon in this excerpt. Support your answer with details from the excerpt.

Vocabulary

DIRECTIONS *Use context clues and your knowledge of prefixes to answer the following questions.*

1. The prefix *un-* in the word *untie* in line 26 most likely means

   A performs an action over again

   B reverses a specified action

   C removes a specific thing

   D goes against something

2. The prefix *em-* means "to put onto." What does the word *embarked* mean in line 36?

   A stayed on shore

   B rowed toward land

   C made a loud noise

   D got onto a ship

3. The prefix *be-* means "to make." The word *befriend* in line 82 means to

   A form a rivalry

   B beg for companionship

   C look for friendship

   D become friends with

4. The prefix *re-* in the word *return* in line 101 most likely means

   A again

   B regarding

   C different

   D more

DIRECTIONS *Use context clues and your knowledge of Latin words and roots to answer the following questions.*

5. The Latin word *spuma* means "foam." What is the most likely meaning of *spuming* as it is used in line 48?

   A bubbling

   B rising

   C shooting

   D raging

6. *Mortal* comes from the Latin root *mer,* which means "to die." What is the most likely meaning of *mortal* as it is used in line 86?

   A short-lived

   B subject to death

   C morbid

   D deadly

7. The Latin root *civ* means "citizen." Which of the following words most likely comes from that root?

   A carrion (line 15)

   B companions (line 16)

   C crew (line 56)

   D cities (line 95)

8. The Latin word *destinare* means "to determine." What is the most likely meaning of *destiny* as it is used in line 97?

   A shame

   B fate

   C privilege

   D misfortune

Writing & Grammar

DIRECTIONS *Read the passage and answer the questions that follow.*

(1) Ithaca, an island west of the Greek mainland, was the home of Odysseus. (2) Today, the island's rugged terrain and other physical features still mirror those described in the *Odyssey.* (3) Ancient ruins lie south of the narrow isthmus that gives Ithaca its distinctive shape. (4) On a hilltop in Pilikáta, you may view the three seas and mountains that Odysseus saw from his palace. (5) The Fountain of Arethusa, mentioned in the *Odyssey,* is a spring located beneath a towering sea cliff. (6) You may visit this spring by hiking along steep mountain paths. (7) Visiting these sites allows a person to trace the ancient travels of Odysseus.

1. Which rewrite of sentence 3 includes a simile?

   A   Ancient ruins lie south of the isthmus that gives Ithaca an hourglass shape.

   B   Ancient ruins lie south of the narrow isthmus that separates Ithaca in two.

   C   Ancient ruins lie south of the narrow isthmus that divides Ithaca like the neck of an hourglass.

   D   Ancient ruins lie south of the narrow isthmus that separates Ithaca into north and south.

2. Which rewrite of sentence 4 includes a metaphor?

   A   A Pilikáta hilltop view offers a scenic landscape of the three seas and mountains that Odysseus saw from his palace.

   B   On a hilltop in Pilikáta the view is a landscape painting of the three seas and mountains that Odysseus saw from his palace.

   C   In Pilikáta, the hilltop view is like the view of the three seas and mountains that Odysseus saw from his palace.

   D   On a hilltop in Pilikáta the view features the three raging seas and towering mountains that Odysseus saw from his palace.

3. Which rewrite of sentence 5 includes a simile?

   A   The Fountain of Arethusa, mentioned in the Odyssey, is a spring located beneath a towering sea cliff that stands like a watchful guardian.

   B   The Fountain of Arethusa, mentioned in the Odyssey, is a spring located beneath a towering sea cliff of jagged rocks.

   C   The Fountain of Arethusa, a spring that flows beneath a towering sea cliff, is mentioned in the Odyssey.

   D   The Fountain of Arethusa, mentioned in the Odyssey, is a cool, fresh spring located beneath a towering sea cliff.

4. Which rewrite of sentence 7 includes a metaphor?

   A   Visiting these sites is like tracking the travels of Odysseus in ancient times.

   B   To visit these sites is to walk through the pages of the Odyssey itself.

   C   Visiting these sites makes one remember the travels of Odysseus.

   D   To visit these sites is to recall Odysseus' travels in ancient times.

UNIT 11
Great Reads

Ideas for Independent Reading

Read more epic tales, and see how Homer's masterpiece has inspired contemporary writers.

The Iliad
by Homer

In the *Iliad,* Homer writes of the events that preceded the *Odyssey*—the actual battles and conflicts during the Trojan War. Menelaus and his brother, Agamemnon, struggle for power; Agamemnon fights with his greatest warrior, Achilles; Achilles shows loyalty to his closest friend, Patroclos; Odysseus commands his powerful army. The *Iliad* shows what the men in the *Odyssey* have left behind them, depicting the greater and smaller aspects of ancient war.

The Aeneid
by Virgil

Odysseus had tremendous difficulty returning home. What was the experience of the Trojans, who no longer had a home? Defeated in the Trojan War, Aeneas and his companions set sail at the instruction of the gods on Mount Olympus. The goddess Venus, Aeneas' mother, has told them they must found a new city. That city will eventually become the center of a new and majestic power—the Roman Empire. However, they are waylaid by storms, the wrath and vengefulness of the goddess Juno, and Aeneas' affection for Dido, the queen of Carthage in northern Africa.

The Epic of Gilgamesh
translated by Stephen Mitchell

The Epic of Gilgamesh is the oldest known piece of writing in the world. Experts believe it preceded the *Odyssey* by at least a thousand years; it was found written on broken clay tablets in the ruined city of Nineveh. Gilgamesh, the great but selfish king of Uruk (modern-day Iraq), has his life transformed by his friendship with Enkidu. Together, the two bring peace to his city, battle monsters similar to those encountered in Homer's work, and go on a quest for immortality.

Omeros
by Derek Walcott

Walcott, a Caribbean-American poet and playwright, resets the *Odyssey* in contemporary St. Lucia. This book-length poem follows contemporary characters—fishermen, a household servant, a seer—who share traits and names with those in Homer's work, as they travel through the Caribbean Islands, Europe, and the United States. Throughout the book, the poet himself addresses Omeros (Greek for "Homer") as a source of inspiration. Like Odysseus' traveling companions, all the characters are, in one way or another, searching for a home.

Cold Mountain
by Charles Frazier

This novel has been called "an American *Odyssey.*" Inman, a Confederate soldier in the Civil War, has been severely wounded and leaves the army, walking home to Ada, whom he loved before going to war. The journey is difficult, and Inman is consistently waylaid by others in the South who have been affected by the war. Like Odysseus, Inman must use all the cunning and determination he has to make it home. Like Penelope, Ada must figure out how to live without the love she had relied upon, knowing he might never return to her.

The Hero with a Thousand Faces
by Joseph Campbell

What makes a hero? Do all heroes embody the same ideals, even in different social contexts? Joseph Campbell examines heroes, looking at sources that range from Greek mythology to fairy tales and Eastern philosophy, and claims that the hero is timeless. No matter how the story changes, Campbell says the hero is a constant figure; his attributes are similar and equally significant through time.

UNIT 12

The Power of Research

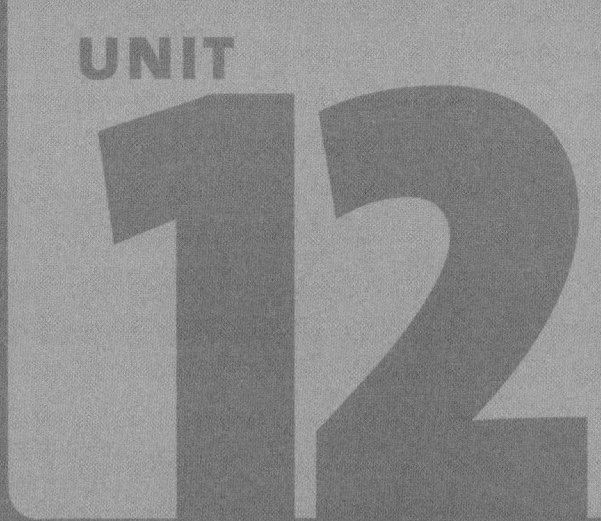

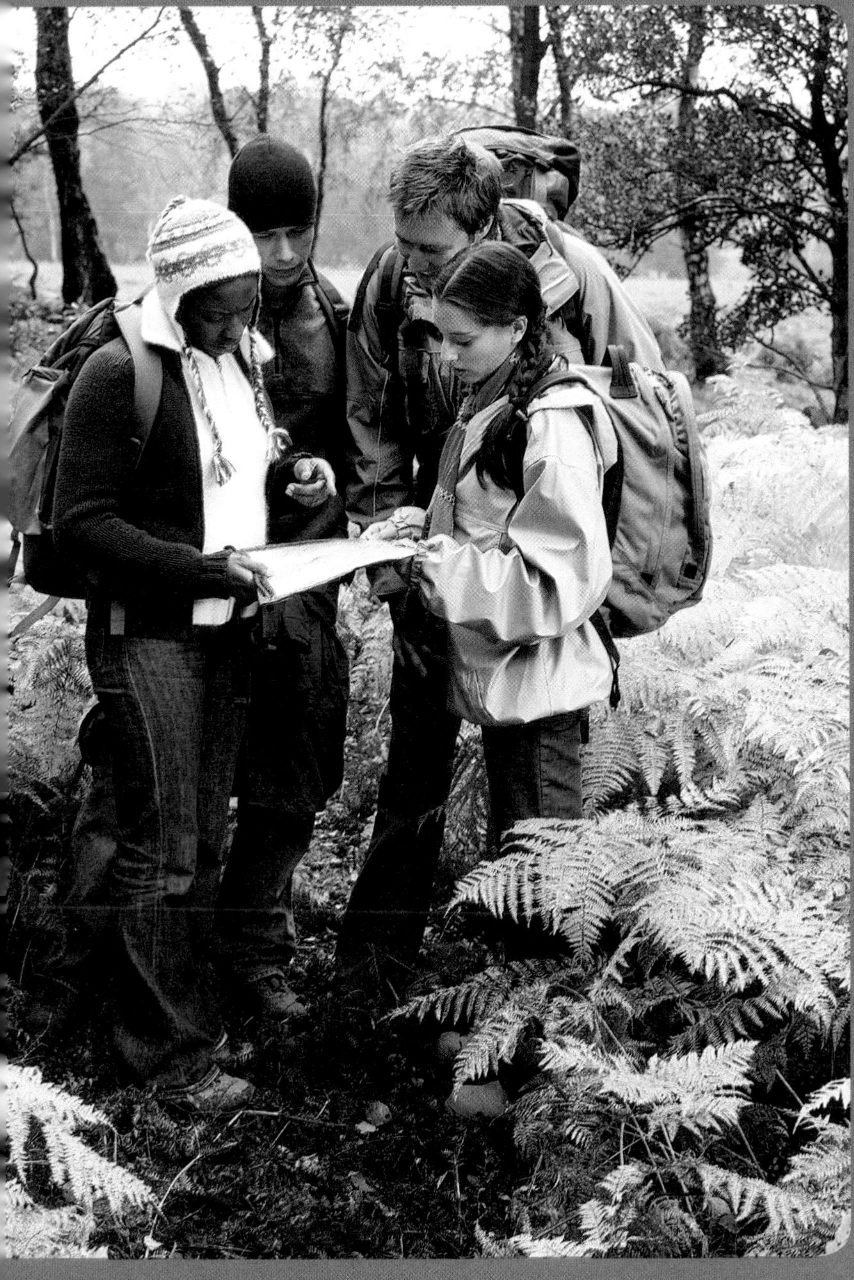

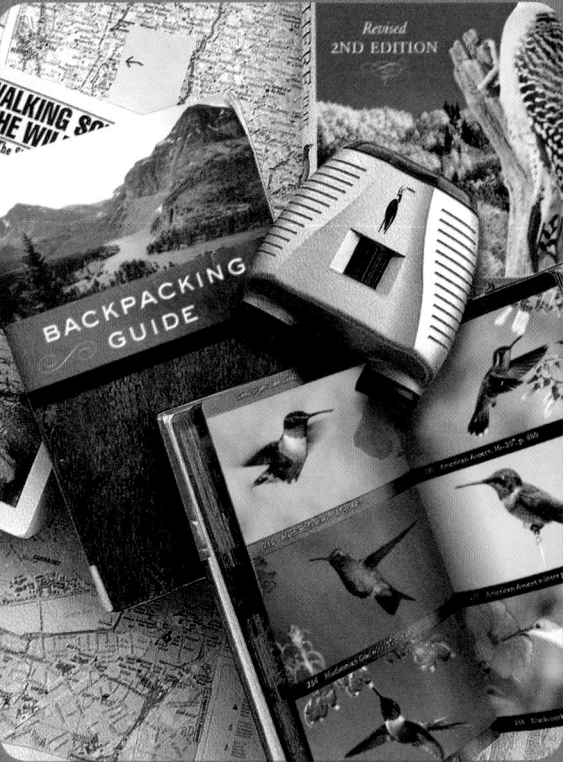

RESEARCH WORKSHOPS

- Research Strategies
- Writing Research Papers

UNIT **12** *Share What You Know*

Why do RESEARCH?

When you look up movie reviews, gather information for a report, or explore careers in computer animation, you are doing **research** to answer questions you have. No matter what your questions are, there are resources available to help you find the answers. You just need to know how to access those resources.

ACTIVITY Make a list of the research challenges or problems you have had over the past week. Next to each question, write the answer and how you found it. Think about topics in the following areas:

- school assignments
- local and national news
- consumer products and services
- movies and television programs

Preview Unit Goals

DEVELOPING RESEARCH SKILLS
- Plan research
- Use library and media center resources
- Distinguish between primary and secondary sources
- Use parts of a book to locate information
- Evaluate information and sources, including nonfiction books, newspaper articles, and Web sites
- Collect your own data

WRITING
- Write a research paper
- Narrow your research topic
- Locate and evaluate sources
- Take notes
- Make source cards
- Summarize and paraphrase
- Quote directly and avoid plagiarism
- Document sources
- Prepare a Works Cited list
- Format your paper

SPEAKING, LISTENING, AND VIEWING
- Create a Web site

VOCABULARY
- research paper
- research topic
- sources
- source cards
- plagiarism
- documentation
- Works Cited list
- Web site

How can I FIND *what I need?*

PENNSYLVANIA STANDARDS

RESEARCH STANDARD
1.8.11.B.2 Evaluate the importance and quality of the sources.

KEY IDEA Finding the information you need can be a challenge. For example, typing a single word or phrase into an Internet search engine could yield tens of thousands of pages to look at. You need to find a way to do **research** efficiently and effectively.

QUICKWRITE Knowing how to do research can help you in many situations. For example, the student handbook pages shown here illustrate a situation requiring research. The skills you will learn in this unit will help you do almost any kind of research. Right now, make a list of subjects that intrigue you. Then choose one or two of them to investigate as you learn research skills.

Graduation Requirement
COMMUNITY SERVICE

All students must complete at least ten hours of community service work by the end of each school year. Service must be completed for

28 STUDENT HANDBOOK

a nonprofit organization within 15 miles of the school. Students must submit a written description of what service they plan to perform, what agency or organization will benefit, and why performing this service would help the community.

STUDENT HANDBOOK 29

Planning Your Research

How Do I Begin? You have a general idea of what you want to accomplish, but you're not sure where to begin. What are the first steps to take?

Getting Started

Just as when preparing for a trip or studying for a test, you will have a better research experience if you make a plan and carry out each step as completely as you can.

CLARIFY YOUR GOAL

What do you want your research to achieve? Your first step is to list your general and specific goals.

> *GENERAL GOAL: find volunteer work with a nonprofit organization*
>
> *SPECIFIC NEEDS:*
>
> **Time:** *Saturday afternoons are best.*
>
> **Preferences:** *working with animals, working outdoors*
>
> **Limitations:** *Where can 15-year-olds volunteer? Check age requirements. Also, I'll have to walk or bike.*
>
> *SPECIFIC GOAL: I want to do volunteer work on weekends, either with animals or in the outdoors, for a nonprofit organization that is near my home.*

GET AN OVERVIEW

Now that you have a goal, the next step is to get a broad overview of your subject.

- **Talk to people.** To explore volunteering, for example, you might talk to students who have already volunteered or to a school counselor.

- **Try the Internet.** Choose **keywords**—specific words and phrases from your goal statement that are related to your subject. For example, you might use the word *volunteer* and the name of your city or town. Plug them into search engines and explore related Web sites.

- **Visit your school's media center or the local public library.** Share your goal with the research librarian.

- **Think creatively.** Does the phone book list places you might call for information? Is there a local business that you might visit?

As you explore your subject, you may decide to change the focus of your research. For instance, Web sites of local volunteer organizations may list opportunities to work with special-needs children, an option you may not have considered.

RESEARCH TOOLS
For research tools and strategies, visit the **Research Center** at **ClassZone.com.**

Focusing Your Research

Now that you have a better sense of what you want to find out, you can direct your research in more specific ways.

DEVELOP RESEARCH QUESTIONS

Develop a set of specific questions to help you narrow the focus of your research. You may think of more key terms as you draft your questions.

> • Which nonprofit organizations in the Sacramento area help stray animals or do animal rescue?
>
> • Which of these organizations are looking for volunteers?
>
> • What requirements do volunteers have to meet? Are there age limitations or time requirements?

CHOOSE A NOTE-TAKING METHOD

To avoid drowning in a sea of facts, figures, and details, record the information you find in a way that matches your purpose. Here are some examples:

- If you are doing research for a formal report, you should probably use **note cards.** See page 1220 to learn more about this method.

- Use a **category chart** to help you compare details.

Name and Address of Animal Shelter	Age Requirements	Hours per Week Required	Other Details
CARE Shelter for Animals, 3832 Bradley Rd.	16+	No minimum	Web site: careshelters.org
Happy Tails, 1560 Broadway	14+	10 hr/week	Saturdays OK

- Consider a **pro-con chart** if you want to examine two options.

Volunteering at CARE Shelter for Animals	
Advantages:	**Disadvantages:**
• can get there on my bike	• must be at least 16 years old, so I'd have to wait until my birthday in January
• no minimum number of hours	• dogs and cats only; no exotic animals
Volunteering at Happy Tails	
Advantages:	**Disadvantages:**
• has dogs, cats, and exotic animals	• have to take two buses to get there
• lets 14-year-olds volunteer	• must volunteer at least one weekday after school and every Saturday

Using the Internet

How Can I Find the Best Online Resources? The Internet is a great place to find a vast amount of information quickly. How can you target your search so that you don't get lost?

Understanding the Web

You probably know that the World Wide Web is accessible through the Internet, a vast system of linked computers. The Web includes literally hundreds of millions of Web sites and billions of Web pages.

Each type of Web site has its own purpose. One clue to the purpose is the URL, or "address," of a Web page. Each Web address includes an abbreviation that tells you what type of site the page is in.

ACADEMIC VOCABULARY FOR THE INTERNET

- World Wide Web
- Web site
- URL (uniform resource locator, also called Web address)
- search engine
- keyword search
- menu
- hyperlink or link
- icon

WEB ABBREVIATIONS AND MEANINGS

.COM commercial organization—product information and sales; some personal sites; some combinations of products and information, such as World Book Online

.EDU education—information about schools, courses, campus life, and research projects; may also include students' personal sites

.GOV U.S. government—official sites of the White House, the CIA, and many other government agencies

.MIL U.S. military—official sites of the armed forces, the Department of Defense, and related agencies

.NET network—product information and sales

.ORG organization—charities, libraries, and other nonprofit organizations; also political parties

SEARCH THE WEB

Keyword Search Start with a **search engine,** a Web site that allows you to look for information by using a phrase or term related to your subject. This kind of search is called a **keyword search.** Here are some search tips:

- Be as specific as possible. Instead of *volunteering*, try *volunteer programs in Sacramento.* Look at your research questions for ideas.

- Some search engines allow you to replace letters at the end of a word with an asterisk. For example, a search for the keyword *volunt** will find sites that contain *volunteer, voluntary,* and *volunteerism.*

- Enclose an exact phrase in quotation marks. For example, a search for *"volunteer with animals"* will find sites that include those three words in that order.

TIP Search engines often have "Advanced Search" or "Search Tips" links that you can click for more information.

Boolean Search A Boolean search allows you to specify the relationships among keywords and phrases.

- **AND search:** The AND tells the search engine to find all documents that contain every word (*volunteer* AND *animals*). Some search engines use a plus sign instead (*+volunteer +animals*).

- **OR search:** The OR broadens the search to include all documents that contain either word (*cats* OR *dogs*).

- **NOT search:** A NOT excludes unwanted terms from the search (*pets* NOT *breeders*). Some search engines use a minus sign (*+pets −breeders*).

SELECT RELEVANT SITES

Your search may result in a list that puts what the search engine considers the most relevant sites at the top of the page. Most search engines base relevance on how often your search terms appear on a particular page and on whether any or all of your search terms appear in the page's URL. However, just because a site is at the top of a list doesn't mean it's the most relevant site for you. Read the full entries in the list, looking for words that are related to your needs.

TRY IT OUT! *Look at Search Engine Results*

A search for volunteer opportunities in one community resulted in a number of possibilities. Which ones would you choose to explore?

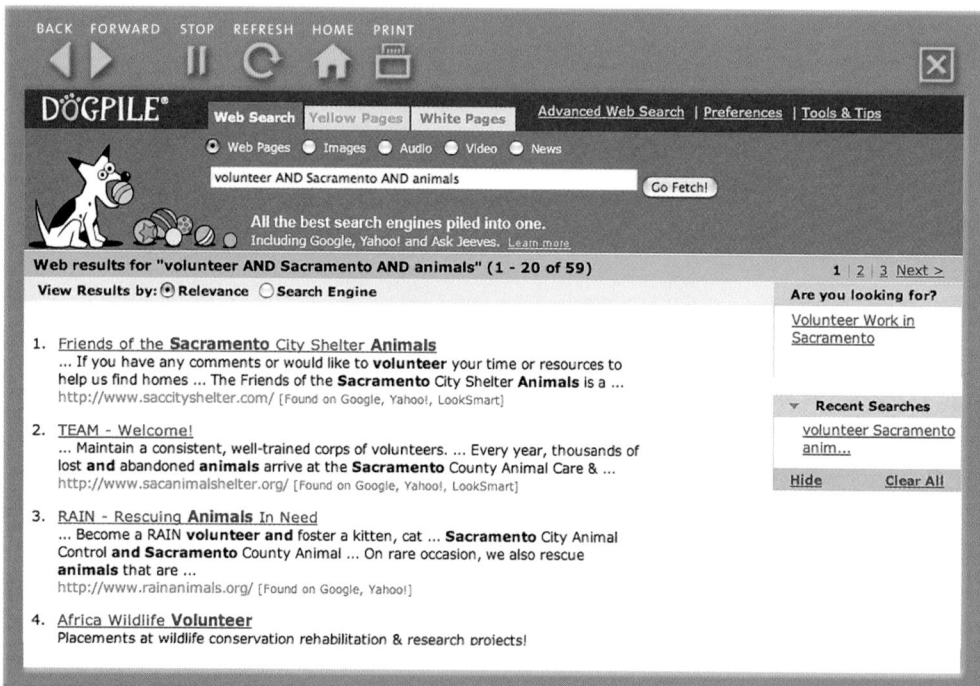

TIP Use a metasearch engine to scan multiple search engines simultaneously. See page 1208 for more information.

INTERACTIVE PRACTICE
For interactive practice of Try It Out! activities, go to the **Research Center** at **ClassZone.com**.

Close Read

1. Which three words were used in this Boolean search? What makes them an effective combination?

2. What was the total number of sites found? Is this a manageable number of sites to open and read? Why or why not?

3. Of the four sites shown, which are relevant to volunteer work with animals in Sacramento? Which one of the sites is not relevant?

EXPLORE WEB SITES

Once you have chosen a site to look at, you have to know how to read it and how to use the special features it contains. Most Web pages have features that aren't used in books.

- **Hyperlinks** are usually underlined or highlighted words. Clicking on a link leads you to related information on another page on the site or on a different site.

- **Icons** are pictures that can be clicked on to take you to another page.

- Most Web pages include at least one **menu,** or list of choices. These are often on one side of the page, at the top, or at the bottom.

TIP To evaluate the usefulness and accuracy of the information on a Web site, use the evaluation guidelines on page 1202.

TRY IT OUT! *Read a Web Site*

Let's say you choose to visit the second site that the search engine listed. Take a close look at the site's home page and see what information you can find.

BACK FORWARD STOP REFRESH HOME PRINT

TEAM

Teaching Everyone Animals Matter

A Non-Profit Affiliate of Sacramento County Animal Care and Regulation

Cat Tales

Go to the Dogs!

About TEAM
Adoption Fees
Dogs & Puppies
Cats & Kittens
SAAC Spay/Neuter Voucher Program
Free Spay/Neuter for Feral Cats
Success Stories
Donations
Volunteer
Finding Lost Pets
Events Calendar

Team Goals

TEAM actively supports efforts designed to:

- **Increase** redemption of lost animals and adoptions of eligible ones
- **Improve** public awareness of animal care and responsibility issues
- **Expand** humane education and humane law enforcement capabilities
- **Provide** foster care and breed rescue assistance
- **Maintain** a consistent, well-trained corps of volunteers.

These are just some of TEAM's objectives More about TEAM.

Team Flyer, Side One
Team Flyer, Side Two

Every year, thousands of lost and abandoned animals arrive at the Sacramento County Animal Care & Regulation.

The County's Board of Supervisors has approved many improvements to be made to the animal shelter facility, including additional field and kennel staff, stainless steel barriers between dog runs, and vaccinations at animal intake.

Adoptions stop one half hour before closing. Please plan accordingly.

Shelter Hours

Tue Thur Fri: 10 - 5
Wed: 10 - 7
Sat: 10 - 4:30
Sun & Mon: Closed

Home | About TEAM | Fees | Dogs | Cats | Success | Donations | Volunteer | Lost Pets | Events
Contact the Shelter | About This Site

Close Read

1. Is this site a useful one for someone looking for volunteer work with animals in Sacramento? Give reasons for your answer.

2. Where would you click to learn more about this organization's objectives and goals?

3. This site has menus on the left side of the page and at the bottom. Which link would you click to find out about volunteer opportunities?

4. Where would you click to find out who created this site and when it was last updated? Why is that information important?

Using the Library or Media Center

What Information Can I Find at the Library? Let's say you find information on animal shelters and begin to volunteer at one. You meet veterinarians and veterinary technicians, and you begin to wonder about a career in veterinary medicine. Now you have a new topic—one that requires in-depth research.

Understanding Today's Library

Libraries and media centers today are information supersources. They offer access to print, audio-visual, electronic, and human resources. Here is a quick look at the many types of information libraries have to offer.

LIBRARY AND MEDIA CENTER RESOURCES

BOOKS

Nonfiction books are organized by subject. See "Library Sleuth" on page 1208 to learn about the two systems for classifying nonfiction books.

Fiction books are organized alphabetically by the authors' last names.

NEWSPAPERS AND PERIODICALS

Periodicals include magazines, newsletters, and scholarly journals.

Microforms are periodicals, newspapers, and reports stored on film (microfilm) or cards (microfiche) and viewable on special machines.

REFERENCE SOURCES

Reference books include dictionaries, encyclopedias, atlases, and almanacs. These usually cannot be checked out of the library.

Search tools include databases, directories, indexes, and the library's online catalog. One search tool that can save you time is an index of abstracts. An **abstract** is a short summary of a journal article. By looking at abstracts, you can determine which articles are most closely related to your topic.

ELECTRONIC RESOURCES

DVDs and videos of documentaries and other films and television shows are available at most libraries for free or for a small fee.

E-books are books available in electronic form. They are readable on a personal computer or on various hand-held electronic devices.

Audio resources include books, music, and speeches on CDs or in MP3 files.

CD-ROMs of encyclopedias, maps, and other resources are available at many libraries.

OTHER RESOURCES

Your library may have a careers section, a college search section, maps, music scores, genealogy resources, and many other items. Most libraries have special sections for both young adults and children.

Finding What You Need

All the different departments and resources in your local library can seem overwhelming. Where should you start? Ask a librarian, or consult the library's online resources.

THE RESEARCH LIBRARIAN

Librarians are experts in finding information. These experts can help you

- define what you need to know
- locate print, electronic, and audio-visual sources of information
- use the library's resources and operate equipment
- use interlibrary catalogs to expand your research to other libraries

THE LIBRARY'S CATALOG

The catalog is your road map to the library's vast resources. There are four ways to search for a source:

- author • title • subject • keyword

In addition to a source's author, title, and publication date, the catalog entry may include a brief summary of its content and the subject categories it addresses. The entry will also indicate where it is shelved and whether it is available.

TRY IT OUT! *Search a Library Catalog*

This example of a catalog entry shows information about a specific book.

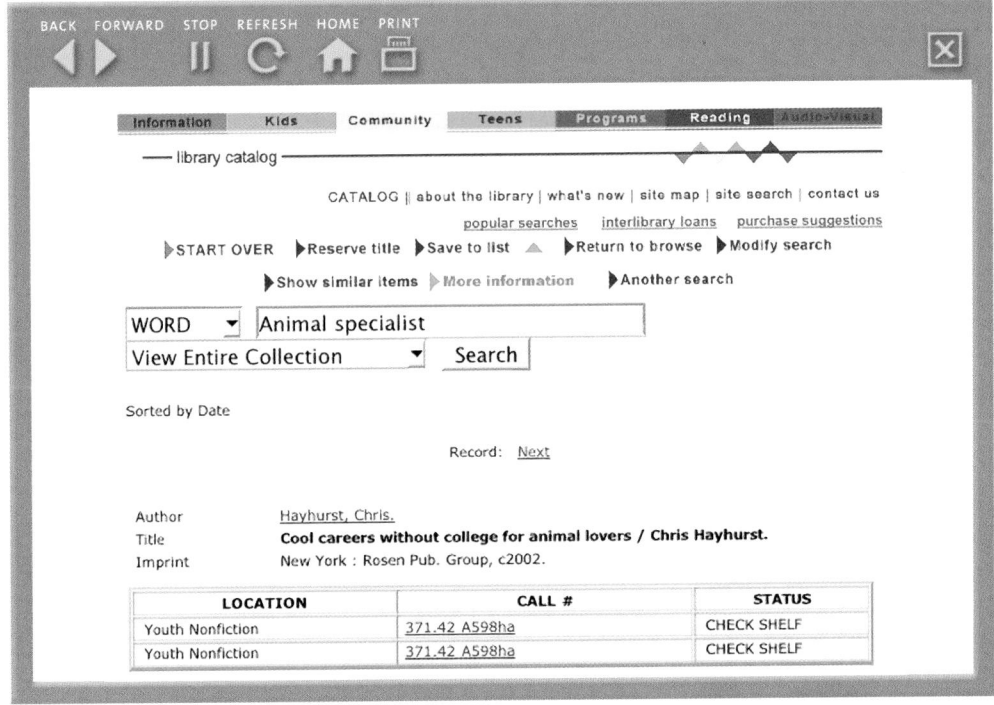

Close Read

1. What search term did this student use? List some other search terms that might produce similar results.

2. Is the book *Cool Careers* available at this library? How can you tell?

3. When was this book published? How do you know?

Choosing Sources

You have arrived at the library and looked at the online catalog. You're amazed at the amount of information available on your subject. How can you find which sources best fit your needs?

PRIMARY AND SECONDARY SOURCES

One of the first steps in choosing a source is to determine whether it is a primary or a secondary source. This chart explains the differences.

PRIMARY SOURCES	SECONDARY SOURCES
Definition: materials written or created by people who were present at events, either as participants or as observers	**Definition:** records of events that were written or created after the events occurred by people who were not directly involved in the events
Advantages: firsthand information; can help the researcher understand the attitudes and beliefs of a particular time period; may contain very specific information	**Advantages:** sometimes include excerpts from many primary sources; often have a broad perspective and many viewpoints; good for getting an overview of a topic
Disadvantages: limited perspective; may need interpretation; may be biased	**Disadvantages:** only as reliable as the sources used; may be biased
Often used when researching: current events, biographical information	**Often used when researching:** complex or technical subjects, ancient history
Examples: letters, diaries, speeches, travelogues, photographs, autobiographies, interviews, e-mails, public documents such as census data, first-person newspaper and magazine articles	**Examples:** encyclopedias, textbooks, biographies, some newspaper and magazine articles, documentaries and other films

REFERENCE SOURCES

A good first step in finding primary and secondary sources is to examine the library's reference collection. Reference works can give you a good overview of a topic and help you identify people, dates, and publications associated with your topic. They can also help you focus your topic and develop research questions. Many types of reference works are available on CD-ROMs and online. Ask a research librarian for help.

REFERENCE SOURCES	EXAMPLES
ENCYCLOPEDIAS **General: Detailed articles on many topics** **Specialized: Articles on topics in a specific field, such as medicine, art, or careers**	*Encyclopaedia Britannica* *The World Book Encyclopedia* *Encyclopedia of Careers and Vocational Guidance*
DICTIONARIES **General: Word meanings, origins, spellings, pronunciations, and usage** **Specialized: Terms used in a specific field, such as medicine or music**	*The American Heritage Student Dictionary* *Delmar's Veterinary Technician Dictionary*
ALMANACS AND YEARBOOKS **Facts and statistics**	*The World Almanac and Book of Facts*
THESAURI **Synonyms and antonyms**	*Webster's New World Thesaurus* *Roget's II: The New Thesaurus*
BIOGRAPHICAL REFERENCES **Detailed information on the lives and careers of noteworthy people**	*Native American Women*
ATLASES **Maps and geographic information**	*Rand McNally Classroom Atlas*
DIRECTORIES **Names, addresses, and phone numbers of people and organizations**	*Telephone books; lists of business organizations, agencies, and publications*
INDEXES **Alphabetical lists of information, usually subjects, authors, and titles**	*Readers' Guide to Periodical Literature* *New York Times Index*

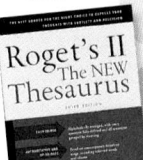

DATABASES

What Are They? A database is a collection of information arranged so that it is easy to search. You may be familiar with some free online databases, such as the Internet Movie Database. Other databases require a subscription, but your local library may have access to them. For instance, InfoTrac is a database of articles from newspapers, magazines, and journals. America's Newspapers contains articles from about 270 American newspapers. The Veterinary Medical Database is a collection of case histories of individual animals that have been given veterinary care.

Why Are They Useful? One advantage to using databases rather than search engines is that database searches are more targeted. Unlike search engines, databases have no advertisements. Also, most databases are collections of specific types of material—only newspaper articles, only scientific papers, and so on.

When Do I Use Them? Use databases when you have narrowed your topic considerably and have a good idea of what information you are seeking. Ask a librarian which databases are available to you.

TRY IT OUT! *Examine a Database*

A search of InfoTrac brought up the following information about veterinary technicians.

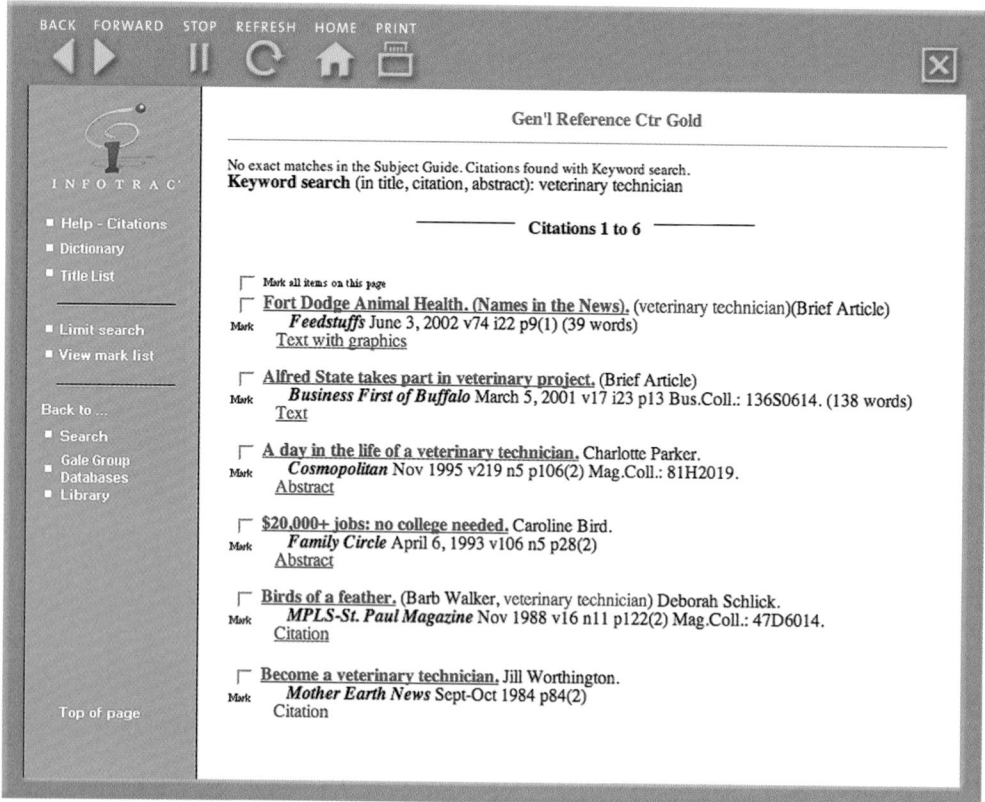

Close Read

1. InfoTrac found six matches for the keywords. Which of these matches might be most useful? least useful? Why?

2. Is the information organized alphabetically or by date? What are the advantages or disadvantages of this organization?

3. Which menu item on the left would you click on to make your search more specific?

NEWSPAPERS AND PERIODICALS

Newspapers are publications that contain news and advertising and that are published daily, weekly, or very frequently. Publications that are issued at regular intervals of more than one day are **periodicals.** Magazines and journals are examples of periodicals.

TYPES OF SOURCES	EXAMPLES
MAGAZINES **General:** For most readers **Specialized:** Articles on specific topics	*Time, Newsweek, Parade* *Horse Illustrated* *Popular Mechanics* 
NEWSPAPERS **General:** For most readers in a particular geographic area **Specialized:** For readers interested in a particular topic, such as finance	*Fort Worth Star-Telegram* *Los Angeles Times* *Wall Street Journal* 
JOURNALS Journals present specialized information and are designed for experts. Journals are usually more formal than magazines and have fewer advertisements.	*American Journal of Veterinary Research* *Journal of Interactive Media in Education* 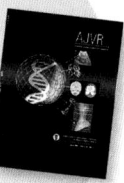

Here are tips to help you find an article on your topic:

- Ask the research librarian about specialized magazines or journals that may contain articles on your topic.

- Use databases of articles, such as InfoTrac, to help you find information on your topic in newspapers and magazines. If the database doesn't provide the full articles, you can ask at the periodicals desk for the specific issues you want to see.

DOCUMENTARIES AND OTHER FILMS

Your list of possible sources may include some titles on DVD or videotape. How can you quickly assess whether these sources are worth watching?

- Is the source **fiction** or **nonfiction?** To identify a nonfiction film, read the library's online catalog description. Look for the word *documentary* or *interview*. A fictional film probably would not have enough factual information to serve as a reliable source.

- Does the film contain the kind of **information** you need? Check the online catalog description and the front and back covers of the DVD or videocassette. Does the film include **primary sources,** such as interviews or speeches?

NONFICTION BOOKS

Your library search may result in a list of book titles and call numbers. How can you quickly determine which books have the information you're seeking?

- Read each book's **title** (and **subtitle,** if there is one) and skim chapter titles and headings to get an idea of the general subject matter.

- Check the **copyright page** for the date of publication. If you need up-to-the-minute information, don't depend on a book that is several years old.

- Examine the **table of contents** at the front of the book and the **index** at the back for terms related to your subject. Is there sufficient information on your subject or very little?

- Many books also have **bibliographies** or lists of **recommended readings.** These can give you ideas for other sources to consult.

- If the book contains difficult technical terms, look for a **glossary** at the back. This section lists specialized terms and their definitions.

TRY IT OUT! *Examine the Parts of a Book*

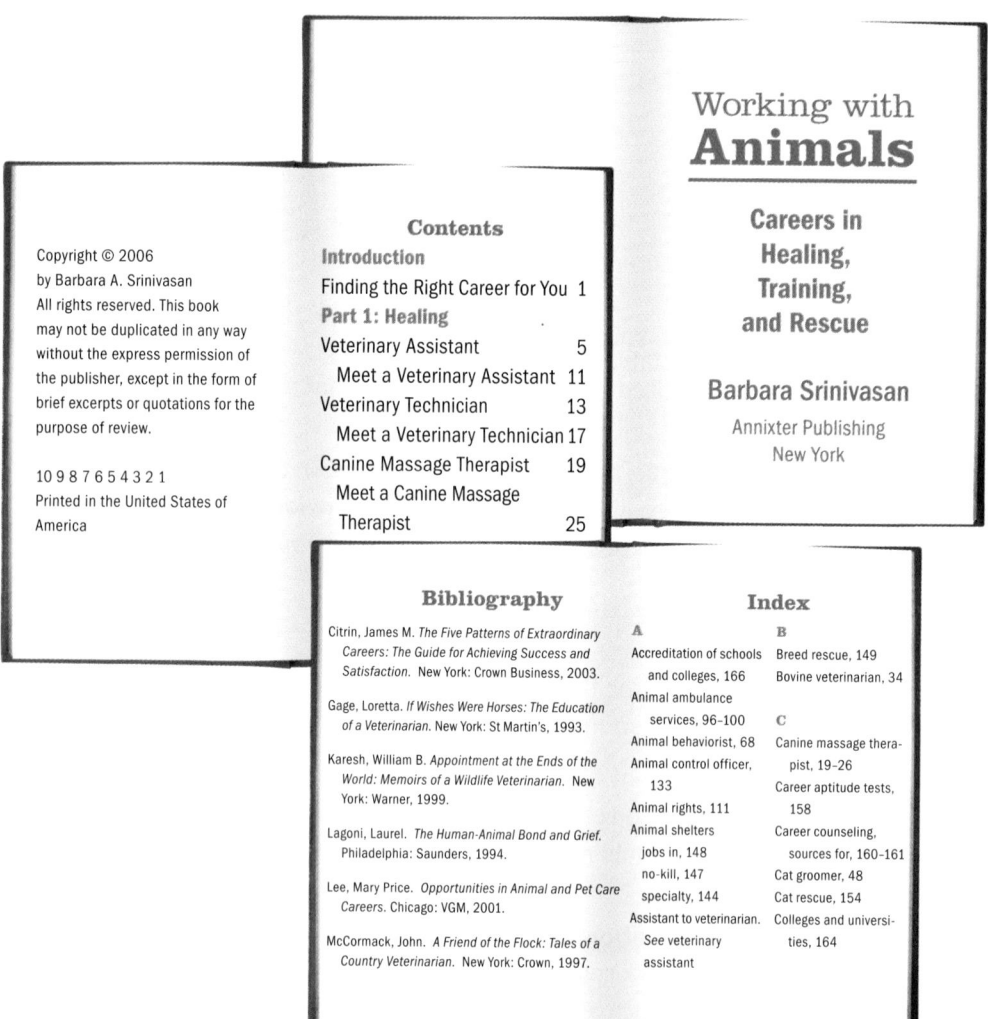

Close Read

1. How does the subtitle of this book help you understand its content?

2. When was this book published? Is it recent enough to be a useful source?

3. Does this book include interviews with people employed in certain jobs? How do you know?

4. Does this book include information on jobs in animal shelters? How do you know?

Evaluating Information

How Can I Tell If the Information I Find Can Be Trusted? Now that you have found a number of useful sources, how can you figure out which ones are credible and reliable?

Applying General Evaluation Guidelines

No matter what kind of source you have chosen—in print or online—or where you have found it, you need to look at it critically before deciding whether you can trust the information it contains.

EVALUATING SOURCES

Is the information up-to-date?	Look for a copyright date or a "last updated" reference. Recent information is critical in some fields, such as science, medicine, and sports. Older publications can be helpful for historical topics.
Is the information accurate?	Can the facts be verified by more than one source? Most print and online encyclopedias, dictionaries, directories, and almanacs are considered reliable because they are updated regularly and go through a rigorous review process.
What are the author's credentials?	Does the author have a position or job title that qualifies him or her as an expert on the topic? Has he or she written other materials on this topic?
What kinds of materials does the publisher produce?	University presses usually publish information that is carefully researched. Magazines that publish trendy articles and gossip are not as reliable as newsmagazines or science magazines.
Could the source be biased?	Why does the source exist? Does the author mention his or her goals in a foreword, preface, or introduction? Is the author's purpose to inform, to persuade, to entertain, or some combination of these? Does the author use loaded language, such as "Millions of people are joining the fight against this unforgivable injustice"?
How much information does the source cover?	Does the source give an overview or detailed information? Does the material support other information you have read or add new information? Start by looking at the table of contents, menu, or index.
Is the source relevant?	Does the source cover aspects of the topic that interest you? Is it written at a level you can understand?

Evaluating Specific Sources

The evaluation guidelines on the previous page apply to every source you use. The questions and tips on these pages will help you evaluate specific types of sources.

EVALUATE WEB SITES

Web sites are often a mix of helpful information and attempts to promote points of view or to sell products or services.

Commercial Web Sites   As you learned on page 1191, sites with URLs containing *.com* or *.net* are sometimes for-profit sites. When you look at a commercial site, ask yourself these questions:

- **Who is the author?** Look for a menu link called "About This Site" or "Contact Us."
- **Why was the site created?** If the site was designed to sell you something, the site creators may have omitted any negative information about the product.

TIP Knowing who created a site can help you figure out why the site exists and whether it is appropriate to use in your research.

Organization (.org) Web Sites   These sites may represent particular points of view. Although many are nonprofit organizations, such as the Red Cross, political parties also have *.org* in their domain names. Ask yourself these questions:

- **Who created the site, and when was it last updated?** Look for a link titled "About Us" or "Mission Statement." If there is no way to identify the creator of the site, then you should be cautious about the content.
- **Are statements of fact supported by examples and evidence?** Look for links to supporting evidence from respected institutions or publications.

Personal Web Sites   Because anyone can post anything on the World Wide Web, there are millions of personal Web sites. Some have misleading URLs. For example, students and faculty members can set up personal Web sites on a university's server, and their Web addresses will contain the university's URL. However, these sites might not be reviewed, evaluated, or in any way sanctioned by the institution.

TIP Not all personal Web sites are unreliable, but be cautious.

- **How can I tell if a site is personal when its address contains the name of an institution?** Look for a forward slash and tilde (/~) and a name or initials following *.edu* in the URL.
- **What does the lack of an official institution logo tell me?** Don't expect the information to have been reviewed or approved by the institution.
- **What does it mean if links in the site don't work or are mostly links to other items by the same author?** The author may be careless, or he or she may lack outside support.

TRY IT OUT! *Examine Web Sites*

Examine this Web site. What does it offer a visitor?

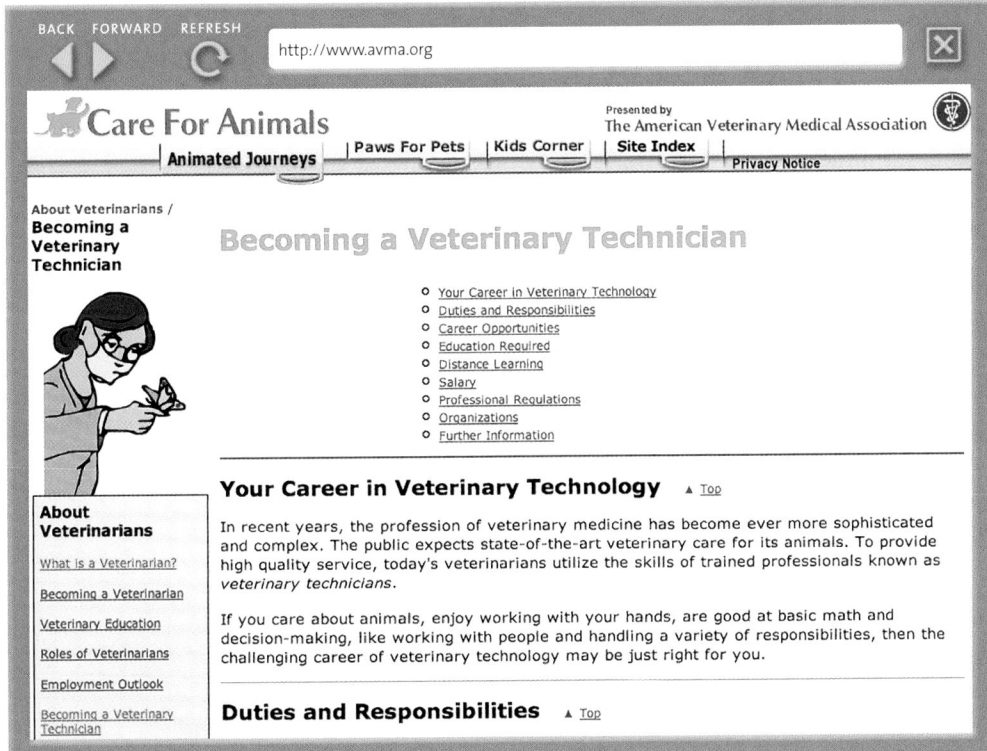

Close Read

1. Who created this site?
2. What is the purpose of the site?
3. Who is the intended audience?
4. What clues tell you that it is a nonprofit site?

TIP To get to a site's home page from a page with a long URL, simply delete everything after the domain name (such as *www.avma.org*) and press Enter. The home page will come up.

Here is an example of a personal Web site. What does it offer?

Close Read

1. How reliable are the statistics about homeless animals? Give reasons for your answer.
2. Does Dunstan Community College support the efforts of the site's creator? How can you tell?

EVALUATE NONFICTION BOOKS

Nonfiction books are one of the best sources of in-depth information.

- **When was the book last copyrighted or updated?** Check the **copyright notice,** which is usually on the back of the title page. Also look on the copyright page or on the cover for a statement such as "revised and updated edition." A book that has gone through many updates and printings is likely to be reliable.

- **What sources did the writer use?** Look for a **bibliography.** Some books include an **appendix**—a collection of additional material on the subject. Notes within the book, such as **footnotes, endnotes,** or **cross-references,** can also give you clues about sources.

- **What are the author's qualifications?** Look for an author's biography on the book jacket or at the beginning or end of the book. The author may have written a **preface,** a short introductory essay that explores the purpose of the book, the intended audience, and the research on which the book is based. If the source is a biography, find out if the author is related to the person he or she has written about.

TRY IT OUT! *Examine a Nonfiction Book*

Use what you have learned about nonfiction books and about the parts of a book (page 1200) to help you evaluate whether this book is a relevant source for someone interested in a career involving work with animals.

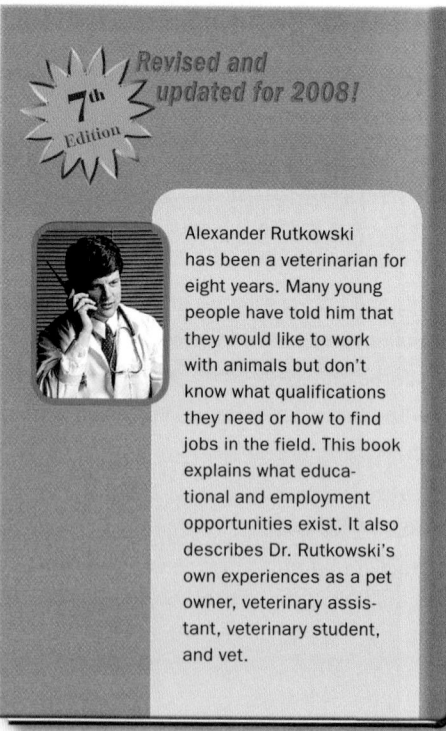

Revised and updated for 2008!
7th Edition

Alexander Rutkowski has been a veterinarian for eight years. Many young people have told him that they would like to work with animals but don't know what qualifications they need or how to find jobs in the field. This book explains what educational and employment opportunities exist. It also describes Dr. Rutkowski's own experiences as a pet owner, veterinary assistant, veterinary student, and vet.

Close Read

1. What is this book about?

2. What qualifies the author to write a book on this topic?

3. Was this book published recently? How do you know?

4. What other parts of the book should you examine to determine if it is a worthwhile source? (Hint: See page 1200.)

EVALUATE NEWSPAPERS AND PERIODICALS

Newspapers and periodicals can be good sources of up-to-the-minute, easy-to-read information. Different publications are available in a print edition, online, or on microfilm or microfiche. Evaluating an article can be tricky, because you need to assess the publication, the author of the specific article, and the content. Here are some basic questions to ask:

TIP Even the most reliable publications may contain errors. Whenever possible, check facts in more than one source.

- **Is the source well-known and respected?** Most large-circulation newspapers and national magazines are reliable sources. Beware of sensationalist publications such as the *National Enquirer,* however.

- **When was it published?** Old is not necessarily bad. Out-of-date newspaper and magazine articles can provide rich information on historical events.

- **Who is the author?** You can usually assume that articles by staff writers or contributing editors are as reliable as the source they're published in.

- **Was the article reprinted from another source?** If so, make sure the original source—for example, *Scientific American* or a news service such as the Associated Press (AP)—is reliable.

- **Can the facts in the article be verified?** Consult other sources, either on paper, online, or in person.

TRY IT OUT! *Examine a Newspaper Article*

Use what you have learned about evaluating sources as you examine this article.

---

from **The Dallas Morning News**

Animal ER

For injured pets, 'round-the-clock clinics provide a haven and hope

BY ALINE MCKENZIE, STAFF WRITER

It's an ordinary night. One of life-and-death situations, tears and relief, small miracles. Meals eaten on the fly, calm during lulls.

Animals don't time their ills and injuries to convenient office hours.

So when regular veterinarians are off duty, the after-hours emergency animal clinics take over. From kennel cough to surgery, every night brings a different mix.

"It's just something I've always wanted to do, just as a kid," says Dr. Michelle Hazlewood, 32. "I've always loved animals."

"Neither of us could go back into a regular day practice," says Dr. Kathleen Bowe, 38. The variety and the excitement beat the ordinary well-animal care of a day job, she says.

The two are the vets on duty this night at the Emergency Animal Clinic of Collin County in Plano, one of a
See ANIMALS, page B2

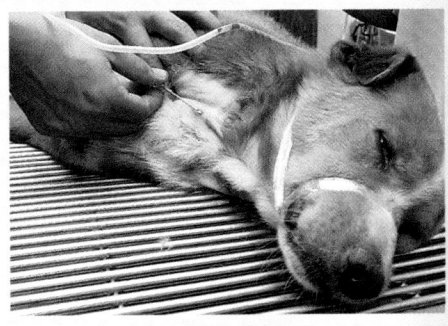
Buster the dog donates blood.

Close Read

1. What kind of veterinary clinic is the focus of this article?

2. Knowing that Dallas is a large city in Texas and that the *Dallas Morning News* is its major newspaper, would you expect this to be a reliable source of information?

3. How could a reader verify the facts in an article like this?

Collecting Your Own Data

What If I Need to Gather Information Firsthand? Sometimes the answers to your questions cannot be found on a Web site or in a library. How can you collect original data?

Using People as Primary Sources

For some topics, your own observations and data will be your best source of information. The following techniques can turn you into your own search engine.

FIELD RESEARCH AND OBSERVATION

Any focused, purposeful observations you make can be considered field research. For instance, you might visit an animal shelter or a veterinarian's office to learn about careers in veterinary medicine, or you might listen to a **lecture** at school about veterinary careers. If you wish to make a visit, be sure to call ahead to ask permission and to make an appointment. For some research projects, you may want to set up a **field study** in which you make observations and collect specific types of data.

Notes on Visit to CARE Shelter for Animals, 10/21/2006

- *staff : 4 full-time employees plus 8 to 12 part-time volunteers*
- *provides medical care for 20 to 30 dogs plus 30 to 40 cats; no rabbits, rodents, wild animals, or exotic animals*
- *Dogs are in individual cages, but most cats are 3 or 4 to a cage.*
- *"no-kill" shelter, which means that animals stay until they are adopted*
- *Jackie Kirchner coordinates all the volunteers. The shelter needs people to clean cages and to feed and exercise the animals.*
- *Ms. Kirchner says that Kyle Faris, their veterinary technician, would probably agree to an interview.*

INTERVIEWS

Try talking with people who have experience in what you are researching. For example, you could interview a veterinary assistant, a veterinary technician, and a veterinarian about their jobs. You might interview someone in person, over the telephone, or by e-mail. First, ask if the person is willing to talk with you, and then set a date and time for the interview. Prepare a list of clear, open-ended questions that must be answered with specific information, not just yes or no. Take thorough notes during the interview. Here are some sample interview questions.

Questions for Kyle Faris

1. *How long have you been a veterinary technician?*
2. *What is the best part of the job? Why?*
3. *What is the worst part of the job? Why?*
4. *What kind of education and work experience would I need to become a veterinary technician?*

See page R81–R82: Interview

If you are able to identify an expert, you may wish to send a politely worded, specific question by e-mail or letter. You can gain an inside track to a group of experts by joining a relevant Internet discussion group, also called a list server. For instance, VETMED is a discussion group about veterinary medicine.

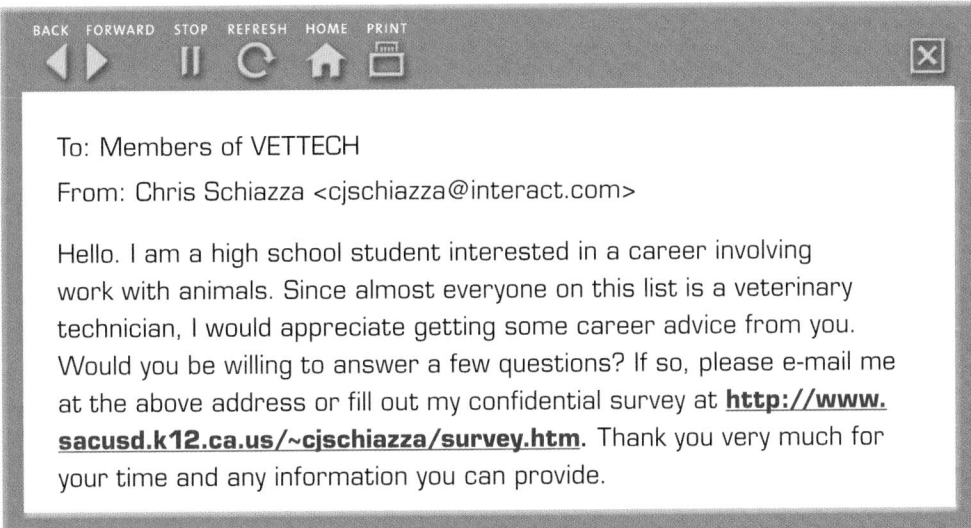

BACK   FORWARD   STOP   REFRESH   HOME   PRINT

To: Members of VETTECH

From: Chris Schiazza <cjschiazza@interact.com>

Hello. I am a high school student interested in a career involving work with animals. Since almost everyone on this list is a veterinary technician, I would appreciate getting some career advice from you. Would you be willing to answer a few questions? If so, please e-mail me at the above address or fill out my confidential survey at **http://www. sacusd.k12.ca.us/~cjschiazza/survey.htm**. Thank you very much for your time and any information you can provide.

SURVEYS AND QUESTIONNAIRES

You can collect survey and questionnaire information by telephone, by mail, by e-mail, through a Web site, or in person. Keep the names of participants confidential to protect their privacy.

TIP Stay safe—give only an e-mail address for people to use in responding to your survey. Do not give your home address or telephone number.

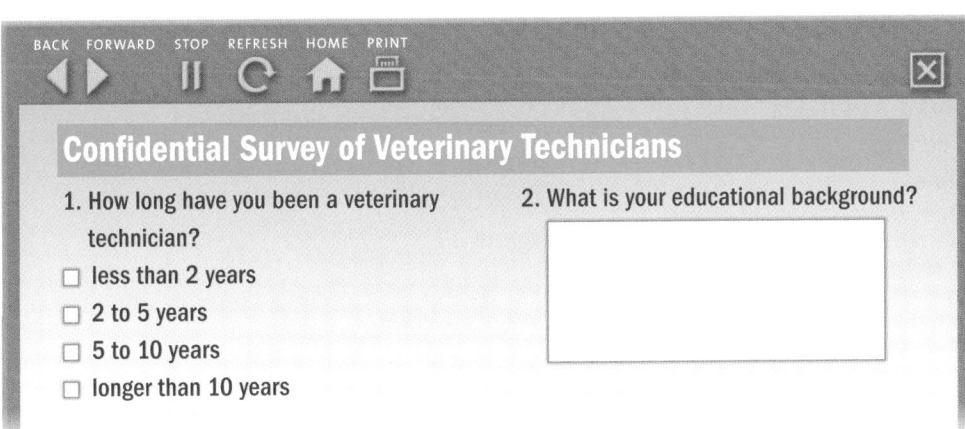

BACK   FORWARD   STOP   REFRESH   HOME   PRINT

Confidential Survey of Veterinary Technicians

1. How long have you been a veterinary technician?
   ☐ less than 2 years
   ☐ 2 to 5 years
   ☐ 5 to 10 years
   ☐ longer than 10 years

2. What is your educational background?

Research Tips and Strategies

Web Watch

Knowing what search tools to use is crucial to finding information on the World Wide Web.

Search Engines

Search engines differ in speed, size of database, method of searching, and other variables. Never use only one search engine.

- Altavista
- Excite
- Teoma
- Google

Metasearch Engines

A metasearch tool can save you time by sending a search to multiple search engines simultaneously.

- Vivismo
- Dogpile
- Metacrawler

Directories

Directories are useful when you are researching a general topic, because they arrange Internet resources into subject categories.

- Galaxy
- About.com
- Yahoo!

Virtual Libraries

At a virtual library, you can look up information in encyclopedias, directories, and indexes. You can even e-mail a question to a librarian.

- Internet Public Library
- Librarians' Index to the Internet

Other Web Resources

Library catalogs: Library of Congress
Encyclopedias: Encyclopaedia Britannica Online
Newspaper archives: New York Times Index
News associations: Associated Press
Specialized databases: Medline

Library Sleuth

Two basic systems are used to classify nonfiction books. Most high school and public libraries use the Dewey decimal system; university and research libraries generally use the Library of Congress system.

DEWEY DECIMAL SYSTEM

000–099	General works
100–199	Philosophy and psychology
200–299	Religion
300–399	Social sciences
400–499	Language
500–599	Natural sciences and mathematics
600–699	Technology (applied sciences)
700–799	Arts and recreation
800–899	Literature and rhetoric
900–999	Geography and history

LIBRARY OF CONGRESS SYSTEM

A	General works
B	Philosophy, psychology, religion
C	History
D	General and Old World history
E–F	American history
G	Geography, anthropology, recreation
H	Social sciences
J	Political science
K	Law
L	Education
M	Music
N	Fine arts
P	Language and literature
Q	Science
R	Medicine
S	Agriculture
T	Technology
U	Military science
V	Naval science
Z	Bibliography and library science

Checklist for Evaluating Sources

☑ The information is relevant to the topic you are researching.

☑ The information is up-to-date. (This point is especially important when researching time-sensitive fields such as science, medicine, and sports.)

☑ The information is from an author who is qualified to write about this topic.

☑ The information is from a trusted source that is updated or reviewed regularly.

☑ The author's or institution's purpose for writing is clear.

☑ The information is written at the right level for your needs. For example, a children's book is probably too simplistic, while a scientific paper may be too complex.

☑ The information has the level of detail you need—neither too general nor too specific.

☑ The facts can be verified in more than one source.

Sharing Your Research

At last you have established your research goal, located sources of information, evaluated the materials, and taken notes on what you learned. Now you have a chance to share the results with the people in your world—and even beyond. Here are some options:

- Use presentation software to create a power presentation for your classmates, friends, or family.
- Publish your research findings on your own Web site.
- Develop a newsletter or brochure summarizing your information.
- Explain what you learned in an oral presentation to your classmates or to people in your community.
- Write up your research in a formal research paper.
  See the following pages. ▶

See pages 1231–1233: Creating a Web Site

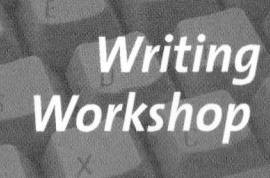

Writing Workshop

Research Paper

Now that you have thoroughly explored a variety of research strategies, you are ready for your next challenge: the formal research paper. Perhaps you will have the opportunity to learn more about people, places, or events in history, science, or art. You can even choose a great literary work and explore one aspect of it in depth. To start your investigation, refer to the **Writer's Road Map.**

WRITER'S ROAD MAP
Research Paper

WRITING PROMPT 1

Writing from Literature Formulate a question about the *Odyssey* or another literary work that you would like to explore in detail. Write a research paper that includes data from at least five sources and has Works Cited list.

Questions Related to the *Odyssey*
- What is the role of women in the *Odyssey*?
- What kinds of weapons, armor, and ships did the ancient Greeks have?
- How did the discovery of the ruins of Troy change our understanding of the *Odyssey*?

WRITING PROMPT 2

Writing for the Real World Write a research paper that investigates an idea or a question that interests you. Your paper should present your own ideas and interpretations as well as factual information. Include data from at least five sources and provide a Works Cited list.

Questions to Investigate
- How has the Internet changed the music industry?
- Are genetically modified foods safe to eat?

 RESEARCH TOOLS
For research help and citation guidelines, go to the **Research Center** at ClassZone.com.

KEY TRAITS

1. IDEAS
- Presents a **thesis statement** that identifies the governing idea of the entire paper
- Supports the thesis with **evidence,** including **quotations** and **paraphrases**
- Synthesizes information from **multiple sources**
- Includes the **writer's own ideas and interpretations**

2. ORGANIZATION
- Has a focused **introduction**
- Has a logical **organizational pattern** and **transition words**
- Includes a satisfying and thoughtful **conclusion**

3. VOICE
- Maintains a **tone** that is appropriate for the topic, audience, and purpose

4. WORD CHOICE
- Uses **precise language** to convey ideas clearly

5. SENTENCE FLUENCY
- Varies **sentence lengths and structures**

6. CONVENTIONS
- Employs **correct grammar and usage**
- **Credits sources**
- Uses **correct formats and style**

Part 1: Analyze a Student Model

WRITING STANDARD
1.4.11.B Write complex informational pieces

Ilona Bergstrom
Mr. Grant
English 9
10 May 2008

The Mystery of the <u>Odyssey</u>

Everybody loves a great adventure story, especially one that has everything—monsters, gods, bloody battles, raging storms, and, finally, a happy ending. The <u>Odyssey</u> by Homer is that kind of adventure story. For modern readers, though, it is also an intriguing mystery.

5 Did the places Homer described really exist? We may never know for certain which places in the <u>Odyssey</u> are real and which are fiction, but investigating the events and geography of Odysseus' wanderings can lead to a better understanding of this great literary work.

As readers begin the <u>Odyssey</u>, we are swept into a journey that is so

10 exciting that we suffer along with Odysseus (or Ulysses, as he is known in Latin) and rejoice when he finally returns home. Only after closing the book do we step back to consider our earlier questions.

The <u>Odyssey</u> is full of fantastic creatures, gods, and events—such as Odysseus' battle with the Cyclops—that seem too amazing to be true.

15 The third-century-B.C. astronomer Eratosthenes, for example, thought that Homer's story was totally imaginary (Knox 25; "Homeric Legend"). Many people throughout history have tried to identify a real setting for the tale, though. The Greek poet Hesiod, who lived in the eighth century B.C., probably not long after the <u>Odyssey</u> was written, thought

20 that Odysseus' wanderings took him around Italy and Sicily. Other

KEY TRAITS IN ACTION

Presents the subject of the report in a clear **thesis statement.**

historians throughout the ages have thought he traveled to other places in the Mediterranean Sea or even the Atlantic Ocean ("Homeric Legend").

25   The debate has continued into modern times. About the only thing people seem to agree on is that Troy existed where Homer said it was and that the Trojan War took place sometime between 1300 and 1200 B.C. (Knox 5; Nardo 20; Wilford D1). The reason they agree is that archaeologists have found proof. Heinrich Schliemann first excavated the ruins of Troy in the 1870s, and other layers of the site have been identified since then (Nardo 16). It is what happened after

30   Odysseus left Troy—and where it happened—that remains a mystery.

Many Theories About <u>Odyssey</u> Locations

To try to solve this mystery, people have to assume that the events reported in the <u>Odyssey</u> actually did happen. Unfortunately, though, Homer's descriptions of places are often vague and confusing. Unlike the

35   events of the Trojan War, which took place on land, Odysseus' sea voyage left no traces (Severin 17; Struck). Therefore, all of the ideas historians have come up with about where the events occurred are just guesses.

Interestingly, these guesses have been literally all over the map, ranging from the North to the South Pole and from Norway to South

40   Africa (Knox 25). One sea captain claims that he identified every location described in the <u>Odyssey</u> along the coast of the Adriatic Sea (Severin 22).

Focus on the Mediterranean

Other historians have looked for the location of the <u>Odyssey</u> closer to Homer's own Mediterranean home. According to the literary expert

Synthesizes information from **multiple sources.** Uses correct parenthetical documentation **formats.**

Subheadings clarify major ideas and provide structure for a logical **organizational pattern.**

Supports main ideas with specific details **paraphrased** from and correctly **credited** to the sources.

Bergstrom 3

45 George Steiner, the story seems to take place in the waters surrounding Greece, Italy, and Egypt, though he admits, "The geography of the tale is a riddle" (9). For example, in Book Four of the <u>Odyssey</u>, Menelaus describes the island of Pharos as "as far out as the distance a hollow ship can make in a whole day's sailing" (Homer 74). However, Pharos is

50 now connected to the mainland of Egypt. Even the Greek geographer and historian Strabo, who lived from 63 B.C. to A.D. 23, was puzzled by Homer's geography (Severin 18).

The explorer Tim Severin compared many theories of Odysseus' route with nautical maps and concluded that "Ulysses' vessel jumps

55 up and down the length of the Mediterranean like the knight on a chessboard. It skips over inconvenient land masses, skids around capes, travels at speeds that would do credit to a modern cruise liner . . . " (22). Between lines 134 and 135 in Book Ten (Homer 155), for example, Odysseus somehow manages to get from one side of the island of Ithaca

60 to the other without stopping off there, "as though he had sailed right by his homeland" (Severin 240). One explanation is that the <u>Odyssey</u> actually describes two separate voyages and that the adventures after line 135 of Book Ten were based on the stories of another Greek hero, Jason, and his Argonauts ("Homeric Legend").

65 **Retracing Odysseus' Route**

Even so, none of the theories Severin examined were formulated by sailors, and he thought that the best way to discover the route taken by Odysseus was to try to retrace it. Using a replica of a Bronze Age ship

Includes a lively **quotation** from the source to support a main idea and add interest.

he had built, Severin set sail from Troy. He took the most direct route
70 to the present-day island of Ithaca, assuming that's what Odysseus
would have done in his haste to return home after the long Trojan War
(Burgess; Severin 22-23). He used both physical landmarks and local
folk tales to help him trace the places and events in Homer's story.

> Severin did manage to locate many places and things mentioned in
75 the <u>Odyssey</u>, such as Scylla and Charybdis, described in Book Twelve:

> On one side was Scylla, and on the other side was shining
> Charybdis, who made her terrible ebb and flow of the sea's
> water. When she vomited it up, like a cauldron over a strong
> fire, the whole sea would boil up in turbulence (Homer 191).

80 Cape Scylla still exists, and Severin found the cave of the monster
that ate six of Odysseus' men. According to Homer, Charybdis was
just across a narrow channel. Today, however, the channel is too wide
to create the violent whirlpools described in the <u>Odyssey</u>. Severin did
locate a narrow channel a little south of Cape Scylla that may have
85 caused whirlpools in ancient times, though (199). It's possible that
Homer used this place as the basis for Charybdis, exaggerating its power
to make the story more exciting. After all, a larger-than-life hero needs
larger-than-life problems to struggle with.

> The land of the Lotus-Eaters also turned out to be where other
90 people had thought it was—past the island of Cythera in Tunisia
(Burgess). Severin used Homer's mention of "wild goats beyond
number" in Book Nine (Homer 140) to locate Odysseus' next stop, the
island of the Cyclopes, on present-day Crete. The savage people

Straightforward tone conveys ideas objectively and understandably.

Correctly indents and documents a long quotation.

Provides the writer's original interpretation and summary of ideas.

Bergstrom 5

described by Homer were nothing like the civilized Cyclopes of
95 folklore, however (Severin 86). On the other hand, Severin failed to
find anything like Calypso's island, Ogygia. For this reason, he agreed
with other scholars that Homer may have created it and Odysseus'
imprisonment there to help explain why the hero had been wandering
for so long (Severin 243).

100   In the end, Severin was unable to trace Odysseus' journey exactly
and found many parts of Homer's tale puzzling. He concluded that "the
geographies of folklore and navigation overlapped" (245). Although he
didn't set out to prove whether the Odyssey was real or imagined, his
findings suggest that it was a mixture of both.

105 **An Unsolved Mystery**
     What conclusions can modern readers draw from these confusing
and conflicting ideas about the Odyssey? Robert Fagles, a well-known
translator and scholar of Homer, gives probably the best summary of the
possibilities—and of the Odyssey's lasting influence and interest:

110   I think it's altogether likely that, however "mythological"
     the Greek experience may seem, it nevertheless stems from
     experience. Was that experience actual or imagined, or a
     combination of the two? I don't think we'll ever know. . . .
     Homer's period in history was in fact a time of exploration
115   and new settlements, and these events survive in the
     [Odyssey], strikingly dramatized by Homer's incorporation of
     the fabulous, the Cyclops, the witches, and the other monsters
     and seductresses. All of it is stranger than fiction, as we'd say,
     and even more compelling than fact.

Transitions show how
ideas are related.

Varied **sentence lengths
and structures** integrate
information from several
sources while creating
interest and flow.

Conclusion provides a
thoughtful summary.

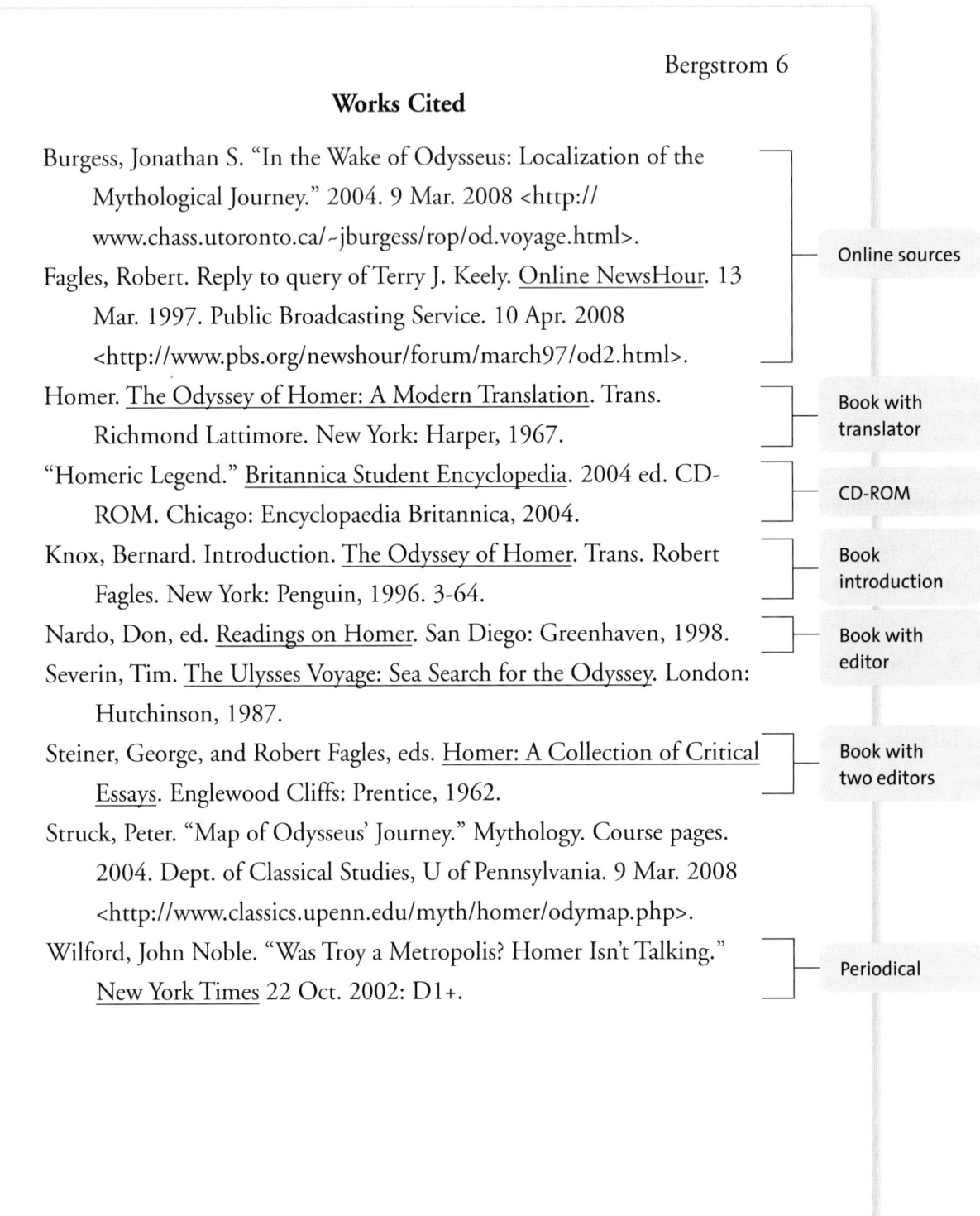

Bergstrom 6

Works Cited

Burgess, Jonathan S. "In the Wake of Odysseus: Localization of the Mythological Journey." 2004. 9 Mar. 2008 <http://www.chass.utoronto.ca/~jburgess/rop/od.voyage.html>.

Fagles, Robert. Reply to query of Terry J. Keely. Online NewsHour. 13 Mar. 1997. Public Broadcasting Service. 10 Apr. 2008 <http://www.pbs.org/newshour/forum/march97/od2.html>.

— Online sources

Homer. The Odyssey of Homer: A Modern Translation. Trans. Richmond Lattimore. New York: Harper, 1967.

— Book with translator

"Homeric Legend." Britannica Student Encyclopedia. 2004 ed. CD-ROM. Chicago: Encyclopaedia Britannica, 2004.

— CD-ROM

Knox, Bernard. Introduction. The Odyssey of Homer. Trans. Robert Fagles. New York: Penguin, 1996. 3-64.

— Book introduction

Nardo, Don, ed. Readings on Homer. San Diego: Greenhaven, 1998.

— Book with editor

Severin, Tim. The Ulysses Voyage: Sea Search for the Odyssey. London: Hutchinson, 1987.

Steiner, George, and Robert Fagles, eds. Homer: A Collection of Critical Essays. Englewood Cliffs: Prentice, 1962.

— Book with two editors

Struck, Peter. "Map of Odysseus' Journey." Mythology. Course pages. 2004. Dept. of Classical Studies, U of Pennsylvania. 9 Mar. 2008 <http://www.classics.upenn.edu/myth/homer/odymap.php>.

Wilford, John Noble. "Was Troy a Metropolis? Homer Isn't Talking." New York Times 22 Oct. 2002: D1+.

— Periodical

RESEARCH STANDARD
1.8.11.C.2 Develop a thesis statement based on research

Part 2: Apply the Writing Process

PREWRITING

What Should I Do?	*What Does It Look Like?*

1. Analyze the prompt. Reread the prompts on page 1210 and pick the one that interests you. (Circle) the words that tell you what to do. <u>Underline</u> the important details about the assignment.

▶ **WRITING PROMPT** <u>Formulate a question about the *Odyssey* or another literary work</u> that you would like to <u>explore in detail</u>. Write a (research paper) that includes <u>data from at least five sources and has a Works Cited list.</u>

I'm supposed to do research and write a paper about some aspect of the <u>Odyssey</u> or another piece of literature. I have to use in-depth information from at least five sources in the body of the paper and list the sources at the end.

2. Brainstorm possible topics and narrow your focus. Use a graphic organizer to explore topics that you'd like to research and write about. Focus on one that can be covered in detail in a short research paper.

TIP Check the catalogs in your school and local libraries, and databases such as InfoTrac, to see how much information is available on your topic. If there's too little, broaden your focus; if there's too much, you may need to limit it.

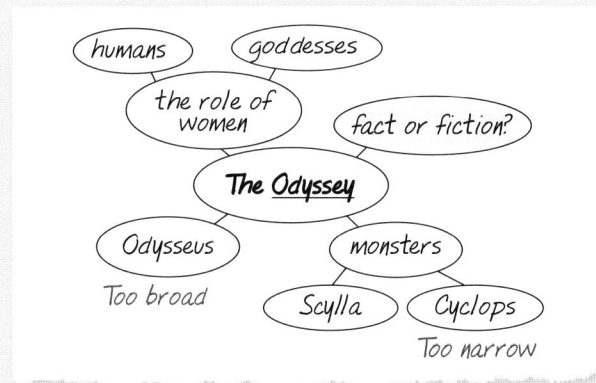

3. Develop research questions. Make a list of questions that you want to answer in your report. Keep these questions in mind as you do your research.

▶ *Research Questions*

1. How much of the <u>Odyssey</u> is real, and how much is made up?

2. If any of the events are real, where did they take place?

3. If events were made up, what were they based on?

4. Has anyone ever tried to duplicate Odysseus' journey?

What Should I Do?

What Does It Look Like?

1. Look for possible sources.
Begin gathering information about your topic by searching the World Wide Web and your school and local libraries. Try to select only those reference materials that are most likely to contain the information you need. For example, you might consult an atlas to trace Odysseus' journey, and refer to an encyclopedia to learn about Homeric legends. Keep a list indicating the name of each source and the place where you found it, adding comments that will help you use the sources later.

After locating and making comments on the sources, go on to the next step—evaluating each source for usefulness and reliability.

See pages 1189–1200 for more information about selecting appropriate reference works and research tools.

Sources	Comments
World Wide Web (bookmarked)	
"Geography in the Odyssey." <u>Wikipedia</u>[1]	lots of info
"Map of Odysseus' Journey"	go to "Background" link
"About the Odyssey." <u>Gradesaver</u> [2]	compares several sources
"In the Wake of Odysseus: Localization of the Mythological Journey"	
"Synesthesia and Homer's World"	far-out theory
"Homer's Odyssey Resources on the Web." <u>Robot Wisdom</u> [3]	guide to other sources
School Library	
"Homeric Legend." <u>Britannica Student Encyclopedia</u> CD-ROM	study "Analysis" section
<u>The Odyssey of Homer: A Modern Translation.</u> Trans. Richmond Lattimore (883 HOM)	easy reading
Public Library	
<u>The Odyssey of Homer.</u> Trans. Robert Fagles (883.01 Homer)	great introduction by B. Knox
<u>Tales from the Odyssey.</u> Mary Pope Osborne [4]	retelling of <u>Odyssey</u>
"Was Troy a Metropolis? Homer Isn't Talking." <u>New York Times</u>	scientific evidence

2. Evaluate each source.
Carefully examine and evaluate each source you have identified. Ask yourself if the information it contains is reliable, specifically addresses your topic, and is the right level for your audience. Eliminate unsuitable sources, noting why you rejected each one.

TIP In considering a source, ask yourself questions such as these: Is this a primary or a secondary source? What are the author's qualifications? What biases might he or she have? How up-to-date is the information? Who is the intended audience? For more information on evaluating sources, see the **Research Strategies Workshop, pages 1201–1205.**

Reasons for Rejecting Sources

[1] Disclaimer says "Wikipedia makes no guarantee of validity."

[2] No credentials given for author of the article; statements may be unreliable.

[3] Site not updated since 2002; also, information really confusing.

[4] Too elementary; should use primary source.

RESEARCHING

What Should I Do?

3. Make source cards.

Once you have sorted through your initial list of sources, record important information about each of the "keepers" on an index card. Include the following information, numbering each card in the top right-hand corner:

World Wide Web source

- author (if given)
- title of Web page or article
- publication information for any print version
- date created or posted
- name of any institution or organization responsible for the site
- date accessed
- URL

Book

- author or editor
- title
- location and publisher
- year of publication
- library call number

Encyclopedia article

- author (if given)
- title of article
- name and year of encyclopedia
- location and publisher (if CD-ROM)

Periodical article

- author
- title of article
- name and date of periodical
- page numbers of article

What Does It Look Like?

World Wide Web source

> ③
>
> Burgess, Jonathan S. "In the Wake of Odysseus: Localization of the Mythological Journey." 2004. 9 Mar. 2008 <http://www.chass.utoronto. ca/~jburgess/rop/od.voyage.html>.

Book

> ⑥
>
> Severin, Tim. *The Ulysses Voyage: Sea Search for the Odyssey.* London: Hutchinson, 1987. 883.01 S49

Encyclopedia article

> ①
>
> "Homeric Legend." *Britannica Student Encyclopedia.* 2004 ed. CD-ROM. Chicago: Encyclopaedia Britannica, 2004.

Periodical article

> ④
>
> Wilford, John Noble. "Was Troy a Metropolis? Homer Isn't Talking." *New York Times* 22 Oct. 2002: D1+.

What Should I Do?

4. Take notes.

Read through your sources, looking for information that addresses your research questions and for new facts and expert opinions. Record each piece of information on a separate index card so that you can try different ways of organizing your ideas as you draft your report. On each card, include

- the main idea
- the number of the source (from its source card)
- a page number, section name, or other way of locating the information

TIP You also might want to add comments to your note cards about information that is puzzling or that supports or contradicts what you already know.

Restatements

Unless you are quoting material from the source directly, be sure to restate it in your own words. There are two ways to do this: in a paraphrase or in a summary.

Paraphrase—captures all the ideas of the original and is about the same length

Summary—presents the main idea of the original; may include key facts and statistics but is shorter because it omits unnecessary details

What Does It Look Like?

▶ **Original source**

The vividly fictional characteristics of the story have not prevented critics, past and present, from seeking to place it in a specific geographic context. Hesiod, who wrote later than Homer, believed that Odysseus and his ships sailed around in the general area of Italy and Sicily, to the west of . . .

"Homeric Legend." Britannica Student Encyclopedia CD-ROM

Paraphrase

Early ideas—Italy and Sicily	①
Although the Odyssey includes many fantastic creatures and events, people throughout history have tried to identify a real setting for the tale. Hesiod, a writer who came after Homer, thought that Odysseus' journey took him around Italy and Sicily. (Section: "Analysis of the Odyssey") NOTE: Who was Hesiod? Look him up.	

Summary

Early ideas—Italy and Sicily	①
The early writer Hesiod believed that the Odyssey took place near Italy and Sicily. (Section: "Analysis of the Odyssey") NOTE: Modern explorer Tim Severin agrees.	

RESEARCHING

What Should I Do?

5. Quote well-stated ideas directly.
Sometimes, information in a source is expressed so powerfully that you want to use the author's own words. In recording direct quotations on your note cards, be sure to copy the material exactly as it appears in the original and to enclose it in quotation marks.

TIP If you want to leave out phrases or sentences within a quotation, insert three ellipsis points (. . .) in place of the omitted material. If you need to add a word or phrase to clarify an idea, enclose it in brackets ([ ]).

6. Avoid plagiarism.
Plagiarism, or the unauthorized use of others' words or ideas, is not honest. To avoid plagiarism, you must document the sources of any ideas that aren't common knowledge. You must do this whether you are paraphrasing, summarizing, or directly quoting the material.

TIP Remember that quoting word for word several sentences or more without documenting the source is not the only type of plagiarism. When you use special phrases someone else wrote, you must credit the source. For example, if your source includes the phrases "Alexandrian geographer," "ports of call," and "wild-goose chase," and you use any of these phrases without citing the source, you are plagiarizing.

What Does It Look Like?

▶

Odyssey's odd geography   ⑥

Explorer Tim Severin compared many theories of Odysseus' route with nautical maps and concluded that "Ulysses' vessel jumps up and down the length of the Mediterranean like the knight on a chessboard. It skips over inconvenient land masses, skids around capes, [and] travels at speeds that would do credit to a modern cruise liner ..." (22).

▶ **Original source**

Odysseus' wanderings in the west have inspired many attempts to plot his course and identify his ports of call. This wild-goose chase had begun already in the ancient world, as we know from ... the great Alexandrian geographer Eratosthenes, who said that you would be able to chart the course of Odysseus' wanderings when you found the cobbler who sewed the bag in which Aeolus confined the winds.

Knox, Bernard. Introduction. *The Odyssey of Homer*. Trans. Robert Fagles

Plagiarized

The great Alexandrian geographer Eratosthenes said that trying to identify Odysseus' ports of call would be a wild-goose chase.

Correctly documented

The third-century-B.C. astronomer Eratosthenes, for example, thought that Homer's story was totally imaginary (Knox 25).

What Should I Do?	What Does It Look Like?

7. Craft a working thesis statement.

Review the material you've gathered from your sources. Write a working thesis statement that describes the main idea you want to explore in your research paper. You may have to rework your statement several times to define a topic that is neither too broad nor too narrow. You'll probably also continue to refine it as you draft your report.

TIP Your paper should not include information that is unrelated to your thesis. If you discover an interesting new angle as you research, then you need to revise your thesis to match it.

Working Thesis Statement

People have come up with many different answers to questions such as these: ~~Who was Homer? Why did he write the Odyssey? Were the characters he described real?~~ Did the places Homer described really exist? We may never know for sure how much of the Odyssey is real and how much is made up, but doing some investigating can help us understand the book better.

I have so much info about places. I should focus on that.

8. Organize and outline your material.

Read through your note cards and collect them into groups that address similar main ideas. Then arrange the main ideas in an order that shows the relationships between those ideas and develops them logically. Try several arrangements to find the one that works best. These main ideas will become the Roman numerals of your outline. Then separate each group of cards into subgroups to create the sublevels of your outline. As you draft, use the entries in your outline to create the topic sentences and supporting details of your report.

TIP You can also outline your material by using a graphic organizer or grouping the ideas into questions and answers.

The Mystery of the Odyssey

I. Great adventure story
  A. Based on real places?
  B. Investigate to understand Odyssey better
II. Early theories
  A. Imaginary
  B. Real
    1. Italy and Sicily
    2. Other Mediterranean sites; the Atlantic
    3. Schliemann proved Troy real
III. Modern ideas
  A. All over the map
  B. Mediterranean (Severin)
    1. Re-created Odysseus' voyage
    2. Identified some sites, not others
IV. Conclusion
  A. Homer's era a time of exploration
  B. Unsolved mystery

DRAFTING

What Should I Do?

1. Draft your introduction.
You've already created a working thesis statement, so that's a good place to begin your report. Don't worry about writing the perfect opening at this stage. The important thing is to clearly state what you want to accomplish in the paper and to get your ideas flowing.

2. Incorporate facts, ideas, and quotations from your notes.
Using your outline as a guide, incorporate the material on your note cards into a draft of your report. As you add information to your draft, include the source and page number of that information. For instructions on how to do this, see "Document your sources" on the next page.

TIP Don't just plop a quotation into the middle of your paper. Use these techniques instead:

• Introduce the quotation.
  As Severin says, . . .

• Insert phrases or words into a sentence.
  The story is "a cunning weave" . . .

3. Share your own ideas and interpretations.
Writing a report involves more than just stringing together the information you found. It also involves analyzing the ideas of others and making your own interpretations. You should, however, use the facts, examples, and other evidence you found to support your ideas.

What Does It Look Like?

The *Odyssey* by Homer is a real adventure story. For modern readers, though, it is also an intriguing mystery. Did the places Homer described really exist?

Note card

Mediterranean ⑤
The story of Odysseus' voyage home is "a cunning weave." It is hard to get into because it is full of complications and irony. The story seems to be set in the waters around Greece, Italy, and Egypt. "The geography of the tale is a riddle" (9).

Draft

Other historians have looked for the location of the *Odyssey* closer to Homer's own Mediterranean home. According to the literary expert George Steiner, the story seems to take place in the waters surrounding Greece, Italy, and Egypt, though he admits, "The geography of the tale is a riddle" (9).

Severin did locate a narrow channel south of Cape Scylla that may have caused whirlpools in ancient times (199). It's possible that Homer used this place as the basis for Charybdis, exaggerating its power to make the story more exciting. After all, a larger-than-life hero needs larger-than-life problems to struggle with.

What Should I Do?

4. Document your sources.
Indicate the source of each specific idea in parentheses at the end of the sentence. This parenthetical documentation will help readers find the original information. In general, include the **author's last name** and the **page number** (Severin 22). Here are some special cases:

- **Author already mentioned in the sentence**—use only the page number (22).
- **Author unknown**—use a shortened title of the work ("Homeric Legend").
- **Multiple authors**—use last names for up to three authors (Steiner and Fagles 12). For more than three authors, use the first author's last name and *et al.* (Greene et al. 45).
- **More than one work by an author**—include the name of the work (Jones, Readings 39).
- **More than one source supporting an idea**—include citations for all sources, separated by semicolons (Knox 5; Nardo 20; Wilford D1).

TIP Highlight each parenthetical citation in color to help you compile your Works Cited list later.

5. Extend and interpret.
As you draft your report, weave together ideas from your various sources. Compare and contrast them and add your own interpretations, observations, and conclusions.

What Does It Look Like?

According to the literary expert George Steiner, the story seems to take place in the waters surrounding Greece, Italy, and Egypt, though he admits, "The geography of the tale is a riddle" (9). — *Author mentioned in sentence*

For example, in Book Four of the Odyssey, Menelaus describes the island of Pharos as "as far out as the distance a hollow ship can make in a whole day's sailing" (Homer 74). — *Basic documentation—author and page number*

One explanation is that the Odyssey actually describes two separate voyages and that the adventures after line 135 of Book Ten were based on the stories of another Greek hero, Jason, and his Argonauts ("Homeric Legend"). — *No page number in source*

About the only thing people seem to agree on is that Troy existed where Homer said it was and that the Trojan War took place sometime between 1300 and 1200 B.C. (Knox 5; Nardo 20; Wilford D1). The reason they agree is that archaeologists have found proof. — *Synthesizes information from multiple sources*

DRAFTING

| *What Should I Do?* | *What Does It Look Like?* |

6. Create a thoughtful conclusion.

An effective conclusion should go beyond restating the facts presented in your report. It should leave readers with something solid and interesting to think about, such as the overall importance of your topic, questions about it that remain unanswered, or suggestions for additional research.

TIP A powerful quotation, an exciting anecdote, or a provocative question can help make your conclusion memorable.

> What conclusions can modern readers draw from these confusing and conflicting ideas about the <u>Odyssey</u>? Robert Fagles, a well-known translator and scholar of Homer, gives probably the best summary of the possibilities—and of the <u>Odyssey</u>'s lasting influence and interest:
>
> > I think it's altogether likely that, however "mythological" the Greek experience may seem, it nevertheless stems from experience. Was that experience actual or imagined, or a combination of the two? I don't think we'll ever know.... All of it is stranger than fiction, as we'd say, and even more compelling than fact.

7. Prepare a Works Cited list.

After you have finished a draft of your research paper, go through it and collect the source cards for all the parenthetical documentation you included. (If you highlighted these references during drafting, they will be easy to find.) Alphabetize the cards by the author's last names (by work titles where the author's names are unknown), and copy the information on the cards onto a list. For instructions on preparing and formatting a Works Cited list, see "MLA Citation Guidelines" on pages 1228–1229.

> ### Works Cited
>
> Burgess, Jonathan S. "In the Wake of Odysseus: Localization of the Mythological Journey." 2004. 9 Mar. 2008 <http://www.chass.utoronto.ca/~jburgess/rop/od.voyage.html>.
>
> Fagles, Robert. Reply to query of Terry J. Keely. <u>Online NewsHour</u>. 13 Mar. 1997. Public Broadcasting Service. 10 Apr. 2008 <http://www.pbs.org/newshour/forum/march97/od2.html>.
>
> Homer. <u>The Odyssey of Homer: A Modern Translation</u>. Trans. Richmond Lattimore. New York: Harper, 1967.
>
> "Homeric Legend." <u>Britannica Student Encyclopedia</u>. 2004 ed. CD-ROM. Chicago: Encyclopaedia Britannica, 2004.

What Should I Do?	*What Does It Look Like?*

1. Make your introduction a "grabber."

- Highlight the first sentence of your introduction.
- Ask yourself if this beginning would "hook" your reader.
- Consider starting with a question, a powerful quotation, or a lively image.

▶ Everybody loves a great adventure story, especially one that has everything—monsters, gods, bloody battles, raging storms, and, finally, a happy ending. The <u>Odyssey</u> by Homer is ~~a real~~ adventure story. For modern readers, though, it is also an intriguing mystery.

_{that kind of}

2. Hone your thesis statement.

- <u>Underline</u> your thesis statement.
- Make sure you have explained clearly and completely what you will investigate or discuss.

TIP Your thesis is the governing idea of your paper. In other words, it sets boundaries on what your paper will cover.

▶ <u>Did the places Homer described really exist?</u> We may never know for certain which places in the <u>Odyssey</u> are real and which are fiction, but investigating the events and geography of Odysseus' wanderings can lead to a better understanding of this great literary work.

3. Show how ideas are connected.

- Ask a peer reader to draw a ☐box☐ around sentences or paragraphs whose logical connection is unclear.
- Add transitions or more information to show how the ideas are related.

  See page 1230: Ask a Peer Reader

▶ Unlike the events of the Trojan War, which
☐ ~~The Trojan War~~ took place on land, Odysseus' sea voyage left no traces (Severin 17; Struck). ☐
Therefore,
All of the ideas historians have come up with about where the events occurred are just guesses.

4. Support your ideas with details.

- Reread your paper. Ask yourself: Did I provide reasons and evidence to support my ideas?
- Add reasons and evidence in places where support is missing.

▶ Many people throughout history have tried to identify a real setting for the tale. The Greek poet Hesiod, who lived in the eighth century BC, probably not long after the <u>Odyssey</u> was written, thought that Odysseus' wanderings took him around Italy and Sicily.

REVISING AND EDITING

What Should I Do?	What Does It Look Like?

5. Document others' ideas correctly.

- (Circle) ideas or quotations from your sources that are not documented.
- Follow guidelines for parenthetical documentation.

▶ In the end, Severin was unable to trace Odysseus' journey exactly and found many parts of Homer's tale puzzling. He concluded that "the geographies of folklore and navigation overlapped" (245). Although he didn't set out to prove whether the <u>Odyssey</u> was real or imagined, his findings suggest that it was a mixture of both.

6. Eliminate unnecessary words.

- Ask a peer reader to draw a wavy line under words or phrases that do not add new information to a sentence or that can be stated more simply.
- Delete unnecessary information and simplify complicated statements.

  See page 1230: Ask a Peer Reader

▶ As readers begin ~~reading~~ the ~~epic poem known as the~~ <u>Odyssey</u>, we are swept into a journey that is so ~~very~~ exciting that we ~~feel suffering~~ along with Odysseus.
  suffer

7. Adjust your tone.

- [Bracket] passages that have an inappropriate tone for a research paper because they are too casual or slangy.
- Substitute words or phrases that are objective and serious, yet lively.

▶ used this place as the basis for Charybdis,
  exaggerating its power
It's possible that Homer∧[~~could've figured out the whole idea of Charybdis from this spot~~]. [~~So weird!~~] [~~Then he just made a mountain out of a molehill~~] to make the story more exciting.

8. Check the parenthetical documentation.

- Look through the paper for all the places you used parenthetical documentation.
- Check that you have punctuated the references correctly.

  See page 1224: Document your sources.

▶ **Incorrect:** (Knox, 25, "Homeric Legend.").
Correct: (Knox 25; "Homeric Legend").

Incorrect: (Knox, 5, Nardo, 20; Wilford, D1).
Correct: (Knox 5; Nardo 20; Wilford D1).

MLA Citation Guidelines

Here are some basic forms for citing sources. Use these forms on your source, or bibliography, cards and in the Works Cited list that appears at the end of your paper.

BOOKS

One author

Severin, Tim. The Ulysses Voyage: Sea Search for the Odyssey. London: Hutchinson, 1987.

Two authors or editors

Steiner, George, and Robert Fagles, eds. Homer: A Collection of Critical Essays.
    Englewood Cliffs: Prentice, 1962.

Three authors

Heubeck, Alfred, Stephanie West, and J. B. Hainsworth. A Commentary on Homer's Odyssey.
    New York: Oxford UP, 1988.

Four or more authors

The abbreviation et al. *means "and others." Use* et al. *instead of listing all the authors.*

Melick, Peter, et al. The Odyssey Explained. New York: Garden UP, 1997.

No author given

Greek Literature: An Overview. New York: Sunrise, 1993.

An author and a translator

Homer. The Odyssey of Homer: A Modern Translation. Trans. Richmond Lattimore.
    New York: Harper, 1967.

An author, a translator, and an editor

La Fontaine, Jean de. Selected Fables. Trans. Christopher Wood. Ed. Maya Slater.
    New York: Oxford UP, 1995.

PARTS OF BOOKS

An introduction, a preface, a foreword, or an afterword written by someone other than the author(s) of a work

Knox, Bernard. Introduction. The Odyssey of Homer. Trans. Robert Fagles.
    New York: Penguin, 1996. 3-64.

A poem, a short story, an essay, or a chapter in a collection of works by one author

Sappho. "He Is More Than a Hero." The Works of Sappho. Trans. Edward Osmond.
    New York: Garden UP, 1990. 53.

A poem, a short story, an essay, or a chapter in an anthology of works by several authors

Solonos, Costa. "Journeys." Trans. Carl Foreman. Greek Voices. Ed. Katharine Greene and
    Gerald Spencer. London: Greenwood, 1985. 83-85.

A novel or a play in a collection

Sophocles. <u>Antigone</u>. <u>The Three Theban Plays</u>. Trans. Robert Fagles. New York: Penguin, 1984.

MAGAZINES, NEWSPAPERS, AND ENCYCLOPEDIAS

An article in a newspaper

Wilford, John Noble. "Was Troy a Metropolis? Homer Isn't Talking." <u>New York Times</u> 22 Oct. 2002: D1+.

An article in a magazine

Severin, Tim. "The Quest for Ulysses." <u>National Geographic</u> Aug. 1986: 194-225.

An article in an encyclopedia

"Homer." <u>The World Book Encyclopedia</u>. 2000 ed.

MISCELLANEOUS NONPRINT SOURCES

An interview

Baldwin, Richard. Personal interview. 9 June 2004.

A video recording

<u>The Odyssey of Troy</u>. Videocassette. A&E Home Video, 1994.

ELECTRONIC PUBLICATIONS

A CD-ROM

"Homeric Legend." <u>Britannica Student Encyclopedia</u>. 2004 ed. CD-ROM. Chicago: Encyclopaedia Britannica, 2004.

A document from an Internet site

Entries for online sources should contain as much of the information shown as available.

Author or compiler   Title or description of document

Fagles, Robert. Reply to query of Terry J. Keely.

Title of site and date of document   Site sponsor   Date of access

Online NewsHour. 13 Mar. 1997. Public Broadcasting Service. 10 Apr. 2008

Complete URL enclosed in angle brackets. Break only after a slash.

<http://www.pbs.org/newshour/forum/march97/od2.html>.

Struck, Peter. "Map of Odysseus' Journey." Mythology. Course pages. 2004. Dept. of Classical Studies, U of Pennsylvania. 9 Mar. 2008 <http://www.classics.upenn.edu/myth/homer/odymap.php>.

Apply the Rubric

A strong research paper . . .

- ☑ has a lively introduction
- ☑ presents the controlling idea of the paper in a clear thesis statement
- ☑ supports the thesis with quotations, paraphrases, and other evidence from multiple sources
- ☑ uses quotations effectively
- ☑ credits sources correctly
- ☑ develops ideas in a logical organizational pattern
- ☑ includes the writer's own interpretations of the material
- ☑ has a tone appropriate for the topic, audience, and purpose
- ☑ uses precise language and varied sentence lengths and structures
- ☑ has a thoughtful conclusion

Ask a Peer Reader

- Which part of my paper did you find most interesting? Why?
- Which ideas need clarification?
- Which aspects of my subject would you like to know more about?

Format Your Paper

Follow these guidelines in preparing the final draft of your research paper:

- Leave one-inch margins at top, bottom, and sides of each page (except for page numbers).

- On separate lines, type your name, your teacher's name, the class, and the date at the top left of the first page.

- On each page, type your last name and the page number one-half inch from the top, aligned at the right-hand corner.

- Double-space all text, including quotations and the Works Cited list.

- Indent paragraphs one-half inch (or five spaces) from the left margin.

- Indent set-off quotations one inch (or ten spaces) from the left margin.

- Begin your Works Cited list on a separate page, and indent the second and subsequent lines of entries one-half inch (or five spaces). End each entry with a period.

See the *MLA Handbook for Writers of Research Papers* for additional formatting guidelines.

Writing Online

PUBLISHING OPTIONS
For publishing options, visit the
Writing Center at **ClassZone.com.**

ASSESSMENT PREPARATION
For writing and grammar assessment practice,
go to the **Assessment Center** at **ClassZone.com.**

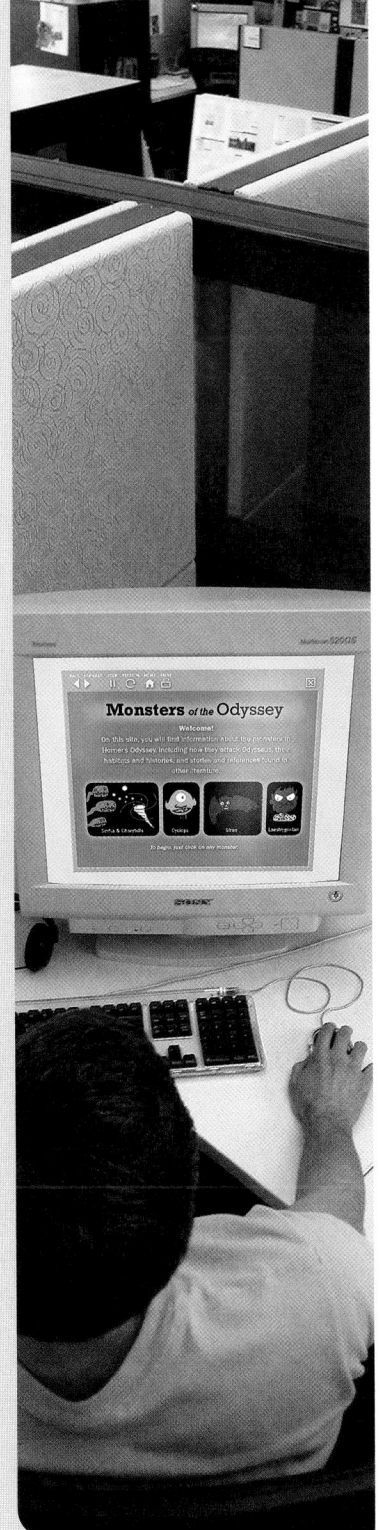

Creating a Web Site

You can use the World Wide Web to share your research with the world. The Web also lets you supplement your research paper with pictures, audio, and video.

Planning the Web Site

1. **Decide on a topic for your Web site.** Choose a subject that interests you and that lends itself to various kinds of media elements. For example, a Web site about monsters in the *Odyssey* could have many different media types: images of the monsters, sound effects, and maps showing the monsters' locations.
2. **Who is your audience?** Other students? People who are unfamiliar with your topic? Will your site inform, persuade, or entertain?
3. **Research your subject.** Find media elements to illuminate your topic. You may find maps, photographs, music, animation—even video clips. Use library resources and at least two Internet search engines.

Organizing the Web Site

1. **Create a flow chart.** A flow chart will help you figure out how to group information, where to make links, how everything will fit together, and how many pages you will need. Here is an example for a site about monsters in the *Odyssey*.

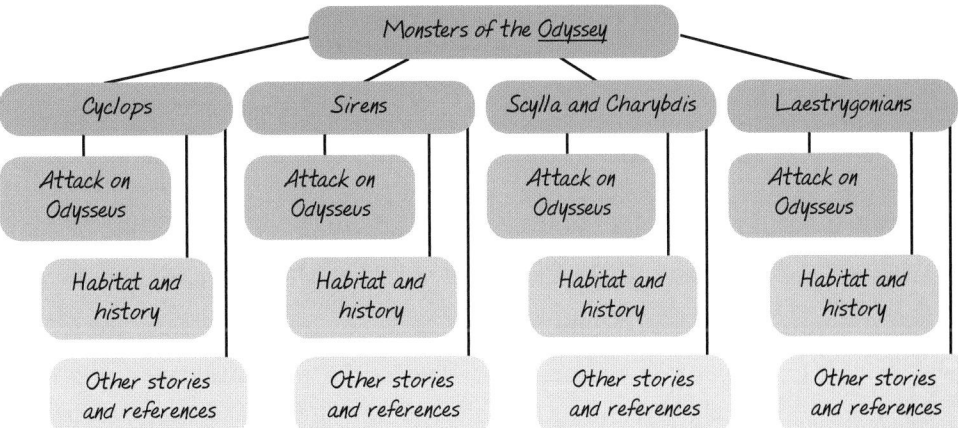

continued

2. **Storyboard the pages.** Draw rough sketches of how you want your pages to look. Each storyboard frame should indicate the placement of text, images, buttons, and links.

   TIP Avoid distractions like flashing text or constant background music. All elements should be relevant to your purpose.

The Sirens

- half bird, half woman
- lured sailors to destruction with the sweetness of their song
- "Square in your ship's path are Sirens, crying / beauty to bewitch men coasting by; / woe to the innocent who hears that sound!" (Book Twelve)

<u>Watch a video</u>
<u>Hear a siren song</u>

PICTURE OF SIREN GOES HERE

(Attack on Odysseus)　　(Habitat + History)　　(Other Stories + References)

(Return to <u>Odyssey</u> Monsters Home Page)

---

3. **Write the text.** Web sites are a mostly visual medium. Try to use visuals to convey your ideas. Charts and bulleted lists can help keep text brief and to the point.

Producing the Web Site

1. **Prepare your research materials for the Web.** Ask your school's computer specialist for help in scanning graphics and saving CD-ROM elements to your project file.

   Note: Be careful when using elements from sources like the Internet, books, and magazines. These sources often contain copyrighted material that must be cited on a Works Cited page. (See page 1225.) Some materials require permission from the creators, and many media elements on the Internet have terms-and-conditions statements. These statements may specify that students can use the media elements in school projects.

2. **Choose an authoring program.** An authoring program allows you to combine media elements into a Web document. Your school may have an authoring program, or you can download a program from the Internet. (Check with your school's computer specialist first.) Import your media elements into the program. Choose colors, fonts, buttons, and layout. Keep these guidelines in mind:

   - Text should be easy to read. Use a font size of 12 points or larger, and choose contrasting colors for the text and the background.
   - Buttons with the same function should have the same design.

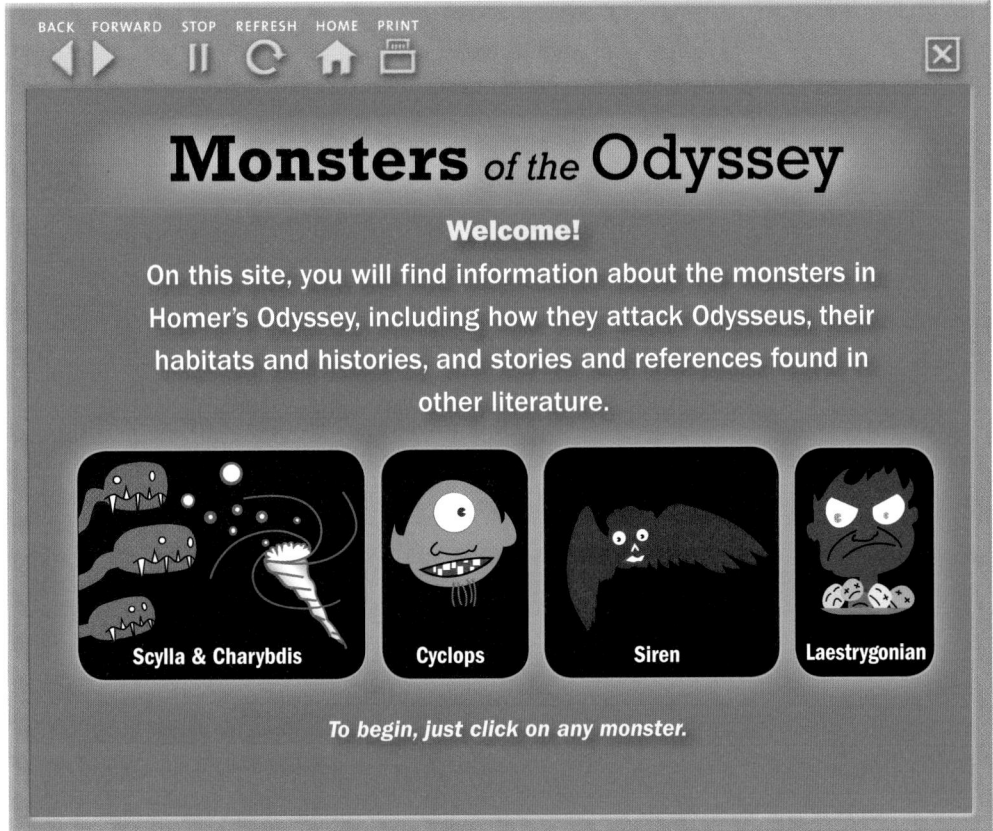

3. **Test and revise your site.** Proofread every screen and check for faulty links. Ask yourself and classmates the following questions: Where is the navigation confusing? Which visual or audio elements are helpful? Which are distracting? Use the feedback to revise and improve your site.

4. **Upload your site.** Make your site available for viewing either on your school's internal server or on the World Wide Web. Ask your school's computer specialist for permission.

Student Resource Bank

Reading any text—short story, poem, magazine article, newspaper, Web page— requires the use of special strategies. For example, you might plot events in a short story on a diagram, while you may need to use text features to spot main ideas in a magazine article. You also need to identify patterns of organization in the text. Using such strategies can help you read different texts with ease and also help you understand what you're reading.

1 Reading Literary Texts

Literary texts include short stories, novels, poems, and dramas. Literary texts can also be biographies, autobiographies, and essays. To appreciate and analyze literary texts, you will need to understand the characteristics of each type of text.

1.1 READING A SHORT STORY
Strategies for Reading

- Read the title. As you read the story, you may notice that the title has a special meaning.

- Keep track of events as they happen. Plot the events on a diagram like this one.

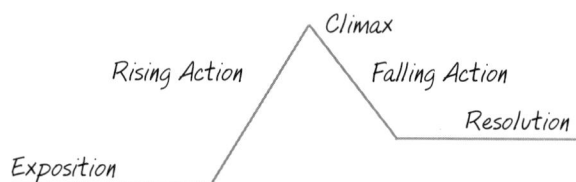

- From the details the writer provides, **visualize** the characters. **Predict** what they might do next.

- Look for specific adjectives that help you visualize the **setting**—the time and place in which events occur.

1.2 READING A POEM
Strategies for Reading

- Notice the **form** of the poem, or the number of its lines and their arrangement on the page.

- Read the poem aloud a few times. Listen for **rhymes** and **rhythms.**

- **Visualize** the images and comparisons.

- **Connect** with the poem by asking yourself what message the poet is trying to send.

- Create a word web or another **graphic organizer** to record your reactions and questions.

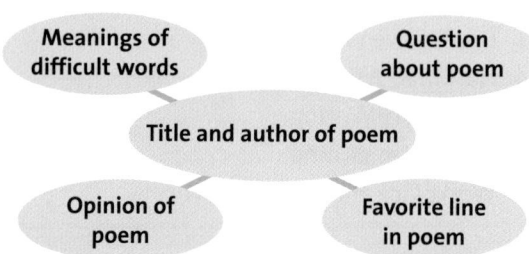

1.3 READING A PLAY
Strategies for Reading

- Read the stage directions to help you **visualize** the setting and characters.

- **Question** what the title means and why the playwright chose it.

- Identify the main conflict (struggle or problem) in the play. To **clarify** the conflict, make a chart that shows what the conflict is and how it is resolved.

- **Evaluate** the characters. What do they want? How do they change during the play? You may want to make a chart that lists each character's name, appearance, and traits.

1.4 READING LITERARY NONFICTION
Strategies for Reading

- If you are reading a biography, an autobiography, or another type of biographical writing, such as a diary or memoir, use a family tree or word web to keep track of the people mentioned.

- When reading an essay, **evaluate** the writer's ideas and reasoning. Does the writer present a thesis statement? identify the main points? support opinions with facts?

❷ Reading Informational Texts: Text Features

An **informational text** is writing that provides factual information. Informational materials, such as chapters in textbooks and articles in magazines, encyclopedias, and newspapers, usually contain elements that help the reader recognize their purposes, organizations, and key ideas. These elements are known as **text features.**

2.1 UNDERSTANDING TEXT FEATURES

Text features are design elements of a text that indicate its organizational structure or otherwise make its key ideas and information understandable. Text features include titles, headings, subheadings, boldface type, bulleted and numbered lists, and graphic aids, such as charts, graphs, illustrations, and photographs. Notice how the text features help you find key information on the textbook page shown.

Ⓐ The **title** identifies the topic.

Ⓑ A **subheading** indicates the start of a new topic or section and identifies the focus of that section.

Ⓒ **Boldface type** is used to make key terms obvious.

Ⓓ A **bulleted list** shows items of equal importance.

Ⓔ **Graphic aids,** such as graphs, illustrations, photographs, charts, diagrams, maps, and timelines, often clarify ideas in the text.

Ⓕ A **caption,** or the text that accompanies a graphic aid, gives information about the graphic aid that isn't necessarily obvious from the image itself.

PRACTICE AND APPLY

1. What are the subheadings on the textbook page shown?

2. What are the key terms on the page? How do you know?

3. What does the illustration tell you about shield volcanoes? Can you find this information elsewhere on the page?

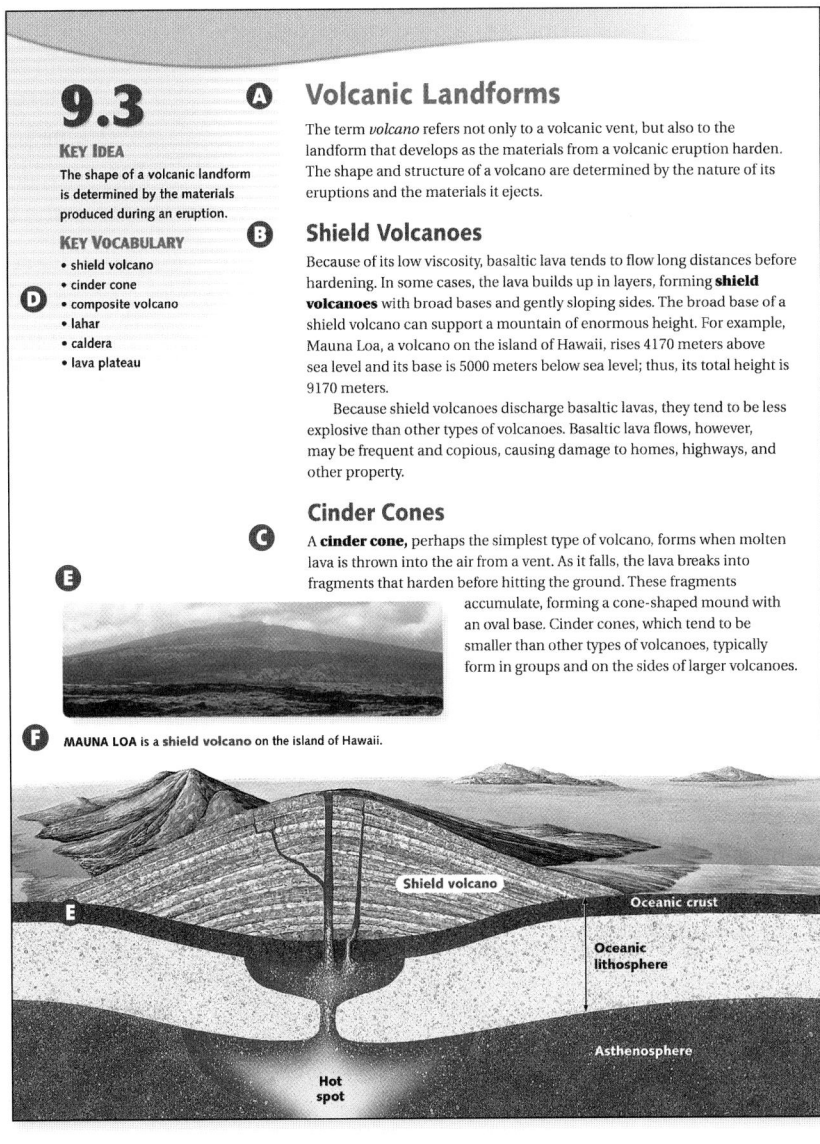

9.3

KEY IDEA
The shape of a volcanic landform is determined by the materials produced during an eruption.

KEY VOCABULARY
- shield volcano
- cinder cone
- composite volcano
- lahar
- caldera
- lava plateau

Ⓐ **Volcanic Landforms**

The term *volcano* refers not only to a volcanic vent, but also to the landform that develops as the materials from a volcanic eruption harden. The shape and structure of a volcano are determined by the nature of its eruptions and the materials it ejects.

Ⓑ **Shield Volcanoes**

Because of its low viscosity, basaltic lava tends to flow long distances before hardening. In some cases, the lava builds up in layers, forming **shield volcanoes** with broad bases and gently sloping sides. The broad base of a shield volcano can support a mountain of enormous height. For example, Mauna Loa, a volcano on the island of Hawaii, rises 4170 meters above sea level and its base is 5000 meters below sea level; thus, its total height is 9170 meters.

Because shield volcanoes discharge basaltic lavas, they tend to be less explosive than other types of volcanoes. Basaltic lava flows, however, may be frequent and copious, causing damage to homes, highways, and other property.

Ⓒ **Cinder Cones**

A **cinder cone,** perhaps the simplest type of volcano, forms when molten lava is thrown into the air from a vent. As it falls, the lava breaks into fragments that harden before hitting the ground. These fragments accumulate, forming a cone-shaped mound with an oval base. Cinder cones, which tend to be smaller than other types of volcanoes, typically form in groups and on the sides of larger volcanoes.

Ⓕ MAUNA LOA is a shield volcano on the island of Hawaii.

Shield volcano

Oceanic crust

Oceanic lithosphere

Asthenosphere

Hot spot

2.2 USING TEXT FEATURES

You can use text features to locate information, to help you understand it, and to categorize it. Just use the following strategies when you encounter informational text.

Strategies for Reading

- Scan the title, headings, and subheadings to get an idea of the main concepts and the way the text is organized.

- Before you begin reading the text more thoroughly, read any questions that appear at the end of a lesson or chapter. Doing this will help you set a purpose for your reading.

- Turn subheadings into questions. Then use the text below the subheadings to answer the questions. Your answers will be a summary of the text.

- Take notes by turning headings and subheadings into main ideas. You might use a chart like the following.

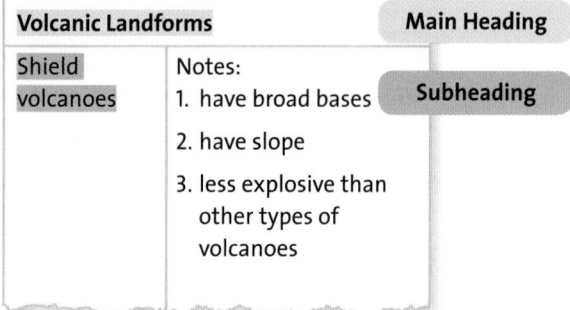

2.3 TURNING TEXT HEADINGS INTO OUTLINE ENTRIES

You can also use text features to take notes in outline form. The following outline shows how one student used text headings from the sample page on page R3. Study the outline and use the strategies that follow to create an outline based on text features.

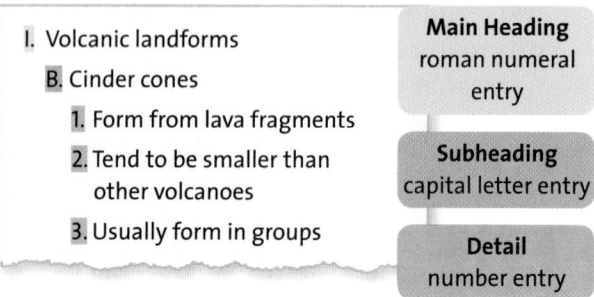

Strategies for Using Text Headings

- Preview the headings and subheadings in the text to get an idea of what different kinds there are and what their positions might be in an outline.

- Be consistent. Note that subheadings that are the same size and color should be used consistently in Roman-numeral or capital-letter entries in the outline. If you decide that a chapter heading should appear with a Roman numeral, then that's the level at which all other chapter headings should appear.

- Write the headings and subheadings that you will use as your Roman-numeral and capital-letter entries first. As you read, fill in numbered details from the text under the headings and subheadings in your outline.

PRACTICE AND APPLY

Reread *The Lost Boys*, pages 548–553. Use text features in the selection to take notes in outline form.

Preview the subheadings in the text to get an idea of the different kinds. Write the headings and subheadings you are using as your Roman-numeral and capital-letter entries first. Then fill in the details.

2.4 GRAPHIC AIDS

Information is communicated not only with words but also with graphic aids. **Graphic aids** are visual representations of verbal statements. They can be charts, webs, diagrams, graphs, photographs, or other visual representations of information. Graphic aids usually make complex information easier to understand. For that reason, graphic aids are often used to organize, simplify, and summarize information for easy reference.

Graphs

Graphs are used to illustrate statistical information. A **graph** is a drawing that shows the relative values of numerical quantities. Different kinds of graphs are used to show different numerical relationships.

Strategies for Reading

Ⓐ Read the title.

Ⓑ Find out what is being represented or measured.

Ⓒ In a circle graph, compare the sizes of the parts.

Ⓓ In a line graph, study the slant of the line. The steeper the line, the faster the rate of change.

Ⓔ In a bar graph, compare the lengths of the bars.

A **circle graph,** or **pie graph,** shows the relationships of parts to a whole. The entire circle equals 100 percent. The parts of the circle represent percentages of the whole.

MODEL: CIRCLE GRAPH

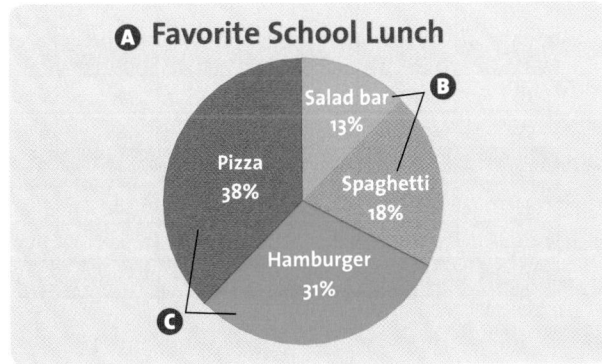

Line graphs show changes in numerical quantities over time and are effective in presenting trends such as attendance at a drama fair from 2003 to 2007. A line graph is made on a grid. Here, the vertical axis indicates quantity, and the horizontal axis shows years. Points on the graph indicate data. The line that connects the points highlights a trend or pattern.

MODEL: LINE GRAPH

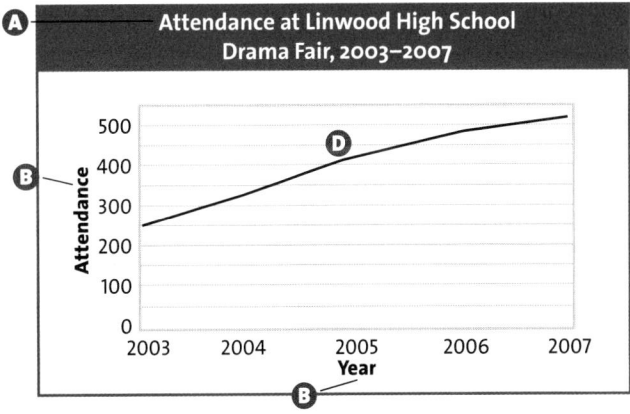

In a **bar graph,** vertical or horizontal bars are used to show or compare categories of information, such as the gestation periods of certain mammals. The lengths of the bars indicate the quantities.

MODEL: BAR GRAPH

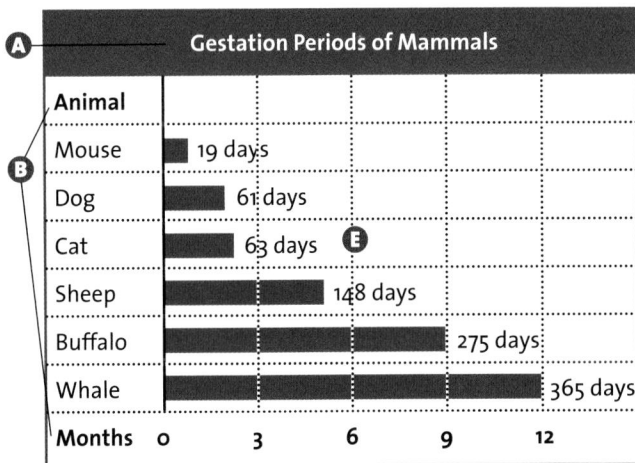

WATCH OUT! Evaluate carefully the information presented in graphs. For example, circle graphs show major factors and differences well but tend to minimize smaller factors and differences.

Diagrams

A **diagram** is a drawing that shows how something works or how its parts relate to one another.

A **picture diagram** is a picture or drawing of the subject being discussed.

Strategies for Reading

Ⓐ Read the title.

Ⓑ Read each label and look at the part it identifies.

Ⓒ Follow any arrows or numbers that show the order of steps in a process, and read any captions.

MODEL: PICTURE DIAGRAM

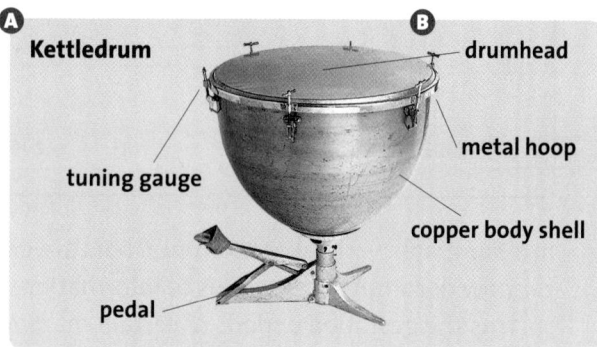

Ⓐ **Kettledrum**
Ⓑ drumhead
metal hoop
tuning gauge
copper body shell
pedal

In a **schematic diagram,** lines, symbols, and words are used to help readers visualize processes or objects they wouldn't normally be able to see.

MODEL: SCHEMATIC DIAGRAM

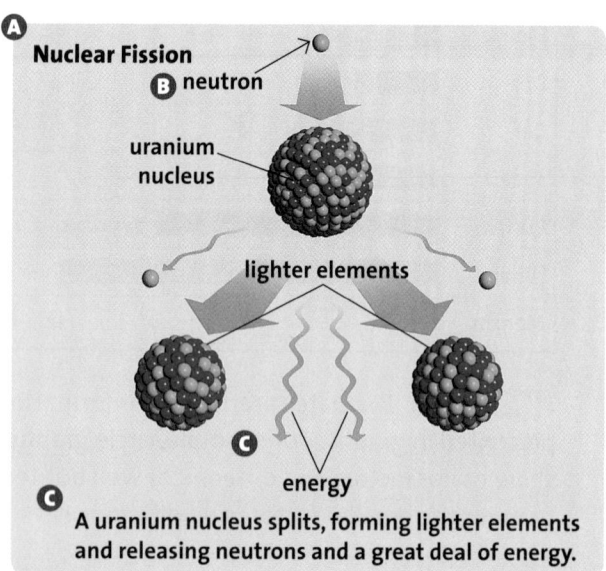

Ⓐ **Nuclear Fission**
Ⓑ neutron
uranium nucleus
lighter elements
Ⓒ energy
Ⓒ A uranium nucleus splits, forming lighter elements and releasing neutrons and a great deal of energy.

Charts and Tables

A **chart** presents information, shows a process, or makes comparisons, usually in rows or columns. A **table** is a specific type of chart that presents a collection of facts in rows and columns and shows how the facts relate to one another.

Strategies for Reading

Ⓐ Read the title to learn what information the chart or table covers.

Ⓑ Study column headings and row labels to determine the categories of information presented.

Ⓒ Look down columns and across rows to find specific information.

MODEL: CHART

Ⓐ Sounds in Poetry	
Ⓑ **Technique**	**Example**
Onomatopoeia	the slow **clip clop** of the ox Ⓒ
Alliteration	**r**ough **r**eaches of **r**anch and sky
Assonance	the c**o**stly t**o**ssing of l**o**st dreams
Consonance	his mea**g**er nu**gg**ets of be**g**rudging praise
Rhyme	A truth that's told with bad **intent** Beats all the lies you can **invent.**

MODEL: TABLE

Ⓐ Bus Route 333: Grand Avenue			Weekday Mornings— EASTBOUND		
Ⓑ Lawrence Station	Chestnut St. Mall	Grand & Lincoln	Memorial Hospital	Grand & Delaware	Three Rivers Station
Ⓒ 4:57 A.M.	5:03 A.M.	5:06 A.M.	5:10 A.M.	5:16 A.M.	5:19 A.M.
5:38	5:44	5:48	5:53	5:59	6:02
5:55	6:02	6:06	6:11	6:18	6:22
6:15	6:22	6:26	6:31	6:38	6:42
6:35	6:42	6:46	6:51	6:58	7:02
7:00	7:08	7:13	7:19	7:28	7:33
7:15	7:23	7:28	7:34	7:43	7:48

Maps

A **map** visually represents a geographic region, such as a state or country. It provides information about areas through lines, colors, shapes, and symbols. There are different kinds of maps.

- **Political maps** show political features, such as national borders.
- **Physical maps** show the landforms in areas.
- **Road or travel maps** show roads and highways.
- **Thematic maps** show information on a specific topic, such as climate, weather, or natural resources.

Strategies for Reading

Ⓐ Read the title to find out what kind of map it is.

Ⓑ Read the labels to get an overall sense of what the map shows.

Ⓒ Look at the **key** or **legend** to find out what the symbols and colors on the map stand for.

MODEL: WEATHER MAP

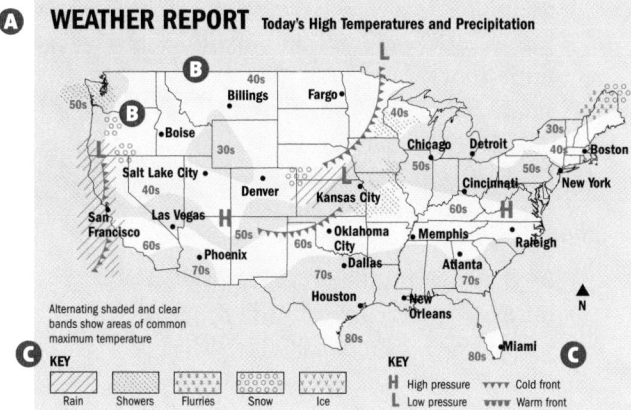

MODEL: POLITICAL MAP

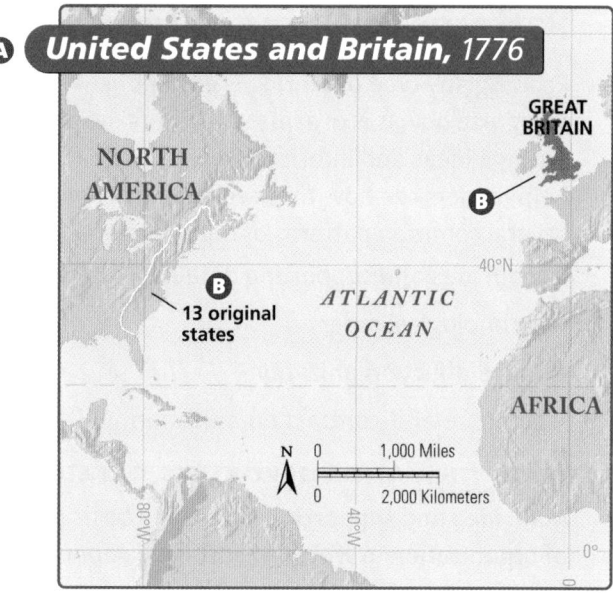

PRACTICE AND APPLY

Use the graphic aids shown on pages R5–R7 to answer the following questions:

1. What was the approximate attendance at the Linwood High School Drama Fair in 2005?
2. Is there more than one tuning gauge on a kettledrum?
3. What is the least favorite lunch according to the circle graph?
4. Write a definition of *alliteration,* using the information in the chart.
5. Use the bus schedule to figure how long your trip would be if you boarded the bus at Lawrence Station at 7:15 A.M. and got off the bus at Memorial Hospital.
6. According to the weather map, which states have temperatures in the 80s?
7. Using the scale on the political map, find the approximate number of miles from the 13 original states across the Atlantic Ocean to Great Britain.

3 Reading Informational Texts: Patterns of Organization

Reading any type of writing is easier once you recognize how it is organized. Writers usually arrange ideas and information in ways that best help readers see how they are related. There are several common patterns of organization:

- main idea and supporting details
- chronological order
- cause-effect organization
- compare-and-contrast organization

3.1 MAIN IDEA AND SUPPORTING DETAILS

Main idea and supporting details is a basic pattern of organization in which a central idea about a topic is supported by details. The **main idea** is the most important idea about a topic that a particular text or paragraph conveys. **Supporting details** are words, phrases, or sentences that tell more about the main idea. The main idea may be directly stated at the beginning and then followed by supporting details or may be merely implied by the supporting details. It may also be stated after it has been implied by supporting details.

Strategies for Reading

- To find a stated main idea in a paragraph, identify the paragraph's topic. The topic is what the paragraph is about and can usually be summed up in one or two words. The word, or synonyms of it, will usually appear throughout the paragraph. Headings and subheadings are also clues to the topics of paragraphs.

- Ask: What is the topic sentence? The topic sentence states the most important idea, message, or information the paragraph conveys about this topic.

- To find an implied main idea, ask yourself: Whom or what did I just read about? What do the details suggest about the topic?

- Formulate a sentence stating this idea and add it to the paragraph. Does your sentence convey the main idea?

Notice how the main idea is expressed in each of the following models.

MODEL: MAIN IDEA STATED IN THE BEGINNING

Some of the most impressive of all human achievements took place during the prehistoric period called the Stone Age. [Main idea] These accomplishments included the invention of tools and pottery, as well as the development of farming. Stone chopping tools date from the early Stone Age—2.5 million to 8000 B.C. Polished tools, pottery, and agriculture were developed during the late Stone Age—8000 to 3000 B.C. [Supporting details]

MODEL: MAIN IDEA IMPLIED BY SUPPORTING DETAILS

Imagine that the 102-story Empire State Building represents the history of the earth. Each story is the equivalent of about 40 million years. The earth was formed at the ground floor. Not until floor 30 or so did the first single-celled organism appear. The first dinosaurs arose at the base of the radio antenna. Mammals appeared on earth about three-quarters of the way up the antenna. The ancestors of modern humans did not appear until the tip of the antenna—about 40,000 years ago. [Supporting details]

[Implied main idea: Humans have existed for only a small percentage of the history of the planet.]

MODEL: MAIN IDEA STATED AFTER IT HAS BEEN IMPLIED BY SUPPORTING DETAILS

Scientists believe that Cro-Magnons planned their hunts carefully. Cro-Magnons studied animals' habits. They also developed advanced language skills, which improved their ability to cooperate and plan. [Supporting details] These survival skills helped the Cro-Magnon population to grow and thrive. [Main idea]

Read each paragraph, and then do the following:

1. Identify the main idea in the paragraph, using one of the strategies discussed on the previous page.

2. Identify whether the main idea is stated or implied in the paragraph.

> It was deeply unnerving. It took us over two hours to cover six-tenths of a mile of trail. By the time we reached solid ground at a place called Bearpen Gap, the snow was four or five inches deep and accumulating fast. The whole world was white, filled with dime-sized snowflakes that fell at a slant before being caught by the wind and hurled in a variety of directions. We couldn't see more than fifteen or twenty feet ahead, often not even that.
> —Bill Bryson, *A Walk in the Woods*

> For many people with Parkinson's managing their disease is a full-time job. It is a constant balancing act. Too little medicine causes tremors and stiffness. Too much medicine produces uncontrollable movement and slurring. And far too often, Parkinson's patients wait and wait for the medicines to "kick-in."
> —Michael J. Fox, testimony before the Senate

3.2 CHRONOLOGICAL ORDER

Chronological order is the arrangement of events in their order of occurrence. This type of organization is used in fictional narratives, historical writing, biographies, and autobiographies. To indicate the order of events, writers use words such as *before, after, next,* and *later* and words and phrases that identify specific times of day, days of the week, and dates, such as *the next morning, Tuesday,* and *on July 4, 1776.*

Strategies for Reading

• Look in the text for headings and subheadings that may indicate a chronological pattern of organization.

• Look for words and phrases that identify times, such as *in a year, three hours earlier, in 202 B.C.,* and *the next day.*

• Look for words that signal order, such as *first, afterward, then, during,* and *finally,* to see how events or steps are related.

• Note that a paragraph or passage in which ideas and information are arranged chronologically will have several words or phrases that indicate time order, not just one.

• Ask yourself: Are the events in the paragraph or passage presented in time order?

Notice the words and phrases that signal time order in the first two paragraphs of the following model.

MODEL
Dynasties of China from 202 B.C. to A.D. 1279

The Han dynasty ruled China from 202 B.C. to A.D. 220. (A dynasty is a series of rulers from a single family.) For more than 350 years after the Han dynasty collapsed, no emperor was able to unite northern and southern China. Then, in 589, Emperor Sui Wendi created a strong central government and laid the foundation for a golden age of China under the Tang and Song dynasties. Literature, poetry, architecture, sculpture, painting, and dance all flourished during this period.

The Tang dynasty ruled China for almost 300 years, from 618 to 907. The first important Tang emperor, Tang Taizong, held the throne from 626 until 649. During his reign, China regained its northern and western lands. After 660 or so, the real power in China was Empress Wu Zhao, although a series of weak emperors actually sat on the throne. Under her leadership, Chinese armies overran

| Events |
| Time words and phrases |
| Order words and phrases |

Korea before 668. By 690, Wu Zhao had become emperor in her own right, the only woman to hold that title.

By the mid-700s, the Tang emperors had begun losing control over their huge empire. Arab armies defeated the Chinese on their far western frontier in 751. For the next 150 years, China suffered attacks on its borders and internal rebellions. Then, in 907, Chinese rebels burned the capital city of Ch'ang-an and murdered the child emperor, ending the Tang dynasty.

Much of China was reunited in 960 under the first Song emperor, Song Taizu. However, in the early 1100s, the Song lost all of northern China to the Jurchen people. The Song established a new capital in the coastal city of Hangzhou, where they continued to rule from 1127 to 1279. During this century and a half, southern China became a prosperous trading center.

The 600 years of Song and Tang rule were years of great growth. Copper coins and paper money came into regular circulation. High-quality schools were established to train government workers. Standard editions of great works of literature were published. Although both dynasties included periods of turmoil, their cultural and economic accomplishments are still impressive today.

PRACTICE AND APPLY

Refer to the last three paragraphs of the preceding model to do the following:

1. List at least eight words in the paragraphs that indicate time or order.

2. Plot the events in the paragraphs on a timeline, using the dates mentioned. Some events may overlap.

3. A writer may use more than one pattern of organization in a text. In the last paragraph of the model, what pattern of organization does the writer use? How does this pattern contribute to your understanding of the passage?

3.3 CAUSE-EFFECT ORGANIZATION

Cause-effect organization is a pattern of organization that establishes causal relationships between events, ideas, and trends. Cause-effect relationships may be directly stated or merely implied by the order in which the information is presented. Writers often use the cause-effect pattern in historical and scientific writing. Cause-effect relationships may take several forms.

One cause with one effect

One cause with multiple effects

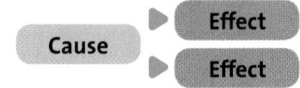

Multiple causes with a single effect

A chain of causes and effects

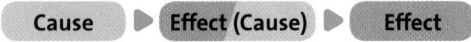

Strategies for Reading

- Look for headings and subheadings that indicate a cause-effect pattern of organization, such as "Effects of Population Density."

- To find the effect or effects, read to answer the question, What happened?

- To find the cause or causes, read to answer the question, Why did it happen?

- Look for words and phrases that help you identify specific relationships between events, such as *because, since, had the effect of, led to, as a result, resulted in, for that reason, due to, therefore, if . . . then,* and *consequently.*

- Evaluate each cause-effect relationship. Do not assume that because one event happened before another, the first event caused the second event.

- Use graphic organizers like the diagrams shown to record cause-effect relationships as you read.

Notice the words that signal causes and effects in the following model.

MODEL

The Lasting Effects of the Krakatau Eruption

In 1883, the massive explosion of a volcano called Krakatau resulted in tens of thousands of deaths as well as long-term changes in climate conditions.

Krakatau, also called Krakatoa, takes up much of a small island called Rakata. Part of the country of Indonesia, Rakata lies between the islands of Java and Sumatra in the Indian Ocean. Until 1883, Krakatau was a huge volcano, with a height of about 6,000 feet above sea level.

At 10:00 A.M. on August 27, 1883, a huge eruption destroyed most of Krakatau. As a result of the explosion, volcanic ash spewed into the air as high as 50 miles above the volcano.

The effects of the explosion were deadly. The blast caused nearly five cubic miles of rock fragments to be released into the air. In the region of the blast, the sun was not visible for the next two and a half days. Burning ash and rocks killed thousands. Tsunamis, underwater earthquakes, struck Java and Sumatra causing waves up to 120 feet. Because of the ash, rocks, and waves, about 36,000 people lost their lives.

The destruction at Krakatau had effects around the world. People in Australia, more than 2,000 miles away, heard the boom. Weather forecasters all over the planet detected sudden increases in atmospheric pressure. A series of tsunamis resulting from the blast reached as far as Hawaii and South America. Some scientists believe that dust from Krakatau may have been the reason the world experienced unseasonably cool weather for months after the eruption.

> Causes
> Signal words
> Effects

PRACTICE AND APPLY

Refer to the preceding model to do the following.

1. Use the pattern of one cause with multiple effects illustrated on page R10 to make a graphic organizer showing the main cause described in the text and at least three effects of that cause.

2. List at least four words and phrases that the writer uses to signal causes and effects in the last two paragraphs.

3.4 COMPARE-AND-CONTRAST ORGANIZATION

Compare-and-contrast organization is a pattern of organization that serves as a framework for examining similarities and differences in two or more subjects. A writer may use this pattern of organization to analyze two or more subjects, such as characters or movies, in terms of their important points or characteristics. These points or characteristics are called points of comparison. The compare-and-contrast pattern of organization may be developed in either of two ways:

Point-by-point organization—The writer discusses one point of comparison for both subjects, then goes on to the next point.

Subject-by-subject organization—The writer covers all points of comparison for one subject and then all points of comparison for the next subject.

Strategies for Reading

- Look in the text for headings, subheadings, and sentences that may suggest a compare-and-contrast pattern of organization, such as "Plants Share Many Characteristics." These will help you identify where similarities and differences are addressed.

- To find similarities, look for words and phrases such as *like, similarly, both, also,* and *in the same way.*

- To find differences, look for words and phrases such as *unlike, but, on the other hand, in contrast,* and *however.*

- Use a graphic organizer, such as a Venn diagram or a compare-and-contrast chart, to record points of comparison and similarities and differences.

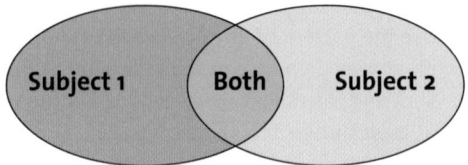

	Subject 1	Subject 2
Point 1		
Point 2		
Point 3		

Read the following models. As you read, use the signal words and phrases to identify the similarities and differences between the subjects and how the details are organized in each text.

MODEL 1

Pyramids in Egypt and the Americas

The pyramid is perhaps the most well-known accomplishment of ancient peoples. When most people think of these amazing structures, they think of Egypt. However, Egypt was not the only place where pyramids were built. Pyramids were also constructed in the Americas, mainly in Central America and South America.

Subjects

Most pyramid construction in Egypt took place between 2686 and 2345 B.C. In contrast, most Central American and South American pyramids were built much later. So far, only one pyramid of the Americas has been found to be similar in age to the Egyptian pyramids. A pyramid in Caral, Peru, has been dated to 2627 B.C.

Contrast words and phrases

Comparison words and phrases

The Pyramid of the Sun at Teotihuacán, Mexico, and the Great Pyramid at Giza, Egypt, measure nearly the same at their base. Egyptian pyramids are taller, however. The Great Pyramid originally reached a height of 481 feet, while the tallest pyramid in the Americas is 216 feet high. Even the pyramid at Caral is only one-eighth the height of the Great Pyramid.

Pyramids in Egypt and the Americas have major structural differences as well. Pyramids in the Americas have receding steps that resemble the layers of a cake. Egyptian pyramids, on the other hand, have smooth sides that connect in a point at the top.

Egyptian pyramids were always part of larger groups of buildings, including temples and houses. Similarly, American pyramids were built in the middle of cities. However, pyramids in the Americas typically served as temples and were the sites of human and animal sacrifices. In contrast, all Egyptian pyramids were built to be royal burial chambers.

Modern scientists are amazed at the size and durability of these structures. Many pyramids took as long as 20 years to build, requiring millions of stone blocks and thousands of laborers. Pyramids in Egypt and in the Americas were both outstanding accomplishments of the civilizations that created them.

MODEL 2

The Governments of Rome and the United States

After fighting the Revolutionary War, Americans were faced with the task of creating a new government. The vision of the new nation as a republic—a government in which citizens rule through their elected representatives—was based on the republic of ancient Rome. The republican governments of Rome and the United States have both similarities and differences.

The guiding principles of the government of Rome were recorded in the Twelve Tables, a list of legal rules. Only adult male landowners could be citizens, and only they could vote. The government was divided into three branches—executive, legislative, and judicial. The executive branch was made up of two consuls, or leaders, chosen by the legislative assembly to serve one-year terms. The legislative branch was divided into three houses: a 300-member Senate chosen from the aristocracy, a Centuriate Assembly of citizen-soldiers, and a Tribal Assembly of general citizens. All assembly members served life terms. The judicial branch consisted of eight judges chosen by the Centuriate Assembly for one-year terms.

Like the republic of Rome, the government of the United States is based on a code of laws, the U.S. Constitution, which gives its citizens the right to select their leaders. However, U.S. citizens now include all native-born and naturalized persons, not just adult male landowners as in Rome. The U.S. government also consists of an executive, a legislative, and a judicial branch. In contrast to the Roman consuls, the U.S. executive is one person—a president elected by citizens for a four-year term. The legislative branch includes only two houses rather than Rome's three—

Subjects

Comparison words and phrases

Contrast words and phrases

a Senate, whose 100 members are elected by the people for six-year terms, and a House of Representatives whose members are elected for two-year terms. These legislators all serve shorter terms than their Roman counterparts. However, the federal judges in the U.S. judicial branch are appointed by the president to life terms, in contrast to the Roman judges' single-year appointments.

PRACTICE AND APPLY

Refer to the preceding models to answer the following questions:

1. Which model is organized by subject? Which model is organized by points of comparison?

2. Identify at least two words or phrases in each model that signal a compare-and-contrast pattern of organization. Do not choose words or phrases that have already been highlighted.

3. List at least three points that the writer of each model compares and contrasts.

4. Use a Venn diagram or a compare-and-contrast chart to identify at least two points of comparison and their similarities and differences in model 2.

4 Reading Informational Texts: Forms

Magazines, newspapers, Web pages, and consumer, public, and workplace documents are all examples of informational materials. To understand and analyze informational texts, pay attention to text features and patterns of organization.

4.1 READING A MAGAZINE ARTICLE

Because people often skim magazines, magazine publishers use devices to attract attention to articles.

Strategies for Reading

A Notice whether **graphic aids** or **quotations** attract your attention. Sometimes a publisher pulls a quotation out of the text and displays it to get your attention. Such quotations are called **pull quotes.**

B Once you decide that you're interested in the article, read the title and other headings to find out more about its topic and organization.

C Notice whether the article has a **byline,** a line naming the author.

D Sometimes an article will be accompanied by a **sidebar,** a short article that presents additional information. This sidebar also has a **title.** Is your understanding of the main article enhanced by the information in the sidebar?

PRACTICE AND APPLY

1. Which graphic aids in the article attracted your attention?

2. What heading other than the title tells you what the article is about?

3. From what part of the article is the pull quote taken?

B Is "youth sports rage" on the rise?

Parents become violent and abusive during kids' games

C by Belinda Liu

The news stories are frightening. In Virginia, the mother of a soccer player assaults a 14-year-old referee and is fined. In Pennsylvania, a "midget league" football game results in a brawl involving about 100 players and spectators. Accounts of "youth sports rage" are reported in Britain, Canada, Australia, and New Zealand.

Are spectators at youth sports becoming more violent? Some observers believe they are.

"There have always been problem parents in kids' sports," explains soccer coach Larry Fiore. "But the vast majority of parents, coaches, and athletes act appropriately."

However, some factors are making the problem worse, believes sports psychologist Theresa Mathelier. "Sports are getting more expensive for parents in terms of equipment, traveling, and coaching," she explains. "The tendency

now is to start kids in organized sports earlier and to get them to specialize in one sport."

As a result, Mathelier says, "a few parents get unrealistic ideas about college scholarships and professional careers in sports. They start to live through their kids, and if something goes wrong, they blow up."

A *"Parents should be role models."*

Fiore and Mathelier both say that it is rarely the athletes who cause the problems. Serena Terell, a 15-year-old soccer player, agrees. "It's so embarrassing when the parents yell and curse," Serena explains, adding that her parents always behave themselves. "Their kids just want them to stop. After all, it's only a game, and parents should be role models."

D STOPPING SPORTS RAGE: STEPS YOU CAN TAKE

Here are steps that some groups have taken to prevent youth sports rage.

• The National Youth Sports Safety Foundation has created a Sport Parent Code of Conduct. Penalties range from a verbal warning to a season suspension for parents.

• Some soccer leagues designate one day as "Silent Sunday." Spectators are not allowed to cheer or even talk until the game is over.

• Some coaches choose one parent to be in charge of crowd control. This parent patrols the bleachers or sidelines, making sure that fans of his or her team behave.

4.2 READING A TEXTBOOK

Each textbook that you use has its own system of organization based on the content in the book. Often an introductory unit will explain the book's organization and special features. If your textbook has such a unit, read it first.

Strategies for Reading

Ⓐ Before you begin reading the lesson or chapter, read any **questions** that appear at the end of it. Then use the questions to set your purpose for reading.

Ⓑ **Read slowly and carefully** to better understand and remember the ideas presented in the text. When you come to an unfamiliar word, first try to figure out its meaning from **context clues.** If necessary, find the meaning of the word in a **glossary** in the textbook or in a dictionary.

For more information, see the ***Vocabulary and Spelling Handbook,*** *pages R68 and R72.*

Ⓒ Use the book's graphic aids, such as illustrations, diagrams, and captions, to clarify your understanding of the text.

Ⓓ Take notes as you read. Use text features such as **subheadings** and boldfaced terms to help you organize your notes. Use graphic organizers, such as cause-effect charts, to help you clarify relationships among ideas.

PRACTICE AND APPLY

1. How would you find the definition of *pyroclastic*?

2. Where on the page can you find out the names of different composite volcanoes?

3. Use the text to answer the second question in the Section Review.

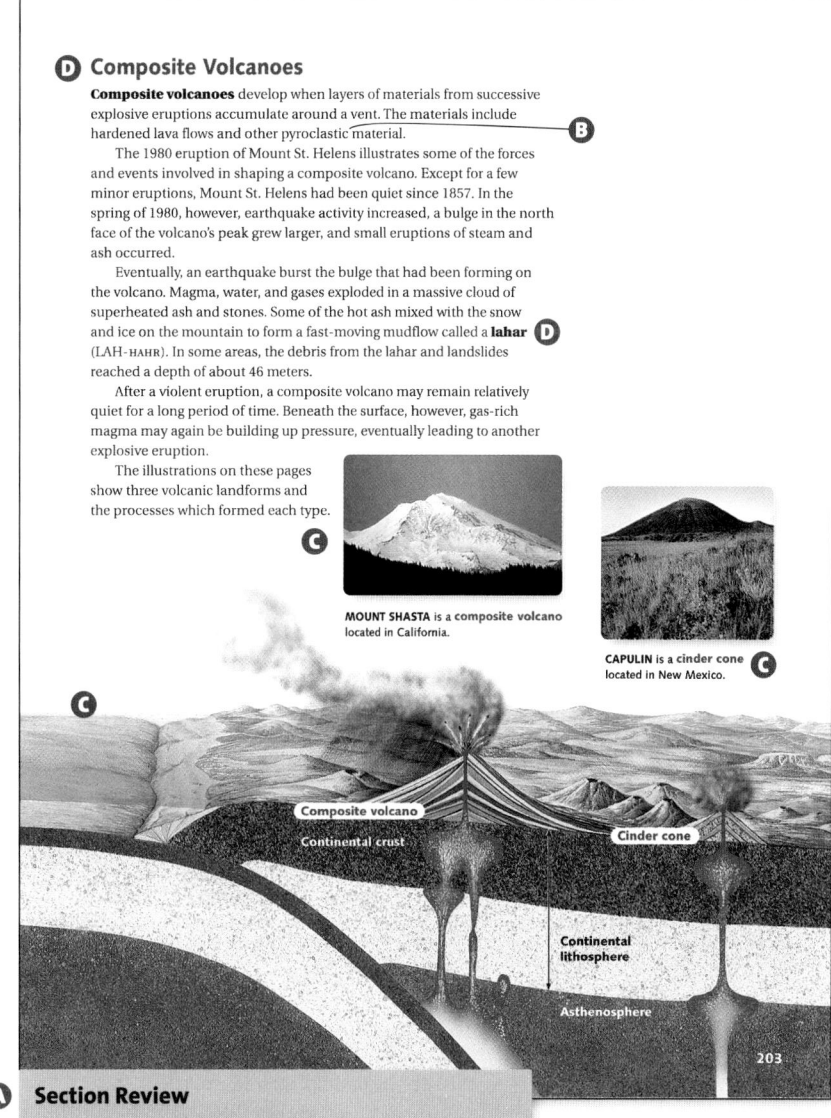

Ⓓ Composite Volcanoes

Composite volcanoes develop when layers of materials from successive explosive eruptions accumulate around a vent. The materials include hardened lava flows and other pyroclastic material. **Ⓑ**

The 1980 eruption of Mount St. Helens illustrates some of the forces and events involved in shaping a composite volcano. Except for a few minor eruptions, Mount St. Helens had been quiet since 1857. In the spring of 1980, however, earthquake activity increased, a bulge in the north face of the volcano's peak grew larger, and small eruptions of steam and ash occurred.

Eventually, an earthquake burst the bulge that had been forming on the volcano. Magma, water, and gases exploded in a massive cloud of superheated ash and stones. Some of the hot ash mixed with the snow and ice on the mountain to form a fast-moving mudflow called a **lahar** **Ⓓ** (LAH-HAHR). In some areas, the debris from the lahar and landslides reached a depth of about 46 meters.

After a violent eruption, a composite volcano may remain relatively quiet for a long period of time. Beneath the surface, however, gas-rich magma may again be building up pressure, eventually leading to another explosive eruption.

The illustrations on these pages show three volcanic landforms and the processes which formed each type.

Ⓒ

MOUNT SHASTA is a composite volcano located in California.

CAPULIN is a cinder cone located in New Mexico. **Ⓒ**

Ⓒ

Composite volcano
Continental crust
Cinder cone
Continental lithosphere
Asthenosphere

203

Ⓐ Section Review

- Compare and contrast the ways in which shield volcanoes and cinder cones are formed.
- **Critical Thinking** Describe the formation of a composite volcano.
- **Writing** The eruption of Mount Rainier, a composite volcano, could pose a serious threat to local residents. Write a description of the potential hazards that people living near Mount Rainier might face.

4.3 READING A CONSUMER DOCUMENT

Consumer documents are printed materials that accompany products and services. They usually provide information about the use, care, operation, or assembly of the products they accompany. Some common consumer documents are contracts, warranties, manuals, instructions, and schedules. Two examples of consumer documents follow.

Strategies for Reading

A Read the **subheadings** to learn what process each section of the instructions explains.

B Look for **numbers** or **letters** that indicate the order in which the steps should be followed. If you do not find letters or numbers, look for signal words such as *first, next, then,* and *finally* to see the order in which the steps should be followed.

C Words that appear in **all capital letters** are often button names or labels that appear on the device you are being shown how to use. If there is an illustration or diagram, try to match the capitalized words in the instructions to words or symbols in the graphic aid.

D Look for **verbs that describe actions** you should take, such as *press, select, set,* and *turn.*

E Pay attention to **warnings** or **notes** that describe potential problems.

INSTRUCTIONS FOR OPERATING A TELEVISION REMOTE CONTROL

A SETTING THE SLEEP TIMER

B **1.** Press the MENU key. The Setup menu will appear on your television.

C **2.** Select the Timer Setup on your screen by using the UP/DOWN arrows on your remote control.

3. Now press the RIGHT or LEFT arrow. A menu of the Timer Setup will appear on the screen.

4. Sleep Timer: Use the RIGHT/LEFT arrows to program the length of time until the TV shuts down. You can select any time from ten minutes to four hours. Press ENTER to return to TV viewing.

A SETTING THE ON/OFF TIMER

5. Follow steps 1–3 above to get to the Timer Setup menu. Using the UP/DOWN arrows on the remote control, select On Time on your screen.

C **6.** Press the RIGHT or LEFT arrow to adjust the time your television will turn on automatically.

D **7.** Press the TIMER button to choose either A.M. or P.M.

8. Repeat steps 5–7 to set Off Time. Use the UP/DOWN arrows to select the On/Off Timer, and activate the timer by pressing a RIGHT/LEFT arrow.

E **WARNING:** The On/Off Timer will not work until the clock on your television has been set.

PRACTICE AND APPLY

Reread the page from the manual for a television remote control and then answer the following questions:

1. What do these instructions explain how to do?

2. According to the instructions, what happens when the Enter button is pressed?

3. What button allows the user to select A.M. or P.M.?

The instructions on this page are from a manual for operating a graphing calculator.

Strategies for Reading

Ⓐ Read the **heading** to learn the kind of operation this section of the manual explains.

Ⓑ Look at any **introductory text** to get an overview of what the numbered steps will cover.

Ⓒ Look for **numbers** that indicate the order in which the steps should be followed.

Ⓓ Look for **verbs that describe actions** you should take, such as *press, position,* and *select.*

Ⓔ Examine **graphic aids** that illustrate steps. If you have trouble completing the process, the graphic aids can help you pinpoint what you are doing wrong.

INSTRUCTIONS FOR OPERATING A GRAPHING CALCULATOR

Ⓐ Zooming on the Graph

Ⓑ You can magnify the viewing WINDOW around a specific location by using the ZOOM instructions, thus making it easier to help identify maximums, minimums, roots, and intersections of functions.

1. Press ZOOM to display the ZOOM menu.

   This menu is typical of TI-82 menus. To select an item, you may either press the number to the left of the item, or you may press ▼ until the item number is highlighted and then press ENTER.

   Ⓔ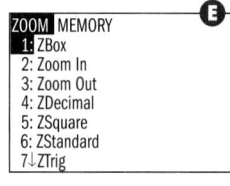

Ⓒ 2. To zoom in, press 2. The graph is displayed again. The cursor has changed to indicate that you are using a ZOOM instruction.

   Ⓓ

Ⓓ 3. Use ◀, ▲, ▶, and ▼ to position the cursor near the maximum value of the function and press ENTER.

   The new viewing WINDOW is displayed. It has been adjusted in both the X and Y directions by factors of 4, the values for ZOOM factors.

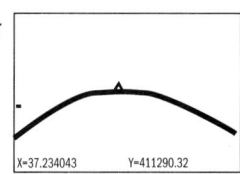

4. Press WINDOW to display the new WINDOW settings.

   ```
   WINDOW FORMAT
   Xmin=24.734042...
   Xmax=49.734042...
   Xsc1=10
   Ymin=348790.32...
   Ymax=473790.32...
   Ysc1=100000
   ```

PRACTICE AND APPLY

Reread the page from the manual and then answer the following questions:

1. What does this page explain how to do?

2. According to the instructions, how do you select a menu item?

3. What key should you press to zoom in?

4. What key should you press to display new window settings?

Refer to the documents on pages R16–R17 to answer the following questions.

5. Compare the document on page R16 with the document on this page. In terms of text features and organization, are they more alike or more different? Support your answer.

6. Do you think the directions for the remote control would be clearer if the steps below "Setting the On/Off Timer" were also numbered 1–4? Why or why not?

4.4 READING A PUBLIC DOCUMENT

Public documents are documents that are written for the public to provide information that is of public interest or concern. These documents are often free. They can be federal, state, or local government documents. They can be speeches or historical documents. They may even be laws, posted warnings, signs, or rules and regulations. The following is one type of public document.

Strategies for Reading

Ⓐ Look at the **title** to determine what the document is about.

Ⓑ Look for **subheadings** to identify main ideas and topics and to determine how the document is organized.

Ⓒ Read the body of the document and examine any **illustrations** or other **graphic aids.** Think about how the text and the images are related.

Ⓓ Check the document to find information on how to contact the creator or source of the document.

Ⓐ Rules of the Road for Cyclists
Follow these rules when you are bicycling in our area.

Ⓑ Be Visible

Don't Ride Against Traffic: Motorists may not see you on the wrong side of the road.

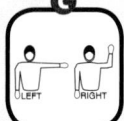
Use Hand Signals: These let drivers know what you plan to do. Be polite—and be safer, too!

Protect Yourself: Local laws require you to wear a helmet while cycling. If you are riding at night, your bike must have a headlight and a rear reflector.

Ⓑ Ride Defensively

Watch for Vehicles: Cars and trucks may pull out suddenly.

Obey Traffic Signs and Signals: They apply to you as well as to drivers. For example, don't go straight in a lane marked "Right Turn Only."

Don't Weave Between Parked Cars: Drivers may not see you as you move back into traffic.

Thank you for being a courteous cyclist!

Ⓓ Buena Vista County Parks Department (602) 555-6367 www.buenavistacounty.az.gov/parksdept
Para los hispanohablantes, llame por favor a (602) 555-6388.

PRACTICE AND APPLY

Refer to the document shown to answer the following questions.

1. Into what two subtopics is the information organized? What are the main ideas covered within each subtopic?

2. What appears to be the purpose of this document?

3. Many people may find the rules of the road for cyclists easier to follow than the directions for operating a TV remote control on page R16 or those for operating a graphing calculator on page R17. How do the text features used in "Rules of the Road for Cyclists" make it effective in communicating its message? In your answer, be sure to address each of the following features:

   - graphic aids
   - subheadings
   - use of color
   - arrangement of words and visuals on the page

For more information, see **Reading Informational Texts: Text Features,** *pages R3–R7.*

4.5 READING A WORKPLACE DOCUMENT

Workplace documents are materials that are produced or used within a workplace, usually to aid in the functioning of a business. These may be documents generated by a business to monitor itself, such as minutes of a meeting or a sales report. These documents may also explain company policies, organizational structures, and operating procedures. Workplace documents include memos, business letters, job applications, and résumés.

Strategies for Reading

A Read a workplace document slowly and carefully, as it may contain **details** that should not be overlooked.

B Notice how to contact the creator of the document. You will need this information to clear up anything that you don't understand.

C **Take notes** to help you remember times, dates, deadlines, and actions required. In particular, note whether you are expected to respond to the document, whether there is a deadline for your response, and to whom you should address your reply.

PRACTICE AND APPLY

Refer to both workplace documents to answer the following questions:

1. Why might the letter from Fred Fenton be classified as a workplace document?

2. According to the details in Fenton's letter, what actions should the yearbook staff take?

3. How does the author of the memo use text features, such as graphics and headings, to get his message across clearly and quickly?

4. What actions is the recipient of the memo expected to take?

LETTER

B **Famous Fred's Bike Store**
7451 East Trenton Boulevard
Cupertino, CA 95014
voice (408) 555-BIKE
fax (408) 555-3658
info@famousfreds.net

January 14, 2008 **A**

Yearbook Staff
James Madison High School
300 Elmwood Avenue
Cupertino, CA 95014

Dear Yearbook Staff:

C I would like to buy an advertisement in your upcoming yearbook. Would you call me at the above number to discuss the layout and cost of the ad. I also need to know whether you require camera-ready copy **A** and art, plus the total measurement, in inches or picas, of a full-page ad. I look forward to hearing from you. **C**

Yours truly,

Fred Fenton
Fred Fenton

MEMO

To: Rayna Jordan
B **From:** Mr. Jeff Kniffen, Yearbook Adviser
Re: Customer Letter
Date: January 21, 2008

C Rayna, please call Mr. Fenton with the prices for the ads for the yearbook. The chart below shows the price breakdown.

Size of ad	Price
1/4 page (3 1/2" W x 5" H)	$75.00
1/2 page (7 1/2" W x 5" H)	$125.00
1 full page (7 1/2" W x 10" H)	$200.00

Also, let him know that we do need camera-ready copy and art. Don't forget to tell him what the deadlines are for submitting the **A** ad and paying for it.

Thanks.

4.6 READING ELECTRONIC TEXT

Electronic text is any text that is in a form that a computer can store and display on a screen. Electronic text can be part of Web pages, CD-ROMs, search engines, and documents that you create with your computer software. Like books, Web pages often provide aids for finding information. However, each Web page is designed differently, and information is not in the same location on each page. It is important to know the functions of different parts of a Web page so that you can easily find the information you want.

Strategies for Reading

A Look at the **title** of a page to determine what topics it covers.

B For an online source, such as a Web page or search engine, note the **Web address,** known as a **URL** (Universal Resource Locator). You may want to make a note of it if you need to return to that page.

C Look for a **menu bar** along the top, bottom, or side of a Web page. Clicking on an item in a menu bar will take you to another part of the Web site.

D Notice any hyperlinks to related pages. **Hyperlinks** are often underlined or highlighted in a contrasting color. You can click on a hyperlink to get to another page—one that may or may not have been created by the same person or organization.

E For information that you want to keep for future reference, save documents on your computer or print them. For online sources, you can pull down the **Favorites** or **Bookmarks** menu and bookmark pages so that you can easily return to them or print the information you need. Printing the pages will allow you to highlight key ideas on a hard copy.

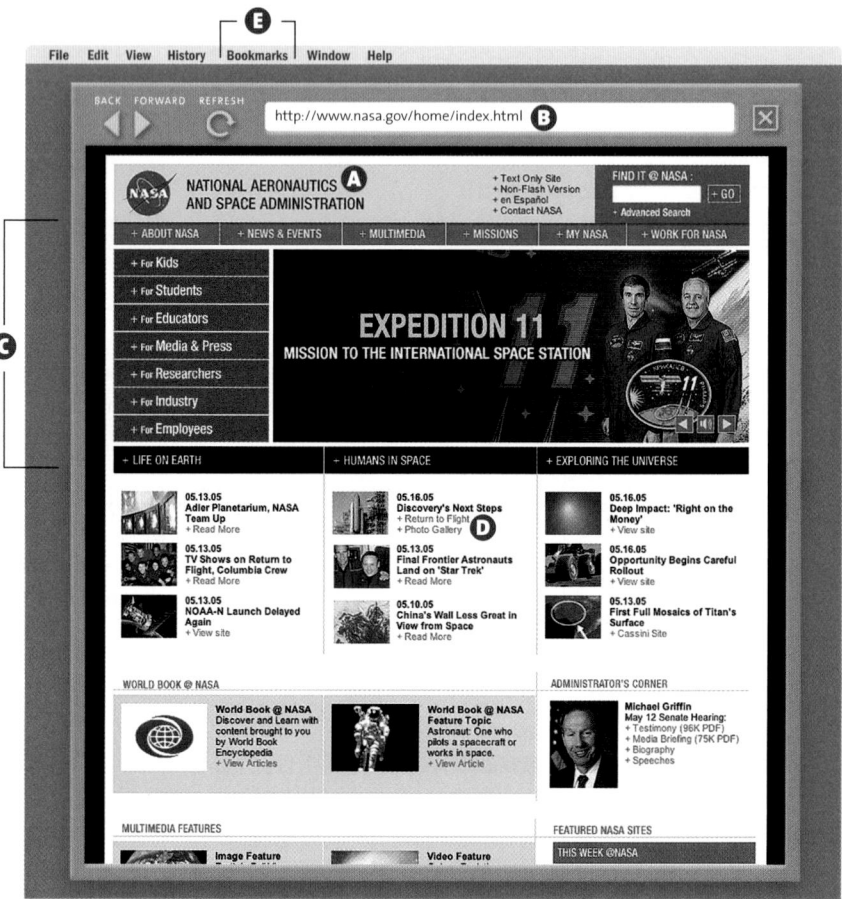

PRACTICE AND APPLY

1. What is the URL of the Web page shown?

2. How do you know that the Web site has information for different audiences?

3. What would you do to view an article about astronauts?

5 Reading Persuasive Texts

5.1 ANALYZING AN ARGUMENT

An **argument** expresses a position on an issue or problem and supports it with reasons and evidence. Being able to analyze and evaluate arguments will help you distinguish between claims you should accept and those you should not. A sound argument should appeal strictly to reason. However, arguments are often used in texts that also contain other types of persuasive devices. An argument includes the following elements:

- A **claim** is the writer's position on an issue or problem.

- **Support** is any material that serves to prove a claim. In an argument, support usually consists of reasons and evidence.

- **Reasons** are declarations made to justify an action, decision, or belief—for example, "My reason for thinking we will be late is that we can't make it to the appointment in five minutes."

- **Evidence** is the specific references, quotations, facts, examples, and opinions that support a claim. Evidence may also consist of statistics, reports of personal experience, or the views of experts.

- A **counterargument** is an argument made to oppose another argument. A good argument anticipates opposing claims and provides counterarguments to disprove or answer them.

Claim	I believe my curfew should be extended from 11 P.M. to midnight on Saturday night.
Reason	I don't have enough time to spend with my friends on weekdays because of homework and my job.
Evidence	On weekends I spend four hours doing homework and four hours at my job.
Counterargument	I know that it's difficult for you to sleep when I'm out late, but you need to trust that I'll be home by midnight and give me a chance to prove it.

PRACTICE AND APPLY

Read the following editorial and use a chart like the one shown to identify the claim, reason, evidence, and counterargument.

On the second Monday in October, Americans celebrate Columbus Day. We honor the Italian explorer who has been credited with discovering the Americas in 1492. Some people, however, think that we need to look more closely at what Christopher Columbus actually did and at his place in our history. I am one of those people.

First of all, although we honor Columbus as the first European to set foot in the Americas, he may not have been the first. Archaeologists have found Norse ruins in Greenland and what is now Newfoundland, dating from around A.D. 1000. This evidence seems to prove that Vikings actually reached the North American continent nearly 500 years before Columbus ever left the shores of Spain.

Second, although Columbus did reach the Americas, he did not discover them. Millions of people were already living here when he arrived.

Defenders of Columbus argue that, in a way, he did discover the Americas. Even if he wasn't the first person, or even the first European, to set foot on the land, his voyages made the rest of the world aware of the Americas. In the years following Columbus' voyages, Europeans came to establish colonies and to explore the land.

I argue that this spread of culture brought great harm as well as great good to the Americas. The Europeans who came to the Americas brought deadly diseases with them. The native people had no immunity to such diseases as mumps, measles, smallpox, and typhus. As a result, hundreds of thousands of them died.

In conclusion, I don't suggest that people should boycott their local Columbus Day parades. I do think, though, that we should create a more balanced picture of the man we're honoring.

5.2 RECOGNIZING PERSUASIVE TECHNIQUES

Persuasive texts typically rely on more than just the logical appeal of an argument to be convincing. They also rely on **persuasive techniques**—devices that can sway you to adopt a position or take an action. Persuasive techniques are used in advertising, political speeches, films, and fundraisers. The chart shown here explains several ways a writer may attempt to sway you to adopt his or her position. Learn to recognize these techniques, and you will be less likely to be influenced by them.

Persuasive Technique	Example
Appeals by Association	
Bandwagon appeal Uses the argument that a person should believe or do something because "everyone else" does	More and more people are making the switch to Discountline long-distance service.
Testimonial Relies on endorsements from well-known people or satisfied customers	Pierre DuPont, world-class rock climber, would be left hanging without DuraTwine rope.
Snob appeal Taps into people's desire to be special or part of an elite group	Treat yourself to Tropical Paradise because after all, you deserve the best under the sun.
Transfer Connnects a product, candidate, or cause with a positive emotion or idea	Freedom . . . you can feel it the instant you put your hands on the wheel of a Farnsworth 4 × 4 SL.
Appeal to loyalty Relies on people's affiliation with a particular group	This car is made in America by Americans.
Emotional Appeals	
Appeals to pity, fear, or vanity Use strong feelings, rather than facts, to persuade	Without more police, we'll be at the mercy of thieves.
Word Choice	
Glittering generality Makes a generalization that includes a word or phrase with positive connotations to promote a product or idea.	A vote for Evan Smith is a vote for democracy.

Identify the persuasive techniques used in the model.

Indiana and Issun Boshi— Building Another Great Team

Indiana is basketball country. Names like Bobby Knight, Larry Bird, and Isiah Thomas have added greatness to the game for over a quarter century.

That's why Issun Boshi, Japan's leading automobile company, chose Indiana as its U.S. teammate. The new plant will produce 150,000 new vehicles a year, built by 25,000 hard-working Hoosiers just like you. In addition, many of those workers will be driving the cars they make at a special discount—that's only fair; that's the American way. It's how we play the game.

Just ask Indiana sportscaster Wally Elliot, who says, "Issun Boshi and Hoosier pride— now that's what I call an expansion team."

5.3 ANALYZING LOGIC AND REASONING

When you evaluate an argument, you need to look closely at the writer's logic and reasoning. To do this, it is helpful to identify the type of reasoning the writer is using.

The Inductive Mode of Reasoning

When a writer leads from specific evidence to a general principle or generalization, that writer is using **inductive reasoning**. Here is an example of inductive reasoning.

SPECIFIC FACTS

Fact 1 The American Society of Composers, Authors, and Publishers (ASCAP) was formed on Friday, February 13, 1914, to collect royalties on copyrighted music.

Fact 2 The licensing of the first female flight instructor took place on Friday, October 13, 1939.

Fact 3 On Friday, February 13, 1948, Orville Wright announced that he was giving the famous flying machine *Kitty Hawk* to the Smithsonian Institution.

GENERALIZATION

Good things can happen on Friday the 13th.

Strategies for Determining the Soundness of Inductive Arguments

Ask yourself the following questions to evaluate an inductive argument:

- **Is the evidence valid and sufficient support for the conclusion?** Inaccurate facts lead to inaccurate conclusions.

- **Does the conclusion follow logically from the evidence?** From the facts listed in the previous example, the conclusion that good things happen only on Friday the 13th would be too broad a generalization.

- **Is the evidence drawn from a large enough sample?** Even though there are only three facts listed above, the sample is large enough to support the claim. If you wanted to support the conclusion that only good things happen on Friday the 13th, the sample is not large enough.

The Deductive Mode of Reasoning

When a writer arrives at a conclusion by applying a general principle to a specific situation, the writer is using **deductive reasoning.** Here's an example.

Journalism that stretches the truth is deceptive.	General principle or premise

▼

Hollywood Snoop Magazine stretches the truth.	Specific situation

▼

Hollywood Snoop Magazine practices deceptive journalism.	Specific conclusion

Strategies for Determining the Soundness of Deductive Arguments

Ask yourself the following questions to evaluate a deductive argument:

- **Is the general principle actually stated, or is it implied?** Note that writers often use deductive reasoning in an argument without stating the general principle. They just assume that readers will recognize and agree with the principle. So you may want to identify the general principle for yourself.

- **Is the general principle sound?** Don't just assume the general principle is sound. Ask yourself whether it is really true.

- **Is the conclusion valid?** To be valid, a conclusion in a deductive argument must follow logically from the general principle and the specific situation.

The following chart shows two conclusions drawn from the same general principle.

All team members wore school colors on Friday.	
Accurate Deduction	**Inaccurate Deduction**
Mara is on the volleyball team; therefore Mara wore school colors on Friday.	Jaime wore school colors on Friday; therefore Jaime is on a school team.

Jaime could have worn school colors in support of a team without being a member.

PRACTICE AND APPLY

Identify the mode of reasoning used in the following paragraph.

> . . . America has digitized, and there's no going back. Worldwide there are almost 200 million people on the Internet. In the United States alone, 80 million. . . . A third of wired Americans now do at least some of their shopping on the Net, and some are already consulting doctors on the Net, listening to radio on the Net, making investments on the Net, getting mortgages on the Net. . . . Each of these activities is impressive, but the aggregate effect is a different kind of life.
> —*Newsweek,* September 20, 1999

Identifying Faulty Reasoning

Sometimes an argument at first appears to make sense but isn't valid because it is based on a fallacy. A **fallacy** is an error in logic. Learn to recognize these common fallacies.

TYPE OF FALLACY	DEFINITION	EXAMPLE
Circular reasoning	Supporting a statement by simply repeating it in different words	Teenagers should avoid fad diets, because it is important for **adolescents to stay away from popular weight-loss plans.**
Either/or fallacy	A statement that suggests that there are only two choices available in a situation that really offers more than two options	**Either** students should be allowed to leave school to have lunch at nearby fast-food restaurants, **or** they should be allowed to choose the cafeteria menu.
Oversimplification	An explanation of a complex situation or problem as if it were much simpler than it is	Making the team depends on **whether the coach likes you.**
Overgeneralization	A generalization that is too broad. You can often recognize overgeneralizations by the use of words such as *all, everyone, every time, anything, no one,* and *none.*	**No one** cares that there is not enough parking downtown.
Stereotyping	A dangerous type of overgeneralization. Stereotypes are broad statements about people on the basis of their gender, ethnicity, race, or political, social, professional, or religious group.	The only thing **the members of that political party** care about is big business.
Attacking the person or name-calling	An attempt to discredit an idea by attacking the person or group associated with it. Candidates often engage in name-calling during political campaigns.	**My opponent is not smart enough** to be mayor.
Evading the issue	Refuting an objection with arguments and evidence that do not address its central point	Yes, I broke my campaign promise not to raise taxes, **but higher taxes have led to increases in police patrols, paved highways, and smaller class size in schools.**
Non sequitur	A statement that uses irrelevant "proof" to support a claim. A non sequitur is sometimes used to win an argument by diverting the reader's attention to proof that can't be challenged.	I know I'll pass math. **Mr. Gray is my math teacher and my football coach.**
False cause	The mistake of assuming that because one event occurred after another event in time, the first event caused the second one to occur	The mayor declared a get-tough crime policy, and sure enough, **crime rates dropped.**
False analogy	A comparison that doesn't hold up because of a critical difference between the two subjects	She walks to the store and back every day, **so surely she can walk in the 10K race.**
Hasty generalization	A conclusion drawn from too little evidence or from evidence that is biased	That corner must be dangerous. **There were two car accidents there last week.**

Look for examples of logical fallacies in the following argument. Identify each one and explain why you identified it as such.

> Watching television causes a child's grades to drop. What other conclusion can be drawn? Money-hungry media moguls produce horrible programming just to sell advertising time. These programs interfere with children's thinking. If you say television isn't bad for children, you would probably say the earth is flat. Parents who care should at least limit their children's viewing. The most responsible parents should turn off the TV—permanently. They can either unplug the TV or expect their children to become uneducated slugs.

5.4 EVALUATING PERSUASIVE TEXTS

Learning how to evaluate persuasive texts and identify bias will help you become more selective when doing research and also help you improve your own reasoning and arguing skills. **Bias** is an inclination for or against a particular opinion or viewpoint. A writer may reveal a strongly positive or negative opinion on an issue by presenting only one way of looking at it or by heavily weighting the evidence on one side of the argument. Additionally, the presence of either of the following is often a sign that a writer is biased:

Loaded language consists of words with strongly positive or negative connotations that are intended to influence a reader's attitude.

EXAMPLE: *The safety of our children depends on our driving the savage criminals out of this horrible neighborhood.* (*Savage* and *horrible* have very negative connotations.)

Propaganda is any form of communication that is so distorted that it conveys false or misleading information. Some politicians create and distribute propaganda. Many logical fallacies, such as name-calling, the either/or fallacy, and false causes are often used in propaganda. The following example shows an oversimplification. The writer uses one fact to support a particular point of view but does not reveal another fact that does not support that viewpoint.

EXAMPLE: *Since the new park opened, vandalism in the area has increased by 10 percent. Clearly, the park has had a negative impact on the area.* (The writer does not include the fact that the vandalism was caused by people who were not drawn into the area by the park.)

For more information, see **Identifying Faulty Reasoning, page R24.**

Strategies for Evaluating Evidence

It is important to have a set of standards by which you can evaluate persuasive texts. Use the questions below to help you critically assess facts and opinions that are presented as evidence.

- **Are the facts presented verifiable?** Facts can be proved by eyewitness accounts, authoritative sources such as encyclopedias and almanacs, experts, or research.
- **Are the opinions presented well informed?** Any opinions offered should be supported by facts, be based on research or eyewitness accounts, or be the opinions of experts on the topic.
- **Is the evidence thorough?** Thorough evidence leaves no reasonable questions unanswered. If a choice is offered, background for making the choice should be provided. If taking a side is called for, all sides of the issue should be presented.
- **Is the evidence biased?** Be alert to evidence that contains loaded language and other signs of bias.
- **Is the evidence authoritative?** The people, groups, or organizations that provided the evidence should have credentials that support their authority.
- **Is it important that the evidence be current?** Where timeliness is crucial, as in the areas of medicine and technology, the evidence should reflect the latest developments in the areas.

Read the argument below. Identify the facts, opinion, and elements of bias.

Why are students who show up late for tests, fill in answers randomly, and then snooze for the rest of the period allowed to jeopardize school test scores and reduce the quality of instruction for motivated kids? The answer is simple—compulsory attendance laws. These laws say that kids must be in school. But a study by economists William Landes and Lewis Solomon found little evidence that such laws increase attendance rates at all. Why not tell poor attenders, who are almost always failing too, "You're done. You don't belong here." Private schools do it, and the ability to expel students contributes to a positive climate.

Strategies for Determining a Strong Argument

Make sure that all or most of the following statements are true:

- The argument presents a claim or thesis.

- The claim is connected to its support by a general principle that most readers would readily agree with. Valid general principle: *It is the job of a school to provide a well-rounded physical education program.* Invalid general principle: *It is the job of a school to produce healthy, physically fit people.*

- The reasons make sense.

- The reasons are presented in a logical and effective order.

- The claim and all reasons are adequately supported by sound evidence.

- The evidence is adequate, accurate, and appropriate.

- The logic is sound. There are no instances of faulty reasoning.

- The argument adequately anticipates and addresses reader concerns and counterclaims with counterarguments.

Use the preceding criteria to evaluate the strength of the following editorial.

According to veterinarian and animal-rights advocate Dr. Michael W. Fox, more than 100 million animals are used each year in laboratory tests. These animals are used to study such things as the causes and effects of illnesses and to test drugs. This unnecessary and cruel animal testing must be stopped.

The most important reason to stop this testing is that it's wrong to make living creatures suffer. Even though they can't talk or use tools as people do, animals have feelings. Zoologist Ann Speirs says that animals may suffer even more than people do, because they can't understand what's happening to them.

People who favor animal research argue that the medical advances gained justify animal experimentation. They also say that the suffering experienced by the animals is minor. People like that are dumber than any guinea pig or rat.

Another important reason to stop this testing is that everybody knows it isn't reliable. Many drugs that help animals are harmful to people. One example is the drug thalidomide. After it was tested in animals in the 1950s and early 1960s, it was given to pregnant women. More than 10,000 of these women gave birth to handicapped babies. The process works the other way, too. Many drugs that help people kill animals. Two common examples are penicillin and aspirin.

Animal testing also affects the environment. The Animal Protection Service says that a quarter of a million chimpanzees, monkeys, and baboons are taken from their natural homes and used in laboratory experiments every year. Those animals will never be able to reproduce, and whole species may become extinct.

A final reason for not using animals in experiments is that there are other research methods available. Two examples are using bits of animal tissue and cells and using computer models.

In conclusion, animal testing has to stop because it just can't go on.

6 Adjusting Reading Rate to Purpose

You may need to change the way you read certain texts in order to understand what you read. To properly adjust the way you read, you need to be aware of what you want to get out of what you are reading. Once you know your purpose for reading, you can adjust the speed at which you read in response to your purpose and the difficulty of the material.

Determine Your Purpose for Reading

You read different types of materials for different purposes. You may read a novel for enjoyment. You may read a textbook unit to learn a new concept or to master the content for a test. When you read for enjoyment, you naturally read at a pace that is comfortable for you. When you read for information, you need to read material more slowly and thoroughly. When you are being tested on material, you may think you have to read fast, especially if the test is being timed. However, you can actually increase your understanding of the material if you slow down.

Determine Your Reading Rate

The rate at which you read most comfortably is called your **independent reading level.** It is the rate that you use to read materials that you enjoy. To learn to adjust your reading rate to read materials for other purposes, you need to be aware of your independent reading level. You can figure out your reading level by following these steps:

1. Select a passage from a book or story you enjoy.
2. Have a friend or classmate time you as you begin reading the passage silently.
3. Read at the rate that is most comfortable for you.
4. Stop when your friend or classmate tells you one minute has passed.
5. Determine the number of words you read in that minute and write down the number.
6. Repeat the process at least two more times, using different passages.
7. Add the numbers and divide the sum by the number of times your friend timed you.

Reading Techniques for Informational Material

Use the following techniques to adapt your reading for informational texts, to prepare for tests, and to better understand what you read:

- **Skimming** is reading quickly to get the general idea of a text. To skim, read only the title, headings, graphic aids, highlighted words, and first sentence of each paragraph. In addition, read any introduction, conclusion, or summary. Skimming can be especially useful when taking a test. Before reading a passage, you can skim questions that follow it in order to find out what is expected and better focus on the important ideas in the text.

  When researching a topic, skimming can help you determine whether a source has information that is pertinent to your topic.

- **Scanning** is reading quickly to find a specific piece of information, such as a fact or a definition. When you scan, your eyes sweep across a page, looking for key words that may lead you to the information you want. Use scanning to review for tests and to find answers to questions.

- **Changing pace** is speeding up or slowing down the rate at which you read parts of a particular text. When you come across familiar concepts, you might be able to speed up without misunderstanding them. When you encounter unfamiliar concepts or material presented in an unpredictable way, however, you may need to slow down to process and absorb the information better.

WATCH OUT! Reading too slowly can affect your ability to comprehend what you read. Make sure you aren't just reading one word at a time. Practice reading phrases.

PRACTICE AND APPLY

Find an article in a magazine or textbook. Skim the article. Then answer the following questions:

1. What did you notice about the organization of the article from skimming it?
2. What is the main idea of the article?

Writing is a process, a journey of discovery in which you can explore your thoughts, experiment with ideas, and search for connections. Through writing, you can explore and record your thoughts, feelings, and ideas for yourself alone or you can communicate them to an audience.

WRITING TOOLS
Go to the **Writing Center** at **ClassZone.com** for interactive models, publishing ideas, and other support.

1 The Writing Process

The writing process consists of the following stages: prewriting, drafting, revising and editing, proofreading, and publishing. These are not stages that you must complete in a set order. Rather, you may return to an earlier stage at any time to improve your writing.

1.1 PREWRITING

In the prewriting stage, you explore what you want to write about, what your purpose for writing is, whom you are writing for, and what form you will use to express your ideas. Ask yourself the following questions to get started.

Topic	• Is my topic assigned, or can I choose it? • What would I be interested in writing about?
Purpose	• Am I writing to entertain, to inform, or to persuade—or some combination of these? • What effect do I want to have on my readers?
Audience	• Who is the audience? • What might the audience members already know about my topic? • What about the topic might interest them?
Format	• What format will work best? Essay? Poem? Speech? Short story? Article? Research paper?

Find Ideas for Writing

- Browse through magazines, newspapers, and Web sites.
- Start a file of articles you want to save for future reference.
- With a group, brainstorm as many ideas as you can. Compile your ideas into a list.
- Interview someone who is an expert on a particular topic.

- Write down anything that comes into your head.
- Use a cluster map to explore subordinate ideas that relate to a general topic.

Organize Ideas

Once you've chosen a topic, you will need to compile and organize your ideas. If you are writing a description, you may need to gather sensory details. Or you may need to record information from different sources for an essay or a research paper. To record notes from sources you read or view, use any or all of these methods:

- **Summarize:** Briefly retell the main ideas of a piece of writing in your own words.
- **Paraphrase:** Restate all or almost all of the information in your own words.
- **Quote:** Record the author's exact words.

Depending on what form your writing takes, you may also need to arrange your ideas in a certain pattern.

For more information, see the **Writing Handbook**, *pages R34–R41.*

1.2 DRAFTING

In the drafting stage, you put your ideas on paper and allow them to develop and change as you write. You don't need to worry about correct grammar and spelling at this stage. There are two ways that you can draft:

Discovery drafting is a good approach when you are not quite sure what you think about your subject. You just start writing and let your feelings and ideas lead you in developing the topic.

Planned drafting may work better if you know that your ideas have to be arranged in a certain way, as in a research paper. Try making a writing plan or an informal outline before you begin drafting.

1.3 REVISING AND EDITING

The revising and editing stage allows you to polish your draft and make changes in its content, organization, and style. Use the questions that follow to assess problems and determine what changes would improve your work:

- Does my writing have a **main idea** or central focus? Is my thesis clear?

- Have I used **precise** nouns, verbs, and modifiers?

- Have I incorporated **adequate detail** and **evidence?** Where might I include a telling detail, a revealing statistic, or a vivid example?

- Is my writing **unified?** Do all ideas and supporting details pertain to my main idea or advance my thesis?

- Is my writing clear and **coherent?** Is the flow of sentences and paragraphs smooth and logical?

- Have I used a consistent **point of view?**

- Do I need to add **transitional words, phrases,** or sentences to clarify relationships among ideas?

- Have I used a **variety of sentence types?** Are they well constructed? What sentences might I combine to improve the rhythm of my writing?

- Have I used a **tone** appropriate for my audience and purpose?

1.4 PROOFREADING

When you are satisfied with your revision, proofread your paper for mistakes in grammar, usage, and mechanics. You may want to do this several times, looking for a different type of mistake each time. Use the following questions to help you correct errors:

- Have I corrected any errors in **subject-verb agreement** and **pronoun-antecedent agreement?**

- Have I double-checked for errors in **confusing word pairs,** such as *it's/its, than/then,* and *too/to?*

- Have I corrected any **run-on sentences** and **sentence fragments?**

- Have I followed rules for **correct capitalization?**

- Have I used **punctuation marks** correctly?

- Have I checked the **spellings of all unfamiliar words** in the dictionary?

TIP If possible, don't begin proofreading just after you've finished writing. Put your work away for at least a few hours. When you return to it, it will be easier for you to identify and correct mistakes.

*For more information, see the **Grammar Handbook** and the **Vocabulary and Spelling Handbook**, pages R46–R75.*

Use the proofreading symbols in the chart to mark changes on your draft.

Proofreading Symbols	
⋀ Add letters or words.	/ Make a capital letter lowercase.
⊙ Add a period.	⌗ Begin a new paragraph.
≡ Capitalize a letter.	⌁ Delete letters or words.
⊂ Close up space.	⋃ Switch the positions of letters or words.
⋀ Add a comma.	

1.5 PUBLISHING AND REFLECTING

Always consider sharing your finished writing with a wider audience. Reflecting on your writing is another good way to finish a project.

Publishing Ideas

- Post your writing on a Weblog.

- Create a multimedia presentation and share it with classmates.

- Publish your writing in a school newspaper, local newspaper, or literary magazine.

- Present your work orally in a report, speech, reading, or dramatic performance.

Reflecting on Your Writing

Think about your writing process and whether you would like to add what you have written to your writing portfolio. You might attach a note in which you answer questions like these:

- Which parts of the process did I find easiest? Which parts were more difficult?

- What was the biggest problem I faced during the writing process? How did I solve the problem?

- What changes have occurred in my writing style?

- Have I noticed any features in the writing of

published authors or my peers that I can apply to my own work?

1.6 PEER RESPONSE

Peer response consists of the suggestions and comments you make about the writing of your peers and also the comments and suggestions they make about your writing. You can ask a peer reader for help at any time in the writing process.

Using Peer Response as a Writer

- Indicate whether you are more interested in feedback about your ideas or about your presentation of them.

- Ask questions that will help you get specific information about your writing. Open-ended questions that require more than yes-or-no answers are more likely to give you information you can use as you revise.

- Encourage your readers to be honest.

Being a Peer Reader

- Respect the writer's feelings.

- Offer positive reactions first.

- Make sure you understand what kind of feedback the writer is looking for, and then respond accordingly.

For more information on the writing process, see the **Introductory Unit,** *pages 16–19.*

2 Building Blocks of Good Writing

Whatever your purpose in writing, you need to capture your reader's interest and organize your thoughts clearly.

2.1 INTRODUCTIONS

An introduction should present a thesis statement and capture your reader's attention.

Kinds of Introductions

There are a number of ways to write an introduction. The one you choose depends on who the audience is and on your purpose for writing.

Make a Surprising Statement Beginning with a startling statement or an interesting fact can arouse your reader's curiosity about a subject, as in the following model.

> **MODEL**
> W. H. Auden is one of the major poets of the 20th century. Until he was 14 years old, however, Auden's greatest interests were machinery and mining. He intended to become a mining engineer.

Provide a Description A vivid description sets a mood and brings a scene to life for your reader.

Here, details about heating the air for a hot-air balloon set the tone for a narrative about a balloon ride.

> **MODEL**
> Whoosh! The red and yellow flame shot up into the great nylon cone. The warm air filled the balloon so that the cooler air below held the apparatus aloft. A soft breeze helped to push the balloon and basket along. The four passengers hardly noticed the noise or the heat as they stared in awe at the hilly farmland and meandering streams below.

Pose a Question Beginning with a question can make your reader want to read on to find out the answer. The following introduction asks a question about the breadth of a popular author's imagination.

> **MODEL**
> Between 1915 and 1973, Agatha Christie wrote 184 works of crime fiction. How was it possible for her to create so many clever plots that depend on intricate puzzles, clues, and solutions?

Relate an Anecdote Beginning with an anecdote, or brief story, can hook your reader and help you make a point in a dramatic way. The following anecdote introduces a firsthand account of a rescue from a burning apartment building.

MODEL

A red light began blinking. A siren started up slowly but built to a screeching pitch. Twenty-five sleepy faces appeared a few at a time in the hallway. As I recall, each of us looked to left and right almost in unison, as if watching an imaginary tennis match that would give some clue to the source of this midnight disturbance.

Address the Reader Speaking directly to your reader establishes a friendly, informal tone and involves the reader in your topic.

MODEL

Find out how to maintain your cardiovascular system while enjoying yourself. Come to a free demonstration of Fit for Life at the community center, Friday night at 7:00 P.M.

Begin with a Thesis Statement A thesis statement expressing a main idea may be woven into both the beginning and the end of a piece of nonfiction writing. The following thesis statement introduces a literary analysis.

MODEL

In "The Great Taos Bank Robbery," Tony Hillerman presents eccentric characters in loving detail. It is clear that he has affection for the hapless criminals as well as for the fascinated, easygoing townspeople.

TIP To write the best introduction for your paper, you may want to try more than one of the methods and then decide which is the most effective for your purpose and audience.

2.2 PARAGRAPHS

A paragraph is made up of sentences that work together to develop an idea or accomplish a purpose. Whether or not it contains a topic sentence stating the main idea, a good paragraph must have unity and coherence.

Unity

A paragraph has unity when all the sentences support and develop one stated or implied idea. Use the following techniques to create unity in your paragraphs:

Write a Topic Sentence A topic sentence states the main idea of the paragraph; all other sentences in the paragraph provide supporting details. A topic sentence is often the first sentence in a paragraph. However, it may also appear later in a paragraph or at the end, to summarize or reinforce the main idea, as shown in the model that follows.

MODEL

Tomás lifted the skimmer baskets and emptied the collection of bugs and leaves. Then he filled the small vials with water and carefully measured four different solutions to test the pH, chlorine, total alkalinity, and acid demand. Next, he got out the equipment for vacuuming. Tomás had not realized that taking care of a swimming pool would require so much time and effort.

Relate All Sentences to an Implied Main Idea A paragraph can be unified without a topic sentence as long as every sentence supports an implied, or unstated, main idea. In the model, all the sentences work together to create a unified impression of baking an apple pie.

MODEL

The chef carefully poured in the mixture of freshly sliced apples, sugar, flour, salt, cinnamon, and nutmeg. Then she floured her hands again before adding strips of pastry in crisscrosses over the top. She dotted some butter all around the top and sprinkled on a little more sugar and cinnamon. Finally she placed the masterpiece in the oven.

Coherence

A paragraph is coherent when all its sentences are related to one another and each flows logically to the next. The following techniques will help you achieve coherence in paragraphs:

- Present your ideas in the most logical order.
- Use pronouns, synonyms, and repeated words to connect ideas.
- Use transitional devices to show relationships among ideas.

In the model shown here, the writer used some of these techniques to create a unified paragraph.

MODEL

Just the name "alligator snapping turtle" brings to mind a ferocious, frightening creature. The alligator snapping turtle can grow to more than 200 pounds. In fact, whereas common snapping turtles rarely weigh 30 pounds, alligator snappers have been recorded with weights up to 300 pounds.

2.3 TRANSITIONS

Transitions are words and phrases that show connections between details. Clear transitions help show how your ideas relate to one another.

Kinds of Transitions

The types of transitions you choose depend on the ideas you want to convey.

Time or Sequence Some transitions help to clarify the sequence of events over time. When you are telling a story or describing a process, you can connect ideas with such transitional words as *first, second, always, then, next, later, soon, before, finally, after, earlier, afterward,* and *tomorrow.*

MODEL

The orchestra members were seated. At first, the sounds conflicted with one another as the players tuned and tested their instruments. Then, the concertmaster stood and played one note on her violin. Next, all the instruments tuned to that tone, so that one great sound on the same pitch filled the auditorium.

Spatial Relationships Transitional words and phrases such as *in front, behind, next to, along, nearest, lowest, above, below, underneath, on the left,* and *in the middle* can help your reader visualize a scene.

MODEL

Gardeners have kept the tall-grass maze in perfect order. They have mowed the paths that weave in and out within the 15-foot diameter of the maze. On the left, a clearly marked entrance invites walkers to try the maze. At the center, a small clump of clover signals to the careful observer that the path winds toward the exit on the right.

Degree of Importance Transitional words such as *mainly, strongest, weakest, first, second, most important, least important, worst,* and *best* may be used to rank ideas or to show degrees of importance.

MODEL

Nathan has several qualifications that make him a good candidate for class representative; his greatest strength is his tolerance of more than one point of view.

Compare and Contrast Words and phrases such as *similarly, likewise, also, like, as, neither . . . nor,* and *either . . . or* show similarity between details. *However, by contrast, yet, but, unlike, instead, whereas,* and *while* show difference. Note the use of both types of transitions in the model.

MODEL

Like dogs, cats are wonderful pets. Dogs give unconditional affection and have a great desire to please. You will find out, however, that there is no substitute for the comfort of a cat's purr.

TIP Both *but* and *however* can be used to join two independent clauses. When *but* is used as a coordinating conjunction, it is preceded by a comma. When *however* is used as a conjunctive adverb, it is preceded by a semicolon and followed by a comma.

Cause and Effect When you are writing about a cause-effect relationship, use transitional words and phrases such as *since, because, thus, therefore, so, due to, for this reason,* and *as a result* to help clarify that relationship and make your writing coherent.

MODEL

Because a tree fell across the electric wires Monday night, we lost our electricity for four hours.

2.4 CONCLUSIONS

A conclusion should leave readers with a strong final impression.

Kinds of Conclusions

Good conclusions sum up ideas in a variety of ways. Here are some techniques you might try.

Restate Your Thesis A good way to conclude an essay is by restating your thesis, or main idea, in different words. The following conclusion restates the thesis introduced on page R31.

MODEL

The kind humor with which Hillerman portrays the would-be bank robbers as well as the curious townspeople in "The Great Taos Bank Robbery" shows his affection for all his characters.

Ask a Question Try asking a question that sums up what you have said and gives your reader something new to think about. This question concludes a request to consider a visit to a place of educational entertainment.

MODEL

If you enjoy science experiments and you like puzzles, shouldn't you plan to visit the Magic House soon?

Make a Recommendation When you are persuading your audience to take a position on an issue, you can conclude by recommending a specific course of action.

MODEL

Today's youth are at risk of damaging their hearing by listening to very loud music. Consider turning down the bass and turning down the volume on your headphones.

Make a Prediction Readers are concerned about matters that may affect them and therefore are moved by a conclusion that predicts the future.

MODEL

If this state continues to permit landowners to drain wetlands, we will see a tremendous decline in the numbers and variety of wildlife.

Summarize Your Information Summarizing reinforces your main idea, leaving a strong, lasting impression. The model concludes with a statement that summarizes a literary analysis of the works of Agatha Christie.

MODEL

Although there are a few examples of unrealistic situations in Agatha Christie's novels, for the most part each story is well crafted, providing an excellent plot and entertaining reading.

2.5 ELABORATION

Elaboration is the process of developing an idea by providing specific supporting details that are relevant and appropriate to the purpose and form of your writing.

Facts and Statistics A fact is a statement that can be verified, and a statistic is a fact expressed as a number. Make sure the facts and statistics you supply are from reliable, up-to-date sources.

MODEL

Female cicadas cut little slits in the bark of twigs and lay their eggs inside the slits. The eggs hatch after 6 to 10 weeks. When the eggs hatch, the nymphs drop from the trees.

Sensory Details Details that show how something looks, sounds, tastes, smells, or feels can enliven a description, making readers feel they are actually experiencing what you are describing.

MODEL

About 4:00 in the afternoon, the racket would begin in earnest. The cicadas must have dozed all day, but they seemed to awake in the heat of the afternoon to begin their persistent mating screeches. In lush suburban areas with large trees, the din was almost deafening.

Incidents From our earliest years, we are interested in hearing "stories." One way to illustrate a point powerfully is to relate an incident or tell a story, as shown in the example.

MODEL

The pavement was slippery from the rain, but I was going to miss the bus if I didn't run. As I rushed toward the bus stop, I tripped and fell on the sidewalk close to the curb. Now I had dirt on my skirt. As I got up from the pavement, the bus roared past me, splashing muddy water on my skirt and shoes.

Examples An example can help make an abstract idea concrete or can serve to clarify a complex point for your reader.

MODEL

Many fiction writers use real locations for their settings. For example, Tony Hillerman uses cities and towns in New Mexico and Arizona for his mystery novels.

Quotations Choose quotations that clearly support your points, and be sure that you copy each quotation word for word. Remember always to credit the source.

MODEL

The sky looks blue because air is not completely transparent. In *The Cosmological Milkshake,* Robert Ehrlich explains that "a fraction of sunlight is scattered by the molecules of the atmosphere, with blue light scattered the most." Even without smog and other forms of pollution, the sky would still look blue.

3 Descriptive Writing

Descriptive writing allows you to paint word pictures about anything, from events of global importance to the most personal feelings. It is an essential part of almost every piece of writing.

> **RUBRIC: Standards for Writing**
> **Successful descriptive writing should**
> - have a clear focus and sense of purpose
> - use sensory details and precise words to create a vivid image, establish a mood, or express emotion
> - present details in a logical order

3.1 KEY TECHNIQUES

Consider Your Goals What do you want to accomplish with your description? Do you want to show why something is important to you? Do you want to make a person or scene more memorable? Do you want to explain an event?

Identify Your Audience Who will read your description? How familiar are they with your subject? What background information will they need? Which details will they find most interesting?

Think Figuratively What figures of speech might help make your description vivid and interesting? What simile or metaphor comes to mind? What imaginative comparisons can you make? What living thing does an inanimate object remind you of?

Gather Sensory Details Which sights, smells, tastes, sounds, and textures make your subject come alive? Which details stick in your mind when you observe or recall your subject? Which senses does it most strongly affect?

You might want to use a chart like the one shown here to collect sensory details about your subject.

Sights	Sounds	Textures	Smells	Tastes

Create a Mood What feelings do you want to evoke in your readers? Do you want to soothe them with comforting images? Do you want to build tension with ominous details? Do you want to evoke sadness or joy?

3.2 OPTIONS FOR ORGANIZATION

Option 1: Spatial Order
Choose one of these options to show the spatial order of elements in a scene you are describing.

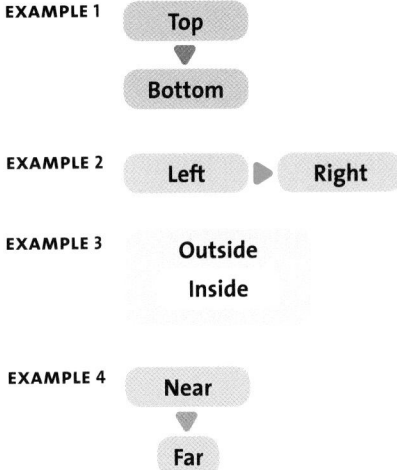

MODEL

The tour group squeezed through the door and into the long, narrow entryway. The leader began describing what they would see when it was their turn to enter the great center room. Some in the group tried to steal a glimpse of the enormous spectacle just ahead of them. At the end of the hall, a light illuminated a magnificent marble sculpture.

For more information, see **Transitions,** *page R32.*

Option 2: Order of Impression
Order of impression is the order in which you notice details.

MODEL

When I first looked at the painting, I saw a brightly illuminated, sophisticated face looking toward me and well-manicured hands turning the pages of a book. The longer I looked at the painting, the more I saw. I noticed that a letter seems to have just been opened, read, and set down. Before long my eyes fastened on bits of paper or maybe flower petals that might have come with the letter. At this point, I studied the expression on the young man's face. He seems very serious, maybe sad or worried. Suddenly, I really wanted to know more about this subject. I stared at the painting a long time.

TIP Use transitions that help readers understand the order of the impressions you are describing. Some useful transitions are *after, next, during, first, before, finally,* and *then.*

Option 3: Order of Importance
You can use order of importance as the organizing structure for a description.

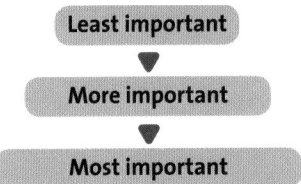

MODEL

Annaliese tried to dredge up from her memory everything about the accident. She remembered unimportant details, like the song that was playing on her radio before the truck loomed up ahead. She remembered her panic as she steered into the guardrail. Gradually she recalled more important information—her conservative speed, the fact that the truck was coming toward her on the wrong side of the road, the driver's long beard. Finally, when she closed her eyes and really concentrated, she could remember the license-plate number at eye level as the truck zoomed by.

For more information, see **Transitions,** *page R32.*

❹ Narrative Writing

Narrative writing tells a story. If you write a story from your imagination, it is a fictional narrative. A true story about actual events is a nonfictional narrative. Narrative writing can be found in short stories, novels, news articles, personal narratives, and biographies.

> **RUBRIC: Standards for Writing**
>
> **A successful narrative should**
> - hook the reader's attention with a strong introduction
> - include descriptive details and dialogue to develop the characters, setting, and plot
> - have a clear beginning, middle, and end
> - have a logical organization, with clues and transitions that help the reader understand the order of events
> - maintain a consistent tone and point of view
> - use language that is appropriate to the audience
> - demonstrate the significance of events or ideas

For more information, see **Writing Workshop: Personal Narrative,** *pages 168–175, and* **Writing Workshop: Short Story,** *pages 384–391.*

4.1 KEY TECHNIQUES

Identify the Main Events What are the most important events in your narrative? Is each event needed to tell the story?

Describe the Setting When do the events occur? Where do they take place? How can you use setting to create mood and to set the stage for the characters and their actions?

Depict Characters Vividly What do your characters look like? What do they think and say? How do they act? What details can show what they are like?

TIP Dialogue is an effective way of developing characters in a narrative. As you write dialogue, choose words that express your characters' personalities and that show how the characters feel about one another and about the events in the plot.

4.2 OPTIONS FOR ORGANIZATION

Option 1: Chronological Order One way to organize a piece of narrative writing is to arrange the events in chronological order, as shown in the following example.

EXAMPLE

Kid Turner is missing from the ranch. Fearing that he is hurt, Jake and Edna Mae set out to search for him.

Introduction
Characters and setting

As a thunderstorm approaches, they find his horse and backtrack up a dry wash.
Event 1

They find Turner just as the storm breaks. He has a broken leg, and he can't drag himself out of the dry wash.
Event 2

They carry him out of the riverbed and find shelter under a rock ledge. As they watch, a flash flood surges over the riverbed where Turner had been lying.
End
Perhaps showing the significance of the events

Option 2: Flashback In narrative writing, it is also possible to introduce events that happened sometime before the beginning of the story. You can use a flashback to show how past events led up to the present situation or to provide background about a character or event. Use clue words such as *last summer, as a young girl, the previous school year,* and *his earliest memories* to let your reader know that you are interrupting the main action to describe earlier events.

Notice how the flashback interrupts the action in the model.

MODEL

At the trials for the first big meet of the school year, Shayna was anxious to prove to the coach that she could be a leader on the track team. During warm-ups, her mind drifted back to her disastrous showing in the final meet last year, when she had dropped a baton in a relay race.

Option 3: Focus on Conflict When a fictional narrative focuses on a central conflict, the story's plot may be organized as shown in the following example.

EXAMPLE

Before a championship basketball game, two players arrive at the school gym an hour before the rest of the team. The players are identical twins, but their personalities couldn't be more different. Mark is outgoing and impulsive, while Matt is thoughtful and shy.

> **Describe main characters and setting.**

As they prepare for the game, Matt notices a man enter the locker room and give Mark a wad of cash. In the first quarter of the game, Matt notices that his brother is missing shots on purpose. He realizes that Mark has taken cash to lose the game.

> **Present conflict.**

- Matt has a chance at a basketball scholarship if they win the championship.
- Mark needs money to buy a car.
- Matt and Mark have always supported each other's goals.

> **Relate events that make conflict complex and cause characters to change.**

During halftime, Matt reminds Mark of a family story in which their grandfather chose honor and integrity over easy money. When the game resumes, Mark plays to win.

> **Present resolution or outcome of conflict.**

5 Expository Writing

Expository writing informs and explains. You can use it to evaluate the effects of a new law, to compare two movies, to analyze a piece of literature, or to examine the problem of greenhouse gases in the atmosphere. There are many types of expository writing. Think about your topic and select the type that presents the information most clearly.

5.1 COMPARISON AND CONTRAST

Compare-and-contrast writing examines the similarities and differences between two or more subjects. You might, for example, compare and contrast two short stories, the main characters in a novel, or two movies.

> **RUBRIC: Standards for Writing**
>
> **Successful compare-and-contrast writing should**
>
> - hook the reader's attention with a strong introduction
> - clearly identify the subjects that are being compared and contrasted
> - include specific, relevant details
> - follow a clear plan of organization
> - use language and details appropriate to the audience
> - use transitional words and phrases to clarify similarities and differences

Options for Organization

Compare-and-contrast writing can be organized in different ways. The examples that follow demonstrate point-by-point organization and subject-by-subject organization.

Option 1: Point-by-Point Organization

EXAMPLE

I. Both women want something that they cannot afford.

> **Point 1**

Subject A Mathilde in "The Necklace": new dress and fancy jewelry to go to a ball

Subject B Della in "The Gift of the Magi": special Christmas present for her husband

II. Both make sacrifices that turn out to be ironic.

> **Point 2**

Subject A Mathilde: works for years to replace a necklace that turns out to be a cheap imitation

Subject B Della: sells her hair to buy a chain for a watch that her husband has sold

Option 2: Subject-by-Subject Organization

EXAMPLE

I. Mathilde in "The Necklace" **Subject A**

Point 1/Wish: new dress and fancy jewelry to go to a ball

Point 2/Ironic Sacrifice: works for years to replace a necklace that turns out to be a cheap imitation

II. Della in "The Gift of the Magi" **Subject B**

Point 1/Wish: special Christmas present for her husband

Point 2/Ironic Sacrifice: sells her hair to buy a chain for a watch that her husband has sold

*For more information, see **Writing Workshop: Comparison-Contrast Essay,** pages 284–291.*

5.2 CAUSE AND EFFECT

Cause-effect writing explains why something happened, why certain conditions exist, or what resulted from an action or a condition. You might use cause-effect writing to explain a character's actions, the progress of a disease, or the outcome of a war.

RUBRIC: Standards for Writing

Successful cause-effect writing should

- hook the reader's attention with a strong introduction
- clearly state the cause-and-effect relationship
- show clear connections between causes and effects
- present causes and effects in a logical order and use transitions effectively
- use facts, examples, and other details to illustrate each cause and effect
- use language and details appropriate to the audience

Options for Organization

Your organization will depend on your topic and your purpose for writing.

Option 1: Effect-to-Cause Organization If you want to explain the causes of an event, such as the closing of a factory, you might first state the effect and then examine its causes.

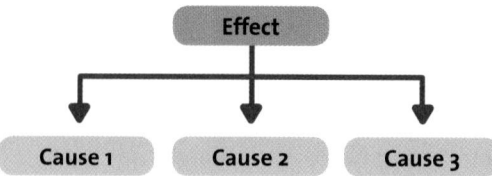

Option 2: Cause-to-Effect Organization If your focus is on explaining the effects of an event, such as the passage of a law, you might first state the cause and then explain the effects.

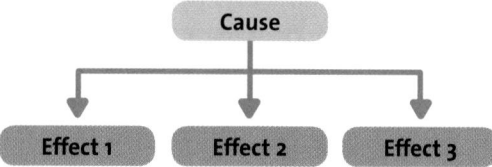

Option 3: Cause-Effect Chain Organization
Sometimes you'll want to describe a chain of cause-effect relationships to explore a topic, such as the disappearance of tropical rain forests or the development of home computers.

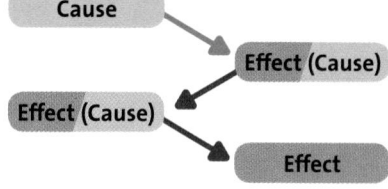

TIP Don't assume that a cause-effect relationship exists just because one event follows another. Look for evidence that the later event could not have happened if the first event had not caused it.

5.3 PROBLEM-SOLUTION

Problem-solution writing clearly states a problem, analyzes the problem, and proposes a solution to the problem. It can be used to identify and solve a conflict between characters, investigate global warming, or tell why the home team keeps losing.

RUBRIC: Standards for Writing

Successful problem-solution writing should

- hook the reader's attention with a strong introduction
- identify the problem and help the reader understand the issues involved
- analyze the causes and effects of the problem
- include quotations, facts, and statistics
- explore possible solutions to the problem and recommend the best one(s)
- use language, details, and a tone appropriate to the audience

Options for Organization

Your organization will depend on the goal of your problem-solution piece, your intended audience, and the specific problem you have chosen to address. The organizational methods that follow are effective for different kinds of problem-solution writing.

Option 1: Simple Problem-Solution

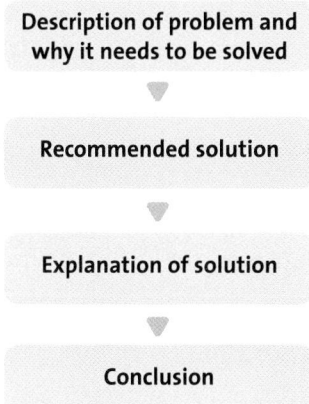

Option 2: Deciding Between Solutions

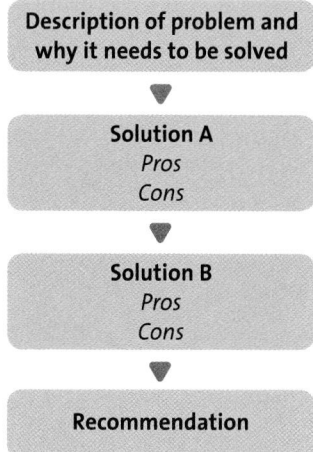

5.4 ANALYSIS

In writing an analysis, you explain how something works, how it is defined, or what its parts are.

RUBRIC: Standards for Writing

A successful analysis should

- hook the reader's attention with a strong introduction
- clearly define the subject and its parts
- use a specific organizing structure to provide a logical flow of information
- show connections among facts and ideas through transitional words and phrases
- use language and details appropriate for the audience

Options for Organization

Organize your details in a logical order appropriate to the kind of analysis you're writing. Use one of the following options:

Option 1: Process Analysis A process analysis is usually organized chronologically, with steps or stages in the order they occur. You might use a process analysis to explain how to bake a pie, prepare for a test, or replace a windowpane.

EXAMPLE

Repairing a window is easy.

> **Introduce process.**

You will need to measure the frame and purchase a new pane. You will also need to buy glazing compound and glazier's points.

> **Give background.**

Step 1: Remove broken glass and clean frame.

> **Explain steps.**

Step 2: Put glazing compound in frame; set new glass.

Step 3: Push in glazier's points to secure glass.

Step 4: Apply glazing compound to space where glass meets frame.

Option 2: Definition Analysis You can organize the details of a definition analysis in order of importance or impression. Use a definition analysis to explain a quality (such as proficiency), the distinguishing features of a sonnet, or the features of a lever.

EXAMPLE

A lever is a simple machine that allows a person to move heavy loads with less effort.

> **Introduce term and definition.**

Feature 1: Force

Feature 2: Fulcrum (pivot point)

> **Explain features.**

Feature 3: Load

Option 3: Parts Analysis The following parts analysis explains the parts of the intestinal tract.

EXAMPLE

The intestinal tract breaks food into particles the body can use.

> **Introduce subject.**

Part 1: Mouth, esophagus, stomach

Part 2: Small intestine

> **Explain parts.**

Part 3: Large intestine, appendix, rectum

For more information, see **Writing Workshop: Analysis of an Author's Style,** pages 812–819.

6 Persuasive Writing

Persuasive writing allows you to use the power of language to inform and influence others. It includes speeches, persuasive essays, newspaper editorials, advertisements, and critical reviews.

> **RUBRIC: Standards for Writing**
>
> **Successful persuasive writing should**
>
> - hook the reader's attention with a strong introduction
> - state the issue and the writer's position
> - give opinions and support them with facts or reasons
> - have a reasonable and respectful tone
> - answer opposing views
> - use sound logic and effective language
> - conclude by summing up reasons or calling for action

For more information, see **Writing Workshop: Persuasive Speech,** pages 650–657.

6.1 KEY TECHNIQUES

Clarify Your Position What do you believe about the issue? How can you express your opinion most clearly?

Know Your Audience Who will read your writing? What do they already know and believe about the issue? What objections to your position might they have? What additional information might they need? What tone and approach would be most effective?

Support Your Opinion Why do you feel the way you do about the issue? What facts, statistics, examples, quotations, anecdotes, or expert opinions support your view? What reasons will convince your readers? What evidence can answer their objections?

Ways to Support Your Argument	
Statistics	facts that are stated in numbers
Examples	specific instances that explain points
Observations	events or situations you yourself have seen
Anecdotes	brief stories that illustrate points
Quotations	direct statements from authorities

For more information, see **Identifying Faulty Reasoning,** *page R24.*

Begin and End with a Bang How can you hook your readers and make a lasting impression? What memorable quotation, anecdote, or statistic will catch their attention at the beginning or stick in their minds at the end? What strong summary or call to action can you conclude with?

MODEL

Beginning

If you want to spend an evening with your neighbors, seeing a live performance or shopping for homemade crafts, will you come to the community center? Probably not. It's too hot!

End

Many people put hours and weeks into providing our town with entertainment. Often only a few people attend these events at the community center because the building is too hot on summer evenings. One "cool" solution would be to purchase an air-conditioning system.

6.2 OPTIONS FOR ORGANIZATION

In a two-sided persuasive essay, you want to show the weaknesses of other opinions as you explain the strengths of your own.

Option 1: Reasons for Your Opinion

> Introduction states issue and your position on it.
> ▼
> Reason 1 with evidence and support
> ▼
> Reason 2 with evidence and support
> ▼
> Reason 3 with evidence and support
> ▼
> Objections to whole argument
> ▼
> Response to objections
> ▼
> Conclusion includes restatement of your position and recommended action.

Option 2: Point-by-Point Basis

> Introduction states issue and your position on it.
> ▼
> Reason 1 with evidence and support
> ▼
> Objections and responses for reason 1
> ▼
> Reason 2 with evidence and support
> ▼
> Objections and responses for reason 2
> ▼
> Reason 3 with evidence and support
> ▼
> Objections and responses for reason 3
> ▼
> Conclusion includes restatement of your position and recommended action.

7 Workplace and Technical Writing

Business writing is writing done in a workplace to support the work of a company or business. Several types of formats, such as memos, letters, e-mails, applications, and bylaws, have been developed to make communication easier.

> ### RUBRIC: Standards for Writing
> **Successful business writing should**
> - be courteous
> - use language that is geared to its audience
> - state the purpose clearly in the opening sentences or paragraph
> - have a formal tone and not contain slang, contractions, or sentence fragments
> - use precise words
> - present only essential information
> - present details in a logical order
> - conclude with a summary of important points

7.1 KEY TECHNIQUES

Think About Your Purpose Why are you doing this writing? Do you want to promote yourself to a college admissions committee or a job interviewer? Do you want to order or complain about a product? Do you want to set up a meeting or respond to someone's ideas? Are you writing bylaws for an organization?

Identify Your Audience Who will read your writing? What background information will they need? What tone or language is appropriate?

Use a Pattern of Organization That Is Appropriate to the Content If you have to compare and contrast two products in a memo, you can use the same compare-and-contrast organization that you would use in an essay.

Support Your Points What specific details might clarify your ideas? What reasons do you have for your statements?

Finish Strongly How can you best sum up your statements? What is your main point? What action do you want the recipients to take?

Revise and Proofread Your Writing Just as you are graded on the quality of an essay you write for a class, you will be judged on the quality of your writing in the workplace.

7.2 MATCHING THE FORMAT TO THE OCCASION

E-mail messages, memos, and letters have similar purposes but are used in different situations. The chart shows how each format can be used.

Format	Occasion
Memo	Use to send correspondence **inside** the workplace only.
E-mail message	Use to send correspondence **inside or outside** the company.
Letter	Use to send correspondence **outside** the company.

TIP Remember that e-mail messages in the workplace require formal language and standard spelling, capitalization, and punctuation.

PRACTICE AND APPLY

Refer to the documents on page R43 to complete the following:

1. Draft a response to the letter. Then revise your letter as necessary according to the rubric at the beginning of this section. Make sure you have included the necessary information and have written in an appropriate tone. Proofread your letter for grammatical errors and spelling mistakes. Follow the format of the model and use appropriate spacing between elements.

2. Write a memo in response to the memo. Tell the recipient what actions you have taken. Follow the format of the model.

7.3 FORMATS

Business letters usually have a formal tone and a specific format as shown below. The keys to writing a business letter are to get to the point as quickly as possible and to present your information clearly.

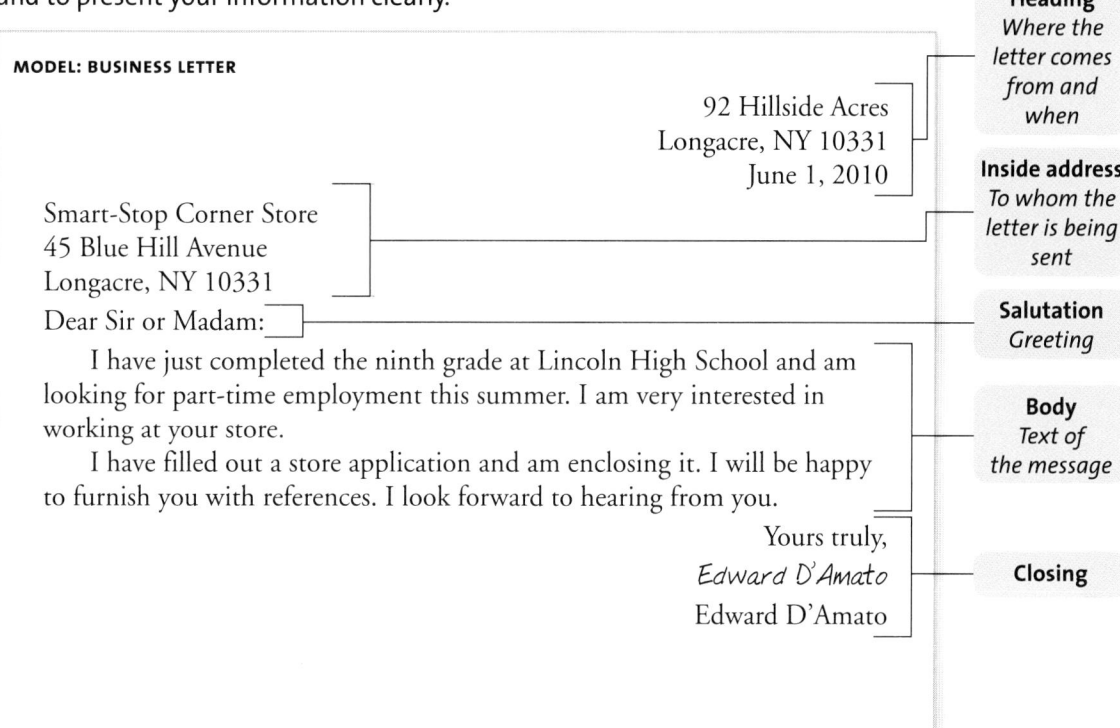

MODEL: BUSINESS LETTER

92 Hillside Acres
Longacre, NY 10331
June 1, 2010

Smart-Stop Corner Store
45 Blue Hill Avenue
Longacre, NY 10331

Dear Sir or Madam:

    I have just completed the ninth grade at Lincoln High School and am looking for part-time employment this summer. I am very interested in working at your store.
    I have filled out a store application and am enclosing it. I will be happy to furnish you with references. I look forward to hearing from you.

Yours truly,
Edward D'Amato
Edward D'Amato

Heading
Where the letter comes from and when

Inside address
To whom the letter is being sent

Salutation
Greeting

Body
Text of the message

Closing

Memos are often used in workplaces as a way of conveying information in a direct and concise manner. They can be used to announce or summarize meetings and to request actions or specific information.

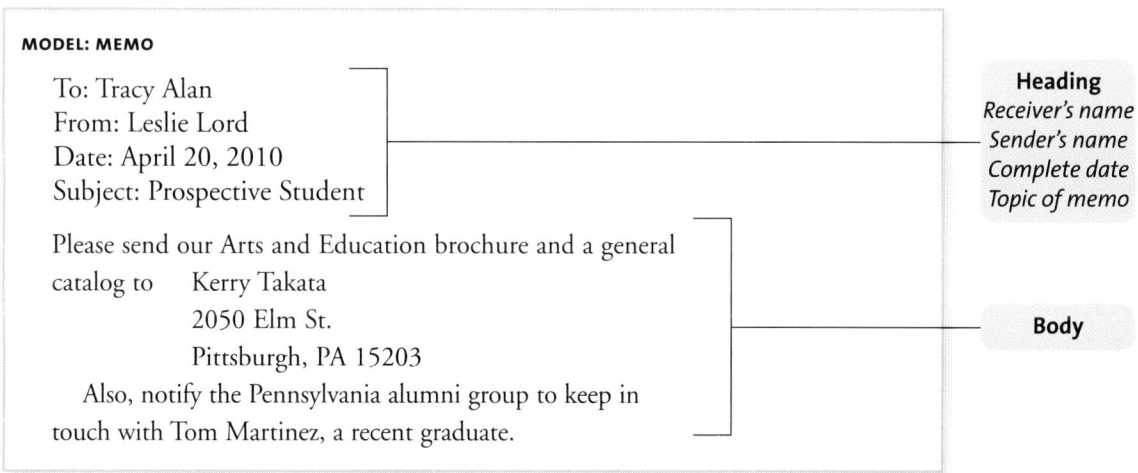

MODEL: MEMO

To: Tracy Alan
From: Leslie Lord
Date: April 20, 2010
Subject: Prospective Student

Please send our Arts and Education brochure and a general catalog to   Kerry Takata
               2050 Elm St.
               Pittsburgh, PA 15203
    Also, notify the Pennsylvania alumni group to keep in touch with Tom Martinez, a recent graduate.

Heading
Receiver's name
Sender's name
Complete date
Topic of memo

Body

TIP Don't forget to write the topic of your memo in the subject line. This will help the receiver determine the importance of your memo.

When you apply for a job, you may be asked to fill out an application form. Application forms vary, but most of them ask for similar kinds of information. (If you are mailing your application, you may want to include a brief letter.)

MODEL: JOB APPLICATION

EASY-STOP CORNER STORE
EMPLOYMENT APPLICATION

Date _June 1, 2008_

Name _Daniel_ _Allen_ _Geraci_
       FIRST   MIDDLE   LAST

Address _53 Sunset Path_ _Austin,_ _Texas_ _75207_
         STREET   CITY   STATE   ZIP

Phone _214-443-9447_   Social Security Number _535-89-7779_

Date of Birth _July 7, 1993_   Place of Birth _Dallas, Texas_

Have you been employed here before? ____ Yes _x_ No

AVAILABILITY
Date You Can Start _June 30, 2010_   Full Time ____   Part Time _x_   Summer _x_

Total Hours Available per Week _20_

If hired, and you are under 16, can you furnish proof of age and/or a work permit?

_x_ Yes ____ No

EDUCATION
Highest Grade Completed (circle one)

Middle 6 7 8   High ⑨ 10 11 12   College 13 14 15 16

College _N/A_   From _N/A_ To _N/A_

High School _James Bowie_   From _2007_ To _2008_

Middle School _Fulmore Middle School_   From _2004_ To _2007_

REFERENCES

1 _____

PRACTICE AND APPLY

Refer to the documents on pages R44 and R45 to complete the following:

1. Visit a business and request an employment application for a job you would like to have. Make sure you understand what each question is asking before you begin to write. Fill out the application as neatly and completely as possible.

2. Write a set of bylaws for an organization that you already belong to or one that you would like to form. Follow the format of the document on page R45.

Sometimes you may have to write technical documents, such as a list of procedures for conducting a meeting, a manual on rules of behavior, or the minutes of a meeting. These documents contain written descriptions of rules, regulations, and meetings and enable organizations and businesses to run smoothly.

These bylaws for a drama club include a description of the organization and detailed information about how the club operates. The writer began each section with a heading, so that readers could easily find information. The writer was also very specific, so that readers would not misunderstand the rules.

MODEL: BYLAWS DOCUMENT

Central High School Drama Club Bylaws

We, the current members of the Central High School Drama Club, create the following laws for our organization. Our members include actors, scenery designers, makeup artists, costume designers, lighting and sound specialists, stagehands, and stage managers.

MISSION STATEMENT: To provide an organization through which members of the dramatic arts program at Central High School heighten awareness of theater in the school and provide entertainment for the community

ACTIVITIES
- Biweekly meetings to talk about concerns and programming
- Publicity for upcoming school productions
- Performances, including two major drama productions

MEMBERSHIP REQUIREMENTS
To qualify for membership in the Drama Club, a candidate must
- be enrolled as a student at Central High School
- complete ten hours of participation in a school or community production

To remain a member of the Drama Club, an individual must
- actively contribute to the goals of the club
- complete a minimum of five hours of production participation each year

OFFICER ELECTION LAWS
Each year the members will vote for a president, a vice-president, a treasurer, and a secretary.
1. Each individual running for office must be nominated by another Drama Club member.
2. To be elected, a nominee must receive a majority of the votes.

RULES OF ORDER FOR MEETINGS
1. All meetings will be conducted according to *Robert's Rules of Order.*
2. A quorum of five members must be present for discussion of business items and voting.
3. The president will call the meeting to order.
4. The secretary will record, distribute, and manage meeting minutes.

Writing that has a lot of mistakes can confuse or even annoy a reader. A business letter with a punctuation error might lead to a miscommunication and delay a reply. Or a sentence fragment might lower your grade on an essay. Paying attention to grammar, punctuation, and capitalization rules can make your writing clearer and easier to read.

Quick Reference: Parts of Speech

PART OF SPEECH	FUNCTION	EXAMPLES
Noun	names a person, a place, a thing, an idea, a quality, or an action	
Common	serves as a general name, or a name common to an entire group	poet, novel, love, journey
Proper	names a specific, one-of-a-kind person, place, or thing	Lewis, Jackson, Pleasant Street, Stanley Cup
Singular	refers to a single person, place, thing, or idea	child, park, flower, truth
Plural	refers to more than one person, place, thing, or idea	children, parks, flowers, truths
Concrete	names something that can be perceived by the senses	roof, flash, Dublin, battle
Abstract	names something that cannot be perceived by the senses	intelligence, fear, joy, loneliness
Compound	expresses a single idea through a combination of two or more words	haircut, father-in-law, Christmas Eve
Collective	refers to a group of people or things	army, flock, class, species
Possessive	shows who or what owns something	Strafford's, Bess's, children's, witnesses'
Pronoun	takes the place of a noun or another pronoun	
Personal	refers to the person making a statement, the person(s) being addressed, or the person(s) or thing(s) the statement is about	I, me, my, mine, we, us, our, ours, you, your, yours, she, he, it, her, him, hers, his, its, they, them, their, theirs
Reflexive	follows a verb or preposition and refers to a preceding noun or pronoun	myself, yourself, herself, himself, itself, ourselves, yourselves, themselves
Intensive	emphasizes a noun or another pronoun	(same as reflexives)
Demonstrative	points to one or more specific persons or things	this, that, these, those
Interrogative	signals a question	who, whom, whose, which, what
Indefinite	refers to one or more persons or things not specifically mentioned	both, all, most, many, anyone, everybody, several, none, some
Relative	introduces an adjective clause by relating it to a word in the clause	who, whom, whose, which, that

PART OF SPEECH	FUNCTION	EXAMPLES
Verb	expresses an action, a condition, or a state of being	
Action	tells what the subject does or did, physically or mentally	run, reaches, listened, consider, decides, dreamed
Linking	connects the subject to something that identifies or describes it	am, is, are, was, were, sound, taste, appear, feel, become, remain, seem
Auxiliary	precedes the main verb in a verb phrase	be, have, do, can, could, will, would, may, might
Transitive	directs the action toward someone or something; always has an object	The storm **sank** the ship.
Intransitive	does not direct the action toward someone or something; does not have an object	The ship **sank.**
Adjective	modifies a noun or pronoun	**strong** women, **two** epics, **enough** time
Adverb	modifies a verb, an adjective, or another adverb	walked **out**, **really** funny, **far** away
Preposition	relates one word to another word	at, by, for, from, in, of, on, to, with
Conjunction	joins words or word groups	
Coordinating	joins words or word groups used the same way	and, but, or, for, so, yet, nor
Correlative	used as a pair to join words or word groups used the same way	both . . . and, either . . . or, neither . . . nor
Subordinating	introduces a clause that cannot stand by itself as a complete sentence	although, after, as, before, because, when, if, unless
Interjection	expresses emotion	wow, ouch, hurrah

Quick Reference: The Sentence and Its Parts

The diagrams that follow will give you a brief review of the essentials of a sentence and some of its parts.

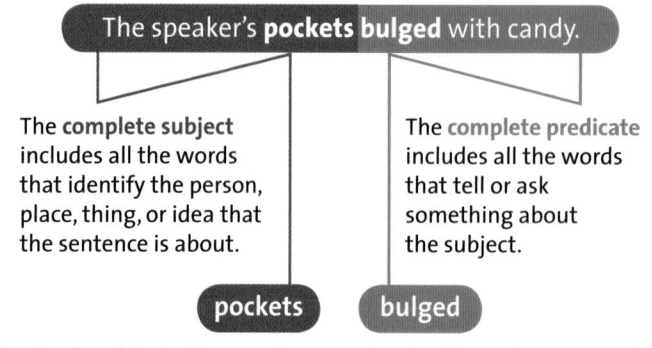

The **speaker's pockets bulged** with candy.

The **complete subject** includes all the words that identify the person, place, thing, or idea that the sentence is about.

The **complete predicate** includes all the words that tell or ask something about the subject.

pockets

bulged

The **simple subject** tells exactly whom or what the sentence is about. It may be one word or a group of words, but it does not include modifiers.

The **simple predicate,** or **verb,** tells what the subject does or is. It may be one word or several, but it does not include modifiers.

Every word in a sentence is part of a complete subject or a complete predicate.

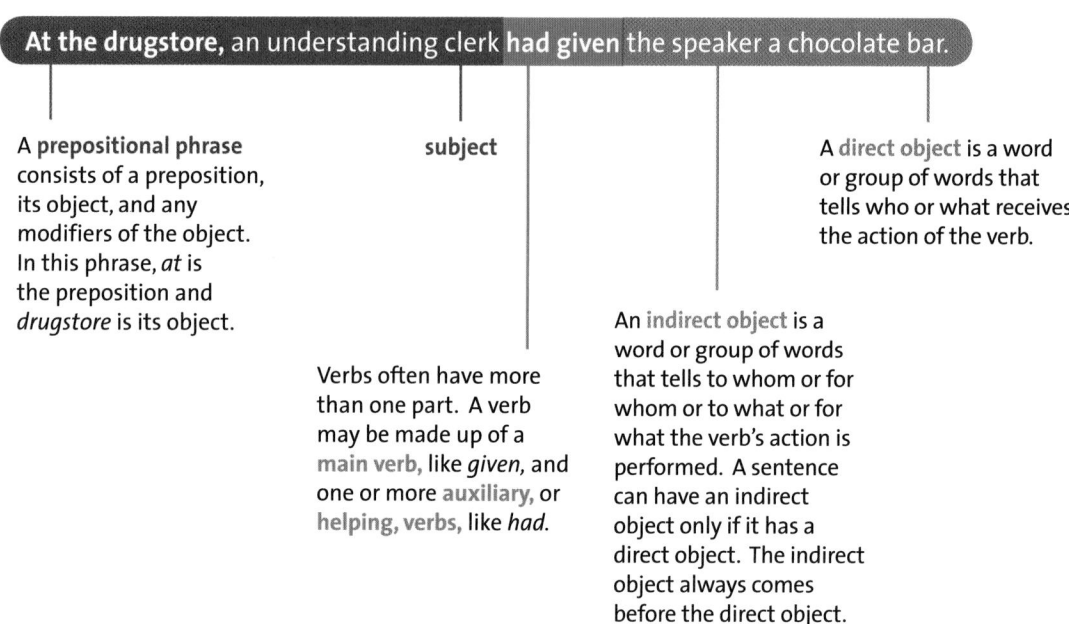

At the drugstore, an understanding clerk **had given** the speaker a chocolate bar.

A **prepositional phrase** consists of a preposition, its object, and any modifiers of the object. In this phrase, *at* is the preposition and *drugstore* is its object.

subject

A **direct object** is a word or group of words that tells who or what receives the action of the verb.

Verbs often have more than one part. A verb may be made up of a **main verb,** like *given,* and one or more **auxiliary,** or **helping, verbs,** like *had.*

An **indirect object** is a word or group of words that tells to whom or for whom or to what or for what the verb's action is performed. A sentence can have an indirect object only if it has a direct object. The indirect object always comes before the direct object.

Quick Reference: Punctuation

MARK	FUNCTION	EXAMPLES
End Marks period, question mark, exclamation point	ends a sentence	We can start now. When would you like to leave? What a fantastic hit!
period	follows an initial or abbreviation	Mrs. Dorothy Parker, McDougal Littell Inc., C. P. Cavafy, p.m., a.d., lb., oz., Blvd., Dr.
	Exception: postal abbreviations of states	NE (Nebraska), NV (Nevada)
period	follows a number or letter in an outline	I. Volcanoes A. Central-vent 1. Shield
Comma	separates part of a compound sentence	I had never disliked poetry, but now I really love it.
	separates items in a series	She is brave, loyal, and kind.
	separates adjectives of equal rank that modify the same noun	The slow, easy route is best.
	sets off a term of address	Maria, how can I help you? You must do something, soldier.
	sets off a parenthetical expression	Hard workers, as you know, don't quit. I'm not a quitter, believe me.
	sets off an introductory word, phrase, or dependent clause	Yes, I forgot my key. At the beginning of the day, I feel fresh. While she was out, I was here. Having finished my chores, I went out.
	sets off a nonessential phrase or clause	Ed Pawn, the captain of the chess team, won. Ed Pawn, who is the captain, won. The two leading runners, sprinting toward the finish line, finished in a tie.
	sets off parts of dates and addresses	Mail it by May 14, 2010, to the Hauptman Company, 321 Market Street, Memphis, Tennessee.
	follows the salutation and closing of a letter	Dear Jim, Sincerely yours,
	separates words to avoid confusion	By noon, time had run out. What the minister does, does matter. While cooking, Jim burned his hand.
Semicolon	separates items that contain commas in a series	We spent the first week of summer vacation in Chicago, Illinois; the second week in St. Louis, Missouri; and the third week in Albany, New York.
	separates parts of a compound sentence that are not joined by a coordinating conjunction	The last shall be first; the first shall be last. I read the Bible; however, I have not memorized it.
	separates parts of a compound sentence when the parts contain commas	After I ran out of money, I called my parents; but only my sister was home, unfortunately.

MARK	FUNCTION	EXAMPLES
Colon	introduces a list	Those we wrote were the following: Dana, John, and Will.
	introduces a long quotation	Abraham Lincoln wrote: "Four score and seven years ago, our fathers brought forth on this continent a new nation. . . ."
	follows the salutation of a business letter	To Whom It May Concern: Dear Leonard Atole:
	separates certain numbers	1:28 P.M., Genesis 2:5
Dash	indicates an abrupt break in thought	I was thinking of my mother—who is arriving tomorrow—just as you walked in.
Parentheses	enclose less important material	It was so unlike him (John is always on time) that I began to worry. The last World Series game (did you see it?) was fun.
Hyphen	joins parts of a compound adjective before a noun	The not-so-rich taxpayer won't stand for this!
	joins part of a compound with *all-, ex-, self-,* or *-elect*	The ex-firefighter helped rescue him. Our president-elect is self-conscious.
	joins part of a compound number (to ninety-nine)	Today, I turned twenty-one.
	joins part of a fraction	My cup is one-third full.
	joins a prefix to a word beginning with a capital letter	Which Pre-Raphaelite painter do you like best? It snowed in mid-October.
	indicates that a word is divided at the end of a line	How could you have any reasonable expect-ations of getting a new computer?
Apostrophe	used with *s* to form the possessive of a noun or an indefinite pronoun	my friend's book, my friends' books, anyone's guess, somebody else's problem
	replaces one or more omitted letters in a contraction or numbers in a date	don't (omitted *o*), he'd (omitted *woul*), the class of '99 (omitted *19*)
	used with *s* to form the plural of a letter	I had two A's on my report card.
Quotation Marks	set off a speaker's exact words	Sara said, "I'm finally ready." "I'm ready," Sara said, "finally." Did Sara say, "I'm ready"? Sara said, "I'm ready!"
	set off the title of a story, article, short poem, essay, song, or chapter	I liked McLean's "Marine Corps Issue" and Roethke's "My Papa's Waltz." I like Joplin's "Me and Bobby McGee."
Ellipses	replace material omitted from a quotation	"When in the course of human events . . . and to assume among the powers of the earth. . . ."
Italics	indicate the title of a book, play, magazine, long poem, opera, film, or TV series, or the name of a ship	*The House on Mango Street, Hamlet, Newsweek, the Odyssey, Madama Butterfly, Gone with the Wind, Seinfeld,* USS *Constitution*

Quick Reference: Capitalization

CATEGORY	EXAMPLES
People and Titles	
Names and initials of people	Amy Tan, W. H. Auden
Titles used before names	Professor Holmes, Senator Long
Deities and members of religious groups	Jesus, Allah, Buddha, Zeus, Baptists, Roman Catholics
Names of ethnic and national groups	Hispanics, Jews, African Americans
Geographical Names	
Cities, states, countries, continents	Philadelphia, Kansas, Japan, Europe
Regions, bodies of water, mountains	the South, Lake Baikal, Mount Everest
Geographic features, parks	Great Basin, Yellowstone National Park
Streets and roads, planets	318 East Sutton Drive, Charles Court, Jupiter, Pluto
Organizations, Events, Etc.	
Companies, organizations, teams	Ford Motor Company, Boy Scouts of America, St. Louis Cardinals
Buildings, bridges, monuments	Empire State Building, Eads Bridge, Washington Monument
Documents, awards	Declaration of Independence, Stanley Cup
Special named events	Mardi Gras, World Series
Government bodies, historical periods and events	U.S. Senate, House of Representatives, Middle Ages, Vietnam War
Days and months, holidays	Thursday, March, Thanksgiving, Labor Day
Specific cars, boats, trains, planes	Porsche, *Mississippi Queen*, *Stourbridge Lion*, Concorde
Proper Adjectives	
Adjectives formed from proper nouns	French cooking, Freudian psychology, Edwardian age, Midwestern university
First Words and the Pronoun *I*	
First word in a sentence or quotation	This is it. He said, "Let's go."
First word of sentence in parentheses that is not within another sentence	The spelling rules are covered in another section. (Consult that section for more information.)
First words in the salutation and closing of a letter	Dear Madam, Very truly yours,
First word in each line of most poetry Personal pronoun *I*	Then am I A happy fly If I live Or if I die.
First word, last word, and all important words in a title	*A Tale of Two Cities*, "The World Is Too Much with Us"

1 Nouns

A **noun** is a word used to name a person, a place, a thing, an idea, a quality, or an action. Nouns can be classified in several ways.

*For more information on different types of nouns, see **Quick Reference: Parts of Speech**, page R46.*

1.1 COMMON NOUNS

Common nouns are general names, common to entire groups.

1.2 PROPER NOUNS

Proper nouns name specific, one-of-a-kind people, places, and things.

Common	Proper
guitarist, museum, lake, month	B. B. King, Rock and Roll Hall of Fame, Lake Pontchartrain, February

*For more information, see **Quick Reference: Capitalization**, page R51.*

1.3 SINGULAR AND PLURAL NOUNS

A noun may take a singular or a plural form, depending on whether it names a single person,

Singular	Plural
stage, city, foot	stages, cities, feet

place, thing, or idea or more than one. Make sure you use appropriate spellings when forming plurals.

*For more information, see **Forming Plural Nouns**, page R74.*

1.4 POSSESSIVE NOUNS

A **possessive noun** shows who or what owns something.

*For more information, see **Forming Possessives**, page R74.*

2 Pronouns

A **pronoun** is a word that is used in place of a noun or another pronoun. The word or word group to which the pronoun refers is called its **antecedent.**

2.1 PERSONAL PRONOUNS

Personal pronouns change their form to express person, number, gender, and case. The forms of these pronouns are shown in the following chart.

	Nominative	Objective	Possessive
Singular			
First person	I	me	my, mine
Second person	you	you	your, yours
Third person	she, he, it	her, him, it	her, hers, his, its
Plural			
First person	we	us	our, ours
Second person	you	you	your, yours
Third person	they	them	their, theirs

2.2 AGREEMENT WITH ANTECEDENT

Pronouns should agree with their antecedents in number, gender, and person.

If an antecedent is singular, use a singular pronoun.
> EXAMPLE: *I lost my new **cell phone**. I may have left it on the bus.*

If an antecedent is plural, use a plural pronoun.
> EXAMPLES: *Take the **snacks** out of the grocery bag and put them in the pantry.*
>
> ***Delores and Arnetta** rode their bikes to the park.*

The gender of a pronoun must be the same as the gender of its antecedent.
> EXAMPLE: *The **man** thought he left his hat in the **room**. He ran back to it to look for the hat.*

The person of the pronoun must be the same as the person of its antecedent. As the chart in Section 2.1 shows, a pronoun can be in first-, second-, or third-person form.
> EXAMPLE: *You folks will have to go to the stadium to buy your tickets for the concert.*

GRAMMAR PRACTICE

Rewrite each sentence so that the underlined pronoun agrees with its antecedent.

1. The story "A Sound of Thunder" tells about a man who travels back in time and <u>its</u> adventures.

2. The man behind the desk warns Eckels, "If you disobey instructions, there will be a stiff penalty upon <u>our</u> return."

3. Eckels panics at the size of the dinosaur and <u>his</u> enormous teeth.

4. Travis looks at Eckels's shoes and notices dirt on <u>it</u>.

5. Travis feels <u>they</u> has to kill Eckels, so he shoots him.

2.3 PRONOUN CASE

Personal pronouns change form to show how they function in sentences. Different functions are shown by different **cases.** The three cases are **nominative, objective,** and **possessive.** For examples of these pronouns, see the chart in Section 2.1.

A **nominative pronoun** is used as a subject or a predicate nominative in a sentence.

An **objective pronoun** is used as a direct object, an indirect object, or the object of a preposition.

SUBJECT   OBJECT

He will lead them to us.

OBJECT OF PREPOSITION

A **possessive pronoun** shows ownership. The pronouns *mine, yours, hers, his, its, ours,* and *theirs* can be used in place of nouns.

EXAMPLE: *This horse is mine.*

The pronouns *my, your, her, his, its, our,* and *their* are used before nouns.

EXAMPLE: *This is my horse.*

WATCH OUT! Many spelling errors can be avoided if you watch out for *its* and *their.* Don't confuse the possessive pronoun *its* with the contraction *it's,* meaning "it is" or "it has." The homonyms *they're* (a contraction of *they are*) and *there* ("in that place" or an expletive) are often mistakenly used for *their.*

TIP To decide which pronoun to use in a comparison, such as "He tells better tales than (I *or* me)," fill in the missing word(s): *He tells better tales than I tell.*

GRAMMAR PRACTICE

Replace the underlined words in each sentence with an appropriate pronoun and identify the pronoun as nominative, objective, or possessive.

1. In "The Necklace," <u>Mme. Loisel</u> was not happy about her life.

2. Mme. Loisel married a clerk but wished <u>the couple</u> could be wealthy.

3. She hated <u>the apartment's</u> dirty walls.

4. One evening <u>Mme. Loisel's</u> husband said, "I have something for you."

5. Mme. Loisel's reaction to the party invitation was puzzling to <u>M. Loisel.</u>

2.4 REFLEXIVE AND INTENSIVE PRONOUNS

These pronouns are formed by adding *-self* or *-selves* to certain personal pronouns. Their forms are the same, and they differ only in how they are used.

A **reflexive pronoun** follows a verb or preposition and reflects back on an earlier noun or pronoun.

EXAMPLES: *He likes himself too much.*

She is now herself again.

Intensive pronouns intensify or emphasize the nouns or pronouns to which they refer.

EXAMPLES: *They themselves will educate their children.*

You did it yourself.

WATCH OUT! Avoid using *hisself* or *theirselves.* Standard English does not include these forms.

NONSTANDARD: *The sniper kept hisself hidden behind a chimney.*

STANDARD: *The sniper kept himself hidden behind a chimney.*

2.5 DEMONSTRATIVE PRONOUNS

Demonstrative pronouns point out things and persons near and far.

	Singular	Plural
Near	this	these
Far	that	those

2.6 INDEFINITE PRONOUNS

Indefinite pronouns do not refer to specific persons or things and usually have no antecedents. The chart shows some commonly used indefinite pronouns.

Singular	Plural	Singular or Plural	
another	both	all	most
anybody	few	any	none
no one	many	more	some
neither	several		

TIP Indefinite pronouns that end in *one, body,* or *thing* are always singular.

> INCORRECT: *Did everybody play their part well?*
> CORRECT: *Did everybody play his or her part well?*

If the indefinite pronoun might denote either a male or a female, *his or her* may be used to refer to it, or the sentence may be recast.

> EXAMPLES: *Did everybody play his or her part well?*
> *Did all the students play their parts well?*

2.7 INTERROGATIVE PRONOUNS

An **interrogative pronoun** tells a reader or listener that a question is coming. The interrogative pronouns are *who, whom, whose, which,* and *what.*

> EXAMPLES: *Who is going to rehearse with you?*
> *From whom did you receive the script?*

TIP *Who* is used as a subject; *whom,* as an object. To find out which pronoun you need to use in a question, change the question to a statement.

> QUESTION: *(Who/Whom) did you meet there?*
> STATEMENT: *You met (?) there.*

Since the verb has a subject (*you*), the needed word must be the object form, *whom.*

> EXAMPLE: *Whom did you meet there?*

WATCH OUT! A special problem arises when you use an interrupter, such as *do you think,* within a question.

> EXAMPLE: *(Who/Whom) do you think will win?*

If you eliminate the interrupter, it is clear that the word you need is *who.*

2.8 RELATIVE PRONOUNS

Relative pronouns relate, or connect, adjective clauses to the words they modify in sentences. The noun or pronoun that a relative clause modifies is the antecedent of the relative pronoun. Here are the relative pronouns and their uses.

	Subject	Object	Possessive
Person	who	whom	whose
Thing	which	which	whose
Thing/Person	that	that	whose

Often short sentences with related ideas can be combined by using a relative pronoun to create a more effective sentence.

> SHORT SENTENCE: *Poe wrote "The Raven."*
> RELATED SENTENCE: *"The Raven" is one of the most famous poems in American literature.*
> COMBINED SENTENCE: *Poe wrote "The Raven," which is one of the most famous poems in American literature.*

GRAMMAR PRACTICE

Write the correct form of each incorrect pronoun.

1. Whom has read "The Gift of the Magi"?

2. Jim needs money for a present for Della, so he takes his watch to the pawnshop hisself.

3. Would anybody else sell their watch to buy a Christmas present?

4. He chooses a beautiful pair of them jeweled combs for Della's hair.

5. Della sells her long hair to buy a watch chain for himself.

2.9 PRONOUN REFERENCE PROBLEMS

The referent of a pronoun should always be clear. Avoid problems by rewriting sentences.

An **indefinite reference** occurs when the pronoun *it, you,* or *they* does not clearly refer to a specific antecedent.

> UNCLEAR: *In the new production of* Romeo and Juliet, *you have more experienced actors.*
> CLEAR: *The new production of* Romeo and Juliet *has more experienced actors.*

A **general reference** occurs when the pronoun *it, this, that, which,* or *such* is used to refer to a general idea rather than a specific antecedent.

> UNCLEAR: *Jenna takes acting lessons. This has improved her chances of getting a part in the school play.*
> CLEAR: *Jenna takes acting lessons. The lessons have improved her chances of getting a part in the school play.*

Ambiguous means "having more than one possible meaning." An **ambiguous reference** occurs when a pronoun could refer to two or more antecedents.

> UNCLEAR: *Odysseus escaped from Cyclops, and he blinded him.*
> CLEAR: *Odysseus escaped from Cyclops, and he blinded Cyclops.*

GRAMMAR PRACTICE

Rewrite the following sentences to correct indefinite, ambiguous, and general pronoun references.

1. In Miss Lottie's yard you don't have any grass.
2. Miss Lottie plants marigolds. This makes her barren yard look strange.
3. Lizabeth and her brother throw stones at the marigolds, which ends Miss Lottie's planting.
4. Miss Lottie stares at Lizabeth as if she is strange.

3 Verbs

A **verb** is a word that expresses an action, a condition, or a state of being.

For more information, see **Quick Reference: Parts of Speech,** page R47.

3.1 ACTION VERBS

Action verbs express mental or physical activity.

> EXAMPLE: *Mr. Cho slept with the window open.*

3.2 LINKING VERBS

Linking verbs join subjects with words or phrases that rename or describe them.

> EXAMPLE: *When he awoke the next morning, his bed was wet from the rain.*

3.3 PRINCIPAL PARTS

Action and linking verbs typically have four principal parts, which are used to form verb tenses. The principal parts are the **present,** the **present participle,** the **past,** and the **past participle.**

Action verbs and some linking verbs also fall into two categories: regular and irregular. A **regular verb** is a verb that forms its past and past participle by adding *-ed* or *-d* to the present form.

Present	Present Participle	Past	Past Participle
risk	(is) risking	risked	(has) risked
solve	(is) solving	solved	(has) solved
drop	(is) dropping	dropped	(has) dropped
carry	(is) carrying	carried	(has) carried

An **irregular verb** is a verb that forms its past and past participle in some other way than by adding *-ed* or *-d* to the present form.

Present	Present Participle	Past	Past Participle
begin	(is) beginning	began	(has) begun
break	(is) breaking	broke	(has) broken
go	(is) going	went	(has) gone

3.4 VERB TENSE

The **tense** of a verb indicates the time of the action or state of being. An action or state of being can occur in the present, the past, or the future. There are six tenses, each expressing a different range of time.

The **present tense** expresses an action or state that is happening at the present time, occurs regularly, or is constant or generally true. Use the present part.

NOW: *That snow looks deep.*

REGULAR: *It snows every day.*

GENERAL: *Snow falls.*

The **past tense** expresses an action that began and ended in the past. Use the past part.

EXAMPLE: *The storyteller finished his tale.*

The **future tense** expresses an action or state that will occur. Use *shall* or *will* with the present part.

EXAMPLE: *They will attend the next festival.*

The **present perfect tense** expresses an action or state that (1) was completed at an indefinite time in the past or (2) began in the past and continues into the present. Use *have* or *has* with the past participle.

EXAMPLE: *Poetry has inspired many readers.*

The **past perfect tense** expresses an action in the past that came before another action in the past. Use *had* with the past participle.

EXAMPLE: *He had built a fire before the dog ran away.*

The **future perfect tense** expresses an action in the future that will be completed before another action in the future. Use *shall have* or *will have* with the past participle.

EXAMPLE: *They will have read the novel before they see the movie version of the tale.*

An auxiliary verb is not used with a past-tense irregular verb, but it is always used with a past-participle irregular verb.

INCORRECT: *I have saw her before.* (*Saw* is the past tense form and shouldn't be used with *have*.)

CORRECT: *I have seen her somewhere before.*

INCORRECT: *I seen her before.* (*Seen* is the past participle form of an irregular verb and shouldn't be used without an auxiliary verb.)

3.5 PROGRESSIVE FORMS

The progressive forms of the six tenses show ongoing actions. Use forms of *be* with the present participles of verbs.

PRESENT PROGRESSIVE: *She is rehearsing her lines.*

PAST PROGRESSIVE: *She was rehearsing her lines.*

FUTURE PROGRESSIVE: *She will be rehearsing her lines.*

PRESENT PERFECT PROGRESSIVE: *She has been rehearsing her lines.*

PAST PERFECT PROGRESSIVE: *She had been rehearsing her lines.*

FUTURE PERFECT PROGRESSIVE: *She will have been rehearsing her lines.*

WATCH OUT! Do not shift from tense to tense needlessly. Watch out for these special cases.

- In most compound sentences and in sentences with compound predicates, keep the tenses the same.

INCORRECT: *His boots freeze, and he shook with cold.*

CORRECT: *His boots freeze, and he shakes with cold.*

- If one past action happens before another, do shift tenses.

INCORRECT: *They wished they started earlier.*

CORRECT: *They wished they had started earlier.*

GRAMMAR PRACTICE

Rewrite each sentence, using a form of the verb in parentheses. Identify each form that you use.

1. Many people (benefit) from the civil rights movement.

2. Martin Luther King Jr. (remain) a towering figure in the history of nonviolent protest.

3. King (become) the leader of the Montgomery bus boycott.

4. When he (speak) to the crowds in Washington, D.C., more than 200,000 people heard his words.

5. Our class (read) his speech "I Have a Dream."

Rewrite each sentence to correct an error in tense.

6. It is a chilly morning as Rosa Parks went to work.

7. She leaves her job early and was preparing to go out of town.

8. She boarded the bus and is taking a seat in the "colored" section.

9. After several more stops, there are no more seats in the front of the bus.

10. Rosa Parks refused to give up her seat and is arrested.

3.6 ACTIVE AND PASSIVE VOICE

The voice of a verb tells whether its subject performs or receives the action expressed by the verb. When the subject performs the action, the verb is in the **active voice.** When the subject is the receiver of the action, the verb is in the **passive voice.**

Compare these two sentences:

ACTIVE: *Richard Wilbur wrote "The Writer."*

PASSIVE: *"The Writer" was written by Richard Wilbur.*

To form the passive voice, use a form of *be* with the past participle of the verb.

WATCH OUT! Use the passive voice sparingly. It can make writing awkward and less direct.

AWKWARD: *"The Writer" is a poem that was written by Richard Wilbur.*

BETTER: *Richard Wilbur wrote the poem "The Writer."*

There are occasions when you will choose to use the passive voice because

- you want to emphasize the receiver: *The king was shot.*
- the doer is unknown: *My books were stolen.*
- the doer is unimportant: *French is spoken here.*

4 Modifiers

Modifiers are words or groups of words that change or limit the meanings of other words. Adjectives and adverbs are common modifiers.

4.1 ADJECTIVES

Adjectives modify nouns and pronouns by telling which one, what kind, how many, or how much.

WHICH ONE: *this, that, these, those*
EXAMPLE: *That bird is a scarlet ibis.*

WHAT KIND: *small, sick, courageous, black*
EXAMPLE: *The sick bird sways on the branch.*

HOW MANY: *some, few, ten, none, both, each*
EXAMPLE: *Both brothers stared at the bird.*

HOW MUCH: *more, less, enough, fast*
EXAMPLE: *The bird did not have enough strength to remain perched.*

4.2 PREDICATE ADJECTIVES

Most adjectives come before the nouns they modify, as in the examples above. A **predicate adjective,** however, follows a linking verb and describes the subject.

EXAMPLE: *My friends are very intelligent.*

Be especially careful to use adjectives (not adverbs) after such linking verbs as *look, feel, grow, taste,* and *smell.*

EXAMPLE: *The bread smells wonderful.*

4.3 ADVERBS

Adverbs modify verbs, adjectives, and other adverbs by telling where, when, how, or to what extent.

WHERE: *The children played outside.*
WHEN: *The author spoke yesterday.*
HOW: *We walked slowly behind the leader.*
TO WHAT EXTENT: *He worked very hard.*

Adverbs may occur in many places in sentences, both before and after the words they modify.

EXAMPLES: *Suddenly the wind shifted.*

The wind suddenly shifted.

The wind shifted suddenly.

4.4 ADJECTIVE OR ADVERB?

Many adverbs are formed by adding *-ly* to adjectives.

EXAMPLES: *sweet, sweetly; gentle, gently*

However, *-ly* added to a noun will usually yield an adjective.

EXAMPLES: *friend, friendly; woman, womanly*

4.5 COMPARISON OF MODIFIERS

Modifiers can be used to compare two or more things. The form of a modifier shows the degree of comparison. Both adjectives and adverbs have **comparative** and **superlative** forms.

The **comparative form** is used to compare two things, groups, or actions.

EXAMPLES: *His father's hands were stronger than his own.*

His father was more courageous than the other man.

The **superlative form** is used to compare more than two things, groups, or actions.

EXAMPLES: *His father's hands were the strongest in the family.*

His father was the most courageous of them all.

4.6 REGULAR COMPARISONS

Most one-syllable and some two-syllable adjectives and adverbs have comparatives and superlatives formed by adding *-er* and *-est*. All three-syllable and most two-syllable modifiers have comparatives and superlatives formed with *more* or *most*.

Modifier	Comparative	Superlative
small	smaller	smallest
thin	thinner	thinnest
sleepy	sleepier	sleepiest
useless	more useless	most useless
precisely	more precisely	most precisely

WATCH OUT! Note that spelling changes must sometimes be made to form the comparatives and superlatives of modifiers.

EXAMPLES: *friendly, friendlier* (Change *y* to *i* and add the ending.)

sad, sadder (Double the final consonant and add the ending.)

4.7 IRREGULAR COMPARISONS

Some commonly used modifiers have irregular comparative and superlative forms. They are listed in the following chart. You may wish to memorize them.

Modifier	Comparative	Superlative
good	better	best
bad	worse	worst
far	farther *or* further	farthest *or* furthest
little	less *or* lesser	least
many	more	most
well	better	best
much	more	most

4.8 PROBLEMS WITH MODIFIERS

Study the tips that follow to avoid common mistakes:

Farther and Further Use *farther* for distances; use *further* for everything else.

Double Comparisons Make a comparison by using *-er/-est* or by using *more/most*. Using *-er* with *more* or using *-est* with *most* is incorrect.

INCORRECT: *I like her more better than she likes me.*

CORRECT: *I like her better than she likes me.*

Illogical Comparisons An illogical or confusing comparison results when two unrelated things are compared or when something is compared with itself. The word *other* or the word *else* should be used when comparing an individual member to the rest of a group.

ILLOGICAL: *The narrator was more curious about the war than any student in his class.* (implies that the narrator isn't a student in the class)

LOGICAL: *The narrator was more curious about the war than any other student in his class.* (identifies that the narrator is a student)

Bad vs. Badly *Bad*, always an adjective, is used before a noun or after a linking verb. *Badly*, always an adverb, never modifies a noun. Be sure to use the right form after a linking verb.

INCORRECT: *Ed felt badly after his team lost.*

CORRECT: *Ed felt bad after his team lost.*

Good vs. Well *Good* is always an adjective. It is used before a noun or after a linking verb. *Well* is often an adverb meaning "expertly" or "properly." *Well* can also be used as an adjective after a linking verb when it means "in good health."

INCORRECT: *Helen writes very good.*

CORRECT: *Helen writes very well.*

CORRECT: *Yesterday I felt bad; today I feel well.*

Double Negatives If you add a negative word to a sentence that is already negative, the result will be an error known as a double negative. When using *not* or *-n't* with a verb, use *any-* words, such as *anybody* or *anything*, rather than *no-* words, such as *nobody* or *nothing,* later in the sentence.

> INCORRECT: *We haven't seen nobody.*
> CORRECT: *We haven't seen anybody.*

Using *hardly, barely,* or *scarcely* after a negative word is also incorrect.

> INCORRECT: *They couldn't barely see two feet ahead.*
> CORRECT: *They could barely see two feet ahead.*

Misplaced Modifiers Sometimes a modifier is placed so far away from the word it modifies that the intended meaning of the sentence is unclear. Prepositional phrases and participial phrases are often misplaced. Place modifiers as close as possible to the words they modify.

> MISPLACED: *We found the child in the park who was missing.* (The child was missing, not the park.)
> CLEARER: *We found the child who was missing in the park.*

Dangling Modifiers Sometimes a modifier doesn't appear to modify any word in a sentence. Most dangling modifiers are participial phrases or infinitive phrases.

> DANGLING: *Looking out the window, his brother was seen driving by.*
> CLEARER: *Looking out the window, Josh saw his brother driving by.*

GRAMMAR PRACTICE

Choose the correct word or words from each pair in parentheses.

1. *The House on Mango Street* gives (better, more better) insight into Mexican-American culture than any other book I've read.

2. Sandra Cisneros's family moved so often that she hardly had (any, no) friends.

3. She felt (bad, badly) that she didn't live in a perfect house like the ones she saw on TV.

4. At one time Cisneros didn't think (nothing, anything) was positive about belonging to a different culture.

GRAMMAR PRACTICE

Rewrite each sentence that contains a misplaced or dangling modifier. Write "correct" if the sentence is written correctly.

1. The house on Loomis Street belongs to Esperanza's family with the broken water pipes.

2. Esperanza has to carry water from the house in empty milk jugs.

3. A nun asks Esperanza where she lived.

4. Feeling bad about the nun's reaction, the house is no longer good enough for Esperanza.

5 The Sentence and Its Parts

A **sentence** is a group of words used to express a complete thought. A complete sentence has a subject and a predicate.

*For more information, see **Quick Reference: The Sentence and Its Parts,** page R48.*

5.1 KINDS OF SENTENCES

There are four basic types of sentences.

Type	Definition	Example
Declarative	states a fact, a wish, an intent, or a feeling	Joan Bauer understands youths.
Interrogative	asks a question	Did you read "Pancakes"?
Imperative	gives a command or direction	Read the story.
Exclamatory	expresses strong feeling or excitement	The story is funny!

5.2 COMPOUND SUBJECTS AND PREDICATES

A compound subject consists of two or more subjects that share the same verb. They are typically joined by the coordinating conjunction *and* or *or.*

> EXAMPLE: *A short story or novel will keep you engaged.*

A compound predicate consists of two or more predicates that share the same subject. They too are typically joined by a coordinating conjunction, usually *and, but,* or *or.*

EXAMPLE: *The class finished all the poetry but did not read the short stories.*

5.3 COMPLEMENTS

A **complement** is a word or group of words that completes the meaning of the sentence. Some sentences contain only a subject and a verb. Most sentences, however, require additional words placed after the verb to complete the meaning of the sentence. There are three kinds of complements: direct objects, indirect objects, and subject complements.

Direct objects are words or word groups that receive the action of action verbs. A direct object answers the question *what* or *whom.*

> EXAMPLES: *The students asked many questions.* (Asked what?)
>
> *The teacher quickly answered the students.* (Answered whom?)

Indirect objects tell to whom or what or for whom or what the actions of verbs are performed. Indirect objects come before direct objects. In the examples that follow, the indirect objects are highlighted.

> EXAMPLES: *My sister usually gave her friends good advice.* (Gave to whom?)
>
> *Her brother sent the store a heavy package.* (Sent to what?)

Subject complements come after linking verbs and identify or describe the subjects. A subject complement that names or identifies a subject is called a **predicate nominative.** Predicate nominatives include **predicate nouns** and **predicate pronouns.**

> EXAMPLES: *My friends are very hard workers.*
>
> *The best writer in the class is she.*

A subject complement that describes a subject is called a **predicate adjective.**

> EXAMPLE: *The pianist appeared very energetic.*

6 Phrases

A **phrase** is a group of related words that does not contain a subject and a predicate but functions in a sentence as a single part of speech.

6.1 PREPOSITIONAL PHRASES

A **prepositional phrase** is a phrase that consists of a preposition, its object, and any modifiers of the object. Prepositional phrases that modify nouns or pronouns are called **adjective phrases.** Prepositional phrases that modify verbs, adjectives, or adverbs are **adverb phrases.**

> ADJECTIVE PHRASE: *The central character of the story is a villain.*
>
> ADVERB PHRASE: *He reveals his nature in the first scene.*

6.2 APPPOSITIVES AND APPOSITIVE PHRASES

An **appositive** is a noun or pronoun that identifies or renames another noun or pronoun. An **appositive phrase** includes an appositive and modifiers of it.

An appositive can be either **essential** or **nonessential.** An **essential appositive** provides information that is needed to identify what is referred to by the preceding noun or pronoun.

> EXAMPLE: *The book is about the author Richard Wright.*

A **nonessential appositive** adds extra information about a noun or pronoun whose meaning is already clear. Nonessential appositives and appositive phrases are set off with commas.

> EXAMPLE: *The book, an autobiography, tells how he began writing.*

7 Verbals and Verbal Phrases

A **verbal** is a verb form that is used as a noun, an adjective, or an adverb. A **verbal phrase** consists of a verbal along with its modifiers and complements. There are three kinds of verbals: **infinitives, participles,** and **gerunds.**

7.1 INFINITIVES AND INFINITIVE PHRASES

An **infinitive** is a verb form that usually begins with *to* and functions as a noun, an adjective, or an adverb. An **infinitive phrase** consists of an infinitive plus its modifiers and complements. The examples that follow show several uses of infinitive phrases.

> NOUN: *To know her is my only desire.* (subject)
> *I'm planning to walk with you.* (direct object)
> *Her goal was to promote women's rights.* (predicate nominative)
> ADJECTIVE: *We saw his need to be loved.* (adjective modifying *need*)
> ADVERB: *She wrote to voice her opinions.* (adverb modifying *wrote*)

Because *to,* the sign of the infinitive, precedes infinitives, it is usually easy to recognize them. However, sometimes *to* may be omitted.

> EXAMPLE: *Let no one dare [to] enter this shrine.*

7.2 PARTICIPLES AND PARTICIPIAL PHRASES

A **participle** is a verb form that functions as an adjective. Like adjectives, participles modify nouns and pronouns. Most participles are present-participle forms, ending in *-ing,* or past-participle forms ending in *-ed* or *-en.* In the examples below, the participles are highlighted.

> MODIFYING A NOUN: *The dying man had a smile on his face.*
> MODIFYING A PRONOUN: *Frustrated, everyone abandoned the cause.*

Participial phrases are participles with all their modifiers and complements.

> MODIFYING A NOUN: *The dogs searching for survivors are well trained.*
> MODIFYING A PRONOUN: *Having approved your proposal, we are ready to act.*

7.3 DANGLING AND MISPLACED PARTICIPLES

A participle or participial phrase should be placed as close as possible to the word that it modifies. Otherwise the meaning of the sentence may not be clear.

> MISPLACED: *The boys were looking for squirrels searching the trees.*
> CLEARER: *The boys searching the trees were looking for squirrels.*

A participle or participial phrase that does not clearly modify anything in a sentence is called a **dangling participle.** A dangling participle causes confusion because it appears to modify a word that it cannot sensibly modify. Correct a dangling participle by providing a word for the participle to modify.

> DANGLING: *Running like the wind, my hat fell off.* (The hat wasn't running.)
> CLEARER: *Running like the wind, I lost my hat.*

7.4 GERUNDS AND GERUND PHRASES

A **gerund** is a verb form ending in *-ing* that functions as a noun. Gerunds may perform any function nouns perform.

> SUBJECT: *Running is my favorite pastime.*
> DIRECT OBJECT: *I truly love running.*
> INDIRECT OBJECT: *You should give running a try.*
> SUBJECT COMPLEMENT: *My deepest passion is running.*
> OBJECT OF PREPOSITION: *Her love of running keeps her strong.*

Gerund phrases are gerunds with all their modifiers and complements.

> SUBJECT: *Wishing on a star never got me far.*
> OBJECT OF PREPOSITION: *I will finish before leaving the office.*
> APPOSITIVE: *Her avocation, flying airplanes, finally led to full-time employment.*

Rewrite each sentence, adding the phrase shown in parentheses.

1. "Daughter of Invention" was written by Julia Alvarez. (a short story)

2. The narrator loves writing. (to record her experiences)

3. She will appear at an assembly. (to give a speech)

4. She finally finishes her speech. (working feverishly for hours)

5. She reads her speech to her parents. (feeling proud)

8 Clauses

A **clause** is a group of words that contains a subject and a predicate. There are two kinds of clauses: independent clauses and subordinate clauses.

8.1 INDEPENDENT AND SUBORDINATE CLAUSES

An **independent clause** can stand alone as a sentence, as the word *independent* suggests.

INDEPENDENT CLAUSE: *Taos is famous for its Great Bank Robbery.*

A sentence may contain more than one independent clause.

EXAMPLE: *Many people remember the robbery, and they will tell you all about it.*

In the preceding example, the coordinating conjunction *and* joins two independent clauses.

For more information, see Coordinating Conjunction, page R47.

A **subordinate clause** cannot stand alone as a sentence. It is subordinate to, or dependent on, an independent clause.

EXAMPLE: *Although the two men needed cash, they didn't get it from the bank.*

The highlighted clause cannot stand by itself.

8.2 ADJECTIVE CLAUSES

An **adjective clause** is a subordinate clause used as an adjective. It usually follows the noun or pronoun it modifies.

EXAMPLE: *Tony Hillerman is someone whom millions know as a mystery writer.*

Adjective clauses are typically introduced by the relative pronoun *who, whom, whose, which,* or *that.*

*For more information, see **Relative Pronouns**, page R54.*

EXAMPLES: *A person who needs money should get a job.*

The robbers, whose names were Gomez and Smith, had guns.

An adjective clause can be either essential or nonessential. An **essential adjective clause** provides information that is necessary to identify the preceding noun or pronoun.

EXAMPLE: *One robber wore a disguise that was meant to fool Taos's residents.*

A **nonessential adjective clause** adds additional information about a noun or pronoun whose meaning is already clear. Nonessential clauses are set off with commas.

EXAMPLE: *The suspects, who drove away in a pickup truck, sideswiped a car driven by a minister.*

TIP The relative pronouns *whom, which,* and *that* may sometimes be omitted when they are objects in adjective clauses.

EXAMPLE: *Hillerman is a writer [whom] millions enjoy.*

8.3 ADVERB CLAUSES

An **adverb clause** is a subordinate clause that is used to modify a verb, an adjective, or an adverb. It is introduced by a subordinating conjunction.

*For examples of subordinating conjunctions, see **Noun Clauses**, page R63.*

Adverb clauses typically occur at the beginning or end of sentences.

MODIFYING A VERB: *When we need you, we will call.*

MODIFYING AN ADVERB: *I'll stay here where there is shelter from the rain.*

MODIFYING AN ADJECTIVE: *Roman felt as good as he had ever felt.*

8.4 NOUN CLAUSES

A **noun clause** is a subordinate clause that is used as a noun. A noun clause may be used as a subject, a direct object, an indirect object, a predicate nominative, or the object of a preposition. Noun clauses are introduced either by pronouns, such as *that*, *what*, *who*, *whoever*, *which*, and *whose*, or by subordinating conjunctions, such as *how*, *when*, *where*, *why*, and *whether*.

For more information, see **Quick Reference: Parts of Speech,** *page R47.*

TIP Because the same words may introduce adjective and noun clauses, you need to consider how a clause functions within its sentence. To determine if a clause is a noun clause, try substituting *something* or *someone* for the clause. If you can do it, it is probably a noun clause.

> **EXAMPLES:** *I know whose woods these are.*
> ("I know *something*." The clause is a noun clause, direct object of the verb *know*.)
> *Give a copy to whoever wants one.* ("Give a copy to *someone*." The clause is a noun clause, object of the preposition *to*.)

GRAMMAR PRACTICE

Add descriptive details to each sentence by writing the type of clause indicated in parentheses.

1. My aunt has an interesting hobby. (adjective clause)
2. She works on her craft at night. (adverb clause)
3. She writes. (noun clause)
4. She has written several books. (adjective clause)
5. I asked her to write a story about me. (adverb clause)

9 The Structure of Sentences

When classified by their structure, there are four kinds of sentences: simple, compound, complex, and compound-complex.

9.1 SIMPLE SENTENCES

A **simple sentence** is a sentence that has one independent clause and no subordinate clauses.

The fact that such a sentence is called simple does not mean that it is uncomplicated. Various parts of simple sentences may be compound, and simple sentences may contain grammatical structures such as appositive and verbal phrases.

> **EXAMPLES:** *Ray Bradbury, a science fiction writer, has written short stories and novels.* (appositive and compound direct object)
> *The narrator, recalling the years of his childhood, tells his story.* (participial phrase)

9.2 COMPOUND SENTENCES

A **compound sentence** consists of two or more independent clauses. The clauses in compound sentences are joined with commas and coordinating conjunctions (*and, but, or, nor, yet, for, so*) or with semicolons. Like simple sentences, compound sentences do not contain any subordinate clauses.

> **EXAMPLES:** *I enjoyed Bradbury's story "The Utterly Perfect Murder," and I want to read more of his stories.*
> *The narrator has lived a normal, complete life; however, he decides to kill his childhood playmate.*

WATCH OUT! Do not confuse compound sentences with simple sentences that have compound parts.

> **EXAMPLE:** *A subcommittee drafted a document and immediately presented it to the entire group.* (Here *and* joins parts of a compound predicate, not a compound sentence.)

9.3 COMPLEX SENTENCES

A **complex sentence** consists of one independent clause and one or more subordinate clauses. Each subordinate clause can be used as a noun or as a modifier. If it is used as a modifier, a subordinate clause usually modifies a word in the independent clause, and the independent clause can stand alone. However, when a subordinate clause is a noun clause, it is a part of the independent clause; the two cannot be separated.

MODIFIER: *One should not complain unless one has a better solution.*

NOUN CLAUSE: *We sketched pictures of whomever we wished.* (The noun clause is the object of the preposition *of* and cannot be separated from the rest of the sentence.)

9.4 COMPOUND-COMPLEX SENTENCES

A **compound-complex sentence** contains two or more independent clauses and one or more subordinate clauses. Compound-complex sentences are, simply, both compound and complex. If you start with a compound sentence, all you need to do to form a compound-complex sentence is add a subordinate clause.

COMPOUND: *All the students knew the answer, yet they were too shy to volunteer.*

COMPOUND-COMPLEX: *All the students knew the answer that their teacher expected, yet they were too shy to volunteer.*

9.5 PARALLEL STRUCTURE

When you write sentences, make sure that coordinate parts are equivalent, or **parallel,** in structure.

NOT PARALLEL: *Erin loved basketball and to play hockey.* (*Basketball* is a noun; *to play hockey* is a phrase.)

PARALLEL: *Erin loved basketball and hockey.* (*Basketball* and *hockey* are both nouns.)

NOT PARALLEL: *He wanted to rent an apartment, a new car, and traveling around the country.* (*To rent* is an infinitive, *car* is a noun, and *traveling* is a gerund.)

PARALLEL: *He wanted to rent an apartment, to drive a new car, and to travel around the country.* (*To rent, to drive,* and *to travel* are all infinitives.)

10 Writing Complete Sentences

Remember, a sentence is a group of words that expresses a complete thought. In writing that you wish to share with a reader, try to avoid both sentence fragments and run-on sentences.

10.1 CORRECTING FRAGMENTS

A **sentence fragment** is a group of words that is only part of a sentence. It does not express a complete thought and may be confusing to a reader or listener. A sentence fragment may be lacking a subject, a predicate, or both.

FRAGMENT: *Waited for the boat to arrive.* (no subject)

CORRECTED: *We waited for the boat to arrive.*

FRAGMENT: *People of various races, ages, and creeds.* (no predicate)

CORRECTED: *People of various races, ages, and creeds gathered together.*

FRAGMENT: *Near the old cottage.* (neither subject nor predicate)

CORRECTED: *The burial ground is near the old cottage.*

In your writing, fragments may be a result of haste or incorrect punctuation. Sometimes fixing a fragment will be a matter of attaching it to a preceding or following sentence.

FRAGMENT: *We saw the two girls. Waiting for the bus to arrive.*

CORRECTED: *We saw the two girls waiting for the bus to arrive.*

10.2 CORRECTING RUN-ON SENTENCES

A **run-on sentence** is made up of two or more sentences written as though they were one. Some run-ons have no punctuation within them. Others may have only commas where conjunctions or stronger punctuation marks are necessary. Use your judgment in correcting run-on sentences, as you have choices. You can make a run-on two sentences if the thoughts are not closely connected. If the thoughts are closely related, you can keep the run-on as one sentence by adding a semicolon or a conjunction.

RUN-ON: *We found a place for the picnic by a small pond it was three miles from the village.*

MAKE TWO SENTENCES: *We found a place for the picnic by a small pond. It was three miles from the village.*

RUN-ON: *We found a place for the picnic by a small pond it was perfect.*

USE A SEMICOLON: *We found a place for the picnic by a small pond; it was perfect.*

ADD A CONJUNCTION: *We found a place for the picnic by a small pond, and it was perfect.*

WATCH OUT! When you form compound sentences, make sure you use appropriate punctuation: a comma before a coordinating conjunction, a semicolon when there is no coordinating conjunction. A very common mistake is to use a comma alone instead of a comma and a conjunction. This error is called a **comma splice.**

INCORRECT: *He finished the apprenticeship, he left the village.*

CORRECT: *He finished the apprenticeship, and he left the village.*

11 Subject-Verb Agreement

The subject and verb in a clause must agree in number. Agreement means that if the subject is singular, the verb is also singular, and if the subject is plural, the verb is also plural.

11.1 BASIC AGREEMENT

Fortunately, agreement between subjects and verbs in English is simple. Most verbs show the difference between singular and plural only in the third person of the present tense. In the present tense, the third-person singular form ends in -s.

Present-Tense Verb Forms	
Singular	**Plural**
I sleep	we sleep
you sleep	you sleep
she, he, it sleeps	they sleep

11.2 AGREEMENT WITH *BE*

The verb *be* presents special problems in agreement, because this verb does not follow the usual verb patterns.

Forms of *Be*			
Present Tense		**Past Tense**	
Singular	**Plural**	**Singular**	**Plural**
I am	we are	I was	we were
you are	you are	you were	you were
she, he, it is	they are	she, he, it was	they were

11.3 WORDS BETWEEN SUBJECT AND VERB

A verb agrees only with its subject. When words come between a subject and a verb, ignore them when considering proper agreement. Identify the subject, and make sure the verb agrees with it.

EXAMPLES: *A story in the newspapers tells about the 1890s.*

Dad as well as Mom reads the paper daily.

11.4 AGREEMENT WITH COMPOUND SUBJECTS

Use plural verbs with most compound subjects joined by the word *and*.

EXAMPLE: *My father and his friends read the paper daily.*

To confirm that you need a plural verb, you could substitute the plural pronoun *they* for *my father and his friends*.

If a compound subject is thought of as a unit, use a singular verb. Test this by substituting the singular pronoun *it*.

EXAMPLE: *Peanut butter and jelly [it] is my brother's favorite sandwich.*

Use a singular verb with a compound subject that is preceded by *each, every,* or *many a*.

EXAMPLE: *Each novel and short story seems grounded in personal experience.*

When the parts of a compound subject are joined by *or, nor,* or the correlative conjunctions *either . . . or* or *neither . . . nor*, make the verb agree with the noun or pronoun nearest the verb.

EXAMPLES: *Cookies or ice cream is my favorite dessert.*

Either Cheryl or her friends are being invited.

Neither ice storms nor snow is predicted today.

11.5 PERSONAL PRONOUNS AS SUBJECTS

When using a personal pronoun as a subject, make sure to match it with the correct form of the verb *be*. (See the chart in Section 11.2.) Note especially that the pronoun *you* takes the forms *are* and *were*, regardless of whether it is singular or plural.

WATCH OUT! *You is* and *you was* are nonstandard forms and should be avoided in writing and speaking. *We was* and *they was* are also forms to be avoided.

INCORRECT: *You was a good student.*

CORRECT: *You were a good student.*

INCORRECT: *They was starting a new school.*

CORRECT: *They were starting a new school.*

11.6 INDEFINITE PRONOUNS AS SUBJECTS

Some indefinite pronouns are always singular; some are always plural.

Singular Indefinite Pronouns			
another	either	neither	one
anybody	everybody	nobody	somebody
anyone	everyone	no one	someone
anything	everything	nothing	something
each	much		

EXAMPLES: *Each of the writers was given an award.*
Somebody in the room upstairs is sleeping.

Plural Indefinite Pronouns			
both	few	many	several

EXAMPLES: *Many of the books in our library are not in circulation.*
Few have been returned recently.

Still other indefinite pronouns may be either singular or plural.

Singular or Plural Indefinite Pronouns		
all	more	none
any	most	some

The number of the indefinite pronoun *any* or *none* often depends on the intended meaning.

EXAMPLES: *Any of these topics has potential for a good article.* (any one topic)
Any of these topics have potential for good articles. (all of the many topics)

The indefinite pronouns *all, some, more, most,* and *none* are singular when they refer to quantities or parts of things. They are plural when they refer to numbers of individual things. Context will usually give a clue.

EXAMPLES: *All of the flour is gone.* (referring to a quantity)
All of the flowers are gone. (referring to individual items)

11.7 INVERTED SENTENCES

Problems in agreement often occur in inverted sentences beginning with *here* or *there*; in questions beginning with *how, when, why, where,* or *what*; and in inverted sentences beginning with phrases. Identify the subject—wherever it is—before deciding on the verb.

EXAMPLES: *There clearly are far too many cooks in this kitchen.*
What is the correct ingredient for this stew?
Far from the embroiled cooks stands the master chef.

GRAMMAR PRACTICE

Locate the subject of each verb in parentheses in the sentences below. Then choose the correct verb form.

1. Many Greeks sail home from Troy, but few (struggles, struggle) as hard as Odysseus to get there.

2. Neither Odysseus nor his men (know, knows) what dangers lie ahead.

3. There (is, are) more dangers awaiting him than there (is, are) gods to save him.

4. Everybody who has read about Odysseus' trials (knows, know) what he endured.

5. There (is, are) few friends who can help him during his ten-year odyssey.

6. The herds of the Cyclops Polyphemus (gives, give) Odysseus an idea for escape.

7. Does anyone (escapes, escape) the spell of Circe?

8. Standing before the hogs that are his friends (is, are) Odysseus.

9. Some of the winds (blows, blow) favorably, but many (blows, blow) ill.

10. Penelope, Telemachus, and the suitors (awaits, await) Odysseus upon his return.

11.8 SENTENCES WITH PREDICATE NOMINATIVES

When a predicate nominative serves as a complement in a sentence, use a verb that agrees with the subject, not the complement.

EXAMPLES: *The speeches of Martin Luther King Jr. are a landmark in American civil rights history.* (*Speeches* is the subject—not *landmark*—and it takes the plural verb *are*.)

One landmark in American civil rights history is the speeches of Martin Luther King Jr. (The subject is *landmark*—not *speeches*—and it takes the singular verb *is*.)

11.9 *DON'T* AND *DOESN'T* AS AUXILIARY VERBS

The auxiliary verb *doesn't* is used with singular subjects and with the personal pronouns *she, he,* and *it*. The auxiliary verb *don't* is used with plural subjects and with the personal pronouns *I, we, you,* and *they*.

SINGULAR: *She doesn't know Martin Luther King's famous "I Have a Dream" speech.*

Doesn't the young woman read very much?

PLURAL: *We don't have the speech memorized.*

Don't speakers usually memorize their speeches?

11.10 COLLECTIVE NOUNS AS SUBJECTS

Collective nouns are singular nouns that name groups of persons or things. *Team,* for example, is the collective name of a group of individuals. A collective noun takes a singular verb when the group acts as a single unit. It takes a plural verb when the members of the group act separately.

EXAMPLES: *Our team usually wins.* (The team as a whole wins.)

Our team vote differently on most issues. (The individual members vote.)

11.11 RELATIVE PRONOUNS AS SUBJECTS

When the relative pronoun *who, which,* or *that* is used as a subject in an adjective clause, the verb in the clause must agree in number with the antecedent of the pronoun.

SINGULAR: *I didn't read the **poem** about fireworks that was assigned.*

The antecedent of the relative pronoun *that* is the singular *poem;* therefore, *that* is singular and must take the singular verb *was*.

PLURAL: ***William Blake and Amy Lowell,** who are very different from each other, are both outstanding poets.*

The antecedent of the relative pronoun *who* is the plural compound subject *William Blake and Amy Lowell*. Therefore *who* is plural, and it takes the plural verb *are*.

The key to becoming an independent reader is to develop a toolkit of vocabulary strategies. By learning and practicing the strategies, you'll know what to do when you encounter unfamiliar words while reading. You'll also know how to refine the words you use for different situations—personal, school, and work.

Being a good speller is important when communicating your ideas in writing. Learning basic spelling rules and checking your spelling in a dictionary will help you spell words that you may not use frequently.

VOCABULARY PRACTICE
For more practice, go to the **Vocabulary Center** at **ClassZone.com.**

1 Using Context Clues

The context of a word is made up of the punctuation marks, words, sentences, and paragraphs that surround the word. A word's context can give you important clues about its meaning.

1.1 GENERAL CONTEXT

Sometimes you need to infer the meaning of an unfamiliar word by reading all the information in a passage.

> *After twelve hours without food, I was so ravenous that I ate four slices of pizza, two bowls of cereal, and an ice-cream sundae.*

You can figure out from the context that *ravenous* means "extremely hungry."

1.2 SPECIFIC CONTEXT CLUES

Sometimes writers help you understand the meanings of words by providing specific clues such as those shown in the chart.

1.3 IDIOMS, SLANG, AND FIGURATIVE LANGUAGE

An **idiom** is an expression whose overall meaning is different from the meaning of the individual words. **Slang** is informal language in which made-up words and ordinary words are used to mean something different from their meanings in formal English. **Figurative language** is language that communicates meaning beyond the literal meaning of the words. Use context clues to figure out the meanings of idioms, slang, and figurative language.

> *The mosquitoes drove us crazy on our hike through the woods.* (idiom; means "bothered")

> *That's a really cool backpack that you're wearing.* (slang; means "excellent" or "first-rate")

> *I was angry. Heat rose under my skin until I felt as if searing flames were threatening to engulf my whole body.* (figurative language; hot skin and flames symbolize anger)

Specific Context Clues		
Type of Clue	**Key Words/ Phrases**	**Example**
Definition or restatement of the meaning of the word	or, which is, that is, in other words, also known as, also called	His first conjecture, **or guess,** was correct.
Example following an unfamiliar word	such as, like, as if, for example, especially, including	She loved macabre stories, **such as those by Edgar Allan Poe and Stephen King.**
Comparison with a more familiar word or concept	as, like, also, similar to, in the same way, likewise	Despite his physical suffering, his mind was as **lucid** as any **rational** person's.
Contrast with a familiar word or experience	unlike, but, however, although, on the other hand, on the contrary	Unlike her **clumsy** partner, she was an **agile** dancer.
Cause-and-effect relationship in which one term is familiar	because, since, when, consequently, as a result, therefore	**Because** this perfume has such a sharp scent, I **will buy** the one with a subtle fragrance.

For more information, see **Vocabulary Strategy: Using Context Clues,** pages 371 and 457.

2 Analyzing Word Structure

Many words can be broken into smaller parts. These word parts include base words, roots, prefixes, and suffixes.

2.1 BASE WORDS

A **base word** is a word part that by itself is also a word. Other words or word parts can be added to base words to form new words.

2.2 ROOTS

A **root** is a word part that contains the core meaning of the word. Many English words contain roots that come from older languages such as Greek, Latin, Old English (Anglo-Saxon), and Norse. Knowing the meaning of the word's root can help you determine the word's meaning.

Root	Meaning	Examples
bi (Greek)	life	biography
gramm (Greek)	letter, something written	grammar
grad (Latin)	step, degree	graduate
man (Latin)	hand	manual
hēadfod (Old English)	head, top	headfirst

*For more information, see **Vocabulary Strategy: Word Roots**, pages 49, 204, 340, 532, and 555.*

2.3 PREFIXES

A **prefix** is a word part attached to the beginning of a word. Most prefixes come from Greek, Latin, or Old English.

Prefix	Meaning	Examples
pre-	before	preschool
ex-	out, from	extend
re-	again, back	return

*For more information, see **Vocabulary Strategy: Prefixes**, page 92.*

2.4 SUFFIXES

A **suffix** is a word part that appears at the end of a root or base word to form a new word. Some suffixes do not change word meaning. These suffixes are

- added to nouns to change the number of persons or objects
- added to verbs to change the tense
- added to modifiers to change the degree of comparison

Suffix	Meaning	Examples
-s, -es	to change the number of a noun	snack + s = snacks
-d, -ed, -ing	to change verb tense	walk + ed = walked
-er, -est	to change the degree of comparison in modifiers	wild + er = wilder fast + est = fastest

Other suffixes can be added to a root or base to change the word's meaning. These suffixes can also determine a word's part of speech.

Suffix	Meaning	Examples
-age	action or process	pilgrimage
-able	ability	enjoyable
-ize	to make	criticize

*For more information, see **Vocabulary Strategy: Suffixes**, page 421.*

Strategies for Understanding Unfamiliar Words

- Look for any prefixes or suffixes. Remove them to isolate the base word or the root.
- See if you recognize any elements—prefix, suffix, root, or base—of the word. You may be able to guess its meaning by analyzing one or two elements.
- Consider the way the word is used in the sentence. Use the context and the word parts to make a logical guess about the word's meaning.
- Consult a dictionary to see whether you are correct.

3 Understanding Word Origins

3.1 ETYMOLOGIES

Etymologies show the origin and historical development of a word. When you study a word's history and origin, you can find out when, where, and how the word came to be.

> **dra•ma** (drä′mə) *n.* **1.** A work that is meant to be performed by actors. **2.** Theatrical works of a certain type or period in history. [Late Latin *drāma, drāmat-,* from Greek *drān,* to do or perform.]
>
> **for•mi•car•y** (fôr′mĭ-kĕr′ē) *n., pl.* **-ies** A nest of ants; an anthill. [Medieval Latin *formīcārium,* from Latin *formīca,* ant.]
>
> **lock**² (lŏk) *n.* **1a.** A length or curl of hair; a tress. **b.** The hair of the head. Often used in the plural. **2.** A small wisp or tuft, as of wool or cotton. [Middle English, from Old English *locc.*]

For more information, see **Vocabulary Strategy: Etymologies,** *page 282.*

3.2 WORD FAMILIES

Words that have the same root make up a word family and have related meanings. The chart shows a common Greek and a common Latin root. Notice how the meanings of the example words are related to the meanings of their roots.

Latin Root	*vid, vis:* "see"
English	**vision** eyesight
	video visual portion of a televised broadcast
	visible possible to see

Greek Root	*phonē:* "sound"
English	**homophone** word that sounds like another word
	phonetics the study of speech sounds
	telephone a device that converts voice into a form that can be transmitted as sound waves

For more information, see **Vocabulary Strategy: Word Family,** *pages 131 and 354.*

3.3 WORDS FROM CLASSICAL MYTHOLOGY

The English language includes many words from classical mythology. You can use your knowledge of Greek, Roman, and Norse myths to understand the origins and meanings of these words. For example, *herculean task* refers to the strongman Hercules. Thus *herculean task* probably means "a job that is large or difficult." The chart shows a few common words from mythology.

Greek	Roman	Norse
Achilles' heel	academy	Thursday
pandemonium	volcano	berserk
muse	cupid	rune
Midas touch	floral	valkyrie

3.4 FOREIGN WORDS

The English language has grown to include words from diverse languages such as French, Dutch, Spanish, Italian, Portuguese, and Chinese. Many of these words stayed the way they were in their original languages.

French	Dutch	Spanish	Italian
ballet	boss	canyon	diva
beret	caboose	rodeo	carnival
mirage	dock	salsa	spaghetti

4 Synonyms and Antonyms

4.1 SYNONYMS

A **synonym** is a word with a meaning similar to that of another word. You can find synonyms in a thesaurus or a dictionary. In a dictionary, synonyms are often given as part of the definition of the word. The following word pairs are synonyms:

happy/joyful   sad/unhappy

angry/mad   beautiful/lovely

4.2 ANTONYMS

An **antonym** is a word with a meaning opposite that of another word. The following word pairs are antonyms:

best/worst   well/ill

light/dark   happy/sad

5 Denotation and Connotation

5.1 DENOTATION

A word's dictionary meaning is called its **denotation.** For example, the denotation of the word *rascal* is "an unethical, dishonest person."

5.2 CONNOTATION

The images or feelings you connect to a word add a finer shade of meaning, called **connotation.** The connation of a word goes beyond its basic dictionary definition. Writers use connotations of words to communicate positive or negative feelings.

Positive	Neutral	Negative
gaze	look	glare
slender	thin	scrawny
playful	active	rowdy

Make sure you understand the denotation and connotation of a word when you read it or use it in your writing.

*For more information, see **Vocabulary Strategy: Denotation and Connotation,** pages 76, 324, and 444.*

6 Analogies

An **analogy** is a comparison between two things that are similar in some way but are otherwise dissimilar. Analogies are sometimes used in writing when unfamiliar subjects or ideas are explained in terms of familiar ones. Analogies often appear on tests as well, usually in a format like this:

bird : fly ::   A) boat : water
                   B) bear : cave
                   C) fish : scales
                   D) fish : swim
                   E) sparrow : wings

Follow these steps to determine the correct answer:

- Read the first half of the analogy as *"bird* is to *fly* as...."
- Read the answer choices as *"boat* is to *water,"* *"bear* is to *cave,"* and so on.
- Ask yourself how the words *bird* and *fly* are related. (A bird can fly.)
- Ask yourself which of the choices shows the same relationship. (A boat can't water and a bear can't cave, but a fish can swim. Therefore, the answer is D.)

7 Homonyms and Homophones

7.1 HOMONYMS

Homonyms are words that have the same spelling and sound but have different meanings.

The girl had to stoop to find her ball under the stoop.

Stoop can mean "a small porch," but an identically spelled word means "to bend down." Because the words have different meanings, each word has its own dictionary entry.

The lawyer argued the case of the missing jewelry case.

Case can mean "evidence in support of a claim." However, another identically spelled word means "container." Each word has a different meaning and its own dictionary entry.

Sometimes only one of the meanings of a homonym may be familiar to you. Use context clues to help you figure out the meaning of an unfamiliar word.

7.2 HOMOPHONES

Homophones are words that sound alike but have different meanings and spellings. The following homophones are frequently misused:

it's/its   they're/their/there

to/too/two   stationary/stationery

Many misused homophones are pronouns and contractions. Whenever you are unsure whether to write *your* or *you're* and *who's* or *whose,* ask yourself if you mean *you are* or *who is/has.* If you do, write the contraction. For other homophones, such as *fair* and *fare,* use the meaning of the word to help you decide which one to use.

8 Words with Multiple Meanings

Some words have acquired additional meanings over time that are based on the original meaning.

> *Thinking of the horror movie made my skin creep.*
> *I saw my little brother creep around the corner.*

These two uses of *creep* have different meanings, but both of them have the same origin. You will find all the meanings of *creep* listed in one entry in the dictionary.

*For more information, see **Vocabulary Strategy: Multiple-Meaning Words,** page 248.*

9 Specialized Vocabulary

Specialized vocabulary is special terms suited to a particular field of study or work. For example, science, mathematics, and history all have their own technical or specialized vocabularies. To figure out specialized terms, you can use context clues and reference sources, such as dictionaries on specific subjects, atlases, or manuals.

*For more information, see **Vocabulary Strategy: Specialized Vocabulary,** pages 263 and 545.*

10 Using Reference Sources

10.1 DICTIONARIES

A **general dictionary** will tell you not only a word's definitions but also its pronunciation, parts of speech, and history and origin. A **specialized dictionary** focuses on terms related to a particular field of study or work. Use a dictionary to check the spelling of any word you are unsure of in your English class and for other subjects as well.

*For more information, see **Vocabulary Strategy: Using a Dictionary,** page 618.*

10.2 THESAURI

A **thesaurus** (plural, thesauri) is a dictionary of synonyms. A thesaurus can be especially helpful when you find yourself using the same modifiers over and over again.

10.3 SYNONYM FINDERS

A **synonym finder** is often included in word-processing software. It enables you to highlight a word and be shown a display of its synonyms.

10.4 GLOSSARIES

A **glossary** is a list of specialized terms and their definitions. It is often found in the back of a book and sometimes includes pronunciations. Many textbooks contain glossaries. In fact, this textbook has three glossaries: the **Glossary of Literary Terms,** the **Glossary of Reading and Informational Terms,** and the **Glossary of Vocabulary in English & Spanish.** Use these glossaries to help you understand how terms are used in this textbook.

11 Spelling Rules

11.1 WORDS ENDING IN A SILENT *E*

Before adding a suffix beginning with a vowel or *y* to a word ending in a silent *e,* drop the *e* (with some exceptions).

> **amaze + -ing = amazing**
> **love + -able = lovable**
> **create + -ed = created**
> **nerve + -ous = nervous**

Exceptions: *change + -able = changeable; courage + -ous = courageous*

When adding a suffix beginning with a consonant to a word ending in a silent *e,* keep the *e* (with some exceptions).

> **late + -ly = lately**
> **spite + -ful = spiteful**
> **noise + -less = noiseless**
> **state + -ment = statement**

Exceptions: *truly, argument, ninth, wholly, awful,* and others.

When a suffix beginning with *a* or *o* is added to a word with a final silent *e,* the final *e* is usually retained if it is preceded by a soft *c* or a soft *g.*

bridge + -able = bridgeable
peace + -able = peaceable
outrage + -ous = outrageous
advantage + -ous = advantageous

When a suffix beginning with a vowel is added to words ending in *ee* or *oe,* the final silent *e* is retained.

agree + -ing = agreeing   **free + -ing = freeing**
hoe + -ing = hoeing   **see + -ing = seeing**

11.2 WORDS ENDING IN Y

Before adding most suffixes to a word that ends in *y* preceded by a consonant, change the *y* to *i.*

easy + -est = easiest
crazy + -est = craziest
silly + -ness = silliness
marry + -age = marriage

Exceptions: *dryness, shyness,* and *slyness.*

However, when you add *-ing,* the *y* does not change.

empty + -ed = emptied   but
empty + -ing = emptying

When adding a suffix to a word that ends in *y* preceded by a vowel, the *y* usually does not change.

play + -er = player
employ + -ed = employed
coy + -ness = coyness
pay + -able = payable

11.3 WORDS ENDING IN A CONSONANT

In one-syllable words that end in one consonant preceded by one short vowel, double the final consonant before adding a suffix beginning with a vowel, such as *-ed* or *-ing.* These are sometimes called 1+1+1 words.

dip + -ed = dipped   **set + -ing = setting**
slim + -est = slimmest   **fit + -er = fitter**

The rule does not apply to words of one syllable that end in a consonant preceded by two vowels.

feel + -ing = feeling   **peel + -ed = peeled**
reap + -ed = reaped   **loot + -ed = looted**

In words of more than one syllable, double the final consonant when (**1**) the word ends with one consonant preceded by one vowel and (**2**) the word is accented on the last syllable.

be•gin´   per•mit´   re•fer´

In the following examples, note that in the new words formed with suffixes, the accent remains on the same syllable:

be•gin´ + -ing = be•gin´ning = beginning
per•mit´ + -ed = per•mit´ted = permitted

Exceptions: In some words with more than one syllable, though the accent remains on the same syllable when a suffix is added, the final consonant is nevertheless not doubled, as in the following examples:

tra´vel + er = tra´vel•er = traveler
mar´ket + er = mar´ket•er = marketer

In the following examples, the accent does not remain on the same syllable; thus, the final consonant is not doubled:

re•fer´ + -ence = ref´er•ence = reference
con•fer´ + -ence = con´fer•ence = conference

11.4 PREFIXES AND SUFFIXES

When adding a prefix to a word, do not change the spelling of the base word. When a prefix creates a double letter, keep both letters.

dis- + approve = disapprove
re- + build = rebuild
ir- + regular = irregular
mis- + spell = misspell
anti- + trust = antitrust
il- + logical = illogical

When adding *-ly* to a word ending in *l,* keep both *l*'s. When adding *-ness* to a word ending in *n,* keep both *n*'s.

careful + -ly = carefully
sudden + -ness = suddenness
final + -ly = finally
thin + -ness = thinness

11.5 FORMING PLURAL NOUNS

To form the plural of most nouns, just add *-s.*

    prizes   dreams   circles   stations

For most singular nouns ending in *o,* add *-s.*

    solos   halos   studios   photos   pianos

For a few nouns ending in *o,* add *-es.*

    heroes   tomatoes   potatoes   echoes

When the singular noun ends in *s, sh, ch, x,* or *z,* add *-es.*

    waitresses   brushes   ditches
    axes   buzzes

When a singular noun ends in *y* with a consonant before it, change the *y* to *i* and add *-es.*

    army—armies   candy—candies
    baby—babies   diary—diaries
    ferry—ferries   conspiracy—conspiracies

When a vowel (*a, e, i, o, u*) comes before the *y,* just add *-s.*

    boy—boys   way—ways
    array—arrays   alloy—alloys
    weekday—weekdays   jockey—jockeys

For most nouns ending in *f* or *fe,* change the *f* to *v* and add *-es* or *-s.*

    life—lives   calf—calves   knife—knives
    thief—thieves   shelf—shelves   loaf—loaves

For some nouns ending in *f,* add *-s* to make the plural.

    roofs   chiefs   reefs   beliefs

Some nouns have the same form for both singular and plural.

    deer   sheep   moose   salmon   trout

For some nouns, the plural is formed in a special way.

    man—men   goose—geese
    ox—oxen   woman—women
    mouse—mice   child—children

For a compound noun written as one word, form the plural by changing the last word in the compound to its plural form.

    stepchild—stepchildren   firefly—fireflies

If a compound noun is written as a hyphenated word or as two separate words, change the most important word to the plural form.

    brother-in-law—brothers-in-law
    life jacket—life jackets

11.6 FORMING POSSESSIVES

If a noun is singular, add *'s.*

    mother—my mother's car   Ross—Ross's desk

Exception: The *s* after the apostrophe is dropped after *Jesus', Moses',* and certain names in classical mythology *(Zeus').* These possessive forms can thus be pronounced easily.

If a noun is plural and ends with *s,* just add an apostrophe.

    parents—my parents' car
    the Santinis—the Santinis' house

If a noun is plural but does not end in *s,* add *'s.*

    people—the people's choice
    women—the women's coats

11.7 SPECIAL SPELLING PROBLEMS

Only one English word ends in *-sede: supersede.* Three words end in *-ceed: exceed, proceed,* and *succeed.* All other verbs ending in the sound "seed" are spelled with *-cede.*

    concede   precede   recede   secede

In words with **ie** or **ei,** when the sound is long *e* (as in *she*), the word is spelled *ie* except after *c* (with some exceptions).

i before *e*	thief	relieve	field
	piece	grieve	pier
except after *c*	conceit	perceive	ceiling
	receive	receipt	
Exceptions:	either	neither	weird
	leisure	seize	

12 Commonly Confused Words

WORDS	DEFINITIONS	EXAMPLES
accept/except	The verb *accept* means "to receive or believe"; *except* is usually a preposition meaning "excluding."	**Except** for some of the more extraordinary events, I can **accept** that the *Odyssey* recounts a real journey.
advice/advise	*Advise* is a verb; *advice* is a noun naming that which an *adviser* gives.	I **advise** you to take that job. Whom should I ask for **advice?**
affect/effect	As a verb, *affect* means "to influence." *Effect* as a verb means "to cause." If you want a noun, you will almost always want *effect*.	Did Circe's wine **affect** Odysseus' mind? It did **effect** a change in Odysseus' men. In fact, it had an **effect** on everyone else who drank it.
all ready/already	*All ready* is an adjective meaning "fully ready." *Already* is an adverb meaning "before or by this time."	He was **all ready** to go at noon. I have **already** seen that movie.
allusion/illusion	An *allusion* is an indirect reference to something. An *illusion* is a false picture or idea.	There are many **allusions** to the works of Homer in English literature. The world's apparent flatness is an **illusion**.
among/between	*Between* is used when you are speaking of only two things. *Among* is used for three or more.	**Between** *Hamlet* and *King Lear*, I prefer the latter. Emily Dickinson is **among** my favorite poets.
bring/take	*Bring* is used to denote motion toward a speaker or place. *Take* is used to denote motion away from such a person or place.	**Bring** the books over here, and I will **take** them to the library.
fewer/less	*Fewer* refers to the number of separate, countable units. *Less* refers to bulk quantity.	We have **less** literature and **fewer** selections in this year's curriculum.
leave/let	*Leave* means "to allow something to remain behind." *Let* means "to permit."	The librarian will **leave** some books on display but will not **let** us borrow any.
lie/lay	To *lie* is "to rest or recline." It does not take an object. *Lay* always takes an object.	Rover loves to **lie** in the sun. We always **lay** some bones next to him.
loose/lose	*Loose* (lo͞os) means "free, not restrained"; *lose* (lo͞oz) means "to misplace or fail to find."	Who turned the horses **loose?** I hope we won't **lose** any of them.
precede/proceed	*Precede* means "to go or come before." Use *proceed* for other meanings.	Emily Dickinson's poetry **precedes** that of Alice Walker. You may **proceed** to the next section of the test.
than/then	Use *than* in making comparisons; use *then* on all other occasions.	Who can say whether Amy Lowell is a better poet **than** Denise Levertov? I will read Lowell first, and **then** I will read Levertov.
their/there/they're	*Their* means "belonging to them." *There* means "in that place." *They're* is the contraction for "they are."	**There** is a movie playing at 9 P.M. **They're** going to see it with me. Sakara and Erin drove away in **their** car after the movie.
two/too/to	*Two* is the number. *Too* is an adverb meaning "also" or "very." Use *to* before a verb or as a preposition.	Meg had **to** go **to** town, **too**. We had **too** much reading **to** do. **Two** chapters is **too** many.

Effective oral communication occurs when the audience understands a message the way the speaker intends it. Good speakers and listeners do more than just talk and hear. They use specific techniques to present their ideas effectively, and they are attentive and critical listeners.

1 Speech

In school, in business, and in community life, a speech is one of the most effective means of communicating.

1.1 AUDIENCE, PURPOSE, AND OCCASION

When developing and delivering a speech, your goal is to deliver a focused, coherent presentation that conveys your ideas clearly and relates to the background of your audience. By understanding your audience, you can tailor your speech to them appropriately and effectively.

- **Know Your Audience** What kind of group are you presenting to? Fellow classmates? A group of teachers? What are their interests and backgrounds? Understanding their different points of view can help you organize the information so that they understand and are interested in it.

- **Understand Your Purpose** Keep in mind your purpose for speaking. Are you trying to persuade the audience to do something? Perhaps you simply want to entertain them by sharing a story or experience. Your reason for giving the speech will guide you in organizing your thoughts and deciding on how to deliver it.

- **Know the Occasion** Are you speaking at a special event? Is it formal? Will others be giving speeches besides you? Knowing what the occasion is will help you tailor the language and the length for the event.

1.2 PREPARING YOUR SPEECH

There are several approaches to preparing a speech. Your teacher may tell you which one to use.

Manuscript	Prepare a complete script of the speech in advance and use it to deliver the speech. Use for formal occasions, such as graduation speeches and political addresses, and to present technical or complicated information.
Memory	Prepare a written text in advance and then memorize it in order to deliver the speech word for word. Use for short speeches, as when introducing another speaker or accepting an award.
Extemporaneous	Prepare the speech and deliver it using an outline or notes. Use for informal situations, for persuasive messages, and to make a more personal connection with the audience.

1.3 DRAFTING YOUR SPEECH

If you are writing your speech beforehand, rather than working from notes, use the following guidelines to help you:

- **Create a Unified Speech** Do this first by organizing your speech into paragraphs, each of which develops a single main idea. Then make sure that just as all the sentences in a paragraph support the main idea of the paragraph, all the paragraphs in your speech support the main idea of the speech.

- **Use Appropriate Language** The subject of your speech—and the way you choose to present it—should match your audience, your purpose, and the occasion. You can use informal language, such as slang, to share a story with your classmates. For a persuasive speech in front of a school assembly, use formal, standard American English. If you are giving an informative presentation, be sure to explain any terms that the audience may not be familiar with.

- **Provide Evidence** Include relevant facts, statistics, and incidents; quote experts to support your ideas and opinions. Elaborate—provide specific details, perhaps with visual or media displays—to clarify what you are saying.

- **Emphasize Important Points** To help your audience follow the main ideas and concepts of your speech, be sure to draw attention to important points. You can use rhyme, repetition, and other rhetorical devices.

- **Use Precise Language** Use precise language to convey your ideas, and vary the structure and length of your sentences. You can keep the audience's attention with a word that elicits strong emotion. You can use a question or interjection to make a personal connection with the audience.

- **Start Strong, Finish Strong** As you begin your speech, consider using a "hook"—an interesting question or statement meant to capture your audience's attention. At the end of the speech, restate your main ideas simply and clearly. Perhaps conclude with a powerful example or anecdote to reinforce your message.

- **Revise Your Speech** After you write your speech, revise, edit, and proofread it as you would a written report. Use a variety of sentence structures to achieve a natural rhythm. Check for correct subject-verb agreement and consistent verb tense. Correct run-on sentences and sentence fragments. Use parallel structure to emphasize ideas. Make sure you use complete sentences and correct punctuation and capitalization, even if no one else will see it. Your written speech should be clear and error-free. If you notice an error in your notes during the speech, you may not remember what you actually wanted to say.

1.4 DELIVERING YOUR SPEECH

Confidence is the key to a successful presentation. Use these techniques to help you prepare and present your speech:

Prepare

- **Review Your Information** Reread your notes and review any background research. You'll feel more confident during your speech.

- **Organize Your Notes** Some people prefer to include only key points. Others prefer the entire script. Write each main point, or each paragraph, of your speech on a separate numbered index card. Be sure to include your most important evidence and examples.

- **Plan Your Visual Aids** If you are planning on using visual aids, such as slides, posters, charts, graphs, video clips, overhead transparencies, or computer projections, now is the time to design them and decide how to work them into your speech.

Practice

- **Rehearse** Rehearse your speech several times, possibly in front of a practice audience. Maintain good posture by standing with your shoulders back and your head up. If you are using visual aids, practice handling them. Adapt your rate of speaking, pitch, and tone of voice to your audience and setting. Glance at your notes to refresh your memory, but avoid reading them word for word. Your style of performance should express the purpose of your speech. Use the following chart to help you.

Purpose	Pace	Pitch	Tone
To persuade	fast but clear	even	urgent
To inform	using plenty of pauses	even	authoritative
To entertain	usually building to a "punch"	varied to create characters or drama	funny or dramatic

- **Use Audience Feedback** If you had a practice audience, ask them specific questions about your delivery: Did I use enough eye contact? Was my voice at the right volume? Did I stand straight, or did I slouch? Use the audience's comments to evaluate the effectiveness of your delivery and to set goals for future rehearsals.

- **Evaluate Your Performance** When you have finished each rehearsal, evaluate your performance. Did you pause to let an important point sink in or use gestures for emphasis? Make a list of the aspects of your presentation that you will try to improve for your next rehearsal.

Present

- **Begin Your Speech** Try to look relaxed and smile.

- **Make Eye Contact** Try to make eye contact with as many audience members as possible. This will establish personal contact and help you determine if the audience understands your speech.

- **Remember to Pause** A slight pause after important points will provide emphasis and give your audience time to think about what you're saying.

- **Speak Clearly** Speak loud enough to be heard clearly, but not so loud that your voice is overwhelming. Use a conversational tone.

- **Maintain Good Posture** Stand up straight and avoid nervous movements that may distract the audience's attention from what you are saying.

- **Use Expressive Body Language** Use facial expressions to show your feelings toward your topic. Lean forward when you make an important point; move your hands and arms for emphasis. Use your body language to show your own style and reflect your personality.

- **Watch the Audience for Responses** If they start fidgeting or yawning, speak a little louder or get to your conclusion a little sooner. Use what you learn to evaluate the effectiveness of your speech and to decide what areas need improvement for future presentations.

Respond to Questions

Depending on the content of your speech, your audience may have questions. Follow these steps to make sure that you answer questions in an appropriate manner:

- Think about what your audience may ask and prepare answers before your speech.

- Tell your audience at the beginning of your speech that you will take questions at the end. This helps avoid audience interruptions that may make your speech hard to follow.

- Call on audience members in the order in which they raise their hands.

- Repeat each question before you answer it to ensure that everyone has heard it. This step also gives you time to prepare your answer.

❷ Different Types of Oral Presentations

2.1 INFORMATIVE SPEECH

When you deliver an informative speech, you give the audience new information, provide a better understanding of information, or enable the audience to use the information in a new way. An informative speech is presented in an objective way.

*For more information, see **Speaking and Listening: Delivering an Oral Report**, page 1177.*

Use the following questions to evaluate the presentation of a peer or a public figure, or your own presentation.

Evaluate an Informative Speech

- Did the speaker have a specific, clearly focused topic?
- Did the speaker take the audience's previous knowledge into consideration?
- Did the speaker cite sources for the information?
- Did the speaker communicate the information objectively?
- Did the speaker explain technical terms?
- Did the speaker use visual aids effectively?
- Did the speaker anticipate and address any audience concerns or misunderstandings?

2.2 PERSUASIVE SPEECH

When you deliver a persuasive speech, you offer a thesis or clear statement on a subject, you provide relevant evidence to support your position, and you attempt to convince the audience to accept your point of view.

*For more information, see **Speaking and Listening: Presenting a Persuasive Speech**, page 657.*

Use the following questions to evaluate the presentation of a peer or a public figure, or your own presentation.

Evaluate a Persuasive Speech

- Did the speaker present a clear thesis or argument?
- Did the speaker anticipate and address audience concerns, biases, and counterarguments?
- Did the speaker use sound logic and reasoning in developing the argument?
- Did the speaker support the argument with valid evidence, examples, facts, expert opinions, and quotations?
- Did the speaker use rhetorical devices, such as emotional appeals, to support assertions?
- Did the speaker hold the audience's interest with an effective voice, facial expressions, and gestures?
- Is your reaction to the speech similar to other audience members'?

2.3 DEBATE AN ISSUE

A debate is a balanced argument covering both sides of an issue. In a debate, two teams compete to win the support of the audience. In a formal debate, two teams, each with two members, present their arguments on a given proposition or policy statement. One team argues for the proposition or statement and the other argues against it. Each debater must consider the proposition closely and must research both sides of it. To argue persuasively either for or against a proposition, a debater must be familiar with both sides of the issue.

*For more information, see **Speaking and Listening: Debating an Issue**, page 915.*

Use the following guidelines to evaluate a debate.

Evaluate a Team in a Debate

- Did the team prove that a significant problem does or does not exist? How thorough was the analysis?
- How did the team convince you that the proposition is or is not the best solution to the problem?
- How effectively did the team present reasons and evidence supporting the case?
- How effectively did the team rebut arguments made by the opposing team?
- Did the speakers maintain eye contact and speak at an appropriate rate and volume?
- Did the speakers observe proper debate etiquette?

PRACTICE AND APPLY

View a political debate for a local, state, or national election. Use the preceding criteria to evaluate it.

2.4 NARRATIVE SPEECH

When you deliver a narrative speech, you tell a story or present a subject using a story-type format. A good narrative keeps an audience informed and entertained. It also allows you to deliver a message in a creative way.

*For more information, see **Speaking and Listening: Presenting an Informal Speech**, page 175.*

Use the following questions to evaluate a speaker or your own presentation.

Evaluate a Narrative Speech

- Did the speaker choose a context that makes sense and contributes to a believable narrative?
- Did the speaker locate scenes and incidents in specific places?
- Does the plot flow well?
- Did the speaker use words that convey the appropriate mood and tone?
- Did the speaker use sensory details that allow the audience to experience the sights, sounds, and smells of a scene and the specific actions, gestures, and thoughts of the characters?
- Did the speaker use a range of narrative devices to keep the audience interested?
- Is your reaction to the presentation similar to other audience members'?

2.5 DESCRIPTIVE SPEECH

Description is part of most presentations. In a descriptive speech, you describe a subject that you are personally involved with. A good description will enable your listeners to tell how you feel toward your subject through the images you provide.

Use the following questions to evaluate a speaker or your own presentation.

Evaluate a Descriptive Speech

- Did the speaker make clear his or her point of view toward the subject being described?
- Did the speaker use sensory details, figurative language, and factual details?
- Did the speaker use tone and pitch to emphasize important details?
- Did the speaker use facial expressions to emphasize his or her feelings toward the subject?
- Did the speaker change vantage points to help the audience see the subject from another position?
- Did the speaker change perspectives to show how someone else might feel toward the subject or place?

2.6 ORAL INTERPRETATION

When you perform an oral reading, you use appropriate vocal intonations, facial expressions, and gestures to bring a literature selection to life.

*For more information, see **Speaking and Listening: Delivering an Oral Interpretation,** page 819.*

Use the following questions to evaluate an artistic performance by a peer or a public presenter, a media presentation, or your own performance.

Evaluate an Oral Interpretation

- Did the speaker speak clearly, enunciating each word carefully?
- Did the speaker maintain eye contact with the audience?
- Did the speaker control his or her volume, projecting without shouting?
- Did the speaker vary the rate of speech appropriately to express emotion, mood, and action?
- Did the speaker use a different voice for the character(s)?
- Did the speaker stress important words or phrases?
- Did the speaker use voice, tone, and gestures to enhance meaning?
- Did the speaker's presentation allow you to identify and appreciate elements of the text such as character development, rhyme, imagery, and language?

PRACTICE AND APPLY

Listen to an oral reading by a classmate or view a dramatic performance in a theater or on television. Use the preceding criteria to evaluate it.

2.7 ORAL RESPONSE TO LITERATURE

An oral response to literature is a personal, analytic interpretation of a writer's story, novel, poem, or drama. It demonstrates to an audience a solid and comprehensive understanding of what that piece means to you.

*For more information, see **Speaking and Listening: Participating in a Panel Discussion,** page 497.*

Use the following questions to evaluate a speaker or your own presentation.

Evaluate an Oral Response to Literature

- Did the speaker choose an interesting piece that he or she understands and feels strongly about?
- Did the speaker make a judgment that shows an understanding of significant ideas from the text?
- Did the speaker direct the audience to specific parts of the piece that support his or her idea?
- Did the speaker identify and analyze the use of artistic elements such as imagery, figurative language, and character development?
- Did the speaker demonstrate an appreciation of the author's style?
- Did the speaker discuss any ambiguous or difficult passages and the impact of those passages on the audience?

PRACTICE AND APPLY

Listen as a classmate delivers an oral response to a selection you have read. Use the preceding criteria to evaluate the presentation.

3 Other Types of Communication

3.1 CONVERSATION

Conversations are informal, but they are important means of communicating. When two or more people exchange messages, it is equally important that each person contribute and actively listen.

3.2 GROUP DISCUSSION

Successful groups assign a role to each member. These roles distribute responsibility among the members and help keep discussions focused.

Leader or Chairperson

- Introduces topic
- Explains goal or purpose
- Participates in discussion and keeps it on track
- Helps resolve conflicts
- Helps group reach goal

Recorder

- Takes notes on discussion
- Reports on suggestions and decisions
- Organizes and writes up notes
- Participates in discussion

Participants

- Contribute relevant facts or ideas to discussion
- Respond constructively to one another's ideas
- Reach agreement or vote on final decision

Guidelines for Discussion

- Be informed about the topic.
- Participate in the discussion.
- Ask questions and respond appropriately to questions.
- Don't talk while someone else is talking.
- Support statements and opinions with facts and examples.
- Listen attentively; be courteous and respectful of others' viewpoints.
- Work toward the goal; avoid getting sidetracked by unrelated topics.

*For more information, see **Speaking and Listening: Participating in a Panel Discussion,** page 497.*

3.3 INTERVIEW

An **interview** is a formal type of conversation with a definite purpose and goal. To conduct a successful interview, use the following guidelines:

Prepare for the Interview

- Select your interviewee carefully. Identify who has the kind of knowledge and experience you are looking for.
- Set a time, a date, and a place. Ask permission to tape-record the interview.
- Learn all you can about the person you will interview or the topic you want information on.
- Prepare a list of questions. Create questions that encourage detailed responses instead of yes-or-no answers. Arrange your questions in order from most important to least important.
- Arrive on time with everything you need.

Conduct the Interview

- Ask your questions clearly and listen to the responses carefully. Give the person whom you are interviewing plenty of time to answer.
- Be flexible; follow up on any responses you find interesting.
- Avoid arguments; be tactful and polite.
- Even if you tape an interview, take notes on important points.
- Thank the person for the interview, and ask if you can call with any follow-up questions.

Follow Up on the Interview

- Summarize your notes or make a written copy of the tape recording as soon as possible.
- If any points are unclear or if information is missing, call and ask more questions while the person is still available.
- Select the most appropriate quotations to support your ideas.
- If possible, have the person you interviewed review your work to make sure you haven't misrepresented what he or she said.
- Send a thank-you note to the person in appreciation of his or her time and effort.

Evaluate an Interview

You can determine how effective your interview was by asking yourself these questions:

- Did you get the type of information you were looking for?
- Were your most important questions answered to your satisfaction?
- Were you able to keep the interviewee focused on the subject?

❹ Active Listening

Active listening is the process of receiving, interpreting, evaluating, and responding to a message. Whether you listen to a class discussion or a formal speech, use the following strategies to get as much as you can from the message.

Listening with a Purpose		
Situation	**Reason for Listening**	**How to Listen**
A friend tells a joke.	enjoyment	Maintain eye contact; react to the joke.
You and a friend are trying to go to a concert.	to make plans	Identify goals and problems; listen closely to each other's ideas.

Before Listening

- Learn what the topic is beforehand. You may need to read background information about the topic or learn technical terms in order to interpret the speaker's message.
- Think about what you know or want to know about the topic.
- Have a pen and paper or a laptop computer to take notes.
- Establish a purpose for listening.

While Listening

- Focus your attention on the speaker. Your facial expressions and body language should demonstrate your interest in hearing the topic. Ignore barriers such as room temperature and noise.
- Listen for the speaker's purpose (usually stated at the beginning), which alerts you to main ideas.
- To help you interpret the speaker's message, listen for words or phrases that signal important points, such as *to begin with, in addition, most important, finally,* and *in conclusion.*
- Listen carefully for explanations of technical terms. Use these terms to help you understand the speaker's message.
- Listen for ideas that are repeated for emphasis.
- Take notes. Write down only the most important points.
- If possible, use an outline or list format to organize main ideas and supporting points.
- Note comparisons and contrasts, causes and effects, or problems and solutions.

- As you take notes, use phrases, abbreviations, and symbols to keep up with the speaker.
- To aid your comprehension, note how the speaker uses word choice, voice pitch, posture, and gestures to convey meaning.

After Listening

- Ask relevant questions to clarify anything that was unclear or confusing.
- Review your notes right away to make sure you understand what was said.
- Summarize and paraphrase the speaker's ideas.
- You may also wish to compare your interpretation of the speech with the interpretations of others who listened to it.

4.1 CRITICAL LISTENING

Critical listening involves interpreting and analyzing a spoken message to judge its accuracy and reliability. You can use the following strategies as you listen to messages from advertisers, politicians, lecturers, and others:

- **Determine the Speaker's Purpose** Think about the background, viewpoint, and possible motives of the speaker. Separate facts from opinions. Listen carefully to details and evidence that a speaker uses to support the message.
- **Listen for the Main Idea** Figure out the speaker's main message before allowing yourself to be distracted by seemingly convincing facts and details.
- **Recognize the Use of Persuasive Techniques** Pay attention to a speaker's choice of words. Speakers may slant information to persuade you to buy a product or accept an idea. Persuasive devices such as inaccurate generalizations, either/or reasoning, and bandwagon or snob appeal may represent faulty reasoning and provide misleading information.

*For more information, see **Persuasive Techniques**, pages 596 and R22.*

- **Observe Nonverbal Messages** A speaker's gestures, facial expressions, and tone of voice should reinforce the message. If they don't, you should doubt the speaker's sincerity and his or her message's reliability.
- **Give Appropriate Feedback** An effective speaker looks for verbal and nonverbal cues from you, the listener, to gauge how the message is being received. For example, if you understand or agree with the message, you might nod your head. If possible, during or after a presentation, ask questions to clarify understanding.

4.2 VERBAL FEEDBACK

At times you will be asked to give direct feedback to a speaker. You may be asked to evaluate the way the speaker delivers the presentation as well as the content of the presentation.

Evaluate Delivery

- Did the speaker articulate words clearly and distinctly?
- Did the speaker pronounce words correctly?
- Did the speaker vary his or her rate?
- Did the speaker's voice sound natural and not strained?
- Was the speaker's voice loud enough?

Evaluate Content

Here's how to give constructive suggestions for improvement:

Be Specific Don't make statements like "Your charts need work." Offer concrete suggestions, such as "Please make the type bigger so we can read the poster from the back of the room."

Discuss Only the Most Important Points Don't overload the speaker with too much feedback about too many details. Focus on important points, such as:

- Is the topic too advanced for the audience?
- Are the supporting details well organized?
- Is the conclusion weak?

Give Balanced Feedback Tell the speaker not only what didn't work but also what did work: "Consider dropping the last two slides, since you covered those points earlier. The first two slides got my attention."

Every day you are exposed to hundreds of images and messages from television, radio, movies, newspapers, and the Internet. What is the effect of all this media? What do you need to know to be a smart media consumer? Being media literate means that you have the ability to think critically about media messages. It means that you are able to analyze and evaluate media messages and how they influence you and your world. To become media literate, you'll need the tools to study media messages.

MEDIA TOOLS

For more information, visit the **Media Center** at **ClassZone.com.**

1 Five Core Concepts in Media Literacy

from The Center for Media Literacy

The five concepts of media literacy provide you with the basic questions you can consider when examining media messages.

All media messages are "constructed." All media messages are made by someone. In fact, they are carefully thought out and researched and have attitudes and values built into them. Much of the information that you use to make sense of the world comes from the media. Therefore, it is important to know how a medium is put together so you can better understand the message it conveys.

Media messages are constructed using a creative language with its own rules. Each means of communication—whether it is film, television, newspapers, magazines, radio, or the Internet—has its own language and design. Therefore, the contents of a message must use the language and design of the medium that conveys the message. Thus, the medium actually shapes the message. For example, a horror film may use music to heighten suspense, or a newspaper may use a big headline to signal the significance of a story. Understanding the language of each medium can increase your enjoyment of it as well as alert you to obvious and subtle influences.

Different people experience the same media messages differently. Personal factors such as age, education, and experience will affect the way a person responds to a media message. How many times has your interpretation of a film or book differed from that of a friend? Everyone interprets media messages through his or her own lens.

Media have embedded values and points of view. Media messages carry underlying values, which are purposely built into them by the creators of the message. For example, a commercial's main purpose may be to persuade you to buy something, but it also conveys the value of a particular lifestyle. Understanding both the core message and the embedded point of view will help you decide whether to accept or reject the message.

Most media messages are constructed to gain profit and/or power. The creators of media messages often provide a commodity, such as information or entertainment, in order to make money. The bigger the audience, the higher the cost of advertising. Consequently, media outlets want to build large audiences in order to bring in more revenue from advertising. For example, a television network will create programming to appeal to the largest audience possible, in the hope that the viewer ratings will attract more advertising dollars.

2 Media Basics

2.1 MESSAGE

When a film or TV show is created, it becomes a media product. Each media product is created to send a **message,** or an expression of belief or opinion, that serves a specific purpose. In order to understand the message, you will need to deconstruct it.

Deconstruction is the process of analyzing a media presentation. To analyze a media presentation you will need to look at its content, its purpose, the audience it's aimed at, and the techniques and elements that are used to create certain effects.

2.2 AUDIENCE

A **target audience** is a specific group of people that a product or presentation is aimed at. The members of a target audience usually share certain characteristics, such as age, gender, ethnic background, values, or lifestyle. For example, a target audience may be males, ages 15 to 20, who live in urban areas and engage in sports.

Demographics are the characteristics of a population, including age, gender, profession, income, education, ethnicity, and geographical location. Media decision makers use demographics to shape their content to suit the needs and tastes of a target audience.

Nielsen ratings are the system used to track TV audiences and their viewing preferences. Nielsen Media Research, the company that provides this system, monitors TV viewing in a random sample of 5,000 U.S. households selected to represent the population as a whole.

2.3 PURPOSE

The **purpose,** or intent, of a media presentation is the reason it was made. Most media have more than one purpose. However, every media message has a **core purpose.** To discover that purpose, think about why its creator paid for and produced the message. For example, an ad might entertain you with humor, but its core purpose is to persuade you to buy something.

2.4 TYPES AND GENRES OF MEDIA

The term *media* refers to television, newspapers, magazines, radio, movies, and the Internet. Each is a **medium,** or means, for carrying information, entertainment, and advertisements to a large audience.

Each type of media has different characteristics, strengths, and weaknesses. Understanding how different types of media work and the role they play will help you become more informed about the choices you make in response to the media.

For more information, see **Types of Media,** *page 12.*

2.5 PRODUCERS AND CREATORS

People who control the media are known as **gatekeepers.** Gatekeepers decide what information to share with the public and the ways it will be presented. The following diagram gives some examples.

Who Controls the Media?

Media Owners
TV networks
Recording companies
Publishing companies

Media Products
Television
Radio
Magazines
Movies
Newspapers
Internet

Media Creators
Actors
Writers
Directors
Webmasters

Media Sponsors
Clothing manufacturers
Fast-food restaurants
Department stores

Some forms of media are independently owned, while others are part of a corporate family. Some corporate families might own several different kinds of media. For example, a company may own three radio stations, five newspapers, a publishing company, and a small television station. Often a corporate "parent" decides the content for all of its holdings.

2.6 LAWS GOVERNING MEDIA

Four main laws and policies affect the content, delivery, and use of mass media.

The First Amendment to the Constitution forbids Congress to limit speech or the press.

Copyright law protects the rights of authors and other media creators against the unauthorized publishing, reproduction, and selling of their works.

Laws prohibit **censorship,** any attempt to suppress or control people's access to media messages.

Laws prohibit **libel,** the publication of false statements that damage a person's reputation.

2.7 INFLUENCE OF MEDIA

By sheer volume alone, media influences our very existence, values, opinions, and beliefs. Our environment is saturated with media messages from television, billboards, radio, newspapers, magazines, video games, and so on. Each of these media products is selling one message and conveying another—a message about values—in the subtext. For example, a car ad is meant to sell a car, but if you look closer, you will see that it is using a set of values, such as a luxurious lifestyle, to make the car attractive to the target audience. One message of the ad is that if you buy the car, you'll have the luxurious lifestyle. The other message is that the luxurious lifestyle is good and desirable. TV shows, movies, and news programs also convey subtexts of values and beliefs.

Media can also shape your opinions about the world. For example, news about crime shapes our understanding about how much and what type of crime is prevalent in the world around us. TV news items, talk show interviews, and commercials may shape our perception of a political candidate, a celebrity, an ethnic group, a country, or a regional area. As a consequence, our knowledge of someone or someplace may be completely based on the information we receive from the television.

❸ Film and TV

Films and television programs come in a variety of types. Films include comedies, dramas, documentaries, and animated features. Televison programs cover an even wider array, including dramas, sitcoms, talk shows, reality shows, newscasts, and so on. Producers of films and producers of television programs rely on many of the same elements to convey their messages. Among these elements are scripts, visual and sound elements, special effects, and editing.

3.1 SCRIPT AND WRITTEN ELEMENTS

The writer and editor craft a story for television or film using a script and storyboard. A **script** is the text or words of a film or television show. A **storyboard** is a device often used to plan the shooting of a film and to help the director envision and convey what the finished product will look like. It consists of a sequence of sketches showing what will appear in the film's shots, often with explanatory notes and dialogue written beside or underneath them, as shown in the example.

*For more information, see **Media Study: Produce Your Own Media,** page 109.*

Shot type: LS (long shot)
Action: Black Rider races dangerously fast.
Audio: Horse screeches. Silence.

Shot type: MS (medium shot)
Action: Camera zooms in to show image of Black Rider. *Audio:* Music plays to indicate danger.

Media Handbook

3.2 VISUAL ELEMENTS

Visual elements in film and television include camera shots, angles, and movements, as well as film components such as mise en scène, set design, props, and visual special effects.

A **camera shot** is a single, continuous view taken by a camera. **Camera angle** is the angle at which the camera is positioned during the recording of a shot or image. Each angle is carefully planned to create an effect. The chart shows what different shots are used for.

Camera Shot/Angle	Effect
Establishing shot introduces viewers to the location of a scene, usually by presenting a wide view of an area	establishes the setting of a film
Close-up shot shows a detailed view of a person or object	helps to create emotion and make viewers feel as if they know the character
Medium shot shows a view wider than a close-up but narrower than an establishing or long shot	shows part of an object or a character from the knees or waist up
Long shot is a wide view of a scene, showing the full figure(s) of a person or group and their surroundings	allows the viewer to see the "big picture" and shows the relationship between characters and the environment
Reaction shot shows someone reacting to something that occurred in a previous shot	allows the viewer to see how the subject feels in order to create empathy in the viewer
Low-angle shot looks up at an object or person	makes a character, object, or scene appear more important or threatening
High-angle shot looks down on an object or person	makes a character, object, or scene seem vulnerable or insignificant
Point-of-view (POV) shot shows a part of the story through a character's eyes	helps viewers identify with that character

Camera movement can create energy, reveal information, or establish a mood. The following chart shows some of the ways filmmakers move the camera to create an effect.

Camera Movement	Effect
Pan–a shot in which the camera scans a location from right to left or left to right	reveals information by showing a sweeping view of an area
Tracking shot–a shot in which the camera moves with the subject	establishes tension or creates a sense of drama
Zoom–the movement of the camera as it closes in or moves farther away from the subject	captures action or draws the viewer's attention to detail

Mise en scène is a French term that refers to the arrangement of actors, props, and action on a film set. It is used to describe everything that can be seen in a frame, including the setting, lighting, visual composition, costumes, and action.

Framing is capturing people and objects within the "frame" of a screen or image. Framing is what the camera sees.

Composition is the arrangement of objects, characters, shapes, and colors within a frame and the relationship of the objects to one another.

3.3 SOUND ELEMENTS

Sound elements in film and television include music, voice-over, and sound effects.

Music may be used to set the mood and atmosphere in a scene. Music can have a powerful effect on the way viewers feel about a story. For example, fast-paced music helps viewers feel excited during an action scene.

Voice-over is the voice of the unseen commentator or narrator of a film, TV program, or commercial.

Sound effects are the sounds added to films, TV programs, and commercials during the editing process. Sound effects, such as laugh tracks or the sounds of punches in a fight scene, can create humor, emphasize a point, or contribute to the mood.

3.4 SPECIAL EFFECTS

Special effects include computer-generated animation, manipulated video images, and fast- or slow-motion sequences in films, TV programs, and commercials.

Animation on film involves the frame-by-frame photography of a series of drawings or objects. When these frames are projected—at a rate of 24 per second—the illusion of movement is achieved.

A **split screen** is a special-effects shot in which two or more separate images are shown in the same frame. One example is when two people, actually a distance apart, are shown talking to each other.

3.5 EDITING

Editing is the process of selecting and arranging shots in a sequence. The editor decides which scenes or shots to use, as well as the length of each shot, the number of shots, and their sequence. Editing establishes pace, mood, and a coherent story.

Cut is the transition from one shot to another. To create excitement, editors often use quick cuts, which are a series of short shots strung together.

Dissolve is a transitional device in which one scene fades into another.

Fade-in is a transitional device in which a white or black shot fades in to reveal the beginning of a new scene.

Fade-out is a transitional device in which a shot fades to darkness to end a scene.

Jump cut is an abrupt and jarring change from one shot to another. A jump cut shows a break in time or continuity.

Pace is the length of time each shot stays on the screen and the rhythm that is created by the transitions between shots. Short, quick cuts create a fast pace in a story. Long cuts slow down a story.

4 News

The **news** is information on events, people, and places in your community, your region, the nation, and the world. The news can be categorized by type, as shown in the chart.

Type	Description	Examples
Hard news	fact-based accounts of current events	local newspapers, newscasts, online wire services
Soft news	human-interest stories and other accounts that are less current or urgent than hard news	magazines and tabloid TV shows such as *Sports Illustrated, Access Hollywood*
News features	stories that elaborate on news reports	documentaries such as history reports on PBS
Commentary and opinion	essays and perspectives by experts, professionals, and media personalities	editorial pages, personal Web pages

4.1 CHOOSING THE NEWS

Newsworthiness is the significance of an event or action that makes it worthy of media reporting. Journalists and their editors usually weigh the following criteria in determining which stories should make the news:

Timeliness is the quality of being very current. Timely events usually take priority over previously reported events. For example, a car accident with fatalities will be timely on the day it occurs. Because of its timeliness it may be on the front page of a newspaper or may be the lead story on a newscast.

Widespread impact refers to the importance of an event and the number of people it could affect. The more widespread the impact of an event, the more likely it is to be newsworthy.

Proximity gauges the nearness of an event to a particular city, region, or country. People tend to be more interested in stories that take place locally and affect them directly.

Human interest is a quality of stories that cause readers or listeners to feel emotions such as happiness, anger, or sadness. People are interested in reading stories about other people.

Uniqueness refers to uncommon events or circumstances that are likely to be interesting to an audience.

Compelling video and **photographs** grab people's attention and stay in their minds.

4.2 REPORTING THE NEWS

While developing a news story, a journalist makes a variety of decisions about how to construct the story, such as what information to include and how to organize it. The following elements are commonly used in news stories:

5 *W*'s and *H* are the six questions reporters answer when writing news stories—*who, what, when, where, why,* and *how.* It is a journalist's job to answer these questions in any type of news report. These questions also serve as a structure for writing and editing a story.

Inverted pyramid is the means of organizing information according to importance. In the inverted-pyramid diagram below, the most important information (the answers to the 5 *W*'s and *H*) appears at the top of the pyramid. The less important details appear at the bottom. Not all stories are reported using the inverted-pyramid form. The form remains popular, however, because it enables a reader to get the essential information without reading the entire story. Notice the following example.

Marcus Albright, star guard for the Streaking Impalas, scored the winning basket in an 87–86 come-from-behind victory over the Rovers.

The Impalas had trailed by as many as 15 points with just over four minutes left in the game.

Albright dominated the last three minutes with four three-pointers.

Angle or slant is the point of view from which a story is written. Even an objective report must have an angle.

Consider these two headlines that describe the same house fire.

The first headline focuses on facts about the family's loss and has a human-interest angle. The second headline focuses on an opinion about the firefighters' response time and has a negative slant.

Standards for News Reporting

The ideal of journalism is to present news in a way that is objective, accurate, and thorough. The best news stories contain the following elements:

- **Objectivity** The story takes a balanced point of view on the issues; it is not biased, nor does it reflect a specific attitude or opinion.
- **Accuracy** The story presents factual information that can be verified.
- **Thoroughness** The story presents all sides of an issue; it includes background information, telling *who, what, when, where, why,* and *how.*

Balanced Versus Biased Reporting

Objectivity in news reporting can be measured by how balanced or biased the story is.

Balanced reporting means that all sides of an issue are represented equally and fairly.

A balanced news story

- represents people and subjects in a neutral light
- treats all sides of an issue equally
- does not include inappropriate questions, such as "Will you seek counseling after this terrible tragedy?"
- does not show stereotypes or prejudice toward people of a particular race, gender, age, religion, or other group

- does not leave out important background information that is needed to establish a context or perspective

Biased reporting is reporting in which one side is favored over another or in which the subject is unfairly represented. Biased reporting may show an overly negative view of a subject, or it may encourage racial, gender, or other stereotypes and prejudices. Sometimes biased reporting is apparent in the journalist's choice of sources.

Sources are the people interviewed for the news report and also any written materials and documents the journalist used for background information. From each source, the journalist gets a different point of view. To decide whether news reporting is balanced or biased, you will need to pay attention to the sources. For a news story on a new medicinal drug, for instance, if the journalist's only source is a representative from the company that made the drug, the report may be biased. But if the journalist also includes the perspective of someone neutral, such as a scientist who is objectively studying the effects of drugs, the report may be more balanced. The following chart shows which sources are credible.

Sources for News Stories	
Credible Sources	**Weak Sources**
• experts in a field • people directly affected by the reported event (eyewitnesses) • published reports that are specifically mentioned or shown	• unnamed or anonymous sources • people who are not involved in the reported event (for example, people who heard about a story from a friend) • research, data, or reports that are not specifically named or are referred to only in vague terms (for example, "Research shows that ...")

5 Advertising

Advertising is a sponsor's paid use of various media to promote products, services, or ideas. Some common forms of advertising are shown in the chart.

Type of Ad	Characteristic
Billboard	large outdoor advertising sign
Print ad	typically appears in magazines and newspapers; uses eye-catching graphics and persuasive copy
Flyer	print ad that is circulated by hand or mail
Infomercial	an extended ad on TV that usually includes detailed product information, demonstrations, and testimonials
Public service announcement	a message aired on radio or TV to promote ideas that are considered to be in the public interest
Political ad	broadcast on radio or TV to promote political candidates
Trailer	a short film promoting an upcoming movie, TV show, or video game

Marketing is the process of transferring products and services from producer to consumer. It involves determining the packaging and pricing of a product, how it will be promoted and advertised, and where it will be sold. One way companies market their product is by becoming media sponsors.

Sponsors pay for their products to be advertised. These companies hire advertising agencies to create and produce specific campaigns for their products. They then buy television or radio airtime or magazine, newspaper, or billboard space to feature ads where the target audience is sure to see them. Because selling time and space to advertisers generates much of the income the media need to function, the media need advertisers just as much as advertisers need the media.

Product placement is the intentional and identifiable featuring of brand-name products in movies, television shows, video games, and other media. The intention is to have viewers feel positive about a product because they see a favorite character using it. Another purpose may be to promote product recognition.

5.1 PERSUASIVE TECHNIQUES

Persuasive techniques are the methods used to convince an audience to buy a product or adopt an idea. Advertisers use a combination of visuals, sound, special effects, and words to persuade their target audience. Recognizing the following techniques can help you evaluate persuasive media messages and identify misleading information:

Emotional appeals use strong feelings rather than factual evidence to persuade consumers. An example of any emotional appeal is, "Is your home safe? ProAlarm systems will make sure it is."

Bandwagon appeals use the argument that a person should believe or do something because "everyone else" does. These appeals take advantage of people's desire to be socially accepted by other people. Purchasing a popular product seems less risky to those concerned about making a mistake. An example of a bandwagon appeal is "More and more people are making the switch to Discountline long-distance service."

Slogans are memorable phrases used in advertising campaigns. Slogans substitute catchy phrases for factual information.

Logical appeals rely on logic and facts, appealing to a consumer's reason and his or her respect for authority. Two examples of logical appeals are expert opinions and product comparison.

Celebrity ads use one of the following two categories of spokesperson:

- **Celebrity authorities** are experts in a particular field. Advertisers hope that audiences will transfer the respect or admiration they have for the person to the product. For example, a famous chef may endorse a particular brand of cookware. The manufacturers of the cookware want you to think that it is a good product because a cooking expert wouldn't endorse pots and pans that didn't work.

- **Celebrity spokespeople** are famous people who endorse a product. Advertisers hope that audiences will associate the product with the celebrity.

Product comparison is comparing a product and its competition. Often mentioned by name, the competing product is portrayed as inferior. The intended effect is for people to question the quality of the competing product and to believe the featured product is superior.

6 Elements of Design

The design of a media message is just as important as the words are in conveying the message. Like words, visuals are used to persuade, inform, and entertain.

Graphics and images, such as charts, diagrams, maps, timelines, photographs, illustrations, and symbols, present information that can be quickly and easily understood. The following basic elements are used to give meaning to visuals:

Color can be used to highlight important elements such as headlines and subheads. It can also create mood, because many colors have strong emotional or psychological impacts on the reader or viewer. For example, warm colors more readily draw the eye and are often associated with happiness and comfort. Cool colors are often associated with feelings of peace and contentment or sometimes with sadness.

Lines—strokes or marks—can be thick or thin, long or short, and smooth or jagged. They can focus attention and create a feeling of depth. They can frame an object. They can also direct a viewer's eye or create a sense of motion.

Texture is the surface quality or appearance of an object. For example, an object's texture can be glossy, rough, wet, or shiny. Texture can be used to create contrast. It can also be used to make an object look "real." For example, a pattern on wrapping paper can create a feeling of depth even though the texture is only visual and cannot be felt.

Shape is the external outline of an object. Shapes can be used to symbolize living things or geometric objects. They can emphasize visual elements and add interest. Shapes can symbolize ideas.

Notice how this movie poster uses design elements:

- **Lines** The reader's eyes are led downward to the cityscape and film's title by the vertical line or ray of light.
- **Shape** The spacecraft's shape immediately suggests a flying saucer. It may also symbolize a friendly or unfriendly visitor.
- **Color** Deep blues and purples lend an air of mystery and also make the central ray of light stand out.

7 Evaluating Media Messages

Being able to respond critically to media images and messages will help you evaluate the reliability of the content and make informed decisions. Here are six questions to ask about any media message:

Who made—and who sponsored—this message, and for what purpose? The source of the message is a clue to its purpose. If the source of the message is a private company, that company may be trying to sell you a product. If the source is a government agency, that agency may be trying to promote a program or philosophy. To discover the purpose, think about why its creator paid for and produced the message.

Who is the target audience and how is the message specifically tailored to it? Think about the age group, ethnic group, gender, and/or profession the message is targeting. Decide how it relates to you.

What are the different techniques used to inform, persuade, entertain, and attract attention? Analyze the elements, such as humor, music, special effects, and graphics, that have been used to create the message. Think about how visual and sound effects, such as symbols, color, photographs, words, and music, support the purpose behind the message.

What messages are communicated (and/or implied) about certain people, places, events, behaviors, lifestyles, and so forth? The media try to influence who we are, what we believe in, how we view things, and what values we hold. Look or listen closely to determine whether certain types of behavior are being depicted and if judgments or values are communicated through those behaviors. What are the biases in the message?

How current, accurate, and credible is the information in this message? Think about the reputation of the source. Note the broadcast or publication date of the message and whether the message might change quickly. If a report or account is not supported by facts, authoritative sources, or eyewitness accounts, you should question the credibility of the message.

What is left out of this message that might be important to know? Think about what the message is asking you to believe. Also think about what questions come to mind as you watch, read, or listen to the message.

Strategies and Practice for the SAT, ACT, and Other Standardized Tests

The test items in this section are modeled after test formats that are used on the SAT. The strategies presented here will help you prepare for that test and others. This section offers general test-taking strategies and tips for answering multiple-choice items, as well as short-response and extended-response questions in critical reading and writing. It also includes guidelines and samples for impromptu writing and essay writing. For each test, read the tips in the margin. Then apply the tips to the practice items. You can also apply the tips to Assessment Practice Tests in this book.

1 General Test-Taking Strategies

- Arrive on time and be prepared. Be sure to bring either sharpened pencils with erasers or pens—whichever you are told to bring.

- If you have any questions, ask them before the test begins. Make sure you understand the test procedures, the timing, and the rules.

- Read the test directions carefully. Look at the passages and questions to get an overview of what is expected.

- Tackle the questions one at a time rather than thinking about the whole test.

- Refer back to the reading selections as needed. For example, if a question asks about an author's attitude, you might have to reread a passage for clues.

- If you are not sure of your answer, make a logical guess. You can often arrive at the correct answer by reasoning and eliminating wrong answers.

- As you fill in answers on your answer sheet, make sure you match the number of each test item to the numbered space on the answer sheet.

- Don't look for patterns in the positions of correct choices.

- Only change an answer if you are sure your original choice is incorrect. If you do change an answer, erase your original choice neatly and thoroughly.

- Look for main ideas as you read passages. They are often stated at the beginning or the end of a paragraph. Sometimes the main idea is implied.

- Check your answers and reread your essay.

2 Critical Reading

Most tests contain a critical reading section that measures your ability to read, understand, and interpret passages. The passages may be either fiction or nonfiction, and they can be 100 words or 500 to 800 words. They are drawn from literature, humanities, social studies, and natural sciences.

Directions: Read the following passage. Base your answers to questions 1 and 2 on what is stated or implied in the passage.

PASSAGE

By global or historical standards, much of what Americans consider poverty is luxury. A rural Russian is not considered poor if he cannot afford a car and his home has no central heating; a rural American is. Most impoverished people in the world would be dazzled by the apartments, telephones, television sets, running water, clothing, and other amenities that surround the poor in America. But that does not mean that the poor are not poor, or that those on the edge of poverty are not truly on the edge of a cliff.

—David Shipler, *The Working Poor*

① stem

1. The (main) idea of this paragraph is that ②
   (A) the definition of poverty can differ from one country to another
   ③ (B) no one in America is really poor
   choices (C) many people in Russia are very poor
   (D) being poor is like falling off a cliff
   (E) running water and central heating are basic amenities

2. What does the author mean when he says that those on the edge of poverty are standing on the edge of a cliff? **⑤**
   (A) Poor people sometimes feel suicidal.
   (B) For poor people, life can be risky and uncertain.
   (C) Being poor is like looking down into a black hole. **④**
   (D) Many poor people are homeless.
   (E) It is hard to pull yourself up out of poverty.

Tips: Multiple Choice

A multiple-choice question consists of a stem and a set of choices. On some tests, there are four choices. On the SAT, there are five choices. The stem is usually in the form of a question or an incomplete sentence. One of the choices correctly answers the question or completes the sentence.

① Read the stem carefully and try to answer the question without looking at the choices.

② Pay attention to key words in the stem. They may direct you to the correct answer. Question 1 is looking for the "main idea." Choices (D) and (E) focus on minor details.

③ Read all the choices before deciding on the correct answer.

④ After reading all of the choices, eliminate any that you know are incorrect. In question 2, you can safely eliminate choice (C), because the passage says nothing about a black hole.

⑤ Some questions ask you to interpret a figure of speech. Poor people are not actually "on the edge of a cliff," but that image reinforces the author's point of view that a life of poverty is filled with risk and uncertainty.

Answers: 1. (A), **2.** (B)

Directions: Base your answers to questions 1 through 3 on the two passages below.

PASSAGE **1**

Contemporary students now sample the once-exotic sounds of African pennywhistle, Tuvian throat singing, or Scandinavian mandolin as casually as they choose between tacos, pizza, and sushi. . . . Madonna's *Ray of Light,* for example, borrowed from bhangra, an Indian-inflected dance music. . . . Some fear that globalization will destroy cultural diversity, resulting in a world ruled by American exports. Yet the world-music scene suggests an alternative, where global popular culture enters our marketplace with help from American youth.

—Henry Jenkins, "Culture Goes Global"

PASSAGE **2**

As the unrivaled global superpower, America exports its culture on an unprecedented scale. From music to media, film to fast food, language to literature and sport, the American idea is spreading inexorably, not unlike the influence of empires that preceded it. The difference is that today's technology flings culture to every corner of the globe with blinding speed. Sometimes, U.S. ideals get transmitted—such as individual rights, freedom of speech, and respect for women—and local cultures are enriched. At other times, materialism or worse becomes the message and local traditions get crushed.

—"In 2,000 Years, Will the World Remember Disney or Plato?"
The Christian Science Monitor

1. Which statement best describes the attitudes of the authors of Passages 1 and 2 toward the spread of U.S. culture to other countries?

   (A) Only the author of Passage 1 sees this trend as positive.

   (B) Only the author of Passage 2 sees this trend as positive.

   (C) Neither author sees this trend as positive.

   (D) Both authors see this trend as positive.

   (E) Both authors see positive and negative aspects of this trend.

2. The author of Passage 1 claims that

   (A) globalization will destroy cultural diversity

   (B) students and musicians are influenced by music from other cultures

   (C) non-Westerners prefer American culture to their own

   (D) American ideals are spreading around the world

   (E) pop musicians fear globalization

3. The author of Passage 2 believes that

   (A) freedom of speech will have a negative effect on local traditions

   (B) international music is a problem for American culture

   (C) local traditions can be crushed by American culture

   (D) other cultures have no interest in American culture

   (E) American influence abroad has been uniformly negative

Tips: Two Passages

Questions are sometimes based on a pair of related passages. Sometimes the passages have completely different views. At other times, the passages describe different aspects of the same subject.

❶ Before reading the passages, skim the questions to see what information you will need.

❷ Look for topic sentences in each passage. Ask yourself whether the passage supports or refutes its topic sentence. Passage 1 refutes its topic sentence, while Passage 2 supports its topic sentence.

❸ Focus on key words, especially ones that are used in both passages (though possibly in different forms). You can figure out that *globe* is the root word of *global* and *globalization*. If *globe* refers to the earth, then *global* means "worldwide," and *globalization* means "the process of making worldwide."

❹ Look for clues about an author's attitude toward a subject in the author's choice of words and examples. In Passage 2, the author's use of the word *flings* suggests that he has some negative feelings about the spread of American culture.

Answers: 1. (E), **2.** (B), **3.** (C)

Directions: Read the following passage. Base your answers to questions 1 through 3 on what is stated or implied in the passage. Then base your answer to question 4 on your knowledge of types of writing.

In the following passage, the narrator recalls her childhood growing up in Puerto Rico.

PASSAGE

❶—I had not meant to start a contest of wills between my parents when I mentioned my dreams of playing the piano to Papi. My hands seemed to yearn for action, moving constantly as I talked, seeking textures when I sat reading a book, digging fearlessly into holes on walls, dipping into containers, drawers, boxes with lids that didn't quite close. Since I loved music, learning to play piano seemed like a good choice, even though I'd never actually seen a piano, let alone had any idea of what it took to play one.

❷ When I mentioned it to Papi, he was excited. The idea of a concert career for me appealed to his vision of himself as a poet and of me as more than a spunky tomboy. He took it upon himself to find me a teacher and ❷—came up with the principal at my new school, an elderly gentleman with thinning hair and a thick mustache that seemed pasted on his delicate features. We wouldn't have to pay anything, Papi said, because "he's willing to give you lessons in exchange for some carpentry on his porch."

On Sunday afternoon I set off with Papi for my first piano lesson. I had never seen a teacher outside of school, and as we neared Don Luis's house, I was scared and dug my thumbnail into the other nails to scrape out any dirt that might have escaped the scratchy bristles of Mami's vegetable brush.

"Buenas!" he greeted us. I held on to Papi's hand as to a lifeline, not ❸ trusting my knocking knees to hold me up. But Don Luis's warm smile soon melted my fear into awe at finding myself in his house, away from the unpleasant implications of a student face-to-face with the school principal.

His house was detached from those around it, surrounded by flowers that bloomed in splendid colors and overwhelming fragrances. The inside ❹ was small but as ornate as the yard, with lace curtains, glass-topped tables, invitingly curvy furniture, and, dominating the back wall, an enormous reddish-brown piano, lustrous and dust free, majestic against a fabric-covered wall. I looked at Papi, who winked at me and smiled. We shared the joy of being in this room, in the home of an artist, a person whose life was gracious and carefree, whose furnishings and decorations were as impractical as ours were utilitarian.

—Esmeralda Santiago, *When I Was Puerto Rican*

Tips: Reading Text

❶ Identify the narrator's point of view. In the first-person point of view, the narrator is a character in the story and describes people and events as he or she experiences them, using the pronouns *I* and *me*. In the third-person point of view, the narrator is outside of the story and uses pronouns such as *he*, *she*, and *they*.

❷ Notice the characters who are presented in a passage. The characters in this passage are the narrator, Papi, and the principal. Look for details about personality such as appearance, feelings, actions, and things that a character owns.

❸ Find words that contribute to the mood or atmosphere of a passage. When the narrator says she held onto Papi's hand "as to a lifeline," she conveys her fear.

❹ Look at details that describe the setting of a narrative passage. The details in this passage take the reader inside the piano teacher's home.

Answers: **1.** (C), **2.** (E), **3.** (A), **4.** (B)

1. What was Papi's vision of his daughter?
   (A) He envisioned her as a poet.
   (B) He saw her as nothing more than a tomboy.
   (C) He believed she could have a musical career.
   (D) He wanted her to become a teacher.
   (E) He thought she was spoiled.

2. How would you describe the narrator's feelings before her first piano lesson?
   (A) She felt that the piano lessons were a mistake.
   (B) She felt humble because her family didn't own a piano.
   (C) She was embarassed because she had never seen a piano.
   (D) She felt proud because her father was able to arrange free lessons.
   (E) She was scared because the piano teacher was the principal of her school.

3. The narrator wanted to play piano
   (A) to find an outlet for her nervous energy
   (B) to impress her father
   (C) to test her will against her parents' will
   (D) to develop discipline by practicing an instrument
   (E) to prove she was not a tomboy

4. The last paragraph of the passage is an example of what kind of writing?
   (A) persuasive
   (B) descriptive
   (C) expository
   (D) dramatic
   (E) analytic

The critical reading section may also feature sentence-completion questions that test your knowledge of vocabulary. They may also measure your ability to figure out how different parts of a sentence logically fit together.

Directions: Choose the word or set of words that, when inserted, best fits the meaning of each of the following sentences.

1. The personal computer, which was a _____ tool just 30 years ago, has had a _____ impact on our lives since then. ❶
   (A) forgotten . . profound
   (B) fledgling . . huge
   (C) whimsical . . significant ❷
   (D) negligible . . munificent
   (E) practical . . healthy

2. Today there is _____ evidence that the earth orbits the sun, (but) before the ❸ telescope was invented, facts to back that claim were _____.
   (A) mammoth . . tenuous
   (B) ample . . unstinting
   (C) dynamic . . credible
   (D) circumstantial . . incalculable
   (E) copious . . scant

3. The island of Alcatraz was once the _____ of an _____ federal prison.
   (A) topography . . idyllic
   (B) portal . . impromptu
   (C) locale . . eclectic
   (D) site . . infamous ❹
   (E) milieu . . illicit

4. The woman left food every day for a colony of _____ cats that lived behind her barn, but they shied away from her nonetheless.
   (A) feral ❺
   (B) affectionate
   (C) fierce
   (D) indoor
   (E) docile

Tips: Sentence Completion

❶ When you are completing sentences with two words missing, look at both blanks and think about what kinds of words will fill them.

❷ If one of the words in an answer choice is wrong, you can eliminate that whole set of words from consideration. In sentence 1, *significant* makes sense, but *whimsical* does not.

❸ Look for key words or phrases that link the ideas in a sentence. The word *but* signals that the two parts of the sentence express contrasting ideas.

❹ A prefix can change the meaning of a word. Someone becomes famous for doing something positive but infamous for doing something negative. An artist might be famous; a criminal would be infamous.

❺ If you don't know the exact meaning of a word, you can look for clues in the sentence. For sentence 4, you can ask yourself: What kind of cat lives outdoors and shies away from people? *Feral* means "untamed" and is the best answer to that question.

Answers: **1.** (B), **2.** (E), **3.** (D), **4.** (A)

3 Writing

To measure your ability to express ideas clearly and correctly, tests ask you to identify errors in grammar and usage and to improve sentences and paragraphs.

> **Directions:** Select the one underlined part that must be changed to make the following sentence correct. There is no more than one error in the sentence. If the sentence is correct as written, select answer choice E.

1. Since the first dinosaur bones <u>collected</u> in 19th-century England,
   (A)
   dinosaur remains—<u>ranging from bone fragments to nearly complete skeletons</u>—
   (B)
   have been <u>unearthed</u> on every continent <u>except</u> Antarctica. No error
   (C)   (D)   (E)

> **Directions:** Determine whether the underlined section of the following sentence needs improvement. If it does, select the best change presented in the choices below the sentence. Note that Choice A repeats the original phrase.

2. The author of a definitive work on Abraham Lincoln, Carl Sandburg is renowned as a biographer <u>as well as for his poetry</u>.
   (A) as well as for his poetry
   (B) as well as a poet
   (C) as well as for being a poet
   (D) and for being a poet
   (E) and also for poetry

> **Directions:** Read the passage below and select the best answer to the question that follows the passage.

> (1) Scott Joplin was an African-American pianist and composer. (2) He is regarded as the father of ragtime, a form of popular music. (3) Joplin wanted to establish his name with more serious music. (4) His opera titled *Treemonisha* received the Pulitzer Prize for music in 1976, 59 years after the composer's death. (5) It is considered the first truly American opera.

3. What is the best way to combine sentences 2 and 3?
   (A) He is regarded as the father of ragtime, a form of popular music, so Joplin wanted to establish his name with more serious music.
   (B) He is regarded as the father of ragtime, a form of popular music; Joplin wanted to establish his name with more serious music.
   (C) He is regarded as the father of ragtime, a form of popular music, but Joplin wanted to establish his name with more serious music.
   (D) Rather than being regarded as the father of ragtime, a form of popular music, Joplin wanted to establish his name with more serious music.
   (E) He is regarded as the father of ragtime, a form of popular music, and Joplin wanted to establish his name with more serious music.

Tips: Grammar and Style

1 Read the entire sentence or passage to grasp its overall meaning. Pay particular attention to any underlined portions.

2 Parenthetical thoughts can be inserted between dashes to interrupt the main flow of a sentence.

3 Use prefixes to help you understand unfamiliar words. In test item 1, *un-*, for example, means "a reverse action." To unearth is to dig up.

4 Don't confuse words that look or sound alike. *Except* means "other than"; *accept* means "to receive willingly."

5 In choosing a revision, read through all of the choices before you and decide which one is best. Choose this answer (A) only if the sentence is correct as it appears originally.

6 Parallelism is an important part of sentence structure. In test item 2, *biographer* and *poet* are both nouns and both descriptions of Sandburg.

7 Know the meanings of conjunctions.

Answers: 1. (A), **2.** (B), **3.** (C)

Some tests may measure your understanding of a passage by asking you to write a response.

Directions: Read the passage. Then answer the questions that follow.

When I was a boy my grandfather died, and he was a sculptor. He was also a very kind man who had a lot of love to give the world, and he helped clean up the slum in our town; and he made toys for us and he did a million things in his lifetime; he was always busy with his hands. . . .

Everyone must leave something behind when he dies, my grandfather said. A child or a book or a painting or a house or a wall built or a pair of shoes made. Or a garden planted. Something your hand touched some way so your soul has somewhere to go when you die, and when people look at that tree or that flower you planted, you're there. It doesn't matter what you do, he said, so long as you change something from the way it was before you touched it into something that's like you after you take your hands away. The difference between the man who just cuts lawns and a real gardener is in the touching, he said. The lawn-cutter might just as well not have been there at all; the gardener will be there a lifetime.

—Ray Bradbury, *Fahrenheit 451*

SHORT RESPONSE

What things does the grandfather say we can create that will live after we die? Write a sentence that names two of those things.

SAMPLE SHORT RESPONSE

The grandfather says we can live on in a book we write or a house we build. **❶**

EXTENDED RESPONSE

What does the grandfather mean when he says, "Everyone must leave something behind when he dies"? Write one or two paragraphs to answer this question.

SAMPLE EXTENDED RESPONSE

The grandfather in this passage believes that people should create things that they will be remembered for. The things we create, whether they are **❸** works of art or the children we raise, express our individuality. Just as we leave fingerprints when we touch something, we leave a part of ourselves in the things we create. A person who creates something of worth or **❷** beauty will be remembered for generations to come. For that reason, the grandfather is urging his grandchild to make a difference with his life.

Tips: Responding to Writing Prompts

❶ Short-response prompts are often fact based rather than interpretive. Get right to the point in your answer, and stick to the facts.

❷ Make sure that you write about the assigned topic. Support your answer with details from the passage, such as a quotation, a paraphrase, or an example.

❸ When you are writing an extended response, build your paragraphs around clear topic sentences that will pull your ideas together.

❹ If you are asked to interpret a passage, don't just copy the author's words. Try to express the ideas in your own words. Express your ideas clearly, so that the reader understands your viewpoint.

❺ Proofread your response for errors in capitalization, punctuation, spelling, or grammar.

4 Essay

To determine how well you can develop and support your thoughts, many tests ask you to write an essay in response to an assignment, or prompt. The essay will represent a first draft and will be scored based on the following:

- **Focus** Establish a point of view in the opening paragraph.

- **Organization** Maintain a logical progression of ideas.

- **Support for ideas** Use details and examples to develop an argument.

- **Style/word choice** Use words accurately and vary sentences.

- **Grammar** Use standard English and proofread for errors.

Think carefully about the issue presented in these quotations and the assignment that follows.

> No slogan of democracy; no battle cry of freedom is more stirring than the American parent's simple statement which all of you have heard so many times: 'I want my child to go to college.' —Lyndon Baines Johnson
>
> Everybody can be great. Because anybody can serve. You don't have to have a college degree to serve. —Dr. Martin Luther King Jr.

Assignment: What is your view on the idea that a college education is needed to be successful in our society? Plan and write an essay in which you develop your point of view on this issue. Support your position with examples from your reading, your experience, or current events.

SAMPLE ESSAY

Some people believe that everyone needs a college degree. Education is important, but I don't think a four-year university education is needed to be successful in our society. **❶**

Electricians, plumbers, and carpenters go through specialized training in their fields. They don't need to be college graduates to do their work. Blue-collar workers are the backbone of our society. Where would we be if no one took vocational training? Who would repair our cars and unclog our sinks? The college-educated professional won't do it. Unskilled work is important, too. Dishwashers and taxi drivers may not have even a high school education, but many people rely on the services they provide. **❸**

On the other hand, a practical education combined with some college **❷** courses in business administration might mean the difference between being an electrician and owning a successful electrical contracting business. Bill Gates is a good example. He started building computers from kits when he was in high school. He went to Harvard for a while, but he dropped out so that he could pursue his own idea of creating an operating system for personal **❸** computers. He invented DOS (disk operating system) and founded Microsoft.

In conclusion, people should have a chance to receive the highest level of education that their potential and effort allow. It's great to have some college experience, because it exposes you to new people and new ideas, but it is not **❹** necessary for everyone to receive a four-year university education.

Tips: Writing an Essay

The SAT test allows only 25 minutes for you to write an essay. So before you begin writing, take a few minutes to gather your thoughts. Write down the main points you want to make. Allow time to reread your essay before you hand it in. Make sure your handwriting is legible.

❶ When you're writing a persuasive essay, state your point of view in the introduction.

❷ Take the opposing point of view into consideration and respond to it.

❸ Use examples in the body of your essay to clarify your points and strengthen your arguments.

❹ Make sure your essay has a conclusion, even if it's just a single sentence. A conclusion pulls your ideas together and lets the reader know you've finished.

❺ Allow enough time to reread what you have written. If you have to make a correction, do so neatly and legibly.

Glossary of Literary Terms

Act An act is a major division within a play, similar to a chapter in a book. Each act may be further divided into smaller sections, called scenes. Plays can have as many as five acts, as in Shakespeare's *Romeo and Juliet*. Neil Simon's *The Sneeze* is a one-act play.

Allegory An allegory is a work with two levels of meaning—a literal one and a symbolic one. In such a work, most of the characters, objects, settings, and events represent abstract qualities. Personification is often used in traditional allegories. As in a fable or a parable, the purpose of an allegory may be to convey truths about life, to teach religious or moral lessons, or to criticize social institutions.

Alliteration Alliteration is the repetition of consonant sounds at the beginning of words. Note the repetition of the *d* sound in these lines.

> Deep into that darkness peering, long I stood there
> wondering, fearing,
> Doubting, dreaming dreams no mortal ever dared to
> dream before
> —Edgar Allan Poe, "The Raven"

See pages 139, 670, 797.
See also **Consonance.**

Allusion An allusion is an indirect reference to a famous person, place, event, or literary work. The title of Maya Angelou's autobiography *I Know Why the Caged Bird Sings* is an allusion to the poem "Sympathy" by Paul Laurence Dunbar.
See pages 238, 608, 837, 933, 1096.

Analogy An analogy is a point-by-point comparison between two things that are alike in some respect. Often, writers use analogies in nonfiction to explain unfamiliar subjects or ideas in terms of familiar ones.
See also **Extended Metaphor; Metaphor; Simile.**

Antagonist An antagonist is a principal character or force in opposition to a **protagonist,** or main character. The antagonist is usually another character but sometimes can be a force of nature, a set of circumstances, some aspect of society, or a force within the protagonist. In "The Most Dangerous Game," General Zaroff is the antagonist.
See pages 370, 930.

Archetype An archetype is a pattern in literature that is found in a variety of works from different cultures throughout the ages. An archetype can be a plot, a character, an image, or a setting. For example, the association of death and rebirth with winter and spring is an archetype common to many cultures.

Aside In drama, an aside is a short speech directed to the audience, or another character, that is not heard by the other characters on stage. In Act Four, Scene 1, of *Romeo and Juliet,* Paris is urging that his marriage to Juliet take place soon. Friar Laurence expresses his uneasiness in an aside.

> Friar Laurence [*aside*]. I would I knew not why it
> should be slowed.—
> Look, sir, here comes the lady toward my cell.
> —William Shakespeare, *Romeo and Juliet*

See pages 939, 1018.
See also **Soliloquy.**

Assonance Assonance is the repetition of vowel sounds within nonrhyming words. An example of assonance is the repetition of the *u* sound in the following line.

> Only their usual maneuvers, dear
> —W. H. Auden, "O What Is That Sound"

Author's Perspective An author's perspective is a unique combination of ideas, values, feelings, and beliefs that influences the way the writer looks at a topic. **Tone,** or attitude, often reveals an author's perspective. Julia Alvarez in "Daughter of Invention" writes from a perspective that reflects her feelings about being an immigrant in America.
See pages 361, 459, 508, 569.
See also **Author's Purpose; Tone.**

Author's Purpose A writer usually writes for one or more of these purposes: to express thoughts or feelings, to inform or explain, to persuade, to entertain. For example, Pat Mora's purposes for writing "A Voice" are to express her feelings and to explain.
See also **Author's Perspective.**

Autobiography An autobiography is a writer's account of his or her own life. In almost every case, it is told from the first-person point of view. Generally, an autobiography focuses on the most significant events and people in the writer's life over a period of time. Richard Wright's *Black Boy* is an autobiography. Shorter autobiographical narratives include **journals, diaries,** and **letters.** An **autobiographical**

essay, another type of short autobiographical work, focuses on a single person or event in the writer's life.

See pages 9, 111, 236.

See also **Memoir.**

Ballad A ballad is a type of narrative poem that tells a story and was originally meant to be sung or recited. Because it tells a story, a ballad has a setting, a plot, and characters. **Traditional ballads** are written in four-line stanzas with regular rhythm and rhyme. **Folk ballads** were composed orally and handed down by word of mouth. These ballads usually tell about ordinary people who have unusual adventures or perform daring deeds. A **literary ballad** is a poem written by a poet in imitation of the form and content of a folk ballad. "O What Is That Sound" is an example of a literary ballad.

Biography A biography is the true account of a person's life, written by another person. As such, a biography is usually told from a third-person point of view. The writer of a biography usually researches his or her subject in order to present accurate information. The best biographers strive for honesty and balance in their accounts of their subjects' lives.

Blank Verse Blank verse is unrhymed poetry written in **iambic pentameter.** That is, each line of blank verse has five pairs of syllables. In most pairs, an unstressed syllable is followed by a stressed syllable. The most versatile of poetic forms, blank verse imitates the natural rhythms of English speech. Much of Shakespeare's drama is in blank verse.

> But soft! What light through yonder window breaks?
> It is the East, and Juliet is the sun!
> —William Shakespeare, *Romeo and Juliet*

See also **Iambic Pentameter.**

Cast of Characters In the script of a play, a cast of characters is a list of all the characters in the play, usually in order of appearance. It may include a brief description of each character.

Character Characters are the individuals who participate in the action of a literary work. Like real people, characters display certain qualities, or **character traits;** they develop and change over time; and they usually have **motivations,** or reasons, for their behaviors.

> **Main characters:** Main characters are the most important characters in literary works. Generally, the plot of a short story focuses on one main character, but a novel may have several main characters.

Minor characters: The less prominent characters in a literary work are known as minor characters. Minor characters support the plot. The story is not centered on them, but they help carry out the action of the story and help the reader learn more about the main character.

Dynamic character: A dynamic character is one who undergoes important changes as a plot unfolds. The changes occur because of his or her actions and experiences in the story. The change is usually internal and may be good or bad. Main characters are usually, though not always, dynamic.

Static character: A static character is one who remains the same throughout a story. The character may experience events and have interactions with other characters, but he or she is not changed because of them.

Round character: A round character is one who is complex and highly developed, having a variety of traits and different sides to his or her personality. Some of the traits may create conflict in the character. Round characters tend to display strengths, weaknesses, and a full range of emotions. The writer provides enough detail for the reader to understand their feelings and emotions.

Flat character: A flat character is one who is not highly developed. A flat character is a one-sided character: he or she usually has one outstanding trait, characteristic, or role. Flat characters exist mainly to advance the plot, and they display only the traits needed for their limited roles. Minor characters are usually flat characters.

See pages 79, 186, 207, 233.

See also **Characterization.**

Characterization The way a writer creates and develops characters' personalities is known as characterization. There are four basic methods of characterization:

- The writer may make direct comments about a character's personality or nature through the voice of the narrator.
- The writer may describe the character's physical appearance.
- The writer may present the character's own thoughts, speech, and actions.
- The writer may present pertinent thoughts, speech, and actions of other characters.

See pages 188, 237, 275.

See also **Character.**

Chorus In early Greek tragedy, the chorus commented on the actions of the characters in a drama. In some Elizabethan plays, such as Shakespeare's *Romeo and Juliet,* the role of the chorus is taken by a single actor who serves as a narrator and speaks the lines in the **prologue** (and sometimes in an **epilogue**). The chorus serves to foreshadow or summarize events.

Climax In a plot, the climax is the point of maximum interest or tension. Usually the climax is a turning point in the story, which occurs after the reader has understood the **conflict** and become emotionally involved with the characters. The climax sometimes, but not always, points to the **resolution** of the conflict. In "American History" by Judith Ortiz Cofer, the climax occurs when Elena encounters Eugene's mother at the door of Eugene's house.
See pages 420, 876.
See also **Plot.**

Comedy A comedy is a dramatic work that is light and often humorous in tone, usually ending happily with a peaceful resolution of the main conflict. A comedy differs from a farce by having a more believable plot, more realistic characters, and less boisterous behavior.

Comic Relief Comic relief consists of humorous scenes, incidents, or speeches that are included in a serious drama to provide a reduction in emotional intensity. Because comic relief breaks the tension, it allows an audience to prepare emotionally for events to come. Shakespeare often uses this device in his tragedies.
Example: In many of Shakespeare's plays, a scene involving a fool, or bawdy interplay among common folks or between a servant and his or her master, provides comic relief. Comic relief in *Romeo and Juliet* is provided by the nurse in Act Two, Scene 5, when she returns to Juliet after learning the wedding plans from Romeo. Although Juliet is anxious to hear of the plans, which the audience already knows, the nurse deliberately withholds the information until the end of the scene.

Complication A complication is an additional factor or problem introduced into the rising action of a story to make the conflict more difficult. Often, a plot complication makes it seem as though the main character is getting farther away from the thing he or she wants.

Conflict A conflict is a struggle between opposing forces. Almost every story has a main conflict—a conflict that is the story's focus. An **external conflict** involves a character pitted against an outside force, such as nature, a physical obstacle, or another character. An **internal conflict** is one that occurs within a character.
Examples: In "The Most Dangerous Game" by Richard Connell, Rainsford is in conflict with General Zaroff. In Doris Lessing's "Through the Tunnel," Jerry is torn between the

safety of familiar beach surroundings and the challenge of swimming through the tunnel.
See pages 24, 53, 54, 328, 761.
See also **Plot.**

Connotation A connotation is an attitude or a feeling associated with a word, in contrast to the word's **denotation,** which is its literal, or dictionary, meaning. The connotations of a word may be positive or negative. For example, *enthusiastic* has positive associations, while *rowdy* has negative ones. Connotations of words can have an important influence on style and meaning and are particularly important in poetry.

Consonance Consonance is the repetition of consonant sounds within and at the end of words, as in "lonely afternoon." Consonance is unlike rhyme in that the vowel sounds preceding or following the repeated consonant sounds differ. Consonance is often used together with **alliteration, assonance,** and **rhyme** to create a musical quality, to emphasize certain words, or to unify a poem.
See also **Alliteration.**

Couplet A couplet is a rhymed pair of lines. A couplet may be written in any rhythmic pattern.

> From what I've tasted of desire
> I hold with those who favor fire.
> —Robert Frost, "Fire and Ice"

See also **Stanza.**

Critical Essay *See* **Essay.**

Denotation *See* **Connotation.**

Dénouement *See* **Falling Action.**

Dialect A dialect is a form of language that is spoken in a particular geographic area or by a particular social or ethnic group. A group's dialect is reflected in its pronunciations, vocabulary, expressions, and grammatical structures. Writers use dialects to capture the flavors of locales and to bring characters to life, re-creating the way they actually speak. In "Two Kinds" by Amy Tan, the narrator's mother uses grammatical constructions that are not common in English and therefore speaks a kind of dialect.

> "Who ask you be genius?" she shouted. "Only ask you be your best. For your sake. You think I want you be genius?"
> —Amy Tan, "Two Kinds"

Dialogue Dialogue is written conversation between two or more characters. Writers use dialogue to bring characters to life and to give readers insights into the characters' qualities, traits, and reactions to other characters. Realistic, well-paced dialogue also advances the plot of a narrative. In fiction, dialogue is usually set off with quotation marks. In drama, stories are told primarily through dialogue. Playwrights use stage directions to indicate how they intend the dialogue to be interpreted by actors.

Diary A diary is a daily record of a writer's thoughts, experiences, and feelings. As such, it is a type of autobiographical writing. The terms *diary* and *journal* are often used synonymously.

Diction A writer's or speaker's choice of words and way of arranging the words in sentences is called diction. Diction can be broadly characterized as formal or informal. It can also be described as technical or common, abstract or concrete, and literal or figurative. A writer for *Scientific American* would use a more formal, more technical, and possibly more abstract diction than would a writer for the science section of a local newspaper.
See pages 515, 605.
See also **Style.**

Drama Drama is literature in which plots and characters are developed through dialogue and action; in other words, it is literature in play form. Drama is meant to be performed. Stage plays, radio plays, movies, and television programs are types of drama. Most plays are divided into acts, with each act having an emotional peak, or climax. Certain modern plays, such as *The Sneeze*, have only one act. Most plays contain stage directions, which describe settings, lighting, sound effects, the movements and emotions of actors, and the ways in which dialogue should be spoken.

Dramatic Irony *See* **Irony.**

Dramatic Monologue A dramatic monologue is a lyric poem in which a speaker addresses a silent or absent listener in a moment of high intensity or deep emotion, as if engaged in private conversation. The speaker proceeds without interruption or argument, and the effect on the reader is that of hearing just one side of a conversation. This technique allows the poet to focus on the feelings, personality, and motivations of the speaker. The poem known as "The Seven Ages of Man," spoken by Jaques, a character in Shakespeare's play *As You Like It,* is a dramatic monologue.
See page 721.
See also **Lyric Poetry; Soliloquy.**

Dynamic Character *See* **Character.**

Elegy An elegy is an extended meditative poem in which the speaker reflects on death—often in tribute to a person who has died recently—or on an equally serious subject. Most elegies are written in formal, dignified language and are serious in tone.

Epic An epic is a long narrative poem on a serious subject, presented in an elevated or formal style. It traces the adventures of a great hero whose actions reflect the ideals and values of a nation or race. Epics address universal concerns, such as good and evil, life and death, and sin and redemption. The *Odyssey* is an epic.

Epic Hero An epic hero is a larger-than-life figure who embodies the ideals of a nation or race. Epic heroes take part in dangerous adventures and accomplish great deeds. Many undertake long, difficult journeys and display great courage and superhuman strength.
See page 1094.

Epic Simile An epic simile (also called a Homeric simile) is a long, elaborate comparison that often continues for a number of lines.

> Just as a farmer's hunger grows, behind
> the bolted plow and share, all day afield,
> drawn by his team of winedark oxen: sundown
> is benison for him, sending him homeward
> stiff in the knees from weariness, to dine;
> just so the light on the sea rim gladdened
> Odysseus.
>
> —Homer, *Odyssey*

See page 1096.
See also **Simile.**

Epilogue An epilogue is a short addition at the end of a literary work, often dealing with the future of the characters. The concluding speech by Prince Escalus in *Romeo and Juliet* serves as an epilogue.

Epithet An epithet is a brief phrase that points out traits associated with a particular person or thing. In the *Odyssey,* Odysseus is often called " the master strategist."
See page 1096.

Essay An essay is a short work of nonfiction that deals with a single subject. Some essays are **formal**—that is, tightly structured and written in an impersonal style. Others are **informal,** with a looser structure and a more personal style. Generally, an **expository essay** presents or explains information and ideas. A **personal essay** is typically an informal essay in which the writer expresses his or her thoughts and feelings about a subject, focusing on the meaning of events and issues in his or her own life. In a **reflective essay,** the author makes a connection between a personal observation or experience and a universal idea, such as love, courage, or freedom. A **critical essay** evaluates a situation, a course of action, or a work of art. In a **persuasive essay,** the author attempts to convince readers to adopt a certain viewpoint or to take a particular stand.

See pages 8, 458, 514, 524, 774, 783.

Exposition Exposition is the first stage of a plot in a typical story. The exposition provides important background information and introduces the setting and the important characters. The conflict the characters face may also be introduced in the exposition, or it may be introduced later, in the rising action.

See page 24.
See also **Plot.**

Expository Essay *See* **Essay.**

Extended Metaphor An extended metaphor is a figure of speech that compares two essentially unlike things at some length and in several ways. It does not contain the word *like* or *as*. For example, in "The Seven Ages of Man" by William Shakespeare, an extended metaphor compares the world to a stage.

> All the world's a stage,
> And all the men and women merely players
> —William Shakespeare, *As You Like It*

See also **Metaphor.**

External Conflict *See* **Conflict.**

Fable A fable is a brief tale told to illustrate a moral or teach a lesson. Often the moral of a fable appears in a distinct and memorable statement near the tale's beginning or end. "The Princess and the Tin Box" by James Thurber is a humorous fable.

See also **Moral.**

Falling Action In a plot, the falling action follows the climax and shows the results of the important action that happened at the climax. Tension eases as the falling action begins; however, the final outcome of the story is not yet

fully worked out at this stage. Events in the falling action lead to the **resolution,** or **dénouement,** of the plot. In "American History" by Judith Ortiz Cofer, the falling action begins when the narrator turns away from the door of Eugene's house.

See page 24.
See also **Climax; Plot.**

Fantasy Fantasy is a type of fiction that is highly imaginative and portrays events, settings, or characters that are unrealistic. The setting might be a nonexistent world, the plot might involve magic or the supernatural, and the characters might employ superhuman powers.

Farce Farce is a type of exaggerated comedy that features an absurd plot, ridiculous situations, and humorous dialogue. The main purpose of a farce is to keep an audience laughing. The characters are usually stereotypes, or simplified examples of individual traits or qualities. Comic devices typically used in farces include mistaken identity, deception, physical comedy, wordplay—such as puns and double meanings—and exaggeration.

Fiction Fiction is prose writing that consists of imaginary elements. Although fiction can be inspired by actual events and real people, it usually springs from writers' imaginations. The basic elements of fiction are plot, character, setting, and theme. The novel and short story are forms of fiction.

See also **Character; Novel; Plot; Setting; Short Story; Theme.**

Figurative Language Figurative language is language that communicates meanings beyond the literal meanings of words. In figurative language, words are often used to symbolize ideas and concepts they would not otherwise be associated with. Writers use figurative language to create effects, to emphasize ideas, and to evoke emotions. Simile, metaphor, extended metaphor, hyperbole, and personification are examples of figurative language.

See pages 703, 791, 991.
See also **Hyperbole; Metaphor; Onomatopoeia; Personification; Simile.**

First-Person Point of View *See* **Point of View.**

Flashback A flashback is an account of a conversation, an episode, or an event that happened before the beginning of a story. Often, a flashback interrupts the chronological flow of a story to give the reader information needed for the understanding of a character's present situation.

Example: In "Where Have You Gone, Charming Billy?" Tim O'Brien uses flashbacks to help capture the thought process of the main character as he copes with the realities of his wartime experience.

Foil A foil is a character who provides a striking contrast to another character. By using a foil, a writer can call attention to certain traits possessed by a main character or simply enhance a character by contrast. In Shakespeare's *Romeo and Juliet,* Mercutio serves as a foil to Romeo.

Foreshadowing Foreshadowing is a writer's use of hints or clues to suggest events that will occur later in a story. The hints and clues might be included in a character's dialogue or behavior, or they might be included in details of description. Foreshadowing creates suspense and makes readers eager to find out what will happen. For example, in Stephen King's teleplay *Sorry, Right Number,* the opening camera close-up and the first line of dialogue seem to hint that the telephone and Bill's health will be important in the play.

Form *Form* refers to the principles of arrangement in a poem—the ways in which lines are organized. Form in poetry includes the following elements: the length of lines, the placement of lines, and the grouping of lines into stanzas.
See also **Stanza.**

Free Verse Free verse is poetry that does not contain regular patterns of rhythm or rhyme. The lines in free verse often flow more naturally than do rhymed, metrical lines and thus achieve a rhythm more like that of everyday speech. Although free verse lacks conventional meter, it may contain various rhythmic and sound effects, such as repetitions of syllables or words. Free verse can be used for a variety of subjects. Billy Collins's poem "Today" is an example of free verse.
See pages 669, 797.
See also **Meter; Rhyme.**

Genre The term *genre* refers to a category in which a work of literature is classified. The major genres in literature are fiction, nonfiction, poetry, and drama.

Haiku Haiku is a form of Japanese poetry in which 17 syllables are arranged in three lines of 5, 7, and 5 syllables. The rules of haiku are strict. In addition to the syllabic count, the poet must create a clear picture that will evoke a strong emotional response in the reader. Nature is a particularly important source of inspiration for Japanese haiku poets, and details from nature are often the subjects of their poems.

> Harvest moon—
> walking around the pond
> all night long.
>
> —Bashō

Hero A hero is a main character or protagonist in a story. In older literary works, heroes tend to be better than ordinary humans. They are typically courageous, strong, honorable, and intelligent. They are protectors of society who hold back the forces of evil and fight to make the world a better place. In modern literature, a hero may simply be the most important character in a story. Such a hero is often an ordinary person with ordinary problems.

Historical Fiction A short story or novel can be classified as historical fiction when the settings and details of the plot include real places and real events of historical importance. Historical figures may appear as major or minor characters, as Napoleon does in Leo Tolstoy's classic novel *War and Peace.* In historical fiction, the setting generally influences the plot in important ways.

Horror Fiction Horror fiction contains strange, mysterious, violent, and often supernatural events that create suspense and terror in the reader. Edgar Allan Poe and Stephen King are famous authors of horror fiction.

Humor In literature, there are three basic types of humor, all of which may involve exaggeration or irony. **Humor of situation** arises out of the plot of a work. It usually involves exaggerated events or situational irony, which arises when something happens that is different from what was expected. **Humor of character** is often based on exaggerated personalities or on characters' failure to recognize their own flaws, a form of dramatic irony. **Humor of language** may include sarcasm, exaggeration, puns, or verbal irony, in which what is said is not what is meant.
See page 775.
See also **Irony.**

Hyperbole Hyperbole is a figure of speech in which the truth is exaggerated for emphasis or humorous effect.

Iambic Pentameter Iambic pentameter is a metrical pattern of five feet, or units, each of which is made up of two syllables, the first unstressed and the second stressed. Iambic pentameter is the most common meter used in English poetry; it is the meter used in blank verse and in the sonnet. The following lines are examples of iambic pentameter.

> My lips, two blushing pilgrims, ready stand
> —William Shakespeare, *Romeo and Juliet*

See pages 725, 932.
See also **Blank Verse; Sonnet.**

Idiom An idiom is a common figure of speech whose meaning is different from the literal meaning of its words. For example, the phrase "raining cats and dogs" does not literally mean that cats and dogs are falling from the sky; the expression means "raining heavily."

Imagery Imagery consists of descriptive words and phrases that re-create sensory experiences for the reader. Imagery usually appeals to one or more of the five senses—sight, hearing, smell, taste, and touch—to help the reader imagine exactly what is being described. The imagery in the poem "Incident in a Rose Garden" by Donald Justice helps the reader to see Death, who wears a black coat, black gloves, and a black hat. Truman Capote uses vivid imagery appealing to multiple senses in order to re-create the childhood of the narrator in "A Christmas Memory."
See pages 145, 273, 304, 309, 379, 677.

Internal Conflict *See* **Conflict.**

Interview An interview is a conversation conducted by a writer or reporter, in which facts or statements are elicited from another person, recorded, and then broadcast or published. "Tim O'Brien: The Naked Soldier" is an example of an interview.
See page 760.

Irony Irony is a special kind of contrast between appearance and reality—usually one in which reality is the opposite of what it seems. One type of irony is **situational irony,** a contrast between what a reader or character expects and what actually exists or happens. The unexpected twist in the outcome of "The Gift of the Magi" by O. Henry is an example of situational irony. Another type of irony is **dramatic irony,** where the reader or viewer knows something that a character does not know. **Verbal irony** exists when someone knowingly exaggerates or says one thing and means another.
See pages 95, 780, 811.

Journal *See* **Diary.**

Limited Point of View *See* **Point of View.**

Line The line is the core unit of a poem. In poetry, line length is an essential element of the poem's meaning and rhythm. **Line breaks,** where a line of poetry ends, may coincide with grammatical units. However, a line break may also occur in the middle of a grammatical or syntactical unit, creating a meaningful pause or emphasis. Poets use a variety of line breaks to play with sense, grammar, and syntax and thereby create a wide range of effects.

Literary Criticism Literary criticism is a form of writing in which works of literature are compared, analyzed, interpreted, or evaluated. Two common forms of literary criticism are book reviews and critical essays.

Literary Nonfiction Literary nonfiction is nonfiction that is recognized as being of artistic value or that is about literature. Autobiographies, biographies, essays, and eloquent speeches typically fall into this category.

Lyric Poetry A lyric poem is a short poem in which a single speaker expresses personal thoughts and feelings. Most poems other than dramatic and narrative poems are lyric poems. In ancient Greece, lyric poetry was meant to be sung. Modern lyrics are usually not intended for singing, but they are characterized by strong melodic rhythms. Lyric poetry has a variety of forms and covers many subjects, from love and death to everyday experiences. Langston Hughes's "Theme for English B" and Pat Mora's "A Voice" are examples of lyric poems.

Memoir A memoir is a form of autobiographical writing in which a writer shares his or her personal experiences and observations of significant events or people. Often informal or even intimate in tone, memoirs usually give readers insight into the impact of historical events on people's lives. *Angela's Ashes* by Frank McCourt is a memoir.
See pages 165, 837.
See also **Autobiography.**

Metaphor A metaphor is a figure of speech that makes a comparison between two things that are basically unlike but have something in common. Unlike similes, metaphors do not contain the word *like* or *as.* In "Ode to My Socks," Pablo Neruda uses metaphors to compare his socks to multiple objects, including "two long sharks of lapis blue."
See also **Extended Metaphor; Figurative Language; Simile.**

Meter Meter is a regular pattern of stressed and unstressed syllables in a poem. The meter of a poem emphasizes the musical quality of the language. Each unit of meter, known as a **foot,** consists of one stressed syllable and one or two unstressed syllables. In representations of meter, a stressed syllable is indicated by the symbol ´; an unstressed syllable, by the symbol ˘. The four basic types of metrical feet are the **iamb,** an unstressed syllable followed by a stressed syllable (˘´); the **trochee,** a stressed syllable followed by an unstressed syllable (´˘); the **anapest,** two unstressed syllables followed by a stressed syllable (˘˘´); and the **dactyl,** a stressed syllable followed by two unstressed syllables (´˘˘).

See pages 671, 721.

See also **Rhythm.**

Mise en Scène *Mise en scène* is a term from the French that refers to the various physical aspects of a dramatic presentation, such as lighting, costumes, scenery, makeup, and props.

Mood In a literary work, mood is the feeling or atmosphere that a writer creates for the reader. Descriptive words, imagery, and figurative language contribute to the mood of a work, as do the sound and rhythm of the language used. In "The Cask of Amontillado," Edgar Allan Poe creates a mood of dread and horror.

See pages 304, 343, 361.

See also **Tone.**

Moral A moral is a lesson taught in a literary work, such as a fable. For example, the moral "Do not count your chickens before they are hatched" teaches that one should not count on one's fortunes or blessings until they appear. In James Thurber's "The Princess and the Tin Box," the moral, like the fable itself, is satirical.

See also **Fable.**

Motivation *See* **Character.**

Myth A myth is a traditional story, usually concerning some superhuman being or unlikely event, that was once widely believed to be true. Frequently, myths were attempts to explain natural phenomena, such as solar and lunar eclipses or the cycle of the seasons. For some peoples, myths were both a kind of science and a religion. In addition, myths served as literature and entertainment, just as they do for modern-day audiences.

Greek mythology forms much of the background in Homer's *Odyssey.* For example, the myth of the judgment of Paris describes events that led to the Trojan War. The goddesses Athena, Hera, and Aphrodite asked a mortal—Paris—to decide which of them was the most beautiful. Paris chose Aphrodite and was rewarded by her with Helen, wife of the Greek king Menelaus.

Narrative Nonfiction Narrative nonfiction is writing that reads much like fiction, except that the characters, setting, and plot are real rather than imaginary. Its purpose is usually to entertain or to express opinions or feelings. Narrative nonfiction includes, but is not limited to, autobiographies, biographies, memoirs, diaries, and journals. *Seabiscuit* by Laura Hillenbrand is an example of narrative nonfiction.

See page 122.

Narrative Poetry Narrative poetry tells a story or recounts events. Like a short story or a novel, a narrative poem has the following elements: plot, characters, setting, and theme. "The Raven" by Edgar Allan Poe is a narrative poem.

Narrator The narrator of a story is the character or voice that relates the story's events to the reader.

See also **Persona; Point of View.**

Nonfiction Nonfiction is writing that tells about real people, places, and events. Unlike fiction, nonfiction is mainly written to convey factual information, although writers of nonfiction shape information in accordance with their own purposes and attitudes. Nonfiction can be a good source of information, but readers frequently have to examine it carefully in order to detect biases, notice gaps in the information provided, and identify errors in logic. Nonfiction includes a diverse range of writing—newspaper articles, letters, essays, biographies, movie reviews, speeches, true-life adventure stories, advertising, and more.

Novel A novel is an extended work of fiction. Like a short story, a novel is essentially the product of a writer's imagination. Because a novel is considerably longer than a short story, a novelist can develop a wider range of characters and a more complex plot.

Example: In John Knowles's novel *A Separate Peace,* Gene's character develops as he struggles with guilt that resulted from the "accident" that crippled Phineas.

Novella A novella is a work of fiction that is longer than a short story but shorter than a novel. A novella differs from a novel in that it concentrates on a limited cast of characters, a relatively short time span, and a single chain of events. The novella is an attempt to combine the compression of the short story with the development of the novel.

Ode An ode is a complex lyric poem that develops a serious and dignified theme. Odes appeal to both the imagination and the intellect, and many commemorate events or praise people or elements of nature.

Omniscient Point of View *See* **Point of View.**

Onomatopoeia Onomatopoeia is the use of words whose sounds echo their meanings, such as *buzz, whisper, gargle,* and *murmur.* Onomatopoeia as a literary technique goes beyond the use of simple echoic words, however. Skilled writers, especially poets, choose words whose sounds intensify images and suggest meanings.

Oxymoron An oxymoron is a special kind of concise paradox that brings together two contradictory terms. In *Romeo and Juliet,* each of the phrases "brawling love," "loving hate," "bright smoke," and "feather of lead" is an oxymoron.

Paradox A paradox is a seemingly contradictory or absurd statement that may nonetheless suggest an important truth.

Parallelism Parallelism is the use of similar grammatical constructions to express ideas that are related or equal in importance.

> Go back to Mississippi. Go back to Alabama. Go back to South Carolina. Go back to Georgia. Go back to Louisiana. Go back to the slums and ghettos of our Northern cities. . . .
> —Martin Luther King Jr., "I Have a Dream"

Parallel Plot A parallel plot is a particular type of plot in which two stories of equal importance are told simultaneously. The story moves back and forth between the two plots.

Parody A parody is an imitation of another work, a type of literature, or a writer's style, usually for the purpose of poking fun. It may serve as an element of a larger work or be a complete work in itself. The purpose of parody may be to ridicule through broad humor, deploying such techniques as exaggeration or the use of inappropriate subject matter. Such techniques may even provide insights into the original work. "The Princess and the Tin Box" by James Thurber is a parody of the typical moralistic fairy tale.

Persona A persona is a voice that a writer assumes in a particular work. A persona is like a mask worn by the writer, separating his or her identity from that of the speaker or the narrator. It is the persona's voice—not the writer's voice—that narrates a story or speaks in a poem.
See also **Narrator; Speaker.**

Personal Essay *See* **Essay.**

Personification Personification is a figure of speech in which human qualities are given to an object, animal, or idea. In "Incident in a Rose Garden" by Donald Justice, death is personified as someone who wears black and grins. In the following line by Shakespeare, morning is personified.

> The grey-eyed morn smiles on the frowning night
> —William Shakespeare, *Romeo and Juliet*

See pages 672, 703.
See also **Figurative Language.**

Persuasive Essay *See* **Essay.**

Play *See* **Drama.**

Plot The sequence of events in a story is called the plot. A plot focuses on a central **conflict** or problem faced by the main character. The actions that the characters take to resolve the conflict build toward a climax. In general, it is not long after this point that the conflict is resolved and the story ends. A plot typically develops in five stages: exposition, rising action, climax, falling action, and resolution.
See pages 24, 79.
See also **Climax; Exposition; Falling Action; Rising Action.**

Poetry Poetry is a type of literature in which words are carefully chosen and arranged to create certain effects. Poets use a variety of sound devices, imagery, and figurative language to express emotions and ideas.
See also **Alliteration; Assonance; Ballad; Free Verse; Imagery; Meter; Rhyme; Rhythm; Stanza.**

Point of View *Point of view* refers to the method of narration used in a short story, novel, narrative poem, or work of nonfiction. In a work told from a **first-person** point of view, the narrator is a character in the story, as in "The Cask of Amontillado" by Edgar Allan Poe. In a work told from a **third-person** point of view, the narrative voice is outside the action, not one of the characters. If a story is told from a **third-person omniscient,** or all-knowing, point of view, as in "The Gift of the Magi" by O. Henry, the narrator sees into the minds of all the characters. If events are related from a **third-person limited** point of view, as in Doris Lessing's "Through the Tunnel," the narrator tells what only one character thinks, feels, and observes.
See pages 186, 193.
See also **Narrator.**

Prologue A prologue is an introductory scene in a drama. Some Elizabethan plays include prologues that comment on the theme or moral point that will be revealed in the play. The prologue is a feature of all Greek drama.

Prop The word *prop*, originally an abbreviation of the word *property*, refers to any physical object that is used in a drama. In the teleplay *Sorry, Right Number*, a telephone is an important prop.

Prose Generally, *prose* refers to all forms of written or spoken expression that are not in verse. The term, therefore, may be used to describe very different forms of writing—short stories as well as essays, for example.

Protagonist A protagonist is the main character in a work of literature—the character who is involved in the central conflict of the story. Usually, the protagonist changes after the central conflict reaches a climax. He or she may be a hero and is usually the one with whom the audience tends to identify. In Judith Ortiz Cofer's "American History," Elena is the protagonist as well as the narrator.

Pun A pun is a joke that comes from a play on words. It can make use of a word's multiple meanings or of a word's sound. In *Romeo and Juliet,* when Mercutio is fatally wounded, he says, "Ask for me tomorrow, and you shall find me a grave man," with a pun on the word *grave,* meaning both "solemn" and "a tomb."

Quatrain A quatrain is a four-line stanza, or group of lines, in poetry. The most common stanza in English poetry, the quatrain can have a variety of meters and rhyme schemes.

Realistic Fiction Realistic fiction is fiction that is a truthful imitation of ordinary life. "Through the Tunnel" by Doris Lessing and "A Christmas Memory" by Truman Capote are examples of realistic fiction.

Recurring Theme *See* **Theme.**

Reflective Essay *See* **Essay.**

Refrain A refrain is one or more lines repeated in each stanza of a poem.
See also **Stanza.**

Repetition Repetition is a technique in which a sound, word, phrase, or line is repeated for emphasis or unity. Repetition often helps to reinforce meaning and create an appealing rhythm. The term includes specific devices associated with both prose and poetry, such as alliteration and parallelism.
See pages 670, 715.
See also **Alliteration; Parallelism; Sound Devices.**

Resolution *See* **Falling Action.**

Rhetorical Devices Rhetorical devices are techniques writers use to enhance their arguments and communicate more effectively. Rhetorical devices include **analogy, parallelism, rhetorical questions,** and **repetition.**
See also **Analogy; Repetition; Rhetorical Questions,** *Glossary of Reading and Informational Terms, page R119.*

Rhyme Rhyme is the occurrence of similar or identical sounds at the end of two or more words, such as *suite, heat,* and *complete.* Rhyme that occurs within a single line of poetry is **internal rhyme.** Rhyme that occurs at the ends of lines of poetry is called **end rhyme.** End rhyme that is not exact but approximate is called **slant rhyme,** or **off rhyme.** Notice the following example of slant rhyme involving the words *care* and *dear.*

> O haven't they stopped for the doctor's <u>care</u>,
>   Haven't they reined their horses, their horses?
> Why, they are none of them wounded, <u>dear</u>.
>   None of these forces.
> —W. H. Auden, "O What Is That Sound"

See pages 670, 716, 791.

Rhyme Scheme A rhyme scheme is a pattern of end rhymes in a poem. A rhyme scheme is noted by assigning a letter of the alphabet, beginning with *a,* to each line. Lines that rhyme are given the same letter. Notice the rhyme scheme of the first stanza of this famous poem.

> Two roads diverged in a yellow wood,   *a*
> And sorry I could not travel both   *b*
> And be one traveler, long I stood   *a*
> And looked down one as far as I could   *a*
> To where it bent in the undergrowth   *b*
> —Robert Frost, "The Road Not Taken"

See page 670.

Rhythm Rhythm is a pattern of stressed and unstressed syllables in a line of poetry. Poets use rhythm to bring out the musical quality of language, to emphasize ideas, to create moods, to unify works, and to heighten emotional responses. Devices such as alliteration, rhyme, assonance, consonance, and parallelism often contribute to creating rhythm.
See pages 670, 791.
See also **Meter.**

Rising Action Rising action is the stage in a plot in which the conflict develops and story events build toward a climax. During this stage, complications arise that make the conflict more intense. Tension grows as the characters struggle to resolve the conflict.

See page 24.
See also **Plot.**

Satire Satire is a literary technique in which ideas, customs, behaviors, or institutions are ridiculed for the purpose of improving society. Satire may be gently witty, mildly abrasive, or bitterly critical, and it often involves the use of irony and exaggeration to force readers to see something in a critical light.

Scansion Scansion is the notation of stressed and unstressed syllables in poetry. A stressed syllable is indicated by the symbol ´; an unstressed syllable, by the symbol ˇ. Using scansion can help you determine the rhythm and meter of a poem.

See page 670.
See also **Meter.**

Scene In drama, the action is often divided into acts and scenes. Each scene presents an episode of the play's plot and typically occurs at a single place and time.

See also **Act.**

Scenery Scenery is a painted backdrop or other structures used to create the setting for a play.

Science Fiction Science fiction is fiction in which a writer explores unexpected possibilities of the past or the future, using known scientific data and theories as well as his or her creative imagination. Most science fiction writers create believable worlds, although some create fantasy worlds that have familiar elements. Ray Bradbury, the author of "A Sound of Thunder," is a famous writer of science fiction.

See also **Fantasy.**

Screenplay A screenplay is a play written for film.

Script The text of a play, film, or broadcast is called a script.

Sensory Details Sensory details are words and phrases that appeal to the reader's senses of sight, hearing, touch, smell, and taste. For example, the sensory detail "a fine film of rain" appeals to the senses of sight and touch. Sensory details stimulate the reader to create images in his or her mind.

See also **Imagery.**

Setting Setting is the time and place of the action of a story. Some stories, such as "The Open Window" by Saki,

have only minimal descriptions of setting. In other works, such as Eugenia Collier's "Marigolds" and Edgar Allan Poe's "The Cask of Amontillado," settings are described in detail and become major contributors to the stories' overall effect.

See pages 302, 309, 361.
See also **Fiction.**

Short Story A short story is a work of fiction that centers on a single idea and can be read in one sitting. Generally, a short story has one main conflict that involves the characters, keeps the story moving, and stimulates readers' interest.

See also **Fiction.**

Simile A simile is a figure of speech that makes a comparison between two unlike things, using the word *like* or *as*.

> I am offering this poem to you,
> since I have nothing else to give.
> Keep it <u>like a warm coat</u>
> When winter comes to cover you
> —Jimmy Santiago Baca, "I Am Offering This Poem"

See pages 672, 703.
See also **Epic Simile; Figurative Language; Metaphor.**

Situational Irony See **Irony.**

Soliloquy In drama, a soliloquy is a speech in which a character speaks his or her thoughts aloud. Generally, the character is on the stage alone, not speaking to other characters and perhaps not even consciously addressing an audience. At the beginning of Act Two, Scene 3, of *Romeo and Juliet*, Friar Laurence has a long soliloquy. Shakespeare makes use of soliloquies in many of his plays.

See also **Aside; Dramatic Monologue.**

Sonnet A sonnet is a lyric poem of 14 lines, commonly written in **iambic pentameter.** Sonnets are often classified as Petrarchan or Shakespearean. The Shakespearean, or Elizabethan, sonnet consists of three quatrains, or four-line units, and a final couplet. The typical rhyme scheme is *abab cdcd efef gg.*

See also **Iambic Pentameter; Rhyme Scheme.**

Sound Devices Sound devices, or uses of words for their auditory effect, can convey meaning and mood or unify a work. Some common sound devices are **alliteration, assonance, consonance, meter, onomatopoeia, repetition, rhyme,** and **rhythm.** The following lines contain alliteration, repetition, assonance, consonance, rhyme, and rhythm, all of which combine to help convey both meaning and mood.

O what is that sound which so thrills the ear
  Down in the valley drumming, drumming:
Only the scarlet soldiers, dear,
  The soldiers coming.
                —W. H. Auden, "O What Is That Sound"

See pages 139, 715.
See also **Alliteration; Assonance; Consonance; Meter; Onomatopoeia; Repetition; Rhyme; Rhythm.**

Speaker In poetry the speaker is the voice that "talks" to the reader, similar to the narrator in fiction. The speaker is not necessarily the poet. For example, in Pat Mora's "A Voice," the experiences related may or may not have happened to the poet.
See pages 269, 673, 715.
See also **Persona.**

Speech A speech is a talk or public address. The purpose of a speech may be to entertain, to explain, to persuade, to inspire, or any combination of these aims. "I Have a Dream" by Martin Luther King Jr. was written and delivered in order to inspire an audience.
See pages 600, 610.

Stage Directions A play typically includes instructions called stage directions, which are usually printed in italic type. They serve as a guide to directors, set and lighting designers, performers, and readers. When stage directions appear within passages of dialogue, parentheses are usually used to set them off from the words spoken by characters.

Jeff *gets up, walks to the window, and looks out into the dark. He's really upset.* Dennis *and* Connie, *in the grand tradition of older brothers and sisters, are delighted to see it.*
                —Stephen King, *Sorry, Right Number*

See pages 7, 150, 934.

Stanza A stanza is a group of two or more lines that form a unit in a poem. A stanza is comparable to a paragraph in prose. Each stanza may have the same number of lines, or the number of lines may vary. "The Road Not Taken" by Robert Frost is divided into four stanzas.
See also **Couplet; Form; Poetry; Quatrain.**

Static Character *See* **Character.**

Stereotype In literature, a simplified or stock character who conforms to a fixed pattern or is defined by a single trait is known as a stereotype. Such a character does not usually demonstrate the complexity of a real person. Familiar stereotypes in popular literature include the absent-minded professor and the busybody.

Stream of Consciousness Stream of consciousness is a literary technique developed by modern writers, in which thoughts, feelings, moods, perceptions, and memories are presented as they randomly flow through a character's mind.

Structure Structure is the way in which the parts of a work of literature are put together. In poetry, structure involves the arrangement of words and lines to produce a desired effect. A common structural unit in poetry is the stanza, of which there are numerous types. In prose, structure is the arrangement of larger units or parts of a work. Paragraphs, for example, are basic units in prose, as are chapters in novels and acts in plays. The structure of a poem, short story, novel, play, or nonfictional work usually emphasizes certain important aspects of content.
See also **Act; Stanza.**

Style Style is the particular way in which a work of literature is written—not *what* is said but *how* it is said. It is the writer's unique way of communicating ideas. Many elements contribute to style, including word choice, sentence structure and length, tone, figurative language, and point of view. A literary style may be described in a variety of ways, such as formal, informal, journalistic, conversational, wordy, ornate, poetic, or dynamic.

Surprise Ending A surprise ending is an unexpected plot twist at the end of a story. The surprise may be a sudden turn in the action or a piece of information that gives a different perspective to the entire story. O. Henry is famous for using this device, as exemplified in his story "The Gift of the Magi."
See pages 96, 146.

Suspense Suspense is the excitement or tension that readers feel as they wait to find out how a story ends or a conflict is resolved. Writers create suspense by raising questions in readers' minds about what might happen next. The use of **foreshadowing** is one way in which writers create suspense.
See page 107.
See also **Foreshadowing.**

Symbol A symbol is a person, a place, an object, or an activity that stands for something beyond itself. For example, a flag is a colored piece of cloth that stands for a country. A white dove is a bird that represents peace.

Example: In "Through the Tunnel" by Doris Lessing, the rocky bay represents challenge, danger, and adulthood; the beach represents safety and Jerry's childhood.

See pages 323, 327, 402, 427, 853.

Tall Tale A tall tale is a humorously exaggerated story about impossible events, often involving the supernatural abilities of the main character. Stories about folk heroes such as Pecos Bill and Paul Bunyan are typical tall tales.

Teleplay A teleplay is a play written for television. In a teleplay, scenes can change quickly and dramatically. The camera can focus the viewer's attention on specific actions. The camera directions in teleplays are much like the stage directions in stage plays.

See page 149.

Theme A theme is an underlying message about life or human nature that a writer wants the reader to understand. It is a perception about life or human nature that the writer shares with the reader. In most cases, themes are not stated directly but must be inferred. A theme may imply how a person should live but should not be confused with a **moral.** The theme of "The Scarlet Ibis" by James Hurst might be expressed as "Pride, love, and cruelty are often intermingled in human relationships."

    Recurring themes are themes found in a variety of works. For example, authors from varying backgrounds might convey similar themes having to do with the importance of family values. **Universal themes** are themes that are found throughout the literature of all time periods. For example, the *Odyssey* and *The Lord of the Rings* both contain a universal theme relating to the hero's search for truth, goodness, and honor.

See pages 107, 402, 467.
See also **Moral.**

Third-Person Point of View *See* **Point of View.**

Tone Tone is the attitude a writer takes takes toward a subject. Unlike mood, which is intended to shape the reader's emotional response, tone reflects the feelings of the writer. A writer communicates tone through choice of words and details. Tone may often be described by a single word, such as *serious, humorous, formal, informal, somber, sarcastic, playful, ironic, bitter,* or *objective.* For example, the tone of "Grape Sherbet" by Rita Dove might be described as tender and loving, whereas the tone of Mary Oliver's essay "A Few Words" might be described as persistent and somewhat angry.

See pages 525, 561, 746, 783.
See also **Author's Perspective; Mood.**

Tragedy A tragedy is a dramatic work that presents the downfall of a dignified character (**tragic hero**) or characters who are involved in historically or socially significant events. The events in a tragic plot are set in motion by a decision that is often an error in judgment (**tragic flaw**) on the part of the hero. Succeeding events are linked in a cause-and-effect relationship and lead inevitably to a disastrous conclusion, usually death. Shakespeare's *Romeo and Juliet* is a tragedy.

Tragic Flaw *See* **Tragedy.**

Tragic Hero *See* **Tragedy.**

Traits *See* **Character.**

Turning Point *See* **Climax.**

Understatement Understatement is a technique of creating emphasis by saying less than is actually or literally true. It is the opposite of **hyperbole,** or exaggeration. One of the primary devices of irony, understatement can be used to develop a humorous effect, to create satire, or to achieve a restrained tone.

See also **Hyperbole; Irony.**

Universal Theme *See* **Theme.**

Verbal Irony *See* **Irony.**

Voice Voice is a writer's unique use of language that allows a reader to "hear" a human personality in the writer's work. Elements of style that contribute to a writer's voice include sentence structure, **diction,** and **tone.** Voice can reveal much about the author's personality, beliefs, and attitudes.

See pages 801, 863.

Word Choice *See* **Diction.**

Glossary of Reading & Informational Terms

Almanac *See* **Reference Works.**

Analogy *See Glossary of Literary Terms, page R102.*

Argument An argument is speech or writing that expresses a position on an issue or problem and supports it with reasons and evidence. An argument often takes into account other points of view, anticipating and answering objections that opponents of the position might raise.
See also **Claim; Counterargument; Evidence.**

Assumption An assumption is an opinion or belief that is taken for granted. It can be about a specific situation, a person, or the world in general. Assumptions are often unstated.

Author's Message An author's message is the main idea or theme of a particular work.
See also **Main Idea; Theme,** *Glossary of Literary Terms, page R114.*

Author's Perspective *See Glossary of Literary Terms, page R102.*

Author's Position An author's position is his or her opinion on an issue or topic.
See also **Claim.**

Author's Purpose *See Glossary of Literary Terms, page R102.*

Autobiography *See Glossary of Literary Terms, page R102.*

Bias Bias is an inclination toward a particular judgment on a topic or issue. A writer often reveals a strongly positive or strongly negative opinion by presenting only one way of looking at an issue or by heavily weighting the evidence. Words with intensely positive or negative connotations are often a signal of a writer's bias.

Bibliography A bibliography is a list of books and other materials related to the topic of a text. Bibliographies can be good sources of works for further study on a subject.
See also **Works Consulted.**

Biography *See Glossary of Literary Terms, page R103.*

Business Correspondence Business correspondence includes all written business communications, such as business letters, e-mails, and memos. In general, business correspondence is brief, to the point, clear, courteous, and professional.

Cause and Effect A **cause** is an event or action that directly results in another event or action. An **effect** is the direct or logical outcome of an event or action. Basic **cause-and-effect relationships** include a single cause with a single effect, one cause with multiple effects, multiple causes with a single effect, and a chain of causes and effects. The concept of cause and effect also provides a way of organizing a piece of writing. It helps a writer show the relationships between events or ideas.
See also **False Cause,** *Reading Handbook, page R24.*

Chronological Order Chronological order is the arrangement of events in their order of occurrence. This type of organization is used in both fictional narratives and in historical writing, biography, and autobiography.

Claim In an argument, a claim is the writer's position on an issue or problem. Although an argument focuses on supporting one claim, a writer may make more than one claim in a work.

Clarify Clarifying is a reading strategy that helps a reader to understand or make clear what he or she is reading. Readers usually clarify by rereading, reading aloud, or discussing.

Classification Classification is a pattern of organization in which objects, ideas, or information is presented in groups, or classes, based on common characteristics.

Cliché A cliché is an overused expression. "Better late than never" and "hard as nails" are common examples. Good writers generally avoid clichés unless they are using them in dialogue to indicate something about characters' personalities.

Compare and Contrast To compare and contrast is to identify similarities and differences in two or more subjects. Compare-and-contrast organization can be used to structure a piece of writing, serving as a framework for examining the similarities and differences in two or more subjects.

Conclusion A conclusion is a statement of belief based on evidence, experience, and reasoning. A **valid conclusion** is a conclusion that logically follows from the facts or statements upon which it is based. A **deductive conclusion** is one that follows from a particular generalization or premise. An **inductive conclusion** is a broad conclusion or generalization that is reached by arguing from specific facts and examples.

Connect Connecting is a reader's process of relating the content of a text to his or her own knowledge and experience.

Consumer Documents Consumer documents are printed materials that accompany products and services. They are intended for the buyers or users of the products or services and usually provide information about use, care, operation, or assembly. Some common consumer documents are applications, contracts, warranties, manuals, instructions, package inserts, labels, brochures, and schedules.

Context Clues When you encounter an unfamiliar word, you can often use context clues as aids for understanding. Context clues are the words and phrases surrounding the word that provide hints about the word's meaning.

Counterargument A counterargument is an argument made to oppose another argument. A good argument anticipates opposing viewpoints and provides counterarguments to refute (disprove) or answer them.

Credibility *Credibility* refers to the believability or trustworthiness of a source and the information it contains.

Critical Review A critical review is an evaluation or critique by a reviewer or critic. Different types of reviews include film reviews, book reviews, music reviews, and art-show reviews.

Database A database is a collection of information that can be quickly and easily accessed and searched and from which information can be easily retrieved. It is frequently presented in an electronic format.

Debate A debate is basically an argument—but a very structured one that requires a good deal of preparation. In academic settings, *debate* usually refers to a formal argumentation contest in which two opposing teams defend and attack a proposition.
See also **Argument.**

Deductive Reasoning Deductive reasoning is a way of thinking that begins with a generalization, presents a specific situation, and then advances with facts and evidence to a logical conclusion. The following passage has a deductive argument imbedded in it: "All students in the drama class must attend the play on Thursday. Since Ava is in the class, she had better show up." This deductive argument can be broken down as follows: generalization—all students in the drama class must attend the play on Thursday; specific situation—Ava is a student in the drama class; conclusion—Ava must attend the play.
See also **Analyzing Logic and Reasoning,** *Reading Handbook, pages R22–R23.*

Dictionary *See* **Reference Works.**

Draw Conclusions To draw a conclusion is to make a judgment or arrive at a belief based on evidence, experience, and reasoning.

Editorial An editorial is an opinion piece that usually appears on the editorial page of a newspaper or as part of a news broadcast. The editorial section of a newspaper presents opinions rather than objective news reports.
See also **Op-Ed Piece.**

Either/Or Fallacy An either/or fallacy is a statement that suggests that there are only two possible ways to view a situation or only two options to choose from. In other words, it is a statement that falsely frames a dilemma, giving the impression that no options exist but the two presented—for example, "Either we stop the construction of a new airport, or the surrounding suburbs will become ghost towns."
See also **Identifying Faulty Reasoning,** *Reading Handbook, page R24.*

Emotional Appeals Emotional appeals are messages that evoke strong feelings—such as fear, pity, or vanity—in order to persuade instead of using facts and evidence to make a point. An **appeal to fear** is a message that taps into people's fear of losing their safety or security. An **appeal to pity** is a message that taps into people's sympathy and compassion for others to build support for an idea, a cause, or a proposed action. An **appeal to vanity** is a message that attempts to persuade by tapping into people's desire to feel good about themselves.
See also **Recognizing Persuasive Techniques,** *Reading Handbook, page R22.*

Encyclopedia *See* **Reference Works.**

Essay *See Glossary of Literary Terms, page R105.*

Evaluate To evaluate is to examine something carefully and judge its value or worth. Evaluating is an important skill for gaining insight into what you read. A reader can evaluate the actions of a particular character, for example, or can form an opinion about the value of an entire work.

Evidence Evidence is the specific pieces of information that support a claim. Evidence can take the form of facts, quotations, examples, statistics, or personal experiences, among others.

Expository Essay *See* **Essay,** *Glossary of Literary Terms, page R105.*

Fact versus Opinion A **fact** is a statement that can be

proved or verified. An **opinion,** on the other hand, is a statement that cannot be proved because it expresses a person's beliefs, feelings, or thoughts.
See also **Inference; Generalization.**

Fallacy A fallacy is an error in reasoning. Typically, a fallacy is based on an incorrect inference or a misuse of evidence. Some common logical fallacies are **circular reasoning, either/or fallacy, oversimplification, overgeneralization,** and **stereotyping.**
See also **Either/Or Fallacy, Logical Appeal, Overgeneralization; Identifying Faulty Reasoning,** *Reading Handbook, page R24.*

Faulty Reasoning *See* **Fallacy.**

Feature Article A feature article is a main article in a newspaper or a cover story in a magazine. A feature article is focused more on entertaining than informing. Features are lighter or more general than hard news and tend to be about human interest or lifestyles.

Functional Documents *See* **Consumer Documents; Workplace Documents.**

Generalization A generalization is a broad statement about a class or category of people, ideas, or things, based on a study of only some of its members.
See also **Overgeneralization.**

Government Publications Government publications are documents produced by government organizations. Pamphlets, brochures, and reports are just some of the many forms these publications may take. Government publications can be good resources for a wide variety of topics.

Graphic Aid A graphic aid is a visual tool that is printed, handwritten, or drawn. Charts, diagrams, graphs, photographs, and maps can all be graphic aids.
See also **Graphic Aids,** *Reading Handbook, pages R5–R7.*

Graphic Organizer A graphic organizer is a "word picture"—that is, a visual illustration of a verbal statement—that helps a reader understand a text. Charts, tables, webs, and diagrams can all be graphic organizers. Graphic organizers and graphic aids can look the same. For example, a table in a science article will not be constructed differently from a table that is a graphic organizer. However, graphic organizers and graphic aids do differ in how they are used. Graphic aids are the visual representations that people encounter when they read informational texts. Graphic organizers are visuals that people construct to help them understand texts or organize information.

Historical Documents Historical documents are writings that have played a significant role in human events or are themselves records of such events. The Declaration of Independence, for example, is a historical document.

How-To Book A how-to book is a book that is written to explain how to do something—usually an activity, a sport, or a household project.

Implied Main Idea *See* **Main Idea.**

Index The index of a book is an alphabetized list of important topics and details covered in the book and the page numbers on which they can be found. An index can be used to quickly find specific information about a topic.

Inductive Reasoning Inductive reasoning is the process of logically reasoning from specific observations, examples, and facts to arrive at a general conclusion or principle.
See also **Analyzing Logic and Reasoning,** *Reading Handbook, pages R22–R23.*

Inference An inference is a logical assumption that is based on observed facts and one's own knowledge and experience.

Informational Nonfiction Informational nonfiction is writing that provides factual information. It often explains ideas or teaches processes. Examples include news reports, science textbooks, software instructions, and lab reports.

Internet The Internet is a global, interconnected system of computer networks that allows for communication through e-mail, listservers, and the World Wide Web. The Internet connects computers and computer users throughout the world.

Journal A journal is a periodical publication issued by a legal, medical, or other professional organization. Alternatively, the term may be used to refer to a diary or daily record.

Loaded Language Loaded language consists of words with strongly positive or negative connotations intended to influence a reader's or listener's attitude.

Logical Appeal A logical appeal relies on logic and facts, appealing to people's reasoning or intellect rather than to their values or emotions. Flawed logical appeals—that is, errors in reasoning—are considered logical fallacies.
See also **Fallacy.**

Logical Argument A logical argument is an argument in which the logical relationship between the support and the claim is sound.

Main Idea A main idea is the central or most important idea about a topic that a writer or speaker conveys. It can be the central idea of an entire work or of just a paragraph. Often, the main idea of a paragraph is expressed in a topic sentence. However, a main idea may just be implied, or suggested, by details. A main idea and supporting details can serve as a basic pattern of organization in a piece of writing, with the central idea about a topic being supported by details.

Make Inferences *See* **Inference.**

Monitor Monitoring is the strategy of checking your comprehension as you are reading and modifying the strategies you are using to suit your needs. Monitoring may include some or all of the following strategies: **questioning, clarifying, visualizing, predicting, connecting,** and **rereading.**

Narrative Nonfiction *See Glossary of Literary Terms, page R109.*

News Article A news article is a piece of writing that reports on a recent event. In newspapers, news articles are usually written concisely and report the latest news, presenting the most important facts first and then more detailed information. In magazines, news articles are usually more elaborate than those in newspapers because they are written to provide both information and analysis. Also, news articles in magazines do not necessarily present the most important facts first.

Nonfiction *See Glossary of Literary Terms, page R109.*

Op-Ed Piece An op-ed piece is an opinion piece that usually appears opposite ("op") the editorial page of a newspaper. Unlike editorials, op-ed pieces are written and submitted by named writers.

Organization *See* **Pattern of Organization.**

Overgeneralization An overgeneralization is a generalization that is too broad. You can often recognize overgeneralizations by the appearance of words and phrases such as *all, everyone, every time, any, anything, no one,* and *none.* Consider, for example, this statement: "None of the sanitation workers in our city really care about keeping the environment clean." In all probability, there are many exceptions; the writer can't possibly know the feelings of every sanitation worker in the city.

See also **Identifying Faulty Reasoning,** *Reading Handbook, page R24.*

Overview An overview is a short summary of a story, a speech, or an essay. It orients the reader by providing a preview of the text to come.

Paraphrase Paraphrasing is the restating of information in one's own words.
See also **Summarize.**

Pattern of Organization A pattern of organization is a particular arrangement of ideas and information. Such a pattern may be used to organize an entire composition or a single paragraph within a longer work. The following are the most common patterns of organization: **cause-and-effect, chronological order, compare-and-contrast, classification, deductive, inductive, order of importance, problem-solution, sequential,** and **spatial.**
See also **Cause and Effect; Chronological Order; Classification; Compare and Contrast; Problem-Solution Order; Sequential Order; Reading Informational Texts: Patterns of Organization,** *Reading Handbook, pages R8–R13.*

Periodical A periodical is a publication that is issued at regular intervals of more than one day. For example, a periodical may be a weekly, monthly, or quarterly journal or magazine. Newspapers and other daily publications generally are not classified as periodicals.

Personal Essay *See* **Essay,** *Glossary of Literary Terms, page R105.*

Persuasion Persuasion is the art of swaying others' feelings, beliefs, or actions. Persuasion normally appeals to both the intellect and the emotions of readers. **Persuasive techniques** are the methods used to influence others to adopt certain opinions or beliefs or to act in certain ways. Types of persuasive techniques include emotional appeals, logical appeals, and loaded language. When used properly, persuasive techniques can add depth to writing that's meant to persuade. Persuasive techniques can, however, be misused to cloud factual information, disguise poor reasoning, or unfairly exploit people's emotions in order to shape their opinions.
See also **Emotional Appeals; Loaded Language; Logical Appeal; Recognizing Persuasive Techniques,** *Reading Handbook, page R22.*

Predict Predicting is a reading strategy that involves using text clues to make a reasonable guess about what will happen next in a story.

Primary Source *See* **Sources.**

Prior Knowledge Prior knowledge is the knowledge a reader already possesses about a topic. This information might come from personal experiences, expert accounts, books, films, or other sources.

Problem-Solution Order Problem-solution order is a pattern of organization in which a problem is stated and analyzed and then one or more solutions are proposed and examined. Writers use words and phrases such as *propose, conclude, reason for, problem, answer,* and *solution* to connect ideas and details when writing about problems and solutions.

Propaganda Propaganda is a form of communication that may use distorted, false, or misleading information. It usually refers to manipulative political discourse.

Public Documents Public documents are documents that were written for the public to provide information that is of public interest or concern. They include government documents, speeches, signs, and rules and regulations.
See also **Government Publications.**

Reference Works General reference works are sources that contain facts and background information on a wide range of subjects. More specific reference works contain in-depth information on a single subject. Most reference works are good sources of reliable information because they have been reviewed by experts. The following are some common reference works: **encyclopedias, dictionaries, thesauri, almanacs, atlases, chronologies, biographical dictionaries,** and **directories.**

Review *See* **Critical Review.**

Rhetorical Devices *See Glossary of Literary Terms, page R111.*

Rhetorical Questions Rhetorical questions are those that do not require a reply. Writers use them to suggest that their arguments make the answer obvious or self-evident.

Scanning Scanning is the process of searching through writing for a particular fact or piece of information. When you scan, your eyes sweep across a page, looking for key words that may lead you to the information you want.

Secondary Source *See* **Sources.**

Sequential Order A pattern of organization that shows the order in which events or actions occur is called sequential order. Writers typically use this pattern of organization to explain steps or stages in a process.

Setting a Purpose The process of establishing specific reasons for reading a text is called setting a purpose.

Sidebar A sidebar is additional information set in a box alongside or within a news or feature article. Popular magazines often make use of sidebar information.

Signal Words Signal words are words and phrases that indicate what is to come in a text. Readers can use signal words to discover a text's pattern of organization and to analyze the relationships among the ideas in the text.

Sources A source is anything that supplies information. **Primary sources** are materials written by people who were present at events, either as participants or as observers. Letters, diaries, autobiographies, speeches, and photographs are primary sources. **Secondary sources** are records of events that were created sometime after the events occurred; the writers were not directly involved or were not present when the events took place. Encyclopedias, textbooks, biographies, most newspaper and magazine articles, and books and articles that interpret or review research are secondary sources.

Spatial Order Spatial order is a pattern of organization that highlights the physical positions or relationships of details or objects. This pattern of organization is typically found in descriptive writing. Writers use words and phrases such as *on the left, to the right, here, over there, above, below, beyond, nearby,* and *in the distance* to indicate the arrangement of details.

Speech *See Glossary of Literary Terms, page R113.*

Stereotyping Stereotyping is a type of overgeneralization. Stereotypes are broad statements made about people on the basis of their gender, ethnicity, race, or political, social, professional, or religious group.

Summarize To summarize is to briefly retell, or encapsulate, the main ideas of a piece of writing in one's own words.
See also **Paraphrase.**

Support Support is any material that serves to prove a claim. In an argument, support typically consists of reasons and evidence. In persuasive texts and speeches, however, support may include appeals to the needs and values of the audience.

Supporting Detail *See* **Main Idea.**

Synthesize To synthesize information is to take individual pieces of information and combine them with other pieces of information and with prior knowledge or experience to gain a better understanding of a subject or to create a new product or idea.

Text Features Text features are design elements that indicate the organizational structure of a text and help make the key ideas and supporting information understandable. Text features include headings, boldface type, italic type, bulleted or numbered lists, sidebars, and graphic aids such as charts, tables, timelines, illustrations, and photographs.

Thesaurus *See* **Reference Works.**

Thesis Statement In an argument, a thesis statement is an expression of the claim that the writer or speaker is trying to support. In an essay, a thesis statement is an expression, in one or two sentences, of the main idea or purpose of the piece of writing.

Topic Sentence The topic sentence of a paragraph states the paragraph's main idea. All other sentences in the paragraph provide supporting details.

Visualize Visualizing is the process of forming a mental picture based on written or spoken information.

Web Site A Web site is a collection of "pages" on the World Wide Web that is usually devoted to one specific subject. Pages are linked together and are accessed by clicking hyperlinks or menus, which send the user from page to page within the site. Web sites are created by companies, organizations, educational institutions, branches of the government, the military, and individuals.

Workplace Documents Workplace documents are materials that are produced or used within a work setting, usually to aid in the functioning of the workplace. They include job applications, office memos, training manuals, job descriptions, and sales reports.

Works Cited A list of works cited lists names of all the works a writer has referred to in his or her text. This list often includes not only books and articles but also nonprint sources.

Works Consulted A list of works consulted names all the works a writer consulted in order to create his or her text. It is not limited just to those works cited in the text.
See also **Bibliography.**

Glossary of Vocabulary in English & Spanish

abject (ăb-jĕkt′) *adj.* exceedingly humble
abyecto *adj.* sumamente pobre

abominably (ə-bŏm′ə-nə-blē) *adv.* in a hateful way; horribly
abominablemente *adv.* de manera odiosa u horrible

abscond (ăb-skŏnd′) *v.* to go away suddenly and secretly
fugarse *v.* huir de repente

abysmal (ə-bĭz′məl) *adj.* very bad
pésimo *adj.* desastroso; atroz

acclimatization (ə-klī′mə-tĭ-zā′shən) *n.* the act of getting accustomed to a new climate or environment
aclimatación *s.* acción de acostumbrarse a un nuevo clima o ambiente

adulation (ăj′ə-lā′shən) *n.* excessive praise or flattery
adulación *s.* halago exagerado

adversary (ăd′vər-sĕr′ē) *n.* an opponent; enemy
adversario *s.* opositor; enemigo

adversity (ăd-vûr′sĭ-tē) *n.* hardship; misfortune
adversidad *s.* infortunio; desgracia

advocacy (ăd′və-kə-sē) *adj.* involving public support for an idea or policy
defensa *s.* apoyo público a una idea o medida

affiliate (ə-fĭl′ē-ĭt) *n.* a person or an organization officially connected to a larger body
afiliado *s.* persona u organización conectada oficialmente con una entidad

aghast (ə-găst′) *adj.* filled with shock or horror
horrorizado *adj.* muy atemorizado

agile (ăj′əl) *adj.* able to move quickly and easily
ágil *adj.* capaz de moverse con rapidez y facilidad

alienation (āl′yə-nā′shən) *n.* a feeling of separation or isolation
alienación *s.* sensación de separación o aislamiento

aloof (ə-lōōf′) *adj.* distant; remote; standoffish
distante *adj.* remoto; indiferente

amenity (ə-mĕn′ĭ-tē) *n.* something that adds to one's comfort or convenience
comodidad *s.* cosa que aumenta el confort

analytic (ăn′ə-lĭt′ĭk) *adj.* using logical reasoning or analysis
analítico *adj.* que usa razonamiento o análisis lógico

annihilate (ə-nī′ə-lāt′) *v.* to destroy completely
aniquilar *v.* destruir por completo

anonymity (ăn′ə-nĭm′ĭ-tē) *n.* the condition of being unknown
anonimato *s.* condición de no ser conocido

anthem (ăn′thəm) *n.* an uplifting song or hymn
himno *s.* composición musical solemne

anthropology (ăn′thrə-pŏl′ə-jē) *n.* the science or study of human beings, including their physical characteristics and cultures
antropología *s.* ciencia que estudia las características físicas y las culturas de los seres humanos

aperture (ăp′ər-chər) *n.* an opening, such as a hole or a gap
abertura *s.* agujero o grieta

aplomb (ə-plŏm′) *n.* poise; self-assurance
aplomo *s.* serenidad; circunspección

appalled (ə-pôld′) *adj.* filled with dismay; horrified **appall** *v.*
asombrado *adj.* pasmado; asustado **asombrar** *v.*

archaic (är-kā′ĭk) *adj.* very old or unfashionable
arcaico *adj.* muy antiguo o pasado de moda

ardor (är′dər) *n.* passion
ardor *s.* pasión

arduous (är′jōō-əs) *adj.* requiring much effort; difficult
arduo *adj.* que requiere mucho esfuerzo; difícil

articulate (är-tĭk′yə-lĭt) *adj.* able to speak clearly and coherently; well-spoken
elocuente *adj.* que se expresa con claridad y convicción

artifact (är′tə-făkt′) *n.* something created by humans, usually for a practical purpose
artefacto *s.* objeto creado por los seres humanos, usualmente con propósitos prácticos

askew (ə-skyōō′) *adj.* crooked; to one side
torcido *adj.* chueco; que se inclina hacia un lado

assertion (ə-sûr′shən) *n.* a statement
aseveración *s.* declaración; afirmación

assuage (ə-swāj′) *v.* to calm or pacify
calmar *v.* tranquilizar o mitigar

awry (ə-rī′) *adj.* off course; wrong
sesgado *adj.* desviado; torcido

baleful (bāl′fəl) *adj.* evil; destructive
    torvo *adj.* funesto; siniestro

banal (bə-năl′) *adj.* commonplace; trite
    banal *adj.* común; trillado

beguiling (bĭ-gī′lĭng) *adj.* charming; pleasing **beguile** *v.*
    encantador *adj.* seductor; atrayente **encantar** *v.*

benign (bĭ-nīn′) *adj.* good; kindly
    benigno *adj.* bondadoso; amable

boon (bo͞on) *n.* a benefit; blessing
    beneficio *s.* gran ayuda; bendición

bravado (brə-vä′dō) *n.* a false show of courage or defiance
    bravata *s.* alarde; demostración falsa de valor o valentía

brazenly (brā′zən-lē′) *adv.* boldly and without shame
    descaradamente *adv.* con descaro y frescura

browser (brou′zər) *n.* a program used to navigate the Internet
    browser *s.* programa para desplazarse en la Internet

buffeted (bŭf′ĭ-tĭd) *adj.* knocked about or struck **buffet** *v.*
    golpeado *adj.* empujado o azotado **golpear** *v.*

cadence (kād′ns) *n.* a balanced, rhythmic flow
    cadencia *s.* repetición regular de sonidos o movimientos

cascade (kă-skād′) *v.* to fall or flow like a waterfall
    precipitarse *v.* caer o deslizarse como una cascada

cavort (kə-vôrt′) *v.* to leap or romp about
    retozar *v.* saltar; divertirse

cede (sēd) *v.* to give up; give way
    ceder *v.* conceder; rendirse

chronicle (krŏn′ĭ-kəl) *n.* a record of events
    crónica *s.* registro de sucesos

clamor (klăm′ər) *n.* a noisy outburst; outcry
    clamor *s.* conjunto de gritos o ruidos fuertes

clarity (klăr′ĭ-tē) *n.* clearness
    claridad *s.* transparencia

commandeer (kŏm′ən-dîr′) *v.* to take control of by force
    confiscar *v.* tomar por la fuerza

compile (kəm-pīl′) *v.* to put together by gathering from many sources
    compilar *v.* reunir de muchas fuentes

condescending (kŏn′dĭ-sĕn′dĭng) *adj.* assuming an air of superiority
    condescendiente *adj.* que asume un aire de superioridad

condiment (kŏn′də-mənt) *n.* a sauce, relish, or spice used to season food
    condimento *s.* salsa o especia para sazonar la comida

condone (kən-dōn′) *v.* to forgive or overlook
    condonar *v.* perdonar, olvidar o ignorar

contemptible (kən-tĕmp′tə-bəl) *adj.* deserving of scorn; despicable
    despreciable *adj.* que merece desdén o desprecio; vil

contrition (kən-trĭsh′ən) *n.* a feeling of regret for doing wrong
    contrición *s.* arrepentimiento por haber actuado mal

correlate (kôr′ə-lāt′) *v.* to figure out or create a relationship between two items or events
    correlacionar *v.* establecer una relación entre dos puntos o sucesos

cosmetic (kŏz-mĕt′ĭk) *adj.* decorative rather than functional
    cosmético *adj.* decorativo más que funcional

coveted (kŭv′ĭ-tĭd) *adj.* greedily desired or wished for **covet** *v.*
    codiciado *adj.* que se desea con envidia **codiciar** *v.*

crass (krăs) *adj.* crude; unrefined
    craso *adj.* burdo; grosero

crevasse (krĭ-văs′) *n.* a deep crack or split in a glacier
    grieta *s.* hendidura profunda, especialmente en un glaciar

cultivated (kŭl′tə-vā′tĭd) *adj.* refined or cultured in manner
    cultivado *adj.* refinado o de modales cultos

daunted (dôn′tĭd) *adj.* discouraged **daunt** *v.*
    amilanado *adj.* intimidado **amilanar** *v.*

debut (dā-byo͞o′) *n.* first public performance or showing
    debut *s.* estreno; primera presentación

default (dĭ-fôlt′) *v.* to fail to keep a promise, especially a promise to repay a loan
    incumplir *v.* no cumplir una promesa, especialmente no pagar un préstamo

deftness (dĕft′nĭs) *n.* the quality of quickness and skillfullness
    destreza *s.* agilidad y habilidad

degenerate (dĭ-jĕn'ər-ĭt) *n.* a corrupt or vicious person
degenerado *s.* persona corrupta o viciosa

degradation (dĕg'rə-dā'shən) *n.* condition of being brought to a lower level; humiliation
degradación *s.* pérdida de status y dignidad; humillación

demeanor (dĭ-mē'nər) *n.* a way of behaving; manner
comportamiento *s.* conducta externa

derisive (dĭ-rī'sĭv) *adj.* expressing contempt or ridicule
desdeñoso *adj.* que expresa burla o ridículo

desolation (dĕs'ə-lā'shən) *n.* lonely grief; misery
desolación *s.* dolor en soledad; desgracia

dialect (dī'ə-lĕkt') *n.* a variety of a standard language unique to a certain region or social group
dialecto *s.* variedad de una lengua que se habla en una región o que habla un grupo social

diffuse (dĭ-fyōōs') *adj.* unfocused
difuso *adj.* vago e impreciso

dilapidated (dĭ-lăp'ĭ-dā'tĭd) *adj.* broken down and shabby
dilapidado *adj.* en ruinas

diminutive (dĭ-mĭn'yə-tĭv) *adj.* very small
diminuto *adj.* muy pequeño

disarming (dĭs-är'mĭng) *adj.* removing or overcoming suspicion; inspiring confidence
apaciguador *adj.* tranquilizador; que elimina sospechas; que crea confianza

disclaimer (dĭs-klā'mər) *n.* a denial of responsibility or knowledge
descargo *s.* repudiación de responsabilidad o conocimiento

disconcerting (dĭs'kən-sûr'tĭng) *adj.* causing one to feel confused or embarrassed **disconcert** *v.*
desconcertante *adj.* que causa confusión, malestar o desconcierto **desconcertar** *v.*

disconsolate (dĭs-kŏn'sə-lĭt) *adj.* extremely depressed or dejected
desconsolado *adj.* extremadamente triste

discordant (dĭ-skôr'dnt) *adj.* having a disagreeable or clashing sound
discordante *adj.* disonante; de sonidos desagradables; sin armonía

dispirited (dĭ-spĭr'ĭ-tĭd) *adj.* dejected
desanimado *s.* abatido

distraught (dĭ-strôt') *adj.* deeply upset
perturbado *adj.* profundamente molesto

doggedness (dô'gĭd-nĭs) *n.* persistence; stubbornness
obstinación *s.* persistencia; tenacidad

droll (drōl) *adj.* amusingly odd or comical
divertido *adj.* gracioso y curioso

encore (ŏn'kōr') *n.* a repeated or additional performance
bis *s.* repetición

engender (ĕn-jĕn'dər) *v.* to bring into existence
engendrar *v.* causar; originar

enthralled (ĕn-thrôld') *adj.* charmed greatly **enthrall** *v.*
cautivado *adj.* encantado **cautivar** *v.*

eradicate (ĭ-răd'ĭ-kāt') *v.* to do away with completely
erradicar *v.* acabar por completo

evanesce (ĕv'ə-nĕs') *v.* to disappear; vanish
desvanecerse *v.* desaparecer; disiparse

exalted (ĭg-zôl'tĭd) *adj.* raised up **exalt** *v.*
exaltado *adj.* elevado **exaltar** *v.*

exhilarate (ĭg-zĭl'ə-rāt') *v.* to make merry or lively
regocijar *v.* alegrar; levantar el ánimo

exhortation (ĕg'zôr-tā'shən) *n.* a communication strongly urging that something be done
exhortación *s.* palabras que inducen a una acción

exodus (ĕk'sə-dəs) *n.* a mass departure
éxodo *s.* partida en masa

exotic (ĭg-zŏt'ĭk) *adj.* excitingly strange
exótico *adj.* extraño; curioso

expansive (ĭk-spăn'sĭv) *adj.* outgoing; showing feelings openly and freely
expansivo *adj.* comunicativo; que muestra sus sentimientos

expendable (ĭk-spĕn'də-bəl) *adj.* not worth keeping; not essential
prescindible *adj.* que no es esencial

exuberance (ĭg-zōō'bər-əns) *n.* condition of unrestrained joy
exuberancia *s.* euforia; exaltación

falter (fôl′tər) *v.* to hesitate from lack of courage or confidence
　　vacilar *v.* titubear por falta de valor o de confianza

fecund (fē′kənd) *adj.* producing much growth; fertile
　　fecundo *adj.* fértil; abundante

fiasco (fē-ăs′kō) *n.* a complete failure
　　fiasco *s.* fracaso total

flay (flā) *v.* to whip or lash
　　desollar *v.* despellejar a latigazos

foreboding (fôr-bō′dĭng) *n.* a sense of approaching evil
　　presentimiento *s.* sentimiento de que algo malo sucederá

fractious (frăk′shəs) *adj.* hard to manage or hold together; unruly
　　quisquilloso *adj.* cascarrabias; rebelde

frenetically (frə-nĕt′ĭk-lē) *adv.* in a frenzied or frantic way
　　frenéticamente *adv.* de modo frenético o desenfrenado

futile (fyōōt′l) *adj.* having no useful result
　　fútil *adj.* inútil; sin resultados útiles

gamut (găm′ət) *n.* an entire range or series
　　gama *s.* serie; variedades

genesis (jĕn′ĭ-sĭs) *n.* the origin or coming into being (of something)
　　génesis *s.* origen o principio de una cosa

goad (gōd) *v.* to drive or urge
　　provocar *v.* urgir; instar

harried (hăr′ēd) *adj.* tormented; harassed **harry** *v.*
　　agobiado *adj.* atribulado; acosado **agobiar** *v.*

heresy (hĕr′ĭ-sē) *n.* an action or opinion contrary to what is generally thought of as right
　　herejía *s.* acto u opinión contrario a lo que se considera correcto

hierarchy (hī′ə-rär′kē) *n.* a body of persons having authority
　　jerarquía *s.* grupo de personas de autoridad

homely (hōm′lē) *adj.* characteristic of home life; simple; everyday
　　casero *adj.* característico de la vida hogareña; sencillo

hypothesis (hī-pŏth′ĭ-sĭs) *n.* an assumption made in order to test its possible consequences
　　hipótesis *s.* suposición que se pone a prueba

illiteracy (ĭ-lĭt′ər-ə-sē) *n.* a lack of ability to read and write
　　analfabetismo *s.* desconocimiento de la lectura y escritura

imminent (ĭm′ə-nənt) *adj.* about to occur
　　inminente *adj.* que está por ocurrir

immolation (ĭm′ə-lā′shən) *n.* death or destruction
　　inmolación *s.* muerte o destrucción

immutable (ĭ-myōō′tə-bəl) *adj.* unchanging
　　inmutable *adj.* que no cambia

imperative (ĭm-pĕr′ə-tĭv) *adj.* absolutely necessary
　　imperativo *adj.* absolutamente necesario

implacable (ĭm-plăk′ə-bəl) *adj.* impossible to soothe; unforgiving
　　implacable *adj.* desalmado; despiadado; que no perdona

impotent (ĭm′pə-tənt) *adj.* powerless; lacking strength or vigor
　　impotente *adj.* sin poder o capacidad; carente de fuerza o vigor

impunity (ĭm-pyōō′nĭ-tē) *n.* freedom from penalty or harm
　　impunidad *s.* falta de castigo, penalidad o daño

inaudibly (ĭn-ô′də-blē) *adv.* in a way that is impossible to hear
　　inaudiblemente *adv.* de modo que no se oye

inaugurate (ĭn-ô′gyə-rāt′) *v.* to make a formal beginning of
　　inaugurar *v.* dar principio o estrenar

incessantly (ĭn-sĕs′ənt-lē) *adv.* without interruption; continuously
　　incesantemente *adv.* continuamente; sin parar

incredulous (ĭn-krĕj′ə-ləs) *adj.* doubtful; disbelieving
　　incrédulo *adj.* no creyente

increment (ĭn′krə-mənt) *n.* a small, slight growth or increase
　　incremento *s.* pequeño aumento o crecimiento

induced (ĭn-dōōst′) *adj.* led on; persuaded **induce** *v.*
　　inducido *adj.* persuadido; convencido **inducir** *v.*

inept (ĭn-ĕpt′) *adj.* generally incompetent
　　inepto *adj.* incompetente

inertia (ĭ-nûr′shə) *n.* tendency to continue to do what one has been doing
　　inercia *s.* tendencia a continuar haciendo lo que se ha estado haciendo

inevitability (ĭn-ĕv′ĭ-tə-bĭl′ĭ-tē) *n.* something that is certain to happen
inevitabilidad *s.* lo que no se puede evitar

inexplicably (ĭn-ĕk′splĭ-kə-blē) *adv.* in a way that is difficult or impossible to explain
inexplicablemente *adv.* de modo difícil o imposible de explicar

inextricably (ĭn-ĕk′strĭ-kə-blē) *adv.* in a way impossible to untangle
inextricablemente *adv.* de manera imposible de descifrar o desenredar

infallibility (ĭn-făl′ə-bĭl′ĭ-tē) *n.* an inability to make errors
infalibilidad *s.* incapacidad para cometer errores

infatuated (ĭn-făch′o͞o-ā′tĭd) *adj.* possessed by an unreasoning love or attraction
encaprichado *adj.* locamente enamorado o atraído irracionalmente hacia una persona

infinitesimally (ĭn′fĭn-ĭ-tĕs′ə-mə-lē) *adv.* in amounts so small as to be barely measurable
infinitesimalmente *adv.* en cantidades tan pequeñas que casi no se puede medir

infuse (ĭn-fyo͞oz′) *v.* to fill, as if by pouring
infundir *v.* llenar

inherent (ĭn-hîr′ənt) *adj.* forming part of the essential nature of something; built-in
inherente *adj.* que por naturaleza es parte esencial de algo

inhospitable (ĭn-hŏs′pĭ-tə-bəl) *adj.* not welcoming; hostile
inhóspito *adj.* hostil; que rechaza

inquisitive (ĭn-kwĭz′ĭ-tĭv) *adj.* curious; inquiring
inquisitivo *adj.* curioso; preguntón

instigate (ĭn′stĭ-gāt′) *v.* to stir up; provoke
instigar *v.* provocar; incitar

insubordinate (ĭn′sə-bôr′dn-ĭt) *adj.* disobedient to a superior
insubordinado *adj.* desobediente a un superior

insurmountable (ĭn′sər-moun′tə-bəl) *adj.* impossible to overcome
insuperable *adj.* insalvable; infranqueable

intuitive (ĭn-to͞o′ĭ-tĭv) *adj.* based on what seems to be true without conscious reasoning; instinctive
intuitivo *adj.* que se conoce sin razonamiento consciente; instintivo

lament (lə-mĕnt′) *v.* to express grief or deep regret
lamentar *v.* expresar dolor o profundo arrepentimiento

lavish (lăv′ĭsh) *adj.* extravagant; more than is needed
espléndido *adj.* extravagante; despilfarrador

leer (lîr) *v.* to give a sly, evil glance
mirar de reojo *v.* lanzar una mirada lasciva o maliciosa

legitimate (lə-jĭt′ə-mĭt) *adj.* justifiable; reasonable
legítimo *adj.* justificable; razonable

malfunctioning (măl-fŭngk′shə-nĭng) *adj.* not working or operating properly **malfunction** *v.*
dañado *adj.* que no funciona bien **dañar** *v.*

maneuvering (mə-no͞o′vər-ĭng) *n.* an action skillfully designed to achieve a goal **maneuver** *v.*
maniobras *s.* acciones diseñadas para alcanzar una meta **maniobrar** *v.*

marauding (mə-rô′dĭng) *adj.* roaming about in search of plunder **maraud** *v.*
saqueador *adj.* que merodea en busca de botín **saquear** *v.*

meager (mē′gər) *adj.* lacking in quantity or quality
escaso *adj.* poco, insuficiente en cantidad y número

meditation (mĕd′ĭ-tā′shən) *n.* the act of being in serious, reflective thought
meditación *s.* reflexión atenta y profunda

mesmerizing (mĕz′mə-rīz′ĭng) *adj.* holding one's attention in an almost hypnotic manner **mesmerize** *v.*
fascinante *adj.* que capta la atención de forma casi hipnótica **fascinar** *v.*

militancy (mĭl′ĭ-tənt-sē) *n.* the act of aggressively supporting a political or social cause
militancia *s.* apoyo enérgico a una causa política o social

misnomer (mĭs-nō′mər) *n.* an inaccurate or incorrect name
incorrección *s.* nombre erróneo o incorrecto

momentous (mō-mĕn′təs) *adj.* of great importance
trascendental *adj.* de gran importancia

monolith (mŏn′ə-lĭth′) *n.* something, such as a monument, made from a single large stone
monolito *s.* monumento u objeto tallado de un solo bloque de piedra

mortified (môr′tə-fīd′) *adj.* very embarrassed; humiliated **mortify** *v.*
mortificado *adj.* avergonzado; apenado **mortificar** *v.*

muted (myōō′tĭd) *adj.* softened or muffled
apagado *adj.* débil o suave

negligible (nĕg′lĭ-jə-bəl) *adj.* not large or important enough to merit attention
insignificante *adj.* que no merece atención; desdeñable

neurological (nŏŏr′ə-lŏj′ĭ-kəl) *adj.* having to do with the nervous system
neurológico *adj.* relacionado con el sistema nervioso

noncommittal (nŏn′kə-mĭt′l) *adj.* not committing oneself; not revealing what one thinks
indefinido *adj.* evasivo; que no revela su opinión o propósito

nonpartisan (nŏn-pär′tĭ-zən) *adj.* not supporting or controlled by any political group
independiente *adj.* no afiliado a un grupo político

nostalgia (nŏ-stăl′jə) *n.* bittersweet longing for things from the past
nostalgia *s.* recuerdo triste del pasado

optimal (ŏp′tə-məl) *adj.* most favorable; best
óptimo *adj.* sumamente favorable; lo mejor

ostensibly (ŏ-stĕn′sə-blē) *adv.* seemingly; to all outward appearances
aparentemente *adv.* en apariencia

paradox (pär′ə-dŏks′) *n.* a statement or an event that sounds impossible but seems to be true
paradoja *s.* afirmación o suceso que suena imposible pero parece verdadero

paramount (pär′ə-mount′) *adj.* of highest importance
primordial *adj.* de suma importancia

paraphernalia (pär′ə-fər-nāl′yə) *n.* the articles needed for a particular event or activity
parafernalia *s.* conjunto de artículos necesarios para una actividad

pauper (pô′pər) *n.* a poor person, especially one who depends on public charity
pobre *s.* indigente; persona que depende de la caridad pública

perfidy (pûr′fĭ-dē) *n.* treachery; betrayal of trust
perfidia *s.* traición; abuso de confianza

persistence (pər-sĭs′təns) *n.* the act of refusing to stop or be changed
persistencia *s.* constancia; perseverancia

pervasive (pər-vā′sĭv) *adj.* spreading widely through an area or group of people
penetrante *adj.* que todo lo invade; dominante

perverse (pər-vûrs′) *adj.* stubbornly contrary; wrong; harmful
perverso *adj.* malvado; vil

petrified (pĕt′rə-fīd′) *adj.* turned into stone **petrify** *v.*
petrificado *adj.* convertido en piedra **petrificar** *v.*

plagiarized (plā′jə-rīzd′) *adj.* copied from someone else's writings **plagiarize** *v.*
plagiado *adj.* copiado de los escritos de otro **plagiar** *v.*

poignantly (poin′yənt-lē) *adv.* in a profoundly moving manner
emocionadamente *adv.* de manera muy conmovedora

ponderous (pŏn′dər-əs) *adj.* heavy in a clumsy way; bulky
pesado *adj.* lento y torpe; sin gracia

posse (pŏs′ē) *n.* a band
banda *s.* grupo; cuadrilla

potent (pōt′nt) *adj.* powerful
potente *adj.* poderoso

precariously (prĭ-kâr′ē-əs-lē) *adv.* insecurely; in a dangerous or unstable way
precariamente *adv.* peligrosamente; de manera incierta o insegura

preclude (prĭ-klōōd′) *v.* to make impossible, especially by taking action in advance
imposibilitar *v.* impedir mediante un acto realizado con anticipación; prevenir

presumed (prĭ-zōōmd′) *adj.* thought to be true **presume** *v.*
supuesto *adj.* presunto; que se cree que es verdad **suponer** *v.*

privation (prī-vā′shən) *n.* the lack of a basic necessity or a comfort of life
privación *s.* carencia de lo básico o de comodidades

prodigy (prŏd′ə-jē) *n.* a person who is exceptionally talented or intelligent
prodigio *s.* persona con inteligencia o talento especiales

profusion (prə-fyōō′zhən) *n.* abundance
profusión *s.* abundancia

promontory (prŏm′ən-tôr′ē) *n.* a high ridge of land or rock jutting out into a body of water
promontorio *s.* altura de tierra que avanza dentro del mar

prosaic (prō-zā′ĭk) *adj.* dull; commonplace
prosaico *adj.* vulgar; corriente

prospects (prŏs′pĕkts′) *n.* chances or possibilities, especially for financial success
perspectivas *s.* oportunidades o posibilidades, especialmente de éxito o ganancia

protégé (prō′tə-zhā′) *n.* a person who is guided or supported by an older or more influential person
protegido *s.* persona guiada o financiada por una persona mayor o de más influencia

prudence (prōōd′ns) *n.* the use of good judgment and common sense
prudencia *s.* juicio y sentido común

quarry (kwôr′ē) *n.* the object of a hunt; prey
presa *s.* objeto de la cacería

rabid (răb′ĭd) *adj.* uncontrollable; fanatical
rabioso *adj.* furibundo; fanático

rancor (răng′kər) *n.* bitter and deep ill will
rencor *s.* sentimiento persistente de animosidad o de resentimiento

ransack (răn′săk′) *v.* to search or examine vigorously
registrar *v.* buscar por todas partes

ravage (răv′ĭj) *n.* serious damage
estrago *s.* daño grave

reconnoiter (rē′kə-noi′tər) *v.* to make a preliminary inspection
reconocer *v.* hacer una inspección preliminar del terreno o de una situación

refute (rĭ-fyōōt′) *v.* to prove false by argument or evidence
refutar *v.* demostrar una falsedad con argumento o evidencia

reiterate (rē-ĭt′ə-rāt′) *v.* to repeat
reiterar *v.* repetir

relapse (rē′lăps) *n.* a worsening of an illness after a partial recovery
recaída *s.* empeoramiento de una enfermedad después de una recuperación parcial

repose (rĭ-pōz′) *v.* to lie dead or at rest
reposar *v.* yacer muerto o en descanso

reproach (rĭ-prōch′) *n.* blame; criticism
reproche *s.* reprimenda; crítica

resigned (rĭ-zīnd′) *adj.* marked by acceptance of a condition or action as unavoidable
resignado *adj.* que acepta algo como inevitable

resilient (rĭ-zĭl′yənt) *adj.* strong but flexible; able to withstand stress without injury
elástico *adj.* fuerte pero flexible; que tolera presión

restitution (rĕs′tĭ-tōō′shən) *n.* a making good for loss or damage; repayment
restitución *s.* reposición que se da por algo perdido o dañado

retaliate (rĭ-tăl′ē-āt′) *v.* to pay back an injury in kind
tomar represalias *v.* contraatacar; responder con agresión

retribution (rĕt′rə-byōō′shən) *n.* something given in repayment, usually as a punishment
castigo *s.* represalia; merecido

retrieve (rĭ-trēv′) *v.* to find and return safely
recuperar *v.* rescatar; salvar

revelry (rĕv′əl-rē) *n.* noisy merrymaking; festivity
juerga *s.* jolgorio; festejo alegre y ruidoso

reverie (rĕv′ə-rē) *n.* a state of daydreaming
ensueño *s.* sueño despierto; ensoñación

revulsion (rĭ-vŭl′shən) *n.* a sudden feeling of disgust or loathing
repugnancia *s.* sentimiento repentino de asco o desprecio

sacrilegious (săk′rə-lĭj′əs) *adj.* disrespectful toward a sacred person, place, or thing
sacrílego *adj.* irrespetuoso hacia una persona, lugar o cosa sagrada

saunter (sôn'tər) *v.* to walk in a slow, relaxed manner
   pasear *v.* caminar de una forma lenta y relajada

scenario (sĭ-nâr'ē-ō') *n.* a description of a possible course of action or events
   panorama *s.* descripción de un curso posible de acción

scruple (skrōō'pəl) *n.* a feeling of uneasiness that keeps a person from doing something
   escrúpulo *s.* malestar provocado por la conciencia o por los principios personales

serene (sə-rēn') *adj.* calm; peaceful
   sereno *adj.* calmo; con paz

sever (sĕv'ər) *v.* to cut off
   arrancar *v.* partir; cortar por completo

singularity (sĭng'gyə-lăr'ĭ-tē) *n.* something peculiar or unique
   singularidad *s.* rareza; peculiaridad

solace (sŏl'ĭs) *n.* comfort from sorrow or misfortune
   solaz *s.* consuelo frente al dolor o el infortunio

solicitously (sə-lĭs'ĭ-təs-lē) *adv.* in a manner expressing care or concern
   solícitamente *adv.* con preocupación e interés

spartan (spär'tn) *adj.* simple, plain, and frugal
   espartano *adj.* sencillo y frugal

squalor (skwŏl'ər) *n.* a filthy, shabby, and wretched condition, as from poverty
   escualidez *s.* condición sucia y miserable

squander (skwŏn'dər) *v.* to spend or use wastefully
   despilfarrar *v.* desperdiciar; gastar o usar algo descuidadamente

stagnating (stăg'nā'tĭng) *adj.* becoming foul or rotten from lack of movement **stagnate** *v.*
   estancado *adj.* putrefacto por falta de movimiento **estancar** *v.*

stalk (stôk) *n.* a stem or main axis of a plant
   tallo *s.* tronco o eje central de una planta

stark (stärk) *adj.* complete or utter; extreme
   marcado *adj.* absoluto; extremo

status quo (stăt'əs kwō) *n.* the existing state of affairs
   statu quo *s.* estado actual

stealth (stĕlth) *n.* cautious or secret action or movement
   secreto *s.* conducta callada u oculta

steel (stēl) *v.* to make hard or strong
   templar *v.* endurecer; fortalecer

stoicism (stō'ĭ-sĭz'əm) *n.* indifference to pleasure or pain; a lack of visible emotion
   estoicismo *s.* indiferencia ante el dolor o placer

subliminal (sŭb-lĭm'ə-nəl) *adj.* below the level of consciousness
   subliminal *adj.* por debajo de la conciencia

subside (səb-sīd') *v.* to decrease in amount or intensity; settle down
   calmarse *v.* tranquilizarse; disminuir

subsist (səb-sĭst') *v.* to support oneself at a minimal level
   subsistir *v.* vivir con lo mínimo

suffuse (sə-fyōōz') *v.* to gradually spread through or over
   envolver *v.* extenderse gradualmente

superannuated (sōō'pər-ăn'yōō-ā'tĭd) *adj.* obsolete with age
   caduco *adj.* que se ha vuelto obsoleto con el tiempo

supplication (sŭp'lĭ-kā'shən) *n.* a humble request or prayer
   súplica *s.* ruego; solicitud o petición humilde; rezo

surrogate (sûr'ə-gĭt) *adj.* serving as a substitute
   suplente *adj.* que sustituye

surveillance (sər-vā'ləns) *adj.* having to do with close observation
   vigilante *adj.* que hace una observación detallada

sustenance (sŭs'tə-nəns) *n.* food or provisions that sustain life
   sustento *s.* alimentos para vivir

tangible (tăn'jə-bəl) *adj.* capable of being touched or felt; having actual form and substance
   tangible *adj.* que puede tocarse o sentirse; que tiene forma o sustancia real

taut (tôt) *adj.* pulled or drawn tight
   tenso *adj.* tirante

termination (tûr'mə-nā'shən) *n.* an end, limit, or edge
   terminación *s.* fin de algo; límite u orilla

torrent (tôr'ənt) *n.* a heavy, uncontrolled outpouring
   torrente *s.* aguacero fuerte

transcend (trăn-sĕnd´) *v.* to pass beyond the limits of
  transcender *v.* ir más allá de los límites

travail (trə-vāl´) *n.* painful effort
  congoja *s.* esfuerzo doloroso

tremulous (trĕm´yə-ləs) *adj.* marked by trembling or shaking
  trémulo *adj.* tembloroso

trepidation (trĕp´ĭ-dā´shən) *n.* nervous fear
  trepidación *s.* incertidumbre; nerviosismo

uncanny (ŭn-kăn´ē) *adj.* so remarkable as to seem supernatural
  extraordinario *adj.* tan asombroso que parece sobrenatural

undulate (ŭn´jə-lāt´) *v.* to move in waves or in a smooth, wavelike motion
  ondular *v.* moverse en olas

unequivocal (ŭn´ĭ-kwĭv´ə-kəl) *adj.* allowing no doubt or misunderstanding
  inequívoco *adj.* que no admite duda o malentendido

unnerving (ŭn-nûr´vĭng) *adj.* causing loss of courage
unnerve *v.*
  desconcertante *adj.* que pone nervioso **desconcertar** *v.*

valorous (văl´ər-əs) *adj.* brave
  valeroso *adj.* valiente

veneer (və-nîr´) *v.* to cover with a thin layer of material
  enchapar *v.* cubrir con una fina capa de un material fino

vestibule (vĕs´tə-byōōl´) *n.* a small entryway within a building
  vestíbulo *s.* pequeña entrada en un edificio

vexation (vĕk-sā´shən) *n.* irritation; annoyance
  molestia *s.* irritación o ira

vigilant (vĭj´ə-lənt) *adj.* on the alert; watchful
  alerta *adj.* atento para evitar un peligro

wry (rī) *adj.* dryly humorous, often with a bit of irony
  irónico *adj.* de un humor seco; sardónico

zealous (zĕl´əs) *adj.* intensely enthusiastic
  fervoroso *adj.* intensamente dedicado y entusiasta

Pronunciation Key

Symbol	Examples	Symbol	Examples	Symbol	Examples
ă	**a**t, g**a**s	m	**m**an, see**m**	v	**v**an, sa**ve**
ā	**a**pe, d**ay**	n	**n**ight, mitte**n**	w	**w**eb, t**w**ice
ä	f**a**ther, b**a**rn	ng	si**ng**, ha**ng**er	y	**y**ard, law**y**er
âr	f**air**, d**are**	ŏ	**o**dd, n**o**t	z	**z**oo, rea**s**on
b	**b**ell, ta**b**le	ō	**o**pen, r**oa**d, gr**ow**	zh	trea**s**ure, gara**ge**
ch	**ch**in, lun**ch**	ô	**aw**ful, b**ough**t, h**o**rse	ə	**a**wake, ev**e**n, penc**i**l,
d	**d**ig, bor**ed**	oi	c**oi**n, b**oy**		pil**o**t, foc**u**s
ĕ	**e**gg, t**e**n	o͝o	l**oo**k, f**u**ll	ər	p**er**form, lett**er**
ē	**e**vil, s**ee**, m**ea**l	o͞o	r**oo**t, gl**ue**, thr**ough**		
f	**f**all, lau**gh**, **ph**rase	ou	**ou**t, c**ow**	**Sounds in Foreign Words**	
g	**g**old, bi**g**	p	**p**ig, ca**p**	KH	*German* i**ch**, au**ch**;
h	**h**it, in**h**ale	r	**r**ose, sta**r**		*Scottish* lo**ch**
hw	**wh**ite, every**wh**ere	s	**s**it, fa**c**e	N	*French* e**n**tre, bo**n**, fi**n**
ĭ	**i**nch, f**i**t	sh	**sh**e, ma**sh**	œ	*French* f**eu**, c**œu**r;
ī	**i**dle, m**y**, tr**ie**d	t	**t**ap, hopp**ed**		*German* sch**ö**n
îr	d**ear**, h**ere**	th	**th**ing, wi**th**	ü	*French* **u**tile, r**ue**;
j	**j**ar, **g**em, ba**dge**	*th*	**th**en, o**th**er		*German* gr**ü**n
k	**k**eep, **c**at, lu**ck**	ŭ	**u**p, n**u**t		
l	**l**oad, ratt**le**	ûr	f**ur**, **ear**n, b**ir**d, w**or**m		

Stress Marks

ˈ   This mark indicates that the preceding syllable receives the primary stress. For example, in the word *language,* the first syllable is stressed: lăngˈgwĭj.

ˌ   This mark is used only in words in which more than one syllable is stressed. It indicates that the preceding syllable is stressed, but somewhat more weakly than the syllable receiving the primary stress. In the word *literature,* for example, the first syllable receives the primary stress, and the last syllable receives a weaker stress: lĭtˈər-ə-cho͝orˌ.

INDEX OF FINE ART

Index of Skills

A

Abbreviations
    periods in, R49
    postal, R49
    Web, 1191
Academic vocabulary, 23, 185, 301, 401,
    507, 593, 667, 743, 829, 925, 1087,
    1187. *See also* Specialized vocabulary.
Act (in a play), 7, R102
Active listening, R82–R83
Active voice. *See* Voice.
Adjective clauses, 243, 249, R62
Adjective phrases, R60
Adjectives, 93, 490, 491, 495, R47, R57
    versus adverbs, R57
    avoiding too many, 205
    choosing, 495
    commas and, R49
    precise, 170, 196, 205, 284, 286
    predicate, R57, R60
    proper, R51
    sensory, 390
Adverb clauses, R62
Adverb phrases, R60
Adverbs, 93, 490, 491, 495, 565, 567, R47,
    R57
    versus adjectives, R57
    choosing, 495
    relative, 249
Advertising, 4, 10, 634–637, R90–R91
    audience and cost of, R84
    billboard, R90
    celebrities in, 635–636, R91
    flyer, R90
    infomercial, R90
    marketing, R90
    persuasive techniques in, 596, 635, R22,
        R91
    political ad, R90
    print ad, R90
    product comparison, R91
    product placement, R91
    promotional posters, 1025
    public service announcement, 634–637,
        R90
    sponsors, R90
    trailer, R90
    types of, R90–R91
Aesthetics and literary criticism. *See* Literary
    criticism.
Affixes. *See* Prefixes; Suffixes.

Agreement
    pronoun-antecedent, R52
    subject-verb agreement, R65–R67
Allegory, R102
Alliteration, 139, 142, 654, 670, 697, 797,
    895, 1098, R102. *See also* Sound devices.
Allusions, 95, 103, 608, 932, 933, 939, 987,
    999, 1017, 1096, 1115, 1119, 1126,
    1138, R102
    author's perspective and, 849
    to make inferences, 837, 843, 847, 849
Almanacs, 1197. *See also* References.
Ambiguity, interpreting, 907
Analogy, 598, 601, 608, 654, R71, R102. *See
    also* Rhetorical devices.
    false, R24
Analysis, writing, 490–497, 608, 726–733,
        812–819, 1051, 1170–1177, R37–R40
    definition, R40
    process, R40
Anapest, R109
Anecdotes, 447, 452, 454, 548, R30–R31
Angle, in news reporting, R89
Anglo-Saxon affix, 1139
Animation, 557, R88
Antagonist, 370, 930, 1033, R102
Antecedent-pronoun agreement, R52
Antonyms, 118, 176, 292, 392, 498, 584,
        658, 734, 820, 916, 1078, 1178, R71
Apostrophes, R50
Appeals
    by association, 596, R22
    to authority, R91
    bandwagon, 596, R22, R91
    emotional, 596, 611, 617, 635, 637, 655,
        656, R22, R91, R116
    ethical, 596
    to fear, 596, R22, R116
    logical, R91, R117
    to loyalty, R22
    to pity, 596, R22, R116
    "plain folks," 596
    to values, 596, R116
    to vanity, R22
Appearance in oral presentations, R77–R78
Applications, job, R44
Appositives, R60
Approaches to literature. *See* Literary
    criticism.
Archetypes, 1094, 1103, 1141, 1150, 1153,
    1164, 1167, R102

Arguments, 601, 602, 606, R115. *See also*
    Appeals; Persuasive writing.
    analysis of, 608, 617, 631, R21, R26
    claim, 594, 601, 608, 909, 911, R115
    counterarguments, 617, 650, 651, 654,
        661, R21, R116
    counterclaims, 650, 651
    deductive, R23, R116
    elements of, 594, 595
    by emotion, 596, 611, 617, 635, 637,
        655, R22, R91, R116
    ethical, 596
    evidence, 594, R21
    faulty, R24
    general principle, R23
    inductive, 631, R22–R23, R117
    logical, R118
    opposing, 908, 909
    reasons, 594, 595, 599, 601, 617, 633,
        653, 655, R21, R41
    strategies for determining strong, R26
    strategies for reading, 594, R21
    support, 594, 601, 608, 911, 912, R21,
        R119
    writing, 633, 851
Art. *See* Visuals.
Articles (part of speech), 220
Articles (written). *See* Feature articles; Journal
    articles; Magazine articles; News
    articles; Newspapers, articles in.
Articulation. *See* Speaking strategies.
Artistic effects. *See* Media presentations.
Aside, 930, 934, 939, 944, 991, R102
Assessment Practice
    reading comprehension, 176–179, 292–
        297, 392–397, 498–503, 584–589,
        658–663, 734–739, 820–825, 916–
        921, 1078–1083, 1178–1183
    vocabulary, 180, 296, 396, 502, 588, 662,
        824, 920, 1182
    writing and grammar, 181, 283, 295,
        297, 395, 397, 489, 501, 587, 589,
        649, 661, 737–739, 823, 825, 919,
        921, 1082, 1083, 1181, 1183, R101
Assonance, 670, 715, 716, 719, 895, 1098,
    R102
Assumptions, R115
Atlases, 1197. *See also* References.
Attitudes, comparing, 205, 231
Audience, 285, 650, 651, 1033
    media, 636, R85
    speaking and listening, 657, 1177, R76,
        R78, R83

target, 635, R85
writing, 16, 635, 908, 909, R34, R41, R42
Authority. *See* Arguments; Sources.
Author's background, 832, 875, 876, 881, 885, 886
Author's intent. *See* Author's purpose.
Author's message, 377, 639–648, R115
Author's perspective, 361, 362, 366, 370, 459, 460, 462, 464, 510, 522, 569, 573, 574, 575, 849, 860, R102
Author's point of view. *See* Author's perspective.
Author's position, R21, R40–R41, R115. *See also* Author's perspective; Author's purpose; Claims.
Author's purpose, 121, 122, 126, 130, 377, 506, 508, 509, 547, 548, 552, 554, 561, 562, 565, 566, 1061, R85, R102
Author's style. *See* Style.
Author's viewpoint. *See* Author's perspective.
Autobiographical essay, R102–R103
Autobiography, 4, 8, 9, 111, 114, 115, R102–R103. *See also* Memoirs.
  characterization in, 237, 238, 242, 245, 247
  dialogue in, 111, 114, 117
  interpreting, 117
  narrative techniques in, 117

B

Ballad, 715, 718, 719, R103
Bandwagon appeal, 596, R22, R91
Bar graphs, R5
Base words, R69
Bias, 621, R115
  analysis, 631
  in evidence, R25
  recognizing, 621, 623, 627, 629, 1201, R25
  in reporting, R90
Bibliography, 1200, 1204, R115. *See also* Works cited.
  MLA citation guidelines, 1228–1229
Biographical context, 247, 273, 323, 901
Biographical essay, 1197
Biographical references, 1197. *See also* References.
Biography, 4, 8, R103
  suspense in, 121, 124, 127, 129, 130
Blank verse, 932, 933, 939, 951, 963, 967, 1051, R103
Boldface type, as text feature, 510, R3
Boolean searches, 1192
Brainstorming, 19, 52, 287, 387, 389, 446, 579, 610, 1173, 1217
Bulleted list, as text feature, R3

Business and technical writing, R42–R43
  audience, R42
  correspondence, R115
  formats for, R43–R45
  key techniques, R42
  rubric for, R42
Bylaws, R45
Bylines, R14

C

Calculator, graphing, R17
Call to action, 652, 908, 910
Camera shots in film and video, 107, 1076
  camera movement, R87
  close-up, 109, 357, 358, 391, R87
  establishing, 391, R87
  extreme long, 109
  high-angle, 107, 108, 109, R87
  long, 109, 771, R87
  low-angle, 107, 108, 109, R87
  medium, 109, 391, R87
  pan, R87
  point-of-view, 107, 108, 109, 771, R87
  reaction, 771, R87
  tracking shot, R87
  zoom, R87
Capitalization
  in outlines, 422
  quick reference chart, R51
  in quotations, 496
Captions
  as text features, 510, 535, 536, R3
  in Web news report, 557
Career-related writing. *See* Business and technical writing.
Case, pronoun
  nominative, R53
  objective, R53
  possessive, R53
Casting, 949
Cast of characters, 934, R103
Cause-and-effect organization, 111, 262, 576, 577, R10–R11, R38, R115. *See also* Patterns of organization.
  setting and, 364
  in Shakespearean tragedy, 934
  in writing, 582, R38
Cause-and-effect relationships, reading, 111, 112, 116, 262
CD-ROMs, of reference works, 1194
Censorship, R86
Chain of events, 342, R38. *See also* Cause-and-effect organization.
Characterization, 235, 238, 242, 243, 245, 533, 873, R103
  across genres, 275, 278, 279, 280, 281
  in autobiography, 237, 247

in biography, 275, 278, 279, 281
methods of, 188, 189, 235, 237, 247, 275, 278, 279, 281, 339, 427, 533, 683, 1016, 1053
in poetry, 275, 280, 281
Characters, 384, 879, 946, 955, 973, 975, 980, 996, 1016, 1041, 1055, R103. *See also* Character types; Characterization.
  actions of, 188, 189, 341, 445
  analysis of, 203, 220, 233, 235, 325, 339, 341, 443, 445, 567, 683, 849, 991, 1017, 1033, 1167
  archetypes, 1103, 1150, 1153, 1164, 1167, R102
  cast of, 934, R103
  comparing and contrasting, 75, 91, 130, 218, 233
  creating memorable, 184, 387
  creating realistic, 167, 387
  describing, 873
  details in creating, 323
  development, 991
  dialogue in revealing, 388
  drawing conclusions about, 323, 480, 485, 840, 849
  evaluating, 93, 872, 1017, 1169, R116
  facial expressions, body language, and actions of, 1053
  humor of, R107
  making inferences about, 270, 353, 427, 428, 430, 432, 433, 434, 437, 441, 569, 570, 572, 575, 680, 991, 1016
  motivation of, 190, 207, 212, 215, 217, 218, 247, 531, 849, 980, 991, 994, 1017, 1018, 1026, 1138, 1158, 1162
  in narrative poetry, 145, 1067
  in narrative writing, R36
  physical appearance of, 188, 189
  plot and, 79, 82, 86, 89, 91
  point of view and, 186–187, 223, 226, 226, 229, 233, R110
  reactions of other, 188
  relationships between, 339, 427, 683, 1016
  settings in influencing, 302, 303
  social context of, 886, 1167
  study, 251, 252, 254, 256, 258, 262
  theme and, 404, 474
  thoughts of, 188, 189
  in tragedy, 931, 1036, 1040
  traits. *See* Character traits.
  for video presentation, 391
  words of, 188, 189
Character study, 251, 252, 254, 256, 258, 262
Character traits, 75, 188–189, 196, 200, 224, 226, 233, 237, 242, 249, 252,

evaluating, 621, 631, 1075, R23, R25
expert opinions, 909
providing, in speeches, R77
tracking, in reading argument, 594
Exaggeration, 765, 766, 769
Exclamation points, 174, R49
Expert opinion, 621, 909, R25, R41
Explanatory writing, 508, 509, 547. *See also*
Expository writing.
Exposition, of plot, 24, 25, 36, R106. *See
also* Plot.
Expository texts. *See* Nonfiction.
Expository writing, student, R37–R40
analysis, 490–497, 726–733, 812–819,
1170–1177, R39–R40
cause and effect, R32, R38
comparison and contrast in, 283,
284–291, 489, 649, 1068–1075, R32,
R37–R38
options for organization, R37–R40
problem-solution, 576–583, R39
research papers, 1210–1233
rubric for, 174, 290, 496, 582, 732, 818,
914, 1076, 1176, 1230, R37
Expressive writing. *See* Narrative writing.
Extemporaneous speeches, R76. *See also* Oral
presentations.
Extended metaphor, 725, 795, R106
External conflict, 24, 456, 761, R104
Eye contact, 819, 915, R78

F

Fable, R106
Facial expression in speeches, 819, 915
Facts, 621, 909, R116–R117. *See also*
Supporting statements.
in elaboration, R33
versus opinion, 623, 624, 626, 628, 630,
631, R25, R116–R117
recognizing, 621
verifying, R25
Fallacy, 914, R24, R117
Falling action, 24, 31, 130, R106. *See also*
Plot.
False analogy, R24
False cause, 914, R24
Fantasy, R106
Farce, 4, 803, 811, R106
Faulty reasoning, R24
Fear, appeal to, 596, R22, R116
Feature articles, 4, 8, 264–267, 422–425,
889, R117
Feedback. *See* Peer response.
Fiction, strategies for reading, 11–15, 831.
See also Reading skills and strategies.
Fiction, types of, 4, 5
fable, R106

fantasy, R106
historical, 831, R107
horror, R107
novellas, 4, 5, R109
novels, 4, 5, R109
realistic, R111
science, 5, 33, 639, 642–647, R112
short stories, 4, 5, 13–14, R112
tall tales, R114
Field research, 1206
Figurative language, 642, 648, 672, 673,
703, 704, 706, 707, 710, 712, 791,
991, 1098, 1103, 1119, 1169, R68,
R106
in descriptive writing, R34
epic similes, 1096, 1097, 1098, 1103,
1106, 1119, 1124, 1138, 1144, R105
epithets, 1096, 1097, 1109, 1113, 1116,
1122, 1138, R105
extended metaphor, 725, 795, R106
hyperbole, 627, 672, 775, R107, R114
metaphor, 672, 703, 707, 712, 793,
1156, 1169, R108
paradox, 281, R110
personification, 117, 672, 703, 710, 712,
907, R110
similes, 672, 703, 706, 1096, 1169, R112
Figure of speech. *See* Figurative language.
Film reviews, 1056–1061
Films, 1199, R86–R88. *See also* Camera shots
in film and video; Media elements and
techniques.
comparing with plays, 1070–1077
differences between text and, 359, 1073
documentaries, 1199
editing of, 107, 108, 391, 583, R88
feature, 4, 10
irony in, 357
mood in, 357, 772, 1054
script and written elements, R86, R112
setting in, 357, 1054
sound in, 107, 1054, 1076, R87
storyboard, 109, 391, 583, R86
style in, 771, 773
suspense in, 106, 107, 109
visual elements in, R87
First Amendment, R86
First-person narrator. *See* Narrators.
First-person point of view. *See* Point of view.
Firsthand and expressive writing. *See*
Narrative writing.
Flashbacks, 26, 27, 751, 759, 761, R36,
R106–R107
Flat characters, 233, R103
Flow chart, 733, 1231
Fluency in writing, 168, 284, 384, 490, 523,
576, 650, 908
Foils (character), 930, 967, R107

Folk ballads, R103
Folktales. *See* Oral tradition.
Foreground, 757
Foreign words in English, 618, R70
Foreshadowing, 26, 33, 34, 36, 37, 48, 121,
166, 443, 967, 996, 1034, 1129, R107
in creating suspense, 26, 33, 37, 75, 121,
166, R107, R113
Form in poetry, 6, 668, 693, 694, 696, 697,
R107
Formal language, 348, 355
Formatting
research paper, 1230
workplace documents, R42–R44
works cited, 1228–1229
Forms of writing. *See* Writing skills and
strategies.
Fragments. *See* Sentence fragments.
Framing (on screen), 668, 1053, R87
Freewriting, 17, 19, 729, 1173. *See also*
Quickwriting.
Free verse, 668, 669, 797, R107
Functional documents, 8. *See also* Consumer
documents; Workplace documents.
Functional reading, R3–R20

G

Generalizations, R117
hasty, R24
making, 267
overgeneralization, 621, 914, R24, R117,
R118
General pronoun reference, R55
Genre, 4, R107. *See also* Drama; Fiction;
Informational texts; Nonfiction; Poetic
forms.
characterization across, 275, 278, 279,
280, 281
comparing across, 274–283, 472–489,
638–649
theme across, 473
writer's message across, 639
Gerunds and gerund phrases, 843, 851, R61
Gestures, R79
Glittering generality, R22
Glossary, 1200, R15, R72
Government publications, R117
Grammar. *See also specific grammar concepts;*
Grammar handbook, R46–R65.
checking, 18, 174, 290, 390, 496, 582,
656, 732, 818, 914, 1076, 1176
style and, 40, 50, 69, 77, 82, 93, 105, 115,
119, 167, 196, 205, 214, 220, 232, 235,
243, 249, 316, 325, 331, 341, 348, 355,
434, 445, 462, 465, 503, 518, 523, 528,
533, 565, 567, 616, 619, 630, 633, 663,

P

Pace, 107, 108, 771, 915, R27, R88
Pacing. *See* Speaking strategies.
Pagination, 1230
Panel discussions, 497
Paradox, 281, R110
Paragraphs, R31–R32
  coherence of, R31–R32
  organizing, R31
  topic sentence in, R31, R120
  transitions in, R32–R33
  unity of, R31
Parallelism, 630, 654, 970, 1051, 1176, R64, R110
  as a rhetorical device, 598, 601, 606, 608, 633
Parallel plot, R110
Paraphrasing, 343, 344, 351, 419, 531, 562, 685, 688, 691, 783, 786, 787, 934, 967, 998, 1034, 1210, 1212, 1220, R118. *See also* Plagiarism.
Parentheses, R50
Parenthetical documentation, 1224, 1227
Parodies, 765, 766, 768, 769, R110
Participles and participial phrases, 683, R61
  dangling, R61
  misplaced, R61
  past, R55
  present, R55
Parts analysis, R40
Parts of a book, 1200
Parts of speech. *See also specific part of speech.*
  reference chart of, R46–R47
Passive voice. *See* Voice.
Past participle verb forms, 683, R55
Patterns of organization, 18, 284, 285, 490, 491, 494, 650, 651, 908, 909, 912, 1070, 1071, R8–R13, R118
  analysis of, 515, 519, 520, 522
  cause-effect, 262, 576, 577, R10–R11, R38, R115
  chronological, 26, 172, 510, 515, R9–R10, R36, R115
  classification, 511, R115
  comparison-contrast, 510, 515, 522, 523, 816, R11–R13, R37–R38, R115
  deductive, R23, R116
  effect-to-cause, R38
  hierarchical, 816, R35
  inductive, 631, R22–R23, R117
  main idea and supporting details, R8–R9
  order of importance, 816, R35
  order of impression, R35
  point-by-point, 288, 489, 1071, 1074, R11, R37, R41
  problem-solution, R39, R119
  reasons for opinion, R41

sequential, R119
  spatial order, R35, R119
  subject-by-subject, 288, 1074, R11, R38
Peer response, 17, 19, 174, 290, 390, 496, 582, 656, 732, 818, 914, 1076, 1176, 1230, R30
Performing arts. *See* Drama.
Periodicals, 1194, 1199, 1205, R118. *See also* Magazines; Newspapers.
Periods, R49
  in abbreviations, R49
  with quotation marks, 290, 496
Persona, R110. *See also* Speakers.
Personal essay, 8, R106
Personal narratives, 168–175. *See also* Narrative writing.
Personification, 117, 672, 703, 710, 712, 907, R110
Perspective. *See also* Point of view.
  analysis of, 237, 240, 245, 247
  author's, 361, 362, 366, 370, 459, 460, 462, 464, 510, 522, 569, 573, 574, 575, 849, 860, R102
  in literary criticism, 262
Persuasion, 592, R118. *See also* Persuasive techniques.
  craft of, 596
  in the media, 597
  in public service announcements, 635
  text analysis of, 599, R25–R26
Persuasive arguments, R21. *See also* Arguments.
Persuasive essay, 8, 908–915, R106
Persuasive language, 908, 910, 912
Persuasive speeches, 597, 650–657, R79, R83
Persuasive techniques, 611, 612, 614, 617, R22, R91, R118. *See also* Persuasion.
  appeals by association, 596, R22
  appeals to loyalty, R22
  appeals to pity, fear, or vanity, 596, 611, R22, R116
  bandwagon appeals, 596, R22, R91
  celebrity ads, 635–636, R91
  emotional appeals, 596, 611, 617, 635, 637, 655, R22, R91, R116
  ethical appeals, 596
  evaluating, 617, R25–R26
  glittering generality, R22
  loaded language, 596, 621, 623, 629, R25, R117
  logical appeals, R91, R117
  "plain folks" appeal, 596
  product comparison, R91
  recognizing, R22
  slogans, 635, R91
  snob appeal, R22
  testimonial, 596, R22
  transfer, 596, R22
  word choice in, 596, R22

Persuasive writing, 508, 547, R40–R41. *See also* Arguments.
  arguments, 631, 851
  essay, 8, 908–915, R106. (*See also* Expository writing.)
  key techniques, R40–R41
  opinion statement, 789
  options for organizing, R41
  rubric for, R40
Philosophical assumptions, R115
Philosophical context, 1017
Photographs, 536, 537, 543, 547, 548, 553, 554, R3, R5, R117, R119, R120
Phrases, R60–R62
  adjective, R60
  adverb, R60
  appositive, R60
  gerund, 851, R61
  infinitive, 713, R61
  participial, 683, R61
  prepositional, 69, 77, 390, R48, R60
  verbal, R60–R61
Plagiarism, 1221. *See also* Parenthetical documentation; Works cited.
Planned drafting, R28
Plays. *See also* Drama.
  comparing films with, 1070–1077
  strategies for reading, 934–935, 939, 967, 991, 1017, 1033, 1050, R2
Plot, 24, 36, 176, 292, 384, 386, 392, 498, 584, 658, 734, 820, 916, 1024, 1078, 1178, R110
  character interactions and, 79, 82, 86, 89, 91
  climax of, 24, 25, 111, 420, R104
  as clue to theme, 404
  complications in, 62, 70, R104
  conflict in, 24, 53, 54, 57, 62, 68, 70, 72, 79, 111, 140, 149, 957, 967, 991, 1008, R104
  development of, 24
  in drama, 149, 166
  in epic poem, 1094, 1141, 1153, 1167
  exposition of, 36, R106
  falling action in, 24, 31, 130, R106
  in narrative poetry, R109
  parallel, R110
  resolution in, 24, 130, 386, 1050
  rising action in, 24, 53, R112
  summarizing, 1141, 1167
Plot chart, 939
Plot diagram, 166, 939
Plot summary, 1141, 1167
Poetic devices and elements, 6, R110. *See also* Poetic forms.
  alliteration, 139, 142, 670, 697, 797, 1098
  assonance, 670, 715, 716, 719, 1098
  consonance, 670, 1098

V

Valid conclusion, R115
Validity of sources. *See* Sources, evaluating.
Vantage points. *See* Oral presentations.
Venn diagrams, 75, 233, 287, R12
Verb agreement. *See* Subject-verb agreement.
Verbal irony, 95, R108
Verbals and verbal phrases, R60–R62
    gerunds, 843, R61
    infinitives, 713, R61
    participles, 683, R55, R61
Verbs, R47, R48, R55–R57
    action, R47, R55
    auxiliary (helping), R47, R48, R56
    with compound subjects, R65
    intransitive, R47
    irregular, R55
    linking, R47, R55
    main, R48
    mood of
    objects of
    plural, R65
    precise, 102, 105, 170, 176, 292, 392, 498,
        584, 658, 734, 820, 916, 1078, 1178
    principal parts of, R55
    in reading consumer documents, R16, R17
    regular, R55
    sensory, 390
    singular, R65
    strong, in series, 115, 119, 176, 292, 392,
        498, 584, 658, 734, 820, 916, 1078,
        1178
    transitive, R47
    vivid, 869, 873
Verb tense, R55–R56
    choosing effective, 325
    errors in, R56
    future, R56
    future perfect, R56
    past, R56
    past perfect, R56
    present, 316, 325, R56
    present perfect, R56
    progressive forms, R56
    shifting, R56
Verifying information, 1205
Verse. *See* Poetic forms.
Video. *See* Media; Technology.
Video-editing software, 391, 583
Video presentations, 391
Viewing skills and strategies
    analyzing techniques, 558
    compare and contrast audience, 636
    comparing formats, 359, 558
    core concepts in media literacy, R84
    deconstructing media, R85
    drawing conclusions, 558
    5 W's and the H questions, 557

    making inferences, 636
    message analysis, 636, R92
    spotting lead, 557
Viewpoint. *See* Author's perspective; Bias.
Virtual libraries, 1208
Visual aids. *See also* Graphic aids.
    in oral presentations, 657, 117, R77
    in persuasive speech, 657
Visual effects, 391
Visual elements
    of film, 107–109, 356–359, 770–773,
        1052–1055, R87
    of TV, 556–559, R87
Visualizing, 12, 13, 53, 56, 57, 58, 63, 74,
        75, 149, 223, 224, 410, 703, 704, 708,
        711, 712, 803, 811, 1098, R120
Visuals, analysis of, 34, 43, 54, 65, 80, 89,
        96, 112, 122, 127, 128, 140, 194, 198,
        208, 213, 216, 224, 228, 238, 241,
        252, 259, 271, 276, 310, 316, 328,
        332, 344, 349, 362, 380, 410, 415,
        428, 436, 448, 460, 474, 516, 521,
        526, 529, 530, 562, 570, 602, 605,
        613, 641, 642, 678, 686, 696, 704,
        716, 723, 752, 757, 766, 776, 786,
        798, 838, 854, 864, 867, 876, 880,
        1064, 1092–1093, 1104, 1106, 1110,
        1127, 1130, 1136, 1142, 1146, 1148,
        1150, 1154, 1156, 1160, 1162
Vocabulary. *See also* Vocabulary skills and
    strategies.
    assessment practice, 180, 296, 396, 502,
        588, 662, 824, 920, 1182
    building your, 15
    in context, 33, 49, 53, 76, 79, 92, 95,
        104, 111, 118, 121, 131, 193, 204,
        207, 219, 223, 234, 237, 248, 251,
        263, 275, 282, 309, 324, 327, 340,
        343, 354, 361, 371, 409, 421, 427,
        444, 447, 457, 473, 488, 525, 532,
        535, 545, 546, 555, 601, 609, 611,
        618, 621, 632, 751, 762, 775, 781,
        783, 788, 837, 850, 853, 861, 875,
        887, 1103, 1139, 1141, 1168
    in writing, 49, 76, 92, 104, 118, 131,
        204, 219, 234, 248, 263, 282, 324,
        340, 354, 371, 421, 444, 457, 488,
        532, 545, 555, 609, 618, 632, 731,
        762, 781, 788, 850, 861, 887, 913,
        1139, 1168
Vocabulary skills and strategies, 15, R68–
    R75. *See also* Vocabulary.
    analogies, 598, 601, 608, 654, R71, R102
    antonyms, 118, R71
    base words, R69
    commonly confused words, R75
    connotation, 76, 324, 444, 781, R71,
        R104

    context clues, 371, 457, R68, R116
    denotation, 76, 324, 781, R71, R104
    dictionary, 618, R72
    foreign words in English, R70
    glossaries, 1200, R15, R72
    homonyms, 788, R71
    homophones, R71
    idioms, 887, R68, R108
    Internet words, 632
    multiple-meaning words, 248, R72
    political words, 609
    prefixes, 92, 762, 1139, R69
    root words. *See* word roots, *below.*
    specialized vocabulary, 263, 545, R72
    suffixes, 421, R69
    synonyms, 118, R70, R72
    word choice, 781
    word families, 131, 354, R70
    word origins, 234, 282, 488, R70
    word parts. *See* Word parts.
    word roots, 49, 104, 131, 204, 219, 340,
        354, 532, 555, 850, 861, 1168, R69
    words from Greek culture, 234
Voice. *See also* Oral presentations; Speaking
    strategies; Style.
    active, 384, 385, 389, 732, R57
    in literature, 746, 801, 812, 814, 849,
        863, 864, 868, 870, 872, 908, R114
    passive, R57
    in writing, 18, 168, 284
Volume. *See* Speaking strategies.

W

Webs (graphics), 52, 104, 204, 219, 236,
    340, 387, 458, 466, 532, 555, 653,
    780, 862, 1217
Web address, 1191, R20
Web sites, 4, 10, R120. *See also* Internet;
    References.
    evaluating, 1202–1203
    organizing, 1231–1232
    planning, 1231
    producing, 1232–1233
    reading, 1193
    writing text for, 1232
Word choice, 18, 576, 746, 765, 781, 812,
    860, 869–873, 1070. *See also* Diction.
    in author's perspective, 510
    compare and contrast of, 907
    in information sources
    making effective, 105
    in persuasive techniques, 596, R22, R91
    precise words, 102, 105, 168, 170, 196,
        205, 284, 286, 578, 726, 728, 812,
        813, 912, 1070, 1170, 1172, 1210
    tone and, 18, 530, 572, 746, 780, 1075,
        1175, R114

Word derivations. *See* Word families; Word parts; Word roots.

Word families, 131, 354, R70. *See also* Word roots.

Word order, 515, 685. *See also* Diction.

Word origins, 234, 282, 488, R70. *See also* Word roots.

Word parts, analyzing
  base words, R69
  prefixes, 92, 1139, R69
  roots, 49, 104, 131, 204, 219, 340, 354, 532, 555, 861, 1168, R69
  suffixes, R69

Word play, 775, 778, 932, 933

Word-processing software. *See* Software.

Word roots, R69
  Anglo-Saxon (Old English), R69
  Greek, 104, 532, 861, R69
  Latin, 49, 131, 204, 219, 340, 354, 555, 850, 1168, R69

Word structure. *See* Word roots.

Workplace and technical writing, R42–R45. *See also* Business writing.
  formats for, R43–R45
  key techniques in, R42
  matching the organization to the content, R42
  rubric for, R42

Workplace documents, 8, R19, R120. *See also* Business writing; Workplace and technical writing.
  strategies for reading, R19

Works cited, 1216, 1224, 1225, R120. *See also* Parenthetical documentation.
  direct quotations, 1213, 1214, 1221, 1223
  formatting, 1228–1229
  MLA citation guidelines, 1228–1229
  preparing list, 1224, 1225

Works consulted, R120

World Wide Web. *See* Internet.

Writer's message, 639, 640, 641, 642, 644, 645, 646, 647, 648. *See also* Author's message.

Writing
  across texts, 50, 220
  audience, 16, 284, 635, R34, R41, R42

format of, 16

goals in, R34

from literature, 168, 284, 384, 490, 576, 650, 726, 812, 908, 1070, 1170, 1210

peer response. *See* Peer response.

prompts, 19, 137, 171, 267, 489, 1217, R100

purpose of, 16

style, R113

Writing about literature, 168, 284, 384, 490, 576, 650, 726, 812, 908, 1070, 1170, 1210

Writing for assessment, 181, 283, 295, 297, 395, 397, 489, 501, 587, 589, 649, 737–739, 823, 825, 919, 921, 1082, 1083, 1181, 1183, R100, R101

Writing modes. *See* Descriptive writing; Expository writing; Narrative writing; Persuasive writing; Writing about literature.

Writing process, 17, R28–R29
  drafting, 17, 172, 288, 388, 489, 494, 580, 654, 729, 730, 816, 912, 1074, 1174, 1223–1225, R28
  evaluating, 17, 174, 290, 390, 496, 582, 656, 732, 818, 914, 1076, 1176, 1230, R34–R42
  peer response in, 17, 19, 174, 290, 390, 496, 582, 656, 732, 818, 914, 1076, 1176, 1230, R30
  prewriting, 17, 19, 52, 94, 148, 171, 206, 222, 287, 387, 493, 579, 653, 729, 815, 911, 1073, 1173, 1217, R28
  proofreading, R29
  publishing, 17, 174, 290–291, 390–391, 496–497, 582–583, 656–657, 732–733, 818–819, 914–915, 1076, 1176, 1231–1233, R29
  reflecting, R29–R30
  revising and editing, 17, 50, 93, 105, 119, 167, 173, 235, 289, 325, 341, 355, 389, 445, 495, 523, 533, 581, 619, 655, 731, 817, 851, 913, 1051, 1075, 1169, 1175, 1226–1227, R29

Writing skills and strategies. *See also* Reading-writing connection.
  analogies, 598, 601, 608, 654, R71, R102
  anecdotes, R30–R31
  cause and effect, 582, R32, R38, R115
  characters, creating, 167, 184, 323
  coherence, R31–R32
  compare and contrast, 284–291, 523, 544, 1061, 1069, R32, R115
  conciseness, 341, 713, 851
  description, 105, 205, R30, R34
  details, 168, 169, 384, 385, 390, 494, 726, 727, 812, 813, R33
  dialogue, 50, 167, 168, 169, 174, 341, 388, 851, R36
  elaboration, 727, 812, 813, 1174, R33–R34
  examples, 284, 286, 289, R34
  humor, R107
  organization. *See* Patterns of organization.
  parallelism, 598, 601, 606, 608, 630, 633, 654, 970, 1051, 1176, R64, R110
  precise language, 102, 105, 168, 170, 205, 284, 286, 578, 726, 728, 912
  quotations, 726, 727, 1210, 1213, 1221
  rhetorical devices, 604, 606, 633, 650, 651, R111
  rhetorical questions, 462, 465, R119
  sentence variety, 18, 168, 169, 214, 220, 284, 285, 445, 490, 492, 495, 578, 726, 728, 731, 789, 812, 814, 817, 908, 910, 1070, 1170, 1171, 1210, 1215
  style, R113
  tone, 18, 168, 173, 289, 490, 492, 495, 726, 727, 746, 1075, 1170, 1171, 1175, 1210, 1214, 1227
  transitions, 288, 731, 908, 910, 1070, 1071, 1074, 1175, 1210, 1215, 1227, R32
  unity, R31
  word choice, 18, 105, 510, 530, 572, 576, 746, 765, 780, 781, 812, 860, 907, 1070, 1075, 1170, 1172, 1175, 1210, R22

INDEX OF TITLES & AUTHORS

Page numbers that appear in italics refer to biographical information.

ACKNOWLEDGMENTS

UNIT 1

Pollinger Limited: Excerpt from *The Splendid Outcast: Beryl Markham's African Stories* compiled and introduced by Mary S. Lovell. Copyright © 1987 by the Beryl Markham Estate. Reproduced by permission of Pollinger Limited and the proprietor.

Eugenia Collier: "Sweet Potato Pie," by Eugenia Collier from *Black World,* August 1972, pp. 54–62. Copyright © 1969 by Eugenia Collier. Reprinted by permission of the author.

Scholastic Inc.: "Checkouts" from *A Couple of Kooks and Other Stories* by Cynthia Rylant. Published by Orchard Books/Scholastic Inc. Copyright © 1990 by Cynthia Rylant. All rights reserved. Used by permission.

Don Congdon Associates, Inc.: Excerpt from "A Sound of Thunder" from *R is for Rocket* by Ray Bradbury. Copyright © 1952 by Crowell Collier Publishing, renewed 1980 by Ray Bradbury. Reprinted by permission of Don Congdon Associates, Inc.

Newsweek, Inc.: "From Here to There: The Physics of Time Travel," by Brad Stone, from *Newsweek,* March 16, 1998. Copyright © 1998 by Newsweek. Reprinted by permission of Newsweek, Inc.

Brandt & Hochman Literary Agents, Inc.: "The Most Dangerous Game" by Richard Connell. Copyright © 1924 by Richard Connell. Copyright renewed 1952 by Louise Fox Connell. Reprinted by permission of Brandt & Hochman Literary Agents, Inc.

Susan Bergholz Literary Services: "Daughter of Invention," from *How the Garcia Girls Lost Their Accents* by Julia Alvarez. Copyright © 1991 by Julia Alvarez. Published by Plume, an imprint of The Penguin Group (USA) and originally in hardcover by Algonquin Books of Chapel Hill. Reprinted by permission of Susan Bergholz Literary Services, New York. All rights reserved.

HarperCollins: Excerpt from *Black Boy* by Richard Wright. Copyright 1937, 1942, 1945 by Richard Wright; renewed 1973 by Ellen Wright. Reprinted by permission of HarperCollins Publishers Inc.

Random House, Inc.: Excerpt from *Seabiscuit: An American Legend* by Laura Hillenbrand. Copyright © 2001 by Laura Hillenbrand. Used by permission of Random House, Inc.

Laura Hillenbrand: "Four Good Legs Between Us," from *American Heritage,* July/August 1998, by Laura Hillenbrand. Copyright © 1998 by Laura Hillenbrand. Reprinted by permission of the author.

WGBH/Boston: Excerpt from "Timeline: Seabiscuit" from the American Experience Web site located at http://www.pbs.org/wgbh/amex/seabiscuit/timeline/timeline2.html. Copyright © 2003 by WGBH/Boston. Reprinted by permission of WGBH Educational Foundation.

NBC News Archives: Excerpt from the radio broadcast "Santa Anita Handicap," by Clem McCarthy and Buddy Twist. Copyright © 1937 by NBC News Archives. Reprinted by permission of NBC News Archives.

Alfred A. Knopf: "Incident in a Rose Garden" from *Collected Poems* by Donald Justice. Copyright © 2004 by Donald Justice. Reprinted by permission of Alfred A. Knopf, a division of Random House, Inc.

Stephen King: "Sorry, Right Number" by Stephen King. Copyright © 1993 by Stephen King. Reprinted with permission.

Simon & Schuster: Excerpt from *On Writing: A Memoir of the Craft* by Stephen King. Copyright © 2000 by Stephen King. Reprinted with the permission of Scribner, an imprint of Simon & Schuster Adult Publishing Group.

Sandra Dijkstra Literary Agency: "Fish Cheeks" by Amy Tan first appeared in *Seventeen* magazine. Copyright © 1987 by Amy Tan. Reprinted and digitalized with permission of the author and the Sandra Dijkstra Literary Agency.

Persea Books: Excerpt from "Piedra," from *The Effects of Knut Hamsun on a Fresno Boy: Recollections and Short Essays* by Gary Soto. Copyright © 1983, 1988, 2000 by Gary Soto. Reprinted by permission of Persea Books, Inc. (New York).

UNIT 2

Random House: Excerpt from *The Chocolate War* by Robert Cormier. Copyright © 1974 by Robert Cormier. Used by permission of Random House Children's Books, a division of Random House, Inc.

HarperCollins Publishers: Excerpt from "Life Without Go-Go Boots," by Barbara Kingsolver from *High Tide in Tucson: Essays from Now or Never.* Copyright © 1995 by Barbara Kingsolver. Reprinted by permission of HarperCollins Publishers Inc.

Excerpt from *To Kill a Mockingbird* by Harper Lee. Copyright © 1960 by Harper Lee. Forward copyright © 1993 by Harper Lee. Reprinted by permission of HarperCollins Publishers.

Bancroft Library: Excerpt from *Picture Bride* by Yoshiko Uchida. Copyright © 1987 by Yoshiko Uchida. Reprinted by permission of the Bancroft Library, University of California, Berkeley.

Sll/Sterling Lord Literistic, Inc.: "Pancakes," by Joan Bauer from *Trapped! Cages of Mind and Body* by Lois Duncan. Copyright © 1998 by Joan Bauer. Reprinted by permission of Sll/Sterling Lord Literistic, Inc.

Harcourt: "The Necklace" by Guy de Maupassant from *Adventures in Reading,* Laureate Edition, Grade 9. Copyright © 1963 by Harcourt, Inc., and renewed 1991. Reprinted by permission of the publisher. This material may not be reproduced in any form or by any means without prior written permission of the publisher.

Naomi Shihab Nye: "Hamadi" by Naomi Shihab Nye. Copyright © 1993 by Naomi Shihab Nye. First published in *America Street,* edited by Anne Mazer. Reprinted by permission of the author.

Random House, Inc.: Excerpt from "Sister Flowers," from *I Know Why the Caged Bird Sings* by Maya Angelou. Copyright © 1969 and renewed © 1997 by Maya Angelou. Used by permission of Random House, Inc.

"Caged Bird," from *Shaker, Why Don't You Sing?* by Maya Angelou. Copyright © 1983 by Maya Angelou. Used by permission of Random House, Inc.

Time: "Blind to Failure" by Karl Taro Greenfeld from *Time,* June 18, 2001. Copyright © 1991 by Time, Inc. Reprinted by permission.

Anne Stein: "A Different Level of Competition" by Anne Stein from *Chicago Tribune,* February 24, 2002. Copyright © 2002 by Anne Stein. Reprinted by permission of the author.

Arte Público Press: "A Voice," from *Communion* by Pat Mora. Copyright © 1991 by Pat Mora. Reprinted with permission of Arte Público Press, University of Houston.

Simon J. Ortiz: "My Father's Song," by Simon J. Ortiz from *Going for the Rain* originally published by Harper & Row Publishers, Inc. Copyright © 1976 by Simon J. Ortiz.

Penguin Group (USA) Inc.: Excerpt from "The Bus Boycott" from *Rosa Parks* by Douglas Brinkley. Copyright © 2000 by Douglas Brinkley. Used by permission of Viking Penguin, a division of Penguin Group (USA) Inc.

Rita Dove: "Rosa" by Rita Dove was first published in the *Georgia Review,* Winter 1998, and subsequently in *On the Bus with Rosa Parks,* published by W.W. Norton. Copyright © 1999 by Rita Dove. Reprinted by permission of the author.

Random House, Inc.: "Powder," from *The Night in Question* by Tobias Wolff. Copyright © 1996 by Tobias Wolff. Used by permission of Alfred A. Knopf, a division of Random House, Inc.

Brooks Permissions: "Description of Maud Martha," from *Blacks* by Gwendolyn Brooks. Copyright © 1945, 1949, 1953, 1960, 1963, 1969, 1970, 1971, 1975, 1981, 1987 by Gwendolyn Brooks Blakely. Reprinted by consent of Brooks Permissions.

UNIT 3

Harcourt, Inc.: Excerpt from *Nineteen Eighty-Four* by George Orwell. Copyright © 1949 by Harcourt, Inc., and renewed 1977 by Sonia Brownell Orwell. Reprinted by permission of the publisher. This material may not be reproduced in any form or by any means without the prior written permission of the publisher.

Arkham House Publishers: Excerpt from "The Music of Erich Zann" by H. P. Lovecraft, from *Masterpieces of Terror and the Supernatural,* selected by Marvin Kaye. Copyright © 1925. Used by permission of Arkham House Publishers, Inc., and Arkham's agent, JABberwocky Literary Agency.

Sabine R. Ulibarrí: Excerpt from "My Wonder Horse/Mi caballo mago." From *Tierra Amarilla: Stories of New Mexico* by Sabine R. Ullibarí, translated from the Spanish by Thelma Campbell Nason. Reprinted by permission of the author.

Random House, Inc.: "A Christmas Memory" by Truman Capote. Copyright © 1956 by Truman Capote. Used by permission of Random House, Inc.

HarperCollins Publishers and Jonathan Clowes: "Through the Tunnel," from *The Habit of Loving* by Doris Lessing. Copyright © 1954, 1955 by Doris Lessing, originally appeared in the *New Yorker.* Reprinted by permission of HarperCollins Publishers Inc. and the kind permission of Jonathan Clowes Ltd., London, on behalf of Doris Lessing.

The Estate of Edward Rowe Snow: Excerpt from "The Roving Skeleton of Boston Bay" by Edward Rowe Snow, from *Yankee* magazine. Reprinted by permission of Dorothy Snow Bicknell on behalf of the Estate of Edward Rowe Snow.

Broadway Books and Doubleday Canada: Excerpt from *A Walk in the Woods* by Bill Bryson. Copyright © 1997 by Bill Bryson. Used by the permission of Broadway Books, a division of Random House, Inc., and Doubleday Canada, a division of Random House of Canada Limited.

Doubleday: "Wilderness Letter" from *The Sound of Mountain Water* by Wallace Stegner. Copyright © 1969 by Wallace Stegner. Used by permission of Doubleday, a division of Random House, Inc.

New Directions: "The Sharks," from *Collected Earlier Poems 1940–1960* by Denise Levertov. Copyright © 1957, 1958, 1959, 1960, 1961, 1979 by Denise Levertov. Reprinted by permission of New Directions Publishing Corp.

Farrar, Straus and Giroux: "The Peace of Wild Things," from *Collected Poems: 1957–1982* by Wendell Berry. Copyright © 1985 by Wendell Berry. Reprinted by permission of North Point Press, a division of Farrar, Straus and Giroux, LLC.

Houghton Mifflin: Excerpt from *The Hobbit* by J.R.R. Tolkien. Copyright © 1937 by George Allen & Unwin Ltd. Copyright © 1966 by J.R.R. Tolkien. Copyright © renewed 1994 by Christopher R. Tolkien, John F.R. Tolkien, and Priscilla M.A.R. Tolkien. Copyright © restored 1996 by the Estate of J.R.R. Tolkien, assigned 1997 to the J.R.R. Tolkien Copyright Trust. Reprinted by permission of Houghton Mifflin Company. All rights reserved.

UNIT 4

PFD: "The Sniper," from *Spring Sowing* by Liam O'Flaherty. Copyright © 1924 by the Estate of Liam O'Flaherty. Reproduced by permission of PFD (www.pfd.co.uk) on behalf of the Estate of Liam O'Flaherty.

Eugenia Collier: "Marigolds," from *Breeder and Other Stories* by Eugenia Collier. Copyright © 1994 by Eugenia Collier. First published by Black Classic Press, Baltimore. Reprinted by permission of the author.

Donna Freedman: "Sowing Change" from *Chicago Tribune,* August 31, 2003, by Donna Freedman. Copyright © 2003 by Donna Freedman. Reprinted by permission of the author.

James Hurst: "The Scarlet Ibis" by James Hurst. Copyright © 1960 by the *Atlantic Monthly* and renewed 1988 by James Hurst. Reprinted by permission of James Hurst.

Naomi Long Madgett: "Woman With Flower," from *Star By Star* by Naomi Long Madgett. Copyright © 1965, 1970 by Naomi Long Madgett. Published originally by Lotus Press, Inc. Reprinted by permission of the author.

Ruth Cohen, Inc.: "Math and After Math" by Lensey Namioka from *Going Where I'm Coming From,* edited by Anne Mazer. Reprinted by permission of Lensey Namioka. All rights are reserved by the author.

Aragi Inc. and Edwidge Danticat: "The Future in My Arms" by Edwidge Danticat, first published in *Ebony* magazine. Reprinted by permission of Edwidge Danticat and Aragi Inc.

Thames & Hudson Ltd.: "Poem on Returning to Dwell in the Country," from *T'ao the Hermit: Sixty Poems by Tao Chien* by Tao Ch'ien, translated by William Acker. Copyright © 1952 by William Acker. Reprinted by kind permission of Thames & Hudson Ltd., London.

UNIT 5

UNIT 6

UNIT 7

New Directions: "I Am Offering This Poem," by Jimmy Santiago Baca from *Immigrants In Our Own Land.* Copyright © 1982 by Jimmy Santiago Baca. Reprinted by permission of New Directions Publishing Corp.

Random House, Inc.: "My Papa's Waltz," by Theodore Roethke from *Complete Poems of Theodore Roethke.* Copyright © 1942 by Hearst Magazines, Inc. Used by permission of Doubleday, a division of Random House, Inc.

BOA Editions, Ltd.: "I Ask My Mother to Sing," from *Rose, poems by Li-Young Lee* by Li-Young Lee. Copyright © 1986 by Li-Young Lee. Reprinted by permission of BOA Editions, Ltd.

Rita Dove: "Grape Sherbet," by Rita Dove from *Museum* published by Carnegie-Mellon University Press. Copyright © 1983 by Rita Dove. Reprinted by permission of the author.

Liveright: "Spring is like a perhaps hand," by E. E. Cummings from *Complete Poems: 1904–1962.* Copyright © 1923, 1925, 1951, 1953, 1991 by the Trustees for the E. E. Cummings Trust. Copyright © 1976 by George James Firmage. Used by permission of Liveright Publishing Corporation.

Houghton Mifflin: "Elegy for the Giant Tortoises," by Margaret Atwood from *Selected Poems 1965–1975.* Copyright © 1976 by Margaret Atwood. Reprinted by permission of Houghton Mifflin Company. All rights reserved.

Random House, Inc.: "Today," by Billy Collins from *Nine Horses.* Copyright © 2002 by Billy Collins. Used by permission of Random House, Inc.

W. W. Norton: "400-Meter Freestyle," by Maxine Kumin from *Selected Poems 1960–1990.* Copyright © 1959 and renewed 1987 by Maxine Kumin. Used by permission of W. W. Norton & Company, Inc.

Harcourt, Inc.: "Bodybuilders' Contest," by Wislawa Szymborska, English translation by Stanislaw Baranczak and Clare Cavanaugh from *View with a Grain of Sand.* Copyright © 1993 by Wislawa Szymborska, English translation copyright 1995 by Harcourt, Inc. Reprinted by permission of the publisher. This material may not be reproduced in any form or by any means without the prior written permission of the publisher.

Scholastic: "The Night Poetry Rocked the House" by Rachel Shapiro from the *New York Times Upfront* magazine, September 4, 2000. Copyright © 2000 by Scholastic Inc. and The New York Times Company. Reprinted by permission of Scholastic Inc.

Al Young: "For Poets" by Al Young. Copyright © 1968, 1992 by Al Young. Reprinted by permission of the author.

University of California Press: "Ode to My Socks," by Pablo Neruda from *Selected Odes of Pablo Neruda,* translated by Margaret Sayers Peden. Copyright © 1990 by Regents of the University of California and Fundación Pablo Neruda. Reprinted by permission of the University of California Press.

Agencia Literaria Carmen Balcells: "Oda a los calcetines," by Pablo Neruda from *Nuevas odas elementales.* Copyright © 1956 by Fundación Pablo Neruda. Reprinted by permission of Agencia Literaria Carmen Balcells, S.A. on behalf of Fundación Pablo Neruda.

Laurel Winter: "egg horror poem," by Laurel Winter from *Nebula Awards: Showcase 2001,* edited by Robert Silverberg. Copyright © 2001 by Laurel Winter. Reprinted by permission of the author.

Random House, Inc.: "O What Is That Sound," by W. H. Auden from *Collected Poems* by W. H. Auden. Copyright © 1937 and renewed 1965 by W. H. Auden. Used by permission of Random House, Inc.

"To be of Use," by Marge Piercy from *Circles on the Water.* Copyright © 1982 by Marge Piercy. Used by permission of Alfred A. Knopf, a division of Random House, Inc.

UNIT 8

Random House, Inc.: Excerpt from *Bird by Bird* by Anne Lamott. Copyright © 1994 by Anne Lamott. Reprinted by permission of Random House, Inc.

Susan Bergholz: Excerpt from "Geraldo No Last Name" from *The House on Mango Street* by Sandra Cisneros. Copyright 1984 by Sandra Cisneros. Published by Vintage Books, a division of Random House, Inc., and in hardcover by Alfred A. Knopf in 1994. Reprinted by permission of Susan Bergholz Literary Services, New York. All rights reserved.

International Creative Management: Excerpt from "Single Room, Earth View" by Sally Ride from *Air & Space,* April/May 1986. Copyright © 1986 by Sally Ride. Reprinted by permission of International Creative Management, Inc.

Tim O'Brien: "Where Have You Gone, Charming Billy?" by Tim O'Brien, from *Redbook,* May 1975. Copyright © 1975 by Tim O'Brien. Reprinted by permission of the author.

Scissor Press: Interview with Tim O'Brien by Douglas Novielli, Chris Connal, and Jackson Ellis. From *Verbicide,* Issue 8. Copyright © 2003 by Scissor Press. Reprinted by permission of Scissor Press.

Barbara Hogenson Agency: "The Princess and the Tin Box," from *The Beast In Me and Other Animals* by James Thurber. Copyright © 1948 by James Thurber. Copyright renewed 1976 by Helen Thurber and Rosemary A. Thurber. Reprinted by arrangement with Rosemary A. Thurber and The Barbara Hogenson Agency. All rights reserved.

HarperCollins Publishers: "Going to Japan," from *Small Wonder: Essays* by Barbara Kingsolver. Copyright © 2002 by Barbara Kingsolver. Reprinted by permission of HarperCollins Publishers Inc.

Harcourt: "A Few Words," from *Blue Pastures* by MaryOliver. Copyright © 1995, 1992, 1991 by Mary Oliver. Reprinted by permission of Harcourt, Inc. This material may not be reproduced in any form or by any means without the prior written permission of the publisher.

Harvard University Press: "A Narrow Fellow in the Grass" and "'Hope' Is the Thing with Feathers" by Emily Dickinson from *The Poems of Emily Dickinson,* edited by Thomas H. Johnson, Cambridge, Mass.: The Belknap Press of Harvard University Press. Copyright © 1951, 1955, 1979 by the President and Fellows of Harvard College. Reprinted by permission of the publishers and the Trustees of Amherst College.

HarperCollins Publishers: "Luxury" and "Kidnap Poem" by Nikki Giovanni from *The Selected Poems of Nikki Giovanni.* Compilation copyright © 1996 by Nikki Giovanni. Reprinted by permission of HarperCollins Publishers, Inc.

Gary N. DaSilva: "The Sneeze" from *The Good Doctor,* by Neil Simon. Copyright © 1974 by Neil Simon, copyright renewed 2004 by Neil Simon. Professionals and amateurs are hereby warned that *The Good Doctor* is fully protected under the Berne Convention and the Universal Copyright Convention and is subject to royalty. All rights, including without limitation professional, amateur, motion picture, television, radio, recitation, lecturing, public reading and foreign translation rights, computer media rights and the right of reproduction, and electronic storage or retrieval, in whole or in part and in any form, are strictly reserved and none of these rights can be exercised or used without written permission from the copyright owner. Inquiries for stock and amateur performances should be addressed to Samuel French, Inc., 45 West 25th Street, New York, NY 10010. All other inquiries should be addressed to Gary N. DaSilva, 111 N. Sepulveda Blvd., Manhattan Beach, CA, 90266-6850.

UNIT 9

The Wylie Agency: Excerpt from "The Names of Women" by Louise Erdrich, originally published in *The Granta Book of the Family.* Copyright © 1995 by Louise Erdrich. Reprinted with permission of The Wylie Agency Inc.

Farrar, Straus and Giroux: Excerpt from "The Son from America," from *A Crown of Feathers and Other Stories* by Isaac Bashevis Singer. Copyright © 1973 by Isaac Bashevis Singer. Reprinted by permission of Farrar, Straus and Giroux, LLC.

Jewish Museum in Prague: Excerpt from "The Butterfly," by Pavel Friedmann from … *I Never Saw Another Butterfly: Children's Drawings and Poems from Terezin Concentration Camp 1942–1944.* Copyright © 1962 by the State Jewish Museum in Prague. Reprinted by permission of the Jewish Museum in Prague.

Alberto Ríos: "The Vietnam Wall," by Alberto Ríos from *The Lime Orchard Woman.* Copyright © 1988 by Alberto Ríos. Reprinted by permission of the author.

Simon & Schuster: Excerpt from *Angela's Ashes* by Frank McCourt. Copyright © 1996 by Frank McCourt. Reprinted with the permission of Scribner, an imprint of Simon & Schuster Adult Publishing Group.

Reader's Digest: Excerpt from "The Education of Frank McCourt," by Barbara Sande Dimmitt published in *Reader's Digest,* November 1977. Copyright © 1997 by The Reader's Digest Association, Inc. Reprinted with the permission of Reader's Digest.

N. Scott Momaday: "Revisiting Sacred Ground," by N. Scott Momaday from *The Man Made of Words.* Copyright © 1997 by N. Scott Momaday. Reprinted by permission of the author.

Random House, Inc.: "Blues Ain't No Mocking Bird," by Toni Cade Bambara from *Gorilla, My Love.* Copyright © 1971 by Toni Cade Bambara. Used by permission of Random House, Inc.

University of Georgia Press: "American History," from *The Latin Deli: Prose & Poetry* by Judith Ortiz Cofer. Copyright © 1992 by Judith Ortiz Cofer. Reprinted by permission of the University of Georgia Press.

Dallas Morning News: Excerpt from "President Dead" by George Carter, from the *Dallas Times Herald,* November 22, 1963. Copyright © 1963 by The Dallas Times Herald. Reprinted by permission of the Dallas Morning News.

Lady Bird Johnson: Excerpt from *A White House Diary* by Lady Bird Johnson. Copyright © 1970 by Claudia T. Johnson. Reprinted by permission of Mrs. Lyndon B. Johnson.

U.S. News & World Report: "Dark Day" by Kenneth T. Walsh from *U.S. News & World Report,* November 24, 2003. Copyright © 2003 by U.S. News & World Report. Reprinted by permission of U.S. News & World Report.

Random House, Inc.: "Theme for English B," by Langston Hughes from *The Collected Poems of Langston Hughes.* Copyright © 1994 by The Estate of Langston Hughes. Used by permission of Alfred A. Knopf, a division of Random House, Inc.

HarperCollins Publishers: "Harvest moon—," "Heat waves shimmering," and "You could turn this way," by Matsuo Bashō from *The Essential Haiku: Versions of Bashō, Buson & Issa,* edited and with an introduction by Robert Hass. Introduction and selection copyright © 1994 by Robert Hass. Used by permission of HarperCollins Publishers, Inc.

Arcade Publishing: "From a tenement," "Twisting violently," and "Standing in the crowd," by Richard Wright from *Haiku: This Other World.* Copyright © 1998 by Ellen Wright, published by Arcade Publishing, New York, New York. Reprinted by permission of Richard Wright.

Aaron Naparstek: "clinton street autos," by Aaron Naparstek from www.honku.org. Copyright © 2003 by Aaron Naparstek. Reprinted by permission of the author.

Random House, Inc.: "Morning commuters," and "When the light turns green" from *HONKU* by Aaron Naparstek. Copyright © 2003 by Aaron Naparstek. Reprinted by permission of Villard Books, a division of Random House, Inc.

Pryor Cashman Sherman & Flynn LLP: Excerpt from *All Quiet on the Western Front* by Erich Maria Remarque. Copyright © 1929, 1930 by Little, Brown and Company, copyright renewed 1957, 1958 by Erich Maria Remarque. *Im Westen Nichts Neus* by Erich Maria Remarque. Copyright © 1928 by Ullstein A.G., copyright renewed 1957, 1958 by Erich Maria Remarque. Reprinted by permission of Pryor Cashman Sherman & Flynn LLP on behalf of the Estate of Erich Maria Remarque.

UNIT 10

Universal Press Syndicate: Excerpt from "Romeo and Juliet" by Roger Ebert, from the *Chicago Sun-Times,* September 17, 2000. Copyright © 2000 by The Ebert Company. Reprinted with permission. All rights reserved.

Harcourt, Inc.: Excerpt from *The Metamorphoses of Ovid: A New Verse Translation* by Allen Mandelbaum. English translation copyright © 1993 by Allen Mandelbaum. Reprinted by permission of Harcourt, Inc. This material may not be reproduced in any form or by any means without the prior written permission of the publisher.

UNIT 11

Farrar, Straus and Giroux: Excerpts from *The Odyssey* by Homer, translated by Robert Fitzgerald. Translation copyright © 1961, 1963 renewed 1989 by Benedict R. C. Fitzgerald on behalf of the Fitzgerald children. This edition © 1998 by Farrar, Straus & Giroux, LLC. Reprinted by permission of Farrar, Straus and Giroux, LLC.

Penguin Group (USA) Inc.: "Penelope," by Dorothy Parker from *The Portable Dorothy Parker,* edited by Brendan Gill. Copyright © 1928, renewed 1956 by Dorothy Parker. Used by permission of Viking Penguin Group (USA) Inc.

UNIT 12

Dallas Morning News: Excerpt from "Animal ER" by Aline McKenzie from the *Dallas Morning News,* January 19, 2005. Copyright © 2005 by The Dallas Morning News. Reprinted with the permission of The Dallas Morning News.

STUDENT RESOURCE BANK

Broadway Books and Doubleday Canada: Excerpt from *A Walk in the Woods* by Bill Bryson. Copyright © 1997 by Bill Bryson. Used by the permission of Broadway Books, a division of Random House, Inc. and Doubleday Canada, a division of Random House of Canada Limited.

Newsweek: Excerpt from "e-Life: How the Internet is Changing America" from *Newsweek,* September 20, 1999. Copyright © 1999 by Newsweek, Inc. All rights reserved. Reprinted by permission.

Center for Media Literacy: The "Five Core Concepts in Media Literacy" may be found in the *CML MediaLit Kit ™/Part I—Literacy for the 21st Century: An Overview and Orientation to Media Literacy Education.* Copyright © Center for Media Literacy. Reprinted by permission of Center for Media Literacy, whose Web site is located at www.medialit.org.

Project Look Sharp: "Six Questions to Ask About Any Media Message," from Project Look Sharp, Ithaca College. Copyright © Project Look Sharp. Reprinted by permission of Project Look Sharp, www.ithaca.edu/looksharp/resources.php.

Copyright Clearance Center: Excerpt from "Culture Goes Global," by Henry Jenkins from *Technology Review,* July/August 2001. Copyright © 1991 by Technology Review. Reprinted by permission of the Copyright Clearance Center.

Christian Science Monitor: Excerpt from "In 2000 Years, Will the World Remember Disney or Plato," from the *Christian Science Monitor,* January 15, 2004. Reprinted by permission of the author.

Don Congdon Associates, Inc.: Excerpt from *Fahrenheit 451* by Ray Bradbury. Copyright © 1953 by Ray Bradbury, copyright renewed 1981 by Ray Bradbury. Reprinted by permission of Don Congdon Associates, Inc.

ART CREDITS

CONSULTANTS

Title page © Brand X Pictures; Photo © Duane McCubrey; Photo © Mark Schmidt; Photo © Bruce Forrester; Photo © McDougal Littell; Photo © Howard Gollub; Photo © Tamra Stallings; Photo © Mark Schmidt; Photo © Robert J. Marzano; Photo © McDougal Littell; Photo © Dawson & Associates Photography; Photo © Gitchell's Studio; © Michael Romeo; Photo © Monica Ani; Photo © William McBride; Photo © Bill Caldwell; Photo © Gabriel Pauluzzi; Photo © Steven Scheffler.

TABLE OF CONTENTS

Contents in Brief verso *top* © Stone/Getty Images; *bottom* © Mary Rhodes/Animals Animals; **recto** *top, Young Man Studying* (Portrait of Langston Hughes) (1932), Hilda Wilkinson Brown. Oil on canvas. Photo by Gregory R. Staley. © Lilian T. Burwell/Howard University; *bottom* © The University of South Carolina Department of Theatre and Dance, Directed by Dennis Krausnick, Scenery by Kim Jennings, Lighting by Jim Hunter, Costumes by Kenneth Wolfe; **Unit 1 verso** *left* © Firefly Productions/Corbis; *right,* © Don Carstens/Brand X/Corbis; **recto** © PunchStock; **Unit 2 verso** *left* © Bettmann/Corbis; *right, Girls from Guadalupita, New Mexico,* Miguel Martinez. Oil pastel on paper, 30″ × 40″. Contemporary Southwest Galleries, Sante Fe, New Mexico; **recto** © PunchStock; **Unit 3 verso** *left* © Stone/Getty Images; *right, La Jolla Cove* (1922), Alson Clark. Private collection. Courtesy of the Laguna Art Museum; **recto** © PunchStock; **Unit 4 verso** *left* © Tom Salyer; *right* © Mary Rhodes/Animals Animals; **recto** © PunchStock; **Unit 5 verso** *left, Brownstones,* Patti Mollica. © Patti Mollica/SuperStock; *right, Farm in Haiti,* Roosevelt. Oil on canvas. Private collection. © SuperStock; **recto** © PunchStock; **Unit 6 verso** *left, A Tempestuous Evening at the Maison de la Culture* (1937), Albert Lafloret. Oil on canvas, 54 cm × 81 cm. Private collection. Photo © Bridgeman Art Library; *right* © Robert W. Kelley/Time Life Pictures/Getty Images; **recto** © PunchStock; **Unit 7 verso** *left, Flower* (1964), Andy Warhol. Screenprint printed on white paper, 23″ × 23″. © Art Resource, New York © 2007 Andy Warhol Foundation for the Visual Arts/Artists Rights Society (ARS), New York; *right* From *Wings* by Christopher Myers. © 2000 by Christopher Myers. Reprinted by permission of Scholastic, Inc.; **recto** © PunchStock; **Unit 8 verso** *left, Tumbling Flowers* (1954), Hyacinth Manning-Carner. © Hyacinth Manning-Carner/SuperStock; *right, Infantry* (1997), James E. Faulkner. Oil on canvas. Collection of Nature's Nest Gallery, Golden, Colorado. Courtesy of the artist; **recto** © PunchStock; **Unit 9 verso** *left* © Images.com/Corbis; *right, Young Man Studying* (Portrait of Langston Hughes) (1932), Hilda Wilkinson Brown. Oil on canvas. Photo by Gregory R. Staley. © Lilian T. Burwell/Howard University; **recto** © PunchStock; **Unit 10 verso** *left* © ArenaPal/Topham/The Image Works; *right* © The University of South Carolina Department of Theatre and Dance, Directed by Dennis Krausnick, Scenery by Kim Jennings, Lighting by Jim Hunter, Costumes by Kenneth Wolfe; **recto** © PunchStock; **Unit 11 verso** *left* © Araldo de Luca/Corbis; *right* Detail from *Ulysses and the Sirens* (1891), John William Waterhouse. Oil on canvas, 100 cm × 201.7 cm. National Gallery of Victoria, Melbourne, Australia. Photo © Bridgeman Art Library; **recto** © PunchStock.

INTRODUCTORY UNIT

1 *left,* From *Wings* by Christopher Myers. © 2000 by Christopher Myers. Reprinted by permission of Scholastic, Inc.; *top right* © MGM/The Kobal Collection; *lower right, Healing* (1996), Daniel Nevins. Oil on wood, 7.4″ × 9.0″. © Daniel Nevins/SuperStock; **2** *left* © ArenaPal/Topham/The Image Works; *right* © Araldo de Luca/Corbis; **3** *left, The Lord of the Rings: The Fellowship of the Ring* © 2001 New Line Productions, Inc. ™ The Saul Zaentz Company, d/b/a Tolkien Enterprises under license to New Line Productions, Inc. All rights reserved. Photo by Pierre Vinet. Photo appears courtesy of New Line Productions, Inc.; *right, Tender Moments* (2000), Francks Deceus. Mixed media. 101.6 cm × 101.6 cm. Haitian. Private Collection. Photo © The Bridgeman Art Library; **8** *top, upper center* © Bettmann/Corbis; *lower center* © Peter Turnley/Corbis; *bottom* Commuter Rail Division of the Regional Transportation Authority, d/b/a/ Metra; **10** *top to bottom* © Universal/The Kobal Collection; News footage of *All 9 Coal Miners Brought to Safety* courtesy of NBC News Archives; © NBC/courtesy Everett Collection, courtesy Kansas Department of Transportation, Bureau of Traffic Safety; © Tony Freeman/PhotoEdit; © Richard Thornton/Shutterstock; **11** © Jaume Gual/Age Fotostock America, Inc.; **15** *top* © Brian Hagiwara/Getty Images (Royalty-Free); *bottom* © Thinkstock/Getty Images; **16** *left* © Corbis; *center* © PhotoDisc; *right, collage left* © Time & Life Pictures/Getty Images; *center* Public Domain; *right* © Norbert Rosing/National Geographic Image Collection; **17** © Brian Mcweeney/Getty Images; **18** © Alain Choisnet/Getty Images; **19** *left* © Brian Mcweeney/Getty Images; *center* © Dex Image/Getty Images; *right* © Flying Colours, Ltd./Getty Images.

UNIT 1

21 *left, Raven* (1994), Jim Dine. Charcoal on wall, 128″ × 98 ¹/₂″. Kunstverein Ludwigsburg, Germany, destroyed. © 2007 Jim Dine/Artists Rights Society (ARS), New York; *right* © Firefly Productions/Corbis; **22–23** © Warner Brothers/The Kobal Collection; **22** *bottom left* From *The Perfect Storm* by Sebastian Junger. © 1997 by Sebastian Junger. Used by permission of W.W. Norton & Company, Inc.; **24** © Stockbyte/Royalty-Free; **32** © Reuters/Corbis; **33** © Bassouls Sophie/Corbis Sygma; **35** © Mary Evans Picture Library; **38** *Orinoco Jungle Life* (1894), A. Goering. Lithograph. © Mary Evans Picture Library; **42–43** Illustration by Steve Kirk/Wildlife Art Ltd. from *A Guide to Dinosaurs* © Weldon Owen Pty Ltd; **51** NASA; **52** AP/Wide World Photos; **53** © Schlesinger Library, Radcliffe College; **55** © Terry Deroy Gruber/Getty Images; **60** © Earl and Nazima Kowall/Corbis; **65** Detail of *Downtime,* Dale Kennington © Dale Kennington/SuperStock; **67** © Bertrand Demée/Getty Images/Amana America Inc.; © Lee Cates/Getty Images; **68** Man © Keith Goldstein/Getty Images/Amana America Inc.; forest © Photodisc/Getty Images; **73** © Wieteke Teppema/Getty Images; **78** © Jeff Greenberg/PhotoEdit; **79** AP/Wide World Photos; **94** © Michael Newman/PhotoEdit; **95** © Bettmann/Corbis; **97** *The Kiss* (1891),

Edouard Vuillard. Oil on paper mounted on board, 23 cm × 16.5 cm. Philadelphia Museum of Art, The Louis E. Stern Collection, 1963. © Philadelphia Museum of Art/Art Resource, New York. © 2007 Artists Rights Society (ARS), New York/ADAGP, Paris (1963-181-76); **101** © Royalty-Free/Corbis; **106** *The Lord of the Rings: The Fellowship of the Ring* © 2001 New Line Productions, Inc. ™ The Saul Zaentz Company, d/b/a Tolkien Enterprises under license to New Line Productions, Inc. All rights reserved. Photo by Pierre Vinet. Photo appears courtesy of New Line Productions, Inc.; **107** *The Lord of the Rings: The Fellowship of the Ring* © 2001 New Line Productions, Inc. ™ The Saul Zaentz Company, d/b/a Tolkien Enterprises under license to New Line Productions, Inc. All rights reserved. Photo appears courtesy of New Line Productions, Inc.; **108** *background* © Stone/Getty Images; *top, bottom, The Lord of the Rings: The Fellowship of the Ring* © 2001 New Line Productions, Inc. ™ The Saul Zaentz Company, d/b/a Tolkien Enterprises under license to New Line Productions, Inc. All rights reserved. Photo appears courtesy of New Line Productions, Inc.; **110** © Eric Gaillard/Reuters News Picture Archive; **111** © Corbis; **120** AP/Wide World Photos; **121** © Lauren Chelec; **123** © Bettmann/Corbis; **124** © Keeneland-Cook Association, Inc.; **126–127, 128, 132** © Bettmann/Corbis; **133** © Morgan Collection/Getty Images; **134** *top* © Hulton Archive/Getty Images; *bottom* © Bettmann/Corbis; **135** *left* © Bettmann/Corbis; *right* © Hulton Archive/Getty Images; **138** © Corbis; **139** *bottom* Photo by Nathaniel Justice; *top* © Bettmann/Corbis; **144** *Red Passion* (1996), Jim Dine. Cardboard relief intaglio. Image size 33 1/8" x 59". Paper size 39 1/2" x 63 7/8". Published by Pace Editions, Inc. Edition of 12 © 2007 Jim Dine/Artists Rights Society (ARS), New York; **145** *The Back of a Man with a Rose*, René Magritte. Private Collection Bloch, Santa Monica, CA. Photo © Superstock, Inc. © 2007 C. Herscovici, Brussels/Artists Rights Society (ARS), New York; **148** © Aaron Horowitz/Corbis; **149** © Seth Joel/Corbis; **151** © Joel Sartore/Getty Images; **153** © William Whitehurst/Corbis; **154** © Photodisc; **157** © Andrea Pistolesi/Getty Images; **161** © Royalty-Free/Corbis; **162** © Lorna Clark/Getty Images; **165** AP/Wide World Photos; **168, 174** © Craig Aurness/Corbis; **175** © Mary Kate Denny/PhotoEdit; **182** © Siede Preis/Photodisc/Getty Images.

UNIT 2

183 *left, Louise Augusta, Queen of Prussia* (1801), Marie Louise Elisabeth Vigée-LeBrun. Pastel, 51 cm × 41 cm. Stiftung Preussische Schlösser und Gärten Berlin-Brandenburg. Photo by J. P. Anders; *right* © BananaStock/Punchstock; **184** *left* Public Domain; *right* © Paul C. Chauncey/Corbis; **184–185** © Pawel Libera/Corbis; **193** Photo by Jim Lundquist; **195** © Peter M. Fisher/Corbis; **198** © Iconica Limited; **201** © Ian Kahn/Iconica; **206** © Mauro Panci/Corbis; **207** © Chris Hellier/Corbis; **221** © Dave Nagel/Stone/Getty Images; **222** © Photodisc Green/Getty Images; **223** Photo by Madison Nye; **236** © Gabe Palmer/Corbis; **237** © Mitchell Gerber/Corbis; **246** © Photodisc/Getty Images; **250** © Peter Turnley/Corbis; **251** © Amy Etra/Time Life Pictures/Getty Images; **253** © Didrik Johnck/Corbis; **255** © Chris Curry/Hedgehoghouse.com; **259, 264** © Didrik Johnck/Corbis; **265** © Adam Pretty/Getty Images; **268** © Jeff Greenberg/Age Fotostock America, Inc.; **269** *top* Courtesy Pat Mora/Photo by Cheron Bayman; *bottom* Photo by David Burkhalter. Reprinted by permission of the University of Arizona Press; **272** *Navajo Power Plant* (1990). © Shonto Begay/Avery Collection of American Indian Painting; **274** white gloves © Photodisc/Getty Images; Empress Michiko © Andy Rain-Pool/Getty

Images; man © Getty Images; frames © Image Farm, Inc.; working glove © Rubberball Productions/Getty Images; **275** *top* AP/Wide World Photos; *bottom* © Fred Viebahn/Rita Dove; **277** © Bettmann/Corbis; **280** From *Americans Who Tell The Truth*, Robert Shetterly. Used by permission of Dutton Children's Books, a division of Penguin Young Readers Group, a member of Penguin Group, Inc. All rights reserved. © Robert Shetterly; **284, 290** © Joseph Sohm; ChromoSohm Inc./Corbis; **291** *left* © Jan von Holleben/Getty Images; *right* © SuperStock, Inc./SuperStock; **298** © Siede Preis/Photodisc/Getty Images.

UNIT 3

299 *left* Burial niches with fresco of Christ Pantocrator. Catacomb of San Callisto, Rome, Italy. Photo © Erich Lessing/Art Resource, New York; *right* © Keith Kapple/SuperStock; **300–301** © Sekai Bunka/Premium/Panoramic Images; **304** © The Kobal Collection; **309** © Slim Aarons/Getty Images; **311** © Getty Images/Royalty Free; **326** © Stanley Chou/Getty Images; **327** © Bettmann/Corbis; **329** *La Jolla Cove* (1922), Alson Clark. Private collection. Courtesy of the Laguna Art Museum; **342** © Photographer's Choice/Getty Images; **343** © Bettmann/Corbis; **345** © Stone/Getty Images; **349** Burial niches with fresco of Christ Pantocrator. Catacomb of San Callisto, Rome, Italy. Photo © Erich Lessing/Art Resource, New York; **350** © Punchstock; **352** © PhotoDisc/Getty Images; **356** © Nik Wheeler/Corbis; **357** *top, center, bottom* Footage from *Edgar Allan Poe: The Soul of Terror, The Cask of Amontillado.* Courtesy of Film Odyssey, Inc.; **358** *background* © Image Source/PictureQuest; *top left, bottom left* Footage from *Edgar Allan Poe: The Soul of Terror, The Cask of Amontillado.* Courtesy of Film Odyssey, Inc.; **359** *top left* © Photodisc; *top center* © Image Farm, Inc.; *top right* © PhotoDisc; *bottom left* © Brand X Pictures/Fotosearch Stock Photography; *bottom center, bottom right* © Photodisc, Inc.; **360** © Paul Katz/Index Stock Imagery/PictureQuest/Jupiterimages Corporation; **361** © Rick Friedman/Corbis; **363** © Patrik Giardino/Corbis; **364–365** © Ric Ergenbright/Ric Ergenbright Photography; **369** © Creatas/PictureQuest; **373** © Margaretta K. Mitchell; **378** © SuperStock; **379** *top* © Christopher Felver/Corbis; *bottom* Courtesy The Land Institute, Prairie Writers Circle; **381** © Kiefner/Premium Stock/PictureQuest/Jupiterimages Corporation; **382** © John Warden/Index Stock Imagery/PictureQuest/Jupiterimages Corporation; **384, 390** © Daryl Benson/Masterfile; **391** © Yang Liu/Corbis; **398** © Siede Preis/Photodisc/Getty Images.

UNIT 4

399 *left, Mama's Cradle,* April Harrison. Mixed media collage on canvas board, 14" × 18". © April Harrison; **400–401** © Richard Cummins/Corbis; **400** © Royalty-Free/Corbis; **402** © Kevin Anthony Horgan/Getty Images; **408** © Digital Vision Ltd./SuperStock; **409** © Olan Mills; **422** *Full Spittoon* (1974), Bob Timberlake. Watercolor. Private Collection. © Bob Timberlake; **423** Chicago Tribune photo by Warren Skalski; **426** FOXTROT © 1997 Bill Amend. Reprinted with permission of UNIVERSAL PRESS SYNDICATE. All rights reserved; **427** Courtesy of James Hurst; **435** © Vincent McIndoe/Images.com/Corbis; **438** © Mary Rhodes/Animals Animals; **442** © Sam Abell/National Geographic Image Collection; **446** © Spencer Grant/PhotoEdit; **447** © Richard McNamee; **449** © Keren Su/Corbis; **450** © Images.com/Corbis; **453** © Dean Conger/Corbis; **458** © Richard T. Nowitz/Corbis; **459** © Getty Images; **466** © Craig C. Sheumaker/PanStock/

PictureQuest/Jupiterimages Corporation; **467** *top* © ChinaStock; *center* The Granger Collection, New York; *bottom* Photo by Barbara Savage Cheresh; **468** *Viewing Plum Blossoms by Moonlight,* Ma Yuan. Southern Sung. John M. Crawford, Jr. Collection. Photo © Wan-go H. C. Weng/ Metroplitan Museum of Art, New York/Art Resource, New York; **469** © Bill Binzen/Corbis; **470** © Tom Salyer; **472** © Pete Saloutos/ Corbis; **473** *top* © Lawrence Lucier/Getty Images; *bottom* © Photo by Paul H. Mark; **475** *top* © Corbis; *left* © Getty Images; *right* © Rykoff Collection/Corbis; **478** *center* © Ed Sullivan Show/Photofest; *bottom* © Trinette Reed/Corbis; **481** © Richard Cummins/SuperStock; **484** © Catherine Karnow/Corbis; **486** © Anthony-Masterson/Foodpix/Getty Images/Jupiterimages Corporation; **490, 496** © Richard Sisk/ Jupiterimages; **497** © Design Pics, Inc./Alamy Images; **504** © Siede Preis/Photodisc/Getty Images.

UNIT 5

505 *left, Cow's Skull: Red, White, and Blue* (1931), Georgia O'Keeffe. Oil on canvas, 39⁷/₈″ × 35⁷/₈″. The Metropolitan Museum of Art, Alfred Stieglitz Collection, 1952. Photo © Georgia O'Keeffe/ Metropolitan Museum of Art (52.203) © 2007 Georgia O'Keeffe Museum/Artists Rights Society (ARS), New York/Art Resource, New York; *right* © Joseph Sohm; Visions of America/Corbis; **506-507** *collage far left* © Creatas Images/Jupiterimages Corporation; *center left* © Karl Weatherly/Getty Images; *center* © Time & Life Pictures/Getty Images; *center right* Public Domain; *far right* © Norbert Rosing/National Geographic Image Collection; **511** © Matthew Frey/Wood Ronsaville Harlin; **513** © Erik Simonsen/Getty Images; **514** © Bryan and Cherry Alexander; **515** © Taro Yamasaki/Time Life Pictures/Getty Images; **524** © Abigail Pope/LuckyPix; **525** © Neville Elder/Corbis; **527** Phillips Collection/AP/Wide World Photos; **529** *Cow's Skull: Red, White, and Blue* (1931), Georgia O'Keeffe. Oil on canvas, 39⁷/₈″ × 35⁷/₈″. The Metropolitan Museum of Art, Alfred Stieglitz Collection, 1952. Photo © Georgia O'Keeffe/Metropolitan Museum of Art (52.203) © 2007 Georgia O'Keeffe Museum/Artists Rights Society (ARS), New York/Art Resource, New York; **530** *Jimson Weed* (1932), Georgia O'Keeffe. The Georgia O'Keeffe Museum, Santa Fe, New Mexico. © Art Resource, New York © 2007 Georgia O'Keeffe Museum/Artists Rights Society (ARS), New York; **534** © Reuters/Corbis; **535** © Corbis Sygma; **536** *top* © National Geographic Society. Reprinted by permission of the National Geographic Society; *bottom* © Hanny Paul/Gamma Press USA, Inc.; **537** *left* © Regional Hospital of Bolzano/South Tyrol Museum of Archaeology www.iceman.it; *right* © South Tyrol Museum of Archaeology; **538** *top* © GeoNova LLC; *bottom* © South Tyrol Museum of Archaeology; **539** © Hinterleitner Gerhard/Gamma Press USA, Inc.; **540–543** Photos from *The Bone Detective.* © Charles Fellenbaum, Boulder, Colorado; **546** AP/Wide World Photos; **549** © Jeff Riedel/Creative Photographers, Inc.; **551** © Hudson Derek/ Corbis Sygma; **553** © Jeff Riedel/Creative Photographers, Inc.; **556** AP/ Wide World Photos; **557** *top* News footage of *All 9 Coal Miners Brought to Safety* courtesy of NBC News Archives; *center* © by CNN. Reprinted by permission of Cable News Network; *bottom* © Getty Images; **558** *top left* News footage of *All 9 Coal Miners Brought to Safety* courtesy of NBC News Archives; *bottom left* Getty Images; *background* © Larry Lee Photography/Corbis; **559** © IT International Ltd./Jupiterimages Corporation; **560** © Andrew McKim/Masterfile; **561** The Granger Collection, New York; **568** © Mike Powell/Getty Images; **569** © Gene Blevins/Corbis; **576, 582** © Daryl Benson/Masterfile; **583** © Lon

C. Diehl/PhotoEdit; **586** © Daily News Leader. All rights reserved. Reproduced with the permission of Gannett Co., Inc. by NewsBank, Inc.; **590** © Siede Preis/Photodisc/Getty Images.

UNIT 6

591 *left, A Tempestuous Evening at the Maison de la Culture* (1937), Albert Lafloret. Oil on canvas, 54 cm × 81 cm. Private collection. Photo © The Bridgeman Art Library; *right* © Bettmann/Corbis; **592–593** © Spencer Platt/Getty Images; **592** *left* © New Voters Project; **597** © Ad Council; **600** © Alex Wong/Getty Images; **601** © Time Life Pictures/Getty Images; **603** © Bettmann/Corbis; **604–605** © Robert W. Kelley/Time Life Pictures/Getty Images; **604** *top left* © Paul Schutzer/Time Life Pictures/Getty Images; **605** *top right* © MPI/Getty Images; **607** AP/Wide World Photos; **610** © Tatsuyuki Tayama/ Fujifotos/The Image Works; **611** © Thierry Orban/Corbis Sygma; **613** © Ron Sachs/CNP/Corbis; **614** © Corbis Sygma; **615** © Ron Sachs/ CNP/Corbis; **616** © Eurelios/Phototake; **620** © Jeffrey Sylvester/Getty Images; **621** © Mike Baldwin/www.CartoonStock.com; **622** © Peter Ciresa/Index Stock Imagery; **624** AP/Wide World Photos; **625** © Reuters/Corbis; **626** © Ed Quinn/Corbis; **629** © The Image Bank/ Getty Images; **630** © Mauro Fermariello/Photo Researchers, Inc.; **634** Courtesy of Kansas Department of Transportation, Bureau of Traffic Safety; *background* © Tony Freeman/PhotoEdit; **635** *top, Billy Thomas* Public Service Announcement courtesy of Boys and Girls Clubs of America; *bottom, How Far Would You Go?* Public Service Announcement courtesy of Peace Corps of America; **636** *top left, Billy Thomas* Public Service Announcement courtesy of Boys and Girls Clubs of America; *bottom left, How Far Would You Go?* Public Service Announcement courtesy of Peace Corps of America; *background* © Layne Kennedy/ Corbis; **637** © Ad Council; **638** © Nicholas Rigg/Getty Images; **639** *top* © Washington Post Writers Group; *bottom* © Bassouls Sophie/ Corbis Sygma; **641** © Chip Simons/Getty Images; **650–656** © J. David Andrews/Masterfile; **657** © Pedro Coll/Age Fotostock America, Inc.; **664** © Siede Preis/Photodisc/Getty Images.

UNIT 7

665 *left* From *Wings* by Christopher Myers. © 2000 by Christopher Myers. Reprinted by permission of Scholastic, Inc.; *right* © Pete Turner/ Getty Images; **666** *right, The Cow Jumped Over the Moon* (1885), Randolph Caldecott. From *R. Caldecott's Second Collection of Pictures and Songs*/Mary Evans Picture Library; *left* The Granger Collection, New York; **676** © Colin Paterson/PhotoDisc: Green/Getty Images; **677** *top* © Bettmann/Corbis; *center* © 2002 Margaretta Mitchell; *bottom* © Fred Viebahn/Rita Dove; **681** *Ice Cream Dessert* (1959), Andy Warhol. Photo © Andy Warhol Foundation/Corbis © 2007 Andy Warhol Foundation for the Visual Arts/Artists Rights Society (ARS), New York; **684** © Kevin Fleming/Corbis; **685** *top* © Bettmann/Corbis; *center* © Touhig Sion/Corbis Sygma; *bottom* © Christopher Felver/ Corbis; **689** *Flower* (1964), Andy Warhol. Screenprint printed on white paper, 23″ x 23″. © Art Resource, New York © 2007 Andy Warhol Foundation for the Visual Arts/Artists Rights Society (ARS), New York; **690** *top* J. P. Beato III/The Battalion © Texas Agricultural and Military University; *bottom* AP/Wide World Photos; **692** AP/Wide World Photos; **693** *top* © Nancy E. Crampton; *bottom* © Wojda/Free/Corbis Sygma; **694–695** © Franco Vogt/Corbis; **698** left, Municipal Bonds (2004), Byron Spicer. Mixed media, 45″ x 45″. © Hespe Gallery; *right* © Franco Vogt/Corbis; **699** © Bob Daemmrich/PhotoEdit; **700** *top*

The New York Times Company; *bottom* © Spencer Platt/Getty Images; **702** Leslloyd F. Alleyne Jr./Journal Inquirer/AP/Wide World Photos; **703** *top* © Christopher Felver/Corbis; *bottom* Photo taken by Colin Beltz and used courtesy of the Red Wing Republican Eagle; *center* © Sam Falk/New York Times Company/Getty Images; **705** From *Wings* by Christopher Myers. © 2000 by Christopher Myers. Reprinted by permission of Scholastic, Inc.; **707, 709** Photo by Sharon Hoogstraten; **711** © Corbis; **714** © Royalty-Free/Corbis; **715** © Harry Redl/Time Life Pictures/Getty Images; **718** *Returning to the Trenches* (1914–15), C. R. W. Nevinson. Oil on canvas, 51 cm × 76 cm. © Gift of the Massey Collection of English Painting, 1946/National Gallery of Canada, Ottawa. Courtesy of the Nevinson Estate/Bridgeman Art Library; **720** © Tobbe/zefa; **721** *top* The Granger Collection, New York; *bottom* National Archives; **726–732** © Jason Ernst/Age Fotostock America, Inc.; **733** © Paul Vozdic/Getty Images; **740** © Siede Preis/Photodisc/Getty Images.

UNIT 8

741 *left, Tumbling Flowers* (1954), Hyacinth Manning-Carner. © Hyacinth Manning-Carner/SuperStock; *right* © Brand X Pictures/Getty Images; **742–743** *The Persistence of Memory* (1931), Salvador Dali. Oil on canvas, 9$^1/_2$" × 13". Museum of Modern Art, New York. © 2000 Foundation Gala-Salvador Dali/VEGAP © 2007 Salvador Dali, Gala-Salvador Dali Foundation/Artists Rights Society (ARS), New York; **746** *left* © Carl Van Vechten/Corbis; *left* © Bettmann/Corbis; *right* © Darryl Bush/Getty Images; **750** © Ron Fehling/Masterfile; **751** © 2002 Marilyn Knapp Linn; **764** CinemaPhoto/Corbis; **765** Berko/Time Life Pictures/Getty Images; **770** © akg-images; **771** *top* © MGM/ The Kobal Collection; *center #1* © Universal/The Kobal Collection; *center #2* © Paramount/The Kobal Collection; *bottom* © Paramount /The Kobal Collection; **772** *background* © Joe McDonald /Corbis; *top left, bottom left, The Birds* © 1963 Alfred J. Hitchcock Productions, Inc., courtesy of Universal Studios Licensing LLLP; **773** *left, right* © MGM/The Kobal Collection; **774** © Lluis Real/Age Fotostock America, Inc.; **775** Photo © Steven Hopp; **777** © Tadashi Miwa/Getty Images; *top right* © Sarma Ozols/Getty Images; **778** *bottom left* © ImageState-Pictor/PictureQuest; *center left* Sushi and chopsticks © Anthony Johnson/Getty Images; *center right* © Stone/Getty Images; *bottom right* © Tadashi Miwa/Getty Images; **782** © Tony Anderson/ Getty Images; **783** Photo by Barbara Savage Cheresh; **785** © 2003 Aflo Foto Agency; **786** *left* © Tom Lazar/Earth Scenes/Animals Animals; *right* Roy Toft/National Geographic Image Collection; **790** © Susan Meiselas/Magnum Photos; **791** The Granger Collection, New York; **796** © Alamy Images; **797** © Mike Simons/Getty Images; **802** © Pete Stone/Corbis; **803** *top* © Bettmann/Corbis; *bottom* © Hulton Archive/Getty Images; **805** © Bettmann/Corbis; **806–810** The Granger Collection, New York; **812, 818** © Alain Choisnet/Getty Images; **819** © Eric O'Connell/Getty Images; **822** © Carsten Peter/ National Geographic Image Collection; **826** © Siede Preis/Photodisc/ Getty Images.

UNIT 9

827 *left, Jazz Player III* (1991), Freshman Brown. Collage. © SuperStock; *right* © Frans Lemmens/Iconica Limited/Getty Images; **828** Reprinted with the permission of Random House, Inc., from *The House on Mango Street* book cover by Sandra Cisneros; © Reprinted by permission of Vintage Books, a division of Random House, Inc. Used by permission of Vintage Books, a division of Random House, Inc. Book design by Cathryn S. Aison, hand lettering by Henry Sene Yee; **828–829** © Margo Cohn; **830** © Charles and Josette Lenars/Corbis; **832** © Bettmann/Corbis; **835** © J Sohm/VOA LLC/Panoramic Images; **836** © The Image Bank/Getty Images; **837** © Michael Brennan/ Corbis; **839** © Aaron M. Priest Literary Agency, Inc.; **842** Courtesy of the *Limerick Leader,* Limerick, Ireland; **845** © Hulton Archive/Getty Images; **852** © Chris Rainier/Corbis; **853** Photo by Loce Momaday/ Courtesy of Royce Carlton, Inc.; **855** © David Muench/Corbis; **857** © Courtney Milne; **863** © The New York Public Library/Art Resource, New York; **874** Photo courtesy Suraiya Nathani; **875** Photo of Judith Ortiz Cofer is reprinted with permission from the publisher Arte Publico Press. © 2005, University of Houston, Houston, Texas; **877, 888** © Bettmann/Corbis; **889** *top* Reprinted with permission of *The Dallas Morning News; bottom* © Bettmann/Corbis; **891** © U.S. News & World Report, L. P. reprinted with permission; **892** © 1963 Bill Mauldin, reprinted with special permission from the Chicago Sun-Times, Inc. 2004; **894** © Ed Kashi/Corbis; **895** © Corbis; **897** © Images.com/ Corbis; **902** © Ryan McVay/Getty Images; **903** *top, Portrait of Bashō,* Kameda Bosai. Hanging scroll in ink and color on paper. Gift of an anonymous donor. © New Orleans Museum of Art (80.181); *center* © Bettmann/Corbis; *bottom* © Charlie Gross; **906** © Digital Vision Ltd./SuperStock; **914, 920** © Sam Barricklow/Jupiterimages; **915** © Michelle D. Bridwell/PhotoEdit; **922** © Siede Preis/Photodisc/Getty Images.

UNIT 10

923 *left, The Proposal* (1872), Adolphe-William Bouguereau. Oil on canvas, 64$^3/_8$" × 44". Gift of Mrs. Elliott L. Kamen, in memory of her father, Bernard R. Armour, 1960 (60.122). © The Metropolitan Museum of Art, New York/Art Resouce, New York; *right* © ArenaPal/ Topham/The Image Works; **924–925** *left to right, A Bridal Couple,* (about 1490). Southern Germany. Oil on wood, 77.5 cm × 51 cm × 7.5 cm. © 2004 The Cleveland Museum of Art; *Francesca da Rimini* (1837), William Dyce. Oil on canvas, 142 cm × 176 cm. National Gallery of Scotland, Edinburgh. © Bridgeman Art Library; The Granger Collection, New York; Clip from *Romeo and Juliet* courtesy of Paramount Pictures; *Romeo and Juliet,* Claire Danes, 1996 © 20th Century Fox/courtesy Everett Collection; **926** The Granger Collection, New York; **927** Illustration by John James/Temple Rogers—Artists' Agents; **928** Much Ado About Nothing poster © Samuel Goldwyn Films, Courtesy Everett Collection; **929** The Granger Collection, New York; **930** © Andrea Pistolesi/Getty Images; **938** © 1993 Jay Ullah/Stern/Black Star; **941** *left* © Dmitrij Matvejev/Anzelika Cholina Dance Theatre, Lithuania; *center left* © ArenaPal/Topham/The Image Works; *center* Chicago Shakespeare Theater's production of Romeo and Juliet toured to 14 communities in the Southeast United States, as part of the National Endowment for the Arts Shakespeare in American Communities initiative. Martin Yurek as Mercutio (left) and Ryan Kitley as Tybalt (right). Photo by: SteveLeonardPhotography. com, courtesy Chicago Shakespeare Theater; *center right* © ArenaPal/ Topham/The Image Works; *right* Marian Hinkle as Juliet and Jay Goede as Romeo in The Shakespeare Theatre's 1993–1994 production of *Romeo and Juliet,* directed by Barry Kyle. Photo by Richard Anderson; **943** © Dmitrij Matvejev/Anzelika Cholina Dance Theatre,

Topham /The Image Works, Inc.; *right* Chicago Shakespeare Theater and Second City Theatrical's production of the *Romeo and Juliet Musical, The People vs. Friar Lawrence, The Man Who Killed Romeo and Juliet.* Nicole Parker as Juliet and Keegan-Michael Key as Romeo. Photo by Michael Brosilow, courtesy Chicago Shakespeare Theater; **954** Jean Stapleton as Nurse and Marin Hinkle as Juliet in The Shakespeare Theatre's 1993–1994 production of *Romeo and Juliet,* directed by Barry Kyle. Photo by Richard Anderson; **959** *top* © Elliott Franks/Arena Pal/Topham/The Image Works, Inc.; *right* © ArenaPal/Topham/The Image Works; *bottom left* © Reuters/Corbis; **962** © Robbie Jack/Corbis; **965** Katie Atkinson as Juliet and Brian Weaver as Romeo in Shakespeare & Company's 2004 Spring Tour Production of *Romeo and Juliet.* Directed by Kevin Coleman. Photo by Kevin Sprague; **969** © ArenaPal/Topham/The Image Works; **974** © Chris Bennion Photography; **979** © Don Pierce/University of Victoria Photographic Services; **985** *top left* © Orlando-UCF Shakespeare Festival; *top right* © Royal Shakespeare Company; *bottom* © The University of South Carolina Department of Theatre and Dance, Directed by Dennis Krausnick, Scenery by Kim Jennings, Lighting by Jim Hunter, Costumes by Kenneth Wolfe; **993** Chicago Shakespeare Theater's production of Romeo and Juliet toured to 14 communities in the Southeast United States, as part of the National Endowment for the Arts Shakespeare in American Communities initiative. Martin Yurek as Mercutio (left) and Ryan Kitley as Tybalt (right). Photo by: SteveLeonardPhotography.com, courtesy Chicago Shakespeare Theater; **998** © Royal Shakespeare Company; **1009** *top left* © Scot J. Mann/Atlanta Stage Combat Studio; *top right* © Chris Bennion Photography; *bottom* © 2004 Susana Raab; **1019** © ArenaPal/Topham/The Image Works; **1025** *left* © Gary Wayne Golden; *center* The Seattle Repertory Theatre's 2003 Romeo and Juliet poster © Sedgwick Rd.; *right* © Wieslaw Walkuski; **1029** © Don Pierce/University of Victoria Photographic Services; **1035** Marian Hinkle as Juliet and Jay Goede as Romeo in The Shakespeare Theatre's 1993–1994 production of *Romeo and Juliet,* directed by Barry Kyle. Photo by Richard Anderson; **1039** *top left* © Royal Shakespeare Company; *right* © Clive Barda/ArenaPal/Topham/The Image Works, Inc.; *bottom left* © ArenaPal/Topham/The Image Works, Inc.; **1044** © ArenaPal/Topham/The Image Works, Inc.; **1049** © Bob Daemmrich/The Image Works; **1052, 1053, 1054** *left* Clip from *Romeo and Juliet* courtesy of Paramount Pictures; *bottom* © Image 100/Alamy / Royalty-Free; **1055** *top* © 20th Century Fox/courtesy Everett Collection; *bottom* Stills from *William Shakespeare's Romeo and Juliet,* courtesy of Twentieth Century Fox. All rights reserved; **1056** left © Dmitrij Matvejev/Anzelika Cholina Dance Theatre, Lithuania; 2nd from left © ArenaPal/Topham/The Image Works; center Chicago Shakespeare Theater's production of Romeo and Juliet toured to 14 communities in the Southeast United States, as part of the National Endowment for the Arts Shakespeare in American Communities initiative. Martin Yurek as Mercutio (left) and Ryan Kitley as Tybalt (right).Photo by: SteveLeonardPhotography.com, courtesy Chicago Shakespeare Theater; center right © ArenaPal/Topham/The Image Works; right Marian Hinkle as Juliet and Jay Goede as Romeo in The Shakespeare Theatre's 1993-1994 production of Romeo and Juliet, directed by Barry Kyle. Photo by Richard Anderson; **1057** Courtesy Everett Collection; **1058, 1059, 1060** Clip from *Romeo and Juliet* courtesy of Paramount Pictures; **1062** © Digital Stock Royalty Free; **1063** *Ovid* (1500–1503). Fresco. Post-restoration. Duomo, Orvieto, Italy. Photo © Scala/Art Resource, New York; **1070, 1076**

© Jupiterimages; **1077** *left* © Comstock Images/Getty Images; *right* © Rosie Hardman-Ixer; **1084** © Siede Preis/Photodisc/Getty Images.

UNIT 11

1085 *left, Scylla and Charybdis,* from the *Ulysses Cycle* (1580), Alessandro Allori. Fresco. Banca Toscana (Palazzo Salviati), Florence, Italy. Photo © Erich Lessing/Art Resource, New York; *right* © Corbis; **1086–1087** © Don Mason/Corbis; **1088** *top* © Corbis/Royalty-Free; *bottom, Procession of Trojan Horse into Troy,* G. D. Tiepolo. The Granger Collection, New York; **1089** Detail of a frieze representing a procession of mythological divinities, muses, graces, etc. Oil on plaster. Chateaux de Malmaison et Bois-Preau, Rueil-Malmaison, France. Photo © Gerard Blot/Art Resource, New York; **1090** *left* © 2004 Warner Bros./Photofest; *right, Homer* (about 150 B.C.). Marble sculpture. Museo Nazionale Archeologico. Photo © akg-images; **1091** © GeoNova LLC; **1092** *top, Ulysses Returns Chryseis to Her Father,* Claude Lorrain. Louvre, Paris. Photo © Scala/Art Resource, New York; **1093** *top left* Plaque with the return of Odysseus (about 460–450 B.C.). Classical Greek. Melian. Terracotta, Height $7\,^3/_8''$. The Metropolitan Museum of Art, Fletcher Fund, 1930. (30.11.9) © 1982 The Metropolitan Museum of Art/Art Resource, New York; *bottom left, Ulysses* (1931–1932), Georges Braque. Pastel, 180.5 cm × 73.5 cm. Private Collection. Photo © Visual Arts Library/Art Resource, New York © 2007 Artists Rights Society (ARS), New York/ADAGP, Paris; *top right, Odysseus Slaying the Suitors* (400s B.C.), Penelope Painter. Attic red figure painting on kylix. Height 20 cm. Inv F 2588. Antikensammlung, Staatliche Museen zu Berlin, Berlin. Photo by Juergen Liepe. © Bildarchiv Preussischer Kulturbesitz/Art Resource, New York; *bottom right* Illustration by Innes Fripp in *Tales of the Gods and Heroes* by Sir G.W. Cox. © Edwin Wallace/Mary Evans Picture Library; **1094** *top to bottom* © Araldo de Luca/Corbis; *Odysseus and Polyphemus* (1896), Arnold Bocklin. Tempera on wood, 65.5 cm × 148.5 cm. Private collection. © akg-images; *Ulysses Returns Chryseis to Her Father,* Claude Lorrain. Louvre, Paris. Photo © Scala/Art Resource, New York; Detail of *Tilla Durieux as Circe* (about 1912–1913), Franz von Struck. Oil on paper, 53.5 cm × 46.5 cm. Private collection. Photo © akg-images; **1105** *The Ship of Odysseus,* Francois-Louis Schmeid. From *Homer, the Odessy,* published Paris (1930–1933). Colour lithograph. Private collection, The Stapleton Collection. © 2007 Artists Rights Society (ARS), New York/ADAGP, Paris. © Bridgeman Art Library; **1100** © Liu Jin/AFP/Getty Images; **1105** *The Ship of Odysseus,* Francois-Louis Schmeid. from Homer, the Odessy, published Paris (1930-1933). Colour lithograph. Private collection, The Stapleton Collection. © 2007 Artists Rights Society (ARS), New York/ADAGP, Paris © Bridgeman Art Library; **1111** © Araldo de Luca/Corbis; **1140** AP/Wide World Photos; **1141** *Penelope Embroidering* (1903), Mrs. H. de Rudder. Photo © Mary Evans Picture Library; **1143** *Athene and Telemach,* from *Odyssey II* (1975), Marc Chagall. Lithograph on Arches paper. 16.9″ × 13″. Photograph by George R. Staley. Courtesy the Georgetown Frame Shoppe. © 2007 Artists Rights Society (ARS), New York; **1149** © Bettmann/Corbis; **1154, 1157** Illustrations by N.C. Wyeth from *The Odyssey of Homer,* translated by George Herbert Palmer. © 1929 by N.C. Wyeth. © renewed 1957 by Carolyn Wyeth. Reprinted by permission of Houghton Mifflin Company. All rights reserved; **1163** Detail of plaque with the return of Odysseus (about 460–450 B.C.). Classical Greek. Melian. Terracotta, Height 7 ³/₈″. The Metropolitan Museum of Art, Fletcher Fund, 1930. (30.11.9) © 1982 The Metropolitan Museum of Art/Art Resource, New York; **1166** © Lindsay Hebberd/Corbis; **1170, 1176** © Neil Emmerson/ Getty Images; **1177** © Charles Gupton/Corbis; **1184** © Siede Preis/ Photodisc/Getty Images.

UNIT 12

1185 *left* © Zac Macaulay/Getty Images; *right, collage, center left to right* Cover of *Walking Softly in the Wilderness* by John Hart. Cover photo by Art Twomey. Reprinted with the permission of The Sierra Club, San Francisco, California; © Getty Images; Courtesy of the National Audubon Society; *cover background* © Brand X Pictures: Four Seasons; *foreground* © Rich Phalin/istockphoto.com; *bottom book pages, left top to bottom* Jupiterimages Corporation; © Brand X Pictures/PunchStock; © Michael and Patricia Fogden/Minden Pictures/Getty Images; *right, top to bottom* Michael and Patricia Fogden/Minden Pictures/Getty Images; © Altrendo Nature/Altrendo/Getty Images; © Jupiterimages Corporation; **1186–1187** © Digital Vision Ltd./SuperStock; **1188** Ken Chernus/Stone/Getty Images; **1192** © 2005 Infospace, Inc. All rights reserved. Reprinted with permission of Infospace, Inc.; **1193** 2005 County of Sacramento, California; **1195** © Skokie Public Library; **1196** *left* © PhotoDisc Green; *right* © Brian Hagiwara/Brand X Pictures; *background* © 1994 Artbeats; **1197** *top to bottom* Cover from *The Concise Geography Encyclopedia.* © Kingfisher Publications Plc 2005. Reprinted by permission of Kingfisher Publications Plc., an imprint of Houghton Mifflin Company. All rights reserved.; Cover of *The American Heritage Student Dictionary* © Houghton Mifflin Company, all rights reserved; Cover images *inset top* © Larry Brownstein/Getty Images; *inset top right* © Digital Vision/Getty Images; *inset center* © Cartesia/Getty Images; *inset bottom left* © Alan & Sandy Carey/Getty Images; *inset bottom right* © C Squared Studios/Getty Images; © McDougal Littel art; Cover of *Roget's II Thesaurus* © Houghton Mifflin Company. All rights reserved; Cover of *Chambers Reference Atlas* (2005), Edited by Editors of Chambers. © Houghton Mifflin Company, all rights reserved, Cover image © Getty Images; **1198** From *InfoTrac,* by Gale Group, reprinted by permission of The Gale Group; **1199** *top to bottom* © Time Life Pictures/Getty Images; © Wall Street Journal; © American Veterinary Medical Association; **1203** American Veterinary Medical Association; **1204** *left to right* © 1996 PhotoDisc, Inc.; © 2001 PhotoDisc, Inc.; © 1999 PhotoDisc, Inc.; **1205** *top* © The Dallas Morning News. Reprinted with the permission of The Dallas Morning News; *bottom* © Reuters/Corbis; **1209** © PictureNet/Corbis; **1210, 1230** © PictureQuest/Jupiterimages Corporation; **1231** © Image Source/ Alamy Images.

STUDENT RESOURCE BANK

R3 *top* © G.R. Roberts Photo Library; *bottom* Illustration by Gary Hincks; **R6** *top* © Getty Images (Royalty-Free); *bottom* Illustration by SlimFilms; **R7** © Mapping Specialists; **R14** *left, right* © Paul Simcock/ Brand X Pictures/PictureQuest; *center* © Photodisc/Getty Images; **R15** *top left* Galen Rowell/Corbis; *top right* David Muench/Corbis; *bottom*

Illustration by Gary Hincks; **R20** NASA; **R84** © Digital Vision/Getty Images (Royalty-Free); **R92** © Coneyl Jay/Getty Images.

BACK COVER

© Brand X Pictures.

PENNSYLVANIA ACADEMIC STANDARDS AND ASSESSMENT ANCHOR CONTENT STANDARDS
Academic Standards

1.4.11 Types of Writing

1.4.11.A Write short stories, poems and plays.
    1.4.11.A.1 Apply varying organizational methods.
    1.4.11.A.2 Use relevant illustrations.
    1.4.11.A.3 Utilize dialogue.
    1.4.11.A.4 Apply literary conflict.
    1.4.11.A.5 Include varying characteristics (e.g., from limerick to epic, from whimsical to dramatic).
    1.4.11.A.6 Include literary elements.
    1.4.11.A.7 Use literary devices.
1.4.11.B Write complex informational pieces (e.g., research papers, analyses, evaluations, essays).
    1.4.11.B.1 Include a variety of methods to develop the main idea.
    1.4.11.B.2 Use precise language and specific detail.
    1.4.11.B.3 Include cause and effect.
    1.4.11.B.4 Use relevant graphics (e.g., maps, charts, graphs, tables, illustrations, photographs).
    1.4.11.B.5 Use primary and secondary sources.
1.4.11.C Write persuasive pieces.
    1.4.11.C.1 Include a clearly stated position or opinion.
    1.4.11.C.2 Include convincing, elaborated and properly cited evidence.
    1.4.11.C.3 Develop reader interest.
    1.4.11.C.4 Anticipate and counter reader concerns and arguments.
    1.4.11.C.5 Include a variety of methods to advance the argument or position.
1.4.11.D Maintain a written record of activities, course work, experience, honors and interests.
1.4.11.E Write a personal resume.

1.5.11 Quality of Writing

1.5.11.A Write with a sharp, distinct focus.
    1.5.11.A.1 Identify topic, task and audience.
    1.5.11.A.2 Establish and maintain a single point of view.
1.5.11.B Write using well-developed content appropriate for the topic.
    1.5.11.B.1 Gather, determine validity and reliability of, analyze and organize information.
    1.5.11.B.2 Employ the most effective format for purpose and audience.
    1.5.11.B.3 Write fully developed paragraphs that have details and information specific to the topic and relevant to the focus.
1.5.11.C Write with controlled and/or subtle organization.
    1.5.11.C.1 Sustain a logical order throughout the piece.
    1.5.11.C.2 Include an effective introduction and conclusion.
1.5.11.D Write with a command of the stylistic aspects of composition.
    1.5.11.D.1 Use different types and lengths of sentences.
    1.5.11.D.2 Use precise language.
1.5.11.E Revise writing to improve style, word choice, sentence variety and subtlety of meaning after rethinking how questions of purpose, audience and genre have been addressed.
1.5.11.F Edit writing using the conventions of language.
    1.5.11.F.1 Spell all words correctly.
    1.5.11.F.2 Use capital letters correctly.
    1.5.11.F.3 Punctuate correctly (periods, exclamation points, question marks, commas, quotation marks, apostrophes, colons, semicolons, parentheses, hyphens, brackets, ellipses).
    1.5.11.F.4 Use nouns, pronouns, verbs, adjectives, adverbs, conjunctions, prepositions and interjections properly.
    1.5.11.F.5 Use complete sentences (simple, compound, complex, declarative, interrogative, exclamatory and imperative).
1.5.11.G Present and/or defend written work for publication when appropriate.

1.6.11 Speaking and Listening

1.6.11.A Listen to others.
    1.6.11.A.1 Ask clarifying questions.
    1.6.11.A.2 Synthesize information, ideas and opinions to determine relevancy.
    1.6.11.A.3 Take notes.
1.6.11.B Listen to selections of literature (fiction and/or nonfiction).
    1.6.11.B.1 Relate them to previous knowledge.
    1.6.11.B.2 Predict solutions to identified problems.
    1.6.11.B.3 Summarize and reflect on what has been heard.
    1.6.11.B.4 Identify and define new words and concepts.
    1.6.11.B.5 Analyze and synthesize the selections relating them to other selections heard or read.
1.6.11.C Speak using skills appropriate to formal speech situations.
    1.6.11.C.1 Use a variety of sentence structures to add interest to a presentation.
    1.6.11.C.2 Pace the presentation according to audience and purpose.
    1.6.11.C.3 Adjust stress, volume and inflection to provide emphasis to ideas or to influence the audience.
1.6.11.D Contribute to discussions.
    1.6.11.D.1 Ask relevant, clarifying questions.
    1.6.11.D.2 Respond with relevant information or opinions to questions asked.
    1.6.11.D.3 Listen to and acknowledge the contributions of others.
    1.6.11.D.4 Adjust tone and involvement to encourage equitable participation.
    1.6.11.D.5 Facilitate total group participation.
    1.6.11.D.6 Introduce relevant, facilitating information, ideas and opinions to enrich the discussion.
    1.6.11.D.7 Paraphrase and summarize as needed.
1.6.11.E Participate in small and large group discussions and presentations.
    1.6.11.E.1 Initiate everyday conversation.
    1.6.11.E.2 Select and present an oral reading on an assigned topic.
    1.6.11.E.3 Conduct interviews.
    1.6.11.E.4 Participate in a formal interview (e.g., for a job, college).
    1.6.11.E.5 Organize and participate in informal debate around a specific topic.
    1.6.11.E.6 Use evaluation guides (e.g., National Issues Forum, Toastmasters) to evaluate group discussion (e.g., of peers, on television).
1.6.11.F Use media for learning purposes.
    1.6.11.F.1 Use various forms of media to elicit information, to make a student presentation and to complete class assignments and projects.
    1.6.11.F.2 Evaluate the role of media in focusing attention and forming opinions.
    1.6.11.F.3 Create a multi-media (e.g., film, music, computer-graphic) presentation for display or transmission that demonstrates an understanding of a specific topic or issue or teaches others about it.

1.7.11 Characteristics and Functions of the English Language

1.7.11.A Describe the influence of historical events on the English language.
1.7.11.B Analyze when differences in language are a source of negative or positive stereotypes among groups.
1.7.11.C Explain and evaluate the role and influence of the English language within and across countries.

1.8.11 Research

1.8.11.A Select and refine a topic for research.
1.8.11.B Locate information using appropriate sources and strategies.
    1.8.11.B.1 Determine valid resources for researching the topic, including primary and secondary sources.
    1.8.11.B.2 Evaluate the importance and quality of the sources.
    1.8.11.B.3 Select sources appropriate to the breadth and depth of the research (e.g., dictionaries, thesauruses, other reference materials, interviews, observations, computer databases).
    1.8.11.B.4 Use tables of contents, indices, key words, cross-references and appendices.
    1.8.11.B.5 Use traditional and electronic search tools.

1.8.11.C Organize, summarize and present the main ideas from research.

> 1.8.11.C.1 Take notes relevant to the research topic.
> 1.8.11.C.2 Develop a thesis statement based on research.
> 1.8.11.C.3 Anticipate readers' problems or misunderstandings.
> 1.8.11.C.4 Give precise, formal credit for others' ideas, images or information using a standard method of documentation.
> 1.8.11.C.5 Use formatting techniques (e.g., headings, graphics) to aid reader understanding.

Assessment Anchor Content Standards

A Comprehension and Reading Skills

A.1 Understand fiction appropriate to grade level.

A.1.1 Identify and apply the meaning of vocabulary.

> A.1.1.1 Identify and/or apply meaning of multiple-meaning words in text.
> A.1.1.2 Identify and/or apply a synonym or antonym of a word in text.

A.1.2 Identify and apply word recognition skills.

> A.1.2.1 Identify how the meaning of a word is changed when an affix is added; identify the meaning of a word from the text with an affix.
> A.1.2.2 Define and/or apply how the meaning of words or phrases changes when using context clues given in explanatory sentences or through the use of examples in the text.

A.1.3 Make inferences, draw conclusions, and make generalizations based on text.

> A.1.3.1 Make inferences and/or draw conclusions based on information from text.
> A.1.3.2 Cite evidence from text to support generalizations.

A.1.4 Identify and explain main ideas and relevant details.

> A.1.4.1 Identify and/or explains stated or implied main ideas and relevant supporting details from text.

A.1.5 Summarize a fictional text as a whole.

> A.1.5.1 Summarize the key details and events of a fictional text as a whole.

A.1.6 Identify, describe, and analyze genre of text.

> A.1.6.1 Identify and/or analyze intended purpose of text.
> A.1.6.2 Describe and/or analyze examples of text that support its intended purpose.

A.2 Understand nonfiction appropriate to grade level.

A.2.1 Identify and apply the meaning of vocabulary in nonfiction.

> A.2.1.1 Identify and/or apply meaning of multiple-meaning words used in text.
> A.2.1.2 Identify and/or apply meaning of content-specific words used in text.

A.2.2 Identify and apply word recognition skills.

> A.2.2.1 Identify and apply how the meaning of a word is changed when an affix is added; identify the meaning of a word from the text with an affix.
> A.2.2.2 Define and/or apply how the meaning of words or phrases changes when using context clues given in explanatory sentences or through the use of examples in text.

A.2.3 Make inferences, draw conclusions, and make generalizations based on text.

> A.2.3.1 Make inferences and/or draw conclusions based on information from text.
> A.2.3.2 Cite evidence from text to support generalizations.

A.2.4 Identify and explain main ideas and relevant details.

> A.2.4.1 Identify and/or explain stated or implied main ideas and relevant supporting details from text.

A.2.5 Summarize a nonfictional text as a whole.

> A.2.5.1 Summarize the major points, processes, and/or events of a nonfictional text as a whole.

A.2.6 Identify, describe, and analyze genre of text.

> A.2.6.1 Identify and/or describe intended purpose of text.
> A.2.6.2 Describe and/or analyze examples of text that support its intended purpose.

B Interpretation and Analysis of Fictional and Nonfictional Text

B.I Interpret, compare, describe, analyze, and evaluate components within and between text.

B.1.1 Interpret, compare, describe, analyze, and evaluate components of fiction and literary nonfiction.

B.1.1.1 Interpret, compare, describe, analyze, and/or evaluate the relationships among the following within or between fiction and literary nonfiction:

B.1.1.1.A Character (may also be called narrator, speaker, subject of a biography):

B.1.1.1.A.1 Interpret, compare, describe, analyze, and/or evaluate character actions, motives, dialogue, emotions/feelings, traits, and relationships among characters within fictional or literary nonfictional text.

B.1.1.1.A.2 Interpret, compare, describe, analyze, and/or evaluate the relationship between characters and other components of text.

B.1.1.1.B Setting:

B.1.1.1.B.1 Interpret, compare, describe, analyze, and/or evaluate the setting of fiction or literary nonfiction.

B.1.1.1.B.2 Interpret, compare, describe, analyze, and/or evaluate the relationship between setting and other components of the text.

B.1.1.1.C Plot (May also be called action):

B.1.1.1.C.1 Interpret, compare, describe, analyze, and/or evaluate elements of the plot (conflict, rising action, climax and/or resolution).

B.1.1.1.C.2 Interpret, compare, describe, analyze, and/or evaluate the relationship between elements of the plot (conflict, rising action, climax, resolution) and other components of the text.

B.1.1.1.D Theme:

B.1.1.1.D.1 Interpret, compare, describe, analyze, and/or evaluate the theme of fiction or literary nonfiction.

B.1.1.1.D.2 Interpret, compare, describe, analyze, and/or evaluate the relationship between the theme and other components of the text.

B.1.1.1.E Tone, Style, Mood:

B.1.1.1.E.1 Interpret, compare, describe, analyze, and/or evaluate the tone, style, and/or mood of fiction or literary nonfiction.

B.1.1.1.E.2 Interpret, compare, describe, analyze, and/or evaluate the relationship between the tone, style, and/or mood and other components of the text.

B.1.1.1.F Symbolism:

B.1.1.1.F.1 Interpret, compare, describe, analyze, and/or evaluate the use of symbolism in fiction or literary nonfiction.

B.1.1.1.F.2 Interpret, compare, describe, analyze, and/or evaluate the relationship between symbolism and other components of the text.

B.1.2 Make connections between text.

B.1.2.1 Interpret, compare, describe, analyze, and/or evaluate connections between text.

B.2 Identify, interpret, describe, and analyze literary devices in fictional and literary nonfictional text.

B.2.1 Identify, interpret, describe, and analyze figurative language and literary structures in fiction and literary nonfiction.

B.2.1.1 Identify, interpret, describe, and/or analyze examples of personification, simile, metaphor, hyperbole, satire, imagery, foreshadowing, flashbacks and irony in text.

B.2.1.2 Identify, interpret, describe, and/or analyze the author's purpose for and effectiveness at using figurative language in text.

B.2.2 Identify, interpret, describe, and analyze the point of view of the narrator.

B.2.2.1 Identify, interpret, describe, and/or analyze the point of view of the narrator as first person or third person point of view.

B.2.2.2 Interpret, describe, and/or analyze the effectiveness of the point of view used by the author.

B.3 Interpret, describe, and analyze concepts and organization of nonfictional text.

B.3.1 Interpret, describe, and analyze the characteristics and uses of facts and opinions in nonfictional text.

B.3.1.1 Interpret, describe, and/or analyze the use of facts and opinions to make a point or construct an argument in nonfictional text.

B.3.2 Distinguish between essential and nonessential information within or between text.

B.3.2.1 Identify and/or interpret bias and propaganda techniques in nonfictional text.

B.3.2.2 Describe and/or analyze the effectiveness of bias and propaganda techniques in nonfictional text.

B.3.3 Interpret, describe, and analyze how text organization clarifies meaning of nonfictional text.

B.3.3.1 Interpret and/or analyze the effect of text organization, including the use of headers.

B.3.3.2 Interpret and/or analyze the author's purpose for decisions about text organization and content.

B.3.3.3 Interpret and/or analyze graphics and charts, and make connections between text and the content of graphics and charts.

The PSSA Informational Scoring Guideline is a rubric that provides a way to evaluate your composition. The rubric outlines the level to which your writing demonstrates your ability to develop ideas, organize information logically, make appropriate word choices, and exhibit a unique style.

The PSSA Conventions Scoring Guidelines on these pages outline the level to which your writing demonstrates a mastery of grammar, usage, and mechanics. Your writing will be compared to both rubrics and scored appropriately.

Writing

PSSA INFORMATIONAL SCORING GUIDELINE

4	**FOCUS**	Sharp, distinct controlling point made about a single topic with evident awareness of task and audience.
	CONTENT DEVELOPMENT	Substantial, relevant, and illustrative content that demonstrates a clear understanding of the purpose. Thorough elaboration with effectively presented information consistently supported with well-chosen details.
	ORGANIZATION	Effective organizational strategies and structures, such as logical order and transitions, which develop a controlling idea.
	STYLE	Precise control of language, stylistic techniques, and sentence structures that creates a consistent and effective tone.
3	**FOCUS**	Clear controlling point made about a single topic with general awareness of task and audience.
	CONTENT DEVELOPMENT	Adequate, specific, and/or illustrative content that demonstrates an understanding of the purpose. Sufficient elaboration with clearly presented information supported with well-chosen details.
	ORGANIZATION	Organizational strategies and structures, such as logical order and transitions, which develop a controlling idea.
	STYLE	Appropriate control of language, stylistic techniques, and sentence structures that creates a consistent tone.
2	**FOCUS**	Vague evidence of a controlling point made about a single topic with an inconsistent awareness of task and audience.
	CONTENT DEVELOPMENT	Inadequate, vague content that demonstrates a weak understanding of the purpose. Underdeveloped and/or repetitive elaboration with inconsistently supported information. May be an extended list.
	ORGANIZATION	Inconsistent organizational strategies and structures, such as logical order and transitions, which ineffectively develop a controlling idea.
	STYLE	Limited control of language and sentence structures that creates interference with tone.
1	**FOCUS**	Little or no evidence of a controlling point made about a single topic with minimal awareness of task and audience.
	CONTENT DEVELOPMENT	Minimal evidence of content that demonstrates a lack of understanding of the purpose. Superficial, undeveloped writing with little or no support. May be a bare list.
	ORGANIZATION	Little or no evidence of organizational strategies and structures, such as logical order and transitions, which inadequately develop a controlling idea.
	STYLE	Minimal control of language and sentence structures that creates an inconsistent tone.

Writing

PSSA CONVENTIONS SCORING GUIDELINE

4	Thorough control of sentence formation.
	Few errors, if any, are present in grammar, usage, spelling, and punctuation, but the errors that are present do not interfere with meaning.
3	Adequate control of sentence formation.
	Some errors may be present in grammar, usage, spelling, and punctuation, but few, if any, of the errors that are present may interfere with meaning.
2	Limited and/or inconsistent control of sentence formation. Some sentences may be awkward or fragmented.
	Many errors may be present in grammar, usage, spelling, and punctuation, and some of those errors may interfere with meaning.
1	Minimal control of sentence formation. Many sentences are awkward and fragmented.
	Many errors may be present in grammar, usage, spelling, and punctuation, and many of those errors may interfere with meaning.